The Sonata in the Classic Era

SECHS SONATEN
FÜR ZWO PERSONEN

AUF

EINEM CLAVIER

VON

FRANZ SEYDELMANN,

CHURF. SÆCHS. CAPELLMEISTER.

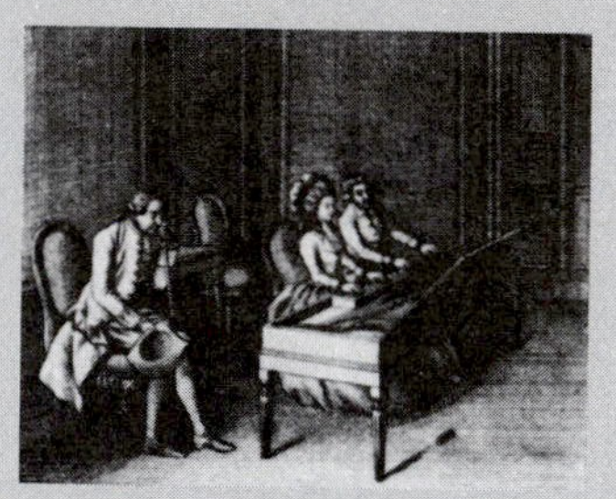

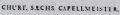

LEIPZIG,

BEY JOHANN GOTTLOB IMMANUEL BREITKOPF.

[illegible]

THE SONATA IN THE CLASSIC ERA

THIRD EDITION

By WILLIAM S. NEWMAN

W · W · NORTON & COMPANY · INC ·
NEW YORK · LONDON

Published simultaneously in Canada by
Penguin Books Canada Ltd,
2801 John Street, Markham, Ontario L3R 1B4.

Printed in the United States of America.

Third edition published 1983 by arrangement with
the University of North Carolina Press

Library of Congress Cataloging in Publication Data

Newman, William S.
The sonata in the classic era.

Bibliography: p.
Includes index.
1. Sonata. 2. Classicism in music. I. Title.
ML1156.N43 1983 781′.52′09033 82-24575

W. W. Norton & Company, Inc., 500 Fifth Avenue,
New York, N. Y. 10110
W. W. Norton & Company Ltd., 37 Great Russell Street,
London WC1B 3NU

ISBN 0-393-95286-X

2 3 4 5 6 7 8 9 0

To

Glen Haydon

Preface

No author can hope to succeed in a project of this size and scope without the generous help of many others in the field, including the wise and experienced counselors, the seasoned readers, the conscientious research assistants, and all those specialists whose particular territories, already staked off, he must invade so summarily. In the present volume, wherever the help has been the sort that can be linked to specific subject matter, my aim has been to acknowledge it at that point in the text. But I do not want to miss the opportunity that a preface affords to bring together, all in one place, the names of those who have helped, including some whose help has been of a more general sort; and to acknowledge my indebtedness and gratitude for certain other kinds of assistance as well.

I am grateful for the valued information contributed on Haffner's *Oeuvres mêlées,* in Chapter VI, by Mr. Roger Kamien of Queens College, New York, who also reviewed all of Chapters XI, XII, and XIII in the typed manuscript; on Galuppi, by Professor Edith Woodcock at the University of Washington, who reviewed all of Chapter VII; on G. B. Sammartini, by Miss Bathia Churgin at Vassar College, who reviewed all of Chapter VIII; on Boccherini, in Chapter VIII, by both Mr. Charles Farrell of New York City and Professor William Klenz at Duke University; on Domenico Scarlatti and possible Madrid associates, in Chapter IX, by Professor Ralph Kirkpatrick at Yale University; on numerous Iberian composers in Chapters IX and X, by Professor Santiago Kastner of Lisbon; on the Platti family, in Chapter XII, by Professor Lothar Hoffmann-Erbrecht of Frankfurt/M; on Emanuel Bach, in Chapter XIII, by Professor Miriam Terry at the University of Washington, who also provided photographs of numerous unpublished sonatas by Bach; on both Haydn and Mozart, by Professor Jan LaRue of New York University, who reviewed all of Chapter XIV; on Beethoven, by Mr. Donald W. MacArdle of Littleton, Colorado, who reviewed all of Chapter XV; on French violin music, by Professor Robert Preston at the University of Oklahoma, who reviewed all of Chapter XVII; on Hüllmandel, by Dr. Rita Benton at the State University of Iowa, who reviewed all of Chapter XVIII; on chamber and solo instrumental music in England, by Mr. Charles Cudworth of Cambridge University and Dr. Stanley Sadie of Wembley, both of whom reviewed all of Chapter XIX; on Clementi, by Sister Alice Eugene, S.L., of Webster College, who reviewed all of Chapter XX; on "the sonata in Ireland," in Chapter XX, by Mrs. Ita Beausang of Dublin; on "the sonata in Sweden," in Chapter XXI, by Professor Ingmar Bengtsson of Uppsala University and his seminar students in the fall of 1960; on certain of the Thomas Jefferson Papers, in Chapter XXI, by Miss Dorothy S. Eaton at the Library of Congress; and on other aspects of musical Americana, by Professor Edgar Alden at the University of North Carolina, who reviewed all of Chapter XXI.

I am likewise grateful to Dr. Otto Kinkeldey, currently in South Orange, New Jersey, for his illuminating critical review of the entire typed manuscript, and to Dr. Lilian Pruett at the University of North Carolina for her careful editorial reading of the entire manuscript; to Dr. Carl A. Rosenthal of New York and Mrs. Ross Scroggs of Chapel Hill for their expert preparation of the music examples and the map, respectively; to the late Dr. Alfred Einstein for the loan of the many Rutini sonatas that he himself had copied by hand, and to Professor Dragan Plamenac at the University of Illinois for making and donating photographs of his unique copy of Rutini's Op. 9; to Dr. Keith Mixter at Ohio State University for bibliographic and related assistance; to Professor Joaquin Nin-Culmell at the University of California for information about the editions by his father, Joaquin Nin, of Herrando's sonatas; to Professor E. Chappel White at Emory University for the loan of Viotti's sonatas in early editions; and to Robert A. Titus at Ohio State University and Professor Loren Bartlett at Arkansas Polytechnic College for information on eighteenth-century clarinet sonatas and bassoon sonatas, respectively.

The institutions that have co-operated with this project by lending books and supplying microfilm of rare sonata holdings are too numerous even merely to list here. But I do want to express once more my warm thanks to the staffs of certain institutions where I have asked for and gotten much kind help in person and/or by way of all too many urgent letters about bibliographic minutiae. These institutions include the main and special music libraries, as well as the Interlibrary Loan Center, at the University of North Carolina; the Library of Congress;

the New York Public Library; the Boston Public Library; the main and special music libraries at Harvard University; the British Museum in London; and the Bibliothèque nationale in Paris.

Furthermore, I naturally welcome this opportunity to cite the Guggenheim Foundation and the University of North Carolina for matching grants that completely freed fifteen months of my time during the final, twenty-two-month sprint on this volume; the American Council of Learned Societies for two successive "grants-in-aid" that provided not only for essential microfilm and travel but for the research assistance of three talented and willing graduate students in musicology, Mr. Lawrence Bernstein and Mr. Thomas Warner at New York University, and Miss Martha Jane Gilreath at the University of North Carolina; and the University of North Carolina Press for the full co-operation of its able staff in all matters pertaining to publication.

A number of publishers have kindly granted permissions to quote from modern editions of various letters, translations, and music scores that they have issued. Most of these permissions are acknowledged individually in the present volume as each quotation appears. But because of the recurring use of certain basic sources, grateful acknowledgment is made instead at this point, to Macmillan & Co., Ltd., of London, and St. Martin's Press, Inc., of New York, for permission to quote from *The Letters of Mozart and His Family* and *The Letters of Beethoven,* both sets being translated and edited by Emily Anderson; and to Barrie and Rockliff of London and Oxford University Press of New York for permission to quote from *The Collected Correspondence and London Notebooks of Joseph Haydn,* translated and edited by H. C. Robbins Landon.

Again, I have put off to the last any mention of my wife's share in this project. It is hard to stand apart and offer objective thanks to the one who has worked with me most closely, patiently, and conscientiously, from start to finish. Suffice it to recall here just one main aspect of her help, which has been the heroic feat of typing, retyping, and correcting the entire volume, with all of its fussy editorial problems and constant detail.

The Third Edition

I am indebted again to W. W. Norton & Company, Inc., for permitting me to do considerable updating and emending, in this Third Edition of this volume. And I am indebted again to numerous colleagues and students, near and far, for supplying much of the needed information from new research they have been doing. The many additions or revisions that could not be fitted into the text proper are keyed by marginal footnotes to the expanded Addenda that begin on page 810. Only a selected few of the new titles and names that now appear could be incorporated in the Bibliography or Index. In the preparation of this edition the help of Ms. Penny Schwarze, doctoral candidate at the University of North Carolina in Chapel Hill, and a grant from the University Research Council to support that help are both gratefully acknowledged.

W. S. N., Chapel Hill, June 1981

Abbreviations and Related Editorial Matters

As in the previous volume, one grand *SIC* will have to do for all the curious word forms and spellings that have been retained here, without a *sic,* from early titles and other sources. Where modern names have alternative spellings the choice here has been made again largely on the arbitrary basis of preferring one standard source to another. The translations are new here unless otherwise credited.

The bibliographic minutiae in the present volume, the many references to specific passages in specific sonatas, and the characteristically prolix titles of Classic sonatas, with their full indications of optional scorings, have necessitated more use of abbreviations and symbols (especially within parentheses and in footnotes) than might be tolerated in a less detailed volume. I can only hope that most of these are self-evident to any reader conversant with the subject at hand, and that the others will quickly become self-evident after only a little use. A less-initiated reader may welcome the following explanations.

All of the bibliographic short titles are listed and expanded in the one approximately alphabetic order of the Bibliography (after Chap. XXI). An "-m" is added to the short title of each publication that consists mainly of music. Specific passages in a sonata are identified by the catalogue number or the opus and set numbers, the movement number (always in a lower-case Roman numeral), and the measure numbers, in that order. Thus, among Mozart's works, K.V. 576/ii/1-4 refers to Köchel's much revised *Verzeichnis,* item 576, second movement, measures one to four. As the context should make clear, hyphenated capital letters are used both to letter the sections of a form, as in the familiar A-B-A design, and to abbreviate the successive movements of a complete cycle in terms of their tempos (in English), as in F-S-M-VF for fast, slow, moderate, and very fast. Also, in keeping with common practice, major keys are indicated by capital letters and minor keys by lower-case letters.

In the scoring designations the most common instruments are indicated by the standard abbreviations that are listed shortly. In addition, three symbols are used to abbreviate the status of any accompanying instrument that may be specified in the title of an accompanied keyboard sonata. A plus sign (+) means that this accompaniment is obligatory (obbligato, *concertante,* and so on). A plus-or-minus sign (±) means that it is optional (ad libitum, *a piacere,* and so on). But a simple ampersand (&) means merely that it is added in the title. Thus, a sonata for P-or-H & Vn-or-Fl ±.Vc is a sonata for piano or harpsichord with violin or flute accompaniment and optional cello accompaniment. As in the previous volume, a setting in which the polarity of one or more melody instruments and thorough bass prevails is referred to as "melo/bass," or more specifically, as "Vn/bass," and so on.

References to the previous volume, abbreviated SBE, are made by page numbers. But because of the risky and costly business of resetting so many lines in the page proofs, the frequent cross references within the present volume, SCE, are made only by chapter number. Knowing the chapter, the interested reader can get the exact page number readily enough from the detailed name-and-subject Index.

W. S. N.

Abbreviations

A	alto (instrument) in an A/bass setting
à 2, à 3-5, etc.	for two players, for three to five players, etc.
acc'd.	accompanied
B	bass (instrument) in a B/bass setting
b.c.	*basso continuo*
dim.	diminished
dom.	dominant
ex(x).	example(s)
F	fast, as in F-S(low)-F
F.	referring to a work as indexed in Falck/BACH
facs.	facsimile(s)
Fl	flute
G.	referring to a work as indexed in Giazotto/VIOTTI
H	harpsichord
H.	referring to a work as indexed in Hoboken/HAYDN
H.W.	referring to a work as indexed in Wohlfarth/BACH
K	keyboard
K.	referring to a work as numbered in Kirkpatrick/SCARLATTI
K.V.	referring to a work as indexed in Köchel/MOZART
L.	referring to a work as numbered in Longo/SCARLATTI-m

M	moderate, as in F(ast)-M-F
ms(s)	measure(s)
mvt(s).	movement(s) of a musical work
obl.	obbligato (accompaniment)
Op., Opp.	opus, opera
opt.	optional (accompaniment)
P	piano (instrument)
S	slow, as in F(ast)-S-F; also, soprano (instrument) in an S/bass setting
son(s).	sonata(s)
suppl.	supplementary volume
T.	referring (by page number only) to a work as indexed in Terry/BACH
V	very, as in F(ast)-S(low)-VF
Va	viola
Vc	(violon-)cello
Vn	violin
W.	referring to a work as indexed in Wotquenne/BACH
WoO	referring to a work without opus number as indexed in Kinsky & Halm/BEETHOVEN

Contents

Music Examples

Tables, Charts, and Map

The Sonata in the Classic Era

Chapter I

Introduction—The Historical Problem

The Period and the Scope

Once more, a discussion of historical problems—that is, another Introduction, Confession, and Apologia—provides the best way of leading into the history itself. *The Sonata in the Classic Era* is the middle (and also the bulkiest) of the three volumes included in "A History of the Sonata Idea." It covers the crucial period of about eighty-five years from the first real flowering of the solo keyboard sonata, starting shortly before 1740, to the last sonatas of Beethoven and Clementi, completed shortly after 1820. In political history the corresponding period includes the long reigns, both starting in 1740, of Frederick the Great in Berlin and Maria Theresa in Vienna; the widespread conflicts known as the War of the Austrian Succession, from 1740 to 1748, and the Seven Years' War, from 1756 to 1763; and the entire convulsive cycle created by the French Revolution, the Napoleonic Wars, and the Congress of Vienna, from 1789 to 1815. In cultural history the same period includes the Enlightenment in France and elsewhere, with its pursuit of "freedom, reason, and humanitarianism," as well as the ensuing, more localized *Sturm und Drang* in Germany, with its rebellion against accepted eighteenth-century standards, especially French literary standards.

Certain style and structural traits might be adduced to reinforce the limits of music's Classic Era as it is viewed here. Thus, at the start, while the solo keyboard sonata began to flower, the introduction of textural devices like the Alberti bass proved to be as seminal to budding Classic styles and forms as the *basso continuo* had been in the Baroque Era or the "um-pah-pah" bass was to be in the Romantic Era. At the close, with the end of Beethoven's and Clementi's sonata output, a significant concept of musical form came to an end, too. That concept embraced a fluid, fluent, and dynamic kind of form in which distinctive conflicts of keys, themes, textures, and syntactic processes were resolved in an ideal co-ordination, if not restraint, of all forces. Other delimitations may be seen in the rise and fall of the accompanied keyboard setting; or in the *galant* style of closely ornamented, short-breathed melody at the start, as against the more universal, balanced, folklike melodies at the end; or in differences of structural rhythm, tonal organization, dynamics, and related traits (SCE VI).

Unfortunately, such delimitations never fail to bring exceptions to mind. For example, the start of the Classic Era is blurred by the continuation of the Baroque *basso continuo* practice right to the end of the century. And the close of the era is still more blurred by the absence even of such innovations in scoring and texture as those at the start.[1] Since history is always in transition, any division into periods, however necessary for the sake of easy reference and simplified perspective, is bound to have something of the arbitrary about it. There may be little disagreement regarding the successive peaks, as defined by the sonatas, say, of Bach and Handel in the Baroque Era, of the Viennese triumvirate formed by Haydn, Mozart, and Beethoven in the Classic Era, or of Schumann and Brahms in the Romantic Era. But where to draw the lines among the intervening men, whose music was often transitory as well as transitional, is always harder to decide. In fact, an overlapping border or fringe area of about two decades must be allowed between each pair of adjacent eras in the present project. Stylistically as well as temporally, men like Hurlebusch, D. Scarlatti, and Platti can be fitted into the late-Baroque Era at least as comfortably as into the pre-Classic Era. They were deferred to the present volume only because they seem more important as harbingers of that keyboard sonata flowering than as terminators of any Baroque development.

As for the border between the Classic and Romantic Eras, many composers are retained in the present volume in spite of certain pre-Romantic traits in their sonatas. Pre-Romantic traits appeared fairly early, for example, in Clementi's fifty-six years of sonata composing. But the more important consideration seems to be that long span itself, which not only encompassed virtually the entire sonata production of Haydn, Mozart, and Beethoven but witnessed close interchanges of style between the Anglo-Italian and each of those Viennese masters in turn. The Parisian admirer of Clementi, J. L. Adam, who did not die until 1848 at the age of ninety, presents a more extreme case, but is kept in the present volume on similar grounds. On the other hand, many a

1. The problem of establishing this latter dividing point is elaborated in Adler/WIENER 793-795.

contemporary or near contemporary of Clementi is saved for the next volume because pre-Romantic traits seem more nearly to dominate his sonata writing—especially preoccupations with wider harmonic and tonal relationships, with a more outspoken yet naïve kind of poetizing, and with a salon type of virtuoso passage work. Clementi died in 1832. Among composers deferred here to the pre-Romantic side of the fringe, Pinto had already died in 1806, Eberl in 1807, and J. L. Dussek in 1812; Steibelt died in 1823, Schubert in 1828, Hummel in 1837, Ladurner in 1839, and J. B. Cramer not until 1858. Schubert, who must be given a special niche in any case, is also included in Einstein's *Music in the Romantic Era,* although neatly classified there as a "Romantic *Classic*" (p. 67).

The subdivisions of the Classic Era will necessarily have fringe areas and something of the arbitrary about them, too. Regarding their limits, like those of the era itself, only a little help can be found in contemporary writings. As will be noted in later chapters, these writings do contain numerous uses of the term *galant* that tally with our pre-Classic subdivision. And the Lyonese teacher Brijon used the word "rococo" in 1763 in a sense that is at least pertinent if not quite the positive one intended by today's music historians: "Compared with the energy and manly swing of the Italian concerto, a sonata of Philip Emanuel Bach is fairly characterized as 'rococo,'" this word signifying, according to a footnote, "an elaborate want of good taste."[2] For that matter, Grétry used the word "Classic" in 1789 in something like its present musical sense,[3] much as Koch and E. T. A. Hoffmann were soon to use "Romantic."[4] But only through the perspective of time and further use have these chance terms acquired enough tangible musical associations to convey meaningful style-period impressions.

Recalling the focal importance of Corelli's music in the three phases of the Baroque sonata, the chief sonatas of Haydn and Mozart, composed within the twenty-two-year span from 1773 to 1795, constitute the reference center for the present volume. In other words, our frequently overlapping subdivisions into pre-, high-, and late-Classic phases might be restated for our purposes as before, during, and after the Classic peak defined by Haydn and Mozart.[5] The "before" is

2. Trans. from Brijon/MUSIQUE 27.

3. According to A. Damerini, as noted in MGG VII 1031 (Blume); but the reference could not be found in a preliminary check of Grétry/MÉMOIRES. No use before 1835 is found in the helpful discussion in Engel/KLASSIK 46-51.

4. MGG VII 1031; Adler/WIENER 793.

5. In Adler/HANDBUCH II 795, W. Fischer preferred a somewhat different, nonoverlapping subdivision of Classic instrumental music into 4 phases, described as pre-Classic transitional, 1730-60 (cf. p. 799), early-Classic, 1760-80, high-Classic, 1780-1810, and early-Romantic, 1810-28 (including Schubert). Cf., also, Engel/KLASSIK 51-52.

constantly concerned with antecedents of that peak, especially with antecedents of the Mozart style, which, to the minds of many, marks at once the essence and acme of musical Classicism. Among the chief sonata composers in this pre-Classic phase are G. B. Sammartini, Boccherini, Soler, J. Stamitz, Emanuel Bach, Schobert, and Christian Bach.

The "during" or high-Classic phase is so brilliantly illuminated by Haydn and Mozart themselves that their contemporaries are all but lost in the shadows, the more so as the *Kleinmeister* or even such then celebrities as Vanhal and Koželuch now no longer offer the historical appeal of leading somewhere. Only men like Clementi, Rust, and Hüllmandel shed enough light of their own to maintain appreciable interest today. And the "after" or late-Classic phase offers a still greater contrast of light and shadow. Beethoven, who represents almost a special era unto himself in any case, so completely dominates his contemporaries that, with the exception of Clementi and Schubert again, scarcely a one still survives sufficiently to attract present-day devotees of the sonata.[6]

This much delimitation of the Classic Era needs to be followed by a few words on the scope of our particular subject matter. In keeping with arguments advanced at some length in the previous volume (SBE 4-8), this second volume continues to focus not so much on the "evolution" of a single principle—that is, "sonata form"—as on the changing meanings and uses that the term "sonata" itself underwent. If the distinction between principle and term proves to be of less actual significance by the time of the Classic Era, it still needs at least to be recalled at this point. Tracing a single principle tends to favor whatever, but only whatever, compositions happen to supply links in the supposed chain leading to that principle. Such an approach can be not only too exclusive but too inclusive, for it is likely to encourage dipping into any or all other instrumental genres of the Classic Era wherever they happen to supply missing links in the chain. On the other hand, tracing the meanings and uses of "sonata" by the Classic composers and writers themselves shifts the burden of historical selection and emphasis to contemporary concepts of the term. If this second or semantic approach lets in a few obviously disparate works called "sonata," like the seven single orchestral movements that originally comprised Haydn's "Seven Last Words," it still helps to avoid treacherous pitfalls in the

6. However, the three Viennese masters should not be quite so isolated from their environment as is implied by the statement in Engel/QUELLEN 285: "There is really no Classic style, but only a style of the Classicists Haydn and Mozart (Beethoven already stands beyond this concept)."

more usual "evolutionary" approach (as noted later in this chapter and examined more fully in Chap. VI on styles and forms).[7]

This semantic approach seems to promote a better historical balance in other ways, too. It permits frequent reference to the *post hoc,* nineteenth-century concept of "sonata form" as a convenient means of comparing procedures, without making this concept a fixed standard for evaluating "progress." It invites as much consideration of the cycle as a whole as of any one movement within that cycle. And it allows for allusions to other Classic genres when the allusions are pertinent—that is, when the sonata actually crossed paths with some other genre, as in the solo and accompanied sonatas by the Parisian clavecinists that the young Mozart arranged as "concertos" (K.V. 37 and 39-41), or the "sinfonies" of Emanuel Bach that were transcribed as solo keyboard "sonatas."[8] However, unlike the search for some one principle, such allusions do not threaten to diffuse our subject beyond recognition by opening the floodgates to all Classic instrumental music. For the Classic sonata does reveal a recognizable identity of its own, not only by virtue of its characteristic solo, accompanied, and small ensemble settings or any distinctions made by contemporaries (SCE II), but as a manifestation of its particular concert and domestic functions, of its exceptional intimacies and caprices, and of several other individualities that are to reappear constantly throughout this survey.

The Ways and the Means

This volume, like its predecessor, is planned in two parts. Part I offers a summary, over-all view of the Classic sonata, organized in terms of its meanings, uses, spread, settings, and forms. Part II, which is nearly four times as long, supplies the evidence for that over-all view in a detailed survey of the individual composers and their works. This latter survey is organized by centers or schools, then by regions or countries during the pre-, high-, and late-Classic Era, and, when necessary, by further considerations such as instrumental medium or national origin. It would be tempting to paraphrase Charles Ives' *Essays Before a Sonata* to the effect that Part I is "for those who can't stand" so much detail and Part II "for those who can't stand" so many generalizations, while "to those who can't stand either, the whole is respectfully dedicated." But more accurately and still more familiarly, the manifest object of this plan is to let the reader have his historical cake and eat it,

7. The values of a semantic approach to music history are developed at length (without emphasis on the son.), in Eggebrecht/TERMINOLOGIE, especially pp. 11-17 and 83-110.

8. Cf. BRITISH UNION I 73.

too. Although such a plan does entail a certain minimum of repetition, that repetition itself may prove to be an advantage in disguise, in that it obviates many cross references and supplies the periodic reorientation needed in such an extended study. There is also the fact that the longer the study, the greater becomes the need for some such tightly organized plan, even to the point where almost no escape may remain from the unadorned methodology of a legal brief or the musty aroma of an academic dissertation. To indulge in one more paraphrase (of the Kirnberger title met later, SCE XIII), there is no short-cut "Method for Tossing Off a Sonata History."

As before, in Part II each composer normally is put in the music center where he did his main sonata composing, regardless of whether this was the place where he was born or trained. In that way he appears where he is most likely to have met and influenced other sonata composers, if not necessarily where he himself was most influenced. At best, this policy makes for an authentic grouping by schools and styles that could hardly be improved through any artificial grouping contrived from our present vantage point. It also helps to establish significant ties and continuity in a survey that might otherwise be limited largely to reference uses.

At worst, this policy does have its shortcomings. But less than might be expected is the danger of obliterating national currents, insofar as they really matter. Wherever there was any significant emigration of sonata composers, as from Czechoslovakia and Germany, it shows up clearly enough in the foreign, nationalist colonies of cities like Vienna and London. Moreover, in those disunited countries and especially in Italy, where the emigration was greatest (as tabulated early in SCE VII), national identities were often more theoretical than real, anyway. More troublesome inconsistencies arise when one attempts to place three other sorts of composers where they lived. Some, like Sarti, traveled so much and so widely, in spite of the almost incredible travel conditions that still existed in many areas (SCE IV), that they can only be put back in their place of birth or training. Others, like Neefe in Leipzig, must be put not where they wrote their sonatas but in yet another center where their influence was demonstrably greater, as was Neefe's on the young Beethoven in Bonn. Still others, like T. A. Arne and Paradisi in London, are put in the same center on the basis of residence, yet must be acknowledged to stand about as far apart in their musical styles as the range of the times permitted.

Part II takes in over four hundred Classic composers, as against over three hundred in the Baroque Era. The survey is intended to be comprehensive, which inevitably means exhuming a certain number of composers who will only slip right back into their obscure graves. As prescient as Burney could be at times, this pioneer historian scarcely allowed for today's musicological zeal when he concluded that he had "spoken of some musicians whose fame is now so much faded, that it is perhaps the last time they will ever be mentioned."[9] More explicitly, the rather optimistic aim here has been to include every Classic composer whose sonatas have seemed interesting for their quality, style, form, or historical significance, or for some study or edition devoted to them; also, every composer who wrote interestingly about the sonata or, like the astronomer Herschel, arouses curiosity through other associations.

In addition, a few composers are included even without such blessings, though usually with no more than passing mention. The reason, purely and simply, is to achieve a certain completeness for the record, in coverage as well as documentation. This latter aim probably needs no further justification in an area that has proved as fruitful as any in music, yet has not previously been surveyed as a whole either in detail or by a single viewer. However inadequate the single view must be over so broad an area, cutting across the full expanse of Classic instrumental music can hardly fail to put the great masters in clearer perspective. It may do little to explain their astonishing isolation in quality or depth (which fact alone is well worth confirming). But at least it can bring the middlemen into better view. And it can turn up enough precedents and antecedents for nearly every facet of the masters' styles to bind them fully to their musical times and environment. To test this observation one only needs to discover how hard it is to tell Haydn from Latrobe when representative passages by each are singled out, or Mozart from Mysliveček, or even Beethoven from Hüllmandel.

The discussion of each composer who gets more than passing mention in Part II generally begins with biographic and bibliographic information, after which comes the consideration of styles, forms, and influences in his sonatas. No more biographic information is given, as a rule, than that needed to relate the composer's sonata output to the main stations and turning points in his life. But the bibliographic information on the sonatas is fuller. In fact, it often introduces considerable fussy detail, as in the new *catalogue raisonné* offered for Rutini's sonatas, or the revised chronological charts provided for the sonatas of each of the three Vienna masters and Clementi. Such detail has an undeniable fascination of its own. For the curious reader, only at this level of detail

9. Burney/HISTORY II 1025.

does the fun really begin—with such questions as where and when the Cimarosa sonatas originated, what Beethoven piano sonata, if any, was ever performed in public during his lifetime, which Rossi wrote the sonatas Michelangelo Rossi could not have written, and whom among Classic sonata composers Thomas Jefferson preferred. However, the detail justifies itself on still more pertinent grounds. Frequently, only by means of it can one incorporate existing research, or reappraise this research when necessary, or report new findings, or merely summarize much of the vast literature on Haydn, Mozart, and Beethoven. Furthermore, it is difficult to discuss the sonatas in historical perspective until the essentials of what, where, and when are clarified. In the short, eighty-five-year span of the Classic Era—especially that era, when it seems to have been a point of honor not to date music or index books—any bibliographic detail that can improve the dating is of particular value. Musical events followed upon each other so closely then that every decade counts, even every year, in the weighing of styles and influences (as with Galuppi or the Sammartini brothers).[10]

In order to avoid undue repetition in Part II of the subject matter in Chapter VI, the discussion of each composer's individual styles, forms, and influences is limited largely to distinguishing traits—that is, those that orient his sonatas historically and identify them musically. In two special chapters, XIV and XV, on Haydn, Mozart, and Beethoven, the emphasis is almost entirely biographic, bibliographic, and historical, with scarcely any consideration of their styles and forms, for these last already constitute the central point of discussion in Chapter VI.

Along with objective summaries and factual observations on styles and forms throughout Part II, subjective and evaluative reactions are offered (as such), recalling again both the advantages and disadvantages of a single view. No Haydns, Mozarts, or Beethovens seem to have gone unrecognized. But a fair number of stimulating surprises await anyone who explores the literally thousands of sonatas left by Classic composers. Some of these surprises bear out or even enhance the good reputations of the lesser masters and a few others bring back names not so well remembered. An idea of those "surprises" may be had from the contents of a proposed collection of seventeen little known, Classic
11a keyboard sonatas, projected as a sequel to an earlier, similar collection:[11]

Seixas, Sonatas in d and e (Kastner/CRAVISTAS-m I nos. 6 and 11), *ca.* 1740

10. The need for more exact bibliographic detail in Classic music is argued further in Picquot/BOCCHERINI 5-6 and Schaeffner/LA LAURENCIE 9.

11. Newman/THIRTEEN-m. Further identifications of the sons. appear under the individual composers in Part II.

Platti, Sonata Op. 4/5 in c, *ca.* 1746
Sorge, Sonata 1 in B♭ from *Erste Lieferung, ca.* 1748
Rutini, Sonata Op. 3/4 in d, *ca.* 1757
Emanuel Bach, Sonata 3 in a, from the "veränderten Reprisen" set (W. 50/3), 1760
Buttstett, Sonata in A (TRÉSOR-m XII no. 1), 1764
Galuppi, Sonata 14 in B♭ (Benvenuti/CEMBALISTI-m no. 8), *ca.* 1770
Séjan, Op. 1/6 in c (without the lost but unnecessary Vn part), *ca.* 1772
E. W. Wolf, Sonata 2 in G from the first set, 1774
Soler, Sonatas 41 and 42 in E♭ (a pair in Rubio/SOLER-m III), *ca.* 1775
Riegel, Sonata Op. 13/3 in D, 1777
Grazioli, Sonata Op. 1/6 in D, *ca.* 1780
Turini, Sonata 4 in g from the first solo set, *ca.* 1780
Seydelmann, Sonata 4 in E♭ for two players at one piano, 1781
Hüllmandel, Sonata Op. 10/3 in g, with an "ad libitum" Vn part that is not dispensable, 1788
Méhul, Op. 2/2 in a, 1788
Rust, Sonata in C (Czach no. 11; d'Indy/RUST-m no. 10), *ca.* 1792

Where other considerations are equal, most of the 126 examples that appear in the composer discussions and the two preceding chapters have been selected from sonatas that do not appear in modern editions. However, for equally obvious reasons, when the modern editions do exist and are applicable, many of the references in the text proper are made to them. Music examples can be very helpful for illustrating styles. But, of course, such short extracts can give only a little idea of the generative techniques of musical form, and no idea at all of the over-all structure of a sonata. The reader who hopes to examine these all-important aspects of the sonata for himself naturally must expect to utilize whatever scores, recordings, and library facilities are accessible to him.

The Sources and the Resources

The lack of an over-all history of the sonata was discussed in the
previous volume.[12] The nearly total lack of even a general history of 12a
the Classic Era is still more conspicuous. Most eligible in this latter respect is Bücken's concentrated survey,[13] which continues to be interesting for its outlines. But this book goes back thirty-five years (as of 1962), before some of the most significant researches in Classic music, and it ranges too widely, in any case, to allow more than an occasional
nod toward instrumental genres like the sonata. On the other hand, as 13a

12. SBE 11-12; cf. DMF XIV (1961) 86-88 (Reimann).
13. Bücken/ROKOKO. Substantial books on the Classic Era are still projected in the Norton and Oxford series. Certainly, the finest style-historical survey within the confines of an encyclopedia is Blume's recent, extended, masterly article, "Klassik," in MGG VII 1027-1090; trans. by M. D. Herter Norton in *Classic and Romantic Music* (New York: W. W. Norton, 1970).

with the Baroque sonata, there is certainly no shortage of raw materials and specific studies waiting to be collected, assimilated, reconciled, and condensed. Early sources, bibliographic compilations, extended monographs, and critical editions abound on the sonata as well as on other facets of Classic music. More than a third of the over eight hundred items in the Bibliography of the present volume apply primarily to the Classic sonata itself.

Among contemporary sources of most value to our subject are the remarkably keen, fruitful travel reports of the early 1770's by Burney and the *History* to which they led, the historical-critical *Lexicon* by Gerber and *Essai* by La Borde, the aesthetic interpretations of the passing musical scene by Avison, Schubart, and Reichardt, and the more discursive of many autobiographies or memoirs, as by Quantz, Ferrari, Kelly, Grétry, Dittersdorf, Moscheles, and Spohr.[14] To these sources may be added the numerous collections of letters and related documents, headed by the scintillating, incomparably rich examples from the Mozart family. There are also the periodicals, including the venerable *Mercure de France,* the *Briefe* and the *Beyträge* published by Marpurg in the pre-Classic Era, C. F. Cramer's *Magazin,* Reichardt's *Kunstmagazin,* and Forkel's *Almanach* in the high-Classic Era, and the large-scale, influential *Allgemeine musikalische Zeitung* (AMZ) edited by Rochlitz of Leipzig in the late-Classic Era. And there are the many theory treatises and instrumental methods of the Classic Era that give some place to the sonata, such as Manfredini's *Regole* or Löhlein's *Clavier-Schule.*

Although some of the early sources remain almost unknown, modern scholars have already sifted, assorted, and published important segments of them that are pertinent here, especially where the Vienna masters are concerned. Outstanding examples are Larsen's facsimile publication of three Haydn catalogues, and the recent editions by Deutsch and Anderson, respectively, of Mozart documents[15] and Beethoven letters. Of course, not a few contemporary sources have been made available (or more widely available) simply by exact photographic reproduction, without editorial additions, notable examples being the "Microcard Publications in Music" issued by the University of Rochester Press in this country and the *Documenta musicologica* series published as "Druckschriften-Faksimiles" by Bärenreiter. At the other extreme are the documentary collections that, through interpretations and supple-

14. The sources not annotated here are self-evident in the Bibliography. Shorter autobiographies of Classic sonata composers are included in Kahl/SELBSTBIOGRAPHIEN and Nettl/FORGOTTEN.

15. Mozart/NEUE-m X/34.

mentary information, attain the continuity of historical surveys, as in Mooser's valuable *Annales* of eighteenth-century music in Russia.

The studies done in modern times that bear directly on the sonata range in scope all the way from monographs on music in single cities, like Engländer's on instrumental music in Dresden, to monumental surveys of an entire slice of history, like La Laurencie's on French violin music, which work is as important to the Classic as to the Baroque sonata. And these studies range all the way from Saint-Foix's many short articles on Parisian pianists to such major investigations as that of Schmid on Emanuel Bach's chamber music, or Kastner on Iberian keyboard music, or Racek on Czech influences, or Closson and Borren on Belgian music, or Schiedermair on the young Beethoven, or Bone on the guitar and its music, or Oberdörffer on the thorough-bass and its decline in the later eighteenth century. Not a few of these studies originated as doctoral dissertations, including fine products from this country like that of Benton on Hüllmandel, or Helm on Abel. But there are still numerous composers of importance whose sonatas have yet to be studied in any detail, as of this writing. Among these are G. B. Sammartini, Boccherini, Soler, Buttstett, J. Stamitz, Filtz, Richter, both M. G. and J. C. Monn, G. Benda, Haydn (except for articles and surveys!), Vanhal, Rosetti, Hässler, Séjan, F. Beck, Riegel, and Paradisi.

Because of the need for precise dating in the Classic Era that was noted earlier, some of the most valuable contributions to sonata literature have been those that help with this problem. Several researchers have felt compelled to wrestle valiantly with it singlehandedly in the course of other projects.[16] But its further conquest has depended on more specialized kinds of attack. These have produced full dated lists of publishers' plate numbers, such as Weinmann has compiled for Artaria and other Vienna firms; exhaustive bibliographies within special areas, such as that of early American secular music (both printed and MS) that Sonneck began and Upton completed; chronological sequences of contemporary music catalogues, such as those of French publishers that Johansson has dated, annotated, and indexed; and dictionaries of con- 16a
temporary publishers, with at least some record of their duration and changing addresses, such as Sartori has written on Italian publishers. Other aids to eighteenth-century (and earlier) dating include Göhler's records of German publishers' fairs prior to 1760, Brenet's well-known chronology of French royal privileges (supplemented by Cucuel), and, of course, the recent *British Union Catalogue of Early Music,* in which

16. As in Oberdörffer/GENERALBASS 174-182.

dates are hazarded for all listings and prove to be especially reliable for British publications. The problem of dating those late-Classic sonatas that were published after 1800 is greater because most catalogues stop with that year. A few lists of plate numbers apply, including Deutsch's. And a *terminus ad quem* is provided by sources like the two Whistling volumes that preceded Hofmeister's yearbooks. But the later first editions of Clementi and even those of Beethoven will continue to pose knotty problems until more bibliographic research is undertaken in the curiously unplowed nineteenth century, where much can still be derived from letters and from periodicals such as AMZ. Beethoven himself already complained about the failure of publishers to insert the year.[17]

Fortunately, the problem of dating Classic MSS arises less, since sonatas were among the most published of all musical genres in that era. When this problem does arise here, it has not been possible to turn to the developing science of watermarks.[18] But more traditional aids frequently have come to the rescue, such as clues in contemporary documents and other writings, or another *terminus ad quem,* that supplied by Breitkopf's dated thematic indices of several thousand contemporary MSS on file. In all these considerations of dates one must keep in mind that the sonatas in question may have been composed anywhere from a short time to many years before they were first published or otherwise made known. This is an obvious fact, one that Torrefranca constantly restates for the Italians but disregards for the Germans in his intensive and ingenious efforts to find Italian examples that antedated Emanuel Bach's first published sonatas in 1742. To be sure, a gap of "many years" is only a good possibility when the known date falls fairly late in the composer's life, as in Scarlatti's *Essercizi* of 1738 or 1739.

Among today's chief music encyclopedias, *Die Musik in Geschichte und Gegenwart* (MGG) has been a constant aid here as far as it has progressed ("PAR" in Vol. X). Other encyclopedias have been of special help for the remainder of the alphabet and for certain more obscure composers in particular regions, including, of course, Eitner's *Quellen-Lexikon, Grove's Dictionary* in England, *Sohlmans Musiklexikon* in Scandinavia, the *Riemann Musik Lexikon* (12th ed.) in Austro-Germany, the *Diccionario de la música labor* in Iberia, and, to a lesser extent, both Fasquelle and Larousse in France. Badly needed are a larger-scale French encyclopedia and the new multivolume encyclopedia scheduled for early publication by Ricordi in Italy; also, the volume on eighteenth-century printed anthologies that will appear from the International Inventory on Musical Sources.

17. As in his letter of March 7, 1821 (Anderson/BEETHOVEN II 916).
18. Cf. La Rue in AM XXXIII (1961) 120-146.

With regard to modern editions of Classic sonatas, the music has not kept pace with the research, any more than in the Baroque Era. About four-fifths of the sonatas examined for the present survey have had to be located in the early editions and MSS that are still extant in the great libraries in London, Paris, Berlin, Bologna, Florence, Naples, Brussels, Washington, and New York, and in several smaller European libraries.[19] The one-fifth that does exist in more recent editions is unpredictable, once the complete sets of the three Vienna masters are given their due. For example, the available editions provide only a spotty picture of the total sonata output of Emanuel Bach, Christian Bach, and Clementi. They do still less for G. B. Sammartini, Boccherini, and Rust, and almost nothing for Hüllmandel, Pugnani, or Reinagle. However unsatisfactory, a nearly complete edition does exist of D. Scarlatti's sonatas. And a few bright spots do appear, such as the Soler edition in progress under Rubio's editorship or the issues that continue to appear in anthologies like *Nagels Musik-Archiv* and *Organum*.[20] But the student still has to go back to the twenty increasingly scarce volumes of *Le Trésor des pianistes,* published by A. and L. Farrenc in Paris between 1861 and 1872, for one of the most reliable and comprehensive collections of lesser known Classic sonatas (among other works).[21] For instance, the largest printed collection of Emanuel Bach's sonatas appears in this set. Short of *Le Trésor,* the chief anthologies of sonatas have been those that go back to the "Old Masters" sets first edited by Köhler, Pauer, and other nineteenth-century pedagogues. In these sets the same few sonatas have appeared time and again, and continue to appear, leaving a very limited, sometimes false impression of their composers, and suffering from excessive editorial "enrichments."

Before we leave this introductory chapter on the historical problems of the Classic sonata, three approaches in the existing literature call for some words of caution. One is the "evolutionary" approach mentioned earlier. As there will be numerous occasions to discover, the search for the "evolution" of a specific "sonata form" in the nineteenth-century textbook sense—especially for a contrasting "second theme" and a recapitulation of the opening idea—so dominates many sonata studies up to about 1940 that all other aspects tend to be undervalued if not totally overlooked. In place of the highly flexible concept of form that under-

19. Much of the comprehensive library built up for the present study (cf. NOTES I [1944] 24-32) consists of photographic reproductions provided through the greatly valued co-operation of these libraries and of numerous private collectors, who are thanked individually in later chapters.

20. Unfortunately, but few examples apply here in the most pertinent vols. of *Das Musikwerk* series (Giegling/SOLO-m, Stephenson/KLASSIK-m, Schenk/TRIOSONATE-m).

21. Cf. the full contents in Heyer/HISTORICAL 110-111 (but listed in 23 vols.).

lies the Classic sonata idea, a single routine design is assumed to be the conscious goal of the eighteenth-century composer. The misleading notion of an "evolutionary" chain leading straight from Kuhnau, to D. Scarlatti, to Emanuel Bach, "the father of sonata form," still obtains.[22] Such an approach allows little place for alternative designs, or for the fantasy element that often pervades the sonatas of men like Galuppi, Emanuel Bach, Soler, and Rust. In fact, several writers have felt obliged to regard certain sonatas of Beethoven as not really being legitimate sonatas, including Opp. 54, 78, 90, 101, 106, and 111![23]

The second, not unrelated approach is the attempt to categorize styles by tracing each to its national origin. Some writers seem to have taken too literally the distinctions that aestheticians like Quantz made between Italian, French, and German styles in late-Baroque music.[24] Although the so-called "Manieren" by which Riemann identified the Mannheim school soon proved to be in the air almost everywhere, authors have continued to designate specific origins for traits that can be found wherever the Classic sonata flourished. Thus, Seiffert still finds in the sonatas of the Dutch composer Hurlebusch the *agréments* of the French clavecinists, the leaps of D. Scarlatti along with other Italian melodic elements, and the bold harmony of a German like Buxtehude.[25]

The third approach is a manifestation of nationalism itself. It occurs primarily in studies bounded by national limits. Such studies may have taken their start from Riemann's sensational "discovery" of the Mannheim school in 1902, Adler's counter "discovery" of the Vienna Classical school, and the various further "discoveries" that were soon proclaimed in other countries (SCE XI). In some of these studies, especially the more chauvinistic ones like Torrefranca's important researches into Italian origins of the Mozart style, one senses continuing repercussions of the eighteenth-century quarrel between the ancients and moderns in its more nationalistic and academic guises. Torrefranca's diatribes on Riemann or La Laurencie's more tempered remarks on Wasielewski[26] almost seem to be transplanted from Burney's hostile references to La Borde, or Mozart's to the French in general, or Schubart's to Burney.[27]

22. As still in GROVE IV 164; or Abert/MOZART I 79-85. Cf. SBE 11.

23. Cf. Prod'homme/BEETHOVEN 208-209 and 250 (quoting Cortot and Wagner); Shedlock/SONATA 176; Nagel/BEETHOVEN II 216.

24. As in Quantz/VERSUCH 306-334.

25. Seiffert/HURLEBUSCH 275. A different kind of example may be seen in the neat derivations worked out for each *Sinfonie* type in Tutenberg/BACH, as on pp. 53-59.

26. E.g., Torrefranca/ORIGINI and La Laurencie/ÉCOLE II 334; also, Dent in MR X (1949) 56.

27. Burney/HISTORY II 981-982; Scholes in BURNEY'S TOURS I 322-326; Anderson/MOZART II 870-872; Schubart/IDEEN 258-259; Scholes/BURNEY I 246-254.

Part One

The Nature of the Classic Sonata

Chapter II

The Concept of "Sonata" in Classic Writings

Its Use as a Title

At the onset of the Classic Era the title "sonata" already bore a fairly specific meaning in music, one that it had gradually acquired during the century-and-a-half of the Baroque Era. That is, it already implied "a solo or chamber instrumental cycle of aesthetic or diversional purpose, consisting of several contrasting movements that are based on relatively extended designs in 'absolute' music" (to repeat the overall definition arrived at earlier, SBE 6-8). What further and more specific connotations "sonata" acquired throughout the Classic Era becomes the primary subject of the present volume, in accordance with the "semantic" approach restated in Chapter I. In this chapter the understanding of the word "sonata" at that time is explored. And in this first section some of the interesting confusions, exceptions, and variants in the use of the word as a title are noted.

In spite of its more precise definition, "sonata" was still used from time to time in the Classic Era in its broadest generic sense, merely to mean an instrumental piece. Gerber referred to assorted instrumental works of Boccherini as "Sonaten" in 1790; Koch grouped the string quartets of Haydn, Mozart, and others under "modern four-voice sonatas" in 1793; Haydn himself used the title "Sonata" for his well-known "Andante con variazioni" in f in the autograph of 1793; and Carpani still spoke of gigues, *ballate,* "and similar sonatas" in 1812.[1] To a lesser extent, this generic sense also obtained when "sonata" was simply equated with another term. Such equating differed mainly with the scoring and the country, except that it occurred less in Italy, the land where "sonata" had first appeared as a title. In English keyboard music "sonata" and "lesson" were equated. Each of the *Eight Lessons,* 1a

1. Gerber/LEXICON I 174; Koch/ANLEITUNG III *326-327*; Hoboken/HAYDN 791-793; Carpani/HAYDINE 55.

Op. 7, by S. Arnold was individually called "Sonata" in the publication of about 1770, whereas the reverse was true about 10 years later in the *Six Sonatas* by S. Webbe. This equation recalls that of *Essercizi* and "Sonata" in D. Scarlatti's first publication, about 1739. In the S/bass sonata in England, and not seldom elsewhere, too, the term "solo," which Quantz had preferred in 1752,[2] was similarly equated with "sonata," as in Giardini's *Six Solos,* Op. 16, published in 1788. The origin of such an equation is obvious in a title like "Sei Sonate a solo" by C. F. Abel (Op. 6, 1765). In 1789 Türk still felt obliged to give a separate definition to "Klaviersolo" as an instrumental type, but indicated little distinction between it and "sonata."[3]

In France a common equation was that of "pièce de clavecin" and "sonate," whether between the over-all and separate titles (as in Beecke's 10 *Pièces de clavecin* published in Paris in 1767) or within the over-all title itself (as already in Mondonville's acc'd. *Pièces de clavecin en sonates,* Op. 3, published in Paris *ca.* 1734). In much the same way we shall find "toccata" equated with "sonata" in Spanish and Portuguese keyboard music (as by Seixas),[4] or "divertimento" equated with "sonata" in Viennese keyboard music (as by Wagenseil, Steffan, and
4a the young Haydn). With regard to this last equation, the definition for divertimento in Bossler's *Elementarbuch* of 1782 is simply "a cyclic sonata for one or more instruments."[5]

Such equations create no special confusion until they bring terms together that usually associate, then as well as now, with different scorings and style traits. The rather frequent equating of "trio" or "duet" and "sonata" (as by Christian Bach) does not strain the limits of typical sonata scorings in the Classic Era. But a title like *Sonates en symphonie* does, as in a trio for clavecin and 2 horns by C. Kayser (1784), or *Sonata o vero sinfonia,* as in an SS/bass trio by Emanuel Bach (W. 156; 1754).[6] And even more confusion results from the indeterminate use of "trio," "partita," "divertimento," "sinfonia," and "sonata" for SS/bass or string quartet settings by the Monns, Wagenseil, and Gassmann, or "sinfonia," "concerto," "trio," "overtura," and "sonata" for small ensembles by G. B. Sammartini and others.[7] In

2. Cf. SBE 278. "Solo" was still preferred for the S/bass setting in 1793, in Koch/ANLEITUNG III 292-293.

3. Türk/KLAVIERSCHULE 391. Cf. Schenk/PAGANELLI 90-91 for more on this distinction.

4. "Sonate" and "Toccate" are treated as synonyms in Marpurg/CLAVIERSTÜCKE-m I 5-6, with the reservation that the latter is more likely to be for organ and in one mvt.

5. As paraphrased in Strunk/BARYTON 228.

6. Facs. of autograph in Schmid/BACH 112.

7. Cf. Cesari/GIULINI 15-17 for further exx.; also, MGG VIII 1415-1416.

1804 the French cellist Bréval still defined the sonata as "a kind of lesson or overture for the pianoforte with or without a few accompaniments."[8] 8a

Among variants of "sonata" or compounds in which it occurs, the title "sonatina," first used early in the Baroque Era (SBE 18, 215), turns up frequently in the Classic Era. One thinks of diverse keyboard sets like Paganelli's "Sonatines" of 1757 or Hook's "Sonatinos" of 1776 and 1779, as well as numerous pre- and high-Classic sonatas variously qualified as "easy," "short," "facile," "kleine," "leichte," "piccole," and "brevi." All these figure among predecessors of the succinct, elementary, pedagogic type of "sonatinas" that became standard with the unsurpassed models left us by Clementi in Op. 36, about 1798. Beethoven's frequent use of the title "Grande Sonate" seems to have meant a large-scale work for recital use, although one wonders, then, why it is missing from a later work like Op. 57 or 81a. Before him W. F. E. Bach had used it in a MS of 1778. A. E. Müller's use of it in 1813, in Op. 36, was probably an imitation of Beethoven's use. The title "Sonate notturne," or even "Sonate o notturne," was used especially in Milan for SS/bass settings, as by G. B. Sammartini, Christian Bach, and Pichl.[9] The title "Sonata da camera" still appears from time to time in the Classic Era, as in a quintet by Dittersdorf.

Some Definitions (*Schulz*)

Among writings on music published in the Classic Era relatively few contain definitions of "sonata" or explanations of its structural procedures in technical terms. Less than two dozen dictionary definitions and perhaps three dozen explanations might be assembled.[10] Of all these, only a few do not merely repeat previous definitions and explanations, and still fewer say enough to be of real consequence. Among the latter the most influential were the article "Sonate" by Rousseau that was first published in 1755 in Diderot's great *Encyclopédie* (1751-72),[11] the article "Sonate" by J. A. P. Schulz that was first published in 1775 in Sulzer/ALLGEMEINE II/2 688-689,[12] the section

8. As quoted in Straeten/VIOLONCELLO 297.

9. There is too little evidence for the identification of this term with a particular style, as implied in Torrefranca/ORIGINI 684.

10. The dictionaries are listed in Coover/LEXICOGRAPHY. A list of theory and related treatises is appended (pp. 167-168) to the first of 2 fruitful articles dealing with the recognition of form problems during the Classic Era, Ratner/HARMONIC and Ratner/THEORIES. Previously, this same topic had been explored with special regard to "sonata form" in Newman/THEORISTS.

11. Vol. XV, p. 348. The identical article is more accessible in Rousseau/DICTIONNAIRE II 217-219.

12. On Schulz's authorship, cf. Riess/SCHULZ 189-194.

"Von der Sonate" published in 1793 in Koch/ANLEITUNG III 315-319, and the article "Sonate" published in 1802 in Koch/LEXIKON 1415-1417.[13] To be sure, the early sources yield considerably more in their definitions and explanations of the Classic symphony[14] than of the sonata, not to mention what they contain on other forms like the concerto and quartet. But while the symphony references often bear significantly on the sonata, we shall find them even more interesting for their frequently explicit distinctions between the two forms.

In the survey that follows, our representative definitions of "sonata" are arranged largely in chronological order, whereas the representative explanations are grouped according to the procedures of style and form that each introduces.

The late-Baroque Era had still subscribed to nothing more concrete or up-to-date in its definitions of "sonata" than emphases on the fantasy element, on the "alternating adagio and allegro" sections, and on the distinction between *da chiesa* and *da camera* types, as discussed chiefly by Brossard and Mattheson earlier in the eighteenth century (SBE 24-27). Mizler, J. S. Bach's learned pupil in Leipzig, said of the sonata, in 1742, only that its purpose is to be pleasing and agreeable.[15] And in the same year the Barcelona theorist Francisco Valls simply lumped it with most of the other current instrumental types under "Estilo Phantástico," in his *Mapa armónico*.[16] Tans'ur in England described it in 1746 as "A Composition only for Instruments."[17] Corrette in Paris called it in 1753 "a suite of 3 or 4 pieces in the same key."[18] Albrecht in central Germany did no more than to copy verbatim in 1761 the bit that J. G. Walther had copied verbatim in 1732 from Mattheson in 1713, about the "alternating adagio and allegro" sections and a preference for violin.[19] And Marpurg in Leipzig merely combined Corrette's and Albrecht's definitions when he observed in 1762 that the movements marked with contrasting tempos often sounded quite like the allemande, courante, and gigue.[20]

13. A wholly new article replaced this last in the better known 2d ed. by Dommer, published in 1865. Koch's contributions are discussed, with emphasis on their prime importance to the understanding of Classic phrase-and-period syntax, in Fétis/BU V 69-70; Riemann/PRÄLUDIEN II 56-70; and Ratner/THEORIES.

14. Sondheimer/THEORIE is a valuable synthesis of much of this material; indexed by J. LaRue & G. Wolf in AM XXXVII (1965) 79-86.

15. Mizler/BIBLIOTHEK II/3 102.

16. Cf. Cat. MADRID I 197, 193. Earlier applications of this term to the son. are cited in SBE 46.

17. Tans'ur/GRAMMAR 153.

18. Corrette/CLAVECIN 92.

19. Albrecht/TONKUNST 121; cf. SBE 26-27. "A species of composition adapted to the violin" is the conservative definition still supplied in the "Index" at the end of Hawkins' *History* (1776).

20. Marpurg/CLAVIERSTÜCKE-m I 5-6.

Meanwhile Rousseau's more extended article of 1755 had appeared. It begins by defining the sonata as

an instrumental piece consisting of three or four consecutive movements of different character. The *sonata* is to instruments about what the cantata is to voices.

The *sonata* is usually composed for a single instrument that plays [while being] accompanied by a *basso continuo*; and in such a piece one seizes upon whatever is the most favorable for showing off the chosen instrument, whether the contour of the lines, the selection of the tones that best suit this sort of instrument, or the boldness of the execution. There are also trio *Sonatas,* which the Italians more commonly call *Sinfonie;* but when they [the sonatas] exceed three parts or one of these is a solo part, they [the sonatas] are called [by the name] concerto.[21]

Then, after going back to Brossard's distinction between the *da chiesa* and *da camera* types, Rousseau shifts to some interesting but negative views of a more general nature, to be noted later in this chapter.

Schulz's article of 1775 became such a standard reference and, in spite of its north German orientation, brought together enough of the views on the sonata expressed by Classic writers, that it deserves to be translated in full here:[22]

Sonata. An instrumental piece [consisting] of two, three, or four successive movements of different character, which has one or more melody parts, with only one player to a part [i.e., "einfach" as against Mattheson's "stark," for multiple performance of the parts; cf. SBE 25]. Depending on the number of *concertante,* melody parts that it has, a sonata is described as [being] *à solo, à due, à tré,* etc.

Clearly, in no form of instrumental music is there a better opportunity than in the sonata to depict feelings without [the aid of] words. The symphony [and] the overture have a more fixed character. The form of a concerto seems designed more to give a skilled player a chance to be heard against the background of many instruments than to implement the depiction of violent emotions. Aside from these [forms] and the dances, which also have their special characters, there remains only the form of the sonata, which assumes [any or] all characters and every [kind of] expression. By [means of] the sonata the composer can hope to produce a monologue through tones of melancholy, grief, sorrow, tenderness, or delight and joy; or maintain a sensitive dialogue solely through impassioned tones of similar or different qualities; or simply depict emotions [that are] violent, impetuous, and [sharply] contrasted, or light, gentle, fluent, and pleasing. To be sure, [even] the weakest composers have such goals in the making of sonatas, among the weakest [being] the Italians and those who imitate them. The sonatas of the present-day Italians are characterized by a bustle of sounds succeeding each other arbitrarily without any other purpose than to gratify the insensitive ear of the layman, [and] by sudden, fantastic transitions

21. Trans. from Rousseau/DICTIONNAIRE II 217.
22. From Sulzer/ALLGEMEINE II/2 688-689.

from the joyous to the mournful, from the pathetic to the flirtatious, without our getting what the composer wants [to say]. And if the performance of these [sonatas] engages the fancy of a few hotheads, the heart and imagination of every listener of taste or understanding will still remain completely untouched.

A large number of easy and hard keyboard [i.e., clavichord] sonatas by our Hamburg [Emanuel] Bach show how character and expression can be brought to the sonata. The majority of these are so communicative ["sprechend"] that one believes [himself] to be perceiving not tones but a distinct speech, which sets and keeps in motion our imagination and feelings. Unquestionably, to create such sonatas requires much genius [and] knowledge, and an especially adaptable and alert sensibility. But they also require a highly expressive performance, which no German-Italian is conditioned to achieve, but which is often achieved by children, who become accustomed early to such sonatas. Likewise, this composer's sonatas for two *concertante* melody parts with bass accompaniment are truly impassioned tone dialogues. Whoever fails to experience or perceive this [quality] in these [trios] should realize that they are not always played as they should be. Among these is one printed in Nürnberg [W. 161/1] that carries on [just] such a dialogue between a Melancholicus and a Sanguineus, which [work] is so remarkable and so full of invention and character that one can regard it as a masterpiece of fine instrumental music. Embryonic composers who hope to succeed with sonatas must take those of Bach and others like them as models.

For players of instruments, sonatas are the most usual and the best exercises. Moreover, there are lots of easy and hard ones for all instruments. After vocal pieces they hold first place in chamber music. And, since they require only one player to a part, they can be played in the smallest music society [or association] without much ceremony. A single artist can often entertain a whole society with a keyboard sonata better and more effectively than [can] the largest ensemble.

Sonatas with two melody parts and a *concertante* or simple accompanying bass are more fully discussed in the article [on the] trio.

We shall return shortly to the aesthetic considerations advanced by Schulz. His article already seems to have influenced the one-paragraph definition of "Sonate" penned by Schubart about 1785, with its emphasis on the "intimate and sociable" conversation of three (rather than two) parts.[23] Schubart also noted the appropriateness of the "arioso, cantabile, recitative, and all kinds of songful and instrumental music" to the sonata, as well as the need for adapting this genre to the particular medium for which it is scored. Türk's discussion of more than a page on the sonata, published in 1789,[24] shows Schulz's influence, too, by its stress on the sonata's special capabilities for varied and intense expression as though through speech. And it shows the influence of an article of 1784 by Forkel to which we shall return, through its com-

23. Schubart/IDEEN 360.
24. Türk/KLAVIERSCHULE 390-391.

parison of the sonata with the literary ode and of the way both depend on law and order for their unity. But Türk introduces new concepts with regard to the setting, especially when he begins, "The sonata belongs in the first place—indeed, with the utmost right—among the compositions designed for the keyboard [i.e., clavichord]." He also mentions, along with sonatas *a due* and *a tre,* those with optional or obbligato accompaniments, those for four hands at one or two instruments (the latter being "Doppelsonaten"), and the little sonata known as a "Sonatine." A little later,[25] Türk notes Sulzer's (i.e., Schulz's) likening of the symphony to an instrumental chorus and the sonata to an instrumental (solo) cantata. Schulz had added that the main line of the sonata, played by only one performer, permits if not demands more ornamentation than the lines played by more than one performer in the symphony; also, that the latter was not "a practice piece like the sonata."[26] Türk suggests somewhat inconsistently that while symphonies for keyboard are rare they are not objectionable in principle and might be used by unskilled players as a means of advancing to larger pieces and an understanding of the "true sonata style."

In 1793 Koch amplified Schulz's article on the sonata's various settings, quoted it on the sonata's adaptability to a full range of expression, and extended the distinction between symphony and sonata to that between a direct symphonic drive and an intimate, sensitive chamber style.[27] He showed a knowledge of Mattheson's and Türk's writings, too, when he went on to complain about the modern, empty sonatas that are "overladen with bluster and difficulties" and are designed for the fingers rather than the heart—that is, for the astonishment of the public and dilettantes rather than for the expression of feelings by connoisseurs. Among the relatively conservative models Koch still cited were the sonatas for keyboard by Emanuel Bach and Türk, for violin by F. Benda, and for flute by Quantz. His important remarks about structure will be noted presently. But we may add here that his dictionary definition of 1802 summarizes all the same general facts and views, and again quotes Schulz.[28] Its main changes are the incorporation of Forkel's ideas on unity and the addition of Haydn and Mozart as models, with only Emanuel Bach retained among the former names. The definition supplied in 1799 by Kollmann, the German organist in London, follows in the same line from Schulz to Türk to Koch without adding any new concepts.[29]

25. Türk/KLAVIERSCHULE 392.
26. Sulzer/ALLGEMEINE II/2 724-725.
27. Koch/ANLEITUNG III 292-293, 315-319.
28. Koch/LEXIKON 1415-1417.
29. Kollmann/ESSAY 9-15.

Some Explanations (Koch)

As for explanations of the Classic sonata's structure, we shall find that Koch's came the closest. Yet at no time during the Classic Era itself did theorists provide comprehensive discussions that take in both the cycle and the single movements, including a systematic treatment of melody types, phrase syntax, bridges, dualistic opposition of themes, "developments," recapitulations, codas, tonal plans, and over-all designs. When A. B. Marx and Czerny finally did publish such discussions,
30a around 1840-50 and for the first time, as Czerny himself asserted,[30] they
succeeded above all in establishing the fixed, textbook concept of "sonata form" that has prevailed ever since. Undoubtedly some such concept existed considerably earlier. In 1803 the Swiss publisher Nägeli referred to a "usual sonata form" when he invited contributions to his forthcoming anthology, *Repertoire des clavecinistes:*[31]

> I am interested primarily in piano solos in the grand manner, of large extent, and with manifold departures from the usual sonata form. Wealth of detail and full texture ought to distinguish these products. Contrapuntal movements must be impregnated with artistic figures for the pianist. Whoever possesses no skill in the art of counterpoint and at the same time is no piano virtuoso will hardly be able to achieve much here.[32]

At least, one gets some idea, from this excerpt, of what the "usual sonata form" was thought not to be. Yet, in the last years of Clementi and Beethoven, most well-reputed writers on music, like Castil-Blaze (1825) and Frederick Schneider (1828),[33] still had nothing more comprehensive and finite to say about what "sonata form" did consist of than the authors who wrote before 1800, in the publications already noted. Needless to say, there is no artistic reason why any conscious recognition of "sonata form" had to precede the composing of Classic sonatas. The sequence of theory before practice would be rare, of course, in the healthiest stages of any art form.[34] Moreover, one gathers from a letter of 1777 written by Emanuel Bach that the teaching of form analysis at that time was generally neglected.[35] But there is even less reason for later writers to impute a conscious recognition of a particular "sonata form" in the Classic Era[36] when no evidence for such a concept can be found.

30. Cf. Newman/THEORISTS 21-22, 28-29.
31. Anth. NÄGELI-m; cf. Newman/THIRTEEN-m 18-19.
32. Trans. from AMZ V (1802-03) Intelligenz-Blatt 97.
33. Schneider/ELEMENTS 120-121; Castil-Blaze/DICTIONNAIRE II 271-272.
34. The often unconscious nature of the composing process is well demonstrated in a recent article, Walker/MOTIVATION.
35. The letter is printed in Bitter/BRÜDER I 348 and trans. in Bach/ESSAY 441.
36. As in Barford/FORMALISM 207.

On the other hand, here and there in Classic writings explanations do occur of individual sonata traits that might be assembled into a fair anticipation of that nineteenth-century concept of "sonata form"—that is, everything but its relative inflexibility. We may take note of those explanations by starting with remarks about the number, order, and interrelationship of the movements, then proceeding to aspects of the individual movements.

Rousseau's, Schulz's, and Kollmann's mentions of from two to four movements of different character in the sonata added only a little to Mattheson's mention in 1713 of "alternating adagio and allegro sections." But Scheibe in 1740 and Quantz in 1752 had already outlined such favorite Baroque cycles as those in the order S(low)-F(ast)-S-F, S-F-F, or S-F-minuet, as well as the F-S-F cycle to be found in the concerto and Italian sinfonia.[37] Within another generation recognition of the F-S-F plan as the one most commonly associated with the sonata was evidenced in a letter, dated April 1, 1773, from Friedrich Bach in Bückeburg to the poet Gerstenberg:[38]

> As to why our sonatas must have two fast movements and one slow [one], I know no other way to answer than this: A fugue is called a fugue precisely because it is worked out according to the prescribed rules. An old *clavecin suite* would not have been so named if our elders were not pleased to call such a compilation of *prelude, allemande,* and the remaining movements a *suite pour le clavecin.* I understand just as little why the order in this sort of composition must progress from the *preludio* to the *allemande,* then to the *currente, sarabanda,* and finally the *gigue.*

In 1787 the French writer and composer Lacépède compared the three movements of a sonata or symphony to the "noble" first act, "more pathetic" second act, and "more tumultuous" third act of a drama.[39] By 1793 Koch left no doubt that he thought of the F-S-F plan as the standard one for the sonata, being like the symphony plan when no minuet was inserted before the finale.[40] In 1797 Grétry noted the F-S-F plan as being almost invariable and asked why the first movement could not be exchanged with the finale, since the former, or "Allegro maestoso," is "the more pompous."[41] Not until 1838 was the plan F-S-minuet-F identified as a standard Classic sonata plan.[42]

The interrelationship of movements in sonata cycles received little

37. Scheibe/CRITISCHER 675-682; Quantz/VERSUCH 301-305.

38. Trans. from the complete letter as quoted by Schünemann in BJ XIII (1916) 21-22.

39. As quoted in La Laurencie/ÉCOLE III 202.

40. Koch/ANLEITUNG III 318-319 and 314-315.

41. Trans. from Vol. III, p. 427, of the reprint of the *Mémoires,* as quoted in La Laurencie/ÉCOLE III 203.

42. Schilling/LEXICON VI 420.

attention from writers beyond the requirement of contrast. Quantz expanded this principle sufficiently to say that the second allegro in the S-F-F plan should differ in meter and character from the first, so that if one were "lively and fast" the other might be "moderate and arioso."[43] Friedrich Bach, in the letter of 1773 just quoted, doubted the value of trying to unify a sonata through a specific verbal program, whether in the SS/bass trio his brother Emanuel had composed (the same that Schulz mentioned) or a sonata on Cleopatra that Gerstenberg evidently was planning to write. On the other hand, Forkel did not object to an analogy between a sonata's three movements and the state of man progressing from melancholy to happiness, or vice versa.[44] However, no one seems to have expressed much interest in the scarcely accidental interrelationship of movements through similar incipits that we shall be encountering now and then from the pre-Classic Era right through Beethoven. About all one finds is a statement such as the French writer Brijon made in 1763 after finding fault with French opera for a lack of connection between the "entr'acte airs" and the previous scene: "But this same lack of liaison and analogy is still less justifiable in a piece as prescribed [unaided by a text?] as is a symphony, a sonata, or a concerto."[45]

With regard to any explanations of the movements, not a few writers were satisfied merely to classify the sonata under a heading like the "Estilo Phantástico" used by Valls and previous writers. The German-Dutch organist and theorist J. W. Lustig (SCE XXI) simply threw the sonata in with the solo, concerto, symphonie, and "caprice," in 1751, as a form wholly subject to the composer's fancy.[46] And it is interesting that in the but four or five instances that Burney troubled to comment on a particular *"sonata"* (always still italicized as a foreignism) in his travel reports of the early 1770's, he found no more to remark about it than its "spirited" and "brilliant passages."[47] Indeed, most of the ostensibly more fruitful and systematic explanations of the sonata by Classic writers amount to nothing more than expatiations of such generalities at a higher sounding level of aesthetic argument. Schulz and Türk were seen to be not free from this sort of argument.[48] But the most bloated, pompous example is the oft-cited article of seventeen pages by Forkel that grows out of a favorable review of Emanuel

43. Quantz/VERSUCH 304-305.
44. Forkel/ALMANACH III (1784) 32.
45. Trans. from Brijon/MUSIQUE 4.
46. Lustig/INLEIDING 332-333.
47. E.g., BURNEY'S TOURS II 117.
48. It permeates Schulz's article on the symphony, too (Sulzer/ALLGEMEINE II/2 724-726).

Bach's Sonata in f, W. 57/6.[49] To be summarized under Forkel (SCE XVI), this article employs the analogies of the literary ode, of the laws of rhetoric and logic, and of the state of man (as just noted) to "explain" the sonata. When the reader finishes reading it, he has gained little more than a truism to the effect that however fine a composer's ideas may be, his sonata still must be unified by the logic, good taste, and inspiration that only the great masters command.[50]

The occasional attempts by such aesthetically minded authors to employ the technical language of music usually resulted in descriptions of styles rather than structures, as in Quantz's comments in 1752 on melody, texture, tempo and mood (SBE 278); or in V. Manfredini's explanation in 1775 of a free, motivic process applicable to all other genres as well as the sonata.[51] But the consideration of the sonata by the theorists who were more matter-of-fact in their treatment, without any inclination toward aesthetic discussions, often proves to be only a short traditional course in the detailed problems of realizing a thorough-bass as these arise in the most characteristic melo/bass settings. In the second volume of Löhlein's *Clavier-Schule,* not published until 1781, the reader is guided patiently through the composition of six Vn/bass sonatas for the sole purpose of showing how to construct a melody over an unfigured bass. In Kirnberger's brief pamphlet of 1783 entitled "Method for Tossing Off Sonatas" (trans. in full in SCE XIII), the curious short cut that he proposes grows directly out of thorough-bass practice. And as late as 1806 and 1808, the French composition treatises of Momigny and Choron, respectively, still come little closer to the structure of the sonata than the thorough-bass and other textural problems posed by its melo/bass settings.[52] 52a

All of this is not to say that there was no recognition of design as such by theorists of the Classic Era. A fair number of references to design can be cited. But these seldom go into any detail and they seldom appear in conjunction with the sonata. Unfortunately, the frequent analogies with the ode in poetry cannot be interpreted literally enough to have any direct bearing on the designs of sonata movements. In 1763, after observing that independent instrumental music could be just as picturesque, pathetic, or imposing as music set to words, Brijon

49. Forkel/ALMANACH III (1784) 22-38.

50. In 1778, in Forkel/BIBLIOTHEK II 278, the same need for unity had been emphasized more briefly, in the course of another long review of E. Bach's sons., this time those in the acc'd. sets W. 90/1-3 and 91/1-4.

51. Manfredini/REGOLE 103-106.

52. Momigny/COURS II 548-553, 698-699 (with comments on recent piano sons.); Choron/PRINCIPES III/6 36 (with a reference to I/2 26-35; cf. Newman/THEORISTS 27).

distinguished the "sonata en *solo*" by its sectional divisions, regarding it as "a type of work that one might call an ode in music."[53] In 1775 Schulz likened an emotive symphony allegro to a Pindaric ode.[54] But in the analogies made by Forkel and Türk (noted previously) neither writer attempted to specify even the type of ode and Türk was careful to insert that an exact comparison was not possible, what with the ode's variety and smaller size.[55] In our final chapter we shall come to a strong sonata by H. O. C. Zink in Copenhagen that he said was inspired by an ode of Stolberg he had set recently, but that certainly shows no structural influence from the purely strophic (or Horatian) form of that ode.

In 1739, in conjunction with the symphony, Scheibe had given a succinct description of the familiar binary design that obtains in so much Baroque instrumental music. The description includes an initial idea, followed by passages or related ideas that lead to a cadence in the dominant or relative key at the repeat sign; a return to this idea at the start of the "second section"; and a general parallelism of the two sections up to a convincing cadence in the home key, although modulations and cadences in foreign keys are permitted "in the middle."[56] Quantz took briefer notice of binary design while describing the first allegro in the S-F-F cycle of a "solo," including the observation that "the first part must be somewhat shorter than the last."[57] In 1757 the Madrid violinist José Herrando called binary design indispensable, adding that the double-bars or repeat signs "are to mark the middle of sonatas, concertos, overtures, minuets, and trios."[58] Tacit recognition of a binary concept is found in the remarks by two composers about observing the repeats. Emanuel Bach called these last "mandatory" when he wrote out the "varied repetitions" in his sonatas of 1760 (W. 50/1-6).[59] Since the allegro movements in these sonatas usually have a clear recapitulation, the design that actually results most of the time is A-A′-B-A-B′-A′. On the other hand, Grétry argued in 1797 against the sense of repeating "each half" (as quoted under Hüllmandel in SCE XVIII). In 1808 Choron still seemed to be thinking in terms of the binary design as described by Scheibe.[60] And, of course, there have been many writers ever since who have preferred to interpret "sonata form" in a binary sense.[61]

53. Brijon/MUSIQUE 2.
54. Sulzer/ALLGEMEINE II/2 725.
55. Türk/KLAVIERSCHULE 390.
56. Scheibe/CRITISCHER 628-629.
57. Quantz/VERSUCH 304.
58. As quoted in Subirá/ALBA 173.
59. Most of his preface is trans. in Bach/ESSAY 166.
60. Choron/PRINCIPES III/6 36.
61. Cf. Ratner/HARMONIC 163.

Ternary design was recognized, too, as it had been far back in the Baroque Era.[62] The Austrian theorist Joseph Riepel printed the upper line of a symphony allegro "by a [German or Italian] master" in which the "beginning of the second part" and the recapitulation are clearly indicated and the latter is duly noted by the pupil.[63] Vogler showed only a slight recognition of an independent "development section" in 1778.[64] But as early as 1770 Reichardt and Schulz seemed to have been thoroughly conscious of the recapitulation as being *"comme il faut"* in sonata movements of the Berlin school (according to Reichardt's own recollection, as quoted in SCE XVI). Furthermore, a ternary interpretation of the tonal scheme is usually evident in late-eighteenth-century writings even when the author still speaks of two sections. Thus, starting with a sentence that shows how important the tonal concept was to the Classic theorist, the German pedagogue J. G. Portmann wrote in 1789:

> The plan or outline of a musical piece is [found in] the skillful arrangement of the main and subordinate keys, the order of these, what comes first, and [what] ought to follow next, thirdly, [and] fourthly. For example, I shall make the outline for the allegro of a keyboard sonata in D. Thus, I establish the main key of D, in which I begin and [from which I] modulate. After this I veer toward the dominant . . . and cadence therein. This [much] constitutes the outline of the first section of the allegro. In the other section I begin with more remote modulations . . . these then take me back to D, in which [key] I repeat the [main] theme and my melodic materials and passages . . . already heard in the subordinate key. I remain and conclude there [in the home key].[65]

Much the same was written still more explicitly by Koch in 1787 and 1793, and, in a more involved way, by Kollmann in 1799.[66]

Certain Classic theorists, notably Koch again, did prove to be fully articulate about problems of syntax, especially phrase-and-period relationships, in the music of their time. In other words, they explored form most successfully by approaching it from this local level rather than by attempting to formulize it in one over-all design. Although their explanations of syntax were seldom made in immediate conjunction with the sonata, there is no doubt about a direct application of the explana-

62. E.g., Printz in *Phrynis* I, Chap. IX, par. 24 (1676) [information kindly supplied by the late Dr. Herman Reichenbach]; Mattheson in *Neu-eröffnete Orchestre*, pp. 170-171 (1713).

63. Riepel/TONORDNUNG 72-74.

64. As quoted in Sondheimer/THEORIE 44 from *Mannheimer Tonschule* II 62.

65. Trans. from the excerpt quoted in Ratner/HARMONIC 161 from Portmann's *Leichtes Lehrbuch der Harmonie*, p. 50.

66. In Ratner/HARMONIC 160-162, three pertinent extracts are quoted from Koch/ANLEITUNG II 223-226, III 311 and 342 (cf., also, III 318-319); and one from Kollmann/ESSAY 5.

tions to the latter. This aspect of Classic form has been illuminated in a fine article by Leonard Ratner, from which the following paragraph largely draws.[67]

Classic theorists were not slow to observe essential syntactic changes in the continuous motivic style that had characterized late-Baroque writing. Marpurg referred in 1763 to the many cadences, and Kirnberger in 1775 to the short phrases, found anywhere and everywhere in the light *galant* style.[68] In the last quarter of the eighteenth century theorists like Kirnberger, Koch, Portmann, and Daube took increasing note of the analogy between phrase syntax and such relationships as the subject and predicate in rhetoric, a favorite musical example being the question-answer complementation of a pair of phrases ending in a half- and full-cadence.[69] Illustrations of how to build phrases into periods and thence into sections usually began with the making of dances, where the simplest and most regular relationships prevailed (4 + 4 mss., 8 + 8, etc.).[70] Löhlein's use of the minuet for this purpose, in 1765, was typical (SCE XII). Ratner develops the important point that Koch used the dance with good musical justification as the starting point for explaining larger forms. Koch actually showed, among many other illustrations, how the material in a regular period of two 4-measure phrases could be extended by repetitions, extensions, sequences, and interpolations into a section of 32 measures.[71] His most detailed explanation of a large form in this manner is that of the first movement of a symphony.[72] Since this explanation in 1793 surpasses any comparable one by other Classic theorists, since it includes some references to differences in the sonata, and since Koch refers back to it in his discussion of the separate sonata movements (p. 318), it calls for a summary paraphrase and some actual translation here (insofar as its involute sentences can be parsed).

The initial allegro, says Koch, is in two sections that may or may not have repeat signs. The first section [or "exposition," in nineteenth-century terminology] contains the main idea in its original form and is a single division lasting up to the cadence in the new key.

67. Ratner/THEORIES, with extracts in trans. and with exx.

68. Marpurg/BRIEFE II 13-14; Sulzer/ALLGEMEINE II/1 226-227 (in the original ed.; regarding Kirnberger's authorship, cf. Riess/SCHULZ 189-194).

69. Cf. Ratner/THEORIES 441-443.

70. Cf. Ratner/THEORIES 443-445.

71. Koch/ANLEITUNG III 226-230. Cf. Ratner/THEORIES 449-451, with Koch's complete ex.

72. Koch/ANLEITUNG III 304-311. One of the earliest ms.-by-ms. analyses, in the manner of program notes, is that published in 1806 on the first mvt. of Haydn's "Drum Roll" Symphony in E♭, H. I/103, in Momigny/COURS II 583-606 and III 245-292 (full score).

> The construction of this section (as with the other sections of the symphony) differs from that of the sonata and the concerto not in the keys to which one modulates [and] not in any special succession or alternation of full- or half-cadences, but in the fact that 1) the melodic ideas are likely to be more extended at their first appearance than in other pieces, and, especially, 2) that these melodic ideas usually relate more to each other and stream forth more compellingly than in the sections of other pieces—that is, they are so drawn together that their cadences are less perceptible.[73]

To continue the paraphrase of Koch, often there is no cadential break, until the nearly related key is attained, whether dominant or relative, and "the rushing, sonorous theme gives way to a more songful theme, generally played with diminished force." Including the third melodic element ["closing theme"?], "the second and largest half of this first section" is in the nearly related key. In the "newer symphonies" this first section often has a slow, serious introduction that differs from the *grave* of the [French] overture in being tied to no one meter or pattern, and cadences in the main key or its dominant after optional modulations.

The second section has two main divisions, Koch continues, of which the first [or "development," in nineteenth-century terminology] has many forms but may be reduced to two chief kinds. Most often this division starts with a literal, inverted, or otherwise altered statement of the main or other theme in the dominant or more remote key (or, if the home key is minor, in the relative major key when the first section ended on the minor dominant, and in the minor dominant when it ended on the relative). After an optional restatement in the home key, some one or more of the melodic ideas are sequenced, repeated, or otherwise expanded and dissected in the course of modulations that may touch on the submediant, supertonic, or mediant keys in the opposite mode and generally lead through a short retransition of like nature back to the home key.

In the other kind of division [or "development"], Koch continues (all in one sentence), some effective theme from the first section, or only an element of it, may be so extended, transposed, or dissected, within the same voice or by exchange with other voices, that it gradually modulates through near and remote keys until the home key is restored at the end of this division, or until the dominant key is reached, after which a return is made that derives from the first section. This kind of division, says Koch, occurs in many symphonies by Haydn and most by Dittersdorf.

The final section ["recapitulation," in nineteenth-century termi-

73. Trans. from Koch/ANLEITUNG III 305-306.

nology] gives preference to the home key, Koch concludes, and "starts most often with the [main] theme, though sometimes with another melodic idea." The preferred ideas are brought together and a modulation is generally made to the subdominant key, but without a cadence and with an early return to the home key. The allegro now ends with the repetition in the home key of the "latter half" of the first section [or "exposition"] from the point where the dominant key was reached.

The flexibility of Koch's explanation of first-movement form in the symphony should be apparent in the foregoing paraphrase and would be even more so in a literal, full translation. His distinction between the symphony and the sonata relates to a similar one between symphonic and chamber styles that we shall have several occasions to observe.[74] A somewhat similar distinction had already been suggested by Avison in 1764 (SCE XIX). Also worth noting is his tangential recognition of a contrasting, gentler idea, yet his tendency still to think of only one main theme, and of tonal movement as the all-controlling force. Note, too, his reference to dissective and imitative techniques as well as mere restatement and transposition in the "development" section, and his disinclination to detail the start of the "recapitulation" exactly and unequivocally. Just such latitudes help to suggest why the nineteenth-century textbook version of "sonata form" can be a distorted measure of progress and why it makes too rigid a concept of Classic sonata form.

Not only Koch's but earlier allusions to a contrasting theme have been singled out by seekers of "sonata form." Thus, as early as 1755, Riepel illustrated and commented on a soft contrasting idea and its recapitulation in a symphony movement.[75] In 1778, Vogler was more specific: "In the symphony there are usually two main themes, the first being the stronger, which supplies the material for development ["Ausführung"], the second being the gentler, which relieves the heated commotion and bolsters the ear with a pleasing contrast."[76] Burney, supposing Christian Bach "to have been the first composer who observed the law of *contrast,* as a *principle,*" said that "his symphonies and other instrumental pieces, as well as his songs, seldom failed, after a rapid and noisy passage to introduce one that was slow and soothing."[77]

But such relatively isolated statements need to be countered with a larger number of others that oppose any contrasting ideas. The article by Schulz that was quoted earlier, in full, emphasized the special stand

74. The distinction is restated and amplified in Koch/ANLEITUNG III 319.
75. Riepel/TONORDNUNG 83-86.
76. Trans. from *Mannheimer Tonschule* II 62 as quoted in Sondheimer/THEORIE 44.
77. Burney/HISTORY II 866-867 (cf. C. Bach in SCE XIX).

that north German writers took on this question by decrying "the sudden, fantastic transitions from the joyous to the mournful, from the pathetic to the flirtatious," in the "sonatas of the present-day Italians." In 1763 Marpurg objected to a second theme in a Symphony in B♭ by Galuppi as sounding like the start of a new symphony without an end to the previous one.[78] The dramatist and critic Lessing wrote, about 1768, "A symphony that expresses different, contradictory passions in its different themes is a musical atrocity; in a symphony only one passion must prevail."[79] Reichardt wrote some 15 years later,

> . . . instead of contenting oneself each time with the expression and the representation of [but] one of these passions [joy or sadness], one mixes the two in a most improper manner in order to show both styles of performance in each instance. Thus originate the most outlandish sonatas, symphonies, concertos, and other pieces in our newer music.[80] 80a

In 1813 Gerber was still referring to previous north German tastes when he gave high praise to the way Haydn wrote symphonies out of "a single main theme," calling this process "the *non plus ultra* in the newest art, the highest and most admirable in instrumental composition."[81]

With regard to the remaining movements of the sonata, eighteenth-century writers found as little to say in direct connection with the over-all cycle as later writers have found. Again Koch wrote more than most, and again he referred the reader to his remarks on the symphony.[82] The "andante or adagio," he says, may simply be in the older binary design with optional repeats, or it may be expanded into something like the three divisions of the first movement except for the less developed treatment of the material that is to be expected in a slower, more expressive movement. Rondo form and variations on a binary andante or adagio melody of sixteen to twenty measures are other possibilities mentioned for this movement. The finale may be like the first movement or it may be in the form of a rondo, or of variations on a dance tune or allegro idea, with episodes interspersed in related keys, in rondo fashion, Koch concludes.

78. Marpurg/BRIEFE II 172.
79. Trans. from *Dramaturgie*, "27. Stücke," as quoted in Päfflin/NARDINI 51.
80. Trans. from Reichardt/KUNSTMAGAZIN I 25. Further quotations illustrating north German objections to more than one *Affekt* in a single piece may be found in Stilz/BERLINER 86-88, 93-96, 118; Sondheimer/THEORIE 34-35; Dennerlein/REICHARDT 93 (from Spazier); Reeser/SONS 40 (from Cramer/MAGAZIN).
81. AMZ XV (1813) 457-463.
82. Koch/ANLEITUNG III 318-319 and 311-315 (symphony).

Some Attitudes and Tastes

When the Classic writers expressed any attitude at all toward the sonata as an art form it was more likely than not to be one of disparagement. Such an attitude reflected, first, a hostility toward instrumental music that still persisted in certain areas, especially France, through the eighteenth century. And it reflected, second, the resistance to progress that is all too familiar to composers of every era. The hostility toward instrumental music in France must be regarded as one kind of resistance to progress in itself, in that it grew as one of the more remote by-products of the quarrel between the ancients and the moderns that the protagonists of both sides kept alive chiefly within that country.[83] In the later, more significant part of Rousseau's article of 1755 on the sonata appeared one of the most representative and influential statements. It includes an early reference to the flippant remark credited to Fontenelle, "Sonate, que me veux-tu?" which remark has never been traced to a written source but was to be much quoted in the writing on music of the next century.[84]

> Now that instruments are making most of today's music, *sonatas* are very much in style, as is every sort of instrumental ensemble [*Symphonie*]. Vocal music is scarcely more than an accessory, and the singing accompanies the accompaniment [probably referring to Mondonville's *Pièces de clavecin avec voix ou violon,* Op. 5, published about 7 years earlier]. We get this [example of] bad taste from those who, wishing to introduce the Italian style of music into a language not susceptible to it, have made us try to do with instruments that which is impossible for us to do with our voices. I dare to predict that such an unnatural taste will not last. Music [that is] purely harmonic [or absolute] is of little consequence. As a means of giving continuing pleasure and of preventing boredom it should be raised to the status of the arts of imitation [or imagery]. But its imitation is not always tangible like that of poetry and painting. The word most often determines the object of the image that music gives us. And it is through the affecting sounds of the human voice that this image arouses the feeling at the bottom of the heart that it ought to arouse. Who does not realize how far from this capability is mere instrumental music, in which one only seeks to show off the instruments? Do all the follies for violin by Mondonville move me the way [but] two sounds from the voice of Mademoiselle le Maure do? Instrumental music enhances the singing and adds to its expression, but it does not replace it. To clarify the meaning of all this jumble of sonatas that overwhelms us, one would have to do as the inept painter did who had to write below his figures, "this is a tree," "this is a man," "this is a horse." I shall never forget the quip of the celebrated Fontenelle, who, finding himself worn out with these eternal instrumental pieces, exclaimed aloud in a fit of

83. Schueller/QUARREL provides an informative discussion of the musical consequences of that quarrel, with emphasis on its repercussions in Great Britain. Cf., also, SBE 30-32.

84. Cf. SBE 353; also, d'Alembert's statement near the start of SCE XVII.

impatience, "Sonata, what do you want of me? [i.e., what good are you to me?]"[85] 85a

In another generation Grétry was to put an answer to Fontenelle's rhetorical question into the mouths of Haydn and Boccherini: "We want a soul and you have but a mind *composed of epigrams and schemes.*"[86] And by the start of the Romantic Era, as will be seen early in our next volume, the attitude toward instrumental music's suitability for imagery was fully reversed. Yet, if Rousseau was fighting a losing battle and if the sonata was, in fact, gaining hold almost everywhere, there were others who saw less chance of its surviving. In fact, as in the Baroque Era, there was a continuing stream of negativists who insisted or implied that the sonata had spent itself. Thus, around 1734 Mondonville himself had written in the dedication to his accompanied clavecin sonatas, Op. 3, "For several years such a prodigious number of sonatas of all types have been brought to light that there is no one who does not believe this genre is exhausted" (SCE XVII). Quantz wrote in 1752, "Today one sees no art [any more] in composing a solo [S/bass son.]."[87] And in 1799, soon after the first review of a Beethoven piano sonata, Rochlitz (?) wrote that "Good piano sonatas are written less often now than formerly."[88]

But even granting the myopia in such statements, one cannot fail to recognize what a small share of the total musical interest the sonata aroused in the eighteenth century, at least among the more articulate writers. In the accounts of the principal travelers and observers—including Burney, Schubart, and Reichardt—it got little but incidental and passing mentions amidst long discussions of the opera and church music that preoccupied the courts at Paris, Mannheim, Berlin, Dresden, London, Vienna, and other main centers. How, after all, could the sonata compete in entertainment value with the charms of a *Così fan tutte* or even of much less worthy operas? Occasionally a writer dropped a remark that suggested a lowly status for the sonata in a more specific way. In 1740, Scheibe had declared it to be of less consequence than the symphony, concerto, or overture.[89] J. W. Hässler said in 1786, "Mere keyboard sonatas I shall not be writing so much anymore, since I am urged on all sides to [compose] more important works."[90]

85. Trans. from Rousseau/DICTIONNAIRE 218-219.

86. Trans. from the quotation in Picquot/BOCCHERINI 28. For other similar reactions, cf. Grétry/MÉMOIRES 353-354; La Borde/ESSAI I xii; La Laurencie/ÉCOLE III 201.

87. Quantz/VERSUCH 302.

88. AMZ I (1798-99) 236; cf. the full paragraph on p. 47 below.

89. Scheibe/CRITISCHER 675.

90. Trans. from Kahl/SELBSTBIOGRAPHIEN 73.

Similar implications are found in the course of the definitions of "sonata" by Schulz and Türk quoted earlier in the present chapter. Moreover, Haydn is said to have wished in his later years that he had composed more music for voices with a text rather than so "many quartets, sonatas, and symphonies."[91]

Other belittlements of the sonata figure in expressions of nationalistic prejudice, whether related or not to the quarrel of the ancients and moderns. An example is the term "rococo" used by the Frenchman Brijon in 1763 to signify bad taste in an Emanuel Bach sonata (as quoted in SCE I). Brijon had negative remarks to make about the Italian sonata, too, complaining that it exploited the shock value of excessive variety, yet induced monotony by repeating one idea and modulating with it too long.[92] In 1752 Quantz had come to similar though less prejudiced conclusions in his more detailed distinctions between French, Italian, and German styles, in both composition and performance and in both operatic and instrumental music of the late-Baroque Era; and he had looked forward, though not without reservations, to the synthesis of these styles—that is, to an international "mixed style"—by the Germans.[93] On the other hand, J. A. Hiller found a loss of individual character through the intermixing of styles when, in 1768, he reviewed Dittersdorf's *Sinfonia nel gusto di cinque nazioni.*[94] The previous year he, too, had objected to the Italian sonata, citing especially the "inharmonious jangle" of the keyboard types (as quoted under Manfredini in SCE XXI). In 1789, fifteen years after Gluck had seriously damaged the prestige of both French and Italian opera in Paris, Grétry was still much less tolerant of Italian instrumental than vocal music, finding in the former little melody, little harmony, and nothing but noise in their fusion.[95] Others expressed their resentments against French music. Well known is Leopold Mozart's letter of February 1-3, 1764, in which he wrote that the "whole of French music is not worth a sou" and that the French were beginning to make their sonatas (and other music) after German models.[96] Burney was a notable Gallophobe in matters musical, aligning himself with Rousseau and those others among the French themselves who had become strongly anti-French and pro-Italian since the "Guerre des bouffons."[97] His

91. Griesinger/HAYDN 63.
92. Brijon/MUSIQUE 4-5.
93. Quantz/VERSUCH 306-334.
94. Originally printed in *Wöchentliche Nachrichten* for Jan., 1768, the review is quoted in Krebs/DITTERSDORFIANA 59.
95. E.g., Grétry/MÉMOIRES 131-138.
96. Trans. in Anderson/MOZART I 54.
97. Cf. Scholes in BURNEY'S TOURS I 322-326.

chief concession was to the harpsichord playing of the French, who, "in point of neatness, precision, and brilliancy of execution, are not excelled by the people of any other country in Europe."[98]

With all these nationalistic likes and dislikes, the wonder is that the attitude toward the sonata and related music became so international as soon as a Classic peak was attained in the works of the great Viennese masters. Of course, the composer himself always had to be adaptable, anyway, to the nationality, style, and idiom favored at the court or other center where he earned his living. Thus, Platti, who probably came from Venice, served most of his life at the German court of Würzburg, yet complied with the fashionable local custom of using French to word the title of his *VI Sonates pour le clavessin sur le goût italien,* published in Nürnberg in 1742. But before Haydn died in 1809 the profoundest respect and utmost enthusiasm for his and Mozart's works was being voiced by writers as well as composers, in all countries where those works were becoming known. The composers showed this respect everywhere by appropriating the traits of the Vienna Classical style as exemplified at its peak in Haydn's and Mozart's works, a style that was at once the most "mixed" and most pure of all international styles.[99] A verbal acknowledgment of the pre-eminent position of Haydn and Mozart among the *cognoscenti* of their day is provided in Dittersdorf's celebrated conversation with the emperor in 1786,[100] five years after the pertinent and equally celebrated encounter between Clementi and Mozart (when Clementi played his "Magic Flute" Sonata in B♭ for the emperor). Warm endorsements of Haydn's instrumental music, such as the unbounded enthusiasm Grétry frequently expressed for his symphonies,[101] were too general and too immediate to require further documentation here. Mozart was not quite so accessible in his own day. Hence, it is a little harder to find an exclamation of joy like that uttered by the Italian opera composer Latilla at the age of 74 (in 1785) when, according to his pupil G. G. Ferrari, he read the fugal finale of Mozart's first "Haydn" String Quartet in G: "Why, it's the most beautiful, most magnificent piece of music I ever saw in my life!"[102]

As we have already seen, resistance to progress in the sonata took the form, especially, of widespread objections to new styles in the Italian sonata. The corollary of that statement might well be that these

98. BURNEY'S TOURS I 4.

99. In 1826, in Nägeli/VORLESUNGEN 158-160, Mozart is still called "a style mixer" and "an impure instrumental composer"; cf., also, Abert/MOZART II 19, 474, 578.

100. As reported in DITTERSDORF 251-253.

101. E.g., Grétry/MÉMOIRES 286-287.

102. Saint-Foix/FERRARI 460.

objections were unintended and unwitting recognitions of the significant role that Italian music was playing in the "evolution" of the Classic sonata. The objections that were made by the English aesthetician Avison in 1752 were characteristic, whether to contrasting ideas, to the dissipation of counterpoint, to technical and ornamental "Extravaganzi," or to the "Extreme of an unnatural Modulation."[103] His list of men "whose Compositions being equally defective in various Harmony and true Invention, are only a fit Amusement for Children" includes Vivaldi, Tessarini, (D.) Alberti, and Locatelli! As late as 1790, Rangoni, himself an Italian dilettante from Modena, was still arguing in much the same vein, although his target was now the Italian modernisms of his own day, such as Lolli's "newer sonatas" as distinguished from his older ones or, better still, from the sonatas of Corelli, Tartini, Nardini, and Pugnani.[104] Similar objections can be found in the writings of Rangoni's contemporaries in France, as in the remark of Framery that sonatas and concertos have no purpose other than to show off the ability of the performer, or that "bravura arias" are nothing but "vocal sonatas."[105]

Thus far the attitudes we have noted in the Classic Era have been largely ones of disparagement toward the sonata. Lest the reader begin to wonder if anything kind was ever said about it, let him be assured that after we leave these generalized attitudes and come to the reviews of sonatas by individual composers in Part II we shall meet with a full measure of favorable and highly favorable comments. Right now we do have at least a few examples of more friendly attitudes to consider. These concern especially the simplicity and originality of the new instrumental style. When the learned German theorists Maichelbeck and Sorge dedicated their first published keyboard sonatas in the 1730's (SCE XI and XII), each made clear that the familiar phrase "in the Italian manner" that appeared in the full titles meant a lighter, thinner, more popular style. Here were starting points in the Classic Era in the trend toward increasing simplicity and clarity. "One of the sure ways . . . to make instrumental music appeal," according to a French essay published in London in 1776, "is to put few notes in it and not to make a lot of technical problems. Anything hard to play is seldom agreeable to hear."[106] Burney found frequent occasions to comment on the increasing simplicity of instrumental music in his time, as in his comparison of the "difficult" harpsichord "lessons" by Handel

103. Avison/ESSAY *passim* (SCE XIX).

104. Rangoni/ESSAI *passim* (as quoted at length in SCE VIII).

105. As cited and quoted in La Laurencie/ÉCOLE III 199 (along with other similar quotations).

106. Trans. from the extract quoted in Reeser/KLAVIERSONATE 16.

and D. Scarlatti with those by Alberti.[107] At one point he quoted a remarkable conjecture by C. F. Abel in London to the effect that Sebastian Bach and his son Emanuel "would have extended their fame, and been indisputably the greatest musicians of the eighteenth century" if instead of serving their respective civic posts they had composed for the stage in such great centers as Naples, Paris, or London. Then, Abel continued, "the one would have sacrificed all unmeaning art and contrivance, and the other have been less fantastical and *recherché*," resulting in "a style more popular, and generally intelligible and pleasing"![108]

The cult of originality per se that pervaded philosophic thought at the onset of the Classic Era[109] affected the sonata, too. Avison, always on the side of "reason," still objected in 1752 to what "the unskilful call Invention."[110] But pleas for more originality had already been uttered, as by the French author Bollioud-Mermet, who complained in 1746 that a musician plays 10 sonatas and the listener thinks they are all the same, so full are they of stock figures, passages, ornaments, and other clichés.[111] A generation later a Parisian critic continued the complaint: "When one comes to our airs, our motets, our concertos, our symphonies, one is tempted to believe that there exists in Europe but one composer for the airs and choruses, [and?] one for the sonatas, the concertos, and all the instrumental music."[112]

In Germany in 1761 and 1762 Marpurg criticized Wagenseil for a lack of originality in some cembalo *divertimenti* just published.[113] Aside from a certain actual sterility in these pieces, one must recognize that Marpurg was writing in Berlin, the city that proved to be a veritable hotbed of the *Affektenlehre* (doctrine of the affections) and of the *empfindsam* (ultrasensitive) style.[114] It was the latter style (SCE VI) that became one of the chief manifestations in music of the *Sturm und Drang* movement in German literature and, correspondingly, the most conspicuous occasion for originality—almost with a vengeance—

107. Burney/HISTORY II 1008; cf., also, pp. 996-997.

108. Burney/HISTORY II 955. For Abel's authorship of this paragraph cf. BACH READER 262.

109. Cf. the interesting summary of this trend in *The Art of Music* by Cannon, Johnson, and Waite (New York: Thomas Y. Crowell, 1960), pp. 287-290.

110. Avison/ESSAY 35.

111. As quoted in La Laurencie/ÉCOLE III 198.

112. Trans. from MERCURE 1780 Jan., p. 33, as quoted in La Laurencie/ÉCOLE III 199.

113. Marpurg/BRIEFE II 141-143 and 476.

114. For a sample of Marpurg's own description of these musical forces cf. the statement of 1749 trans. by Mitchell in Bach/ESSAY 81.

in the sonata.[115] Yet when E. Wolf in Weimar started by imitating the sonatas of the prime representative of the *Empfindsamkeit,* Emanuel Bach, he was criticized for his lack of originality by Schubart and by none other than Goethe (SCE XII). According to Wolf's own response, "since Goethe's arrival everything has become original with us. Thereupon thought I, you too [i.e., I myself] must try to be original." Burney's warm praise of Haydn's music in 1789 stressed its originality, combining familiar arguments for its acceptance with sentences that show the *empfindsam* influence was still alive:

> Indeed, his compositions are in general so new to the player and hearer, that they are equally unable, at first, to keep pace with his inspiration. But it may be laid down as an axiom in Music, that "whatever is *easy* is *old,*" and what the hand, eye, and ear are accustomed to; and, on the contrary, what is *new* is of course *difficult,* and not only scholars but professors have it to learn. The first exclamation of an embarrassed performer and a bewildered hearer is, that the Music is very *odd,* or very *comical*; but the queerness and comicality cease, when, by frequent repetition, the performer and hearer are at their ease. There is a general cheerfulness and good humor in Haydn's allegros, which exhilarate every hearer. But his adagios are often so sublime in ideas and the harmony in which they are clad, that though played by inarticulate instruments, they have a more pathetic effect on my feelings, than the finest air united with the most exquisite poetry. He has likewise movements that are sportive, *folâtres,* and even grotesque, for the sake of variety; but they are only the *entre-mets,* or rather *intermezzi,* between the serious business of his other movements.[116]

115. For more on the aesthetic of the *Affektenlehre,* the *empfindsam* style, and the *Sturm und Drang* (not always interrelated as here) cf. Emanuel Bach's own typical statement about expressive performance of the different affections in Bach/ESSAY 152-153; also, Lang/WESTERN 585-591 (one of the most useful, comprehensive summaries); Bücken/ROKOKO 94-96; Hoffmann-Erbrecht/STURM (on the keyboard music). A fuller, balanced study is much needed. A significant, somewhat iconoclastic probing of the "Storm and Stress in Music" by Max Rudolf appears in *Bach, the Quarterly Journal of the Riemenschneider Bach Institute* III (1972) 1-28.

116. Burney/HISTORY II 959-960.

Chapter III

The Sonata in Classic Society

Amateurs, Dilettantes, and "le beau sexe"

The important question in this chapter is how the sonata figured in the general social and cultural life of the Classic Era. One might furnish a preliminary, summary answer simply by listing its chief uses, proceeding from the most to the least frequent. The sonata provided a main staple in the diversional diet of the musical amateur or dilettante, an essential stepping stone in the career of the professional performer and composer, an ideal vehicle for the training of student instrumentalists, a rather frequent ingredient in private and public concerts, and a useful embellishment of the church service. Throughout the Classic Era writers still distinguished, both functionally and stylistically, between those same three uses of music that had been categorized since early in the Baroque Era—that is, music's uses at court, in church, and in the theater.[1] However, as regards the sonata itself, the church now seems to have found less use for it, and to have limited that use to the most conservative types; the theater seems to have found no use for it unless possibly as an *entr'acte* diversion;[2] and only court society, among these three categories, continued to cultivate it to any significant extent. 2a
Fortunately, information about the sonata's uses is not quite so scarce for the Classic as for the Baroque Era.[3] But it still consists largely of random bits that must be pieced together and that may or may not be specific enough for our purposes. Further studies into such sociologic aspects of music history remain one of the principal challenges to music research.[4]

1. E.g., cf. Avison/ESSAY 105-108; cf., also, Rowen/CHAMBER 5-14, including a pertinent paragraph on p. 7 that is trans. from Koch/LEXIKON 820-821 (1802).
2. Cf. Engländer/DRESDNER 14.
3. Cf. SBE 33. Brief, representative discussions that concern the uses of instrumental music in the Classic Era, although not the son. in particular, occur in Rowen/CHAMBER 5-14; Gradenwitz/STYLE 266-270; Mersmann/AUFFÜHRUNGSPRAXIS 104-105.
4. Loesser/PIANOS, cited at several points in our later chapters, is notable for

The broad role that the amateur or dilettante played in the cultivation of the Classic sonata becomes increasingly evident throughout the era. One discovers this role in titles or dedications, and senses it, in any case, in the ever more facile, fluent, and popular writing. Most conspicuous in this latter trend was the *galant* style (SCE VI), the term which came into use early in the eighteenth century to mean a relaxing of severe counterpoint but depreciated during the next half century until it connoted cheapness and superficiality.[5] Mattheson had introduced the "galant homme" in 1713 in the full title of *Das neu-eröffnete Orchestre,* implying an up-to-date dilettante in the best sense of the word; and he had already identified "Galanterie" in that book with a newer homophonic style (e.g., p. 137). J. S. Bach listed various dances and other "Galanterien" in the full title of *Clavier-Übung* I, which he published in 1731. In 1745 Spiess used "Galanterie-Musik" to mean chamber music in his *Tractatus* (p. 161).[6] Meanwhile, looking back to 1723, Quantz had extended the meaning of *galant* to a "melodic style, ornamented with many small figures and fast passages. . . ."[7] Quantz's *Versuch* of 1752 shows much interest in this style, as in his observation that a (SS/bass) "trio involves less fussy working out than a quartet . . . one can introduce more *galant* and more pleasing ideas than in the quartet, since there is one *concertante* part less."[8] Among many further references are those by Marpurg and Kirnberger to syntactic aspects of the style (SCE II), including the latter's statement in 1775, now derogatory, that "It is a very serious error when the composer allows himself to be seduced by the applause that unpracticed and inexperienced listeners give to the pleasant so-called *galant* pieces, and thereby introduces small, chopped-up dainty music instead of beautiful music into serious works and even into church music."[9]

The word *galant* appears often in eighteenth-century sonata titles. One early example is the set called *Six Sonates en quatuors*[,] *ou conversations galantes et amusantes* by Guillemain (Op. 12, 1743). Another, translated, is ". . . a [keyboard] Sonata well composed according to the present *galant* taste" by F. G. Fleischer (1745). For whom were such

its pathbreaking sociologic approach as well as for an entertaining style that all but conceals its solid scholarship. Hans Engel's recent survey, *Musik und Gesellschaft* (Berlin: Max Hesse, 1960), covers too wide a range of subject matter to have any immediate applications here.

5. The early history of this term and associated style traits is summarized in Bücken/GALANTE; Torrefranca/ORIGINI 337-341; Rowen/CHAMBER 108-119.

6. Cf. Torrefranca/ORIGINI 339-340.

7. From his "Autobiography" as trans. in Nettl/FORGOTTEN 294-295.

8. Trans. from Quantz/VERSUCH 302.

9. Sulzer/ALLGEMEINE II/1 227, as trans. from a later ed. in Ratner/THEORIES 440.

sonatas intended? J. Steffan's keyboard sonatas Op. 3 (*ca.* 1763) were dedicated to the "*dilettanti* of music,"[10] and Boccherini's *Sei Conversazioni a tre,* Op. 7 (1770), to the "*amatori* of music." Nor are the ladies overlooked in these titles, although the mention of them usually carried the uncomplimentary, cavalier implication that the sonatas are easy enough even for them to play. Thus, in 1757 appeared Paganelli's *Divertissement de le beau sexe ou six sonatines,* and in 1770 Emanuel Bach's sonatas "à l'usage des Dames" (W. 53), recalling a title Nichelmann had used in 1745. Vanhal's keyboard sonatas were said by both Schubart and C. F. Cramer (in 1774 and 1786, respectively) to have the graceful and charming melodies that would attract amateurs, "especially ladies."[11]

Of course, making his sonatas easy to play was one of the composer's surest ways of appealing to the amateur and dilettante. Typical was the listing of some Spanish sonatas of 1764 as "muy fáciles y de buen gusto."[12] In the 1780's J. W. Hässler even specified various levels of difficulty with such qualifying terms as "easy," "very easy," or "half easy, half hard."[13] Rutini's sonatas Op. 7, dedicated in 1770 "To the *Signori dilettanti* of the cembalo," have a preface indicating the composer "sought to avoid confusion, trying to make them natural and without difficult keys. It seems to me I have achieved what I wanted to, since a little girl ten years old plays them all without finding anything beyond her ability . . ." (SCE VII).

The "half easy, half hard" in Hässler's title was but one of numerous variations on Emanuel Bach's title for six sets of sonatas and other keyboard pieces published between 1779 and 1787—"für Kenner und Liebhaber," meaning "for connoisseurs [or even "professionals"] and amateurs." Türk opposed these terms similarly and at about the same time, but went a step further to indicate which term applied to which sonatas.[14] And Haydn seemed to have this distinction in mind when he complained to a publisher in 1785 about the careless engraving of some accompanied sonatas: "Even a professional would have to study before disentangling this passage, and then where would the dilettante be?"[15]

The term "conversations" in the titles by Guillemain and Boccherini that we have noted suggests another aspect of the dilettante's interest, the social and diversional pleasure of ensemble playing. Thus, in 1760 Avison wrote in the preface ("Advertisement") to his harpsichord so-

10. Cf. the facs. in the frontispiece of Gericke/WIENER.
11. Cf. Dewitz/VANHAL 63-64.
12. Cat. MADRID I 337.
13. Kahl/SELBSTBIOGRAPHIEN 48-49.
14. Cf. Hedler/TÜRK 64 and 72.
15. As trans. in Landon/HAYDN 51.

natas Op. 7, with accompaniments for 2 violins and a cello, "This Kind of Music is not, indeed, calculated so much for public Entertainment, as for private Amusement. It is rather like a Conversation among Friends, where Few are of one Mind, and propose their mutual Sentiments, only to give Variety, and enliven their select Company." Toeschi's use of "Conversation" and "dialoguées" in titles for ensemble sonatas of the next decade had similar implications. When, in 1777, Burney prefaced his set of the first keyboard duets to be published, he barely mentioned "the *Amusement* which such experiments will afford," preferring to stress their didactic and exercise values. Yet there is no doubt that the social pleasure afforded by playing duets with his daughter Fanny prompted the composition of these duets.[16] And similar motivations undoubtedly explain much of the sonata literature in various popular ensemble settings that we shall be discussing in Chapter V, including keyboard with violin accompaniment, three hands at one piano, and so on. As but one of many examples may be cited the note on L. Adam's *Grande Sonate pour le forté-piano,* Op. 12: "At the request of a large number of amateurs, the author has just added to this sonata an accompaniment for violin and bass that may be used *ad libitum.*"[17]

Before leaving the dilettante's use of the sonata we should not fail to note a dilettante type of sonata composer. This type was characteristically an individual of higher social station, better means, and broader cultural background than our average professional composer. But, just as characteristically, his sonatas are deficient in professional skill, their compensations, if any, being the unspoiled, naïve technical exuberance and the almost unwitting originality of the enthusiastic avocationalist. Among representatives of the dilettante composer whom we shall meet in later chapters are the German keyboardists Dalberg, Münchhausen, and Herschel. Beecke and Latrobe belong in this class, too, although their greater training, skills, and experience put them nearer the professionals.

The Professional Musician At Large and At Court

In any discussion of the sonata's place in Classic society the professional musician's own use for it must not be overlooked. Thus, the point was made earlier (SBE 30) that a set of sonatas published as "Opera prima" was a fine and frequent way for him to get off to a good start on his career, however far from this genre his further musical activities might take him. Gluck's first work to be published in full, his

16. Cf. Sonnedecker/DUETS 219.
17. Cf. Newman/ACCOMPANIED 341-342.

set of six SS/bass sonatas that appeared in London in 1746, was a case in point. Thereafter, he went on to "more important works," to borrow the unflattering expression of Hässler that was quoted in our previous chapter. In superintending the start of his little son's precocious career, Leopold Mozart knew very well the value of getting some sonatas right into print.[18] A cynical recognition of such values, along with some practicalities of publication that will come up in our next chapter, appeared in 1799 at the start of a verbose review of three piano sonatas by Wölfl, Op. 6:

> Good piano sonatas are written less often now than formerly, when the tendency of every musician who wanted public recognition as an active composer was to begin his career with piano pieces, especially solo sonatas—solo sonatas that may not have shown our present superior taste but still had to excel in craftsmanship if the composer hoped to come off with some distinction for his work. Although piano sonatas were generally less cultivated then, they had relatively more good in them than now, when everyone who knows that 3/5/8 is a triad writes any old way, as the spirit moves him. This composition mania is now gone so far that in nearly every town of any size music publishers are or will be established that, in order to supply nothing but novelties, accept and publish everything they can engrave. There are always [those] little men who will buy anything without looking so long as it is new. Such works cost nothing more than about a dozen free samples as an honorarium, [plus] paper and ink, whereby the publisher is satisfied. The author sees his name printed, nice and big, in an elegantly flourished title, whereby he has achieved his main purpose.[19]

After that unsubtle gambit, the reviewer (Rochlitz?) proceeded to show what exceptions Wölfl's sonatas were to this general rule.

As with the young Mozart's first published sonatas, the initial publication of many a Classic sonata composer had to be "Printed for the Author."[20] In other words, the composer had to start with a personal financial investment somewhat comparable to that expended by pianists on a Town Hall début in present-day America. His need to make such an investment increased with his gradual emancipation from almost total dependence on the court and the church for his income and security. Diverse evidences of this economic trend and of corresponding cultural trends are seen both in the failure of Mozart's efforts to find a satisfactory court position and in the success of Beethoven's arrangements to get along without one,[21] or in the public concerts that spread as fast as the newly independent burgher or middle-class society did, or in the expansion of the composer's intellectual horizons, such as the literary,

18. E.g., cf. Anderson/MOZART I 54, 77-78, 80, 82.
19. Trans. from AMZ I (1798-99) 236-237.
20. Cf. Köchel/MOZART 12 (K. V. 10).
21. Cf. GROVE VIII 779 (Roger, Wellesz, and Rutz).

philosophic, and legal training at the University of Leipzig that men like J. A. Hiller, Neefe, and Reichardt enjoyed before embarking on their careers. Naturally, the sonatas composed at this time were bound to be affected by the newer trends, both in kind and quality, quite as were all other music genres then in favor. However, we shall find such trends affecting not only some of the greatest Classic sonatas, but many of the slightest as well. In the latter regard, several able sonata composers—including Clementi in London, Hoffmeister in Vienna and Leipzig, and Pleyel in Paris—seemed to influence their own as well as others' styles by becoming music publishers themselves. Publishers had to meet the popular tastes of the time in order to succeed, whether with their own or others' works. Thus, the Spanish sonata composer Sor, called by Fétis "the Beethoven of the guitar," wrote in his *Mémoires* that when he arrived in Paris about 1813 or 1814,

> publishers said to me, "Make us some easy tunes." I was very willing to do so; but I discovered that easy meant incorrect, or at least incomplete. A very celebrated guitarist told me that he had been obliged to give up writing in my manner, because the publishers had openly told him: "It is one thing to appreciate compositions as a connoisseur, and another as a music seller, [and] it is necessary to write silly trifles for the public. I like your work, but it would not return me the expense of printing." What was to be done? An author must live.[22]

Of course, the composers who were virtuoso performers, as most were, had another way of capitalizing on the sonatas they wrote. They could use them, like concertos, as their own best vehicles for impressing their private or public audiences. Boccherini and Mozart did just that. So did Viotti, La Houssaye, A. Bruni, J. P. Duport, and many others. Such débuts led to more interest in the playing of sonatas for some, as for D. Ferrari, and to more interest in the composing of them for others, as for Beethoven.

All in all, however the Classic composer pursued his professional career, he was under constant and varied pressures that did indeed influence the kind and quality, as well as the quantity, of the sonatas he composed. When he was at court he served in a dictatorial establishment run "entirely at the will and expense of an aristocratic patron."[23] His position often carried with it either an implied or stipulated obligation to compose. For example, Burney said of the English harpsichordist Kelway that he "thought it necessary, as music-master to her Majesty [the Queen, in London], to publish a book of harpsichord

22. As trans. in Bone/GUITAR 338.
23. GROVE I 531 (McNaught).

lessons. . . ."[24] As "Director and Concertmaster" at the court in Berleburg, from 1753, B. Hupfeld's creative obligations were prescribed rather specifically by the ruling prince: "He must be fluent in his compositions and make sure that he frequently submits any new ones to us. And although we fix no precise number of concertos to be composed by him, he must still . . . compose and supply us with at least four dozen concertos or other musical pieces."[25]

In our previous volume we had occasion to note how circumscribed was Quantz's composition of sonatas and concertos within the celebratedly severe regime at Frederick the Great's court in Potsdam.[26] We shall have occasion later to see how Emanuel Bach lost favor by not toeing this same line more submissively. Other composers as important as Boccherini in Madrid or Haydn at Esterház not only received but obeyed orders to adapt ensemble compositions for their respective patrons so that the latter, as participating dilettantes, could have the main melodic interest yet be able to manage the technical problems in these pieces.[27] How menial was the composer's relation to his patron might be recalled by quoting one of those fawning, high-flown prefaces, this one from the London edition of M. Vento's "3d Book" of accompanied harpsichord sonatas:

Sir [Charles, Hereditary Prince of Brunswick Lunebourg]

The Honour Your Serene Highness has done me in permitting me to Dedicate the following Sonatas to you, must be of that Consequence on the Publication of them that I am at a Loss to express myself for so Distinguish'd a Mark of your Highness's Favour, if on the Perusal I shou'd be so happy as to meet with your Highness's Approbation of them I then can have no Doubt the reception they must meet with from the Publick whose Favour I shall be ever Ambitious of gaining next to that of leave to Subscribe my self

Your Serene Highness's
Most Dutiful
Most Humble and
Most Obedient Servant
Mathias Vento

Other kinds of pressures also influenced the sonatas (and other music) of even the greatest Classic composers. Haydn did not comply when Frau von Genzinger asked him to change some hand-crossing in his piano Sonata 49/ii that she found difficult.[28] But he did agree to add variations to an accompanied sonata (or piano trio, H. XV/13) at

24. Burney/HISTORY II 1009.
25. Trans. from the extract quoted in MGG VI 966 (Engelbrecht).
26. SBE 277-278, 299-300. Cf., also, BURNEY'S TOURS II 180-182; Helm/FREDERICK 158-160, 167-173, 175.
27. Cf. Picquot/BOCCHERINI 59-60; Strunk/BARYTON 221-222, 229, 244-245.
28. Cf. Landon/HAYDN 108.

the request of the publisher Artaria.[29] And Beethoven was astonishingly ready to let Ries do almost anything with the order and number of movements in the "Hammerklavier" Sonata in B♭, Op. 106, in order to insure its sales in London.[30]

Essercizi, Lessons, and the "Sonata scolastica"

Uses of the sonata as pedagogic material, especially the solo keyboard sonata, turn up often in any survey of Classic instrumental music. We have already met several allusions to such uses, including Schulz's statement in 1775 that "for players of instruments, sonatas are the most usual and the best exercises" (SCE II). The most obvious evidences come from titles. In the previous chapter we noted the equating of sonatas with "Essercizi," as by D. Scarlatti about 1739, or with "Lessons," as by Arne in 1756. Among other sample titles might be cited G. J. J. Hahn's "Keyboard Exercise, consisting of a light and short sonata, with a clarification of the figures and practical examples added, which prove very desirable for use by a keyboard and thorough bass" (*ca.* 1750); or Hoffmeister's *Sonata scolastica* for piano (*ca.* 1790); or Viguerie's *Trois Sonates précédées de préludes ou exercises pour forte-piano* (*ca.* 1800).[31] Pedagogic values are implied, too, in the sonata titles by Löhlein, E. W. Wolf, Friedrich Bach, Emanuel Bach, and nu-
31a merous other composers we shall be meeting.

Nicolai's *XXIV Sonates pour le clavecin sur les 24 tons de la musique* (*ca.* 1780) established an academic procedure already familiar in other, shorter instrumental forms.[32] By 1789, Türk provided teachers and students with a list of composers arranged according to the difficulty of their sonatinas and sonatas, though restricted somewhat to music intended for clavichord rather than piano.[33] After naming some compilers of the easiest song arrangements he says, "Now it is time to move on to little sonatinas, which are currently available in great quantity." As the least difficult among these he puts two sets of his own, then those by E. W. Wolf, Sander, and S. Schmiedt. Eventually and by degrees the student can progress to Gressler, Gruner, [J. L. T.] Blum, G. Benda, Sander's larger pieces, Zink, Vierling, Haydn, E. W. Wolf's larger pieces, Hässler, and Emanuel Bach. Türk also recom-

29. Cf. Landon/HAYDN 82; Hoboken/HAYDN 695.

30. Cf. Anderson/BEETHOVEN II 804-805; Kinsky & Halm/BEETHOVEN 296.

31. Eitner/QL IV 477, Cat. SCHWERIN I 411, and BRITISH UNION II 1042, respectively.

32. BRITISH UNION II 729. The first 2 "Sonatinen," in C and a, in a similar series by Diabelli, Op. 50, are praised for their elementary instructive worth in AMZ XXVIII (1826) 659.

33. Türk/KLAVIERSCHULE 16-17.

mends the practice of sonatas for two players at one or two keyboards, including—note how up-to-date he was—those by P. Schmidt, Mozart, Seydelmann, Koželuch, Vanhal, and E. W. Wolf.

D. Scarlatti's only hint of actual pedagogic intentions in his *Essercizi* of about 1739 comes in the first line of his preface to the "Reader": "Whether you be Dilettante or Professor, in these Compositions do not expect any profound Learning, but rather an ingenious Jesting with Art, to accommodate you to the Mastery of the Harpsichord."[34] But about 1785 one of the first of Scarlatti's less faithful editors in England and elsewhere assured the buyer that a more general knowledge of Scarlatti's "lessons" has

> been greatly retarded by the many superfluous and studied difficulties with which they abound.—In Manuscript, their obscurity was not without an intention;—as they were expressly composed for the Practice of a very brilliant Performer, the Infanta MARIA, to whom Scarlatti was Master of Music; every opportunity was taken by the Author to introduce difficult and affected Passages, for no other use or reason than merely as extraordinary exercises for the eminent ability of his Pupil.
>
> To remove these Obstacles . . . the present Editor . . . has selected the most beautiful movements—such as are of distinguished excellence—divested them of their pedantic difficulties, and arranged them in distinct Lessons . . . . Among the enthusiastic admirers of SCARLATTI'S Lessons, was the late Dr. Arne, who always considered them, with the "Suites de Pieces" of HANDEL, as the best calculated Performances to compleat the Practical Part of a Musical Education. . . .[35]

Of course, this trend toward preoccupation with pedagogic values infected composers as well as editors. Around 1755 Dittersdorf was still content to find his violin exercises among the then passé sonatas of the late-Baroque Era, much as the modern pianist looks back at Mendelssohn's piano concertos as "student concertos." He said that Locatelli's "sonatas may sound old-fashioned nowadays, but I would earnestly recommend them to every beginner on the violin—for practice, not for show pieces."[36] But, as implied in our remarks on the dilettante, less than a generation later Rutini was explaining on his own behalf that "In these sonatas I have aimed at [still] more brevity and ease, in order, I hope, to better satisfy the inclinations of the students" (from Op. 9, SCE VII); Hässler was disclosing the pedagogic philosophy that underlay his first set of "leichte Sonaten";[37] and Burney was rationalizing the first published keyboard duets with the statement that students will

34. As trans. in Kirkpatrick/SCARLATTI 102.

35. Extracted from the complete preface by A. Pitman as quoted in Newton/SCARLATTI 154-155.

36. DITTERSDORF 28.

37. His "Vorbericht" is part of the insert in NAGELS-m No. 20 (Glöder).

find them to be "reciprocally useful, and necessary companions in their musical exercises . . . [, which] may be made subservient to two very useful purposes of *improvement,* as they will require a particular attention to *Time* and to that clair-obscure which is produced by different degrees of *Piano* and *Forte.*"

Concerts, Private and Public

To what extent did the sonata figure in the concert life of the Classic Era? No one simple answer can be given to that question. As we move from center to center in Part II we become increasingly aware of a great variety in the kind, amount, and significance of the concert life. Private and public support for concerts was about equally divided during the later eighteenth century in cities like Milan and Berlin. But in some centers much of the concert life was the private sort that was reserved for the local court establishment and the salons of the related aristocracy—for example, in Madrid, Vienna, Mannheim, Dresden, Mecklenburg-Schwerin, and St. Petersburg. In other centers, a more vigorous concert life developed outside the court milieu, as in London, Paris, Leipzig, Hamburg, Danzig, Copenhagen, and Stockholm. In fact, the Classic Era saw a rapid mushrooming of public concerts, including such different sorts as those of the Bach-Abel subscription series in the London "concert rooms," the Concert spirituel in Paris (which had now become more secular than sacred), the Collegium musicum and its successors in the coffee houses and other town meeting places of Leipzig, or the Tonkünstler-Societät in Vienna (not until 1781).[38]

One tends to think of a concerto as being more of a concert vehicle than a sonata, at least for soloists.[39] Yet it will be recalled (SCE II) that, in 1775, Schulz considered the sonata to be ideal not only as an exercise but as a performance piece in any "music society," small or large. How much it was actually heard that way is another question. Always surprising to recall is the fact that only one solo piano sonata and but a very few ensemble sonatas by Beethoven seem to have been played even once in public during his lifetime (SCE XV). To be sure, as we shall see (SCE XIV and XV), the correspondence and other contemporary records not only of Beethoven but of Haydn and Mozart contain references to private performances of sonatas by each. But, at least before 1800, the Vienna public supported relatively few public

38. Cf. MGG VII 1590-1592 (Schaal) for a concise summary of 18th-century concert life.

39. Cf. Loesser/PIANOS 150-163, 174-182; Scholes/BURNEY II 178.

concerts and showed still less interest in hearing sonatas when these concerts did occur.[40] By contrast, it is just as surprising to recall how often—nearly one hundred times, in fact—the sonata or "lesson" or "solo" appeared in public concerts in America up to 1800 (SCE XXI). Of course, here there were no courts and far less incentive of any other sort for private concerts.

In any case, although the sonata did qualify primarily as intimate diversional and domestic music before 1800, it found its way into concerts enough to deserve notice of that fact here. The whole study of eighteenth-century concert life has been furthered significantly by numerous recent monographs on single cities and centers, such as those in the Arno Volk-Verlag's *Beiträge zur rheinischen Musikgeschichte*. If the pickings still seem lean when one attempts to glean "sonatas" from the many itemized programs that these studies reproduce, they are nevertheless too many for more than a small sampling here. Some further gleanings will be introduced in our later discussions of individual composers. And many more performances of sonatas undoubtedly remain veiled in those early programs by such frequent, general listings as "solo" or "and other pieces."

With regard first to private concerts, the very fact that these concerts were private and that they were more likely to be informal than formal when they included sonatas may well explain why the records of them are so seldom specific and so often of an anecdotal character. Thus, we must be content merely to assume that the child Mozart performed the keyboard parts of his earliest, accompanied sonatas at the royal courts in Paris, London, and The Hague for which they were written, since neither Leopold nor he ever says exactly that.[41] We do know that Clementi played his "Magic Flute" Sonata in B♭ before the emperor in Vienna, in 1781, but only through the anecdotal reports of his celebrated contest with Mozart that began to circulate twenty-four years later (SCE XX). As another example, when Burney heard Frederick the Great in a private flute concert at the Sans Souci palace in 1772, he reported that that particular program consisted of nothing but three flute concertos; however, elsewhere he supplies at least the fact that sonatas, too, had their share in the routine pattern of these exclusive, almost nightly recitals.[42]

A better idea of the sonata's use in private concerts, or rather of what sonatas may have been played, can be had from records of the

40. Cf. Thayer/BEETHOVEN I 163-173.

41. E.g., cf. Anderson/MOZART I 48, 51, 66, 67, 86-87; Mozart/NEUE-m X/34 (Deutsch) 30, 31, 39-40 (also, p. 47).

42. BURNEY'S TOURS II 181 and 183.

library holdings of various patrons of music. For instance, in his valuable study of the Parisian nobleman La Pouplinière, Cucuel could find no itemized programs of specific concerts that were given. But he did learn that the library of this leading patron included "a very fine collection of music, both printed and manuscript, of the most celebrated French, Italian, and German composers. . . . It consists of concertos, symphonies, trios, sonatas for all kinds of instruments, and ariettes." In another report a few of the works were actually specified, including the sonatas for keyboard by D. Alberti and those for cello (and *b.c.*) by Graziani. And Cucuel was able to point to collections maintained in other, contemporary private salons in Paris that included late-Baroque and pre-Classic names mainly identified with the sonata, such as Loeillet, Pepusch, de Fesch, Schickhard, Chédeville, Blavet, Dauvergne, Guillemain, Naudot, Boismortier, and d'Herbain.[43]

In Madrid, according to the rich monograph by Subirá, the library of the Duke of Alba once contained sonatas or related chamber works by Locatelli, F. M. Veracini, Brunetti, Manalt, Herrando, and some less known Spanish composers.[44] And in Dresden, Engländer has compiled an exceptionally complete list of over 125 composers and the categories of their instrumental works, from solo keyboard to orchestral, that were used between about 1777 and 1810.[45] Sonatas in various settings comprise nearly half of this list, including some by such main names as Emanuel Bach, Boccherini, Clementi, J. B. Cramer, Dittersdorf, Grétry (?), Hässler, Haydn, Koželuch, Mozart, Naumann, Pleyel, Sacchini, Schuster, Seydelmann, Sterkel, Vanhal, and A. Wranitzky.

In Vienna, according to a report from Leipzig in 1808, the musical amateurs abounded as in few other cities.

> Throughout the winter there are countless so-called private academies ([making] music in aristocratic homes). There is no birthday, no anniversary that is not celebrated musically. Most [of the concerts] are pretty much alike. First [comes] a quartet or symphony, which is regarded essentially as a necessary evil and hence lost in [general] chattering. Then comes one young lady after another, [who] puts up her piano sonata and plays through it as best she can, [and] then come others [who] similarly sing some arias from the newest operas. . . . Every refined girl, talented or not, must learn piano playing or singing, first [because] it's the custom and second [because] it's the most convenient way to come out nicely in society and, with good luck, make a strong match.[46]

43. Cucuel/LA POUPLINIÈRE 356-361. For an amusing account in 1757 of private concerts in Paris, including the boredom of having to please parents by applauding the "budding talents" that perform "sonatas and vocal pieces," cf. Loesser/PIANOS 313.

44. Subirá/ALBA *passim*.

45. Engländer/DRESDNER 26-35.

46. Trans. from most of the complete quotation in Hanslick/WIEN I 66-67.

And, the report continues, the sons must do likewise, for somewhat the same reasons.

Information about public concerts in the Classic Era has proved to be both more available and more specific than for private concerts. The researchers who have troubled to dig it up usually depend on the printed programs and journalistic publicity that such concerts require for their success. Again only samples can be given. In Vienna Hanslick's voluminous study turned up almost no sonatas in many itemized programs, including those of the "mixed concerts," vocal and instrumental, given by the Akademie der Tonkünstler-Societät up to 1800. Though symphonies and quartets were done often, Hanslick had to call attention to the general absence of sonatas from concerts until well into the 1830's.[47] Of course, there were a few exceptions, such as one of the public concerts given in the home of the Aurnhammer family, in 1781, when, according to Mozart's letter of November 24 to his father, "We played the concerto a due and a sonata for two claviers [K.V. 375a], which I had composed expressly for the occasion and which was a great success."[48] And there were those half-dozen performances of ensemble sonatas by Beethoven that occurred in Vienna between 1800 and 1816 (SCE XV).

Mozart has also left us a record of a characteristically long public concert in Augsburg, in 1777, consisting entirely of his own works and including two piano sonatas: "Now what does Papa think that we played immediately after the symphony? Why, the concerto for three claviers. . . . Then I gave a solo, my last sonata in D, written for the Baron Dürnitz [K.V. 205b], and after that my concerto in B♭. I then played another solo, quite in the style of the organ, a fugue in C minor, and then all of a sudden a magnificent sonata in C major, out of my head [K.V. 300h?], and a Rondo to finish up with. There was a regular
din of applause. . . ."[49] 49a

Schletterer gives twelve sample programs from the first two years of the Concert spirituel series that Reichardt instituted, after the Paris model, in Berlin in 1783.[50] Only two of these programs have any sonatas actually so called, there being a violin sonata by F. Benda in one and a cello sonata by Duport in the other. The program in which the latter occurs may be listed in abbreviated form here, as typical of "mixed concerts" in the late eighteenth century:

47. Hanslick/WIEN I 30-35, 24, 92-93.

48. As trans. in Anderson/MOZART III 1161.

49. As trans. in Anderson/MOZART II 497-498. The identification of K. V. 300h is discussed in SCE XIV.

50. Schletterer/REICHARDT 654-656.

Part II of the *Miserere* by Leo and Bertoni
Symphony by Dittersdorf
Scene from *Armida* by Reichardt
Oboe concerto by Stamitz
Aria, "Non temer bell' idol mio," by Bertoni
Cello sonata by Duport
Symphony by Reichardt

Sittard's study of Hamburg concert life reveals the performances of only a few sonatas, among these last being one each for keyboard by Zink, Haydn, Koželuch, and Mozart (4 hands). Otherwise, one finds only vaguer titles like "solo" or "Clavierstücke."[51]

Brenet's pioneer investigation into French concert life before the Revolution gives only rare bits and hints about the sonata itself, mostly with regard to the Concert spirituel. Pertinent here are the performances by J. Stamitz of his viola d'amore sonata in 1754 and by Cifolelli of a mandolin sonata in 1760, the unprecedented performance of a piano duet in 1784 (at the first concert of La Societé académique des enfants d'Apollon), the general use of "symphonie" to mean almost any ensemble, and the frequent appearances of many instrumentalists primarily associated with the sonata.[52] In La Laurencie's detailed survey of French violin playing (La Laurencie/ÉCOLE), presumptive if not conclusive evidence is provided for the playing of sonatas at the Concert spirituel by not a few of the residents or visitors in Paris whom we shall be meeting in later chapters, including Mondonville, Gaviniès, Pugnani, Boccherini, Capron, Le Duc, Janson, Duport, Séjan, and Riegel. Burney reported a program of the Concert spirituel in 1770 in which he heard two Italian concertos sandwiched between four sacred French vocal works, finding the former to be well played yet insufficiently appreciated by the French audience, and the latter to be quite the converse.[53] In another French city, Lyon, sonatas were certainly not unknown in public concerts of L'Académie des beaux-arts. Thus, in a concert in 1765, between the usual symphonies, ariettes, and opera extracts, a sonata for violin and another for harpsichord were both performed by their composer, "the celebrated virtuoso" designated as "le Signor Schmid." The fine library of the academy once included sonatas by many of the chief Italian and French sonata composers of the time.[54]

In English centers, the exceptionally healthy concert life was again focused mainly on the orchestra rather than on chamber groups or

51. E.g., Sittard/HAMBURG 125, 128, 136, 137, 90, 107, 182.

52. Brenet/CONCERTS 223 and 248, 271, 367, 250-251, 289-294 and 309-313, respectively.

53. BURNEY'S TOURS I 16-17.

54. Vallas/LYON 124, 161, 165-166.

soloists.[55] Yet it is hard to believe that sonatas were not played fairly often in public, what with the prevalence of virtuoso as well as dilettante sonatas and with the many virtuoso instrumentalists then resident in London. But the readily verifiable instances are few, chiefly being those when Clementi's music was heard in London before (and only before) the turn of the century.[56] A program of 1786 in which Clementi played one of his own sonatas may be quoted as given by Unger, with the sonata placed near the middle as usual.[57]

Act I.	Act II.
Symphony, Haydn;	Symphony, Clementi;
Song, Harrison;	Concerto, Graff;
Concerto, Salomon;	Song, Harrison;
Song, Mara;	Concerto, Mara;
Sonata, Clementi.	Song, Mara.

As elsewhere the sonata reached its lowest ebb as a concert staple in England around the end of the Classic Era.[58] Contributing to Rees's *Cyclopedia* in the early nineteenth century, Burney commented to the effect that "solos" were "wholly laid aside" in favor of orchestral music.[59]

Sittard believed that solo recitals were not yet known in the eighteenth century.[60] However, between 1775 and 1800 a whole series of these seem to have taken place in the then Prussian center of Königsberg.[61] Although the programs are not itemized in available records, one can safely assume that the sonata contributed its full share. Furthermore, several keyboard recitals, including duets, were given in Stockholm that justify the same assumption.[62] Other concert programs in Stockholm from 1762 on, do specify sonatas from time to time, including, for instance, sonatas for violin, for harp with cello accompaniment, for carillon, for piano (?) with accompaniment, and for two mandolins.[63]

In the Church Service

Contemporary references to the use of the sonata in church during the Classic Era turn up fairly often and in most of the main countries of the sonata. But these references are seldom more than generaliza-

55. Cf. Sadie/CONCERT 17.
56. E.g., cf. Unger/CLEMENTI 15, 43, 67, 70, 71, 80, 86-87; JAMS XXV (1972) 306n.
57. Unger/CLEMENTI 69.
58. Cf. Temperley/DOMESTIC 37-38.
59. Cf. Scholes/BURNEY II 178.
60. Sittard/HAMBURG 84.
61. Güttler/KÖNIGSBERG 170-178.
62. Vretblad/STOCKHOLM 243-246.
63. Vretblad/STOCKHOLM 165 and 210, 245, 256, 259 and 265, and 273, respectively.

tions or hints that reveal nothing specific about how the sonata or related instrumental music figured in the service.[64] One of the most explicit statements about instrumental music during the service concerns the symphony rather than the sonata, although the statement is certainly applicable. It comes from the guitarist Sor again, as a recollection of his life at Montserrat monastery near Barcelona, where he arrived about 1790 at the age of twelve: "The morning Mass was accompanied by a small orchestra composed of violins, violoncellos, contrabasses, and oboes. All of these were played by children, the oldest of them being no more than fifteen or sixteen. During the Offertory they performed the Introduction and Allegro of one of the symphonies of Haydn in the key of D; during the Communion the Andante was played, and at the last Gospel, the Allegro."[65] There follows here a representative sampling of such meager information about the sonata in church as has turned up during the present survey. The sonatas themselves that are referred to are generally conservative or anomalous works that, for all the worth of a few of them, have no bearing on main trends of the Classic sonata.

Maichelbeck's eight keyboard sonatas in his Op. 1, published in 1736, were offered "for use as well on church as on domestic keyboard instruments"; they could be played not only as diversional music but during the new, "light" type of Masses "in Italian style" and after the Vesper service (SCE XI). Paganelli's *XXX Ariae pro organo et cembalo* of 1756, from which he drew more than half of his "Six Sonatines" the following year, are decidedly *galant* pieces, yet were designated not only for the amateur's pleasure but for use during the Elevation (of the Host) in the Mass, if not more generally in the Offertory and Vespers.[66] Cherubini composed a "Sonata" for two organs in 1780, for use in the Mass.[67] Haydn's seven one-movement orchestral "sonatas" that comprise *The Seven Last Words of Our Saviour on the Cross* (H. XX) resulted in 1785 from a request "by a canon of Cádiz . . . to compose seven adagios to last ten minutes each," each one to follow a pronouncement of one of the sacred words by the bishop.[68] And Mozart's seventeen "Epistle Sonatas," composed between about 1772 and 1780 for various instrumental groups and organ, are short pieces now believed to have been used between the Epistle and Gospel, chiefly on special fast days (SCE XIV).

64. The 19th- and 20th-c. references to this question have usually gone no further, as in Engländer/DRESDNER 14-15, Hanslick/WIEN I 64, or MGG VI 1526-1530 (Mompellio; in a discussion of 18th-c. Italian church music).

65. As trans. in Sasser/SOR 40.

66. Cf. Schenk/PAGANELLI 143, 84-85.

67. Cf. Frotscher/ORGELSPIEL II 1240.

68. Cf. Geiringer/HAYDN 77.

Chapter IV

The Spread of the Classic Sonata

Its Main Centers

The spread of the Classic sonata depended, first, on the musical centers where it was cultivated or transmitted, and second, on the publishers in those centers by whom it was printed or reprinted. These two factors are the main concerns, then, of the present chapter. In the Baroque Era the sonata had originated in a very few centers of northern Italy and gradually spread to much of musical Europe. In the Classic Era it followed almost the opposite trend. From the start it appeared in many centers, whether in its traditional or its newer styles and settings; then less gradually it narrowed, in its finest examples, to the masterworks distilled in the "melting pot" of the Vienna Classical school. But the two eras did have in common the marked, progressive influence of Italian music at the start of each and the unsurpassed masterworks from Austro-German centers at the end. (In the Romantic Era the sonata was to spread once more from few to many centers, yet remain largely within the Austro-German hegemony.)

At the start of the Classic Era there were actually so many centers of the sonata—or of all music, for that matter—that their sheer number plus their complex interrelationships have created the chief obstacles to an adequate understanding and survey of that era as a whole. Moreover, even the fact of this diversity and confusion was obscured for some time by oversimplified explanations—that is, by the zealous nationalistic claims of early twentieth-century scholars for the absolute priority and unquestioned influence of this or that one center. As discussed later (SCE XI), Riemann started the melee by heralding the symphonic and related instrumental music of the Mannheim school as the long missing prototype of that by the Viennese masters. Then Adler countered with similar claims for the pre-Classic school in Vienna itself. Soon Torrefranca did much the same for Italian keyboard music, La Laurencie and Saint-Foix for symphonists in Paris, and so on, until nearly every main center of Classic music had its champion. The ultimate conclusion is obvious, that pre-Classic styles, forms, and trends must have been "in the air," everywhere and at about the same time.[1] Yet, the notion of some one center as the prime source for Classic music has continued to dominate concepts of sonata, as of other music, history. In particular, it has tended to beget categorical and oversimplified theories about derivations. For example, a preoccupation with composers from North German centers seems to have caused Falck to trace a single line in the keyboard sonata that excludes both Haydn and Mozart, yet extends right from Friedemann Bach through Emanuel Bach, Müthel, and Rust to Beethoven.[2]

At the same time, one must not overlook such distinctions within, and differences between, musical centers as did actually inhere in the local concert life, the patron's tastes, the skills and talents of the individual musicians, and the social and economic environment. Thus, Mannheim was outstanding as a center of orchestral playing, especially as a training ground for string players. Its composers would be expected to cultivate, and did cultivate, not only the symphony but the ensemble sonata in all its most popular settings, the latter being for the private diversion of the elector palatine Karl Theodor and his family. But, rejecting Riemann's attempts to relate Schobert and Edelmann, we find in Mannheim little of the occasion, incentive, or talent for composing solo keyboard sonatas that, say, the imperial court in Vienna offered in the same period. At this court, during retrenchments in the war-burdened economy, a main post was that of *Hofklaviermeister* to Maria Theresa and her children, with Wagenseil and J. Steffan being among the outstanding incumbents. Similarly, one might point to such indigenous or near-indigenous factors of concern to the sonata as the Castillian dance and guitar music in Madrid, or the *Affektenlehre* in Berlin, or the accompanied *pièces de clavecin* in Paris, or the benevolent yet despotic control of the arts, as of all else, by Catherine the Great at her imperial court in St. Petersburg.

Moreover, while discarding the idea of a single source for Classic music, one must not overlook those influences of one center or composer upon another that are clear-cut enough to leave no doubt. Thus, Paris —a host to numerous influences, anyway—was under the direct influence of Mannheim through the many symphonies, concertos, and chamber

1. This conclusion was already reached at least tentatively in Fischer/WIENER 84 in 1915.

2. Falck/BACH 81 (Müthel was inadvertently put ahead of Emanuel Bach by Falck).

works by J. Stamitz and other Mannheimers that were both published and performed there. It was under the direct influence of Strasbourg through the composition, performance, and publication of sonatas or related pieces by several Alsatian clavecinists who moved to Paris, including Honauer, Edelmann, and Hüllmandel. And it was under the direct influence of Torino through a number of violin virtuosos and composers resident in Paris who had studied with G. B. Somis and his pupil Pugnani, including both Leclair and Viotti.

More of these interrelationships will come up in the next section of this chapter. The map on p. 62 should help the reader to visualize the spread of the musical centers that concern us here. Except for the four American centers indicated on the inset, the map is bounded roughly and irregularly by Lisbon and Madrid on the southwest, Dublin and Edinburgh on the northwest, Copenhagen and Stockholm on the north, St. Petersburg (Leningrad) on the northeast, Königsberg (Kaliningrad), Breslau (Wroclaw), and Vienna on the east, and Naples on the southeast. The number of resident sonata composers whom we shall be meeting in each city, in Part II, appears in parentheses beside the city when that number is 5 or more. Out of some 85 centers with over 400 composers, it will be noted that Paris led with 75, followed by London with 53, Vienna with 49, and Berlin with 24. These figures are commensurate not necessarily with quality, of course, but with publishing activities, concert life, and popular (or dilettante) interest in the sonata. The greatest number of centers was in Germany, where, however, our more than 105 sonata composers were spread rather thinly because of the large number of separate little states, duchies, principalities, and the like.[3]

Besides the map of musical centers, another kind of visual aid can help to clarify the spread of the Classic sonata. That aid is a chart (p. 63) showing where and when some of the main composers wrote and/or published their sonatas (insofar as the places and years can be pinned down in this fashion). Such a graphic view should give at least an inkling of how much did go on concurrently in sonata history and how much the new styles and tastes do seem to have taken hold almost everywhere at about the same time.

Emigrants and Immigrants

We shall be getting a closer look at the main individual centers of the sonata when we consider, in Part II, what factors in each may have

3. Though in need of revision, Brenet/CLASSIQUES 1014-1018 still provides a useful summary of these German centers.

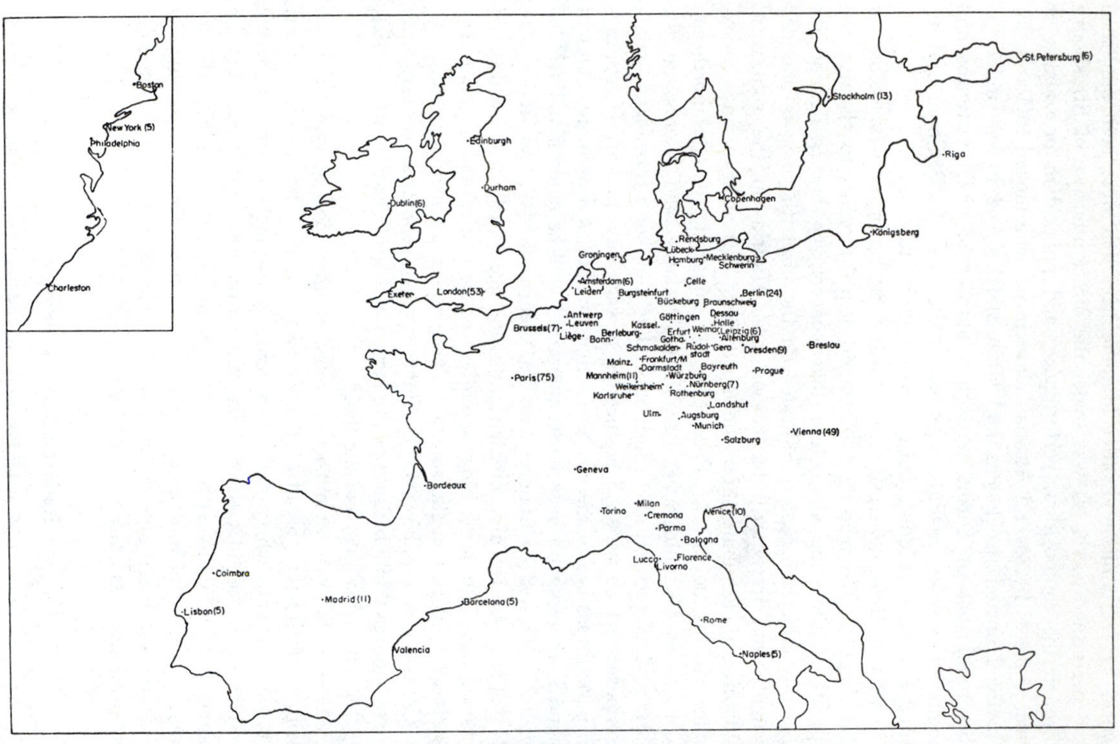

The Musical Centers in Which Classic Sonatas Were Composed and/or Published

Centers and Production Spans of Some Main Classic Sonata Composers

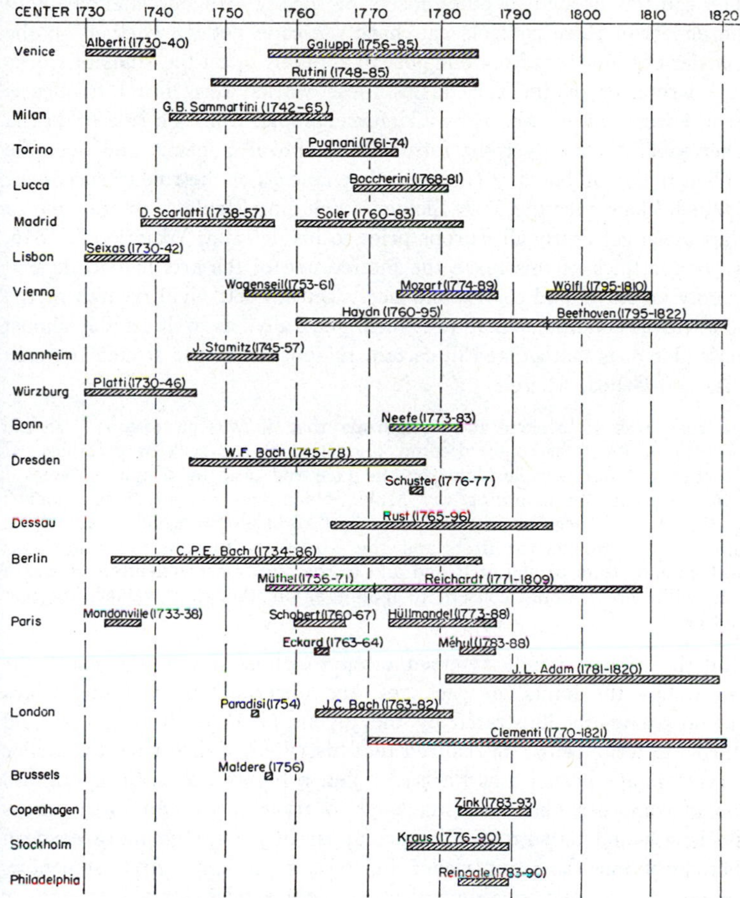

been most conducive, or least so, to the cultivation of the sonata. At the moment, in keeping with the over-all view of Part I, we are concerned with more of those general influences and movements between musical centers such as were just noted in Mannheim, Vienna, and Paris. Perhaps the first point to stress should be that so much intercourse between centers did take place. This intercourse was stimulated by the crosscurrents in a maze of political controls. It was, in fact, a fortunate gain for the arts among the many frustrating limitations that such controls created in other facets of society. In our later chapters the effects of these controls can hardly escape notice, whether on the transfer of composers from one post to another, or on the kinds of works they wrote, or on the very tastes these works were meant to please. Such effects will be seen to result, for example, from the rule of Maria Theresa in Vienna over the former kingdom of Bohemia and over the Italian region of Tuscany (among other lands), or the rule of successive Spanish kings over the Two Sicilies (including Naples), or the rule of Napoleon over nearly all Europe prior to his defeat at Waterloo in 1815.

In the thick of this maze the intercourse of the arts had to depend heavily on travel and correspondence. Burney left vivid records of the poor travel conditions that prevailed generally, as well as the almost incredible ones that existed in certain regions, as at one stretch between Pisa and Genoa, where

> the road was so broken and dangerous that it was necessary I should alight, give the Mule to the Pedino, and cling to the rock or precipice. I got three or four terrible blows on the face and head by boughs of trees I could not see. In mounting my Mule, which was vicious, I was kicked by the two hind legs on my left knee and right thigh, which knocked me down, and I thought at first, and the Muleteers thought my thigh was broken, and began to pull at it and add to the pain most violently. It was a long while ere I would consent to mount again, though I walked in great misery.[4]

And the Mozart family referred often to difficulties of the mail—the censorship, the limits on packages, the uncertainties, and the delays (as so poignantly illustrated by the joyous birthday greeting Leopold started to write before he realized that his wife had died ten days earlier in Wolfgang's presence in Paris).[5] Yet, a highly successful opera and sonata composer like Sarti managed to travel back and forth across the length and breadth of Europe, apparently with no more concern than busy musicians experience in today's jet age. And, somehow, composers managed to communicate rapidly enough for a front-ranker like Beethoven to get a sonata published in three different countries all within a year of its completion.[6]

With regard to the transfer of musicians, no one fact stands out so clearly in the Classic Era as the preference for Italian composers, especially opera composers, in nearly every major court of Europe including that in St. Petersburg. Consequently, the emigration of Italians

4. BURNEY'S TOURS I 306.
5. Letter of July 12-13, 1778 (Anderson/MOZART II 839-843).
6. E.g., Op. 53 in 1805 (Kinsky & Halm/BEETHOVEN 125).

continued to be as widespread, at least up to the last quarter of the eighteenth century, as it had been in the Baroque Era.[7] The emigrants included almost all of Italy's best sonata composers (and many others, as listed near the start of SCE VII). D. Scarlatti and Boccherini went to Madrid, Viotti to Paris, and Paradisi and Clementi to London. Furthermore, Galuppi, Rutini, Pugnani, and Nardini, all of whom we do meet later in Italian centers, were active abroad during much of their careers. Only Tartini in Padua and G. B. Sammartini in Milan stayed home most of their lives. Their cities and the region of Tuscany were among the few centers that still paid appreciable attention to independent instrumental music in a land that was fast becoming a full-time nursery of opera. Even Italy's fine tradition of keyboard playing was losing ground at home. Burney recognized this fact, though he may have overstated when he wrote, "I have neither met with a *great* player on the harpsichord, nor an *original* composer for it throughout Italy. There is no accounting for this but by the little use which is made of that instrument there, except to accompany the voice. It is at present so much neglected, that it is difficult to say whether the instruments themselves, or the performers are the worst."[8] It is true that Alberti, Paganelli, Bertoni, and several other Italian composers of keyboard sonatas were what Torrefranca has called "singer-cembalists,"[9] whose "songful" playing started with their primary interests in the opera.

One notes in Italy that except for the Bohemian violinist Mysliveček there were no immigrant sonata composers of consequence to counterbalance the many emigrants. Italian centers simply did not hold the opportunities for the immigrants. Yet for one important reason foreign musicians did get to Italy in large numbers, and that reason was to do their advanced training. Christian Bach, Mozart, Rust, Schuster, and Guillemain are among the many sonata composers who trained there and, more to the point, who show the distinctly Italianate effects in their music. Even more widely recognized than the Torinese violinists G. B. Somis and Pugnani mentioned earlier, two Italian masters became the most sought after teachers of the pre-Classic Era, Tartini (1692-1770) in Padua and Padre Martini in Bologna (1706-84).[10] The reverence for Martini on the part of Christian Bach, Mozart, and Gluck is well known. Less well known may be the large number of violinists who went to Tartini, from as far off as Rotterdam (Hellendaal), Stockholm

7. Cf. the map of this emigration up to 1750 in Lang/WESTERN 464-465.
8. BURNEY'S TOURS I 236.
9. Torrefranca/ORIGINI 396-397, 506, *et passim.*
10. The sons. by each were discussed in SBE 189-192 and 181-183.

(Wesström), and St. Petersburg (if Khandochkine actually did study with him).

The second greatest emigration of Classic sonata composers (and other musicians) was that of Bohemians, Moravians, and Silesians from Czechoslovakia. This emigration will become especially evident when we get to composers such as J. Stamitz and Richter in Mannheim, or Vanhal and Koželuch in Vienna. Like the Italians, the Czechs were going where they could find the patronage, the interest, the concert life, and the publishers.[11] One indirect piece of evidence lies in the almost total absence of resident sonata composers in Prague itself during the Classic Era (SCE XXI). For the same reason, if to a somewhat lesser extent, the Belgians left Antwerp or Brussels, and the Dutch left Amsterdam or Rotterdam to go to Paris, London, and various German centers. Only the French musicians did very little emigrating, at least until the Revolution compelled many of them to flee from their homeland to London or other near-by centers. The chief English emigration that we shall have occasion to notice is that to this country, both before and after the American Revolution (SCE XXI).

Being single united monarchies of long standing, France and England differed from Italy and Germany in concentrating nearly all of their international art activities in their respective capitals of Paris and London. As already suggested, throughout much of the Classic Era these two cities were the great hosts to all Western music. The foreign colonies were especially large in London, where, for example, we meet more Italians than in any other center, not excluding Italian cities.

Although Clementi and Viotti alone almost counterbalanced the trend, the Italian influence on instrumental music abroad tended to lessen in the later eighteenth century for several reasons. In the first place, the number of Italians primarily interested in independent instrumental music was decreasing rapidly. The long line of professional violinists who wrote melo/bass sonatas, reaching back more than a century-and-a-half, was coming to an end in Nardini and Pugnani. Most of the other professionals were being absorbed by the craze for opera. In the second place, Italianate predilections abroad, both at court and in public, were giving way to the nationalistic tastes fostered by such divergent forces as the *Sturm und Drang,* the French Revolutionary spirit, and the resistance to the Napoleonic campaigns. Symptoms of these tastes may be found as far apart artistically as Kocžwara's "Battle of Prague" sonata[12] and Beethoven's frequent preference for German

11. Cf. the map of this emigration, from 1700-75, in Lang/WESTERN 624-625; also, MGG V 1815-1816 (Quoika); GROVE V 739 (Howes).

12. Cf. Loesser/PIANOS 243-244.

inscriptions in his late sonatas.[13] And in the third place, the amateur music associations that were springing up everywhere in middle class society were feeding more and more on local talent as well as, or even in place of, imported composers and performers.

Furthermore, in Vienna, the imperial court had to reduce its Italian importations and turn to native talent, for financial reasons. (When the Vienna Classical school is called a "melting pot" of international styles, one must think not so much of the rather provincial composers actually living there before Haydn, Mozart, and Beethoven, as of the great absorptive powers those three masters possessed for assimilating any and all styles that suited their different kinds of genius.) In Paris, the rapidly deteriorating government and the increasing pressures from the even more rapidly growing society of intellectuals compelled Marie Antoinette to switch her allegiance from Italian to French composers (as in her last-minute rejection, in 1786, of Sacchini's *Oedipe*[14]). In Berlin, the sharp reduction of Frederick the Great's musical activities, after the Seven Years' War, led to much less employment for the Italians. But in any case, resistance to the newer Italian styles was being voiced in that center by theorists and aestheticians like Schulz and Reichardt (SCE II); and all instrumental composers of consequence in Berlin were devoting themselves to the *empfindsam* style, that peculiarly north German extension both of the *galant* mannerisms in music and of the *Sturm und Drang* spirit in literature.

Some of the nationalistic resistance manifested itself within the ranks of the musicians themselves. Avison had still welcomed Italian influences in English music in 1752, as Purcell had 69 years before.[15] The first resistance began to appear not among the English so much as among foreigners other than the Italians. From Berlin, Marpurg got word in 1754 that German keyboard players in London were unable to compete with the Italians, whose impress had to be on all music and who were getting all the entrees with the ladies.[16] With regard to Germany herself, Leopold Mozart evidently was pleased to tell his son in 1777 that "the stage for these Italians does not extend very much further than Munich and practically comes to an end there. In Mannheim, for instance, everyone except a few castrati is already German. . . ."[17] But he did not express himself spitefully here in the way that both he and his son did about the French. It will be recalled

13. E.g., cf. Anderson/BEETHOVEN II 657.
14. Cf. GROVE VII 348 (Marshall).
15. Avison/ESSAY 80-81; cf. SBE 307-308.
16. Marpurg/BEYTRÄGE I 167-168.
17. Anderson/MOZART I 430; cf., also, II 530.

that Leopold had written in 1764, among other things, that the "whole of French music is not worth a sou" (SCE II); and again from Paris, in 1778, his son referred to "these stupid Frenchmen" and how "I tremble from head to foot with eagerness to teach the French more thoroughly to know, appreciate and fear the Germans."[18]

Some Quantitative Aspects of Publication

The extent to which MSS were copied and circulated in the Classic Era is often surprising. Yet it must be obvious that only through publication could the sonata spread as widely as it did. Just how widely calls for some consideration of the sheer quantities involved. About how many sonatas were composed in the Classic Era? What is the ratio between this total and that of other, related types of instrumental music composed at the same time? What is the ratio of MS to published sonatas of the time? Among the total published sonatas, in what proportion is each of the main settings found? How large were the editions of sonatas? To what extent did the published sonatas achieve contemporary re-editions? Obviously, over-all answers to these questions can be only educated guesses at best. Quantitative studies, intelligently interpreted, are badly needed in the field of musicology. But it is possible to take statistical samplings here that are at least representative.

Regarding the number of separate, so-called sonatas composed during the Classic Era (*ca.* 1735-1820), even the roughest estimate is complicated at once by the question of borderline composers. The best that can be offered here is the fact that about 3,200 sonatas, whether separate or within sets, have been examined for the present survey (or almost a third more than for our previous volume), and that these represent scarcely a fifth of all those, extant or not, for which listings could be culled from old or new catalogues, dictionaries, and other bibliographic sources. As to the ratio between sonatas and related instrumental types, the following table gives percentages computed from a total of works listed in four representative sources. These sources are all international in scope and, together, embrace the pre, high, and late phases of the Classic Era. First is the "Fonds Blancheton" in the library of the Paris Conservatoire, which contains MSS dating from about 1720 to 1740. The statistics that we need for these MSS were prepared by La Laurencie in 1931.[19] Second is the catalogue of the

18. As trans. in Anderson/MOZART I 53 (cf. II 781) and II 871-872.

19. La Laurencie/BLANCHETON II 107; but his statistics are slightly altered here to exclude one "ballo," one capriccio, and one minuet.

enterprising publisher in Nürnberg, Johann Ulrich Haffner, which
dates from about 1742 to 1766, and has been pieced together largely by
the German scholar Hoffmann-Erbrecht.[20] Third is the extensive
thematic catalogue issued by the important publisher in Leipzig, J. G.
Breitkopf, which dates from 1762 to 1787 (with 16 nearly annual supplements) and lists MSS in his keeping, including some that he eventually published.[21] About ten per cent of these MSS date as far back as
1720, though they do not seem to affect the percentages derived here.
And fourth is the virtually complete catalogue of publications by the
outstanding firm of Artaria in Vienna, which dates from 1778 to 1858
and has been compiled by the Viennese bibliographer Alexander Weinmann.[22] Only Artaria's publications up to 1820 have been included in 22a
the present tabulation. The total number of instrumental works tabulated in each source is listed in parentheses under the name of that
source.

The Sonata and Related Instrumental Types

Source (Total works)	*Blancheton* (298)	*Haffner* (505)	*Breitkopf* (9,595)	*Artaria* (1,856)
Sonatas	9 per cent	60 per cent	23 per cent	36 per cent
Duets		1	9	21
Trios	6	1	12	7
Quartets			12	27
Quintets				2
Partitas, suites, and *divertimenti*		23	3	
Concertos	41	5	16	2
Symphonies and overtures	44	10	22	3
Other			3	2

The wide variations in the foregoing percentages are only partly
explained by different tastes in different times and locales, or by what
actually got published as against what remained in MS. Although this
sampling appears to be the broadest yet taken, it still is much too spotty
to permit a reliable estimate.[23] Mainly, one can see that even when the 23a

20. Hoffmann-Erbrecht/HAFFNER (including a statistical summary on p. 125 that is different in kind from the one prepared here); supplemented in Newman/HAFFNER.

21. BREITKOPF MS. Cf. Meyer/BREITKOPF.

22. Weinmann/ARTARIA.

23. Larger samplings might be taken from Eitner/QL, HOFMEISTER 1815 and 1828 (Whistling), or the fullest library catalogues, including BRITISH UNION, Cat. BRUXELLES, and the PUBBLICAZIONI series. Each would have its own limitations, of course. Pertinent here is Nef's analysis of 1241 MSS only partially extant in Basel, in which 37 per cent of 813 cyclic instrumental works are SS/- or S/bass

"sonatas" are limited to works that actually bear the title (as here and elsewhere in the present survey), they represent a very substantial portion of the total instrumental output in the Classic Era. This reminder is necessary primarily because so much attention has been paid to the symphonies and/or concertos of pre-Classicists like G. B. Sammartini, J. Stamitz, the Monn brothers, and J. C. Bach that almost none has been left for their equally numerous and often equally interesting if very different sonatas.

It is useful to compare the corresponding figures for the three Viennese masters. Sonatas comprise about 47 per cent of the approximately 600 larger, cyclic instrumental works by Haydn, 33 per cent of the 275 by Mozart, and 44 per cent of the 130 by Beethoven.[24] But the percentage for Haydn would be reduced considerably if we were to exclude every "sonata" that was also called a "divertimento," "trio," or other title in some other source.

None of the foregoing figures include vocal works or smaller instrumental pieces. One can only hazard the impression that substantially more vocal than instrumental music was still being composed in the Classic Era, but that, especially among the more extended works, the instrumental music was achieving publication at least as much as the vocal. Naturally, the cost of printing was less and the prospects for sales better when, say, a complete set of accompanied keyboard sonatas was published than a complete opera in reduced, vocal score. Arthur Loesser has analyzed a 1789 catalogue from the London firm of Longman & Broderip, in which 20 per cent of the 1664 items are for single, accompanied voice and 34 per cent are for piano alone, including 18 per cent of the total that are "sonatas" or "lessons."[25]

The further impression has been received here that a good third of the Classic sonatas known to have existed at one time, if not recently, did achieve publication. However, since the sonatas that remained in MS were far more likely to disappear over the years, this estimate, too, is subject to drastic revision. It is pertinent to recall that even a piano sonata by Beethoven (in C) that got published has completely disappeared.[26]

---

sons. (ZIMG IV [1902-1903] 385-389); also, Boyden's analysis of 958 cyclic string ensembles in a MS collection mostly by Tartini and his immediate descendants, in which over 40 per cent are Vn/bass and over 22 per cent are SS/bass sons. (MQ XLVI [1960] 318-320).

24. Based mainly on the totals of such works recognized as authentic in Hoboken/HAYDN, Köchel/MOZART, and Kinsky & Halm/BEETHOVEN. The somewhat different figures in SCE XIV and XV include all categories of their instrumental works.

25. Loesser/PIANOS 229-231.

26. Hess/VERZEICHNIS no. 52.

Regarding the proportions in which the different settings of the Classic sonata were composed, the Haffner, Breitkopf, and Artaria catalogs may be utilized again for representative samplings from the pre-, high-, and late-Classic Era, respectively.

The Settings of the Sonata

Source	*Haffner*	*Breitkopf*	*Artaria*
(Total sonatas)	(303)	(2198)	(664)
Solo keyboard	78 per cent	27 per cent	42 per cent
Accompanied keyboard		28	47
SS/bass	4	24	
S/bass	14	12	2
Other	4	9	9

A more detailed consideration of the varieties and characteristics of the settings is reserved for our next chapter. Here this tabulation helps to illustrate the spread of the sonata by pointing up a quantitative trend from the melo/bass to the still more popular accompanied settings. It also shows the exceptional interest that Haffner took in the solo keyboard sonata, an interest shared by Schmid and other publishers in Nürnberg, too (as shown on the check list early in our next chapter).

To illustrate the international character of sonata publishing in the Classic Era two other kinds of lists may be helpful. One is a list by cities or court centers of the 67 composers of 114 sonatas that one man, Haffner, published between 1755 and 1766 in the 19 volumes of his 3 important keyboard anthologies.[27] Most of the composers are now obscure. But their spread throughout much of Europe is another reminder of how general the interest in the sonata was at this time. (Where they differ, Haffner's spellings but not his locations are changed to conform with those in the present survey, which touches on most of his composers in Part II. Initials or Christian names are given only where needed.)

The Spread of Composers in Haffner's Sonata Anthologies

Altenburg
  Krebs
Augsburg
  Seifert
Berleburg
  Hupfeld
Berlin
  Bach, Emanuel
  Benda, G.
  Busse
  Fasch, C. F. C.
  Janitsch
  Kirnberger
  Krause
  Le Fevre
  Marpurg
  Rackemann
  Roth
  Schaffrath
  Wenkel
Bologna
  Sales
Braunschweig
  Zachariae

27. Anth. HAFFNER COLLECTION-m; Anth. HAFFNER OM-m; Anth. HAFFNER RACCOLTA-m. Cf. SCE XI.

Brussels
Krafft
Bückeburg
Serini
Coburg
Fischer, J. N.
Copenhagen
Palschau
Scheibe
Cremona
Chiarini
Dresden
Binder
Weber, C. J.
Florence
Martini
Rutini (as though 3 different men!)
Lübeck
Kunzen
Madrid
Paganelli
Scarlatti, D.
Mainz
Zach
Mecklenburg
Hertel

Milan
Paladini
Munich
Stadler
Nürnberg
Agrell
Brand
Kehl
Kleinknecht
Spitz
Paris
Schobert
Pavia
Martino
Scarlatti, Giuseppe
Prague
Fischer, P.
Rendsburg
Appel
St. Petersburg
Araja
Salzburg
Adlgasser
Eberlin
Mozart, L.
Stockholm
Johnsen

Stuttgart
Daube
Hardt
Tournai
Le Roy
Ulm
Walther, J. C.
Venice
Bertoni
Galuppi
Pampani
Peroti
Pescetti
Vienna
Hengsberger
Martinez
Monn, J. C.
Timer
Wagenseil
Weikersheim
Buttstett
Weimar
Bach, J. E.
Würzburg
Umstatt

The remaining list gives some idea of the spread not of the composers but of the publishers.[28] It applies to the late-Classic Era and consists of 53, or most but not all, of the early publishers and republishers of some 35 sets containing 123 sonatas by Clementi, first issued between 1773 and 1821. (Variants of the same company are not given here, but would increase the total number of publishers by almost a third.) Further lists showing a similarly surprising amount and spread of publishing activity could be prepared for Haydn, Koželuch, Hoffmeister, Pleyel, Beethoven, and not a few other highly successful composers of the time.

Clementi's Publishers

Berlin
Hummel
Bonn
Simrock

Dublin
Hime, M.
Lee, J.

Edinburgh
Corri & Co.
Hamburg
Boehme

28. Among valuable recent studies, directories, and catalogues of Classic publishers utilized in the present volume are those listed in the Bibliography under Johansson, Hopkinson, Humphries & Smith, Hill, Weinmann, Gericke, Hoffmann-Erbrecht, Wiberg, and Sartori.

Leipzig
- Breitkopf & Härtel

London
- Babb
- Birchall, R.
- Blundell
- Broderip & Wilkinson
- Clementi
- Dale, J.
- Davis & Collard
- Harrison
- Kerpen
- Longman & Broderip
- Preston, J.
- Royal Harmonic Institution
- Thompson, S., A., and P.
- Walker, G.
- Welcker, J.

Lyon
- Garnier
- Naderman

Mainz
- Artaria
- Schott

Mannheim
- Haeckel

Milan
- Carulli

Munich
- Falter

Naples
- Settembre e Negri

Offenbach/M
- André

Paris
- Bailleux
- Baillon
- Boyer
- Cornouaille
- Erard
- Imbault
- Le Duc
- Le Menu
- Lobry
- Magasin de musique
- Naderman
- Pleyel
- Pollet
- Porro
- Richault
- Sieber

Speyer
- Bossler

Vienna
- Artaria
- Cappi
- Mollo
- Torricella

Zürich
- Nägeli

It will be noted that the large number of publishers in Paris and London (including Clementi himself) is in proportion to the large number of sonata composers active in those cities. Conversely, the small number in Italian cities reflects the little such activity there. Thus, no independent instrumental music seems to have been published in Rome after 1745 in the eighteenth century.[29] As we shall see (SCE X), Burney overstated when he wrote about Venice in 1770 that the "art of engraving music there seems to be utterly lost, as I was not able to find a single work printed in the manner we print music in England."[30] He was to overstate even more in 1772 in a similar remark about Vienna.[31] But Venice certainly had dropped a long way from its pre-eminent position as a publishing center in the Baroque Era (as had Amsterdam). And Vienna was only on the threshold of its lively publishing activity in the late-Classic Era.[32]

Of course, the number of copies in an edition of sonatas enters into these largely quantitative considerations. Whereas a comparable edi- 32a
tion today is small if it numbers 1,000 copies, the Classic edition was more likely to fall within the 150 to 600 copies that an average Baroque

29. None can be found in Sartori/DIZIONARIO.

30. BURNEY'S TOURS I 139. Besides several publications of sons. in Venice that we shall be noting, interesting counterevidence from 1787 is cited in Torrefranca/ORIGINI 723.

31. BURNEY'S TOURS II 121 and 124.

32. Gericke/WIENER traces a relatively thin stream of activity up to 1778, after which Weinmann/WIENER shows a rapid increase.

edition had contained (SBE 46). But we read of larger editions on occasion. Brenet mentions Paris editions of 1,500 copies around the mid-eighteenth century.[33] The subscription lists prepared by composers who found it more advantageous to undertake their own publishing give us some of the best information on sizes of editions. For example, the set of six keyboard sonatas that E. W. Wolf published in Leipzig in 1774 shows 165 copies going to 150 names, starting with 12 to the "Crown Prince of Prussia." (Patrons could expect as many as 24 copies, as with Rutini's Op. 2.[34]) The six volumes of Emanuel Bach's *Kenner und Liebhaber* series started with 519 subscribers in the first volume and dropped to 288 by the last.[35] N. G. Gruner's first set of keyboard sonatas appeared in Leipzig in 1781 with no fewer than 1365 subscribers' names,[36] including 37 Hungarians and 74 Austrians as well as many Germans. And the first volume of G. Benda's *Sammlung vermischter Clavierstücke,* which he brought out in Gotha in 1780, seems to have topped all other reported totals for collections containing sonatas, with over 2,000 subscribers.[37] No figures have been found here on the size of re-editions. But one assumes that the successes that led to them must often have encouraged the publishers to make them larger than the original editions. Among the editions represented by the foregoing list of Clementi's publishers are as many as nine re-editions of a single set.[38] A glance at BRITISH UNION, HOFMEISTER, and other major catalogues is sufficient to reveal that such a large number of re-editions was not rare for the most successful composers, although nothing can be cited for the Classic Era that quite equals the 78 (or more?) re-editions of Corelli's five sets of sonatas during his own lifetime (SBE 156).

Some Further Aspects of Publication

When a composer's sonatas did not get published, the reason was not necessarily any lack of skill on his part or any shortcoming in the music. On the contrary, the very fact of his skill and of the music's appeal may have kept his sonatas from publication. His patron may have wanted to keep such plums by the artists in his establishment to himself, whether for his personal use or as show pieces to produce on special occasions. In our previous volume we saw that the sonatas of Zelenka in Dresden

33. Brenet/LIBRAIRIE 411.
34. Torrefranca/MAESTRO 245.
35. Cf. Bitter/BRÜDER I 212-230.
36. Cf. Eitner/QL IV 395-396.
37. Gerber/NEUES I 133 (reduced from "well over 3,000" in Gerber/LEXICON I 134).
38. Cf. MUSICA XIV (1960) 117.

and of Quantz in Berlin had to remain in MS because the royal patrons of each composer guarded these works jealously, not allowing them either to be copied or to be published (SBE 274 and 277).

It is significant that the least published category of Emanuel Bach's sonatas was that in melo/bass settings, for these settings are the ones with prominent flute parts and with the more conservative style traits that were most likely to appeal to Frederick the Great's own tastes. Also in this monarch's service, Franz Benda wrote in his autobiography that he was paid by some (unnamed) "friend" to keep his sonatas "from becoming generally known through print" (SCE XIII). Sometimes the composer had his own reason for not wanting his sonatas to be copied or published, especially the virtuoso who preferred not to have his thunder stolen in this way. Dittersdorf tells in his autobiography how the outstanding violinist D. Ferrari rewarded his accompanist (Dittersdorf's teacher) by allowing him "to copy his [Ferrari's] finest concertos and sonatas."[39]

Such methods of protecting a composer's works were necessary in this golden century of forgeries and plagiarisms and a century that knew no effective copyright, nor anything closer to it than a "royal privilege." Very frequent, and far from a falsely modest excuse for publication, was the sort of statement that Guénin added to a catalogue of his works inserted in his accompanied sonatas Op. 5, published in 1781:

> Besides some of the works [catalogued] above that have been plagiarized and crammed with errors, several things have been engraved elsewhere under the author's name that are not by him and about which he knows nothing. Being informed of these things, he has the honor to caution the respected amateurs who wish to have his music that he has brought out nothing but the works in the above catalogue and that they should suspect all the copies that may be presented to them under his name unless these have the present warning in front signed in his hand.[40]

We shall get a further idea of what Guénin and other composers feared when we come to Jozzi's plagiarism of Alberti's sonatas, or Pellegrini's plagiarism of sonatas by several other Italians, or the crediting of sonatas to Pergolesi that were probably composed much later, or the confusion
surrounding some "trios" by Haydn (H. XV/3-5) or Pleyel, if either, 40a
or even the grand hoax that involved F. W. Rust posthumously.

A "Privilège du Roy" was granted in France right up to the start of the Revolution. But this required permission to publish often could be side-stepped by little-known composers (and was unsystematic enough, in any case, to be only a partial help in present-day efforts to establish

39. DITTERSDORF 41.
40. Trans. from the original French as quoted in Reeser/KLAVIERSONATE 133.

dates).[41] England's Copyright Act of 1709 and her royal privileges granted up to at least 1763 did little to stop piracy in that country (and, again, were too uncertain to serve as precise dating tools today).[42]

In the present and previous chapters we have already seen that a published "Opera prima" of sonatas made a good start for the young composer or performer, that this publication was often undertaken at his own expense, that sometimes he preferred to continue publishing in this way by getting subscribers, and that otherwise his only reimbursement, all too often, might be a few free copies. This last fact resulted partly from the relatively high cost of printing and, hence, the relatively high price that had to be charged for the music.[43] Even more than today, only the composers most respected and most in demand could pretty well set their own fees. Thus, where Vento in London had to depend on his students to subsidize his publications,[44] Emanuel Bach, Haydn, and Beethoven could stipulate exact charges for sonatas and other works in their many business letters. Bach made it clear in 1786 that six new sonatinas (W. 63/7-12) composed for his *Essay* would have to be the one-movement kind, since the three-movement "kind could not be made for 18 thalers . . . and would, on account of the expense, rather impede the sale. . . ."[45] Haydn seems to have established an approximate ratio of fees in the 1780's of 6:6:5:4 for symphonies, string quartets, accompanied piano sonatas (P & Vn & Vc), and solo piano sonatas, respectively, although his fees fluctuated considerably.[46] Beethoven evaluated his Septet, Op. 20, Symphony No. 1, Piano Concerto No. 2, and Piano Sonata Op. 22 in the respective ratio, surprisingly, of 2:2:1:2, partly because "I do not consider it [the concerto] to be one of my best concertos."[47] But his prices fluctuated even more sharply than Haydn's.[48]

Another frequent concern in the many letters that Haydn and Beethoven wrote their publishers is that about the carelessness of the

41. Cf. Brenet/LIBRAIRIE 411-412.

42. Cf. Humphries & Smith/PUBLISHING 23-24; Terry/BACH 78-79 (including a lengthy privilege of 1763 for J. C. Bach, quoted in full).

43. Cf. Leopold Mozart's letter of Feb. 12, 1781, to Breitkopf (Anderson/MOZART II 1054); Hoffmann-Erbrecht/HAFFNER 125-126; Loesser/PIANOS 453.

44. Burney/HISTORY II 884.

45. From the complete trans. in Plamenac/BACH 567.

46. Cf. his letters in Landon/HAYDN 45, 47, 83, 84, 85, 94, *et passim*. Cf., also, Deutsch's relevant discussion of Schubert's income and Austrian currency in ML XXXVI (1955) 165-166; and the note on "money values" in Anderson/BEETHOVEN I xlvii-xlviii.

47. Letter of *ca.* Jan. 15, 1801, as trans. in Anderson/BEETHOVEN I 47-48.

48. Cf. the interesting, fuller schedule of his rates in about 1804, in MacArdle & Misch/MINOR 446-448. In that year he could write, ". . . people give me up to 60 ducats for a single sonata for pianoforte solo" (Anderson/BEETHOVEN I 117).

engraving.[49] Beethoven had an especially bad time with his late piano sonatas. Mozart left very few letters to publishers that are known, mostly because so much less of his music was published during his lifetime. But he said enough to make clear his general dissatisfaction with engravers of the time.[50] The engraving by the larger firms seems to have been about equally poor and hasty in the three main centers, Paris, London, and Vienna.[51] 51a

A few words may be added about the nature of the scores as they were published. The use of different clefs in Classic keyboard scores was never as great as it had been in, say, the MS sonatas of B. Marcello, dating from about 1710-20. But the tenor, alto, and baritone clefs still occasionally replace the bass clef in the left-hand staffs of pre-Classic scores. And the soprano C-clef lasted so long that as late as 1789 Emanuel Bach's widow had to advertise the "Kenner und Liebhaber" sets as being available "in the keyboard [C] as well as the violin [G] clef,"[52] and Türk had to advise students that "the learning of the G- or Violin-clef has now become more necessary."[53] Yet, as early as 1757 Haffner had discarded the C- for the G-clef (Anth. HAFFNER OM-m III).

The large majority of eighteenth-century chamber works appeared in separate parts rather than in score. Not a few of the optional violin-or-flute parts in accompanied sonatas are missing in present-day libraries that would be known had they been scored above the piano part.[54] English publishers generally led the way in such uses of scores as did occur. Thus, the accompanied keyboard sonatas of Christian Bach and Abel, among others, appeared originally in score. Avison, whose concertos were published "for the Author" in score in 1758 by Johnson in London, had urged the use of cues, in 1752, in the parts for which no score could be supplied.[55] However, cues are not present in his own published sonatas. Not until Beethoven's cello sonatas Op. 102 were published in 1817 did a chamber work by that master appear in score,[56] which fact was warmly greeted by the reviewer (SCE XV). Sonatas in SS/bass settings were not published in score, although usually submitted in score by the composer, to judge from extant MSS.[57]

49. E.g., cf. Landon/HAYDN 51-52; Anderson/BEETHOVEN II 796-805 (Op. 106) and III 1037-1054 *passim*.
50. E.g., cf. Anderson/MOZART II 928 and III 1261.
51. Cf., also, Humphries & Smith/PUBLISHING 26-29.
52. Miesner/NACHLASS 162.
53. Türk/KLAVIERSCHULE 16-17; cf., also, Hedler/TÜRK 95 regarding Türk's more positive statement in 1798.
54. Cf. Newman/ACCOMPANIED 329-330.
55. Avison/ESSAY 131-138.
56. Kinsky & Halm/BEETHOVEN 283.
57. E.g., cf. the facs. of an Emanuel Bach autograph in Schmid/BACH 113.

Most sonatas continued to appear in sets throughout the eighteenth century, as they had appeared in the Baroque Era. But they tended to group in smaller and smaller sets. The earlier melo/bass sonatas often appeared in sets of 12, or 2 sets of 6 each. (At the end of Herrando's first of 2 sets of 6 SS/bass sonatas, in a MS of the 1750's, the composer wrote, "Others follow.")[58] Paradisi still published 12 keyboard sonatas in his set of 1754. Beginning only about six years later, Schobert's accompanied sonatas became among the first to appear mostly in sets of but two or three each.[59] The child Mozart may have been following this precedent in his "Op. 1" and "Op. 2" (K.V. 6-7 and 8-9), although "Op. 3" (K.V. 10-15) and several subsequent sets contained 6 sonatas each, again. When a single sonata first appeared alone, it usually did so in default of the rest of the set, as did Friedemann Bach's Sonata in D in 1745 (F. 3). But by the end of their careers, Haydn, Mozart, Beethoven, and Clementi were all publishing their sonatas singly (beginning with Mozart's K.V. 457 in 1785). Yet it is interesting to recall that Beethoven still published his two cello sonatas Op. 102 as a set in 1817 and that he originally wrote to Schlesinger in Berlin about the publication of Opp. 109-111 as "a work consisting of three sonatas."[60]

In numerous instances sonatas in different settings were mixed in the same set. Among the examples we shall meet in later chapters are English editions in which duet and accompanied or duet and solo keyboard sonatas are mixed, both groupings being found in some sets of Christian Bach and Clementi. Sometimes in the pre-Classic, as in the Baroque Era, the last "sonata" still tops off a set by ending with a "Minuetto con variazioni" (Eckard, Op. 1/6/ii) or a song with words (Rutini, Op. 8/6/ii), or by being an opera medley (Pescetti, No. 10) or a rondo (Emanuel Bach, W. 50/6), or by offering something else special. Sets with 6 or more sonatas usually reveal a planned distribution of keys, as in Mozart's set of 6 piano sonatas K.V. 189d-h and 205b, in C, F, B♭, E♭, G, and D.

The opus number generally was not assigned to a set of sonatas until the set was published. Throughout most of the Classic Era the publisher ordinarily made up his own chronological sequence of opus numbers for each of his composers, regardless of what numbers one or more other publishers may have assigned to their editions of the same works.[61] Apparently some publishers made a special point of changing the opus

58. Subirá/ALBA 179.
59. Cf. David/SCHOBERT 21 and 70 (chart).
60. Anderson/BEETHOVEN II 893.
61. Cf. Sondheimer/SAMMARTINI 90; MGG VI 927 (Schaal).

numbers in order to appear to be issuing different or new works. The resulting confusion for modern bibliographers becomes a recurring theme in the present survey. Schobert's and Rutini's opus numbers are somewhat exceptional in the pre-Classic Era in providing fairly clear sequences (though by no means free of other bibliographic problems). The opus numbers for Haydn's and Mozart's sonatas are too confused to have any over-all value. Those for Clementi's sonatas are confused enough to warrant a new numbering system. But those for Beethoven's sonatas survived in surprisingly good order, the more so when one considers all the entanglements of his negotiations with publishers.

Opus numbers were sometimes assigned to the successive volumes in a published anthology, too, as in the five volumes of Anth. HAFFNER RACCOLTA-m, Opp. 1-5. Until sonatas appeared singly, these anthologies provided almost the only means by which a composer could publish one sonata at a time.[62] Whether he ever received more than the honor and a free copy for his trouble is another question. In many later anthologies, publishers capitalized on previous successes by reprinting particular sonatas that had appeared originally in complete sets. But in his especially valuable anthologies of the pre-Classic Era, Haffner adhered almost entirely to his intention of publishing only original works.[63] Several anthologies appeared on a subscription basis—for example, *Bland's Collection of Sonatas, Lessons, Overtures. . .* , a "periodical" founded in London about 1790[64]—and sometimes sonatas and related instrumental music were issued on a loan basis by publishers.[65]

62. For a representative list of anthologies, see under "Anth." in the Bibliography, *infra;* also, cf. Cat. BRUXELLES II 343-347 and BRITISH UNION II 613 and 962-964.

63. Cf. Hoffmann-Erbrecht/HAFFNER 125.

64. Cf. the facs. in Newman/ACCOMPANIED 347.

65. Cf. Reeser/KLAVIERSONATE 29; Hopkinson/PARISIAN 19.

Chapter V

Instruments and Settings

The Harpsichord and the Clavichord

Intimately bound up in the nature of the Classic sonata, of course, are the kinds and combinations of instruments that were preferred then. The present chapter explores these aspects of musical science and composition insofar as they bear directly on sonata history.

Much as the stringed instruments, especially the newly cultivated violin, had been central to the scoring of the Baroque sonata, so the keyboard instruments, especially the newly cultivated "fortepiano," were central to the Classic sonata.[1] Indeed, the preliminary definition and demarcation of the Classic Era in our first chapter might well have been made in terms of the trends in keyboard types and styles during those approximately 85 years. The start of the era is rather clearly defined by the conspicuous flowering of the harpsichord and clavichord sonata around 1740. The transition from pre- to high-Classic phases of the era is similarly well defined by the momentous transition from harpsichord to piano in the 1760's and 1770's. And the onset of the late-Classic phase in the 1790's can be identified partly by the new exploitation of the piano's idiomatic techniques and sonorities, although this exploitation had been anticipated two decades earlier in Clementi's early sonatas.

Because the flowering of the keyboard sonata around 1740 was so significant to Classic trends, a check list of pertinent publications is in order here. The list includes all original publications of solo keyboard sonatas between about 1732 and 1749 that are noted in either the present or previous volume.[2] The importance of the Nürnberg publishers to this flowering was already noted in our previous chapter. Relatively few composers would be added to this list if sonatas were included that are

1. This idea is expanded in Torrefranca/ORIGINI 63-66.

2. Cf., also, Newman/EARLIEST, which stops at 1738 but starts with the first known publication, in 1641 (Del Buono).

known only in MSS of the same period. Among those composers are Pergolesi (if he actually wrote sonatas), Seixas, Hasse, Roman, C. H. Graun (if the MSS are really his), Rutini, and Galuppi (if the MSS are that early).

Solo Keyboard Sonatas Published from about 1732 to 1749

Year	*Composer*	*Place of publication*	*Identification if any*	*Chap. in* SCE *or p. in* SBE
1732	Giustini	Florence	Op. 1 (for piano!)	SBE 195
1732	Handel	Amsterdam	"Sonata" in C	SBE 293 (cf. Newman/EARLIEST 212)
1732?	Durante	Naples	6 *Sonate*	SBE 199
1732 or *ca.* '37	Lustig	Amsterdam	Op. 1	SCE XXI
1735	Sorge	Nürnberg	first set	SCE XII
1736	Maichelbeck	Augsburg	Op. 1	SCE XI
ca. 1736	Telemann	?	*VI neue Sonatinen*	SBE 287
1738-39	D. Scarlatti	London	30 *Essercizi*	SCE IX
1739	Pescetti	London	*Sonate*	SCE XIX
ca. 1739	Sorge	Nürnberg	second set	SCE XII
ca. 1740	Renotte	Liège	*Six Sonates*	SCE XXI
1742	Platti	Nürnberg	Op. 1	SCE XII
1742	Emanuel Bach	Nürnberg	"Prussian" set	SCE XIII
1742	Martini	Amsterdam	12 *Sonate*	SBE 182
1742?	Barrière	Paris	Book 6	SBE 388
1744	Emanuel Bach	Nürnberg	"Württemberg" set	SCE XIII
1745	Friedemann Bach	Dresden?	F. 3	SCE XII
1745	Fleischer	Nürnberg	*Clavier-Übung*	SCE XIII
ca. 1745	Nichelmann	Nürnberg	Opp. 1 and 2	SCE XIII
ca. 1745	Sorge	Nürnberg	third set	SCE XII
1746?	Hurlebusch	Amsterdam	Opp. 5 and 6	SCE XXI
1747	Nares	London	first set	SCE XIX
1747	Martini	Bologna	6 *Sonate*	SBE 182
1748	D. Alberti (posthumous?)	London	Op. 1	SCE VII
1748	Agrell	Nürnberg	*Sei Sonate*	SCE XI
ca. 1748	Sorge	Nürnberg	*XII Sonaten*	SCE XII
1749	Schaffrath	Nürnberg	Op. 2	SCE XIII

Regarding the harpsichord's use, only a few essentials need to be recalled here. Until it was finally replaced by the piano, the harpsichord continued to be the principal stringed keyboard instrument wherever sonatas were composed. The dearth of good instruments and players that Burney deplored in Italy in 1770 (SCE IV) must not hide the fact that even in that opera-minded country there was at least a steady trickle of expert keyboard playing, from the harpsichordists B. Marcello, Della Ciaja, and both A. and D. Scarlatti near the start of the century to the pianists Turini, Clementi, and Pollini near the end.[3] Known by various names in the sonata titles of different countries—especially clavicembalo,

3. Burney himself found good players from time to time, such as C. A. Campioni's wife in Florence (BURNEY'S TOURS I 187 and 190), who perhaps could play her husband's 6 virtuoso H sons. of 1763.

gravicembalo, or cembalo in Italy, *crave* or *clavicordio* in Spain, clavecin in France, *Flügel* in Germany, and harpsichord or spinet in England—the harpsichord was also known in many shapes and sizes. Generally it could have one or 2 keyboards and from one to 4 strings per note that were plucked by jacks of quill or leather. With its jacks of 2 different materials, its "lute" and other stops, its 8-, 4-, and 16-foot registers, its 5-octave range (often from FF to f'''), and its devices to couple the keyboards, the larger eighteenth-century harpsichord was capable not only of "the precision, the clarity, and the brilliance" that Couperin had attributed to it in 1717[4] but of surprising contrasts of color and dynamics. Furthermore, by these means, by the slight but not negligible control of touch that was often possible, and by the composer's or performer's thinning or thickening of the texture, the dynamics could be graduated to at least a slight extent not usually thought possible.[5]

The clavichord is specified much less often in Classic sonatas. Its only real remaining stronghold was in Germany, especially north
6a Germany in the important sphere of Friedemann and Emanuel Bach.[6] After 1750 the usual German designation for it was the generic term "Clavier," although Quantz, Emanuel Bach, Türk, and others were careful to be more specific when they wrote about it.[7] The clavichord attained about the same five-octave range that the harpsichord did in the eighteenth century but, of course, did not have the latter's different stops, registers, or keyboards. Even the eighteenth-century *bundfrei* type, with its separate pair of strings for each note, was a much simpler instrument than the harpsichord, calling for little more in the way of mechanical complexities than "pressure-strokes" on the strings by brass tangents, and suitable damping of the strings. This very simplicity was at once the clavichord's chief virtue and failing. By bringing the performer into more intimate control of the string itself than was possible on any other stringed keyboard instrument, the clavichord permitted subtle dynamic gradations and even a subtle control of pitch, including vibrato (*Bebung*). But its principle of "pressure-strokes" could not produce enough volume for use either in concerts or ensemble accompaniments. Although the clavichord's champions acknowledged

4. *L'Art de toucher le clavecin* (p. 22 in the Breitkopf & Härtel reprint of 1933).

5. Cf. the well-known statements in Quantz/VERSUCH 230-232; Bach/ESSAY 149-150, 368-369. Cf., also, GROVE IV 99, 100-101, 106, 109-10 (Donington); MGG II 962-963 (Neupert).

6. "The French are not well acquainted with the clavichord . . ." (Bach/ESSAY 106).

7. E.g., Quantz/VERSUCH 231; Bach/ESSAY 37-38 and 369; Türk/KLAVIERSCHULE 4 (with "Klavier" used thereafter).

its inadequacy for accompaniments,[8] they were strong in their praise for its songful, expressive qualities. The instrument was peculiarly suited to the intense, probing subtleties of the north German, *empfindsam* style. We shall be coming to numerous examples of the praise for it in this latter sense in the sonata prefaces and related comments of Emanuel Bach, G. Benda, Neefe, Zink, and others. Here it may be interesting to add the opinion still held as late as 1785 by Schubart, the rapturous German aesthetician, poet, and musician, of the *Empfindsamkeit:*

> *Clavichord,* this lonely, melancholy, inexpressibly sweet instrument surpasses the harpsichord or piano when it is made by a master [craftsman]. Through the pressure of the fingers, through the oscillation and vibrato of the strings, through the strong or gentler touch of the hand, can be determined not only the immediate musical colorings but the middle tints, the swelling and dying away of the tone, the expiring trills melting away under the fingers, the portamento or glide—in a word, all the qualities out of which feeling is comprised. Whoever does not prefer to bluster, rage, and storm; whosever heart overflows often and readily in sweet feelings—he passes by the harpsichord and piano, and chooses a clavichord . . .[9]

The Early Piano

In Florence in 1732, only about 23 years after Cristofori made his
first piano in that city, Giustini published the first set of sonatas to
specify the piano as the instrument (SBE 194-196). In 1725 Mattheson 9a
had already quoted a description of Cristofori's invention.[10] Further
early interest in the piano is reflected in J. S. Bach's trial of the
Silbermann pianos at the court of Frederick the Great in 1747; also, in
the serious consideration that both Quantz and Emanuel Bach gave to it
within the next six years.[11] But the earliest records of public performances on the piano and the earliest sonatas that call for it after
Giustini's isolated example do not date before the 1760's. Its first
known use in a London concert was in 1767, in an accompaniment to a
song, followed in 1768 by its first use alone, in a "Solo on the Piano
Forte by Mr. [Christian] Bach."[12] Its first known use in a Paris 12a

8. E.g., Bach/ESSAY 36, 368-369.

9. Trans. from Schubart/IDEEN 288-289. Recall the oft-cited description in 1772 of Emanuel Bach playing at the clavichord, "animated and possessed," in BURNEY'S TOURS II 219-220. Auerbach/ CLAVICHORDKUNST contains more information pertinent to the present survey (as noted in later chaps.) than the similarly valuable studies of the harpsichord by Neupert, Harich-Schneider, and others.

10. Parrish/PIANO 5; this diss. on the early piano is especially rich in quotations from contemporary sources, some of which are included in Parrish/ CRITICISMS and Parrish/HAYDN.

11. BACH READER 176, 259, 305-306; Bach/ESSAY 36, 112, 172, 317, 369; Quantz/ VERSUCH 225, 231.

12. Terry/BACH 113.

concert occurred in the latter year, 1768, probably in a solo piece and as a consequence of its use in England.[13] Shortly before these concerts, in Paris in 1763, Eckard published his six "clavecin" sonatas Op. 1, in which frequent indications of graduated dynamics and an explicit preface make clear that either clavichord or piano would be preferable to harpsichord here (SCE XVII). The title of his next set, published the following year as Op. 2, actually offers the choice of "le clavecin ou le piano forte." The first English set of keyboard sonatas to contain graduated dynamics and to specify the piano as an alternative (to both harpsichord and organ) seems to be the charming set by John Burton published in London in 1766 (SCE XIX). Christian Bach's Op. 5, *Six Sonates pour le clavecin ou le piano forte,* appeared in London about two years later.[14]

If the records of the early piano's use do not begin until the 1760's, the transition from the harpsichord to the piano must have started at least a decade earlier, soon spreading almost everywhere.[15] Quantz and Emanuel Bach seem to have taken the "new" instrument for granted in the early 1750's. But, largely because of the Seven Years' War and the devotion to the clavichord, the piano made its way in Germany a little more slowly than elsewhere. Müthel published duets in 1771 for two clavichords, harpsichords, or pianos. Four years later, in spite of the preference for clavichord that he had expressed in 1773, Neefe specified "per Pianoforte con flauti" in a MS,[16] and by 1780 Emanuel Bach himself specified "Forte-Piano" for some pieces in the second set of his "Kenner und Liebhaber" series. Leopold Mozart heard from his wife in 1777 that the piano was in general use in Mannheim, where Mozart played it "as no one had heard it before."[17] In Madrid, D. Scarlatti evidently knew early pianos of the Cristofori type,[18] although the piano may not have been specified in any Spanish piece before 1774.[19] As early as 1760 a piano was built in Portugal.[20] In Italy it-

13. Brenet/CONCERTS 292-293. Several evidences that the piano was imported from England are cited from the early 1770's in Reeser/KLAVIERSONATE 40; cf., also, BURNEY'S TOURS I 27. In turn, the piano may have been brought to England around 1760 by Germans escaping the Seven Years' War (GROVE VI 731 [Harding]), although Burney said the first English piano was made by an English monk in Rome (Scholes/BURNEY I 189).

14. BRITISH UNION I 76.

15. The transition and the introduction of the piano in Germany, England, France, and America are ably described and documented in Loesser/PIANOS 96-112, 218-223, 314-318, and 440-446, respectively.

16. Leux/NEEFE 122-123.

17. Letter of Dec. 28, as in Mueller von Asow/MOZART II 274 (but wrongly trans. in Anderson/MOZART II 644; cf. Loesser/PIANOS 96).

18. Kirkpatrick/SCARLATTI 176, 178.

19. Nin/ESPAGNOLS-m I iii.

20. Kastner/CONTRIBUCIÓN 282.

self, Burney reported a piano of the Cristofori type in Bologna in 1770,[21] the same year that Rutini's keyboard writing introduced dynamics and other traits of the piano style (Op. 7; SCE VII). Only a year later a piano was heard in America, in a public concert in Boston, although it was not specified in the performance of a sonata until 1785.[22]

The gradual changes in Classic sonata titles supply a useful record in themselves of the transition from harpsichord to piano, as well as some indication of the use of the clavichord and organ.[23] The option "per organo ed cembalo" in the seventeenth century had become "per cembalo o piano forte" in the eighteenth century. An average of the dates in several countries would show that the option of harpsichord or piano became general about 1770, that the converse, piano or harpsichord, began to be general only about ten years later, and that by 1785 harpsichord began to disappear from titles.[24] Of course, the titles were not wholly accurate indications of either the meaning or the application of the term. Mozart used the terms "clavier" and "cembalo" in most of the MSS of his keyboard sonatas and in most of his correspondence about them. Most of his publications for or with keyboard from 1778 are "pour le Clavecin ou le Pianoforte." But internal and circumstantial evidence suggest that he was already thinking of the piano in the sonatas that he composed in 1774-75 (K.V. 189d-h and 205).[25] Similarly, Haydn used "cembalo," "clavicembalo," or "clavier" in all his sonata titles but H. XVI/49 in E♭ "per il Forte-piano," yet piano seems to have been intended from H. XVI/20 in c. And Beethoven generally offered the option of "Clavecin ou Pianoforte" through Op. 27 (still writing "Cembalo" in the inscription over Op. 101/iii), though there can be little doubt that the piano was intended exclusively right from Op. 2.

By contrast, some titles were exceptionally precise. Roeser's pioneer use of "forte piano" without any alternative about 1774 (SCE XVIII) proves to apply merely to conservative *pièces de clavecin*. But Beecke's MS sonata of about 1780 that is designated for two pianos and a harpsichord[26] can leave little doubt that a definite distinction between

21. BURNEY'S TOURS I 152.

22. Sonneck/AMERICA 265, 81. Cf. Loesser/PIANOS 441-442 for other references to the piano in America from as early as 1771.

23. For sample lists, cf. Allorto/CLEMENTI 69-136 (1765-1821); Favre/FRANÇAISE 173-181 (1771-1820); "Hoffmeister" in Eitner/QL V 182-183; Weinmann/ARTARIA 14-122 (1778-1822); also, the analysis of 109 items "for or with clavier" in Cramer/MAGAZIN I (1783), as given in Broder/MOZART 427-428.

24. The statistics compiled by A. G. Hess, in *The Galpin Society Journal* VI (July, 1953) 75-94, tend, in spite of their limited scope, to support the average dates determined here.

25. As concluded in Broder/MOZART.

26. Munter/BEECKE 596.

instruments was intended.[27] Similarly unequivocal are clarifying inscriptions within the sonata like "grand et petit clavier" for the two manuals of the harpsichord, as by Edelmann.[28]

Ordinarily no style distinction at all was intended by the optional titles used during the transition from harpsichord to piano. The composer and publisher naturally wanted the sale to reach as wide a market as possible. For this reason, organ was not seldom added to the title, too, as in John Garth's several sets of "Sonatas for the Harpsichord, Piano-Forte, and Organ, With Accompanyments for Two Violins and a Violoncello."[29] But during the transition, style distinctions began to show up in the music itself that help to explain why the piano ultimately replaced the harpsichord. Most obvious was the insertion of "cresc.," "decresc.," and related terms or signs to indicate graduated dynamics. These tended to be used profusely at first, as in 1777 in Burney's *Sonatas or Duets For two Performers on One Piano Forte or Harpsichord,* but only sparingly in Mozart's keyboard sonatas, with most in K.V. 189d-h and 205b,[30] and not liberally again until Haydn's last sonatas and Beethoven's Op. 2. A second editorial distinction was the more detailed indication of articulation through slurs and staccato dots or wedges. We shall see in our next chapter that the niceties of articulation were among essential traits of the high-Classic sonata style.

But the indications for both dynamics and articulation were also characteristic of the *empfindsam* clavichord sonatas (e.g., those in Emanuel Bach's "Kenner und Liebhaber" series). One must remember that the first attraction of the new "piano forte" was its expressive capabilities rather than its potential as a concert instrument. Burney recommended in 1772 that children study not "a monotonous harpsichord" but a clavichord or piano for "expression."[31] Mozart's enthusiastic letter of October 17-18, 1777, after trying Stein's pianos in Augsburg, mainly concerns his delight with the touch control, especially its evenness and its damping and escapement action.[32] The later eighteenth-century piano that was not merely a rebuilt clavichord or harpsichord fitted with hammers and assorted "stops" could well be the type associated with Mozart—wing shaped, about 7 feet long, narrow in width and in its compass of about 5½ octaves, equipped with a very light action, thin wire strings, and leather-covered hammers, and char-

27. For further titles of this sort, cf. Saint-Foix/PIANISTES V 195; Favre/FRANÇAISE 15; Broder/MOZART 428.
28. Cf. Saint-Foix/PIANISTES V 190.
29. BRITISH MUSEUM I 361.
30. Cf. Broder/MOZART 429-430.
31. BURNEY'S TOURS II 96.
32. Cf. Loesser/PIANOS 100-102.

acterized by "a clear, singing tone, sonorous and vibrant in the bass and silvery in the middle and upper octaves."[33] By the end of the Classic Era the piano was still a wood-frame instrument in which the tone had but little of the depth, roundness, penetration, and sustaining power of that in today's best instruments. Yet it had now acquired many of its ultimate essentials, including thicker strings (wound in the bass), unisons made up of two or three strings, larger hammers, and a wider compass (extending to 6½ octaves, CC-f'''', in Beethoven's Op. 106).[34] Also, by the end of the Classic Era, two main trends in piano manufacture were already distinguishable—that stemming from the Vienna type just described, which was preferred by Haydn, Hummel, Weber, and Czerny, and was characterized by its delicate, easy action and its bright clear sound; and that of the Broadwood type such as Beethoven got from London in 1818, characterized by greater power, heavier action, and orchestral resonance.[35] 35a

To return to the question of what style traits distinguished the early piano music from contemporary harpsichord music, the eighteenth-century writers recognized the fact of the distinction without clarifying
it very much. An anonymous German writer objected in 1782 to the 35b
indefinite title "Sonaten fürs Clavier" because each of the three stringed keyboard instruments must be treated differently according to its character and function, the clavichord being best suited to beginners, composers, and the playing of intimate solos; the piano to accompanying singers and small chamber groups; and the harpsichord only to *b.c.* realization by an opera or concert orchestra conductor.[36] Hüllmandel, the fine Alsatian pianist and sonata composer in Paris, published an encyclopedia article in 1791, much to the same effect, on the "Clavecin." His words reflect the dissatisfaction that finally led to the harpsichord's discard:

> The harpsichord lacks nuances. No way was found, after the addition of the second keyboard, of augmenting or diminishing the volume . . . [except by complications that] denote the imperfection of the harpsichord. It requires too much skill from craftsmen and too much patience from performers . . . Moreover, should we seek to cling to false and puerile imitations? An instrument in which evenness and purity of sound and all the desired degrees of strength and gentleness speak to the heart without hurting the ear, fulfills the aim of music to a much greater degree. (See the article *Piano-forte.*)

As instrumental music was perfected, the style of the harpsichord went

33. Cf. King/MOZART 244-245.
34. Cf. Parrish/CRITICISMS 430.
35. Cf. MGG VII 1105 (Neupert); Schlesinger/CRAMER 26-27; also, the fine photographs in Rosenberg/BEETHOVEN 281 and 349.
36. Parrish/CRITICISMS 437-438.

through several changes. Sixty years ago it felt the effect of these developments even more than did the style of organ music. Since then a clearer distinction has been made between the two instruments. To harpsichord music was assigned the role of harmony and execution, gracefulness and lightness, which are suitable to it. Alberti, Scarlatti, Rameau, Müthel, and then Schobert, have almost simultaneously effected this revolution. The different styles of these composers have served, during more than twenty-five years, as a model for their successors who have composed for the harpsichord. . . . [Now various authors,] by giving to their music graduated nuances, contrasts, and a melody suited to the tone and resources of the piano, have prepared or determined the downfall of the harpsichord.[37]

Carl Parrish reports one of the rare style distinctions between clavichord and piano to be made by an eighteenth-century writer. It occurs in a review published in 1783 of the fourth set in Emanuel Bach's "Kenner und Liebhaber" series and would appear to belie Bach's partial change to "Forte-Piano" in the title (as noted earlier). The German author also seems to be objecting to the very kind of damping problem in the action that Mozart found so well solved in the Stein pianos.

The E major Rondo, as well as the preceding second Sonata, is definitely intended for the clavichord, and only that instrument can bring to it the expressive nuances which it demands. The piece is made suitable for this first of instruments by the flow and the closeness of its melodic intervals, the light and shadow with which it is suffused, the use of certain musical *chiaroscuro,* and the almost complete abstention from those arpeggios and passages consisting of mere broken chords which, as I am well aware, occur too often in these new collections of the *Herr Kapellmeister* to suit some connoisseurs. The remarks of these latter are, considered abstractly, perhaps not without reason; but actually they lose much of their force when one recalls that these Rondos, Sonatas, etc., are, according to the title page, intended for the piano and that adjacent melodic notes make a bad effect on this defective instrument, since no player has springs in his fingers. Composers must, therefore, change the character of their melodies so that the intervals are wider, in order to lessen the untimely sounding together of notes already heard.[38]

From our present standpoint it is often impossible to find any traits that distinguish the writing for piano from that for harpsichord or for clavichord while the latter two instruments were still in common use. After all, throughout most of their careers both Mozart and Haydn continued to have uses for the harpsichord and to enjoy composing at the clavichord.[39] But by the turn of the century, when the piano had won the competition anyway, enough evolutionary change in keyboard writing itself had taken place to produce a clearly identifiable piano

37. Quoted from the complete article as trans. in Benton/HÜLLMANDEL 307-308 and 312-315.

38. From Cramer/MAGAZIN I (1783) 1238 as trans. in Parrish/CRITICISMS 439.

39. Cf. Broder/MOZART 423-424; James/HAYDN 315.

style. We may note, for instance, some striking examples of piano writing that are striking for the very reason that they appeared so long before 1800. Clementi's *Six Sonatas for the Harpsichord or Piano Forte . . .*, Op. 2, published by Welcker in London, were not remarkable in 1779 for their modest dynamic and articulation markings, their occasional cantabile lines, or any other expressive values. But they did prove to be remarkable for their idiomatic uses of the keyboard. These 39a
uses anticipate the more brilliant writing in the sonatas of Beethoven and other late-Classic writers, although not of Clementi himself, since he eventually turned to a simpler, purer, thinner style, probably under Mozart's influence. In Op. 2 we find the double-note passages that Mozart decried (SCE XIV), as well as advanced scale and arpeggio passages, prolonged series of rapid octaves, broken octaves such as Beethoven used in Op. 2/3/i, and tricky chordal figures. Precedents might be cited for any one of these, but not for all of them in the same sonata nor in such abundance (Ex. 1).

Other Instruments

Other instruments used in the Classic sonata require less notice here than the stringed keyboard instruments, both because they figured in it less often or importantly and because they underwent no corresponding transitions in their types and use at this time. The organ was not included with the other keyboard instruments because the relatively few organ sonatas left in the Classic Era are of but minor consequence. Maichelbeck presumably had the organ in mind along with the harpsichord and clavichord when he designated his sonatas of 1736 "for use as well on church as on domestic keyboard instruments." But the style differences implied by now between the wind and stringed keyboard instruments were too great for us to attach much significance to such alternative titles other than the publisher's desire, again, to reach the widest possible market. After the early examples left by Maichelbeck and Padre Martini (1742), most of the sonatas with alternative titles have the thin, light textures of *galant* harpsichord music, as by D. Hasler (1759? Haffner plate no. CI), L. de Rossi (between 1773 and 1782), and numerous others. More of the polyphonic, traditional organ style is found in Scheibe's organ "trio" sonatas (i.e., for two manuals and pedalboard) and Janitsch's organ sonatas (*ca.* 1760). But such organ sonatas as those by Emanuel Bach (1755-58; W. 70) and I. Cirri (*ca.* 1770) are again light music suitable for harpsichord, even though this alternative is not mentioned in the titles.[40]

40. Regarding all these organ sons. and others, cf. Frotscher/ORGELSPIEL 717, 788-795, 799, 1099-1100; also, Geiringer/BACH 358.

Ex. 1. From the first movement of Sonata in B♭, Op. 2/6, by Muzio Clementi (after TRÉSOR-m X/3).

In the MSS of Spanish keyboard sonatas at the Montserrat monastery and elsewhere the organ is often the alternative or even the only instrument designated, and its registrations are sometimes indicated in the music. Yet the light texture and character of the *galant* harpsichord sonata prevail here, too.[41] But Soler has anachronistic movements in his

41. Cf. Pujol/MONTSERRAT-m II viii.

stringed keyboard sonatas that go back to the severe liturgic organ "intento" of the seventeenth century (SCE IX). Although it has occasional solo passages, the organ in Mozart's so-called "Epistle" or "organ" sonatas serves mainly to realize the *b.c.* As noted earlier (SCE III), these sonatas had a liturgic function. So did Cimarosa's "Sonata" for two organs (1780), G. D. Catenacci's "Sonate d'organo" (1792), and, probably, two sonatas for three organs and *b.c.* that Frotscher reports.[42]

The violin did not experience any advances or transitions in the Classic Era comparable to those in the Baroque Era. Technically, it had already attained such heights in the sonatas and concertos of Locatelli and Leclair that it had little to add in range, bowings, multiple stops, and special effects during the near century before Paganini. Furthermore, the violin was not the main instrument of the greatest sonata composers in the Classic Era as it had been for many of them in the Baroque Era. Haydn, Mozart, and Beethoven all knew and wrote extremely well for the violin, of course, but none of these men gave to it as a solo instrument what they gave to the piano. Those Classic musicians who did excel on the violin were generally among our less important sonata composers, like Lolli, D. Ferrari, La Houssaye, and W. Cramer. Pugnani and Nardini might be classified as exceptions. But these and other fine Italian violinists still made their chief contribution to the traditional melo/bass settings, as Viotti did in 1782, shortly after he reached Paris. The French and German violinists who preferred to compose in the newer sonata settings contributed still less from the standpoint of violin music. For they wrote mainly accompanied keyboard sonatas in which the violin parts were too subordinate and elementary to be interesting in their own right, as discussed shortly. Such parts were not meant for the professional violinist, anyway. They were meant for that largely anonymous body of dilettantes, who wanted to participate in musical ensembles, but with the least effort. Only when these ad libitum accompaniments graduated into the obbligato parts of the true duo, late in the Classic Era, did the sonata once more attract the professional violinists.

Though the viola appeared but rarely as the solo instrument in the Classic sonata, the cello appeared somewhat more in this way. As we shall see in the next section, the cello's main change of status at this time revolved around its ultimate emancipation from the *b.c.* part. Here may be noted how it continued to serve in a small but not unworthy body of
Vc/bass sonatas, as it had served in the late Baroque Era. Graziani, 42a

42. Frotscher/ORGELSPIEL II 795-796, 799.

Duport, Bréval, and Tricklir were among the Classic contributors to this setting. As discussed later (SCE VIII), G. B. Sammartini belongs here, too, if the Vc/bass sonatas ascribed to him are authentic; and Boccherini, if his sonatas in question actually originated in that setting. Though neither Haydn nor Mozart cultivated the "solo" cello sonata, Beethoven added immeasurably to the cellist's literature at the end of the Classic Era with his genuine duet sonatas for piano and cello.

Haydn came closest to sonatas in the cello range when he wrote duos or trios with Prince Esterházy's baryton as the solo instrument, accompanied by cello and often viola. Exclusive even then, this simultaneously bowed and plucked instrument was soon to disappear from view, as was the viola da gamba, which C. F. Abel brought to one final peak of solo playing in his sonatas. A single statement by Burney on the viola da gamba that actually covers the baryton and its sympathetic strings, too, reflects the more progressive eighteenth-century view, in which these instruments were regarded as musical archaisms. Said Burney, the viola da gamba

> was practised longer in Germany than elsewhere; but since the death of the late Elector of Bavaria, who next to Abel was the best performer on the viola da gamba I had ever heard, the instrument seems laid aside. The late M. Lidl, indeed, played with exquisite taste and expression upon this ungrateful instrument [now meaning the baryton], with the additional embarrassment of base strings at the back of the neck, with which he accompanied himself, an admirable expedient in a desert, or even in a house, where is but one musician; but to be at the trouble of accompanying yourself in a great concert, surrounded by idle performers who could take the trouble off your hands, and leave them more at liberty to execute, express, and embellish the principle melody, seemed at best a work of supererogation. The tone of the instrument will do nothing for itself, and it seems with Music as with agriculture, the more barren and ungrateful the soil, the more art is necessary in its cultivation. And the tones of the viola da gamba are radically so crude and nasal, that nothing but the greatest skill and refinement can make them bearable. A human voice of the same quality would be intolerable.[43]

A small number of composers, such as Hochbrucker in Paris, or S. Webbe the Younger in London, left a fair number of light sonatas for harp, whether solo or accompanied. In other sonatas the harp is designated as an alternative to harpsichord or piano, as in Anth. VENIER-m I. More numerous are the light sonatas for guitar by the several virtuosos who won high renown toward the end of the eighteenth century, especially on the Spanish guitar and its variants.[44] Sor,

43. Burney/HISTORY II 1020.

44. A convenient summary of the instrument and its history may be found in the diss. Sasser/SOR.

Molitor, and Giuliani were the strongest composers among these virtuosos. We find sonatas not only for guitar alone, but for guitar and *b.c.* (as by Noferi), guitar and piano (as by J. M. Kraus), guitar with other accompaniments (as by Matiegka), and guitar arranged from some other setting (as by Viotti). The guitarists represented such a special clique of dilettantes, performers, and composers (as they still do today) that they have made but a small mark if any on general histories of music. The more social-minded historians will undoubtedly want to pay more attention to the widespread interest in this instrument around 1800.[45] Beethoven himself wrote two "sonatines" for the guitar's popular near relative, the mandolin, with keyboard accompaniment (WoO 43 and 44).[46]

Beethoven also contributed to the relatively few Classic sonatas for wind instruments, with the sonata for horn or cello, Op. 17, and another for flute if authentic.[47] We meet the transverse flute or "German" flute as it was still called, especially in flute ensembles (as by Hook) and as a frequent alternative—now more frequent than the oboe—to the violin in SS/bass or similar settings. But there are more distinctive solo uses of it, such as the Fl/bass and unaccompanied flute sonatas by
Hugot.[48] The newly popular clarinet was employed as the solo instru- 48a
ment in a few late-Classic sonatas, chiefly some rather slight S/bass
examples by F. Devienne and J.-X. Lefèvre, and a somewhat more
developed sonata for piano and clarinet by Vanhal (1806).[49] Similarly, 49a
only a few sonatas with bassoon as the solo instrument can be found
in the Classic Era, including examples by Mozart (K.V. 196c), Boismortier, Devienne, Oginsky, and Paxton.[50] All in all, wind instru- 50a
ments had solo responsibilities much less often in the Classic sonata than in the Classic concerto.

Before leaving the subject of individual instruments, we should note the use of the carillon in occasional sonatas by Scandinavian and British composers, as by J. Worgan, and especially the use of the delicate,

45. One need only glance at Weinmann/ARTARIA or the two Whistling catalogues of 1815 and 1828 (preceding HOFMEISTER) to get an idea of the quantity of guitar music being published at that time.

46. Cf. Bone/GUITAR 21-26; Buchner/BEETHOVEN.

47. Cf. Hess/ERSTDRUCK.

48. For a survey of 17th- and 18th-c. Fl sons. and related music cf. the diss. Jones/FLUTE.

49. Warm thanks are owing to Dr. Robert A. Titus at Ohio State University for information on this subject. Chap. VIII in the diss. Titus/CLARINET is on solo clarinet music with keyboard.

50. Information on the last 4 may be found on pp. 56-61 and 73-78 in the diss. Bartlett/BASSOON (most of which consists of a detailed catalogue and thematic index of 18th-c. bassoon concertos and sons.).

ethereal glass harmonica, chiefly in sonatas by Naumann (SCE XVI). In a report dated 1796, J. G. A. Kläbe wrote that Naumann's

> favorite instrument, to which he was wholeheartedly devoted, was the bewitching harmonica, whose idiomatic traits he sought to exploit to best advantage through his manner of treating them. He has published various sonatas for this instrument that are but hints [of how he treats it]; otherwise he generally improvises freely according to his heart's mood at the moment and to his listener's taste, without limiting himself to prescribed music, for to him his [method] is the right way to treat this instrument.[51]

Melo/bass Settings in Decline

Having considered the instruments individually, we are ready to take note of the main ensemble settings of the Classic sonata. The only literal solo settings aside from the large number for keyboard instruments were the few in the select but limited literature for unaccompanied violin—including examples by Rust, Reichardt, J. Stamitz, Nardini, and Bertheaume (the last two in *scordatura*)—and in the still more limited literature for unaccompanied flute, including the examples by Hugot mentioned earlier and one by Emanuel Bach (W. 132). As suggested by the statistic samplings in our previous chapter, the favorite Classic sonata settings were the S/- and SS/bass, the solo keyboard, and the accompanied keyboard, with the trend from pre- to late-Classic being in that order. At the end of the era (1821) the French aesthetician and lexicographer Castil-Blaze showed an awareness of this trend when he wrote:

> The sonata is composed for a single instrument that plays [while] accompanied by a bass or viol if this [single] instrument, such as the violin or flute, has not the means of making a complete harmony heard. But the piano, the harp, and even the guitar can get along without this support. In a composition of this sort one tries for whatever will display most effectively the instrument one is using, whether by the turn of the melody, or the choice of the tones that resonate the best, or the daring of the [feats required in] execution.
>
> The sonata suits the piano best of all, on which one can play three or four distinct voices at the same time, and even more. It is also on this instrument that it [the sonata] has gone the furthest in its astonishing progress.[52]

History and the dictates of today's "standard repertoire" have placed rather different values on the main Classic settings of the sonata.

51. Trans. from the quotation in Engländer/DRESDNER 56. Cf., also, GROVE I 204-206 (King).

52. Trans. from Castil-Blaze/DICTIONNAIRE II 271-272. Recall that the keyboard setting of the son. had already been given first place in Türk/KLAVIERSCHULE 390, in 1789 (SCE II).

They have given an easy first place to the piano sonata, especially the finest examples by the three Viennese masters. But they have given second place to the relatively few actual duos for piano and violin or piano and cello, especially selected examples by Mozart and Beethoven. The duo comes closer to what are now regarded as the ideal settings of Classic instrumental music—that is, the string quartet and the orchestra of which it had become the nucleus.[53]

It is probably because of epigonic traits that even the best Classic sonatas in melo/bass settings are seldom heard today. Insofar as **53a**
melo/bass sonatas are still played, the Classic examples are certainly heard less than Baroque sonatas in the same settings. It is still more probable that the dilettante traits and the thoroughly obsolete settings of the accompanied keyboard sonata have kept it from being heard today. Only when the optional accompaniment has been discarded have some sonatas of this sort survived, such as Mozart's K.V. 547a[54] or Clementi's Op. 4, now known only in the two sets of solo "Sonatinas" Opp. 37 and 38. This procedure is quite the opposite of that in the late-Classic Era itself, when editors and publishers sometimes felt obliged to add an accompaniment in order to insure a sonata's success. Thus, it was probably the publisher André or Artaria who added a violin part to Mozart's K.V. 570 in B♭, and Burney who added accompaniments to several of Haydn's piano sonatas.[55]

As just suggested, the melo/bass settings in the Classic Era were taken over from Baroque settings. The term "melo/bass" was coined in our previous volume "to designate that general opposition of melody and *b.c.* parts so characteristic of Baroque scoring," or what Bukofzer has called "the polarity . . . between harmonic support and a new type of melody dependent on such support" (SBE 50-51). The use and realization of *b.c.* parts persisted longest—in fact, well into the nineteenth century—in the support of vocal music, especially certain church music and the recitative of opera. With regard to independent instrumental music, the *b.c.* tradition persisted longest in the tuttls of concertos and in the Vn/bass sonata. Viotti in Paris was the last composer of consequence to make his début with Vn/bass sonatas, in 1782 and 1784 (SCE XVIII). But further examples continued to appear in the 1790's, by G. Conti and P. Fux in Vienna, and Lolli and Nardini (posthumous)

53. Cf. Adler/WIENER 788-793 and Adler in KONGRESS 1925 (Leipzig) 35-43; MGG VII 1076-1080 (Blume).

54. Cf. Marguerre/KV. 547.

55. Cf. Köchel/MOZART 719; MR II (1941) 155; Hoboken/HAYDN 727-728, 733 *et passim.* André published Christian Bach's solo K sons. Op. 17 as Op. 1, "con un Violino ad Libitum composto dal Editore."

in Italy, among others; and perhaps as late as 1805, by G. A. Capuzzi in Italy (SCE X).

By contrast, the SS/bass sonata setting largely disappeared by about 1775 and the late examples, except for those by Uttini, Pugnani, and a few others, hardly seem important enough to cite here. This setting appears to have given way to several more progressive types, including the string trio (SSB or SAB), the accompanied keyboard sonata (K & Vn) or the incipient piano trio (P & Vn & Vc), and the unaccompanied duo (SS). The melo/bass settings also appeared throughout at least the pre-Classic Era in sonatas that specify less conventional choices and groupings of instruments—for example, harp and *b.c.* (as by Kunzen), or two horns and *b.c.* (as by G. Comi). Otherwise, the *b.c.* tradition was maintained chiefly in theory treatises such as were noted earlier (SCE II).

The factors that contributed most to the gradual obsolescence of the *b.c.* part contributed quite as much to the progress of the Classic
56a sonata.[56] One was the inability of the increasingly numerous amateurs to cope with its intricacies, intricacies that were brought at once to their highest and last stage of refinement in Emanuel Bach's *Essay*. Another was the debilitating effect that the new, more regularly phrased melody exerted on a constantly moving bass line, for this type of melody engendered a much slower harmonic rhythm with a more static kind of supporting bass (as in Ex. 2, by a renowned Mannheim flutist). And a third was the growing need for more textural precision than even the best improvised realization could provide, this need being most evident in the *concertante* exchanges of a fine Haydn string quartet, with their wealth of dynamic and articulatory detail.[57] In the publications of the later eighteenth century, one finds ample evidence for the decline of the *b.c.* practice. The bass figures become more and more careless and incomplete. They differ in different editions, or are added entirely by the publisher (as by Hummel of Amsterdam in Filtz's Opp. 3 and 5, and Christian Bach's Op. 2 [our D. 1; SCE XIX]).

Naturally, as the main vehicle of the *b.c.* line, the cello part is the one to watch first for the discard of the *b.c.* practice. There are rare instances of a return to the seventeenth-century *concertante* bass part, in which the cello elaborates the simpler *b.c.* line played by some other bass instrument (SBE 51-53). Thus, Pugnani was using such a part when he scored a sonata movement in SSB/bass setting (Zschinsky-Troxler/

56. The decline of the *b.c.* in 18th-c. instrumental music is the subject of the enlightening diss. Oberdörffer/GENERALBASS, with exx. (summarized briefly in MGG IV 1720-23).

57. This aspect of Haydn's quartets is a central topic in Sondheimer/HAYDN.

Ex. 2. From the opening of Sonata in D, Op. 5/1, by Johann Baptist Wendling (after the original Napier ed. of 1772 at the British Museum).

PUGNANI no. 58/ii).[58] But the main trend was toward the discard of *b.c.* figures altogether. A halfway stage exists in a set like Giardini's Op. 3 for cembalo and violin or flute, published in London in 1751 (SCE XIX). When the violin takes a clear lead it is supported by a figured *b.c.,* and when the cembalo takes the lead it is written out. Cello parts begin to appear without any figures in the 1760's, an early example being a set of six SS/bass sonatas in a Milan MS by Maldere (SCE XXI).

More frequent are the sonatas for violin and bass, or cello and bass, in which the bass is actually an unfigured cello part that constitutes a duet partner quite as much as a harmonic support. In such duets the upper part is often designed to be played by either violin or cello. Then the duet usually appears in score, with the upper part in the treble clef, obviously to be read an octave lower if played on the cello, and the lower part in the bass clef, playing enough chordal outlines or actual multiple-stop chords to serve at once as a bass, a realization, and a complement

58. Cf., also, Abel's Op. 9 in BRITISH UNION I 3.

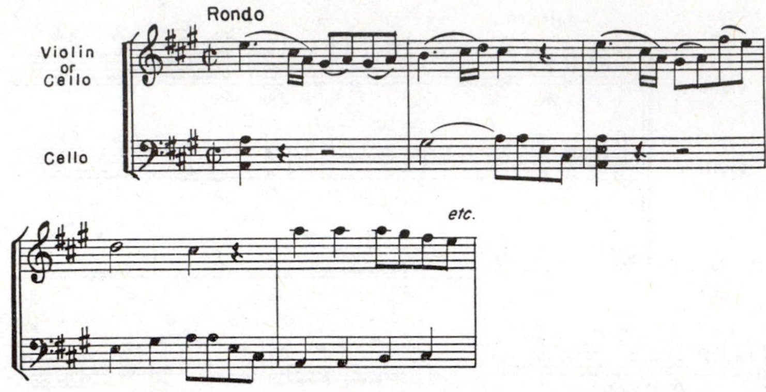

Ex. 3. From the finale of Sonata in A, Op. 3/4, by Jean Pierre Duport (after the Imbault reprint, *ca.* 1790, at the British Museum).

to the other part (Ex. 3). Boccherini's fine set of six duets in this category leave some question as to whether a choice between cello and violin or just one of these was originally intended. The two earliest editions, about 1770-71, are both in score, one with violin specified and a treble clef in the upper part, and the other with cello specified and a bass clef in the upper part (SCE VIII, with ex.). In MSS of these and similar sonatas by Boccherini there are editorial indications over the lower part, such as "sul ponticello," that help to confirm the cello's use as more than a *b.c.* instrument.[59]

The Accompanied Keyboard Setting

The accompanied keyboard sonata—or "the accompanied Sonata for the Harpsichord," as Avison already referred to it in 1764, in the preface to his Op. 8 (SCE XIX)—was a genre peculiar to the Classic Era. In it, typically, the keyboard took the lead, a violin or flute played a subordinate part, often distinguished as "ad libitum" or "obligato" (i.e., obligatory),[60] and a cello could be added to double the keyboard bass. As suggested earlier, this genre is rarely revived today because of its dilettante traits and obsolete scoring. Few violinists or cellists are historically minded enough to take pleasure in the elementary, uninter-

59. Information kindly supplied by Professor William Klenz at Duke University
60. This much of the definition is already stated in Türk/KLAVIERSCHULE 391.

esting parts it usually relegates to them. Even the historians have paid only modest attention to it.[61] Yet this genre flourished almost from 61a
the start to the end of the Classic Era as defined in the present survey, to become one of our most tangible delimiters of that era in terms of the sonata. Indeed, it became the most numerous representative of the published Classic sonata, as may be seen almost at a glance in BRITISH UNION, Cat. BRUXELLES, and the catalogues of other libraries with rich instrumental holdings from the eighteenth century. We shall become especially aware of it in the quarter century overlapping the pre- and high-Classic phases, from about 1760 to 1785, when it touched virtually every main sonata composer, including Boccherini, both Emanuel and Christian Bach, Haydn, Mozart, and Clementi. Indeed it was such a standard setting at that time that a composer who preferred not to write an accompaniment sometimes felt obliged to make special mention of that fact, as in Benser's *Sonata; the Storm; for the Pianoforte ONLY* (1781).[62]

Reports of harpsichordists being "accompanied" by a violinist go as far back as 1727 in Rome and 1729 in Paris.[63] Since the light *galant* style, characteristic of the accompanied keyboard sonata in its heyday, hardly prevailed in the 1720's, one can only guess that these reports concerned ancestral settings. Perhaps they merely referred to a doubling of the keyboard lines such as Telemann allowed in his lost sonatinas of about 1736, which "can be played on the keyboard, or by a violin or flute and thorough-bass" (SBE 287).[64] Or perhaps they referred to a setting best known in J. S. Bach's "Sei Suonate à cembalo certato e violino solo, col basso per viola da gamba accompagnato se piace," to use Bach's own title (*ca.* 1720; Schmieder nos. 1014-1019a)—that is, the setting with violin in which the keyboard had a realized part except for short passages of *b.c.* (SBE 65, 272). This frequently severe, three-part setting, supplied by one line for each of the keyboardist's two hands and one for the violinist, was commonly described as being "en trio," as it still was in Clément's *Sonates en trio pour un clavecin et un violon* of

61. Among discussions and studies devoted to it, nearly all with exx., are DDT-m XXXIX viii-x and DTB-m XV/1 xvii-xix (both Riemann, with reference to Mannheim composers and Schobert); Studeny/VIOLINSONATE 79-85; La Laurencie/ÉCOLE II 412-414 and III 147-152 (in Paris); Torrefranca/ORIGINI 569, 587-598, and 628-631 (with unsound claims for Italian precedence); Cesari/TRIO (on the origins of the piano trio); Reeser/KLAVIERSONATE (in Paris; a diss., the most detailed study to date); Newman/ACCOMPANIED (general survey); Fischer/MOZART (on the transition to the true duo and trio).

62. Cf., also, Köchel/MOZART 264.

63. Cf., respectively, Cudworth in KONGRESS 1952 (Utrecht) 129; La Laurencie/ÉCOLE I 232.

64. For an extant ex. of this setting that goes back to 1662 and includes a "Secondo Violino à Beneplacito," cf. the first Cazzati entry in Cat. BOLOGNA IV 99.

1743 (SCE XVII). But the influence of the accompanied keyboard setting was such that in its last years Nägeli entitled the first edition (*ca.* 1804) of Bach's same sonatas, *Clavier-Sonaten mit obligater Violine.*[65]

Other settings ancestral to the accompanied keyboard type were the sort more likely to be improvised, such as the keyboard solo made by dividing the S/bass setting between the two hands,[66] or the "accompanied" keyboard solo made when the keyboardist "realized" the *b.c.* merely by playing either upper part of an SS/bass setting in his right hand while the violinist played the other (SBE 58-60). Although Mondonville, Guillemain, Clément, and other Parisian pioneers proclaimed their innovations in highly quotable prefaces, much of the writing in their "pièces de clavecin en sonates, avec accompagnement de violon," dating from the 1730's and 1740's, still points back more or less to the three-part writing that Bach used (SCE XVII, with exx.). The lighter examples by Simon, Giardini, and others, which began to appear from about 1750 in the two chief hotbeds of the genre, Paris and London, must be traced to more immediate influences. Among the latter were the need to fill in the thin keyboard writing of the *galant* style, to reinforce weak tones both before and after the piano was introduced in the 1760's, to provide a part simple and unexposed enough for the less skilled, dilettante violinist or flutist to play when he wanted to join in the fun,[67] and merely "to find something new," as Mondonville had put it in the preface to his Op. 3 (*ca.* 1734; SCE XVII). The articulate French pioneers variously stressed each of these needs, too, in their prefaces.

If the ad libitum practices of Baroque instrumental music (SBE 57-60) narrowed considerably in the Classic Era, the accompanied keyboard sonata still offered four main options. First there was the option of including or omitting the accompaniment itself. Corrette had already offered this option in his accompanied keyboard sonatas Op. 25, published about 1742 (SCE XVII). But Schobert may have been the first to put that familiar phrase in the title, "qui peuvent se jouer avec l'accompagnement du violon," as in his Op. 1 of about 1760, or "avec accompagnement du violon ad libitum," as in his Op. 5. Second, there was the option of flute or violin in the accompaniment, if not some

65. HIRSCH MUSIKBIBLIOTHEK III, item 77.

66. Mozart's sons. K.V. 46d and 46e are still listed uncertainly in Köchel/MOZART 86-87 as being "for violin (?) and bass or keyboard."

67. Recall the statement by L. Adam early in SCE III. But the dilettante seems to be the pianist in an advertisement printed in the *Wiener-Zeitung* in 1789: "Wanted by nobleman a servant who plays the violin well and is able to accompany difficult piano sonatas" (as trans. in Geiringer/HAYDN 38).

other instrument in the same range.[68] In his accompanied set of about 1755 d'Herbain troubled to write different notes for the flute and the violin when necessary, and to explain these in the full title (SCE XVII). But in Hook's Op. 16, published about two decades later, no adjustment is made for the flute when there are double-notes or notes below its range, on the G-string. The English publishers seem to have added the option of flute to the title as a matter of course.

A third option concerns the use of the cello to reinforce the keyboard bass. This instrument may be specified without any option, as in Abel's *Six Sonatas for the Harpsicord With Accompanyments for a Violin or German Flute and Violoncello,* Op. 2 (1760). Or it may be optional, as in Eichner's *Three Sonatas for the Harpsichord or Forte Piano With Accompanyments for a Violin and Bass ad libitum,* Op. 3 (1771). Or it may be specified in the title yet not be published, as in Vento's Op. 4, which appeared in 1768 only as a keyboard-and-violin score. Or, finally, it may be published yet not be specified in the title, as in the Toricella edition of Eichner's Op. 1. Yet, specified or not, optional or not, printed or not, the cello rarely did more than double the keyboard bass, and its use to this extent seems to have been taken for granted whenever it was available. Thus, Mozart's mother must simply have been echoing the jargon around her when she referred to her son's six sonatas for keyboard and violin K.V. 293a-d, 300c, and 300l as "six new trios."[69]

Finally, the fourth main option that the accompanied keyboard sonata offered was that of harpsichord or piano (but rarely clavichord), as would be expected in this period of transition from one to the other. Often the option was broader, an example being Rosetti's *Six Sonates pour la harpe ou le clavecin ou piano-forte avec accompagnement de violon,* Op. 2 (*ca.* 1785). However, one gets the impression that the piano soon became the preferred keyboard instrument in this setting. Sometimes the piano's new technical idiom permeated the more usual, light-textured, facile writing of the genre (as in Séjan's Op. 1, *ca.* 1772; SCE XVII). But the piano's clear and pliant tone and its expressive capabilities must have held more immediate attractions. Dynamic and articulation markings are often present in abundance in accompanied keyboard sonatas. And the composers give not a few hints of the keyboard's "weak tone," which certainly suggest the piano rather than harpsichord. Thus, in Rosetti's accompanied sonatas Op. 6 (H-or-P & Vn),

68. Among rarer accompanying instruments is the keyboard itself, as in P.-J. Meyer's *Two Sonatas for the Harp, With an Accompaniment for the Piano-forte, or Two Violins, Viola, and Violoncello* (*ca.* 1800). Vn with P accompaniment is still rarer, as noted under Viotti (SCE XVIII).

69. Letter of Jan. 11, 1778 (Anderson/MOZART II 658).

published about 1781, the violin is marked one dynamic degree softer than the keyboard much of the time.[70] As late as 1826 Nägeli objected to the "senseless" ad libitum accompaniments of sonatas in which "the stronger instrument—that is, the violin—takes long sustained notes or figuration while the weaker instrument—that is, the piano—gets the main part and is drowned out."[71] But this conjecture about the early piano's weak tone must be qualified by the fact that Mondonville,[72] Corrette, Guillemain, and d'Herbain all left instructions before 1760 that the violin must be played softly or muted in order that it does not cover the tone of the "clavecin" (SCE XVII).[73]

Dedicating his twelve solo clavichord sonatas of 1773 to Emanuel Bach, Neefe objected to the way keyboard "pieces usually are provided with the accompaniment, often arbitrary, of a violin, and [they] become just as playable on many other instruments as on the keyboard" (SCE XII). In reality, some of the accompaniments prove to be quite superfluous, as do most of those by Rust (SCE XVI). One assumes the same of the accompaniments in Séjan's Op. 1, for though they are lost they are in no sense missed in those fine sonatas. Sometimes the accompaniment actually seems to obstruct the keyboard part, as in Op. 14/3/ii by Schobert. The subordinate but persistent afterbeat figures of the violin part in this movement are only tolerable when the violin is muted. In the strong first movement of that same Schobert sonata, as in several sonata movements by Edelmann, the violin is simply left out or marked "tacet." It is noteworthy that a "Celebrated Sonata" with accompaniment by Sarti was reprinted about 1795 as a solo "in which all the obligato violin passages are adapted for the piano-forte" (SCE VIII).

But in many more examples than not, the accompaniment is missed in the texture if it is omitted, even though it is marked "ad libitum" and is not essential to either the melodic continuity or the harmonic clarity. Emanuel Bach himself wrote that the violin and cello parts could be left out of the seven "easy" accompanied keyboard sonatas that he published in two sets, by subscriptions, in 1776 and 1777 (W. 90/1-3 and 91/1-4; SCE XIII). But the early reviewers, Forkel included, felt the accompaniments were necessary to the total effect,[74] and a repre-

70. Cf. Newman/ACCOMPANIED 340, with ex.
71. Nägeli/VORLESUNGEN 176.
72. Cf. Newman/ACCOMPANIED 339.
73. It is more understandable that Canobbio's guitar sons., published in 1797, specify that the accompaniment is for "violin with mute" (SCE XXI).
74. Bach's letter of Sept. 25, 1775, and 2 Hamburg reviews of 1777 are printed in Bitter/BRÜDER I 209-210. Cf., also, Forkel/BIBLIOTHEK II 278-279, with ex. (but the rest of the long, glowing review, pp. 275-300, is largely confined to the keyboard part, with exx.).

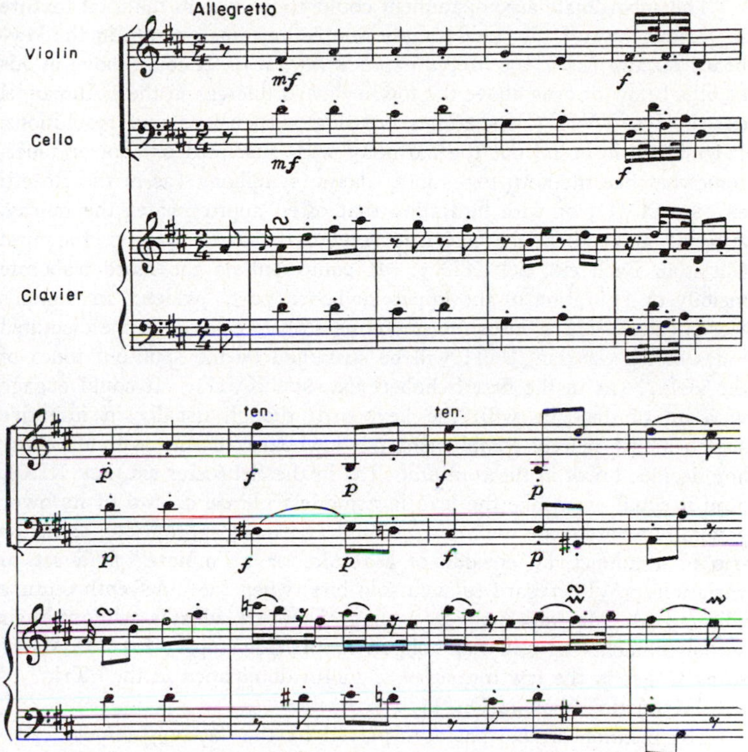

Ex. 4. From the opening of Emanuel Bach's Sonata 4 in D, W. 91/4 (after the facs. of the autograph score in Schmid/BACH 144).

sentative example quoted here should confirm that the clean, precise texture would suffer without these parts (Ex. 4).

Burney found a somewhat different reason for retaining the accompaniments in Christian Bach's sonatas. He said Christian had had to make his piano parts "such as ladies can execute with little trouble" because his own playing had slipped over the years; in consequence, his pieces "lose much of their effect when played without the accompaniments, which are admirable, and so masterly and interesting to an audience, that want of hand or complication in the harpsichord part, is never discovered."[75]

75. Burney/HISTORY II 866 (quoted more fully in SCE XIX). Burney changes from "piano forte" to "harpsichord" for no apparent reason in this paragraph.

The subordinate accompaniment could contribute to the total texture in various ways.[76] It could simply double any line or note in the keyboard texture (as in the Méhul ex., SCE XVIII). It could move in 3ds or 6ths below or even above the top keyboard line (as in the Hüllmandel ex., in SCE XVIII), sometimes creating suspensions and resolutions. It could fill in or fill out the harmony with sustained or shorter tones, somewhat like the horn tones in a Classic symphony (as in the Rosetti ex., SCE XVI), or with figuration that often approximates the murky, Alberti, and other characteristic keyboard basses (as in the first Christian Bach ex., SCE XIX). It could outline the more elaborate melody or figuration of the upper keyboard part, "which," in Simon's words (SCE XVII), "loses the smoothness of its contour in the disunited tones of the clavecin, [but] will be sustained by the spun-out tones of the violin" (as in the first Schobert ex., SCE XVII). It could engage in a bit of dialogue with the keyboard, though usually in imitative snatches that merely complement the keyboard rhythm without filling any decided break in the continuity (as in the Schroeter ex., SCE XIX). And it could even take the lead in a modest phrase or two of its own, generally where some such novelty might be most appropriate, as in the trio of a minuet, an episode of a rondo, or a "minore" in a set of variations. With regard to such solo bits, when the nineteenth-century editor J. A. Mereaux published some Schobert sonatas without their accompaniments he still felt obliged to provide a part for "3e Main" so as to get in the few measures of violin dominance in the "Trio" of the "Menuetto" finale in Op. 14/3 in E♭.[77]

The mention of solo passages played by the "accompaniment" prepares us for the first true duos of keyboard and violin (or other instrument). As suggested earlier, in the sense of the more conservative, three-part writing, there was scarcely any stylistic or temporal interruption in the "progress" from such sonatas for realized harpsichord and violin as Bach wrote to those by Mondonville (Op. 3, *ca.* 1734), Guillemain (Op. 13, 1745), Schaffrath (Op. 1, 1746), Gruber (*ca.* 1750), Scheibe (Op. 1, *ca.* 1758), and Richter (first Walsh ed. of acc'd. sons., 1759). But these diverse successors to Bach's models seem not to have pointed directly to the later duo, in spite of the newer titles of the accompanied sonata that some of them bore. In a more significant generative sense, it was the purely subordinate, optional accompaniment that led to the true duo of piano and violin. To effect this change, the violin had to graduate into the role of an obligatory and equal partner.

76. Cf. the exx. of each in Newman/ACCOMPANIED 343-346.
77. DDT-m XXXIX (Riemann) ix and 33.

Giardini's accompanied keyboard sonatas Op. 3 of 1751 (H & Vn-or-Fl), with some sections of solo violin supported by *b.c.* and some of realized cembalo accompanied by the violin, marked a halfway stage not only in the discard of the *b.c.* but in the evolution of the duo. The first 77a
important signs of the true duo appeared in 1768 in Boccherini's accompanied set Op. 5 (K & Vn; SCE VIII), especially in Sonata 3 in B♭. Other early examples include Friedrich Bach's set of 1777 (H. W. VIII/3; SCE XIII), J. Schuster's six *Divertimenti* of about the same year (SCE XIV and XVI), and Mozart's "Mannheim" set of 1778 (K.V. 293a-d; 300c, and 300l; SCE XIV). It is interesting that these first examples already contain the exchange between keyboard and violin of entire phrases and periods. Such exchanges occurred originally at main dividing points in the form, then spread throughout the movement. As late as 1783, in his review of Mozart's "Auernhammer" set of 1781 (K.V. 296, 317d, 373a, 374d-f), C. F. Cramer was still reacting to the equal responsibility of the violin as an innovation.[78]

One of the first to label the violin part "obligé" in this newer sense was the Parisian organist Charpentier. His Opp. 3, 4, and 8, dating from about 1774 to 1778, contain several sonatas "dans le gout de la simphonie concertante," as the full titles read (SCE XVII). But if no one can question that the "Violino obligato" in Beethoven's "Kreutzer" sonata, composed in 1802-03, is a full partner in a true duo (SCE XV),[79] 79a
the fact must also be noted that the term "obligato" was applied on occasion, even that late (as by Steibelt), to parts that were clearly subordinate and sometimes superfluous. Beethoven's two sonatas with "Violoncelle obligé" Op. 5, composed in 1796, were the first known duos for piano and cello. W. A. Mozart "the Younger" left a *Grande Sonate* in E, published in 1820, that has alternative "obligé" parts for either violin or cello (SCE XVI, with ex.). His father's trios, sometimes still published as *Sonate per il clavicembalo o forte-piano con violino e violoncello* (e.g., K.V. 502, 542, and 548), give enough independence to the cello as well as the violin part to qualify these works as the first important examples of the piano trio.

Further Settings, Arrangements, and Practices

Other settings of the sonata enjoyed a distinct popularity in the Classic Era, even though less numerous than the solo, melo/bass, and accompanied types considered thus far. Burney's "Preface" to the first

78. Cramer/MAGAZIN I 485 (as quoted in SCE XIV).

79. Most mod. eds. still list Beethoven's "Sonatas for Pianoforte and Violin" rather than the converse.

of his two sets of *Four Sonatas or Duets for Two Performers on One Piano Forte or Harpsichord,* published in 1777 and 1778, declares at once and rightly that "the following pieces are the first that have appeared in print." In these pieces there is already a good awareness of the problems of balance, dialogue, and texture that duets pose (SCE XIX, with ex.). Duets had been left in MS by Christian Bach and Mozart from about the time of their first meeting in London in 1764, and perhaps by others (as discussed under Mozart, SCE XIV). Among many duet publications that followed soon after Burney's precedent were those by Christian Bach in 1778 (T. 340), Clementi about 1780 (Op. 3; SCE XX), Seydelmann in 1781 (SCE frontispiece and XVI, with ex.), C. H. Mueller in 1782 (with the charming title, *Drey Sonaten fürs Clavier, als Doppelstücke für zwo Personen mit vier Händen;* BRITISH UNION II 714), Rutini about 1782 (Op. 13/6; SCE VII), and Mozart in 1783 (K.V. 123a and 186c; SCE XIV). Furthermore, Séjan and Charpentier are known to have played a duet at a public concert in Paris in 1784.[80] Performances of duets were still described as a rarity in Germany in 1780.[81] But by 1789 Türk treated one- as well as two-keyboard duets as standard settings.[82] And by 1800 a reviewer was already theorizing on the special skills in harmonic doubling and voice-leading that the duet composer must have, and the need for intelligent handling of the dialogue problem if monotony was to be avoided.[83] Haydn composed no known sonatas in this setting and Beethoven contributed only one example, of minor consequence, in Op. 6. But Clementi and Mozart left outstanding examples, the latter's Sonata in F of 1786, K.V. 497, being one of the strongest in the literature. We shall also be coming upon occasional sonatas for three hands at one piano, as by Hässler and Metzger (SCE XVI and XVIII), or even five hands, by Dalberg (SCE XVI).

In the same preface of 1777 Burney did acknowledge earlier, German publications of duets for two keyboard instruments. Perhaps he had in mind Müthel's "Duetto" for two clavichords, harpsichords, or pianos, published in 1771 (SCE XIII). In any case, though this setting was cultivated less than the one-keyboard duet, its history goes back to Mattheson's publication of about 1705 and even earlier MSS by Pasquini (SBE 289-290, 160). Two examples in MS by Schaffrath probably date from around 1750 (SCE XIII), and two more by Grétry from not much later (now lost; SCE XVII). Among other composers of the two-key-

80. Brenet/CONCERTS 367.
81. Cf. Scharnagl/STERKEL 78-79.
82. Türk/KLAVIERSCHULE 391.
83. AMZ II (1799-1800) 680-681.

board duet may be named C. Stamitz and Vogler (about 1790 and 1794, respectively; SCE XVI).[84] Again, the chief masterpieces come from Clementi (Opp. 1a/6 and 12/5) and Mozart (K.V. 375a). A sonata in MS for two pianos and harpsichord was left by Beecke (SCE XI), and examples of sonatas for two pianos with the option of piano and harp were left by both G. G. Ferrari, about 1795,[85] and Pollini, in 1807 (SCE X).

Duets played on a pair of stringed or wind instruments without accompaniment continued to be as popular in the Classic as in the late-Baroque Era, especially the violin or flute type in France.[86] One evi- 86a
dence of this popularity is the number of sonatas for two violins or two flutes that were arranged from other settings. For example, Lolli's six Vn/bass sonatas Op. 6 became his *Premier Livre de duos* for two violins.[87] Moreover, there were numerous duet sonatas for different stringed or wind instruments, such as Haydn's six sonatas for violin with viola accompaniment, composed around 1766-74 (H. VI/1-6; SCE XIV). Also published as Vn/bass sonatas and violin duos, they recall the duets for violin and unfigured cello discussed and illustrated earlier in this chapter. Pleyel was an especially prolific composer and arranger of unaccompanied duets, trios, and quartets in all the popular styles. His samples examined here are typical of this general category of Classic instrumental sonata in their ingratiating lightness, contrapuntal dexterity, and routine content (Ex. 5).

The title "sonata" was applied occasionally to the string quartet setting—for example, by Gassmann, Albrechtsberger, Rolla, C. F. Müller, and C. G. Kuhlau. By contrast, Kleinheinz seems to have arranged one or more of Beethoven's piano sonatas in string quartet setting. Boccherini's accompanied keyboard sonatas were arranged variously in trio and quintet settings, and his trios and quintets were arranged variously in more familiar "sonata" settings (SCE VIII).

We had occasion earlier to note several contemporary views, as by Schulz, Türk, and Koch, on the similarities and differences between the orchestral symphony and the keyboard sonata (SCE II). The mention of arrangements brings us once more to this relationship, for there are many times when at least the lighter, more direct and routine sort of keyboard sonata—which is to say, the commonest sort—seems like nothing more than a watery reduction of the lightest, most direct and

84. Friedemann Bach's "Sonate für 2 Klaviere," as it is called in mod. eds., is actually Brahms' arrangement of an early concerto by Bach (SCE XII).

85. BRITISH UNION I 331.

86. Cf. Studeny/VIOLINSONATE 85-91; DDT XV/1 xv-xvi (Riemann); SBE 65, 376.

87. MGG VIII 1132 (Mell).

Ex. 5. From the finale of Duo in a, Op. 59/4, by Ignaz Joseph Pleyel (after David/PLEYEL-m 11).

routine sort of symphony. Transcriptions of symphonies for keyboard were, in fact, often made in the Classic Era. One of the earliest and most important collections of these transcriptions, Anth. SINFONIE-m, was published by Breitkopf in 1761-62.[88] In this collection, the publisher inserted movements from original keyboard sonatas to fill out each eight-page signature. He also wrote a "Nachricht," to the effect that simple arrangements are the best means of popularizing the symphony and that filler material may be introduced, according to the abilities of the keyboardist or an accompanying violinist, in order to replace *concertante* elements that had to be left out of the reductions (Ex. 6).

It will be remembered that Türk spoke of the keyboard sinfonia almost as a separate genre and as a training piece by which the less skilled player might advance to the "true sonata style."[89] Actually, original keyboard pieces seem not to have been called symphonies except when there are optional accompaniments, and these accompaniments usually consist of enough instruments to bring the "symphonies" closer to concertos, as in Schobert's Opp. 9 and 10. Pieces of the latter sort also may be called "Sonates en symphonie" or "Sonata o vero sinfonia" (SCE II). Many of the symphonies transcribed for keyboard alone do retain their original title. Thus, using the frequent English equivalent of overture for symphony (and recalling the many "periodical overtures in eight parts"), Abel retained the title "Overture" when he transcribed

88. Described in Menicke/HASSE 73-74. The significance of such transcriptions to K music is emphasized in Torrefranca/ORIGINI 527-534, 635; cf., also, Engländer/DRESDNER 82-83, 113.

89. Türk/KLAVIERSCHULE 392; SCE II.

Ex. 6. From the opening of Georg Christoph Wagenseil's Sinfonia in D, arranged for clavicembalo (after Anth. SINFONIE-m III/10).

his six symphonies Op. 1 for keyboard.[90] But not seldom is the title changed to "sonata," as in the duet arrangements of Haydn's Symphonies in C and B♭, H. I/97 and 98,[91] or Gelinek's excellent transcription of Mozart's Symphony in g, K.V. 550 (SCE XVI). A further relationship between the sonata and the symphony is suggested in a series of similar Paris publications by Mannheim or related composers that started with J. Stamitz's *Six Sonates à trois parties concertantes qui sont faites pour exécuter ou à trois, ou avec toutes l'orchestre,* Op. 1 (*ca.* 1755; SCE XI).

Similar if less frequent relationships between the concerto and the sonata will come to our attention in later chapters. A title like *Grande Sonate pour le piano, avec accompagnement de l'orchestre* (before 1822), by Beczwarowsky,[92] merely suggests a misnomer for concerto. More to the point are such works as the two brilliant solo piano sonatas Clementi arranged from his own concertos (Opp. 32/3 and 34/1; SCE XX) or, conversely, the seven early keyboard concertos that the child

90. Helm/ABEL 297-298.
91. Cf. BRITISH UNION I 469.
92. BIBLIOGRAPHIE MUSICALE 226.

Mozart made from solo or accompanied keyboard sonata movements by Christian and Emanuel Bach and by the Parisian clavecinists Raupach, Honauer, Eckard, and Schobert.[93]

This chapter should not be concluded without some further reference to the several performance practices involved in the various aspects of instruments and settings that have been considered here. Some of these have already been noted, including the options of solo and accompanying instruments in the accompanied keyboard sonata, the option of single or multiple performance in works like J. Stamitz's sonatas "for a trio or an orchestra," the gradual decline of the *b.c.* practice, and the increase in signs for dynamics and articulation. A little more may be added here regarding the question of filling out the keyboard texture and a couple of other practices.

The evidence for filling in the thin, two-part keyboard texture turns up fairly often.[94] When the left hand of a solo keyboard sonata has *b.c.* figures, as it has occasionally in *galant* keyboard music, there can be no
94a doubt of the practice (Ex. 7). There also can be no doubt, when the

Ex. 7. From the first movement of Sonata in G by Giovanni Marco Placido Rutini, Op. 9/4 (after the original, unidentified ed. owned and kindly supplied by Professor Dragan Plamenac at the University of Illinois).

performer is invited to fill in the texture, as in Anth. SINFONIE-m just noted, or in Maichelbeck's keyboard sonatas of 1736. Of course, the accompanied keyboard setting was evidence in itself that some sort of

93. Cf. Simon/MOZART, with tables and exx.; also, Torrefranca/ORIGINI 562-566.

94. Among representative discussions are Gerstenberg/SCARLATTI 94-99; Raabe/GALUPPI 21; Schaefer-Schmuck/TELEMANN 59-60 (valuable).

filler was regarded as necessary.[95] One assumes that the filling-in occurred more often in slower movements, where there is more time to enrich the texture. 95a

In the Classic Era all options of performance were gradually reduced from their free use in the Baroque Era.[96] We shall come upon F. Benda's elaborations of the lines in the slow movements of his sonatas (SCE XIII, with ex.), but in the pre-Classic Era this practice seems to have been rare and still to have stemmed from the past. Although (or because) complaints were voiced at this time against the many excessive decorations of French and Italian instrumental music, both rhythmic and melodic (SCE II), the *galant* style tended to retain only a few types of ornaments. These last were run into the ground at first, it is quite true. But one of the most salutary effects of high-Classic melodic trends was to rid much sonata (and other) melody of even these abuses (SCE VI). A license that did seem to thrive in high-Classic music was the free improvising of cadenzas at focal points in any or all movements. Though associated mainly with the concerto, this practice was evidently common in virtuoso sonatas, too, according to evidence gathered for both Haydn and Clementi.[97]

95. Cf. Studeny/VIOLINSONATE 79-85.
96. Cf. SBE 57-60; MGG VI 1119-1123 (Ferrand).
97. Cf. Steglich in ZFM XCIX (1932) 293-294; Berger/CLEMENTI.

Chapter VI

Style and Form

Approaching the Problem

In Chapter II the Classic writers' own statements on the sonata's structure were summarized. In this last chapter of Part I, a new, coordinated view of the Classic sonata's structure is sought—that is, a view that relates the sonata's essential style or generative traits to its over-all form. Our constant points of reference in this view are the sonatas by Haydn, Mozart, and Beethoven, especially those for piano. In other words, as the principal focuses of the Classic sonata, these masterworks provide starting points for the present discussion of form much as the violin sonatas of Corelli provided starting points for our earlier discussion of Baroque form (SBE 67). Of course, the superiority of form in the Viennese masterworks is so marked that a consideration of them alone could hardly give a balanced view of form in the Classic sonata as a whole. They do span nearly the entire Classic Era, from the earliest examples by Haydn, before 1760, to the last by Beethoven, in 1822. But sonatas by other representative Classicists must be brought into the discussion, too, especially by way of establishing antecedents, concurrents, or consequents of the Viennese masterworks. In any case, the intention here has been to give these other sonatas their just due in Part II, on the individual composers, at least with regard to their distinguishing traits of style and form. Only the sonatas of Haydn, Mozart, and Beethoven receive their main discussion, from this standpoint, in the present chapter, for which reason Chapters XIV and XV on these three composers are confined to the factual—that is, the biographic and bibliographic—circumstances of their sonatas.

In this first section of Chapter VI the object is to summarize certain traditional approaches and pitfalls that may affect any approach to Classic form, leaving the rest of the chapter free for considerations of the music itself. It is also necessary to restate the bases of the present approach, already defined earlier (SBE 67-68). Within the extensive literature, both general and specific, on form in the Classic sonata, the tendency here has been to prefer those approaches that transcend the labeling of themes and chords in order to explore broad functional relationships (as in Schenker's writings), that avoid Procrustean classifications of form in favor of more flexible interpretations (as in Tobel/KLASSISCHEN), and that pay at least as much attention to the generative processes of rhythm, melody, and texture as to the total structural result of these processes (one example being Blume's lucid yet penetrating article, "Klassik," in MGG VII 1027-1090, and another being the creative approach in Kirkpatrick/SCARLATTI 251-279). However, in no instance has it been possible here to adopt fully either the approach or the specific analyses of another writer. If it were only a matter of accepting and crediting his biographic and bibliographic discoveries, there usually would be no problem, since these ordinarily appear as incontrovertible facts. But the chance of being able to accept his approach to form and his analyses is much less, if only because the most objective approach must always fall back on subjective conclusions in the face of such simple questions as, when is a modulation, or a "second theme," or a contrapuntal texture, or, even, a separate movement (as against a contrasting section).[1] Moreover, though the reader, with his score in hand, may learn much from another's analysis, the writer must prepare his own, in order to keep his approach consistent, to formulate and word his analyses in the terms of his particular study, and, most important, to experience the music for himself.

As suggested earlier, the approach developed here is based on a consideration of essential style traits as generative elements, or even as form determinants, the aim being a view of the Classic sonata that is both dynamic and flexible. In particular, a distinction is made between two mutually opposed styles of progression, leading, typically, to two mutually opposed structural results.[2] In its purest state, "motivic play"—that is, the continual passing about of a distinctive but fragmentary "clause"—tends to generate a monothematic (or monomotivic), cursive form. Its most characteristic traits are its polyphonic texture, fast harmonic rhythm, proselike meter, and constant tonal flux. An ideal or relatively pure example might be the opening movement of J. S. Bach's Sonata 2 in A for harpsichord and violin (Schmieder 1015). By diametric contrast and in its purest form, "phrase grouping"—that is, the apposition, opposition, or other juxtaposition of relatively complete

1. Among numerous pertinent exx. of decidedly personal analysis might be cited 2 very different approaches to Mozart's sons., H. Keller's in Landon & Mitchell/MOZART 90-94, and that in Dennerlein/MOZART (e.g., pp. 315-319).

2. A detailed exposition of this approach to musical form appears in Newman/UNDERSTANDING Chaps. 8-11.

"sentences"—tends to generate a polythematic, hierarchic design of sections within sections. Its most characteristic traits are its homophonic texture, slow harmonic rhythm, verselike meter, and broad tonal plateaus. An "ideal" example might be the "Alla Turca" finale from Mozart's Sonata in A, K.V. 300i.

Our "ideal" examples suggest a generalization, and rightly so, to the effect that in the Baroque sonata at its peak the most characteristic styles and forms are those growing out of motivic play, whereas in the Classic sonata at its peak they are those growing out of phrase grouping. Certainly this is a safer generalization than one that distinguishes merely between Baroque polyphony and Classic homophony (quite apart from the important resurgence of polyphony in the finest Classic sonatas). But it is a generalization still fraught with perils. Mainly, we must bear in mind that the ideal examples are rare extremes and that most of the sonata movements we shall encounter lie somewhere along the transitional path between them. The next section of this chapter defines the main stages along that historically unpredictable path by summarizing and illustrating the most characteristic style traits of each. And the remaining sections take up the structural results of these traits. In the meantime it is necessary to add to our thesis regarding the interdependence of style and form, starting with some propositions that are fast becoming axioms among present-day students of musical form.

Careful analysts may try to distinguish between three main concepts of form: (1) that of the particular generative process "inherent" in a particular set of materials or ideas, (2) that of the particular structural result growing out of a particular generative process, and (3) that of the standardized design, generalized mold, or textbook abstraction most applicable to a particular structural result. In the first movement of Beethoven's Sonata in E♭, Op. 31/3, for example, (1) a particular sort of irregular phrase grouping seems to inhere in the particular character of the initial idea, (2) a particular over-all structure seems to grow out of that sort of phrase grouping, and (3) the standardized design most applicable as a generalization of that result is "sonata form" (with quotation marks). The third concept has prevailed in much nineteenth- and twentieth-century analysis, partly because ready-made classifications, however inadequate and inaccurate, are far quicker and easier to make than all the particularizing required to show in what ways a certain process or structural result is, in fact, particular.

There are two main reasons why the approach to form as a scheme of standardized designs cannot be adequate for our survey of the Classic
2a sonata. In the first place, the number of such designs that are funda-

mentally different, whether based on motivic play or phrase grouping, is remarkably small. But the variants, of course, are countless. To force each analysis into one of those few prime designs does damage not only in the rough Procrustean sense but in the finer qualitative sense that everything original and individual about the work in question must give way to everything routine and standard about music in general. In the second place, the attempt to classify musical works largely in terms of standardized designs attaches too much significance to the fact itself of the design.[3] Actually, for all its convenience, the design concept is the least significant of the three concepts of form. To exalt it unduly is tantamount to saying that one only needs to "fill up" the same design, with the same number of measures in each subdivision, in order to produce another "Pathétique" sonata.

Both objections to the design concept lead to the same tautologic and self-evident conclusion, which is that the significance and distinction of a particular work lie more in its individualities than in its generalities. By way of analogy, one might recall the tendency in recent copyright suits over literary works of art, to give more weight to the particular treatment of a plot than to the basic plot itself. There is only one real danger that accompanies the fuller consideration of form as a generative process and as the structural result of that process. It is the usual danger of carrying any approach too far. Thus, one must not start to make organic inevitabilities out of aesthetic tendencies, as though he were observing the growth of a particular seed into a particular plant, or as Reti does by insisting that, necessarily, "in the great works of musical literature the different movements of a composition are connected in thematic unity—a unity that is brought about not merely by a vague affinity of mood but by forming the themes from one musical substance. . . . the different themes of *one* movement—in fact all its groups and parts—are in the last analysis also but variations of one identical thought."[4] There need not be anything inevitable about the fact that certain ideas lend themselves best to certain processes, or that these in turn tend to generate certain structures. Consciously or unconsciously,[5] strong, imaginative composers neither hesitate nor lack the "free will" to contradict these tendencies when they please.

This much of an excursion into the general problems of form analysis is made necessary by the great importance that writers have

3. Cf. Edmund Rubbra's excellent statement to this effect as quoted in MR XXI (1960) 149.

4. Reti/THEMATIC 4.

5. In Walker/MOTIVATION the composer's need to be conscious of his methods is denied.

attached to the nineteenth-century textbook concept of "sonata form" for more than a century. A concise but representative example of that familiar concept may be quoted from *Musical Forms* by the German pianist, editor, and pedagogue, Ernst Pauer.[6]

> *First part.* Chief or principal subject, transition to second subject. Final group. Repeat. [The corresponding key scheme is] Tonic. Modulation into the dominant or a relative major key; or rarely, if the chief subject is in a minor key, to the minor key of the fifth above.
>
> *Middle part.* Thematic working out or development of both the subjects of first part; called also the Free Fantasia, because unrestricted as to form. [With regard to the tonality] Free modulations return to the tonic.
>
> *Repetition* [i.e., recapitulation]. Chief subject. Transition ["a short passage," Pauer says elsewhere] to second subject. Final group. Recollection ["the coda, or summing up"]. Finale ["with some concluding chords." As for the key] Reign of the tonic.

Pauer, himself a student of W. A. Mozart "the Younger," introduced these remarks by a statement (p. 116) that was also representative, with its serious misunderstanding of both Emanuel Bach's and Mozart's contributions as we now view them (SCE XIII and XIV): "It was Emanuel Bach, the second son of the great Sebastian Bach, who fixed the present form of the sonata; even the greatest works of this kind by Beethoven are founded or built on Emanuel Bach's original plan. Joseph Haydn, an enthusiastic admirer of Emanuel Bach, improved the sonata to such an extent, that we could pass from Haydn's sonatas directly to those of Beethoven, without the intervention of Mozart's sonatas as a connecting link."

It is true that thoughtful writers of textbooks on musical form, such as Marx, Hadow, Parry, Goetschius, and Leichtentritt, have added to the standard concept of "sonata form" the caution that many variants are to be found in the masterworks of music literature. Yet, nearly all of the many historians who have selected and evaluated sonatas on the basis of that concept have placed special emphasis on its three most characteristic features—that is, the "second" or "contrasting" theme, the "development" or "working out" section, and the return of the main theme in the tonic key where the recapitulation is expected to begin. The mention of these three features is significant here because, as will be seen later in this chapter and, in fact, throughout the rest of the book, they prove to be the very features of "sonata form" that remain its most flexible, fluid, and unpredictable aspects well into the late-Classic

6. The book was first published in London in 1878; the description appears in the text and in a chart on p. 117. Cf. the slightly fuller chart in Hadow/SONATA 91.

Era.[7] Before that time the number of scattered examples that happens to satisfy the textbook concept in all its main features is not few. But its percentage is never sufficient to suggest that it marks a prime goal of either pre- or high-Classic trends.

Then, of what importance, one may well ask, are the ever earlier examples of "sonata form" reported by this or that researcher? Not a few of these go back to the high-Baroque Era or earlier, such as Abaco's SS/bass Sonata Op. 3/6/i of about 1714.[8] But such examples actually sound no more like high-Classic movements in "sonata form" than a dance in binary form by J. S. Bach might sound like one by Beethoven. As we have seen (SCE II), even the late eighteenth-century writers who troubled to write about structure were concerned much less about design itself than about such means of design as tonal organization and phrase syntax. It is in just those respects that attempts to find early precedents for "sonata form" seem meaningless. An interesting illustration is found by comparing the first movements from one representative keyboard sonata each by J. S. Bach's three greatest sons (Friedemann's Son. in E♭, F. 5; Emanuel's Son. in g, W. 65/17; Christian's Son. in B♭, Op. 17/6[9]). Progressing from Friedemann to Christian, the style and feel (or treatment) of these sonatas bring us closer and closer to that of the high-Classic sonata, but their designs, if those same three features are judged literally, actually regress more and more from the requirements of "sonata form." In fact, in such a literal sense the first movements of Beethoven's Sonatas in A and E, Opp. 101 and 109, would have to be regarded as distinct regressions from those of his Sonatas in f, A, and C, Op. 2/1-3!

As already suggested (SCE I), the search for "sonata form" became the chief basis for innumerable "evolutionary" approaches to sonata history that have been published and still prevail as encyclopedia articles, introductions to monographs, sections in more general histories, and separate short surveys.[10] These approaches, it must be both acknowledged and emphasized, are seldom found acceptable as such, here, notwithstanding the valuable single bits of information sprinkled

7. A pertinent M.A. thesis is Serrins/TEXTBOOK, in which the last string 7a
quartets of Haydn and Mozart are measured, point for point, against textbook concepts of "sonata form" (with conclusions similar to those reached here).

8. SBE 262-263. Several other exx. are cited in Fischer/INSTRUMENTALMUSIK 801; Raabe/GALUPPI 26-27.

9. Mod. ed. of all 3 sons., Newman/BACH-m, with preface.

10. Typical are Parry's original article on the "Sonata," written nearly a century ago and still used almost intact in GROVE VII 886-907; the introduction, pp. 10-26, to the diss. Stauch/CLEMENTI; Hadow's Chap. VII on "C. P. E. Bach and the Growth of the Sonata" in OXFORD HISTORY V; and the separate survey, Eitner/SONATE, based largely on the popular collection Pauer/MEISTER-m.

throughout them. They are too often characterized by a high degree of selectivity, in order to provide a chronological path to the preconceived concept, yet by an overly wide range of music, even extending to vocal music on occasion, from which the selections are made. One gets the sense of constant historical groping toward the ultimate concept. There is a tendency to establish an evolutionary chain of form types, as in the idea that the suite was the direct ancestor of the sonata, although these types generally developed concurrently, not successively. Within the form types further chains are made to lead from simple binary to complex ternary designs. This last succession is often illustrated by a series of diagrams in which the ideas and sections are lettered. (Apart from the questionable or false historical implications of the series, such diagrams can, of course, be of much graphic value.) Thus, using a and b for the main ideas, 1 and 2 for the main keys, and c3 for development in other keys, Hadow traces the following evolution:

a1-b1 || a2-b1
a1-b2 || a2-c3-b1
a1-b2 || a2-c3 || a1-b1[11]

In such approaches, the sonata cycle as a whole, which at best gets much less attention than "sonata form" in the first quick movement, is usually introduced at random and without sufficient distinction between the two problems. But attempts are made, too, to find an evolutionary trend in the number of movements. These attempts meet with more varied and less successful results[12] than the approaches to "sonata form," because even with selective methods a writer is hard pressed to bring order out of this frequently haphazard phenomenon.

Related to the "evolution" of "sonata form" are the numerous attempts to derive this design from the *da capo* or other aria forms.[13] Bukofzer has drawn parallels between the various "stages" of design in the Classic aria and sonata, illustrating each with detailed diagrams. But he is careful to disclaim any more vital relationship or any derivation of the sonata from the aria.[14] Although there can be little question about interchanges of style between the aria, with, say, its melodic

11. OXFORD HISTORY V 191, 193, 195. A somewhat similar series of diagrams still appears in Engel/QUELLEN 289-290; cf., also, Engel/KLASSIK 58-59. An exceptionally complex and arbitrary series appears in Bousquet's article tracing "sonata form" from Torelli in 1698 to Emanuel Bach in 1742, in RIM I/5-6 (1939) 853-862.

12. As in Eitner/SONATE.

13. As in Dent/OPERA and, again by Dent, in MR X (1949) 56; Abert/MOZART I 242-245; Helfert/SONATENFORM 138-141; Tovey/ANALYSIS III 3-26. The short definition of the son. in Kollmann/ESSAY 9 includes the statement that it "may be compared in Instrumental Music, to what an *Air* is in Vocal Music."

14. Bukofzer/CLASSIC 5-12.

lyricism or *buffa* piquancy, and the sonata, with its technical virtuosity,
there is not much likelihood of a cause-and-effect relation between the
over-all design of the aria and that of "sonata form," if only, again,
because they developed concurrently, not successively. For that matter, 14a
the opera composer Grétry saw the opposite relation in the several
instances when he cited instrumental music as the model for operatic
music.[15] In any case, instrumental and vocal forms had progressed too
far along their separate ways by the time of the pre-Classic Era for there
to be anything like the close relationship that existed between the
symphony or concerto, on the one hand, and the sonata, on the other
(SCE II and V).

The Style Shift

In the past generation or so, writers on musical form have come to
interest themselves more in its stylistic or generative traits than in its
architectonics or over-all design. A pioneer study in 1915 was W.
Fischer's on style in Vienna Classical instrumental music (Fischer/
WIENER), with special emphasis on melodic traits. Since about the
same time basic studies have also appeared on the sources of the Mozart
style, as by Wyzewa and Saint-Foix, Torrefranca, Abert, Racek, Engländer, Fischer, and Engel. Less has appeared, however, on the sources
of the Beethoven style (as by Schiedermair) or the Haydn style (as by
Abert). As we have already seen, tracing the sources and styles of 15a
the great masters should itself make the ideal approach to the subject
of design. For it reveals the steps by which the musical climate became
more and more favorable to "sonata form" or any related design, to the
point where a minor figure like Graziani could fall into these designs
in the 1760's (SCE VIII) just as naturally as, and even before, Haydn
or Mozart did.

Our object in this section, then, will be to summarize and illustrate
the main style shifts in the history of the Classic sonata, beginning with
late-Baroque traits that still persisted at the start of the era, proceeding
to the *galant* style and its offshoot in the *empfindsam* style during the
pre-Classic Era, continuing to the high-Classic style of Haydn and
Mozart, and concluding with the late-Classic style of Beethoven and his
contemporaries. Throughout this summary it is essential to note the 15b
separate elements of musical style—melody, texture, syntax, rhythm,
tonality, and concomitants like articulation, scoring, dynamics, and
harmonic vocabulary. It is also essential to keep in mind the several 15c

15. Grétry/MEMOIRES 353-354, 415-416, 422, 460; cf. CM XXVIII (1979) 19-29.

philosophic and literary influences noted earlier (SCE II), including the not wholly compatible urges toward originality and simplicity.

The **Baroque style traits and processes** that were still cultivated well into the pre-Classic Era, by the more conservative composers and in the more conservative settings, are mainly those associated here with motivic play. Integral to the later Baroque style is the continuously spun-out melody, which parallels the *b.c.* in melo/bass settings and tends to grow intensively rather than extensively out of the sequences, transpositions, inversions, and other free reiterations of a motive or stock figure. Often this melodic line shifts from one voice to another by motivic exchanges in a relatively polyphonic texture. In turn, the overlapping or dovetailing of these exchanges makes for a plastic, proselike rhythm still somewhat independent of barline meter. And the texture itself favors a rapid harmonic rhythm. The tonal organization is usually defined by the sphere of nearest related keys, as attained by one drive-to-the-cadence after another. Characteristic of these drives-to-the-cadence is sequential progress in chains of dominant or mediant harmonies. The total impression is that of a continual push and pull on one idea within the scope of one main key, one main flow, and one relatively unbroken arch. Except in fugal episodes and certain development sections, the sonatas of the Viennese masters no longer reveal any consistent dependence on Baroque styles. But insofar as any one example can be representative (along with the other examples scattered throughout our later chapters), it may still be found in the slow middle movement of an early keyboard sonata (1739?) by Friedemann Bach (Ex. 8).

The term *galant* was in favor long enough to undergo considerable change in its musical connotations—in fact, long enough to necessitate
15d a distinction here between a first and a second **galant style.** The first *galant* style paralleled or coincided with the Rococo style in music and painting during the late-Baroque Era. Among its chief exponents were Couperin "le Grand," Telemann, D. Scarlatti, and Tartini. And its most characteristic trait, along with Couperin's wealth of refined ornamentation, was the relaxation, though not yet the abandonment, of the several processes we have grouped under "motivic play." By contrast, the second *galant* style, which reached its peak in the 1750's and 1760's, cannot be said to have derived so clearly from Baroque music, for it was distinctly anti-Baroque both in concept and character. In this sense it suggests negativistic foundations for the Classic Era not unlike the anti-Romantic beginnings of the Modern Era (but without a close parallel in the transition from late-Classic to pre-Romantic music). Yet in the pertinent works of Galuppi, Rutini, G. B. Sammartini, Boccherini, Soler,

Ex. 8. From the second movement of Sonata in E♭, F. 5, by Wilhelm Friedemann Bach (after TRÉSOR-m VI 28).

Christian Bach, early Haydn, and early Mozart, it is more positive and crystallized as a style than the first *galant* style. And it is what is intended in later chapters when reference is made to the "*galant* style" without further qualification.

The departure from Baroque music in the second *galant* style relates especially to the new keyboard music and reveals itself first of all in the melody. The long continuous line becomes fragmented in a series of restless, short-winded clauses marked off by half-cadences and rests. The object was a simpler, more "natural" style in place of the "turgid," "confused," and "artificial" melody such as Scheibe had already found in J. S. Bach's music in 1737.[16] But *galant* melody soon revealed at least a superficial complexity of its own with its almost incessant short trills. It revealed further decided mannerisms, too, with its frequent series of triplets in 16th-notes, its delicate appoggiatura "sighs," its syncopations, "Scotch snaps," and other dotted figures, as well as its new refinements of both articulation and dynamics.

Coupled with these *galant* melodic traits were a watery thin, two-

16. BACH READER 238; cf., also, SCE II and III; Bücken/GALANTE (including further distinctions between a first and second *galant* style).

voice texture (except as this texture may have been filled out in practice; SCE V) and a variety of chordal and even more rudimentary accompaniments. These last supplied an essential but unobtrusively fluent motion in relatively slow harmonic rhythm. When they supported a lyrical, often tuneful type of melody, the result was the "singing-allegro" style, something very different from the older melo/bass style in which the motion is created by a "running" bass and the fast harmonic rhythm that it engenders (SBE 139). Most characteristic of the *galant* chordal accompaniments was the Alberti bass—specifically, the 4-note figure in 16th- or 8th-notes that oscillates in closed position (cf. Alberti, SCE VII, with exx.).[17] In this literal form, this highly influential but eventually much abused device was used so rarely before the 1740's (as by Pescetti in 1739, SCE XIX) that its appearance makes a convenient dating aid. Other characteristic accompaniments included non-oscillating chordal figures in 8th- or 16th-note triplets or 16th-note quadruplets, and broken octaves or mere repeated notes and double-notes known as "murky" and "drum" basses, usually in steady 8th-notes.

Among still other characteristics of the second *galant* style are the return to a harmonic orbit defined largely by the primary triads; the frequent stop at an abrupt half- or full-cadence introduced by a I^6_4 chord, to the point where this formula becomes an irritating cliché;[18] and the sense of contrasting key areas achieved by actual plateaus of tonality rather than the twisting and turning resulting from continual drives-to-the-cadence. Added to these traits is the syntactic tendency of *galant* music to fall into two-measure units that now unfold extensively rather than intensively. This structural organization becomes disturbing in the earlier sonatas of the second *galant* style when the successive units change enough to vitiate any motivic unity, yet not enough to implement clear phrase grouping. One can almost hear the sighs of relief as the composers of these sonatas lapse, on occasion, into the secure comforts of Baroque motivic play (as in the second Alberti ex., SCE VII).

The traits of the second *galant* style as a whole are summed up very well in the earliest keyboard sonatas by Haydn, where the influences on him still seem to be more Italian (by way of Wagenseil, Porpora, and others) than north German (SCE XIV). A representative example may be quoted from a Sonata in A composed not later than 1763 (Ex. 9).

The concurrent **empfindsam** (or ultrasensitive) **style,** which was the musical expression of the *Sturm und Drang* spirit, may be regarded

17. The definition is looser in Marco/ALBERTI.
18. Cf. Bücken/GALANTE 425 and Cudworth/GALANTE, both with exx.

Ex. 9. From the opening of Franz Joseph Haydn's Sonata in A, H. XVI/5 (after Martienssen/HAYDN-m II 108, but without the editorial additions).

as a special case of the *galant* style (SCE II). More to the point, it is an intensification and exaggeration of the latter, sometimes carried to extremes of eccentricity, as in certain sonatas by Emanuel Bach and all
sonatas by Müthel (both SCE XIII, with exx.). Emanuel and, to a 18a
lesser extent, his older brother Friedemann were prime agents of the *Empfindsamkeit,* which prevailed especially in north Germany. In spite of its close affinity with the *galant* style, the *empfindsam* style reveals a clearly distinguishable character of its own. In fact, it must be called the most individual style of the Classic Era. Its melodic lines give the effect of being even more fragmented than those of the *galant* style, owing to the greater number of rests, diversity of rhythms, and variety
of ornaments. Furthermore, the sighs are intensified by wider leaps, 18b
up or down, to more dissonant appoggiaturas. The phrase endings are subtilized by the indirection of constant deceptive cadences. The texture is somewhat enriched, with less use of the Alberti and other chordal basses. The harmonic vocabulary, dynamic fluctuations,[19] and articulatory minutiae are all increased. And the tonal outlines are colored by surprising key contrasts. One main result of all these excesses (by high-Classic standards) proves to be a frequent quality of fantasy, especially when recitative and parlando passages appear or when the tempo changes, whether gradually or abruptly. Only one keyboard sonata by Haydn exhibits the *empfindsam* style sufficiently to be quoted on this account here. It is his fine Sonata in c, which marked a turn toward more subjective writing on his part about 1771 (Ex. 10).

19. Cf. Hoffmann-Erbrecht/STURM.

Ex. 10. From the first movement of Franz Joseph Haydn's Sonata in c, H. XVI/20 (after Martienssen/HAYDN-m III 16, but without the editorial additions).

The **high-Classic style** represents, above all, the peak at which the ideal and most purposeful co-ordination of Classic style traits obtained. In four respects, that generalization applies directly to our further remarks. First, the very fact of an ideal co-ordination of style traits implies a shift in emphasis from generative processes to structural results. In other words, there will be at least as much to say on this co-ordination in the subsequent sections of this chapter, dealing with the over-all and separate forms of the Classic sonata. Second, the ideal co-ordination implies, quite rightly, a new naturalness and universality (or internationalism) of style that tends either to assimilate or eliminate any regional distinctions. Third, the universality implies, in turn, a new widespread popularity, which is reflected not only in the greater simplicity and appeal for the dilettante but in the greater absorption of dance and folk elements. And fourth, as we have seen (*supra* and SCE II), the ideal co-ordination and the universality must not be taken to imply the arrival at a state of structural formulization. Structural fluidity still prevails in the high-Classic sonatas of Haydn, Mozart, early Beethoven, Clementi, and their best contemporaries. In fact, the originality and personality per se of these composers, especially in their melody and rhythm, are among the many points of distinction between them and the relatively impersonal Baroque masters. Only the most unimaginative of the *Kleinmeister* fail to show this originality and personality. But that, of course, is why they are *Kleinmeister*. It is they, as we shall be reminded more than once in later chapters, who are always ready and waiting to reduce current masterworks to lifeless formulas and stereotypes.

In the incomparably songful, fresh melodies of Haydn, Mozart, and their best contemporaries, the folk and dance elements require some comment first.[20] Earlier in this century Fischer and Adler planted the hypothesis that the Classic masters, especially Haydn, drew heavily on folk music for their melodic materials.[21] But any assumption that folk melodies were generally taken over intact is misleading. Such literal transfers occurred only infrequently and, except for an occasional well-known example like the "Theme russe" in Beethoven's Quartet Op. 59/1/iv, they occurred not in the symphonies, quartets, and sonatas that best represent Classic music but in actual folk settings, variations on folk melodies, and a few dance tunes in lighter instrumental works. Furthermore, as in the "Surprise" theme of Haydn's "Surprise" Symphony in G, one cannot even be sure that the theme did not originate with the master and only later become known as a folk melody. As Wiora observes, the composer may try deliberately to create folklike naïveté as he might try to create any other effect.[22] It is both more applicable and more accurate to think of the composer as adapting to his artistic uses certain characteristic melodic elements, scale types, and phrase-and-period structures that had become common property. Thus, hints of Austrian, Hungarian, and Czech folk elements seem to abound in the high-Classic instrumental music of the Viennese masters.

Among 20 illustrations of melodic elements derived from folk music sources, Wiora includes the opening phrase of Mozart's piano Sonata in A, K.V. 300i, and another in his 2-piano Sonata in D/iii/121-124, K.V. 375.[23] To this kind of adaptation of folk elements the high-Classic sonata lends itself well, especially where the need is for a complete characterful theme rather than a pithy motive suitable for development. Most often one finds folklike ideas in a contrasting, second theme of the first movement, or in the main theme of a minuet and trio, or in the

20. This paragraph is based largely on the excellent discussion in Wiora/VOLKSMUSIK 104-133, with further bibliography.

21. Fischer/WIENER 29; Adler/WIENER 772-773.

22. Wiora/VOLKSMUSIK 106-107.

23. Wiora/VOLKSMUSIK 227, 221.

refrain of a rondo. But actual identification of such ideas with specific folksong sources is difficult and seldom demonstrated convincingly. The same may be said for dance rhythms, which perhaps leave little doubt in the hearer's mind of their folk and dance origin, as in the Spanish sonatas of D. Scarlatti and Soler (SCE IX), yet may be almost impossible to trace to specific dances.

The ideal co-ordination of style traits in high-Classic music is evident at once in its lucid melodic organization, which often reveals a folklike balance of antecedent and consequent phrases. One favorite means of attaining such organization is the compounding of motives by sequential or freer repetition so that they add up to clear phrases, as in Mozart's piano Sonata in B♭, K.V. 315c/i/1-4.[24] The motives submit to this superior organization by recurring throughout the phrase in the same metric position, with the same articulatory refinements, within the same tonal arch, and perhaps as graduations in one and the same crescendo. Further definition and direction is often given to the initial phrase of a high-Classic sonata movement by its division into two distinct members that are sharply contrasted in every respect including dynamic levels.[25] The start of Mozart's "Jupiter" symphony is one of the most familiar examples. But J. Stamitz, Wagenseil, and others had already followed a *forte* opening clause in unisons or bare octaves, *à la* concerto grosso, with a harmonized clause. This characteristic dualism within the opening theme is analogous to the dualism between contrasting themes that will be discussed presently as part of the first quick movement. Whereas the antecedent phrase in an opening sonata theme is usually a regular one of four measures, its one or more consequent phrases are likely to be extended in the most subtle manner by Haydn and Mozart. Thus, the opening theme stretches into 4 (2 & 2) + 7 (2 & 5) measures in Haydn's Sonata in E♭, H. XVI/45, and into 4 + 8 (4 & 4) in Mozart's Sonata in B♭, K.V. 570.

The high-Classic piano texture generally returns to three-part writing after the two-part writing of the second *galant* style. "Singing-allegro" passages are still just as prevalent, with the use of literal Alberti bass being more frequent in Mozart's than Haydn's or (early) Beethoven's sonatas. Only gradually does the bass regain a thematically more significant role in Classic music. Its importance increases in this respect in direct proportion to the return to polyphonically enriched

24. Cf. the discussion of this process in Kolneder/MOTIVISCHE (including the opening of Mozart's Son. in F, K.V. 300k).

25. Cf. Heuss/DYNAMIK (in Mannheim music) and Heuss/DYNAMIK II (in Mozart's K.V. 284b/ii); Fischer/INSTRUMENTALMUSIK 806 (with exx. from symphonies); F. K. Grave, "'Rhythmic Harmony' in Mozart," in MR XLI (1980) 87-102.

textures, which become more and more evident in the sonatas of the three Viennese masters and Clementi (as in the first mvts. of Haydn's Son. in F, H. XVI/47, Mozart's Son. in F, K.V. 533, Clementi's Son. in f♯, Op. 25/5, and Beethoven's Son. in A, Op. 2/2).

The high-Classic sonata imparts a heightened sense of harmonic richness and color. Yet the harmonic vocabulary is another factor that increases only gradually, the chief gains being in the subtle use of passing chromatic chords. Examples of the latter may be seen in Haydn's outstanding Sonata in E♭, H. XVI/52/i/11-16, with "borrowed" tones from the parallel minor key, and especially in Mozart's equally outstanding Sonata in D, K.V. 576/i/83-96, in which passing dissonances also figure.[26] Increasingly pungent dissonance is another main factor in the new sense of harmonic color. A particularly telling example occurs just after the inner double-bar in the middle movement of Mozart's Sonata in B♭, K.V. 315c, where a biting double appoggiatura resolves upward into a V^6_5 that leads deceptively to VI. In all such examples, the impeccable voice-leading constitutes one of the most tangible evidences of the great masters' superior craftsmanship, just as their rhythmic ingenuity and accurate timing constitute the most tangible evidences of their superior creativity and structural perspective. Other considerations, like the slower harmonic rhythm, the broader, wider-ranged tonal schemes, and a new modulatory use of enharmony, will come up in our discussion of the separate forms. By way of illustration, the opening of Mozart's strong Sonata in c, K.V. 457, which anticipated Beethoven's *Grande Sonate pathétique* by 14 to 20 years (SCE XIV and XV), incorporates as many of the high-Classic style traits discussed here as any single example that comes to mind (Ex. 11).

The universality of the high-Classic style gave way to the striking individualities of the **late-Classic style.** The latter was universal only in the epigonic sense that facile, stereotyped sonatas were now being formulated, published, and sold by countless *Kleinmeister* of the times. But there is nothing stereotyped about the best works of the two chief late-Classic composers, Beethoven and Clementi. Indeed, for all the similarities of style that have been noted between these two men (SCE XX), relatively few generalizations can be made that apply to both. Perhaps the safest generalization is one to the effect that the late-Classic individualities can usually be viewed as extensions, intensifications, or even exaggerations of high-Classic norms.

The introduction of complete folk or other melodies that were cur-

26. Cf. the interesting argument over b♮ or b# in Mozart's Son. in B♭, K.V. 315c/i/44 in MUSICA X (1956) 333 and 680-681.

Ex. 11. From the opening of Wolfgang Amadeus Mozart's Sonata in c, K.V. 457 (after MOZART WERKE-m XX 160).

rently popular was not unusual in the dance or variation movements (as by Wölfl, SCE XVI) or throughout all of the movements in some very light "tune sonatas" of the late-Classic Era. But, as Wiora observes, the fact that composers now turned consciously to the use of such ma-

terials could itself be a sign of epigonic trends.[27] Beethoven did not introduce outright folk melodies in his sonatas; nor did Clementi in his more artistic, serious ones. However, there are melodies in the sonatas of each that are decidedly folklike in their refreshing simplicity and their clearly balanced periods (as in the hand-crossing "trio" of Beethoven's Op. 10/3/iii or the symmetrical tune hidden in the oscillating accompaniment to the third theme in his Op. 10/1/i/56-69). In their 27a
later works both Beethoven and Clementi drew more and more away from such melodies as they cultivated increasingly complex phrase groupings, especially those with two or more consequent phrases that are greatly elongated through the reiteration and cumulative contraction of a motive (as in the grouping of 4 [2 & 2] + 13 [4 & 9] in Beethoven's Op. 106/i/1-17, or 16 [8 & 8] + 14 [4 & 10] + 16 [8 & 8] in Clementi's Op. 50/3/i).

Even more of the late- than of the high-Classic style must come under the province of structure. Here we may note how, besides motivic cumulation, Beethoven had other means of intensifying if not actually peculiarizing the melodic, rhythmic, and harmonic flow in his sonatas. (Clementi is dealt with further in SCE XX.) The metric drive in his quick movements may be heightened by the almost inexorable persistence of simple accompaniment figures, as in Op. 13/i/11-27, where the impelling broken octaves that set up the hot pulse are scarcely recognizable as the erstwhile lowly murky bass. In his scherzo movements (e.g., Op. 27/1/ii), the pulsation may become so persistent and uniform that all suggestions of dance influences disappear, not to mention the minuet style that his scherzo style replaced. At the same time, tension may be added to the metric drive by unexpected thrusts on the "weak" beats, as by the right-hand syncopations in the same theme of Op. 13, or by the right-hand *sforzando* octaves (mss. 27-28 and 31-32) in the bridge that follows. And, in turn, these thrusts may be pointed up by stinging harmonic dissonances, as by the double appoggiaturas on the offbeats in the continuation of that bridge (mss. 45-49). Moreover, the increasingly refined articulation may contribute to the headlong rush by further defining the shifts of accents, as in the development section of the same movement, where left-hand, two-note slurs convert adjacent pairs of beats from weak-strong to strong-weak (mss. 149-158). And the dynamic markings may contribute, whether they see a crescendo to its logical climax (mss. 137-139) or "disappoint" it in a "Beethoven *piano*" (mss. 207-211). With this many details to concern them, it is no

27. Wiora/VOLKSMUSIK 133.

wonder that composers became so much more meticulous in their editing by the end of the Classic Era.

Other style shifts in the late-Classic Era might come under the heading of increased color rather than metric drive. In a few later sonatas, both Beethoven and Clementi carried the resurgence of polyphonic interest to an extreme in recherché fugues or canons. But both men seem to have been more preoccupied with the textural enrichment than the structural results in their polyphony. Beethoven even experimented with new, oblique, dissonant relationships in certain imitative passages (as in Op. 81a/i/230-234). When he did extend such processes into complete forms he apparently still preferred to bend them to the sectional kinds of structures that usually result more naturally from homophonic (or phrase-grouping) processes, as in the fugal finales of Opp. 101 and 110. However, in most of their sonata movements, Beethoven and Clementi preferred to heighten the color in other ways, especially by exploring new technical idioms (SCE V) and by creating new, quasi-orchestral sonorities at the piano—for example, in Op. 31/2/i/21-28, where one might imagine the dialogue as being played, say, by cellos, basses, and bassoons in octaves against a clarinet and a flute in octaves in the upper part, and with a rhythmic filler taken by the violas.[28] Beethoven's evident association of particular moods and styles with particular keys and modes undoubtedly influenced these dispositions.

Minute variations in the melodic, harmonic, rhythmic, and textural make-up of an idea can in themselves be of color as well as structural significance. Even more than Haydn and Mozart, Beethoven became increasingly absorbed with variation techniques, applying them not only in his formal sets of variations (as in the incredibly sublime finale of Op. 111) but throughout his sonata movements (as in Op. 54/i or 106/iii), to the point where, so to speak, he could scarcely keep his hands off his own music. Indeed, variation treatment underlies much of the free fantasy that adorns his last sonatas (as in Op. 109/i), marking a kind of final obeisance to the *empfindsam* style.

Above all, harmony and tonality served Beethoven as agents of color as well as form. Like such factors as syntax and tempo, his modulations, mediant and enharmonic relationships, "false returns," and enlarged tonal horizons will have to await their discussion under structure. But here we may recall Beethoven's extraordinarily telling placement of certain expressive or climactic chords in spite of the surprising preference he showed for the simple primary triads throughout much of his music.

28. Recall the orchestral timbres linked with Op. 53/i/98-99 and Op. 57/iii/342-343 and 348-349, in the 19th-c. Bülow-Lebert ed. of Beethoven's sons.

The gentle arrival at V_6 in the dominant-major key in Op. 81a/ii/15, or the smiling yet tearful reference to the Neapolitan harmony in Op. 106/iii/14, or the momentary digression to the submediant harmony in Op. 101/ii/30-32—each is just as telling in its way as, for instance, the climactic I^6_4 in Op. 27/2/iii/183.

Every serious reader will have his complete Beethoven sonatas at hand, in which he is likely to be familiar not only with the examples of late-Classic style traits already cited but numerous others like them. As a single example of several of these traits, the first "Allegro" theme may be quoted from Op. 81a (Ex. 12).

Before we leave this section on style shifts, two other distinctions should be recalled from earlier discussions. One is the distinction between the chamber and symphonic styles that Koch already observed late in the eighteenth century (SCE II) and that we shall observe when we come to G. B. Sammartini, Boccherini, J. Stamitz, Emanuel Bach, and others. In spite of their designations, both styles can be found in ensemble sonatas, and solo sonatas too, often by the same composer. The distinction is really that between the variegated, delicate, easygoing *galant* style, or even the more sentimental, probing *empfindsam* style, and that businesslike, efficient, purposeful, economical kind of writing associated especially with the pre-Classic symphony in Mannheim and Vienna. The first movements of Haydn's piano Sonatas in B♭ and e, H. XVI/18 and 34, might be cited as examples of the chamber and symphonic styles, respectively.

The other distinction is that between national styles such as Quantz argued in the interest of an ultimate "mixed" style (SCE II). As already suggested (SCE IV), eighteenth-century writers attributed general styles to Italy, France, and Germany, and twentieth-century pioneers like Riemann have attributed more specific traits to more specific locales. But at least in the sonata, both the general and the specific styles were actually so much in the air everywhere by the time of the pre-Classic Era, depending more on the individual composer than on the place, that attempts to categorize them are contradicted at every turn. Perhaps the most clearly regionalized style is that of the *Empfindsamkeit* in north Germany. Otherwise, one might point to such tentative and temporary distinctions as the use of Alberti bass primarily by Italians during its first decade, or the syntactic method frequently used by later eighteenth-century Spanish composers of literal repetition rather than the free unfolding of an idea, or the conservative, three-part writing still found in the early accompanied keyboard sonatas by Parisian sonata composers, or those elusive Austrian, Czech, and Hungarian folk elements in pre-

Ex. 12. From the opening movement of Ludwig van Beethoven's Sonata in E♭, Op. 81a (after BEETHOVEN WERKE-m XVI/3 9).

Classic Viennese music. But specific traits like the "sighs," "rocket" themes, and dynamic markings that Riemann ascribed to Mannheim composers have proved especially vulnerable to contradiction (SCE XI). In any case, by the time of the high-Classic Era, such regional distinctions as did exist were largely amalgamated, when they were not boiled off, in the "melting pot" of the Vienna Classical school—that is, in the Classic style we now regard as "universal." The individualities of the late-Classic style suggest no further national distinctions. Not until the full bloom of the Romantic Era does a more positive kind of nationalism obtain in music.

The Cycle as a Whole

The point was made in the first section of this chapter that the Classic sonata cycle as a whole and its inner and final movements as individual pieces have been neglected by most writers because of a preoccupation with "sonata form" in the first quick movement. In view of the manifest importance that the composers themselves attached to it, the first movement obviously deserves to be considered as at least the equal of any other part of the sonata. But, just as obviously, there is also a need to give systematic attention to the cycle as a whole and to the other individual movements. The object of this section is to consider the cycle from the standpoints of the number, order, and length of its movements, the choice of main and subsidiary keys, the thematic, programmatic, and structural relationships, if any, and the center of gravity or dynamic curve of the whole cycle. To arrive at safe generalizations about most of these points presupposes some statistical compilations. A number of such compilations have been prepared, especially with regard to tonality. A few of these are cited here. But as with the analysis, much of the statistical material has had to be prepared anew here in order that it may apply to our particular approach.

Most Classic sonatas are in two, three, or four movements. In spite of numerous efforts by past writers to find chronological trends in the number of movements, no such trend can be validated here. But there can be no question that by far the largest number of sonatas are in three movements. The percentages for the main keyboard sonatas by the Viennese masters are as follows:

	Haydn (49 sonatas)	*Mozart* (19 sonatas)	*Beethoven* (32 sonatas)
2 movements	20 per cent	0 per cent	22 per cent
3 movements	76	100	44
4 movements	4	0	34

Beethoven comes nearest to an even distribution, with more of the four-movement cycles dating from the earlier part of his career and more of the two-movement cycles from the later part. Haydn's sonatas in two and four movements are scattered throughout his production. Mozart made no exception to the three-movement cycle (i.e., among his 19 solo keyboard sons.), unless he did not mean to include the present finale of K.V. 547a (SCE XIV). In the 72, largely German keyboard sonatas of Anth. HAFFNER OM-m, published from 1755 to 1766, 76 per cent are in 3 movements, 19 in 4, 3 in 2, and one in one movement.[29] The three-movement cycle holds almost as great a majority in the thirty, largely Italian keyboard sonatas of Anth. HAFFNER RACCOLTA-m, although there are now more two- than four-movement sonatas in the minority. We shall also find that the three-movement cycle has more or less of a lead in the sonatas, whether ensemble or solo keyboard, by Pugnani, Friedemann and Emanuel Bach, Rust, Clementi, and most of the other composers second only to the Viennese masters.

On the other hand, enough pre-Classic Italian composers, including especially Alberti and Paradisi, wrote enough two-movement sonatas to give rise today to the term "Italian sonata" for this type. Actually, the two-movement sonata has only a slight edge over the three-movement type in the works of Galuppi and Rutini, the two types run about the same in G. B. Sammartini's works, and the edge is on the other side in Boccherini's. In France and England, as well as Italy, the two-movement cycle is characteristic especially of lighter sonatas, such as those designated for pedagogic or dilettante use, or those in the popular accompanied keyboard, SS, or SS/bass settings. For example, Rutini changed from predominantly three- to predominantly two-movement cycles in his later, lighter sets. But Christian Bach, the Italian-trained composer in London, favored the two-movement cycle not only in almost all his accompanied keyboard sonatas but in most of the solo keyboard and some of the SS/bass sonatas as well. Furthermore, many of the sonatas by the three S's of Iberian keyboard music—Seixas, D. Scarlatti, and Soler—now appear to have been intended as two- rather than the one-movement works they have long been taken for. At least, pairs of movements in the same key occur much too often in the extant MSS (none of them autographs) to be only coincidental, not to mention an occasional verbal or other clue of a more tangible nature (SCE IX). Otherwise, one-movement sonatas, as by Emanuel Bach and G. Benda, are neither numerous nor consequential enough to represent more than a minor category of the Classic sonata. As for cycles in more than four movements—in fact, in over twice that many, sometimes—these occur chiefly in the earliest pre-Classic sonatas, especially those that are still

29. Warm thanks are owing to Mr. Roger Kamien of Queens College, New York, for supplying a variety of statistical data on this important anthology (SCE XI).

close to the Baroque suite, as by Agrell, Maichelbeck, Hurlebusch, and Lustig.

In the three-movement cycle, the most frequent **order of movements** is F(ast)-S(low)-F, or F-M(oderate)-F. This plan is also preferred by each of the three Viennese masters. Haydn and Beethoven show a 30a
slight preference for a slow middle movement and Mozart for a moderate (i.e., andante) movement. Otherwise, their three-movement plans are too varied to generalize, including even the plan F-F-F (as in Beethoven's Op. 10/2). Haydn uses a minuet as the middle or final movement in more than half his three-movement sonatas. Mozart uses it only twice, as the middle movement, and Beethoven not at all in his three-movement sonatas, though he does use a scherzo or quasi-scherzo in several instances, as in Op. 27/2/ii. In the three-movement sonatas of all three masters, "sonata form" or some approximation of it prevails in the first movements and rondo form in the finales. In centers other than Vienna, when the three-movement cycle is not built on the favorite F-S-F or F-M-F plan (as it is so regularly in Germany), it sometimes reverts to the late-Baroque plan of S-F-F. Otherwise, the variety of movement plans is so great that often we shall be able to note only the frequency of the minuet finale, the fondness for rondos and variations, the need for contrast between movements, and perhaps a tendency to step up the meter (or fractional time signature) from one movement to the next.[30]

The chief two-movement plans are M-F, F-F, F-rondo, and F-minuet. These types account for most of Haydn's two-movement sonatas and most of Beethoven's, too, although it is a bit difficult to think of Op. 90 in the same category as Alberti's Op. 1/2 on this account alone. A slow movement in two-movement sonatas is rather rare. Haydn's and Beethoven's four-movement sonatas generally insert a minuet or scherzo, in the high-Classic symphony manner, on either side of the middle movement in the F-S-F or F-M-F plan. But Beethoven uses both a minuet and a scherzo, side by side, between the outer fast movements of Op. 31/3. Examples of four-movement sonatas by other Classic composers are not infrequent—there are 14 among the 72 sonatas in Anth. HAFFNER OM-m—but they are scattered and show no special trend toward the Haydn and Beethoven types.

An introduction in slow or moderate tempo to the first or last movement is not always readily distinguishable from a separate, additional movement. Beethoven used introductions in several of both his solo keyboard and ensemble sonatas. His introductions to the first move- 30b

30. Cf. Müry/PUGNANI 12-13.

ments in Opp. 5/1, 5/2, 13, 47, 81a, and 102/1, and to the finales in Opp. 53, 69, 101, 102/1, and 110, all lead directly, through transitional harmonies, to what follows, yet all have more or less independent interest of their own. Haydn and Mozart did not use slow introductions in their keyboard sonatas, notwithstanding the use of them in their symphonies. The big "Fantaisie" in c, K.V. 475, with which Mozart published his Sonata in c, K.V. 457, can hardly be reduced to that classification. But he did use slow introductions to the first movements in some of his sonatas for piano and violin, whether long and nearly independent (K.V. 385e) or short and unquestionably dependent (K.V. 454). Slow or moderate, dependent introductions (stemming from the first or third movements in the S-F-S-F plan of the Baroque church sonata) are less rare in pre-Classic sonatas (as by Neefe and Barbandt) than has generally been supposed. There are even precedents for Beethoven's sort in Op. 13—that is, the sort that reappears in the following allegro movement (as in Binder's Son. in G published in 1761 in Anth. HAFFNER OM-m VIII/2).

With such a wide variety in the number and order of the movements and such a wide difference in their structural scope and aesthetic import, it is less surprising that the **length of the Classic sonata** varies all the way from, say, the 71 measures, lasting 100 seconds, in a one-movement preludial Sonata in a, by Seixas (Kastner/CRAVISTAS-m II/11) to the 1,167 measures, or at least 37 minutes, in Beethoven's enormous four-movement Sonata in B♭, Op. 106. Of course, the length of the sonata tended to increase as the thematic, rhythmic, and tonal means of extending its structural arches increased. We get only a rough idea of this increase by comparing the numbers of measures, since these differ in length and tempo (not to mention the question of repeats). But it is still interesting to note that Haydn's keyboard sonatas ranged from 93 to 479 measures, averaging 255; Mozart's from 221 to 561, averaging 417; and Beethoven's from 242 to 1,167, averaging 562. That the string quartets and symphonies by these men average from a fourth to a third longer than the solo sonatas is explained only partly by the regular use of four movements in the former and partly by the greater length that a greater variety of instrumental color permits. Even Beethoven's piano and string sonatas average almost a third longer (710 measures), although the "Kreutzer" sonata, Op. 47, with 1,373 measures, still takes about 5 minutes less to play than the "Hammerklavier," Op. 106. Of course, to anyone who knows the extraordinary compression of the first movement in Op. 101, containing only 102 measures, the fact hardly need be added that great length is no prerequisite to aesthetic worth and depth.

With regard to **tonality,** the individual statistics in our later chapters will show repeatedly what a remarkably large percentage of the Classic sonata output is limited to major keys, and to those of not more than four sharps or flats. Mozart himself used keys of not more than three sharps 30c
or flats, with scarcely a tenth of his sonatas in the minor mode. Haydn stayed entirely within the four sharps or flats and used the minor mode still less. Even Beethoven passed the limit of four sharps or flats only once, in his piano Sonata in F♯, Op. 78, but he did prefer the minor mode in more than a fourth of his sonatas, especially those for piano alone. The percentage of minor keys in all of Mozart's works is still smaller than that for his sonatas.[31] But even for this age of major-key preferences, the percentages for Haydn's and Mozart's music are unusually low. The over-all ratio for the Classic Era is close to four uses of major to one of minor, at least for the sonata, and applies even to the pre-Classic Era.[32] It is not unusual to find that each set of three to six sonatas contains one sonata in minor.

Of course, there were individual composers who showed a greater preference for minor keys, like Pescetti, who wrote as many minor as major sonatas. Such individual preferences seem to account for more use of minor keys than a force like the *Sturm und Drang,* which is often credited with stimulating its use.[33] But it is true that, as in Mozart's own late output, the use of minor keys increased in the later phases of the Classic Era. A point worth noting, though not necessarily in the sonatas of the Viennese masters, is the fact that time and time again the relatively few uses of minor account for some if not all of a composer's best sonatas.[34] *Sturm und Drang* or not, the minor mode, especially d, g, and c, seems to have aroused the composer's most intense, dramatic, and expressive feelings. We shall come to many examples of this phenomenon, as by Rutini, Galuppi, Christian Bach, Hüllmandel, Séjan, and Clementi.

Besides the choice of home key the other main question that concerns the tonality of the cycle as a whole is the **choice of key for any movement not in the home key.**[35] This question applies almost entirely to one inner movement in sonatas of three or four movements, and, more specifically, to an inner movement that is moderate or slow rather than

31. Cf. Dennerlein/MOZART 96; Engel/MOZART 67-68.
32. Cf. Faisst/CLAVIERSONATE 60 and 69; La Laurencie/BLANCHETON II 107.
33. As in Engel/MOZART 68.
34. Cf. Tenschert in KONGRESS 1956 (Vienna), pp. 640-642.
35. Cf. the illuminating discussion of key choice by Bach, Haydn, Mozart, and Beethoven, in Einstein/MOZART 130, 157-163.

a minuet or scherzo or a fast movement, as in the S-F-F plan. Sonatas in which the finale is put in a different key (as by Galuppi, SCE VII), or in which all three movements are put in different keys (as by Emanuel Bach, SCE XIII), or in which more than one inner movement is put in a different key (as by Umstatt, SCE XII), are all too rare to matter here. The only change in sonatas of two movements is the occasional one of mode, nearly always to major, as in Beethoven's three piano sonatas that change their mode in the finale—for example, Op. 90 in e and E.

In Haydn's 39 keyboard sonatas with 3 or 4 movements, over 40 per cent have no change either of key or mode in any of the movements. Nearest to such a change is the use of the opposite mode in the trios of most of the minuets, changes of this sort being, incidentally, one of the compensations for so little other use of minor keys by Classic composers. None of Beethoven's 25 sonatas in more than 2 movements and only 10 per cent of Mozart's 19 sonatas are without a change of key or mode in an inner movement. But as in nearly 18 per cent of Haydn's same sonatas, 32 per cent of Beethoven's reveal only the change of mode in an inner movement. For the rest, Haydn and Mozart show a decided preference for the subdominant and Beethoven for the submediant among nearly related keys. In 2 instances, Opp. 101 and 106, Beethoven goes further afield to the lowered submediant. And, as is well known, Haydn chooses the raised tonic in one extreme instance, H. XVI/52. This last recalls Clementi's Op. 47/2, in which the slow introduction begins in C, in a "Neapolitan" relationship to the home key of b. In the pre-Classic Era there is a still greater tendency to keep all movements in the same key. But there were some surprises then, too, as in a 4-movement sonata by Sorge with an inner movement in the supertonic key (SCE XII).

An interesting question is the extent to which the movements of the Classic sonata are united by factors over and above consistency of key and idiom. Three factors call for our attention—melodic or other stylistic relationships, programmatic continuity, and structural interconnections. On the whole, none of these can be called a major factor in the unity of the Classic sonata. We shall be finding more instances of **melodic relationships** between movements in the pre- and late- than in the high-Classic Era, those in Beethoven being the most notable. A first problem is always to decide whether the relationships are valid—not necessarily whether they were intended by the composer, since the creative process can operate at least in part at a subconscious level,[36] but whether they really represent something more than the accidental

36. Cf. Walker/MOTIVATION.

similarity of figures in a language all too often limited to conventions and clichés.[37] Sometimes, the more distinct relationships help to validate the more subtle ones in a composer's works. These relationships are most likely to occur between the incipits of the outer movements in a three- or four-movement sonata, although Friedemann Bach uses the same closing figure in all three movements of a Sonata in D (F. 3; SCE XII). Similar incipits in two-movement sonatas are rare. One might expect a greater cultivation of melodic interrelationships in the Berlin sonata because of the emphasis on one *Affekt* by Berlin writers (SCE II). But this emphasis pertained only to any one movement and does not seem to have influenced the treatment of the whole cycle.

Mozart's sonatas reveal only occasional, tentative melodic relation- 37a
ships between movements (as between K.V. 315c/i and iii). About a fourth of Haydn's sonatas, chiefly from his earlier output, contain possible interrelationships. But these are very tentative, too. The incipits rising from c″ to g″ in each of the three movements of H. XVI/10 give about as clear an example as any (Ex. 13). Beethoven's

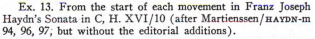

Ex. 13. From the start of each movement in Franz Joseph Haydn's Sonata in C, H. XVI/10 (after Martienssen/HAYDN-m 94, 96, 97; but without the editorial additions).

use of this unifying device is more tangible and more frequent than has
generally been recognized.[38] Moreover, there can be no doubt that he 38a
used it consciously, at least in certain later works, in view of his belated
addition of the introductory measure in Op. 106/iii in order to make
all four movements start with a rising 3d (SCE XV). Actually, the 38b
interrelationships are even clearer and more numerous in the earlier

37. Cf. the melodic relationships adduced in Engel/KLASSIK 75-79 and Engel/QUELLEN 300-304 with the questions raised in LaRue/RESEMBLANCE; also, SBE 78-79, 372-374.

38. It is explored especially in Mies/SKETCHES 114-130 and Rosenberg/BEETHOVEN, both with many exx.

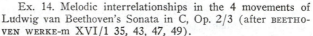

Ex. 14. Melodic interrelationships in the 4 movements of Ludwig van Beethoven's Sonata in C, Op. 2/3 (after BEETHOVEN WERKE-m XVI/1 35, 43, 47, 49).

sonatas. One example, based on a simple turn, will have to suffice here (Ex. 14; one of the internal ideas also based on this turn is illustrated in Ex. 15 *infra*).

But Beethoven often discloses still **other ways to bind the movements** of a sonata. Whereas the corresponding movements in many, though not the most important and individual, sonatas by Haydn or Mozart could be transposed and interchanged without conspicuous effect on the unity of the cycle, the movements in Beethoven's sonatas generally reveal textural and stylistic affinities that would be missed through any such interchange. Examples are the thin texture, light character, and angular motives throughout much of Op. 10/2, or the slower harmonic rhythm, more passive character, and pedal bass throughout much of Op. 28, or the decorative, persistent rotary figures throughout much of Op. 78.

Beethoven also comes to mind before any other Classic composer as regards the binding of movements through programmatic unity. Writers in the nineteenth and early twentieth century have imputed far more specific programmatic content to his sonatas than his vague references to "The Tempest" in Opp. 31/2 and 57 would seem to justify (SCE XV). One recalls the various stories invented for the "Pathétique" sonata (his title), or the "Moonlight" and "Appassionata" sonatas (not his titles). The only sure "programme" in the "Pathétique" sonata, which, in any case, has no lack of thematic and stylistic bonds, is that of the nobler passions it so consistently probes. More definitely characterized, of course, is the programme of "farewell, absence, and return" in the three successive movements of Op. 81a, along with the "Le-be-wohl" motive's variants in the first movement.[39] By analogy, at most, the programme of Clementi's Op. 50/3, "Didone abbandonata, Scena tragica," cannot be translated beyond the moods of departure, absence, and desperation in its three successive movements (SCE XX). Neither Clementi nor Beethoven wrote the sort of programmatic literalities in their sonatas that Beethoven wrote in his *Sinfonia pastorale*.

Mozart and Haydn showed no interest in programmatic content in their sonatas. But a number of programmatic sonatas by other Classic composers will be met in our later chapters, none of them of appreciable consequence to the mainstream of sonata history.[40] In some, the programme hardly goes beyond the title, as in "Sonata; the Storm" by Benser (SCE XX) or a "Sonate sentimentale" for guitars and lyre entitled "Les Amours d'Adonis et de Venus."[41] Others, like "The Battle of Prague, A Favourite Sonata," by Kocžwara, are ridiculously literal (SCE XX). In between are such varied types as sonatas with a religious programme (MGG VII 1642), a clavichord sonata with imitations of other instruments (Rust, SCE XVI), a sonata about a marital quarrel and reconciliation (Vogler, SCE XVI), a sonata that describes travels (Graziani, SCE VIII), and a sonata about man's despair and hope (Emanuel Bach, SCE XIII). The numerous British sonatas based on "favorite airs" (as by Dibdin, SCE XIX), which are programmatic only insofar as they reflect the subject matter of the airs' texts, are of even less consequence to any significant trend in sonata history.

The Classic sonata also reveals considerable interconnecting and interlocking of movements as a means of furthering the unity of the whole cycle. Thus, we shall be meeting numerous instances, throughout most of the era, of a movement that ends on a suspensive chord and proceeds directly ("attacca") to the next movement (as in Op. 57/ii-iii by Beethoven) or proceeds without any break in the continuity (as in Op. 81a/ii-iii by Beethoven). This kind of connection usually links only the penultimate movement with the finale, as also in many Classic and Romantic concertos. But it links all four movements in Beethoven's first "Sonata quasi una fantasia," Op. 27/1. And a three-movement sonata by Guénin continues from beginning to end without repeats within its movements or breaks between them (SCE XVIII). Haydn interconnects his movements, too (as in H. XVI/34/ii-iii), but Mozart does this only in his piano and violin sonatas and only at the ends of

39. But hardly in ii and iii as illustrated in Rosenberg/BEETHOVEN II 333 and 335.

40. Among contemporary discussions of the programmatic son. that are trans. or summarized in the present survey, those of Rousseau (SCE II) and Zink (SCE XXI) are especially pertinent here.

41. BIBLIOGRAPHIE MUSICALE 180.

slow introductions or of internal contrasting sections. Beethoven also supplies the most notable uses of interlocking movements (among other examples being the structural experiments by D. Scarlatti, Soler, and others in Spain [SCE IX, with diagrams]). Thus, during the introductory matter of the finale in Beethoven's Op. 101 the start of the first movement is recalled. And the interlocking of arioso-fugue-arioso-inverted fugue is so intimately conceived in Op. 110 that it provides the chief argument for hearing the highly distinctive slow material as an introduction to the finale in that work rather than as a separate movement.

Finally, with regard to the cycle as a whole, some remarks may be made on the **dynamic or climactic curve** that it describes.[42] The idea of one over-all climax in the cycle seems not to have taken hold in the Classic Era, except in certain of Beethoven's last works, in the way it was to take hold in the Romantic works of Liszt, Wagner, Brahms, Bruckner, Rachmaninoff, and others. One thinks of the climax as having to come somewhere near the end of a "time art" like music if there is not to be an excessive anticlimax.[43] In this sense, a finale like that in Beethoven's Op. 13 must be regarded as something of a letdown, whereas that of his Op. 27/2 or 110 certainly marks the peak of the cycle.[44] Evaluating the climax curve depends to a large extent on subjective judgments, since such a variety of considerations must be balanced against each other. The climax may or may not coincide with what might be called the center of gravity in the sonata. The driving, fateful finale of Beethoven's Op. 57 makes a stunning climax, but the calm, arabesque variations of the slow movement may well seem like the "center of gravity" to many hearers. Only in the numerous instances when a light minuet or other dance concludes the sonata is there likely to be general agreement that the climax must be found in some earlier movement.

With the foregoing considerations in mind, an attempt was made, during the present survey, to pick out the one or two "strongest" movements in each of the keyboard sonatas by the three Viennese masters. The chart that follows indicates the percentage of sonatas in which the main strength seems to lie (1) in both outer movements (as in Op. 81a, to cite Beethoven's better known examples), or (2) in one inner movement (as in Op. 10/3), or (3) in one outer and one inner movement (as in Op. 31/2), or (4) in the first movement (though not in any

42. Climax structure in music in general is the subject of the detailed diss. Muns/CLIMAX (with many Classic instrumental analyses).
43. Cf. Newman/CLIMAX; Newman/UNDERSTANDING 137, 203.
44. Cf. Tovey/BEETHOVEN 177.

sufficiently clear example by Beethoven), or (5) in the finale (as in Op. 27/2), or (6) in all but an inner dance in a 4-movement sonata (as in Op. 2/1), or (7) about equally in all movements (as in Op. 14/2). Insofar as this single subjective view has any validity, the chart suggests that none of the three composers was especially interested in creating a rising dynamic curve that climaxes in the finale. All three seem to have given first place to cycles in which all the movements have about equal importance, although Haydn and Beethoven show a fair distribution throughout the other dispositions, too.

The "Strongest" Movements in the Vienna Classic Sonata

	Haydn	*Mozart*	*Beethoven*
Both outer movements	17 per cent	0 per cent	6 per cent
One inner movement	6	11	19
One outer and one inner movement	21	5	3
First movement	23	0	0
Finale	4	0	9
All but an inner dance	1	0	25
All movements	28	84	38

The First Quick Movement

We have already noted what a large proportion of interest in the sonata, both historic and analytic, has been concentrated on the first quick movement. As the foregoing chart suggests, Haydn placed special emphasis on this movement and both Mozart and Beethoven treated it at least on a par with the "strongest" movements in a large majority of their sonatas. Our approach here will be to consider, first, this movement's design and tonality as a whole, then to add some remarks regarding its individual elements in the order in which they most often appear. The "sonata form" concept will serve us regularly as a convenient reference outline but not (the point has now been made sufficiently) as a standard for evaluating progress. In fact, as noted earlier, the three most characteristic features of this concept—the contrasting theme, development section, and return of the initial idea—must be considered not for any growing consistency but for the continuing flexibility of their treatment. 44a

The question of a return to the initial idea is pertinent at once because it focuses attention on the larger question, often debated though too seldom illuminated, as to whether "sonata form" is a **binary or ternary design.** In its usual, simpler form, the first quick movement can hardly be described as anything but binary. Each "half" is marked off by repeat signs and the two halves are roughly complementary, both thematically and tonally. That is, the first half usually presents an initial idea, an extension through phrase groupings, passage work, and sequential modulations to the dominant or relative key, and a closing figure in that key; and the second half usually begins with the initial idea in the new key, continues with transpositions and sequential modulations that return circuitously to the home key from its underside, as it were, then literally repeats the corresponding dominant or relative measures and closing figure of the first half, in the home key.

The ternary concept of the first quick movement becomes more plausible, of course, as a sense of genuine departure and return increases. In more complex forms of this movement the portion from the inner double-bar to the restoration of the tonic takes on the sense of a departure more and more as it gains independence through greater extent, through sectional, motivic, or other structural interest of its own, through avoidance of any appreciable emphasis on the tonic key, and even through the introduction of new material. The restoration of the tonic takes on the sense of a return more and more as it gains emphasis through another statement of the initial idea at that point, through adequate harmonic, rhythmic, and dynamic preparation for this idea, and through the idea's placement far enough after its restatement at the double-bar and before the closing figure's restatement to sound like the start of a third independent section. In short, with the departure and return sufficiently defined, a sense of A-B-A design should obtain, rather than A-B design or what might be diagramed as ||:A → dominant (or relative):||:A → tonic:||. Writers have shied away from any view of "sonata form" quite so simplified as A-B-A, especially if it implies a static and new B section rather than a dynamic and derived one. However, at least as regards the last point, in the better Classic sonatas it is not only the B section that is dynamic and compelling but the entire form.

In practice, many fascinating phenomena affect the binary-ternary question. One is forced to conclude that this basic question itself remains one of the most fluid and flexible aspects of "sonata form" throughout most of the Classic Era, and, furthermore, that each case must be decided on its own merits. To begin with, there is the matter of repeats, including the questions of when they were used. When repeats for both "halves" were written in, the indicated design was A-A-B-B or A-A-B-A-B-A, depending on whether the effect was binary or ternary. That the repeats were usually taken is suggested by Emanuel Bach's need to write out "varied repetitions" in 1760 and Grétry's objections to the practice in 1797 (p. 654, *infra*), as well as by a few men who seemed to make a point of leaving out the repeat signs in certain sonatas (e.g., Hüllmandel, Edelmann, and Sacchini). 44b

In all but their last sonatas, Haydn and Mozart enclosed each of the two "halves" of their first quick movements within repeat signs. In the last sonata by each (H. XVI/52 and K.V. 576), and in all but eight of Beethoven's sonatas only the first "half" is enclosed in repeat signs. Beethoven's greater use of the coda is undoubtedly one of the reasons why he generally did not repeat the second half, although he did do so in one movement without coda (Op. 10/2/i), one with a short coda (Op. 78/i), and one in which the final repeat precedes the coda (Op. 79/i).[45] He put no repeats at all in his five most intimate first movements—Opp. 27/2, 90, 101, 109, and 110, all of which can be construed as "sonata forms" by some reading between the lines—and none in Op. 57/i. But one should recall his physically exhausting, rarely played repeat of only the second "half," before the coda, in Op. 57/iii.[46]

As suggested earlier, the location of the tonic return to the initial idea can affect the binary-ternary question materially. In many pre- 46a
and high-Classic sonatas, the sense of a departure that begins, after the inner double-bar, with a dominant or relative restatement of the initial idea or some related material, virtually disappears when a new statement of the initial idea follows immediately in the home key (as in Op. 5/3/57-68 by Boccherini, Op. 17/5/42-49 by Christian Bach, or H. XVI/13/31-40 by Haydn). The fact that modulatory passages quickly leave the key again usually does little to restore the lost sense of departure. Actually, there is more of a sense of departure when the restatement at the double-bar begins right in the home key and soon veers off in a new direction, as in Clementi's Op. 32/1/i/61-69 in A or Beethoven's Op. 31/1/i/112-122. But there is a lessening of the sense of departure again when not the initial idea but a continuation of the closing figure occurs after the inner double-bar, making for a smooth transition rather than a clear break, as in Mozart's K.V. 284c/i/38-55.

The binary-ternary question may be affected by variants in the final, tonic section, too. Often the restoration of the home key begins not with a restatement of the initial idea but at a later point corresponding to the arrival at the related key in the first "half," as in many sonatas by Mannheim composers or D. Scarlatti. This incomplete return is most likely to occur in sonatas in which a clear contrasting idea

45. Representative present-day arguments for the taking of repeats in Classic sons. and other music, largely based on tonal and other structural factors, are advanced in Tovey/BEETHOVEN 56; Blom/BEETHOVEN 52-56 (cf., also, GROVE VII 125-126); and by Leonard Marcus in *The Juilliard Review* IV/3 (Fall, 1957) 6-16.

46. Cf. Tovey/BEETHOVEN 185-186.

has marked the arrival at the related key in the first "half" and a clear restatement of the initial idea has marked the start of the second "half." Essentially, the thematic result then becomes the complementary binary plan :||:A → B (related key) :||:A (related key) → B (home key) :||, as in H. XVI/5/i by Haydn. Sometimes the return occurs where it is expected, but not in the home key. Thus, it occurs in the subdominant in Mozart's K.V. 545/i, in the submediant in Beethoven's Op. 10/2/i, and in the subtonic in Clementi's Op. 16/i. And not seldom the return occurs so late that there is only time left for the closing figure (as in Op. 1/5/i/150 by J. Stamitz). In the latter connection, one is less conscious of a return in the ternary sense when the final section reverses the order of themes, displaying what has been called the M-N-O-N-M or mirror form, as in K.V. 284c/i by Mozart.

The sheer factor of relative sectional lengths plays its part in that same binary-ternary question, which is leading us into nearly every main aspect of the over-all design. Thinking now in terms of 3 sections—exposition, development, and recapitulation—we may note that in 54 per cent of 41 piano "sonata forms" by Beethoven these sections, including any introductions and codas, fall on the average into a ratio of 10 : 8.8 : 12.5, and in about 37 per cent they fall into a much less balanced ratio of 10 : 4.1 : 13.[47] The relatively shorter development sections are compensated in a thematic sense by the growing tendency to "develop" each idea as it is introduced, throughout the "sonata form" (as in Op. 90/i). Of course, Beethoven's coda, like his introduction, sometimes attains such proportions and independent significance in itself that it constitutes a separate development section, or what d'Indy and others have called a "terminal development,"[48] as in Op. 57/i/203-262 (over 22 per cent of the mvt.). The resulting sectional form might be lettered A-B-A-C. The 3 sections in Haydn's "sonata forms" tend to fall into proportions that are in a ratio of 10 : 8 : 10.6, while Mozart's show even smaller development sections proportionately, in a ratio of 10 : 5.5 : 10.8.

It will be observed that in all the foregoing ratio averages (though not in every individual movement) the order of size from largest to smallest is recapitulation, exposition, and development. The use of an introduc-

47. The bases for the proportions given in this paragraph are the detailed statistics in Abbott/FORM 29, 73, 76, 112, 119, 189; this diss. consists largely of such helpful compilations, mainly on tonal relationships and dimensions in 18th- and 19th-c. piano son. forms. Cf., also, the brief, similar statistics on symphony mvts. cited in Engel/KLASSIK 67. The several theories of the "golden mean" in son. form proportions—e.g., as ridiculed in Torrefranca/ORIGINI 92 (1:2 as 2:1 + 2 + 3!) and as defended by Douglas Webster in ML XXXI (1950) 238-248
47a (5:8:13, etc.)—have not proved here to have any consistent validity.

48. D'Indy/COURS II/1 283-286 *et passim.*

tion and/or coda naturally affects this average, but the development still tends to be shorter than the other two sections. From the standpoint of the binary-ternary question, when the development is very short and when it concentrates on the dissection of but one idea and the attainment of but one tonal goal, it gives more the impression of a retransition, as in Beethoven's Opp. 13/i and 31/2/i, than an independent section, as in the long, multiform development of his Op. 57/i. Yet in Op. 31/2/i, in which the 3 sections have a ratio of 10 : 5.4 : 9, Beethoven still seems to confirm a ternary concept by announcing each of the 3 sections with the same introductory material.

Finally, the **tonal organization,** to which we have alluded so much by now, must be considered in its own right. For it ranks, along with the structural rhythm, or timing, as one of the two most basic factors in the over-all concept of "sonata form," profoundly affecting both the binary-ternary question and the dynamic flow. In Classic music especially, this tonal organization is a prime means of achieving the tension and relaxation, the variety within unity, and that push and pull of the main ideas that are essential to all valid works of art. It accounts for much of the vivacity and wit of Haydn's music, the purposefulness and drive of Mozart's, and the "inexorable fate" of Beethoven's. Indeed, the tonal organization must be said to have preceded, even engendered the thematic organization of the sonata cycle and its separate movements, particularly the first quick movement. The sonatas of Christian Bach and the early ones of Haydn, like those of many less known pre-Classicists, are filled with busy passages that say little or nothing thematically yet say much tonally by heading toward a well-defined goal and being constantly on the go. Repeatedly we come to what "should" be a "second theme" but proves to be only a neatly attained tonal plateau (as in Christian Bach's Op. 5/3/i/16-27). When a distinct idea does mark this spot it may prove to be only a new version of the initial idea, anyway, meaning that the sense of contrast still depends on the tonal rather than the thematic organization (as is often true in Haydn's sonatas—e.g., H. XVI/52/i/17-18).

To perceive the tonality of the sonata form to best advantage, one does well to start with the largest possible view—perhaps with d'Indy's idea of a "grand cadence" in mind,[49] or with a flexible application of Schenker's *Ursatz* (basic framework) that also takes rhythmic organization into full consideration.[50] D'Indy made much of Beethoven's balance between keys on the bright and dark (or sharp and flat) sides

49. D'Indy/COURS II/1 45 and 286.

50. Cf. the penetrating analyses of all 3 mvts. of Beethoven's Op. 109 in Forte/MATRIX.

of the home key.[51] For instance, by emphasizing the subdominant and still more "somber" keys in both the development and "terminal development" of Op. 53/i (from mss. 86 and 245), Beethoven counterbalances his emphasis on the bright mediant and submediant keys in the exposition and recapitulation. One thinks, too, of the extraordinary color effects he achieves through unexpected tonal contrasts, as at the quick turn of the development in Op. 13/i/137 to the minor mode on the bright-yet-sinister raised mediant of c, or the start of the development in Op. 57/i/67 on the bright-but-calm leading tone of f, followed soon by a brusque change to the minor mode.

As for the tonal plan, statistical tabulations bear out distinct differences in the "sonata forms" of the three Viennese masters, with Beethoven's tonal plan being the least predictable and most experimental, and Haydn's next in order.[52] All three men naturally show a decided preference for going to the dominant key as the goal of the exposition, or to the relative key when the home key is minor. But, for example, Beethoven's penchant for the submediant (as already in Op. 10/3/i/23) or the mediant (Op. 31/1/i/66) as the goal in about a fifth of the opening "sonata forms" sets him apart from the others. Likewise, Mozart's penchant for starting the development with a change of mode (as already in K.V. 189d) sets him apart, as does Haydn's for starting that section in a new key (e.g., in the submediant in H. XVI/33/i/69-78, after a cadence on the dominant). Typically, all three composers guide their modulations into minor keys soon after the development sections start in sonatas in major keys.

Pre-Classic composers and writers seem to have taken special pleasure in modulations for their own sake. The *empfindsam* composers used them for their shock value as they indulged in one "sea of modulations" after another (to use Burney's term for Emanuel Bach's improvisations, SCE XIII). Haydn still seems to have the shock value uppermost in mind when, in his Sonata in E♭, H. XVI/52/i/67-68, he jumps directly from V in c to I in E (i.e., to the raised tonic, the same distant key in which the second mvt. is placed). But the high- and late-Classic Era saw an advance in the two chief means of making smooth, uninterrupted modulations to the remoter keys. These means are the change of mode[53] and the use of enharmony.[54] A representative example of the former is the change from A to a, which then functions as

51. D'Indy/COURS II/1 251-261.

52. Cf. Abbott/FORM 187-192, 35, 36, 40, 82, 112, 128, 129, 141, 152.

53. Wise/MODE is a diss. on this process in 18th- and 19th-c. music.

54. Late-18th-c. theorists are quoted on enharmony by Pfrogner in KONGRESS 1956 (Vienna), pp. 471-476.

an altered vii leading chromatically to a V_7-I cadence in B♭, in K.V. 576/i/58-63 by Mozart. Beethoven's Op. 106 proves to be a veritable mine of enharmonic as well as chromatic modulations. The D♭ chord that turns out to be V-of-V in b provides an unquestioned example of enharmony (Op. 106/i/263-268). But the astonishing retransition from B to B♭ (Op. 106/i/201-227) is either a chromatic or enharmonic modulation depending on the long argued question of whether A or A♯ should be read (mss. 224-226).[55]

It is almost paradoxical that, throughout the Classic Era, as the extent of the "sonata form" increases (*supra*), the organization of tonality and structural rhythm grows broader and simpler. One might 55a
expect that as the architecture grows higher, wider, and deeper, the systems of rafters, joists, and girders must become more numerous and complex. But the reference here is not to the enlarged tonal horizons nor to the enrichments of the design in the longer high- and late-Classic "sonata forms." It is rather to the broad, simple arches that are described by increasingly broad tonal plateaus. The trend may be said to begin partly with slower harmonic rhythm. As the harmonic rhythm slows, the phrases grow longer, and hence the phrase groupings (recall Beethoven's new theme in Op. 57/i/36-51). These last, in turn, make for the bigger sections that correspond to broader tonal plateaus. Of course, the greater extent must also be credited to other sorts of expansion, too, especially the tendency to develop each idea as it enters (*supra*). But the total outline or "grand cadence" is still remarkably broad and simple. It is so, for example, in spite of the harmonic surprises and rich figuration in H. XVI/52/i in E♭ by Haydn,

||: I — V — :||: → (VI — vi — IV — N6th) — I — :||
(measure) 1 17 43 46 57 61 68 79 116

or the contrapuntal enlivenment in K.V. 576/i in D by Mozart,

||: I — V — :|| → (♭VI — iv — vi) — I — :||
(measure) 1 27 58 63 70 86 99 160

or the continual sense of development in Op. 111/i in c by Beethoven.

||: i — VI — :|| → (v — iv) — i — I — :||
(measure) 2 43 69 72 82 92 116 158

Where does the dynamic curve in such movements reach its climax, or what may be called its catastasis in the protasis, epitasis, and catastrophe of the sonata drama? The climax, when there is one, occurs most

55. Cf. the summary statement in Tovey/BEETHOVEN 230-231.

often at the shift to the dark or subdominant side of the tonal orbit in the coda. And it often reaches a secondary peak in the retransition to the home key at the start of the recapitulation. Beethoven seems to be especially conscious of these crucial moments. Thus, a main and a secondary climax may be heard, respectively, at measures 210-239 and 123-136 in Op. 57/i. Needless to say, to hear these moments as climaxes depends greatly on the over-all perspective of the performer. Of paramount importance is his finding and maintaining of a tempo that will permit full attention to both the over-all and local organization. It is no accident that the tempo inscriptions became more and more precise in the high- and late-Classic Era, culminating in Beethoven's unsatisfactory attempt to specify a few exact tempos in his late works by means of metronomic indications (SCE XV). A thoroughly co-ordinated design requires a consistent prevailing tempo. The more the composer deliberately changes the tempo within the movement, as in certain pre-Classic, *galant* sonatas by Friedemann Bach and Soler (SCE XII and IX), or as still in Beethoven's Op. 109/i, the more that movement becomes a fantasy in character.

The **separate elements of "sonata form"** have been observed thus far in their relation to the whole. They call for some individual comment, too, in the order in which they most often appear. Whereas the initial idea in the late-Baroque sonata serves primarily as an energizer of the motivic and motoric discourse that ensues, the initial Classic idea comes more and more to be a full-fledged "theme" that constitutes not only a fund of elements subject to development but an aesthetic fact in itself. We have already remarked and illustrated the characteristic dualism of this theme, which still stands out clearly in Beethoven's Op. 106/i/1-16
55b but almost disappears from Op. 110/i/1-11. We have also remarked this theme's characteristically complex syntax, with one or more elongated consequent phrases. Among the many qualitative factors that distinguish the sonatas of the few great masters from those of the many little ones are the distinctive character, unending variety, and telling proportions of the opening themes. For example, the opening theme in Op. 17/6/i/1-16 by Christian Bach unfolds additively into three successive phrases of 6 + 4 + 4 measures, each of which phrases keeps turning around itself without melodic distinction, textural interest, or tonal movement. By contrast, the similar, possibly derived opening theme in K.V. 315c/i/1-10 by Mozart unfolds into an antecedent of four measures and a consequent of six measures, each phrase being sharply defined by its melodic and harmonic arch. Broad melodic curves, a bit of melodic chromaticism, feminine endings, syncopations, and an

independent rhythm in the thin but accurate accompaniment all contribute to a distinctively lyrical yet piquant character in this theme. Furthermore, the two phrases are tightly integrated by the two-note groups and scalewise lines of 16th-notes that are common to both.

One could carry this comparison into the second element of "sonata
form," the bridge. Whereas Bach makes his bridge to the new key by
adding still another new phrase (mss. 16-19), Mozart takes advantage of
the bridge to restate the start of his first phrase, placed effectively an
octave lower. And he continues to draw on material from his opening 55c
theme to make the rest of the bridge (mss. 10-22). These two very
different procedures bring our attention to this important but highly
variable structural member.[56] The bridge or transition, which had little 56a
separate identity in the constant tonal flux of Baroque music, is itself a distinguishing feature of Classic "sonata form." There it serves to set off the tonal plateaus, with their corresponding thematic groups, by leading from one to the next both in the exposition and, even though the plateaus are the same, in the recapitulation. The bridge may derive from foregoing material (as in the Mozart ex. just cited), or be new (as in the Bach ex.), or be partly new and partly derived (as in H. XVI/49/i/13-24 by Haydn). In the exposition it may modulate to a half-cadence in the new key (as in Beethoven's Op. 31/3/i/25-45), to a deceptive cadence in the new key (though rarely, as in Beethoven's Op. 101/i/16), or not at all (often,[57] as in K.V. 189e/i/26 by Mozart). It may come to a stop on the half-cadence, frequently in the hammer-stroke pattern of 3 repeated chords and a rest (as in H. XVI/19/i/18 by Haydn), or it may lead directly into the new theme (as in Beethoven's Op. 53/i/35).

Among other solutions in the recapitulation, the bridge may follow its analogue in the exposition, yet change enough to remain in the home key (as in K.V. 300k/i/176), or it may repeat the exposition bridge literally when the latter is nonmodulatory anyway (as in H. XVI/43/i/112-121), or it may be entirely new (as in mss. 159-171 of the shortened recapitulation of Beethoven's Op. 31/2/i). It is interesting that Mozart preferred not to repeat the bridge literally but to expand it in K.V. 545/i/46-57, although his return to the initial idea in the subdominant key (ms. 42) had given him the ideal opportunity for a literal repetition. Haydn tended to write more extended and varied bridges than either

56. The remainder of this paragraph adapts several conclusions in the thoughtful and thorough diss. Tangeman/TRANSITION, which is devoted largely to the 3 Viennese masters (with detailed statistics in Vol. I, pp. 193-221, and exx. in Vol II).

57. Cf. Abbott/FORM 112 on Mozart's use of the bridge.

Mozart or Beethoven. But in general the bridges in solo and small-ensemble sonatas are less developed than those in the works for larger ensembles.

The new tonal plateau and thematic group to which the bridge customarily leads is, in effect, the "second theme." Understandably, this structural member has been one of the most discussed and heralded
57a features of "sonata form." In the many instances when it is actually independent and different enough to provide a sharp, dualistic contrast with the initial theme it does indeed represent one of the most conspicuous features of that form. But, like the binary-ternary question, it is also one of the most variable, unpredictable members, with just as many instances that have to be evaluated subjectively and on their own merits. Of course, in the sense that dualism is but another term for the polarity of variety and unity, some kind of dualism must exist in all music.[58] It is not the fact of it but how it is achieved that distinguishes the dualism of Classic "sonata form."

In motivic play and variation form much of the unity and variety is achieved simultaneously, since in both processes something must change while something remains constant. Naturally, in the hands of the great masters, these processes go on in Classic "sonata form," too. And they are essentially what the pre- and some high-Classic sonata composers in Berlin seem to have had in mind still when they insisted on but one *Affekt* in a movement (SCE II). But to a large extent the unity and variety in Classic "sonata form" are achieved alternately rather than simultaneously, and in relatively large blocks, these last being the tonal plateaus with their more or less distinctive thematic groups. To be sure, this alternate-block kind of dualism, or pluralism, also occurs at other levels in the Classic sonata. We have already seen it within the initial theme itself and, at the other extreme, between the movements of the whole cycle.

Various approximations and kinds of second themes that were mentioned earlier may be summarized here along with some others, under the not mutually exclusive headings of identity, contrast, character, extent, and separation. Thus, the identity (or identifiableness) of the member loosely classified under "second theme" may range from nothing but a new tonal landmark in the prevailing passage work (as in Schobert's Op. 14/3/i/15-18), to the same with a fleeting turn to minor,[59] to a bare hint of a new idea (as in Beethoven's Op. 101/i/17-25), to an unequivocally clear idea (as in Beethoven's Op. 2/2/i/59-83). Aside

58. Cf. Newman/UNDERSTANDING 134-135, 150-152, 186-188.

59. As in the second Boccherini ex. quoted in SCE VIII. Cf. the further exx. in Fischer/INSTRUMENTALMUSIK 805.

from the tonal change, the degree of contrast between the second and first themes may range from very little difference when the initial idea is transposed almost literally to the related key (as in H. XVI/38/i/13-14 by Haydn), to a difference only of notes but not of character (the German *Nebenthema,* as in K.V. 189e/i/27-34 by Mozart), to a decided contrast of style and character (as in Beethoven's Op. 14/1/i/23-38), and to a contrast that is more subjective in nature (as in Beethoven's Op. 90/i/55-67).[60]

The character of the "second theme" varies more widely, of course, than is implied by the "feminine" in the masculine-feminine dualism that Romantic writers associated with the principal themes of "sonata form." For example, "feminine" does seem to fit the gentle, lyrical, 60a
expressive contrasting theme in K.V. 576/i/42-53 by Mozart. And it is a not inappropriate adjective for the coquettish theme in K.V. 300h/i/19-34, or for the deeply felt progression of line and harmony in Op. 53/i/35-49. But it seems much less appropriate to the crisply punctuated theme (derived from the initial idea, anyway) in H. XVI/50/i/30-37 by Haydn. The character of the second theme has a bearing on the latter's extent and structure. In fact, when one thinks of it in this feminine sense of being the most lyrical, often the most folklike theme in the sonata, he usually has in mind the most regular phrase grouping, too. Some second themes do fall into a simple 4-measure antecedent and 4-measure consequent (as in K.V. 284b/i/35-42 by Mozart). But others range from the momentary pause for reflection in the headlong drive of Beethoven's Op. 111/i (mss. 50-55) to a whole complex of ideas unfolding right to the double-bar, as in his Op. 31/2/i/41-92.

Finally, we may note that the degree of separation of the second theme from its context varies widely, too. In Beethoven's Op. 7/i/41-59, this theme enters without a break in the continuity and at a harmonic tangent, on V_7 in the new key. In his Op. 2/3/i/27-39, it enters after a full break and on the new tonic harmony. This last instance may be quoted here (Ex. 15), among numerous other pertinent examples throughout our later chapters, because it also illustrates a change to the minor mode and a remote derivation, by way of its turn, from the incipit of this movement that was quoted in the previous example. Haydn actually changes the key signature for a second theme that begins, after a clear break, in the minor mode (H. XVI/5/38). And from instances by L. Mozart, D. Scarlatti, and other pre-Classicists to Beethoven's Op. 109/i/9, there are not a few freer-type movements in

60. Cf. G. Donath on the subjective factor in the dualism of the Classic "sonata forms," in KONGRESS 1956 (Vienna), pp. 139-142.

Ex. 15. From the first movement of Ludwig van Beethoven's Op. 2/3 (after BEETHOVEN WERKE-m XVI/1 35-36).

which a complete change of tempo demarcates what would still have to be called the "second theme."

Contrary to the history of the second theme, the so-called "closing theme" appears clearly defined throughout the Classic Era and, in fact, far back into the Baroque Era. The genesis of both themes lies in their enhancement of tonal functions. But the cadential function came before that of a contrasting tonal plateau and is less ambiguous, in any case. In fact, the closing theme is not seldom the most characterful of all the sonata themes, as any devotee of D. Scarlatti's sonatas knows (e.g., K. 361 or L. 247, mss. 35-47) and as is suggested by the frequent instances when the Viennese masters chose elements from this theme to concentrate on in development sections (e.g., K.V. 284c/i by Mozart). The closing theme only tends to lose its identity when the second theme gains in individuality, especially when the latter keeps unfolding, as in the example from Beethoven's Op. 31/2/i just cited. Then, in the absence of a modulatory bridge or any clear break in the continuity, it may be hard to say just where one theme ends and the other begins. Assuming that any thematic distinction is intended, one can usually distinguish the closing theme by its strongly cadential outline, as in the I^6_4-V-I-V-I . . . in H. XVI/52/i/39-45 by Haydn. The closing theme may well take up more measures than the second theme, since it is even more likely than the latter to comprise, in reality, an additive succession or veritable patchwork of ideas, as in K.V. 315c/i/39-63 by Mozart, with no fewer than four ideas strung together in six phrases.

In all phases of the Classic Era, various approximations of "sonata form," often including second themes, or returns to the initial idea, or both, are easy to find, whatever their actual significance may be. But there are two qualitative aspects of "sonata form" that remain rare except in the works of the chief masters. These are distinctive initial ideas, as mentioned earlier, and true developments that work the ideas in some motivic or organic fashion, by dissecting, reforming, compounding, or interchanging them. One aspect depends partly on the other. That is, true development presupposes a germinal, aphoristic idea capable of development. (At least, this is the usual assumption. But the great masters seem to have had no difficulty in developing the most rudimentary, innocent figures with imagination and resourcefulness. How much potential for development can inhere in a musical idea itself is an iconoclastic though moot question!)

But two other, related factors also seem to have delayed the mastery of the development processes. One was the general spread of the *galant* style, a style inimical to the motivic techniques required in these processes. The other was the particular trend of the sonata toward dilettantism, with all its emphasis on simplicity of means and content (SCE III). While these forces were at work, most "development" sections were likely to contain nothing more than restatements or transpositions of the initial idea and modulatory passage work. Brief, isolated instances of something akin to true development did appear in pre-Classic sonatas as early as those of D. Scarlatti, Agrell, and Paradisi (SCE IX, XI, and XIX). But only with the further cultivation of larger ensembles like the quartet and symphony did that resurgence of polyphonic interest occur that was so essential to the Viennese style of development.[61] Significantly, even those late-eighteenth-century writers who penetrated the subtleties of high-Classic phrase syntax wrote very little that was articulate about the processes of development (SCE II).

Haydn and Beethoven seem to have been born with a sense of true development. Mozart acquired this sense a little later in his short
career. We have seen that all three composers eventually applied the 61a
processes of development not only in their development sections but in their bridges, codas, and even the extensions of themes. An example of the dissection process in a development section may be seen in Beethoven's Op. 28/i/165-256, where the initial idea appears twice in full, at 2 pitch levels; then the last half of it appears 4 times at ever lower pitch levels and against a new contrapuntal line in 8th notes; then the last quarter appears 4 times during interchanges with the new line; then only the penultimate measure of that quarter appears, now 33 times,

61. Cf. Fischer/WIENER 71-73; MGG VII 1060-1062 (Blume).

in different combinations with the new line and with further, syncopated contractions of itself; and, finally, only one note of the initial idea remains, to be sounded 13 times as its value lengthens. An example of the reforming and compounding of ideas as well as their dissection may be seen in Beethoven's Op. 13/i/137-194, where the short development begins with an impetuously elided, 6-measure phrase that fuses the main bridge motive with an accelerated adaptation of the main motive of the slow introduction. After a transposition one step down of this fused phrase, only the bridge motive repeats in the bass, against a furious right-hand tremolo that had been the murky bass of the exposition. This bridge motive contracts into a single note, too, after which comes the retransition on a dominant pedal, made up of another bridge figure alternating with the initial allegro idea. The reworking of these ideas is made all the more "organic" by the close relationship that already exists between them in the introduction and exposition.

As in the rest of the "sonata form," the fundamental organizing agent of the development section is its tonal outline. This section may begin where the exposition left off or in another key, as already noted. Then, to achieve its typically purposeful drive, it often proceeds by dominant and third relationships to the point where it can return to the home key through the latter's dominant or secondary dominant harmony. The two to four main tonal areas that it usually emphasizes define the subsections into which the development characteristically divides. Minor keys tend to be favored in the sonatas in major keys, not only in true development sections but in those "developments" that consist only of restatements, transpositions, and modulatory passage work. These uses of the minor mode may be added to those in second themes, in trios of minuets and scherzos, and in "minore" variations or rondo episodes, to complete the list of partial compensations for the relatively little use of minor as the home key in the Classic sonata.

"True" development sections often include subsections of purely chordal, modulatory passage work, too, as in Beethoven's Op. 2/3/i/96-108. But one tends to think of imitative exchanges in contrapuntal textures as being a prevailing trait of these sections, as in K.V. 457/i/75-99 by Mozart. A representative instance may be quoted here from one of Haydn's most entertainingly developed sonatas (Ex. 16). Sometimes the polyphony is carried to the point of a fugato, as in Beethoven's Op. 106/i/138-176. Whether the development concentrates on but one idea in but one of these processes, as in Beethoven's Op. 81a/i/70-109, or discusses several elements of the exposition in turn, using more than one process, as in his Op. 57/i/67-135, the tightly

Ex. 16. From the first movement of Haydn's Sonata in C, H. XVI/50 (after Martienssen/HAYDN-m IV 82, but without the editorial additions).

organized tonal outline imparts a sense of one cumulative drive to the whole section. Only the introduction of new material—for instance, the neat double-period, related but remotely to the exposition, in K.V. 547a/i/79-94 by Mozart—tends to mitigate this drive.

Much of what would need to be said here about the recapitulation and coda in "sonata form" has already been covered in our discussions of the binary-ternary question, the comparative dimensions of sections, the inclusion and location of a return, the bridge, the tonal plan, and the dynamic or climax curve. There remain a few incidental observations to make. The retransition to the recapitulation was seen often to be climactic. The actual moment of return to the home key itself provides a main opportunity for the release of tension in the sonata form. A powerful example occurs in the enormous architecture of Beethoven's Op. 53/i, with the double-*forte* climax on the dominant pedal and the double-*piano* release when the initial idea returns (mss. 142-156). Sometimes a detail of the development is carried over to the recapitulation in order to assure an unbroken and meaningful connection, as with the dominant-pedal triplets that become the bass pattern for 15 measures

of the recapitulation in Beethoven's Op. 57/i/134-150. At other times the recapitulation begins only after the development has slowed to a *fermata* and rest, as in H. XVI/35/i/99-104 by Haydn. When the recapitulation does not begin in the home key, it may start as a "false return" tonally—for example, in the submediant key for the first 16
61b measures in Beethoven's Op. 10/2/i. Or it may start in the opposite, minor mode, as in a number of French sonatas, by Séjan, Hüllmandel, and others.

The great masters were not satisfied to write perfunctory recapitulations that merely repeat the exposition except for its essential tonal adjustments. With their sense of the dynamic and their strong penchant for variation treatment they went out of their way to make new tonal and thematic experiences out of what the textbooks usually show as nothing more than a whole section repeated in, or transposed to, the tonic key. Mozart's "mirror" form in K.V. 284c/i has already been mentioned. Beethoven even puts his second themes in a kind of axis tonal relationship between exposition and recapitulation when he answers mediant with subdominant in Op. 13/i/51 and 221, or mediant with submediant in Op. 53/i/35 and 196. Haydn's fine sense of tonal and structural balance causes him simply to omit the second theme in the recapitulation of several first movements when it had been largely derived from the first theme in the exposition and thus would offer no contrast if it were to be restated in the home key (as in H. XVI/36/i). The need to counterbalance the bright keys of the exposition and development may be met by excursions in the subdominant key when the movement has no coda (as in H. XVI/41/i/135-137). When it does have a coda, the latter is used, especially by Beethoven, not only to round out the tonal outline but to exploit some of the previous thematic elements in a new light. The coda may have all the surprise and charm, then, of a punch line in a short story, as in the fetching leaps that grow wider and wider as they toy with the cadence of the initial idea in Op. 28/i/445-455.

The Slowest Movement

In not a few Classic sonatas most or even all of the movements come nearer to "sonata form" than to any other classification. For example, all three movements approximate "sonata form" in H. XVI/47 by Haydn, K.V. 189e by Mozart, and Op. 31/2 by Beethoven. Rarely, no movement is of this type, as in Beethoven's Op. 26. But in the majority of cycles there is at least one such movement plus from one to three other design principles in the other movement or movements. Naturally, much in the previous discussions of this chapter on style, the cycle as a whole, and the structural traits in the first quick movement applies to the later movements. It is for this reason that only brief remarks are added in the rest of this chapter, and not because of any necessarily lower value placed on these later movements such as was objected to earlier. In other words, there remain to be considered only those traits of style and form that are peculiar to these later movements.[62]

More often than not, the slowest movement in the Classic sonata is no slower than moderato (with "andante" understood in that sense). In fact, movements labeled "Andante," "Moderato," "Grazioso," "Affettuoso," and the like represent one of the relaxations inherent in the *galant* style, for they mark a compromise between the high-Baroque extremes of adagio and allegro. The noble, deep, introspective sort of adagio that we associate first of all with Beethoven does indeed come largely from him. It appears already in Op. 2/1/ii in a maturer style
and form than in any other type of his early movements. Nearest to 62a
this sort by other composers are the slow movements in the late sonatas of Haydn, Mozart, and Clementi. Beethoven knew those sonatas well, of course. His Op. 10/1 and Op. 13, both in c, contain several unmistakable recollections of all 3 movements in Mozart's K.V. 457 in the same key, and especially its slow movement. None of his slow movements relates to any of Haydn's quite so clearly, say, as the "fate motive" in his Op. 57/i/235-238 recalls that in H. XVI/49/i/109-117 by the latter. But there is certainly a strong emotional kinship between a decorative, songful movement such as his Op. 2/1/ii and H. XVI/50/ii in the same key of F by Haydn, or his Op. 10/3/ii in d and Clementi's earlier but slightly more intimate slow movement, Op. 25/5/ii in b.

The earlier "slow" movements of Haydn and, especially, Mozart are actually moderate movements that flow along gracefully in the manner of cantabile Italian opera arias (as in K.V. 189h/ii by Mozart). Beethoven's nearest approaches to Italian song are his lovely quasi barcarolles, Opp. 22/ii and 79/ii. Haydn's movements seem to have deepened gradually in the direction of fantasy under the influence of such a rhapsodically expressive product of the *Empfindsamkeit* as W. 65/17/ii by Emanuel Bach. But Mozart's later slow movements retain the symmetrical phrase balance of the aria, avoid Bach's abandon, and keep pace with Haydn's slow movements only in their generally slower tempos and increased ornamentation. Otherwise they seem to result from the maturing of feeling and subtilizing of both melodic and harmonic styles

62. In any case, separate, up-to-date studies of the individual slow, dance, and final movements are much to be desired.

Ex. 17. From the middle movement of Wolfgang Amadeus Mozart's Sonata in D, K.V. 576 (after MOZART WERKE-m XX 198).

that went on right within his own writing (Ex. 17). Before Emanuel Bach's slow movements, there was the Baroque heritage of preludial or partly polyphonic introductions in the church sonata, and both the saraband and siciliana in the suite. The siciliana remained popular throughout much of the Classic Era and still left its clear mark in the lilting pattern, tenderly expressive lines, minor mode, and simple phrase grouping of movements like H. XVI/47/ii by Haydn.

The variety of structural designs that the Viennese masters employed in their slow movements is small. Furthermore, the syntax tends to be more regular and simple than in the quick "sonata forms," and there is often less development in the motivic, organic sense. But that symphonic sort of development does occur, too, as in K.V. 300d/ii/43-51 by Mozart or the rather similar passage in Op. 31/1/i/41-53 by Beethoven. Frequently, the developmental interest is more accurately that of variation treatment, especially in the recurring sections of A-B-A and rondo forms. Or it occasionally is expressed in an unfolding of ideas very close to free fantasy, as in H. XVI/39/ii by Haydn or the introductions to Opp. 53/ii and 101/iii by Beethoven. The large majority of Haydn's slow movements divide about equally between binary designs (as in H. XVI/24/ii) and incipient "sonata forms," sometimes with not much more than a short retransition for a "development section" (as in H. XVI/34/ii). Mozart prefers "sonata forms" (as in K.V. 533/ii), with somewhat less use of A-B-A designs (as in K.V. 300k/ii) or rondo designs (A-B-A-C-A, as in K.V. 570/ii). And Beethoven prefers A-B-A designs (Op. 7/ii), with somewhat less use of "sonata forms" (Op. 22/ii) and variation forms (Op. 57/ii). But it is the variation forms, treated inwardly and freely, that underlie two of his greatest slow movements, Opp. 109/iii and 111/ii. And it is an arabesque kind of variation treatment that accounts for one of the most expressive pages in his most extended slow movement, Op. 106/iii/88-103.

Dance Movements

Almost every kind of dance or related movement known to the suite can be found in scattered instances in the pre-Classic sonata. This variety narrows, by the time of the high-Classic Era, to the point where the minuet and scherzo are the main survivors. The scherzo had only an occasional and very distant ancestor in the Baroque sonata (e.g., cf. SBE 232-235). But the minuet derived directly from its French, Italian, and German ancestors in the Baroque sonata and other instrumental music.[63] Italian and Spanish composers of the pre-Classic Era (including Galuppi and Rutini) still often used the French spelling "minué." The trio that almost always appears in the minuet had Baroque precedents, too, but only became usual in sonata minuets during the pre-Classic Era.[64]

The minuet served as the finale in countless pre-Classic and not a few high-Classic sonatas. Thus, over a fourth of both Christian Bach's and Haydn's keyboard sonatas still end with this type of movement. The minuet also begins to appear early if less frequently as an inner movement. Clément already uses it in 1743 as the penultimate of four movements (SCE XVII). Only rarely does it serve as the opening movement, as does the variation minuet in Beethoven's Op. 54. This last example recalls the frequent combination of dance types with other form principles. For instance, in numerous Spanish and French rondos the refrain is a minuet (as in exx. by Soler, SCE IX).

The minuet must be admitted to be not only one of the commonest of Classic sonata movements but one of the most commonplace. Moreover, it generally ranks not only as the shortest and slightest movement,

63. SBE 75, 137 (with ex.), *et passim*; also, cf. MGG X 106-110 (Marcel-Dubois).
64. Cf. Torrefranca/ORIGINI 533, 658, 663; Torrefranca/SAMMARTINI 284-286.

but as the movement with the most regular syntax and routine design. Undoubtedly, we miss some of the dance and folk associations (as in H. XVI/1/iii by Haydn) when we read these minuets today—associations that must have made the same old formulas more than tolerable to the dilettantes and amateurs who kept the minuet in fashion for so long. But only rarely does a minuet stand out for its special charm (as by Nares, SCE XIX) until we come once again to the much more creative examples by the Viennese masters—for instance, H. XVI/36/iii by Haydn, K.V. 300i/ii by Mozart, or Op. 10/3/iii by Beethoven.

Haydn uses minuets in more than half of his sonatas, dividing them about equally between inner and final movements. The trio, or "Menuetto II" (H. XVI/43/ii), is only rarely absent (as in H. XVI/25/ii, a "Tempo di Menuetto"). It varies considerably in style, ranging from bare, smooth, quarter-note lines in octaves, as in H. XVI/5/ii, to energetic 16th-note figures, as in H. XVI/32/ii. In the "Minuetto al Rovescio," H. XVI/26/ii, both the minuet and the trio consist of two eight-measure repeated periods, the second period in each double-period being the exact backwards statement of the first. Mozart uses the minuet only twice in his solo keyboard sonatas, but more often in his keyboard sonatas with violin. Beethoven has four minuets in his piano sonatas besides that free variation minuet with which Op. 54 begins. The four examples are all inner movements in the simple ternary plan of minuet-trio-minuet (or *da capo*), each section usually being a binary design with repeated halves. Three of these examples appear well after the first scherzo in Beethoven's piano sonatas, Op. 2/2/iii.[65] Hence, the scherzo cannot be said quite to supercede the minuet in his sonatas. He returns to the minuet in his works that may already be called neo-Classic, or, rather, neo-high-Classic, as in Op. 31/3/iii.

Although there are relatively early, so-called scherzos that are not distinguishable from minuets in style and character (as in Haydn's Quartets Op. 33), the scherzo as it is chiefly viewed in retrospect must be thought of more as a mere physical than a stylistic successor to the minuet. It is perhaps most often identified today with driving staccato quarter-notes in 3/4 meter, as in Ex. 18 or in the more motivic, polyphonic "Scherzo" in Beethoven's Op. 2/3. But a surprising number of "scherzos" are in duple meter and reveal considerable differences of style, as in Beethoven's Op. 31/3/ii. It is interesting that this last example as well as the "Scherzo" in H. XVI/9/iii and the "Scherzando" in H. XVI/36/ii by Haydn, both also in 2/4 meter, all appear right alongside minuets in their respective sonatas. There is a novel pro-

65. Not including the early "Scherzando" mvt. in 2/4 meter, in WoO 47/3.

Ex. 18. From the second movement of Ludwig van Beethoven's Sonata in E♭, Op. 27/1/ii (after BEETHOVEN WERKE-m XVI/2 4).

cedure of style or texture in almost every trio of Beethoven's scherzos, such as the 6 different harmonizations of nearly the same 5- or 6-note scale figure in Op. 28/iii/71-94. But whereas the clodhopping, hand-crossing trio in the minuet of Op. 10/3 can sound downright funny, the meaning of "joke" in the word scherzo actually gives way more and more to a sense of something sinister, as in the "Presto" trio episode in 2/4 meter, with a change of mode to minor, in Op. 106/ii.

The driving, persistent style associated with the scherzo can be found occasionally in pre-Classic sonatas, as in those by Pescetti (SCE XIX). Its association with the title "Scherzo" comes later in the century, as in a sonata of 1785 by J. M. Kraus (SCE XXI). Whether Clementi actually anticipated Beethoven in this notable style depends on dates of composition in the early 1790's that cannot now be fixed exactly (SCE XX). Aside from the 2 examples by Haydn that were cited, neither he nor Mozart left any so-called scherzos in their keyboard sonatas. Beethoven left 6 in his 32 piano sonatas, plus at least 4 more movements that might well have received this title (e.g., Op. 27/2/i).

Among other dances that survived the pre-Classic Era, the gigue and *caccia,* or *chasse,*[66] still leave their marks in the rollicking style and compound meter of a finale like Beethoven's Op. 31/3/iv. And the polonaise or "polacca," used by Zach, Platti, Rutini, Neefe, Riegel, and many others, sometimes along with and sometimes in place of the minuet, still appears as the "Polonaise en Rondeau" in K.V. 205b/ii by Mozart. March movements continue to be popular, too, as in Mozart's celebrated "Alla Turca," K.V. 300i/iii, and Beethoven's somber "Marcia funèbre sulla morte d'un Eroe," Op. 26/iii.

Finales Other Than Dance Movements

Along with dance movements, the most frequent finales are the rondeaux and rondos, the sets of brilliant display variations, the incipient or larger-scale "sonata forms," about on a par with the first quick movements, and various combinations of these. A relatively small number of fugal finales can be found in sonatas throughout the Classic Era, including exceptionally strong examples by Christian Bach, Rust, Pugnani, and Wölfl, among others. One recalls that the publisher Nägeli was still commissioning fugues in the early 1800's (SCE II). The culmination of this trend comes, of course, with the great fugal finales in Beethoven's Opp. 101, 106, and 110. For all Clementi's increasing devotion to thin, polyphonic writing he includes canonic movements in his sonatas (SCE XX) but not complete fugues.

The rondo finale is as prevalent as the minuet finale in the Classic
66a sonata, as is evident again, for example, in the works of Christian Bach. Although Burney complained that there were *too* many rondos,[67] the rondo, with its characteristically fetching refrain, seems to have maintained its individuality better than the minuet. In fact, some of the most enchanting, original themes in the Classic sonata occur in the rondos (Ex. 19). The rondo designs range from the archaic, square, alternating couplets in the additive French rondeau to the more complex and highly integrated forms by Haydn, Mozart, and Beethoven. These last are often called "sonata-rondo" forms because they bring rondo and "sonata form" so close. Thus, Beethoven's Op. 7/iv has the frequent over-all plan, A-B(dominant)-A-C(submediant)-A-B(tonic)-A-coda, with A always in the home key. Aside from the decidedly tuneful refrain theme, this plan differs from "sonata form" only in the return to A in the home key before the middle section, plus the fact that the middle section is an independent subform in itself rather than a development of previous material. The absence of a development is made up partly

66. Cf. Ringer/CHASSE 153-154.
67. In the German ed. of his travel reports (cf. MGG III 1188).

Ex. 19. From the finale of Wolfgang Amadeus Mozart's Sonata in B♭, K.V. 570 (after MOZART WERKE-m XX 190).

in the coda. However, the differences are still basic enough to give the rondo its effect of sectional alternation as against the one broad curve of an ideal "sonata form."

In other sonatas, as in Beethoven's Op. 28/iv/79-113, the C section of the rondo is more in the nature of a development section. Further, representative instances of "sonata-rondo" forms by Haydn and Mozart may be seen in H. XVI/48/ii and K.V. 300k, respectively. In five rondos Beethoven leaves out the final A by merging the final B with the coda, as in Op. 2/3/iv. And in several instances all three Viennese masters also omit the final B. This is what Beethoven does in Op. 53/ii, with its long "terminal development," and it is what Mozart does in K.V. 576/iii, which is another variant of "sonata-rondo" form. The combination of minuet refrain and rondo form that was mentioned earlier may be seen in Beethoven's Op. 49/2/ii. The rondo also incorporates other dances in this way in the Classic sonata, as in a "Rondo alla polacca" movement by Reichardt (SCE XVI) or the movement by Mozart already noted, K.V. 205b/ii.

Haydn uses various approximations of "sonata form" more than any other form type in his finales. Next come the rondos and minuets, after which he seems to delight in a special kind of variation form that sounds almost as much like a rondo. In this form his theme is the sort of tune that would be ideal for a rondo refrain except that it divides into two equal or unequal, repeated "halves." Since the B part of this theme makes a clear tonal and melodic contrast to the A part, each variation on the A-B theme starts by giving the impression of a return to a refrain (A). The variations are of a relatively brilliant sort, suitable in a finale, and full of syncopations, figural elaborations, and articulatory refinements. Two examples often played are H/XVI/27/iii and 28/iii.

Mozart gives first place to the rondos in his finales, after which come a variety of "sonata forms." Among other form types he uses are decorative variations, in two instances (K.V. 205b/iii and 547a/iii). Like Haydn, Mozart uses a binary theme with each half repeated and he writes melodic variations of a purely extrinsic sort. But he does not get a similar rondo effect because the themes he uses do not have quite the angular clarity of Haydn's refrain tunes and because he does not return to the most distinctive outlines of his themes in each variation quite as Haydn does. Beethoven also gives first place to the rondos and second place to a variety of "sonata forms." Like these types, his other preferred types, the variation forms and fugues, were noted earlier. But one should add that, as in H. XVI/42/ii by Haydn and K.V. 570/iii by Mozart, there are movements in Beethoven's sonatas apart from the free introductory types—for example, Op. 54/ii, a *moto perpetuo*—that defy classification in terms of standard designs. They can only be regarded as intuitive solutions to the problem of making sectional forms based on phrase grouping.

Part Two

The Composers and Their Sonatas

Chapter VII

The Keyboard Sonata in Italy From About 1735 to 1780

Background and Sources

The land of Italy, from which came several of our most interesting pre-Classic composers of sonatas, was still only a "geographical expression" in the mid-eighteenth century, and was to remain so until Garibaldi and his compatriots rallied all of Italy to the successful Risorgimento more than a century later. With the general repartition of Italy that accompanied the Peace of Aix-la-Chapelle in 1748, Emperor Francis I and Maria Theresa of Austria retained Milan, Mantua, and Tuscany, the future Charles III of Spain acquired the kingdom of the Two Sicilies, his brother Don Philip controlled Parma and Piacenza, and Louis XV of France became the protector of Modena. Only the region of Piedmont in the northwest, ruled by the ancient house of Savoy, could be called a true Italian state, although Venice, Lucca, and Genoa were still nominally independent republics. It is hardly necessary to recall what an important bearing this variegated political scene had on international cultural exchanges, on the employment and movements of the many highly itinerant Italian musicians, and even on such details of concern here as the numerous sets of sonatas dedicated to Maria Theresa by composers in Milan and the Tuscan center of Florence.

The same political disposition held throughout the period covered in these next two chapters and until the repercussions of the French Revolution were felt. During this period Italy did enjoy a degree of prosperity and security that were conducive to artistic enterprise. But her collective emotional state was hardly one of calm passivity. Rather was it a state of restless excitement and fermentation as the Enlightenment and other intellectual forces from abroad aroused Italians to mixed reactions of increasing intensity, and as ultimate political unity became more and more of a conscious need and goal. It may be harder to find valid symptoms of this fermentation in those arts that had passed their peaks in Italy, including architecture, sculpture, and painting, but the symptoms can be found readily enough in literature and music. They occur, for example, in the diverse writings by men of letters like the anti-Voltairian expatriate G. Baretti, the pro-Dantean G. Gozzi, or those two Arcadian poet-dramatists from whom came the most successful Italian opera librettos of the time—the mellifluous melodramatist Metastasio and the graceful comedian Goldoni. And such symptoms were still occurring somewhat later in the poetry of Parini and Monti, emulators, respectively, of authors in the Enlightenment and the *Sturm und Drang* movements; and in continuing offshoots of the great quarrel over the ancients and moderns, as in the conservative appraisal of three violinist-composers by the musical dilettante Rangoni that is quoted later (SCE VIII).

In the instrumental music of the time, symptoms of Italy's emotional state can be felt through moods that contrast sharply and crop up often (as we shall discover)—fantasy, bravura, melancholy, drama, gaiety, exuberance, pathos.[1] Together those moods help to explain Italy's particular brand of the *galant* style, the style that was then almost universal. It is only within the range of this style and within the general period of pre-Classic music that Italian instrumental music made its significant contribution to the imminent high-Classic sonata. For as opera came increasingly to occupy the whole and not just the center of musical interest in that country, as Vienna became more and more of a maelstrom in which the most important instrumental trends of all countries were converging, the cultivation of the sonata in Italy diminished to mere eddies of attention and achievement. To be sure, one must acknowledge that even during the pre-Classic period a fair share of her efforts in the sonata was exerted or directed abroad. Neither the dearth of good cembalists nor the decline of printing could have been so bad in that country as Burney reported them (SCE IV). But the fact remains that much of the attention and patronage came from abroad, and abroad is where many of the sonatas were composed and most of them published. In this connection, it is significant that among sonata composers active in Italy only one of consequence has been found in the present study who was foreign born, he being Mysliveček from Bohemia.

The strongest interest in the pre-Classic sonata within Italy seems to have been the sort that carried over from the Baroque Era—in other

1. Further remarks on the cultural environment of 18th-c. Italian instrumental music occur in MGG VI 1530-1533 (Barblan).

words, an interest in the melo/bass string sonatas as kept alive by the descendants of Corelli and Tartini. But unlike Corelli and Tartini themselves, these stringsmen usually stayed home no more than the cembalists (or the "singer-cembalists," as most of them are shortly to be classified). Many traveled too widely to be placed anywhere but in their Italian city of birth or of chief training as the "operating" locale. And some, like Sarti, traveled so widely and so often in their international crisscross patterns as to challenge credibility, the more so when one recalls the gruesome, equally incredible difficulties of travel that Burney digressed to relate, after his famous tours (SCE IV). Since the present study follows the general method, when practical, of placing the composer where he wrote his sonatas, it may be advisable at this point at least to list the Italian-born expatriates. The following are the main sonata composers of the Classic Era who were born in Italy (in the cities indicated parenthetically) but do not appear in these next two chapters or Chapter X because each established a sufficiently permanent residence at some foreign center to be placed there, instead. One can see at a glance what a large Italian colony of sonata composers there was then in London.

Italians Abroad

L. Borghi (Bologna?), London
V. L. Ciampi (Piacenza), London
G. B. Cirri (Forli), London
M. Clementi (Rome), London
D. Dall'Oglio (Padua), St. Petersburg
G. G. Ferrari (Rovereto), London
I. Fiorillo (Naples), Braunschweig
F. de Giardini (Torino), London
T. Giordani (Naples), London
F. Guerini (Naples), The Hague
P. A. Guglielmi (Massa Carrara), London
G. Jozzi (Rome), London
A. Lucchesi (Treviso), Bonn
V. Manfredini (Pistoia), St. Petersburg
G. B. Noferi (?), London
P. D. Paradisi (Florence?) London
F. Pellegrini (Pesaro), London
G. B. Pescetti (Venice), London
G. Platti (Bergamo?), Würzburg
V. Rauzzini (Camerino), London
F. P. Ricci (Como), London
A. Sacchini (Florence), London
P. P. Sales (Brescia), Augsburg
Giuseppe Sammartini (Milan), London
D. Scarlatti (Naples), Madrid
G. B. Serini (Cremona), Bückeburg
G. F. Tenducci (Siena), London
C. G. Toeschi (Padua), Mannheim
F. Uttini (Bologna), Stockholm
M. Vento (Naples), London
G. B. Viotti (Fontanetto da Po), Paris
F. Zanetti (Volterra), London

The twenty-one pre-Classic composers here to be placed in Italy fall into two rather well-defined groups. In the present chapter are discussed eight cembalists or singer-cembalists, and in the next eleven stringsmen (along with two very minor keyboard composers related more by locale). This division may be expressed somewhat more loosely as that between the newer solo or accompanied keyboard sonatas and the more conservative melo/bass string settings. However, there was an overlap of the two categories later in the period when several of the stringsmen conceded to popular French and English tastes by writing accompanied sonatas, too. And any such dichotomy of keyboard and melo/bass settings must be qualified further with regard to that majority of later melo/bass sonatas in which the *b.c.* part had become, as we have seen in Chapter V, only a vestige of past practices. The *b.c.* part found little justification in the new, simpler, more homophonic textures and their slower harmonic rhythm. As with the dichotomy of court and church sonatas around 1700, this dichotomy of settings discloses more fusion than fission, its common ground being the *galant* style.

Another somewhat looser way of classifying our two composer groups might have been found under the headings of the two Italian teachers most influential and most sought after in their day, the sage of Bologna, Padre Martini, and the king of violinists, Giuseppe Tartini (SBE 181-183, 189-192). Composition was taught along with violin by Tartini and was, of course, the main subject the keyboard composers studied with Martini. Although some of our composers went to neither teacher and certain of the violinists went also or only to Martini, it is surprising how consistently the lines were drawn that divided the cembalists and Martini on the one hand from the stringsmen and Tartini on the other. Perhaps a geographical parallel can be suggested that relates here, too. The main centers of the keyboard composers were Venice and Naples, in each of which cities we shall find at least a tentative new school of cembalo playing, apparently tied in with operatic activities. The main centers of the violin composers were Milan (in Lombardy), Torino (in Piedmont), and the region of Tuscany, where the Austrian dominated courts were especially favorable to chamber and orchestral music. "Everybody plays the violin here [in Lombardy], with all the arpeggiations and all the position shifts," observed a traveler in 1758; "even the village church services have all the air of a concert."[2]

Throughout the present chapter and in later references to Italian keyboard composers one study is cited more than any other. It is Fausto Torrefranca's 779-page prize-winning book of 1930 on "The Italian Origins of Musical Romanticism,"[3] made up almost entirely of separate studies on the Italian keyboard sonata that had appeared in the *Rivista musicale italiana* as far back as 1909. Torrefranca's main theses are four, in brief: (1) The modern (Classic) instrumental style that

2. Grosley/MEMOIRES I 94-95.

3. See Torrefranca/ORIGINI in the Bibliography, with references to some main reactions and rebuttals by other authors.

culminated in Beethoven is of Italian origin, beginning in the Venetian school in the period from Vivaldi to Galuppi (p. 119). (2) The style changes involved in this historical development are revealed most intimately and embodied most comprehensively in the Italian cembalo sonata, which even gave new life to the violin sonata (in the accompanied keyboard setting, that is; pp. 60-61). (3) This Italian cembalo sonata led off in two different (though not wholly clarified) paths that eventually rejoined in the Classic sonata of Clementi (pp. 526-529). Up to about 1760 and during "a second *galant* style" (pp. 340-341, 507) it was a starting point for later "piano" technique (p. 278) and an "impressionistic" synthesis of the entire musical scene at the time, whether vocal or instrumental, pastoral or dramatic. And from about 1750 to 1775, along with its tendency toward a more regularized metric drive (p. 509) it became a synthesis of the *tutti-soli* oppositions of the concerto and the structural plan of the chamber and opera symphony. (4) In particular, the origins of the Mozart style are primarily Italian (pp. 722-723).

In pursuit of these four theses Torrefranca devotes at least as much effort to the rejection of two corollary anti-theses (p. 48). One is the idea that Italy arrived at a state of complete musical decadence in the eighteenth century—"To the vogue of Italian opera [in the period after Padre Martini and D. Scarlatti] must be attributed the decadence of our instrumental music, which, unable to continue in its [past] styles and forms, generally turned to the [operatic] styles of the moment as a means of sure success," as his own countryman Torchi had put it.[4] The other is the idea that the modern (Classic) instrumental style is of German origin (pp. 502-504), especially that this style was born in the Mannheim school under Stamitz. Where Torchi had accepted his German training Torrefranca disavowed any such. One does not have to read far to realize how greatly Torrefranca's arguments are motivated by chauvinism. Starting with "Platti, il grande," a veritable fetish is revealed in the ingenious but strained efforts to date one composer's sonatas after another's "around 1740 and 60 years before Beethoven"—that is, a precious two years ahead of the first published set of "Ph. E. Bach, il piccolo." Dropping back by easy stages from facts to probabilities, to possibilities, to mere suppositions, Torrefranca only comes to rest each time on the earliest conceivable date, there to remain for all further references. Moreover, past and present authorities of whatever nationality are evaluated only in accordance with the support or contradiction each happens to have given to his (Torrefranca's)

4. Torchi/ISTRUMENTALE 257 (-259).

arguments. If a "sonata form" is regular (as with D. Alberti) it is a remarkable anticipation of the high-Classic sonata; if it is conspicuously irregular (as with Ferradini) it is a remarkable evidence of how free the creative spirits of those Italians could be. And so on, and so on. There are also considerable repetition and evidences of haste to contend with.

But one would hesitate to bother over these undeniable shortcomings were Torrefranca's book still not one of the most important contributions to sonata history (and the Classic Era in general). We must grant that it has helped to right a one-sided historical perspective and that it does restore considerable music of real interest, some of it not yet sufficiently recognized. Furthermore, it brings together much factual material of value (even though some of the clever dating must be corrected in the light of newer, better sources) and it offers many keenly perceptive discussions and analyses of musical style. Nor should one overlook the large number of music examples, most of them facsimiles of early editions and some of them extended nearly to complete movements.

Other sources cited repeatedly in the present chapter are BURNEY'S TOURS (basic, as always), La Borde/ESSAI, Mooser/ANNALES, BRITISH
4a UNION and Johansson/FRENCH for bibliographic aids, and David Stone's helpful dissertation on the Italian keyboard sonata throughout the eighteenth century.

Venice (Alberti, Paganelli, Galuppi)

Venice was the starting locale for each of our three chapters on the Italian sonata in the Baroque Era. Once more it makes a good starting locale, this time for the individual discussions of Italian, and indeed of all, sonata composers in the Classic Era. In the 1730's, where we begin, Venice, still at least nominally an independent republic, continued as one of the most brilliant, active centers and crossroads of music in Europe; and it was to continue so throughout much of the era.[5] To be sure, by the late 1730's the careers were ending of its chief luminaries in the earlier eighteenth century—Vivaldi, Lotti, Albinoni, and Marcello—and by then the stage and church music of such Venetians were already succumbing to influences from the newly pre-eminent forces in Naples. But Venice's four main *ospitali* or conservatories continued to thrive, as ever, by feeding its broad, musically hungry environs with a steady stream of young graduates skilled as singers, instrumentalists, and

5. Burney's description of musical Venice, first published in 1771 (BURNEY'S TOURS I 108-140), is unsurpassed among contemporary accounts; the account in Grosley/MEMOIRES II 52-56 is shorter but similarly informative (*ca.* 1758). Cf., also, GROVE VIII 719 (Sartori).

composers;[6] and its own opera continued to thrive, especially in the fresh *opere buffe* of Galuppi.

Perhaps still more to our purpose though certainly less conspicuous at the time, Venice, like Naples, was becoming the nursery for its own new "school" of cembalo players and composers, including Marcello, Pescetti, Platti, Alberti, Galuppi, Paganelli, Grazioli, and some lesser names to be noted soon. (Marcello was discussed earlier [SBE 174-179]; Pescetti will appear in pre-Classic England, Platti in pre-Classic Germany, and Grazioli among later Italians, in Chap. X.) Torrefranca says that this "scuola veneziana del clavicembalo" has been totally ignored (prior to his own writings), "since neither Alberti nor Marcello can be called legitimate representatives."[7] Yet both the latter were examples of the "singer-cembalists" he finds so significant, here and elsewhere in Italy, to the subsequent Mozart style.[8] Not being tied to Torrefranca's search for a particular "stile nuovo," we can more generally include both as belonging rightfully with their Venetian kin, artistically as well as civically.

In fact, **Domenico Alberti** (*ca.* 1710 to at least 1739) makes an ideal Venetian with whom to begin these individual discussions. His writing hovers between motivic techniques cast in Baroque textures of the immediate past and remarkably newer idioms that caused Torrefranca to see in it a prime landmark in the evolution of Mozartean and even Beethovian styles. His sonatas are scored no longer for the violin family but come right at the start of that steady stream of Italian and other sonatas for keyboard that was to swell to the peak of the Classic piano sonata and beyond. His consistent two-movement plan is the one adopted often enough in keyboard sonatas by eighteenth-century Italians to have been dubbed "sonata italiana."[9] And in several of the separate movements he seems to anticipate "sonata form," at least to the extent that a moderately clear return makes for ternary design.

Recognizing these many innovational trends, one can only hope that, eventually, enough definite information about Alberti's life will turn up to confirm or disprove the approximate dating of his sonatas in the later 1730's. His year and place of death can be guessed only from the last of his three known opera productions, *Olimpiade* in Rome in 1739.[10]

6. Cf. Pincherle/OSPITALI; MGG VII 1460 (Schaal).
7. Torrefranca/ORIGINI 83.
8. Cf. "cantante cembalista" in Torrefranca/ORIGINI 396-397, 506, *et passim.*
9. As in DIZIONARIO RICORDI 20.
10. DIZIONARIO RICORDI 20 gives 1739 (based on what source?) and most dictionaries of the past (including Fétis/BU I 53) give Rome as the place where Alberti composed his operas, though some give Venice (including La Borde/ESSAI III 162 and Schilling/LEXICON I 125-126). Alberti is not listed among composers of operas produced at the time in Venice, in Wiel/CATALOGO 117-142. The assump-

The year of birth is even more conjectural, based merely on the assumption that he must have died very young since his first known opera production occurred only three years earlier, *Endimione* in 1737, and since his only extant music to be published separately, the set of *VIII Sonate Per Cembalo* first known in (the younger) John Walsh's edition of 1748,[11] appeared with the label "Opera Prima." Torrefranca prefers 1710 for the approximate birth year,[12] rather than 1717 as formerly given.[13] For, he says, a 23-year-old would hardly have had time to write three operas, some motets, and 36 keyboard sonatas; and to be a dilettante virtuoso (at the keyboard), a (potential) rival of the great Farinelli (in singing), a minor diplomat (page to the Venetian ambassador in Madrid), and a (busy) traveler. In any case, he adds with his usual effort to claim priority for the Italians and his usual sarcastic wit, he will not argue the time of birth if only "i signori tedeschi" will concede that Alberti must have written his sonatas at least shortly before he died in (presumably) 1740!

Still further biographical digressing is needed, for our purposes, in Alberti's case. In spite of his alleged successes as performer and composer,[14] it has not been possible here to find even one mention of him made during his supposed lifetime. Perhaps a search on the scene—especially in Rome, Venice, or Madrid—will ultimately turn up pertinent archival material. But the first literary mention known to this study is the fleeting, supposedly posthumous one of 1752, already disparaging, in *An Essay on Musical Expression* by the Englishman Charles Avison (SCE XIX) and in the letter from Dr. J. Jortin added to Avison's second, 1753 edition.[15] The first actual account of Alberti's life seems not to have appeared for another 27 years, or until some 40 years after he is thought to have died, in La Borde's *Essai* (1780).[16] In the early 1770's Burney had already given passing mention twice to Alberti in his travel reports,[17] but his own main biographical account, apart from several other mentions in the final two volumes (both 1789) of his *History,* clearly derives from La Borde.[18] Thereafter, in an exceptionally imaginative process of anecdotal accretion, subsequent historians and lexicographers have expanded on the information supplied by those

tion that he was in Paris in 1753 (as in Mennicke/HASSE 81) is based on a probable error (cf. Cucuel/LA POUPLINIÈRE 372).

11. Newly dated in BRITISH UNION I 16.
12. Torrefranca/ORIGINI 506-507.
13. Since Fétis/BU I 53 (without source).
14. Cf. La Borde/ESSAI III 161-162.
15. Cf. Burney/HISTORY I 103; LC EARLY (Suppl.) 5.
16. III 161-162.
17. BURNEY'S TOURS I 236 and II 87.
18. Burney/HISTORY II 910; cf., also, pp. 981-982.

two men.[19] Among the first of the subsequent writers, by the way, the German E. L. Gerber in 1790 already recognizes "the so-called Alberti bass" and deplores its abuse,[20] thus establishing the unjustly restricted niche in which Alberti generally has been confined and nearly forgotten to this day.[21]

Burney's several other contributions to the Alberti story in his *History*,[22] plus an encyclopedia article he prepared on Alberti in his seventy-fifth year or later,[23] all center around an act of plagiarism that takes us directly to Alberti's keyboard sonatas, and an act that seems to have done more for the Italian's posthumous renown than any lifetime success. Bringing us, as no other writer, almost within grasp of Alberti's own time, Burney is able to report that he himself had been a witness to this act.[24] In 1745 he had attended a London benefit concert by the great violinist F. M. Veracini on behalf of the Roman *castrato* Giuseppe Jozzi (*ca.* 1720-*ca.* 1770). A former pupil of Alberti, Jozzi also took part, for "besides being an opera singer, [he] was likewise a celebrated performer on the harpsichord; and executed at this benefit several of Alberti's lessons, which he passed for his own. . . ." Later,[25] Burney adds that Jozzi then went so far as to print and sell Alberti's lessons

> for his own, at a guinea each book; till detected by a gentleman coming from Venice, who had been personally acquainted with Alberti, and was in possession of a manuscript copy in his own hand writing; which, in order to expose the impudence and plagiarism of Jozzi, he gave to Walsh, who printed and sold the eight elegant and graceful lessons of the original composer, for six shillings. Jozzi, though not the author of these charming pieces, which were the first of a style ["quite new in England"[26]] that has been since too much imitated, but never equalled, had the merit of playing them with a neatness and precision that was truly admirable. The harpsichord having neither sostenuto nor expression, maintained its reputation by brilliant execution; and there was an accent, a spring, and smartness in Jozzi's touch, which I had then never heard. Handel's harpsichord lessons and organ concertos, and the first two books of Scarlatti's lessons, were all the

19. Cf. Gerber/LEXICON I 20-21, supplemented in Gerber/NEUES I 51 and 810; Schilling/LEXICON I 125-126; Fétis/BU I 53; etc.

20. Gerber/LEXICON I 21, apparently following the lead in 1783 of Cramer/MAGAZIN I 1377-1379. Similar remarks published posthumously in 1806 in Schubart/IDEEN 199 (including a mention of Alberti's successes in Vienna) could have been written still earlier, though not before 1761, when a derogatory reference was made in Marpurg/BRIEFE II 143 to the "usual Italian style" of bass broken into 4 16th-notes.

21. Cf. Shedlock/SONATA 109-110; Klauwell/SONATE 44; Seiffert/KLAVIERMUSIK 428-429; Villanis/CLAVECINISTES 812; GROVE I 93-94 (Parry).

22. Burney/HISTORY II 405, 996-997, and 1008.

23. Rees/CYCLOPEDIA I (under "Alberti," without pagination); quoted in full in Stone/ITALIAN I 146-147.

24. Burney/HISTORY II 451; cf. p. 843.

25. Burney/HISTORY II 1008.

26. Burney/HISTORY II 451.

good music for keyed-instruments at that time in the nation; and these were original, difficult, and in a style totally different from those of Alberti.

Still later,[27] Burney tells us that Jozzi soon beat a precipitate retreat to Holland, "where he practiced the same trick [again], but not with equal profit."

Jozzi's original printing of Alberti's sonatas is no longer known, although his plagiarism in Holland is—in fact, in two Amsterdam editions of 1761 or later.[28] Walsh's original edition of the eight sonatas of Op. 1 in 1748 under Alberti's own name has survived in numerous copies,[29] which fact helps to confirm their popularity at the time. An edition of this set also appeared in Paris about 1760, which was but one of the evidences of Alberti's considerable popularity in that city.[30] The contents of all the editions of Op. 1 is the same, although the order of sonatas is changed in the two Amsterdam editions.[31] Some of these same sonatas and a few different ones appear in certain printed keyboard anthologies of the later eighteenth century.[32] Sometimes they occur alongside still others under Jozzi's name, leaving the question of whether Jozzi did actually write some sonatas of his own, too. Furthermore, there are several eighteenth-century MSS that add new sonatas or separate movements by Alberti, including some that raise this question of authorship again. We can be grateful to the German researcher Wilhelm Wörmann for collating twenty extant sources available to him and preparing a thematic index of all the sonatas in them that he could identify with some assurance as Alberti's.[33] He finds a total of 38 movements, or 14 complete two-movement sonatas (the first 8 of which are Sons. 1-8 in the Walsh edition) and 10 separate movements of which several may or may not have been paired originally as complete sonatas.[34]

27. Rees/CYCLOPEDIA I, under "Alberti."
28. Cf. MGG VII 221 (Cudworth); Eitner/QL V 307.
29. E.g., cf. the listing of 15 copies alone in BRITISH UNION I 16. Mod. eds.: Son. 5 in A in facs., cf. MGG I 296; Son. 8 in G, Newman/THIRTEEN-m, no. 3, with preface, pp. 6-8; Son. 2 in F, Giegling/SOLO-m 78.
30. Cf. Cucuel/LA POUPLINIÈRE 368-373, including a thematic index of this French edition; BIBLIOTHÈQUE NATIONALE II 226. La Borde's interest is a further evidence.
31. The incipits of the first mvts. of Jozzi's Amsterdam edition of 1761 (not Walsh's 1748 edition) are quoted in Eitner/QL I 84; cf. Wörmann/ALBERTI 94. It could have been Walsh who changed Alberti's original order (cf. Haas/CAT. 20, nos. 438 and 441).
32. In Anth. VENIER-m I alone are 11 mvts.
33. Wörmann/ALBERTI 92-98.
34. There appear not to be any other Alberti sons. among the 5 listings totaling 18 "sonate" and 21 "toccate" grouped under his name and classed as 22. 1. 25. in PUBBLICAZIONI NAPOLI 545-546. However, it would be interesting to add a consideration of these pieces to Wörmann/ALBERTI, for they include variants in the

The 38 sonata movements now known may be more or less than the 36 "Sonates" that La Borde reported to be hidden in the sole possession "d'un particulier de Milan,"[35] depending on whether La Borde counted 72 paired or 36 separate movements. In this presumed MS hangs another mystery. Were the "particulier de Milan" and his MS (La Borde) the same as the "gentleman coming from Venice" and his MS in Alberti's "own hand writing" that "he gave to Walsh" (Burney)? Wörmann guesses so,[36] and goes on to surmise that the MS of 21 "Sonate [separate mvts.] d'Intavolatura" in the British Museum[37] and the MS of 28 "Sonate [separate mvts.] per Cembalo" in Münster[38] are both contemporary copies of this original MS, now lost. Moreover, he notes that both MSS are dated 1746, and that the former copy is inscribed "ad uso d'Alessandro Scafa" while the latter frequently has "SC" or "S.C." inscribed beside the titles. Thus, this apparent dedicatee may well have been the hitherto unidentified "gentleman" of the original MS.

Only now, after this exceptional digression into matters of biography and bibliography, can we get to the music itself of Alberti's sonatas.[39] These deserve full attention on historical if not purely musical grounds. All 14 of the "complete" sonatas that are extant are in two movements. The keys are always the same in each pair of movements. In none of these or the other movements does Alberti exceed three sharps or flats, and only once does he use a minor key (Son. 4 in g[40]). The paired movements usually balance in length, ranging from 40 to over 100 measures each in the different sonatas. Every first movement is in simple duple or quadruple meter, whereas 8 of the 14 second movements identifiable as such are in simple triple meter and three more are in compound duple or quadruple meter. Most of these second movements

---

text, different juxtapositions of the mvts. in a few instances, several tempo marks missing elsewhere, and answers to some details questioned by Wörmann. There is no basis at present for deciding whether any of these MSS are autographs. But the last item, 16 (not 17) *toccate* (MS 35977), seems to contain no piece by D. Alberti. The later syntax and more advanced keyboard writing (including hand-crossing), plus the absence of even one incipit provided by Wörmann, make Alberti very unlikely as the composer.

35. La Borde/ESSAI III 162.

36. Wörmann/ALBERTI 90-93; but direct use is not made of either author's statement, resulting in some minor confusions. Cf., also, Torrefranca/ORIGINI 506.

37. Add. 14245, ff. 34-57b (BRITISH MS III 130).

38. No. 36 in the Santini-Bibliothek (cf. Wörmann/ALBERTI 92).

39. The chief discussions (with extended exx.) are two already cited, Torrefranca/ORIGINI 504-526 and Wörmann/ALBERTI; cf., also, Stone/ITALIAN I 146-156 and III no. 4 (Son. 4 in g, complete).

40. The numbering used here corresponds to the Roman numbering of the thematic index in Wörmann/ALBERTI (but XXV/1 in Wörmann's "Quellen" 5, 8, and 11, pp. 93 and 94, evidently should be corrected to XXIV/1).

are dances, often in title ("Menuet" or "Giga") and still more often in spirit. Furthermore, the tempo marks, inserted in most of the movements and ranging largely from moderate to fast, differ more often than not in pairs of movements. Thus, heard as cycles these sonatas ordinarily afford adequate contrast between movements. But both Torrefranca and Wörmann seem to give too much credit to Alberti for the establishment of this two-movement plan in the pre-Classic keyboard sonata. In the first place, unless Alberti's sonatas date from still earlier than the late 1730's, they were anticipated consistently in this plan by Durante's six *Sonate* of about 1732 (SBE 199-200), and probably were paralleled if not anticipated by the keyboard sonatas of the presumably older Italian Paradisi.[41] In the second place, one hesitates to attach undue importance to a plan that proves to have been "more honored in the breach than in the observance" (SCE VI).

On the other hand, the present tendency to demote Alberti from innovator to popularizer of the "Alberti bass" may be detracting from credit that he does deserve, and in more than one sense. What sort of precedents are to be found for his familiar device? Although previous writers on keyboard music have frequently called attention to antecedents, only recently (1959) did anyone make a systematic search.[42] The conclusion was the expected one. It verified that keyboard accompaniments have been derived by arpeggiating chords almost, if not ever, since chords have been played on keyboard instruments. In fact, contemporary theorists remind us how often the arpeggiations were improvised when not so written.[43] However, in the experience of this study the Alberti bass proper needs to be defined as a more particularized figure. Ordinarily it should not include the mere consecutive arpeggiation of three- or four-note chords,[44] the embellishing of octaves, or still other means of enlivening a slow harmonic rhythm. Rather it should be limited largely to those four-note figures in 16th- or 8th-notes that oscillate within any closed position of triads or 7th-chords and within a prevailing metric beat, as in Ex. 20.

Obvious as it may now seem in its construction, this particular figure, which is a broken chord but not a literal, consecutive arpeggiation, did occur but rarely and only momentarily before Alberti's time. Hence, within our present knowledge, Alberti's immediate and abundant use of it does make him its virtual inventor. Nor must its ultimate

41. Cf. Torrefranca/ORIGINI 482-484.
42. Marco/ALBERTI.
43. E.g., cf. Bach/ESSAY 159-160, 316 (on Italian practice), and 421-422.
44. As implied in Apel/DICTIONARY 21.

Ex. 20. From Sonata 13/ii by Domenico Alberti (after MS 35973 in the Biblioteca del R. Conservatorio di Musica in Naples).

abuse belie its real significance to Classic styles and forms.[45] One thinks first of all, naturally, of the ideal support it gives to the singing-allegro style, with its busy yet unobtrusive activation of a slow harmonic rhythm (SCE VI). But he may also note how in its oscillations there is a characteristic rhythmic pattern, and how, in turn, this pattern tends to bring out the voice-leading of the individual strands as the chordal outline changes. Furthermore, in the oscillations and closed-position chords lies a convenient technique that is idiomatic to the keyboard in spite of its eventual transfer to stringed and wind instruments (especially in accompanied sonatas). That technique undoubtedly relates to the new neatness, precision, accent, spring, and smartness that Burney remarked in Jozzi's playing (as quoted earlier).

But now the fact must be noted that the Alberti bass is by no means the only or even the predominant style of accompaniment in Alberti's sonatas. Hardly is a complete view provided by one writer, who tabulates only its maximum uses; he finds it in 37 out of 46 measures in Sonata 2/i and in 38 out of 46 in Sonata 6/i.[46] Even in its broader

45. Cf. Kenyon/HARPSICHORD 120-121.
46. GROVE I 94 (Parry).

senses, the Alberti bass may be said to predominate as an accompaniment in only 5 of the 16 movements of Op. 1, all of them first movements (Sons. 2, 3, 4, 6, and 8). Among other styles of accompaniment there are simple repeated notes (2/ii), "murky" basses (in broken octaves; 6/ii), "running" basses in steady 8th-notes (5/ii), and slower bass lines, both conjunct and disjunct, that provide one harmonic support per beat (4/ii). Moreover, in occasional movements Alberti uses the loose, pseudopolyphonic texture of the *galant* style (5/i); and in others he alternates the hands rapidly (5/ii), thus employing one of the most idiomatic of keyboard techniques. This last disposition, however, does not invalidate Burney's implication (quoted earlier) that idiomatic as Alberti's writing is, the demands on the performer are still elementary compared with those of Handel and Scarlatti.

Of course, as was stressed in the previous chapter, varieties of texture make for varieties of structural method, ultimately influencing the over-all design. Alberti is clearly at his best in the more traditional styles of progression. In Ex. 21 the drive-to-the-cadence is made convincing enough by the overlapping reiterations of the upbeat motive. It is extended by diminutions in the penultimate measure and embellished

Ex. 21. From the first movement of Sonata 5 in A by Domenico Alberti (after the Walsh ed. in 1748 in the Library of Congress).

by the typically *galant* trills. Here Alberti is close to his senior compatriots, Marcello and D. Scarlatti, in sound and feel, as he also is in his fast-galloping yet fluent "Giga" finales (as in Son. 4). His writing is certainly competent, not "amateurish" (in the depreciated sense by which that word has been applied to Alberti), even though it is not favored by the original genius that constantly inspired Scarlatti. Its most original moments in the latter sense, especially some daring harmonies (as in the sequence based on deceptive resolutions in Son. 6/i/26-38), bring it closer to Marcello.

However, from our present perspective, the novelty of the "singing-allegro" style, with its new type bass, seems to have confronted Alberti with a special problem, that of finding a suitable continuation once the initial idea is stated.[47] As Ex. 20 revealed, the opening idea falls into a clear, if piecemeal, organization. Its "singing-allegro" style moves well so long as the idea itself lasts (as also at the start of the second half of some mvts.—e.g., Son. 6/i/18-26, with all four measures supported only by one dim.-7th chord). But the unadulteratedly homophonic texture of this style makes poor soil for the motivic process that still was Alberti's only sure means of continuation. To reiterate a simple motive at the same pitch level and within the tonal plateaus so common to this texture quickly grows tiresome. Alberti's usual compromise was to alter the motive a little with every other repetition. But, again from our present perspective, the compromise is generally ineffectual. The motive itself ordinarily lacks character and proves to be more of a mere technical figure. Hence the alternations are also likely to lack melodic weight. Nor do they afford sufficient pitch, rhythm, or tonal contrast to maintain a sense of compelling motion. In short, a certain monotony and static effect result from the fact that the ideas are not distinctive enough to provide strong unity, while the contrasts are not sharp enough to provide clear variety.

Three clues tend to confirm this structural dilemma of Alberti. One is the restored sense of motion that results when a harmonic sequence occurs (as in Son. 6/i/27-31)—that is, when tonal contrast does occur. Another is the tell-tale lapses of phrase symmetry where symmetry would be likely in later, Classic music (as at the three-measure phrase in Son. 3/i/5-7), which simply suggests that Alberti was not fully aware yet of this broader means of organization (and hardly subtle enough yet to be challenging the "tyranny of the bar"). And a third clue is Alberti's apparent inexperience in the handling of the new

47. In the detailed analysis of Son. 12/i (reproduced in full) in Wörmann/ALBERTI this essential aspect of Alberti's style is ably examined.

texture itself as compared with the more conservative textures. Especially does there seem to be a disregard, at times and in later terms, of the four-part harmony outlined by the Alberti bass and the (soprano) melody, as when the melody moves in octaves with an inner strand (Son. 3/i/8) or resolves into it from a 9-8 appoggiatura (cf. mss. 2 and 1 in Son. 6/i). With regard to all three clues, Sonatas 6 in G, 12 in B♭, and 13 in E♭[48] seem to fare better than many of the others.

Alberti's continuation of the "singing-allegro" style in this pseudomotivic process (as it might now be called) is apparently what Torrefranca heralds as an extreme example of "l'involuzione ritmica,"[49] by which he means persistent metric drive with minimal changes in the rhythmic pattern and harmonic changes mainly on the first beats. To him, "rhythmic involution" is an essential of the "second *galant* style" (from about 1755-65), leading ultimately to the more plastic Mozart style. From our own standpoint he seems to be reading too much historical prescience into an experiment made somewhat gauche by rapidly obsolescing processes. Unless one singles out details like the Mozartean feminine cadences in the charming "Menuet" movements (e.g., Son. 3/ii/12), the openings in which an initial melodic idea "sings" over an Alberti bass still remain the most advanced aspects of these sonatas from a historical standpoint—more so, too, than the anticipations of ternary, or even "sonata form."

With regard to the over-all form, in the first movements each half is enclosed by repeat signs in the usual Baroque manner, with the second half of the movement always leading into modulations and being longer than the first. The initial idea does return frequently in the second half (in 6 out of the 8 first movements of Op. 1; also, 4 of the finales). But this return is generally too casual to seem like a clear landmark in the over-all form. Mainly it is not set apart by its rhythmic placement (in 5/i and 7/i it shifts to the weaker half of the measure) or by its tonal orientation (in 8/i the home key has already been in force for at least 19 measures). Furthermore, these factors, the static nature of Alberti's "pseudomotivic" process, the lack of any true development of his ideas, and the absence of clear contrasting ideas all tend to make the approximations of "sonata form" in his sonatas more discernible to the enthusiastic scholar's eye than to the blasé musician's ear.

Unlike Alberti in two main respects, another "singer-cembalist," **Giuseppe Antonio Paganelli** (1710 to at least 1762[50]), did leave clear

48. Most of 13/i is reproduced in Torrefranca/ORIGINI 519-523.

49. Torrefranca/ORIGINI 507 and 509.

50. Paganelli's last verifiable composition is the only present basis for approximating his death year, which differs here from most recent sources for the reasons given below.

biographical traces and did find satisfactory styles of progression, both in extent and drive, for the newer idioms in his sonatas. Although serious gaps and confusions still exist, enough is known about Paganelli's life to relate these sonatas to it in time and place.[51] But he moved about too often to be identified primarily with one city, hence must be placed somewhat arbitrarily here in Venice, the city of his home country in which he was most active. He was born in Padua where he may well have been introduced to the *galant* style in composition studies with Tartini, though he seems never to have excelled as a violin virtuoso.[52] That he did excel early as a cembalist is suggested by his employment as such at the age of 23 in opera productions in Augsburg (Bavaria), one year after he had made his debut as an opera composer in Venice. In 1737-38, except for another half year in Venice, Paganelli served as "Kammer-Musik-Meister" at court in the central-German town of Bayreuth, and for some or all of the next three years he seems to have served similarly in some less official way[53] and as "compositeur des operas italiens de S. A. S. Monseigneur le Duc Régnant de Brunswick Lunebourg," still farther north in Braunschweig. It is in the latter's service that Paganelli identifies himself in the titles of all his published ensemble sonatas that are now known.[54] In 1743-44 and perhaps longer he was producing operas again in Venice,[55] and for a few years from about 1747 he may have been in Munich and elsewhere in Germany again. He then served, presumably in his last years, as "Directeur de la Musique de Chambre de S. M. C. Roi d'Espagne" in Madrid. At this post. where he certainly appeared by 1756 (according to the full title of his *XXX Ariae pro organo et cembalo*) and where he may even have succeeded the ailing Scarlatti in 1754 just after the latter had "retired,"[56] he seems to have written all his keyboard sonatas and other keyboard music. He was still and last reported at this post about 1762 in the title of the Sonata in F that appears as No. 5 in Anth. HAFFNER RACCOLTA-m IV.[57]

51. The comprehensive doctoral dissertation Schenk/PAGANELLI is the chief source on both the man and his music (including a thematic index).

52. Cf. Schenk/PAGANELLI 12-15.

53. Cf. Schenk/PAGANELLI 42-43.

54. Cf. Schenk/PAGANELLI 146-151.

55. Cf. Wiel/CATALOGO 137-145.

56. Cf. Kirkpatrick/SCARLATTI 127, but without mention of Paganelli. No report on Paganelli's activities in Spain has been discovered in the present study, notwithstanding numerous inquiries.

57. In Schenk/PAGANELLI 51, Paganelli's last extant publication is assumed to be his set of S/bass sons. Op. 16, probably because 16 is the highest op. no. of his that is now known. But the year 1765 suggested for this publication (and hence for the approximate time of death) must be at least 20 years too late (cf. BRITISH UNION II 754; also, BIBLIOTHÈQUE NATIONALE VII 100 for Op. 13). For that

In short, Paganelli seems to have written most if not all of his ensemble sonatas in the early 1740's in north Germany (with all publications appearing in Paris[58]), and his keyboard sonatas in the late 1750's in Madrid (with publications in Augsburg, Amsterdam, and Nürnberg). The ensemble sonatas include three sets of six each (Opp. 4, 5, and 13 [derived largely from Opp. 4 and 5]). These sonatas are in that duet setting of two unaccompanied violins or flutes that was so popular throughout the eighteenth century, especially in France, as attested in this instance by the many reprints of Paganelli's sets. The ensemble sonatas also include six for flute and *b.c.,* Op. 16, plus four more in MS, called "Sonata" or "Solo"; and six for two violins or flutes and *b.c.,* Op. 7, plus nine more in MS, called "Trio." The keyboard sonatas are better known today (insofar as Paganelli is remembered at all), although they make up only the last fifth of the total of about sixty extant sonatas. Among the keyboard sonatas is the set by Paganelli most often cited, *Divertissement de le beau sexe ou six sonatines* (1757).[59] Ten, or more than half, of the seventeen short movements in these "sonatines" he took almost without change from his *XXX Ariae pro organo et cembalo,* which had appeared the previous year.[60] Three

---

matter, the dating of nearly all Paganelli's instrumental ensemble music in Schenk/PAGANELLI 78-79 seems too late in the light of newer sources, and probably should be moved back from 1753-65 to the early 1740's (thus falling once more within the period 1733-58 originally given for all Paganelli's works in Gerber/LEXICON II 58). Schenk's later dates are based mainly on "privilèges du roi" of 1751 and 1765 in Brenet/LIBRAIRIE 446 and 454, but evidently apply to reprints, especially Paganelli's three sets of Sons. for 2 Vns or Fls alone (Opp. 4, 5, 13), which appeared variously in at least 15 French catalogues up to at least 1797 (as indexed in Johansson/FRENCH [Facs. 50, De la Chevardière, 1765, includes the (flute) "Duetti" of 1764 mentioned in Saint-Foix/MOZART I 60]). Aside from the many records that have since been lost, the "privilège" was often disregarded or evaded by composers and publishers, as made clear in Brenet/LIBRAIRIE 411-412. The announcement in MERCURE 1774 July I 180 of "*Six Sonates* aisées pour le pianoforte & le clavecin" by Paganelli, issued by Boivin in Paris, undoubtedly means a reprint of the *Six Sonatines* of 1757, therefore should not be taken (as in Saint-Foix/SCHENK 303) either as a reason for extending the death date or as a source for the Son. in F in Pauer/MEISTER-m V 80.

58. But Op. 7 (SS/bass) is one set that may not have been printed until after 1753 (cf. Schenk/PAGANELLI 44, 78, and 155).

59. Discussion (with exx.) in Torrefranca/ORIGINI 143-150 (originally in RMI XVII [1910] 785-792, but neither Schenk nor Torrefranca mentions the other's work on Paganelli). Mod. ed., complete: Tagliapietra/PAGANELLI-m; a further ed. is listed in HOFMEISTER CVI/1 (1957) 258.

60. The reverse derivation in Schenk/PAGANELLI 84 (cf., also, pp. 141-145) seems to be contradicted by the year 1757 supplied for the "Sonatines" in Scheurleer/CATALOGUS II 326. That the young Mozart was influenced by the *XXX Ariae* while in Augsburg with his father in 1763 is assumed in Saint-Foix/MOZART I 33 and 73 but discredited in Schenk/PAGANELLI 83-84. There is a more tangible connection through Leopold Mozart, whose *Violinschule* was published in the same year by the same publisher in this city (Lotter) and whose light keyboard pieces, similar to Paganelli's *Ariae,* were published 3 years later (1759) by Lotter (cf. DTB-m IX/2 [Seiffert] xli and lvi).

other, more extended keyboard sonatas by Paganelli, in G, F, and F, complete this summary. These occur in Anth. HAFFNER RACCOLTA-m II no. 3, III no. 2, and IV no. 5, respectively (1757-62?).[61]

All of Paganelli's sonatas are in three movements except "Sonatine" 6 and the first two in Anth. HAFFNER RACCOLTA-m, these last three being further Italian examples of the two-movement keyboard type. The movements follow no one order of tempos, but the two most frequent plans of the late Baroque Era prevail in the ensemble cycles—S-F-M (slow-fast-moderate) or S-F-F in the S/bass settings, and F-S-M or F-S-F in the others—while the order in the keyboard cycles is limited only by the typical absence of true slow movements in Italian keyboard sonatas. The finale is often the usual pre-Classic "Menuetto" or "Tempo di Menuetto," sometimes with its alternate "Menuetto II." This and the other moderate movements, mostly marked "Andantino" or "Grazioso," recall similar movements in contemporary French sonatas such as Leclair's, with their delicate ornamentation, their concise and neatly balanced ideas, and their frequent repetitions. The keys of all but four sonatas are major and do not exceed three flats or four sharps. Within many of the sonatas the movements are all in the same key, but the middle movements do appear in the relative, subdominant, or minor dominant keys, and the alternate tonic modes in as many other sonatas.[62] It proves possible to find subtle yet not too equivocal relationships between two or all three of the movement incipits in several of the ensemble sonatas (e.g., Opp. 4/4, 5/6, or 16/2), as was still often true in the late Baroque Era (SBE 78-79).

The forms of Paganelli's first movements are in keeping with the relatively free binary plans of pre-Classic music. Most stable among the features are, in the first half, the initial idea, modulating directly to a nearly related key; a shorter second idea, often tending toward contrast; and a distinctive close in the new key, prior to the repeat sign; in the second half, modulations of a limited range, which start and extend this half; a return more often to the second than the initial idea; and a close in the home key that closely parallels that of the first half in the related key. Paganelli's other forms are simpler though still not reduced to formulas. They include the expected binary designs of the dances (minuet and *giga*), sets of variations on the melody and within

61. Mod. eds. of the first 2: Benvenuti/CEMBALISTI-m nos. 5 and 6; Tagliapietra/ANTOLOGIA-m XII nos. 11 and 12. The Son. in G was overlooked in the thematic index of Schenk/PAGANELLI. Mod. ed. of the third of these sons.: Pauer/MEISTER-m V 80.

62. Two finales in different keys from the other 2 mvts. (cf. Schenk/PAGANELLI 92 and 149) seem more likely to have been interchanged at some point in the copying process.

the supporting harmony of minuet themes, and a rondeau (Op. 4/2/iii) near to the sort Couperin wrote.

Although Paganelli's ensemble sonatas are still scored in the favorite melo/bass and SS settings of the Baroque Era, these as well as the keyboard sonatas all exhibit the new light idiom of the *galant* style—the essentially homophonic texture, enhanced only by pseudo-counterpoint if any (especially in the relatively independent parts of the SS and SS/bass settings); the emphasis on details, including brief but rhythmically fussy ideas, frequent rests, and frequent precise ornaments; and the progression by generally short arches. If this style was already present in Paganelli's operas of the late 1730's it may relate to some derogatory criticism from his superiors,[63] particularly that calling the "accompaniments mostly faulty and hard on the ear." At any rate, Paganelli's own awareness of the newness and purely diversional character of his style is evident enough in titles like "Galante" for two of his sonata movements ("Sonatine" 4/iii and duet Op. 5/3/iii), "Sonatines," "Divertissement de le beau sexe," and "Trattenimento" (i.e., diversion or amusement, as each individual SS/bass sonata of Op. 7 is subtitled). The same light quality is present (though without such titles) even in the *XXX Ariae pro organo et cembalo,* from which so many of the "Sonatine" movements derive, in spite of the primarily liturgical function emphasized in this set's full title.[64]

The texture of Paganelli's keyboard sonatas is not unlike that in Scarlatti's sonatas or Telemann's *Fantaisies pour le clavessin,* although its slower harmonic rhythm gives a still more homophonic effect. The crossing and alternating of hands, scalewise and chordal passages, and leaps all show a somewhat greater exploitation of the keyboard than Alberti made. But nothing in Paganelli's sonatas seems to betray any influence of his late residence in Spain.[65] In all but one of them (the third Haffner son.) the music achieves continuation by unfolding in a constant succession of short, ever-changing ideas or less distinctive figures. But the latter process is not static, as in much of Alberti's writing. Rather, the changing figures possess enough rhythmic vitality and enough contrast, they fit clearly enough into balanced phrases (Ex. 22), and these in turn contribute clearly enough to a simple, over-all tonal organization, to maintain a sense of purposeful flow in most instances.

Naturally, by these means it is Paganelli's shortest forms that become the most convincing ones. The movements of the "Sonatines,"

63. Cf. Schenk/PAGANELLI 40-41.
64. Cf. Schenk/PAGANELLI 143 and 83-86; SCE III.
65. Cf. Kastner/CONTRIBUCIÓN 292.

Ex. 22. From the first movement, second half, in Giuseppe Antonio Paganelli's Sonata in G for cembalo (after Anth. HAFFNER RACCOLTA-m II no. 3).

ranging from only 14 to 38 measures, progress purposefully from one easily perceived goal to the next. But in the longer keyboard sonatas the composer risks losing sight of those structural goals. Both the tonal plans and the ideas seem too elementary to be extended so greatly by such means. Or put conversely, these movements seem too long for what they have to say. Most vulnerable of all to this problem is the longest keyboard sonata, that third one in Anth. HAFFNER RACCOLTA-m, in which each of the outer movements extends beyond 120 measures. But this sonata is surprisingly different in two further ways that also tend toward monotony. First, the Alberti bass appears in nearly half of the initial, longest movement, whereas it is totally absent except for rare hints in all of Paganelli's other keyboard music. Second and more important from a structural standpoint, only in all three movements of this Sonata in F is the method of continuation not an unfolding of ever-changing figures but a concentration on a minimum of ideas in rather exceptional examples of economy of materials. Although other traits of the style are not essentially different, one still begins to question seriously whether Haffner was correct in ascribing this sonata to Paganelli. The question is of more than passing interest, since it is this very sonata to which Eitner called attention as containing remarkable antecedents of the Mozart style.[66] However, as with Alberti, it is primarily the use of the "singing-allegro" style here, rather than the structural method, that would seem significant in Mozartean terms.

Our third Venetian to be discussed here was, if still not on Scarlatti's level, one of the main Italian composers of eighteenth-century keyboard sonatas—**Baldassare Galuppi** (1706-85), known in his own day as "il Buranello" after his birthplace Burano near Venice. Primarily, of course, Galuppi was celebrated for the *opere buffe* he set to librettos by Goldoni, making him a kind of "Rossini of the eighteenth century."[67] With him there is no problem of finding references made contemporaneously,[68] but as usual the main interest was in the opera. No contemporary reference to Galuppi's sonatas has been found, although Burney, who visited him in Venice in 1770, did at least make the pertinent remark that he was "a good harpsichord player."[69] And two previous reports, of his St. Petersburg service (1765-68), probably apply to the sonatas when they touch on the precision and virtuosity with which he played his own keyboard pieces.[70]

In today's historical perspective and occasional revivals of his music, the interest has broadened markedly, with considerable attention being

66. Eitner/SONATE 179-180. Cf., also, Torrefranca/ORIGINI 84, 115, 405-406.

67. Torrefranca/ORIGINI 184.

68. E.g., many are cited in Piovano/GALUPPI (the main biographic and bibliographic study), CHIGIANA GALUPPI (reports assembled for the Galuppi festival in Siena in 1948), and Mooser/ANNALES II 69-86 *et passim* (with much new information on Galuppi's stay in St. Petersburg, 1765-68); cf., also, Raabe/GALUPPI 11, 47.

69. BURNEY'S TOURS I 133.

70. Cf. Raabe/GALUPPI 17; Mooser/ANNALES II 72.

paid to Galuppi's sonatas, and lately some to his keyboard concertos, other instrumental works, and the *seria* side of his opera output.[71] Again the chief promoter of the Italian keyboard sonata has been Torrefranca, who makes Galuppi one of his main heroes in articles totaling nearly 150 pages, most of which he has brought together in his principal study.[72] And again a German has responded, too, only to view the contribution more cautiously and scientifically.[73] There is also the Englishman's view of Galuppi's sonatas, an enthusiastic appreciation by Eric Blom.[74] It is entitled "Brave Galuppi" in nice reference to *A Toccata of Galuppi's* by Browning (but it is not one of those foredoomed attempts to link the poem with a particular piece[75]).

It is possible here to account for a total of about ninety keyboard sonatas by Galuppi.[76] The total has jumped significantly in each of four main installments of a thematic index that was begun in 1909 and now awaits final editorial reorganization and consolidation in a single publication.[77] Less than a fourth of the sonatas were published during 77a
Galuppi's lifetime, the remainder being MSS scattered in a surprising number and spread of libraries throughout Europe (like the MSS of his older co-citizen and onetime mentor Benedetto Marcello[78]). Both Torrefranca and Raabe have argued at length for dating the bulk of all these sonatas between 1740 and 1760 if not earlier.[79] But the better information now available makes 1755-85 the more likely period and tends to invalidate the division into "early" and "late" sonatas on which both

71. Cf. Raabe/GALUPPI 53; CHIGIANA GALUPPI 75; MGG IV 1345-1348 (Bollert).

72. Torrefranca/ORIGINI 136-142, 180-278, and elsewhere (with copious exx.); cf., also, Torrefranca/GALUPPI. An impetus for his studies on Galuppi had existed in Torchi/ISTRUMENTALE 259-262.

73. Raabe/GALUPPI.

74. Blom/STEPCHILDREN 23-30.

75. Cf. Torrefranca/ORIGINI 277 and 688; Borren/GALUPPI 367; Stone/ITALIAN I 115-116; PMA XXXIX (1912-13) 46 and 52-53 (J. A. Fuller-Maitland).

76. The totals have varied widely in reference works from a modest 12 in BAKER'S DICTIONARY 533 to a very unlikely 250 in DIZIONARIO RICORDI 508.

77. Its present order is largely arbitrary, complicated by misattributions, duplications, differences, and unclear juxtapositions of movements in the MSS that remain to be clarified (cf. the descriptive list in Raabe/GALUPPI 50-52; also, Torrefranca/ORIGINI 196-197). In Torrefranca/GALUPPI are the themes of Sons. 1-28. Along with additions to the previous entries, Sons. 29-33 are indexed in Borren/GALUPPI, 34-51 in Raabe/GALUPPI (but 45 and 46 are actually Op. 1/8 and 1/11 by L. Giustini), and around 25 others in an index prepared, in conjunction with a proposed ed. of selected Galuppi sons., by Professor Edith Woodcock at the University of Washington in Seattle. Finally may be added the 12 sons. to be mentioned shortly in 2 MS sets dated 1782 and '85 but not yet indexed. Warm thanks for providing microfilm and other materials are owing to Professor Woodcock, whose work on Galuppi has included the finding of the 25 (or more) additional sons. in MSS in 7 libraries of Italy, Spain, England, and Germany.

78. Cf. SBE 176; CHIGIANA GALUPPI 20 and 51.

79. Torrefranca/ORIGINI 185-194; Raabe/GALUPPI 17-20.

men based their style discussions.[80] Apart from Torrefranca's eagerness at all times to find Italian precedents around 1740 for the first published sonatas of Emanuel Bach, both he and Raabe had assumed that Galuppi's opera activities in London in 1741-43 were the occasion for Walsh's editions of the only two sets of sonatas by Galuppi to reach publication. However, though Galuppi may well have shown his skill as cembalist at that time, perhaps even leaving several early sonatas with Walsh or some other Londoner, Walsh did not first publish the two sets of six sonatas each, Opp. 1 and 2, until 1756 and 1759, respectively.[81] The few sonatas or separate movements by Galuppi that were published singly in his lifetime all first appeared no earlier than these two sets
82a and not more than ten years later.[82] Only two sets (not yet indexed) of Galuppi's MS sonatas can be dated with any certainty, and both came very late in his life.[83] One set of 6 *Sonates* was composed "in a few days" in his 76th year (1782) for his former generous patron in St. Petersburg (1765-68) when the latter passed through Venice (incognito as Conti del Nort),[84] and the other, final set of 6, *Passa Tempo* [*Pastime*] *al Cembalo,* was composed in his last year, 1785, in the all
85a but illegible, trembling hand of a very feeble but still creative old man.[85]

The larger number of Galuppi's sonatas that is now available naturally permits more secure statistics regarding their general make-up, but the conclusions do not run counter to the related ones by Torrefranca and Raabe. Unlike Alberti, Galuppi kept the cycle flexible, even within sets, by not settling predominantly on any one number or sequence of movements. Nearly 80 per cent of about 85 sonatas that could be tabulated here are two- and three-movement cycles, the former

80. Torrefranca/ORIGINI 189, 196, 250; Raabe/GALUPPI 20, 56. Cf. Hoffmann-Erbrecht/KLAVIERMUSIK 92.

81. BRITISH UNION I 360. Op. 1 contains Sons. 30, 11, 34, 35 (in D, not E), 36, 19, respectively, in the cumulative index; Op. 2 contains Sons. 1-6. Mod. ed.: Son. 35 (in D) Köhler/MAÎTRES-m II 20, Oesterle/TREASURY-m V 58, etc.

82. These include, among others, Son. 33, in Anth. HILL LESSONS-m no. 5 (cf. BRITISH UNION II 613); Son. 35, in several reprintings (Op. 1/4; cf. "Lesson [in D]," BRITISH UNION I 360; Borren/GALUPPI 366); Sons. 49, 50, and 14, in Anth. HAFFNER RACCOLTA-m I no. 1, II no. 2, and V no. 2, respectively); other separate movements in Anth. VENIER-m I and II (cf. Borren/GALUPPI 366-368; Raabe/GALUPPI 49). Mod. eds.: Sons. 49 and 50, Pauer/MEISTER-m V nos. 49 and 48, Oesterle/TREASURY-m V 40 and 48, Benvenuti/CEMBALISTI-m 20 and 14, etc.

83. The earlier dating of various other MSS in Raabe/GALUPPI 50-52 is too conjectural to use here. Among mod. eds.: 12 of the sons. especially liked by Torrefranca (28, 50, 26, 16, 27, 17, 10, 14, 25, 12, 13, 9), Benvenuti/GALUPPI-m (with added mvts.); 4 separate mvts. from Sons. 15, 17, 4, 37, Piccioli/GALUPPI-m. Cf., also, MGG IV 1347.

84. Cf. Caffi/STORIA I 412; Torrefranca/GALUPPI 872; Torrefranca/ORIGINI 192 (was the MS preserved in St. Petersburg [Leningrad]?); Mooser/ANNALES II 84.

85. Mod. ed.: GALUPPI/facs.-m; cf. CHIGIANA GALUPPI 12, 75.

having only a slight majority. The remainder are divided between one-, four-, and even five-movement cycles, in that order. The tempos are marked in about two-thirds of the movements and can be guessed in several of the others by their meter, style, and position (as in the quasi-gigue finale of Son. 45). They show the clear majority of fast movements in Italian keyboard music of the time, with about half as many moderate movements, and relatively few slow movements. Fast movements occur side-by-side often, moderate movements occasionally, and slow never. Except for the sequence M-F-F, in only about ten scattered sonatas, and the fact that the minuet, gigue, or variation form most often occurs as a finale, the sequence of movements is too variable—intentionally, one almost suspects—to permit even of any generalization.

Over 80 per cent of Galuppi's sonatas are in major keys and a similar proportion do not go beyond keys of two sharps or flats (four of either being the maximum). About 90 per cent of the sonatas with three or more movements have both or all movements in the same key and mode, the few exceptions having an inner movement in the relative, dominant, or subdominant key or in the opposite tonic mode. Only rarely are the movements of any one sonata related by similar incipits, suggesting that even these relationships may have been merely fortuitous ones (e.g., Sons. 19, 25, and 34).

To stop a bit longer on external traits, we find that most of Galuppi's separate movements have repeat signs near the middle and at the end. The shorter ones (e.g., Son. 5/i), including the dance and dancelike finales, are ordinarily in the simple binary design still prevalent, with its modulation to a nearly related key in the first half, and its more indirect modulations back to the tonic and a parallel closing figure in the second half. The longer movements, especially when they are the first moderate or fast movements of a cycle, usually have the well-prepared and well-spaced returns of the initial idea that qualify them as clear ternary designs. But Galuppi still left these designs in a fluid state, with many variants and no stereotypes. Though they sometimes come surprisingly close to "sonata-allegro" form as it was later codified in nineteenth-century textbooks (SCE II and VI), they always happen to "lack" some feature or aspect that would make it "complete." In Sonata 28/i the arrival at the dominant key is marked by an idea that relates too clearly to the first to make a clear contrast, and serves in its place for the subsequent return. Sonata 26/ii gives the impression of being monothematic except for its closing figure; the tentative figure introduced in the dominant key is too much a part of its context (the foregoing cadence and the ensuing passages) to have an identity of its own. Sonata 17/i has the requisite theme distribution, including even a clear break before the adequately contrasted second theme, but its "development" section is simply the series of transpositions and modulatory passages that Galuppi more often employs in this region of the form. Except that their "second themes" afford less distinct contrast, both the first and second movements of Sonata 14 come as close as any by him to meeting all the textbook requirements. Both of these movements fall into three nearly equal divisions (16 + 14 + 12 mss. and 39 + 27 + 37 mss., respectively) and both do discuss and dissect their materials in ways bordering on Classic development techniques.

Galuppi's several minuets (e.g., Son. 1/iv,[86] "Minuetto") and quasi-minuets (Son. 10/iii, "Allegretto") are in 3/8 more often than 3/4 meter and have no separate trio or second minuet, although at least one has a short middle section (Son. 17/iii, "Minúè"). Their identification with French origins and styles is suggested by their purely homophonic texture, their niceties of rhythm and articulation, their thetic openings, their square-cut phrases and periods, and the deliberate pace dictated by their precise ornamentation. The gigues (e.g., Son. 35/iv, "Giga") and quasi-gigues (Son. 2/ii) are similarly homophonic and regular in their structure, and they are fluent and fleet rather than rollicking or rhythmically complex. Other forms in these sonatas include a single instance of a siciliana;[87] a rondo (Son. 45/iii); at least three sets of variations, consisting of melodic and chordal elaborations of simple, square-cut themes (as in *Passa Tempo* no. 6/ii); a quasi-French overture (Son. 51); and at least one fugal movement (Son. 10/ii, "Presto"), an effective, driving piece for all its contrapuntal laxness.

Galuppi displays a good variety of melodic styles, both lyrical and tuneful. Among them, the cantabile melodies over Alberti or other chordal basses provide some further Italian precedents for the Mozart style (Ex. 23). These melodies are notable for their sensitively planned contours, supple rhythmic organization, and frequent appoggiaturas in feminine rhythms. In more conservative textures the melodic line, always on top, is less likely to fall into distinct phrases than to unfold in an equally supple and a still more florid and broad contour (Son. 26/i), lasting through much of a whole section (Son. 35/i). Such melodic dispositions, occurring mainly in moderate to slow introductory movements, often recall Baroque "solo" or "trio" settings with a "running" type of *b.c.* in steady 8th-notes and perhaps a note-for-note

86. In Anth. VENIER-m I no. 2; also, Paoli/ITALIANE-m 12. Cf. Borren/GALUPPI 366.

87. Raabe/GALUPPI 28; but the saraband mentioned here comes from the Son. in A, 45/i, that is actually Giustini's Op. 1/8/i.

Ex. 23. From the start of Sonata 1 in *Passa Tempo* by Baldassare Galuppi (after GALUPPI/facs.-m).

filler line. But not infrequently this "*b.c.*" remains static for a measure or more (Son. 34/i) instead of moving stepwise or less conjunctly, meaning that the melody is then accompanied in much slower harmonic rhythm than could ordinarily be expected in Baroque accompaniments. When there are no filler notes, the thin two-voiced texture may suggest their insertion by the performer in the supposed manner of the times (SCE V). This practice is actually indicated by occasional *b.c.* figures in the Galuppi MSS and by a modest filling out of the parts in some of his publications.[88] But the enrichment is excessive in nineteenth-century editions.[89] While on the subject of melody, we should also note Galuppi's ability to write short, piquant, *buffa* ideas of much charm, like the coquettish closing figure *à la* Mozart in Sonata 14/ii (mss. 27 ff.),[90] or complete, forthright tunes, like that used as the theme of variations in Sonata 1/iii. This last movement is another blood relative of

88. Cf. Raabe/GALUPPI 20-22.
89. For comparative exx. see Stone/ITALIAN 109-111.
90. In general, Galuppi's possible influences on Mozart seem to be dismissed on insufficient grounds in Saint-Foix/MOZART I 340.

that "celebrated Gavotte" by Corelli (Op. 5/10) that became common property throughout the eighteenth century (SBE 171-172 *et passim*).

For the most part, Galuppi's harmony is skillful and adequately varied without being conspicuous in its own right. But there are some surprises, often pathetic in character.[91] Sonata 4/ii/49-50 makes a sudden shift from an f- to a d-minor triad. Sonata 1/ii/28-32 sequences downwards by whole-steps, each step being approached through its own dominant (as implied by the appropriate dim.-7th chord). Some deceptive cadences, enharmonic dominants, and major-minor shifts occur in Sonata 12/i and ii that are unexpectedly Schubertian in flavor (Ex. 24).

Ex. 24. From Sonata 12/i by Baldassare Galuppi (after Benvenuti/GALUPPI-m 104, but without the editorial additions; by permission of the publisher, Francesco Bongiovanni in Bologna).

And considerable chromaticism occurs in isolated instances, harmonic (Son. 26/ii) as well as melodic (Son. 12/iii). There are also the surprises occasioned by progressions that have some precedent in the sonatas of the Venetians, including Marcello and Alberti, but in terms of the peak Vienna Classicists seem harsh, even crude. Such are the forceful sequences by major and minor 7th chords (e.g., Son. 1/i/7-9), the unprepared 9th in the opening theme of Sonata 11 (ms. 2), the weak-beat suspension in the opening theme of Sonata 14 (ms. 5), the several prominent cross relations (Son. 4/ii/13), the hidden octaves (Son. 12/i/35-36), and the parallel 5ths as well as anticipated resolutions in the treatment of the Alberti bass (Son. 1/ii/3-11). A device that is not gauche but becomes irritating in its excessive use is the cadential formula

91. Cf. Della Corte/GALUPPI 21-22.

made up of I^6_4, a trilled dotted note, and two notes of resolution (as at nearly every main pause in both mvts. of Son. 19).

One further trait in Galuppi's keyboard sonatas can hardly go unmentioned, and that is his expert, varied, and often novel use of the keyboard. The reference here is to idioms beyond the "*b.c.*" and Alberti bass settings noted earlier. Although Galuppi's obvious inclination toward fluency keeps his technical requirements from ever seeming inordinate—harder passages occur, for example, in the writing of both Marcello and Scarlatti—there are few idiomatic treatments known up to his time that cannot be found in his sonatas. One of his favorite treatments, used with great variety, is the division of a line, figure, or rhythm through interchanges between the hands (e.g., *Passa Tempo* no. 3/i/1-7). The mere division of the Alberti bass in this manner (Son. 11/34-44) adds a new rhythmic and even thematic interest to that device,[92] especially when it includes hand-crossing (Son. 2/iii/66-78). A maximum of hand-crossing occurs during the quasi-gigue finale of Sonata 28 (mss. 26-33) in a tuneful phrase group that seems to anticipate the "Trio" of Beethoven's Op. 10/3/iii. Double thirds make the interchanges more difficult in Sonata 13/iii/13-14. In Sonata 1/ii/14-16 there are rapid repeated notes and in Sonata 12/ii/38 there are broken octaves in both hands. Although the left hand is usually much less active, it has its share of the rapid scale passages in Sonata 11 in one movement (mss. 107-109). Arpeggios are another of Galuppi's specialties,[93] in one instance (Son. 4/i) rivaling those of the well-known study in Czerny's *Art of Finger Dexterity,* Op. 740, No. 2. In the form that they take in Sonata 12/i they anticipate Schubert's Impromptu in A♭, Op. 90, No. 4. If any further evidence be needed of Galuppi's devotion to the keyboard per se it can be found in free flights of virtuosity such as the extended ending of Sonata 1/ii or the veritable cadenzas in which the one-movement Sonatas 11 and 3 culminate.

Viewed in the light of the style traits discussed here, the first and even the second set of Galuppi's sonatas that Walsh published in 1756 and 1759 do hint at an earlier origin for at least some of them—unless, indeed, the conservatisms of these were custom-made to the mercenary Walsh's order, a not unlikely possibility then any more than it would be today. One notes in these sets the greater frequency of the "*b.c.*" settings described previously, and of bass parts in general that serve only as the barest harmonic supports; of long, purely mechanical sequences made from empty scalewise or chordal figures; of pseudopo-

92. Cf. Torrefranca/ORIGINI 138.
93. Cf. Torrefranca/ORIGINI 139-141.

lyphony; and of the harmonic "crudities" and cadence clichés listed earlier. One also notes in these two sets the lesser frequency of florid lines, of harmonic color, and of certain refinements of ornamentation and expressive markings that abound in *Passa Tempo,* the last set.

But these arguments might be countered, in turn, by a main strength in Galuppi's music, one that is not necessarily brought out by the mere tabulation of his chief style traits and one that reveals itself at least as clearly in the two Walsh sets as in any other Galuppi sonatas. It is his superior grasp of form. By treating his materials intensively rather than extensively—that is, by repeatedly returning to a few ideas rather than constantly evolving new ones—and by taking a large, uncomplicated view of tonality, he creates forms of exceptional unity and breadth. It is true that this important virtue of unity can at the same time be a chief fault, for not seldom do Galuppi's ideas seem somewhat flat in their lack of contrast and individuality. Yet, exceptional unity without the benefit of distinguished ideas seems to account for the success of two of his most convincing sonatas. These are the two in one movement, with long "cadenzas," in the Walsh sets, Sonatas 11 (Op. 1, No. 2) and 3 (Op. 2, No. 3).

It is noteworthy that Torrefranca, who had not been able to learn the contents of Walsh's first set, tentatively classified Sonata 11 as the most mature and perhaps latest of Galuppi's sonatas in spite of its admitted conservatisms.[94] In fact, this sonata inspired him to make comparisons not only with Beethoven, as usual, but with Wagner and Berlioz. However, even without the chauvinism that lies behind so much of Torrefranca's enthusiasm, one cannot help but find a special excitement in Galuppi's Sonata 11. The ideas and passage work do indeed lack interest in themselves. But these are distributed so logically and consistently, and kept moving by such forceful rhythmic and tonal direction (somewhat in the sweep of a "Toccata," as this piece was called in a contemporary MS[95]), that the form reaches its conclusion with a touch of the dramatic, fatalistic inevitability we know so well in Beethoven's more driving sonata movements.

In general and in the experience of this study, Galuppi ranks with the few best of our pre-Classic sonata composers in all countries. Of course, with the later dating of his sonatas by at least fifteen years he becomes not quite so "pre-" or so much of a forerunner as Torrefranca argued. But even in the 1750's and 1760's sonatas like Galuppi's three

94. Torrefranca/ORIGINI 271-277.

95. It is the third of 3 Galuppi "Toccate" in Cat. BRUXELLES II no. 6017 and a chief candidate for the piece Browning allegedly had in mind (cf. Borren/GALUPPI 367).

that rightly found their way into the "old masters" sets (Sons. 50, 49, and 35) are not often equalled by those of contemporary composers. One is tempted to attribute much of Galuppi's superiority to his long and successful experience as an opera composer. And the "beauty, clearness, and good modulation" by which he broadly defined "good music" for Burney[96] does seem to apply to the many cantilena melodies, nicely proportioned and appropriately harmonized, that occur in his sonatas as well as in his operas (insofar as one can still find examples[97]). However, another remark, credited to him by La Borde,[98] seems even more pertinent to the sonatas. It was to the effect that opera, chamber, and keyboard music each raises its own very different problems (in composition). The keyboard seems to have brought out especially a fantasy element in Galuppi's writing, not only in those two "cadenzas" of Sonatas 11 and 3 but in many decorative passages and free extensions in the second "half" of the longer movements. This fantasy element could well have been another factor, along with the *opera buffa* style, in the enthusiasm for Galuppi expressed by that master of fantasy, Emanuel Bach. Bach singled him out in his "Autobiography" after Galuppi had visited him in Berlin on his way to St. Petersburg.[99]

Our last in this group of pre-Classic Venetians, **Ferdinando Giuseppe Bertoni** (1725-1813), may be noted more briefly. Bertoni was born in Salò near Venice but studied primarily with Padre Martini in Bologna. A successor to Galuppi at St. Mark's as *maestro di cappella* in 1784, and the teacher of his nephew Ferdinando Turini and of G. B. Grazioli, both of whom we shall be meeting in Chapter X among composers in Venice and Padua, he was another singer-cembalist who made his chief and successful career in opera.[100] The extant instrumental music by him, less than Galuppi's, includes 6 sinfonias, 6 String Quartets Op. 2, one solo keyboard Sonata in E♭ in Anth. HAFFNER RACCOLTA-m no. 1,[101] and one set of 6 accompanied keyboard sonatas (the first we have met by a Venetian). The complete set (H-or-P & Vn) was published as Op. 1 in London during Bertoni's first period of opera

96. BURNEY'S TOURS I 134.
97. E.g., *Il Filosofo di campagna* in CLASSICI-m I No. 13.
98. La Borde/ESSAI III 189.
99. Kahl/SELBSTBIOGRAPHIEN 37. Cf. Della Corte/GALUPPI 23-24.
100. Haas/BERTONI is a recent, thorough diss. from Vienna, with much new biographic material, a full list of works, and a thematic index and full discussion of the instrumental works (the sons. are treated on pp. 84, 89, 92-93, and 204-251). Cf., also, Schmidl/DIZIONARIO I 172 and Suppl. 91-92; GROVE I 689-690 (Loewenberg). Caffi/STORIA I 419-444 (i.e., all of Chap. 50) concerns his life and choral works only, both sacred and secular.
101. Mod. ed.: Benvenuti/CEMBALISTI-m no. 1.

activities there, 1779-80, and in Paris shortly after.[102] It was also published in the next few years as Op. 9 and as Op. 11 (surprisingly enough for that time, right in Venice, by A. Zatta).[103]

Bertoni's solo sonata is in three movements, M-M-F, whereas all six sonatas in Op. 1 are in two movements in various pairings of moderate and fast tempos. The finales in this set include rondo, minuet, and gigue types. The *galant* style still prevails to the extent of thin texture, ornamental detail, and short-winded ideas. Binary design also prevails. Even in the larger movements there are not the clear returns to the initial idea that are needed to confirm ternary design. Otherwise, the regular period structures, balanced forms, use of the Alberti bass, and general keyboard style are about as progressive as Galuppi's. But Galuppi's original turns of melody and harmony, and his fantasy extensions are lacking. The competent, lighthearted, but undistinguished music that results, together with the hybrid position of the accompanied sonata in music literature, must explain the relatively little interest thus far expressed in Bertoni's sonatas. Certainly, the timid violin part adds no interest of its own. In those few instances when it does not simply double the top of the keyboard part or parallel it a 3d or 6th below, it attempts only the most fleeting imitations or plays intermittent chords in order to punctuate phrase endings and other cadences. In short, one is tempted to apply Burney's polite dictum on Bertoni's operas, based on firsthand experiences:[104] "Though the invention of this master is not very fertile, his melody is graceful and interesting; and though he never had perhaps sufficient genius and fire to attain the sublime, yet he is constantly natural, correct, and judicious; often pleasing, and sometimes happy." La Borde and Gerber came to remarkably similar conclusions.[105]

En route to our next locale, Naples, some 350 miles south, we should stop to visit our one composer in this volume who was active primarily in Rome, the more so as Venetian ties are still hinted. The obscure abbot Don **Lorenzo de** (or De) **Rossi** (1720-94), one of the innumerable Rossis waiting to ensnare unwary lexicographers,[106] was

102. Listed in BRITISH UNION I 105; BIBLIOTHÈQUE NATIONALE III 65; Johansson/FRENCH II Facs. 8, etc. Cf. Stone/ITALIAN I 201-209 (discussion with exx.), II 5 (thematic index), and III no. 16 (copy of entire Son. 5 in B♭, but without the Vn part).

103. Cf. BRITISH UNION I 105; Sartori/DIZIONARIO 171. There is no other set of acc'd. sons. by Bertoni, contrary to the articles on him in reference works.

104. Burney/HISTORY II 890.

105. La Borde/ESSAI III 168; Gerber/LEXICON I 152-153.

106. In Eitner/QL VIII he is "Rossi, Romano" on p. 321 but not "Rossi, Lorenzo" the Florentine, p. 323, who wrote late-18th-century symphonies. Nor should he be confused with another clerical Rossi who left keyboard sonatas about the same time—Ildefonso Rossi (cf. Gerber/LEXICON II 328; HIRSCH MUSIK-

another singer-cembalist, apparently above average in his skills.[107] Burney may actually have heard him in 1770 when he wrote, "The Abate Rossi is reckoned the neatest harpsichord player at Rome. . . . But, to say the truth, I have neither met with a *great* player on the harpsichord, nor an *original* composer for it throughout Italy."[108] There follows the highly pertinent footnote, "It seems as if Alberti was always to be pillaged or imitated in every modern harpsichord lesson." This Rossi has had the historically blank fate of composing only two pieces that have won any renown, then missing almost all recognition for them. His "Andantino and Allegro" have often been remarked and reprinted over the past ninety years under the name of the seventeenth-century Roman organist Michelangelo Rossi,[109] then readmired under the name of another Roman, Giuseppe de Rossi,[110] after the glaring centurial anachronism was recognized,[111] and finally relegated to almost total oblivion once the true source and its author were brought back to light.

This true source is *Sei Sonate per cembalo da esequirsi ancora coll'Organo, composte dal Sig. Abbate De Rossi Romano.*[112] The place of publication was Venice, the dates can now be given as between 1773 and 1782,[113] and, although no Christian name is given, Giuseppe had died about 1720,[114] leaving Lorenzo as the very likely if not only "Abbate De Rossi" active in Rome at any time near the style period concerned.[115] In this set Sonata 3 is made up of the known "Andantino and Allegro," all six sonatas being in the two-movement plan that we found to prevail in Alberti's sonatas. In his teens Rossi could well have known

BIBLIOTHEK III 150). The identification is not yet clear in Torrefranca/ORIGINI 459-460.

107. Cf. Schmidl/DIZIONARIO II 402-403 (the only recent account known here).

108. BURNEY'S TOURS I 236.

109. Cf. SBE 155. Among many eds.: Pauer/MEISTER-m III 56.

110. Since Torrefranca/ORIGINI 115 (originally in RMI XVII [1910] 353).

111. Werra/ROSSI.

112. Listed in full in Cat. BOLOGNA IV 41 and reported as the source in the complete mod. ed. (editorially enriched): Tenaglia/ROSSI-m 10. A MS copy (autograph?) is listed in PUBBLICAZIONI PISTOIA 93. The first half of Son. 5/i is reprinted in Schökel/BACH 154-155 (with discussion).

113. Inside the cover is a catalogue of Marescalchi and Canobbio (Torrefranca/ORIGINI 153 [with the 1740's suggested, as usual]), but these men were associated in Venice only between 1773 (not 1774) and 1782 (Sartori/DIZIONARIO 96; cf., also, p. 6).

114. Eitner/QL VIII 323.

115. The name needs some such confirmation because it appears unquestioned in what is merely a pseudo-facsimile designed as the title page for Tenaglia/ROSSI-m, with the wording slightly altered and without the original publisher or place. Apparently only from this source or by error Schmidl/DIZIONARIO II 403 gives Rome as the place of publication (*ca.* 1750), but Sartori/DIZIONARIO mentions not a single publisher of instrumental music in Rome after 1745 (cf. p. 49) in the 18th century!

Alberti while the latter was in Rome.[116] Burney's implication that the styles are similar seems justified, including several (but not too many) "singing-allegro" passages with Alberti bass (especially Sons. 2/i and 6/i). But now this style reveals the better control of a later generation. Although the forms themselves are short and binary in design—Torrefranca discusses them as ideal sonatinas[117]—the lines and syntactic relationships are broader, and the ideas are fewer and more dominating. In general, Rossi's music is light, fresh, skillful, convincing within its scope, and altogether representative of the decade in which it can now be dated.

Naples (Rutini)

By the mid-eighteenth century Naples had long been, as it still is, the radiating center of music in southern Italy.[118] Contemporary reports are even stronger: "I hardly need to repeat what all the world knows, which is that Naples is the center of the best music in Italy and the *non-plus-ultra* of performance."[119] Even more than Venice it depended for its musical sustenance on its four main conservatories, which chiefly supplied the church, and its theaters, especially the San Carlo, where opera flourished so significantly. Instrumental music was never so important in Naples as it was in Venice, especially if we recall that the authenticity and period of works traditionally attributed to the Neapolitan Pergolesi have been seriously questioned (SBE 196-199). Yet Naples had its school of cembalists, too—mainly singer-cembalists again, but not all sonata composers. Like the Neapolitan opera, this school may be said to have begun with Alessandro Scarlatti (whose chamber sonatas were noted in the previous volume). It includes Leo and Durante (also noted in the previous volume), Domenico Scarlatti (to be met in Madrid, in Chap. IX), Ferradini, Rutini, Prati, Guglielmi and Paradisi and Vento (to be met in London), the opera rivals Cimarosa and Paisiello (to be met among later Neapolitans, in Chap. X), and Piccinni (to be met among later composers active in Paris).

A very minor figure may be noted before we come to Rutini. The obscure Neapolitan **Antonio Ferradini** (*ca.* 1718-1779) is assumed here to have been a cembalist simply because his only known sonatas are for keyboard and because they reveal idiomatic keyboard writing. Prior

116. In Torrefranca/ORIGINI 584 there is even mention of a "misteriosa scuola romana del cembalo," known to Boccherini and brought to maturity by Clementi.
117. Torrefranca/ORIGINI 152-159, with exx.
118. Cf. MGG IX 1328-1336 (Mondolfi).
119. Grosley/MEMOIRES 92-93 (1758).

to World War II[120] these "Sei Sonate per il Clavicembalo" were in MS 41 of the former Königliche Öffentliche Bibliothek in Dresden, where Ferradini could have been active before moving to Prague in 1748.[121] Torrefranca assumes that the sonatas must have originated at least before 1756 and the start of the Seven Years' War, since they are dedicated (from Prague?) to an unspecified Saxon elector who was probably Frederick Augustus II, and since this indolent ruler but devoted patron of the arts is known to have fled from Dresden to Poland when the war began. But Torrefranca then goes on to hazard an even earlier date for the sonatas, suggesting a time when the composer could have been in Dresden or, as usual, "about 1740." Now his argument is the doubly shaky one that the use of the term "alla francese" (interesting in itself) over the presumably allegro movements in three of the sonatas (the "less expressive" ones, naturally!) ties in with the term "allegro alla francese," which he assures us was current about then.[122]

Ferradini's sonatas are described as being in from four to seven movements, which generally are short and are interconnected by suspensions extending from the cadence of one movement to the start of the next. The finale of Sonata 6 has the programmatic title of "La Chasse." In the longest of the sonatas is a "Minuetto" with nine variations. Although Torrefranca finds in these sonatas no unusual distinction in the musical ideas or their treatment, he does make special points of the freedom from formalism in the allegro movements and the expressive depth of the slow movements.[123]

Much more important—in fact, another of the main, pre-Mozartean heroes—in Torrefranca's writings is **Giovanni Marco** (or Maria) **Placido Rutini** (1723-97).[124] Although Rutini began and completed his life in Florence, and spent most of his active career outside of Italy, he is placed in Naples here by virtue of the training he is thought to have received from Fago and Leo in that city.[125] Sundry biographical dates, locations, dedications, and other information can be derived or deduced from some twenty publications that contain sonatas and from

120. Cf. GROVE V 172 (Cudworth).

121. Cf. Eitner/QL III 420; Torrefranca/ORIGINI 172-178, with exx. The biographical sources conflict, but Ferradini's operatic activities (cf. GROVE III 69 [Loewenberg]) suggest that Ferradini either returned to Italy in the 1750's or did not leave until about 1760. Neither Fürstenau/SACHSEN II nor Engländer/DRESDNER mentions Ferradini in Dresden.

122. The Spanish composer Misón used this term before 1766 (SCE IX).

123. Torrefranca/ORIGINI 173-175 and 176-177, respectively.

124. Cf. Torrefranca/ORIGINI 164-171, 461-478, 598-625, *et passim*, with many exx.; Torrefranca/MAESTRO. For the birth year cf. Schmidl/DIZIONARIO Suppl. 672.

125. Torrefranca/MAESTRO 243.

several cantatas and successful operas in print or MS. They show Rutini probably to have been in Naples from 1739-44, in Prague from
125a 1748 (at the same time as Ferradini), in Dresden in 1754, in Berlin and back in Prague in 1756, in St. Petersburg in 1758-61 (four years before Galuppi's stay), in Bologna in 1762 (in time to become a member of the Accademia dei Filarmonici and study with Padre Martini), in Florence and Venice in 1763 as well as Livorno and Genoa in 1764,[126] in Modena from 1766 to at least 1782,[127] and finally back in Florence.

The student who wishes to explore Rutini's sonatas in detail must first grope his way through a fascinating maze of bibliographic perplexities. Torrefranca led the way with a detailed list of Rutini's works in order to show that the different Christian names variously used by Rutini (or his publishers) can only refer to one man,[128] not to the supposed two or even three men formerly confused in another of those almost unravelable "brother problems."[129] The main argument, incidentally, was that coincidence alone could hardly explain the neat complementation in one series of the opus numbers that had been assigned to "each man," and confirmation has come recently with the discovery in St. Petersburg of a MS opera by "Rutini" in which all three Christian names precede the family name.[130] In 1936 Torrefranca improved on his own list of Rutini's works in an article with the somewhat ambitious title of "Il primo maestro di W. A. Mozart (Giovanni Maria Rutini)."[131] With this information plus still further
132a details that have been added since,[132] or can be added now, it becomes possible—indeed, necessary—to consolidate at least in very abbreviated fashion certain available facts of Rutini's sonata publications. (The known MSS of Rutini sonatas appear not to include any that did not achieve publication).

Rutini's Published Sonatas

Op. 1, 6 cembalo sons.; signed in Prague in 1748 (cf. Cat. BOLOGNA IV 63) though quite possibly not published until later, since this set appears to be the first of "2 Tom." announced at the Leipzig fair in the fall of 1757

126. Cf. Schmidl/DIZIONARIO II 423 and Suppl. 672.

127. Schmidl/DIZIONARIO II 423 gives 1766-74 as the Modena dates, but in Op. 14 (RUTINI/facs.-m), which is not likely to have appeared before 1782 (the latest date for Op. 13), Rutini still calls himself "Maestro di Capella di S. A. S. di Modena." He probably maintained connections in both Modena and Florence (cf. Torrefranca/ORIGINI 476-478) until the early 1780's.

128. Torrefranca/ORIGINI opposite p. 462, discussed pp. 461-467.

129. Cf. Eitner/QL VIII 368-370; Torchi/ISTRUMENTALE 257-258.

130. Mooser/ANNALES I 278 (with other new information, pp. 278-281).

131. Torrefranca/MAESTRO.

132. Especially in Schmidl/DIZIONARIO Suppl. 672 and Hoffmann-Erbrecht/HAFFNER.

(Göhler/MESSKATALOGEN III item 385 [386 being Rutini's Op. 3]). No publisher given, but probably Haffner in Nürnberg and at the composer's expense (cf. Torrefranca/MAESTRO 243-244). Mod. ed., complete but with excessive editorial "enrichment": CLASSICI-m I No. 27. Copied in full in Einstein/RUTINI-m XI (the late Dr. Alfred Einstein's generous loan of the 7 sets of Rutini's sonatas that he copied by hand in connection with his Mozart studies has been an invaluable help to the present discussion).

Op. 2, 6 cembalo sons.; signed in Prague, with dedication (reproduced in Cat. BOLOGNA IV 63) but no date. Haffner plate no. 82, *ca.* 1757 (evidently the 2d of the "2 Tom." noted under Op. 1). Mod. ed., entire (cf. Op. 1): CLASSICI-m I No. 27.

Op. 3, 6 cembalo sons.; signed in Prague, with dedication (in Cat. BOLOGNA IV 63) but no date. Haffner plate no. 96, *ca.* 1757; announced at the Leipzig fair in the spring of 1758 (Göhler/MESSKATALOGEN III item 386). Mod. ed., much "enriched": Sons. 3-5, Perinello/RUTINI-m.

"Op. 4," see Op. 5.

Op. 5, 6 cembalo sons.; signed in St. Petersburg, with dedication (in Cat. BOLOGNA IV 64) to Count Nikolaus Esterházy (Haydn's patron in Vienna from 1762) but no date. Haffner plate no. 104, *ca.* 1759; announced September 14, 1759, in the *Gazette de Saint-Pétersbourg* (Mooser/ANNALES I 279; but the mention here of "Août 1758" in the dedication to Op. 5 merely repeats an error that crept into the first list and discussions in Torrefranca/ORIGINI 472 and opposite p. 462). As discussed in complex detail in Torrefranca/MAESTRO 244-249, the Bolognese publisher Della (or dalla) Volpe used an "avviso" in his 1765 ed. of Rutini sonatas to make a retroactive correction in the opus numbers that Haffner had used and thus to fill the gap between Opp. 3 and 5:

Haffner's Op. 5 should be Op. 4.
Haffner's Op. 6 should be Op. 5.
Dalla Volpe's 1765 ed. becomes "Op. 6" (*q.v.*).

These "corrections" are adopted in the remainder of Torrefranca/MAESTRO *but not here,* since Haffner's original numbers still appear on the extant copies. Haffner himself had failed to follow the usual procedure of giving a separate series of opus numbers to the instrumental sets, for he gave Op. 4 to Rutini's cantata *Nò, non turbati* (1759). Actually, the copy of Op. 5 listed in Cat. BOLOGNA IV 64 is corrected in "old ink" to "Op. 4," perhaps by Rutini himself, since this could well be the set he supposedly presented along with Opp. 2 and 3 to Padre Martini (cf. Torrefranca/MAESTRO 245). Mod. ed., much "enriched": Sons. 1 and 5, Perinello/RUTINI-m. Copied in full in Einstein/RUTINI-m XI.

Op. 6, 6 cembalo sons.; undoubtedly dedicated in St. Petersburg (cf. Mooser/ANNALES I 279-280), though without place or date. Haffner plate no. 108, *ca.* 1760 (but Haffner's plate nos. hardly followed regularly enough to justify the "certain" conclusion in Mooser/ANNALES I 279 that Op. 6 appeared "almost immediately" after Op. 5). Cf. our entries for Op. 5 and for "Op. 6" of 1765. Mod. ed.: Son. 6/iii, Davison & Apel-m II no. 302. Copied in full in Einstein/RUTINI-m XI.

"Op. 6," 6 cembalo sons. Bologna: Lelio dalla Volpe (cf. Sartori/DIZIONARIO 59), 1765 (listed in Cat. BOLOGNA IV 62). This set was wrongly listed as "Op. VII?" in Torrefranca/ORIGINI 470 and opposite 462, but its claim to "Op. 6" is mentioned only in Della Volpe's retroactive correction of Haffner's plate numbers (cf. our entry for Op. 5; also, Torrefranca/MAESTRO 244-247). As it happens, when Della Volpe added that this set is "da me per la seconda volta ristampate" he seems to have meant that except for 4 new mvts. it is simply a reprint of Haffner's Op. 6. One can only assume that Della Volpe's "Op. 6" has the same contents as the publication by him once in Carlo Schmidl's valuable library (cf. Schmidl/DIZIONARIO II 423; also, DIZIONARIO RICORDI 958 and 1064), which is actually labelled Op. 6, has a different dedicatee, and only "accademico Filarmonico" after Rutini's name to suggest the date. Further complications are suggested by a Della Volpe ed. of 6 Rutini cembalo sons. labelled Op. 5 (!) and dated *ca.* 1756 as listed in Scheurleer/CATALOGUS II 328.

Op. 7, 6 cembalo sons. Bologna: Lelio dalla Volpe, 1770 (listed in PUBBLICAZIONI AMBROSINI 60-61). "Op. 7" does not appear in the title but is implied in the composer's note to the "Signori Dilettanti di Cembalo" when he refers to this set as "the seventh that I have offered" to them. In some but not all copies of Op. 7 (cf. BRITISH UNION II 909; WOLFFHEIM MUSIKBIBLIOTHEK I item 1472) a folio was later inserted, perhaps by Rutini himself (cf. Torrefranca/MAESTRO 247), with his portrait engraved on the right (reproduced in Mooser/ANNALES I Fig. 50) and a letter printed on the left that the famous poet Metastasio wrote to him February 18, 1771. Copied in full in Einstein/RUTINI-m XI.

Op. 8, 6 cembalo sons. Florence: Allegrini, Pisoni (cf. Sartori/DIZIONARIO 6), 1774 (listed in PUBBLICAZIONI FILARMONICA 26). No dedication. Mod. ed.: Son. 1, Paoli/ITALIANE-m 30. Copied in full in Einstein/RUTINI-m XII.

Op. 9, 6 cembalo sons. No date or publisher (but Zatta in Venice is named in an apparently different ed. of Op. 9 by "Ruttini" in the Archivio Musicale di Montecassino [listed in Dagnino/MONTECASSINO 295]). Signed by Rutini in Florence as "Maestro di Capella di S. A. S. il Principe Ereditario di Modena," with dedication to "il Signor Marchese di Priero." (This set, listed in PUBBLICAZIONI FIRENZE 279 but not previously explored in recent studies, has been made available here in a photographic copy very kindly provided by Professor Dragan Plamenac at the University of Illinois, who owns a copy of the original edition.)

Op. 10, (6?) K & Vn sons., evidently signed in Florence by 1780. Known only through a listing in BREITKOPF MS Suppl. XIV (1781) 49 and a reference in Prosniz/HANDBUCH I 127 to Opp. 10 and 11 as being in an Artaria catalog of 1780, though no listing of any Rutini work occurs in Weinmann/ARTARIA (cf. p. 5). In Torrefranca/ORIGINI 467-468 the attempt to relate Rutini's 4-hand *Divertimenti* in MS to Op. 9 (unknown then) or Op. 10 is proved wrong, in any case, now that a printed edition of the *Divertimenti* is known as Op. 18 (*q.v.*).

Op. 11, 6 K + Vn sons., "Incise in Firenze da Ranieri del Vivo" (cf. Op. 10). Listed only in Cat. BOLOGNA IV 144 and with the cembalo part missing. The dedicatee, "la Signora Contessa Eleonara di Colloredo," was a sister-in-law of Mozart's unfriendly patron in Salzburg, Archbishop Hieronymus, Count of Colloredo. A MS of 6 K + Vn sons. listed in

PUBBLICAZIONI PISTOIA 93 is probably this set. Cf., also, BREITKOPF MS Suppl. XIV (1781) 49.

Op. 12, 6 cembalo sons. Florence: Stecchi (cf. Sartori/DIZIONARIO 152) e Del Vivo, not after 1782 (cf. Eitner/QL VIII 369). An ed. by Zatta in Venice is listed in Dagnino/MONTECASSINO 295 as being in the Archivio Musicale di Montecassino. Cf., also, BREITKOPF MS Suppl. XIV (1781) 40.

Op. 13, 6 cembalo sons.; without publisher, place, date or dedication (listed merely as "Ruttini J. M." in MUSIKFREUNDE WIEN Suppl. 31), but not after 1782 (cf. Eitner/QL VIII 369). Copied in full in Einstein/RUTINI-m XII.

Op. 14, 3 K + Vn sons.; without publishers or date, but presumably not before the 1782 announcement of Opp. 12 and 13 (*q.v.*). Dedicated to the "Arci-Duchessa Maria Teresa d'Austria" and still signed by Rutini as "Maestro di Cappella di S. A. S. di Modena." Preserved in the Archivio Musicale di Montecassino (cf. Dagnino/MONTECASSINO 295). Mod. ed., entire: RUTINI/facs.-m (in score).

Opp. 15-17?

(Op. 18, *XII Divertimenti facili e brevi per cimbalo a 4 mani o arpe e cimbalo,* without place, date, or publisher. Listed in PUBBLICAZIONI NAPOLI 633.)

5 cembalo sons., one each in Anth. HAFFNER RACCOLTA-m I no. 5 (G), II no. 4 (C), III no. 4 (A), IV no. 6 (C), V no. 4 (G), 1756-65. (No vol. VI was published in this collection, contrary to Torrefranca/ORIGINI opposite p. 462.) Mod. eds.: Sons. in vols. II, III, IV, Pauer/MEISTER-m VI nos. 58, 57, 56, respectively; Sons. in vols. I, II, III, Benvenuti/CEMBALISTI-m nos. 13, 12, 11; Son. in vol. III, Tagliapietra/ANTOLOGIA-m XIII no. 12.

2 H-or-P + Vn sons., Anth. STEFFANN-RUTINI-m nos. 2 (D) and 4 (G), 1772 (Cf. Saint-Foix/MOZART II 167). Both sons. are extensive revisions (mainly so the Vn can participate) of movements from Op. 5 (no. 2 from Op. 5/1/i and Op. 5/3/iii [transposed]; no. 4 from Op. 5/6/i and iii).

Obviously Rutini was much more successful than the more celebrated and original Galuppi at getting his sonatas into print, the two men having written almost exactly the same number in the same years and in several of the same locales. Noteworthy is the interest in Rutini that the Nürnberg publisher Haffner maintained almost up to his last year (1767).[133] Added together, our list accounts for 88 published sonatas by Rutini.[134] Leaving out Opp. 10 and 11, 76 of the sonatas are extant and complete, although about 6 of these are duplications (in "Op. 6" and Anth. STEFFANN-RUTINI-m). Rutini still showed a preference of nearly four to one (11 out of 14 sets) for the solo as against the accompanied keyboard sonata, the latter appearing only relatively late in his production. Two departures from either of these settings occur

133. Cf. Hoffmann-Ebrecht/HAFFNER.

134. A thematic index of Op. 2 and the 7 sets copied in Einstein/RUTINI-m XI and XII (Opp. 1, 3, 5, 6, 7, 8, and 13) is provided in the useful master's thesis Hieronymus/RUTINI 99-125 and in Stone/ITALIAN II 74-88.

as characteristic novelties at the end of two of the later sets. The finale of Op. 8/6 is a setting of the tune "Clori amabile" (one of Rutini's own opera arias?), complete with words, while all of Op. 13/6 is a 4-hand duet.

In some 60 sonatas examined for the present study about 50 per cent are in 2 movements, 45 in 3, and only 5 in 4 movements. Except for the absence of one-movement sonatas and the preponderance of the 2-movement type in the later, lighter sets, the number of movements seems to be almost as indeterminate as in Galuppi's sonatas. Nor can the order of the movements be stated much more conclusively, especially through Op. 6. As with Galuppi, moderate and fast movements prevail; slow movements do not occur side-by-side nor as finales; and the many literal or quasi-gigues and minuets serve most often as finales. Only one finale is a set of variations (Op. 7/6/iii). Certain arrangements of the movements do occur fairly consistently within the later sets. Thus, in every sonata of Opp. 7 and 9 the first movement is tonally prepared by a short, cadential, free "Preludio." Apart from this introduction, the 2-movement plan of F-F or F-M obtains throughout Op. 7, and the 3-movement plan of M or F-"minúè"-*balletto* obtains in 4 sonatas of Op. 9. All 9 sonatas of Opp. 8 and 14 are in 2 movements, 7 of the finales being called "Rondo," or "Tempo di minuet" (if not "Minuet"), or both. Interrelations between the movements within a cycle are achieved by generally effective contrasts of style and meter, by an occasional ending on a half cadence (Op. 3/4/i also ends with the words "Attaca subito la Giga"), and by a few of those loose but probably intentional relationships of incipits that turn up at least infrequently in many a Classic composer's sonatas (as in the outer mvts. of Op. 3/3 or the first 2 mvts. of Op. 3/4, or all 3 mvts. in Op. 5/4 and 5/5).

Only rarely are Rutini's sonatas in keys of as many as 4 sharps or flats and only about 15 per cent of the keys are minor. With regard to key schemes, this composer, like Galuppi, keeps the movements in the same key within each of most of his sonatas. Infrequently, and chiefly in the earlier sonatas, one movement is in the alternate tonic mode or in the relative or dominant key. Somewhat more often the trio (or second minuet) of a *da capo* minuet design is in the alternate tonic mode. Op. 13/4/iii is a *da capo* minuet with a "Giga" in the tonic minor as its middle section. Exceptional, too, is Op. 5/5/iii (the finale of 3 movements all in f), which is a *da capo* "Presto," this time with a "Minuetto" in the tonic major as the middle section.

As already hinted, distinct style trends can be observed when

Rutini's sonatas are examined in their chronological order from Op. 1 to Op. 14. They fall rather clearly into three groups, quite apart from a rather steady advance in craftsmanship in the first half-dozen sets. In Opp. 1 and 2 the material is treated somewhat repetitiously and without clear structural perspective, both because the language is still motivic and because the composer had not yet gained control of his means. Opp. 3, 5, and 6 mark the unquestionable peak in Rutini's sonatas, Op. 5 in particular being a set that deserves a chance to be known again, in a careful, ungarnished modern edition. A tight motivic consistency is still present but the harmonic rhythm is slower and the motive's repetitions are balanced in appositions and oppositions that now permit distinct phrase and period relationships to prevail much of the time. And even more conspicuous in these sets than the changes in style of continuation are the new imagination, seriousness, sentiment, and drama. But the latter advances were soon abandoned by Rutini. Either he had gone as far in these respects as his talents could reach or he found himself in an environment where such efforts could not be appreciated. For after a slight tapering off in Op. 6 there is an abrupt shift in Op. 7 to a facile, popular, routine style that would be more likely to attract the musical public at large and that Rutini adopted thereafter. Whatever the reason, like Emanuel Bach and most of the other pre-Classic figures, Rutini slipped back instead of trying to surmount the further artistic obstacles, which were later overcome by the three great masters of Vienna.

It will be pertinent to sample the styles in each of Rutini's three groups of sonatas. But first, certain more objective traits may be noted that remained fairly constant throughout his production. Insofar as these traits apply, Rutini's music does not quite attain the moments of interest that were noted in Galuppi's music. To start with Rutini's musical ideas, we may note that these are almost always fragmentary, whether they are single motives (Op. 2/1/i), composites of motives (Op. 14/3/i), or merely successions of idiomatic keyboard figures (Op. 6/6/iii). The rests that separate the motives, the variety of pointed rhythms that occur within them, and the frequent short or long trills, turns, and appoggiaturas (Op. 5/1/i; also, Ex. 25, *infra*) do not keep the ideas from being tuneful (Op. 9/4/ii) but do rule out the long songful lines such as Galuppi often wrote. Thus, even when Rutini's ideas are set in the "singing-allegro" style with Alberti bass (Op. 2/3/i) they do not seem especially to call Mozart's writing to mind. This relationship is more likely to be suggested when the fragments are symmetrically ordered and when they cadence on chromatic appoggiaturas (Op. 8/1/i).

Rutini's harmony is always appropriate but never exceptional for its period. As usual, it is most compelling in the dominant chains of sequential passages, but neither in vocabulary nor dissonance treatment does it disclose the surprises and occasional near crudities found in Galuppi's sonatas. Rutini's textures also show skill and variety but no exceptional treatments.. The bass is mostly of the simplest sort—a single or double note repeated statically (Op. 6/6/i), octaves broken in "murky" fashion (Op. 8/2/ii), or chordal figures (with little else in Op. 1/5/iii/48-57). However, except in Op. 8 the literal Alberti bass is used less than might be expected and then chiefly for what seem to be deliberately stylized effects (as in Op. 5/3/ii, a movement with much tuneful charm). In the thinnest, 2-part writing (Op. 6/5/i) one can safely assume that the performer was expected to fill out the texture, the surest evidence being that specific figures are given for a filler part throughout much of Opp. 8, 9, and 13 (SCE V, with ex.). Only rarely does the left hand carry the main thematic interest (Op. 2/4/ii/17-20), but it does often engage in simple imitations with the right hand (Op. 5/6/iv/"Trio"). Such imitations, of course, become the main resource of the "Secondo" in Op. 13/6 and the violin parts in the accompanied sonatas (as a comparison of the arrangements in Anth. STEFFANN-RUTINI-m with the originals in Op. 5 so instructively demonstrates). They represent Rutini's nearest approaches to polyphonic writing. It is not that this student of Padre Martini and translator of part of the French edition of Marpurg's *Traité de la Fugue*[135] could not have gone further. But, as we saw in the previous volume,[136] even his scholarly teacher had already made similar concessions by 1747 to the new lighter style.

In Rutini's use of the keyboard there is good understanding and variety, although again he failed to attain quite the interest and imagination found in Galuppi's sonatas. Runs, arpeggios, and hand-crossing are frequent, as can be seen in such starts toward virtuosity as the quasi-gigue finale of Op. 1/6, the toccata-like "Preludio" of Op. 3/1, and the generally tricky "Allegretto" that concludes Op. 3/5. "Cembalo" is the instrument specified through Op. 13, although the preface from Op. 7 to be quoted shortly, the melody in right-hand octaves in Op. 8/1/50-52, the figures calling for a filler part from Op. 8 on, the word "crescendo" first in Op. 13/1/29-30, and the actual alternative of "Forte

135. Cf. Torrefranca/ORIGINI 473-474.
136. SBE 183; cf., also, Torrefranca/ORIGINI 735-736.

Piano" in Anth. STEFFANN-RUTINI-m suggest that Rutini was up-to-date in thinking of the piano as well as the harpsichord in his later sets.

In the matter of Rutini's structural designs, the ternary plan is made conspicuous by its relative absence. When it does appear, complete with contrasting idea (as in Op. 6/4/i and Op. 7/5/ii [one of the most telling movements in Op. 7]), it is just purposeful enough to suggest that Rutini saw the possibility, though he generally preferred other solutions. His forms are still fluid, but, especially in the more extended, faster ones, three practices tend away from the sense of "sonata-allegro" form. One is the gradual reduction of the initial idea to modulatory motivic play, thus effacing the clear syntax within sections. Another is the return to the initial idea too soon after the double-bar—that is, after too brief a departure—to sound like a return. And the third is the placing of this return in the tonic key, giving the rather undynamic effect of parallelism rather than opposition between the two "halves." The first movement of Sonata 5 in C, in Anth. HAFFNER RACCOLTA-m IV no. 6, is typical. Its initial idea is stated in mss. 1-2 (Ex. 25),

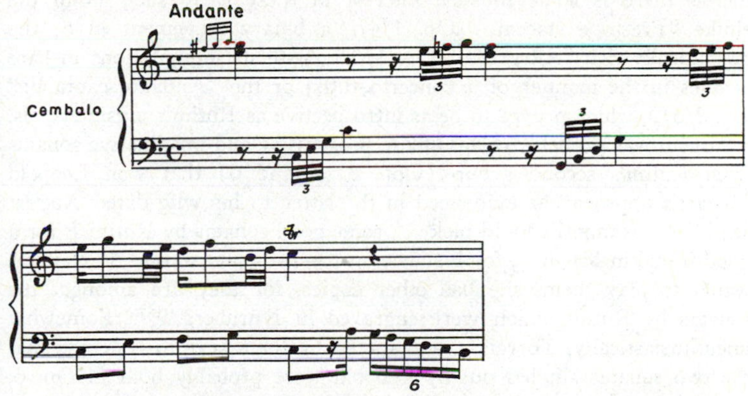

Ex. 25. From the opening of Giovanni Marco Placido Rutini's Sonata in C in Anth. HAFFNER RACCOLTA-m IV/6 (after Pauer/MEISTER-m VI 38).

repeated an octave lower in mss. 3-4, then reduced and recast in several forms during the modulation to the dominant key, mss. 5-12. A second idea, affording exceptional contrast for Rutini, is stated in the new key in mss. 13-14 and repeated with enrichments, mss. 15-17, prior to the double-bar. Beginning the second half (an exact half), the initial idea is stated intact in the new key, mss. 18-19, then repeated at once in the tonic key, mss. 20-21. Sequential exchanges on the scalewise and chordal figures within this idea effect a digression to the relative minor key, mss. 22-25; but reductions of it like those in the first half restore the home key, mss. 26-29. An exact transposition of the complete second idea into this key, mss. 30-34, closes the second half as the first half had been closed.

Coming back to Rutini's three style groups, a sample of the indeterminate motivic writing in the first (Opp. 1 and 2) may be cited almost at random. For example, in Op. 1/4/i in A repetitions or variants of the initial motive occur in almost every measure, falling mostly into two-measure units. These short-breathed units and a fast harmonic rhythm inherent in the motive itself result in tonal movements that spend themselves quickly. Hence, in place of one broad shift from tonic to dominant in the first "half" of this movement, there is the vacillating effect of no fewer than three shifts to-and-fro. The fact that the rest of the movement happens to complete a literal A-B-A design means that this process is almost certain to become monotonous. Nevertheless there is some musical interest in these early sets, as in the elflike "Presto e staccato" Op. 1/4/i, a binary movement in c; the thematically rich "Allegretto" Op. 1/5/ii, with its interruptions in bare octaves in the manner of a concerto tutti; or the "Andante cantabile" Op. 2/3/ii, which proves to be as introspective as Rutini's music ever is.

But it was probably certain more progressive and imaginative sonatas from Rutini's second group (Opp. 3, 5, and 6) that won Leopold Mozart's approval, as evidenced in the letter to his wife dated August 18, 1771: "Nannerl should pick . . . some good sonatas by Rutini ["for a good friend in Milan"], for instance, in E♭, in D and so on. If Nannerl wants to play them, she has other copies, for they are amongst the sonatas by Rutini which were engraved in Nürnberg."[137] Somewhat unenthusiastically, Torrefranca is forced by their keys to conclude that the two sonatas singled out by Leopold were probably both in Op. 6, specifically Nos. 2 in D and 6 in E♭.[138] These two sonatas do have Mozartean charm, if more in Leopold's than Wolfgang's vein, especially in the almost naïve directness of Op. 6/2/i and Op. 6/6/ii. But Torrefranca obviously would have preferred, as most others probably would, to single out the three sonatas in minor keys in Rutini's second group, one in each set. These are Op. 3/4 in d, Op. 5/5 in f, and Op. 6/5 in

137. As trans. in Anderson/MOZART I 281; cf. the German original in Mueller von Asow/MOZART I 197. In Torrefranca/MAESTRO 242-243, the date, recipient, and key of E♭ are all given incorrectly, but fortunately "E" is later argued to mean "E♭" anyway (pp. 252-253).

138. Torrefranca/MAESTRO 252-253, with "op. V" still meaning Haffner's original Op. 6.

g.[139] The keys themselves are ones we have found to be reserved for some of the most affective of the pre-Classic sonatas (SCE VI), and so they are in Rutini's music.

In Op. 3/4/i there are dramatic traits of a surprisingly Beethovian turn, including abrupt *forte-piano* (or *-dolce*) contrasts in a genuine opening "theme" (Ex. 26), reiterated *sforzando* syncopations (marked

Ex. 26. From the opening of Giovanni Marco Placido Rutini's Sonata Op. 3/4/i (after Einstein/RUTINI-m XI).

"for:" each time), driving sequential modulations after the double-bar, and a lingering before an abrupt *forte* close. The driving "Giga" that follows without break and the tender "Tempo di Minuetto" finale, both in rondo form, are worthy companions to this superior example of the pre-Classic Italian sonata. Even stronger, and the Rutini sonata that is considered his best here, is Op. 5/5 in f. The opening "Andante" in this work moves logically through a fragmented melodic line made up of tremulous sighs and accompanied by a steadily oscillating bass that is effective for all its simplicity. The Allegro that follows is another dramatic movement, one of those several anticipations of the spirit if

139. For the Sons. in f and g cf. Torrefranca/ORIGINI 603-609 and 619-623, including extended exx.

not the melodic shapes of Beethoven's Op. 2/1/i in f. And the finale is a lean "Presto" in 3/8 meter, neatly managed by alternating hands and relieved in its rush by the central "Minuetto" in the tonic major key. This movement has a bit of the suppressed intensity of a swift Brahms scherzo. Op. 6/5/i is especially interesting as a rondo constructed nearly in the square manner of the Couperin rondeau except for its forcefully extended retransitions. Among much else of interest in Rutini's second group are movements like Op. 5/3/i, a fine display of keyboard dexterity that Torrefranca would like to call "La Caccia";[140] Op. 5/4/ii, a wistful, folklike piece; and Op. 6/4/i, a rapid, deft piece in e, with sudden darts and thrusts quite in the manner of a Mendelssohn scherzo.

Rutini's third group (Opp. 7-14) is at times almost too light and elementary to consider seriously. The movements are shorter (averaging in the first fast movements 30-40 instead of the 75-100 measures in the second group), new lighter dance titles appear (especially "Balletto"), the use of the keyboard is simplified, and the dramatic, affective writing is gone. More interesting here is Rutini's declared change-over to the new style. In his preface to Op. 7, addressed, significantly, "To the *Signori dilettanti* of the cembalo," he notes the cembalist's need to sight-read well, if only so he can accompany; the cembalist's problem of reading two staffs at once and the greater clarity of printed music; the hope that his (Rutini's) sonatas will bring public approval; and the fact that, in these sonatas,

> I have sought to avoid confusion, trying to make them natural and without difficult keys. It seems to me I have achieved what I wanted to, since a little girl ten years old plays them all without finding anything beyond her ability when she studies them. I have tried to make them charming so far as my little talent has allowed me to. In order to please the [more conservative?] students I have introduced a Preludio in every sonata, since we see so few of them [now]. In order to get the [right] effect on the cembalo [pianoforte?] one has to [be able to] soften the tone abruptly and keep the hand agile. . . .[141]

Metastasio's polite acknowledgement of a copy of Op. 7 that Rutini sent him is interesting for its concurrence as to the "ease of execution" of these sonatas and their appeal to the student.[142] Furthermore, in the dedication of Op. 9 Rutini added a more positive aesthetic reason, or what might be called a Classic justification, for his change of style:

140. Torrefranca/ORIGINI 612-617.

141. Quoted (except for minor revisions and additions made here) from Hieronymus/RUTINI 76, where the whole preface is trans. after the copy of the original in Einstein/RUTINI-m XI.

142. The original and translation are given in Einstein/MOZART 240-241.

"In these sonatas I have aimed at [still] more brevity and ease, in order, I hope, to better satisfy the inclinations of the students. I have made sure that the style is songful, judging that any instrument that approaches the voice becomes more attractive to the extent the graces of nature triumph over the fussy embellishments of art."

In Naples and in this chapter there remains at this point only to give a passing mention to **Alessio Prati** (1750-88), pupil of Piccinni (though Prati's sonatas were composed earlier than the latter's) and another singer-cembalist. Born in Ferrara he is placed in Naples by virtue of his conservatory training there and because in the but twenty years left to him after graduation—to recall the eighteenth-century musician's often hectic career—he was active in Naples, Bologna, Paris, St. Petersburg, Vienna, Munich, Ferrara, and Venice.[143] He left at least four sets of a total of fifteen accompanied sonatas (K-or-harp & Vn), published in Berlin and Paris in French titles and probably composed mostly in the late 1770's while he was in Paris[144] and before his stay in St. Petersburg (1782-83). The three sonatas that could be examined here (Op. 6) are purely homophonic, with lyrical but stiffly phrased melodies, double-notes and interchanges of the hands, and nothing but Alberti bass or repeated-note accompaniments. They suggest little reason for further study in spite of the considerable interest in Prati's operas in his own day.

143. Cf. Eitner/QL VIII 51-52; Mooser/ANNALES II 398-400, III Fig. 76 (portrait).

144. Cf. Johansson/FRENCH II Facs. 66, 75, etc.

Chapter VIII

The Ensemble Sonata in Italy From About 1740 to 1780

At the start of the previous chapter the division of subject matter between that and this chapter was discussed. Aside from history's inevitable crossing of lines, these two chapters separate keyboard composers active primarily in Venice and Naples, often under Padre Martini's influence, from string composers active primarily in Milan and Tuscany, mostly under Tartini's influence. Since the string composers cultivated chiefly the melo/bass settings and since such settings were more traditional than the solo and accompanied keyboard types, the chapters may seem to be out of chronological order. However, we have seen that the melo/bass settings were fast becoming mere carry-overs of former practices, barely disguising the same newer textures and styles that were taking hold in most other music of the time. Furthermore, this chapter takes us on to certain composers, notably Boccherini, whose "pre-Classic" output paralleled rather than preceded the high-Classic output of Haydn and Mozart.

In the previous chapter it was possible to cite basic studies on the sonatas of each of our main composers. In the present chapter it will be possible to do the same for Nardini and Pugnani. But, surprisingly enough, no such studies, completed or in progress, can be reported on the sonatas of two of our Italians most important to Classic instrumental music, G. B. Sammartini and Boccherini.

Milan (G. B. Sammartini)

Under Austrian control through most of the eighteenth century, Milan, capital of Lombardy, seems to have struck visitors as the most "German" in musical character among Italian cities.[1] From the standpoint of instrumentally minded Germans and Austrians like Gluck, J. C. Bach,

1. Cf. Saint-Foix/MOZART I 336.

and the Mozarts, father and son, one reason is not hard to find. Milan, lacking the native opera (though not the strong musical interests[2]) of Venice, Bologna, and Naples, was peculiarly open and fitted to the cultivation of instrumental groups and activities.[3] There were no distinguished singer-cembalists to mention, but the chamber groups and opera orchestra were outstanding.[4] In these activities two guiding stars were certainly the brothers Sammartini, the elder being Giuseppe the oboist, who by 1727 had already gone to London (where we shall meet him), and the younger being the lifelong church organist in Milan whom we shall now meet, **Giovanni Battista Sammartini** (or San Martini, Martini of Milan, etc.; *ca.* 1700-75).

Of French extraction, G. B. Sammartini began primarily as a church composer, but from the time of his oratorio "Sinfonia" in 1724, he paid increasing attention to instrumental music.[5] In this latter capacity he made his chief mark in his own day[6] and has aroused much interest in recent times. This interest has led to several valuable studies shortly to be cited, with Torrefranca leading the way again but with scholars in other countries responding, too, and in the main with equal enthusiasm. Quite apart from the music itself, such interest is not surprising when one recalls that G. B. Sammartini was the influential teacher of Gluck for four years,[7] and one model for Mozart,[8] J. C. Bach,[9] and Haydn (controversial as the nature of this last influence may be[10]), among others.

The writing done on Sammartini in recent times started with his symphonies,[11] but soon extended to his equally important chamber music.[12] Within the latter category, of course, come his works identified by the title "sonata." But we shall see that he sometimes made this term interchangeable with sinfonia, as also with the terms overture and concerto, in one of those not infrequent survivals of Baroque

2. Cf. BURNEY'S TOURS I 64-85.
3. Cf. Torrefranca/ORIGINI 361-362; GROVE V 752 (Barblan).
4. Cf. the reports by Quantz (Kahl/SELBSTBIOGRAPHIEN 142-143), L. Mozart (Anderson/MOZART I 256), and Burney (BURNEY'S TOURS I 67, 71-72, 74). Cf., also, Carse/XVIIIth 82-83; Cesari/GIULINI 19-22.
5. Cf. pp. 5 and 6 in Sartori/SAMMARTINI (with further new biographic information).
6. Cf. Burney/HISTORY II 454, 924; La Borde/ESSAI III 233; Carpani/HAYDINE 58-62.
7. Cf. Einstein/GLUCK 14-17; SBE 334-335.
8. Cf. Einstein/MOZART 171; also, Anderson/MOZART I 165, 257.
9. Cf. SCE 708, *infra;* also, Schökel/BACH 64-72.
10. Cf. Carpani/HAYDINE; Griesinger/HAYDN 12; Torrefranca/SANMARTINI (XXI) 304-308.
11. Torrefranca/SANMARTINI. Cf., also, Barblan/SANMARTINI.
12. Sondheimer/SAMMARTINI; Mishkin/QUARTETS.

terminological confusion.[13] In fact, this observation brings us indirectly to yet another bibliographic muddle based on a "brother problem" —by now, one of the better known "brother problems" of the eighteenth century—and yet another realization that any attempt to pin down a composer's styles and influences must presuppose a knowledge of what he actually wrote, when he wrote it, and in what order. The problem arises here, in both publications and MSS, when the Christian name is missing, or even when it is present in earlier works, since some of these have been shown to bear the wrong brother's name. Unacknowledged transcriptions by one brother of the other's music, and conflicting or duplicate opus numbers merely thicken the muddle. To be sure, some of this problem has been resolved, at least as regards the published works, in two pioneer studies,[14] so that little else but the conclusions, and only those that concern the sonata, need to be summarized here. As for the many more works in MS, which complete what Burney called G. B. Sammartini's "incredible number of spirited and agreeable compositions, [composed] between the years 1740 and 1770,"[15] little beyond estimates can be given as yet. But it is encouraging to learn
16a that new studies and the long needed thematic index are in progress.[16]

G. B. Sammartini's separate sets of extant published sonatas include, in order of quantity, at least seven in SS/- or SSS/bass settings, four in SS settings, two in S/bass settings, and one set of the accompanied keyboard type. There are also numerous sonatas in published anthologies, including at least six examples for keyboard solo, bringing the total to over one hundred sonatas in publications alone.[17] A digest list follows, with the numerous "trio" and "quatuor" settings coming first:

G. B. Sammartini's Published Sonatas

A. 12 SS/- and SSS/bass sons., Op. 2. Paris: Le Clerc, 1742 or earlier. Although "Giuseppe" is specified in the title, all 12 sons. appear in further sources that are credited to G. B. Sammartini, "Martini," or Brioschi, and are variously called "Trio," "Overtura," "Concertino," and "Sinfonia." (For that matter, only "Giuseppe" is named in all the early Sammartini

13. Cf. Cesari/GIULINI 15-17.

14. Saint-Foix/SAMMARTINI; Mishkin/SAMMARTINI.

15. Burney/HISTORY II 454. In Fétis/BU VII 389 is a debatable hint of more than 2,800 works by G. B. Sammartini.

16. At the time of this writing (1960) Miss Bathia Churgin of Vassar College is completing a dissertation at Radcliffe College on the symphonies of G. B. Sammartini and is preparing a thematic index of his instrumental works in collaboration with Mr. Newell Jenkins of New York City. Her contributions to the present discussion, including new information and the loan of the Le Clerc ed of Op. 5 (our item C. below) on microfilm, are gratefully acknowledged.

17. Although extant copies are widely dispersed and the ascriptions remain confused, BRITISH UNION II 919-921 gives the most comprehensive listing of the son. publications of the two brothers.

publications in France, but G. B. is not invariably intended, as was first maintained in Saint-Foix/SAMMARTINI 310, then contradicted for Giuseppe's Opp. 1 and 3.) Sons. 2, 6, 10, and 12 are ascribed to another Milanese instrumental composer of the time, Antonio Brioschi (cf. La Laurencie/BLANCHETON I 43). Thematic index of first mvts. in Saint-Foix/SAMMARTINI 311-312.

B. 6 SS/bass sons., Op. 1. London: Simpson, 1744; later reprints by Cox and Bremner. Son. 3 is by another composer, probably Brioschi (according to information from Miss Churgin), but is credited to G. B. Sammartini in the mod. ed. COLLEGIUM MUSICUM-m No. 28.

C. 12 SS/- and SSS/bass sons., Op. 5. Paris: Le Clerc, *ca.* 1748. "Giuseppe" is specified in the title and defended as the actual composer in Mishkin/SAMMARTINI 368-371; but G. B. Sammartini's authorship is argued in Saint-Foix/SAMMARTINI (and accepted here, on the bases both of style and of "numerous" MS copies of sons. in this set that do have the latter's name [according to detailed information from Miss Churgin]).

D. 6 SS/bass sons., Op. 5. London: I. Walsh, 1756.

E. 6 SS/bass sons. (*Sei Sonate notturne a due violini e basso*), Op. 7. Paris: Le Clerc, *ca.* 1760. Mod. ed., complete but much "enriched": CLASSICI-m I No. 28. The same sonatas comprise the 6 SS/bass "trios," Op. 5 (wrongly corrected to Op. 6 in Saint-Foix/SAMMARTINI 313?) published by Huberty in Paris in 1766 (not 1760; cf. Johansson/FRENCH I 46). 17a

F. 6 SSS/bass "Sonatas called Notturnis," Op. 9. London: Walsh, 1762 (Saint-Foix/SAMMARTINI 321).

G. 6 SS/bass sons., without op. no. London: A. Hummel, 1762 (Saint-Foix/SAMMARTINI 320).

H. 3 or 4 SS/bass sons. in 2 anthologies with Lampugnani, published by Walsh as Opp. 1 and 2, 1744 and 1745 (cf. BRITISH UNION II 593; SBE 335-336), including Son. 3 in Op. 1 and Sons. 1 (or Brioschi?), 3, and 5 in Op. 2. But in the anthology with Brioschi published as a "3d set" by Walsh, 1746, Sons. 3, 5, and probably 4 are by Brioschi, while the others may or may not be by G. B. Sammartini (according to information from Miss Churgin).

I. 24 of the then popular unaccompanied duet sons. (Fl or Vn), 6 each in 4 sets published by Walsh as Op. 4, 1748; Op. 5, 1756; Op. 7 (and as a later Op. 5!), "A second set. . . ," 1757; Op. 10, "A third set. . . ," 1763. Cf. BRITISH UNION II 919.

J. 6 S/bass "Solos" (Fl or Vn), Op. 8. London: Walsh, 1759 (same as 6 S/bass "Sonatas" published without op. no. by Hummel in 1765? cf., also, Cucuel/DOCUMENTS 388).

K. 6 "easy" S/bass "Solos" (Fl or Vn), no op. no. London: Bremner, 1765.

L. 6 acc'd. sons. (K & Vn), dedicated to the "Marchesana di Rockingamme" by the Milanese singer (and publisher?) Ercole Ciprandi, dated 1766 in London. Also published in the same year by Venier in Paris (Saint-Foix/SAMMARTINI 316, 323; cf. Johansson/FRENCH I 161).

M. 6 solo keyboard sons. in Anth. JOZZI-m I nos. 2 and 3, II nos. 2 and 4, III nos. 2 and 3 (1761-64; cf. Saint-Foix/SAMMARTINI 320; BRITISH UNION II 613). Mod. ed.: Son. in C, no. 2 in vol. II, Saint-Foix/SAM-

MARTINI-m (with preface). In 1954 Curci in Milan published 2 other, one-mvt. keyboard Sons. in C (Maffioletti), neither from this source (according to information from Miss Churgin).

The many MS sonatas attributable to G. B. Sammartini are widely scattered, mostly undated, often duplicated, and hard to chronologize. They fall into the same categories as the published sets and in about the same quantitative proportions, starting with over 135 "trio" sonatas.[18] Of these last, about 40 are in the Sarasin collection in Basel,[19] comprising the corpus examined by Sondheimer, who concluded that Sammartini's chamber music is of even more historical significance to Classic music than his symphonies.[20] There are 36 melo/bass compositions attributed to Sammartini in the Blancheton collection in Paris,[21] of which 2 are clearly concertos for soloist and an orchestral group whereas the remaining 34 are of that pre-Classic sort that could be played one to a part as chamber music or doubled and multiplied into one of those English "overtures-in-8-parts" (SCE V). The 34 titles seem to have little distinction with regard to setting (SS/-, SSS/-, SSA/bass, etc.), style, or form. They include 11 uses of "Concertino," 9 of "Sinfonia," 9 of "Overtura," 3 of "Sonata," and 2 of "Trio." Until recently, remarkably few Sammartini MSS were thought to have survived in Italy.[22] In fact, in Sammartini's own city of Milan only one MS—not an autograph, at that—could be found by the Milanese scholar Gaetano Cesari, this being another set of 6 SS/bass *Sonate notturne,* similar to but different in content from the published item E. listed earlier.[23] (This MS set had been handed down through the still active family of Sammartini's dilettante pupil Giorgio Giulini, himself an interesting composer of symphonies.[24])

Among other extant MSS by G. B. Sammartini that are pertinent

18. According to Miss Churgin.
19. Cf. Cat. BASEL 74.
20. Sondheimer/SAMMARTINI, with extended exx. Mod. eds.: Sons. in C and E♭ (*ca.* 1740 and 1755, Sarasin 81 and 223), SAMMLUNG SONDHEIMER-m Nos. 37 and 38.
21. Cf. La Laurencie/BLANCHETON II 27-47, with thematic index. According to Miss Churgin 7 of these compositions are probably by Brioschi or others.
22. Cf. Eitner/QL 408-410. Actually, there is "a large collection" of his "trios" in the Noseda collection of the Milan Conservatory, according to information from Miss Churgin.
23. Cesari/SANMARTINI, with thematic index of first mvts.; the alternative version of Son. 2 described on p. 482 is the one printed in SAMMLUNG SONDHEIMER-m No. 38. Our item F., being SSS/bass, is probably not the same as either E. or Cesari's set. Roncaglia/SAMMARTINI simply reports the "discovery" of still another "Trio" (cf. PUBBLICAZIONI MODENA 492, but SS/bass!), in the same setting and general plan though not called "Sonata notturna"; this is the same as our D./2, *supra,* according to information from Miss Churgin.
24. Cf. Cesari/GIULINI.

here are some twelve S/bass "solos" for flute and/or violin and eight keyboard sonatas in one or more movements.[25] That this Sammartini left sonatas originally for cello and *b.c.*, as is usually supposed by virtue of the nineteenth- and twentieth-century editions ascribed to him,[26] now seems somewhat doubtful. The best known example, the one in G, has been identified as Joseph dall'Abaco's (SBE 338); the only known publication, now lost, was actually ascribed to Giuseppe,[27] whose near-Handelian style would, in any case, seem closer to the cello sonatas in question; and Eitner's listing of MS cello sonatas in Padua appears to be in error.[28] However, there do seem to be those cembalo sonatas in MS, including five in Bologna,[29] one of which is the Sonata in C in Benvenuti/CEMBALISTI-m no. 15.[30] Since this last is simply a transposition of the keyboard part of Sonata 2 in D (K & Vn) in our item L., the other sonatas in Bologna may relate similarly to item L.[31]

For the present survey some three dozen "trio" and accompanied sonatas were available (especially our items B., C., E., H., L., and M.), along with several symphonies for comparison.[32] As we have generally noted in other pre-Classic Italian sonatas, Sammartini's cycles divide about equally between those in two and those in three movements, moderate and quick tempos prevail in no set order, the movements in even meter usually precede those in triple meter (with the finale most often being a minuet in name or spirit), major keys up to three flats or sharps serve almost exclusively, and a central movement occurs only occasionally in a different key from that of its outer movements. Sammartini's sonatas of only two movements predominate in his later sets. Cycles with movements related by similar incipits are frequent, especially in the earlier sets (as in item B., with the more obvious relationships being the main argument, as usual, for supposing that the more subtle or conjectural ones, like those in Ex. 27, *infra,* are not merely fortuitous).

When Henry Mishkin made his illuminating analysis of five Sam-

25. According to information from Miss Churgin.
26. Cf. Weigl/VIOLONCELL 79; Altmann/KAMMERMUSIK 270.
27. Saint-Foix/SAMMARTINI 313.
28. Eitner/QL VIII 409; they are not listed in Tebaldini/PADOVA.
29. Cat. BOLOGNA IV 28 and 64. But the listing in Eitner/QL VIII 409 of 6 cembalo sons. in "Neapel Turchini" cannot be found in PUBBLICAZIONI NAPOLI.
30. Reprinted in Tagliapietra/ANTOLOGIA-m XII no. 10.
31. Could the absence of the Vn part explain the opinion that these pieces are "mediocre" in Torchi/ISTRUMENTALE 257?
32. E.g. (besides the many extended excerpts in Torrefranca/SANMARTINI), Nef/SINFONIE 318; SAMMLUNG SONDHEIMER-m Nos. 13, 49; *Sinfonia in do maggiore,* enlarged score by Torrefranca (Milan: Carisch, 1936); La Laurencie/BLANCHETON II music suppl. 13.

martini "string quartets" composed in the late 1760's,[33] one main object was to define a late style as opposed to an early-to-middle style such as the Blancheton collection of the 1740's might reveal.[34] However, after Mishkin made his broader, bibliographic study of Sammartini's published instrumental works he felt that he had found "a new Sammartini in whose homogeneous succession of publications there are no longer any stylistic lapses or inconsistencies"—that is, a composer who did not change over from the "Handelian trio sonata style" (and forms so strongly characteristic of his older brother's writing) but "even at the beginning of his career . . . is already firmly and confidently at home in the new *galant* style."[35] This second view has seemed more just in the present study, too. In fact, it might be extended here, and in two senses, one pertaining to Sammartini's evolution within the *galant* style, and the other to two continuing but opposed facets of his own writing within that style.

The evolution concerns that simple but profound shift in pre-Classic sonatas, especially in the first allegro movements, from the fast harmonic rhythm still to be found in Sammartini's early works (Ex. 27) to the relatively slower harmonic rhythm in his later ones (Ex. 29, *infra*). As we have seen (SCE VI), the important effect of this shift, not only then but extending right into Beethoven's sonatas, was to channel many diverse tonal progressions into a few broad, structurally significant directions.

As for the two opposed facets of Sammartini's style to be found throughout his instrumental writing, these chiefly concern his approach to melody. They might be described as the chamber and symphonic facets (SCE II), although each overlaps the other's category just as his terminology overlaps. Or they might even be linked to his slower and faster tempos, respectively, again with some overlapping. Whatever the designations, the most characteristic melodic line in the "Affettuoso" or "Larghetto" movement that so often opens Sammartini's sonatas is one that roams widely through a rapid, almost kaleidoscopic succession of varied rhythms and fussy ornaments (Ex. 28). Typical of the rhythms are the dotted (especially Lombardian) figures, the syncopations, the triplets, the bursts of 32d-notes, and the frequent rests. But in the "symphonic" or "allegro" facet of his writing Sammartini's melodic approach is quite the opposite. Or rather, it might be

33. Mishkin/QUARTETS. In SSSB and SSAB settings, each is an autograph MS entitled "Concertino a 4° stromenti soli." All 5 are in the Paris Conservatoire but not in the Blancheton collection; 4 have dates, 1763 and '67.

34. The basis for dating this collection is given in La Laurencie/BLANCHETON I 13.

35. Mishkin/SAMMARTINI 374.

Ex. 27. From the opening of each movement in Giovanni Battista Sammartini's "trio" Sonata 6, Op. 1, 1744 (after the later, Bremner ed. of *ca.* 1765).

said to yield to the tonal drive, for here it becomes all simplicity and directness (Exx. 27 and 29). Its continuation now depends not on ornate changing patterns but on the reiteration of a single short pattern or motive. Indeed, the compounding of reiterated patterns into effective structural rhythms is one of the most artful procedures in Sammartini's "symphonic" writing, although, or partly because, he was no addict of the square phrase. On the other hand, we should note in his sonatas

Ex. 28. From the opening of Giovanni Battista Sammartini's "trio" Sonata 7, Op. 5, *ca.* 1760 (after the original Le Clerc ed. in the Bibliothèque nationale).

that neither facet of his style produces pre-Mozartean examples of "singing-allegro" melodies or themes based on sharp *forte-piano* contrasts, even the near exceptions being conspicuously rare (e.g., the openings of our item C./4/i and C./2/i, respectively).[36]

36. More detailed though somewhat inconclusive discussions of these aspects of Sammartini's style may be found in Sondheimer/SAMMARTINI (with perhaps too much emphasis on thematic dualism) and Schökel/BACH 64-71 (especially regarding our item E.) But his chamber music still remains an inviting field for a comprehensive dissertation.

Several varieties of scoring and texture occur in Sammartini's sonatas. Strict counterpoint is absent and, of course, would have been out of place in the *galant* style. But imitations are not infrequent and are carried out with the superior craftsmanship to be expected from such a rich background in church music. They occur especially in the *concertante* interchanges of flute and first violin in the SSS/bass settings (Sons. 9-12) of our item C., and in some SS/bass movements (e.g., item E./3/ii, in which the bass also participates). But always in the SSS/- and much of the time in the SS/bass settings the second violin plays an alto filler part, the contrast being especially pronounced in item D.[37] The violin part in the accompanied sonatas (item L.) makes imitations and occasional independent statements above the keyboard part, but mainly serves to fill out rests and harmonies in the usual manner (Ex. 29). With regard to technical demands, along with the

Ex. 29. From the opening of Giovanni Battista Sammartini's Sonata 4 for cembalo and violin (after the original London ed. of 1766).

ornamental treatments there are scales, arpeggios, and certain more idiomatic techniques. Examples of the latter are the cembalist's hand-crossing in item L./4/i, the one real use of Alberti bass in L./5/i, and rapid alternation of the hands in the first movement, notably marked

37. According to information from Miss Churgin.

"Brillante," in L./6. But virtuosity for its own sake is not a trait of this music. There is no time for it or for fantasying in such solidly organized forms. Nor do even Sammartini's simplest lines—for instance, in the quasi-gigue, "Presto" finale of E./2—provide quite the fluency that is a usual prerequisite of virtuosic performance and that we found in the contemporary cembalo sonatas of both Galuppi and Rutini.

The broad but simple tonal organization and the efficiency of Sammartini's forms have already been mentioned. Together they define his main strength. Clear ternary designs, with distinct tonal departures and well prepared returns, are achieved often (e.g., E./1/i). They occur not seldom in the minuet finales, too (C./4/ii), although Sammartini's minuets do not ordinarily have the trios (an exception being the "Minore" in E./6/ii) that often constitute middle sections in other minuets of the time.[38] One or more contrasting themes are also to be found in the longer movements. Only the relatively neutral quality of Sammartini's ideas keeps these contrasts from having more structural significance. In other movements, chiefly shorter or slower ones, well balanced forms are achieved that are just as clearly binary rather than ternary. These often have contrasting themes, too (E./2/i). The important fact to realize is that Sammartini's formal procedures are still flexible and fluid, seeming to grow very logically out of their material. Thus, in Sonata 3/i of our item E. the opening passage in unisons and octaves sounds like the *tutti* of a concerto grosso and, indeed, reappears three more times in ritornello fashion.

A later and more progressive example of flexible procedures, in one of the most progressive and "symphonic" of all Sammartini's sonatas examined here, is item L./4/i. Its successive, well defined sections include a chordal, proclamatory opening theme (Ex. 29, *supra*); a bridge to a dominant cadence (mss. 7-16); a second theme with but slight melodic contrast, in the dominant key (mss. 17-24), followed by a third of little more contrast (mss. 25-30); some passages reconfirming the dominant key (mss. 30-40) and a fourth fairly neutral theme that closes the "exposition" in the key (mss. 40-49). In Sammartini's most frequent manner, the "development" starts with material only indirectly related, modulates through nearly related keys in derivative passages that are made tonally affective by their emphasis on diminished 7th and subordinate minor harmonies, and works compellingly up to the dominant harmony prior to the return. But the "recapitulation" gives the chief evidence of a form by no means standardized, yet by no means compromised in its total force. The sole reference to any "contrasting"

38. Cf. Torrefranca/SANMARTINI (XXI) 284-286.

theme occurs on a dominant pedal just before the clear return to the main theme in the home key.[39] Thereafter, only the bridge and other passage work is recalled prior to a repetition of the fourth or closing theme in the home key.

All in all, the impression made here by G. B. Sammartini is that of a peak exponent of the *galant* style in his decorative "chamber" writing, a capable, pert incipient Classicist in his straightforward "symphonic" writing, but no significant forerunner as regards the pre-Romantic traits of Classic music—with, for example, little of the dramatic element in Rutini's best keyboard sonatas or the fine sentiment in Galuppi's.

Besides the mention already made of Brioschi, Lampugnani, and Giulini, one other contemporary of Sammartini in Milan may be noted, in passing, as a minor contributor to the sonata. **Giuseppe Paladini,** who composed many oratorios performed in Milan from at least 1726 to 1743,[40] was a young rival of Sammartini[41] and is known for one three-movement cembalo sonata in Anth. HAFFNER RACCOLTA-m III no. 3 [42] (suggesting that he was still active *ca.* 1759). The latter is mildly interesting for its *galant* figuration and the broad ternary outline of its first movement. But it is so generally chordal and so devoid of any of the melodic, harmonic, or expressive interest found in contemporary sonatas, that the attention previously paid to it is hard to understand.[43]

Bologna (Mysliveček, Sarti)

Bologna, home of the revered Padre Martini (SBE 181-183) and the Accademia dei Filarmonici, saw much opera activity in the later 18th century but nothing like the interest in the sonata that had been shown there in the previous 100 years. In fact, the only native Bolognese to name, **Giovanni Battista Predieri,**[44] is too obscure and inaccessible to discuss in spite of occasional mentions given to his cembalo and accompanied cembalo sonatas.[45] But the Bohemian violinist and gifted composer **Josef Mysliveček** (1737-81) may be placed in Bologna, where he was admitted to the Accademia, supposedly under Martini's tutelage, in 1771, and where Mozart had first met him the year before. Otherwise, he might have been placed in Venice, where he studied with

39. This procedure also occurs in several of G. B. Sammartini's later symphonies, according to information from Miss Churgin.
40. Schmidl/DIZIONARIO Suppl. 585.
41. Carpani/HAYDINE 58-59.
42. Mod. ed.: Benvenuti/CEMBALISTI-m no. 7.
43. Torrefranca/ORIGINI 128-136, with exx.; Stauch/CLEMENTI 18.
44. Cf. Schmidl/DIZIONARIO II 313; Cat. BOLOGNA IV 61; Eitner/QL VII 362 (Perdieri!).
45. E.g., Torchi/ISTRUMENTALE 169; Torrefranca/ORIGINI 178.

Pescetti in 1763, in Naples, where he had his first operatic success in 1767, or in Milan in 1779, where he reportedly made his oft-quoted statement about Sammartini's symphonies being the true source of
46a Haydn's style.[46] Along with two sets of 6 SS/bass "trios" each, Opp. 1 and 4 (1768 and 1772),[47] Mysliveček left 6 accompanied sonatas (K & Vn, London, *ca.* 1775),[48] some related chamber and solo keyboard publications,[49] and several keyboard sonatas in MS.[50]

Mysliveček's accompanied keyboard sonatas are all in two movements (as against three in the "trios," Op. 1) in the order allegro-minuet (with trio or "minore") except Sonata 2 ("Andantino"-minuet). Mozart played them in Munich and found them "very easy and good to the ear," advising his sister to learn them from memory and perform them "with much expression, gusto, and fire," for they would be sure to please everyone "if played with the necessary precision."[51] It is no surprise to read this endorsement after discovering how remarkable is the anticipation—one might almost say, full attainment—of the "Mozart style" right from Mysliveček's first publication. In Mysliveček's delightful melodies, both slow and fast, Jan Racek finds an element of Czech folksong that seems to carry over to Mozart.[52] But there are more specific syntactic and textural resemblances, such as the *forte-piano* dualism within a single theme,[53] the cumulative line built from motives stated in pairs, the thetic appoggiaturas that provide melodic chromaticism, the homophonic accompaniments of repeated 8th-notes and Alberti basses, and the cadential hammer strokes after a dominant pedal. Only Mozart's greater depth, imagination, harmonic range, formal logic, skillful voice-leading, and all else that distinguishes the master explain why this immediate predecessor's charming music remains scarcely known (all too much so!). His music is, indeed, almost too Mozartean before the fact to have an identity of its own.

Born in Faenza, thirty-five miles southeast of Bologna, the violinist

46. Haydn himself is said to have ridiculed the statement. Cf. GROVE V 1047-1048 (Grove); Carpani/HAYDINE 59; Saint-Foix/MYSLIWECZEK; Pincherle/FEUILLETS 103-109; Mueller von Asow/MOZART I 152; MAB-m No. 31 (Racek) xiii-xv (preface, with new information and further references).

47. Cf. Johansson/FRENCH II Facs. 53 and 82. Mod. ed.: Op. 1/4 in B♭, COLLEGIUM MUSICUM No. 20.

48. Listed in BRITISH UNION II 722. Mod. ed., complete, Prague, 1938 (cf. Racek/TSCHECHISCHEN 513, but without mention of the Vn part); Son. (6) in D (without the Vn part), MAB-m No. 17 (plus other mvts.).

49. Cf. BRITISH UNION II 722; Racek/TSCHECHISCHEN 514-515 (with confusions in titles and dates).

50. Cf. Eitner/QL VII 8.

51. Letter to his father of Nov. 13, 1777 (Mueller von Asow/MOZART II 162).

52. Racek/TSCHECHISCHEN 495-497, 513, 517.

53. Cf. Einstein/MOZART 219.

Giuseppe Sarti (1729-1802), like Mysliveček, may be placed in Bologna because of his study with Padre Martini,[54] although he travelled even more widely than the Czech composer. The popularity of his operas and oratorios, the far-off demands for his services, and the many honors heaped on him as a scholar and inventor are evidence enough for his lifetime successes. But his niche in history, however small, has been made secure rather by the fact that he taught Cherubini, by Mozart's friendly interest in his music,[55] and, paradoxically enough, by his own harmonically unperceptive censure of Mozart's music. (The last, made in a mock "esame acustico," pertained to the openings of Quartets 6 ["Dissonance"] and 2 dedicated to Haydn in 1785, and included the remark, usually translated more freely, "When barbarians attempt to compose music, some passages stand out that make us shudder.")[56]

It was while Sarti was serving in Copenhagen that his first two publications of concern to us appeared, a set of three harpsichord sonatas (London, 1769)[57] as well as a (lost?) set of six Fl/bass sonatas (Paris, 1772).[58] And it was while he was serving in St. Petersburg and elsewhere in Russia, after meeting both Haydn and Mozart in Vienna, that his Op. 3 was published, consisting of three accompanied sonatas (H-or-P & Vn, Vienna, 1786), followed by another, like set, Op. 4 (Vienna, 1788).[59] Sarti also published two accompanied "sonatas" (H-or-P & Vn) based on successful opera tunes and reprinted widely. One of these, *Giulio Sabino ed Epponina, Sonata caratteristica,* Op. 1 (Vienna, 1785), was based on his chief serious opera (1781). It reappeared, in a kind of reversal of the accompanied-sonata practice, as *The celebrated sonata . . . , in which all the obligato violin passages are adapted for the piano-forte* (London, *ca.* 1795).[60] The other, Op. 2, was based on the tunes of several *opere buffe* (Vienna, 1786).[61]

Sarti's first set of harpsichord sonatas (1769) reveals no musical or structural distinction that seems exceptional alongside much other

54. Martini's help is questioned in the useful article in GROVE VII 412-415 (Chouquet), but adequate proof was cited in Eitner/QL VIII 431.

55. Letter of June 9, 1784 (Anderson/MOZART III 1312; but cf. Fischer/SARTI).

56. Cf. AMZ XXXIV 373-378; Mooser/ANNALES III 742-743 (Fig. 133 for Sarti's portrait); J. A. Vertrees in CM XVII (1974) 96-114.

57. Listed in BRITISH UNION II 922. Cf. Stone/ITALIAN I 230, II 92 (thematic index). Mod. eds.: Son. 2/ii, Malipiero/ITALIAN-m 23; son. 3/iii, Pauer/MEISTER-m IV 16.

58. Cf. Johansson/FRENCH I 113, II Facs. 82 and later.

59. The dates are in Weinmann/ARTARIA plate nos. 95 and 215. Thematic index of Op. 4 (without the Vn part) in Stone/ITALIAN II 92-93. Title page of Op. 4 reproduced in Newman/ACCOMPANIED opposite p. 346 (with ex. from Son. 2/ii).

60. Cf. BRITISH UNION II 922-923.

61. Weinmann/ARTARIA plate no. 103; probably the same as all or part of the "6 Sonate . . . dell'opera Buffa . . ." in a Dresden MS listed in Eitner/QL VIII 431.

music of its day. All three sonatas begin with a toccata-like "Preludio," followed by one allegro movement in the first and two allegro movements in the other two sonatas, always in the original key. In the allegro movements are typically *galant* mannerisms, including tortuously decorative lines and incessant triplets. The change of style in the accompanied sets, after little more than fifteen years, is noteworthy. These sonatas, in two or three movements, now have the cantilena melodies, regular phrases, and broad tonal movements of much high-Classic music (Ex. 30). Interesting is the change from the minor key of the movement

Ex. 30. From the opening of Giuseppe Sarti's Sonata Op. 4/2/i (after the Artaria ed. of 1788 in the Library of Congress).

just quoted to tonic major in the remaining two movements ("Allegro" and "Rondeau Allegretto"). Here is an instance of the progression from minor to major that was to occur often in nineteenth-century sonata cycles.

Last here to be related to Bologna, through both Padre Martini's instruction and admission to the Accademia dei Filarmonici (1761), is **Filippo Maria Gherardeschi** (1738-1808). But the birth, various posts, and death of this organist and esteemed church composer all occurred just across the Apennines in the region of Tuscany.[62] His set of three sonatas "per Cembalo o Forte-piano" was published in the early 1770's by Ranieri Del Vivo in Florence, as was a set of six accompanied sonatas (K + Vn) by his nephew Giuseppe, both sets being dedicated to Tuscany's Austrian empress Maria Theresa.[63] Filippo's sonatas were not available here but should be worth investigating. According to L. G. Tagliavini,[64] their numerous nuances and other expression marks indicate that the piano was intended, and they are pieces with elegance, pre-Romantic traits, and charms pointing to Haydn.

Tartini's Descendants and Other Stringsmen (Nardini, Pugnani, Boccherini)

We come now to our other main group of Italians in this chapter, the group more often viewed as post-Baroque than pre-Classic in spite of many progressive tendencies. This is the group of string players whose main sonata output was still of the melo/bass type and whose main "locale" was the sphere of Tartini's influence.[65] Geographically, its locale was more Tuscan than any other, although Tartini himself (1692-1770) lived in Padua, west of Venice, and most of these men were traveling virtuosos. Florence, seat of the grand ducal court of Tuscany, home of lively theaters and musical "accademie," saw exceptional instrumental activity in the later eighteenth century, what with the residence at various times of F. M. Veracini, Campioni, Nardini, Rutini, and Cherubini, among others.[66]

The more conservative side of the Italian sonatas about to be discussed is reflected in the *Essai* (1790) of the Modenese dilettante Rangoni.[67] This critic helped to perpetuate the long-time quarrel be-

62. MGG V 57 (Tagliavini).

63. Both sets are listed in PUBBLICAZIONI FIRENZE 269. Filippo's 3 MS sons. in Cat. BOLOGNA IV 49 are presumably the same H-or-P set (preserved by his teacher?). The rough date is suggested by the time when Del Vivo published other like works (cf. Sartori/DIZIONARIO 60).

64. MGG V 58.

65. Cf. SBE; Brainard/TARTINI (a new diss.).

66. Cf. MGG IV 388-390 (Becherini).

67. Cf. Schmidl/DIZIONARIO Suppl. 639.

tween proponents of ancient and modern art (SCE II) by his deprecation of imaginative Italian modernisms, which he traced to French music.[68] As surviving models of the more conservative, rational styles from which he felt music had otherwise strayed he selected three violinists more or less descended from Tartini—Nardini, Lolli, and Pugnani:

In the creative arts, such as music and poetry, the author's first ideas are the most alive and heartfelt [that he has], for at the start his fiery, rich imagination discovers new charms in [the very act of] painting new pictures. However, since all music revolves around but seven notes, combined and varied infinitely according to the composer's wish, [those ideas] ultimately [must] reduce to [the] trifling modulations—dull, without substance or expression—that signify an exhausted inspiration. So it is with the sonatas now in style: much motion and little tenderness; much fluency and little feeling or depth; much of this extravagant and bizarre [sort of] difficulty that astonishes without moving, [but] not that [sort] that depends on the basic rules of counterpoint and good taste such as one admires in the rationally composed sonatas by Corelli or Tartini, and in the more precious though less profound sonatas by Messieurs Pugnani, Giardini, etc. . . . I see nothing in the newer sonatas of Lolli that can compare with the beauties to be found in his earlier works. . . . What success can a piece ever have that subordinates taste to agility? . . . Monsieur Nardini reveals this truth in his new sonatas. Unlike so many other composers, he never seeks to achieve pleasure through pain by conceiving passages of a difficult sort that is disagreeable to the taste and hard on the ear. On the contrary, he disregards difficulty, but produces it unintentionally because it is in the nature of the great master to do nothing that is easy. The style of his sonatas is maintained, the ideas in them are clear, the motives [are] introduced well and treated still better, the modulations comply with the strictest laws of composition, and the sentiments are expressive and natural but in keeping with the composer's serious nature. All his music is bound up with the art of bowing, which he controls to the last degree of perfection. It is by the magic of this art that he produces those unnamable, indefinable sounds. That is why his sonatas do not have the same effect when not played according to his method. It also explains why one plays the music of all composers yet fails in that of Nardini and of his teacher Tartini. Besides, the many accidentals, ornaments, chromatic passages, trills of whatever sort, [and] chords and arpeggios, while making this music very expressive and harmonious, at the same time make it very difficult. . . . Without some knowledge of Monsieur Nardini's art, to hear him play one would think his sonatas are easy. . . .

Among the top-ranking violinists I distinguish Pugnani by the animated and vibrant eloquence throughout his melody. This great sonata composer, who derives as much from the magic of his impassioned lyricism as from that of his performance, sacrifices . . . stylistic elegance to the sentiment that consumes him, and often enraptures the spirit with the fancies of the imagination. His music is ruled by neither the art of bowing nor the

68. Rangoni/ESSAI 22-28. The *Essai* is also published (in French only) in Pincherle/FEUILLETS 50-71.

problem of the hand, [both of] which he subordinates entirely to the communication of the sentiment . . . his modulations are clear, concise, and energetic, like the sentences of a philosopher and an orator. Free of extraneous matter they convey only [genuine] feelings; and the ideas by following in orderly fashion never lose track of the original motive. In short, this able musician achieves in his compositions that perfect unity that results when divers elements combine into an indivisible whole.[69]

First of the Tartini descendants to name, in approximate order of publications, was his violin student **Carlo Antonio Campioni** (1720-88). Campioni was born in Livorno on the Ligurian Sea, probably traveled at least to Paris in 1762, and moved finally to Florence in 1763 (preceding Nardini and Rutini at court as *maestro di cappella*).[70] 70a
There, as the inhabitant of "an elegant house, well furnished," the husband of "a lady who paints very well, and who is likewise a neat performer, on the harpsichord," the owner of "the greatest collection of old music, particularly Madrigals, of the sixteenth and seventeenth centuries, Padre Martini's excepted, that I ever saw," and the composer of much church music that included "curious canons, and ingenious contrivances"—there Burney met and identified him as the man "whose trios have been so well received in England."[71] And well he might, for between 1758 and 1765 Campioni published in London and Amsterdam six SS/bass sets, Opp. 1-6, totaling thirty-six sonatas;[72] a set of six *divertimenti* or duets "for violin & violoncello or harpsichord," Op. 7 or 8; and a set of "Six sonatas or duets for two violins," Op. 8 or 7; each of which editions achieved from one to four re-editions variously in London, Paris, and Amsterdam.[73] Campioni also left an interesting set of six harpsichord sonatas (London, 1763).[74]

It will be helpful to look first at this last set, the one that seems not to have achieved any re-editions. All six harpsichord sonatas in this set are of the two-movement type, in the order of an allegro, followed by a gigue, minuet, or "La Caccia" (Son. 3). The Alberti bass is overdone, especially in the long first movements, but the melodies are appealing in their disarmingly forthright, open contours and in the dolorous quality created by turns to subordinate minor triads and other colorful harmonies. Most interesting is the novel, often virtuoso treat-

69. Rangoni/ESSAI 30-62 *passim.*

70. In a recent unpublished diss. from Vienna, Floros/CAMPIONI, are to be found new biographic information, a full list of works, and detailed analyses of the sons. (pp. 46-115, especially the SS/bass sons.).

71. BURNEY'S TOURS I 187, 190. But there is no mention of Campioni in Burney/HISTORY. Cf., also, Bonaventura/LIVORNESI 2-4.

72. A chronology of these sets is suggested in Floros/CAMPIONI 44-45.

73. Cf. the detailed, collated list in BRITISH UNION I 157.

74. Cf. Torrefranca/ORIGINI 587-598, with several exx. This set is largely disregarded in Floros/CAMPIONI.

ment of the keyboard, which increases in the later sonatas to the point where the printed page is dazzling in itself (e.g., Son. 5/i). Bold leaps, wide hand-crossing, rapid alternations of the hands, and elaborate arpeggios abound. There are no dynamics signs, octaves, or other clues that point particularly to the piano as yet. But obviously Campioni (or his wife?) knew the harpsichord as well as he knew the violin. Torrefranca calls him "the Liszt of his day."[75] "Paganini-Liszt" might be more appropriate in those passages on one staff where the hands overlap and divide repeated notes in the manner of the violinist's bariolage (e.g., Son. 2/i) or of Paganini's Caprice No. 1 in E, as transcribed by Liszt. Sonata 6 adds a part for "violino obbligato." This part merely outlines the keyboard figuration much of the time. But it becomes genuinely obligatory during dialogic exchanges with the keyboard, during its own technical effusions (wide leaps across the strings, double-stops, rapid runs) such as only a violinist might write, and during actual "solos" with only a figured bass for the keyboard player.

Regarding the "trio" sonatas, insofar as examples could be scored for this study one is inclined to share Moser's wonder that so little interest was taken by those nineteenth-century editors of "old chamber music."[76] These sonatas differ from those for harpsichord in having three movements (all in the same key) S-F-F or S-F-M, in having detailed dynamics and bowing marks, and in generally following the ensemble practice of concentrating more on structure than on display. The second violin part is primarily a harmonic filler, but it often answers the first part, too, and with good effect, as in the opening of Op. 4/3/i in g, where the answer occurs in pre-Schubertian fashion in the major submediant key. Op. 3/4/ii in b (another of Campioni's infrequent uses of minor keys) is a skillful "Fuga" in the upper parts, enriched in the customary SS/bass manner by a few entries in the bass part. Ex. 31 from the same sonata illustrates the charming, well-proportioned tunes to be found in the moderate-tempo finales, reminiscent of tunes in similar movements by Tartini (SBE 192, Ex. 39). The finale of Op. 4/6 introduces another charming tune with a brief quasi-recitative marked "Adagio assai." Campioni's movements often reveal distinct ternary designs, although a tonic statement of the opening idea just after the dominant one that begins the "development" section weakens the force of the eventual true return.

A second Tartini pupil to name was the composer and widely heard

75. Torrefranca/ORIGINI 596-597.

76. Moser/VIOLINSPIEL 413. One SS/bass Son. in g is in Moffat/TRIOSONATEN-m No. 26. Numerous short exx. are included in the analyses in Floros/CAMPIONI 46-102.

Ex. 31. From the finale of Op. 3/4 by Carlo Antonio Campioni (after the original Walsh ed. in the British Museum).

violinist **Domenico Ferrari** (1722-80), who was born in Piacenza some forty miles southeast of Milan. Ferrari was a colleague of Nardini and younger brother of an esteemed cellist and composer of cello sonatas, Carlo Ferrari.[77] Domenico left six sets of S/bass and at least one of 77a
SS/bass sonatas published in Paris and London between about 1758 (not 1750) and 1762.[78] Dittersdorf's lively, well-known remarks on

77. Cf. Burney/HISTORY II 446, 454; MGG IV 74-75 (Barblan), including a page in facs. from an SSA/bass son. in MS.

78. Several are listed in BRITISH UNION I 330; for the dates also cf. Cat.

Ferrari include high respect for the "solo" sonatas, apparently mainly for their display value.[79] This last they certainly have, with their harmonics ("sons harmoniques" are indicated already in Op. 1/5/i, soon after Mondonville's use) and their further pyrotechnics, more in the manner of Locatelli than Tartini. But, on other grounds as well, these sonatas deserve the study they have not yet had. There is much of interest in their variety of movements (usually three in any order and thematically interrelated), their simple phrases and out-and-out homophony in spite of the survival of the *b.c.*, their fresh rhythms and harmonies, and especially their melodiousness, all of which show Ferrari to have been something of an eighteenth-century Dancla.

The violinist most celebrated as a Tartini pupil and the one praised even above Lolli and Pugnani by Rangoni (*supra*) was **Pietro Nardini** (1722-93). Nardini's contribution to the sonata has been thoroughly explored in a dissertation (completed in 1930) that is a model of care and good sense,[80] leaving little to be done here beyond summarizing the findings and adding the more exact publication dates to be found in newer sources. The most essential biographical findings and corrections should be restated first,[81] since they tie in with his publications and for the most part have yet to make their way into music dictionaries. Born in Livorno, Nardini advanced to the study of violin and composition with Tartini in Padua at the age of twelve (1734), returned to Livorno by 1740, traveled to Vienna in 1760 and probably to Dresden before returning in 1762, and joined the Neapolitan opera composer Jommelli, the Bergamo violinist Lolli, and the French ballet master Noverre in Stuttgart from late 1762 (not 1753) to early 1765 (not 1767[82]) except for trips home each of the two summers. After a stay at the Braunschweig and perhaps other German courts in 1765, he was back in Livorno in 1766. He then played in Rome, Pisa, and Naples (presumably among many other Italian cities), visited Tartini in 1769 during the latter's last illness, and moved to Florence late that year or early the next. There he continued to play (often in association with the remarkable "Improvisatrice" Corilla) and teach until he died (refusing a call to St. Petersburg in 1778[83]). Nardini was strongly praised for his playing—especially his tender, pathetic, lyrical, pure, even tone in slow

BOLOGNA IV 27 and Johansson/FRENCH I 45. For mod. eds., of "solo" sons. only, cf. Schmidl/DIZIONARIO I 535; Altmann/KAMMERMUSIK 236.

79. DITTERSDORF 40-43. Cf. Moser/VIOLINSPIEL 281-283.

80. Pfäfflin/NARDINI, including thematic index of first mvts.

81. Pfäfflin/NARDINI 58-78.

82. Nor 1764 as in MGG VIII 1130 (Mell). Cf. Pfäfflin/NARDINI 62.

83. Mooser/ANNALES II 214.

movements—by expert contemporaries, including Leopold Mozart,[84] Burney,[85] and Schubart.[86] The young Mozart got to hear and know him in 1763[87] and 1770.[88] The chief contemporary opinion of his music is the conservative view by Rangoni quoted earlier.

Besides string quartets, violin concertos, and orchestral overtures, a total of some 62 sonatas by Nardini is known, 48 in S/bass, 7 in SS/bass, and 2 in SS settings, plus 4 for keyboard alone and one for violin alone.[89] Of the S/bass sonatas 25 were published (and republished) around his time, including an early set of 6, about 1760 (before his first known departure from Italy) by Walsh in London; a second set of 6 ("Op. 5"), in 1769 (after his return to Italy) by Fougt in London; a third set of 6 ("Op. 2"), about 1771 by Hummel in Amsterdam;[90] and a fourth set of 6, later 7, "Sonatas avec les Adagios bordés," posthumously (1798-1801) by Cartier in Paris (in Anth. CARTIER-m [all 3 eds.] and separately[91]). Other publications include a set of 6 SS/bass sonatas, about 1770 by Bremner in London; 2 SS "Sonatas or Duets" in an anthology (nos. 1 and 2) with D. Ferrari, about 1765 by Walsh; 2 keyboard sonatas in Anth. HARPSICHORD-m II (1763); and the unaccompanied violin sonata, in Anth. CARTIER-m.

Nardini's unaccompanied violin sonata and that by Geminiani (SBE 322-323) are the only two such sonatas by Italians that are known prior to the twentieth century. "Sonate énigmatique" is Nardini's title in Anth. CARTIER-m, referring not only to the use of *scordatura* (almost as infrequent by Italians) but the disposition on two staffs as if here were an S/bass score (with this bass understood an octave higher).[92] The motivic, occasionally imitative writing and the free "cadanza" in the first movement, as well as the slight melodic interest in all three movements ("Largo," "Minuetto Vivace," "Allegro"), suggest an early composition date. The keyboard "lessons" also have slight melodic interest, showing the string composer's frequent tendency to think primarily in terms of

84. Cf. Anderson/MOZART 33-34.
85. BURNEY'S TOURS I 185.
86. Quoted in Päfflin/NARDINI 65.
87. Cf. Saint-Foix/MOZART I 34 (with a portrait of Nardini reproduced opposite p. 316).
88. Cf. Anderson/MOZART I 184-185.
89. Cf. the "Thematischer Katalog" in Pfäfflin/NARDINI, including locations and mod. eds.; also, Altmann/KAMMERMUSIK. Most of the published sets are listed in BRITISH UNION II 724.
90. Plate no. 338; cf. Deutsch/NUMBERS 15.
91. The reference in this source to an earlier Venice ed. of 1760 is probably an error at least in the date; cf. Pfäfflin/NARDINI 27.
92. Cf. La Laurencie/ÉCOLE III 20-21; Pfäfflin/NARDINI 30-31 (but "senza basso" is not in the title); Gates/SOLO 130-136 (discussion) and 312-314 (reproduction in full).

figuration and passage work when he turns to the keyboard.[93] These works and Nardini's SS duos are in only two movements, moderate or fast. Both types are light in character, as are his SS/bass sonatas, which are all in three movements, S-F-F or S-M-F. The S/bass sonatas are almost all in three movements, too, with the almost invariable plan of S-F-F. But as with Tartini's sonatas these "solos" are considerably richer and more serious in content than the "trios."

Nardini's epigonic position in the temporal and stylistic shadow of Tartini helps to explain the relatively little interest shown toward him in recent times. So does the fact that his faster movements, even the quasi-minuet and rondo finales, generally lack the tuneful spark of Tartini's. The evolution in his style from continuous motivic progression to the sectional structure of phrase grouping, the frequent tonic returns in the second "halves" of the longer movements, and the technical problems (chiefly double-stops and varied bowings) are hardly enough in themselves to draw attention to the music. It is the more extended, slow movements that have kept alive such interest as does exist (as evidenced in the separate editions of them in collections of "violin classics"), and for the very reasons quoted earlier from Rangoni (Ex. 32). There is also practical interest in the plain and ornamented versions of the adagios that appear superimposed over the bass in three staffs in the Cartier set.[94] If this rich and complex ornamentation was not by Nardini himself it was, of course, of contemporary origin in any case.

The second of the trio of post-Tartini violinists to be appraised by Rangoni (*supra*), albeit with the least enthusiasm, was **Antonio Lolli** (*ca.* 1730-1802). Lolli was probably born in Bergamo northeast of Milan and only about 100 miles from Tartini in Padua, though his actual formal training (if any!) is not known.[95] As one of the most itinerant, colorful, and sensational of eighteenth-century performers[96] he has added spice to almost every history of violin playing; however, his importance as a sonata composer is much less. Even among his contemporaries, who

93. Cf. Pfäfflin/NARDINI 34-36; Stone/ITALIAN I 221 (discussion) and III no. 8 (copy in full of Lesson in G from Anth. HARPSICHORD-m II).

94. In David/VIOLINSPIEL-m I 70 is reprinted Son. 2 in D with only the ornamental version of the "Adagio" (somewhat simplified; cf. Moser/VIOLINSPIEL 272), and with another slow, optional movement inserted (making S-F-S-F), which is the "Larghetto" transposed to A from Son. 7 in B♭.

95. His identification as a Venetian by one of his students (AMZ I 578) suggests possible early residence much closer to Tartini (but cf. MGG VIII 1130 [Mell]).

96. Cf. MGG VIII 1130-1134. New material on his intermittent stay in St. Petersburg (1774-83) is given in Mooser/ANNALES II 161-168 and III Fig. 37 (silhouette). On Lolli's successes in Paris in 1764 cf. La. Laurencie/ÉCOLE II 316-317.

Ex. 32. From the opening of Pietro Nardini's Sonata Op. 5/6 (after the original Fougt ed. in the Library of Congress).

looked on with much relish, there was already a remarkably wide consensus in this mixed view.[97] Burney's short statement in English will be sufficient illustration here:

The celebrated performer on the violin, LOLLI, came into England in the beginning of 1785; but by a caprice in his conduct equal to his performance, he was seldom heard. And then so eccentric was his style of composition and execution, that he was regarded as a madman by most of his hearers. Yet I am convinced that in his lucid intervals he was, in a serious style, a very great, expressive, and admirable performer. In his freaks nothing can be imagined so wild, difficult, grotesque, and even ridiculous as his compositions and performance. After playing at the oratorio, and making the grave and ignorant laugh at very serious difficulties upon

97. Cf., Burney/HISTORY II 1020-1021; J. Uriot, as quoted in Pfäfflin/NARDINI 87; DITTERSDORF 125-127, 226-227, 231-233, 248; Cramer/MAGAZIN II (1786) 902, as quoted in Hanslick/WIEN I 107; AMZ I 577-584, 609-613; Gerber/LEXICON I 820-821, emended in Gerber/NEUES III 252-254; Schubart, as quoted in Wasielewski/VIOLINE 209-210.

which he had perhaps but ill bestowed his time, he suddenly left the kingdom, *à la sourdine;* perhaps, at last, to shun difficulties of another kind.

In short, Lolli was a kind of later-eighteenth-century Paganini, with perhaps still more of the dissolute charlatan and less of the composer in him. Such a parallel was already drawn soon after Paganini's own career had ended.[98] But along with continuing nineteenth-century interest in Lolli's performance exploits, there came a tendency to exaggerate his compositional shortcomings, culminating in Wasielewski's declaration that his compositions were "the most valueless and characterless products of eighteenth-century violin literature."[99] Subsequently, Andreas Moser argued that this evaluation was much too severe, which, indeed, is the conclusion reached here.[100]

Lolli left a considerable number of concertos, sonatas, and shorter pieces in print, including at least five sets of six S/bass sonatas each, and a set of SS duos, published variously in London, Paris, Amsterdam, and Berlin between about 1765 and 1795.[101] The number of these publications and re-editions alone is evidence enough that his music was popular in its day. His Op. 1 of six S/bass sonatas[102] recalls Nardini's general style, although his adagios (here and in the later sets) do not achieve the melodic elegance or serious import of Nardini's.[103] If it is true that Lolli had to have help with his *b.c.* parts and was guilty of harmonic gaucheries, these weaknesses do not show through in the original edition.[104] Furthermore, the quick movements may reveal no melodic or harmonic flashes of genius but they move along melodiously and logically enough in clear phrase groupings (e.g., the "Rondo" finale of Sonata 5). The order of movements in Op. 1 is M-S-F or F-S-F, with two inner movements in the dominant rather than the tonic key. The technical requirements include double-stops (nearly all of the "Adagio" of Op. 1/1 is in thirds) and rapid passages. But it is in this realm that the later sets begin to break down. These, it is indeed true, are overrun with double-stops (including 10ths), passages carried to the highest positions on the E-string or confined only to the G-string, movements in scordatura, Russian tunes (Op. 3), and other devices that "astonish without moving" (to adapt Rangoni's complaint).

98. Hanslick/WIEN I 107.
99. Wasielewski/VIOLINE 208 (as part of an extended evaluation, pp. 204-212).
100. Moser/CORELLI, especially pp. 424-425.
101. Cf. MGG VIII 1132-1133 (with a reproduction of the title page of Op. 2); BRITISH UNION II 626-627.
102. Mod. ed., entire: Gatti/LOLLI-m. For a few mod. eds. from other sets cf. MGG VIII 1134.
103. But they are not unduly short; cf. Moser/CORELLI 422.
104. Cf. Moser/CORELLI 422-423.

The third of Rangoni's three violinists, **Gaetano Pugnani** (1731-98), is, along with G. B. Sammartini and the cellist Boccherini, one of the most interesting stringsmen in this chapter from the standpoint of pre-Classic trends. Born in Torino, in the Piedmont region, he began to play there professionally at the age of ten and, at about the same time, to be introduced to the heritage of Corelli by way of his senior co-citizen, the violinist G. B. Somis (SBE 187-188). But whether he later studied with Tartini, too, as is still maintained in nearly all music dictionaries, now seems at least very doubtful in spite of an early posthumous anecdote that assumes this relationship.[105] There is no known mention of such a relationship during his lifetime and no early unaccounted period, before this headstrong, high-spirited young man[106] himself became a recognized virtuoso, when he might have made a prolonged visit to Padua. On the other hand, in 1792 Gerber already spoke of Pugnani as being "from the Tartini school,"[107] thus giving credence to certain hints that he might have taken some violin lessons from Pasquale Bini ("Pasqualino"), one of Tartini's most important pupils, during Pugnani's 11 months in Rome from 1749-50.[108] If so, Pugnani could be said to bring together the two chief schools of Italian violin playing up to that time. From 1750 to 1754 and from 1770 to his final year, Pugnani again settled in Torino, although this busy and popular performer, composer of widely published instrumental music and moderately successful operas,[109] leader of orchestras, and teacher of Viotti (among others), kept on the go in the main centers of Europe throughout most of his life.[110] As a result, there were few important contemporaries whom he did not meet at one time or other, including Burney, Dittersdorf, Christian Bach, and probably the Mozarts.[111]

As with Nardini, Pugnani's sonatas have been the object of careful, thorough study in recent years (although neither's sonatas are readily accessible in any editions, old or new). Indeed, two excellent books have been devoted primarily to Pugnani's instrumental music and its

105. Choron/DICTIONNAIRE II 182 (first published in 1810).
106. Cf. the anecdotes in AMZ XV (1813) 562-567.
107. Gerber/LEXICON II 200-201.
108. Cf. Pamparato/PUGNANI (the main documentary study of Pugnani's life) 48-49, 53-54.
109. Cf. Burney/HISTORY II 875.
110. Presumptive evidence that Pugnani got to London in his supposed travels during the biographical gap from 1754-67 is found on the title page of an R. Bremner ed. of the first set of "trio" sons. "Op. 1," *ca.* 1762 ("Somerset House in the Strand"), at the Library of Congress: "N. B. This Edition has been Carefully Corrected by the Author." On his visit to St. Petersburg in 1781 cf. Mooser/ANNALES II 309-310, III Fig. 61 (silhouette).
111. Cf., respectively, BURNEY'S TOURS I 59; DITTERSDORF 47; Terry/BACH 113; Saint-Foix/MOZART I 275.

pre-Classic aspects, Zschinsky-Troxler/PUGNANI and Müry/PUGNANI. In one of those curiously frequent coincidences of scholarship, these generally compatible studies were completed and published quite independently, yet within two years (1939 and 1941), of each other, there being only time in the latter for a tribute to the former and a few emendations.[112] By consolidating their findings and adding a few more (chiefly dates), we may begin by summarizing some over-all facts.

Along with quartets, quintets, symphonies, and concertos, at least 75 of some 90 sonatas reported to be by Pugnani are still extant, dispersed in about 35 European and U. S. libraries. Around three-fourths of these achieved publication, originally appearing in the 15 years from about 1761 to 1774, mostly in Paris. Up to 8 or more re-editions per set followed, in Paris, London, and Amsterdam, appearing as late as the 1790's.[113] The different published sets, each containing 6 sonatas, may be summarized here by scoring types and in the supposed chronological order of the first editions. For convenient reference to the sets, the numbering of the sonatas in the thematic index of Zschinsky-Troxler/PUGNANI must be used, since the original opus numbers are typically confused or missing. In extant SS/bass scorings there are 4 sets (Sons. 47-52,[114] 59-64,[115] 53-58, 65-70; *ca.* 1761-71) plus 7 sonatas in MS, but not including 9 *divertimenti* (nos. 78-80f), which are much lighter, more conservative, less developed, 2-movement cycles,[116] with orchestral leanings.[117] In S/bass scorings there are 3 sets (Sons. 100-105, 106-111, 112-117;[118] 1761-*ca.* 1774) plus 2 sonatas in MS. Furthermore,

112. Zschinsky-Troxler/PUGNANI is more detailed, including a thematic index of first mvts., illustrations, and charts, but unfortunately few music exx. Müry/PUGNANI (with no exx.) has more complete titles in its list of publications, re-editions, and mod. eds., and somewhat more systematic, objective analyses and evaluations.

113. Since the two Pugnani studies appeared, several further re-editions have turned up in recent bibliographies, as well as at least one (lost?) set probably not previously reported (cf. the listings of duos in Johansson/FRENCH I 79 and 142 II Facs. 66).

114. The Vendôme and De la Chevardière eds. listed separately in Zschinsky-Troxler/PUGNANI 83 (cf. p. 25) and Müry/PUGNANI 97 (cf. p. 3) appear to be one and the same, which was first announced, and listed in a De la Chevardière catalogue, in 1761 (cf. Johansson/FRENCH I 65 and II Facs. 47). Although Pugnani's dedication (reprinted in Pamparato/PUGNANI 228) to his patron in Torino, the Duca di Savoia, mentions "this first product of my feeble talent," the assumption that publication occurred in 1754, during Pugnani's first visit to Paris, cannot be supported. Besides the mod. eds. listed in Müry/PUGNANI 97, Son. 50 in B♭ occurs in Schenk/TRIOSONATE-m 63.

115. Published *ca.* 1761 in Paris; overlooked in Müry/PUGNANI.

116. Cf. Müry/PUGNANI 34-35; Zschinsky-Troxler/PUGNANI 135.

117. The Venier ed., *ca.* 1769, adds "corni et obboe ad lib" (cf. Johansson/FRENCH I 164, II Facs. 122).

118. In Müry/PUGNANI this last set is put first, perhaps because it is "oeuvre 1" in the Janet et Cotelle ed., but it seems to be Pugnani's latest son. publication,

there is a set of SS duos (Sons. 118-123, *ca.* 1765) plus 12 more sonatas of this type in MS, and a set of accompanied sonatas (K & Vn-or-Fl & Vc, 82-87, *ca.* 1766[119]). Two solo keyboard sonatas reportedly composed for Empress Maria Theresa in 1782 and 1783 are now lost.[120]

Nearly all of Pugnani's published sonatas are in three movements (as against four or five in most of the quartets, quintets, and sinfonias). The chief exceptions are the duos, which are in two movements. There is some consistency within the sets, but overall the plan of the movements is so varied that only the predominance of moderate tempos and minuet or quasi-minuet finales (with or without trio) can be generalized, and then chiefly in the later sets. The theme-and-variations (usually headed "Amoroso," with three or four variations over a repeated *b.c.*) is a frequent finale, too (e.g., Son. 109, S/bass), as is the rondo or rondeau (Son. 83, acc'd.). A quasi-gigue finale, called "Caccia" in the frequent pre-Classic manner, occurs in the only four-movement sonata (52, SS/bass), and one of the very few actual fugues serves as a finale (Son. 58, S/bass). Thematic interrelationships are frequent between any two or all three movements (Son. 50, SS/bass), although sometimes these seem to result merely from the habitual use of certain melodic patterns to be noted. The usual restriction to keys of four sharps or flats and few minor modes obtains, but with B♭ exceptionally favored and D used only once in the published sonatas. In about a fourth of the sonatas the middle movement is in either the dominant or subdominant key, or at least changes to the tonic minor mode.

Pugnani has interesting approximations of "sonata form" more often than not in the first fast movements, and frequently in the first slow or moderate movement, although at least one "standard" ingredient of this form is usually missing. There is generally more than one subordinate idea in the related key that provides a degree of contrast (Son. 105/ii, S/bass). It is most often tentative and cadential in character (Son. 65/i/20-30, SS/bass), but proves to be complete in itself on occasion (Son. 114/ii/32-44, S/bass). The middle section is likely to begin with a complete transposition of the opening idea, after which it goes only so far toward development of the material as to transpose shorter sections and modulate by relatively slight sequencing on still smaller fragments. As a rule there is a clearly prepared return, though it often comes too near the end to include much more than the opening idea

for none of its editions can be dated much before 1774 (J. J. Hummel in Amsterdam).

119. Dated a little late (1770) in Zschinsky-Troxler/PUGNANI 113, as being among "the mature works" (p. 171); cf. Johansson/FRENCH I 73.

120. Pamparato/PUGNANI 365 and 368.

itself (Son. 113/i, S/bass). Sometimes the return occurs only at a harmonic tangent (Son. 51/i, SS/bass), and sometimes not at all (as in all 3 mvts. of Son. 49, SS/bass). In short, once more the salient fact is that the time is ripe and the environment right, but the form is still fluid.

Once more, too, one realizes that it is not what the plot is but how it is told that distinguishes the individual composer's style. Pugnani's more individual traits are evident from the start, although they become more pronounced in the later sets. Already in his earliest sonatas (47-52, SS/bass) the bass figuring, which he came to use less and less without ever abandoning the *b.c.* part itself, is made superfluous by the homophony and generally slow harmonic rhythm, including frequent pedal points. The second violin part is distinctly subordinate in range and thematic importance, having only occasional exchanges with the first, except, of course, in the fugues (as in Son. 52/ii, SS/bass). Even in the fugues the bass has very little melodic responsibility. But the bass—or, rather, cello—does participate in melodic exchanges when it has a part separate from the *b.c.* (e.g., Son. 58/ii) in the manner of the *concertante* parts in seventeenth-century SSB/bass scorings (SBE 51-53). The most difficulties—double-stops, upper positions, rapid passages—naturally occur in the "solo" sonatas. But they are sufficiently present in the "trio" sonatas, especially in the first violin part, to make these above average in difficulty, too. In the accompanied sonatas (82-87) all the parts are relatively easy to play. The keyboard writing at its most advanced level (Son. 83) is still rather elementary for the time. Nor does it dominate the violin part very often as it does in most accompanied sonatas. The cello doubles the keyboard bass as usual (except for passages in Son. 87/i).

Pugnani's harmony is seldom distinctive in its use or rich in its vocabulary, the chief points of interest being the tonal shifts after the middle double-bar in some of the sonatas (e.g., Son. 53/i). Rather is it the melodic treatment that gives his music its individuality. The melodic line itself is generally not notable. In fact, it palls after any prolonged exposure to the sonatas, with its tendency to center around diatonic tetrachords and to overdo certain patterns or formulas like the anacrustic opening on a rising 5th. But the treatment of the melody shows a peak of refinement in the *galant* style.[121] Enhanced by detailed bowing and dynamic markings, it abounds in two- or three-note groupings, appoggiaturas and short trills, melodic sighs and chromaticisms, borrowed tones from the tonic minor mode, fussy rhythmic alterations

121. Cf. the discussion of pre-Romantic traits in his style in Barblan/PUGNANI 24-26.

Ex. 33. From the start of Sonata 65/ii in E♭ by Gaetano Pugnani (after the Welcker ed. in the Library of Congress).

and syncopations, and piquant unprepared dissonances. Melodic continuation is achieved largely by successions of one- or two-measure units usually stated twice. Since the process is one of derivation rather than contrast, even when there are *forte-piano* changes within the same "theme" there is little sense of thematic dualism (Son. 53/i).

Although no one passage in this rather attenuated music embodies all the foregoing traits, a representative example can be taken from Pugnani's last published set of "trio" sonatas (65-70), the one about which the publisher Welcker seems rightly to have written on the title page (*ca.* 1771), "NB These Trios gained such Reputation when the Author was in London as to be called his most capital Work" (Ex. 33). Not only the frequent slow movements of the sort illustrated here but the moderate and fast ones in Pugnani's "trio" sonatas show that, unlike Tartini and Nardini, he took this setting if anything more seriously than the S/bass setting. Yet his S/bass sonatas are still very similar in style (Ex. 34). They are still about as far removed as they can be from that only piece by which "Pugnani" has been made known to today's concert audiences. This is the bold, neo-Handelian "Praeludium and Allegro" passed off as his until Fritz Kreisler revealed his celebrated hoax in 1935.[122]

If some doubt still remains about Pugnani, there is no doubt that the Neapolitan violinist **Emanuele Barbella** (1718-77) was a pupil of Tartini once removed, and by way of Tartini's same pupil Pasquale Bini.[123] Barbella was a good violinist (to judge from Burney's somewhat qualified, firsthand account[124]) and the composer of at least five different sets of melo/bass sonatas and other chamber music that enjoyed several publications in London and Paris in the 1760's and 1770's.[125]
126a The first of two sets of S/bass sonatas (without op. nos.)[126] is optionally scored as *Six Solos for a Violin and Bass or two Violins, Composed for Gentlemen Performers* (1765).[127] These and Barbella's six SS/bass sonatas Op. 1 are mostly in three movements in no special order, often

122. Cf. Lochner/KREISLER 295-308 for a summary of the controversy that followed.

123. Cf. Barbella's autobiographical statement in Burney/HISTORY II 452 (with a reprinting of his well-known "Tinna nonna" or "Lullaby" for Vn). The birth year is newly reported in DIZIONARIO RICORDI 102.

124. BURNEY'S TOURS I 264, 282.

125. Cf. BRITISH UNION I 83; PUBBLICAZIONI NAPOLI 557-558; Johansson/FRENCH II Facs. 4-8, 10, 12. Some English titles (including "Publish'd for the Author" in Op. 1) have suggested a stay in London (cf. Eitner/QL I 335), though it is conspicuously absent from any of Burney's several references to Barbella (cf. especially Burney/HISTORY II 451).

126. One son. was reprinted in Anth. CARTIER-m. Mod. eds.: Son. in g, Moffat/VIOLIN-SONATEN-m No. 19; Son. in E♭, Alard/VIOLIN-m No. 25.

127. Listed in full in WOLFFHEIM MUSIKBIBLIOTHEK I item 1259 (but cf. BRITISH UNION I 83 for the date).

Ex. 34. From the start of Sonata 111/i in G by Gaetano Pugnani (after the Huberty ed. in the Library of Congress).

with colorful titles (e.g., "Alla Napolitana, Sul Fare di Puscinella") but not with the detailed, witty programmatic inscriptions such as appear in his SS *Duos*. The music is a competent imitation of Tartini's in both style and form, though without either the virtuosity or inspiration of the latter's "solo" sonatas.[128]

This chapter's penultimate stringsman is **Luigi Boccherini** (1743-1805). By general consensus both past and present, Boccherini be-

128. It seems to be overrated in Moser/VIOLINSPIEL 239-240.

longs, along with his nearest artistic predecessor G. B. Sammartini, among the most original and historically significant of pre-Classic instrumental composers. Although this gentle, unopportunistic artist was allowed to die in the most abject poverty, there was widespread recognition of his importance in his own day, probably even more than there has yet been in today's revival of interest, except on the part of the relative few who have troubled to delve adequately into his music. Only sixteen years before Boccherini's death Burney wrote of the "revolution in violin-music" effected by him, Haydn, Pleyel, Vanhal, and others, which made the music of Tartini's day "totally tame and insipid" by comparison.[129] This generally cautious historian rated Boccherini in particular as second only to Haydn and "among the greatest masters who have ever written for the violin or violoncello," with a style "at once bold, masterly, and elegant."[130] Three years later Gerber wrote in much the same vein, praising Boccherini's harmony, modulations, and lyricism, and adding—with an outlook quite different from that of the early twentieth century—"Haydn is the only one we Germans can set against this Italian."[131] To be sure, Burney and Gerber both had reference mainly to Boccherini's quintets, which were on the way to becoming his most distinctive and prolific genre (some 120 by 1802[132]). But the sonatas, although they constitute an earlier and smaller part of his production, had been widely valued in their own right, too, as evidenced once more by the many re-editions, in Paris, London, Amsterdam, Mannheim, Vienna, and Riga. The earlier dates of the sonatas and the fact that Boccherini never quite outgrew his *galant* mannerisms nor overstepped the delicately poetic content are the reasons for grouping him here with the pre- rather than the high-Classic composers, whose contemporary he actually was.

By the time he was eighteen (1761) Boccherini had studied cello and composition in his home town of Lucca (in Tuscany), gone to Rome for further study of both (1757), made two trips to Vienna, composed one set each of string trios, quartets (contemporary with Haydn's earliest), and duos, and returned to establish himself in
133a Lucca.[133] But before his actual employment at the Lucchese chapel in

129. Burney/HISTORY II 449-450.

130. Burney/HISTORY II 455.

131. Gerber/LEXICON I 174. Gerber/NEUES I 433-436 adds more praise, a fuller list of works, and what seems to be the first layer of a choice anecdote subsequently much intensified (cf. Picquot/BOCCHERINI 64-66).

132. Cf. Bonaccorsi/CONTRIBUTO 200-201.

133. The two main studies of the man and his music are Picquot/BOCCHERINI (a precocious adventure in musicology of 1851, republished with emendations in 1930 by Saint-Foix; cf. pp. 1-7; but also, cf. Lindsay & Smith/BOCCHERINI 79-80 [with mention, p. 78, of a new "life and works" in progress as of 1943]) and

1764[134] he performed abroad, wrote some church music, and may have visited or even studied with G. B. Sammartini in Milan.[135] In any case, he came to know the latter and symphonies by him when, in 1765 (not 1767), he played first cello in a festival orchestra of sixty members headed by Sammartini and divided between Cremona and Pavia.[136] It must have been around 1766-67[137] that Boccherini became a member in near-by Florence of, reportedly, the first established string quartet.[138] Included in this notable, all-Tuscan group were his inseparable traveling companion and co-citizen, the violinist Filippo Manfredi (1729-77), a pupil of both Nardini and Tartini and himself the composer of at least a dozen S/bass sonatas;[139] the Livornese violinist (violist?) Giovanni Giuseppe Cambini (1746-1825), a pupil of both Manfredi and Nardini and a pioneer quite as Boccherini was in the writing of the Classic *concertante* type of string quartet and quintet;[140] and, of course, Nardini himself. With Manfredi, Boccherini probably reached Paris in 1767, the year his earliest *sinfonie/quartetti* and trios were published there.[141] At any rate, in Paris during the next year, while the two were playing to both favorable and unfavorable criticism,[142] Boccherini wrote the first set of his sonatas to be published (Op. 5, acc'd.) and perhaps the second set (Vc/bass). But probably not until well after he and Manfredi followed up the Spanish ambassador's invitation to visit Madrid (by early 1769[143]) did he compose the third set. It was in Madrid that Boccherini ran afoul of Nardini's pupil Gaetano Brunetti (1753-1808), whose own extensive instrumental music (including symphonies and sonatas) suggests a promising field of exploration.[144]

Bonaventura/BOCCHERINI. Schletterer/BOCCHERINI largely repeats Picquot, with a few additions to both the life and catalogue. Recent information is brought together in Bonaccorsi/BOCCHERINI (bibliography); Bonaccorsi/CONTRIBUTO; Solar-Quintes/BOCCHERINI (Madrid documents).

134. Cf. Bonaventura/BOCCHERINI 13-14 and (for further details on the next year) Bonaventura/CANTATA.

135. Cf. Picquot/BOCCHERINI 55-56, 9-10.

136. Cf. Barblan/ORCHESTRE 19-20; Sartori/SAMMARTINI 17. Further information has been supplied by Miss Bathia Churgin of Vassar College.

137. I.e., after Nardini's return from Stuttgart and before Boccherini's departure for Paris.

138. DIZIONARIO RICORDI 169-170, 234.

139. Cf. Eitner/QL VI 297; Schletterer/BOCCHERINI 138; Bonaccorsi/BOCCHERINI 227: Bonaccorsi/CONTRIBUTO 202.

140. Bonaventura/LIVORNESI 11-13; Roncaglia/CAMBINI (with exx. and a reference to a "very agreeable" S/bass son. by Cambini, p. 269); Roncaglia/QUARTETTISTA, with exx.; Bonaccorsi/QUINTETTI, with exx.

141. Not 1761, as in Lindsay & Smith/BOCCHERINI 75; cf. Picquot/BOCCHERINI 107, 109, 13; Johansson/FRENCH I 161-162, 10-11.

142. Cf. Picquot/BOCCHERINI 56-57, 11; Bonaventura/BOCCHERINI 16-17; Brenet/CONCERTS 291.

143. Picquot/BOCCHERINI 58; Solar-Quintes/BOCCHERINI 92-93.

144. Cf. Picquot/BOCCHERINI 62-64; Subirá/ALBA 159-164.

Boccherini left a careful thematic index in MS of the first movements of 61 of his instrumental and 3 of his vocal works, listed, with their early publishers or as being "inedita," in a single series of 64 opus numbers (which the publishers often changed) and by year of composition from 1760 to 1802.[145] However, only one (Op. 5) of the 3 original, published sets (of 6 sons. each) and none of his unpublished sonatas appear in that list. In the list that Louis Picquot expanded to 485 (original and other) items in 1851, appear the other 2 original sets, plus 9 published sets of accompanied "sonatas" (27 in K & Vn and 7 [not 9] in K & Vn & Vc-or-Va settings) that Pleyel, F.-J. Hérold, and others made from Boccherini's trios and quintets in the 1780's and 1790's.[146] Furthermore, some 16 additional sonatas in MSS to be noted shortly have been found in the present century, bringing the total of extant original sonatas to 34. This total does not include "trios" or "duos" later called "sonatas" in English editions.[147] Obviously, a new, comprehensive, collated, thematic index of Boccherini's entire out-
148a put is much needed.[148]

Boccherini's sonata output, which, it should be remembered, has yet
148b to be studied in detail, may be summarized here by types. Of the original accompanied sets, the first, Op. 5 (K & Vn), is the one composed while Boccherini was in Paris in 1768, where it first appeared late that year,[149] probably before he left. It was republished about a dozen times before the end of the century. Doubtless aimed at the prevailing craze in Paris for the accompanied setting, this set was dedicated to a favorite Parisian clavecinist, Madame Brillon de Jouy, whom Burney called "one of the greatest lady-players on the harpsichord in Europe."[150] The second accompanied set (no op. no.; K & Vn &

145. Printed in Bonaventura/BOCCHERINI 197-203, but without the themes except for a facs. (after p. 104) of the portion from 1792-96 found in another autograph MS (also in BBM V [June, 1930] 33-36); cf. Picquot/BOCCHERINI 107-108, 3-7. What has happened to the complete original of this index?

146. Picquot/BOCCHERINI 110-111, 141, 142, 143-144, 149, 183-184 (but 13, not 15, "Sonates ou Trios").

147. Cf. the good, partially collated list of publications in BRITISH UNION I 116-118; also, PUBBLICAZIONI NAPOLI 563.

148. A thematic index that Walter Upmeyer had prepared by 1943 (Lindsay & Smith/BOCCHERINI 80) has not appeared in print. Mr. Charles Farrell of New York City is completing such an index at the time of this writing (1960); besides contributing new bibliographic information on the cello concertos, in the master's thesis Porter/BOCCHERINI, and on the quintets, in Bonaccorsi/BOCCHERINI 200-201, he has submitted considerable information bearing on the present discussion, which is gratefully acknowledged here.

149. Not 1769; cf. Johansson/FRENCH I 162.

150. BURNEY'S TOURS I 27-28. The set is discussed, with many exx., in Torrefranca/ORIGINI 569-587; cf., also, Picquot/BOCCHERINI 110-111, 13-14; Schletterer/BOCCHERINI 147 (citing Boccherini's re-use of Sons. 2 and 6 in a trio and quintet); Bonaventura/BOCCHERINI 74-85. Mod. ed., entire, with helpful "appendice": CLASSICI-m II No. 4 (Polo).

Vc), first published in Paris in 1781, was among several sets classed as "supposées" by Picquot; but it was later regarded as authentic by Saint-Foix.[151] In the present study, too, both the style and quality of this set have seemed too close to that of the first set to leave any question of authenticity.

Boccherini's third set, which appeared between the other two, is his only published set of melo/bass sonatas, although even in it the bass part is not figured. The interesting question is whether its solo part was originally for violin or for cello, if, indeed, it was not meant for either when the set was first composed. Picquot chose violin in his listing, though with uncertainty.[152] It is true that the probable first edition appeared in that form, about 1770 from De la Chevardière in Paris,[153] followed by the cello edition in 1771 from Bremner in London.[154] However, all other evidence points toward the cello as the instrument originally intended.[155] The cello was Boccherini's instrument; he is known already to have performed a cello sonata of his own at the Concert spirituel in early 1768;[156] it is hardly accidental that the solo part in the violin version is almost always written more than an octave above the bass and above the best tenor portion of the cello's range; the solo part must have posed rewarding challenges to cellists (to judge by other cello music of the time)[157] but would have seemed tame to violinists (hence more salable in that version?); and, finally, no other "solo" violin music by Boccherini can be confirmed (aside from the still controversial, pre-Mozartean Concerto in D[158]). Certainly, these sonatas have only survived as cello pieces, in the reasonably faithful "revisions" that Piatti made of all six,[159] as well as the unconscionably free concert adaptations by Grützmacher (compiler of the *pasticcio* that has become "Boccherini's" best known cello concerto, the one in B♭[160]) and others.[161]

Among Boccherini's MSS are twenty cello sonatas in Milan that seem to include the published set of six, two others (in B♭ and C) made

151. Picquot/BOCCHERINI 141-142, 14.
152. Picquot/BOCCHERINI 141; on calling this set Op. 7, cf., also, Schletterer/BOCCHERINI 147.
153. Contrary to Haas/CAT. 20 item 86. Cf. Johansson/FRENCH II Facs. 54.
154. Listed in BRITISH UNION I 118 (but "1770?" here for the Vn [re-]ed. by Le Duc ["Rue du Roule, à la Croix d'Or"] must be some 15 years too early [cf. Johansson/FRENCH I 86]).
155. Although the discussion is confused and inconclusive, cello is the instrument preferred in Bonaventura/BOCCHERINI 90-97.
156. Picquot/BOCCHERINI 11.
157. Contrary to Schletterer/BOCCHERINI 117, 137.
158. Cf. Bonaventura/BOCCHERINI 97-105.
159. Piatti/BOCCHERINI-m.
160. Cf. Porter/BOCCHERINI 103-111.
161. Cf. Weigl/VIOLONCELL 58; Altmann/KAMMERMUSIK 267.

known in CLASSICI-m I No. 3 (Toni), and two in MS in Florence.[162] There are also some "Sonate per Viola e Basso" in Milan[163] and a "Sonata a due Violoncelli" in C, Op. 35, in Naples.[164] But the six "sonate per cembalo" recently "discovered" by C. Mola, who writes of their "great beauty and thematic wealth" without divulging the location of the MS,[165] should certainly prove to be none other than those in the second published accompanied set (1781), copied as in the published editions, separately from the cello and violin parts. Their description, origin in Spain, and both choice and order of keys (C, e, E♭, D, B♭, and g) all fit exactly.

Boccherini's two accompanied sets are equally divided between sonatas in two and three movements, all of them moderate or fast except for two slow movements (Op. 5/1/ii and 5/2/ii). The cello set is made up entirely of three-movement cycles, with the first or middle movement of each being slow. About half of the finales are minuets or quasi-minuets (seldom with trios) and a "Rondo, Tempo di Minuetto" (Op. 5/4/ii; with "Minore"). The fugues and sets of variations to be found occasionally in his trios and other chamber music do not happen to occur in the published sonatas, but the finale of a MS cello sonata (CLASSICI-m I No. 3, Son. 2) is a minuet with four variations. The movements headed "Minuetto Militare" (2d acc'd set/4/iii) and "All.° alla Militare" (cello/3/ii) recall a descriptive term used elsewhere by Boccherini, too. Otherwise, in the sonatas he used no terms more revealing than "Cantabile" or "Affettuoso." Thematic relationships between movements are infrequent, and then only between outer movements (Op. 5/2). But sometimes one movement leads to the next through a half-cadence, such as that approached by an augmented-$^6{}_5$ chord and couched in poetic cadenzas at the end of Op. 5/4/i.

Only keys with signatures of less than four sharps or flats are used in Boccherini's sonatas, there being a moderate preference, as with Pugnani, for the flat keys. Minor keys are still the exception and major the rule, with the usual ratio of only about one sonata in minor per set of six sonatas. Indeed, in two of the two-movement sonatas, after an opening movement in minor the finale is in major—the tonic major in one instance (e to E, 2d acc'd. set/2) and relative major in the other (g to B♭, 2d acc'd. set/6). When, but only when, the middle of three

162. Cf. Bonaventura/BOCCHERINI 91 (Crepas and Zanon republished Sons. 2, 4, and 5 in the original set), 210.

163. Bonaventura/BOCCHERINI 210.

164. Cf. PUBBLICAZIONI NAPOLI 563; RM XVII (March, 1936) 213 (review of performance); Bonaccorsi/INEDITA, with exx. and a newly found portrait.

165. Cf. Bonaccorsi/BOCCHERINI 227, under C. Mola. Could the unidentified MS be the "Sonate VI Per Cembalo o Pianof." listed in PUBBLICAZIONI NAPOLI 563?

movements is slow is it usually in another key, ordinarily the subdominant rather than the dominant.

The forms of Boccherini's sonata movements are notable for their absence of formalism and their varied, supple adaptations to the nature of the content. They range from the simplest binary outline of tonic-to-dominant-and-back—as in the unbroken, ornamental yet songful "Adagio" that opens one of his most effective and best known sonatas, the last in the cello set, in A—to complete "sonata forms" such as Sonata 3/i (E♭) of the second accompanied set, in which the three sections are disposed in the usual manner although without real development of material in the middle section. Special freedom is exhibited in the recapitulations of the "sonata forms." The main themes in Op. 5/4/i/59-70 and 5/4/ii/90-121 return in the tonic minor and lowered mediant (F), respectively, before going back to the original key of D for the contrasting themes. There is no return to the initial idea, only to subsequent material from the exposition, in that same cello Sonata in A (ii) or Op. 5/3/i. The return is clear enough in Op. 5/3/ii/84, but it seems to be of only secondary importance in what amounts to a simple but original rondo structure based on only three main ideas. Such procedures recall the similarly original plans reported in Boccherini's symphonies, quintets and trios.[166]

As against the thematically simpler rondo procedure there is an embarrassment of melodic riches in many of these forms. In the "Minuetto" finale of the first cello sonata (B♭) in CLASSICI-m I No. 3 there is the equivalent of two trios, one in the relative and the other in the tonic minor key, followed by a *da capo* return: A-B-C-A. But each of the repeated subdivisions introduces new material, with the result that the total effect is much more additive than integrated: A(ab)-B(cd)-C(efg)-A(ab). Instances are frequent in the larger, quasi-"sonata forms," too. In the well-known cello sonata mentioned earlier (Son. 6/ii/52-57) a characteristic, quizzical theme on the dominant harmony (presaging the spirit of that lovely idea in Schubert's String Quartet in G/i/65-68) is added just before the return to A.

Boccherini's instrumental writing and handling of texture show considerable variety, too. Torrefranca interested himself in Op. 5 primarily to argue not only that "Boccherini is the most important precursor of Mozart" but that "he, and not Clementi, should be considered as the true founder of the piano style."[167] This latter aspect of Boccherini's writing, which Torrefranca places in the direct line that had led from

166. Cf. Sondheimer/BOCCHERINI 571; Sondheimer/SINFONIE 98; Picquot/BOCCHERINI 40-42.

167. Torrefranca/ORIGINI 569.

Ex. 35. From Luigi Boccherini's Sonata in D, Op. 5/4/i (after the Longman, Lukey ed. [labeled Op. 3] in the Library of Congress).

Alberti through Galuppi, has not generally been stressed. Yet with the two sets of accompanied sonatas and the keyboard concerto recently discovered in a Dresden MS[168] one begins to attach more importance to Gerber's assumption that Boccherini was a "virtuoso" at the keyboard as well as on the cello.[169] Although his keyboard writing itself is never purely virtuosic in the way that Campioni's sometimes is, the runs, passage work, hand crossing and interchanges, ornaments, and efficient accompaniments (including Alberti basses) bespeak the experience behind them. The violin accompaniments are usually subordinate in range and/or melodic interest (as throughout the excellent sonata Op. 5/5 in g). Then the violin part can be omitted without serious loss. It can also be omitted when it merely supplies melodic bits that provide rhythmic complements and punctuation for the keyboard part, although the imitations that result bring Boccherini as close as he gets to motivic development of his ideas (Ex. 35). Less often the violin part, though never as rich as the solo part in the cello/violin set, has an indispensable solo, as at the start of Sonata 4 in the second accompanied set or

168. Cf. Eitner/QL II 75.
169. Gerber/LEXICON I 174.

throughout most of Op. 5/3. This last is a real duo, for which reason and for its melodic first movement and sprightly finale it becomes one of the most usable of Boccherini's accompanied sonatas in present-day recitals. The cello part in the second accompanied set, as would be expected, doubles the keyboard bass except for infrequent moments of independence (e.g., after the start of Son. 1/ii). There is actually more independent melodic interest, from time to time, in the "bass" (cello) of the cello/violin set. The fact that this bass is unfigured suggests that these sonatas could be and were done as virtual duos of two cellos, as well as melo/bass settings with keyboard filler.[170] Indeed, the setting of the MS "Sonata a due Violoncelli" mentioned earlier reveals quite the same melo/bass relationship between the two parts as do the "solo" and "bass" parts of the published cello/violin set.

Boccherini's lines are formed by motivic repetition, whether literal, sequential, or still freer. In the quicker, gayer movements a single motive is likely to persist in distinct repetitions, even imitations (as in the movement from which Ex. 35 was taken). In the less quick, more lyrical movements the motives are joined skillfully, almost imperceptibly, into separable phrases and periods. One motive serves throughout a phrase or period, and in most instances the material is handled so economically that two or three motives suffice for a whole section of phrases and periods, even when they are hidden behind the decorative lines of the cello sonatas. Outstanding examples of long untroubled lines fashioned in this manner may be found in Op. 5/3/i and Op. 5/5/ii. Heard in succession, such lines produce complete forms in a remarkably few, simple, broad strokes. Large relationships over and above the phrases and periods are pointed up by Boccherini's unerring tonal organization, which becomes as solid a foundation for his forms as for those of his nearest artistic ancestor, G. B. Sammartini. Merely the device of changing the mode at a new theme or section, which he applies frequently, affords a telling contrast. Ex. 36 illustrates a minor theme introduced abruptly after the arrival at the dominant from the original key of F (major). It is copied here in the less familiar violin version, for purposes of comparison with the more accessible cello version.

It is Boccherini's persistence with single motives that explains, as much as any one factor explains, the similarity of his and Haydn's styles.[171] But if the violinist Puppo's oft-cited designation of Boccherini

170. Cf. MGG IV 1721 (Oberdörffer) on the appearance of bass figures in Boccherini's string trios Op. 9.

171. It may also explain that favorite anecdote about a first-violin part by Boccherini in which "ut, si, ut, si" repeats so continually that the Spanish prince who played it (without hearing the changing texture in which it occurred) was

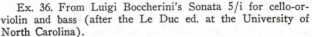

Ex. 36. From Luigi Boccherini's Sonata 5/i for cello-or-violin and bass (after the Le Duc ed. at the University of North Carolina).

as "the wife of Haydn" makes any sense,[172] it is the psychological one of gentle sensitivity as opposed to bold virility.[173] For Boccherini's best known piece, the "Minuetto" in A (from Quintet Op. 13, No. 5, in E), is as truly representative of at least this main facet of his style as Kreisler's afore-mentioned piece is not representative of Pugnani. Actually, though Boccherini and Haydn did know each other,[174] their known contact in 1781 came too late and their works were composed too nearly at the same time for clear influences either way to be demonstrated. There is more chance that Boccherini could have influenced Mozart, although here no contact has been proven,[175] the thematic relationships that have been argued[176] seem too fragmentary and too characteristic of melodic styles that were then "in the air" to be significant, and there is generally less common ground stylistically between them than there is between Boccherini and Haydn or, say, either Mysliveček or Christian Bach and Mozart. Spohr's contemptuous dismissal of Boccherini's music in 1821[177] seems to have been made mainly on the ground that Boccherini was *not* Mozart. In any case, the sonatas, to which we have had to confine ourselves here, show Boccherini to have been an individual musician in his own right and right from the start—a gentle, poetic musician, with a fresh turn of phrase, a subtle touch of fantasy, and a fine sense of clear form.

The last composer to mention in this chapter was another cellist, **Carlo Graziani** (?-1787). Born in the Piedmont region, this inadequately-known composer was active in London, Frankfurt/M, and Berlin. In the last city, at the Potsdam court of the future King Fried-

driven nearly to throw Boccherini out of the palace window (Picquot/BOCCHERINI 64-65).

172. Cf. Picquot/BOCCHERINI 95.
173. Cf. Farnsworth/PSYCHOLOGY 109.
174. Cf. Pohl/HAYDN II 180-181.
175. Cf. Picquot/BOCCHERINI 20-22.
176. Zschinsky-Troxler/BOCCHERINI; Keller/BOCCHERINI.
177. Schletterer/BOCCHERINI 142.

rich Wilhelm II, he preceded Boccherini (who was there from 1787-97) and the French cellist Jean-Pierre Duport (elder of the Duport brothers and presumed participant in Boccherini's quintets). Three published sets of six sonatas each for cello and bass are known by Graziani (Opp. 1-3, London, Paris, and Berlin, *ca.* 1760-70[178]). There is also another sonata by him in this setting, a programmatic travel sonata in MS, with the biographically useful title of "Il viaggio da Berlino a Breslavia con l'affettuoso ricevuta di S. A. R. 1778."[179] The sonatas of Graziani's Op. 3 show a uniformity of plan both in the cycles as a whole and the individual movements that is quite the opposite of the flexible variety throughout the sonatas of the same period by Galuppi, Rutini, and Boccherini. Each sonata has three movements in the order of F-S-M or F-S-F, with a complete "sonata form" for the first movement, an unbroken binary design in a nearly related key for the second movement, and one of the customary dancelike forms for the finale. In this uniformity of plan and in the broad arches that define his ideas Graziani was already more of a high- than a pre-Classicist. Nor do his figured basses necessarily suggest a more conservative side in his writing. Frequently they support purely homophonic textures in slow harmonic rhythm by skipping from root to root of primary triads, repeating the same note, or even falling into an Alberti bass figure (as in Son. 1/i/63-66). The freest, most expressive writing—ranging from *grazioso* to dramatic—naturally occurs in the melodious slow movements, while the chief, somewhat limited technical display occurs in the finales with variations (as in Son. 5/iii/109-144, where the high double-stops make the thumb position almost mandatory). These sonatas are put together with good craftsmanship. Although, as with Padre Martini, Graziani was limited by a somewhat stultified imagination, his music lies well though often high for the cello, it makes clear structural sense, and it has both the melodic pathos and harmonic pull that promise well for the cellist seeking to expand the early Classic side of his repertoire.

178. Cf. WOLFFHEIM MUSIKBIBLIOTHEK I 245, for Op. 1; BRITISH UNION I 398, for Opp. 2 and 3; Johansson/FRENCH I 112-113, II Facs. 82 etc., for re-editions. Mod. ed., Op. 3 in full, with "appendice" containing the only discussion [summarized in MGG V 749]: CLASSICI-m II (Benvenuti).

179. Cf. Cat. HAUSBIBLIOTHEK 87 (including the MSS of the published sons.).

Chapter IX

The Iberian Peninsula From About 1735 To 1780

Circumstances and Influences

During the period under discussion, Portugal and Spain were far from being the world powers that both countries had been in the sixteenth century. Yet Portugal enjoyed a certain prosperity under the absolutist rule of John V (from 1706) and his successor Joseph (from 1750). And Spain could at least relax somewhat after the War of the Spanish Succession was resolved in favor of Bourbon rule (1714), even though this French influence continued to increase under Philip V (from 1700), Ferdinand VI (from 1746), and Charles III (from 1759). In the realm of music, eighteenth-century Italian influences in the Iberian Peninsula are of special interest. Although under Philip V (or, rather, his wife Elizabeth Farnese) Spain regained her longtime control of Naples and Sicily (1735), in music it was the Italy of these and other centers that prevailed over both Spain and Portugal, especially in Madrid and Lisbon. Italy prevailed by providing a preferred training ground, as for the Spanish opera composers of the eighteenth century;[1] by providing a fund of preferred instrumental music, as in court chamber groups;[2] and by being the source for many of the musicians actually present in Spain. We have already had occasion to note the presence of Alberti, Paganelli, and Boccherini, among many others who could be named. To the disadvantage of native talents, such men were preferred by the kings of both Portugal and Spain, and sought out by their ambassadors.

It was, in fact, the Portuguese ambassador in Rome who induced Domenico Scarlatti to move to Lisbon. From the standpoint of the

1. Cf. Chase/SPAIN 138-139.

2. Chamber works by Locatelli, Veracini, and Brunetti were among early publications and MSS in the library of the Duke of Alba in Madrid, according to Subirá/ALBA Chap. 2.

keyboard sonata, Scarlatti was the vital link between Italy, Portugal, and Spain. More significantly, he had direct contact with the two other main composers discussed in this chapter, for he was at the royal court in Lisbon part of the time that Seixas was there, and he was at the royal court in and about Madrid part of the time that Soler was near by at the Escorial monastery. Together, these three composers represent the main centers of concern to us here. We shall meet only minor names at two other, eastern centers of musical interest, the town of Valencia and the Montserrat monastery near Barcelona.

As one of the original geniuses of keyboard music and as the first resident in the Iberian Peninsula to have a book of keyboard sonatas published, Scarlatti is naturally assumed to have exercised a direct influence on native Iberian composers for the keyboard. But we shall see that this particular influence was probably less than might be supposed at first hearing. Seixas and Soler were original creators, too, with their own subtle but significant individualities of style (which recent editions of their music are making more and more evident). One must realize that those traits of keyboard writing most obviously common to Scarlatti, Seixas, and Soler were also more or less present about the same time in the comparable keyboard music of Marcello, Durante, Rameau, Emanuel Bach, and others still farther away. Moreover, in the sense that Scarlatti took as much from his environment as he gave to it, he shared with Seixas and Soler the respective heritages of Portugal and Spain—the sights and sounds, the folklore, the dances, the art music. After all, these countries had had their own backgrounds of keyboard music quite as distinguished as that of Italy (or any other country). Cabezón and Cabanilles in Spain were certainly the peers of their respective Italian contemporaries A. Gabrieli and Pasquini, as M. R. Coelho in Portugal was the peer of Frescobaldi. The Iberians had their literature of the *tiento* and toccata equivalent to that of the *ricercare* and toccata in Italy. Furthermore, it may be recalled that the first known use of the word "sonata" as an instrumental title had been made by the Spanish vihuelist Luis Milan in 1535 (SBE 18). And at the point where we begin now, Spanish theorists were not much behind other theorists in their definitions of the sonata, which were still less definitions than classifications. In 1742, for example, the sonata continued merely to be identified, as it and nearly all other instrumental types then in vogue had been identified for more than a century (SBE 22-24), under the heading of "Estilo Phantástico."[3]

Joaquín Nin, one of the first in recent times to explore the eighteenth-

3. Cat. MADRID I 197; cf. p. 193.

century keyboard music of Spain, has stated that the form of the sonata as Scarlatti knew it persisted without essential change right through the
4a first third of the nineteenth century.[4] But we shall find in this and the next chapter that the Spanish sonata, if never on a qualitative par with that of the three Viennese giants, kept pace with the times at least as regards the nature of the styles and forms. The remarkably close contacts that were maintained with Italy, France, and other European countries seem to have more than made up for the outlying, westernmost position of the Iberian peninsula. Thus, as early as 1764, only seven years after Paganelli's *Sonatines* had appeared in Madrid but before the first lighter sonatas of Rutini (1770) or those "à l'usage des Dames" of Emanuel Bach (1770), we find Spanish sonatas in which ease of performance and the new style are offered, "muy fáciles y de buen gusto."[5] Nin also believed that prior to the 18th century the harpsichord had been neglected in Spain, chiefly because the more intimate and expressive vihuela and perhaps the clavichord had been preferred.[6] On the other hand, in the works of Scarlatti and of others we shall meet, the ranges and keyboard treatment seem to confirm that the frequent word *clavicordio* in the titles was to be taken in its more literal Spanish meaning of harpsichord.[7] In any case, the instruments in Spain kept pace with the times, too. Scarlatti himself had good opportunity to know some of the earliest pianos, those of the Cristofori type.[8] Nin finds the piano actually specified (in a piece by Juan Sessé) in 1774,[9] as it first was in most other countries about this time. In Portugal a piano is known to have been built 14 years earlier, in 1760.[10] Not a few of the sonatas, including those "de buen gusto" that were just mentioned, specify both "clave y órgano." Although it is hard to imagine some of the more idiomatic harpsichord passages on the organ, such titles seem to combine the opposite poles of churchlike severity and lighthearted gaiety in the manner discoverable in so much Spanish art. At any rate, it is remarkable how many of our Spanish sonata composers were both organists and clerics (most often from the northeastern region of Catalonia). And it is also remarkable, while on this point, how few sonatas there are to report for instruments other than keyboard, especially in Portugal.

Of special help here have been the pioneer, almost single-handed

4. Nin/ESPAGNOLS-m I iii.
5. Cat. MADRID I 337.
6. Nin/ESPAGNOLS-m I i-iii.
7. Cf. Kirkpatrick/SCARLATTI 186; Dart/KIRKPATRICK.
8. Cf. Kirkpatrick/SCARLATTI 176, 178.
9. Nin/ESPAGNOLS-m I iii.
10. Kastner/CONTRIBUCIÓN 282.

researches on Seixas and on Iberian keyboard music in general by Santiago Kastner in Lisbon, which have borne fruit in several studies and editions cited repeatedly in this chapter.[11] Other help has come from the numerous studies on Scarlatti and their culmination in Ralph Kirkpatrick's fine book, and from informative but too few specialized studies by Spanish scholars. Among the latter are Subirá's lavish account of the significant musical activities at the home of the Duke of Alba in Madrid. Without this account and its excellent facsimiles of documents, title pages, and score pages we could not even know how much was lost when the Alba library was completely destroyed during the Spanish Civil War of 1936-39. Probably that loss, several fires at the Escorial monastery, and the great earthquake in Lisbon in 1755 go far to explain why not a single autograph MS of the keyboard sonatas by Scarlatti, Seixas, or Soler seems now to be extant. In any case, the Iberian MSS become of first importance here because publications of sonatas within Spain or Portugal were so rare that not more than five instances can be cited in this and the next chapter.

Domenico Scarlatti in Lisbon and Madrid

Our first and most notable "Iberian" to bring up is, of course, the Italian cembalist **Domenico Scarlatti** (1685-1757), who was active in both Portugal and Spain. Because the keyboard sonata around 1740 marks the start rather than the end of a trend in sonata history, the consideration of Scarlatti's sonatas was deferred here from the previous to the present volume. In any case, his position on the arbitrary border line between two eras seems to have cost him some of the attention he might otherwise have received from historians of these eras. He marks a post stage in Bukofzer/BAROQUE 236-239, a preliminary stage in Bücken/ROKOKO 17-19, and only an occasional, early point of reference in Torrefranca/ORIGINI 56 (*et passim*). On the other hand, his importance to sonata history per se undoubtedly has been overstated ever since the earliest accounts in the nineteenth century, which put him between Kuhnau and Emanuel Bach in that "single chronological line leading directly to 'sonata form'" (SBE 11). Except for certain style traits encountered several times in this volume and except for his teacher-pupil relationship with Padre Soler,[12] any appreciable influence by Scarlatti on the course of sonata history is not easily demonstrated,[13]

11. Acknowledgment should be made here, too, of much general help provided by Professor Kastner through correspondence.

12. This relationship, generally recognized since 2 tentative proofs were offered in Nin/SOLER 101-102 (1930), is actually confirmed by Soler himself in a letter to Padre Martini published in Kastner/SOLER 237.

13. One questionable example is a set of 6 sons. by the English Scarlatti en-

least of all in his homeland, where his music seems scarcely to have been noticed in the later eighteenth century.[14] If his writing is generally more *galant* than that of his exact contemporaries Handel and J. S. Bach, it is certainly less so than that of others, like D. Alberti, who were writing sonatas about the same time with nothing of the high content yet much more of the future in them. Today Scarlatti occupies a tangential but more secure niche in music history—along with Frescobaldi, Chopin, and remarkably few others—as one of the most genuine, poetic, and original creators for the keyboard. In that sense he must be regarded more as an intriguing digression than a main theme, or bridge, or development, or even coda in the "sonata form" of the present study.

Starting with reports from the ubiquitous Burney and other near contemporaries, it has taken two centuries and the devoted efforts of many researchers to supply such information, still inadequate, as we now have about Scarlatti and his music. One recalls with special gratitude the strides made during the present century in the biographic and bibliographic studies on various members of the Scarlatti family by scholars like E. J. Dent, Luciani, Walker, Solar-Quintes, Newton, Luise Bauer,[15] Chase, Kastner, and Sartori; and one recalls the first basic study of the music itself in the valuable dissertation by Walter Gerstenberg. More recently, in 1953, nearly all that is essential in these previous studies was ably recapitulated and assimilated in the handsomely printed monograph by the American harpsichordist Ralph Kirk-
15a patrick. Only the researcher hoping to fill gaps or expand topics in uncharted territory should need to go back over the earlier material. Furthermore, Kirkpatrick himself has been able to contribute essential information at several basic points in Scarlatti's career. And where virtually all personal information was lacking about this apparently unassuming, even reticent artist, he has sought, in a convincing manner, at least to recapture the sights, sounds, smells, and feel of the different environments in which Scarlatti matured. Without this much atmosphere it would be difficult to orient ourselves properly to Scarlatti's music, for the known facts of his life in the later years are still few indeed.

Born of a Sicilian family in Naples, under Spain's kingdom of the "Two Sicilies," Scarlatti visited Florence in 1702, stayed in Venice for

---

thusiast Joseph Kelway, "which are, perhaps, the most crude, awkward, and unpleasant pieces of the kind that have ever been engraved [1764]," as cited in Burney/HISTORY II 1009 (cf. Newton/SCARLATTI 149; SCE XIX). Less pertinent here are arrangements such as the concertos Avison made from Scarlatti's sonatas in the 1740's (cf. BRITISH UNION II 925; Kirkpatrick/SCARLATTI 404-405).

14. Cf. Kirkpatrick/SCARLATTI 123-125.

15. Unpublished dissertation (Munich, 1933); cf. AFMF III (1938) 335.

four years from 1705 to 1709, served in Rome for ten years until 1719, then probably went directly to Lisbon (rather than by way of London[16]). In Lisbon one of his main duties was to teach the daughter, Maria Barbara, as well as the younger brother of King John V of Portugal. When Maria Barbara married into the Spanish royal family in 1729, Scarlatti followed in her service to Seville in the southern Spanish region of Andalusia, and from there to Madrid in the central kingdom of Castile in 1733, where he remained until his death, including the period after Maria Barbara's husband succeeded to the Spanish kingship as Ferdinand VI in 1746. Before Scarlatti left Italy he seems to have come under the influence of his father, Alessandro, in Naples,[17] of Gasparini (pupil of both Corelli and Pasquini) in Venice, and perhaps of Pasquini (pupil of Frescobaldi) in Rome during the year before Pasquini died (1710). Scarlatti probably knew B. Marcello (pupil of Gasparini) and Handel in Venice, and the latter again in Rome, where the legendary contest between the two could have occurred.[18] In Lisbon he knew the brilliant harpsichordist Carlos Seixas and in Madrid he was a close associate during his last twenty years of that most famous of *castrati,* Farinelli. Kirkpatrick emphasizes the idea that Scarlatti only came into full, independent maturity and creative emancipation after the death of his father in 1725 and after his first marriage in 1728.[19] During some or all of this period of emancipation he was back in Rome and Naples on leave from his Lisbon post.

More than a dozen operas and several church compositions are known to have been composed by Scarlatti before he first left Italy,[20] and reports of his exceptional keyboard prowess—in fact, the only such reports, mostly by way of Burney—all date from his Italian days.[21] Yet none of his keyboard compositions can be placed with any certainty before the time of his "emancipation" around the age of forty and his service in Portugal;[22] no publication can be confirmed before his celebrated *Essercizi per gravicembalo* appeared in late 1738 or early 1739 in London,[23] in his fifty-third year and nine years after he had moved to

16. Cf. Kirkpatrick/SCARLATTI 65-66, 70, 333-334.

17. Cf. Keller/SCARLATTI 11-12, with exx. (a still more recent monograph [1957], which adds no new material other than an occasional difference of concept).

18. Mainwaring/HANDEL 51-52, 59-62.

19. Kirkpatrick/SCARLATTI 75-76.

20. Cf. the lists in Kirkpatrick/SCARLATTI 413-424; also, the recent report of the only complete opera score (not autograph) to be discovered in recent times (*Tetide in Scirlo,* 1712), in RAM XXVII (1957) 281-289 (Della Corte).

21. Burney/HISTORY II 704 and 1009 (from Roseingrave); BURNEY'S TOURS II 119 (from Hasse) and 191 (from Quantz; cf., also, Kahl/SELBSTBIOGRAPHIEN 133).

22. Cf. Kirkpatrick/SCARLATTI 150-151.

23. Kirkpatrick first reported his solution to the much debated date and place in

Spain; and, apart from two MS volumes dated 1742 and 1749, the large part of his sonatas cannot now be dated with any certainty earlier than the thirteen further volumes of MSS made during the last five years of his life, from 1752-57 or his sixty-seventh to seventy-second years![24] As with all of Pasquini's keyboard MSS, which cannot be dated before his sixtieth year,[25] it is hard to say whether Scarlatti's were composed mainly at the end of his career or composed throughout his life and simply copied in final form during his last years, perhaps by royal request or as part of putting his affairs in final order.[26] In Scarlatti's case the problem is not lessened by the total absence of autographs among his known keyboard MSS.[27] The MS copies exist in many libraries,[28] but much the most important are the four huge collections, with much overlapping of contents, in Venice, Parma, Münster, and Vienna. The last two of these were gathered, and the last was largely copied by one of the most avid collectors of sonatas and of other music in the early nineteenth century, the Abate Fortunato Santini from Rome.[29] And the largest part of the first two of these four collections may actually have been copied by Scarlatti's pupil Soler.[30]

A detailed account of the printed editions over more than two centuries would make an interesting story in itself. Up to the time of Clementi's *Selection of Practical Harmony* (1803-15) well over three dozen publications can be traced that contain sonatas, or concertos transcribed from sonatas, actually or allegedly by Scarlatti.[31] Altogether these editions introduced around 125 different, separate pieces that are authentic.[32] In the nineteenth century this number was con-

---

MQ XXXVII (1951) 145; cf., also, Humphries & Smith/PUBLISHING 27. The doubts still voiced in Keller/SCARLATTI 31 overlook certain arguments in Kirkpatrick/SCARLATTI 405, 402, 403; and Keller's mention of but 2 extant eds. of the *Essercizi* must be corrected to at least a dozen, of which 8 alone are listed in BRITISH UNION II 925. A complete facs. of this superbly engraved 18th-c. ed. is much to be desired (cf. illustrations 32-34 in Kirkpatrick/SCARLATTI: Subirá/ALBA after p. 128). Such a facs. was pub. by Gregg International Press of Farnborough, England, in 1967; cf., also, fn. 37a to p. 265.

24. Cf. Kirkpatrick/SCARLATTI 137-141, 399-401; also, the dated table of the Venice MSS in GROVE VII 460 (Blom).

25. Cf. Shedlock/SONATA 72-73, 75-76, 81; SBE 160.

26. Cf. Kirkpatrick/SCARLATTI 144-145, 114-116.

27. Cf. Kirkpatrick/SCARLATTI 139-141.

28. Cf. Kirkpatrick/SCARLATTI 399-401; also, for sample listings, BRITISH MS III 122-123 and indexed items.

29. Cf. Schmidl/DIZIONARIO II 446; Gerstenberg/SCARLATTI 8-9. The selected list in Stassoff/SANTINI is limited almost entirely to church music.

30. Cf. Kirkpatrick/SCARLATTI 140; one should recall, too, that Soler was near Scarlatti only from 1752 on, the very years when the 13 main volumes were copied.

31. Cf. Newton/SCARLATTI; Kirkpatrick/SCARLATTI 401-411, 425-427; Johansson/FRENCH (for possible editions not previously listed).

32. Or more than twice the number estimated in Keller/SCARLATTI 32.

siderably extended by three main editions, each including all 30 of the original *Essercizi*—Czerny's selection of 200 pieces (1839; including 5 misattributions),[33] Breitkopf & Härtel's "unedited" collection of 60 pieces (1866-67),[34] and the 152 similarly "unedited" pieces distributed in 7 of the 20 volumes in Farrenc's *Trésor des pianistes* (1861-72).[35] But the smaller editions of Bülow, Tausig, and Sauer came into much greater use, and still prevail to this day. Undoubtedly these free adaptations and "enrichments" of the originals better suited nineteenth-century tastes and relieved what Schumann seemed to regard as a certain ineptness and dryness (in his review of the Czerny edition[36]). 36a

In 1906 G. Ricordi in Milan issued the only "complete" collection of Scarlatti's sonatas thus far published, under the editorship of the Italian pianist, sonata composer in his own right, and founder of a Scarlatti
society (1891), Alessandro Longo.[37] With 545 separate sonatas in 11 37a
volumes, this edition, for all its editorial lacks and licenses, has been a landmark in Scarlattiana that can only be topped when and if a new and better "complete" edition appears. The thematic index to Longo's edition that Ricordi issued in 1937, arranged "in order of key and meter," is also still the only one of its kind.[38] In recent years a few other, partial collections have appeared, as well as at least a dozen
sonatas not previously published.[39] As an adjunct to his monograph, 39a
Kirkpatrick has prepared the first *Urtext* edition in which several of the primary sources are collated, consisting of 60 single pieces selected to exemplify the entire range of Scarlatti's art.[40] These pieces follow

33. ". . . less carefully annotated, hence less disturbing than his editions of Bach" (Kirkpatrick/SCARLATTI 412).

34. Breitkopf SCARLATTI-m; photolithographed by Kalmus in this country (1953?); nos. 1-30 are the *Essercizi* in their original order.

35. TRESOR-m II (including an astute preface and sources), V, VIII, XI, XIII, XVI, and XIX.

36. Schumann/SCHRIFTEN I 400-401.

37. Longo/SCARLATTI-m. Cf. Gerstenberg/SCARLATTI 39-41; Della Corte & Pannain/STORIA I 979-980; Kirkpatrick/SCARLATTI 237-241, 305, 412; Schmidl/DIZIONARIO 859-860.

38. Apart from the separate thematic index in each vol. of the later reprintings of Longo/SCARLATTI-m.

39. Among these last are one (K. 417) in Oesterle/TREASURY-m II 142 (cf. Benton/SCARLATTI 265); 5 in Gerstenberg/SCARLATTI-m; 4 published by Newton (Oxford, 1939), but all since regarded as spurious (cf. Gerstenberg/KIRKPATRICK 344; Kirkpatrick/SCARLATTI 426 [regarding Newton/SCARLATTI 152-153]); one in Paoli/ITALIANE-m 15 (also [though not "hitherto unnoticed"] in Kirkpatrick/SCARLATTI 152); one in Kirkpatrick/SCARLATTI 150; and 5 out of 7 in Lee/SCARLATTI-m. A thematic index of 12 sons. not in mod. eds. (as of 1933) is in Gerstenberg/SCARLATTI 153-158 (but cf. Bukofzer/BAROQUE 238-239; Kirkpatrick/SCARLATTI 407, 425-426). On 12 Scarlatti or other sons. wrongly credited to Clementi cf. SCE XX under Clementi.

40. Kirkpatrick/SCARLATTI-m, with preface and facs.; recorded in full by Kirkpatrick for Columbia; cf. Boyden/KIRKPATRICK. This and Breitkopf SCARLATTI-m have 14 sons. in common (Kirkpatrick 1 = Breitkopf 3, 2 = 7, 3 = 16, 4 = 18,

the presumed chronology that Kirkpatrick has worked out in detail in the valuable, complete catalogue and collation of main sources appended to his monograph (pp. 442-456).[41] This chronology depends on several plausible clues—among others, the order in which the sonatas were copied in the main MS volumes, the limitations of a quasi-melo/bass texture in the earliest sonatas, an increased keyboard range in the latest dated MSS, the discontinuation of most of the hand-crossing in those latest MSS, and a general style trend from youthful flamboyancy to more mellow, adult lyricism and poetry, and then to late "digested maturity."[42] The chronological order and other improvements in Kirkpatrick's catalogue certainly justify the change to "K." rather than "L." numbers for the identification of Scarlatti sonatas,[43] except as reference must be made to Longo's edition (for which Kirkpatrick supplies a conversion table, pp. 457-459).

Longo made his own free, though not musically unreasonable, groupings of the sonatas into 5-movement suites centered around one key (e.g., L. 366-370 in d-d-A-D-d = K. 1, 5, 26, 145, 10). These and other groupings by other editors bring us to the important question of single movements or cycles,[44] and hence to the music itself. Mainly in the primary MSS copied from 1752 on (K. 148 ff.), Kirkpatrick finds 388 sonatas that follow in pairs by virtue of tonal, metric, tempo, character, or stylistic relationships, as well as occasional verbal instructions that confirm the association. And he finds 12 others that similarly indicate 3-movement cycles. If all these cycles are recognized and if 8 probable melo/bass sonatas (to be noted later) are subtracted, Scarlatti's known output totals 345 rather than the 555 keyboard sonatas usually given in terms of "single movements."[45] No serious reason remains for

5 = 28, 6 = 29, 7 = 49, 20 = 41, 29 = 58, 43 = 35, 56 = 50, 58 = 55, 59 = 51, 60 = 52); a comparison is instructive, especially when the facs. MS is at hand, too (e.g., mss. 10-20 in Kirkpatrick Son. 60, etc.). Keller & Weismann/SCARLATTI-m is a new ed. of 150 sons. that goes back to the MSS and is arranged only by level of difficulty and key (without consideration of the grouping in the MSS).

41. Minor emendations are offered in Gerstenberg/KIRKPATRICK 344. The earlier, less complete and less developed cat. in Gerstenberg/SCARLATTI 10-31 (cf. pp. 130-132; also, Kirkpatrick/SCARLATTI 440-441) is collated with the Czerny ed.; both cats. include Longo/SCARLATTI-m.

42. Cf. Kirkpatrick/SCARLATTI 144-146, 151, 155, 161, 164-165, 169-173. BURNEY'S TOURS II 87 is the source for the familiar story that (by 1756) Scarlatti became "too fat to cross his hands, as he used to do," but Kirkpatrick rightly asks (p. 171) if it wasn't rather Maria Barbara or even Burney's raconteur L'Augier who became too fat.

43. Unfortunately, the change is not yet made (because of too many "K.'s"?) in Keller/SCARLATTI.

44 Raised by Dent and Gerstenberg (cf. Gerstenberg/SCARLATTI 99) and pursued in Kirkpatrick/SCARLATTI 141-143.

45. Actual separate mvts. total 586 (Keller/SCARLATTI 75). In the Venice MSS 2 larger cycles are also hinted, one being a succession of 5 sons. in the

still regarding the MS groupings merely as the product of an orderly copyist.[46] We have seen how characteristic was the 2-movement sonata and how relatively infrequent the single-movement sonata in the keyboard music by Italians at this time (SCE VI; SBE 199). And, on the other hand, we have seen a general unconcern as to whether sonata cycles were performed as a whole or in part, and a frequent habit of numbering all the pieces in a MS in a single series regardless of how they might group into sonata cycles (SBE 186, 246). In this last regard, it is pertinent to note that all but one section of 4 early Scarlatti sonatas not grouped in later MSS once existed under the over-all heading of "Tocata."[47] Furthermore, scattered throughout the first three-fifths of Kirkpatrick's catalogue are 5 "single-movement" sonatas (e.g., K. 170, L. 303) each of which actually consists of 2 separate movements no different in relationship or extent from those in the paired sonatas.

Undoubtedly, after enough performers follow Kirkpatrick's conclusions and example, the recital hall will have helped to test the validity of the MS groupings.[48] Of course, one should not expect any more by way of internal bonds between movements in Scarlatti sonatas than in most other pre-Classic sonatas. In each of his groupings the tonic remains the same, although in about fifteen per cent the mode changes from minor to major, or conversely. The use of similar incipits—uncommon in contemporary two-movement sonatas, in any case—is too rare and inconclusive to be considered here.[49] In well over half the two-movement groupings the typical succession of a duple- and a triple-metered movement obtains. In a still larger majority both movements are fast. But there are also many movements in moderate tempos, thus making possible the usual unpredictable variety of movement plans. On the other hand, out of all the movements only one is inscribed "Adagio" (K. 109, L. 138), and even this seems to "feel" better at a deliberate andante tempo. Still more than usual for most Italian and Iberian keyboard music of the time, slow movements seem to be eschewed in Scarlatti's sonatas. In any case, a genuinely slow tempo would seem out of place in his relatively undecorated, straightforward writing, and foreign to the spirit behind it. Thanks to tempo inscriptions over almost

---

relatively infrequent key of f (K. 183-187) and the other a succession of 4 sons. in that same key (K. 204a and 204b, Gerstenberg/SCARLATTI nos. 3 and 4).

46. As implied in Keller/SCARLATTI 34.

47. Kirkpatrick/SCARLATTI 141, 400.

48. Performers might have been nudged a bit further over the psychological barrier of tradition if Kirkpatrick had found it possible to show each grouping under one number in his catalogue (as is now apparently intended by K. 204a and 204b).

49. Cf. K. 308-309 (L. 359, 454); K. 490-492 (L. 206, 164, 14).

every movement, there is little doubt about Scarlatti's general intentions in these matters.[50]

With further regard to these inscriptions, the main title of each of the 30 *Essercizi* and of each of the 496 pieces or movements separately numbered in the principal, Venice MS is "Sonata." Only in certain other sources is "Sonata" sometimes equated with or replaced by such frequent alternatives of the time as "Toccata," "Lesson," "Pièce de clavecin," or "Caprice."[51] But besides the tempo inscriptions a few other subtitles occure from time to time, both in the grouped and the independent movements, that point to the few external differentiations Scarlatti made in his forms. "Minuet" or "Minuetto," the most frequent example (as in K. 471, L. 82), occurs 14 times (insofar as the conflicting sources can be reconciled), and there are at least as many more quasi-minuets (K. 210, L. 123), sometimes with elements of the Spanish jota in them.[52] These are simple, steady pieces without trios or other structural extensions. Other dances of the suite occur with subtitles only rarely and in the earliest sonatas—"Allemanda" (K. 4, L. 390[53]), "Gigha" (K. 78, L. 75), and "Gavota" (K. 64, L. 58; almost the opposite number, in minor and duple meter, of Handel's "Hornpipe" from the *Water Music*). The saraband exists only in spirit (K. 87, L. 33).

Six of Scarlatti's sonatas are subtitled "Fuga"[54] (as in K. 93, L. 336), while at least one other is similar in form (K. 287, L. Suppl. 9),[55] and in two others "fugato" is used as part of the subtitle, though in scarcely more than the literal sense of "fleeting" (as in "Veloce è fugato," K. 387, L. 175). Scarlatti's fugal writing is the loose but effectively timed sort in which Corelli had excelled (SBE 83-84). The best known of his fugues—of all his pieces, in fact—is "the celebrated Cat's Fugue" (K. 30, L. 499), which soon must have acquired its programmatic title (for its stalking, wide-spaced chromatic subject), since Clementi was already referring to it in this way around 1805.[56] The remaining subtitles, all good clues to the content, include an "Aria" (K. 32, L. 423), a "Capriccio" (K. 63, L. 84), and three "Pastorales" (as in K. 446, L. 433). But the familiar "Pastorale" and "Toccata," both in d (K. 9 and 141, L. 413 and 422), were only, though appropriately, so called in the free transcriptions of Tausig and others.

50. Cf. the table of tempos in Keller/SCARLATTI 62-63.
51. Cf. Gerstenberg/SCARLATTI 7-8; Kirkpatrick/SCARLATTI 141, 402-411; Keller/SCARLATTI 38-39; SCE III.
52. Cf. Chase/SPAIN 111.
53. The title is missing in some sources (Gerstenberg/SCARLATTI 86).
54. Cf. Kirkpatrick/SCARLATTI 153-155, 141.
55. Cf. Benton/SCARLATTI 265-266.
56. Clementi/HARMONY II 135; also, Newton/SCARLATTI 156.

Scarlatti's fugues are, as would be expected, cursive and uninterrupted in form (not to mention somewhat long for their narrow pitch and tonal ranges). His one set of variations (K. 61, L. 136), two organ voluntaries (e.g., K. 288, L. 57 [but with the first repeat sign added]), and four rondos (e.g., K. 284, L. 90) follow their expected forms, too.[57] But the other, subtitled pieces just noted, whatever their more inborn traits of style and character, all follow the one structural principle that, strictly or freely, underlies the great majority of Scarlatti's sonatas as it does most other light instrumental music of the time. This is the binary design with repeated halves.[58] Because Scarlatti, in his extraordinarily original and refreshing manner, handles and adapts this design with the utmost flexibility, writers have been hard pressed to reduce it to a few procedures that can be generalized, and often too inclined to evaluate it only in terms of subsequent, Classic "sonata form."

Gerstenberg (pp. 76-83) divides the binary designs into (1) those that are monothematic and usually symmetrical (as in L. 32, K. 67), (2) those that are polymotivic (or chains of motives) and usually asymmetrical (as in L. 42, K. 217), and (3) those that are incipient Classic "sonata forms," with a return only to the later portions of the "exposition" (as in L. 220, K. 475). The sonatas he cites are interesting extremes for Scarlatti in each instance. In another chapter (p. 131) he attempts to link the third type to Scarlatti's late sonatas. Rita Benton, after a preliminary description of the non-binary forms, also seeks, though with somewhat different emphasis, to establish a "hierarchy" of three categories that progress from the simplest binary designs to types just short of Classic "sonata form."[59] Her first category, including about 6 per cent of all the binary designs (e.g., L. 358, K. 95), is the most rudimentary sort, thematically and tonally. Her next category, about 10 per cent (e.g., L. 433, K. 446), hints at a second subject. And her third category, about 82 per cent, has a "definite" second subject of more or less contrast ("tonal, thematic and affective," as at ms. 17 in the familiar Son. in D, K. 29, L. 461; also, Ex. 37b, *infra*); this subject is likely to be in the dominant, mediant minor, dominant minor, or relative minor (in that order for major keys); the "development" averages only about half the length of the "exposition"; and in only one sonata does the "recapitulation" mirror the exposition exactly (L. 104, K. 159). Left over are another 2 per cent too free to be "systematically categorized" (e.g., L. 269, K. 333). Keller, deliberately avoiding yet another frontal attack on the problem of form in Scarlatti's sonatas, acknowl-

57. Cf. Benton/SCARLATTI 266-267.
58. Cf. Kirkpatrick/SCARLATTI 269.
59. Benton/SCARLATTI 267-273.

edges the great variety of treatment but generally concludes that Scarlatti was "behind" his times. He was "behind" Bach because he did not make the returns to his initial ideas that Bach did on occasion, and he was not a pathbreaker among pre-Classic composers because he was not striving toward Classic "sonata form" (!).[60]

Kirkpatrick (Chap. 11) has taken an approach that naturally would be preferred here, since it is also meant to steer clear of analysis made only in terms of Classic "sonata form" (p. 253) and since it, too, is utilized mainly to show form in action—that is, through its dynamic tensions and resolutions (p. 255). Coining new terms to suit his brave assault on traditional analysis, Kirkpatrick's method is to determine what the binary designs have in common, then discuss how they may otherwise differ. What the designs have in common is a parallelism of cadential material in each of the tonally complementary halves, from the "crux" or moment when "the closing tonality is made clear"
60a to the double-bar (p. 255). How they may differ is, of course, much harder to generalize. But Kirkpatrick has attempted to enumerate the successive subdivisions of material that may or may not be used to expand any particular sonata, both in the parallel cadential sections and in the parallel or nonparallel opening sections that lead sooner or later into the "crux." Considerable emphasis is placed, and rightly, on the tonal outline (pp. 258-260), including the "excursion" in the second half. This last may modulate in astonishing ways and to the most distant keys (as in K. 215, L. 323—from f♯ to a♭, b♭, B, e, etc.) and may actually "develop" the material (K. 216, L. 273).

An especially complex, free, and interesting group of larger structures is found in those sonatas that transcend the binary design through the addition or interpolation of other sections, which usually contrast in meter, tempo, and key. Such structures could be regarded as further examples of cycles except for the unusual interlocking or integration of the sections in various ways. In one Sonata in E (K. 162, L. 21) the total plan might be diagramed as follows (with lower-case letters for successive ideas):

||:Andante-$^{3}_{4}$: w (ton. → dom.), x (dom. → V-of-dom.); Allegro-$^{4}_{4}$: y (dom.) :||
||:y′ & z (dom. → dom.-of-ton.); Andante-$^{3}_{4}$: w & x (ton. minor → dom.);
Allegro-$^{4}_{4}$: y (ton.) :||.

This plan ultimately reduces to ||:A-B:||:B-A-B:||. In a Sonata in b and *alla breve* meter (K. 282, L. 484) an Andante section in $^{3}_{4}$ meter occurs during the second half, so that the total effect (disregarding repeats) is A-B-A.

60. Keller/SCARLATTI 76-80.

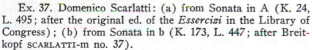

Ex. 37. Domenico Scarlatti: (a) from Sonata in A (K. 24, L. 495; after the original ed. of the *Essercizi* in the Library of Congress); (b) from Sonata in b (K. 173, L. 447; after Breitkopf SCARLATTI-m no. 37).

With regard to his melodic and figural ideas, Scarlatti's position on the border between eras also puts him on the border between the processes of motivic play and phrase grouping. Much of the time he drives forward on a single motive or figure (Ex. 37a), but there are many times when more distinct phrases take precedence over the figure (Ex. 37b). Writers have used various terms to describe essentially the same categories of melodic processes, including the sequential or other reiteration of a single motive (as in K. 238, L. 27), the continuous unfolding into new ideas (K. 545, L. 500), and the division into phrases or sections that are integrated (K. 485, L. 183), or largely additive (K.

395, L. 65).[61] But in Scarlatti's melodies there are also some environmental influences to be considered. There are those "many pages . . . in which he imitated the melody of tunes sung by carriers, muleteers, and common people"[62] (as in the charming Neapolitan Christmas "Pastorale" in K. 513, L. Suppl. 3 [63]). And in keeping with such elements of folksong there is often some clear sign of local color, such as the imitation of the Spanish guitar (K. 215, L. 323), or of flutes and bagpipes (K. 513, L. Suppl. 3), or of trumpets and horns (K. 358, L. 412), or of bells (K. 482, L. 205).[64]

In one of Kirkpatrick's several important chapters related to performance (Chap. 9), he supplies new information on the harpsichords Scarlatti presumably used. Among other things, he concludes that remarkably few pieces (such as K. 109 and 110, L. 138 and 469) were unequivocally intended for a two-keyboard instrument, that Scarlatti's late sonatas were written mostly for a Spanish harpsichord with one 5-octave keyboard and two 8-foot stops, that along with the few pieces known to have been intended for organ (e.g., K. 328, L. Suppl. 27) several others may have been intended for it as well as the harpsichord, and that not much evidence remains of any interest on Scarlatti's part either in some early Cristofori-type pianos at the Spanish court or in the clavichord.[65] There is plausible evidence for suggesting that eight of the earlier sonatas were intended as "solos" for violin and *b.c.* The evidence includes the actual figures in the bass part,[66] the restriction of the upper part to the violin's lowest tones and entirely to single notes except for a few double-stops and chords easily played on the violin, some slurs that suggest bowings, a general sense of melo/bass opposition in the conduct of the two parts, and the fact that five of the sonatas (K. 81, 88-91; L. 271, 36, 211, 106, 176) are complete cycles of three or four movements in or close to the S-F-S-F sequence in the older type of ensemble church sonata.[67]

Quantz, who had heard Scarlatti in Rome in 1724 or 1725, recalled him as "a *galant* [-style] keyboard player in the manner of that time."[68]

61. Cf. Gerstenberg/SCARLATTI 76-78, 140-144; Kirkpatrick/SCARLATTI 276-279; Hoffmann-Erbrecht/KLAVIERMUSIK 69-71.

62. BURNEY'S TOURS II 87.

63. Cf. the editor's note in Longo/SCARLATTI-m Suppl. p. 15.

64. Cf. Kirkpatrick/SCARLATTI 199-206.

65. But on the latter cf. Dart/KIRKPATRICK and the reply pp. 397-398.

66. Deleted in Longo/SCARLATTI-m. In Gerstenberg/SCARLATTI 95-96 the *b.c.* is thought rather to indicate a filling out of the keyboard part, in the manner we have seen in Rutini's sonatas, but the instances cited other than Rutini's are often debatable.

67. Cf. Salter/SCARLATTI. Mod. ed. of all 8 sons. arranged for Vn & K: Salter/SCARLATTI-m.

68. Cf. Kahl/SELBSTBIOGRAPHIEN 133; Quantz's concern with the *galant* style (pp. 123-124) seems to justify the present translation rather than "elegant."

Scarlatti's keyboard writing does exhibit the pseudopolyphony (especially in the opening imitations), the use, though rare, of Alberti bass (K. 517, L. 266), and a little of the syntactic and ornamental detail (K. 490, L. 206) that we have seen in such abundance in the more developed *galant* style of later Italians. But his importance must be restated here as that not so much of a pioneer in the *galant* style as of a highly individual genius of the keyboard—a writer of études as resourceful and artistic in their way as Chopin's in their way. Who else but one so intimately acquainted with the keyboard—its sonorities, resonances, idiomatic voice-leadings, and virtuoso techniques—could create (and "get away with") the novel chains of dissonant 7th chords that he writes (K. 409/75-144, L. 150), or the mixed superimposed chords (K. 132/27-28, L. 457), or the series of parallel 5ths (K. 394/76-81, L. 275), or the biting acciaccaturas (K. 175/25-32, L. 429), or the internal "pedals" (K. 26/36-47, L. 368), or the textures in which voices are added and dropped at will (throughout his sonatas)?[69] And who else could use to such a degree and to such good effect the favorite show devices of the time—the reckless hand-crossing and leaps (K. 120, L. 215), the repeated notes (K. 435, L. 361), the octaves and other
double-notes (K. 487, L. 205), and the fast passages (K. 173, L. 447)?[70] 70a

Seixas and Other Composers in Portugal

In the probably six years that Scarlatti was actually present in Lisbon (between 1719 and 1729) he must have associated closely with the organist and harpsichordist **Carlos de Seixas** (1704-42), who came from Coimbra to the royal chapel of King John V in 1720 when he was only sixteen. Portugal's most important composer for the keyboard in the eighteenth century, Seixas left at least 150 pieces for keyboard, including some 90 sonatas in one or more movements and around 60 separate minuets. He also left an overture, a sinfonia, and a harpsichord concerto, as well as several sacred choral pieces. None of this music was published in his lifetime; and, as with Scarlatti, no autographs of the keyboard pieces are known, only MS copies. In the present day, the one full-length study on Seixas, and nearly all of the discussion and
publication of his music have been the work of Santiago Kastner.[71] 71a

69. Cf. Kirkpatrick/SCARLATTI Chap. 10 (but read "stepwise" for "diatonic" on p. 220 *et passim*).

70. Cf. the diverse exx. in Keller/SCARLATTI 39-58. The possibility that B. Marcello influenced Scarlatti in the use of these devices is discussed in Newman/MARCELLO (with exx.).

71. Kastner/SEIXAS 137-143 itemizes the contents of 5 keyboard MSS in Lisbon and Coimbra; new MSS and identifications of anonymous pieces are likely to raise the totals (pp. 144, 138). 24 sons. (12 in each vol.) are printed in Kastner/CRAVISTAS-m I (some without their minuets?) and II, with prefaces.

Although "Tocata" is the more frequent title, it and "Sonata" are equated and otherwise used without differentiation in the Seixas MSS.[72] More than half of the sonatas are in the familiar two-movement plan of an allegro followed by a minuet, sometimes with related incipits (e.g., Kastner/CRAVISTAS-m I no. 12). Less than a third seem to be single, unattached movements in the MSS. The remainder show the usual variety of two-, three-, and even four- and five-movement plans, with their order determined apparently only by the basic need for contrast, the tendency to step up the meters from duple and simple to compound and/or triple, and the growing popularity of the minuet finale. In the sonatas of more than two movements an inner movement is sometimes in a key other than the home key. And there are at least two more of those instances where the minuet finale is in a new key (unless the original copyist meant each minuet to stand alone in the MS).[73]

Besides recalling Seixas' important predecessors in Iberian keyboard music, especially Coelho and Cabanilles, Kastner pays particular attention to certain Italians still closer to Seixas in time and idiom, among them Pasquini and A. Scarlatti (both of whose works exist in early Portuguese MSS), and Giustini (whose sonatas "di piano, e forte" of 1732 were dedicated to Don Antonio, younger brother of John V, over the signature of one Giovanni de Seixas).[74] But the first interest, of course, is in the relationship between Carlos de Seixas and D. Scarlatti. Seixas may actually have studied with this colleague, who was his senior by nineteen years. But that possibility seems to be contradicted in the one bit of information that comes down to us regarding their relationship (as recalled perhaps a half century later by a lexicographer in Lisbon who himself may have been among the Italian musicians brought in by John V):[75]

The Most Serene Senhor Infante D. Antonio asked the great Escarlate [Scarlatti], who was in Lisbon at the time, to give Seixas some lessons, guided as he was by the erroneous idea that whatever the Portuguese do they cannot equal foreigners, and sent him to Scarlatti. Hardly did Scarlatti see Seixas put his hands to the keyboard but he recognized the giant by the finger [so to speak], and said to him, '*You* are the one who could give *me* lessons.' Upon encountering Don Antonio, Scarlatti told him, 'Your Highness commanded me to examine him. But I must tell you that he is one of the best musicians I have ever heard.'[76]

A "complete" ed. of Seixas' works is in progress (as of 1960; according to a letter from Professor Kastner).

72. Kastner/SEIXAS 135-137 (contrary to Newman/EARLIEST 202).
73. Cf. Kastner/SEIXAS 91-92.
74. Kastner/SEIXAS 41-45, 82-83 (cf. SBE 194-196).
75. Mazza/DICIONÁRIO 32; cf. p. 10.
76. As translated and clarified in Kirkpatrick/SCARLATTI 73.

More to our purpose is a comparison of the sonatas of the two men.[77] If the best sonatas from throughout the production of each are compared, there can be little disagreement that Scarlatti ultimately went well beyond Seixas in nearly everything their sonatas have in common—technical exploitation of the instrument, sound effects, melodic scope, harmonic daring, structural diversity. But if reciprocal influences must be considered, only the sonatas Scarlatti is thought to have composed during his Lisbon period can be included, which limitation leads to different comparisons and brings us right back to the perennial problem of undated MSS. What had each man written before Scarlatti left in 1729? No dates more specific than the twenty-two-year period up to his death in Lisbon (1742) can be ventured for Seixas' MS sonatas. If before 1729 Scarlatti wrote only the few pieces found in old Portuguese MSS,[78] then it is he who seems to have profited most from the association. But if by then he also composed some or all of the thirty *Essercizi* published later, the opposite relationship seems more correct again.

However, in the experience of the present study, the sonatas of the two men are more profitably contrasted than compared. Their points of similarity—the binary designs, the angular motives with incisive rhythms, the persistent repetitions of these motives, the chromatic harmony, the generally thin, two-part texture, and the wide sweeps over the available keyboard range—are all fairly common at this time (as in the sonatas of Durante, Marcello, and Giustini). In fact, these similarities seem largely extrinsic in nature next to the differences, for Seixas was very much an individual, with the mark both of his own creative personality and of his Lusitanian environment in his music. Certain differences are obvious almost at once. At a time when major keys still prevailed over minor in a ratio of about 5 to 1 for composers in general (SCE VI), or 3 to 1 for Scarlatti in particular,[79] the ratio was more than 1 to 1 in favor of minor keys for Seixas.[80] As against Scarlatti's single "Adagio" inscription, which is not wholly convincing at that, there are around a dozen movements so inscribed that are genuinely adagio in character among Seixas' sonatas (e.g., Kastner/CRAVISTAS-m II no. 3/ii). In contrast to the profuse flow of ideas and the exact parallelism of the closing sections that characterize Scarlatti's larger binary designs, Seixas' opening allegro movements generally reveal a greater concentration on the initial idea, a more consistent return

77. Cf. Kastner/SEIXAS 56-60, 64-79, 96-98, 101.
78. Cf. Kastner/CONTRIBUCIÓN 261-277 (with exx.).
79. Cf. the table in GROVE VII 459 (Blom).
80. Based on the full lists in Kastner/SEIXAS 137-143, although the ratio is stated to be equal on p. 113.

to this idea at the start of the second half, and, after the usual modulations, a larger portion of the remainder that parallels the first half, though now much less exactly (e.g., II, no. 6/i, which achieves almost symphonic drive). Whereas Scarlatti's minuets have no second minuets (trios), Seixas' sometimes do (I no. 8/ii).

With respect to the more individual style traits, it is risky to specify anything by Seixas as not occurring at least somewhere in all of Scarlatti's amazingly varied output. However, Seixas often seems even more direct and open in his expression of ideas than Scarlatti. Thus, the melodies of the minuets and adagios are marked by frank, forthright sentiment (Ex. 38). The texture is reduced to a bare

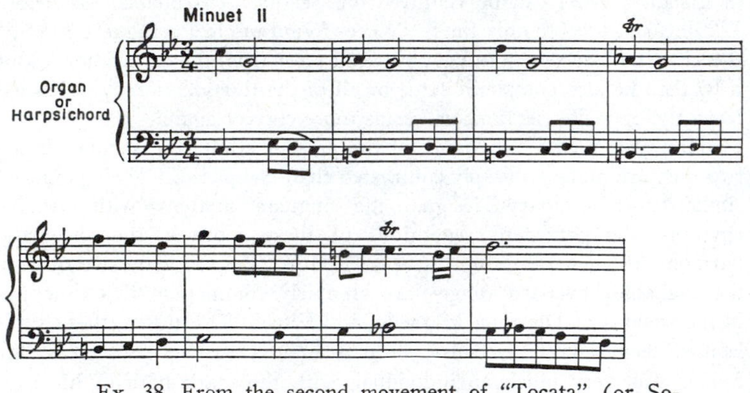

Ex. 38. From the second movement of "Tocata" (or Sonata) in c by Carlos de Seixas (after Kastner/CRAVISTAS-m I no. 8 [but without the editorial additions]; by kind permission of the original copyright owners, B. Schott's Söhne, Mainz, and Associated Music Publishers, Inc., New York).

minimum, as in the "Fuga" (II no. 15), which here only hints at entries or recollections of the elementary "subject." In other instances the two-part writing has a curious way of slipping into nothing more than parallel octaves (I no. 10/i/22-23). Sometimes the sequential modulations are achieved merely by a simple sideslipping of chromatic harmonies without common tones or suspensions (II no. 9/i/69-74). Folk elements of almost naïve rhythmic and melodic charm crop up often (Ex. 39).

But these various simplicities of style must not be taken as signs of a weak invention or, for that matter, of an inability to treat the material more richly in other ways. The adagio movements can be florid and ornamental (as in the instance cited earlier, II no. 3/ii). The rhythmic

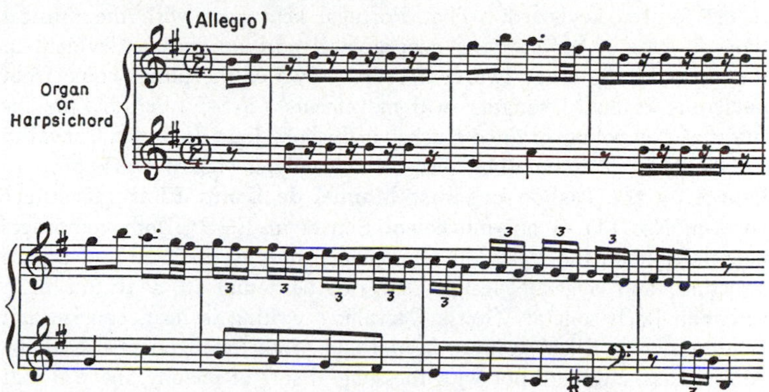

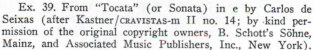

Ex. 39. From "Tocata" (or Sonata) in e by Carlos de Seixas (after Kastner/CRAVISTAS-m II no. 14; by kind permission of the original copyright owners, B. Schott's Söhne, Mainz, and Associated Music Publishers, Inc., New York).

patterns can be complex (I no. 7, mss. 39-47; or throughout II no. 9, with its artful suggestions of guitar strumming). The pace can be furious and relentless (II no. 12), and the technical demands considerable (II no. 7; but hand-crossing is notably absent from this mvt. and was used only modestly by Seixas, as in II no. 14, where most of the apparent crossing is really only overlapping). There is the dignity of a Baroque concerto grosso in some of the movements (as in I no. 14/i, which recalls Vivaldi's Op. 3/6/i) and there are clear traces of the *galant* style in others (as in all 3 mvts., F-S-F, of II no. 3). Certainly, among Seixas' sonatas there are several (e.g., I nos. 6 and 11; II nos. 6, 11, 12, and 14) that can add much musical distinction to the repertoire of today's recitalists. All these need is the chance to be tried and heard by perceptive musicians.

Besides the sonatas of Seixas, Kastner's publications enable us to examine those of three other Portuguese composers for keyboard in the eighteenth century. The "sonatas" (or "toccatas") of these three were also left only in MS. Two one-movement sonatas in binary design, each in d, provide our only knowledge of **Frei Jacinto** (Kastner/CRAVISTAS-m I no. 2, II no. 2).[81] But they are enough to reveal a vigorous, imaginative composer. In brief, both pieces may be described as conservative in style, preludial, monothematic, fuller in texture than Seixas' pieces, rich in compelling chromatic harmony, and knowingly

81. Possibly the same as one Frei Jacinto de Sacramento, according to a letter from Professor Kastner. Cf. Kastner/CONTRIBUCIÓN 277-278.

scored for the keyboard. That Portugal kept pace with the musical times in spite of her outlying geographical position becomes evident in the pieces by the other two composers. Two of the pieces come from numerous keyboard sonatas in 3 movements (F-S-F) left by the influential, Neapolitan-trained teacher in Lisbon, **João de Sousa Carvalho** (1745-98).[82] And another piece is the only keyboard work hitherto known by the Lisbon organist **Manuel de Santo Elias** (Kastner/SILVA-m No. 13), a one-movement Sonata in E♭.[83] Both composers take us right to the stages of homophony, fluency, melodic and phrase structure, and over-all design that can be found in a Rutini or a Christian Bach sonata. Sousa Carvalho's writing is neat, concise and delicate; Santo Elias' is more figural and prolix, with much use of the Alberti bass, although not with the songful sort of melody above it that is essential to the "singing-allegro" style. An investigation has yet to be made into extant keyboard or other sonatas by certain other composers in Portugal, including Eusebio Tavares Le Roy (of French descent?), José Joaquim dos Santos, Davide Pérez (1711-80; a Spaniard born in Naples, active in Lisbon), João Cordeiro da Silva (trained in Naples), José de Mesquita, Frei José de Santa'Ana, Francisco Xavier Baptista, and Pedro Antonio Avondano (?-1782, violinist and composer of 12 Vn/bass sons.).[84]

Soler and Other Keyboard Composers in Spain

The earliest so-called "Sonata" by a Spanish-born composer that is known is a single movement in F, in a MS dated 1744, by Padre
85a **Vincente Rodriguez** (*ca.* 1685-1761).[85] A contemporary of Scarlatti and Seixas, Rodriguez succeeded Cabanilles as organist in Valencia in 1713, belonging with José Elías and Martinez de Oxinaga among the pupils and/or followers of Cabanilles.[86] The sonata itself is a binary design interesting less for its somewhat neutral ideas than for the

82. "Toccata" in g, in Kastner/CRAVISTAS-m I no. 16; "Allegro" (final, 3d mvt.) from Son. in D, in Kastner/SILVA-m (with preface) no. 12. Cf. DICCIONARIO PORTUGUEZES I 228-236; Kastner/CONTRIBUCIÓN 281-282.

83. A letter from Professor Kastner reports the recent discovery (1960) of further sons. by this composer. Cf. DICCIONARIO PORTUGUEZES II 272-273.

84. These names were kindly supplied for the present study by Professor Kastner, who also calls attention to a fine collection of virtually unknown sonatas by 18th-century Portuguese composers, owned by Dr. Ivo Cruz, Director of the Lisbon Conservatório Nacional de Música. At the time of this writing, a Vn/*b.c.* son. by Baptista was to be published, but details were still lacking; the style and incipient "sonata form" in his keyboard sons. are briefly discussed in Kastner/CONTRIBUCIÓN 279-281. Brief information on Santos, Pérez, Cordeiro da Silva, Baptista, and Avondano is given in DICCIONARIO LABOR.

85. Mod. ed.: Nin/ESPAGNOLS-m II no. 1; cf. pp. i-ii.

86. Cf. Kastner/CONTRIBUCIÓN 260-262.

developed sense of structure it reveals as it progresses resolutely from one broad, well-defined tonal area to the next. The word "eco" in measure 14 suggests a two-keyboard harpsichord. Hand-crossings with rapid leaps up to four octaves occur several times. The quick wit is lacking but the clipped speech is of the general sort to be found in Scarlatti's and Seixas' sonatas. However, although it is possible that Rodriguez already knew some of Scarlatti's sonatas, perhaps even the published *Essercizi,* it is more likely that this cleric, at his restricted post, was giving good evidence of how far such forms and styles had developed in the Peninsula independently of Scarlatti's arrival.

Padre **Antonio Soler** (1729-83), Spain's chief native composer of sonatas in the eighteenth century, was a Catalan born the very year Scarlatti followed Maria Barbara to Spain.[87] After early instruction at the Montserrat monastery under Cabanilles' pupil José Elías, Soler became a monk in 1752 at the age of twenty-three and at the same time was appointed to his permanent post as organist and choirmaster at the famed Escorial monastery, northwest of Madrid. It was during the first five years at this post that he must have studied with Scarlatti, and it was there that he also studied with the organist José de Nebra, uncle of the Blasco de Nebra whom we shall meet in our next chapter. Presumably, Soler wrote most of his sonatas for the Infante Gabriel of Bourbon,[88] to whom he gave harpsichord lessons each fall season while the royal court stayed at the somber Escorial palace.

A versatile composer and theorist, Soler's output is being more broadly investigated today, although he is still best known for his keyboard sonatas.[89] Lately these last have been enjoying a sudden flurry 89a
of attention, with good progress toward at least one if not two "complete" editions.[90] Until we can know that one of the editions has actual- 90a

87. Pedrell/SOLER is a pioneer study of Soler's life and output. New biographic information and a valuable itemized list of Soler's music, both MS and published, are given in H. Anglès' preface in Anglès & Gerhard/SOLER-m. A full "biographical and critical study" by S. Rubio is reported in progress in the preface to Rubio/SOLER-m.

88. Cf. Anglès & Gerhard/SOLER-m ix; also, p. xviii for a statement to this effect in a contemporary MS.

89. Cf. Klaus F. Heimes, *Antonio Soler's Keyboard Sonatas* (M.M. thesis, University of South Africa, 1965), Pretoria: University of South Africa, 1969. Shorter discussions occur in Mitjana/ESPAGNE 2182-2185, Nin/ESPAGNOLS-m I & II, and Nin/SOLER.

90. As of this writing (1960), Rubio/SOLER-m has reached 90 sons. in 5 vols., with prefaces, sources, and thematic indices of first mvts. Only the 21 sons. in the first 2 of the 10 vols. projected (since 1957) in Marvin/SOLER-m have appeared (including 8 sons. not yet in Rubio/SOLER-m and 2 MS pp. in facs.). Kastner/SOLER-m (with preface) adds 2 pairs of sons. Hill/SOLER is a helpful evaluation of these and other eds. Nin/ESPAGNOLS-m I and II contain 12 and 2 sons., respectively, by Soler, of which 9 come from MSS that may no longer be accessible for other eds. (cf. Anglès & Gerhard/SOLER-m xxii); the other 5 sons., which do also appear in the unaltered Rubio ed. (Nin I nos. 1-4 and II no. 3 =

ly been brought near to "completion," the number of sonatas Soler wrote can only be estimated at between 130 and 220.[91] But even these uncertain figures are made still less meaningful by the fact that some of Soler's numerous sonatas in more than one movement are listed by separate movements and some under one title. None of Soler's sonatas was published in his lifetime and, as with Scarlatti and Seixas, only MS copies are extant, not autographs. However, Soler is known to have given an autograph of 27 sonatas to Lord Fitzwilliam of Cambridge in 1772, from which came the posthumous and only eighteenth-century publication of Soler's sonatas, that issued by Birchall in London, probably in 1796.[92] Besides that year of 1772 there are dates in a few of the MSS[93] (referring sometimes to the copying and sometimes to the composition itself) that range between 1779 and 1783. Furthermore, in 1765 Soler mentioned pieces he had already written in a set, now lost, of "Quatro libros de Clavicordio" (presumably meaning harpsichord, here), "in all the keys, and in all styles."[94] Some or all of these pieces were probably sonatas, too, which may or may not now be extant in other MSS. Thus, one cannot now suggest more than rough bracketing dates for most of Soler's sonatas—that is, from about 1760-83.

Thanks to the new editions of these sonatas, it is becoming possible not merely to sample them but to get that much broader view without which no composer can receive a fair evaluation of his music.[95] After sufficient exposure to this broader view, one is compelled to reject the typical polite acknowledgment of Soler as the composer of charming, neat little one-movement sonatas that are relatively innocuous copies of Scarlatti's sonatas.[96] In the first place, as with Seixas, the similarities come to seem inconsequential alongside the differences.[97] And, in any case, these similarities reflect more than just the influence of the forty-

---

Rubio nos. 24, 21, 2, 15, and 19, respectively), reveal Nin's insertions of copious (excessive) editorial markings, doublings, and shifts of register; the further alterations of text that are implied in several references to this ed. occur in these 5 sons. only in Nin's I no. 2, in which a total of 7 mss. of cadential reiterations is added in the 2 halves (unless there could actually be these differences in the sources). Vols. VI of Rubio/SOLER-m (Sons. 91-99) and III of Marvin/SOLER-m (Sons. 22-34) were available too late for inclusion in the present discussion (cf. Freedman in NOTES XIX [1962] 513-514).

91. Cf. Hill/SOLER. Not counting such duplications as could be detected, around 115 sons. are identified in various MSS in Anglès & Gerhard/SOLER-m xiv-xxiv.

92. Cf. Nin/SOLER 102; Kirkpatrick/SCARLATTI 123-124; BRITISH UNION II 962. Rubio/SOLER-m nos. 1-27 correspond to this ed.

93. Cf. Anglès & Gerhard/SOLER-m, especially p. xix.

94. Cf. Anglès & Gerhard/SOLER-m viii.

95. Credit must also be given to fine recordings by enterprising and dedicated performers, such as those that Frederick Marvin has made for Decca of the sons. thus far published in Marvin/SOLER-m (cf. Speer/MARVIN).

96. As somewhat in Georgii/KLAVIERMUSIK 76-77.

97. Some differences are brought out in Kastner/CONTRIBUCIÓN 290-297.

four-year-older Italian. They owe at least as much to a common heritage of international styles (such as we found in Marcello or Durante, too) and of indigenous Hispanic elements (such as the bright bolero rhythms in Rubio/SOLER-m no. 4).[98] In the second place, Soler's range of forms, styles, and expressions is nearly the equal of Scarlatti's, including big as well as small, old as well as new, and dramatic as well as pastoral. Thirdly, Soler is quite as much of an individual as Scarlatti is, but with his own, different brands of poetry, novelty, folklore, and exaltation. And finally, though Soler is seldom quite as far advanced toward high-Classic styles as his Italian contemporaries Galuppi and Rutini, he does not live in the past. When he is not indulging in fantasy too personal to permit comparison (Rubio/SOLER-m no. 81) he often writes a movement that is certainly as far along, and not very different from, a Mannheim symphony allegro (Ex. 40).

The majority of Soler's available sonatas appear to fall into groups of two or more movements. About a fifth of the groups, in two to four

Ex. 40. From the second movement of Antonio Soler's Sonata in C (after Rubio/SOLER-m no. 66, by kind permission of Union Musical Española, copyright owners, and Associated Music Publishers, Inc., New York).

98. Cf. Mitjana/ESPAGNE 2182-2184, with a choice ex.; but this emphasis on Hispanic elements is regarded as too strong in Nin/ESPAGNOLS-m I iv.

movements, come under single titles, leaving no doubt as to the groupings; and at least half of the remaining sonatas are paired about as definitely as are the sonatas in the Scarlatti MSS—that is, by key (with an infrequent change of mode), by some contrasts of tempo and/or meter, and by occasional indications such as "sigue" after the first of a pair[99] or the use of related incipits (Rubio/SOLER-m nos. 10 and 11, or 40 and 41). In the separate movements one also finds the same preference that Scarlatti and other keyboard composers around the mid-eighteenth century show for the faster tempos. There are only about half as many moderate tempos and, except for one "Adagio" again (Marvin/SOLER-m no. 17), there is no movement marked slower than a broad andante ("Largo andante," no. 16). But, more than Scarlatti, Soler seems to mean what he says in his slower tempos. Sometimes the ornamentation and rhythmic activity are sufficient to compel a relatively slow performance of a movement with a faster tempo (as in the "Allegretto," Rubio/SOLER-m no. 80). Soler's keys are like Scarlatti's rather than Seixas' in showing a ratio of 3 to 1 in favor of major, and in extending to F♯ and D♭ (one flat more than Scarlatti uses).

As with Scarlatti, Soler uses the binary design with repeats almost always, and, as with Scarlatti, his variants within this design are almost endless. The broad tonal outline, typically, includes a modulation to the nearly related key in the first half, a restatement of the opening idea in the longer second half, some modulations, and a return to a parallel close, exact or free, in the second half (no. 27 [in Rubio/SOLER-m, except as otherwise specified]). But immediately the variants appear. Soler puts into practice his novel principles of key relationships and abrupt versus gradual, stepwise modulations, as discussed and illustrated in Chapter 10 of his important, controversial theory treatise, *Llave de la modulacion* (published in Madrid in 1762).[100] These principles may well have come directly from Scarlatti, but Soler applies and refines them in ways of his own. During the first half of a Sonata in G (no. 4) an unexpected, partial cadence is reached on V of V (ms. 14), but before this tonality is continued (ms. 21) there is an abrupt interlude starting on the lowered subtonic harmony (F) and its dominant (mss. 15-20); the corresponding interlude in the second half starts on the lowered mediant harmony (B♭; mss. 48-53). In the "Cantabile" movement of a Sonata in F♯ (no. 79) there is an interlude in E♭ in the first half,

99. Cf. the "Introduction" to Kastner/SOLER-m.

100. Cf. the illuminating summary, with exx., in Kirkpatrick/SCARLATTI 243-247. On the sharp, productive controversy that this treatise aroused, cf. Anglès & Gerhard/SOLER-m vii-ix. Carroll/SOLER is a new diss. (1960) on this treatise and Soler's application of his modulatory techniques in his sons. and other works.

a return to F♯ and a cadence on the dominant (C♯), a start in that key in the second half, then a series of sections in e♭, F (ending on V of d), and A before the return to F♯.

Sometimes Soler bases an entire sonata on a single idea, especially the fast kind of sonata that explores a particular étude-like figure (as in nos. 13 and 43, both marked "Allegro soffribile," or "as fast as bearable"). One such sonata (no. 70), a dexterous exploit in scales, could pass as an ideal parody, before the fact, of a Czerny étude. More often, Soler prefers a plurality of ideas, but he tends to keep track of these more faithfully than Scarlatti does (no. 53). The initial idea may return when the second half starts (no. 23), or some other idea may enter here (no. 86). A return to the initial idea after the modulations is rarely made by Soler, although the sense of this return is usually achieved by the strong retransition to the home key (no. 88). Yet the soil is now ready for a thematic return. In fact, one is not unduly surprised to come on a remarkably modern sounding, chance example of textbook "sonata form," complete with all the main themes, a real development section (though based on a new idea), and a full recapitulation (no. 41; cf. Ex. 41, *infra*). But many other designs turn up, too. One binary design in G, in 2/4 meter, is interlocked with another in d and g, in 6/8 meter (no. 30: $||{}^{2}_{4}x[G]\rightarrow{}^{6}_{8}y[d]:||:{}^{6}_{8}y[d]\rightarrow{}^{2}_{4}x[G]\rightarrow{}^{6}_{8}y[g,G]:||$). Equally involved in different ways are numerous other designs that come still closer to the rondo principle, as their titles suggest—for instance, "Minue di rivolti" (no. 61/iii [cf. i, too]), or "Rondon" (no. 62/i).

In the examples already cited, the fact that Soler speaks a somewhat later language than Scarlatti becomes clear enough. Soler's ideas range from brief, crisp motives (Ex. 41a) to lyrical arches more extended and broadly organized than any found here in Scarlatti's sonatas (Ex. 41b). When Soler builds his lines in short, separate, ornamented phrases over an Alberti bass or similar chordal figure in relatively slow harmonic rhythm, he becomes a true exponent of the *galant* style in its fullest bloom (no. 66/i and ii). Other signs of this style and a later generation than Scarlatti's are the comical bits of melody in the deep supporting basses (no. 10), cadential trills on penultimate dominant notes (as at the double-bars in no. 3), and the melodic appoggiaturas and feminine endings (as in ms. 1 and at the double-bars in no. 56, another remarkably modern sounding, complete "sonata form"). At the same time, Soler, always a first-rate craftsman, tends to be more literal about voice-leading than Scarlatti. Even in the freer keyboard styles he accounts for each part somewhat more consistently. In this treatment

Ex. 41. From (a) the "development" section, and (b) the second theme, in the first of a pair of movements in E♭ by Antonio Soler (after Rubio/SOLER-m no. 41, by kind permission of Union Musical Española, copyright owners, and Associated Music Publishers, Inc., New York).

he perhaps reflects certain neo-academicisms that appear from time to time, such as the words "en modo dorico" over each of a pair of sonatas in c (with 2 flats); or, more pertinent here, such as his several contrapuntal forms, which are considerably more severe than any of the fugues Scarlatti wrote for keyboard. One example is the "Intento" finale (no. 66/iii) that concludes the very movements just cited for their *galant* traits. And another is the finale of the previous sonata (no. 65/iii), which begins as an "Intento con movimiento contrario" and changes to a "Fuga en octava." These *tientos,* essentially like the Italian *ricercare,*[101] come after the lighter, modern movements as archa-

101. Cf. Kastner/CONTRIBUCIÓN 151-152 *et passim.*

isms in homage to the seventeenth-century organ masters, like Cabanilles,[102] who were Soler's artistic ancestors.

Soler uses every idiomatic technique of the keyboard that Scarlatti uses, and in as advanced a manner, whether it be repeated notes (no. 43), double-notes (no. 17), a glissando (no. 66/i/18), skips and octaves (no. 78), or hand-crossing plus nearly every other device (no. 10). Yet even in this respect the effects are noticeably different from Scarlatti's, chiefly because Soler's devices are incorporated into larger, more regularized and symmetrical phrase groupings. However, it is not by further comparisons of Soler and Scarlatti that we can find what does most to place Soler, in the experience of this study, among the chief pre-Classic composers of the sonata. Soler only rarely used programmatic titles.[103] But his most individual movements are the more subjective ones, in which fantasy is allowed free play. Now dreamy, now introspective and brooding, now impassioned, this sort of music by Soler, though more delicate and subtle, has a surprisingly close affinity with the *empfindsam* fantasying of Emanuel Bach (Ex. 42).

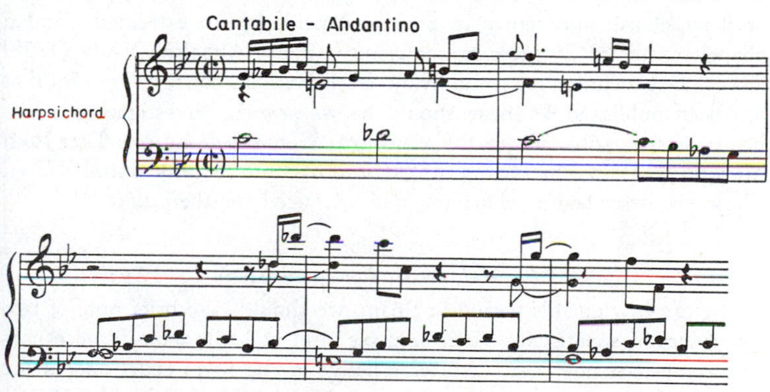

Ex. 42. From the first of a pair of movements in B♭ by Antonio Soler (after Kastner/SOLER-m, by kind permission of the original copyright owners, B. Schott's Söhne, Mainz, and Associated Music Publishers, New York).

There have been made available three sonatas for keyboard by the obscure Catalan composer **Freixanet** (*ca.* 1730-?)[104] and one sonata by the Valencian organist from Aragon, Padre **Rafael Anglés** (ca. 1731-

102. Cf. the *tientos* printed in Cat. BARCELONA II 77-87.
103. Cf. Mitjana/ESPAGNE 2185.
104. Sons. in G and A, Nin/ESPAGNOLS-m II nos. 4 and 5; Son. in B♭, Kastner/SILVA-m no. 11.

105a 1816).[105] These sonatas are all single movements in binary design, close to Soler's in idiom though lighter in texture and content. They are enhanced by suggestions of Spanish dance rhythms, but show no special originality. More prolific was the outstanding organist from Barcelona, Padre **Narciso Casanovas** (1747-99), who spent most of his life at the Catalan monastery of Montserrat. Eight keyboard sonatas have been made available out of at least twenty-four sonatas that are extant.[106] Three of those not yet published are rare Classic examples of sonatas for "clarini" (trumpets). At least the first two of Casanovas' sonatas now available seem to make a pair (since they are both in A, have similar incipits, and occur together in two of the MS sources). His sonatas come still closer in texture and technical idiom to those of Soler, but they lack both the force and structural integration of ideas. In each half of the binary design one new folklike idea follows another in a static fashion and in peculiarly regular but disjointed phrases. The result is hardly that dynamic unity that has proved so essential to the sonata idea in all eras.

It has not been possible here to see thirteen MS sonatas for organ or harpsichord, apparently in one movement, by an esteemed Catalan chapel master at Montserrat monastery, Padre **Anselma Viola** (1738-98).[107] But to judge from the lively, fresh bassoon concerto by him that has been published,[108] these should be well worth investigating. Nor has it been possible to see the keyboard "Sonatines" by one Don **Juan Moreno y Polo** (including a "Minuetto" movement dated 1774).
109a These are described as charming and advanced for their time.[109]

The Melo/bass Sonata in Spain

Before leaving this period in Spain, we should take brief note of two composers of sonatas for violin and *b.c.* and at least name three others whose music is now lost. All were active at the royal court and in the musical circle of the twelfth Duke of Alba in Madrid in the 1750's, during the later years there of Scarlatti and Farinelli. One was **Francisco Manalt,**[110]whose *Obra harmónica en seis sonatas de cámara de violin y bajo solo* was dedicated in 1757 and published, presumably

105. Son. in F (along with other, more interesting pieces), Nin/ESPAGNOLS-m II no. 8.

106. Pujol/MONTSERRAT-m I 222-256 (no. 4 = Nin/ESPAGNOLS II no. 6); cf. the itemized lists of undated MSS, pp. x-xi.

107. Cf. DICCIONARIO LABOR II 2236. Listed in Pujol/MONTSERRAT-m II vii and preserved at Montserrat.

108. Pujol/MONTSERRAT-m II 3-67.

109. Mitjana/ESPAGNE 2185.

110. Cf. DICCIONARIO LABOR II 1464.

the same year, right in Madrid. So far as has been learned in the present study, this set contains the first sonatas not for guitar to be published by any composer of either Spanish or Portuguese nationality, the only melo/bass sonatas from either nationality to be published in the eighteenth century, and the only sonatas to be published inside either Spain or Portugal in the pre-Classic Era. Actually, Manalt may also have published a second set of six sonatas under the same title, but only this "Parte primera" is known, from which two sonatas have been made available.[111] Both of the latter are in three movements, in the order of S-F-minuet. But the finale of the second is actually a kind of rondeau, with several alternations of a "Larghetto maestoso" in *alla breve* and a "Tempo di minuetto affectuoso" in 3/4 meter, the latter ultimately culminating in an "Allegretto piu che di Minuetto." Double-stops raise the only technical problem for the violinist. The harmony is often chromatic, sometimes shifting abruptly between major and minor modes (e.g., near the end of Son. 1/i). As for the forms, there is a certain diffuseness, probably because the writing poses much the same dilemma that Alberti seemed to be facing (SCE VII). The ideas are of the tuneful, metrically distinct sort that makes for clear contrasts and invites grouping into phrases and periods. But this latter tendency is still largely denied (as in Son. 1/iii) by a continuous melodic unfolding such as had characterized Baroque motivic play.

A second composer was the more renowned first violinist of the royal chapel, **José Herrando,** whose violin method was published in Paris in 1756 (not 1757), not long after Mozart's, but who probably was not a
pupil of Corelli as was formerly supposed.[112] Four sets of sonatas and 112a
a set of viola "Lecciones" by Herrando, all MSS supposedly of the 1750's, were extant until destroyed during the Spanish Civil War of the late 1930's.[113] These included two sets of twelve S/bass sonatas each (the second with the over-all title "Tocattas") and two sets of six SS/bass sonatas each (under the over-all title "Trios").[114] A fifth, curious set is still preserved (in an autograph MS dated 1754) and wait-

111. Subirá & Donostia/MANALT-m, with an informative preface by Subirá on Manalt and his environment.

112. Herrando is said to report this relationship in his method, in both Mitjana/ESPAGNE 2187 and Subirá/ALBA 167; but no such statement can be found, according to Pincherle/CORELLI 142 and 200, and it surely would have been mentioned, if it exists, in Cat. MADRID III 131.

113. Cf. Subirá & Donostia/MANALT-m iii. A set of 3 duos is still listed in Cat. MADRID III 193-194.

114. Cf. Subirá/ALBA 165-189, with descriptions of each mvt. and interesting facs. of the title page and first page of score ("Allegro" in G) of the first SS/bass set, and of an engraving of Herrando playing the violin. Mod. ed. of 10 S/bass mvts.: Nin/HERRANDO-m (with preface, realization, "enrichments," and added titles; cf. Subirá/HISTORIA 452).

ing to be investigated in Bologna[115]—six "Sonatine a solo per violino di V corde, per divertimento del Sig. D. Carlo Broschi Farinelli" (i.e., unaccompanied sonatinas for a violin with five strings, for the diversion of Farinelli). Most of the S/bass sonatas are (or were) in three movements, F-S-F or F-S-M, with the slow movement often in the tonic or relative minor key; but three of them return to the church sonata sequence of S-F-S-F through the addition of an introductory slow movement. The finales include examples of the minuet, variations on a recurring bass, fugue, and gigue. In the "trio" sonatas the character is lighter and there are often only two rather than three movements, many of them being minuets or other dances. On the basis of the but limited view of Herrando's music that can now be had, the writing is more on the expressive than the virtuosic side and rather elementary, in any case. However, a more dramatic style and such devices as harmonics and deliberate parallel 5ths are known to have been used on occasion. The language is still that of the Baroque continuous line, spun out somewhat as by Vivaldi.

No complete sonatas remain, since the Civil War, from the MSS of three other composers. **Francesco Montali** (?-*ca.* 1782[116]), a violinist born in Naples, left a set of twelve "trio" sonatas (1751) and three sets of six Vn/bass sonatas each (1752, 1754, 1759). The dilettante **Colonello D. Bernardo di Castro e Ascarrega,** Duke of Conquista, left one set of six Vn/bass sonatas (1754). And **Luis Misón** (?-1766), esteemed court flutist and oboist (probably from Barcelona), left a set of twelve sonatas for flute, *concertante* viola, and *b.c.*[117] In the sonatas of all three composers the plan of movements and general style have been described as similar to those of Manalt and Herrando. Montali wrote several finales of the composite sort that we noted in a Manalt sonata. As the finale of Misón's last sonata one still finds an "Allegro à la francesa," which does indeed recall the simple regularity of the seventeenth-century French chanson.[118]

115. Listed in Cat. BOLOGNA IV 108 under "Errando, Giuseppe."
116. The year of death is deduced in Subirá/ALBA 140-141.
117. Descriptions of each mvt. and facs. of a title page and page of score are given for each of these 3 composers in Subirá/ALBA 137-157, 205-208, and 191-204, respectively.
118. Facs. opposite p. 201 in Subirá/ALBA.

Chapter X

Italy and the Iberian Peninsula From About 1780 to 1825

Some Trends During the High-Classic Era

The political climate in much of Italy, Spain, and Portugal grew more turbulent while music's Classic Era was coming to a peak. In all three countries—as elsewhere, of course—the humiliating governmental collapses, territorial redistributions, and other climactic events were tied in with the French Revolution and the Napoleonic wars. But neither these crises nor the political deterioration that followed can be blamed directly for the concurrent decline of interest toward the sonata in those countries, for there was no corresponding decline in the opera. If anything, the opera was coming to dominate the musical scene still more completely. At most the political climate can be blamed only indirectly for the sonata's vicissitudes, in the sense that it made its mark on current styles and tastes, which, in turn, became more and more inimical to the essential problem of the sonata—that is, the problem of a dynamic form in the medium of absolute music.

Paul Lang has quoted a choice passage from *L'Histoire de l'art dramatique en France* by Théophile Gautier (1858-59) that bears purely on this aesthetic problem of the sonata in Italian instrumental music at the turn of the century.[1] The passage is apropos even though it happens to refer to orchestral music.

> Italian music can only be produced by a genius; the facility of the formulas, the mechanical habits, open too large a field to mediocrity. It is easy to speak without saying anything in Italian, and it is only with superior genius that one can escape from this enervating banality; you must be a Rossini, else you run an infernal risk of being Coppola.
>
> Certainly Cimarosa did not consider himself an incomparable genius; he quite naïvely wrote charming music with some basses and fiddles for accompaniment. But how that music moves, how it leaps, how it roars with

1. MQ XXXII (1946) 605.

laughter! . . . [and its] instrumentation . . . is so simple that, in order to perform it, a third of the orchestra suffices.

Actually, we shall see that the Italian and Iberian sonata had at least some near Rossinis in this period, when we come to Grazioli, Ferdinando Turini, Cherubini, and Blasco de Nebra. But in any case, its decline must not be categorized solely as a qualitative one. To some extent this decline should be recognized rather as a matter of decreasing historical significance to the mainstream of the sonata after about 1780—that is, after all the international tributaries had converged in Vienna. As the great Viennese masters mature, our attention is naturally diverted more and more from the subordinate streams that kept flowing independently for a while.

In the sonata of Spain and Portugal still another sort of decline has been deplored by writers from both countries. Thus speaks Nin:[2]

With [the Sonata in D, about 1813, by the Spaniard Mateo] Ferrer we reach an unqualified period of national regression. In this respect the annihilative policy of Philip V [giving preference to Italian over native musicians] had borne its fruits. Spanish music, which had held firm behind the rampart of the tonadilla up to the end of the 18th century, was in [a state now of] total lethargy. The opera, [that] incurable soreness of Spain, had to be Italian or it could not be. The devotees of chamber music revolved around Luigi Boccherini; the old hands spoke of Haydn, who had been one of the idols of musical Spain, as of an outmoded memory.

But here Nin not only contradicts, by implication, his earlier statement that the Spanish sonata did not go beyond the Scarlatti type of structure (SCE IX); he also does an injustice to his national ancestors. At least as regards the sonata, the question was no longer one of Italian or other foreign versus native influences. By now the Spanish sonata was simply sharing in the crystallization of international influences such as marks the classic peak of any era. Furthermore, when a Spanish composer strong enough to speak individually came along, like Blasco de Nebra, or Soler before him, his individuality did express itself by subtly indigenous means. What more could be desired? The acknowledged Spanish flavors in the music of these men are generally surprisingly hard to identify specifically. But anything more tangible that might be introduced from the local dances, the tonadilla, or other popular sources would be likely to conflict increasingly with that very problem of creating dynamic forms in absolute music (as it still does conflict in the five early, forgotten piano sonatas composed before 1887 by Isaac Albéniz).

In the present chapter it is interesting already to be meeting two of the professors, Rolla and B. Asioli, in the newly founded Milan Con-

2. Nin/ESPAGNOLS-m I vi; cf., also, Kastner/CONTRIBUCIÓN 310.

servatory (1807) and to be finding sonatas already published by G. Ricordi (founded in 1808). But for the most part the sonata continues to be cultivated, more or less, in the Italian and Iberian centers where the pre-Classic sonata chiefly flourished—in Venice in the sphere of Galuppi, in Florence in the environment of Rutini and Nardini, in Naples as a minuscule side issue to the opera, in Lisbon only in one instance that could be included here, in Madrid in the wake of Scarlatti and Soler, and at the famed Monserrat monastery near Barcelona. Only two foreigners are included among some twenty-five composers that are brought up, one each resident in Venice and Livorno. A small but distinct flurry of local sonata publishing will be noted in Venice and Florence, and there would be more than one further edition to report in Madrid if, as evidence suggests, several publications had not since been lost. It is partly for the latter reason that nothing but sonatas for the keyboard (chiefly the piano, by now) can be reported in Portugal and Spain,[3] although it is true that even in Italy there are only hints of other settings, like violin and guitar, in this period. The melo/bass sonata as a significant type has virtually disappeared by the end of the eighteenth century. The guitar sonata is much more alive—in fact, is enjoying a resurgence of interest.[4] But, as we shall see when we come to Carulli in Naples or, in other chapters, to M. Giuliani (from Bologna) in Vienna, or Sor (from Barcelona) in Paris, little of the music has survived and this little still needs to be related more sympathetically to other music of the time, if only for its sociological importance.

Some of the music to be discussed in this chapter has been made available in modern editions but none of it has been explored in special studies. Torrefranca would surely have taken much interest in Grazioli and Turini if he had not been so preoccupied with precedents for Mozart. As before, Nin has led the way in Spain.

Northern Italy in the Wake of Galuppi and Others (*Grazioli, Turini, Asioli*)

In Venice itself, where for two centuries there had been so much of importance to discuss here, there was but a single composer of even minor consequence to the sonata in the high-Classic Era—namely, G. B. Grazioli. One other composer, a very obscure foreigner who seems to have been active in Venice, among other places, may be mentioned briefly

3. E.g., cf. the listing of 2 lost Madrid publications of sons. by the Pamplona organist José Ferrer in DICCIONARIO LABOR I 899, a set of 6 for piano alone (1780) and a set of 3 with Vn added (1781).

4. Cf. GROVE III 847-848 (Hipkins and others); also, the quantities of guitar sonatas listed in HOFMEISTER 1815 and 1828.

for a few details of purely bibliographic interest. **Jean Michel Pfeiffer,** whose music titles are sometimes in French and once include "di Franconia,"[5] published a sonata for four hands at one keyboard, along with twelve smaller pieces (1784); another, "once very popular" duet sonata,[6] with the title "Il Maestro e Scolare" that Haydn similarly used by 1778;[7] still another, with the title "Il y a de la malice dedans"; a set of six sonatas for two violins "per esercizio a contratempi" (1785); and a successful keyboard method, *La Bambina al cembalo* (*ca.* 1785). A few single accompanied sonatas and some other instrumental items were left in MS. The two duets that bear titles were both published in Mannheim, but the other publications were all issued in Venice. This last fact alone, at a time when instrumental publications were so few in Venice, is reason for supposing that Pfeiffer spent some time in that city,[8] although the only reference that mentions a locale puts him in London in his last years.[9]

Giovanni Battista Grazioli (1746-*ca.* 1820) came to Venice at an early age (from his birthplace about 75 miles west, on Lake Garda).[10] In Venice he trained under F. G. Bertoni, followed the latter as organist at St. Mark's in 1778, and became first organist there in 1785 when Bertoni succeeded Galuppi (who died in 1785) as *maestro di cappella.* Thus, Grazioli was close to two Venetian sonata composers discussed in Chapter VII. He left 18 sonatas in 3 sets of 6 each, Opp. 1-3. Before being issued in separate volumes (though numbered 1-6 and 7-12) the sonatas of Opp. 1 and 2 originally appeared in one volume as *XII Sonate per cembalo,* and this is how they are published in a fine edition that has been newly prepared.[11] Op. 3 (not seen here) adds a violin accompaniment (K + Vn).[12] All of these editions were published by Zatta e figli in Venice, probably in the 1780's.[13]

5. Cf. Eitner/QL VII 406-407; Gerber/LEXICON II 123; Gerber/NEUES III 691.
6. Thayer & Riemann/BEETHOVEN I 80.
7. Hoboken/HAYDN I 807. A mod. ed. of this son., published by A. J. Heuwekemeijer, is announced in NOTES XVIII (1961), 327.
8. Cf. the listings in BRITISH UNION II 777; also, the article on the Venetian publishers Alessandri e Scattaglia in Sartori/DIZIONARIO 6.
9. Thayer & Riemann/BEETHOVEN I 80.
10. The chief source is the "Appendice" (by G. Benvenuti, according to MGG V 751 [Sartori]) in CLASSICI-m II No. 12 (Gerlin); cf., also, Caffi/STORIA I 452.
11. CLASSICI-m II No. 12 (cf. pp. 149-150; also, the listing of the original ed. in BRITISH UNION I 398).
12. Cf. the listing in Cat. BOLOGNA IV 115.
13. At present, this dating cannot be more than an educated guess based on the start and end of Grazioli's service at St. Mark's (1778-89), the date of Bertoni's later sons. (Op. 11, 1790; also published by Zatta e figli), Grazioli's relatively conservative style and keyboard writing, and the fact that by 1796 a set of sons. by his son Alessandro had already appeared in Venice (H-or-P & Vn, Op. 1; publisher not given [cf. Schmidl/DIZIONARIO Suppl. 377]).

Grazioli's sonatas inherit the clarity of organization, small and large, of both Galuppi's and Bertoni's sonatas. He also knows how to write the finely molded, cantilena lines that we saw in Galuppi's sonatas. But he does not have the latter's imaginative freedom or fantasy; and he makes only a minimal use of the keyboard's idioms, primarily because in both slow and fast movements his main, often sole, interest seems to be in the cantilena melodies. Yet these limitations may be attributed only partly to a more circumscribed (but not undistinguished) creative talent. They also reflect the greater emotional restraint and sense of structural propriety that marked the classic phase of the Classic Era much as such restraint and propriety in Corelli's sonatas marked the classic phase of the Baroque Era. One evidence is Grazioli's standardization both of the cycles and of the designs of the separate movements. All twelve sonatas in Opp. 1 and 2 are in three movements. The order of movements is F-S-F except for moderate tempos in two first movements (Sons. 7 and 11) and in two finales (Sons. 2 and 11, quasi-minuet and minuet). All twelve sonatas are in major keys (of not more than three sharps or two flats), with a change of key or mode in all twelve middle movements, of which eight are in the subdominant, three are in the relative minor, and one is in the tonic minor key. Except for the outer movements of Sonata 4, there is no relationship of incipits in these sonatas, and this exception could be purely fortuitous.

Grazioli's tendency toward standardized forms is further made evident by his employment of the universal binary design in every one of the thirty-six movements in Opp. 1 and 2, with repeat signs in all but one of them (Son. 2/ii). There is no other design—no rondo, no fugue, no set of variations, nor even a trio added to either of the movements in minuet style (Sons. 2/iii and 11/iii). To be sure, within those binary designs one finds that same flexible diversity in the disposition of the thematic material that obtains in the more resourceful treatment of "sonata form" throughout the Classic Era. To generalize, one can say that the requisites of textbook "sonata form" are usually present in the first movements, and they are usually lacking only the return to the initial idea in the second half of the other movements. But from this point there are increasing exceptions and variants. Thus, the complete requisites are present in all three movements of Sonata 11 (the sole Grazioli sonata that has won a place in the "Old Masters" anthologies[14]), whereas a return is lacking in all three movements of Sonata 5. The second half usually begins with a restatement of the initial idea in the

14. E.g., Köhler/MAÎTRES-m II 40; Pauer/MEISTER-m IV no. 5; RICORDI ARTE-m IV 52.

related key, but when it starts with some other idea (always derived from the exposition) the initial idea is sure to return later in the home key (as in Son. 6/iii).

In other words, Grazioli's individuality begins to emerge when we get down to his treatment of the thematic material. Aside from an excessive use of the Alberti bass or related accompaniments and a tendency to fall back on certain melodic patterns (such as the descending figure at the start of Sons. 2/i, 5/ii, 10/i, and 11/i), he shows this individuality increasingly in the more detailed aspects of his writing—the rhythmic and melodic refinements, the precise voice-leading, and the careful balance of phrases and periods. The broad cantilena themes predominate in "singing-allegro" fashion in the first movements (Ex. 43), although

Ex. 43. From the opening of Giovanni Battista Grazioli's Sonata 3/i (Op. 1; after CLASSICI-m II No. 12 [but without the editorial additions], by kind permission of Leo S. Olschki, publisher, in Florence).

motivic play prevails in Sonata 6/i, and passage work in 9/i. Passage work is the mainstay of the finales, sometimes bridged by a gay tune (Son. 12/iii/17-32). Whatever its nature, the basic material is always kept in view and closely integrated. In a few movements the ideas contrast clearly (Son. 6/iii); at other times they do not, because they either resemble each other in character (Son. 3/i) or simply represent essentially the same idea in contrasting keys (Son. 7/i). At the start of the second half the initial or other idea usually undergoes a brief but genuine development (Son. 2/i/42-55).

Grazioli's harmony is sensitive and accurate without being conspicuous, except for dissonances that are occasionally striking, such as a long suspension in the bass (Son. 4/ii/24) or a biting cross relation (Son. 11/i/47). The texture is thin enough to call for an improvised filler part in a few instances (Son. 10/i), but more often it is as close and full, say, as Mozart's. Besides the general affinity of styles, Grazioli gives us specific reminders of Mozart's keyboard writing in such details as the hammer-stroke and feminine cadences (Sons. 5/i/94-95 and 4/ii/21), the chromatic appoggiaturas (Son. 2/iii/9-10), and the contraction of the texture into octaves (Son. 8/ii/7). As with Mozart, there are still traces of the *galant* style, especially in the ornamented, fragmented lines of certain of the "Adagio" movements, which contain Grazioli's most expressive writing (Sons. 6, 7, 11[15]).

Another in the same general circle of composers was **Ferdinando Turini** (or Turrini) "detto Bertoni" (*ca.* 1749-*ca.* 1812), who was the nephew of Ferdinando Bertoni and, like Grazioli, his pupil.[16] When Turini became blind at twenty-three (1772) he quit a short-lived position in Venice and entered upon his main career, as church organist in Padua, there to remain until the threat of military invasion in 1800 compelled him to flee back to his birthplace of Brescia. He wrote a few comic operas and sacred choral works, but the only works that have kept the memory of him even faintly alive today are a complete Sonata 6 in D♭ and a "Presto" in g (Son. 4/i) that have been included in several of the "Old Masters" series.[17] These come from a set of six *Sonate per cembalo* published around 1780, while Turini was still in
Padua, but without indication of place, date, or publisher.[18] Apparently 18a
following this set, a set of six accompanied sonatas (K & Vn, with a

15. The "Adagio" of Son. 11 has also been printed separately, as a cello solo (transposed from g to f); cf. CLASSICI-m II No. 12, pp. 150-151; Weigl/VIOLONCELL 69; Eitner/QL IV 355 (with high praise).

16. Cf. Schmidl/DIZIONARIO I 627 and Suppl. 745; Caffi/STORIA I 440.

17. E.g., Köhler/MAÎTRES-m II 98; Pauer/MEISTER-m III 64 and 60; RICORDI ARTE-m IV 40 and 36.

18. The MS and publication are listed, respectively, in PUBBLICAZIONI NAPOLI 642 and BRITISH UNION II 1024; "c. 1780" seems too early for this remarkably advanced, mature music; yet the dedication notes that it was composed "at the time fatal blindness struck in the best years of my life." In PUBBLICAZIONI PISTOIA 94 (wrongly listed under "Francesco Turrini") the place of publication is given as Venice. Mod. ed. of 5 sons., considerably "enriched": CLASSICI-m I no. 33 (Pedron), in which no. 1 in A = no. 2 of the original ed., no. 2 in E♭ = no. 5, no. 3 in G = no. 1, no. 4 in E = no. 3, no. 5 in D♭ = no. 6, and no. 4 in g of the original ed. is omitted.

"Fuga" added for cembalo alone) was published in Venice in 1784 by Alessandri e Scattaglia. But not until after his return to Brescia did there appear his set of twelve "Sonate per il Cembalo" (Milan, 1807), dedicated, interestingly enough, to Clementi. Unfortunately, no copy of the accompanied sonatas and only the first three sonatas in the set of 1807 could be located in the course of the present study, meaning that only nine of the twenty-four sonatas attributed to Turini may be
19a extant.[19]

One only hopes that the memory of Turini has not grown faint to the point of becoming irretrievable. What music remains ought to be sufficient incentive for continuing the search to find more, especially the rest of the set of 1807. Indeed, the reader who is immersed in this period and locale of the sonata will be struck at once with an unexpected rhythmic vigor, a boldness in the melodic leaps and harmonic dissonance, a resourcefulness of development, an advanced use of the keyboard (surely the piano by now), a full texture, and a rich vocabulary of chromatic chords that immediately differentiate Turini's sonatas from the generally more frail, lyrical, formalized sonatas of Bertoni and Grazioli. In all these respects Turini's music sounds more like an anticipation of Clementi's and Dussek's pre-Romantic styles. Turini has something in common with Galuppi in the latter's moments of fantasying, but his style could hardly be farther from that of the other two and still be so close in time and place.

By comparison with Grazioli's sonatas, Turini's earlier keyboard sonatas are notable for their freedom from standardization and their diversity of treatment. The number of movements varies between two and three again. Different forms are used in the finales, including a driving "Presto" quasi-gigue (Son. in E), a true rondo without the title (Son. in G), a multisectional, scherzo-like "Allegro" in 2/4 meter (Son. in E♭), and a "Larghetto" with three variations (Son. in A). Dramatic pauses on suspensive harmonies interrupt and mark off the sonata forms, with the music usually resuming in an unexpected tonal direction. At the moment of recapitulation in the Sonata in D♭/i the pause is made on V of b♭ but the music resumes in the home key. On the other hand, at the same moment in the Sonata in E♭ the pause is again on the dominant of the relative minor key (c) but the recapitulation, if its freedom permits that term, begins on the major submediant key (C) instead of the tonic. Note should also be taken of the expressively flowing "Andante" between the two driving, fast move-

19. Both sets are listed in Eitner/QL IX 474, but the 1784 set, once in the Königliche Bibliothek in Berlin, seems to have disappeared during World War II, and no location is given for the complete 1807 set.

ments of the Sonata in D♭; and of the varied interest in the left-hand part (seldom a literal Alberti bass) throughout Turini's sonatas.

The first three sonatas in Turini's set of 1807 take us right into pre-Romantic music for the moment. They prove to be a little more discursive than the earlier sonatas, reflecting somewhat greater interest in expressive, lyrical writing and rhythmic refinements, and less interest in abrupt, dramatic contrasts. A table of ornaments and frequent indications for "lento" or "stretto" trilling, which should be known to performers of music from this period, are further evidences of Turini's concern for the expressive aspect of this music. In Sonata 2, all in E, the plan of movements is unusual not only for being in the order S-F-S but for the fact that the finale, approached by a half cadence at the end of the middle movement, is a free repetition of the opening movement. Because it has a little of the contemplative, philosophical quality of a late Beethoven slow movement, the opening of this sonata may be quoted here (Ex. 44).

The other composers to be named in northern Italian cities can, at best, receive only honorable mention in this attempt at a comprehensive

Ex. 44. From the opening of Sonata 2 in Ferdinando Turini's set of 1807 (after the copy in the Bayerische Staatsbibliothek in Munich).

survey. They are minor, late-Classic virtuosos and teachers who paid but incidental attention to the sonata, and to less common types of it, at that. Two of these men were of chief importance as violinists in their day. One was **Giuseppe Antonio Capuzzi** (or Caputi; 1755-1818), another Brescian-born pupil of Bertoni in composition, a descendant of Tartini by way of the violinist A. Nazari, and a prolific composer active in Bergamo and Venice (where he played Haydn quartets in the early 1780's). Among a wide variety of instrumental and vocal works, Capuzzi left some late examples of the sonata for violin and *b.c.* (Venice and Vienna, *ca.* 1800-05) such as only the professional violinists were still writing.[20] Even more prolific was **Alessandro Rolla** (1757-1841), a violinist whose rather difficult duos still figure at least in the teaching material of string players today.[21] Active chiefly in Parma and Milan,
21a Rolla is also remembered as one main teacher of Paganini. His many works for strings (*ca.* 1800-20), both pedagogic and concert, include a sonata in string quartet setting, another for viola and cello duet (Op. 3, 1818), a set of ten sonatas for two violins unaccompanied, and several sonatas for violin and viola in duet. During his own day these pieces were cited for their good taste, tricky figurations, and excessive adagios.[22] Another composer of sonatas in Milan was the pianist **Francesco Pollini** (1763-1846), who is recorded in history as a pupil of Mozart in Vienna, as the dedicatee named in *La Sonnambula* by Bellini, as the author of a successful keyboard method (1808), and as the first to use three staffs in keyboard writing (1820).[23] His sonatas include three for piano solo (before 1803) and several in that growing literature for two players at one and at two pianos (or piano and harp, 1807). In Germany the three solo sonatas were rather harshly reviewed except for the "Adagio" of No. 2; objections were made to weak harmony, and to empty passage work in the rondos (where can be found some first signs of the or-
24a chestral and pre-Lisztian textures that were to require three staffs).[24]

A little more should be said about **Bonifazio Asioli** (1769-1832), a widely renowned composer, theorist, and performer who served in Venice, Milan, and other northern Italian cities.[25] Besides operas and

20. Cf. Caffi/STORIA II 66, 68, 69, 83; Schmidl/DIZIONARIO I 292 and Suppl. 158; Weinmann/ARTARIA item 1643.

21. Cf. Moser/VIOLINSPIEL 291-292.

22. Cf. AMZ V (1803) 766, XII (1809-10) 144, XV (1813) 282-283, XXV (1823) 232-233; Eitner/QL VIII 285-286; Schmidl/DIZIONARIO II 387; Weinmann/ARTARIA item 2546; PUBBLICAZIONI PISTOIA 93.

23. But the last is actually an "honor" that should go to the Abbé Vogler (died 1814; cf. Georgii/KLAVIERMUSIK 476, 284).

24. Cf. AMZ V (1803) 491-492, XII (1809-10) 501, XLIX (1847) 268; Schmidl/DIZIONARIO; GROVE VI 842 (Lincoln); Weinmann/ARTARIA item 1943.

25. Cf. GROVE I 241-242 (Loewenberg; but Asioli did get to London, by 1814, as confirmed in AMZ XVI [1814] 621); Schmidl/DIZIONARIO I 77-78.

another piano method, Asioli wrote three sonatas for four hands at one piano as a prodigy of eight, a four-movement sonata in f for two pianos, twelve solo piano sonatas, a harp sonata (the first example to be noted here of many composed in the late-Classic Era), and a four-movement accompanied sonata in C (K + Vc), all between 1777 and 1800.[26] 26a
Of these, at least a set of three solo piano sonatas (Op. 8) and the two-piano sonata were published in London around 1805-15,[27] while the accompanied sonata was an early publication of G. Ricordi in Milan (*ca.* 1815).[28] The London editions may have been arranged by Asioli's presumed brother, the tenor Luigi Asioli (*ca.* 1767-1815), who arrived in London in 1804. Under Luigi's own name two very similar piano sonatas were published (*ca.* 1806), one for duet.[29]

The three solo sonatas of Bonifazio (Op. 8) and the one of Luigi that were available to this study are, in fact, so much alike—in their naïve harmonic shocks, their abrupt pauses, their editorial sentiments, their new virtuosic figuration, and other pre-Romantic auspices—that one wonders if Luigi did not give his own reputation and name to his younger brother's sonatas in order to get them published in London. If differences are sought, they can be found for these particular sonatas in a somewhat more intricate and continuous figuration on the part of Bonifazio as against intermittent spans of melody in Luigi's writing—a frank, direct sort of melody such as a tenor might most welcome in his arias. In any case, Bonifazio is a knowing composer, with most of the resources of the music of the time at his command. It is not surprising to learn that old Haydn would recommend him as the best teacher for Mozart's older son Carl, in 1806, when the latter was in Milan.[30]

Indeed, Haydn may have found in this relatively young man's music some of his own independent, imaginative approach to harmony and form. Thus, the opening "Allegro" of a Sonata in E by Bonifazio, Op. 8/3, seems to work in conscious defiance of the procedures that were more usual by now. The form is binary, without double-bars or repeat

26. Cf. the biographic-bibliographic summary of his compositions in AMZ XL (1820) 667-670; also, the special Asioli collections listed in PUBBLICAZIONI MODENA 525-531. The composition dates are given in the incomplete list appended to the biography Coli/ASIOLI 114-115 (with no further information on the sons.).

27. Based on the dates of Asioli's other London publications as given in BRITISH UNION I 60-61, and on information in Humphries & Smith/PUBLISHING 74, 257. But no Asioli sons. are listed yet in Gerber/NEUES 171-172 (1812) or HOFMEISTER 1815 (Whistling), leaving the dating in the first 2 decades of the 19th c. as uncertain as it often is.

28. A thematic index of these publications is given in Stone/ITALIAN II 3-4 (but read B., not L., Asioli after the first son. on p. 3), A mod. ed. of a solo piano son. Op. 5 is reported in Schmidl/DIZIONARIO Suppl. 43.

29. Listed in PUBBLICAZIONI MODENA 530; cf. GROVE I 242 (Gehring); Eitner/QL I 220-221. Thematic index of the 3-mvt. solo son., in c, in Stone/ITALIAN II 3.

30. Cf. Hummel/SÖHNE 37-44, with new information on Asioli as a teacher.

signs but with the second half mirroring the first to the extent of restating the thematic material in very nearly the same order while reversing the tonal order. Yet the composer does not merely go back to the binary design common more than a century earlier, for the ideas fall into clear phrases and contrast sharply, there is considerable development of the second idea after it has been reached in each half, and the opening section reappears in the tonic key at the end of the movement to provide a satisfying coda: x(I) → y(V) → x(V) → y(I) → x(I). The second movement, "Andante piu tosto Allegretto," is a rondo form. As one of its episodes, a theme is stated in dialogue fashion by the right hand playing first below then above the left hand, in a manner opposite to that made well known by Beethoven (e.g., Op. 31/3/281-301). The "Prestissimo" finale, a fluent movement in triplets and in *alla breve* meter, does happen to be a complete "sonata form."

In and About Florence and Naples (*Cherubini, Cimarosa*)

Farther south, in Florence, where last we met Rutini, Campioni, and Nardini, among other sonata composers, the one name of any significance to us now is that of **Luigi Cherubini** (1760-1842). This famous, highly skilled composer of operas and church music, this Fux of the Classic Era just one century after Fux himself, left as a very incidental and early part of his output a set of *Sei Sonate per cembalo* first published right in Florence about 1785 (Poggiali) and again in London about 1792 (Longman and Broderip).[31] He also left a seventeen-page sonata in MS that is scored, exceptionally, for two organs and was intended as an instrumental adjunct to the Mass in the manner of Mozart's "Epistle
32a Sonatas."[32] According to Cherubini's own catalogue of his works he had composed these works in 1780.[33] At that time he was still a student of Sarti in Milan and had yet to go on to London and finally to Paris (1788), where he wrote music of so much greater importance that biographers understandably have scarcely mentioned the sonatas. Still, the cembalo sonatas, in spite of their conservative style (more like Clementi's than Sarti's style in the same period), their structural laxity, and their frequently flat, unprepossessing ideas (Son. 2/ii), do already hint at the superior composer yet to come in their thorough craftsmanship, fine sense of rhythm, and occasional sparks of melodic and harmonic

31. Both eds. are listed in BRITISH UNION I 186, and the Florence ed. is in PUBBLICAZIONI FIRENZE 264 (cf. Sartori/DIZIONARIO 123). Mod. ed., complete (editorially "enriched"): Buonamici/CHERUBINI-m (with facs. of title page and dedication).

32. Cf. Frotscher/ORGELSPIEL II 1240. Eitner/QL II 421 reports the autograph in the (former) Berlin Königliche Bibliothek.

33. Bellasis/CHERUBINI 381; cf., also, p. 13.

wit. In fact, they already point to the six string quartets written at the other end of Cherubini's life (four of them in his seventy-fourth to seventy-seventh years), which are certainly tighter knit and more resourceful, yet are similar in style and diversional character.[34]

All six of Cherubini's cembalo sonatas are in two movements in the order of a moderate or allegro "sonata form" followed by a moderate or allegro rondo; and they are all in major keys, up to three flats and two sharps.[35] Sonata 3 in B♭, which has appeared in several "Old Masters" sets,[36] is representative of the entire set. In it as in the other sonatas the first movement hardly reveals the structural tension that the composer later achieved in his "Overture" to *Anacréon*. There is a superfluity of ideas, a lack of dynamic contrast between these ideas, and a disproportionate amount of mere passage work. This particular sonata happens to have little more than a retransition in place of a "development." However, except for Sonata 6, which has an actual motivic development of an earlier idea and, in any case, is built on a somewhat larger design, the "development" sections consist only of transpositions and passage work (as in Sons. 1 or 5). The "second theme" in Sonata 3/i (mss. 35-42) is one of Cherubini's more inspired bits of melody in these sonatas, a coquettish, chromatic sort of melody such as might come right out of a Mozart *opera buffa*. The rondo theme of Sonata 3/ii is not quite so fetching (but see that of Son. 4). Yet it is given a spark of life by its supple rhythmic extensions, falling convincingly into a phrase group (or period) of 4 + 6 + 7 measures. The experienced, varied keyboard writing by this son of a cembalist lends enough additional verve and interest to keep these sonatas fresh. They still make good keyboard diversion.

The now obscure Florentine Abate **Vincenzo Panerai** (?-*ca.* 1800), a church composer and theorist, also published sonatas in Florence, which may be placed about the same time as Cherubini's.[37] These appeared in twenty-two separate fascicles of one sonata each, but with a single pagination for the whole series. They include not only sonatas "per cimbalo o piano-forte" solo but some for four hands and others with violin accompaniment.[38] Probably in the 1790's in Florence appeared three piano sonatas as the "prima giovanile produzione" of G. M. P.

34. Cf. Mansfield/CHERUBINI.

35. These sons. are briefly discussed as a point of departure in Egert/FRÜHROMANTIKER 11-12, 31-34.

36. Köhler/MAÎTRES-m II 2; Pauer/MEISTER-m II 40; RICORDI ARTE-m VI 54; etc.

37. Cf. Schmidl/DIZIONARIO Suppl. 588. The date "1750" in Eitner/QL VII 309 for perhaps the first ed. of Panerai's treatise *Principi di musica* is probably an error, since the several other eds. come from the end of the century and later.

38. Cf. the partial, different listings in PUBBLICAZIONI FIRENZE 275; BRITISH UNION II 761; Cat. BOLOGNA IV 59.

39a Rutini's son, **Ferdinando Rutini** (1767-1827).[39] And in near-by Livorno, the learned German-born theorist **Johann Paul Schulthesius** (1748-1816) published two sets of three and four accompanied sonatas, respectively (H-or-P + Vn; Op. 1, Livorno, 1780 and London, *ca.* 1780; Op. 2, London, *ca.* 1785).[40] A Protestant minister to a Dutch and German colony in Livorno, Schulthesius published almost nothing else but sets of piano variations, the last of which is dedicated to Asioli's pupil Carl Mozart.

The last composers in Italy to be noted in this chapter are three in Naples, two of them being rival masters of the *opera buffa* and the other a popular guitarist now all but forgotten. **Giovanni Paisiello** (1740-1816) and **Domenico Cimarosa** (1749-1801) both left sonatas
40a only in MS, and both seem to have written most of their sonatas during their respective terms of service in the more instrumental-minded environment of St. Petersburg. Paisiello was in that city from 1776-84, during which time he wrote cembalo sonatas with and without accompaniment for his cembalo pupil Grand Duchess Maria Féodorovna,[41] and some accompanied sonatas for Princess Maria Theresa in Vienna (while he was looking about for a new post in 1783).[42] But it was probably not until after his return that he wrote some sonatas for violin and cello and some others for harp (by 1801). All these sonatas and perhaps other sorts exist in at least half a dozen inadequately listed MSS in Naples, Parma, Bologna, and Paris,[43] along with rondos, concertos, and other instrumental music, most of which is still waiting to be collated and examined. Only six one-movement sonatas have been made available, "for the first time," in print, from an unidentified MS of nineteen solo cembalo sonatas.[44]

In the letter to his father of January 16, 1782, Mozart mentions without further pertinent comment that "The Grand Duchess [then visiting the Imperial court in Vienna] produced some sonatas by Paisiello (wretchedly written out in his own hand), of which I had to play the Allegros and Clementi the Andantes and Rondos. We then selected a

39. Cf. GROVE VII 339 (Loewenberg); Cat. BOLOGNA IV 63.

40. Cf. AMZ XVIII (1816) 393-395 (including mention of sons. in German eds.); GROVE VII 595-596 (Stainer); Scharnagl/STERKEL 75 and 105; BRITISH UNION II 934. A study of this composer's music should prove fruitful.

41. Cf. his own recollection of this experience as relayed in Kelly/REMINISCENCES I 239.

42. Cf. Mooser/ANNALES II 360-361, 355 (with much new information in pp. 191-362, *passim*); III Figs. 68 and 69 (facs. of title page and dedication of Paisiello's keyboard method, 1782).

43. Cf. Eitner/QL VII 292; PUBBLICAZIONI NAPOLI 622; Cat. BOLOGNA IV 58; PUBBLICAZIONI PARMA 255; Saint-Foix/PAISIELLO 247; Villanis/CLAVICEMBALO 213; Della Corte/PAISIELLO 259, 262.

44. Mola/PAISIELLO-m (with preface).

theme from them and developed it on two pianofortes."[45] These remarks cause Saint-Foix to speculate on the nature of Paisiello's instrumental music, the examination of which "remains to be done; we shall be astonished if no expressive gift, no 'romantic' tendency is revealed in this writing."[46] The newly printed sonatas could well be from the group Mozart tried. But if so, Saint-Foix would surely have been disappointed with them. They are static forms that come nearer to the rondo than to any other principle, or rather to the older rondeau, since the sections are usually disconnected and without bridges or retransitions. The simple refrain melodies give the impression of coming right out of Paisiello's *opere buffe,* although none of them has the charm of his immensely popular aria from *La Molinara* (1788), "Nel cor più," which became the "favorite air" for so many sets of instrumental variations (as in Asioli's Son. in G, Op. 8/2/i). The episodes are a little more active in their rhythms and figurations. But the use of the keyboard is unimaginative, the part-writing is often crude, and the harmony is often tenuous almost to the point of nonexistence. Devices, ideas, stock cadences, and constant repetitions that must have succeeded very well in support of witty texts and stage action fail almost totally as "absolute" music. In short, these particular "sonatas," even if not viewed in the then more usual senses of the term, have seemed here to be anything but the "rare and precious gems" their editor proclaims them to be.[47]

By comparison, Cimarosa's sonatas seem outstanding, although by more normal qualitative standards they must be regarded as but indifferent examples of their kind—not quite the leaping, roaring, laughing music that Gautier had in mind. Perhaps the most practical evidence for that observation is the absence of these pieces from recitals, in spite of their attractiveness and playability at first sight, the readily available edition of thirty-two solo piano sonatas prepared by Felice Boghen,[48] and every performer's natural curiosity about instrumental music by one so celebrated for his charm and good humor as was the composer of *Il Matrimonio segreto* (1792). Boghen prepared for his edition by announcing his "find" in 1924 and briefly describing the score.[49] But, with

45. As trans. in Anderson/MOZART III 1182.

46. Saint-Foix/PAISIELLO 247-249.

47. These negative comments cannot, of course, be extended to include a more deserving, extended, instrumental work like Paisiello's *Concerto a cinque* in B♭, which the Virtuosi di Roma have recorded so ably (Decca DL 9730). Yet, it could not have been modesty alone that compelled Paisiello himself to acknowledge that outside the theater, "when it comes to real music, I proclaim myself a complete zero . . ." (as trans. in Saint-Foix/FERRARI 457-458).

48. Boghen/CIMAROSA-m.

49. Boghen/CIMAROSA, with "Allegro alla francese" printed in full, which may be compared with Boghen/CIMAROSA-m no. 17 for modest editorial markings added in the latter; cf. Saint-Foix/LONDRES 525.

that frustrating secrecy or indifference of all too many editors, he did not divulge the location of this source, which omission must help to explain why no biographer or lexicographer has paid more than the most fleeting attention to these sonatas since they were found.[50] The source proves
51a to be a MS volume (not autograph) in Florence,[51] "Raccolta di varie sonate per il fortepiano." This music was probably composed in the decade between 1788 and 1798, either while Cimarosa was in St. Petersburg (1788-91), whence he brought back a little piano given to him by Catherine the Great;[52] or after his return to Naples (1793) and before his serious illness in 1798.[53]

There are 81 pieces on 88 pages in the Florence MS of Cimarosa's keyboard music, mostly in moderate and fast tempos. The separate pieces are only headed by tempo inscriptions, except for "Perfidia" (Boghen/CIMAROSA-m III no. 8) and "Giga" (III no. 12). But now the over-all title of "sonate" goes a little beyond the mere generic sense of "instrumental piece" that it seems to have had for Paisiello. Cimarosa's pieces vary considerably in length and style. There are several motivic pieces in binary design that last only one page (I no. 5) and a few that last as many as five pages (I no. 1), including one that divides without a break into an "Andantino" in b♭ and an "Allegro assai" (quasi-gigue) in B♭ (II no. 20, one of the most interesting pieces from a musical standpoint). Other pairings may have been intended by the
53a juxtapositions of pieces in the MS, as with Scarlatti, and others. The longer forms have no repeat signs or double-bars but usually do have returns and clear phrase-and-period syntax. However, the piling up of new separate sections leaves an effect not so much of an integrated, developed "sonata form" as of the additive succession of stanzas in a song. The initial idea is seldom more than a figure or motive, of little interest in itself. In the few instances that a second idea enters (as at I no. 6, ms. 12) no distinct contrast is afforded. The keyboard writing, mostly two-part, is idiomatic and fluent, though never advanced. Its variety of styles within these limits provides the chief interest in Cimarosa's sonatas.

50. Two sentences in Chiesa/CIMAROSA 260 suggest that the keyboard sonata was not this composer's natural vehicle of expression.

51. Listed in PUBBLICAZIONI FIRENZE 264. A group of 6 other sons. mvts. is in a Milan MS (Fondo Moseda E. 18. 1 of the Conservatorio della musica G. Verdi, according to information kindly supplied by Mr. Charles Cudworth at the University in Cambridge, England).

52. Cf. Mooser/ANNALES II 455, III Figs. 87 and 86 (pictures of the piano and of Cimarosa playing another keyboard instrument).

53. As suggested by the chapter heading in Chiesa/CIMAROSA 260. But note that no. 16 in Boghen/CIMAROSA-m II is a reduction of the "Sinfonia" to Cimarosa's *Il Fanatico* of 1777 (information from Mr. Cudworth).

Ferdinando Carulli (1770-1841), a self-taught guitarist, became one of the greatest virtuosi of his day, ranking with Giuliani and Sor.[54] He lived mainly in Naples until he moved to Paris in 1808. His guitar method of 1810 and some exercises, variations, and other pieces are still known. But his many sonatas and sonatinas for one and two guitars, widely published between about 1805 and 1825, are virtually
forgotten today.[55] A further Neapolitan to cite—for numerous sonatas 55a
of minor interest (organ, Vc duo, bass duo)—was the highly prolific, successful opera composer **Nicola Antonio Zingarelli** (1752-1837).

A Solitary Portuguese (Portugal)

In Portugal during the high-Classic Era the only name of consequence known here in connection with the sonata is that of the highly successful opera composer and conductor in Lisbon, **Marcos Antonio Portugal** (or Portogallo; 1762-1830).[56] Also an organist, and a pupil of Sousa Carvalho (SCE IX), Portugal may have undergone his chief exposure to the sonata during eight years in Naples and other Italian cities (1792-1800). At any rate, at least one such work can be reported by him, a work that is unusual in several ways. At the Library of Congress (M23-P85) is a hitherto unnoticed "Sonata e variacoens" in a MS of 22 pages that is certainly a contemporary copy if it is not an
autograph. This is one of those rare sonatas (we shall meet another by 56a
Emanuel Bach) in which each of three movements is in a different key (D, C, E♭). In the first movement, obviously fast though unmarked, the initial idea in octaves, its return only near the end, the more frequent returns of an alternating idea, and the absence of a double-bar all suggest the concerto grosso first movement. But the neat fluency (recalling Portugal's teacher) and the square-cut phrases that cadence consistently every two measures, often repeating, give more the impression of the opera-tune sonatas by Paisiello, although on a higher level of composition. Longer, more diversified phrases and more advanced keyboard passage work occur in the other two movements. The "Rondó Andantino" that comes next has a ten-measure refrain that subdivides into $4 + 2 + 4$ measures (Ex. 45). The refrains are more ornamental and free, with cadenzas. In the finale, an andante theme is treated in six variations that show ingenuity in both the rhythmic and technical patterns.

54. Cf. Bone/GUITAR 70-75.

55. Cf. HOFMEISTER 1815 (Whistling), pp. 241 and 251-252, and 1828, pp. 358-359 and 293-294; also, AMZ XIV (1812) for a review that describes some sons. and other pieces by him as good "exercises and diversion for guitar players."

56. Cf. DICCIONARIO PORTUGUEZES II 191-230; GROVE VI 887 (Grove & Trend).

Ex. 45. From the start of the second movement of Marcus Antonio Portugal's "Sonata e variacoens" (after the MS at the Library of Congress).

Madrid and Related Centers In the Wake of Soler (*Blasco de Nebra*)

In Spain the first and much the most distinctive composer to bring up is Don **Manuel Blasco de Nebra** (*ca.* 1750-1784), about whom we know merely that he was the nephew and reportedly the pupil of his uncle José de Nebra in Madrid, that he knew well the organ music of his uncle's friend and Cabanilles' pupil José Elías, and that he served before the end of his short life as "Organista de la S. Yglesia Cathedral de Sevilla."[57] The single known work by Blasco de Nebra is a set of
58a *Seis Sonatas para Clave, Y Fuerte Piano,* Op. 1, published in Madrid.[58] His death at 34 in 1784 plus the "Fuerte Piano" and "Obra Primera" in the title suggest a date for this set around 1775-80. Insofar as has been discovered in the present study, it is the only extant set of stringed-keyboard sonatas by an Iberian composer that was published in Spain up to the end of the eighteenth century. It is also the first set of Iberian sonatas known here to specify the piano (as well as the harpsichord or clavichord). There are no dynamic or other editorial markings except for minimal tempo indications, but the use of the piano is made likely by long tones that must be sustained in order to project songful lines (Son. 5/i), by searching, dissonant harmony that seems to call for the most subtle nuances (Son. 1/i), by rapid passages in octaves for each

57. Cf. Mitjana/ESPAGNE 2181; DICCIONARIO LABOR II 1619.

58. An apparent unicum in the Library of Congress, the set was kindly brought to the attention of this study by Mr. Richard Hill when it was acquired by that institution in 1940. Mod. eds.: Son. 1 in c, Newman/THIRTEEN-m no. 7 (with preface); Son. 5/ii in f♯, Davison & Apel-m II no. 308.

hand (Sons. 4/ii and 2/ii), by ever-changing textures, and by relatively few of those ornaments that might be used to emphasize particular tones on the harpsichord. The fact that the range exceeds five octaves, using every chromatic tone from FF (Son. 2/ii) to g‴ (Son. 1/ii), would not necessarily point to any one instrument at that time.

All six of Blasco de Nebra's sonatas are in two movements in the order slow-fast. The first movement is always an introspective "Adagio" in quadruple meter, while the second is a hard-driving piece in 3/4, 6/8, or quadruple meter, progressing in its tempo marks from "Allegro" in the first two sonatas to "Allegro molto" in the next two and "Presto" in the last two. There are as many minor as major sonatas, the keys being, respectively, c, B♭, A, g, f♯, and E. No thematic relationship can be found between incipits of the paired movements. In every one of the twelve movements "sonata form" is approximated within the usual binary design and its repeated halves, though always with some variant and never with a real motivic working out of ideas in the "development" sections. Most often, all the other essentials are present except some kind of bridge between the first and second ideas in the recapitulation. A modulatory bridge is always present in the exposition and it is this material that usually opens the second half. But sometimes the initial idea returns only to open the second half and not later, as in Sonata 2/ii, in which a gigue style makes this procedure the expected one, anyway. Sonata 3/ii has no return of the initial idea. Sonata 3/i starts on V of IV[59] and the return occurs with the proper tonal complement, but in minor (V of i).

Blasco de Nebra's ideas generally contrast clearly, by virtue of distinctive melodic outlines as well as tonal and textural differences. Most of the ideas are identified by bold leaps, strong, often chromatic appoggiaturas, and effective rhythmic organization within a broad arch (Ex. 46). Sonata 1/ii starts with the strident leap of a minor 9th, which, in this free texture, gives the impression of belonging to a 2-3 (9-10) suspension. The first contrasting idea in Sonata 6/ii (as at ms. 29) begins without preparation on the major 7th above a single bass note and is not "explained" until, after several beats, it resolves into a I^6_4 chord on that note. In another place (Sonata 5/ii/31) a double appoggiatura, made by a major 7th followed by a major 2d in the melodic line, disorients the listener during a moment when it seems to be confusing the I and V chords. And the material that closes each half of Sonata 3/i includes several minor 10ths approached by leaps of major 9ths. Such foreign tones greatly intensify both the more driving

59. The g♯ in mss. 1 and 2 undoubtedly should be g♮.

Ex. 46. From the opening of Sonata 5 by Manuel Blasco de Nebra (after the original ed. at the Library of Congress).

portions of the fast movements and more expressive, florid lines of the slow movements. But not all the ideas are so intense. The main contrasting idea in both the fast and the slow movements (as in Sons. 6/ii and 4/i) is usually a warmly tender one, repeated several times in the gently persistent manner of a Schubert second theme.

We can already see to what extent Blasco de Nebra's distinctive use of appoggiaturas is also an important qualifier of his harmony. It accounts for much of the harmonic dissonance and chromaticism. And it may complicate the voice-leading, especially when both hands are playing appoggiaturas, with the risk of parallelisms or other traps unless the performer finds contrapuntally satisfactory solutions.[60] Other harmonic

60. E.g., cf. Newman/THIRTEEN-m 68 mss. 6-10.

traits include acciaccatura chords such as Scarlatti and Soler used (Son. 5/ii/40), and a delectable, tonally upsetting interplay between tonic and subdominant harmonies along with their respective applied dominants, in several closing sections (as in Son. 11/i or Ex. 47, *infra*). The texture of this music often seems so ideally suited to the guitar that one must remind himself of the harpsichord and piano specified in the title. Voices drop in and out in *freistimmig* fashion, ranges shift abruptly, wide intervals, especially 10ths, are frequent, and much the greater responsibility is taken by the right hand. The left hand does assume nearly equal importance at times by paralleling the right (Son. 5/i/14-17) or alternating with it (Son 5/ii/63-66, each hand leaping 10ths!), and by getting an occasional share in the melodic burden, including an ornament here and there (Son. 3/i/46-57). Even when it only has repeated notes these are given flavor by an ornament or two and the harmonic and rhythmic play above (Son. 1/i/16-19). But much of the time the left hand plays only single, deep supporting notes, in the manner of a guitar bass (Son. 3/ii/1-8). The chief right-hand difficulty beyond the general requirements of arpeggios, scales, and other passage work in the fast movements is the stretching of broken octaves and 10ths in figuration (e.g., Son 6/i/13-15) that recalls the middle section of Brahms' "Intermezzo" Op. 116/2. Hand-crossing is notably absent from this music.

Quite as much as Scarlatti and Soler, Blasco de Nebra seems to enjoy "dancing" to infectious Spanish rhythm. Representative are certain syncopated patterns in $^{6}_{8}$ meter (Son. 2/ii/15-20, 33-36) or $^{4}_{4}$ meter (Son. 4/ii/17-19), and such a pattern as that made by steady 8th-notes in $^{4}_{4}$ meter with bass quarter-notes accenting the last and first beats (Son. 5/ii/16-20), although none of these patterns can be identified exclusively with any one dance. Blasco de Nebra's rhythmic excitement extends to his well-defined phrase syntax, too. Thus, Sonata 2/ii starts with two phrases of seven measures each (divisible into 4 + 3), then two of five each (3 + 2), and two of four each (2 + 2). In one of those tonally ambivalent codettas mentioned earlier, this same movement ends with a phrase of five measures (4 + 1) and (by a half-measure shift) another phrase of six measures (4 + 2; Ex. 47). Only at the next structural level is there sometimes a certain rhythmic monotony. Rather too often for the expected continuity of form in fast sonata movements, the separate phrases or groups of phrases end in full cadences marked off by rests (Son. 3/ii/8, 27, 30, etc.).

In this last respect Blasco de Nebra may suffer somewhat by comparison with Scarlatti and Soler. But otherwise, insofar as his one

Ex. 47. From the end of Blasco de Nebra's Sonata 2/ii (after the original ed. in the Library of Congress).

youthful set of sonatas permits us to know him, he has seemed here to be the peer of these men in originality, force, and depth of expression. His language is certainly no closer than Soler's to that of the high-Classic masters. In fact, his biting, sometimes anguished dissonance suggests more the earlier style of the Italian organist Della Ciaja (SBE 193-194). He is like Scarlatti chiefly when he persists in the repetition of a short figure. But his ideas are more likely to extend into complete themes, he treats them more intensively than Scarlatti, and he arrives at a more regularized form than either Scarlatti or Soler, with a freer texture but none of the structural fantasy or experimentation found in the latter's sonatas. A complete modern edition of Blasco de Nebra's sonatas would substantially enrich the literature of the Spanish keyboard sonata and, for that matter, of keyboard music in general.

José Lidón (1746-1827) relates indirectly to Blasco de Nebra by way of the latter's uncle, José Nebra, whom Lidón succeeded as organist at the royal chapel in Madrid in 1768.[61] Lidón published *Seis Piezas*

61. The birth year of 1746 rather than 1752 comes from new information in DICCIONARIO LABOR II 1409; cf., also, Mitjana/ESPAGNE 2148, 2180.

o sonatas para órgano in Madrid in 1792[62] and left some others in MS. One of the MS sonatas, a single movement in d, has been made available —"Sonata de 1° tono para clave o para órgano con trompeta real."[63] This is a tightly knit, harmonically strong piece in binary design that whets the appetite for more in spite of its conservative, motivic style and close resemblance to many of the shorter, more concentrated pieces of Scarlatti. Lighter and more perfunctory is the one sonata known by **Mateo Pérez de Albéniz** (?-1831), chapel master in northern Castile (Logroño and San Sebastián). This piece, a single binary design in D, was found by Nin in a MS volume that puts it in high company, including keyboard sonatas by Soler, Haydn, Edelmann, and an unidentified son of J. S. Bach.[64] Nin finds elements of the lively *zapateado* dance in the patterns of its $^6_8$ meter. The short, persistent figures recall Scarlatti again, but not the rather cut-and-dried phrases, hammer-stroke cadences, or lack of significant tonal movement.

Two other keyboard sonatas brought to light by Nin should be mentioned here, although nothing is known about their composers, not even where they were active. One **Cantallos** left a single-movement sonata in c[65] that similarly recalls Scarlatti as well as the *zapateado*. This is an effective piece, with more textural and thematic fiber, more tonal and keyboard enterprise than that of Albéniz. Its "sonata form," which abruptly assumes keys as far afield as g♯, treats a series of nuclear ideas that are more related than contrasted. The one-movement Sonata in B♭ by a **Blas Serrano**[66] is decidedly more advanced in style and syntax, suggesting the homophony and cantabile themes of Christian Bach in spite of its surfeit of short trills. Presumably on the basis of style alone, Nin volunteered approximate dates for the sonatas of Albéniz, Cantallos, and Serrano that he printed—1790, 1795, and 1810, respectively. But there is nothing even in Serrano's music that cannot already be found in Soler's (before 1783). In any case, Serrano's sonata is one more evidence that Iberian styles did not lag seriously behind those on the rest of the continent.

Montserrat and Other Catalan Centers

Padre **Felipe Rodríguez** (1759-1814) was born in Madrid.[67] At 17 he became a monk and organist at the Montserrat monastery north of

62. Reportedly listed in Marcellán's *Catalogo musical de la Capilla Real de Madrid* (1938), a publication that could not be found during the present study.
63. Kastner/SILVA-m no. 14.
64. Mod. ed.: Nin/ESPAGNOLS-m I no. 13 (cf. pp. v-vi).
65. Nin/ESPAGNOLS-m I no. 14 (cf. p. vi).
66. Nin/ESPAGNOLS-m I no. 15 (cf. p. vi).
67. The only information beyond life dates is supplied in Pujol/MONTSERRAT-m II viii-x.

Barcelona (where Soler had first trained) and at some unknown time later returned to Madrid to serve there in the affiliated Montserrat church. At the monastery is preserved a MS collection (presumably not autograph) that includes eighteen sonatas in one to three movements and sixteen rondos by Rodríguez (insofar as unassigned pieces can be identified and disconnected movements related).[68] Some or all of these may have been copies of a collection by him that was published in Madrid, perhaps around 1800, but that no longer exists. At any rate, the fact of the publication itself is worth noting. The MS sonatas are designated for organ. However, in spite of an indication of registration in one of the rondos, the term "organ" has to be understood here (as for Casanovas, Viola, Seixas, and other eighteenth-century Iberians) to be scarcely more restricted in meaning than "keyboard." These pieces are not *tientos, versos,* and fugues; they are light sonata movements with Alberti basses and those related chordal accompaniments that are actually much more appropriate for stringed keyboard instruments. Thanks to Pujol/MONTSERRAT-m (II 71-229), fifteen of the sonatas are available for examination in a modern edition.

The sonatas of Rodríguez are unregularized cycles except for an almost invariable rondo or rondo-minuet finale. Most often this finale is preceded by a moderate and a quick movement or by only one of these. The keys, up to four sharps or flats, do not change within a cycle. Apart from the rondos the forms are binary, variable, and usually without an unqualified return during the second half. As for style, *galant* mannerisms, ornaments, and textures are here in full bloom (e.g., Son. 2/i). These traits and frequent spots of melodic chromaticism (Son. 3/i/2) give a Boccherini or pre-Mozartean flavor in spite of the frequency of cadences in masculine rhythms. There are some original turns in the melodic lines (Son. 1/i/1-4) and some jocose harmonic surprises in Haydn's manner (Son. 5/ii/17-19). But more often these aspects of Rodríguez's writing are routine. Furthermore, the part-writing is sometimes gauche (Son. 1/iii/60-61), and there are many empty passages of mere arpeggiating (Son. 9/ii/87-89). One can be thankful for a further opportunity to know this stylistic stage of Spanish keyboard music, even though from a qualitative standpoint Rodríguez's sonatas do not stand outside the average of the time.

From another monk and organist at Montserrat, Padre **Josep Vinyals** (1771-1825), there remains a group of five sonatas written at the age of sixteen and a more mature Sonata in E♭.[69] The latter is in

68. Only a Rondo in B♭ appears in Nin/ESPAGNOLS-m II no. 11 (cf. p. iii).
69. Mod. ed.: Son. in E♭, Pujol/MONTSERRAT-m II 237 (cf. pp. x-xi).

two movements, a "Presto" with all the essentials of "sonata form" and an extended "Rondo, Tempo di menuetto." More thinly scored, with a minimal, purely harmonic accompaniment, and more formalized than Rodríguez's sonatas, this music can still be rated as more successful in three respects that are basic, of course, to the Classic sonata idea. Vinyals uses fewer ideas, makes more of them, and organizes them into simpler, broader forms.

Padre **José Gallés** (1761-1836), another Catalan monk and organist, served as chapel master at the cathedral of Vich, north of Barcelona. In Barcelona there remains a MS volume of twenty-three keyboard sonatas by Gallés[70] from which Nin selected six for publication.[71] These six sonatas are all single moderate or fast movements in binary designs, without returns to the initial idea after the start of the second half. The relatively broad plateaus of tonality, usually marked off by full cadences and rests, give the impression of structural breadth. But the ideas themselves are fragments (without melodic or rhythmic distinction). The means of continuing these fragments is one frequently met in these Spanish sonatas, though it is not ordinarily carried this far. In place of a motivic working out, each fragment is often simply repeated—usually one more time than the listener believes possible—until the repetitions or but slight alterations add up to the phrases and periods needed to fill out a section. When the section ends, with the usual full cadence, a different but related fragment is started on *its* repetitions, which will constitute the next section, and so on (e.g., Son. in f, throughout). This one process does more than anything else to bring Scarlatti to mind so often in these sonatas. Otherwise, except for a few unconventional if not awkward modulations (e.g., Son. in A♭, mss. 31-33), Gallés is another composer without the individuality and force needed to separate him from his confreres.

The stylistically most advanced sonata printed by Nin and the last work in Spain to mention here is a movement in D by the Catalan organist, director, and church composer in Barcelona, **Mateo Ferrer** (1788-1864).[72] The date of the movement (*ca.* 1814, according to Nin) and its style, which once more shows Spain abreast though not ahead of the times, still justify its mention under the Classic Era, even though

70. Listed in Cat. BARCELONA II 310 (with Pedrell's warm praise of the music).
71. Nin/ESPAGNOLS-m II 43-75 (cf. p. iii). In Marchi/SPAGNOLI-m (an anth. of 8 sons. also to be found among the 33 sons. published by Nin) Gallés' Sons. in c and f (with facs. of a cover and a score page) are printed more faithfully according to the same MS source (giving an opportunity to know the editorial "enrichments" made by Nin); but the editing of the other 6 sons. (by Soler, etc.) appears to be only a futile attempt to restore the *Urtext* by pruning Nin's editions.
72. Nin/ESPAGNOLS-m I 68 (cf. p. vi); cf., also, DICCIONARIO LABOR 900.

Ferrer lived far beyond and into the Romantic Era. But one is at a disadvantage in any attempt to comment on this one known example of its sort by Ferrer. What Nin may have done in an editorial way is hard to guess. His general remarks give no details of the MS source other than that he had a copy "assez ancienne." Nor does he quite make clear whether he is presenting a first movement excerpted from a "grande sonate" in more than one movement or a separate piece in the "grande," fully developed manner of the Classic first movement.

Ferrer's opening idea, with its rising, declamatory octaves, is indeed theatrical beyond anything we have heard in Spain, and the repeated-note figure that follows does at least remotely recall, as Nin suggests, the repeated-note figures in the first movement of Beethoven's "Sonata appassionata." However, the potential of this material is but little realized. Except for abrupt shifts of tonality, the movement soon lapses, by a curious stylistic retreat, into the neater, more impersonal idiom of a Christian Bach. Perhaps the eventual, needed study of Ferrer will throw more light on this inadequate but provocative sample.

Chapter XI

South Germany and Austria From About 1735 to 1780

The Austro-German Scene

The extraordinary peak that the sonata attained in Vienna under Haydn, Mozart, and Beethoven became, of course, the focus of all sonata activities in the Classic Era, much as it continues to be the focus of all sonata history. But whereas the interest in the sonata decreased toward the end of the eighteenth century in Italy, in the Iberian Peninsula, and, to a lesser extent, in France and England, it remained high not only in Vienna but in most other centers throughout Austria and Germany. The mere fact that these next six chapters (XI-XVI), all on the Austro-German sonata, fill more than 40 per cent of our Part II, on composers, should give some idea of the relative extent and importance of that interest. A total of 160 composers are surveyed in these six chapters. To be more specific, in this and the following two chapters we meet 11 pre-Classic composers active in Austria, 26 in south Germany, 19 in central Germany, and 31 in north Germany. Then, after the separate chapters that naturally must be reserved for the Vienna three, we meet some 70 additional composers active in those four regions during the high- and late-Classic Era. Most of these last 70 composers are treated more briefly, all within a final Austro-German chapter, because they were the minor composers who no longer explored new paths but were content to repeat what by now had become Classic stereotypes.

Three political forces stand out on the Austro-German scene during the near century covered by these six chapters (*ca.* 1735-1825). One is the long reign, from 1740-86, of Frederick the Great of Prussia, whose headquarters were in Berlin and near-by Potsdam. Another is the almost parallel reign, from 1740-80, of Maria Theresa, who became

Empress of Austria at the Hapsburg court in Vienna. And a third is the series of cataclysmic French events that started in 1789 with the Revolution, culminated in 1812 when the Napoleonic Empire had overrun almost all Europe, then subsided during the ensuing three years of defeats that led to the Congress of Vienna in 1815 and a greatly revised map of Europe. There were few musicians living in the third quarter of the eighteenth century whose lives were not upset by the Seven Years' War (1756-63), that complex struggle in which Prussia and Austria were the principal antagonists and the earlier War of the Austrian Succession was the starting point. And there were few musicians living in the early 1800's who did not know the anxieties and effects of the Napoleonic conquests (as any reader of Beethoven's life in Vienna will recall).

Culturally, the strongest force in Germany of the later eighteenth century was the literary *Sturm und Drang* movement. This movement had been preceded by the influential poetry of Gottsched and Gellert, and prepared by the poetry of Klopstock and the dramas of Lessing, all of whom lived in Leipzig, Berlin, or Hamburg. Chief figures in the highly emotive, rebellious, anti-rationalistic outbreak were Herder, Schiller, and the young Goethe. And the chief manifestation of the *Sturm und Drang* in instrumental music of the time was the *empfindsam* style (as discussed in Chapter II). We become increasingly aware of this style as we approach its main centers, first those in central Germany where the influence of J. S. Bach was still strong, and above all in north Germany where Bach's sons were active. No composer surpassed Emanuel Bach as an exponent of the *Empfindsamkeit*.

Music's centers in Germany were still many in this period because Germany, like Italy, was still only a conglomeration of principalities, duchies, kingdoms, cities, and ecclesiastic states, large and small. Some consolidation did take place by the end of the period we are considering. But to the brilliantly maintained courts at centers like Mannheim and Dresden may be added many littler, lesser known courts, which continued to be remarkably active for their size, such as those at Öttingen-Wallerstein, Weimar, Burgsteinfurt, or Mecklenburg-Schwerin. Music's largest centers in Austro-Germany were naturally the same as the main centers of the political world and of other cultural activities. Not only did the same power and money that controlled politics also control culture, but many of the musicians we shall meet, especially in central and north Germany, were also law students at the University in Leipzig, men of letters in their own right, participants in the lively intellectual circles of the time, or even—insofar as their inferior social stations could possibly allow—confidants at court. Moreover, although of less direct concern to the sonata, the ties between letters and music were furthered by the close collaboration of poet and composer in songs, opera, and choral music. At any rate, it was not only the music but the sum of the music and these other cultural forces in north Germany upon which the great Viennese masters drew for certain qualities that are neither indigenous nor Mediterranean in their music. To be sure, close connections, often of a more tangible sort, can also be demonstrated between Austrian composers and composers in the near-by districts and states of south Germany. Leopold Mozart, Adlgasser, and Eberlin were all actually Bavarian-born, Leopold's connections with Augsburg being maintained throughout his life.

French was often the language spoken and even written by elite society at such centers as Mannheim, Würzburg, and Potsdam (as by Frederick the Great). Italian and French were still the languages most used, in that order, in music titles, dedications, and prefaces, at least during the earlier pre-Classic Era. But this continued homage to Italian and French tastes cannot be taken as a clue to the actual presence of foreign sonata composers in Austro-Germany at that time. In these next six chapters we meet scarcely a single resident Frenchman, and we meet remarkably few Italians, considering how important Italian opera continued to be in many of the centers we shall visit. To be more specific, there are only ten Italians to be mentioned, or scarcely six per cent of the total in Austria and Germany, of whom only Platti in Würzburg can now be regarded as a figure of any real significance. In 1777 Leopold Mozart wrote his son that the region where Italians could be found "does not extend very much further than Munich and practically comes to an end there."[1] Much more prevalent were the Bohemians, as we shall see—not only the considerable number that were brought to Mannheim by the elector palatine Karl Theodor and his predecessors, but single representatives in many other centers. Also to be met are an occasional Pole, Hungarian, Hollander, Dane, and Swede. On the whole, the native Germans and Austrians themselves seem to have done less traveling and less emigrating than their Italian contemporaries, probably because the former were less disposed to the career of the traveling virtuoso.

Besides the cultivation of the sonata in conjunction with the musical life at court—the formal concerts, the dilettante chamber music, the private lessons given to the patron and members of his family—three other kinds of support for the sonata will come increasingly to our at-

1. As trans. in Anderson/MOZART I 430: cf., also, II 533 on Mannheim.

tention. These were all discussed in Chapters III or IV but deserve at least to be recalled here. One was the growth of public concerts, especially in a city not like Dresden or Vienna but like Nürnberg or Leipzig, where a municipal rather than a royal government tended to favor the participation of the student and burgher classes.[2] Another was the growing interest in the sonata as a diversional or teaching piece for the amateur or ensemble of amateurs, quite as in Italy at this time. And a third was the enterprise of several publishers, notably Haffner in Nürnberg and Breitkopf in Leipzig in the pre-Classic Era, followed by Artaria, Hoffmeister, Bureau des Arts et d'Industrie, and other Viennese firms in the high-Classic Era. Thanks to these and not a few other publishers, Germans and Austrians who composed sonatas had a much better chance of seeing them issued in their homeland than their ancestors had had in the Baroque Era Only the most successful composers now had their sonatas published abroad, a good share of them being the Mannheim musicians, whose reputation was so well established in Paris and London through the renown of their outstanding orchestra.

The literature on the sonata, especially the pre-Classic sonata, in Austria and Germany is, in a word, vast. It is vast not only with regard to the Viennese masters, as would be expected, but in the sense that few aspects have been left unexplored beyond the most obscure names. And even many of those names are being brought out of obscurity as *Die Musik in Geschichte und Gegenwart* advances steadily through the alphabet and as each new young crop of scholars digs deeper and deeper to find topics suitable for monographic treatment. A few plums remain to be plucked—the sonatas of J. Stamitz or J. G. Seifert, for example, or even those of Haydn, if the treatment is to be thorough enough—but not for long, one suspects.

The literature bearing on the Classic sonata in Austria and Germany was already extensive in the eighteenth century, the musicians of these countries being quite as articulate and disposed to scholarship then as later. The letters of Mozart, the autobiography of Dittersdorf, the criticisms by Marpurg, the poetic exaltations by Schubart,[3] the aesthetic observations of Reichardt, the treatise of Emanuel Bach—all these are exceptional in quality but far from unique as types. We even have such bibliographic tools from the eighteenth century as dated thematic

2. An interesting survey of court and concert life in Austro-Germany may be found in Brenet/CLASSIQUES 1014-1018.

3. The travels and observations reported in Schubart/IDEEN (posthumous, 1806; written down in 1784-85, according to P. A. Merbach [p. 271 in the 1924 reprint by Wolkenwanderer in Leipzig]) date before Schubart's 10 years in jail from 1777-87.

indices of the thousands of MSS then on deposit with Breitkopf,[4] many of them sonatas and many of them no longer known in any other source. And, of course, from outside of Germany but immediately translated into German, we always have the incomparably succinct and honest observations of the ubiquitous traveler Burney.

Since the eighteenth century the stream of literature pertinent to the Classic Austro-German sonata has been steadily swelling. In the nineteenth century it is marked especially by the fundamental biographic studies of Haydn, Mozart, and Beethoven that were carried far in the writings of Pohl, Jahn, and Thayer, respectively. In the twentieth century the opening salvos were Riemann's epochal publications on the Mannheim school and such outgrowths or reactions as the brilliant, sprawling, erratic dissertation by Mennicke on Hasse and the Graun brothers, or the studies of Adler and W. Fischer on the Vienna Classical school. These special studies were followed by still more specialized ones —on regions, as by Lange on the southwestern German keyboard sonata; on cities, as by Engländer on Dresden instrumental music, or Stilz on the Berlin keyboard sonata; on single composers, as by Leux on Neefe; on a particular contribution of a single composer, as by Schmid on Emanuel Bach's chamber music; and so on and on. Understandably, the editions of music and the bibliographic tools have not quite kept pace with these studies. But certainly the Denkmäler series and the more "practical" series like *Nagels Musik-Archiv, Organum,* and *Hortus musicus* have done more to make the more obscure Austro-German sonatas available than any similar series has done for the lesser known sonatas in any other country. And such bibliographic tools as the monumental thematic indices of Mozart and, at last, Haydn and Beethoven hardly find their equals in any similar tools for composers of other nationalities.

The Southernmost German Centers (*Maichelbeck*)

Coming up from the Mediterranean countries to Germany, we will find the transition smoothest, both geographically and stylistically, if we begin with southern Germany, in the area eventually comprehended by the predominantly Catholic states of Baden and Bavaria. In particular, we may begin at the southwest corner in the Baden archiepiscopal see of Freiburg (in Breisgau). There there was a staff priest (*praesentiarius*), "professor of the Italian language," organist, and theorist, of immediate interest to us, **Anton Franz Maichelbeck** (1702-50).[5]

4. Cf. Meyer/BREITKOPF.

5. The chief biographical source is Werra/ORGELSPIEL 28-30. Cf., also, GROVE V 519 (Milne); MGG VIII 1506-1507 (Hoffmann-Erbrecht).

Maichelbeck himself gives us nearly that much information plus some that is still more pertinent in the collection that primarily concerns us here, his "Opus I" published in 1736 in Augsburg.[6] The typically lengthy German title is worth translating at least in part:

> The Cecilian playing at the keyboard and pleasing the ear; that is, 8 Sonatas, composed by rule and taste in the current Italian manner, for use as well on church as on domestic keyboard instruments [Zimmer-Clavieren], and grouped into diverse pieces gratifying to [both] soul and ear, consisting therein, I, of a Praeludio, Allegro, Variatio, Buffone, and Gigga; II, of . . . etc.

In his ensuing dedication to three patrons in Freiburg, Maichelbeck explains in Italian his predilection for the Italian manner. He thanks them, with this offering "dei primi frutti della mia Composizione," for financing his musical training in Rome. And in the periphrastic German preface "To the kind music lover" that follows, he adds, in effect, that he has kept these "modern pieces," especially the bass, within the student's range; that those who are able may fill out the chordal texture when it seems too thin; that this music will be more satisfying, on the organ as well as the cembalo, if the "tremulen, mordanten, trillern, etc." are not neglected (whether indicated or implied, presumably); and that these keyboard pieces might also be used during the new, lighter, Italian-style Masses, or following the Vesper service.

Maichelbeck's sonatas vary in number of movements from three to six, neither the order nor type of which is fixed. Not merely because of this indefiniteness of the cycles but for several other reasons, these "sonatas" would now be classified rather as "suites." Most of the first movements, as is usual in the suite, are improvisatory in style and cursive in form (with titles like "Preludio," "Capriccio," "Toccata"). The other movements are all binary designs without reprises. And the majority of these binary designs are the usual Baroque dances ("Allemande," both "Gigue" and "Gigga," "Sarabanda," and so on). In its consistent motivic play, its fast harmonic rhythm, its involute lines that shift between two pitch levels, and its two- or three-part texture, Maichelbeck's writing is certainly closer to that, say, in J. S. Bach's French Suites (1722) than to that in D. Alberti's sonatas or even in D. Scarlatti's or Marcello's sonatas. To be sure, the texture is a little more open and homophonic than Bach's (with less melodic interest in the bass and more sectionalization through cadential breaks) but not than Telemann's in his keyboard Fantaisies from about the same year

6. Discussed briefly, with exx., in Seiffert/KLAVIERMUSIK 331-334. But the quality and historical interest of Maichelbeck's contributions invite a detailed study. Mod. ed., Sons. 1 and 2: Weckbecker/MAICHELBEK-m (with preface).

(*ca.* 1738). What, then, did Maichelbeck bring back from Italy? Where is the "current Italian manner" in his writing? It is these questions rather than the undeniably good quality of his music, both technical and musical, that have elicited the only interest in him shown by music historians.

Of course, any influence from Italy that might bear on the dawning of pre-Classic instrumental music in Germany is always of interest, especially in Bavaria, where predecessors like Gottlieb Muffat had established much closer ties with Austria. Maichelbeck could have been in Rome early enough to know Domenico Scarlatti and students of the late Pasquini, or late enough to know D. Alberti. But there is too little tangible evidence in his music. Seiffert quotes the few short passages that have any bearing,[7] yet these are neither typical of the rest of the music nor significant in themselves. The alternating hands and "Scarlatti-like leaps" up to (only) a 13th (in Son. 6/i and vi, where most of the writing of this sort occurs) are modest at this time. And the sole brief use of Alberti bass (4 mss. in each half of "Variatio 4" in Son. 3/i) could neither have derived from or influenced D. Alberti's writing, as implied both ways by Torrefranca and others.[8] It is a sequential passage with a change of harmony on every beat and no songful line in the upper part. To return to our question, one must conclude that Maichelbeck did not derive anything significant from Italian styles. At most, he seems to have identified the "current Italian manner" with lighter, secular music, which in his own writing would mean his still substantial sonatas as against the sort of organ preludes, fugues, and versets that he put in the third part of his theoretical treatise published the next year. And even these last are not any more strict in texture than the relatively contrapuntal "Toccata" that opens his Sonata 7.

Much more Italian influence might be found less than a generation later and some eighty miles to the northeast, in Stuttgart, where another learned theorist and linguist was active. **Johann Friedrich Daube** (1733-97), "Cammer-Theorbist" and "Flaut-Traversist" at court, may never have gotten to Italy, but at the age of eleven he had already been a "Theorbist" in Emanuel Bach's circle at the often Italianate court of Frederick the Great in Berlin.[9] Among his works Daube left some solo and ensemble sonatas that were published for the most part anonymously in *Der musikalische Dillettant* but are all assumed to be by him since it was he who put out this weekly periodical (in 1770-73,

7. Seiffert/KLAVIERMUSIK 332-334.
8. Torrefranca/ORIGINI 346, 468, 507, 723.
9. Cf. MGG III 27-29 (Reichert), incl. a facs. of an autograph MS page of a Symphonia.

just after he moved to Vienna).[10] However, the only sonata by Daube that has been explored in recent years is one in F, published in 1765 in Nürnberg among the latest of the many sonatas in Haffner's *Oeuvres mêlées* that we shall be noting in this chapter.[11] This sonata is in three movements without key change—a "sonata form" marked "Vivace"; a more motivic, expressive, cursive "Andante"; and a "Vivace" finale in binary design. Its ideas are slight and the keyboard treatment is elementary. But Daube's sense of form is secure and convincing, chiefly because the phrases fall regularly into well-defined units of two and four measures and because the tonality progresses by clear, simple steps from one structural goal to the next (as would be expected of one whose treatise, *General-bass in drey Accorden* [1756], is a practical exposition of Rameau's chordal system). The flavor of Daube's sonata is near *galant,* what with its melodic subdivisions, its rather frequent, simple ornaments, its dynamics and articulation markings (more than average for Anth. HAFFNER OM-m), and its Alberti, repeated-note, or other harmonic bass. How Italianate and *galant* Daube's sonata is may be appreciated readily if it is compared with the more conservative, motivic, and weighty *Trio a Liuto, Traverso e Basso cont.* by him that has been published from a MS in Rostock.[12]

At the onetime, small but musically lively court of Öttingen-Wallerstein (about 60 miles east of Stuttgart) we meet **Ignaz von Beecke** (1733-1803)[13] in the present chapter and F. A. Rosetti in a later chapter. Beecke, a professional soldier, is remembered as an enthusiastic dilettante who was at home, too, in Paris, Vienna, Berlin, and Mannheim; who composed in nearly every category of music both secular and sacred; who was close to Jommelli, Gluck, Hasse, Haydn, and Mozart, among many other notables in music; and who excelled as a brilliant, self-taught pianist. Schubart actually ascribed to him a new "Beeckische" school of playing, which is reflected in his keyboard pieces and which is characterized by "a particularized fingering, short, somewhat affected thrusts of the fist, a distinct execution, a playful spirit in the passage work, and, especially, a magnificent pralltriller."[14] The

10. Cf. Eitner/QL III 150. A lost publication of 6 lute sons. "dans le gout moderne" (1746) is listed in Göhler/GESCHICHTSFORSCHUNG 333.

11. Anth. HAFFNER OM-m XI/2. Portions of mvts. 1 and 3 appear in the exx. (pp. 5-7, 8) appended to Lange/SÜDWESTDEUTSCHEN (with discussions, pp. 10-11, 12).

12. Edited by H. Neemann (Berlin: Viewek, [1926]).

13. Schiedermair/WALLERSTEIN, a documentary study of the musical activities at this court from 1747 to 1833 (especially during the reign of Kraft Ernst, 1773-1802), includes considerable information on Beecke, pp. 107-114. Cf., also, MGG I 1501-1506 (Schmid).

14. Schubart/IDEEN 166; but cf. the several (jealously?) derogatory opinions by the Mozarts in Anderson/MOZART I 445, II 497, 528, 541, 644, 668, 676, 703, 821.

laudatory Schubart also refers to Beecke's keyboard sonatas, calling them some of "the best of this sort that we have." But there is more restraint in another reference to them, made in 1799,[15] and Mozart calls one of them that he read at sight in Augsburg in 1777, "rather hard and *miserabile al solito* [wretched as usual]."[16]

Beecke left about thirty of these sonatas, of which a set of six, Op. 2, was published in Paris in 1767.[17] With neither this set nor any of the scarce MSS available to the present study, we may consult the helpful, detailed summary of an unpublished dissertation, completed in 1921, on Beecke's instrumental music.[18] Here we learn that twenty-six of the sonatas are diminutive, elementary, early works for cembalo solo, predominantly in two movements of simple binary design. They are weaker than the competent piano concertos, quartets, and symphonies that Beecke later wrote under Haydn's influence. But two of three duet sonatas and another scored exceptionally for two pianos and a harpsichord (the model being Mozart's Concerto in F of 1776, K.V. 242) show more substance, with stirring melody (Beecke is previously cited for the warmth of his slow movements), some ornamentation, good structure, and good solutions to the ensemble problems.

Moving nearer to Munich, we find five composers now generally forgotten yet each worth a mention. These men were all as active and widely traveled as Beecke but they did not have the important associations by which his name, at least, has been kept alive. Active in Ulm from 1751 to 1770, the organist **Johann Christoph Walther** (1715-71), son of the learned lexicographer J. G. Walther, left at least four keyboard sonatas, of which only the one in Anth. HAFFNER OM-m II/6 (1756) is extant.[19] This last leads one to hope the other three sonatas will eventually turn up, not because of any significant advances toward the Classic sonata but because of its rich, original, expressive keyboard figuration and its surprising harmony. It is in three movements, F-S-F, in E♭, e♭, and E♭. Walther's obvious predilection for experiments in the flat keys shows up in whole passages all in double-flats, and in his visits to such remotely spelled keys as c♭ (ten flats!), the literal submediant of e♭ at the start of the second half of the middle movement.

Pietro Pompeo Sales (*ca.* 1729-97), a Brescian opera composer

15. AMZ II (1799-1800) 186.
16. Anderson/MOZART II 480. There is general praise for Beecke's keyboard music in BURNEY'S TOURS II 76, and a mention of its popularity in Vienna in Burney/HISTORY II 962.
17. MGG I 1503. Op. 2 is listed in Cat. BRUXELLES III 484.
18. Munter/BEECKE, especially 590-596.
19. Cf. Eitner/QL X 170-171.

and member of the Bologna Accademia dei Filarmonici,[20] spent much of his life in Augsburg and other south German centers.[21] In Anth. HAFFNER RACCOLTA-m III no. 5 (*ca.* 1759) is his only known sonata, which is in C and in three movements, "Conspirito," "Andante," and "Tempo di minuetto."[22] Its neutral ideas, clear designs, affective turns to the tonic minor mode, and ornamental *galant* style (with triplets going almost constantly in both the passage work and chordal bass) all bring it close to the more placid but developed sonatas of Rutini.

Also a resident of Augsburg, **Johann Gottfried Seifert** (or Seyfert; 1731-72) studied under Emanuel Bach in Berlin, at the same time becoming an admirer and close imitator of (J. G.?) Graun's music.[23] Besides eighteen ensemble sonatas in three sets (K + Vn-or-Fl & Vc, 3 Fls or 2 Vns/bass, Fl & Vn/bass), published between about 1762 and 1770 in Augsburg, Leipzig, and London, Seifert left a four-movement cembalo Sonata in F in Anth. HAFFNER OM-m V no. 5. At least one of the ensemble sets is extant[24] and should be worth scoring for further study if the cembalo sonata is representative. The latter begins to pass the *galant* style in its lean texture and consistent drive. Moreover, bearing out the composer's fortunate training, it is above average in the quality of its ideas, the vitality of its rhythms, the interest of its accompaniment, and, above all, the development of its material. In the outer fast movements, separated by a minuet with second minuet and an "Andante," this development goes on not only in the "development" sections but in much of the rest of the incomplete "sonata forms," too. Ex. 48 is a central portion of the cumulative, pre-Beethovian "development" section in the first movement.

In Munich and in Freising twenty-five miles north, the priest and *Kapellmeister* **Placidus von Camerloher** (1718-82) composed much vocal and instrumental music, including over twenty-five SS/bass sonatas in MSS in Darmstadt and Modena, a Fl/bass sonata in a MS copied in 1753 by Le Clerc (the publisher), and a lost set of sonatas Op. 1.[25] His "trio" sonatas were reportedly composed mostly before the death of the prince-bishop Johann Theodor in 1763, himself a participant in chamber music at the Freising court.[26] These may not show the

20. According to the heading in Anth. HAFFNER RACCOLTA-m III no. 5.

21. For assorted bits of information cf. Gerber/LEXICON II 367-368; Gerber/NEUES IV 6-7; Eitner/QL VIII 392-393; Schmidl/DIZIONARIO II 433-434; DIZIONARIO RICORDI 935.

22. Mod. ed.: Benvenuti/CEMBALISTI-m no. 14.

23. Gerber/LEXICON II 507-508; Eitner/QL IX 132.

24. BRITISH UNION II 939.

25. Cf. MGG II 722-724 (Fellerer), with reference to a diss. of 1916 and other sources; Eitner/QL II 293.

26. Mod. ed. of 4 SS/bass sons.: Hoffmann/CAMERLOHER-m.

Ex. 48. From the first movement of Johann Gottfried Seifert's Sonata in F (after Anth. HAFFNER OM-m V no. 5).

skill or Haydnesque charms of his later symphonies but they are fresh and interesting enough to be heard again. Three of the four available sonatas have four movements in the older church sonata plan, S-F-S-F, the fourth being without the initial slow movement. Whether the three parts move in block chords or carry on imitations *concertante* style (or canonic in Son. 2/iii), over a fairly active *b.c.*, they bow to more modern trends by converging in a distinct cadence at the end of almost every phrase, which itself is almost always in four measures. The ideas are motivic, passing from one variant to another without significant contrast, so that the total effect is still monothematic.

In Landshut, another twenty-five miles northeast, lived the organist **Johann Anton Kobrich** (1714-91), whose enormous choral and instrumental output aroused contemporary reactions both pro and con.[27] It includes "Musical Delights, Consisting of Four [keyboard] Sonatas," published in 1752 by Haffner, who also published several other harpsichord and organ collections by Kobrich.[28] Kobrich's instrumental music awaits a co-ordinated study, but these only reported sonatas by him have been examined for their anticipations of "sonata form" and quoted at sufficient length[29] to permit a preliminary judgment of them. They appear to be tuneful, elementary in their use of the keyboard, and up-to-date in their tendency toward sectional forms based on phrase grouping, though revealing little development of the material beyond literal sequences.

The Mannheim School (*Stamitz, Filtz, Richter*)

Not only in south Germany but in all Europe no pre-Classic music center was more celebrated and respected than the Mannheim court during the residence from 1743-78 of the art-loving elector palatine Karl Theodor.[30] It was in 1902 that Hugo Riemann first proclaimed the "discovery" of an epochal "Mannheim School."[31] Here he found, among other things, "the long sought forerunner of Haydn," in the person of Johann Stamitz; and the origins of the Classic symphony, with its minuet now the third of four movements in the order F-S-M-F, with its largely homophonic, realized texture replacing the more contrapuntal texture and the *b.c.* of Baroque music, with its variety of *Manieren* and its graduated as well as terrace dynamics, and with its contrasting "second theme" (though not necessarily with a reprise of the initial idea, which is found even less consistently in Mannheim than elsewhere at the time). But Riemann's discoveries scarcely had time to impress the scholarly world before they were contested. In 1908 Guido Adler

27. Cf. MGG VII 1287-1288 (Scharnagl).
28. Cf. Hoffmann-Erbrecht/HAFFNER 121 *et passim*.
29. Lange/SÜDWESTDEUTSCHEN 9, 17-18, 21-22; and pp. 2-3, 13-15, and 16 of the exx.
30. Cf. MGG VIII 1594-1601 (E. Schmitt & J. Tröller), with full bibliography.
31. DTB-m III/1 ix-xxx, followed by further claims and information in VIII/2 (1906) vii-xxvi. Mennicke/HASSE 65-73 summarizes and develops the same theses. Cf. Thoor/RIEMANN (with summary in German).

came forth to challenge their significance in the course of his own proclamations on behalf of M. G. Monn and other *native* Austrian pioneers of the "Vienna Classical School."[32] Within a year Lucian Kamieński sought to establish priority for the *Manieren* and dynamics in music by the Italianized Hasse, and by Jommelli and other Italian immigrants in Austro-Germany. And at the same time, Fausto Torrefranca began his studies in Italian keyboard music, which were to feed on the belittlement not only of Mannheim but of all German pre-Classic music as a source for the Viennese masters (SCE VII). In succeeding years, La Laurencie and Saint-Foix extended these "discoveries" and claims to French symphonists, including Gossec;[33] Vladimír Helfert extended them to the Bohemian opera composer František Václav Miča;[34] others extended them to G. B. Sammartini, to Boccherini, to Emanuel Bach, to Christian Bach, and so on.

Naturally, as the number of participants in this scholarly melee began to grow, and as more and more musical riches fortunately came to light, the collective understanding of eighteenth-century instrumental music grew, too. An inescapable conclusion was forming to the effect that the change-over to Classic styles was a transitional process going on throughout the musical world, not a sudden inspiration on the part of one group. This conclusion is one, of course, that the present book should help to fortify. In retrospect, one might safely ask why such a conclusion was not evident from the start, considering how Riemann overextended his Mannheim group to an international "circle" that touched Bohemia, Austria, Italy, France—in fact, nearly all of this musical world, even including composers who seem never to have visited Mannheim. At any rate, the effect of cutting that circle down to size has been to put the Mannheim court in a truer light as a lively center of opera, as the home of a renowned, unexcelled orchestra, as a fine training ground for string players, and more incidentally as the residence of a talented, up-to-date, though not pre-eminent group of composers, whose connection with the court and its orchestra all but insured the publication of their works abroad. In the opinion of one near contemporary, the leadership that perfected the orchestra and sent its members out into the world was "worth more than a hundred engraved sonatas."[35]

In 1914 and 1915 Riemann added to the three volumes of Mannheim symphonies that he had published by editing two of chamber music,

32. DTÖ-m XV/2 ix-xxvi, followed by W. Fischer in XIX² (1912) vii-xxiv. Cf. the rebuttal in DTB-m VIII/2 vii-xiv. J. A. Hiller already recognized both a "Steinmetzchen Schule" and a "Wiener Schule" in 1767 (Mennicke/HASSE 66-67).

33. La Laurencie & Saint-Foix/SYMPHONIE.

34. Helfert/SONATENFORM; cf. Racek/TSCHECHISCHEN 504-507.

35. AMZ I (1798-99) 882 (signed "S**.")

with quartets and quintets in the fourth and sonatas or other smaller ensembles in the fifth volume.[36] Only his own thoroughness, his more reserved judgments, and the deflation that the school's historical reputation has undergone can explain why so relatively little has been done to follow up this portion of his "discoveries." Further studies of the symphonies have been made, among them Sondheimer's penetrating analyses of pre-Beethovian thematic processes[37] and Waldkirch's dissertation, which emphasizes not so much the embryonic forms as the new melody and its *Sturm und Drang* subjectivity.[38] But "The Sonata in the Mannheim School" remains an open topic for a dissertation, as
38a of the present writing. More important, it remains a worthwhile topic in spite of the swing of the pendulum away from this center.[39] The sonatas are generally different enough from the symphonies to have an independent, though not necessarily lesser, interest of their own. As we shall see, this very difference may be another reason for their relative neglect.

There are sonatas to discuss by every important Mannheim symphonist except Ignaz Holzbauer (1711-83), and even he gave the title "Sonata da camera" to an affective, four-movement string quartet in f, left in MS,[40] and he published a set of "trios," Op. 4, though the latter is now lost.[41] Much of the extensive Mannheim sonata literature is of the melo/bass rather than the accompanied or duo type. One favorite option, "for a trio or an orchestra," provides a meeting ground for the symphonic and chamber styles. There are almost no solo keyboard sonatas from pre-Classic Mannheim, for this was not a keyboard center. The noted Mannheim soprano Franziska Dorothea Lebrun (1756-91) was also a skilled cembalist, but her two sets of accompanied keyboard sonatas (London, *ca.* 1780) are too weak to take up here.[42] The clavecinists Edelmann and Schobert, whom Riemann drew into the wider Mannheim circle but whom we shall meet in Paris, cannot be shown ever to have been in Mannheim. The sonatas of our first three Mannheim composers —Johann Stamitz, Filtz, and Richter—were all first published in the short seventeen-year period from 1755-72. A new lighter group of sonatas by Wendling and others began to appear around 1765. We shall meet some further Mannheim composers when we come to a younger generation in Chapter XVI.

36. DTB XV (with preface pp. ix-xxiii) and XVI (with list of published works and thematic index of first mvts.).
37. E.g., Sondheimer/SINFONIE and Sondheimer/BEETHOVEN (both with exx.).
38. Waldkirch/SINFONIEN (cf. p. 137).
39. E.g., cf. Lang/WESTERN 608-610.
40. Mod. ed.: EDMR-m XXIV (Lehmann, with preface) 89.
41. Cf. DTB-m XVI xvii.
42. Cf. BURNEY'S TOURS II 34; BRITISH UNION II 605; MGG VIII 420-423.

Johann Stamitz (or Stamic; 1717-57), the historically renowned violinist and composer of Styrian-Bohemian descent, was brought to Mannheim in 1741, two years before Karl Theodor's reign started.[43] About 166 works are credited to him, including 23 that are thus far lost, but not including several choral works. This total breaks down into some 70 symphonies, 43 concertos, 39 sonatas (nearly one fourth), and 14 "trios."[44] The extant sonatas need to be itemized by sets and types, since new sources have added new information and since, despite (or because of?) Stamitz's renown as a symphonist, an organized study has yet to be done on this neither small nor inconsequential portion of his output. Bibliographic confusion with the works of sons Carl and 44a
Anton remains a problem still not fully resolved. The fact should be noted that all but the first of Johann's publications appeared posthumously.

Johann Stamitz's Sonatas

A. *Six Sonates à trois parties concertantes* [2 Vns/*b.c.*], *qui sont faites pour exécuter ou à trois ou avec toutes l'orchestre,* (Op. 1); Paris: Mlle Vendôme, *ca.* 1755 (cf. DTB-m III/1 xxxiv and xxiii; Cucuel/LA POUPLINIÈRE 322). This set appeared in several further eds., in London and Paris, and also in Nürnberg if not Leipzig, for it does prove to be identified with at least one of 2 eds. known to Riemann only through old references (DTB-m III/1 xxxiv); the Nürnberg ed. is that of Haffner (no. 116, 1761?) listed in HIRSCH MUSIKBIBLIOTHEK IV (with facs. of title page) and BRITISH UNION II 973, in spite of its title "Sei Sonate da camera . . ." and the absence of this apparent unicum in Hoffmann-Erbrecht/HAFFNER. Among mod. eds.: Son. 1, DTB-m III/1 3; Sons. 1-6, COLLEGIUM MUSICUM-m Nos. 1-6 (with the *b.c.* figuring omitted).

B. *Sei Sonate da camera a violino solo col basso,* Op. 4. Paris: De la Chevardière, *ca.* 1760 (i.e., between this publisher's issue of Op. 1 in 1759 and Op. 6 in 1761, as in Johansson/FRENCH II Facs. 44 and 46). This listing and the incipits of the first mvts. are given in DTB-m XVI xx and xlv-xlvi (Op. 3/6 should read Op. 4/6). But further references to the contents are rare (one being Moser/VIOLINSPIEL 345), Op. 4 does not appear throughout the excellent run of 20 De la Chevardière catalogues in Johansson/FRENCH

43. The main biographic source, augmenting Riemann in DTB-m III/1 xxv-xxvi and VII/2 ix-x, is Gradenwitz/STAMITZ, from which new (especially, ancestral) findings are summarized in Gradenwitz/FAMILY and GROVE VIII 41-43. More would be known about the life of Stamitz (as of Filtz and of Holzbauer) if, as Riemann points out (DTB-m III/1 xx), Marpurg had not thought it sufficient in his biographical sketch simply to write after the name, "is known well enough."

44. Superseding the entries for J. Stamitz in Riemann's valuable indices (DTB-m III/1, VII/2, and XV [including sons.]), the "Thematic Catalogue" that was to be vol. 2 of Gradenwitz/STAMITZ is still unpublished (1960), but a copy is in the New York Public Library. Its totals, most fully summarized in Gradenwitz/SYMPHONIES 362-363, are changed here mainly because of slight reclassifications and the identification of a "lost" set as another ed. of Op. 1. In Racek's preface to MAB-m No. 28 no basis is given for some loose but very different estimates, including 100 "trio" sons.

II (yet Op. 6, *infra,* is in almost every one), and no present-day listing has been found here to confirm that it is still extant (not even in Cat. BRUXELLES III or IV, where the onetime Wagener copy would presumably be listed; nor in Gradenwitz/STAMITZ II, under "Op. IV. B.") although the score was once in the former Berlin Staatsbibliothek. No mod. ed.

C. *Sei Sonate da camera a violino solo col basso,* Op. 6. Paris: De la Chevardière, 1761 (cf. Op. 4, *supra*). Listed in BRITISH UNION II 973. Mod. eds.: Son. 1 in G, MAB-m No. 28 (Brož); cf., also, Altmann/KAMMERMUSIK 242; Son. 2/i in C, Schering/BEISPIELE-m no. 305; Son. 4 in A, DTB-m XVI 35.

D. *Six Solos for a violin with a thorough bass for the harpsichord* (without op. no.). London: Longman & Broderip, *ca.* 1780 (cf. BRITISH UNION II 973). Presumably this is the set for which Riemann could only quote the incipits (DTB-m XVI xlv-xlvi; cf. p. xx) that he found in BREITKOPF MS Suppl. 1 (1766) 26. No mod. ed.

E. 4 more Vn/*b.c.* sons. in MS (Gradenwitz/SYMPHONIES 362).

F. 6 Vc/*b.c.* sons. in MS (Gradenwitz/SYMPHONIES 362).

G. *Sonata* [in F] *for the harpsichord, with an accompaniment for the violin.* London: C. & S. Thompson, *ca.* 1770 (BRITISH UNION II 973). Since Johann did not otherwise write acc'd sons. and both Carl and Anton did, investigation may prove this son. to be misattributed, on stylistic as well as bibliographic grounds. On the other hand, it could be one of the posthumous arrangements published 2 years earlier (1768) as *Six Sonates pour le clavecin avec accompagnement d'un violon, tirées des ouvrages de Jean Stamitz* (Johansson/FRENCH I 27). The 4-hand keyboard "duett" listed under Johann in BRITISH UNION II 973 is definitely Carl's.

H. "M. Stamitz joua une sonate de viole d'amour de sa composition" at a Concert spirituel Sept. 8, 1754 (as quoted from MERCURE 1754 Oct. 185 in Cucuel/LA POUPLINIÈRE 321). There is no other record of this work, but it is worth noting as a precedent for similar works by son Carl (cf. Altmann/KAMMERMUSIK 250).

I. *Deux Divertissements* [or *Sonates* in a Hoffmeister ed.] *en duo pour un violon seul sans basse* (i.e., "duo" in the sense of double-stops for violin unaccompanied). Paris: Huberty, 1762 (as Op. 7; cf. Johansson/FRENCH II Facs. 25; DTB-m XVI xx and xlv-xlvi; complete facs. in Gates/SOLO 290-299). Among mod. eds., both sons. (except 2/iv): Alard/VIOLON-m Nos. 5 and 35.

All six "trio" sonatas of Stamitz's Op. 1 are in major keys and have four movements, mostly with similar incipits, in the order of fast, andante (or slower), minuet with trio, and very fast. (The same order obtains in at least two of several other orchestral trios that do not happen to be called "sonata."[45]) When there is a change of key the slow movement is in the dominant and/or the minuet trio is in the subdominant; or either may simply be in the tonic minor mode. The forms in all the movements are essentially binary designs with each half repeated, but especially in the outer movements, after the double-bar, there are the

45. Cf. DTB-m XVI xx; COLLEGIUM MUSICUM-m Nos. 7, 48, 49.

modulatory extensions and transpositions (though not the actual development) of the material that point to the ternary concept of "sonata form." Although the initial idea almost always returns at the double-bar, only in one instance when it is not heard there does it return later (Son. 5/i/150), and then too near the end to leave an over-all impression of ternary design. The closing idea, which appears as usual at the end of each half, is readily identified. On the other hand, to speak of a clear "second theme" implies more individuality in most of Stamitz's ideas and more contrast at that point in the form than ordinarily can be found. The contrast is chiefly one of a simplified texture rather than a marked melodic change, Stamitz being bound to his opening idea as much as Haydn is. Sometimes the contrast takes place before any modulation has started (Son. 5/i/14) and sometimes it coincides in the expected manner with the arrival at the dominant key (Son. 6/i/21). The fact of a *piano* indication at the moment of contrast is not as significant as might be supposed, since Stamitz often alternates *forte* and *piano* within sections, too (quite apart from the editorial accretions in "mod. eds.").

Of course, Riemann regarded Stamitz's "trio" sonatas, Op. 1, not only as chamber music (which is how the set was listed in the catalogues of De la Chevardière) but as his first and most important symphonies, not to be surpassed in his own works or soon in the works of any other Mannheim composer.[46] In other words, these *Six grand Orchestra-Trios proper for small or great concerts,* as their title reads in the Bremner edition of 1763, are just as effective when their three parts are multiplied by a full orchestra. Gradenwitz has similarly included them among Stamitz's most mature symphonies but he does not also consider them as chamber sonatas and he does introduce another question by regarding them as being chronologically late, too.[47] With "stylistic peculiarities" as his "only clues," Gradenwitz sees "the greater part of the [other] sonatas and chamber music" (concluding with the Vn/*b.c.* set Op. 6) as belonging to an earlier creative period completed about 1745. However, there are now reasons both factual and stylistic for taking a nearly opposite view. Granted that there were sonatas among the MSS left in Bohemia before Stamitz was called to Mannheim, and that Op. 1 was composed relatively late in his short life, it still seems probable that he had Op. 1 in his pocket when he arrived in Paris late in 1754, shortly before the set was engraved, but that he did not compose his other published sonatas until he was encouraged to do so by the acclaim in Paris. There, as we know (SCE IV), the interest in such things was much greater than in Mannheim.

46. DTB-m VII/2 vii-viii, XV ix-x.
47. Gradenwitz/SYMPHONIES 359-360 ("Ex. 1" is from Op. 6/2/ii, not i).

By way of factual evidence, here is an instance where the order of opus numbers relates at least to the order of publication. When the same publisher issues three sets in the same category (sonatas) in the order of their own opus numbers (1, 4, and 6), one can disregard the usual hodgepodge of publishers and categories. Even the fact that Opp. 4 and 6 were published posthumously does not alter the conclusion that these two sets were probably submitted if not composed after Op. 1. To be sure, if they did exist sooner, the statistical evidence (SCE IV) suggests that the "trio" setting of Op. 1 would still have been one of the main types preferred by De la Chevardière as a first from a relatively new luminary.

But of greater interest here is the stylistic aspect of a Stamitz chronology. Mainly, it seems unsound to conclude that the differences in the other sonatas (again, excluding Op. 1) necessarily mean that those sonatas are earlier and, by inference, less skillful or original works. The differences do exist. With regard to structure they lie chiefly in a less concentrated thematic treatment and in smaller cycles, the S/bass sonatas of Op. 4 being in two or three movements and those of Op. 6 always in three movements in the order of slow, fast, and minuet with trio. More significant are differences in the writing itself. In the sonatas this writing is not the spare, efficient sort associated with Stamitz's symphonies (including Op. 1 this time; Ex. 49) but the more elaborated sort characterized by copious ornaments, triplets, and rhythmic niceties, as well as a looser texture. These are the traits that spell the *galant* style in full bloom. In short, we are in the presence of two different preparations for high-Classic music, the more robust, direct, propulsive symphonic style as against the more intimate, ornate, but easygoing chamber style. One style does not necessarily precede the other. We have seen the two styles co-exist in the music of G. B. Sammartini, Boccherini, and others, and we shall see them co-exist again in the music of Emanuel Bach and still others. The scoring and lighter social function of the S/bass sonatas, as well as the idiomatic capabilities of the solo violin, such as harmonics[48] and rapid arpeggios (Op. 6/4/ii), all tend to dictate the structures and styles of these sonatas. Pertinent to this observation are some still different structures and styles in answer to still other requirements inherent in Stamitz's two "duetti" for unaccompanied solo violin,[49] like a pseudopolyphonic "Fuga" finale (No. 1/iii) or a tuneful melody with its minimal harmonic accompaniment

48. In the 2d variation of the "Menuett" from Op. 4/5, according to Moser/VIOLINSPIEL 345. Op. 6 is discussed in Studeny/VIOLINSONATE 62-63.

49. Discussed in Studeny/VIOLINSONATE 85, 90-91 (but No. 2 actually has 4 mvts., including a minuet finale); Gates/SOLO 167-171.

Ex. 49. From the opening of Johann Stamitz's "grand orchestra trio" in D (Op. 1/4/i; after the Bremner ed. in the Library of Congress).

Ex. 50. From near the start of Johann Stamitz's second "Divertissement en Duo pour un violon Seul sans Basse" (after the facs. of the original Huberty ed. in Gates/SOLO 295).

(Ex. 50). In a somewhat different connection, it is interesting to find in these pieces and Op. 6 (also Op. 4?) none of the *forte, piano, crescendo,* or other dynamic signs that appear so often in the symphonies (again including Op. 1). Yet there is an equal abundance of all those "rocket" figures, C-D-E-D-C ornaments, "sighs," and other *Manieren* that Riemann regarded as identifying traits of Stamitz and his successors,[50] but that subsequent scholars, from Adler on,[51] have shown to be almost universal.

The short-lived cellist **Anton Filtz** (Filz, etc.; *ca.* 1730-60) was once second in renown only to J. Stamitz as an exponent of the new Mannheim school. But the biographical haze that obscures him today permits one to say only tentatively that he came from Bohemia, perhaps by way of another post in Bavaria; that he himself was a pupil of Stamitz ("Dissepolo di Giovan Stamitz" is in the title of Filtz's Op. 3), and that he spent only his last 6 years in Mannheim, from 1754.[52] Besides 41 symphonies, Filtz left 6 sets of 33 ensemble sonatas and "trios" first published in Paris between 1760 and 1772, and republished in Paris, London, and Amsterdam; and he probably left other sonatas in the MSS of his works that are widely scattered in European libraries.[53] As with Stamitz, the sets that concern us here were nearly all published posthumously and first by De la Chevardière, the "Sonatas" by which he made his debut were in "trio" setting, and a first set of "Symphonies" is on the border between orchestral and chamber music (Op. 1, in quartet setting, not discussed here). The sonata sets include

50. DTB-m VII/2 xv-xxv.
51. DTÖ-m XV/2 x-xii; cf. DTB-m VIII/2 (Riemann) vii-xiv.
52. Cf. DTB-m III/1 xxviii-xxix, XV xi-xii; MGG IV 202-205 (Komma).
53. Riemann has listed the publications in DTB-m XVI xv-xvi, with thematic index xxxv-xxxvi; 5 of these can be found in BRITISH UNION I 334-335. For some of the MSS cf. Eitner/QL III 447-448; Cat. BRUXELLES II 374-375, IV 101; Cat. HAUSBIBLIOTHEK 61-62.

4 in "trio" scorings and one each in accompanied and S/bass scorings: Opp. 2 (1765, 2d ed.?),[54] 3 (1760), and 7 (1768) for 2 Vns-or-Fls/*b.c.*; Op. 6 (1772?) for Vc & Fl-or-Vn/*b.c.*; Op. 4 (1763) for K & Vn & Vc; and Op. 5 for Vc-or-Vn/*b.c.*[55]

Riemann makes a special point of the absence of *b.c.* figures in Filtz's "trio" sonatas Op. 3 (referring to the original edition [of De la Chevardière] as well as his own editions).[56] He regards them as early string trios, even though not yet in the scoring of violin, viola, and cello that Boccherini helped to establish. Actually, this "basse" part still serves mainly as a harmonic support in *b.c.* style. Moreover, in the re-edition by Hummel in Amsterdam (1768, plate no. 95) it does have copious figuring and even some indications for "Tasto solo" (e.g., Son. 1/iv/19-20). In Filtz's accompanied sonatas Op. 4 the cello part merely doubles the left hand of the keyboard part in the usual manner, while the violin is mostly subordinate to the keyboard right hand but sometimes takes an indispensable lead (especially in the trios of the minuets). The alternative of cello or violin in Op. 5 recalls the two versions of Boccherini's sonatas first published about seven years later by De la Chevardière (SCE VIII). As a cellist, Filtz naturally wrote more enterprisingly and knowingly for the strings, in Op. 5 and in the "trio" sonatas, than he did for the keyboard, which is treated in a rather elementary and unidiomatic manner in the accompanied sonatas Op. 4.

Even more than Stamitz, Filtz seems to distinguish between symphonic and chamber styles. Whereas his symphonies[57] are largely the effective bluster of chordal progressions well scored and well organized, both dynamically and tonally, the sonatas are more subjective, colorful, experimental, and folklike. The sonatas lead one to think of Filtz as a diamond in the rough and as a talent that might have grown enormously with more time. Op. 3 may be cited, in particular, for it contains some of his most varied and extended sonatas. In this set he shows himself not to have the solid foundation of Stamitz. The three fugal finales (Sons. 2, 3, 6[58]) were hardly meant to be academic fugues (Son. 2/iv is labeled "Fuga con Stylo mixto"), but, even so, the weak counterpoint, the frequent recourse to a particular sequence pattern (as in Son. 3/iv/29-40), and numerous barren spots betray inexperience.

54. Thanks once more to Johansson/FRENCH, it becomes possible to date the earliest known editions; for Opp. 2-7, see vol. II Facs. 50, II Facs. 45, I 67, I 68, II Facs. 56, and I 12 (Bailleux), respectively.

55. Mod. eds.: Op. 3/2 in A, DTB-m XVI 50; Op. 3/5 in E♭, COLLEGIUM MUSICUM-m No. 17; Op. 4/3 in C, DTB-m XVI 59.

56. DTB-m XV xi-xii.

57. As in DTB-m III/1 135 ff., VII/2 93; Carse/SYMPHONIES-m (cf. Carse/SYMPHONIES 52).

58. In the Hummel ed., which interchanges Sons. 1 and 6 of the original ed.

On the other hand, Filtz's procedures are less standardized than Stamitz's. The order, number, and key plan of movements is generally like that in the latter's orchestral "trios," but with some variant in almost every sonata, such as a slower movement at the start (Son. 6), or the omission of the minuet (Son. 5), or the placing of both inner movements in the subdominant key (Son. 3). The themes are often bold and novel, as in the dramatic series of separate iambic thrusts at the start of Sonata 4 in f, or the succession of wide leaps at the start of Sonata 5 in E♭, which for a moment sounds like a source for the opening theme of Schumann's Piano Quintet in the same key. Of special charm are the three nonfugal finales, which anticipate the polka and other dances in an authentic manner that is better evidence than any fact now known for Filtz's Bohemian origin (Ex. 51).

The Bohemian violinist and singer **Franz Xaver Richter** (1709-89) was eight years older but joined the Mannheim court six years after J. Stamitz, in 1747, there to remain until 1769.[59] He wrote much during his long life, including nearly 70 symphonies, a set of string quartets, a set of piano concertos, at least 7 sets of 42 ensemble sonatas, a theory treatise and, especially after he left Mannheim, considerable church music. Six published sets of 6 sonatas each are known, which first appeared chiefly in London between 1759 and 1765, and one MS set of 6 "trio" sonatas, possibly Op. 1, is now known only by its incipits.[60] Extant are 2 "accompanied" sets (K with Fl-or-Vn & Vc), 2 "trio" sets (Opp. 3 & 4, 2 Vns/bass), one set of unaccompanied duos (2 Fls or Vns), and one S/bass set (Fl-or-Vn/*b.c.*).

If, among the first generation of Mannheim composers, Filtz may be considered bolder, lighter, and more original in style than Stamitz, Richter must be placed nearly on the other side as the most traditional, weighty, and conventional of the three. But within Richter's own works the difference between the symphonic and chamber styles does prove this time to be that between progressive and conservative tendencies. More specifically, this difference lies as much as anything in that basic factor of musical style, the rate of the harmonic rhythm. The rate is relatively slow in Richter's symphonies,[61] which permits simple prolongated triads in open texture to have aesthetic values in their own right and to progress in phrases and periods not necessarily enhanced by distinctive

59. Cf. DTB-m III xxvi-xxviii.

60. The list in DTB-m XVI xviii-xix (with thematic index on pp. xli-xliii) is incomplete; e.g., it does not have a Huberty ed. of Op. 3 (*ca.* 1765), a Leclair ed. of Op. 4 (*ca.* 1770), and a 2d Welcker set of acc'd sons. that probably only partly duplicates the Haffner ed. called Op. 2. Cf. BRITISH UNION II 890, where most of the London dates can now be found.

61. E.g., in DTB-m III/1 95-131, VII/2 77.

Ex. 51. From the finale of Sonata in D, Op. 3/1, by Anton Filtz (after the Hummel ed. at the Library of Congress).

themes. The rate is much faster in the sonatas, tending to engender a more active, even polyphonic, texture in which motives and lines become of paramount interest. Now the progress is achieved more by continuous unfolding than by opposition of sections. Somewhere between these extremes Richter's fine quartets might be placed.[62] It is worth noting that the externals of "sonata form," as with Stamitz and Filtz, are not especially affected by these differences, being about equally com-

62. All 6 quartets in Op. 5 are in DTB-m XV 1-60.

plete or incomplete in symphonies, quartets, and sonatas. Nor is there any less use in one type than another of the rather sterile "Rosalie" that Burney understandably deplored in Richter's otherwise able writing.[63]

Actually, it is only the most conservative side of his sonatas that has been made known in recent years, through several editions that all come from but one set, that of six accompanied sonatas (or keyboard trios) published by Haffner.[64] In this set, although the cello merely doubles or outlines the keyboard bass, the flute still plays an independent part, called "concertato" in the Haffner edition, more often than the newer type "accompanyment" indicated in the English editions of these sonatas. Indeed, since the keyboard right hand is realized most of the time and the left hand has its own melodic interest some of the time, there are sections of rich, skillful three-part counterpoint (as in Son. 2/i) that go back some forty years to J. S. Bach's violin sonatas with realized keyboard. Richter's keyboard writing is idiomatic enough (as in the hand-crossing of Son. 6/i), though it is not as advanced as his violin writing in the two sets of "trio" sonatas, with their "Allegro brillante" movements (Op. 4/2/iii) and such technical problems as wide-ranged arpeggios and bariolage (Op. 4/6/i). These sonatas also show a little more tendency toward phrase grouping and homophony.

The majority of all of Richter's instrumental cycles are in three movements, include a minuet, and include a tender, moderately slow movement (with "Grazioso," "Andante amoroso," "Affettuoso," or a similar title). Nearly half of the sonatas end in a fugal (often binary) movement such as could well have been the source for Filtz's less-skilled fugal movements. There is a greater variety of movement types in the "trio" sonatas, among these types being dances—Op. 3/4/iii is a "Gavotte," Op. 4/5/iii a "Siciliano," Op. 4/1/iii a "Giga"—and a "Scherzo Allegro" in *alla breve* meter (Op. 4/4/iv). The dynamic indications and graduations are also more profuse, to the point where one feels the composer is merely rejoicing in a new trick, in spite of the genuinely expressive quality of much of this music. In one instance (Op. 4/2/ii/42-44) and only in the first-violin part a single sustained note is marked to be played "FP FP FP."

Other Mannheim composers of the pre-Classic Era must be mentioned more briefly. The Mannheim-born violinist and conductor **Christian Cannabich** (1731-98) was a pupil of J. Stamitz, of Jommelli in Rome, and possibly of Sammartini in Milan.[65] He left two sets of six

63. BURNEY'S TOURS II 240.

64. Sons. 1-3, HORTUS MUSICUS-m No. 86 (Upmeyer); Son. 2, SCHOTT ANTIQUA-m No. 3709 (Zirnbauer); Son. 3, COLLEGIUM MUSICUM-m; Son. 6, DTB-m XVI 1.

65. Cf. MGG II 751-759 (Komma).

"trio" sonatas each,[66] along with his many dramatic ballets, symphonies, concertos, quartets, and further chamber works. Not explored in recent times, these sonatas were first published in Paris (De la 66a
Chevardière) and Mannheim about 1767 and 1770.[67] The former set, composed in 1766, provides another example, like Stamitz's, of the designation "à trois ou avec tout l'orquestre." To judge from the unimaginative, weak quartet that Riemann reprinted (DTB-m XV 93), Cannabich's fine training and historical renown are no guarantee that any effort to score his "trio" sonatas will be adequately rewarded.

The outstanding Bohemian violinist **Georg Tzarth** (or Czarth, or Zarth; 1708 to at least 1778) was close to his contemporary and compatriot Franz Benda prior to his arrival in Mannheim in 1758, the year after J. Stamitz's death.[68] Among the relatively few works by him that are reported, one set of six Fl/bass and another of six Vn/bass sonatas were published by Boivin in Paris as Opp. 1 and 2, presumably before 1754.[69] If these sets can still be found they should be worth investigating, for the one "Allegro" movement available to this study (from Op. 2/5 in g[70]) discloses virtuosity, warmth, and charm, albeit still in the cursive motivic style of a Leclair.

One of the principal eighteenth-century German flutists besides Quantz,[71] **Johann Baptist Wendling** (*ca.* 1720-97) was in Mannheim from 1753-78.[72] At least eight sets of sonatas by him are reported, in S/bass, SS/bass, and SS settings with flute as the main solo instrument.[73] These were first published in Paris, Amsterdam, and London—all cities where his playing won favor—approximately in the decade from 1765-75. An examination of the six sonatas in Op. 5 for flute, violin, and *b.c.* (London: Napier, 1772) shows them to be like the quartet Riemann has reprinted (DTB-m XV 70) in their unperturbed fluency, clear phrase syntax, good craftsmanship, detailed articulation and dynamics markings, and unresourceful, run-of-the-mill, largely stepwise ideas. In Op. 5 the flute part is technically more advanced,

66. Listed in DTB-m XVI xi (with thematic index pp. xxvii-xxviii).
67. Cf Johansson/FRENCH II Facs. 52; BRITISH UNION I 159.
68. DTB-m VII/2 xi-xii. Cf. Benda's own remarks in Nettl/FORGOTTEN 214-220; Marpurg/BEYTRÄGE I 547.
69. Cf. DTB-m XVI xxiv; but the only S/bass sons. in the thematic index, p. lviii, are 4 MSS. The incipit of a "Trio" for Fl, Vn, & *b.c.* in G is given in Cat. SCHWERIN II 265. In Hopkinson/PARISIAN 14 the last known Boivin catalogue is dated 1754.
70. Anth. CARTIER-m 72-73. A MS Fl/bass "Sola" is listed in Cat. BRUXELLES IV 116.
71. Cf. Schubart/IDEEN 143-144.
72. Cf. Eitner/QL X 225; DTB-m XV xiv.
73. Cf. DTB-m XVI xxv (with thematic index, lxi-lxii); BRITISH UNION II 1066-1067.

while the other two parts are relegated more to harmonic support (SCE V, with ex.). The last four sonatas have only two movements, an allegro in incomplete "sonata form" and a minuet with trio. Lacking is the fast finale of the other two sonatas and the quartet.

Wendling's sonatas are representative of much light, stereotyped music by the Mannheim composers who began to publish around 1765, only five to ten years after the first sonatas of Stamitz, Filtz, and Richter had appeared. The Italian-born violinist **Carlo Giuseppe Toeschi** (*ca.* 1732-88), in Mannheim from 1752-78, belongs with that group, as may be seen in Riemann's reprints of a quartet, a quintet, and an accompanied "Sonata en trio" by him (K with Vn & Vc, Op. 4/4, 1766).[74] Among some four other sets of duos and "trios" published by Toeschi in the next four years are his *Six Conversation Sonatas for Two Violins and a Bass,* Op. 7 (London: Welcker, *ca.* 1770). In these three-movement, tuneful pieces, seldom without their minuets, the three instruments do not participate *concertante* fashion, as the title, or "dialoguées" in another of Toeschi's titles, might suggest. The title simply means music that is purely diversional, with the two lower instruments assigned, again, to little more than the accompaniment of the first violin part.

The short-lived bassoonist **Ernst Eichner** (1740-77) may be grouped with the Mannheimers. He was born in Mannheim and much about his music bears out the reasonable assumption that he was trained there. But his chief orchestral post was at the smaller, Zweibrücken court fifty-five miles southwest of Mannheim, from 1762 to 1772. Thereafter, this still young man gave successful recitals in Paris (where he had already visited in 1770) and London, perhaps wrote most of his sonatas for the eager publishers in these cities, and spent his remaining five years at the Berlin court of Frederick the Great's nephew and successor Prince Frederick William.[75] Eichner's approximately forty sonatas, all first published in the earlier 1770's, have in common the central place they give to "le Clavecin ou le Pianoforte." There are two sets of solo keyboard sonatas or sonatinas, a set of duos (originally called "Sonates") for violin and viola, and five sets of accompanied sonatas (one for K ± Vn and four for K ± Vn & Vc).[76]

74. DTB-m XV 79-92, XVI 44 (with lists and thematic index on pp. xxiii-xxiv and lvi-lvii); cf. VII/2 xii. Cf., also, GROVE VIII 490 (Loewenberg); BRITISH UNION II 1013-1014; MGG XIII 452-458 (R. Münster).

75. Cf. MGG III 1185-1189 (Komma). The unpublished diss. Volk/EICHNER (1943), on the man and his chamber music and concertos, includes biographic material and contemporary statements (pp. 25-37) and a survey discussion of the solo and acc'd. K sons. (pp. 38-61), but no *catalogue raisonné.*

76. Cf. the list in DTB-m XVI xv (with thematic index pp. xxxiv-xxxv); also, BRITISH UNION I 313. The sons. are discussed (inappropriately) in Stilz/BERLINER 77-80. Mod. eds.: 2 sons. for K ± Vn & Vc (Op. 1/3 in c and 2/1 in

All of Eichner's sonatas follow the popular Italian plan of two movements, with a slow or moderate first movement followed by a fast movement or more moderate minuet-with-trio, rondo, or "scherzando." The violin accompaniments are usually subordinate and are often duplicated by 3ds in the right hand of the keyboard part. But there are moments marked "Solo" in almost every movement of the accompanied sonatas without cello, especially near the end, where the violin plays indispensable solo bits. The cello accompaniments always double the keyboard bass at the octave or unison. In the slowest movements the form is sometimes cursive, the long, earnest melodic lines in these movements providing Eichner's most expressive music. Otherwise, relatively simple binary designs with repeated halves prevail except in the rondos. In these movements the chief if not the only interest is in the clear, melodious, balanced phrases, which bring Christian Bach's rounded melodic ideas to mind. The harmonic interest is slight. The modulations are few and plain. There is virtually no development of ideas. And the bass is of the simplest, whether Alberti, repeated notes, or isolated chord roots. One can understand the reservations about Eichner's music that were made by Burney, Schubart, and, more recently, Riemann and Bücken.[77]

Finally, the equally prolific Dutch-born violinist, flutist, and harpsichordist **Friedrich Schwindel** (1737-86) may be grouped with these composers, too, at least in style. Geographically he can be placed no closer than Karlsruhe, thirty miles south, and only there toward the end of his wide travels and many moves.[78] But it is surprising that Riemann did not include him in the "Mannheim circle,"[79] considering how far he stretched this circle in other instances (e.g., to include Maldere and Schobert). Schwindel published at least three sets of "trio" and one set of accompanied sonatas in the decade from 1765-75, along with much other instrumental music.[80] The last of these sets is that of four accompanied sonatas Op. 8 (K with Vn & Vc; London: Longman, Lukey, *ca.* 1775). In this set only the presence of rondo and variation movements differentiates the sonatas from those by Mannheim residents that we have examined. Today one can still agree

A): DTB-m XVI 68; 6 duos, NAGELS-m Nos. 125 and 128 (both Altmann, with prefaces); the "Sonata" in F for Vn & K in SAMMLUNG SONDHEIMER-m No. 15 is an arrangement of a symphony.

77. All are quoted in MGG III 1188-1189. For a comparison of Eichner and Schobert to the latter's disadvantage, cf. DDT-m XXXIX xii (from Junker/COMPONISTEN 89-94).

78. Cf. Eitner/QL IX 116-117.

79. Cf. GROVE VII 657 (Antcliffe).

80. Cf. BRITISH UNION II 936.

with Burney's judgment of Schwindel as "the author of some pretty pieces for harpsichord" and "admirable compositions for violins, which are full of taste, grace, and effects. . . ."[81]

Nürnberg and Near-by Centers (*Agrell, Buttstett*)

For our purposes, the most important individual in pre-Classic Nürnberg was not any of the few resident composers of sonatas, although the music of Agrell will have some interest for us. Rather it was the publisher Johann Ulrich Haffner (1711-67), a lutist and perhaps a composer himself, who, during the twenty-three years from 1742-65, did as much as any other German, including J. G. I. Breitkopf
82a in Leipzig, to propagate the sonata.[82] We have already had occasion to note the importance of his keyboard sonata anthologies issued between 1755-66 (SCE IV), including the twelve volumes mostly by Austro-German composers in *Oeuvres mêlées,* the two mostly by Germans in *Collection recreative,* and the five mostly by Italians in *Raccolta musicale.*[83] In Haffner's small but select and artistically engraved output of some 150 items, chiefly first editions, more than half are for keyboard alone (including 114 sonatas in the anthologies), and several other, ensemble items consist of sonatas. Haffner's interest in the *galant* style is suggested in the title of still another keyboard anthology of sonatas "et altri Pezzi di Galanteria."[84] With regard to his influence, it should be noted that he both represented and was represented by other publishers and dealers in several of the main European music centers.

The Swedish-born violinist, cembalist, and theorist **Johann Joachim Agrell** (1701-65) served in Kassel from about 1722 and travelled as far south as Italy before coming to Nürnberg in 1746 as "Stadtcomplementarius" or leader of the town orchestra.[85] That same year Haffner published a set of six symphonies, Op. 1, that Agrell had composed, reportedly, in 1725.[86] Two years later, in 1748, Haffner published Agrell's *Sei Sonate per il cembalo solo accompagnate da alcune ariette*

81. BURNEY'S TOURS II 234. The estimate in Schubart/IDEEN 231-232 is similar.
82. Cf. MGG V 1305-1307 (Hoffmann-Erbrecht); Hoffmann-Erbrecht/HAFFNER (with additions in Newman/HAFFNER). In Eitner/QL IV 473, the set of 6 Fl/bass sons. ascribed to Haffner is probably only Haffner's ed. of C. F. Döbbert's sons. (plate no. 41).
83. For detailed lists of the contents of each set cf. Eitner/QL IV 473; Cat. BRUXELLES IV 331 (in which the 6 anonymous sons. in vol. I of Anth. HAFFNER OM-m are fortunately identified as being by Agrell, G. A. Appel, Emanuel Bach, J. J. Brand, Kleinknecht, and Wagenseil, respectively).
84. Hoffmann-Erbrecht/HAFFNER 123. Is this set lost?
85. The chief biographic source is Valentin/AGRELL (in Swedish, summarized in Newman/THIRTEEN-m 10-11).
86. Lindfors/AGRELL (a style study based chiefly on the symphonies; in Swedish) p. 104.

polonesi e menuetti, which Walsh reprinted (with a table of ornaments) in London in 1758.[87] Haffner may also have been the original publisher of Agrell's set of six SS/bass sonatas that Walsh published as Op. 3 in 1757.[88] Another cembalo sonata has been identified as Sonata I in A in the first volume (1755) of Haffner's *Oeuvres mêlées,* this being the one of the twelve volumes that gives no composer names. Also known are a published flute duo (1751), two Vn/bass sonatas apparently published as early as 1734 by one Johann Valentin in "Meyell"[89] (possibly Meyel or Meiel in the southeast Netherlands), and two other solo cembalo sonatas in MS, as well as many cantatas, keyboard concertos, and other works that this busy composer left.[90]

The seven published solo sonatas by Agrell, which are those that could be examined here, have from four to six movements. The order of movements is determined by nothing more fixed than a need for tempo contrasts and the preference for a "Polonese" or a minuet-with-trio as the finale. Two of the sonatas are in minor keys and most of them have an inner slow movement in the subdominant or dominant key. In Agrell's symphonies, one Swedish writer has found both Baroque and *galant* traits, the former especially in motivic progression by repetition and sequence, the latter in chromaticism, triplets, and instances of the Mannheim *Manieren.*[91] Much the same can be said for the sonatas. The sequences are well contrived, harmonically and contrapuntally, but certainly excessive as a principal means of continuation. They are made all the more conspicuous by the stock I^6_4-V-I cadences with which they almost invariably conclude and which tend to sectionalize the forms.

Agrell's most characterful ideas are the enunciatory ones in octaves at the start of some of the allegro movements (Ex. 52). Perhaps it is the suggestion of the concerto grosso in these ideas that explains why they in particular are most likely to be restated both at the double-bar, in the related key, and later, in the tonic. However, the feeling of "sonata form" is not here yet. The ideas are still simply energizers of the motivic process, not thematic landmarks. Furthermore, they are generally too angular in their shape and metric organization to be

87. Cf. Lange/SÜDWESTDEUTSCHEN 13-14, 17, 21 (with exx.) for anticipations of "sonata form." Mod. eds.: Son. 4 in e, Newman/THIRTEEN-m 56 (cf. pp. 10-12); Son. in G (Op. 2/2?), cf. SOHLMANS I 39.

88. Cf. BRITISH UNION I 9.

89. According to information kindly supplied by Professor Ingmar Bengtsson in Uppsala. A copy is in the Kungliga Musikaliska Akadamien in Stockholm. The 3-mvt. Son. in A for Vn & P listed under "Agrell, John" in Altmann/KAMMERMUSIK 233 and reprinted by Augener in 1933 is not one of these.

90. Cf. Eitner/QL I 55-56.

91. Lindfors/AGRELL 110.

Ex. 52. From the start of the third movement of Johann Joachim Agrell's Sonata in D, Op. 2/5/iii (after the Walsh ed. at the British Museum).

lyrical. During the sole brief uses of Alberti bass (in Anth. HAFFNER OM-m I/1/ii, seven years after Walsh published Alberti's sonatas) there is not the songful line above it that is essential to the "singing-allegro" style. Nor is the keyboard writing ever florid, the nearest instance being the figuration (including hand-crossing) in the "Aria con [4] Variazioni" that ends Op. 2/6.

These conservatisms rather than any serious lack of expressive content are apparently the reason for Schubart's estimate of Agrell as an able but cold, calculating composer, who is supposed to have said, "Music is concealed arithmetic."[92] Yet when Agrell comes closest to Baroque styles he can write a movement that is musically convincing throughout (as in the "Giga," Op. 2/6/iii). His sonatas did succeed well enough to turn up in some far corners, including an entry for the "trio" sonatas Op. 3 on the purchase lists of Thomas Jefferson that are preserved in the Massachusetts Historical Society (SCE XXI, with ex.). Leopold Mozart thought enough of Agrell's keyboard sonatas to copy the third movement of Op. 2/4 as the last piece in the "Nannerl-Notenbuch" (1759).[93]

The only other composer to mention in Nürnberg itself is **Georg Wilhelm Gruber** (1729-96), who succeeded Agrell as town *Kapellmeister*.[94] A virtuoso violinist who had studied with Domenico Ferrari while the latter was in Nürnberg,[95] Gruber published at least four accompanied sonatas after his return to this city about 1750 from a period of training in Dresden. Although efforts to examine these sonatas (last reported in Munich) have been unsuccessful in the present study, there is some point in calling attention to their interesting titles, which

92. Schubart/IDEEN 208-209. The estimate is briefer but similar in BURNEY'S TOURS II 238-239.

93. As noted in Lerma/NANNERL 4 (but "Ex. 6" does not apply to this piece). Cf. Valentin/NANNERL-m no. 41.

94. Cf. Eitner/QL IV 391-392.

95. Cf. Schubart/IDEEN 209.

all read about the same: "Sonata a cembalo obligato, [flauto] traverso o violino concertato con violoncello accompagnato." What probably is signified is a keyboard "trio" with the cello doubling the keyboard bass.

In Weikersheim and Rothenburg, west of Nürnberg, lived the organist **Franz Vollrath Buttstett** (1735-1814), grandson of the important Baroque organist J. Heinrich Buttstett, probable student of J. S. Bach's pupil J. F. Doles in Leipzig, and composer of what are here regarded as three of the best sonatas from south Germany during the pre-Classic Era.[96] These sonatas, in three of the last four volumes (*ca.* 1763-66) of Anth. HAFFNER OM-m,[97] are all that remain of some forty solo and accompanied sonatas by Buttstett, a large part of whose extensive sacred and instrumental compositions is now lost. All three sonatas are in three movements, headed only by tempo marks, in the order of F-S-F, with the slow movements of the sonatas in A and E♭ in the tonic minor key and that of the Sonata in B♭ in the subdominant. Subtle relationships seem to be intended between the incipits of at least the outer movements in each sonata. In all the fast movements and the "Andante" of the Sonata in B♭ the form is "binary," with each half repeated; with the initial idea usually restated twice right after the double-bar, in the related and home keys, and a third time during the second "half"; with some tendency toward actual development of this idea after the double-bar; and with only occasional hints of a clear contrasting idea except for the closing figure. The slow movements of the sonatas in A and E♭, both marked "Adagio," are cursive in form.

Buttstett deserves his rescue from near oblivion by German scholars in recent years. His fresh ideas, harmonic depth, resourceful treatment, and structural acumen all make for much better music than might be expected from a name now so obscure. But in spite of his late dates, the sonatas themselves still belong in the pre-Classic Era both in time and style. In this respect they closely resemble his cantatas.[98] They are not yet the fluent, direct, transparent products of the high-Classic Era. Rather are they especially interesting here as introducing us, for the first time among composers discussed in the present volume, to the subtle indirections of the *galant* as deepened by the *empfindsam* style. This composite style, which we shall meet regularly in the sonatas of Emanuel Bach, Georg Benda, and others resident chiefly in north

96. Cf. MGG II 540-542 (Blume).

97. Son. in B♭, IX 10; Son. in A, X 10; Son. in E♭, XII 8. The last 2 of these are reprinted in TRÉSOR-m XII (not XIV). Kern/BUTTSTETT is primarily a study of the cantatas, but includes brief discussions of Anth. HAFFNER OM-m (pp. 61-64) and Buttstett's 3 sons. (pp. 64-68, with thematic index pp. 92-93).

98. Kern/BUTTSTETT 64.

Germany, is revealed especially in Buttstett's first and second movements. Along with some of the more usual *galant* traits—the triplets, ornaments, rhythmic minutiae, and melodic fragmentation—there is the extremely sensitive play of emotions effected by changes of tempo, by frequent dynamic contrasts, by rich harmony that leads repeatedly to deceptive cadences and numerous fermate, and by a profusion of different rhythms (Ex. 53). We might attribute Buttstett's monothematic

Ex. 53. From the reprise in the first movement of Franz Vollrath Buttstett's Sonata in A (after Anth. HAFFNER OM-m X 11).

tendencies to north-German influences, too, since one principle of the more conservative *Affektenlehre* was to avoid treating of more than a single affect in a single piece (SCE II). On the other hand, his fast finales certainly come closer than Emanuel Bach's or Benda's to the steady drive and froth of the Italian finales.

Four other obscure composers in the Nürnberg area may be given brief mention for six further sonatas contributed to Haffner's *Oeuvres mêlées*. In three or four movements, all these sonatas are purely *galant* in style and show competent workmanship as well as an idiomatic knowledge of the keyboard, but lack the depth and originality that have justified a closer look at Buttstett's sonatas. Little is known about two of the composers, **Johann Jakob Brand** and **"Enrico Felice" Spitz,** "Dilettante di Cembalo" (Anth. HAFFNER OM-m I no. 4 and VIII no. 6, respectively).[99] A third composer was a flutist and violinist at the Bavarian court, **Jakob Friedrich Kleinknecht** (1722-94), who also published six Fl/bass *Sonate da camera,* Op. 1 (Haffner, 1748) and six SS/bass "trios" (Walsh, 1760).[100] The most interesting detail in Kleinknecht's two keyboard sonatas (Anth. HAFFNER OM-m I no. 5, II no. 6) is the opening of the finale of the second one on $V^6{}_5$-of-iv, with the i chord not heard until measure 4. Here was a near precedent for the opening of Beethoven's First Symphony about 45 years later. The remaining composer was the cellist and organist **Johann Balthasar Kehl** (1725-78), to whose four sonatas in *Oeuvres mêlées* (no. 3 in each of vols. IX-XII, 1762-65) may be added another solo and an accompanied sonata published in Nürnberg (after 1773 and 1764).[101] Kehl was active at the Bavarian court 45 miles north in Bayreuth, where much of musical interest went on during the residence of Margravine Wilhelmine (died 1758), a respected cembalist and a sister of Frederick the Great.[102] We have already noted the sonatas of one of Kehl's predecessors, Paganelli (SCE VII), and of one of his pupils, Schulthesius (SCE X). Other sonata composers in Bayreuth include his teacher, the violinist **Johann Pfeiffer** (1697-1761),[103] and two of his colleagues, the lutist **Adam Falckenhagen** (also 1697-1761) and the flutist **Christian Friedrich Döbbert** (?-1770).[104]

The Pre-Classic Vienna School (M. G. Monn, Wagenseil, J. C. Monn)

The period in Viennese musical life that is about to occupy us coincides with the reign (in effect) of Maria Theresa from 1740-80. When the future empress succeeded her father Karl VI, a new order began, in music quite as in the more general affairs of state. A new generation of composers sprang up, with changing views of the Mass, oratorio, opera, and instrumental music, all of which had flourished in such Baroque pomp under Fux, Conti, Caldara, and others. If there was no name of comparable importance in pre-Classic Vienna—except,

99. Regarding Spitz, cf. Mooser/ANNALES I 193, II 32.
100. Cf. MGG VII 1209-1210 (Kaul).
101. Cf. MGG VII 777-779 (Krautwurst).
102. Cf. MGG I 1455-1456 (Kaul), VI 585-586 and 595 (portrait)-597.
103. In BREITKOPF MS IV (1763) 13, there are listed 4 ensemble sons. by him.
104. Cf. Schenk/PAGANELLI 24-35 (with analyses of the sons. and other works by these 3 men), 160-164 and 166-167 (thematic index).

of course, that of Gluck, whose "reform" operas first succeeded there, from 1762—it is not simply because the changing styles and forms were still too new to lead to another peak so soon. (We know how imminent that peak was, anyhow, in the mature works of Haydn and Mozart.) It is also because the Hapsburg imperial court, partly on account of economic retrenchments, was becoming more provincial in its make-up. Whereas Italian musicians had predominated and native Austrians, notably Schmelzer and Fux, had been exceptional in the Baroque Era, the Austrians now became the rule, including the Monn brothers, Wagenseil, and others soon to be mentioned.

When Guido Adler countered Riemann's claims for the pre-Classic Mannheim school with similar claims for the almost exactly contemporary Viennese composers,[105] he made a special point of the argument that the latter were exclusively Austrian in nationality. Of course, that question of nationality is complicated by the confused, intertwined history of Austria, Hungary, Bohemia, and Moravia, as well as by the fact that Johann Stamitz and some other Mannheim composers were as much Austrian as Bohemian in their ancestry. Even so, to show that Viennese Classical music had its main origins in the art and folk music from in and around Vienna itself was the intention of Adler and his pupils, Horwitz, Riedel, and Fischer.[106] But this ostensibly logical hypothesis is certainly challenged by both the Viennese and Salzburg sonatas examined here. Most of these, including Leopold Mozart's, do not begin to approximate the styles and procedures of Haydn and Mozart as closely as many examples we have already seen or shall see later from composers much farther away than the boundaries of Austria. Rather is it easier to accept that first part of Adler's discussion in which the mature Vienna Classical school is implied to be an international melting pot supplied by the best from many schools. And it is much easier to show that the intermediaries through whom the native music was thus enriched were none other than the chief exponents and natives, Haydn and Mozart themselves. For who else was there that profited so greatly as these masters from healthy exposure—the one through enterprising self-guidance, the other through grand guided tours—to the international panorama of current idioms, styles, and trends?

The sonata had about the same relative importance in the pre-Classic

105. DTÖ-m XV/2 (1908) ix-xiii.

106. For Fischer, cf. the preface to DTÖ-m XIX/2 (1912). However, the subsequent basic style study Fischer/WIENER (1915) also allows for the influence of Emanuel and Christian Bach, certain Mannheim composers, and Pergolesi (the last being questioned in SBE 196-199).

instrumental music of the Vienna school as in that of the Mannheim school, and it has been similarly less investigated than the symphony. The Viennese composers were not as well known in their day for the very reasons that they stayed at home more and their music largely remained (and still remains) in MS. During his visit to Vienna in 1772 Burney remarked, "As there are no music shops in Vienna the best method of procuring new compositions is to apply to copyists . . . none is printed."[107] Actually, music publishing was then just beginning in earnest (from about 1770); as late as our present limit of 1780, only Artaria started to publish music among the main publishers of the Classic masters.[108] Unlike any Mannheim composers, both Viennese and Salzburg composers did have sonatas published in the Nürnberg Anth. HAFFNER OM-m. This fact is simply evidence once more of Haffner's enterprise, of the relative marketability of keyboard music, and of considerable keyboard activity in Vienna and Salzburg such as did not exist in Mannheim. But the chief if most conservative keyboard composer in pre-Classic Vienna, the organist Gottlieb Muffat (1690-1770), happens to have left no keyboard sonatas. He did leave a "Sonata pastorale" in SS/bass setting (in a MS copy dated 1727), which has not been explored.[109] The only other Viennese instrumentalist of consequence who did not leave "sonatas" was the violinist Josef Starzer (1726-87).[110]

All the conjectures about **Mathias Georg Monn** (Georg Matthias Mann, etc.; 1717-50) reduce to little more information about his life than that he was an organist in Vienna and in the near-by Klosterneuburg monastery, and that he died at only thirty-three after a long illness.[111] During this short life he managed to compose much music, including the symphonies that have brought his chief recognition, masses, concertos, chamber music, and keyboard music for cembalo and for organ, none of which was published during or soon after his lifetime. This music may be dated approximately in the decade from 1740 to Monn's death, since his life was so short and since the few MSS that do have dates all fall then. Within the chamber and keyboard categories are six quartets, about a dozen SS/bass cycles variously called "Partita," "Divertimento," or "Sinfonia," three Vn/bass sonatas, and fourteen

107. BURNEY'S TOURS II 121 and 124.
108. Cf. Weinmann/WIENER 7 and 14. A few publications of sons. before 1770 do turn up in Gericke/WIENER, a new study (1960) of Viennese music publishers and dealers from 1700 to '78.
109. Cf. MGG IX 919-924 (Riedel).
110. Cf. DTÖ-m XV2 xxii-xxv and 94-117 (2 SSA/bass *divertimenti* in score).
111. Cf. DTÖ-m XV/2 (Horwitz & Riedel) xx, XIX/2 (Fischer) vii-xii; MGG IX 470-472 (Kollpacher; with full bibliography).

112a cembalo sonatas.[112] The French overtures with which two of the *partite* open exist in separate parts with the title "Sonata" (nos. 18 and 21 in Fischer's thematic index). Another "Partita," or "Trio," or "Sonata," as it is differently called in different MSS, has been made available in score,[113] permitting a description of it as a strong, motivic work in four movements (counting the opening "Adagio" and "Fuga" as one French overture), with distinct recollections throughout of Fux's sonatas (SBE 257-258). The three Vn/bass sonatas (nos. 32-34), not available to the present study, have three, one, and four movements, with tempo titles only.

In the over-all plans of Monn's fourteen cembalo sonatas there could
113a hardly be more freedom and diversity. The number of movements varies from one to seven. These movements, usually binary with repeated halves, may all be standard dances of the suite (no. 50), they may have only tempo titles (no. 49), or they may be mixed, as in most of the sonatas (no. 58). In one sonata more *galant* in style than most of the others (no. 53), three of the four movement titles add programmatic inscriptions, in French and in the French manner—"Andante: La Jonquille," "Presto: L'homme de colère," "Menuetto" and "Trio," and "La Personne galante." In another, decidedly more driving sonata, in f (no. 49), the movements follow without any full break between them, and each of the outer movements is itself a perpetual motion. Movements with related incipits can be found in several of the sonatas (no. 45).

The predominantly two-part texture in Monn's keyboard sonatas is naturally not as enriched by imitations as that of his "trio" settings or even much of his symphonic writing.[114] However, his keyboard music, even in the lighter dances, is still based much more on the continuous unfolding of motivic play than on the sectional oppositions of phrase grouping. In such music the fact that various stages of "sonata form" may be staked out means relatively little. But the good use of the keyboard within this style does seem worth noting. The writing is more than idiomatic, for at times it presupposes a surprising command of relatively advanced techniques, such as double-3ds and -6ths during contrapuntal passages for both hands (no. 52/i), or rapid hand crossing by each hand (no. 57/i and iii). One of the earliest extended uses of a

112. Cf. the thematic index of all movements and sources, in DTÖ-m XIX/2 xxv-xxxi. MS 14631, containing the 14 cembalo sons., is now in the Westdeutsche Bibliothek in Marburg/Lahn. A study of Monn's sons. is needed.

113. No. 29 in A, in DTÖ-m XV/2 60.

114. The largely chordal, homophonic Symphony in E♭ in DTÖ-m XV/2 68 is not representative and was later stated not to be by this Monn (DTÖ-m XIX/2 xiii).

true Alberti bass other than by Alberti himself occurs in one of these movements, although not in what can be called a "singing-allegro" passage (no. 52/v).

If M. G. Monn's keyboard sonatas do not keep us fired with the genius of a Scarlatti they still reveal a superior musician with the courage of his musical convictions. Monn knows how to prolong his lines through deceptive cadences and graduated progress toward more distant goals (no. 54/i and iii), and he knows when to alter or halt a sequence so that this vital prop of motivic writing is not abused, both of which skills help him to write long movements that do not become overly long (no. 51, in one mvt.). Besides an ornate "Adagio" (no. 54/ii) or a movement in full, active texture (no. 52/i), he can write a movement with a simple line that is kept interesting by equally simple imitations, extensions, shifts of range, and slight variations (Ex. 54). He can use leaps to good advantage (no. 47/ii), or melodic chromaticism (to depict "l'homme de colère" in No. 53/ii), or a free concluding cadenza (no. 57/i), or the rhythmic device of hemiola (no. 50/ii, a "courante"). One wishes Monn had indicated not only the slurs but the dynamic

Ex. 54. From the third movement of a Sonata in G (no. 46) by Mathias Georg Monn (after MS 14631 at the Westdeutsche Bibliothek in Marburg/Lahn).

changes in these sonatas (as he does indicate them in the orchestral and chamber music), by which we might be surer of his own expressive concept of the sonata.

Monn's chief contemporary as a symphonist in Vienna was **Georg Christoph Wagenseil** (1715-77), a pupil of Fux and Gottlieb Muffat who served at the imperial court from at least 1736 to the end of his life.[115] Succeeding Muffat as teacher of the future Empress Maria Theresa, Wagenseil became the official "Hofklaviermeister" in 1749. His keyboard prowess, which Burney and Schubart still praised,[116] may explain travels of more than two years from about 1756-59, taking him to Berlin, then probably to Milan and Paris among other centers.[117] Thus, he could have known Emanuel Bach, G. B. Sammartini, Christian Bach, Gossec, and other pre-Classic symphonists. In the long list of Wagenseil's MS and published music, which touches all the main vocal and instrumental categories then in favor, there is still much need for
118a collation and consolidation.[118] Some ninety or more works concern us here, dating from 1753-61 and including at least twelve SS/bass sonatas, symphonies, *divertimenti,* or trios, as they are variously called,[119] of which a set of six was published in London about 1760;[120] at least two sets of six accompanied sonatas each (K & Vn) published as Opp. 1 and 2 in London about 1760-61;[121] and at least six sets of six cembalo *divertimenti* or sonatas each, of which three sets appeared, from 1753 on, among the early publications of the dealer Agostino Bernardi in Vienna.[122] Two other cembalo "sonatas," in C and F, are in Anth. HAFFNER OM-m I no. 6 and II no. 5 (1755-56), and some thirty other single "sonatas," or even sets of "sonatas," remain to be identified.[123]

115. The chief biographic source is still DTÖ-m XV/2 xvi-xviii. Cf., also, MGG IX 920 (Riedel).

116. BURNEY'S TOURS II 112; Schubart/IDEEN 77-78.

117. Sondheimer/THEORIE 64-65.

118. Cf. Eitner/QL X 148-151.

119. Mod. eds.: "Symphonie in D-dur," DTÖ-m XV/2 28 (cf. pp. xix-xx); Son. in F, UNIVERSAL CONTINUO-m No. 10657 (Geiringer, with preface).

120. Listed in BRITISH UNION II 1052.

121. Listed in BRITISH UNION II 1052. Cf., also, Johansson/FRENCH II Facs. 23 and 26 (1760 and '64) for early Paris eds. Mod. ed.: Son. in F (Op. 1/3), Pauer/MEISTER-m II 60 (but without the Vn part).

122. The published sets are listed in Gericke/WIENER 130-131 and Cat. BRUXELLES IV 222; all 6 sets are presumably still at the Gesellschaft der Musikfreunde in Vienna; 5 sets are in MS Mus. 3042 T/1 at the Sächsische Landesbibliothek in Dresden. The preface of the first set and a brief summary of all 6 sets may be found in Abert/HAYDN 556. On Bernardi, cf. Weinmann/WIENER 48-49. Mod. ed.: 4 *divertimenti,* NAGELS-m No. 36 (Blume, with preface).

123. The unpublished diss. Pelikant/WAGENSEIL (1926) refers unclearly (pp. 1-6) to 17 cembalo suites or sons. and 49 cembalo *divertimenti* or sons. as being listed in an otherwise unidentified (work-sheet?) thematic index. The conclusion in this diss. is that Wagenseil accomplished a "transition" from the suite to the son. and that his music was a main influence on the young Haydn.

One author has made the point that Wagenseil uses the term *divertimento* not in Mozart's sense of a brightly colored orchestral suite [of up to ten movements, as in K. 159c] but entirely in the sense of the then more nearly monochrome, three-movement keyboard sonata.[124] This point might have been carried one step further with the fact that Wagenseil actually used *divertimento* and sonata synonymously, as we shall see that Haydn was to do in many of his keyboard sonatas.[125] Thus, Haffner in Nürnberg published one set (the fourth?) of Wagenseil's *divertimenti* as Op. 1 in 1756, with the title *Divertissement musical contenant vi sonates pour le clavessin.*[126] This set could be the same as the "Opera III" published in London first as "Sonatas" (*ca.* 1760) and later as "Lessons" (*ca.* 1775).[127] Furthermore, it is quite possible that the needed collation of Wagenseil's music will show the two accompanied sets merely to be drawn from the cembalo *divertimenti,* with the unessential and suspiciously extraneous accompaniments grafted on by the London publishers, as again we shall find to be true of several Haydn sonatas.[128]

Nearly all of nineteen Wagenseil sonatas available to this study are in three relatively short movements of binary design, arranged in the order of F-S-minuet or F-minuet-F. Occasionally in these or other sonatas there are two or four movements, and occasionally there is a gigue, polonaise, or other dance.[129] The movements are not related by similar incipits. In the first movements, as in Wagenseil's symphonies,[130] tentative "sonata forms" are usually to be found, with more likelihood of a clear reprise than of a clearly contrasting second theme. (Abert preferred to think of Wagenseil's forms as typically south-German in their "fanciful play of changing ideas and moods."[131]) Some of the slower movements are urbane, graceful andantes (Son. 5/ii in the London Op. 3) and others are more decorative, rhythmically fussy andantes or larghettos (Son. 4/iii in the London Op. 1, with a very elementary Vn part). The minuets usually lack trios. In spite of Wagenseil's renown as a cembalist his keyboard writing offers less challenge to the performer than M. G. Monn's. The left-hand part, which is unimaginative at best, only rarely is given an actual Alberti bass (no. 1/i/39-40 in the Nagel ed.). More often, and at worst, it plays what

124. Hausswald/WAGENSEIL.
125. Cf. Pelikant/WAGENSEIL 1-6; MGG III 600-601 (Engel).
126. Listed (only?) in WOLFFHEIM MUSIKBIBLIOTHEK I 280; cf. Hoffmann-Erbrecht/HAFFNER 122.
127. Both London sets are listed in BRITISH UNION II 1052.
128. Cf. Hoboken/HAYDN I 733.
129. Hausswald/WAGENSEIL 47-48.
130. Cf. DTÖ-m XV/2 xviii-xx and 16, XIX/2 xix-xx; also, SCE V, with ex.
131. Abert/MOZART I 83-84.

might be called a murky bass in intervals less than octaves (Op. 3/1/i). In recognition of this latter technique Torrefranca jeeringly placed Wagenseil among the chief exponents of the German "Sonata col pum pum."[132]

The simple clarity of texture and structure in Wagenseil's music, the fairly obvious, unimposing ideas, and a greater tendency than in Monn's music to group these ideas in phrases and periods may help to account for the reported attraction to him by Mozart as a six-year-old child.[133] Occasionally Wagenseil spoke with some force, though chiefly when he turned back to continuous, preludial forms in minor keys (as in no. 4/i in f, in the Nagel ed.). An instructive example is Op. 3/4/i (London) in c, which begins in the same key with the same strong dotted rhythm and even with much the same line to be found in a Schobert sonata published not much later.[134] But Wagenseil's example is instructive for the very reason that he fails to maintain the tension as Schobert does, lapsing instead into a trill figure over that "pum pum" bass. In spite of Wagenseil's reputation as a main forerunner of the great Vienna Classicists,[135] he cannot be elevated above the *Kleinmeister* when musical interest itself is the first criterion. After a sufficient reading of his music one can understand why nearly every commentator since his own day has felt obliged to express similar reservations. Indeed, it was in 1761 and 1762, not long after Wagenseil's Berlin trip, that two generally unfavorable reviews appeared (from Marpurg's own pen, presumably), following the publication of some of his cembalo *divertimenti*.[136] The critic suggested that Wagenseil ought to stick to cembalo playing, in which field he promised to succeed very well, but that his composing was "pretty mediocre," following the rules, yet without the originality so essential to any art work.

Florian Leopold Gassmann (1729-74) was a Bohemian-born harpist, violinist, and singer who studied with Martini in Bologna among others, made his first mark as an opera composer in Venice (from 1757), and renewed his activities there from time to time after moving to the
137a Viennese imperial court in 1763.[137] Besides his operas, ballet music,

132. Torrefranca/ORIGINI 117-118; cf., also, pp. 294-300.

133. Abert/MOZART I 41.

134. The latter is reprinted in DDT-m XXXIX 25.

135. As in Sondheimer/SINFONIE 91-92. It is almost easier to argue a pedagogic connection, at least to the extent that one of Wagenseil's pupils in counterpoint, Johann Schenk, was one of Beethoven's teachers of counterpoint, as Schenk himself relates in a most interesting report on each (Nettl/FORGOTTEN 267-268).

136. Marpurg/BRIEFE II 141-143 (including a slightly disadvantageous comparison with the similar *divertimenti* of J. A. Steffan) and 476.

137. Cf. MGG IV 1431-1435 (Komma and LaRue).

and sacred works, he wrote much chamber music for two, three, four, and five stringed instruments.[138] Reported among publications or MSS in the latter category are some twenty-three works in various trio settings called "sonate," "trii," or "divertimenti," dating chiefly between 1766 and 1769; several "sonates a quatre instruments" in Milan that are incipient symphonies;[139] six *Duetti a violino e violoncello,* 1773; and a cembalo *divertimento* in F. Although a comparison of ensemble and solo keyboard music can easily be misleading, the five diminutive "trio sonatas" by Gassmann that could be examined here (for flute, violin, and viola[140]) point to a composer both more resourceful and more imaginative than Wagenseil. Planned similarly to the latter's sonatas in three movements (but without change of key), these five sonatas may have more contrapuntal interest and a more songful type of melody primarily because they are ensemble music. But they also reveal a concept of dualism both within and between the ideas, a sense of rhythmic organization both small and large, and an ability to extend and develop even the simplest figures that together make for fresh, compelling sonata forms, whether actual "sonata forms," minuets-and-trios, or rondos. One can well understand Mozart's reported interest in Gassmann's chamber music.[141]

Johann Christoph Monn (or Mann; 1726-82), younger brother of Mathias Georg, is known to have taught in Prague in 1750, to have been recognized as a "Virtuoso di Musica in Vienna" in 1765 in the one publication of his music that has been found—a cembalo Sonata in F in Anth. HAFFNER OM-m XI no. 4, and to have taught keyboard students in that city "with much success and acclaim,"[142] yet to have died in extreme poverty.[143] Eleven more keyboard sonatas, and one S/- and 10 SS/bass *divertimenti* are among the relatively few instrumental works that he left.[144] One can only guess from the Haffner publication and some MS minuets dated 1766 that most of these works come from the late 1760's. On the threshold of the high-Classic sonata in Vienna, J. C. Monn's sonatas are remarkable for still being so free from standardization, like those of his older brother, and for still being so much further

138. Leuchter/GASSMANN is a detailed, careful diss. (unpublished, 1926) on the chamber music, divided about equally between a critical thematic catalogue and a style study (with many exx.).

139. Saint-Foix/MOZART I 477.

140. Mod. ed.: ORGANUM-m III Nos. 45, 48, 51, 53, 55. Cf. MGG IV 1435 for 2 other mod. eds., both SS/bass.

141. Saint-Foix/MOZART I 477 and 511.

142. Gerber/LEXICON I 855.

143. DTÖ-m XIX/2 xi-xii (Fischer); MGG IX 470-472 (Kollpacher).

144. A nearly complete thematic index of all mvts. is in DTÖ-m XIX/2 xxxiv-xxxix, plus an SS/bass *Divertimento* in D, in score, p. 107. MS 13480, containing 6 cembalo sons., is now in the Westdeutsche Bibliothek in Marburg/Lahn.

from the imminent Mozart style than the sonatas of contemporary *Ausländer* like Galuppi, Mysliveček, or Boccherini.

Most of J. C. Monn's sonatas have four movements, but a few have
144a three or five. The order of these movements is determined only by the need for contrast, the preference for a moderate to quick finale, and the international fondness for minuets. As for the minuet, only one sonata is without it (no. 91 in Fischer's thematic index) and, as if to make up for this lack, the sonata in Anth. HAFFNER OM-m ends with two unrelated minuets in succession—a "Minuetto" and "Trio" in 3/4 meter as the 3d movement (after an "Allegro assai" and an "Andante mà non troppo") and a "Tempo di Minuetto" in 3/8 meter as the finale. Monn's Sonata in A (no. 97) affords an unusual example of interlocking movements, on a larger scale than the experimental designs by Scarlatti and Soler noted earlier (SCE IX) and not unlike present day experiments by Hindemith and others. There are three groups of interlocking movements, with the movements interconnected in each group by half cadences and actual melodic bridges. The three groups may be diagramed as follows:

||:U. Adagio, 2/4, A → E:||;
V. Allegro assai, 3/8, E;
U. Adagio, 2/4, E → A, cadence on V;
V. Allegro assai, 3/8, A.
||:W. Minuet di gallanteria, 3/4, A → E:||:E → A:||;
||:X. Allegro Paese (rural), 2/4, a → c:||: → a, cadenza on V:||;
W. "Subito e Menuet Da Capo."
Y. Rondo, Allegro mà un poco, 2/4, A → E;
Z. Minore, 2/4, a, cadenza on V;
Y. Rondo, Tempo Primo, 2/4, A.

J. C. Monn's ideas are attractive and well defined. They are stated in the first phrase or two, after which there may be a variety of derived and related figures, but not contrasting ideas. The method of continuation is still more motivic than phrasewise, with the nearest approach to consistent phrase syntax being the succession of ever-changing, two-measure units that we have found in the sonatas of Alberti and other pioneers of pre-Classic idioms. It is understandable that MSS signed only "Monn" still leave something of a "brother problem," but there is not the sharp style distinction between M. G. and J. C. Monn that there is between their near contemporaries Friedemann or Emanuel Bach and Christian Bach. It is also understandable that J. C. Monn's individuality and relatively conservative style do not happen to yield either the divisions or proportions of "sonata form" in most of the first allegro movements, which fact could account for the neglect of this interesting composer by historians only concerned with that phenomenon.

J. C. Monn's keyboard writing is even more varied and advanced than his brother's. There are double-thirds (no. 94/iii), hand-crossing (no. 98/iii/Trio), and rapid leaps of nearly two octaves (no. 96/i). The most brilliant writing occurs in the first two movements of a Sonata in E♭ (no. 98). The first of these is an "Aria Scocese" (Scotch) with one variation, the theme actually being the Irish air "Gramachree" or "The Harp That Once through Tara's Halls." Monn's slow movements are not deep or introspective but they are songful and sometimes very florid. In Ex. 55 a songful melody, over one of his infrequent

Ex. 55. From the second movement of a Sonata in G (no. 91) by Johann Christoph Monn (after MS 13480 in Westdeutsche Bibliothek in Marburg/Lahn).

Alberti-bass accompaniments, is becoming freer as it leads to what will be an extended concluding cadenza of fourteen more measures in C.

Two other pre-Classic composers in Vienna are represented in Anth. HAFFNER OM-m. **Franz Ferdinand Hengsberger** "von Engelsberg" left a Sonata in F in four movements, interrelated by similar incipits (vol.

VIII, no. 3, 1761). Well scored for keyboard, this sonata is interesting for having a "Scherzo, Presto" finale, in 2/4 meter, as well as the "Minuetto" with "Trio" that precedes it. It is also interesting for the skill by which a minimum of rather indifferent material is stretched into full-sized forms, well marked off by clear sections and by a broader tonal organization than we have yet seen in this chapter's survey of the Viennese sonata. The imperial court musician ("Ajutante di Camera") **Joseph Ferdinand Timer** left three sonatas in Anth. HAFFNER OM-m X no. 5, XI no. 5, and XII no. 6 (1764-66); a set of twelve solo cembalo sonatas, 1762;[145] and a set of twelve Vn/bass sonatas, *ca.* 1761.[146] A stay in Venice is hinted in the publication of both sets, by one Joseph Wagner (not Wagener) in that city. The violin sonatas were reviewed in 1761, presumably by Marpurg, as having "much old, little new," with excessive sequences and careless workmanship.[147] In the three Haffner sonatas, each in three movements in the order of fast-minuet-fast, the carelessness is not evident but the sequences do occur in excess and the writing does prove to be conservative in its extreme insistence on a single motive in each movement. On the other hand, the motivic repetitions are used not for contrapuntal imitations but as a means of building phrases, sometimes giving the impression of a high-Classic "development" section (as near the start of the last of these three sonatas).

Joseph Steffan (1726-97), born in Bohemia, succeeded his teacher Wagenseil as one of two or three *Hofklaviermeister,* numbering among his pupils the future French Queen Marie Antoinette.[148] Besides some church music, his highly regarded *Lieder* (1778-82), and several concertos, he left in print and MS at least twenty-four and perhaps many more sonatas for cembalo, the printed ones dating from about 1759 to
149a 1776.[149] These last immediately bring Steffan's teacher to mind, since they represent a similar equating of the cembalo *divertimento* and sonata. Indeed, in another generally unfavorable review, the presumed Marpurg found the keyboard music of the two men so close in style that he wondered which might have supplied the model for the other.[150] He lists two sets by Steffan that, like Wagenseil's, were published by Agostino Bernardi in Vienna, the date of the review (Oct. 25, 1761) incidentally permitting us to fix the terminal year of 1761 for this many of Steffan's sonatas. The first set is headed *Sei Divertimenti* and the

145. Listed in BRITISH UNION II 1010.
146. Eitner/QL IX 409-410; Gerber/LEXICON II 653.
147. Marpurg/BRIEFE II 153.
148. Cf. Riemann/LEXIKON II 1755.
149. Cf. Eitner/QL IX 261-262. Of 8 publications listed in Gericke/WIENER 128-129, one contains 6 divertimenti, one contains 6 sons., and the other 6 contain one son. each.
150. Marpurg/BRIEFE II 143-145.

second *Sei Sonate,* Op. 2. The reviewer did note some minor differences between the two composers, finding Steffan's writing a little more serious and full-textured, with more use of chordal basses—the Alberti bass is described without being so named—as well as murky and drum basses, but also with some harmonic and melodic mannerisms and gaucheries, of which convincing illustrations are inserted.

Little doubt can remain that it was Steffan's pieces that were modeled after Wagenseil's. It is not only that Wagenseil's first appeared in 1753 and that he was the older man, the teacher, and the precursor at court. But Steffan's pieces come nearer to a high-Classic ideal of dualistic themes that are presented in lucid phrases and periods, effectively contrasted, and creatively worked out (Ex. 56)—all within

Ex. 56. From the "development" section of Sonata I in C by Joseph Steffan (after Anth. STEFFANN-RUTINI-m [1772] but without the Vn accompaniment, which may have been added by the publisher).

simple, purposeful structures that are tonally if not thematically ternary. As for qualitative distinctions, the reviewer might well have given the edge still more to Steffan's writing. One notes the latter's major-minor alternations and other harmonic refreshments, the charm and individuality of his ideas, and especially the skillful timing of their entries. In fact, a study of the instrumental music of Steffan, insofar as that music can still be brought together, would be likely to win much the same respect for this composer that his songs have won.[151] The four sonatas available to the present study are those included in Anth. STEFFANN-RUTINI-m, which was published, with a violin accompaniment added

151. Cf. Riemann/LEXIKON II 1755.

perhaps by the publisher, in Paris in 1772. Three of these sonatas are in three movements and the other is in two, but the usual minuet is missing from none of them.

One other name to mention in pre-Classic Vienna is that of the Czech-born organist **Anton Zimmerman** (1741-81), who left among many other instrumental works at least two sets of six accompanied sonatas each (K & Vn), an S/bass sonata in Anth. CARTIER-m, and a "trio" sonata (1764).[152] One of the accompanied sets was published as Op. 1 in 1779 among the earliest issues of the important firm of Artaria in Vienna,[153] and the other of these sets as Op. 2 eleven years earlier (1768) by Huberty in Paris.[154] The violin parts in both sets are almost always elementary and subordinate. In Op. 2 each of the sonatas is in two movements, an andante or similarly modern movement in monothematic ternary design followed by a minuet with trio. The writing is fluent and ornamental, the ideas are songful if rather bland, and the scoring for keyboard is idiomatic without posing any undue technical demands.

Salzburg (L. Mozart)

After a century and a half of increased activity that had included music by Baroque composers of Biber's and Georg Muffat's stature (SBE 217-222), the west-Austrian city of Salzburg reached a musical peak during the Classic Era, a peak defined especially by the Mozarts, father and son, and by Joseph Haydn's younger brother Michael.[155] Located near the border of southeast Germany and set apart as the seat of the archbishopric and the archducal court, this city became as much of a musical as a geographic crossroads. Naturally, church and dramatic compositions were the principal staples in its musical diet. But most of the prevailing instrumental types enjoyed some attention, too. Only the sonata itself seems to have played a relatively small role in pre-Classic Salzburg music—that is, prior to the compositions of Salzburg's most illustrious citizen, Wolfgang Mozart. It should be noted that throughout the Mozart family's residence in this city the successive, all-powerful prince-archbishops were consistently pro-Italian in their tastes, which fact is but one of the reasons for the antagonism Leopold and Wolfgang felt toward Hieronymus, Count von Colloredo, who was the archbishop from 1772.[156]

152. Cf. Eitner/QL X 351-352; Riemann/LEXIKON II 2081; BRITISH UNION II 964.

153. Cf. Weinmann/ARTARIA item 5.

154. Cf. Johansson/FRENCH I 47-48. Op. 2/3/i is in Anth. CARTIER-m no. 54.

155. The chief source on music in Salzburg is Schneider/SALZBURG, with 3 chapters on Rococo and Classic music, pp. 100-142.

156. Cf. Kenyon/MOZART 7, 146-147.

At the age of eighteen, in 1737, **Leopold Mozart** (1719-87) left his Swabian birthplace of Augsburg in west Bavaria to enter the Benedictine university in Salzburg.[157] Six years later (1743) he joined the Salzburg court chapel as violinist, advancing to the moderately important posts of "Hof- und Cammer-Componist" in 1757 and "Vicecapellmeister" in 1762. Leopold is honored primarily as the wise and devoted if somewhat opportunistic teacher and counselor of his son, and as the author of *Versuch einer gründlichen Violinschule*. The latter, originally published in Augsburg in the very year of Wolfgang's birth (1756), is important both as the first comprehensive treatise on violin playing in German and, along with the keyboard *Versuch* that Emanuel Bach had started to publish three years earlier, as one of the chief sources on eighteenth-century performance practices.[158]

As for Leopold's compositions, insofar as they are remembered at all today, the church works are more highly regarded than the instrumental music for orchestra, chamber groups, and keyboard. Leopold himself held this view in 1757.[159] Yet it was only certain instrumental works, chiefly all of the 9 sonatas by him now known, that achieved publication in his lifetime. The sonatas include an early SS/bass set of 6 "per Chiesa e da Camera," which he published at his own expense at the age of 21 (1740) and dedicated, in the usual effusive manner, to a Salzburg patron. And there are 3 sonatas for keyboard, published some 20 years later in the ever-present Anth. HAFFNER OM-m V/4, VI/5, and IX/4 (*ca.* 1759-63).[160] There are also 9 other SS/bass pieces ("divertimenti" and "trios") that belong in the category of the "trio" sonatas.[161]

All of Leopold Mozart's known sonatas and the majority of his other cyclic instrumental works are in three movements in the order F-S-F or F-S-minuet with trio.[162] This is the instrumental plan he seems

157. The extended preface in the anthology of his works that Seiffert edited, DTB-m IX/2, is still the chief study, although considerable information has been added in special studies and in pertinent literature on Wolfgang (as summarized and listed in MGG IX 692-698 [Schmid]).

158 Alfred Einstein's illuminating "Preface" to the English translation, Knocker/MOZART, discusses the background of this work and orients Leopold himself both to his Salzburg environment and to music history at large; cf., also, Kenyon/MOZART 3-47 (with exx.); Schenk/MOZART 3-33.

159. In the terse autobiographic notice printed in Marpurg/BEYTRÄGE III 184-185. Cf. DTB-m IX/2 ix; Knocker/MOZART viii.

160. Cf. DTB-m IX/2 ix-x, xlix-li, lvi (discussions); xliv and xli (in the "complete" thematic index); 49 and 3 (mod. ed. of SS/bass Son. 2 and all 3 keyboard sons.). For a mod. ed. of SS/bass Son. 4 in G cf. MGG IX 696.

161. Cf. DTB-m IX/2 xliii-xliv and the mod. ed. of 4 of these on pp. 37 and 57 ff.

162. In MGG IX 698 is listed a partial publication of a diss. completed in 1943 on Leopold's instrumental music by E. L. Theiss, but the publication could not be found here.

to have taken for granted, as he himself implied in referring to an opera "Overtura" by Wolfgang.[163] In the early SS/bass sonatas nearly all the melodic "interest" occurs in the first violin part, with only occasional, tentative imitations in the second part and little more than repeated notes in the bass. The music progresses by two- and four-measure units that change without providing distinctive contrasts. Even for so young a man, these pieces are surprisingly sterile, faltering, and inept. The keyboard sonatas suffer from thematic short-windedness and sterility, too, as well as the curse of too much sequencing. But they show more experience and resourcefulness in their greater concentration on fewer ideas, their idiomatic use of the keyboard (especially in hand alternations and crossings), and their more adroitly managed structural rhythm. Conspicuous are the *galant* mannerisms, such as triplets, ornaments, and a surfeit of different rhythmic patterns. "Sonata form" is approximated in most of the movements, variously including a clear "second theme" (Son. in C/i/24-27), a degree of actual "development" after the double-bar (Son. in F/i), and a return of the initial idea both in the related key at the double-bar and the home key during the second "half" (Son. in B♭/i). The *galant* mannerisms and near "sonata forms" are, in fact, the chief traits mentioned in the brief discussions that have been written on these sonatas.[164] But it seems farfetched to find a particularly clear auspice of the "second theme" when an "Andante grazioso" episode in 3/4 meter alternates with the "Presto" 2/4 meter in Sonata in F/iii, appearing once in the dominant and once, at the end, in the tonic key. Leopold was simply contributing another of those many free, experimental forms to be found at this time.

One must acknowledge that Leopold's sonatas are interesting only for any influence they may have had on Wolfgang's. Melodic and figural resemblances do occur between the father's keyboard sonatas and the son's first accompanied sonata, from the same period (K.V. 6, 1762-64).[165] But a revealing device like the Alberti bass, which runs throughout Wolfgang's first two movements, was not used by Leopold in his sonatas. It does occur intermittently in the realized cembalo part of his "Trio" in A/i and iii,[166] which fact plus a broader melodic continuity suggest a considerably later date than "1750" for this work, and even the possibility of the son's influence on the father. Occasionally Leopold attains more harmonic depth than is usual in *galant* writing

163. Letter to his wife, Aug. 31, 1771 (Mueller von Asow/MOZART I 201).

164. E.g., Faisst/CLAVIERSONATE 70-71; Friedlander/MOZART; Saint-Foix/MOZART I 4-6.

165. Cf. DTB-m IX/2 1; Saint-Foix/MOZART I 41. No significant anticipations are recognized in Paumgartner/MOZART 90.

166. DTB-m IX/2 57; cf. p. lvi.

(as in "Minuetto II" from the last and best of the keyboard sons., in C). But there is scarcely a hint of Wolfgang's expressive writing, not even in the infrequent moments of chromaticism resulting from major-minor alternations (keyboard Son. in B♭/i/27-37) or melodic decorations (keyboard Son. in F/ii/13-14).

The creative differences between father and son must be less surprising to the reader who has browsed at any length in their respective letters—in the detailed, orderly, circumspect, provident, single-purposed essays of Leopold as against the shorter, frank, pungent, carefree, often capricious, yet remarkably perspicacious revelations by his son. Still, the father was certainly perceptive and alert to the times in his musical comments, as we have noted before (SCE VII) and as we shall note again especially in his shrewd observations concerning Christian Bach. Perhaps more significant for us is the attitude toward the sonata that these comments reveal. To Leopold, as to many another composer of his day, the sonata was first of all an expedient starting point, convenient to perform, welcome in society, appropriate for dedication to a prospective patron, useful as revenue, and promising as the aspiring neophyte's means of getting an "Opera prima" into print.[167] Of course, Leopold also recognized the sonata's pedagogic value. Although he found but little place for it yet in his fairly elementary "notebooks" for Nannerl and Wolfgang (1759 and 1762; *supra* and SBE 280), he subsequently prescribed for Nannerl the recent sonatas of Rutini, Paradisi, Christian Bach, and Wolfgang himself, much as the last was to recommend sonatas by Mysliveček to her, or caution against others by his rival Clementi.[168]

Two other Bavarian-born musicians in Salzburg, both primarily organists and church composers, are represented by two sonatas each in Anth. HAFFNER OM-m, **Johann Ernst Eberlin** (1702-62; Sons. in G and A, IV/3 and VI/3, *ca.* 1758-60) and **Anton Cajetan Adlgasser** (1729-77; Sons. in A and B♭, V/1 and VIII/1, *ca.* 1759-61).[169] Like Leopold Mozart, Adlgasser was a pupil of Eberlin, who had come to Salzburg in 1724. Musically and socially the three families were closely related.[170] Eberlin's and Adlgasser's sonatas are similar to Leopold's in their *galant* mannerisms, in their elementary, often murky bass parts (with the Alberti bass used only in Adlgasser's Son. in B♭/i), in their good use of the keyboard, and in their three-movement plans (except for a loosely constructed "Fuga" added to Eberlin's Son. in A).

167. E.g., cf. Anderson/MOZART I 77-78, 80, 82.

168. E.g., cf. Anderson/MOZART I 281, 364, 366; II 544, 638; III 1267-1268.

169. Cf. Schneider/SALZBURG 102-105, 108-111; MGG III 1057-1060 (Haas), I 88-89 (Valentin).

170. Cf. the many references indexed in Anderson/MOZART.

But, although their style is scarcely any more suggestive of Wolfgang's than that of Leopold's sonatas, they do have more musical interest. The ideas are meaningful and the music moves well. Eberlin's harmony is more colorful than Adlgasser's, and sometimes adventurous (Son. in G/ii). Adlgasser's rhythms are more complex, including some examples of anacrustic slurs (Son. in A/i) that should interest the student of articulation in music. Although he had not yet visited Italy (1764-65) he was able to project a line with considerably broader, Italianate lyricism than can be found in the sonatas of the other two men (Ex. 57).

Ex. 57. From the middle movement of Anton Cajetan Adlgasser's Sonata in A (after Anth. HAFFNER OM-m V/1).

Chapter XII

Central Germany From About 1735 to 1780

From Würzburg to Mainz (Platti)

One of the most interesting sonata composers in pre-Classic central Germany, **Giovanni Benedetto Platti** (1697-1763), brings us back to Torrefranca (SCE VII) and to the Italian he championed longest (since 1910), most ardently, and with the most heated show of anti-Teutonicism.[1] According to such evidence as has been pieced together, 1a
Platti was born in Venice or possibly Bergamo, and he probably trained in Venice. By 1722 he may already have been in Mainz, near his future wife Teresa, a celebrated lyric soprano. He moved to Würzburg in 1722, perhaps at the instigation, suggests Torrefranca, of one Fortunato Chelleri (for Keller in German), who had been composing operas in Venice, also wrote keyboard sonatas, and arrived about the same time in Würzburg, to take charge of the orchestra.[2] There Platti served at a relatively high salary until at least 1761,[3] as a teacher, composer, and "Virtuoso di camera" on the oboe, violin, cello, cembalo, and flute, and as a tenor! He died in Würzburg.[4]

Largely in deference to Torrefranca's claims for Platti as a significant pre-Classicist, consideration of this composer was postponed in our previous volume, although it might well have been given there on the basis of dates and styles (SBE 265). In that volume was noted the question newly raised by Hoffmann-Erbrecht as to whether one man

1. Torrefranca/ORIGINI 72-83 and 85-103 (concerning Opp. 1 and 4, with exx.), 436-458 (biographic speculations; also, Platti's violin concerto, with exx.), 535-547 (Sons. 13-16, with exx.); Torrefranca/PLATTIANO (cello music, with exx.). The chief biographic sources are Kaul/WÜRZBURGER 22-23 (summarized in Torrefranca/ORIGINI 778-779), DIZIONARIO RICORDI 854, and the summary of new findings by Fritz Zobeley and others in Hoffmann-Erbrecht/KLAVIERMUSIK 82.

2. Cf. Torrefranca/ORIGINI 449-455.

3. According to BREITKOPF WERKE II 37 (1761).

4. In Moser/LEXIKON II 967 appears the first notice (1955) known here of the death date Jan. 11, 1763, but with no source other than the late Torrefranca's name. For that source as well as the source of the birth year see fn. 1a to p. 365, *infra*.

could have excelled in so many capacities and whether the "Jean Platti" who published six sonatas in 1742 as "Oeuvre premiere" and as a first set "pour le Clavessin"[5] might not actually have been a son now known to have been born some time after 1722. Because the Würzburg birth registrations and other pertinent records were destroyed in World War II, this question may never get a final answer. Of course, the designation "Oeuvre premiere" is hardly proof in itself of a new young composer, since opus numbers ordinarily were assigned only to publications, and this Op. 1 is the first known publication by any Platti. But some support for the idea of two different composers is seen in the absence of so much as a single keyboard piece among some eighty diverse instrumental works by "Platti" at the Schlossbibliothek in Wiesentheid
5a (about fifteen miles east of Würzburg). On the other hand, "Platti's" twelve cello sonatas copied in MS in 1725 are closer in style to those keyboard sonatas in Op. 1 than the latter are to "his" later keyboard sonatas. For the present we must still speak of but one Platti.

Among a few sacred and dramatic works and about 120 instrumental compositions,[6] including concertos for cembalo, for violin, and for cello, Platti reportedly left at least 56 sonatas. In MSS in Würzburg are copied the 12 cello sonatas in 2 sets, composed in 1725 or earlier, and, apparently, 20 "trio" sonatas.[7] In a Dresden MS are copied 2 sets of 6 keyboard sonatas each, Opp. 1 and 4; in a Darmstadt MS, lost in World War II, 4 other keyboard sonatas are copied, it is worth noting, in the hand of J. S. Bach's contemporary, J. C. Graupner (SBE 284-285); and reportedly in Torrefranca's possession were still 2 others in MSS not otherwise known.[8] Only 4 of Platti's instrumental sets were published, all between 1742 and about 1746 among the earliest issues of Haffner in Nürnberg.[9] These include Op. 1 (plate no. 2, 1742), which

5. The usual fawning dedication (in search of a new post?), to Maria Theresa, and the full title are given in Torrefranca/ORIGINI 78-79.

6. According to Zobeley's preface in HORTUS MUSICUS-m Nos. 87 and 88.

7. On the cello sons., cf. Torrefranca/PLATTIANO (with exx.); 2 in MS are listed in BREITKOPF WERKE II 55 (1761). The "trio" sons. are not known here except for a mention of them in DIZIONARIO RICORDI 854 and a listing of a MS son. for 2 oboes and bass in Eitner/QL VII 471.

8. Cf. Hoffmann-Erbrecht/KLAVIERMUSIK 82-83. It is the above total of 18 known keyboard sons. that Torrefranca was preparing for publication at least as far back as 1939, to be vol. 7 in ISTITUZIONI-m. One very much hopes this vol. is still scheduled for publication, especially since it will preserve the 4 Graupner copies and, reportedly, introduce further information about Platti (but cf. fn. 1a to p. 365 *supra*). No record has been found here of an ed. by Malipiero of 12 keyboard sons. in the CLASSICI-m I series (1920), referred to by Hoffmann-Erbrecht as being much altered. If the reference is not in error, the ed. may have been Quaderni 97-103, missing in Heyer/HISTORICAL 59 and perhaps discarded when the series was bound in 36 vols.

9. Cf. Hoffmann-Erbrecht/HAFFNER 119 and 124.

still exists in at least 5 copies, and Op. 4 (*ca.* 1745), which seems not to have survived in print;[10] *VI Sonate a flauto traversière solo con violoncello overo cembalo,* Op. 3 (plate no. 6, *ca.* 1743);[11] and 6 cembalo concertos, Op. 2 (1742). 11a

Assuming that all these sonatas do come from the same man and granting that they have distinct style traits in common, one is the more surprised by how much Platti's early and late sonatas differ. However, if his sonatas are read in chronological order—that is, the fifteen now available plus the generous excerpts from a few others that Torrefranca has inserted in his discussions—a well graduated transition may be observed from one stylistic extreme to the other. The traits these sonatas have in common include mainly the crisp, angular, wide-spaced ideas that set the pace for driving fast movements; the sensitive, florid, and similarly wide-spaced lines that characterize several deeply expressive slow movements; the constant attention to rhythmic detail; the full vocabulary of harmonic colors; and the monothematic effect of a continuous unfolding or succession of related rather than contrasting ideas. The differences between the early and late sonatas may be defined roughly as those that distinguish high-Baroque from early-*galant*
writing, or, say, Vivaldi from Friedemann Bach. The early cello sonatas 11b
are described by Torrefranca as still having much of Corelli and Vivaldi in them, including one more of the many paraphrases of Corelli's "celebrated Gavotte" (Op. 5/10/iv).[12] The latest keyboard sonatas, which by their stylistic advancements must be the four that Graupner could
have copied any time up to his death in 1760,[13] already show the telltale 13a
triplets and light ornaments, the thinner textures, the slower harmonic rhythm, the less active basses, and the two-measure cadential units of the young *galant* style.

All of Platti's early, relatively short cello sonatas (which are much like his four *ricercate* for violin and cello that have been made avail-

10. Mod. eds.: 12 sons. Opp. 1 and 4, MDMA-m I/3 and 4 (Hoffmann-Erbrecht, with prefaces; further discussion in Hoffmann-Erbrecht/KLAVIERMUSIK 83-89); Op. 1/1 in D, Newman/THIRTEEN-m no. 2 (with preface); Op. 1/2/iv in C, Davison & Apel-m no. 284 (cf. p. 291).

11. Mod. eds.: Sons. in e, G, and A (with changes), SCHOTT ANTIQUA-m Nos. 376, 377, 2457 (Jarnach, with preface). No confirmation could be found here of a "Möseler" ed. cited in Moser/LEXIKON II 967.

12. Cf. Torrefranca/PLATTIANO 203 and 209; SBE 171-172.

13. I.e., Sons. 13-16 in Torrefranca's numbering, which is used here and starts with the 12 sons. in Op. 1 and 4. Sons. 7, 8, 10, 11, and 13 in this numbering are the same as nos. 3, 5, 2, 4, and 1, respectively, of 7 MS sons. listed as a set in Breitkopf/WERKE II 37 (1761) and separately, by their first-mvt. incipits, in Breitkopf/MS IV 7 (1763). Probably nos. 6 and 7 in this Breitkopf set account for 2 of the other 3 sons. that Graupner copied, although they are not so identified in the (confused) statement in Torrefranca/ORIGINI 455-456.

able[14]) and nearly all of his Op. 1 and Op. 3 (Fl/bass) follow the older, four-movement plan, S-F-S-F, of the church sonata. But the sonatas in Op. 4 are more variable, including three in the two most prevalent three-movement plans—F-S-F (Sons. 9 and 10) and S-F-F (Son. 11). Sonatas 3 and 12 for keyboard and the one in e for flute come closer to being four-movement suites. Along with that majority of movements that have mostly slow or fast, rather than moderate, tempo designations, five dance types occur, at least in style when not in name, including the minuet-with-trio, the gigue, the saraband, the siciliana, and the polonaise. Platti chooses keys as far around the circles as E or E♭, and e or c, with about a third, or more than the usual proportion, being in minor. Inner slow movements are in the opposite mode (as are the minuet trios) or in the relative key. Exceptional in one minuet (Son. 3/iii) is the use of the minor dominant key for the "Trio alternativement." The movements of these sonatas are not interconnected by harmonic overlaps nor interrelated by similar incipits. In most of the non-dance movements, even in an occasional slow movement that has no inner double-bar or repeat signs (e.g., Son. 1/i), ternary design is present. That is to say, the initial idea divides the form into three approximately equal sections by reappearing in a related key and again, with good preparation, in the home key. But the lack of sharp contrasts and distinctly separated phrases in Platti's process of thematic unfolding (not to mention the lack of dynamic or any other performance indications except a few slurs) still keeps these movements rather far from a high-Classic sense of "sonata form."

Like Torrefranca, Pincherle has also remarked the similarity of the melodic ideas in the quick movements of Platti's sonatas to those in the concerti grossi of his older co-citizen Vivaldi.[15] One might add that Platti's pert ideas, with their repeated notes, their energetic metric groupings, their wide skips and shifts of range (suited even better to the violin than to the keyboard), and their bare settings in octaves, also bring to mind the neat, thin, buoyant conversation of a Pergolesi *opera buffa*. Understandably, the ideas in the flute and the cello sonatas are more often songful in character (as in the flute Son. in G/ii/8-13). But the later keyboard sonatas begin to have moments of such writing, too (Son. 13/i/22-28).[16] And there is certainly no dearth of lyricism in the opening ideas of the slow movements for keyboard (e.g., Sons. 2/iii and 13/ii, both in a, with instructive differences as well as similarities), or in the finely, often boldly spun-out lines that follow (Ex. 58).

14. HORTUS MUSICUS-m Nos. 87 and 88.
15. Pincherle/VIVALDI I 229.
16. Much of Son. 13 is quoted in Torrefranca/ORIGINI 536-544.

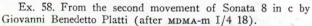

Ex. 58. From the second movement of Sonata 8 in c by Giovanni Benedetto Platti (after MDMA-m I/4 18).

In both his quick and slow movements, Platti's ability to extend his opening ideas into sections of up to fifteen or more measures is one of his chief melodic strengths. He is able to pay out more and more fresh material without abusing the devices either of sequence or of literal repetition (as in Sons. 11/ii and 11/i). Basic to this process is his developed sense of rhythmic organization and the force of his syncopations and other rhythmic patterns (Ex. 59). Sometimes his fast movements are homogeneous because they are almost entirely preludial or toccata-like, as is the excellent "Fantasia" that opens Sonata 8. At other times there are hints of the contrasts out of which "second themes" are made. But these hints are only tangential episodes, usually marked by a new harmonic twist (Ex. 60), not new independent ideas of a different character.

Up to Sonata 12 Platti used an actual Alberti bass only in one movement (Son. 10/i) and only in chance bits totalling scarcely five measures. But in the "later" sonatas 13-16—and this is one good basis for calling them "later"—he used this device more often, more continuously, and more idiomatically in anticipation of the "singing-allegro" style. For the rest, his textures offer considerable variety and interest, including a fair amount of activity in the left hand (Son. 8/iii/42-48), although there are no fugal movements among the "solo" sonatas such as occur in Platti's concertos.[17] Compared with Scarlatti, Platti exploits the keyboard only modestly. Yet his knowledge of the keyboard is amply 17a
demonstrated in some of Scarlatti's favorite devices, including alter-

17. Cf. Torrefranca/PLATTIANO 205.

Ex. 59. From the opening of the fourth movement of Sonata 5 in c by Giovanni Benedetto Platti (after the original Haffner ed. at the Library of Congress).

nations, overlappings, and crossings of the hands (as in Platti's sons. 11/ii, 4/ii, and 13/i).

In the more than seventy-five pages of discussion that Torrefranca devotes to Platti he stresses most of the musical values noted here. He also stresses some others, like the pre-Beethovian scherzo style that he finds in many of the finales (e.g., Son. 4/iv[18]). And he stresses a few values that seem less defensible, such as the appearance of clearly contrasting themes. His most extreme and most hostilely received assertions (as noted in the preface to our Chapter VII) concern Platti's "anticipations" of Beethoven and the ways in which he is alleged to have

18. Cf. Torrefranca/ORIGINI 95-97.

Ex. 60. From the first movement of Sonata 13 in C by Giovanni Benedetto Platti (after Torrefranca/ORIGINI 536).

both antedated and outclassed "Ph. E. Bach, il piccolo." With regard to Beethoven's sonatas, Platti's Sonata 11/ii (an undeniably outstanding movement) is asserted to reveal

> the same freedom, the same native force and originality, the same fertility of invention, the same inherent need for polythematism, the same attention to the meaning of every single beat—only the breathing spans and the impetuosity of the speech are different. Above all, the style of modulating is analogous to Beethoven's and not to the more academic style of Mozart, of Haydn, and of that same Ph. E. Bach. And modulation, next to the style of the themes, is the [most] essential determinant of a composition's character. . . . [Also, Platti's "Fantasia," Son. 8/i] surpasses in grandeur, structure, and lyrical impulse any [other] piece of the sort prior to Beethoven.[19]

Such assertions almost compel the reader to enumerate his exceptions. With regard to Torrefranca's other assertions, Platti's music may be said actually to resemble Emanuel Bach's, as well as Friedemann Bach's, more than that of Alberti, Galuppi, and other co-citizens or compatriots who remained in Italy. Comparing Platti's and Galuppi's music,

19. Trans. from Torrefranca/ORIGINI 83 and 86.

Torrefranca finds the former more austere, universal, abstract, sharply defined, and broadly conceived in the structural sense, and the latter more intimate, amiable, sensitive, delicate, and urbane.[20] Platti himself (using the French often spoken at the Würzburg court, as at the Berlin and Mannheim courts) entitles his Op. 1, "VI Sonates pour le Clavessin Sur le Goût Italien." Nevertheless, in what might be called simply its greater meatiness, especially its compactness of material and richness of harmony, his music does seem to relate more to current German than Italian styles.

The first sets of keyboard sonatas by both Platti and Emanuel Bach originally appeared in Nürnberg in that same year of 1742 (from Haffner and Schmid, respectively; SCE XIII), after which either composer conceivably might have been influenced by the other. Yet no such influence can be pinpointed in the second set of either (both of which sets were published by Haffner, *ca.* 1746 and 1744, respectively). Each man was too well in command of his musical resources and too strong as a musical individual to be readily influenced at this point in his career. Thus, Emanuel Bach started with the clear thematic contrasts that are not characteristic of Platti's sonatas. But Platti did not follow him in this, and Bach himself soon veered in other directions, often marked, as we shall see, by increasing individuality, even to the point of eccentricity.

One must add that Platti's music loses almost more than it gains in the competitive light by which Torrefranca views it. Whereas he finds some of the richest slow movements a bit "studied," he sees Sonata 13 in C as Platti's most "characteristic and important" sonata,[21] chiefly for the ways in which it points to the symphonic style of another favorite Italian, G. B. Sammartini. The fast outer movements of Sonata 13 do prove interesting in this sense, but as with so much other pre-Classic music, the style advances are made at the expense of the musical content. Purely in the latter sense, almost any of Platti's previous sonatas, in which he was more at home in somewhat more traditional techniques, seem both more interesting and more representative. In that sense his music is one of the bright spots—as is, for example, Buttstett's—in the necessarily large amount of only average music that must be explored in a study of the present sort.

A full, up-to-date and unbiased study of Platti's music has yet to be done and is obviously much needed. Such a study is likely to put the composer back among his late-Baroque contemporaries, historical classi-

20. Torrefranca/ORIGINI 182-183.
21. Torrefranca/ORIGINI 86 and 535.

fications being the necessary evils that they are. (Perhaps it is because Haffner viewed his music in that way that, after starting with three collections, he did not see fit to include any of it in his later, decidedly *galant* anthologies.) Meanwhile, a little further idea of the range of Platti's styles might be given by drawing a few, more specific, familiar analogies. Sonata 6/iv, a "Minuet con Variazioni" in E, recalls the techniques and even the lines in the variations of Handel's "Harmonious Blacksmith" in the same key. Sonata 7/iv, a "Minuetto" in F with "Trio" in f, is surprisingly Mozartean, with appoggiaturas and feminine cadences in the "Minuetto" that recall Mozart's early "Menuett" in the same key (K. V. 2). Sonata 4/ii, a "Presto e alla breve" in g, has sections of passage work much like that in Emanuel Bach's "Solfeggio" in c (W. 117/2). And Sonata 4/iii, an "Adagio" in B♭, has the decorative, expressive line and the 8th-note accompaniment of the slow movement in J. S. Bach's "Italian Concerto."

In one of his later keyboard anthologies Haffner did include a lighter sonata by the only other composer in Würzburg (and near-by Bamberg) to be mentioned here, **Joseph Umstatt.**[22] Umstatt is identified as being a *Kapellmeister* there about 1758, in which capacity he had also been employed in Dresden in 1747.[23] At one time, among a few church works and further instrumental works, five other keyboard sonatas and a sonata in quartet setting by him were known. The sonata Haffner published is in five movements, more than average because of a fugue that is inserted. In its opening "Allegro," in 3/4 meter, the form is binary, the initial idea merely outlines the tonic chord as it descends, but the scales and other fluent figures that comprise the body of the movement make ingenious uses of the keyboard and are enhanced by fresh harmonies and a good sense of timing in the rhythmic flow. Much the same may be said of the "Adagio" that follows, which opens with an inconsequential idea and becomes chiefly interesting for its passage work. The third movement is the well contrived if rather academic "Fuga Allegro." After it, comes the *da capo* sequence of "Minuetto" I-II-I in a movement of slightly more melodic interest, followed by a "Presto" finale in 4/4 meter that is similar in form and style to the first movement. Aside from the good keyboard diversion this sonata offers, it is worth noting for its tonal scheme, which includes three nearly related keys in the successive movements—F, C, a, F-d-F, F.

In Darmstadt, sixty miles west of Würzburg, the Bohemian-born, Italian-trained instrumental director **Johann Georg Lang** (1724 to at

22. Anth. HAFFNER OM-m IV no. 6.
23. Cf. Gerber/LEXICON II 699; Eitner/QL X 9-10.

least 1794) contributed four more sonatas to Anth. HAFFNER OM-m
23a (IV/4, VI/4, VII/3, VIII/4; *ca.* 1758-61). Here and in Koblenz during the next twenty-five years he also published (among early issues by André in Offenbach) *Sei Sonate à quatro parti obligate* (K, Fl, Vn, Vc-or-Va); six accompanied sonatas, Op. 6 (K & Vn & Vc); and *Quatres grandes Sonates pour le clavecin ou piano forte, dont l'une est à quatre mains, avec l'accompagnement d'un violon et violoncelle,* Op. 7.[24] Lang's four solo keyboard sonatas in Anth. HAFFNER OM-m come as close to the Mozartean high-Classic style as anything we have met thus far in the pre-Classic Austro-German sonata. All of these are in three movements, in the order F-S-F or F-S-Minuet (with variations) except for one sonata (VI/4) in the order M-F-VF. Especially in the outer movements of the last of these sonatas, in C (VIII/4), both the essentials and the feel of Classic "sonata-form" are present.[25] Mozart's writing is suggested by the melodic chromaticism and the "singing-allegro" style of the texture and melody.[26] Notable is the sense of dualism both within and between the main themes (VIII/4/i) and the sense of actual development (VIII/4/iii). Lang's typical theme begins with a melodic turn. After a phrase or period it dissolves into passages that prolong the tonal movement in a sustained, symphonic, quasi-crescendo drive toward the next cadential landmark in the structure. The total result is convincing enough, even if it is still far from the depth, originality, and expressive range of the high-Classic masterpieces. In this instance, Schubart's warm praise may be taken as only moderately excessive:

> *Lang,* a universally popular and really excellent musician. He brings glory to himself in more than one way. Especially are his *keyboard pieces* eagerly sought throughout Germany, and performed here and there with ever increasing applause. His concertos and sonatas are certainly not unusually difficult, nor [too] deeply conceived. Rather do they stand out for their lovely melodies and for brilliant keyboard passages. The wonder is that Lang can write such beautiful keyboard pieces yet himself play only so-so at the keyboard.[27]

One can only add, what a promising, virgin field of study Lang's music should prove to be for the researcher in pre-Classic styles.

In Mainz, not twenty miles west of Darmstadt, the Bohemian or-

24. The last 2 sets are listed in Cat. SCHWERIN II 2. Cf. the list in MGG VIII 178-179 (Hoffmann-Erbrecht); the MS sons. in this list apparently correspond to the publications.

25. The finale is analyzed in Lange/SÜDWESTDEUTSCHEN 15-16 and its development section is printed on p. 11 of the exx.

26. That the Mozarts knew Lang is evidenced in Anderson/MOZART II 537.

27. Trans. from Schubart/IDEEN 228-229.

ganist and violinist **Johann** (or Jan) **Zach** (1699-1773) was active from 1745-56. He had trained in Prague under Černohorský and later was to go to Italy and Tirol before spending his last days probably in Munich (but not in an asylum in Bruchsal).[28] Out of a sizable quantity of music that Zach is known to have left, much is now lost and only a few sonatas can be reported here. These include a four-movement Sonata in A in Anth. HAFFNER OM-m V/6 (*ca.* 1759),[29] a MS "Sonata a 3 Stromenti" (2 Vns and *b.c.*) that was brought to light recently,[30] two accompanied sonatas in MS (K & Vn & Vc, K & Fl & Vn),[31] and a set of six accompanied sonatas (K & Vn-or-Fl) published in Paris in 1767.[32] Whereas Zach's sacred choral and organ music is described as still conveying the grandeur of the Baroque Era, his symphonies, concertos, chamber music, and solo pieces were clearly written in the modern styles that would most please the public.

Zach's keyboard sonata—made up of an allegro, andante, allegro, and polonaise—is an example of the *galant* style in its more ornamental state. Like Umstatt's sonata, it offers more passage work than tangible melody. In the first movement most of the focal melodic statements occur in the home key, but a ternary division is created by putting the middle section in the tonic minor mode. The "trio" sonata, similar to two "Triosinfonie" of 1755 that have also been published,[33] is a little simpler and more straightforward than the keyboard sonata, with four shorter, purely binary movements (M-F-M-Minuet). Some of its melodies have a folklike quality and may indeed be based on popular Czech tunes, as suggested by the modern editor. The chief hint that a composer of greater force and imagination existed behind these sonatas occurs in occasional harmonic shocks, such as the reiteration of a minor 3d, F♯-A, over a G pedal until "resolutions" follow on V_7 and I^6_4 in C (keyboard son./ii/9-10, 11-12, etc.).

The later violinist **Georg Anton Kreusser** (1743-1810) was in Mainz from 1773 to about 1792. Well known to the Mozarts, he pub-

28. Cf. GROVE IX 392-393 (Černušak); MAB-m No. 9 (preface by Racek and Němec); HORTUS MUSICUS-m No. 145 (preface by Gottron). Komma/ZACH is a study of Zach in Mainz, with a chapter on styles, numerous exx., and a thematic index of his works. A condensed discussion of Zach and his music also occurs in Gottron/MAINZER 129-137.

29. The first movement is analyzed and quoted at length in Lange/SÜDWESTDEUTSCHEN 9-10, 20-21, and 3 and 15 in the exx.

30. MAB-m No. 9; not listed in Komma/ZACH.

31. Cf. Gottron/MAINZER 133-134.

32. The existence of the last is known here only through a listing in "Catalogue No. 62" (Nov., 1959), item 300, of The First Edition Bookshop (kindly brought to the attention of this study by Professor Jan LaRue at New York University); it is not in Komma/ZACH. The date comes from Johansson/FRENCH II Facs. 15.

33. HORTUS MUSICUS-m No. 145.

lished at least five sets of SS/bass "Sonates," "Trios," and "Divertissemens," reportedly in a light popular style, between about 1770 and 1785.[34] These seem not to have been examined closely in recent times.

Bonn and Berleburg (Neefe)

We meet the popular Singspiel composer and able clavierist **Christian Gottlob Neefe** (1748-98) in Bonn because his niche in music history now ties him mainly to that city,[35] as the principal teacher of Beethoven. The young genius worked closely with Neefe from about 1781 up to the meetings with Mozart and Haydn that prompted Beethoven's move to Vienna in 1792. How warm was the mutual respect of teacher and student is well known from the written tributes of each.[36] But two-thirds of Neefe's forty reported sonatas had already been composed and published before he had reached Bonn in 1779—in fact, during his years of legal training and subsequent conversion to music in Leipzig, farther north, from 1769-76. In 1782 Neefe completed a short, affecting, and socially illuminating autobiography, supplemented by his widow in 1798 and since published in part or in full at least a half-dozen times.[37] In this source, in letters, in dedications of his compositions, and in contributions to periodicals, this cultured, idealistic, hypochondriacal man left an exceptionally articulate and full record of his Leipzig training, music impressions, philosophies, and aesthetic judgments. Much of this material has been brought together in the detailed dissertation that Irmgard Leux finished in 1921 on the man and his instrumental music (complete with a chronology and thematic index of this music, and with Neefe's autobiography in its original form), and more of it has turned up in the ever-growing literature on Beethoven.[38]

In Neefe's autobiography we learn that his earliest publications were all composed under the guidance of the musician who most influenced him in Leipzig, the Singspiel pioneer J. A. Hiller.[39] These publications include two sonatinas for keyboard that appeared in Hiller's early musical weekly, *Wöchentliche Nachrichten und Anmerkungen,* when Neefe was only twenty (1768); and a set of *Zwölf Klaviersonaten*

34. Cf. Anderson/MOZART I 250, II 559 and 897; MGG VII 1772-1774 (Gottron).
35. Cf. Thayer/BEETHOVEN I 1-41 on Bonn at that time.
36. Cf. Thayer/BEETHOVEN I 68-70.
37. Including an English transl. in Nettl/FORGOTTEN 246-264 of the shortened version that originally appeared in AMZ I (1798-99) 241-245, 257-261, 273-278, 360-364.
38. Especially in Schiedermair/BEETHOVEN 140-162. Cf., also, MGG IX 1345-1350 (Kahl).
39. Leux/NEEFE 193.

dedicated to Emanuel Bach and published by Schwickert in Leipzig five years later (1773).[40] In the informative dedication to Bach that 40a
appears in this 1773 set as well as in the autobiography and in later tributes, we learn how much Neefe also felt he owed to the theory and keyboard instruction in Bach's *Versuch* and to the latter's published sonatas.[41] Marpurg's several "Anleitungen" are cited in the autobiography, too. And Neefe dedicated his *Sechs neue Klavier-Sonaten,* which appeared the next year (1774, from the same publisher), to J. S. Bach's onetime pupil J. F. Agricola. In short, Neefe's background largely reflects a second generation of J. S. Bach's sphere of influence in Leipzig.

To the three publications mentioned thus far may be added another composed by Neefe while he was still in Leipzig,[42] this time a set of six accompanied sonatas (K ± Vn), issued in the year of his departure, 1776, by Günther in Glogau (Silesia). After he reached Bonn he published one more accompanied sonata, similarly scored, and one more solo keyboard sonata in a Leipzig collection of 1780 (*Vademecum für Liebhaber des Gesangs und Klaviers*). And probably in Bonn he composed the twelve sonatas in two sets now lost. One was "VI. Sonate . . . a Cembalo e Violino," which existed at least in MS when its incipits were listed in 1781.[43] The other was "Sechs Sonaten am Clavier zu singen," which Neefe listed as published in a letter of March 2, 1783.[44] The accompaniment in Neefe's two sets of accompanied sonatas may well have been added as an afterthought at the publisher's request if not by his own doing. That in the 1776 set is purely subordinate, necessitating no change in the keyboard part from the texture to be found in the solo sonatas. Moreover, Neefe had written in his dedication to Emanuel Bach of 1773:

> Since the time that you, dearest *Herr Kapellmeister,* gave to the public your masterly ["Prussian" and "Württemberg"?] keyboard sonatas, worked

40. Neefe's solo keyboard sonatas are discussed in Leux/NEEFE 122-155 (with exx.). All of Neefe's son. publications except that of 1768 are listed in BRITISH UNION II 726. As of this writing (1961), the only mod. ed. of any of his sons. is that of Son. 9 in c from the 1773 set, Newman/THIRTEEN-m 64 (with preface, pp. 12-13). A further mod. ed. that gives at least a representative selection from Neefe's several sets of sons. should be welcomed both by Beethoven researchers and by elementary piano students.

41. Cf. Leux/NEEFE 24, 121, 128, 142, and Auerbach/CLAVICHORDKUNST 35 for portions of the long dedication; Schiedermair/BEETHOVEN 154 for a more detailed evaluation by Neefe of E. Bach's keyboard music as ideal material for the student; Schmid/BACH 62-64.

42. Cf. Leux/NEEFE 171-175; Studeny/VIOLINSONATE 108.

43. BREITKOPF MS Suppl. XIV (1781) 44; but wrongly listed as "für Cembalo und Klavier" in Leux/NEEFE 203.

44. Cramer/MAGAZIN I 382; recognized in Thayer/BEETHOVEN I 36 but not in Leux/NEEFE 117-118.

out with true taste, almost nothing has appeared especially for this instrument. Most of the composers have occupied themselves up to now with symphonies, trios, quartets, etc. And if the keyboard does get attention now and then, the pieces usually are provided with the accompaniment, often very arbitrary, of a violin, and [they] become just as playable on many other instruments as on the keyboard.

In the foregoing statement Neefe would seem to be overlooking the considerable output of idiomatic solo keyboard sonatas (including those that he must have known in Anth. HAFFNER OM-m) during the years immediately preceding. However, in the same dedication he soon makes clear that he is using "Klavier" in that more limited and popular sense of the later eighteenth century, to mean clavichord rather than harpsichord or the newly popular pianoforte: "These sonatas are *Klavier*-sonatas. I mean by that that they are only to be played on the *Klavier,* for most [of them] will have little effect on the *Flügel* or *Pianoforte,* since neither of the two is as capable of cantabile and the various modifications of tone as the *Klavier.*" Yet, as with the accompanied scoring, Neefe seems to have changed his mind about the keyboard instruments, for two years later (1775) he specified "per il Pianoforte con flauti" in two MS "partitas" that were to become sonatas 5 and 6 in the accompanied set.[45]

Aside from a few two- or four-movement works, including the two early sonatinas of 1768 (which are elementary little cycles of four movements each), Neefe's sonatas are all in three movements. The order is usually F-S-F or F-S-Minuet, but occasionally the first movement serves as the slow introduction to two fast movements (as in the set of 1774/2/i). Although Neefe shows little interest in relating the movements of a sonata by similar incipits he does sometimes interconnect them with free modulatory passages that lead from one to the next (1774/1/i-ii). He uses keys of not more than four sharps or flats and prefers major to minor in a ratio of eight to one.

The considerable variety of structural procedures in Neefe's sonatas recalls another statement in the dedication of his 1773 set: "Yet, the majority of clavichord amateurs find interest and satisfaction in nothing but solos. To please them have I written the present sonatas during my spare time. . . . The taste of the amateur, like his understanding, varies in the extreme. Hence I have sought to give as much diversity as possible to my sonatas, in more than one sense."[46] In the first movements, "sonata form" is sometimes approximated (1773/11/i), but just as often are to be found purely binary forms (1774/5/i) or unclassified experi-

45. Cf. Leux/NEEFE 122-123.
46. Quoted in Auerbach/CLAVICHORDKUNST 35.

ments in theme dispositions and "developments," such as that in the first movement of the 1780 solo Sonata in F: ||: x in tonic, y in tonic, z in dom. :||: x developed during modulations from c to F, y in tonic but altered, z unaltered in tonic :||.[47] Neefe's slow movements are usually simple cursive or A-B-A forms. Besides the minuet and incipient "sonata forms," the rondo (1773/10/iii) and *polacca* occasionally serve as finales. But only in one movement (1776/5/iii) does Neefe use the variation form that figures so often in his other keyboard music.

The main ideas in Neefe's sonatas are phrases and periods rather than motives (Ex. 61). These and his closing ideas are often of a

Ex. 61. From the opening of Christian Gottlob Neefe's Sonata 4 in c, from *Zwölf Klaviersonaten,* 1773 (after the original ed. in the Library of Congress).

fetching, songful character (as at the end of 1773/6/ii). In another paragraph from his dedication to Emanuel Bach, Neefe himself says: "Some art critics will perhaps condemn me for sometimes being too songful in certain ways—I mean, in the little sections and closes. But I do not see why one may not at times allow that on the keyboard that true song otherwise allows." Neefe's songful writing, however, is more akin to his Singspiel style than to Mozart's "singing-allegro" style. Except for rare instances in the later sonatas, he does not employ the literal Alberti bass associated with the latter style. He does, however, make characteristic if limited use of the keyboard in hand interchanges and crossings, and in a certain amount of decorative display in the solo sonata of 1780.

The over-all impression made by Neefe's keyboard sonatas is one of

47. Cf. the detailed description with exx. in Leux/NEEFE 152-154.

naïve sincerity effected by expressive, somewhat rudimentary writing in compact, often diminutive forms. J. S. Bach comes to mind only in certain mannerisms, such as Neefe's frequent use (1773/9/i/4-6) of the motive that underlies the Prelude in f from *The Well-Tempered Clavier* II. Emanuel Bach is suggested chiefly by a few sudden, dramatic modulations in slow movements, such as two abruptly *fortissimo* shifts to e, one from E♭ (1774/1/ii[48]) and the other from G (1774/5/ii). As for Beethoven, except for some modulations of this same sort (Op. 13/i/124-127) and a few superficial resemblances that have been noted in structure and terminology,[49] it is only remarkable how far beyond Neefe's expressive and technical range the young student already went in his three early "Kurfürsten" sonatas of 1782-83. At most one can thank Neefe for making *The Well-Tempered Clavier* known to Beethoven, and point to certain incipient Beethovian qualities in Neefe's music —for example, a bare hint of the c-minor drive (as in Sons. 4/i and 9/i of the 1773 set) that was to prove so fateful and relentless in some of Beethoven's best known "sonata-allegro" movements (e.g., Opp. 13, 18/4, 67, 111).

Another possible influence on the young Beethoven in Bonn was that of the organist and cembalist **Andrea Lucchesi,** who succeeded Beethoven's grandfather as court *Kapellmeister* in 1774.[50] Trained in Venice, Lucchesi met the Mozarts there in 1771, the year he had first come to Bonn. Among the many choral and instrumental works that he left are a set of six accompanied sonatas (K & Vn) published as Op. 1 in Bonn in 1772, and another, separate accompanied sonata published there the next year, as well as a set of six one-movement "Sonatines" for keyboard in a MS dated 1769 at the Library of Congress.[51] In Op. 1 the sonatas are reported to have three movements each, mostly in the order F-S-F and often "fresh and original," with interesting development of the material.[52] To judge further from Sonatina 6 in C, from Leopold Mozart's recommendation of Lucchesi's harpsichord concerto to Nannerl,[53] and from Neefe's and Burney's estimates of his music,[54] his sonatas are light, facile, pleasing, and *galant* in style.

In Berleburg, some sixty-five miles to the northeast of Bonn, lived

48. Quoted in Shedlock/SONATA 163.
49. Cf. Shedlock/SONATA 162-163.
50. Cf. MGG VIII 1251-1252 (Stephenson), with mention of new findings by A. Henseler in 1937.
51. For the "Sonatine" cf. Stone/ITALIAN I 228-229 (discussion), II 34-35 (thematic index), III 69-70 (copy of no. 6 in C). There are no mod. eds. of Lucchesi's music.
52. Studeny/VIOLINSONATE 108-109.
53. Cf. Anderson/MOZART I 365.
54. Cf. Thayer/BEETHOVEN I 34 (for Neefe); BURNEY'S TOURS II 25.

another contributor to Anth. HAFFNER OM-m, **Bernhard Hupfeld** (Houpfeld, etc.; 1717-96). Hupfeld, who also wrote symphonies and chamber music, was a violinist, trained by Agrell (in Kassel) and Domenico Ferrari (in Cremona), among others.[55] But the two (not three) sonatas published by Haffner (II/3 and III/4) show an advanced knowledge of the keyboard, too. Each is in four movements, the order being "Preludio"-F-S-F and F-S-Minuetto I and II-F, respectively. In the first sonata, the arpeggiations in all but the first and last measures of the modulatory, rhythmically free "Preludio" seem to set the style for the other three movements, which, as in the keyboard sonatas of Umstatt and Zach, consist much more of passages than of distinct melodic ideas. However, Hupfeld's second sonata is different in this respect, with clear tunes in every movement. The method of continuation after the tunes are stated is chiefly motivic reiteration, the forms being largely monothematic. The somewhat imitative texture, especially in the "Larghetto," and the varied harmony are handled with skill.

Weimar and Near-By Centers (*Wolf, Ernst Bach*)

Weimar, near the very center of Germany, was the site of the long established court orchestra to which J. S. Bach had belonged. From 1761 at this same court, soon to lead this same orchestra, a superior pre-Classic composer is discovered, one unjustly disregarded today. **Ernst Wilhelm Wolf** (or Wolff; 1735-92), also a clavierist and theorist, was regarded highly enough in his own day.[56] Besides contemporary tributes to be cited, one evidence is the publication, mostly during his lifetime, of almost all his large instrumental output, including symphonies, concertos, quintets, quartets, and at least seventy sonatas. Naturally, much less could be published from his dramatic and sacred output (chiefly operas and oratorios). Most of the sonatas, which began to appear in 1774, exist in fourteen publications, issued in Leipzig by Breitkopf and by Schwickert, in Weimar "at the author's expense," and in Lyon by Guéra (who, in keeping with French taste, issued Wolf's one accompanied set).[57] These sonatas all

55. Cf. MGG VI 965-967 (Engelbrecht).

56. Brockt/WOLF is a partial printing of a diss. (1927) on the man and his music, without the chronological list of his works; biographic corrections by E. W. Böhme appear in ZMW XV (1932-33) 171-172. Cf., also, the exceptionally full articles in Gerber/LEXICON II 824-827 (with other contemporary references) and Gerber/NEUES 605-606.

57. Nearly all of these publications are listed in Cat. BRUXELLES II 341-342 and 345, IV 110-111 and 251; BRITISH UNION II 1087-1088. Cf., also, the detailed list in Eitner/QL X 291-294 (with duplications). For Guéra, cf. Hopkinson/PARISIAN 129.

have the keyboard as the solo or main instrument. As with Neefe, keyboard meant clavichord or piano, to judge from the dynamic markings, the scoring, the more intimately expressive sections, and the known influence of Emanuel Bach. But only in two posthumous sets is the option "Clavicord ou le Forte-Piano" actually specified, rather than "clavicembalo" or "clavier." In more detail, Wolf's sonata publications include five sets of six solo sonatas each (1774, 1775, 1779, 1781, 1789) and the two posthumous sets of three solo sonatas each;[58] four sets of six "kleine" or "leichte" sonatas (sonatinas) each (1779, 1783, 1786, 1787);[59] two separate duet sonatas (4 hands at one keyboard; 1784, 1785); and the set of six accompanied sonatas (K & Vn & Vc; 1779).[60]

In view of his training and early experience in Gotha, Jena, Eisenach, and Leipzig, Wolf may be grouped with Neefe among composers who worked in the second generation of J. S. Bach's influence. He, too, started as an enthusiastic disciple of Emanuel Bach. In fact, we shall see him coming much closer in his early writing than Neefe did to the styles and forms of Bach's earlier sonatas. Furthermore, he changed his direction in his later writing much as Bach did. That is, he compromised his conspicuous talent in order to write lighter, less original but more salable pieces that are primarily interesting to young students. Even the later sonatas not qualified by "kleine" or "leichte," such as those in the set of 1789, prove to be sacrificed on the altar of Mammon. Reduced to a formula of three short, similarly constructed movements in the order F-S-F, those sonatas in themselves would hardly justify any further attention here.

Unfortunately, it is from these later works that nearly all of the very
61a few modern editions of Wolf's sonatas have been taken.[61] One such edition revives a witty but trifling description, with words, of a marital quarrel and reconciliation, a not rare topic for programmatic sonatas of the eighteenth century (SCE VI). In this instance the modern editor simply deletes the third movement, since he finds in it no further bearing on the programme![62] Moreover, it is mostly from the standpoint of the lighter sonatas that the partly qualified and partly contradictory judgments of Wolf seem to have been written by his contemporaries.

58. The first-mvt. incipits of the 1774, 1775, and 1779 sets are in BREITKOPF MS Suppls. X (1775) 18 and XII (1778) 31.

59. Cf. BREITKOPF MS Suppl. XIII (1779-80) 23 for the 1779 set.

60. This last set is in BREITKOPF MS Suppl. XII (1778) 38.

61. Cf. HOFMEISTER 1930 p. 197 for a Son. 2 in C, from "Eine Sonatine, vier affectvolle Sonaten . . ." (1785). Other mod. eds.: duet Son. in C (1784), Kreutz/VIER-m 2 (with postscript); Sonatine in c (1783), Kreutz/SONATINEN-m 16 (with preface); Sonata in d (1779), Kreutz/SONATEN-m no. 2 (with preface); 6 "leichte Sonaten" (1786), ORGANUM-m V Nos. 7, 21, and 25.

62. Kreutz/SONATEN-m no. 2, with preface.

Sometime before 1777 the roving Schubart (who began his ten-year jail sentence in that year) must have concluded that Wolf was lacking in that "genius" (originality and subjective interpretation) that became such a basic requisite of later eighteenth-century art: "*Wolf, Kapellmeister* in Weimar, distinguishes himself more through profound learning than through the force of genius. He is a very good keyboard player, performing with the utmost purity and precision, remaining always the same, never becoming fiery . . ."[63] Goethe, already a celebrated young poet when he moved to Weimar in 1775, is known to have found Wolf empty and not "original"; he even tried to have Wolf replaced by Goethe's still younger friend in Frankfurt/M and Zürich, Christoph Kayser (himself the composer of *Deux Sonates en symphonie pour le clavessin et deux cors,* published in Zürich in 1784).[64] One understands, then, some remarks that Reichardt made in the biographical notices that he published in 1794 and 1795 (after the death of Wolf, to whom he had been related by marriage):

> Wolf . . . followed the Bach school entirely in his early years, and his early works belong to the best imitations of the masterpieces by our Emanuel Bach. But later he turned with much success to the newer *galant* style and finally understood how to combine very happily the variety and charm of the newer forms with the serious and more meaningful character of the earlier great school. . . . When I spoke with him about the happy change in his style, he said to me very naïvely, "I have long believed that there is nothing greater in the world than [E.] Bach, and [that] a keyboard composer can and must not even think otherwise than to imitate him. But now since Goethe's arrival everything has become original with us. Thereupon thought I, you too must try to be original." With this change, as not before, he became somewhat piquant even in his playing—he was a great virtuoso in the [E.] Bach manner . . .[65]

Gerber also seems to have had Goethe's criticism in mind when he praised Wolf, about three years earlier, by implying a distinction between excellence and originality. Wolf, he said, "ranks today not only among our classic and best composers in every aspect, but he is also *original.*"[66]

Wolf's earliest sonatas, in the set of 1774, are regarded here as the ones most interesting and worthy of note.[67] In the broader perspective that two centuries allow us, those sonatas do not seem to be quite

63. Schubart/IDEEN 119; cf. further Schubart remarks as quoted in Schmid/BACH 82-83.
64. Cf. E. W. Böhme in ZMW XV (1932-33) 172; Eitner/QL V 330-331; Schubart/IDEEN 219-220.
65. Trans. from the excerpt quoted in Kreutz/VIER-m 24. For another favorable comment by Reichardt, cf. Brockt/WOLF 46.
66. Gerber/LEXICON II 824.
67. Discussed in Brockt/WOLF 46-67, with exx.

the slavish imitations of Emanuel Bach's sonatas that Reichardt and Wolf himself declared them to be. As already suggested, they actually differ in ways that now seem much more original than any changes Wolf later made after his conscious decision to become "original." To take note first of the ways in which Wolf's sonatas of 1774 are like Bach's, we can point to the same general plan of three-movement cycles in the order F-S-F. The first movements similarly disclose all the essentials of "sonata form" at one time or another, clearly though no more consistently than in the works of most other pre-Classic composers. The second movements similarly proceed in cursive, fantasy style, with dramatic outbursts and pauses, subtle harmony, and surprising enharmonic modulations. And the finales similarly fall into relatively simple binary forms, based on curt pecking ideas such as Haydn also used in finales, and divided into short—often abruptly short—phrases that are separated by partial cadences and rests. In Wolf's earlier writing the *galant* mannerisms have made inroads to about the same partial extent as in Bach's, including the triplets, the thin textures, and certain ornaments made known especially in Bach's *Versuch* (e.g., the *prallende Doppelschlag* or trilled turn).[68]

The differences between Wolf's and Bach's earlier sonatas may be less tangible for the very reason that they pertain more to intrinsic aspects of the styles than to extrinsic features of the structures. But for that same reason the differences are at least as significant as the likenesses. In broad terms, what is highly subjective, fanciful, sometimes eccentric and cumbersome writing in Bach's sonatas becomes sufficiently more ordered and fluent in Wolf's sonatas to implement, not disrupt, the over-all structure. Bach is a bold leader of the North German *Empfindsamkeit* school where Wolf anticipates rather remarkably the more compliant but equally subjective pre-Romantic art of the early nineteenth century. All of Sonata 3 in Wolf's set of 1774 comes closest to the dash and drama of Bach's freer fantasy style, without ever losing the sense of dynamic organization and drive that we associate with the Classic sonata. On the other hand, Sonata 1/i and most of Sonata 6 in this set come closer to the Mozart style. Sonata 6 is a more suave, easygoing work than its fellows, anyway, with a more flowing "slow" movement, marked "Commodetto," and a "Rondeau, Allegretto" finale that introduces an exceptional number of ideas but has only one recurrence of its opening theme.

In more specific terms, Wolf binds his cycles more closely than Bach does by almost always ending the slow movement on a half-

68. Bach/ESSAY 121-125.

cadence that leads into the finale (a procedure that Bach had tried only occasionally before 1774—e.g., in one "leichte" son. of 1766, W. 53/6). Wolf creates melodies that tend to involve fewer different patterns, to describe more regular arches, and to invite contrasting phrases more than motivic continuation. Related to his patterns is Wolf's greater refinement of his rhythms and greater exploitation of them. The fact that he is less inclined toward motivic writing than Bach may explain why only occasionally his "development" sections (1774/4/i) actually develop the material as much as Bach's do. On the other hand, he creates figurations in his passage work that make for more interesting and more modern keyboard writing than Bach's. At times this passage work, the chromatic harmony, and the effective use of diminished-7th chords brings Mendelssohn's good keyboard writing to mind (1774/1/iii). An example may be quoted from Sonata 2/i in G that includes some of the "development" and a quasi-recitative before the recapitulation starts (Ex. 62). But since no excerpt can give more than a hint of a sonata's larger structural aspects and none can be hoped to include all of the different aspects just noted, a modern edition is needed that will restore Wolf's earlier sonatas to view, at least those in the set of 1774.

Also active in Weimar, as well as in his near-by birthplace of Eisenach, was the organist **Johann Ernst Bach** (1722-77), the first of five members of the Bach family we shall meet in the present volume. Ernst was in the Erfurt line of the family, his great-great-grandfather being J. S. Bach's great-grandfather.[69] But he was related much more closely to the Baroque master as his godson and as his supposed onetime student and boarder in Leipzig. The nine sonatas now known by this hard-working soul include three for keyboard, of which one in A was left in MS[70] and two, in F and G, are in Anth. HAFFNER OM-m (V/3 and VI/1; *ca.* 1759 and *ca.* 1760); and three sonatas each in two accompanied sets (K + Vn; published by Griessbach in Eisenach, 1770 and 1772).[71] All of these sonatas are in three movements in the order F-S-F except the keyboard Sonata in G, which adds a "Minuetto con III. Variazioni" before the finale. Apart from an occa-

69. He is no. 41 on the genealogy chart in MGG I 910 (Benecke). The chief biographic source is DDT-m XLII v-xii (Kretzschmar); cf., also, Löffler/'BACHE' 114-118; Geiringer/BACH 200, 451-454; MGG I 960-962 (Kraft).

70. Cf. DDT-m XLII xv.

71. The published sons. are briefly discussed in DDT-m XLII xiv-xv and Geiringer/BACH 456-457. Among other extant copies, the first acc'd. set is at the Library of Congress and the second at the British Museum. Mod. eds.: acc'd. Son. 1 in D, NAGELS-m No. 2 (Küster); acc'd. Son. 2 in F/ii and iii, Geiringer/BACH-m 159 (with preface).

(Allegro)
Clavichord
Adagio
Allegro

Ex. 62. From the first movement of Sonata 2 (1774) by Ernst Wilhelm Wolf (after the original Breitkopf ed. at the British Museum).

sional half-cadence leading to the finale, the inner movements remain in the home key.

Ernst Bach betrays the discomforts that he and not a few of his contemporaries experienced in the transition from Baroque to Classic styles. Preferring not, or failing, to take the *galant* way out, he was too able and independent a musician not to find some other way of keeping up with his times. Today, his answer often seems somewhat stiff, stilted, and spare. He is obviously most at ease in the solo keyboard sonatas when he still writes motivically (Son. in G/ii/13-20, etc.) and imitatively (Son. in F/iii, which is not unlike a two-part invention). When he denies these processes he falls into those disjunct two- and four-measure units that we have met frequently in other, usually earlier pre-Classic sonatas. The additive effect of these units and their ever-changing rhythms is partly countered by the occasional references Ernst remembers to make to earlier material. However, his efforts to slow the harmonic rhythm so as to achieve the greater tonal breadth of the new style frequently result in bare repeated notes in the left hand, since he scarcely uses the more fluent Alberti bass. Although the ideas themselves are not devoid of interest, there is not much warmth when the rhythm does not flow and the texture remains so bare.

With further regard to texture, Ernst's accompanied sonatas have been viewed as early examples of true duos in which the violin has already graduated from its function as a mere accompaniment.[72] We have seen valid examples of the Classic duo in even earlier sonatas by Boccherini (Op. 5, 1768). But it would be more accurate from the

72. Geiringer/BACH 456-457.

standpoint of historical styles to think of Ernst's sonatas as still relating to his godfather's sonatas for violin with realized keyboard (SBE 272), in which the violin has not yet been relegated to the status of an accompanying instrument. In the true Classic duo the violin reverts to its accompaniment techniques when it is not taking the lead. In Ernst's sonatas these techniques are not yet present to any appreciable extent, for the violin and upper keyboard parts still intertwine, interchange, and intercross almost constantly as the upper parts did in the old Baroque "trio" sonata. Ernst's special technique, which is of some interest, is to let each instrument follow its natural bent, the keyboard often playing more rapid passages while the violin plays more lyrical lines in longer note values (as in much of Son. 1).

Johann Nikolaus Tischer (1707-74), an organist and pianist in Schmalkalden (forty miles southwest of Weimar), left a Sonata
72a in F in Anth. HAFFNER OM-m VII/6 (1761). He was another supposed student of J. S. Bach,[73] whom Gerber called "one of the most pleasing and enjoyed composers for amateurs and connoisseurs of his time,"[74] and from whose unusual number of keyboard suites and like pieces issued by Haffner (at least ten sets, 1746-53) Leopold Mozart included a "Polonoise" in his *Notenbuch* for Wolfgang.[75] Tischer's Sonata in F is a curious work in two movements that, like Ernst Bach's sonatas, avoided or missed the *galant* transitional style. In spite of some agreeable figures and a euphonious texture largely in 3ds and 6ths, it suffers from excessive sequences, loose structure, and inane ideas. The first movement, "Animoso," is one of the longest movements in Anth. HAFFNER OM-m (about 160 mss.). Toward the end and before a final "allegro" section it dissolves into nearly a page of fantasying marked "andante" and "adagio molto," which may have been substituted for a separate slow movement. The ensuing "Presto assai" is a shorter form, with repeated "halves" and a reprise.

The organist **Georg Andreas Sorge** (1703-78), who served from his nineteenth year in Lobenstein (about fifty miles southeast of Weimar), holds his place in present music dictionaries chiefly as the theorist who wrote on combination tones (1745-47) before Tartini (1754) and who maintained a bitter, lifelong feud with Marpurg and other writers over such theoretical questions. After going into this side of Sorge's career, Gerber found space only to list his compositions, while Eitner and some succeeding lexicographers went further to dis-

73. Riemann/LEXIKON II 1848; but cf. Paulke/VIERLING 441.
74. Gerber/LEXICON II 655-658, including a detailed list of Tischer's works.
75. Abert/WOLFGANG-m 43.

miss his compositions as being of little significance.[76] Insofar as the three keyboard sonatas examined here are representative, Sorge has been wronged; these are skillful, sincere, warm, telling works. They immediately bring to mind those of another theorist and organist, Maichelbeck (SCE XI), for Sorge's sonatas began to appear about the same time (two years later, in 1738), among the earliest sonatas discussed in the present volume. Moreover, they are similarly closer to Baroque than Classic styles and forms, and they similarly include acknowledgments of the current Italian manner in their titles.

Among numerous works for organ or harpsichord by Sorge, the publications that interest us here were all issued by Schmid in Nürnberg between 1738 and *ca.* 1748.[77] These include three sets of six 77a
one-movement "Sonatinen" each (1735, *ca.* 1739, and *ca.* 1745), written "nach italienischem Gusto" and dedicated to J. S. Bach;[78] a set of *Sonatinen, Fantasien, Toccatinen und Sinfonien vors Clavier im neuern Styl gesetzet;* and an *Erste Lieferung* [containing 3] *von XII Sonaten vor die Orgel und das Clavier im neuen Styl gesetzet* (*ca.* 1748).[79] The three sonatas in the last-named set were examined here except for the first movement of Sonata 2, which movement appears to be missing from what may be the only surviving copy of this set, at the British Museum. These sonatas may also be the only known "sonatas" by 79a
Sorge in more than one movement. In the first two sonatas, in B♭ and F, there are four movements in the order of "Moderato" (Son. 2/i?), "Andante," "Aria," and "Fugetta" or "Fuga." In Sonata 3, in d, there are but three movements, the finale being a "Fuga" again, preceded by an "Andante" and a "Larghetto." Sonata 2/ii is in the tonic minor mode while Sonata 3/ii is the only movement in a different key from its fellows, the key chosen being the common one of the subdominant. In the nonfugal movements the traditional binary form with repeat signs is used, sometimes with a clear reprise during the second "half" (Son. 1/i).

One implication in Sorge's rather unctuous, catty, and presumptuous dedication of his "Sonatinen" to J. S. Bach is that the latter was writing learned music for connoisseurs while he, Sorge, was writing a simpler, more popular kind of music for amateurs. The implication would seem to apply equally to the three sonatas in question, which are less in Bach's concentrated, involute style than in the more open, homophonic,

76. Gerber/LEXICON II 531-535; Eitner/QL IX 206-209.
77. Plate nos. 6, 12, 22, and 29, dated here according to Deutsch/NUMBERS 21.
78. The long dedication is quoted in full in Schletterer/WIDMUNG 65-66.
79. The MSS listed in Eitner/QL IX 209 may duplicate some of the publications. The reference in Gerber/LEXICON II 534 to a set of 6 keyboard sons. as Sorge's first publication, in 1738, cannot be reconciled here with the foregoing information.

Ex. 63. From the start of the second movement of Sonata 1 in B♭ by Georg Andreas Sorge (after the original *Erste Lieferung* in the British Museum).

Mediterranean style of Handel. These sonatas would, in fact, provide material of considerably more appeal and artistic value for today's young students—were they to be reintroduced in a modern edition—than many another piece from the same period that has been disinterred apparently for no better reason than the notion that it must be good because it is old. Sorge's writing has the advantage of achieving unusual melodic, expressive, and textural interest for so few notes. A contributing factor is his expert command of harmony, which even Eitner troubles to illustrate in spite of his previous reservation about Sorge's compositions.[80] The result is a surprising sureness of purpose and breadth of outline (Ex. 63), with none of the obscurity that Eitner finds in Sorge's theoretical writings. The fugues, based on similarly
80a attractive ideas, are well worked out in relatively unserried counterpoint.

Leipzig (*Löhlein*)

As we have drawn nearer to Leipzig, both geographically and environmentally, the significance of this center has become increasingly

80. Eitner/QL 209.

apparent.[81] We have already seen or shall be seeing the direct or indirect influence of J. S. Bach on Neefe, E. W. Wolf, Ernst Bach, Sorge, Emanuel Bach, and Reichardt, all of whom but Sorge actually got some of their training in Leipzig. The musical forces at work here in the later eighteenth century were several and of long standing. Among these one only needs to recall the regular and festive performances of the St. Thomas Kirche and its Thomasschule (under J. S. Bach's pupil J. F. Doles from 1756), as well as the other orthodox Lutheran establishments; the Collegium musicum that thrived, at least up to the Seven Years' War (1756-63), on the stimulating student life at the University; the public "Liebhaber-Concerte" (forerunners of the Gewandhaus concerts), which, at the war's end, were given new importance under the direction of J. A. Hiller; and the music publications that were issued (in movable type from 1756) by J. G. I. Breitkopf and his successors in the eventually great firm of Breitkopf & Härtel. At the same time, a musician like the pioneer of the Singspiel, Johann Adam Hiller (1728-1804), who himself added little to the sonata[82] but participated in nearly every other branch of music, and poets and philosophers on the order of Gellert, Gottsched, the young Goethe, and Schiller exercised powerful influences on Leipzig's intellectually disposed artists.

Yet, in spite of all these forces and the good encouragement they gave to instrumental as well as vocal music, they did not lead to any significant cultivation of the sonata by composers actually resident in Leipzig. As with Hiller's varied posts there was not the local need for the sonata that there was at the posts occupied by the outlying composers who had come within the Leipzig sphere of influence, or that we shall be finding in Dresden and especially in Berlin. Furthermore, as Burney wrote in 1772, "nor did I find, upon enquiry, that this city [Leipzig] is at present in possession of many performers of the first class, upon any instrument."[83] Even in the high-Classic Era the most important sonata composer we shall be able to find in Leipzig will be only A. E. Müller.

In the pre-Classic Era our only resident in Leipzig to note here is the pianist and teacher **Georg Simon Löhlein** (1725-81), a colleague

81. Cf. the excellent account of music in 17th- and 18th-century Leipzig in MGG VIII 545-560 and 569-573 (Eller), with full bibliography; also, the firsthand account in BURNEY'S TOURS II 153-157.

82. There are 2 keyboard sons. in his collection *Loisir musical* (Breitkopf, 1762; listed in BRITISH UNION I 482) and 5 in MS that, according to Hoffmann-Erbrecht, "can be compared with the best of their time in the abundance and originality of their invention and technique" (MGG VI 418). The affectionate encomium in Schubart/IDEEN 106-108 includes no mention of these or his few other instrumental works. A facile 3-mvt. "Sinfonia" in C by him is transcribed for keyboard in Anth. SINFONIE-m II no. 12 (1761).

83. BURNEY'S TOURS II 156.

of Hiller. Löhlein came to Leipzig to enroll in the University at the late age of thirty-eight (1763), after having succeeded E. W. Wolf as director of the Collegium musicum at the University of Jena (and after serious wounds had ended some fifteen years of forced service in Frederick the Great's vaunted Prussian guard of tall soldiers).[84] He is best known for one of the most successful and influential keyboard methods of the later eighteenth and early nineteenth centuries. Much of this *Clavier-Schule,* the two volumes of which first appeared in 1765 and 1781, was derived from Emanuel Bach's *Versuch.* But it is simplified for younger students, organized by progressive steps, and kept clear of the "musical labyrinth" of Marpurg's and Sorge's theories, as the author explains in his preface.[85] Similarly derived from Leopold Mozart's *Versuch* is Löhlein's *Anweisung zum Violinspielen,* which, however, was less successful.

Löhlein's compositions, largely for keyboard,[86] include some 25 solo or accompanied sonatas, nearly all published by Breitkopf. Among these are six in Anth. MAGAZIN-m (1756);[86a] a set of *Sei Sonate con variate repetizioni per il clavicembalo,* Op. 2 (1768), modeled after Emanuel Bach's similarly titled sonatas of 1760 and regarded as Löhlein's best sonatas;[87] a set of six sonatas of which three are accompanied (Op. 6, 1776; H-or-P±Vn & Vc);[88] and six S/bass (not accompanied) sonatas in Vol. II of the *Clavier-Schule,* which, to be more specific, is subtitled: "wherein is given a complete course in the accompaniment of the unfigured bass . . . as explained through six sonatas with the accompaniment of a violin."

Löhlein's sonatas are light, fluent, agreeable, well-written pieces, closer in style to the sonatas of Christian Bach or still later composers than to the sonatas of Emanuel.[89] Those in Op. 6, for example, can already be grouped with the pleasant, similarly skilled sonatinas of Diabelli, Clementi, Kuhlau, and Pleyel. They are in three movements, mostly F-S-F, with a short, slow introduction in Sonata 5. In the first movements a reprise is the rule, a clearly contrasted second theme is less frequent (Op. 6/1/i), and there is little actual development of

84. Glasenapp/LÖHLEIN is the chief source on the man, his music, and his writings, with thematic index and other aids. Cf., also, MGG VIII 1093-1097 (Hoffmann-Erbrecht).

85. Löhlein/CLAVIER-SCHULE I "Vorbericht."

86. The incipits of 3 SS/bass "trios" are given in Cat. SCHWERIN II 20 (as well as Glasenapp/LÖHLEIN 228-229).

86a. Glasenapp/LÖHLEIN 224-225.

87. Cf. Glasenapp/LÖHLEIN 67-75, with interesting contemporary comments.

88. The title page of Op. 6, artfully engraved by Löhlein himself, is reproduced in MGG VIII 1095.

89. The sonatas are discussed in Glasenapp/LÖHLEIN 54-75 and 91-99.

ideas in the "development" section. The "slow" movements are gentle, flowing pieces in moderate tempo. And the finale may be a rondo, minuet, or other light type.

More interesting to us are the detailed observations Löhlein devotes to the six sonatas in Vol. II of his *Clavier-Schule*.[90] These observations remind us again (SCE II) how far the theorists still were, at this time, from codifying a "sonata form." In Vol. II Löhlein does not go beyond what his subtitle suggests—chiefly, specific advices on voice-leading and dissonance treatment as they are made necessary when a melody is composed over a bass. However, he does take a step or two into the then uncharted realm of sonata designs, in the last chapter of Vol. I, which, like the last chapter in Part Two of Bach's *Versuch,* is on "fantasying." First he acknowledges that, as in the arts of poetry and painting, the art (as well as the science) of music must be subject at least to certain rules, so that there may be some agreement between phrases, metric organization, and harmonic outline. Next he marks off the regular phrases and periods in a minuet. Finally, he lays out some alternative tonal excursions into nearly related keys, adding a few devices of modulation, after which the student must construct a melody within these progressions. From this point the student is left to the mercy of his good artistic judgment, the author concludes (though in less blunt terms).[91]

The organist **Johann Gottfried Krebs** (1741-1814) was the son of the better known organist Johann Ludwig Krebs, who had been a pupil of J. S. Bach in Leipzig.[92] Primarily a composer of vocal music, Gottfried was active in Altenburg, about thirty miles south of Leipzig, when a keyboard Sonata in E♭ by him appeared in the last volume of Anth. HAFFNER OM-m (as no. 4; 1766). This work is in four movements, of which the first is a rather ungainly, disjointed "Allegro" in *galant* style, the last two are slight binary dances ("Minuetto" I and II, and "Polonoise"), and the second is the redeeming grace. This last is rightly marked "Affetuoso, Largo," for it contains a broad affective line, enhanced by tasteful ornaments, expressive harmony, romantic pauses and dynamic contrasts, and structurally satisfying repetitions of the cadences.

Dresden (Friedemann Bach)

Throughout much of the eighteenth century, Dresden was the foremost musical center in middle Germany.[93] Two periods stand out in

90. Discussed at length in Glasenapp/LÖHLEIN 110-181.
91. Löhlein/CLAVIER-SCHULE I 179-190.
92. Cf. SBE 285; Eitner/QL V 433-434; MGG VII 1726, 1734, 1735 (Tittel).
93. Cf. MGG III 771-776 (Schnoor and Laux); Engländer/DRESDNER 11-23.

particular. One was the reign of the Saxon Elector Friedrich August II from 1733 to 1763, during which the Italianate melodist Hasse (SBE 278-279) brought Dresden opera to an internationally high peak. The other was the succeeding reign of Elector Friedrich August III from 1763 to 1806, in the course of which J. G. Naumann (*Kapellmeister* from 1776, whom we shall meet later) gave a new impetus to nearly all aspects of performance and composition, now in a more modern guise. During Hasse's ascendancy Dresden was the residence, for shorter or longer periods, of renowned instrumentalists like F. M. Veracini, Pisendel, Quantz, Pantaleon Hebenstreit (the virtuoso of the enlarged dulcimer, or "Pantaleon" as Louis XIV called it), and two men we have yet to meet—Friedemann Bach and C. F. Abel. Yet at that time independent instrumental music had little of the *raison d'être* such as was given it by the Collegium musicum or public concerts of the students and burghers in Leipzig, for Dresden's music was then cultivated almost exclusively as the province of the court chapel and opera. During Naumann's ascendancy, the cultivation of instrumental music for its own sake was little more systematized. But with drastic economies forced by the devastating Seven Years' War and with the new young elector not only a devotee of the arts like his father but a good (if shy) clavierist,[94] the climate was certainly more favorable to this cultivation. Interesting evidences may be found in Burney's graphic description of a varied instrumental concert he attended in Dresden in 1772,[95] and in an impressive list of instrumental composers, from near and far, complete with the form types by which they were represented at court from 1777 (when regular records were first kept) to 1810. This list has been compiled in Engländer's fruitful study of Dresden instrumental music contemporary with high-Classic music by the Viennese masters.[96] Nearly half of the pieces on the list were called sonatas, by the way (SCE III).

The Dresden composers discussed at this point still came entirely or partly within Hasse's period. **Wilhelm Friedemann Bach** (1710-84), eldest of J. S. Bach's eleven sons and first of the three important sons to be met in the present volume, wrote most of his sonatas and other instrumental music while he served as organist at the Sophien-Kirche and taught in Dresden from 1733 to 1746.[97] His training had

94. Cf. BURNEY'S TOURS II 141.

95. BURNEY'S TOURS II 144-145.

96. Engländer/DRESDNER 29-33 (cf. Simon/ENGLÄNDER).

97. Since 1913 the dissertation Falck/BACH has remained the chief study of the man and his music, superseding previous studies and including a thematic index. Further biographic and bibliographic detail and a somewhat more balanced historical perspective are offered in GROVE I 321-324 (Terry); Reeser/SONS 7-23; MGG I 1047-1056 (Blume); Geiringer/BACH 154-155, 191-194, 303-335.

been done mainly under his father in Leipzig, supplemented by a year of violin study in Merseburg under J. G. Graun (himself a pupil of Pisendel and Tartini). When the frustrations in Dresden became too great for this increasingly complex, embittered, eccentric, indolent (but not dissolute) man, he took a post in Halle, where he wrote most of his vocal music. He quit this post in 1764 and left Halle in 1770, drifting aimlessly during another fourteen years, including a final ten years in Berlin (1774-84).

In spite of the careful bibliographic study that has been devoted to them, Friedemann's sonatas still raise numerous questions of authenticity. There is no need to repeat all the details here, but we may 97a
recall that most of his works were left in MSS, with the usual problems of conflicting versions in different hands, misattributions by copyists, anonymous scores, confusions with works by other members of the family (J. S. and Emanuel) and by near contemporaries (e.g., J. W. Hässler), and even a little, apparently deliberate juggling of identifications by Friedemann himself. A total of about eighteen works actually called "sonata" are now accepted as his without much question.

Of the eighteen sonatas, nine are for solo keyboard,[98] the dating of which needs some explaining. In 1745, three years after the set of six "Prussian" sonatas by his younger brother Emanuel was issued, Friedemann's first publication appeared. This was but a single "Sonata I" in D (F. 3), although the title page reads "Sei Sonate per il Cembalo . . . In Verlag zu haben 1. bey dem Autore in Dresden, 2. bey dessen Herrn Vater in Leipzig, und 3. dessen bruder [Emanuel] in Berlin."[99] A second single, similarly sponsored publication, "Sonate pour le Clavecin" in E♭ (F. 5), followed in 1748[100] (and was reprinted in 1763 with nothing but the dedicatee changed, not even the reference to its availability through "his [late!] father in Leipzig").[101] The music historian J. N. Forkel, who befriended Friedemann after the Halle years, wrote at the time of the latter's death that the first sonata had been published to see whether the rest of the "Sei Sonate" would sell, "but

98. Discussed in Falck/BACH 65-81; Newman/BACH 236, 237, 239-244. Among mod. eds.: all 9 sons., NAGELS-m Nos. 63, 78, 156 (Blume, with individual prefaces); F. 1A (i.e., item 1A in Falck's thematic index) = NAGELS-m No. 156/8 (the alternate version 1B = Pauer/MEISTER-m III 15, Oesterle/TREASURY-m V 110, etc.), 2 = 156/7, 3 = 78/4, 4 = 78/5, 5 = 78/6 (also in TRÉSOR-m VI 26, with preface; Newman/BACH-m 4, with preface), 6A = 156/9, 7 = 63/1, 8 = 63/2, 9 = 63/3.

99. The title page is reproduced in WOLFFHEIM MUSIKBIBLIOTHEK I Tafel 5; also, along with the first music page, in MGG I 1051. The dedication is quoted in Falck/BACH 66.

100. The title page is reproduced in Reeser/SONS 17. The dedication is quoted in Falck/BACH 68-69.

101. Cf. Miesner/GONNER 106-107.

nobody would buy it because nobody could play it."[102] Martin Falck reasons that the second publication was meant for this set, too—in fact, as "Sonata II," since it is in a key one letter higher, and Friedemann, much as his father had done in the Inventions and *The Well-Tempered Clavier,* later arranged his set of twelve Polonaises and most of his fugues for keyboard in the alphabetic order of their keys.[103] By the same reasoning the MS sonatas in F, G, A, and B♭ (F. 6-9) are assumed to have been meant as the remaining four of the "Sei Sonate" and to have been completed by 1745 when "Sonata I" appeared.

Regarding the other three of the nine solo keyboard sonatas, the MS Sonata in C (F. 1) that is frequently reprinted in "Old Masters" series is thought by Falck to date from about the same time, too. But later dates are suggested by the decidedly simpler and more fluent writing in another Sonata in C (F. 2, the 2d and 3d mvts. of which are reworked in the first Fantasia in c of 1784)[104] and in another Sonata in D (F. 4), one copy of which is dated about 1778. Besides doubtful and spurious works, the only other keyboard "sonata" to note here is Friedemann's early "Concerto â duoi Cembali Concertati" in F (F. 10; *ca.* 1733), known since the first publication of it, which Brahms anonymously prepared for Rieter-Biedermann in 1864, as "Sonate für 2 Klaviere."[105]

In the category of chamber music,[106] the authentic works that pertain are two "trios," one incomplete "trio," and one "sonata" in B♭ (before 1762)—all for two violins or flutes and *b.c.* (F. 47-50);[107] and nine duos for two unaccompanied instruments, of which four "sonatas" for two flutes probably stem from the Dresden period (F. 54, 55, 57, 59), whereas another "sonata" and a "duetto" for two flutes (F. 58, 56) as well as three similar "duetti" for two violas (F. 60-62) may not have been written until Friedemann was in Berlin.[108] Finally, three Fl/bass sonatas are lost today except for their incipits (F. 51-53, before 1761).[109]

102. Quoted from Forkel's *Almanach* for 1784, p. 202, in Mennicke/HASSE 88.
103. Falck/BACH 65.
104. Cf. Falck/BACH 78 and 86.
105. Cf. HOFMEISTER XIII (1864) 37. Regarding the existence of this work in J. S. Bach's hand (the first page is reproduced in MGG I 1033), its inclusion in Bach/WERKE-m XLIII 27 as a first ed. (1894!), and its authentication as Friedemann's, cf. Falck/BACH 62-65; Geiringer/BACH 321-322.
106. Cf. Falck/BACH 114-121 and Geiringer/BACH 328-329, both with exx.
107. For mod. eds., cf. Altmann/KAMMERMUSIK. In Cudworth/SPURIOSITY 535 the Trio in G attributed in HORTUS MUSICUS-m No. 57 to W. F. E. Bach (1759-1845; no. VIII in MGG I 907) is thought rather to be by Friedemann, but the style seems too late and evidence would be needed to refute Falck/BACH 116.
108. Among mod. eds.: all six Fl duos, Walther/BACH-m; Fl duo in F/ii and iii (F. 57), Geiringer/BACH-m 110, with preface; cf., also, MGG I 1056.
109. BREITKOPF MS III 2; BREITKOPF WERKE 60.

Friedemann's sonatas, all relatively short, are nearly all in three movements in the order F-S-VF. But in one of the early flute duos (F. 59) a "Gigue" is added; in certain versions of two early keyboard sonatas (F. 1A and 6A) the second movement is a minuet, and in one of the late viola duos (F. 60) it is a "Scherzo" in 3/4 meter; two of the "trios" (F. 48 and 50) put the slow movement first; and one of the keyboard sonatas (F. 7) starts with two measures marked "Andantino" that recur twice in the movement. The "slow" movements vary in markings from "Adagio" to a moderate "Andante," with a few having less definite indications like "Lamento," "Grazioso," or "Amoroso." All the sonatas are in major keys but three, and all are within three flats or sharps except the late flute duo in f (F. 58). The middle movements, which never lead directly into the finales, are most often in the relative key, the few others being in the subdominant, the original key, or its opposite mode. Similar incipits are rare in the outer movements (F. 4 and 56), and occur only once in all three movements (in the "trio" F. 47). But a cyclical effect is achieved when a characteristic motive in the early keyboard Sonata in D (F. 3) becomes the closing figure for each of the three movements. A surprising stylistic affinity between the outer movements of several of the sonatas (e.g., F. 5) may also be mentioned.

Friedemann's forms reveal considerable flexibility and variety of procedure, though usually not of a sort that can be distinguished by standard classifications. There is an occasional canonic or fugal movement, especially in the relatively conservative ensemble sonatas (F. 59/ii and iii); or there may be a quasi-toccata (F. 9/iii). But there are no sets of variations, no clear rondos, no unequivocal A-B-A designs (apart from the isolated examples of minuet-trio-*da capo,* as in F. 6A/ii). The cursive, motivic process is still too strong here to permit such distinct sectional designs, other than the venerable binary type with repeated "halves," which occurs in most of the fast and a few of the slow movements. In all these "binary" movements, and in the remaining slow movements, too, the initial idea can usually be expected to return from one to three times in the home or nearly related keys, suggesting one conventional basis for classifications. However, other factors, stylistic rather than structural, seem to bear more directly on the sense of Friedemann's forms—namely, texture, thematic diversity, and tempo. In these factors can be found the best bases for differentiating his first-, second-, and third-movement types.

Friedemann's first movements, especially those in the earlier keyboard sonatas, are characterized above all by their *empfindsam* style, the one trait throughout his music that has most interested the explorers—at least, the ones not too busy hunting out embryonic "sonata forms." In Friedemann's music the *empfindsam* style is still a deeply intimate, sensitive, subjective style, full of sentiment without a trace of sentimentality.[110] Its effect is one of extreme, almost nervous volatility, like that of the mercurial facial expressions made by a highly sensitive actor. To play such music the performer must be able and willing to follow every inflection, every surprise, every pause, yet maintain a sense of continuity. At most this continuity can hardly approach his ideal of unperturbed Classic fluency But, as Forkel remarked, "when performed with delicacy, as he himself [Friedemann] performed them, they [his pieces] cannot fail to enchant every connoisseur."[111]

In the more scientific language of texture, thematic diversity, and tempo, Friedemann's *empfindsam* style includes the most familiar *galant* mannerisms—the fragmentary ideas and the frequent rests, triplets, and ornaments (F. 8/i/1-10). But it is a style of obviously greater depth, owing mainly to more three- than two-part writing, more use of imitation, richer harmonies, a greater profusion of ideas, and a greater elasticity in the rhythmic flow. One begins to realize that those who—to recall Forkel—could not play "Sonata I" probably could not understand it either, for the difficulties are as much of an inner as of an outer nature. The texture in this work is as hard to grasp mentally as physically. In Ex. 64 there are not only the double-notes to contend with, but the several measures of canon, the rhythmic disposition of the ornaments, the oblique harmonies that result when dissonances resolve into dissonances, and a typical appoggiatura that starts with the E♯ suspended on a weak beat and resolves upward to a ii_6 (in A) never quite completed.

It would require too long a quotation to illustrate the part that thematic diversity can play in Friedemann's *empfindsam* style. However, a reader with the score in hand can see how organically this composer's ideas may unfold from one into the next. For example, in the first Sonata in C/i (F. 1A), after the opening idea is stated and confirmed an octave lower (mss. 1-6), a one-measure pattern is derived (ms. 7), which is extended into a two-measure unit (mss. 8-9) that repeats in sequence (mss. 10-11); another one-measure pattern (ms. 12) derives from the basic syncopation (ms. 2) in the opening

110. Cf. the discussion of *Empfindsamkeit* in Lang/WESTERN 585-591, which remains one of the most helpful in any language; cf., also, Bücken/ROKOKO 94-96; Hoffmann-Erbrecht/STURM.

111. BACH READER 333.

Ex. 64. From the first movement of Wilhelm Friedemann Bach's Sonata in D (F. 3; after the original ed. at the British Museum).

idea (starting what would have to be the "second theme" if a literal "sonata form" is to be heard in this movement); this new pattern changes slightly in each of the next two measures (13 and 14), the change itself becomes the pattern (from ms. 15), and so on. As for that other factor mentioned in Friedemann's style, elasticity of tempo is achieved both by *fermate* (F. 5/i/5) and actual changes of pace (F. 9/iii/5, etc.). One only wishes that Friedemann had given some clues as to the delicate accelerandos and ritardandos that must also associate with this style and that could help to clarify its expressive force. But he left neither these nor dynamic markings except for a few alternations of "piano" and "forte" in a late slow movement that is less concerned with the *empfindsam* style (F. 4/ii).

In other first movements by Friedemann, especially the later ones, and in most of his slow movements and finales, whether early or late, the treatment is more intensive than extensive—that is, concentration on a single motive tends to replace the organic unfolding of changing ideas. Consequently, in the slow movements, where we might expect the most extreme uses of the *empfindsam* style (as often in Emanuel Bach's sonatas), the expressive flow is single-purposed, direct, steady, and sustained, almost concealing the amount of polyphonic activity in the texture (Ex. 65; cf., also, F. 5/ii [SCE VI, with ex.] and F. 9/ii). In the fast movements this concentration frequently lapses into mere arpeggiations, producing passage work that sometimes seems elephantine (F. 5/iii/28-32) by comparison with Christian Bach's, yet becomes more fluent in the later sonatas (F. 2/i). Other fast movements stick

Ex. 65. From the second movement of Wilhelm Friedemann Bach's "Sonata a 2 Flauti" in E♭ (F. 55; after Walther/ BACH-m I 16, but without the editorial additions).

closer to the initial motive, such as the hearty quasi-gigue finale of the fine keyboard Sonata in G, which achieves variety, among other ways, in delightfully persistent syncopations (F. 7/iii/50-53, etc.).

It becomes evident that "sonata form" can be read or not read into Friedemann's movements almost as one pleases. All the essentials except a true "development" can be found in the early keyboard Sonata in E♭ (F. 5/i), and even that can be found in another sonata. (F. 6A/iii/33-75). But surely in the former those essentials are obscured by the *empfindsam* preoccupations en route. Reprises do occur in most of the movements, slow as well as fast. In the slow movement of the

Sonata in E♭ (F. 5/ii) the reprise is very subtle because the departure is only a tonal one (ms. 16) and the return occurs in the subdominant key. In other movements there is a superfluity of returns in terms of "sonata form," though not quite giving the sense of rondo form. Thus, in one movement (F. 4/iii) the initial idea returns in the dominant at the double-bar, as usual; then soon after in the tonic, as was also common in this period; then in more fragmentary transpositions by way of development; and finally in the tonic again (ms. 72). The initial idea is generally pregnant enough in itself to produce a "sonata form," what with its syncopations, leaps, and almost spasmodic patterns.[112] Some movements also have one or more contrasting ideas, however slightly they may stand out from the context (F. 8/i/9 and 53, in the dominant and supertonic keys). Others restate the initial idea in the related key (F. 3/i/15). And, as a significant indication of how little Friedemann felt the need for such things, both of the later keyboard sonatas (F. 2 and 4) abandon all use of contrasting ideas other than closing figures. Somewhat more regular phrase grouping does occur in the later sonatas, but only in the minuets are the phrases consistently square, and even in them the squareness is hidden by overlapping imitations or strict canon (F. 1A/ii/both "Minuetto I" and "Minuetto II").

As for Friedemann's historical place, one would have to distinguish between influences and values. The influences would be hard to demonstrate, since he wrote relatively little and published such a small proportion even of that little. His organ playing was highly praised in his day,[113] but not his compositions. Falck sees a direct line of influence from Friedemann to Müthel, to Emanuel Bach, to Friedemann's pupil F. W. Rust, to Beethoven, by-passing Haydn and Mozart.[114] This tenuous artistic genealogy may be wrong at the very start. Emanuel, not quite four years younger and more independent than Friedemann, was fourteen years ahead of him with his first publication (W. 111, 1731). Eventually Emanuel was represented in seven of the twelve volumes in Anth. HAFFNER OM-m, Friedemann in none. It is even possible that Friedemann's "Sei Sonate" were not all completed when "Sonata I" appeared in 1745, and that a somewhat mollified *empfindsam* style to be noted in the last four of these sonatas reflects the reverse influence of Emanuel if not

112. For an analysis of the ideas in Friedemann's keyboard sons., cf. Hoffmann-Erbrecht/KLAVIERMUSIK 112-116, with exx.

113. Cf. Schubart/IDEEN 89-90 ("Unquestionably the greatest organist in the world!"); also, Forkel in BACH READER 312-313.

114. Falck/BACH 81. But in Nys/MOZART a brief is built up for influences of Friedemann on Mozart quite contrary to more traditional views (as in Einstein/MOZART 117 and 119).

some pointed comments by Sebastian himself. In his canonic and fugal writing, his wealth of harmony, and his introspective slow movements, Friedemann was still very much the son of his father, the same who had provided for him the *Klavierbüchlein* (with its inventions and its preludes from *The Well-Tempered Clavier*) as well as the six organ sonatas.[115] Writers have suggested that the tragedy of Friedemann's unhappy life was to have been born in the transitional period between great giants of music at either end.[116] Undoubtedly he was too close to his father for his own complete independence. Yet others—Stamitz or Galuppi, for example—succeeded, each in his own way, about the same time and in the face of similar style problems. On the other hand, if it is the value that is questioned, there are those who would say that Friedemann was more successful; at least those susceptible to what Riemann called his "Sinnigkeit und Innigkeit"[117]—for example, the pre-Schumannesque Romanticism that is found in the opening of his keyboard Sonata in G (F. 7). The cultivated musician who chooses the esoteric, precious music of Friedemann in place of the lighter, more popular, standardized music of Christian, is akin to the literate who choses Sterne's *Sentimental Journey* or one of Klopstock's followers in place of the more pedestrian writings of a C. F. Nicolai.

Christlieb Siegmund Binder (1723-89) spent his whole life in Dresden.[118] Although he started his career by playing the Pantaleon under Hebenstreit's tutelage, he is remembered as the chief keyboard player and composer in Dresden around 1760,[119] in the generation that followed Friedemann Bach's thirteen years there and overlapped the reigns of Friedrich August II and III. Several contemporary reports, including one by Burney, attest to his skill as organist and cembalist.[120] Binder left at least twenty-eight cembalo sonatas in the two decades from about 1756-76. These include a printed set of six, "Op. I" (1759), and four others published in contemporary anthologies.[121] He also left SS/bass "trios" and other "trios" in J. S. Bach's sense of two parts for the keyboard and one for a high orchestral instrument,

115. Cf. Forkel in BACH READER 331 and 446.
116. E.g., cf. Blume in MGG I 1054.
117. Riemann/SÖHNE 179.
118. Fleischer/BINDER is a diss. (1940) on the man and his instrumental music, with many exx. and an annotated thematic index. Cf., also, MGG I 1857-1858 (Hausswald).
119. Cf. Engländer/DRESDNER 109-111.
120. Cf. Fleischer/BINDER 25-27; BURNEY'S TOURS II 147-149.
121. There are 2 sons. in Anth. HAFFNER OM-m VIII/2 and X/1 (1761 and '64), one in Anth. HILL LESSONS-m no. 1, and one in Anth. MAGAZIN-m. The keyboard sons. are discussed (almost entirely for traits of "sonata form") in Fleischer/BINDER 29-71, with many exx. For mod. eds., cf. MGG I 1858.

including a set published in 1763 (K & Fl-or-Vl) both as "Sechs Trios" and "Sei Sonate."[122]

In nearly all of Binder's sonatas the number and order of movements are the same that we have met most often in Germany—three, F-S-F or F-S-M (minuet or "rondeau"). However, a dance, polonaise or minuet, is added to the F-S-F cycle in each of the six sonatas that comprise his earliest set (*ca.* 1756). There are free sections in other sonatas that might be construed as added movements, too (e.g., the "Moderato" introduction and interludes in Anth. HAFFNER OM-m VIII/2/i). Binary design with repeated halves is present in almost every movement. But in all these movements the music keeps flowing on so uninterruptedly, as though in a constant state of development, that any further talk of "sonata form" or other sectional designs must be largely academic. Perhaps it is a sense of the almost inescapable garrulity in this process that lies behind the slightly backhanded compliment by which J. A. Hiller of Leipzig began a laudatory statement in 1768: "Mr. Binder in Dresden is to be praised not only for the quantity but for the quality of his works. Melody, invention, and an extraordinary degree of feeling are found throughout. His things appear to be written especially for the harpsichord ["Clavicimbel"], on which they also sound best."[123]

Placed beside that of his more significant contemporaries, the content of Binder's music does not seem to be more overvalued by Hiller than is the rule in most contemporary statements. But it is principally its style that is interesting now, even though (or because) it is off the main line leading to the Classic style. To keep the flow going so continuously Binder variously employs sequence, motivic reiteration, and melodic evolution. If the result does prove to seem garrulous it is at least made more attractive at best (as in Son. 1/i of the 1759 set) by rather wide-ranging, equally continuous modulations. At times we have an "endless melody" a century in advance of Wagner's. At other times there are breaks created by suspensive cadences. There is never quite the concentration, depth, metric irregularity, or volatility that we found in Friedemann Bach's *empfindsam* style. But there is more harmonic depth and metric pliancy than one expects to find in the *galant* style, the chief mannerisms of which are present here, too. The sharp dynamic contrasts that are called for in most of the slow movements are the main hints of the *Empfindsamkeit*. In these move-

122. Cf. Fleischer/BINDER 166-167, 71-76. Mod. ed.: MS Trio in G, HORTUS MUSICUS-m No. 62 (Hausswald).

123. Quoted in Fleischer/BINDER 27.

ments imitations often occur in the bass. Otherwise the bass part is of the simplest, not often being the Alberti type.

It is interesting to find the same continuous style in a two-movement sonata (M-F) by another, more obscure Dresden cembalist of the same period, **Constantin Joseph Weber** (?-*ca.* 1764).[124] Again the source is Anth. HAFFNER OM-m (X/6, 1764, the same year that Haffner also published six cembalo sons., Op. 1, by Weber). The sonata in question is more fluent, songful, and resourceful in its use of the keyboard than any by Binder examined here.

124. He is not mentioned in Engländer/DRESDNER. Cf. Gerber/LEXICON II 770; Eitner/QL X 190.

Chapter XIII

North Germany From About 1735 to 1780

From Burgsteinfurt to Braunschweig (Friedrich Bach)

Leaving central Germany, we may approach Berlin geographically by first taking brief note of a few composers spread from west to east across the southern strip of north Germany. All of these composers are now obscure but Friedrich Bach. Near the western border, at about the same latitude as Berlin, the Bentheim-Steinfurt court in Burgsteinfurt was the site of much activity in chamber music and much interest in Mannheim composers during the reign (1750-80) of Graf Karl Paul Ernst, and again during his son's reign (1780-1817). One of the most productive composers on the scene was the pianist **Johann Friedrich Klöffler** (1725-90), who published many symphonies, concertos, and chamber works in the period from 1767 to 1788.[1] These 1a
include one set of six sonatas for two flutes and *b.c.,* Op. 5, and another of six sonatas, Op. 6, "pour le Clavecin," both published by Hummel in Amsterdam about 1770 (plate nos. 305 and 314).[2] The quantity and 2a
success alone of Klöffler's publications warrant the study that was recently reported to be under way.

In Bückeburg seventy miles to the east, music reached a peak at court during the reign (1748-77) of the highly artistic and intellectual Graf Wilhelm.[3] That the court's predilection was for Italian music is evidenced by the number of Italian works performed and the employment of Italian musicians. One of these last was **Giovanni Battista Serini,** a composer about whom almost nothing is known except that he came from Cremona and that he left Bückeburg at the start of the Seven Years' War in 1756.[4] Besides a quantity of choral and other 4a

1. Cf. MGG VII 1234-1237 (Neumann), with mention of a Münster diss. in progress (as of 1958, by U. Götze) and further literature, but no mod. eds.
2. Cf. BRITISH UNION I 573 (with later dates, but 1770 derives from Deutsch/NUMBERS 15). The title page of Op. 5 is reproduced in MGG VII 1235.
3. Cf. Schünemann/BACH 47-50, 52; MGG II 427-428 (Schramm).
4. Cf. Eitner/QL IX 143-144; Schmidl/DIZIONARIO II 498; Schünemann/BACH 52-54.

instrumental music Serini left several keyboard sonatas, of which three
5a were published in Haffner's Italian anthology between 1756 and 1759.[5] The latter are not pretentious works, but they are appealing, well-conceived, and varied enough to represent a near compendium of current styles and forms. The seeker of "sonata form" will find a clear contrasting theme (1/i/12), a recurrence of the opening theme as a "contrasting" theme in the dominant key (2/i/17), a well projected reprise (2/iii/77), a reprise that begins only with the contrasting idea (3/i/78), and a real "development" (3/i/43-77), though not all in the same movement. The seeker after other forms will find a slow binary movement without repeats (1/ii) and a fast one with repeats (3/iii), a quasi-minuet with trio (1/iii), a quasi-rondo (1/iv), a quasi-gigue (2/iii),[6] and a lively, effective "Fuga." And the student of styles can enjoy everything from the most typical *galant* mannerisms (3/iii) and some athletic sweeps over the keyboard (3/i) to the stricter writing of the "Fuga" and the close imitations in an expressive slow movement (2/ii).

The best known name at the Bückeburg court in the eighteenth century is, of course, that of the "Bückeburg Bach," ninth son of J. S. Bach, younger half brother of Friedemann and Emanuel, older brother of Christian, and third of the five Bachs to be met in the present volume **Johann Christoph Friedrich Bach** (1732-95) planned to study law in Leipzig after the thorough musical training that he received from his father and his distant cousin Johann Elias Bach, but he could not pass up the desirable job as chamber musician in Bückeburg that came to
7a him in 1750, perhaps through Emanuel's good offices.[7] There he remained to the end of his life, in the exceptionally congenial environment created by warmly receptive patrons and stimulating associates (including the writer Herder from 1771-76), and with scarcely more absence than a trip with his son W. F. E. Bach to visit Emanuel in Hamburg and Christian in London in 1778. Only in his later life was the strong interest in Italian music at the Bückeburg court substantially intermixed with performances of music by Gluck, Haydn, the Mannheim composers, and other Germans.

Friedrich's large output includes oratorios, cantatas, songs, and further vocal music; symphonies, concertos, and at least forty sonatas, dating from about 1763 to 1791, among numerous chamber and key-

5. Anth. HAFFNER RACCOLTA-m I/6, II/6, and III/6. Mod. ed.: all 3 sons., Benvenuti/CEMBALISTI-m 120.

6. Cf. Danckert/GIGUE 137-138, with ex.

7. The primary study of the man and his music is Schünemann/BACH, with further biographic information in Hey/BACH. Cf., also, MGG I 956-960 (Benecke); Geiringer/BACH 378-403; GROVE I 327-328 (Terry); Reeser/SONS 44-52.

board works.[8] Included in the extant keyboard works are five solo sonatas and one sonatina published separately in contemporary anthologies (1770, 1787, and 1788),[9] two sets, respectively, of six and three "leichte Sonaten fürs Clavier oder Piano-Forte" (1785 and 1789), and two sonatas for four hands at one keyboard (1786 and 1791). Among the extant chamber works, mostly in MSS and contemporary anthologies, are three SS/bass sonatas (1763, 1768, and 1769),[10] four accompanied sonatas for cembalo or piano and two other instruments (Vn & Vc-or-Va-or-Fl), three accompanied sonatas for cembalo or piano and one other instrument (Vn-or-Fl; H.W. IX/3 is dated 1787) plus six more in a set published in Riga in 1777,[11] and two sonatas for cello and *b.c.* (H.W. X/3 was published in Hamburg in 1770).

Friedrich was another sonata composer who almost always used the three-movement cycle in the order F-S-F in his sonatas.[12] His outer movements fall into no one design beyond the usual division into two repeated "halves." In his earlier sonatas of about 1770 clear "sonata form" was but one of the designs he chanced upon (e.g., H.W. XI/2/i). The main ideas in these outer movements are less interesting as melodic entities in their own right than as harborers of the kind of germ cells that Beethoven was able to enlarge upon so fruitfully (Ex. 66). Friedrich keeps track of his ideas but seldom works them in any intense fashion in the "development" sections themselves. Nevertheless, through purposeful modulations and some unexpected harmonic twists he generates his most heated passages in those rather long sections (H.W. XI 1/i). The slow movements have more sustained melodic interest than the outer movements, and more of the *empfindsam* spirit that pervaded the current thinking and writing at Bückeburg much as elsewhere in central and northern Germany.[13] They offer more poetry, contrast, climax, and harmonic color than the outer movements, a lovely example being the "Andante innocentamente" in the keyboard Sonata in F dated 1770 (H.W. XI/1/ii).

Friedrich's keyboard writing is patently based on much experience

8. Schünemann published a thematic index of Friedrich's works in DDT-m LVI ix-xvii. But the sons. are referred to here by the numbering in the new list (abbreviated H.W.) in Wohlfarth/BACH (1960), which corrects and augments Schünemann's index, specifying works lost in World War II, present locations, mod. eds., and new finds reported in Geiringer/BÜCKEBURGER.

9. Among mod. eds. not in Wohlfarth/BACH: 4 Sons. in F, C, G, and F (H.W. XI/1, 2, 5, 6), TRÉSOR-m XVII 2, 12, 28, and 36.

10. A "Quartetto" in C for Fl, Vl, Va, and *b.c.* (H.W. VI/3) is reprinted as "Sonata in C" in Geiringer/BACH-m 192.

11. H.W. VIII/3; the only known copy is at the Library of Congress.

12. The sons. are discussed chiefly though only briefly in Schünemann/BACH 122-124 and Geiringer/BACH 386-392, both with exx. A fuller study is needed.

13. Cf. Geiringer/BACH 381-383.

Ex. 66. From the opening of Sonata in C (H. W. XI/2) by Johann Christoph Friedrich Bach (after TRÉSOR-m XVII 12).

at the keyboard (H.W. XI/1/iii), although it never quite challenges the player enough to reinforce the contemporary statement that his "playing knew almost no further difficulties" or Friedemann's assertion that Friedrich was the strongest player among the brothers and the best versed in the performance of their father's music.[14] The texture often consists of 3ds or 6ths in the right hand over single notes in the left (rather than an Alberti or other chordal bass), thus is usually not thin enough for the freest uses of the keyboard. Nor does it ever require the filling out by the performer that so much other keyboard music of the time seems to need. Just as Friedrich straddled the Italian and German styles at court, so he straddled the techniques of Baroque and Classic writing. The same transitional position is seen, too, in the familiar *galant* mannerisms and in details drawn from Emanuel, such as the trilled turn; and it is seen in Friedrich's unbridled phrase structures, which usually start as though a square phrase were the object, but extend several more measures through the most supple applications of meter and harmony (recall Ex. 66). To be sure, the foregoing remarks apply primarily to his earlier sonatas. The sonatas he wrote after his visit to Christian and after he brought back the "englisches Pianoforte" that pleased him so much,[15] are not yet quite so fluent and light as the sonatas Christian had already composed. But even those sonatas not called "leicht" are now shorter, sparer, more efficient and regularized,

14. Cf. MGG I 959.
15. Cf. Reeser/SONS 48-51 for exx. and contemporary statements.

more objective, more frankly directed toward pedagogic use, and, for all these reasons, of somewhat less musical and historical distinction. The finale in these later sonatas is usually a minuet or tuneful rondo.

Although only three sons of J. S. Bach—Friedemann, Emanuel, and Christian—are usually singled out for special attention, Friedrich was no poor fourth in either the quality or appeal of his music. In one noteworthy respect he was ahead of most of his contemporaries, and that is the equal share he gives to the one or more orchestral instruments in his "accompanied" sonatas. The six sonatas in the set of 1777 for keyboard and flute or violin are true duos and not merely accompanied keyboard solos or the older three-part writing such as we found in Johann Ernst Bach's "accompanied" sonatas (SCE XII). In the set of 1777 the keyboard always takes the lead at the start, but the violin soon answers it or interchanges themes with it, and elsewhere is itself the first to state the theme (as in No. 1/iii, which, like the other finales, is a minuet with subdominant trio). Similarly the sonatas for keyboard with one high and one low instrument reveal the various oppositions of instruments to be found in the true piano trio (Ex. 67), and not merely the sort that Haydn wrote, in which the cello doubles the keyboard bass.

Braunschweig (or Brunswick), sixty miles east of Bückeburg and one of Germany's oldest music centers, was the site of brilliant court opera productions throughout the seventeenth and eighteenth centuries, influenced partly by close ties with similar productions in Hamburg and Berlin.[16] In the later eighteenth century the court music was supplemented, significantly for instrumental music, by the college students and townspeople who shared in the public concerts (from 1746) of the Collegium Carolineum. Friedemann Bach was among the visiting performers (from 1773). The minor poet **Justus Friedrich Wilhelm Zachariae** (1726-77), another of our numerous law students in Leipzig and a follower of Gottsched, only began to devote himself seriously to music at the age of twenty-five.[17] While he was a member of the Carolineum a Sonata in C by him was published in Anth. HAFFNER OM-m XI/6 (1765). More properly a sonatina in length, technical range, and musical scope, this is an attractive, melodious, clearly phrased work in three movements (F-S-"Minuetto I" and "II").

Another composer close to the activities of the Carolineum was the highly esteemed clavierist **Friedrich Gottlob Fleischer** (1722-1806), who had trained in Leipzig, perhaps under J. S. Bach's pupil and suc-

16. Cf. MGG II 231-237 and 241 (Sievers), with further bibliography.
17. Cf. Eitner/QL X 318-319.

(Allegro)
Violin
Viola
Cembalo
or
Piano

Ex. 67. From the first movement of Johann Christoph Friedrich Bach's "Sonata II per il Cembalo ô Piano-Forte, Violino e Viola" (H.W. VII/5; after the mod. ed., Schünemann/BACH-m).

cessor J. F. Doles.[18] Five keyboard sonatas are known by Fleischer, of which the first was published in 1745, by "Weigl jr." in Nürnberg, with the charming and revealing title, *Clavier-Übung: Erste Partie bestehend in einer nach heutigem galanten Gusto wohl ausgearbeiteten Sonata.*[19] The other four sonatas are the first items in the second edition, "about twice as large," that was published in Braunschweig in 1769 of a collection of minuets, polonaises, and other keyboard pieces originally issued in 1762.[20] These four sonatas suggest Italian influences, whether in the two-movement plan of the "Un poco andante" and the "Rondeau, vivace" that comprise Sonata 1, or in the typical complex of couplets, repeat signs, and *da capo* indications by which this "Rondeau" and the quasi-rondo finale of Sonata 4 are abbreviated, or, especially, in the Classic feel of the full-length, songful themes and the broad sense of direction that they impart, unobstructed by the poetizing of the *Empfindsamkeit.* The skillful keyboard writing bears out Fleischer's reputation as a fine clavierist although it poses no unusual problems. Today's young pianists would enjoy and profit from a chance to train on his forgotten pieces.

One other composer in Braunschweig was **Johann Gottfried Schwanenberger** (1740-1804), *Hofkapellmeister* from 1762, a man

18. Cf. MGG IV 300 (Sievers); BURNEY'S TOURS II 237; Schubart/IDEEN 159-160; Gerber/LEXICON I 419.

19. Listed in Cat. BRUXELLES II 308 (the wording is incorrect in MGG IV 300).

20. The first ed. is listed in Cat. BRUXELLES II 308, the 2d in BRITISH UNION I 339.

concerned chiefly with opera, but also an "extremely neat and accomplished keyboardist."[21] Nearly two dozen solo keyboard sonatas and three SS/bass sonatas (1767) by this onetime student of Hasse were found by Eitner in various MSS.[22] One of the keyboard sonatas may be seen readily enough, since it crept into Karl Päsler's edition (1918) of Haydn's sonatas.[23] Rudolph Steglich has shown with fairly convincing evidence that this three-movement Sonata in B♭ (F-S-F) originated as Sonata 6 in an undated MS copy entitled "VIII Sonate per cembalo di Giov. Schwanberg [*sic*],"[24] and that it may have been deliberately modeled, at least in its opening, after a sonata in the same
24a key, Op. 17/6, by Christian Bach (1779). It is certainly less fluent than the latter's sonatas and more fluent but less original, concentrated, or fresh than the average of Haydn's earlier sonatas.

Emanuel Bach in Berlin

In Berlin[25] we come to a center matched in the quality and surpassed in the quantity of its sonata composers only by Vienna, London, and Paris during the Classic Era. As always, the extent of the activity is explained not only by the composers but by the patrons, opportunities, and incentive provided in the particular locale. The patron of patrons in Berlin was, of course, Frederick II ("the Great"), who indulged his musical interests especially from the start of his reign in 1740 up to the interruptions created from 1756 on by the Seven Years' War, although some of the former musical life was continued or resumed during the remainder of his long reign (to 1786).[26] In our previous volume we had an opportunity to notice his own musicianly though circumscribed flute sonatas, as well as the sonatas of his celebrated flute teacher Quantz and of the Graun brothers (SBE 297-300). Other contemporary and slightly younger composers in that same sphere of Frederick the Great were deferred to the present volume mainly because they con-

21. According to Reichardt (Schletterer/REICHARDT 153-154).

22. Eitner/QL IX 104-105 (with errors). The incipits of 3 MS keyboard sons. appear in Cat. SCHWERIN 224-225.

23. Haydn/WERKE-m XIV/1 no. 17.

24. MS 20509/3 in the former Berlin Staatsbibliothek. Cf. Steglich/SCHWANENBERGER, with ex. The work is still present in Hoboken/HAYDN I 746-747, annotated by what seems here to be insufficient acknowledgment of Steglich's arguments.

25. Cf. MGG I 1708-1714 and 1743-1745 (Sasse), with further bibliography. A full study of 18th-century music in Berlin has yet to be done. Pertinent here are 2 diss., Hoffmann/TRIOSONATE (1927) and Stilz/BERLINER (1930; on the keyboard son. except for chief names like Emanuel Bach).

26. A new survey of "music at the court of Frederick the Great" is provided in Helm/FREDERICK. Included are accounts of several of the figures to be mentioned here, with some references to and exx. of their sons. as well as other music.

tributed primarily, though not entirely, to the more progressive idiom of the solo and accompanied keyboard sonata rather than to the more traditional, melo/bass types. But all of these composers were subject to the same peculiar, unvarying concert regimen and restricted tastes of the king (who found little interest either in church music or the *Empfindsamkeit,* for example); and all lived in the same milieu of predominantly Italianate opera at court, of a well staffed orchestra in the king's new chapel, of learned music theorists like Agricola, Marpurg, and Kirnberger (all steeped in Mattheson's treatises), of renowned writers and intellectuals like Lessing, C. F. Nicolai, and Moses Mendelssohn, and of growing musical activities among the townspeople. These activities included the new Berlin *Liederschule* (from the 1750's) as well as a modest start toward amateur chamber or orchestral music organizations and public concerts (such as J. G. Janitsch's "Friday Academy," from 1740; C. F. Schale's "Monday Assembly," from 1752; and J. F. Agricola's "Saturday Concerts," from 1770).[27]

The most notable sonata composer in the Berlin of Frederick the Great was also the composer who, since the 1840's, has been given more credit than any other for the "perfection" of the pre-Classic sonata, **Carl Philipp Emanuel Bach** (1714-88).[28] As J. S. Bach's second surviving son, Emanuel was born three years before his family moved from Weimar to Köthen and nine before they settled in Leipzig. "In composition and keyboard playing I have never had any other teacher than my father," he wrote in his eleven-page "Autobiography" (supplied for the edition of Burney's *Travels* that was published in German in 1773[29]). After three years of university training 29a
in law and philosophy in Leipzig (1731-34) and four more in Frankfurt/O (1734-38), he became informally attached in 1738 to Crown Prince Frederick's court in Rheinsberg (45 miles northwest of Berlin). Then, in 1740, when the 28-year-old Frederick succeeded his father as the new Prussian King, the 26-year-old Emanuel became officially attached to the Berlin court as first cembalist. He stayed there for 28 years, accompanying the king's almost nightly recitals at the Sans-Souci

27. Recall the lengthy, vivid account of music in Berlin in BURNEY'S TOURS II 158-207. The glories of the Berlin composers are "sung" and poetized in Reichardt/BERLIN, partly in reply to Burney's "one-sided" report (Schletterer/REICHARDT 140). Cf., also, MGG VI 1704 (Becker).

28. E.g., cf. Becker/HAUSMUSIK 39 (1840); Faisst/CLAVIERSONATE 83-85 (1845). If read with caution, Bitter/BRÜDER (1868) is still a valuable source on Emanuel. Recent summary accounts of the man and his music, each somewhat different, include MGG I 924-942 (Schmid); Reeser/SONS 24-43; GROVE I 324-327 (Terry); Geiringer/BACH 336-377.

29. Kahl/SELBSTBIOGRAPHIEN 34; besides this facs. and some incomplete reprints (e.g., Nohl/BRIEFE 59-62), a partial English trans. is in Wallace/LETTERS 51-56; in Burney/HISTORY II 955 is a summary in one efficient paragraph.

Palace in near-by Potsdam, especially in the earlier years, and teaching in high Berlin society. Not until 1767 could he break away from what became an increasingly constrictive routine for him, aggravated by pointed regal disinterest in his music and too little outlet for it. In 1768 he succeeded the late Telemann at a more congenial post in Hamburg, where during his last 20 years he thrived spiritually and financially under heavy church assignments not unlike his father's in Leipzig.[30] He also played, composed, taught, consorted with some of the most prominent intellectuals of his day, as he had in Berlin, and corresponded with an ever-widening circle of national and international associates, who were drawn to him chiefly by his publications. These publications included not only more than a half of his sonatas but one of the most influential of 18th-century treatises, his *Essay on the True Art of Playing Keyboard Instruments,*[31] the two volumes of which first appeared in 1753 and 1762.

Two bibliographic tools dating back to Emanuel Bach's own time are the starting points for any full study of his music. One of these is (to translate) the "Catalogue of the Musical Estate Left By the Late Capellmeister Carl Philipp Emanuel Bach," published in Hamburg in 1790 and valuable especially for the composition and revision dates of most of his instrumental works as well as a partial thematic index of those left in MS.[32] The other is the careful, comprehensive thematic index prepared in MS by Emanuel's devoted follower in Hamburg, J. J. H. Westphal (died in 1825, not 1835), who is reported to have worked on it with Emanuel himself and whose almost complete collection of Emanuel's music passed through Fétis to the Bibliothèque du Conservatoire royal in Brussels.[33] With only minor changes Wotquenne published this index in 1905, though apparently not in cognizance of
34a the 1790 catalogue.[34] Except for the MSS, Wotquenne usually gives only publication dates, which often differ considerably, in both time and order, from the composition dates. Also to be noted are two more recent lists of the sonatas or closely related types, one for the chamber

30. Recall Burney's well-known, firsthand report of his meetings with Emanuel while he visited Hamburg in 1772, in BURNEY'S TOURS 211-212, 213-214, 215-221.

31. Bach/ESSAY, ably trans. into English by W. J. Mitchell, includes a helpful, pertinent "Introduction."

32. Reprinted in full and annotated in Miesner/NACHLASS (with Emanuel's instrumental works in the first installment). The chronologies and overviews prepared largely from the original catalogue in Bitter/BRÜDER I 36-42, 196-201, and II 91-94, 325-344 give a useful perspective in spite of errors and omissions.

33. Cf. Eitner/QL X 245 (with errors); Bitter/BRÜDER II 342-344; Schmid/BACH vii; Miesner/NACHLASS (BJ XXXV) 103; MGG I 930; Cat. BRUXELLES, *passim;* BRITISH UNION I 71-74 (for further rich holdings). Valuable MSS of Emanuel's music are also to be found in the Library of Congress.

34. Wotquenne/BACH, abbreviated to W. here for music references.

and the other for the keyboard works, including sources, concordances with the foregoing lists, corrections and new finds (16 keyboard sons. not in Wotquenne!), and (many) modern editions. These two lists come at the end of two dissertations, important to us here, on the chamber and keyboard sonatas, respectively.[35] 35a

A survey of Wotquenne's index readily indicates the extent and diversity of Emanuel's music. Among over 900 items are some 345 keyboard works, 75 concertos, 125 chamber works, 20 symphonies, 290 sacred and secular songs, and 50 choral works.[36] There are around 265 sonatas or sonatinas, touching every main instrumental category and including about 170 for stringed keyboard solo,[37] 7 for organ, one for harp, 29 in "accompanied" settings (K & 1 or 2 other instruments), 15 in solo/bass settings, 22 in duo/bass settings, 3 in the class of unaccompanied duets (SS alone), 12 in the class of miniature concertos, and 6 in the class of wind ensembles. A summary listing of the sonatas follows, with Wotquenne numbers and such dates, places, and other bibliographic information as are essential to the ensuing discussion. Only the original composition dates (not the revision dates) and only the first of up to four 18th-century editions are given. Also, only the main modern editions are given and only those for the ensemble sonatas that are not already in Schmid/BACH, Altmann/KAMMERMUSIK, or MGG. The arrangement is by scoring types and only partly by order of composition. The ensemble works raise problems of conflicting terminology, especially Emanuel's 37 melo/bass works. "Solo" or "sonata" is used as the title for the 15 S/bass works (W. 123-131, 133-138) and "trio," "sonata," or "sinfonia" for the 22 duo/bass works (W. 143-160, 161/1 and 2, 162, 163). Thus, the duo/bass work labeled "Sinfonia" on the autograph score (W. 156) is called "Sonata o vero Sinfonia" on its title page.[38] Furthermore, a group of Emanuel's symphonies were

35. Schmid/BACH 161-176 (1931; fundamental) and Beurmann/BACH 118-148 (1952). The latter, which is unpublished, is summarized in Wyler/BACH 25-27; it includes discussions of bibliography (both books and music, pp. 6-16), of the over-all and separate forms (pp. 17-36), and of related contemporary problems. The chronological list at the end of the diss. of Canave/BACH (1956; cf. Newman/CANAVE) derives largely from Beurmann. Mod. eds. are also listed in MGG I 939-941 (up to 1949) and GROVE I 326 (selected keyboard eds. only), the largest number of the keyboard sons. being in TRÉSOR-m I, II, III, VI, VII, VIII, XI, XIII (65 sons.); NAGELS-m Nos. 6 and 15, 21-22, 65, 90 (24 sons.); and Krebs/BACH-m (18 sons.). But a *Gesamtausgabe* is still sorely needed.

36. Compounded from the totals given in Geiringer/BACH-m 129-130.

37. The chronological "Sonatenkatalog" in Beurmann/BACH lists 146 keyboard sonatas (nos. 1-16 in the Leipzig-Frankfurt/O period, nos. 17-127 in the Berlin period, and nos. 128-146 in the Hamburg period) plus 15 more that may or may not be authentic; differences in classification account for about 10 others in the present figure of "about 170."

38. A photograph of this title page is in Schmid/BACH 112.

transcribed for harpsichord as "sonatas," in English editions.[39] A few duplications occur in this list when the same work exists in different scorings (as with the acc'd. sons. W. 92).

Emanuel Bach's Sonatas

6 "Prussian" sons. for cembalo (i.e., dedicated to the new Prussian
39a king); composed in 1740-42; Nürnberg: Schmid, 1742; the Haffner ed. no. 15 that is cited uncertainly in Eitner/QL I 284, Torrefranca/ORIGINI 76 (in a specious argument for Platti's priority), and MGG I 930 as being still earlier proves to be not this but the next set to be listed here; W. 48/1-6 (numbers are also given here to Wotquenne's unnumbered subitems). Cf. Bitter/BRÜDER I 51-54 for the title and dedication in the original Italian and in German trans., and for the publication of Son. 5 under J. S. Bach's name. Mod. ed.: all 6 sons. and preface, NAGELS-m Nos. 6 and 15 (Steglich); also, TRÉSOR-m I.

6 "Württemberg" sons. for cembalo (i.e., dedicated to his pupil at the Berlin court, Duke Carl Eugen of Württemberg), Op. 2; composed in 1742-44; Nürnberg: Haffner (plate no. 15; cf. HIRSCH MUSIKBIBLIOTHEK
39b III 13), 1744; W. 49/1-6. Cf. Bitter/BRÜDER I 54-56 for the title and dedication in the original Italian and in German trans. Mod. ed., complete, with preface: NAGELS-m Nos. 21-22 (Steglich); also, TRÉSOR-m I.

Achtzehn Probe-Stücken in sechs Sonaten (i.e., 18 demonstration pieces grouped into 6 three-mvt. sons.; recall Telemann's *6. Sonaten, in 18. melodischen Canons* [1738]), published as a suppl. to Vol. I of the *Essay*; Berlin: Winter, 1753; W. 63/1-6. Mod. ed.: Doflein/BACH-m; also, Sons. 2-6 (not 1-5), TRÉSOR-m II.

6 keyboard sons. "mit veränderten Reprisen" ("with altered reprises"), sometimes called the "Amalian" sonatas because of the dedication to Frederick's sister and Emanuel's patroness, Princess Amalia; composed in 1758-59; Berlin: Winter, 1760; W. 50/1-6. There is no complete mod. ed. of this important set; among single issues: Son. 1 in F, Fischer/SONATE-m
39c 22; Son. 5 in B♭, Herrmann/BACH-m no. 11.

"Fortsetzung" (i.e., another set) of 6 keyboard sons.; composed in 1750-60; Berlin: Winter, 1761; W. 51/1-6. Although "Fortsetzung" relates to the previous set of 1760, except for W. 51/5 neither this set of 1761 nor the next in 1763 actually continues with the "altered reprises," as might be construed from the listings in BRITISH UNION I 72-73 and else-
39d where. Mod. ed.: Son. 3 in c, Herrmann/BACH-m no. 8.

2d "Fortsetzung" of 6 keyboard sons.; composed in 1744-62; Berlin: Winter, 1763; W. 52/1-6. Mod. ed.: Son. 3 in g, Herrmann/BACH-m no. 10.

6 "leichte" keyboard sons.; composed in 1762-64; Leipzig: B. C.
39e Breitkopf, 1766; W. 53/1-6.

6 keyboard sons. "à l'usage des Dames," Op. 1; composed in 1765-66; Amsterdam: J. J. Hummel, 1770, W. 54/1-6.

39. Cf. BRITISH UNION I 73.

18 keyboard sons. in the 6 sets variously titled "für Kenner und Liebhaber" ("for connoisseurs and amateurs"), which include separate rondos in sets 2-6 and fantasias in sets 4-6; composed 1758-85; Leipzig: "im Verlag des Autors," 1779, '80, '81, '83, '85, and '87; W. 55/1-6; W. 56/2, 4, 6; W. 57/2, 4, 6; W. 58/2, 4; W. 59/1, 3; W. 61/2, 5. Mod. ed.: all 6 sets complete, Krebs/BACH-m (originally issued in 1895); also, 10 of these sons. are in TRÉSOR-m IV, VI, VII, and XI (cf. GROVE I 326). From sets 1 and 3 come all but one of the 6 sons. in the infamous Bülow ed., originally published in 1862 (W. 57/6 and 2; W. 55/4 and 6; W. 57/5; W. 49/2) and already censured in the 19th c. for its gross "enrichments" and "corrections" (Bitter/BRÜDER I 218-219; Shedlock/SONATA 96-100), although the choice of sons. is certainly outstanding.

6 "neue Sonatinen" for keyboard; composed in 1786; published as a further supplement to Vol. I of the *Essay* in its 4th (not 3d) ed.; Leipzig: Schwickert, 1787; W. 63/7-12. Mod. ed.: NAGELS-m 65 (Vrieslander), nos. 19-24.

"Una Sonata per il Cembalo"; composed in 1766; Leipzig: J. J. E. Breitkopf, 1786; W. 60. The date is based on Hase/BACH 101.

25 keyboard sons. published in various contemporary anthologies (including Anth. HAFFNER OM-m I/3, III/1, IV/2, V/2, IX/2, XI/1, XII/1), 1755-70; composed 1731-69; W. 62/1-24 and no. 7 in e in the sons. newly 39f
discovered in Beurmann/BACH 146-147. Among mod. eds.: 16 sons., TRÉSOR-m II, IV, VII (cf. GROVE I 326); W. 62/11, ORGANUM-m V No. 11; one son. from Anth. MANCHERLEY-m, cf. NOTES XVIII (1961) 484-485.

71 keyboard sons. left in various MSS, composed between 1731 and '86. These include a set of 6 sonatinas, composed in 1734 and revised in '44, W. 64/1-6 (mod. ed.: W. 64/1, Kreutz/BACH-m no. 1, with "Nachwort"); 50 sons., W. 65/1-50 (4 of which were actually published [cf. MGG I 930]; mod. eds.: 20 sons., TRÉSOR-m VI, VIII, XIII [cf. GROVE I 326]; W. 65/17, Newman/BACH-m no. 2); 16 sons. not in Wotquenne/BACH, but 15 are listed in Beurmann/BACH 146-147 (mod. ed.: Son. in E♭, Kreutz/BACH-m no. 2). P. Friedheim of Harpur College, N.Y., adds: A (pirated) ed. (Paris: Ceron, after 1752) includes W. 62/8; W. 65/10, 22, 13, 9, 18. 39g

One MS "Sonata per il Cembalo a due Tastature" (i.e., for a 2-manual harpsichord); composed in 1747; W. 69.

7 organ sons. in MS, 6 without and one with pedal; composed in 1755-58; W. 70/1-7; W. 70/1-2 published in contemporary anthologies; W. 70/1-6 published posthumously (1790; W. 265; cf. BACH READER suppl. in MQ XXXVI [1950] 509). Mod. eds.: W. 70/3, TRÉSOR-m XIII 483; W. 70/1-6, cf. MT CII (1961) 45.

One harp son. in MS; composed in 1762; W. 139.

10 acc'd. sons., K & Vn (W. 71, 75-78) or K & Fl (W. 83, 85-88); left in MSS dated from 1731-66. Among mod. eds.: W. 83 (1745), FLORILEGIUM-m No. 3.

6 acc'd. sons., H-or-P & Vn & Vc; composed *ca.* 1775; London: Bremner, 1776; W. 89/1-6. Mod. ed.: W. 89/2/i and ii, Geiringer/BACH-m 133.

7 acc'd. sons., K & Vn & Vc, in 2 sets of 3 and 4 sons., respectively; composed in 1775 and '77; Leipzig: "im Verlage des Autors," 1776 and '77; W. 90/1-3 and 91/1-4. Reviewed at length in Forkel/BIBLIOTHEK II 275-300. Mod. ed.: W. 90/3, HORTUS MUSICUS-m No. 46 (Oberdörffer), with preface. Photographs of title page (W. 90) and autograph (W. 91/4) are given in Schmid/BACH 136 and 144; cf. SCE V, with ex. Bitter/BRÜDER I 208-211 gives pertinent correspondence and 2 early reviews.

6 "kleine" acc'd. sons., K & clarinet & bassoon; left in an undated MS; W. 92/1-6. Nos. 1, 2, 4, and 5 reoccur in other keys as nos. 1, 5, 3, and 2, in the 6 sonatas for wind instruments W. 184.

One son. for unaccompanied Fl; composed in 1747; Berlin: Winter, 1763; W. 132.

3 unaccompanied "duetti" (Fl & Vn, 2 Vns, 2 clarinets); left in 3 MSS composed in 1748, '52, and ?; W. 140-142. Among mod. eds.: W. 140 and 142, NAGELS-m No. 35 (Stephan), with preface.

15 solo/bass "soli" or sons., the "solo" instrument being Fl (W. 123-131, 133, 134), oboe (W. 135), Va da gamba (W. 136, 137), or Vc (W. 138); left in MSS composed between 1735 and '86. Among mod. eds.: W. 123, 124, 128, 131, HORTUS MUSICUS-m Nos. 71 and 72 (Walther).

11 duo/bass "trios" (etc.), the upper parts being Fl & Vn (W. 143-153), 2 Vns (W. 154-161/1), Vn & Fl (161/2), 2 Fls (W. 162), and bass Fl & Va (W. 163); left in MSS dating from 1731-55 (only W. 161/1 and 2 published, Nürnberg: Schmid, 1751). Autograph score pages of W. 149 and 156 are reproduced in Schmid/BACH 126 and 113.

7 sonatinas "a Cembalo concertato," with "2 corni, 2 flauti, 2 violini, viola e basso"; left in MSS dated 1762-64; W. 96-100, 102, 103.

3 sonatinas "a Cembalo concertato" and "2 flauti traversi, 2 violini, violetta e basso"; composed in 1763-64 (cf. W. 101, 104, and 105); Berlin: Winter, 1764 (3 separate issues); W. 106-108. A photograph of the title page of W. 106 is given in Schmid/BACH 152.

2 sonatinas "a II Cembali concertati," with 16 and 8 orchestral instruments, respectively; left in MSS dated 1762 & '63; W. 109, 110.

6 "piccole" sons. for 7 wind instruments; left in MSS composed in 1775; W. 184/1-6. Mod. ed.: entire set in score, Janetzky/BACH-m.

About half of Emanuel Bach's 265 or more sonatas were available for the present discussion, including a cross section, both printed and MS, from all categories, and a nearly complete representation of the sonatas that have always attracted the most attention to his music—that is, those in the main sets for keyboard published during his lifetime.[40] In turn, about half of this half, or a sampling of about sixty-

40. Warm thanks are owing to an experienced student of Emanuel's sonatas, Professor Miriam Terry at the University of Washington in Seattle, for supply-

five sonatas, was used as the basis for a fresh statistical survey of the external facts of Emanuel's sonatas. Such facts are a necessary starting point for any attempt to evaluate or re-evaluate his position in sonata history.[41] With regard to the cycles as a whole, there is uniformity in the use of three movements in nearly all the sonatas. The chief exceptions include the six "neue Sonatinen" in one movement each (W. 63/7-12); the one-movement rondo that tops off the "veränderte Reprisen" set as "Sonata VI" (W. 50/6); about four two-movement sonatas for keyboard (e.g., W. 56/4 and W. 65/44); a few actual suites for keyboard, such as W. 62/12 and W. 65/4, in five dances or freer movements each; and the twelve orchestral sonatinas with one or two harpsichords (W. 96-100, 102, 103, 106-110), these being little *divertimenti* in five to eight movements that often recur and interlock.[42] There is also uniformity in the order of the three movements, which is almost always F-S-F. This time the chief exceptions are among the solo/bass works, most of which follow the older plans S-F-F (as in W. 125-131) or S-F-M (as in W. 123, the finale being a minuet).[43] The two-movement plans are variable, W. 56/4, for example, being "Andantino" and "Presto."

More than a third of all Emanuel's keyboard sonatas are in minor keys, a high proportion for the time.[44] In the majority of his three-movement sonatas the middle movement is in the opposite mode or in the relative, subdominant, or submediant key (in that order of frequency). In most of the quasi-suites and *divertimenti,* and in the melo/bass sonatas with the plan S-F-F or S-F-M, the movements are all in the home key. When the mode of the relative key is changed (as from b to g rather than G in W. 55/3) the contrast becomes striking. At least six three-movement sonatas have each movement in a different key, including five of the first *Essay* set (W. 63/1, 2 and 4-6). In this set the reason must have been largely pedagogic, since the keys jump or drop by 3ds in most of the sonatas—for example, b-D-f♯ in Sonata 4—, thereby taking in nearly all of the major and minor keys up to four sharps or flats, within the eighteen "Probe-Stücke." Yet the composer did not seem to mind putting the outer movements in different keys in a few other sonatas, such as W. 58/2, with its three

ing photographs of 19 keyboard sons. left in MSS and early published anthologies not otherwise available to the present study.

41. Newman/BACH is a re-evaluation of Emanuel in relation to his brothers Friedemann and Christian, and to Haydn and Mozart.

42. For detailed plans of the mvts. in this last group cf. Uldall/KLAVIERKONZERT 59-66, with exx.; Schmid/BACH 150-152.

43. Cf. Schmid/BACH 92.

44. Cf. Beurmann/BACH 20.

movements in G, g, and E. Tonal interconnections between movements occur only infrequently, mainly in several sonatas within the six important "Kenner und Liebhaber" sets, and more often, curiously, between the first two movements rather than the last two. The interconnection may occur as a simple cadence on the dominant (W. 55/3/ii → iii); or as a modulatory passage leading directly into the next movement (W. 55/2/i → ii). As an extreme example, the first movement of W. 59/1 is in e and modulates to C in an improvisatory ending, while the second movement modulates from C to E and leads directly to the finale in that key. Thematic interconnections between the movements, conjectural at best, are also infrequent, chiefly between the outer movements in a few of the earlier sonatas (W. 48/2), although it is the first two movements that seem to be so related in W. 48/6. More intrinsic are the stylistic bonds that link the movements of the sonatas—the dotted patterns and scalewise runs in all three movements of W. 63/4, the opening of each movement on a suspensive or foreign harmony in W. 55/5, or the complexity of melody and texture throughout W. 59/3 as against their simple directness throughout W. 50/3.

To carry the statistical conclusions a bit further, the usual "binary" design, with each half repeated, prevails in the outer movements of Emanuel's sonatas, whereas a continuous cursive form is usual in the slow movement. In the first movements one or more of the textbook traits of "sonata form" can be expected with about the same considerable flexibility and variability that we have found in most other pre-Classic sonatas.[45] The trait that is met most consistently is the return of the initial idea in the home key during the second "half," although it then often veers quickly to the subdominant as though beginning a coda (e.g., W. 48/6/i/89, W. 49/5/i/83). This return gives all the more sense of ternary form because it follows, at a suitable distance, just as consistent a statement of the initial idea at the inner double bar, most often
45a in the dominant or relative key. But a "second theme" is found much less consistently. It is missing in some of Emanuel's most driving first movements, where a dualistic contrast might be most expected (W. 57/2/i). In fact, a clear "second theme" is the exception rather than the rule, which conclusion is not surprising in view of the opposition to a mixing of one "Affekt" with another that was voiced at this time by Berlin writers (SCE II and VI). Hence, it is also not surprising that

45. Wyler/BACH is a newly published diss. (influenced by Tobel/KLASSISCHEN) on the first mvts. in Bach's "Prussian," "Württemberg," and "Kenner und Liebhaber" sons.; the variability and flexibility of structure are noted by Wyler, too, although he gives more credit to Bach for the establishment of "sonata form" than is given here.

among the "second themes" that do appear, some of the clearest are those that do little more than restate the initial idea in the nearly related key (W. 55/4/i/13), or invert it (W. 49/2/i/15), or at least start as it does (W. 57/4/i/17). When there does seem to be a contrast, as in the very first "Prussian" sonata (W. 48/1/i/18), it is likely to be less of an independent thought than the sort of subtle, fleeting shift to the minor mode that we saw in the sonatas of E. W. Wolf and others, or a momentary dominant pedal (W. 57/6/i/16-20). As for the "development" sections, a true working out of a single idea is rare (W. 57/6/i/34-63). One would expect more of this from a composer who indulges so often in motivic play. Nor does Emanuel contribute much in the way of a coda. Occasionally he adds a measure or two without changing his tack (W. 55/5/i/28-29), or a few measures of tonal transition (W. 56/6/i/33-41) of the sort noted earlier.

In that majority of Emanuel's slow movements that are cursive in form, the method of progression may be like that of a recitative alternately *accompagnato* and *secco* (W. 48/1/ii),[46] or a florid cantabile aria (W. 63/5/ii), or an expressive, motivically concentrated three-part invention (W. 48/3/ii), or a lilting "Siciliano" dance (W. 65/5/ii), or a gently flowing prelude (W. 63/3/ii), or a mere modulatory transition (W. 51/3/ii). Occasionally the initial idea returns in the tonic key with sufficient projection to suggest an A-B-A form (W. 57/6/ii/28). With regard to the finales, those that do not have a tonic return to the initial idea during the second half (as does W. 49/3/iii) are likely to be in the simpler, purely binary design that returns to somewhat later material (W. 48/5/iii). Several finales are quasi-gigues (W. 61/2/iii), but relatively few are in those other styles or forms that proved most popular in current finales, such as the minuet (W. 63/1/iii) or rondo (W. 55/3/iii, with Emanuel's typically free refrains). One can also find a two-part invention (W. 49/6/iii), an "Allegro Siciliano e scherzando" (W. 63/4/iii), a rhapsodic "Allegretto arioso ed amoroso" (W. 63/5/iii), and a quasi-toccata (W. 55/6/iii), among still other types.

In coming closer to the music itself of Emanuel's sonatas, one is impressed above all by the extraordinary diversity and breadth of styles, by the originality and force of the ideas, and by the authority and skill with which all these are executed. The great skill surprises no one who has followed this composer's patient, thoroughgoing analyses of one fine point of harmony after another in the *Essay*. Emanuel had a right to chide other composers for their lack of a solid foundation, in his last

46. This aspect of his writing is the subject of Schering/REDENDE.

revision of this treatise.[47] Even in the brief, comparatively simple, first "Prussian" sonata (composed when he was twenty-six) there can be no question of "Ph. E. Bach, il piccolo," as Torrefranca put it,[48] or of any "debolissimo Talento mio," as Emanuel himself put it, in the obsequious manner of the neophyte's first dedication. There are two closely related bases for at least a partial division in the styles. One basis, that of music written to order as against music written to his own taste, was defined by Emanuel himself when he wrote in his "Autobiography,"

> Because I have had to compose most of my works for specific individuals and for the public, I have always been more restrained in them than in the few pieces that I have written merely for myself. At times I even have had to follow ridiculous instructions, although it could be that such not exactly pleasant conditions have led my talents to certain discoveries that I might not otherwise have come upon.
>
> Since I have never liked excessive uniformity in composition and taste, since I have heard such a quantity and variety of good [things], since I have always been of the opinion that one could derive some good, whatever it may be, even if it is only a matter of minute details in a piece, probably from such [considerations] and my natural, God-given ability arises the variety that has been observed in my works. . . . Among all my works, especially for keyboard, there are only a few trios, solos, and concertos that I have composed in complete freedom and for my particular use.

The second, related basis for dividing Emanuel's styles is that of works written not to order but in the interest of sure sales, as against those other works, again, written for his own artistic satisfaction.

Examples of Emanuel's works written to order are found especially among the melo/bass sonatas, most of which give prominence to a virtuoso solo part for the flute of Frederick II,[49] reveal the "restraint" of the monarch's Baroque taste notwithstanding their high skill and expressive worth, and suggest exclusive royal ownership in their failure to reach publication. It may even be that Emanuel's SS/bass "Trio" in c of 1751 (W. 161/1) was an attempt to comply with "ridiculous instructions," for both he and his brother Friedrich (to whose patron in Bückeburg it was dedicated) later questioned the validity of this chief programmatic venture and experiment in the realm of the *Affektenlehre*.[50] Neither felt that the idea of Sanguine's ultimate

47. The paragraph in Chap. 41, Section 12 of the 1797 ed. of Part 2 is quoted (incompletely) in Schmid/BACH 84-85.

48. Torrefranca/ORIGINI 103-112.

49. Cf. Schmid/BACH 91-92, 123-124.

50. Cf. pp. 137 and 165-170 in Mersmann/BACH (an extended study of this work, with the detailed programme quoted in full and several exx.); Schmid/BACH 57-60, 115-116, and 80 (reproduction of the title page).

winning over of Melancholy (represented by the first and second violin, respectively) could be conveyed through the music without the aid of the explicit programme that was supplied. Examples of Emanuel's works written to insure sales come especially from his later years. They include the six "leichte" sonatas of 1766, the six sonatas "à l'usage des Dames" of 1770, the six "piccole" sonatas for winds of 1775, and the six "neue Sonatinen" of 1787, which, as he wrote to the publisher Schwickert, "consist together of [only] 6 pieces and not of 18 pieces, like other sonatas, made up of 3 movements each. The latter kind could not be made for 18 thalers; they would constitute not a supplement to a book but a whole in themselves, and would, on account of the expense, rather impede the sale, deter[-ring prospective] buyers instead of alluring them."[51] Thus, whereas the works written to order reflect conservative tastes and fall largely in the Berlin period, those written in the interest of sure sales reflect popular tastes for lightness, brevity, and simplicity (though they are never cheap or inferior in craftsmanship) and fall largely in the Hamburg period.[52]

Of course, what interests us still more are the works written to satisfy Emanuel's own aesthetic tastes. It is not always easy to draw the line, for he labeled no sonata as he did his highly subjective, unpublished "Fantasie" in f♯ of 1787, "Very sorrowful and ever slow; C. P. E. Bach's feelings [*Empfindungen*]."[53] But to judge from the latter and from his position as the chief exponent of the musical *Empfindsamkeit,* during the heightening *Sturm und Drang,*[54] we would certainly include those sonatas—and there are more than he implied, among them perhaps a fourth of all the keyboard sonatas—that most obviously reveal the *empfindsam* style. Although these are scattered 54a
throughout his works, he composed less instrumental music in this style after he left Berlin. One reason may have been his increasing mercenariness in later years,[55] another his increasing preoccupation

51. As translated on p. 567 in the illuminating article Plamenac/BACH. In 1786 Emanuel sent a sonata (W. 60) to J. G. Breitkopf with the remark, "It is entirely new, easy, short, and almost without an Adagio, since such a thing is not the fashion anymore" (as quoted in Hase/BACH 101).

52. The latter conclusion is already reached in Schubart/IDEEN 179 and Rochlitz/FREUNDE IV 197; cf., also, Schmid/BACH 80-82.

53. Left both as a keyboard solo (W. 67) and with violin added (W. 80; cf. Studeny/VIOLINSONATE 71-72; Schmid/BACH 148-149, including a reproduction of the first page of the autograph score); published by Schering as "Phantasiesonate" (cf. MGG I 940).

54. Cf. his own espousals of this style in Bach/ESSAY 152-153 (from Part 1, Chap. 3, Sections 13-15); and in statements quoted from 1762 in Schmid/BACH 14, and 1788 in Schering/REDENDE 17.

55. Cf. Plamenac/BACH 568-569.

with sacred choral music,[56] and a third a certain sophisticated tempering of the ardor that had already reached a peak in the "Württemberg" sonatas. As soon after this set as the "Essay" and "veränderte Reprisen" sets, there are several sonatas that show a marked condensation and simplification of style (e.g., W. 63/1). There are more in the fine "Kenner und Liebhaber" sets, too (e.g., W. 55/1), alongside some of his best known and most impassioned sonatas (e.g., W. 57/67). In any case, in these sets published by the composer himself, the sonatas, a third of which were composed before he left Berlin, can hardly be said to stem from motives primarily mercenary, if only because the subscription list of 519 names for the first volume shrank to 288 by the sixth and last one.[57]

The *empfindsam* style in Emanuel's sonatas exists partly in the *Affekt* of the main idea itself, which idea may be bold (W. 57/2/i/1-8), piquant (W. 49/5/iii/1-10), dualistic (W. 49/1/i/1-5), fragmentary (W. 49/4/1-6), complex (W. 57/2/iii/1-8), tuneful (Ex. 68, *infra*), squarely phrased (W. 57/2/ii/1-4), or merely germinal (W. 50/5/ii).[58] However, this *empfindsam* style is still more concerned with the treatment of these ideas, especially when not one kind of treatment—for example, consistent motivic play or strict variation techniques—but a variety of treatments is applied, freely and plastically.[59] Consistent motivic play is found chiefly in the melo/bass sonatas (W. 157/iii) and in a few of the steadier slow movements for keyboard (W. 49/4/ii). Strict variation techniques seem to have interested Emanuel relatively little, anyway.[60] They occur in his sonatas mainly in the outer movements of the "veränderte Reprisen" set[61] (except Son. 6, which is the one-mvt. rondo mentioned earlier, and Son. 5/iii, a "Tempo di Minuetto" that is more freely varied), as well as in an oc-

56. Cf. the discussion of Emanuel's 3 creative periods (1731-37, 1738-67, 1768-88) in Geiringer/BACH 352-354.

57. Cf. Bitter/BRÜDER I 212-230, with interesting details and contemporary documents regarding each vol.

58. The ideas in the sons. are discussed in Hoffmann-Erbrecht/KLAVIERMUSIK 116-122.

59. This last aspect of Emanuel's writing is the subject of the well conceived, unpublished diss. Randebrock/BACH (1953), which contains many specific analyses and exx. Previously, a similar approach had been taken in the analyses of W. 49/1/i, W. 65/20/i, and related works that occur in Steglich/BACH 116-123.

60. In Fischer/BACH, a study of this topic, the list (pp. 5-7) of independent sets of variations among his instrumental works includes only the one-mvt. acc'd. son. W. 91/4 (cf. Fischer/BACH 18-19; Schmid/BACH 148-150). This piece also exists in 2 keyboard versions (W. 116/23 and W. 118/10).

61. Beurmann/REPRISENSONATEN (largely extracted from the diss. Beurmann/BACH 93-117) is a study of this set and of freer variation techniques used by Emanuel. Still more elaborate variants that Bach added in his private English ed. of this set are reported in Barford/BACH.

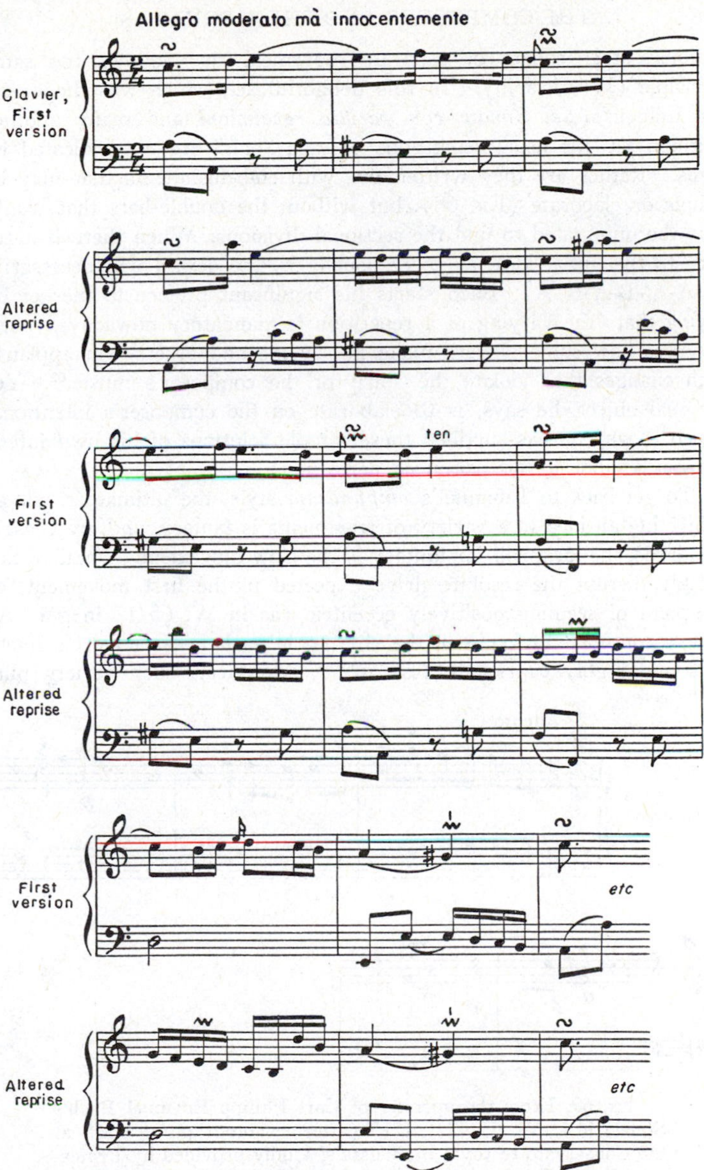

Ex. 68. From the opening theme and its "altered reprise" in a Sonata in a, W. 50/3/iii, by Carl Philipp Emanuel Bach (after the Rellstab re-ed. of 1785, at the Library of Congress).

casional other sonata or separate movement that follows the same principle (W. 61/5/iii). In this delightful set, which was the model for Löhlein's *Sei Sonate con variate repetizioni* and many another German set, the usual repetitions of each "half" are not indicated by signs. Rather are they written out with embellishments that may be simple or elaborate (Ex. 68), but without the double-bars that would help the uninitiated to find the sectional divisions. When there is a return to the initial idea, as there usually is, the design will necessarily be A-A'-B-A-B'-A'. Bach starts his significant preface to the set by saying that "the varying of a repetition is mandatory nowadays," then observes how some players make no change and others win applause with changes that violate the spirit of the composer's music.[62] Yet the real object, he says, is to elaborate on the composer's intentions, which is why he has supplied these sample solutions of his own intentions as a guide to inexperienced performers.

To get back to Emanuel's *empfindsam* style, the ultimate result of subjecting an idea to a variety of treatments is fantasy, and, by Classic standards, the ideal soil for fantasy is the slow movement. Fantasy can quickly disrupt the resolute drive expected in the first movement, to the point of seeming positively eccentric (as in W. 65/17 in g). At best, a continual toying with the rhythm in such faster music is likely to sound highly capricious (Ex. 69). Moreover, such variety plus

Ex. 69. From the opening of Carl Philipp Emanuel Bach's Sonata in C, W. 65/47/i, 1775 (after a photograph of a MS at the Conservatoire royal in Brussels, kindly provided by Professor Miriam Terry of the University of Washington in Seattle).

62. Most of the original preface (quoted in full in Bitter/BRÜDER I 68-69, with errors; Fischer/SONATE-m 21-22; Schmid/BACH 153; Haas/AUFFÜHRUNGS-

the truncated phrases, ornaments, abrupt pauses, "Scotch snaps," tempo gradations,[63] free *fioriture,* and deceptive cadences characteristic of the *empfindsam* style sometimes tend toward that same elephantine "fluency" (as in the "altered reprises" of W. 50/4/iii) that was remarked previously in Friedemann's earlier sonatas. This remark must be made in spite of Emanuel's ability to write in the most fluent Classic manner when he chose to (W. 55/4/i)[64] and of his unsurpassed knowledge of the keyboard, often leading to resourceful combinations (as in W. 55/4/iii, W. 55/6/i, W. 57/2/i, or W. 65/29/i) that point directly to the writing of Haydn (as in H. XVI/52/i and iii) and Beethoven (as in Op. 2/2/i and iii).

But in the slow movements one is allowed enough time to digest the variegations of the *empfindsam* style. Consequently, here are found some of Emanuel's most convincing creations—for example, the several slow movements cited before, or W. 49/2/ii, which has songful lines of triplets like those in the "Andante" of his father's Violin Concerto in a; or W. 63/6/ii in A♭, which brings to mind the philosophical serenity at the start of Beethoven's Op. 110/i, or W. 55/4/ii in f♯, which has a melodic affinity with the "Andante" of Mozart's Concerto in A, K. V. 488. Playing these slow movements helps one to understand Burney's oft-quoted description of Emanuel's own playing at the clavichord, when he "grew so animated and *possessed,* that he not only played, but looked like one inspired. His eyes were fixed, his under lip fell, and drops of effervescence distilled from his countenance"; or Reichardt's description of how "he could become immersed and lost for hours together in his ideas, in a sea of modulations"; or the similar descriptions by C. F. Cramer, Schubart, and others.[65] After these descriptions one is less surprised to find Emanuel's friend, the poet Gerstenberg, grafting the texts both of Hamlet's "Soliloquy" and his own version of Socrates' death to the ruminative, partially unbarred "Fantasia" in c that concludes the last *Essay* sonata (W. 63/6/iii).[66] Emanuel's slow movements—for example, the one in G from a MS Sonata in g of 1746 (W. 65/17), with its tenderly dissonant opening theme and its soaring melodic climaxes—also help one to understand his preference for the

---

PRAXIS 243-244) is translated in Bach/ESSAY 166. The preface is summarized and the music praised in Marpurg/BEYTRÄGE 560-561.

63. Cf. Emanuel's own remarks on W. 49/6/ii in Bach/ESSAY 160-161.

64. In Beurmann/BACH 56 a distinction is made between *empfindsam* and symphonic styled sons. by Bach comparable to that made earlier here in the sons. of G. B. Sammartini, Boccherini, J. Stamitz, and others.

65. BURNEY'S TOURS II 219; Reichardt/SELBSTBIOGRAPHIE 28; Cramer/MAGAZIN II (1786) 870; Schubart/IDEEN 177-178. Cf., also, Schmid/BACH 60.

66. Cf. Bitter/BRÜDER I 110-112 (with the texts); Geiringer/BACH 357 (with exx.); also, Wotquenne/BACH item 202M and p. 93n.

intimacy and subtle expressive capabilities of the clavichord,[67] and his consuming interest in the songful treatment of this instrument:

> My main efforts especially in recent years have been directed toward playing and composing as songfully as possible for the clavichord, notwithstanding its lack of sustaining power. This is not at all easy, if the ear is not to be left too empty and if the noble simplicity of the song [line] is not to be disturbed by too much bustle.
>
> To me, music primarily must touch the heart, and the keyboardist can never do that through mere bluster, drumming, and arpeggiating—at least I can't.[68]

Emanuel practiced what he preached and generally eschewed such modernisms as the Alberti bass (though not the usual *galant* mannerisms). He could command more original means of keeping his musical textures constantly alive and fresh. Even in his relatively conservative chamber works he had shown his concern with the problem of texture. Thus, in the programme trio and its companion (W. 161/1 and 2), the full title allows the alternative of transferring one of the upper parts to the cembalist's right hand.[69] In that sense his "accompanied" sonatas are actually "trios," too. The texture in the solo keyboard works is enhanced by the contrapuntal activity, which is often considerable (W. 48/3/ii) in spite of his avowed contempt for "learned" music in later years.[70] It is enhanced, too, by the rich harmony in comparatively rapid harmonic rhythm (which Riemann unjustly dismissed as a succession of half cadences every few measures[71]), by refined ornamentation, and by carefully scaled dynamic markings[72] (Ex. 70). Musicians who trouble to explore this music sufficiently are greeted by one tonal surprise after another, whether it be a deceptive cadence on the lowered supertonic step (W. 55/6/ii/27), a bold series of parallel 5ths created by chromatic passing tones (W. 48/1/iii/25-32), subtle chromatic inflections both melodic and harmonic (W. 63/5/ii/68), alternation of the major and minor modes (W. 48/3/i/1-22), chromatic and enharmonic modulations involving the remotest key relationships (W.

67. E.g., cf. his own fine distinctions between the clavichord, harpsichord, and piano in Bach/ESSAY 35-36 and 106; his letter to Forkel of Feb. 10, 1775 mentioning 6 sons. composed for a particular clavichord, as quoted in Shedlock/SONATA 93-94; his frequent indications of *Bebung,* as in W. 55/2/i/21-24; also, the pertinent recollections in Rochlitz/FREUNDE IV 180, 195-196, 199-200.

68. Kahl/SELBSTBIOGRAPHIEN 44. Cf., also, Bach/ESSAY 149-150.

69. Cf. the title page as reproduced in Schmid/BACH 80; also, Emanuel's related instructions in another publication (1758), as reprinted in Cat. SCHWERIN II 364-365.

70. Cf. Plamenac/BACH 586-587.

71. Riemann/SÖHNE 174. This source and Mennicke/HASSE 79-88 led a hostile sect in Emanuel Bach criticism around the turn of this century.

72. Regarding these markings and Emanuel's use or implication of "cresc." only in his later works cf. Hoffmann-Erbrecht/STURM 469-470.

Ex. 70. From the slow movement of Sonata 2 in Carl Philipp Emanuel Bach's first "Kenner und Liebhaber" set, W. 55/2/ii (after Krebs/BACH-m I 10-11).

58/2/ii/28-59), or a whole movement generally characterized by highly expressive, even recherché harmony (W. 59/3/ii).

From a historical standpoint and considering the unexcelled quality, widespread influence, and sheer quantity of Emanuel's sonatas, it now seems absurd, without any reflections on Platti, to worry any longer over the competition that Torrefranca set up between these two men (SCE VII). It seems equally absurd to brand him any longer as "*the* father of 'sonata form,'" or words to that effect.[73] The latter assumption probably traces in a very loose fashion to the high regard for Emanuel's music in his own day as demonstrated and voiced not only by lesser masters like Neefe,[74] Wolf, Müthel, and others met in the present chapter, but by Haydn, Mozart, and Beethoven.[75] Though there may be some question about the fact or significance of Mozart's

73. Cf. Newman/BACH 236-240.

74. Cf. Schiedermair/BEETHOVEN 154.

75. The tributes by the last 3 men originally appeared, respectively, in Griesinger/HAYDN 11, Rochlitz/FREUNDE IV 202, and Beethoven's letter to G. C. Härtel of July 26, 1809 (as in Anderson/BEETHOVEN I 235).

tribute,[76] the music itself of Haydn and Beethoven, especially in the writing techniques and the more introspective or dramatic slow movements, is evidence enough of their indebtedness. In fact, in 1784 an English critic went so far as to assert that Haydn deliberately parodied Emanuel's (*empfindsam*) style in two sets of sonatas ("Opp. 13 and 14" or H. XVI/21-32, particularly 22/ii and all of 23) as a way of answering alleged defamations against him by Emanuel, a charge the
77a latter soon took pains to contradict (1785).[77] In any case, it *is* the *empfindsam* style and the writing techniques that spell Emanuel's chief importance. Moreover, it is these factors that already brought complaints in his own day regarding how "*long, difficult, fantastic,* and *far-fetched*" his music could seem,[78] and that still keep it pretty well out of the concert hall. But understood in its own terms, as more recent writers have been discussing it,[79] and not subjected to the academic criteria of later "sonata form," the music of Emanuel's sonatas can rightly take its place with some of the most meaningful and representative sonata music of the eighteenth century.

Other Berlin Composers (Franz and Georg Benda, Müthel, the theorists)

The more conservative side of Emanuel Bach's sonatas may be followed up first, with two composers who left melo/bass sonatas almost exclusively. One of these was the Polish Silesian **Johann Gottlieb Janitsch** (1708-63), who became a "contraviolinist" in Crown Prince Frederick's service in 1736. Janitsch is remembered especially today as the founder of the "Friday Academy," one of the first of those several amateur chamber music organizations in eighteenth-century Berlin. Besides two harpsichord and four organ sonatas, reportedly of lesser interest but published in contemporary anthologies (*ca.* 1760),[80] he left some twenty-five melo/bass sonatas in several undated MSS, variously scored in SS/-, SSA/-, and SSAB/bass settings.[81] The only one of these that has been made available is a "Suonata da camera

76. On the unreliability of Rochlitz cf. Einstein/MOZART 15. On Emanuel's actual influence cf. Schmid/BACH 65-66.

77. Regarding the details of this incident and the whole subject of Emanuel's important influence on Haydn, cf. the valuable article Schmid/HAYDN; also, Burney/HISTORY II 955; Bitter/BRÜDER II 104-107 (with errors); Shedlock/SONATA 114-115; Steglich/BACH 125-126; Geiringer/HAYDN 203-204.

78. BURNEY'S TOURS II 218; cf., also, Schmid/BACH 82-84. Burney is listed among the subscribers to the "Kenner und Liebhaber" sets and could have had in mind such fairly abstruse sons. as W. 55/6 and W. 56/6.

79. In Randebrock/BACH 1-5 this approach is urged.

80. Cf. Stilz/BERLINER 83; Frotscher/ORGELSPIEL II 1100.

81. Cf. MGG VI 1704-1706 (Becker).

a 4. strom.," Op. 8 (Fl, oboe-or-Vn, Va/*b.c.*), with the added title of "Echo" (referring to imitations by the high instruments at the start of the finale).[82] Composed in three movements, in the order S-F-F that predominated in Berlin "trio" sonatas,[83] this is an ornamental, melodious work with a texture of Handelian transparency. While one solo instrument states a main, recurring idea the others answer with secondary motives. The finale, an "Allegretto" in 6/8 meter, has a folklike quality in its square-cut metric patterns.

Among Emanuel Bach's closest associates at the Berlin court were as many as four brothers in the musically important Benda family from Bohemia.[84] After Georg Benda left in 1749, the most notable brother still present was the oldest, **Franz Benda** (1709-86). Franz was an outstanding violinist who had started as a singer and found his adventurous way to Dresden in 1733, entered the service of Frederick about the same time as Janitsch, followed Frederick to Berlin in 1741 as a member of the royal orchestra, and by 1763 could write in his colorful autobiography that he had already accompanied the royal flutist in more than 10,000 concerts![85]

As a onetime pupil of J. G. Graun (and Pisendel?) in violin and composition, as a close associate of Quantz and many others at the star-studded Berlin court, and as the father-in-law of Reichardt and E. W. Wolf, Franz was in the thick of German musical activities. But his own works seem not to have been widely circulated, both the MSS and few publications being very scarce today.[86] Besides concertos, at least one symphony, and some smaller violin pieces, he left about 110 sonatas—91 for violin and *b.c.*,[87] 3 for flute and *b.c.*, 6 "accompanied" sonatas of the older "trio" type that Emanuel Bach wrote (K & Fl-or-Vn), and 9 SS/bass trios. The publications from among these works include 6 Vn/bass sonatas issued as "Op. 1" by Huberty in Paris in 1763; also, probably 6 "trios" issued as "Op. 1" by Hummel in Berlin about 1780, one set of 3 "accompanied" sonatas (Op. 3) from the same publisher, and another such set (Op. 5) from Longman and Broderip in London

82. COLLEGIUM MUSICUM-m No. 68 (Wolff).
83. Hoffmann/TRIOSONATE 69.
84. Cf. Marpurg/BEYTRÄGE I 76-77.
85. The complete autobiography is trans. in Nettl/FORGOTTEN 204-245 (cf. p. 234; it is condensed in BURNEY'S TOURS II 173-177, with some details added). The chief study of the man and his music is the diss. Berten-Jörg/BENDA. Cf., also, MGG I 1621-1624 (Wirth); GROVE I 613-614, with further bibliography (Loewenberg).
86. E.g., cf. Cat. BRUXELLES II 267-268 and 355, III 433, IV 44 and 216.
87. The incipits of 48 of these (8 sets of 6 each) are given in BREITKOPF MS II 2-5 (1762); the incipits of 18 "solos" and "trios" are given in Cat. SCHWERIN I 143-146.

(about 1786).[88] How much earlier these and the other sonatas were composed generally cannot now be ascertained, the more so as all the extant MSS are copies, not autographs. But one clue is provided in the only category of Franz's music that has received any appreciable attention, that of his "solo" sonatas. Writing in the same year in which
89a the publication of the "solo" set can now be placed, 1763,[89] he said,

> The number of my compositions is not so great, because I only began very late to work seriously on them; moreover, the last 12 years I was unable to work on anything new—with the exception of a few violin sonatas which I was willing to have printed on demand of more than one music lover—, since my daily duties as well as my (for many years) weak constitution did not permit much work. In regard to my intention of having those [other?] sonatas published, one of my dearest and best friends prevented this; under the condition that I would teach his son, he paid for them very generously to keep them from becoming generally known through print.[90]

The last statement may be at once an explanation and an excuse for the small number of Franz's publications.

Nearly all of Franz Benda's solo/bass sonatas are in three movements, in the order S-F-F or F-S-F. Occasionally a minuet replaces the fast finale. The middle movement remains in the home key or, in some of the F-S-F cycles, changes to a nearly related key. Similar incipits in the outer or in all three movements are frequent. The *b.c.*, the relatively fast harmonic rhythm, the frequently continuous lines, and the sequential passages still suggest Baroque styles. But newer traits are present, too, in melodic folk elements that may go back to his youth as a Bohemian *Bierfiedler*,[91] and in *galant* mannerisms shortly to be noted. Ternary designs created by a return to the initial idea in the home key are frequent in both the slow and fast movements, but the "second themes" that have been noted[92] rarely make a pronounced contrast. The strength of this music—for it does have strength—lies not in its rather limited harmony and counterpoint. "I am not ashamed to confess publicly that I cannot be placed among the great con-

88. The only lists, in Eitner/QL I 433-434 and Berten-Jörg/BENDA 60-61 and 30-31, are inadequate, with errors, duplications, omissions, understandable confusions with other Bendas, and locations that no longer apply. The "trios" Op. 1 and the acc'd. set Op. 5 are listed, apparently wrongly, under Friedrich Wilhelm Heinrich Benda, Franz's oldest son, in BRITISH UNION I 99 and GROVE I 616; the son did, in any case, write the conservative 4-hand son. credited to him there (cf. AMZ I [1798-99] 816; Stilz/BERLINER 83 and 117).

89. Johansson/FRENCH 45; not "um 1770" as in the caption to the reproduction of the title page of this publication in MGG I 1625. Among the few mod. eds.: Son. 2 in A, Moffat/VIOLIN-SONATEN-m No. 22; Son. 4 in a, Jensen/VIOLIN-m No. 7433; cf., also, Altmann/KAMMERMUSIK 234.

90. As trans. in Nettl/FORGOTTEN 233-234.

91. Cf. Nettl/FORGOTTEN 210.

92. Berten-Jörg/BENDA 32-33.

trapuntists," Franz wrote.[93] Rather does its strength lie in the well spaced and well timed melodic lines. "The fact that I did not master [the keyboard] made me shy away from composing 'strong' ['starken'—i.e., multivoice] things and fugues. Knowing my limited possibilities I endeavored all the more to write violin sonatas in a skilful and singable manner."[94] Burney adds, in his long account of Franz,

> His style is so truly *cantabile,* that scarce a passage can be found in his compositions, which it is not in the power of the human voice to sing; and he is so very affecting a player, so truly pathetic in an *Adagio,* that several able professors have assured me he has frequently drawn tears from them in performing one.[95]

This aspect of Franz's music must also explain Burney's later remark that among all the Berlin composers, including Quantz and Graun, "Carl P. E. Bach, and Francis Benda, have, perhaps, been the only two, who dared to have a style of their own."[96]

With comparatively less harmonic interest, with considerable use of Alberti bass in the "accompanied" sonatas, and with ostensibly simpler and steadier melodic lines, Franz Benda's sonatas would seem to be remote from Emanuel Bach's.[97] Yet they are brought closer to these and to the *galant* style through the embellishments that every performer was expected to improvise in the melodic lines. By good fortune, in the MSS of more than a third of Franz's "solo" violin sonatas an elaborated version of the violin part is written out on an
added staff,[98] supplied by the copyist if not by the composer himself. 98a
This version is different from the elaborations that had been supplied for Corelli's adagios (SBE 158-159) in that it usually appears in all three movements. But naturally it is most developed in the slow movements, especially at the end, where a cadenza was expected at the *fermata* over the cadential $^6_4$ chord.[99] Occasionally there are two staffs added, providing two stages of elaboration (Ex. 71). Sometimes both the original line and its elaboration get into the high positions, double-stops, rapid passage work, and tricky bowings for which Franz was also recog-

93. Nettl/FORGOTTEN 244.
94. Nettl/FORGOTTEN 244.
95. BURNEY'S TOURS II 173. Cf., also, Studeny/VIOLINSONATE 56-59; Moser/VIOLINSPIEL 320-325.
96. BURNEY'S TOURS II 206.
97. The only mention of the latter that has come down to us from Franz is not in his autobiography but in an anecdote about parallel 5ths in a new "solo" by Frederick; cf. Berten-Jörg/BENDA 24-25.
98. Mersmann/AUFFÜHRUNGSPRAXIS is a discussion primarily of these sons., with many exx., including one nearly complete Son. in a (pp. 126-133).
99. Cf. Bach/ESSAY 143-146.

Ex. 71. From the original "solo" part and its 2 successive elaborations (A, B, and C, respectively) in the slow movement of a MS Sonata in A for violin and *b.c.* by Franz Benda (after Mersmann/AUFFÜHRUNGSPRAXIS 111-112).

nized.[100] At other times the original line is actually pruned rather than elaborated.[101] The purpose of the added staff may have been pedagogic and it may have been to demonstrate "altered reprises," as by Emanuel

100. Nissel-Nemenoff/BENDA is a detailed diss. (1930) on Franz's violin technique, with many exx., but the emphasis is on his Vn capriccios.
101. Cf. Mersmann/AUFFÜHRUNGSPRAXIS 121.

Bach. But no more than with Emanuel are the elaborations merely realizations of ornament signs. They are real variations that usually intensify the original lines with scales, arpeggios, and leaps, and often fragmentize it by injecting rests, triplets, dotted patterns, and other rhythmic minutiae. The surprising consequence of the latter procedure is a conversion of late Baroque to *galant* styles of writing.[102] A representative edition of Franz's elaborated sonatas would considerably advance our present understanding of eighteenth-century performance practices.

Trained in Bohemia, **Georg Benda** (1722-95) became a second violinist in the Berlin royal orchestra when, in 1742, Frederick II arranged for the whole Benda family to join Georg's eldest brother Franz.[103] Only seven years later, in 1749, he moved to Gotha in central Germany. During the next twenty-eight years he directed the Gotha court orchestra, became proficient as an oboist and keyboard player,[104] enjoyed a stimulating cultural environment, took time off for travels in Italy with F. W. Rust in 1765-66, and composed cantatas, oratorios, instrumental music, and, especially, the Singspiels and melodramas that in later years brought him his chief reputation.[105] "Not only the greatest among all his brothers but one of the foremost composers that ever lived—one of the epoch makers of our time! . . . What glory does not this immortal man spread over the musical history of our fatherland!" So wrote Schubart at the start and end of a lengthy panegyric.[106] Georg's sonatas were actually published during this Gotha period and even after he left for Hamburg and Vienna in 1778. But he is still grouped here with the Berlin composers because of his close ties to Emanuel Bach, which lasted well beyond his Berlin days.[107]

Quite the opposite of Franz Benda's sonatas, Georg's 55 or more sonatas have received little study but are almost entirely restored in

102. Cf. Haas/AUFFÜHRUNGSPRAXIS 78-79 and 84, with exx.

103. Cf. Nettl/FORGOTTEN 225-226. The most useful and accessible biographic sources are GROVE I 614-615 (Loewenberg) and the prefaces to MAB-m Nos. 24 and 37 (both Racek), with references in each to Vladimír Helfert's standard biography (2 vols., incomplete, 1929 and 1934) and other sources for readers of Czech. Benda's instrumental music is undervalued and wrongly listed in MGG I 1624-1628 (Wirth).

104. Gerber/NEUES I 330.

105. The fullest list of his compositions is in Eitner/QL I 436-439, but includes sons. by both Franz and F. W. H. Benda.

106. Schubart/IDEEN 112-115. Sentences nearly as strong occur in the otherwise more balanced article in Gerber/LEXICON I 134-136 and in its revision (over twice as long and replete with charming anecdotes) in Gerber/NEUES I 330-336.

107. Cf. MAB-m no. 24 xviii. "Madame Benda" was among the subscribers to the fifth of Emanuel's "Kenner und Liebhaber" sets (1785); Georg must have renewed his acquaintance with Emanuel in Hamburg, perhaps going there for that purpose.

good modern editions. They are mainly for keyboard,[108] including a set of 6 sonatas published by Winter of Berlin in 1757 as well as 11 sonatas and 33 one-movement "sonatinas" that appeared in Gotha and Leipzig from 1780 to 1787 (about when Emanuel Bach's 6 "Kenner und Liebhaber" sets appeared) under the general title of *Sammlung vermischter Clavier- und Gesangstücke für geübte und ungeübte Spieler* (*Collection of Assorted Keyboard and Vocal Pieces for Skilled and Unskilled Players*).[109] Other sonatas include one in Anth. HAFFNER OM-m VI/2 (*ca.* 1760), 3 in MSS (2 for solo and one for 2 keyboard instruments),[110] and at least one "trio" (SS/bass).[111] That the clavichord was generally the keyboard instrument intended by Georg is suggested in a note on one of his sonatas, "I have written this Sonata in c primarily for the clavichord ["Clavier"], or [rather] for the few players who know the superiority that this instrument has in expression, over the harpsichord ["Flugel"].[112]

Most of Georg Benda's sonatas, including the more conservative, contrapuntal "trio," have the usual north German cycle of three movements in the order F-S-F. Among exceptions are a two-movement sonata in the order M-minuet (MAB-m No. 37/9), a three-movement sonata that ends with an "Andante con [3] variazioni" (MAB-m No. 24/8), and another in the order M-M-minuet. The single-movement "sonatinas" may take the form of a minuet with trio (No. 37/28), "Rondeau" (No. 37/32), minuet with variation (No. 37/11), or binary design (No. 37/20, with return to the initial idea). The middle movements of the three-movement sonatas are usually in the subdominant or relative key, the latter reflecting Georg's fondness for third relationships. In the outer movements, especially the finales, the various approximations of "sonata form" include the return during the second "half" to the initial idea, although often casually and at a harmonic tangent (No. 24/2/iii/51); a moderate degree of actual development in the development sections (No. 24/3/iii); and a moderate degree of contrast in not merely a "second theme" but a veritable succession of somewhat contrasted themes (No. 24/12/i).

108. The only survey of consequence is that in Stilz/BERLINER 45-54, with a numbered list of publications and MSS.

109. Cf. the listings in BRITISH UNION I 100. Mod. ed.: all 50 sons., MAB-m No. 24 (in which the first 6 sons. are the set of 1757) and No. 37, including all the sons. previously printed in Nos. 14 and 17, with prefatory lists of other mod. eds. (all duplicated here). Among previous mod. eds.: the 6 sons. of 1757, TRÉSOR-m VII, with preface; Son. 1 in B♭ in the 1757 set, Newman/THIRTEEN-m no. 4, with preface; one son. and 12 sonatinas, Oberdörffer/BENDA-m.

110. Stilz/BERLINER 45.

111. Mod. ed.: "Trio" Son. in E, MAB-m No. 2 (Helfert, Kaprál, and Nopp).

112. Quoted in Stilz/BERLINER 101, though it is not in MAB-m No. 24/7 in c (1780); cf., also, Branberger/KLAVIERKUNST.

With regard to the style of Georg Benda's sonatas, the resemblance to the models already established by Emanuel and Friedemann Bach is so close that one might do better to look for the differences. Burney gives a hint of one main difference, in his customary pithy, astute manner, when he says, "His compositions are in general new, masterly, and learned; but his efforts at singularity, will by some be construed into affectation."[113] In his earlier sonata publications, the ones that Burney could have known, Georg reveals quite as much of the *Empfindsamkeit* and the *galant* style as the Bachs do. There is the same *empfindsam* volatility and a near record use of suspensive and deceptive cadences to mark the constant shifts of direction (No. 24/2/ii). But lacking quite the melodic genius or structural sense of the Bachs, Georg sometimes does risk the monotony of too much surprise by producing more of *Affekt* than substance.

Again, the volatility seems more tolerable in the slow movements (as in No. 24/6/ii).[114] It is less, in any case, when some other trait predominates, such as the siciliana pattern (No. 24/3/ii) or scale figures (No. 24/4/iii). It also becomes less in Georg's later sonatas, which, like those of the Bachs and E. W. Wolf, are lighter, simpler, and generally more accessible to the "unskilled" performer. In these sonatas, the harmonic rhythm is slowed, occasional uses of "Alberti bass" in the "singing allegro" style now occur (No. 37/18/33-34), the thematic concentration is greater (making for fewer rather than more instances of contrasting themes; No. 37/7), the technical exploitation of the keyboard, which was also considerable in the 1757 set, becomes more varied and fluent (No. 24/9/i), and the Bohemian folk elements attributed to Georg's sonatas[115] seem to be more in evidence (Ex. 72). On the other hand, there is no sacrifice in quality in the later sonatas (No. 24/7 in c is an exceptionally expressive work throughout) and no loss in the wealth of harmonic interest (in No. 24/12/ii, for example, the modulations progress from E♭ and e♭ to F♯, g♯, b♭, f, and back to E♭).

A further, extreme cultivation of the *empfindsam* style is seen in the four published sonatas by the expert keyboardist sometimes distinguished as J. S. Bach's last pupil, **Johann Gottfried Müthel** (1728-88).[116] Müthel was close not only to the father, in 1750, but to 116a

113. BURNEY'S TOURS II 237.

114. Cf. Gerber/LEXICON I 135, in which Georg's adagios are especially praised.

115. Cf. MAB-m No. 16 xix; also, Racek/TSCHECHISCHEN 507-512.

116. Cf. MGG IX 914-915 (Hoffmann-Erbrecht); no document is cited in this or the few previous sources (e.g., BJ xxxii [1935] 64) that give 1728 rather than 1718 as the year of birth, but in Eitner/QL VII 115 the objection to "1729" in

Ex. 72. From the start of Georg Benda's Sonatina in G in the fifth set of "vermischter Clavier- und Gesangstücke" (after Oberdörffer/BENDA-m 4).

Friedemann and Emanuel. His actual contact with the latter in Berlin in the early 1750's, his further correspondence with him after moving to Riga in Latvia (*ca.* 1755), and Emanuel's obvious influence on his style are the chief reasons for including Müthel here among the Berliners. Besides a Fl/bass sonata, five other keyboard sonatas (all authentic?),[117] and some further instrumental MSS, Müthel left three solo keyboard sonatas published by Haffner in 1756 (plate no. 87) and a *Duetto für 2 Claviere, 2 Flügel oder 2 Fortepiano* published by the
118a similarly enterprising Hartknoch in Riga in 1771.[118] In spite of the
choices allowed in the "Duetto," the clavichord, with its then greater

Gerber/LEXICON I 585 is based on 1738 rather than 1747 for the Mecklenburg-Schwerin appointment that Gerber loosely put in "seinem 17. Jahre."

117. The opening of the autograph of a Son. in C is reproduced in MGG IX plate 58/2.

118. No full study of Müthel's music is known here, but there are discussions of the sons. in Hoffmann-Erbrecht/KLAVIERMUSIK 123-127 and Hoffmann-Erbrecht/STURM 470-476 (both with exx.), and in the prefaces to the 2 mod. eds.: the 3 sons. of 1756, MDMA-m I/6 (Hoffmann-Erbrecht); the "Duetto" of 1771, NAGELS-m No. 176 (Kreutz).

dynamic range and volume, was probably the instrument Müthel preferred for the sensitive shading and tone quality that his sonatas require.

Each of Müthel's four published sonatas has three longer-than-average movements in the order F-S-F. A sense of form is imparted in each movement by not one but several returns to the initial idea, whether in the home key or some other key. But clear contrasts and clear divisions, other than the breaks between the repeated "halves" of the outer movements, are largely lost in the almost continual atmosphere of highly ornamented, stop-and-go fantasy. Even the finales have only slightly more regular motion and less fantasy (the most straightforward being the quasi-gigue in Son. 1 of the 1756 set). One result of so much fantasy is to reduce almost all the motion, fast or slow, to one loose, leisurely rate of pulse. In the "Duetto" one instrument plays at a time, or interjects comments during the other's solo, more often than the two instruments combine homophonically or polyphonically. But there is no lack of harmonic or contrapuntal skill in Müthel's writing, and his good knowledge of the keyboard is apparent in nearly every measure. On the other hand, mixed with various harmonic subtleties, often at cadences (e.g., "Duetto"/i/75), there is a surfeit of half-cadences that now seem trite (e.g., same mvt., mss. 42 and 46). Müthel's particular and most frequent method of continuation can be described as a succession of waves formed by the rise and fall of scales, arpeggios, or related figures.

Even in the later "Duetto," there is no abatement of Müthel's fantasy style, which grows irritating in the protracted doses that he offers. His own explanation of his style is pertinent, as found in a letter published with the enlarged account of Müthel that appeared in the German translation (1773) of Burney's travels in Germany *et al.* He said, in effect, that he wrote little because he wrote only when the mood and time were right, and when the spirit moved him; the composer who writes without letup, and without this means of thinking and writing in a new and impassioned manner, permits his spirit to grow "weary, indolent, and dull," and he soon finds that he is repeating himself.[119] Literal repetition is certainly not carried to a fault by Müthel, although excessive variety can lead to monotony, too. Burney himself writes on Müthel's music more favorably than on Georg Benda's, not disapproving its novelty but stressing its difficulties for the performer, which are indeed considerable.[120] Our Ex. 73 quotes a main idea, the rise of a "wave," and a series of appoggiaturas that seems to occur in

119. The letter is printed in Hoffmann-Erbrecht/KLAVIERMUSIK 123.
120. BURNEY'S TOURS II 240-241.

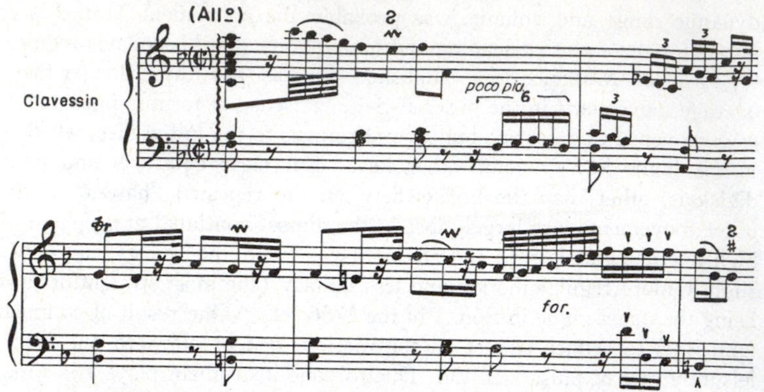

Ex. 73. From the first movement in Sonata 1 (1756) by Johann Gottfried Müthel (after the Preston re-ed., *ca.* 1795, at the Library of Congress).

just this melodic and rhythmic disposition as a nearly universal *empfindsam* mannerism.

At this point, brief note should be taken of the few, little known sonatas, chiefly for keyboard, by four Berliners much better remembered as theorists today. The writings of **Friedrich Wilhelm Marpurg** (1718-95), who was opposed by Kirnberger as well as Sorge (SCE XII) for the espousal of Rameau's theories and other alleged progressivisms that followed his acquaintance with Rameau in Paris in 1746-49,[121] are cited often in the present volume. Marpurg left a set of *Sei Sonate da Clavicembalo* that was published in 1756 by B. Schmid's widow in Nürnberg, another keyboard sonata in MS, and another in Anth. HAFFNER COLLECTION-m I/5 (*ca.* 1760).[122] **Johann Friedrich Agricola** (1720-74), a pupil of J. S. Bach and Quantz, a pro-Italian, conservative arbitrator in the controversies between Sorge and Marpurg,[123] and a composer of Italianate intermezzi, left one keyboard sonata in F, composed in 1762, in Anth. MANCHERLEY-m II 97.[124] **Johann Friedrich Wilhelm Wenkel** (1734-91) was a more obscure colleague of these other theorists, who involved himself in a controversy over C. H. Graun's *Oden* of 1761. Among other light pieces he left one sonata in Anth. HAFFNER OM-m IX/6.[125] And **Johann Philipp Kirnberger**

121. Cf. MGG VIII 1668-1673 (Hoke).
122. Cf. Stilz/BERLINER 74-75.
123. Cf. MGG I 160-163 (Blume).
124. Cf. Stilz/BERLINER 82-83. The middle mvt., "Larghetto," is reprinted in Herrmann/LEHRMEISTER-m II 26.
125. Cf. Eitner/QL X 226 and IV 350.

(1721-83), pupil of J. S. Bach, violinist in the orchestra of Frederick II (from 1751), and a more prolific composer than Marpurg or Agricola, left at least one set of six SS/bass sonatas (before 1763?[126]) and at least five keyboard sonatas, including one in Anth. HAFFNER COLLECTION-m II/5 (*ca.* 1761) and two in one movement each in Marpurg/CLAVIERSTÜCKE-m I and II (1762).[127] Most of the keyboard sonatas by these three men follow the three-movement plan of F-S-F, are somewhat elementary in scope and keyboard treatment, and reveal the expected skill, the expected tendency toward conservative, contrapuntal, motivic writing (apart from considerable free passage work in the first, freer movement of Agricola's sonata), and the expected sterility.[128] Marpurg's skillful harmony conveys a little more warmth, especially in his slow movements, which at least have *empfindsam* titles such as "Sospirando" and "Tenerezza."

More interesting here than the music of these theorists is a remarkable little pamphlet written by Kirnberger as the highly successful teacher. This pamphlet, dated 1783, and his last publication while he lived, has the title (translated), "Method for Tossing Off Sonatas."[129] Some have regarded this pamphlet as being satirical or facetious,[130] as they have his better known, earliest publication, based on dice throwing, "The Ever-Ready Polonaise- and Minuet-Composer" (1757).[131] But when one recalls Kirnberger's longtime emphasis on the *b.c.* as the determinant of the melody, on harmony as the source of contrapuntal figuration, and on mathematics as the means of solving compositional problems,[132] the sonata pamphlet can only be regarded as a contribution made in dead earnest. It is, in fact, distantly related to the discussion we found in the second volume of Löhlein's *Clavier-Schule,* published two years earlier (SCE XII), and it is curiously anticipative of Joseph Schillinger's "systems" 150 years later. There is justification, both in what is and is not said, for (freely) translating (and, it is hoped, clarifying) all of this awkwardly written pamphlet:[133]

126. Cf. Eitner/QL V 375.

127. Cf. Stilz/BERLINER 73-75. The chief study of the man, his music, and his writings is Borris/KIRNBERGER, including only a summary listing of the sons. (p. 40) and discussion (pp. 45-49 and 58). Mod. ed.: Son. in G in one mvt., Frey/SONATINA-m 52.

128. Cf. Burney/HISTORY II 957 and even Schubart/IDEEN 85, on Kirnberger's pedantry.

129. Kirnberger/SONATEN. Cf. Newman/THEORISTS 25-26; Ratner/THEORIES 446. Reprinted in Fischer/SONATE-m 19 (cf. p. 17).

130. E.g., Moser/LEXIKON I 616.

131. Cf. Guttler/WÜRFELSPIEL.

132. Cf. MGG VII 954-955 (Dadelsen).

133. Grateful acknowledgement is made to G. Schirmer, Inc., of New York, for permission to reprint this translation from Newman/KIRNBERGER.

Method for Tossing Off Sonatas

It is surely no small matter to toss off sonatas, so to speak; and we get so many of them every day that I can assume the nature and essence of a sonata are generally known. But to make something better understood that is so widely appreciated, to solve it as if it were a given problem, to make public the key to it—[all this] means disclosing musical secrets. And I believe that whatever honors the world has credited me with thus far, and still may allow me, that much honor is due me for this accomplishment alone. In the following sentences, therefore, I shall put together the method by which one can most easily compose sonatas.

The task is this: One has to make a piece, for whatever instruments, in three or four movements, portraying in these the [various] emotional humors, so that listeners of different temperaments are [kept] entertained. And the solution to this most important problem, which extends to still other instrumental pieces—for example, trios, symphonies, partitas, [and French] overtures (only excepting the fugue of the overture)—can be had as follows.

One takes a piece by a good master or—if one wants to excel more—by oneself, and constructs an entirely different melody over its bass. Now since a note can have manifold values, a change in the note values already will remove any similarity to the previously known melody; yet this [new] melodic beauty will be strengthened and enhanced still more by the changes made [in connection] with the bass line. Furthermore, one [next] makes a [new] bass for the newly found melody, so that now neither the bass nor melody line remains similar to the original.

This method is [applicable] so universal[-ly] that it meets the most severe tests. For instance, it can even be reversed by fitting a different bass to a melody, and to this in turn a different melody.

The rules for this procedure are very easy, reducing to the following precepts. One needs to employ no further knowledge than that of composing to a thorough bass[134] and that of introducing imitations as desired. If one wants to do something further, one can give the sonata still more weight through [the use of] double counterpoint, if necessary calling to mind the rules for this in my *Kunst des reinen Satzes* published by Mr. Decker [1774-79]. Then, too, one can still better conceal the similarity and derivation [of the source material in one's sonata] by changing a piece from even to odd meter and, conversely, from odd to even meter; also, by putting a piece, already entirely altered, into another key—thus, for instance, might the appended example by the late J. S. Bach ["Gigue" from the 6th "French Suite"] be transposed from E to D, E♭, or F, so that even the composer would fail to recognize it—; [and] finally, in some appropriate passages of several measures, one may add to the source melody a new harmony in place of the source bass, especially since, as is well known, a melody lends itself to many harmonizations. Only in songs does the use of this method bring on difficulties.

With regard to trios, *Kapellmeister* [J. A. P.] Schulz, in the service of His Royal Highness Prince Heinrich at the time of his study with me, showed what could be done with a trio by the late *Kapellmeister* [C. H.]

134. For this translation of "des reinen Satzes" cf. MGG VII 954.

Graun. That is, he kept the bass of the Graun trio and composed wholly different melodies in place of Graun's two upper lines for flute and violin. If I should get the permission of Mr. Schulz I shall publish this Graun [-derived] trio in my periodical.[135] For the time being, the appended "Gigue" by the late J. S. Bach and my alterations of its melody and harmony may serve as a practical example of the described method.

The important issue that arises here as to whether the melody originates in the harmony, or vice versa, may be answered by pure theory, to this effect. Whereas I can tell by the melody whether the harmony agrees, it does not follow as a corollary that the harmony must derive from the melody. Now the question stands in clear perspective: How can one achieve a wealth of melody if he is in the mood neither for it nor the writing [of it]? Besides the diverse possibilities already indicated from changes of the melody and harmony, experience shows us the way. Namely, one takes a few tones from different harmonies and, after having composed a few measures by this means, gets inspired, forgets the few harmonic tones, and becomes his own creator. But even these few measures may be furnished, and for that [purpose] F. Geminiani's *Dictionaire harmonique* may serve, which was published in Amsterdam in 1756, in 34 pages, and can be had from the town dealer Hummel.[136] And the rich possibilities of a single succession of harmonies may be gleaned from page 103 in the first part of my *Kunst des reinen Satzes,* while on page 101 in the same, [it is shown that] even two tones permit great variety.

Sapienti sat!

Other Berliners may now be mentioned whose sonatas appeared mostly in the 20 years from 1750 to 1770 and reveal, like those of the theorists, styles that are rational rather than *empfindsam.* Several of these sonatas appeared in contemporary anthologies, especially those, again, of Haffner in Nürnberg and Breitkopf in Leipzig. **Christoph Schaffrath** (1709-63) was a keyboardist in the service of Frederick II from 1735, while the latter was still a crown prince. He later joined the service of Frederick's sister Princess Amalia.[137] Besides symphonies and concertos, he left over 45 chamber and solo or duo keyboard sonatas, some of which can no longer be found. The sonatas include at least 11 in "trio" and other melo/bass scorings in MS, and a published set of *VI Duetti a cembalo obligato e violino ò flauto traverso concertato,* Op. 1 (Haffner, 1746);[138] a set of *VI Sonates pour le clavessin,* Op. 2 (Haffner, 1749);[139] one sonata each in Anth.

135. What periodical is meant is not clear, but Kirnberger did not live to do any further publishing.

136. Originally published in 1742 by J. Johnson in London as *Guida armonica, o Dizionario armonico.*

137. Cf. Eitner/QL VIII 467.

138. Cf. Hoffmann/TRIOSONATE 120; Hoffmann-Erbrecht/HAFFNER 120. The incipits of the melo/bass sons. are in BREITKOPF MS III 10, 25, and 31.

139. The keyboard sons. are listed and discussed in some detail in Stilz/BERLINER 23-34, Schaffrath being one of the chief *Kleinmeister* in this study.

HAFFNER OM-m VII/5 and Anth. VENIER-m II/10; and 2 "Duetti" for 2 keyboard instruments, in MS.[140]

All of Schaffrath's keyboard sonatas follow the three-movement plan of F-S-F except for Op. 2/6, which inserts a "Fuga" between the first and slow movements. In the binary, outer movements there is usually a return in the second half only to later material in the first half. The ideas tend to be motivic and angular, while the style of progression is that continuous sort, common in the 1740's, in which one irregular, separable unit follows after another, with constant changes but no sharp contrasts. The texture is two-part and the left-hand support rudimentary much of the time, the total effect being straightforward, somewhat pedestrian and prosaic, and as far from the *empfindsam* style as any contemporary music could be. Yet Schaffrath shows that he could make fuller use of the keyboard on occasion (Op. 2/6/i),[141] his slow movements do reveal expressive warmth, however constrained, and there is certainly no lack of skill in the "Fuga" or in the convincing modulations that appear regularly in the second half of the binary forms.

Christoph Nichelmann (1717-62) was a pupil of both J. S. and Friedemann Bach in Leipzig, acquiring his keyboard mastery chiefly
142a from the son.[142] He also lived in Hamburg and visited France and England before studying with Quantz in Berlin and officially entering the service of Frederick the Great in 1745. Serving mainly as composer, he lost or quit the court post in 1756 (though he did not leave Berlin), two years after he had been made second cembalist to Emanuel Bach. The cause may have been a literary quarrel over Nichelmann's treatise on melody (1755), his opponent being one "Caspar Dünckelfeind," a pseudonym, supposedly, for Emanuel himself.[143] Nichelmann left about twenty keyboard sonatas and three SS/bass "sonatas" or "trios."[144] The titles of his two principal keyboard publications suggest the

---

Op. 2 is listed in Cat. BRUXELLES IV 279; cf. Hoffmann-Erbrecht/HAFFNER 120 for the date. Mod. ed.: Sons. 5 in B♭ and 6 in g, TRÉSOR-m XX.

140. The incipits of 5 solo keyboard sons. in MS are in BREITKOPF MS IV 8.

141. The slow mvt. of cembalo Concerto in B♭ is printed in part in Mersmann/AUFFÜHRUNGSPRAXIS 134-140 as another example, like Franz Benda's, of the then elaboration of melodic lines.

142. Döllmann/NICHELMANN is a diss. (1938) on the man and his music, of which the biographical section (pp. 7-17) derives largely from the contemporary account in Marpurg/BEYTRÄGE I 431-439, while the discussion of the keyboard sons. (pp. 49-63) largely supersedes that in Stilz/BERLINER 36-41. Cf., also, MGG IX 1441-1443 (Langner).

143. Cf. Döllmann/NICHELMANN 14-15 and 26-28; Bitter/BRÜDER I 27; Eitner/QL VI 142 (under "Leopold, G. . .").

144. Detailed lists are given in Döllmann/NICHELMANN 91-94 and 97-99 (mod. eds.).

reason, and the numerous anthologies in which his keyboard sonatas were represented give proof,[145] for his popularity. *Sei breve Sonate da cembalo massime all' uso delle Dame* and a second set (Op. 2) . . . *all' uso di chi ama il cembalo massime delle Dame* were both originally published about 1745 by Schmid in Nürnberg.[146] 146a

Except for two one-movement keyboard pieces called "Sonata," all of Nichelmann's sonatas are in three movements. And except for two of the SS/bass sonatas, in which the movements follow the order of S-F-F that was still preferred for that setting in Berlin, the sequence of movements is always F-S-F.[147] In most of the slow movements of the second keyboard set the nearly related key leads directly to the home key of the finale. Some of these finales are quasi-gigues. The SS/bass sonatas (2 Fls & *b.c*) are more conservative in styles and forms than the keyboard sonatas, as usual, although even the SS/bass fugal movements are light-footed and melodious in their open counterpoint. The keyboard sonatas are somewhat conservative, too—at least, more so than their early use of *galant* titles would suggest. But their fluency belies the extent of their contrapuntal activities, for the two-part writing in these short movements is so deft that the motivic play and, indeed, canonic passages, can easily pass unnoticed. Life is breathed into these light pieces where it often is not in Schaffrath's (Ex. 74).

Nichelmann's immediate predecessor as second cembalist at the Berlin court was the cellist and organist **Christian Friedrich Schale** (1713-1800), who had previously served Prince Heinrich (from 1735).[148] Of some twenty-two keyboard sonatas by Schale that are known,[149] eighteen occur in three sets of "brevi sonate per cembalo," published by Schmid's widow in Nürnberg about 1758-61.[150] These prove to be similar to Nichelmann's sonatas in their general plan, brevity, and lightness. But they are less contrapuntal and more stereotyped, with more use of minor keys, more tendency toward *galant* mannerisms and *empfindsam* slow movements, and considerable dependence on repeated-note or "drum" basses ("Trommelbässe").

145. Cf. Cat. BRUXELLES II 343-345.

146. Listed in Cat. BRUXELLES IV 133 and II 326, respectively. The *Six Short Sonatas or Lessons* listed in BRITISH UNION II 729 is a London reprint (*ca.* 1770) of Op. 2. The approximate date for the 2 Schmid eds., previously given as 1749 and before 1760, is based on the probable chronology of plate nos. XXIV and XXVI in Deutsch/NUMBERS 21. (There is no mention of Schmid's widow on Nichelmann's title pages, such as did appear after 1749). Among mod. eds.: Sons. 3-6 in the first set, all of the 2d set, and a Son. in a (1762), TRÉSOR-m XI.

147. Cf. Döllmann/NICHELMANN 65-69.

148. Cf. Eitner/QL VIII 467-468; Bitter/BRÜDER I 27.

149. They are listed and discussed in Stilz/BERLINER 42-45.

150. Plate nos. XLIV, XLVII, and LIV.

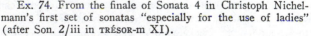

Ex. 74. From the finale of Sonata 4 in Christoph Nichelmann's first set of sonatas "especially for the use of ladies" (after Son. 2/iii in TRÉSOR-m XI).

Two "sonatas" in published anthologies (1762-63), two MS "solos" for keyboard, and an accompanied sonata (K + Vn) are known by **Johann Heinrich Rolle** (1716 [not 1718]-85).[151] Rolle was a violist at Frederick II's court from 1740 to 1746, between posts as organist in Magdeburg (75 miles southwest of Berlin). His success as a composer of many highly esteemed oratorios, cantatas, and Passions is not hard to understand when the sonatas are examined. These are notable for

151. Kaestner/ROLLE is a diss. (1931) on the man and his music but the list of works and mention of the sons. is too brief to be of value here, and there are no exx. Cf., also, Eitner/QL VIII 287-290; Stilz/BERLINER 80-82. The 2 published sons., in G and E♭, are in Anth. ALLERLEY-m VII and VIII. The incipit of the acc'd. son. is given in Cat. SCHWERIN II 162. Among mod. eds. of the Son. in E♭, Pauer/MEISTER-m III 22 and Köhler/MAÎTRES-m I 202.

their harmonic depth, especially in the slow movements, and for their broad, purposeful tonal outlines. (In the Son. in E♭/ii/45-71, see the telling modulations, by means of dim.-7th chords and enharmony, from c to A♭, f, c♯, e♭, b♭, A♭, and back to c.) The main ideas are interesting enough in their own right, but much of the writing, though not fantasy-like, is preludial, modulatory, and loosely polyphonic, such as an organist might improvise.[152] Whereas the two "sonatas" each have three rather long movements in the order F-S-F, the two "solos" are reported to have four and two movements, mostly in binary design and more suitelike in character.

Not deserving of more than passing mention are four further composers in the Berlin area who were all represented in Anth. HAFFNER COLLECTION-m (II/6, I/3, I/6, and I/5, respectively; *ca.* 1760-61). These are the song composer and aesthetician in the Berlin *Liederschule,* **Christian Gottfried Krause** (1719-70);[153] a violinist in Prince Heinrich's service and pupil of both J. G. Graun and Emanuel Bach, **Jakob Le Fevre** (*ca.* 1723-77);[154] the organist and song composer in Berlin and Halle, **Wilhelm August Traugott Roth** (*ca.* 1720-64);[155] and a violinist in Prince Heinrich's service, **Friedrich Christian Rackemann** (1735-?).[156]

Christian Friedrich Carl Fasch (1736-1800), who was trained in violin, keyboard, and composition by his illustrious father J. F. Fasch (SBE 282-284), succeeded Nichelmann at Frederick II's court in 1756, not merely as second but as alternate cembalist to Emanuel Bach.[157] With the immediate interruption of the Seven Years' War and the lessening of court musical activities that followed, he gave himself more and more to teaching, composition, further intensive contrapuntal studies, and, in 1790, the foundation of the subsequent Berlin Singakademie for which he is chiefly remembered. Because he was so severe a self critic from his earliest days, he destroyed much of his own music. But besides sacred choral works, songs, a symphony, and two sets of keyboard variations, at least seven keyboard sonatas are still extant, most of which originally appeared in contemporary anthologies

152. Cf. the approving remarks in BURNEY'S TOURS II 239.
153. Cf. MGG VII 1717-1721 (Becker). Besides another published keyboard son., in a contemporary French anthology, a MS set of 6 keyboard sonatas by "Krause," with no forename, is also discussed under this Krause in Stilz/BERLINER 75-76.
154. Cf. Eitner/QL VI 109-110.
155. Cf. Eitner/QL VIII 331.
156. Cf. Eitner/QL VIII 109.
157. The main biographic source is still Zelter/FASCH (1801), which is digested in MGG III 1857-1861 (Adrio); it contains no list of works or discussion of the sons.

dating from 1760-70.[158] These sonatas are in the customary three movements, F-S-F, except for the Sonata in B♭, in which a minuet finale is added, and the Sonatina in G, which apparently was intended only as a single movement.[159]

Although Emanuel Bach's influence must have been felt strongly,[160] Fasch's sonatas have a steady, compelling drive that is no longer congruent with the emotional vacillations of the *empfindsam* style. On the other hand, they are often conservative in their dependence on a motivic, preludial continuation. Certainly the composer is happier in this style of continuation than in the movements where themes and sections stand out more clearly.[161] His themes may tend to be a little gauche and plain, but he is a minor master of choice harmony, secure tonal movement, and accurate voice-leading. In all his sonata movements, even when the main idea returns, Fasch shows a marked and skilled avoidance of exact repetition for more than a few notes at a time, no doubt with Emanuel Bach's altered reprises much in mind. He varies his ideas with some of the pliability and imagination to be found in Beethoven's later writing. In that connection, it is interesting to read how the young Beethoven visited Fasch at the Singakademie in two successive weeks in the summer of 1796, improvising on a theme of Fasch to the delight of all present.[162]

Finally, among Berlin composers may be mentioned the widely traveled writer and song and opera composer **Johann Abraham Peter Schulz** (1747-1800), who was in Berlin from about 1765-68 and 1773-80.[163] The important article on the sonata that Schulz wrote for the last part of Sulzer's *Allgemeine Theorie* (1775) was quoted earlier (SCE II). Here we are concerned with his *Sonata per il clavicembalo solo* in E♭ (published by Hummel in Berlin and Amsterdam in 1778;

158. The sons. are discussed only in Stilz/BERLINER 54-60; both the list on p. 54 and that in MGG III 1860 have errors and omissions; J. F.'s and Carl's works were confused in Eitner/QL 394. Carl's published sons. include 2, in G and B♭, in Anth. HAFFNER COLLECTION-m I/2 and II/3; 2, in F and C, in Anth. VIELERLEY-m (mod. ed. of both: TRÉSOR-m XIV); one, in F, in Anth. BACH-m; and a Sonatina in G in Anth. MANCHERLEY. The first 5 of the foregoing sons. and a MS Son. in b♭ were all published posthumously by Rellstab of Berlin in 1805 (a copy of the full set is at the Library of Congress). A MS of 6 sons. is listed in Cat. BRUXELLES II item 5988.

159. Stilz/BERLINER 55.

160. In Reichardt/KUNSTMAGAZIN 25 Fasch and Franz Benda's son Karl are called the only true followers in the style of (Emanuel) Bach and (Georg) Benda.

161. The 2 styles are illustrated in the Sons. in F and C, respectively, that are reprinted in TRÉSOR-m XIV, the one in C being more successful than Fasch's other sons. of this type.

162. Cf. Thayer & Riemann/BEETHOVEN II 17.

163. Riess/SCHULZ is the main biographic study, incorporating autobiographic fragments, Reichardt/SCHULZ, Gerber/LEXICON II 471-474 (revised in Gerber/NEUES IV 142-158), and much else.

plate no. 165). It is possible that a few accompanied and SS/bass sonatas by him still exist, although the "trio" sonata that was his first publication (*ca.* 1770?) is lost.[164] The keyboard sonata has the standard sequence of three movements, F-S-F, but could hardly have been composed according to the "method," quoted earlier, of Kirnberger, Schulz's teacher and close associate in Berlin. Its unusual qualities will surprise anyone who troubles to examine any of the copies still to be found in numerous libraries.[165] The first movement has a chordal bluster and dash more reminiscent of the Mannheim symphonic style than the Berlin school of the sonata (Ex. 75). Its ideas have some of the

Ex. 75. From the opening of Johann Abraham Peter Schulz's Sonata in E♭ (after the original ed. at the Library of Congress).

thematic pungency of Haydn, whom Schulz admired and had met in Esterház. There are thematic contrasts and a clear return to the opening (cf. SCE XVI for Reichardt's remark on this). But it is the cumulative passages that make the strongest impression and, at the same time, become the weakness of this movement. For they go on too long, especially in the "development" section, and they find no counter interest in the excessively plain repeated-note or Alberti bass. The "Adagio" is one of the most decorative, recitative-like, florid, and harmonically active examples of the *empfindsam* style (by now somewhat dated) that we have seen. The "Vivace" finale in 6/8 meter is

164. Cf. Reichardt/SCHULZ 12; Riess/SCHULZ 195-196 and 188; Gerber/NEUES IV 157.

165. However, it gets only brief mention in Stilz/BERLINER 83 and 85; cf., also, David/SCHOBERT 66.

similar in style to the first movement, but short. Of incidental interest at the end is a table of ornaments that indicates the trills (wavy lines) are to start on the principal rather than the upper tone. The other ornament solutions follow those in Emanuel Bach's *Essay*.

Hamburg and the Other Northernmost German Centers

Hamburg, where Handel, Mattheson, and Telemann had been active earlier, was still a considerable center of opera and church music, and still the scene of much concert life, both private and public, after Emanuel Bach succeeded Telemann in 1767.[166] However, we have already found that Emanuel himself gave somewhat less to the sonata after he reached Hamburg, and of sonatas by others in Hamburg at this time there is but little to report. In fact, our one other composer who can be identified with Hamburg spent most of his career elsewhere in the north. Most of what there is to report in these northernmost German cities turns up, again, in Haffner's publications.

The violinist and organist **Adolph Carl Kunzen** (or Kuntzen; 1720-81), member of a family active in music for more than a century, trained in Hamburg and spent most of his later years at the Mecklenburg-Schwerin court, in London, and in Lübeck.[167] In addition to the songs and church music for which he was chiefly recognized, Kunzen left over 50 sonatas in print or MS, which may be placed roughly in the 15 years from 1755-70. These include 12 for the unusual combination of harp and *b.c.*,[168] 17 for violin and *b.c.*,[169] 24 in 4 sets (of "sonatas" or "sonatinas") for harpsichord, plus (only) one sonata each in Anth. THOMPSON LESSONS-m (1762) and Anth. HAFFNER OM-m VII/2 (1761).[170] Available to the present study were the *XII Sonatas for Harpsichord,* Op. 1, published by John Johnson of London in 1757, and the Haffner sonata. Within their somewhat limited technical, expressive, and pitch ranges these sonatas show the earlier pre-Classic varieties of style and structure that indicate no stereotype had yet been reached. Furthermore, although the music falls into fairly well-defined phrases the fast harmonic rhythm and "running" bass (in steady 8th-notes) that still predominate tend to block any sense of broad sectional organization. Besides the three-movement plan of F-S-minuet, which occurs most often, there are other plans, including S-F-Aria with

166. Cf. MGG V 1389-1399 (Stephenson); BURNEY'S TOURS 208-222; Sittard/HAMBURG 82-203.

167. Cf. MGG VII 1904-1906 (Karstädt).

168. Listed in Eitner/QL V 476.

169. 2 incipits appear in Cat. SCHWERIN I 478.

170. Cf. the listings in BRITISH UNION I 583 and II 613.

variations, S-F-S-F, and F-S-"Fuga"-minuet with variations (Op. 1/10, 4, and 12, respectively). The melodic ideas sometimes take a fresh, original turn (as in Anth. HAFFNER OM-m VII/2/i). Chordal and repeated-note basses occur (Op. 1/9/ii), though not the literal Alberti bass. Among movements that must have been designed to catch the public ear and eye are a "Siciliano" (Op. 1/8/ii), an exploit in tricky rhythm and hand-crossing (Op. 1/9/i), a purely figural "Fantasia Allegro" (Op. 1/7/i), and the 12 mostly showy variations that top off the last sonata in Op. 1 (after which a "teaser" appears: "The remaining 12 variations [on this same minuet theme?] follow in Op. 2").

The obscure organist **Georg Albert Appel,** active in Rendsburg (fifty-five miles north of Hamburg) in the later 1750's, is known only for three sonatas, in Anth. HAFFNER OM-m I/2, II/1, and IV/1, plus a symphony and keyboard suite left in Schwerin.[171] All three sonatas are in three movements, F-S-F. They are modestly conceived works at most, yet not uninteresting for their compelling harmony, for their fresh melodic ideas, which are naïve somewhat as Neefe's are, and for the stylistic trends they disclose even during the short three years in which they were published (1755-*ca.* 1758). As compared with the extensive (rather than intensive) motivic treatment in the first sonata, the other two sonatas show progressively more homophonic texture, figurate lines, experimental harmony, and emotional intensity.

Johann Wilhelm Hertel (1727-89) was a violinist and keyboardist who numbered among his illustrious teachers a pupil of J. S. Bach in Eisenach (J. H. Heil), Franz Benda, C. H. Graun, and Emanuel Bach. He knew the last three in Berlin. In 1754 he succeeded Kunzen at the lively Mecklenburg-Schwerin court, and he remained in Schwerin for the rest of his life. Unfortunately, his lengthy, genial, often witty autobiography (1783-84) contributes no direct information on his sonatas nor helps to unravel the confused references to his numerous keyboard, Fl/bass, Vn/bass, organ, oboe, and other ensemble sonatas.[172] His printed sonatas include only his first publication, *Sei Sonate per cembalo,* Op. 1 (Haffner, 1756; plate no. 86), and a Sonata in B♭ in Anth. HAFFNER OM-m III/3.[173] The available key-

171. Eitner/QL I 179.

172. The 3 MS versions of the autobiography are annotated in detail in Schenk/HERTEL; but Schenk's "Werksverzeichnis" (pp. 66-71), like that in MGG VI 284-288 (Kahl), does not attempt to itemize the raw list of sons. in Eitner/QL V 129-130.

173. Op. 1 is listed, along with a MS cembalo son. (after 1774) and 2 melo/bass sons. (one dated 1761), in Cat. SCHWERIN I 397-398 and II 375 (dedication in full). Mod. ed.: Op. 1/3 in d, HORTUS MUSICUS-m No. 49 (Erdmann) with

Ex. 76. From the slow movement in g of Christian Franz Severin Hägemann's Sonata 3 in B♭ (after the original MS in the Kreisbibliothek Eutin).

board sonatas are in three movements, F-S-F. The slow movements of those in Op. 1 have something of the florid lyrical breadth in Franz Benda's slow movements, while that in the Haffner sonata has a little of Emanuel Bach's more changeable, precious *empfindsam* style. For the rest, these are rather simple, unprepossessing pieces, still based on short motives that unfold into sequences and changing patterns in relatively fast harmonic rhythm. One wonders whether a study of the later sonatas (when Hertel switched his allegiance from the clavichord to the new Silbermann piano[174]) might not reveal some of the strengths,
175a skill, and virtuosity that have been found in his concertos.[175]

Christian Franz Severin Hägemann (*ca.* 1724-1812) was a trumpeter and violinist in the Schleswig-Holstein court in Plön (fifty miles north of Hamburg) from 1744 to 1776, except for a period of playing

preface; for mod. eds. of a Vn/bass Son. in C and a light, 3-mvt. "Sonata a quattro" for 2 horns and 2 bassoons, cf. Altmann/KAMMERMUSIK 238 and NOTES XVII (1960) 472, respectively.

174. Cf. Schenk/HERTEL 39 and 88.

175. Cf. Uldall/KLAVIERKONZERT 96.

under the direction of G. Sarti in Copenhagen about 1770.[176] He left in MSS at least a set called "Clavier Versuche in sechs Sonaten" (1777) and a set of six accompanied sonatas called "Trios" (in the sense of the keyboard and violin making three parts). Both sets have the usual three-movement plan, F-S-F. The accompanied set is reported to be relatively elementary, perhaps pedagogic in intent. The keyboard solo sonatas are more adventuresome, tuneful, and rhythmically fresh. As is often true in the north German sonata, the slow movement achieves the most expressive interest (Ex. 76).

176. Cf. MGG V 1228-1229 (Holm).

Chapter XIV

Haydn and Mozart

Some Preliminaries

In this and the next chapter, three of the greatest sonata composers the world has known are discussed—Haydn, the self-made court musician of peasant stock; Mozart, the cultured but ill-fated "hothouse fruit" (to use Einstein's term); and Beethoven, the neurotic, rugged individual. The subject matter in these two chapters is confined to the backgrounds, sources, and circumstances of their sonatas. Earlier, in Chapter VI, the "Vienna Classical" styles and forms of their sonatas were dealt with separately, since in these peak works, naturally, lies the central point of attack on the whole question of style and structure in the Classic sonata. In other words, we are about to look into the what, where, when, and sometimes why of the sonatas by Haydn, Mozart, and Beethoven, but we shall not be looking further into the how. The question of influences on and of these three masters is dealt with only where it has immediate application in the next two chapters, since it, too, comes up elsewhere, especially under the individual, lesser composers who exerted or underwent these influences.

The proportion of detail in these two chapters is greatest for the keyboard sonatas. This emphasis is supported by the greater interest in these works on the part of performers ever since the Classic Era itself, by the more extensive literature on these works, and by the greater freedom and more innovational character of the music itself. Regarding the interest that performers have shown, there are practical reasons why the ensemble sonatas by Haydn and the earlier ones by Mozart are seldom heard today. One is the accompanied keyboard style that still prevails in them and would discourage all but the most historically minded students. Another is the extinction of the baryton, which is the main instrument in so many of Haydn's ensemble sonatas. Only a few music examples are provided in these two chapters, chiefly facsimiles made from fine autographs now at the Library of Congress and the New York Public Library. Because the sonatas of the three masters are so widely available and because it is so futile, anyway, to try to illustrate their well-knit structures with short excerpts, it has seemed better to hope that the reader will have his score in hand where necessary.

Out of the enormous literature on the three masters, the primary sources and the studies basic to the sonata are summarized early in the discussion of each man and of each main category of his sonatas. It will be noted that though the literature on Beethoven is the most extensive, it is at the same time, in many respects, the least up-to-date and the least organized. The Mozart literature is in the best state. The Haydn literature is somewhat less voluminous, but conspicuous progress has been made in recent years toward filling the gaps, even the sorely needed complete edition of the music being nearer to a full realization than ever before.

The respective periods in which the sonatas of our three masters were composed might best be compared by drawing the life lines of each (which together bridge the entire Classic Era). Clementi's long span of sonata production is added for purposes of later comparison.

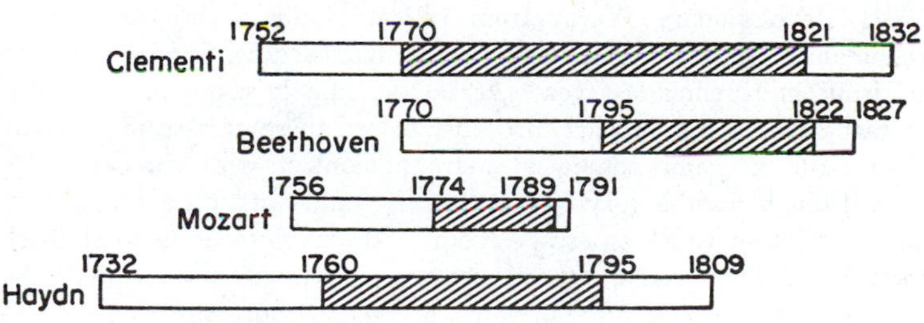

The Creative Spans of Four Classic Masters

As is well known, Haydn's longer life and longer creative span permitted him both to influence and be influenced by Mozart. Beethoven, who started writing sonatas (other than his very early works) about when Haydn stopped, soon effected a "marriage" of his two great predecessors by drawing upon the resources and styles of each. In the discussions that follow, each of the three men's careers is subdivided into its main creative periods, based partly on recent or new considerations. Furthermore, the sonatas of each are tabulated in approximately chronological order, again aided by recent or new considerations. Haydn and Mozart are both shown to have reached maturity in their sonata writing during the 1770's. They came along, that is, about when the Austro-German sonata otherwise had begun to settle into a light, facile formula. The almost precipitate advance in depth, quality, and originality that their sonatas brought about continued right through the sonatas of Beethoven and Schubert. In a broad survey of the present sort it is possible to find precedents for almost every detail of style in Haydn's and Mozart's music and for much in Beethoven's. But, of course, it is much harder to establish any kind of historical continuity that explains this new depth, quality, and originality. In short, the genius of these three men remains as much a mystery as that of any other great artists in any other era.

We shall see that the spirit of the *Sturm und Drang* movement was still a potent force in Beethoven's sonatas, and that it already was present in certain sonatas of his important predecessors. Beethoven's interest in Schiller and Goethe is well known. Since he was closer to Romanticism, too, both in time and spirit, it is not surprising that he was also more affected by current sociopolitical forces. Haydn was shielded all his life by his connection with the Esterházy family. He was in London during much of the early Austrian involvement in the French Revolutionary Wars (from 1792). Only during the French occupation in 1805 and Napoleon's actual bombardment and occupation of Vienna in Haydn's last year (1809) did Haydn come very close to the realities of war. Mozart died just before these catastrophic events began. But he came somewhat more in contact with current sociopolitical forces for the very reason that he could not find a satisfactory court position in which to escape them. His inability quite to stomach the menial status of the eighteenth-century court musician as Haydn did in his earlier career is not unrelated to certain more pronounced Romantic traits in his sonatas. Beethoven was the first great composer to divorce himself entirely from this status, and the bumps he suffered in his constant fight to cope with the world around him may have left their marks still more clearly in his works, even though we shall find the actual evidence to be less tangible than for Mozart.

Haydn and Mozart knew each other well, as did Haydn and Beethoven. But except for their uncertain acquaintance in 1787, Beethoven knew Mozart only through his music. Haydn did not move permanently to Vienna from his secluded residence in the Esterházy castle (45 miles south) until 1790 (at the age of 58), but he visited the city increasingly from the late 1770's. Mozart did not quit his Salzburg post and move to Vienna until 1781 (at the advanced age for him of 25). Beethoven did not move from Bonn to study with Haydn in Vienna until 1792 (at the age of 21). Thus the three never lived in Vienna at the same time. In Vienna two facts should be added to the early mentions of this city (SCE XI).[1] First is the springing up of music publishers, just in time and almost as if to accommodate our three masters (though the London publishers and Breitkopf & Härtel in Leipzig also figured importantly in their publications). One thinks especially of firms like Toricella, Artaria, Hoffmeister, Cappi, and Bureau des Arts et d'Industrie.[2] The other fact is the continued restriction of most concert life in Vienna to the imperial court and to the private homes of the nobility and wealthy citizens. How rare were the opportunities to hear sonatas in public will be noted when we come to Beethoven.

Haydn: Sources, Periods, Works

We start with the earliest of the three Viennese masters in order of birth and historical styles, **Franz Joseph Haydn** (1732-1809). Haydn was also the longest-lived of the three, his 77 years stretching from 18 years before J. S. Bach's death to the year of Mendelssohn's birth. Prior to the bicentennial, in 1932, of Haydn's birth, the research that had been done on him, voluminous by any other standards, had hardly kept pace with that on Mozart or Beethoven, and it had been still more disorderly. Mainly responsible for both the delay and the disorder were not only the complexities of a changing style that bridged two eras, but the serious gaps in the records of Haydn's life; the exceptional problems of telling authentic from spurious compositions that have arisen among the multitudinous MSS and publications credited to him; the wide dispersal of this music, which is still turning up in some Austrian monastery, Czech museum, Hungarian library, German archives, or other of the countless repositories, private or public, that exist throughout the civilized world; and not least, the sheer quantity of all this material that awaits further study.[3] The most important studies before 1932 had been those by the German scholar Carl Ferdinand Pohl, in-

1. Valuable descriptions of musical and social life in Vienna while Beethoven was there are given in Thayer/BEETHOVEN I 163-173; II 1-3, 42, 51-52, 143-146, 165-166 (regarding the exceptional worth of Reichardt's Vienna reports in his *Vertraute Briefe* of 1808-09). Cf., also, Deutsch/SCHUBERT xxi-xxix (including map).

2. Cf. Weinmann/WIENER. The activities of earlier music publishers and dealers in Vienna are ably catalogued in Gericke/WIENER.

3. Cf. Larsen/ÜBERLIEFERUNG 9-21; Geiringer/HAYDN 179-187.

cluding *Mozart und Haydn in London* (1867) and the biography of Haydn (1875-82, completed by H. Botstiber in 1927). Pohl's biography, which started with the valuable but largely anecdotal accounts that Griesinger, Dies, Carpani, and others had published soon after Haydn's death, introduced all the documentary material that could then be found, supplied a still very incomplete thematic index of the works, and provided running, though sketchy comments on the music
3a itself.

Following the international flood of individual studies around 1932, a break-through in Haydn research came in 1939 with the mature, published dissertation by the Danish scholar Jens Peter Larsen.[4] In this study the groundwork was laid for determining authentic works and their chronological dating, chiefly through confirmed autograph MSS, MS copies of reliable origin, contemporary publications issued with Haydn's knowledge, and three main contemporary thematic indices prepared or acknowledged by him. In 1941 the value of this study was increased still more by Larsen's publication of the three thematic indices in facsimile,[5] of which two are pertinent here—the so-called "Entwurf-Katalog," dating mostly from *ca.* 1765-85, and the "Haydn-Verzeichnis," prepared in 1805 by Haydn's copyist Elssler. Elssler used the "Entwurf-Katalog" he had helped to make, all the 48 sonatas, "trios," and other pieces in the first 9 (of the 12) volumes in Haydn/OEUVRES-m that had been published from 1800-03 by Breitkopf & Härtel,[6] Pleyel's Paris edition of the "complete" string quartets, and other sources. In 1955 Larsen added further to his contributions as a leading Haydn specialist by heading the newly founded Joseph Haydn-Institut in Köln, which since 1958 has already made better progress toward the badly needed "complete edition" (Haydn/INSTITUT-m) than either of the two previous, abortive projects in the present century (Haydn/WERKE-m, 1908-33, and Haydn/WORKS-m, 1950-51, the latter overseen by Larsen, too).[7]

Three other milestones recently passed in Haydn research are also pertinent here. One is the book on his symphonies by the American scholar H. C. Robbins Landon,[8] a precocious, exhaustive study that indirectly contributes as much to an understanding of Haydn's sonatas

4. Larsen/ÜBERLIEFERUNG.
5. Larsen/KATALOGE, with preface. Cf. Landon/SYMPHONIES 4-12.
6. Cf. Larsen/ÜBERLIEFERUNG 298-299.
7. As of this writing (1961) most of the baryton "trios" in *Reihe* XIV of Haydn/INSTITUT-m have appeared; the keyboard "trios," the other accompanied sons., and the solo keyboard sons. are scheduled to be in *Reihe* XVIII-XX. The editor of the keyboard sons. was to be Georg Feder.
8. Landon/SYMPHONIES (1955).

as any study yet dedicated expressly to that subject. Another is the collection (and translation into English) of Haydn's entire available correspondence and his "London Notebooks" or diaries (1791-95),[9] 9a
all in a single volume that follows other less complete but somewhat different collections of documents.[10] And a third is the first, instrumental volume in the long awaited, complete thematic index of Haydn's works, an enormous lifetime project undertaken by the veteran Dutch collector of Haydn (and other) first and early editions, Anthony van Hoboken.[11] Other significant Haydn research that bears on the sonata, such as that of Schmid, Geiringer, and Abert, will be noted where each applies in the following pages. 11a

In their recent, excellent joint article on Haydn, Larsen and Landon have suggested new subdivisions of his creative life that are defined, more than in previous solutions to this problem, by apparent turning points in his style and in his outer life.[12] These eight subdivisions or periods do not contradict the broader, tripartite division into youth (to 1760), adulthood (to 1790), and old age that must apply to any full life span. The *earliest creative period,* about 1750-60, covers Haydn's second decade in Vienna, from his dismissal as a choirboy at St. Stephen's Cathedral to his first court appointment. In the works preserved from this decade Larsen and Landon find that there is already a fresh originality in spite of Haydn's obvious ties with the past. The *second period,* about 1760-65, covers the start of Haydn's employ in the Esterházy family, to whom he remained attached for the rest of his life, although it was chiefly during the twenty-eight years of Prince Nikolaus's reign (1762-90) that he served this family. In the works of these years are noted a new depth of purpose and, if anything, increased tokens of a Baroque heritage. The *third period,* about 1766-72, begins with Haydn's promotion to full *Kapellmeister* and the removal

9. Landon/HAYDN (1959).

10. Among these are Reich/HAYDN (1946) and Rutz/HAYDN (1953). A complete collection of Haydn documents is still much to be desired. New documentary material can be expected in *The Haydn Year-book,* announced for publication, under the editorship of Larsen and Landon, in ML XLII/4 (Oct., 1961).

11. Hoboken/HAYDN (1957), here abbreviated H. when a reference to a specific music item is made. O. E. Deutsch's acerb review of this work in MR XVIII (1957) 330-336 discovers some undeniable flaws among its myriad details and rightly raises some broader questions of policy, but fails to emphasize its vast improvement over anything previously available. Until Hoboken's index is completed, the fullest and most convenient lists of all categories of Haydn's music remain those in GROVE IV 166-205 (Scott) and in MGG V 1886-1893 and 1910-1922 (Larsen, Landon, and Schaal).

12. MGG V 1897-1909. In Geiringer/HAYDN (a completely new book after Geiringer's previous biography in German [1932], and one of the best over-all accounts of the man and his music) the subdivision is made somewhat arbitrarily but not ineffectively by decades.

of the family from Eisenstadt (twenty-five miles south of Vienna) to their spectacular new castle, Esterház (some twenty miles further south). In these musically critical years, or the period of what has often been called Haydn's "romantic crisis," there may be noted a still further turn away from a light diversional style to be found in the first period, the tendency now being toward the *empfindsam* or pre-Romantic style of the *Sturm und Drang*. The *fourth period,* about 1773-79, starts around the time of Empress Maria Theresa's visit to Esterház and is characterized by greater interest in sacred choral and operatic music, with a more routine, though ever-skillful, approach to the symphony and sonata, and no attention to the string quartet.

The *fifth period,* about 1779-84, is ushered in approximately by the start of Haydn's dealings with the publisher Artaria and his supposed attachment to Luigia Polzelli. It is marked by a new experimentalism in styles (including the Quartets "Op. 33," written "auf eine ganz neue besondere Art"[13]), in forms, and in settings, as reflected by a groping for new depths, a certain insecurity, and a certain unevenness of quality. The *sixth period,* about 1784-90, is defined chiefly by closer *rapprochements* with Viennese and other musicians, especially Mozart (including the well-known remark of Haydn to Leopold and the dedication by Wolfgang to Haydn, both in 1785[14]). It ends with Haydn's relief from official duties after the death of Prince Nikolaus. In this period Larsen and Landon find a restored security and a still greater clarification and mastery of style, form, and expression, evident above all in the chamber music and symphonies. The *seventh period* takes in the two highly fruitful London visits arranged by the impresario Salomon, in 1791-92 and 1794-95. For and during these visits Haydn wrote some of his finest symphonies, chamber music, and piano sonatas, which owed much of their immense popular appeal to their greater structural breadth and their melodic directness (including the use of Croatian and other folk material). The *eighth and last period,* 1796-1803, follows Haydn's return to Vienna. Although it includes the two oratorios and six Masses that brought him some of his greatest glories, there seem to be no significant instrumental works to report other than quartets and a few last accompanied sonatas (piano trios). Actually, it is only in this last period that solo keyboard sonatas were not composed.[15] As the recounting of these will show, they were spread rather

13. Cf. Landon/HAYDN 33.
14. Cf. Landon/HAYDN 49-50.
15. Haydn did intend to write further "pianoforte Sonatas" after the *Seasons* was finished (cf. Landon/HAYDN 171 and 179), but none is known.

regularly throughout all of his previous creative life, being second in this respect only to the symphonies.[16]

The 107 symphonies, 83 string quartets, and all other instrumental works that Hoboken actually credits to Haydn, including some that are now lost, total around 950, of which about 600 fall into the category of cyclic or other extended works, while the other 350 consist mostly of separate marches, minuets, and other dances.[17] Of the extended works, 283, or nearly half, belong to various settings to which the title "sonata" is given at least in some of the Haydn sources. Thus, on the rough assumption that Haydn's vocal production was about equal to his instrumental, he may be said to have devoted nearly a fourth of his more extended creative efforts to the sonata. Broken down by settings, his sonatas (or *divertimenti,* or trios, or *duetti,* etc.) include 126 trios and 25 duos in which the baryton is the solo instrument (or about 53 per cent of all the sons.), 57 solo keyboard sonatas (or about 20 per cent), 41 accompanied sonatas or piano trios (mostly K & Vn & Vc; about 14 per cent), 21 trios mostly for 2 violins and cello (about 7 per cent), 6 duos for violin and viola (about 2 per cent), and the 7 single-movement orchestral "sonatas" in *Musica instrumentale sopra le sette ultime parole del nostro Redentore in Croce.* The foregoing totals do not include many of the numerous arrangements that Haydn's more popular works underwent, whether made by himself or, much more often, by others. Such, for example, are the solo keyboard sonatas arranged from "The Seven Last Words" set just listed (H. XX/1/c), or the four-hand keyboard sonatas arranged from most of the "London" 17a
symphonies (e.g., H. I/97/f), or 7 accompanied sonatas for keyboard and optional violin that were arranged from 4 solo keyboard sonatas, a *divertimento a 6,* and 2 string quartets (H. XIV/24-26 and 43bis, II/11 [cf. XVI/15], and III/81-82).

Haydn's Keyboard Sonatas

Musically, popularly, and historically, Haydn's most important sonatas are those for solo keyboard and those for keyboard with violin and cello accompaniments. The 12-volume *Oeuvres complettes* (Haydn/

16. Cf. Landon/SYMPHONIES 171-173 (although the periods are not yet those defined in the MGG article).

17. In Griesinger/HAYDN 7 the summary of extended instrumental types, based on the "Haydn Verzeichnis," totals 456 "and still many" more; in Carpani/HAYDINE 97 the total is 527. Both figures suggest how much Haydn himself must have forgotten that he wrote, in his later years. He certainly knew still less of the almost as many works that Hoboken and the other specialists have had to reject as spurious. Cf. the statement made by Härtel in 1810, as trans. in Landon/SYMPHONIES 8; also, Larsen/ÜBERLIEFERUNG 256-260. Recall the related statistics in Chap. IV, *supra.*

OEUVRES-m) that Breitkopf & Härtel issued in 1800-06 included among other works 34 solo keyboard sonatas and 4 more to which violin accompaniments were added, making much the largest of the many editions of his keyboard sonatas published in his lifetime.[18] Innumerable further editions followed in the 19th century. But the first to contain all 49 of these sonatas now known to be extant, as well as 3 more that do not belong there,[19] is the edition prepared by Karl Päsler in 1918, making the keyboard sonatas the only category to be completed as of
20a this writing, in any of the projected sets of Haydn's "complete works."[20]
Päsler's numbering of the sonatas in an approximately chronological order is the one used by Hoboken and in the present survey. Some such numbering is required in any case, since the many original editions, re-editions, piracies, anthologies, and arrangements in which Haydn's works already appeared in his own lifetime made for more than the usual eighteenth-century confusion of opus numbers. But tables and collations have been needed to relieve at least as much confusion created by many different numbering systems, both in older editions and in the two main editions that have followed and derived from Päsler's. For the reader's use in the present discussion, as well as in Chapter VI, a table is given below that collates Päsler's numbering with that in the early Haydn/OEUVRES-m and in the more recent editions of H. Zilcher for Breitkopf & Härtel (1932; 42 sons. in 4 vols.) and C. A. Martienssen for Peters (1936-37 and 1952; 43 sons. in 4 vols. and 6 "Divertimenti"
21a in a 5th vol.).[21] The dates of composition and/or first 18th-century

18. On the history of this ed. and unauthorized changes in it, in spite of Haydn's stamp of approval, cf. Larsen/ÜBERLIEFERUNG 138-144; Parrish/HAYDN 29.

19. Or, in all, 29 more sons. than were listed in the "Haydn-Verzeichnis" (contrary to Landon/SYMPHONIES 9); cf. Larsen/KATALOGE 87-95 and 135; Larsen/ÜBERLIEFERUNG 297-303.

20. Haydn/WERKE-m XIV/1-3 (reprinted in Lea Pocket Scores in 1960). Among the relatively few extant autographs, that of Son. in A, H. XVI/26 is reproduced in HAYDN/facs.-m (Larsen); cf., also, Ex. 77, *infra,* from Son. in E♭, H. XVI/52. With regard to the 3 extra sons., Son. 15 in Päsler's ed. is an arrangement of 3 mvts. from *Divertimento* H. II/11, Son. 16 is of unlikely authenticity on both bibliographic and stylistic grounds (SCE XIII, under Schwanenberger; Steglich/SCHWANENBERGER 79; Larsen/ÜBERLIEFERUNG 302), and Son. 17 is now attributed to Schwanenberger (Steglich/SCHWANENBERGER). In the "Entwurf-Katalog" are given the incipits for 8 further sons. (each called "Divertimento") now not otherwise known (cf. Haydn/WERKE-m XIV/1 xiv-xv, Larsen/KATALOGE 22-24, Hoboken/HAYDN 733 and 735-736 [but H. XVI/2f should not be the same as H. XVI/14!]; all 3 sources with the incipits). The 3 "Göttweiger Sonaten" that were published in 1934 as Haydn sons. newly discovered by E. F. Schmid were reported 3 years later by the same ed. to be by F. A. Hoffmeister, instead (SCE XVI; Schmid/GÖTTWEIGER).

21. Further tables and collations may be found in Pohl/HAYDN II suppl. pp. 7-8; Challier/TABELLE 6-7 (excellent for the 19th century); Cuming/HAYDN 374-375 (a convenient summary of Haydn resources as of 1949); Mitchell/HAYDN. All of the foregoing include thematic incipits except Cuming.

publication, as well as the most used opus number, are included insofar as each is known (according to information given variously in Päsler's 3 prefaces, Hoboken/HAYDN 733-780, and MGG V 1890-1891 or 1910-1916). The chronology, as revised here, differs considerably from either Päsler's or Martienssen's.[22]

No detailed, comprehensive study of Haydn's keyboard sonatas has been published (up to 1961),[23] although numerous articles have 23a
been done on them, of varying worth and scope. The most important of the articles is still the one in two installments that H. Abert wrote in recognition of Päsler's edition,[24] with special consideration of the possible influences by Wagenseil, Emanuel Bach, and others. Päsler's own helpful prefaces had dealt mainly with sources and performance practices.[25] Previously there had appeared only such running descriptions of these sonatas as Pohl and Shedlock had supplied.[26] Since Abert's article, a few discussions of the structural aspects have appeared, chiefly as individual analyses of the late sonatas.[27] In the present discussion certain historical circumstances of the keyboard sonatas may be brought together, by way of supplementing the investigation into Haydn's structural procedures in Chapter VI.

There are hints in early records that some of Haydn's first compositions to attract attention, those written in his early twenties, were keyboard sonatas.[28] However, these may well be the very sonatas known only by their incipits today. In any case, the keyboard sonatas were ten years behind the quartets or symphonies in reaching publication. In the extant autographs, Haydn actually used the title "Partita" for his first two keyboard "sonatas" that are known, and "Divertimento" (as

22. The order of the last 3 sons. follows the fascinating arguments in Strunk/HAYDN. Not included in the following list is the well-known "Andante con variazioni" in f, which was headed "Sonata" in the original autograph of 1793 and subsequently referred to as "1 Sonata in F minore" by Haydn (cf. Landon/HAYDN 309; Hoboken/HAYDN 791-793). An important new source for Sons. 3, 14, 19, 27, and 47 is described in Larsen/QUELLE.

23. Not available here was an unpublished diss. listed in MGG V 1930-1931 as H. Schulze-Reimann, "Stud. zur Formbildung in den Haydnschen Kl.-Son." (Erlangen, 1943).

24. Abert/HAYDN.

25. Haydn/WERKE-m XIV/1-3; Aulabaugh/HAYDN is an unpublished diss. (1958) that goes much further into the performance problems.

26. Pohl/HAYDN II 310-316; Shedlock/SONATA 113-120. Similar descriptions were supplied more recently in Dent/HAYDN, Radcliffe/HAYDN, and Vignal/HAYDN.

27. Westphal/HAYDN and Noske/HAYDN concern the second theme in Haydn's "sonata forms." Detailed analyses may be found of Son. No. 49/i in E♭, in Mersmann/PHÄNOMENOLOGIE 256-262; of Son. No. 35/i in C and No. 52/i in E♭, in Schenker/TONWILLE IV (1923) 15-18 and III (1922) 3-21 (including graphs in the appendices); and of No. 52/i-iii, in Tovey/ANALYSIS VII 93-105.

28. Cf. Pohl/HAYDN I 188-189 and 128.

Haydn's Keyboard Sonatas

Päsler (1918)	Key	Year of composition (*at latest)	First 18th-century edition (as a keyboard solo)	Haydn/ OEUVRES-m (*Vn added)	Zilcher/ HAYDN-m (1932)	Martienssen/ HAYDN-m	Revised chronology of composition
1	C	*1760				D. 1	1
2	B♭	"			40	22	2
3	C	*1765				D. 2	7
4	D	"				D. 3	8
5	A	*1763			41	23	6
6	G	*1766		XII/2	36	37	14
7	C	*1760				D. 5	3
8	G	*1760				D. 4	4
9	F	*1760			42	D. 6	5
10	C	*1765				43	9
11	G	*1765			31	11	10
12	A	*ca.* 1765		XI/11	28	29	11
13	E	"		XI/12	18	18	12
14	D	"		XII/3	15	15	13
(15)	C	(arranged)					
(16)	E♭	(spurious?)					
(17)	B♭	(spurious?)	Op. 53, Artaria, 1788		(30)		
18	B♭	*ca.* 1770	"	I/8	19	19	20
19	D	1767	"	I/7	9	9	18
20	c	1771?	1780, with nos. 35-39	II/6	24	25	21
21	C	1773	(Op. 13), Kurzböck, 1774	XI/7	16	16	22
22	E	"	"	XI/8	39	40	23
23	F	"	"	XI/9	21	21	24
24	D	"	"	*X/6	32	31	25
25	E♭	"	"	*X/7		32	26
26	A	"	"	*X/8		33	27
27	G	1774-76	Op. 14, Hummel, 1778	XI/1	12	12	28
28	E♭	"	"	XI/2	13	13	29
29	F	"	"	XI/3	14	14	30
30	A	"	"	XI/4	35	36	31
31	E	"	"	XI/5	29	30	32
32	b	"	"	XI/6	38	39	33
33	D	*1783	(Op. 41), Birchall, 1783	XII/1	20	20	39
34	e	*1783	(Op. 42), 1783, with no. 33	I/2	2	2	40
35	C	*1780	Op. 30, Artaria, 1780	II/1	5	5	34
36	c#	"	"	II/2	6	6	35
37	D	"	"	II/3	7	7	36
38	E♭	"	"	II/4	34	35	37
39	G	"	"	II/5	17	17	38
40	G	1783 or '84	Op. 37, Bossler, 1784	IV/1	10	10	42
41	B♭	"	"	IV/2	26	27	43
42	D	"	"	IV/3	27	28	44
43	A♭	*1783	(Op. 41), 1783, with nos. 33-34	*XII/5	11	41	41
44	g	*ca.* 1766	Op. 54, Artaria, 1788?	I/4	4	4	15
45	E♭	1766	"	I/5	25	26	16
46	A♭	*ca* .1768	"	I/6	8	8	19
47	F	*ca.* 1766	Op. 55, Artaria, 1788	IV/6	33	34	17
48	C	*1789	(Op. 89), Breitkopf, 1789	IV/4	23	24	45
49	E♭	*1790	Op. 66, Artaria, 1789	I/3	3	3	46
50	C	*1794	Op. 79, Caulfield, *ca.* 1800	2d mvt. XII/4	22	42	49
51	D	1794?	(Op. 93, Breitkopf, *ca.* 1804)	XI/10	37	38	48
52	E♭	1794	Op. 82, Artaria, 1798	I/1	1	1	47

Wagenseil had) for the next eighteen (in our revised chronology). Only at the end of his third creative period, with the newly sensitive, pre-Romantic Sonata in c (H. XVI/20; SCE VI, with ex.), did he adopt the title "Sonata." And it is with this sonata that he may have started to compose for the piano rather than the harpsichord, to judge by the first appearance of dynamic signs as well as by the character.[29] 29a

The twelve sonatas that followed in the next (fourth) period (H. XVI/21-32) comprised the first two sets to be published by Haydn, the success and appeal of which were confirmed by their many reprints. It was the sonatas in these two sets, Opp. 13 and 14, that were denounced by an English critic in 1784 as deliberately parodying Emanuel Bach's style (SCE 430). Previously (1780), a German critic had qualified his commendation of the first set only in terms of Haydn's other works (much as subsequent critics have qualified the sonatas to this day): "One does not find here the strong and original mood that prevails in the composer's new *Quattros* and *Quintettos* but [does find] a highly pleasing mood and entertaining wit."[30] There are increasing evidences in the two sets that the piano was intended. It is true that Haydn used only the terms "cembalo," "clavicembalo," or "clavier" throughout his titles, except for Son. 49 in E♭ (i.e., H. XVI/49), which is called "Sonata per il Forte-piano . . ." in the autograph. Furthermore, Haydn is reported to "have composed the greater part of my 'Creation'" on a clavichord.[31] But the graduated levels of dynamic markings, the use of "cresc." (Son. 29/i/22), and the option of "le clavecin ou le pianoforte" in the first edition of Op. 14 leave little doubt as to the predominant intention.

In Haydn's fifth period, the fine set published by Artaria as Op. 30 (H. XVI/35-39 and 20), containing several of his sonatas that have been the most taught and played ever since, won the warm praise of Reichardt and Gerber.[32] It might be interesting to quote in full a 32a
sample letter from Haydn to Artaria in this period, one that shows his constant concern with the accuracy of the engraving, with the success of the sale, and with the critics' reactions:[33]

Estoras [Esterház], 25th February 1780

Most highly respected Gentlemen!

I send you herewith the corrected proofs of all 6 Sonatas, and ask you to study them as carefully as possible: those numbers marked in red are

29. Cf. Parrish/HAYDN 29 and 33 (but H. XVI/18 does not seem to have been called "Sonata pour le Pianoforte" by Haydn); Aulabaugh/HAYDN 6-8, 43-44; G. Kinsky in ZMW XIII (1930-31) 500-501.
30. As quoted in Pohl/HAYDN II 315.
31. James/HAYDN 315.
32. Both men are quoted in Pohl/HAYDN I 315.
33. As trans. in Landon/HAYDN 25.

the most urgent of all. The approval of the *Demoiselles* von Auenbrugger [the dedicatees] is most important to me, for their way of playing and genuine insight into music equal those of the greatest masters. Both deserve to be known throughout Europe through the public newspapers.

Incidentally, I consider it necessary, in order to forestall the criticisms of any witlings, to print on the reverse side of the title page, the following sentence, here underlined:

Avertissement

Among these 6 Sonatas there are two single movements in which the same subject occurs through several bars; the author has done this intentionally, to show different methods of treatment.

For of course I could have chosen a hundred other ideas instead of this one; but so that the whole *opus* will not be exposed to blame on account of this one intentional detail (which the critics and especially my enemies might interpret wrongly), I think that this *avertissement* or something like it must be appended, otherwise the sale might be hindered thereby. I submit the point in question to the judicious decision of the two *Demoiselles* Auenbrugger, whose hands I respectfully kiss. Please send one of the six copies you promised me to Herr Zach von Hartenstein [Austrian postal official] through the Royal Bavarian post-office, but the other five are to be addressed to [me at] Estoras.

I hope soon to receive an answer to the above point, and have the honour to be, most respectfully,

Your most obedient servant,
Joseph Haydn

The "Avertissement" did appear approximately as requested, but could not the striking similarity of themes in Sonatas 36/ii and 39/i actually have been an accident caught too late by a busy composer whose erratic memory was notorious?[34] Although Haydn had felt only the Berlin critics were too hard on him,[35] it was a Parisian critic who remarked in 1781 on the new traits in Op. 30 (perhaps including the Hungarian melodic elements that have been noted in Son. 37/ii and iii) and on the bold turns, hoping certain movements would be eliminated that hardly came up to the reputation of this composer and that revealed errors and a harshness of style.[36]

Coming at the start of the sixth period, Sonatas 40-42, Op. 37, are masterpieces often undervalued. In their superb craftsmanship and fresh invention these concentrated two-movement miniatures do honor to their dedicatee, the newly married "Princesse Marie Esterházy, née Princesse de Lichtenstein." As C. F. Cramer observed in a review

34. Regarding his memory, cf. Landon/SYMPHONIES 6, 7, and 13. To be sure, other instances of similar thematic relationships do occur (Strunk/BARYTON 243-245).

35. Cf. his autobiographical sketch (Landon/HAYDN 20).

36. Cf. Hoboken/HAYDN 761 and 762.

of 1785, they are different from but no less worthy than their predecessors, and harder to play than they first seem, requiring the greatest precision and delicacy.[37] A different version of Sonata 47 was recently discovered, in E rather than F and with a different finale,
leaving the question of which is to be preferred.[38] Sonata 48 in C was 38a
all that came out of C. G. Breitkopf's original request for six new sonatas from Haydn, and out of some confusing correspondence that followed.[39] Sonata 49 in E♭, the most Mozartean of Haydn's keyboard sonatas, was completed just before the first London trip and ranks with the three outstanding sonatas to follow.[40] From the several letters about it that remain[41] we learn of Haydn's embarrassment resulting, apparently, from promising it to two different ladies,[42] of his anger over Artaria's clandestine acquisition and publication of it, and of some details about the work itself. To quote an excerpt from Haydn's letter of June 20, 1790:[43]

> This Sonata is in E flat, brand new, and was written especially for Your Grace [Maria Anna von Genzinger, by whose last name it is sometimes known] to be hers forever, but it is a curious coincidence that the last movement is the very same Minuet and Trio which Your Grace asked me for in your last letter. This Sonata was destined for Your Grace a year ago, and only the Adagio is quite new, and I especially recommend this movement to your attention, for it contains many things which I shall analyze for Your Grace when the time comes; it is rather difficult but full of feeling. It's a pity, however, that Your Grace has not one of Schantz's [Wenzel Schanz's] fortepianos, for Your Grace could then produce twice the effect.
>
> N. B. *Mademoiselle* Nanette [Anna de Jerlischek, later Madam Tost] must know nothing of the fact that this sonata was already half completed, for otherwise she might get the wrong impression of me, and this might be very disadvantageous for me, since I must be very careful not to lose her favour. Meanwhile I consider myself fortunate to be at least the means of providing her with some amusement; especially since the sacrifice is made for your sake, dearest Frau von Genzinger. Oh! how I do wish that I could only play this Sonata to you a few times; I could then reconcile my staying for a while in this wilderness. . . .

Frau von Genzinger replied, in the course of a letter written July 11:[44] "I . . . leave it entirely to you to choose me an excellent fortepiano . . . I like the Sonata very much, but there is one thing I wish could be

37. The review is reprinted in Pohl/HAYDN II 315, along with the qualification (p. 316) made by a correspondent that they are "zu schwer im Ausdruck."
38. Larsen/QUELLE, with facs. of the new MS finale.
39. Cf. Landon/HAYDN 81 and 83-85.
40. Cf. the laudatory review of 1792 quoted in Pohl/HAYDN II 316.
41. Landon/HAYDN 102-103, 105, 106, 108, 132.
42. Cf. Hoboken/HAYDN 775.
43. As trans. in Landon/HAYDN 105 and 108.
44. As trans. in Landon/HAYDN 108.

changed (if by so doing it does not detract from the beauty of the piece), and that is the passage in the second part of the Adagio, where the hands cross over; I am not used to this and thus find it hard to do, and so please let me know how this could be altered." It is noteworthy that, whatever he may have tried to do about the dedication, Haydn did not, at this later point in his life, acquiesce in the matter of the hand-crossing.

We owe the main story of the last three piano sonatas (all apparently written in Haydn's seventh period near the end [1794] of his second London visit) to the expert and intriguing sleuthwork of Oliver Strunk.[45] Starting with the autograph of the unexcelled, warmly personal Sonata 52 in E♭,[46] which the Library of Congress acquired in 1933, Strunk notes its date of 1794 as well as its original dedication to Therese
46a Jansen (as in Ex. 77). Then he is able to show that the dedicatee was none other than the future Mrs. Gaetano Bartolozzi (an esteemed pianist and pupil of Clementi), that her marriage occurred in 1795, and that Haydn himself witnessed it. Also, he shows that the Longman, Clementi & Co. edition of this sonata (late 1799 or early 1800) was "composed expressly for Mrs. Bartolozzi" and based on the autograph, whereas the Artaria first edition of 1798, dedicated to Fräulein von Kurzböck, is less accurate and perhaps was based on a pirated copy after Mrs. Bartolozzi's visit to Vienna, presumably late in 1798. Furthermore, Strunk conjectures that Sonatas 50-52 were the "3 Sonates for Ms. Janson" that Haydn catalogued in his fourth London diary,[47] that they were intended as a set, and that their chronological order of composition must be 52, 51, 50. The only "internal evidence" offered for this last conjecture is that Son. 50/iii introduces the "additional keys" to the traditional 5-octave keyboard, the same keys that Beethoven introduced in the "Waldstein" Sonata in 1805. However, if all 3 sonatas did originate about the same time, this argument would hardly seem to be conclusive in itself.

Haydn's Ensemble Sonatas

In turning to Haydn's ensemble sonatas we need to keep the original settings separate from the many arrangements. As already indicated, seven of the eight accompanied sonatas (K & Vn) published collectively by Breitkopf & Härtel, Peters, and others[48] are taken from

45. Strunk/HAYDN.
46. It was reviewed in AMZ I (1798-99) 520 as one of the most original of Haydn's sons. and the most difficult to perform.
47. Cf., also, Landon/HAYDN 309 and 310; Hoboken/HAYDN 776-780.
48. Cf. Altmann/KAMMERMUSIK 206-207.

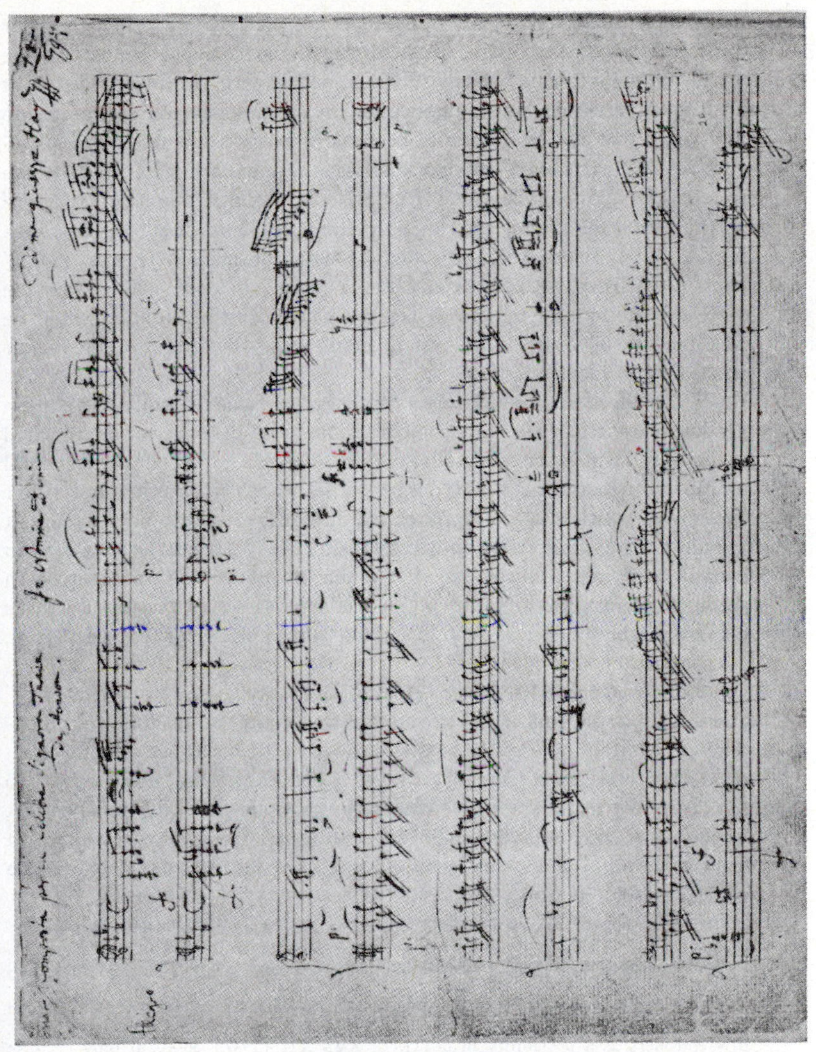

Ex. 77. From the opening of Sonata 52 in E♭ by Joseph Haydn (facs. of the autograph at the Library of Congress).

many more such arrangements of keyboard sonatas and other chamber music. It was none other than Burney who composed most of the violin parts for the keyboard sonatas, which parts were included first in English, then in other publications.[49] The only sonata for piano and violin that has traditionally been accepted as authentic is one in G (H. XV/32), but even this work appears to have originated as a piano trio—that is, *Sonata for the Piano-Forte, with Accompaniments for a Violin & Violoncello,* according to the title of the first, Preston edition of 1794.[50] Another so-called "sonata for pianoforte and violin" from 1794, listed by Haydn as "The Dream," is lost.[51] This was the piece reportedly designed to deflate a certain boastful violinist when he first read it, by compelling him to climb ever upward into the higher
51a positions of "Jacob's ladder."

If the literature on Haydn's keyboard sonatas is modest, that on
52a his keyboard trios is microscopic.[52] The trios deserve to be elevated to their rightful place among Haydn's chief categories of instrumental music. Furthermore, they deserve the same recognition for their significant position at the start of the literature for the piano trio that Haydn's string quartets have within their class.[53] It is true that Haydn usually referred to these pieces by the title "sonata for piano with accompaniments for a violin and a cello," or merely "sonata," in his correspondence and in the few extant autographs (for which reason, as usual, they are included in the present survey). The publishers generally used these titles, too, even though "capriccio," "divertimento," "terzetto," and "concerto" are the terms more often found in contemporary MS copies. It is also true that the cello is seldom independent of the piano bass (as it is in H. XV/9/i), though not so
54a seldom as is usually stated.[54] But with the violin generally independent of the piano and with the cello often different from the piano bass at least in its note values and octave range, the feel of the real piano trio is clear enough at times (Ex. 78).

49. Cf. Hoboken/HAYDN 727-728, 733, *et passim;* AMZ I (1798-99) Intelligenz-Blatt 17 and 57-58 (on an interesting spurious set, actually by a Haydn pupil).

50. Cf. Hoboken/HAYDN 717-718 and 681; Landon/HAYDN 133, 309, and 310-311.

51. Cf. Pohl/HAYDN III 84-85; GROVE IV 157-158; Hoboken/HAYDN 727 and 705. It could not be the Son. in G (H. XV/32) just mentioned, which Klaus G. Roy considers as a possibility in BULLETIN AMS XII (1947) 38-40, if only because Haydn himself listed the 2 works separately (cf. Landon/HAYDN 309 and 311).

52. Little more than warm appreciations are Tovey's comments in COBBETT I 542-543, Scott/HAYDN 215-217, Bell/HAYDN, or the few earlier contributions.

53. Cf. Cesari/TRIO 193.

54. Cf. the rejoinder to Scott/HAYDN in MT LXXIII (1932) 741-742. On the other hand, in 1803 Haydn answered a request for a new sonata by simply turning over a Trio in e♭ without the cello part (H. XIV/31; cf. Hoboken/HAYDN 716 and Landon/HAYDN 221).

Ex. 78. From the first movement of Joseph Haydn's Sonata in E♭ with Violin and Cello Accompaniment H. XV/22 (after Hermann/HAYDN-m III 4).

Hoboken credits Haydn with 10 more than the usually accepted number of 31 piano trios, one being the Sonata in G mentioned shortly before (H. XV/32), 2 being lost, and the other 7 being involved in the usual complexities of Haydn bibliography. The previously accepted group of 31 is not free of such complexities, either. One trio actually originated as a larger ensemble (H. XV/2), 2 others (H. XV/3 and 4) may have been composed by Joseph's brother Michael or by Ignaz
55a Pleyel (either of whom would be preferred here on stylistic grounds),[55]
and 3 or 4 others appear to have originated with the flute intended rather than violin (H. XV/14-17). Again there is a problem of numbering the trios. The chronology worked out by Larsen[56] has been adopted in recent references, but still needs to be collated (as by him) with the standard editions of Ferdinand David for Breitkopf & Härtel (1852)
57a and of Friedrich Hermann for Peters (1876).[57] The opus numbers
in the early publications are too variable and numerous to list here.

Haydn's Sonatas for Piano With Violin and Cello

Larsen	1	2	3	4	5	6	7	8	9	10	11	12	13	14	15	16
key	g	F	C	F	G	F	D	B♭	A	E♭	E♭	e	C	A♭	G	D
Peters	19	26	12	27	28	25	10	24	15	20	16	7	14	11	31	30
Breitkopf	16	25	26	27	28	23	21	22	9	17	11	10	8	24	31	30
Larsen	17	18	19	20	21	22	23	24	25	26	27	28	29	30	31	
key	F	A	g	B♭	C	E♭	d	D	G	f#	C	E	E♭	E♭	e♭	
Peters	29	13	17	9	21	23	22	6	1	2	3	4	5	8	18	
Breitkopf	29	7	14	13	18	20	19	6	1	2	3	4	5	12	15	

The first 3 of these 31 trios date from Haydn's first and second periods; all the others date from the sixth to perhaps the start of the eighth periods (or little more than a decade, 1784-96), with at least the last 4 trios being composed after Haydn's return to Vienna from his second London visit (i.e., H. XV/27-30[58]).

55. Briefly, Joseph sent H. XV/3-5 to Foster in London as his own (published *ca.* 1785 as Op. 40); he identified no. 3 as Michael's in 1803; no. 4 is obviously close to no. 3 in style, and both are more like Mozart's than Joseph's music; no. 5 is clearly by Joseph. Cf. Pohl/HAYDN II 318; Saint-Foix/TRIOS; Larsen/ÜBERLIEFERUNG 117 and 141-144; Hoboken/HAYDN 685-686; Landon/HAYDN 55-56. Still more recently, in Tyson/HAYDN, strong circumstantial evidence is adduced in favor of Pleyel's authorship, even though the many misattributions to Pleyel suggest caution here. New light would be thrown on the question if there actually were a much earlier De la Chevardière ed. containing these trios in Haydn's name, as listed in BRITISH UNION I 467 (first entry); but information kindly supplied by Mr. R. J. Hayes, Director of the National Library of Ireland (Dublin), indicates that the trios in this ed. are not the same.

56. As in Larsen/KATALOGE 138.

57. Other collations may be found in Cuming/HAYDN 368 and Bell/HAYDN 197. Cf., also, MGG V 1891.

58. In Strunk/HAYDN 203, H. XV/30 is shown, with sufficient evidence, to

Before the set of trios 6-8 appeared in 1786 Haydn was compelled to write Artaria one of his bitterest letters about the quality of the engraving—"Even a professional would have to study before disentangling this passage, and then where would the dilettante be?"[59] The extract reminds us how much he had the dilettante in mind in this music. Furthermore, Haydn responded readily enough to the color of the publisher's money and to the publisher's ideas of what the public wanted. In connection with the set of trios 11-13 he wrote to Artaria, "Many thanks for the 25 ducats which you sent me. The zeal I shall bestow on the 3 pianoforte Sonatas with accompaniment of a violin and violoncello which you want, shall be a guarantee of my wish to retain your friendship in the future." Later he asked for further payment because, "In order to compose your 3 pianoforte Sonatas [the same trios] particularly well, I had to buy a new fortepiano." And still later he wrote, "I send you herewith the 3d Sonata, which I have rewritten with variations [H. XV/13/i], to suit your taste."[60] The trios did meet the public taste, as the many reprints and the enthusiastic though few reviews bear witness.[61] Especially popular then, as ever since, was the "Rondo all'Ongarese" ("Gypsy Rondo"), which is the finale in the second of the 3 trios dedicated to the widow Schroeter, one of Haydn's closest friends in London (H. XV/24-26).[62] Trios 27-29, like the piano sonatas 52, 50, and probably 51, were dedicated to Therese Jansen-Bartolozzi, making her and Princess Marie Esterházy the most rewarded of Haydn's lady dedicatees.

More on the fringe of our subject, Haydn's twenty-one works in SS/- or SA/bass setting, four of which are now lost, stem from his earliest creative periods. Called "divertimento" and "trio" in the source MSS, those that were published appeared chiefly as "Sonates en trio."[63] These "trios" are relatively slight and objective, but as diversional pieces they have more attraction than Pohl implies.[64] The large number of trios for baryton, viola, and cello (H. XI) and the duos for baryton and cello (H. XII) are similarly light and diversional

---

have been composed in 1796 and not 1795 (cf. the pertinent letters in Landon/HAYDN 147-148); furthermore, the set H. XV/27-29 may well have been composed later than no. 30, meaning that the end of Larsen's chronology would have to be changed to 26, 31, 30, 27, 28, 29.

59. As trans. in the letter of Dec. 10, 1785, in Landon/HAYDN 51.

60. In the letters of Aug. 17 and Oct. 26, 1788, and March 29, 1789, as trans. in Landon/HAYDN 77-78, 79, and 82.

61. Cf. Pohl/HAYDN II 319-320, where 3 reviews are quoted at length.

62. The abundant literature on this one movement is noted in Hoboken/HAYDN 710.

63. For numerous mod. eds. cf. MGG V 1919-1920.

64. Pohl/HAYDN I 344-347. Cf., also, Geiringer/HAYDN 193-194, 204-205.

in character, with much melodic charm and not a few surprises.[65] Stemming from Haydn's second and third periods (*ca.* 1762-75), these "divertimenti" were written to order as accompanied solos[66] for the private use of Prince Nikolaus and for an unusual instrument that is scarcely known today and was highly exclusive even then. (The baryton or viola di bordone, with its appearance of a viola da gamba and its average of six gut strings supplemented by two to three times as many underlying, sympathetic strings, was unusual in that the player could pluck his own bass accompaniment with his left thumb as he bowed the melody.[67]) Because its use was so restricted, the baryton music remained unpublished in its original form, but much of it did appear in other arrangements, mostly unauthorized.

Haydn's six solos or sonatas for violin with viola accompaniment (H. VI/1-6), as they were originally called, are placed in the years from 1766-74 by Pohl[68] (or probably in the third period). They were first published in 1775 as S/bass sonatas (Bailleux in Paris), but among numerous later editions also appeared as "Six Duo dialogués pour deux violons" (André in Offenbach a/M, in 1790).[69] Actually the two styles of setting implied by these titles are found about equally. The freshness and originality of this music cannot fail to give pleasure to the string players who trouble to play it. Pertinent here only as an important example of a late use of "sonata" for single orchestral pieces, is Hadyn's "Seven Last Words" (H. XX).[70] This music, composed in 1785, originally consisted of an introduction, seven slow, deeply expressive, one-movement sonatas (each prefaced by the appropriate words of the Saviour and programmatic to that extent[71]), and a postlude. It was first published in 1787 both for orchestra and in Haydn's own arrangement for string quartet. In the latter form it is best known today, rather than as an orchestral work or as the oratorio into which Haydn later converted it.

65. Strunk/BARYTON is an illuminating study of the history, styles, forms, and bibliography of this music, with many exx. Cf., also, Pohl/HAYDN I 249-257 and II 304-307; Geiringer/HAYDN 205-207; Hoboken/HAYDN 591-593.

66. Cf. the anecdotes transmitted in Pohl/HAYDN I 252-253.

67. Cf. the pictures in Strunk/BARYTON after p. 216; GROVE VIII Plate 67/2; also, the descriptions of specific instruments on pp. 10-16 of Fruchtman/BARYTON (an unpublished diss. [1960] on baryton music by colleagues of Haydn at the Esterházy court—especially Joseph Burksteiner, one Neumann, and Luigi Tomasini—with 9 complete exx).

68. Pohl/HAYDN II 285-286. Saint-Foix/VIOLON is a brief article on this set.

69. Cf. Hoboken/HAYDN 512-514.

70. The interesting genesis of this work may be found in Sandberger/HAYDN, supplemented by new information in Hoboken/HAYDN 844-848. Cf., also, Haydn's own statement of its origin, as trans. in Geiringer/HAYDN 77.

71. Cf. Haydn's letters of Feb. 14 and April 8, 1787, as in Landon/HAYDN 57 and 59-60; SCE V.

Haydn's Place in Sonata History

Viewed alongside his quartets and symphonies, the main works to which Haydn applied the term "sonata" must be acknowledged as of lesser significance. That evaluation already obtained in his own day, as we saw in the review of 1780 that was quoted earlier,[72] as was made clear by his first biographers,[73] and as Haydn himself indicated in his correspondence, if only by the relative prices for which he offered his works to his publishers.[74] Furthermore, Haydn reportedly came to feel he should have written more vocal music, supported by a text, rather than so "many quartets, sonatas, and symphonies"; and that he could do much more than he had already done if he only were allowed to live still longer.[75] Perhaps in this way Haydn would have removed the one supposed deficiency that Sondheimer has found in his instrumental music. Sondheimer, in a penetrating, psychological, highly idiosyncratic study based on the quartets, concludes that "Haydn restored the technical handling of music to a position of preponderant importance, . . ." but, "though the great dialectician in music, . . ." he "was not, at the same time, its great philosopher, in which capacity alone he could have justified his display of dialectic."[76] Sondheimer's term "dialectic" refers specifically to Haydn's quartet writing, and would be translated here as the development of an idea through "motivic play." Moreover, Sondheimer finds a tangible distinction between a quartet concept and a sonata concept by Haydn's time.[77] But—to skirt the precarious metaphysical issues that are raised—his conclusion that Haydn's greatness begins and ends in a consummate yet wholly intellectual craftsmanship would apply just as well to Haydn's sonatas.

Curiously, it seems to be a failure to appreciate just that craftsmanship in the sonatas that keeps all but a few from being played today. The last piano sonatas are appreciated more for their romanticism and imagination, much as all Haydn's instrumental music was appreciated by his earliest biographers.[78] But the earlier sonatas no longer bring the popular response they once did. Is the superior skill of handling that was praised in almost every contemporary review of these earlier sonatas too subtle and different to be enjoyed today? It is undoubtedly less easy to perceive when it is exercised within the less familiar, pre-

72. The early estimate in Schubart/IDEEN 226-227 is also pertinent.
73. E.g., Carpani/HAYDINE 95-96.
74. Cf. Landon/HAYDN 45, 47, 66-67, 77, 83, 85, and 94, *et passim*. Allowances must be made, of course, for actual differences in the labor involved.
75. Griesinger/HAYDN 63 and 7.
76. Sondheimer/HAYDN 174.
77. Sondheimer/HAYDN 78 and 149.
78. E.g., Carpani/HAYDINE 101.

Classic idioms that still prevail in the earlier sonatas. All of which reminds us that for all his self-training, his lonely seclusion from city life at Esterház, and his striking originality—another quality stressed in almost every contemporary review[79]—Haydn was still very much a man of his times. He was remarkably so, in fact, for it is possible to see a wide variety of influences in his music. We have already noted his repeatedly avowed reverence for Emanuel Bach when the latter was discussed, a reverence that started with his study at an early age of some of Emanuel's first published sonatas and was still being demonstrated in the last year of Emanuel's life (1788), when Haydn was again ordering his sonatas.[80] Haydn's sonatas are certainly more like Emanuel's than Mozart's are. One can point to the introspective slow movements, to the rhythmic versatility—rhythmic virtuosity might be added, too—to the originality sometimes for the sake of originality, to the unexpected harmonies, or to several other traits that Emanuel and Haydn have in common. But the relationship of two such strong individuals could go only so far. And there were practical differences, as between Emanuel's unexcelled command of the keyboard and Haydn's indifferent command. Perhaps more than anything else Haydn got from Emanuel the idea itself of writing sonatas of real worth.

We might know more of other influences on the young Haydn if so much of his earliest music were not lost. Abert states categorically that Wagenseil, living right in Vienna, and not Emanuel Bach, was the chief (early) influence, in structural procedures as well as the use of the title "divertimento."[81] But we also know the value Haydn himself placed on the help of Porpora,[82] and how he has been linked variously with Gluck, Dittersdorf, Sammartini, Boccherini, and others (SCE VIII and XVI). Even in his later years, at least until he started complaining of his waning powers, the ever-young Haydn seems to have undergone almost as much influence as he exerted. If the influence could only have worked one way with regard to the younger men Dussek, J. B. Cramer, and Hummel, it is more likely to have been reciprocal with regard to Clementi.[83] Above all we have the evidence, internal and external, of the reciprocal influences between Haydn and

79. Cf. Burney/HISTORY II 959-960.

80. Cf. Landon/HAYDN 75.

81. Abert/HAYDN 556. Melodic influences on Haydn, from this point to his relative independence in the mid 1770's, are traced in Feder/HAYDN. Cf. SCE VI, with ex.

82. Cf. his autobiographical remark in Landon/HAYDN 19.

83. Saint-Foix/HAYDN considers only Haydn's influence on Clementi, but cf. Abert/HAYDN 550, Strunk/HAYDN 199, and Haydn's own praise of Clementi's sons. in 1783 (Landon/HAYDN 42).

the man to whom we are about to turn, Mozart.[84] These interinfluences, which have been examined with such acumen by Einstein, Blume, Schmid, Wirth, and certain previous writers,[85] have been discussed in the present study, insofar as the sonata is concerned, chiefly in Chapter VI on structure.

Mozart: Comparisons, Periods, Sources, Works

Mention has just been made of the interinfluences experienced by Haydn and **Wolfgang Amadeus Mozart** (1756-91). These two men certainly met by the early 1780's, as we have seen, and may even have begun to notice each other's music as early as the 1760's.[86] But though paired by proximity of time and place, by mutual affection and esteem, and by historical tradition, they actually disclose at least as much that separates as relates them. Like almost all the other pairs of music's greats that come to mind, from Palestrina and Lassus to Stravinsky and Schoenberg, Haydn and Mozart stood about as far apart as their common heritage and interests permitted. To recall the more general, purely circumstantial differences is perhaps the best way to initiate the brief biographic orientation that must suffice for our purposes.

Where Haydn was born into a poor family of simple peasant stock, in a little Austrian frontier village, Mozart was born into a cultured family, living in relative comfort and serving an aristocratic society at the archiepiscopal court in Salzburg. Where Haydn was born while Baroque styles were still in full swing—in fact, while Fux, Vivaldi, and Bach were all still going strong—Mozart was born during the full bloom of the *galant* style, after all these men had passed on and a new, less illustrious generation had succeeded them. Where Haydn grew up amidst Hungarian, Croatian, Gypsy, and German folk music, the young Mozart was nurtured on cultivated art forms that included folk music only in stylized adaptations, such as the Swabian dances that his father transmitted to him in the "Notenbuch für Wolfgang" of 1762.[87] Furthermore, Haydn largely taught himself, he traveled but little until his final years, and he matured remarkably slowly, spending most of his life perfecting much the same idioms and styles with which he began. By contrast, Mozart enjoyed the skillful, devoted, worldly guidance of his father right from the start of one of the most precocious careers

84. Among warm tributes by Haydn, cf. Landon/HAYDN 50, 73-74, 125. In Westrup/HAYDN Dénes Bartha's doubts as to Haydn's actual esteem for Mozart are answered convincingly.

85. Einstein/MOZART 128-131 *et passim;* Blume/MOZART, and MGG IX 751-752; Schmid/MOZART; Wirth/MOZART.

86. Cf. Schmid/MOZART 150-154.

87. Cf. Abert/WOLFGANG-m (preface); Schmid/MOZART 146-148.

the world of art has ever known, and he spent the first two-thirds of that career in an almost unbroken succession of "grand tours" throughout much of Europe, all the while advancing eclectically into his own inimitable world of high-Classic styles. Finally, the deliberate, patient, kindly Haydn made his way in the world with ever-increasing success, while the lively, sensitive, alert, compulsive Mozart followed a course that led from initial successes to ever-increasing frustration.[88]

The 30 creative years that filled nearly all of Mozart's short life have been variously divided by biographers, with the 3 longest tours and the final decade in Vienna providing the chief landmarks. The division most pertinent here is that carefully worked out by Hans Dennerlein in his detailed, fresh, iconoclastic study of Mozart's keyboard music (1951, with revisions in 1955).[89] As in Larsen's and Landon's division of Haydn's career, Dennerlein finds 8 periods within the usual 3 broader phases, the latter falling logically enough into 3 consecutive decades—1762-71 (the prodigy and his basic training), 1772-81 (the formative years), and 1781-91 (full maturity, in Vienna). The *first period,* 1762-66, is that of the prodigy, including first the trial visits to Munich and Vienna that he made with Leopold and his older sister Maria Anna ("Nannerl"), then the grand tour of more than 3 years that the family made to Paris, London, The Hague, and other cities in the Netherlands, Germany, and Switzerland. The *second period,* 1767-71, completes the first decade with serious study under Leopold and with the 2 trips during which father and son visited nearly every important center in Italy, one high spot being Wolfgang's admission to the Accademia dei Filarmonici in Bologna under Padre Martini's enthusiastic supervision.

Mozart's second decade, during which he wrote more sonatas than at any other time, is subdivided by Dennerlein into 3 periods. The first of these, or Mozart's *third period,* 1772-77, includes further visits to Vienna (where he reportedly heard Haydn's "Sun" quartets) and Munich (where the much discussed "clavier contest" with Ignaz von Beecke took place),[90] as well as a third, final visit to Italy. But this period is notable mainly for his feverish composition activity at home during the early rule of the increasingly hostile Archbishop Hieronymus,

88. In Burney/HISTORY II 958-960 (1789) the joy at discussing Haydn can hardly be restrained but Mozart is still noticed chiefly and briefly as the former wonder child.

89. Dennerlein/MOZART, especially pp. 282-287 and the 6 supplementary charts (in which the whole of Mozart's output is tabulated in detail). This valuable book, called "Der unbekannte Mozart," has so far remained virtually the unknown Dennerlein.

90. Cf. Schenk/MOZART 159-160 and 189-190; Dennerlein/MOZART 50.

Count von Colloredo. The *fourth period,* 1777-79, covers the grand tour of 16 months that Mozart made partly with his mother (up to her death in 1778), including important stays in Munich, Augsburg, Mannheim, and Paris (where for the second time he met Christian Bach, his elder friend from his early London visit). The *fifth period,* 1779-81, including some time in Munich and Vienna again, is mainly defined by the crisis and final break with Archbishop Hieronymus, whose *Konzertmeister* and organist he had been in Salzburg.

Mozart's third and last decade, spent largely in Vienna, also subdivides into three periods. His *sixth period,* 1781-83, takes in his probable first meetings with Haydn, his growing interest in Bach and Handel through his first participation in the study sessions of the musical amateur Baron Gottfried van Swieten, and his marriage to Constanze Weber. His *seventh period,* 1784-87, includes mainly the two gratifying trips to Prague to attend "The Marriage of Figaro" and "Don Giovanni." And the *eighth period,* 1788-91, finds Mozart taking two last trips, first to the main northern centers and then to the main southern centers in Germany, before the final months of composing and illness.

With regard to the vast, ever-swelling literature on Mozart, some mention should be made of the most basic and pertinent items before reviewing the output and circumstances of his sonatas. The contrast that was drawn between Haydn and Mozart might well be extended to the interest that has been shown toward each over the past 170 years or so since their maturest instrumental music was written. Where the interest in Haydn's music declined rapidly after his death and has only recently become strong enough again to support major studies and publications, that in Mozart's music underwent a vigorous spurt right after his death and has continued more or less strong ever since, being
scarcely equalled today by the interest in any other composer.[91] Con- 91a
sequently, it is not surprising that the basic tools of Mozart research were developed much earlier and have had that much more time to undergo improvements and refinements. Köchel's chronological thematic index, which Einstein augmented by more than 80 per cent in the second revision (1937)[92] and which is already in the process of
another complete revision,[93] first appeared no less than a century ago. 93a

91. Cf. King/MOZART 1-54, an excellent survey of this subject, followed by intriguing chapters on more specific aspects of Mozart bibliography.

92. Köchel/MOZART (cf. pp. xxiv-xli), abbreviated K.V. here for references to specific works according to Einstein's revised numbering. Cf., also, King/MOZART 55-65.

93. Cf. MGG IX 827 (Lippmann). Convenient summaries of the K.V. listings are provided in Paumgartner/MOZART 628-651; GROVE V 958-982 (Blom); Einstein/MOZART 473-483; Landon & Mitchell/MOZART 377-386; MGG IX 739-751;

Köchel was also the instigator of the first "complete," critical edition of Mozart's music (1877-1905),[94] which had been preceded by Breitkopf & Härtel's "Oeuvres complettes" (1798-1806) and numerous less complete sets,[95] and which today is being replaced by an entirely new set.[96]

The basic biography of Mozart is still the three-volume set published by Otto Jahn in 1856-59, followed by a second edition in 1867 that incorporated Köchel's findings.[97] The bulky, cumbersome revision of this work by Hermann Abert (6th ed., 1923-24; with further revisions by his daughter Anna Amalie Abert in 1955-56) greatly enriches Jahn's inadequate discussions of the music, but the time is now ripe for an entirely new basic study of the man and his music.[98] Such a project would be more fruitful than a similar one for Haydn, since—to introduce another point of contrast—, as against the serious gaps in the records of Haydn's first fifty years, exceptionally detailed records have survived for much of Mozart's life. One thinks first of the rich collections of family letters and related correspondence, which provide an authentic inside view of motives, attitudes, and personalities
99a hardly to be matched by any other source.[99] At the time of this writing (1961), other first hand documents, like the travel diaries kept by Leopold for the years 1763-71[100] and the many contemporary reviews, had just been published by O. E. Deutsch in what is much the fullest
101a collection yet assembled.[101] Further, more specialized studies will be cited where they apply. But this summary of the most pertinent tools for Mozart research must not omit that epochal study of sources, in-

---

Dennerlein/MOZART, in the 6 charts (with some new dates), plus conversion tables (pp. 306-314) for the original and revised numberings.

94. MOZART WERKE-m. Cf. King/MOZART 57-62.

95. Mozart/OEUVRES-m. The contents of this and other sets up to 1905 are itemized in Köchel/MOZART 910-926 and HIRSCH MUSIKBIBLIOTHEK IV 375-385.

96. Mozart/NEUE-m (since 1955; originally headed by the late E. F. Schmid). Cf. MGG IX 825-826. By 1961, among works pertinent here had appeared the 17 "organ" sons. (Series VI) and the four-hand works for one and two keyboard instruments (Series IX).

97. Cf. King/MOZART 66-70 and 16-17. Jahn/MOZART is an English trans. of this second ed.

98. Cf. King/MOZART 70-77. Among important, recent, one-vol. biographies are Paumgartner/MOZART and Schenk/MOZART. Einstein/MOZART, though organized topically rather than chronologically, gives a remarkably coherent and illuminating overview of both the man and the works.

99. The chief collections are Schiedermair/MOZART (in the original German, with an extra vol. containing pictures and documents) and Anderson/MOZART (English trans., with annotations and a valuable preface; scheduled for early reprinting, as of 1961). Cf., also, MGG IX 830; an entirely new German ed., prepared by Bauer and Deutsch, is scheduled for early publication in Mozart/NEUE-m (cf. X/34 vii). Mueller von Asow/MOZART (1949) got only to 1779.

100. Published in facs. in Mozart/REISE.

101. Mozart/NEUE-m X/34. Bory/MOZART surveys Mozart's life tellingly through pictures and facs. A still more complete collection of pictures has appeared in 1961 in Mozart/NEUE-m X/32 (Zenger & Deutsch).

fluences, and styles of which the first two volumes appeared under the joint authorship of Wyzewa and Saint-Foix in 1912 and the last of the other three, by Saint-Foix alone, did not appear until 1946.[102] Especially valuable here (and elsewhere in the present volume) are the first two, more objective volumes, not only for their analyses of Mozart's earlier music (through his third period) but for their emphasis on the sonatas and related music by other composers that presumably became known to him at home and during his early travels.[103] With regard to the latter, Eduard Reeser's study of the accompanied sonata in Paris must also receive special mention.[104]

Allowing for recent revisions, the Köchel-Einstein *Verzeichnis* now credits Mozart with some 635 authentic, extant works, complete or incomplete, large or small (sometimes including several short pieces, as in K.V. 15a-ss or 315g). This output is certainly less than half of what Haydn composed in nearly twice as many years, but includes a larger proportion of instrumental to vocal works (about 2 to 1). A considerably smaller proportion of Mozart's than of Haydn's works was published during their respective lifetimes, although for our purposes it is interesting that the proportion of keyboard to other publications (about 1 to 3) was, if anything, greater for Mozart. The fact that there were fewer re-editions makes the problem of plagiarisms and misattributions not so great for Mozart, but it is still very much present, as sample problems will indicate shortly. Among about 410 instrumental works presently credited to Mozart, 90 (or about 22 per cent) are sonatas, 58 are concertos, 52 are symphonies, 25 are string quartets, and 185 make up all the other types. The 90 sonatas divide into 44 (or 49 per cent) for keyboard and violin, 21 (23 per cent) for keyboard alone, 7 for 4 hands at one or 2 keyboard instruments (8 per cent), 17 for organ and other instruments (19 per cent), and one for bassoon and cello (K.V. 196c). The 8 piano trios are not included among these 90 "sonatas." They qualify less than Haydn's trios as accompanied sonatas because of their increasingly independent cello, as well as violin, parts. And Mozart did not call them "sonatas" except for 2 that seem to have originated as solo keyboard sonatas (K.V. 496 and 564, 1786 and 1788).[105]

102. Saint-Foix/MOZART.

103. Starting from these 2 vols., G. E. Muns's M.A. thesis (Univ. of N.C., 1950) and the diss. Lerma/MOZART emphasize, respectively, the sources of the keyboard sons. and of (all) the works of Mozart's first 10 years.

104. Reeser/KLAVIERSONATE.

105. Cf. Köchel/MOZART 629-630 and 713-714; Einstein/MOZART 260-263; Fischer/MOZART 20-21. Recall the related statistics in SCE IV.

Mozart's Solo Piano Sonatas: Overview

Although, true to his times, Mozart wrote about twice as many sonatas for keyboard and violin as for keyboard alone, the latter must get first consideration here, in keeping with their greater popularity ever since he wrote them. These solo sonatas have also received the lion's share of attention within the growing literature devoted expressly to one or another category of Mozart's sonatas. However, the most detailed discussions of the individual solo sonatas still occur in the course of Saint-Foix/MOZART and in Dennerlein/MOZART (which also covers all his other solo [stringed] keyboard music and, more cursorily, the chamber and orchestral works with [stringed] keyboard).[106] At least two textbooks have been devoted entirely to measure-by-measure
107a analyses of the separate solo sonatas in terms of standardized designs.[107] There are also a few discussions of specific problems in specific sonatas (to be noted where they apply) and, of course, numerous articles on style traits throughout Mozart's music that have a direct bearing on the sonatas.[108]

Furthermore, two books and several articles on performance practices in Mozart's music bear directly on the keyboard sonatas, including the question of when he began to compose for the piano.[109] Regarding this question, Nathan Broder has concluded that Mozart probably had the piano in mind right from the first (extant) solo keyboard sonatas (K.V. 189d-h and 205b), composed in 1774-75, apparently for the instruments he expected to play in Munich. No clue is provided by the compass, which remained at 5 octaves (FF-fff') through most of his lifetime; and but little clue is provided by the terms used in letters and MS titles, which are most often "clavier" or "cembalo," applied in the broadest sense. But increasingly clear evidence is provided by the sudden multiplication of dynamic indications in the first sonatas (e.g., the "cresc." and "decresc." in K.V. 189f/i/2-4), by Mozart's often published letter of October 17-18, 1777 relating his delight with the Stein pianos he tried in Augsburg,[110] by the phrase "pour le Clavecin

106. Among brief surveys, in addition to the short notice given to nearly every son. in Abert/MOZART, are King/PIANO and Hutchings/MOZART.

107. Tobin/MOZART and Marks/SONATA. Among articles, Merian/MOZART concentrates on the use of "sonata form" and Cherbuliez/MOZART on the use of sequence.

108. The MOZART-JAHRBUCH and the flurry of publications in the Mozart bicentennial of 1956 have added many such articles, especially in MQ XLII, KONGRESS 1956 (Vienna), and MR XVII.

109. Brunner/MOZART, Badura-Skoda/MOZART 19-38, and the articles Russell/MOZART, Broder/MOZART, and King/MOZART 242-259 (with further references on p. 244).

110. Anderson/MOZART II 472-482; cf., also, I 45 and 148, II 460-462, 495, 537,

ou le Pianoforte" in most of his publications with keyboard from about 1778, and by the actual use of "pianoforte" in the title of an occasional later autograph. Of course, the narrow, wood-frame "Mozart piano," even with the pedal keyboard that was constructed so that he could reinforce the bass tones,[111] was a much slighter, gentler, more songful instrument than the modern grand piano—closer in some ways, in fact, to the clavichord.[112] The mention of Broder should not be made without also calling attention to his recent edition of Mozart's solo keyboard sonatas and fantasias, based more reliably than any previous edition on autographs and the earliest publications.[113] 113a

A somewhat revised chronology of the solo keyboard sonatas follows, which will also serve here for the conversion of Köchel's original numbers, Einstein's revisions, and the still different chronological catalogue evolved in Saint-Foix/MOZART. (In every reputable edition of re- 113b
cent times the K.V. numbers are inserted.[114]) The original publisher and opus number are added for works printed during his lifetime. Sources are given chiefly for the several dates and places conjecturally revised since Einstein's last changes. Page references are given for the main (but inadequately indexed!) discussions in Dennerlein/MOZART (D/M). Not included are 4 lost sonatas composed about 1766 (K.V. 33d-g), an incomplete first movement in B♭ (K.V. 372a, completed by M. Stadler), some further, late sketches (K.V. 569a and 590a-c), 2 conservative little sonatas supposedly for violin and bass or for keyboard (K.V. 46d and e),[115] the 2 sonatas known only in arrangements as piano trios (K.V. 496 and 564), and several other arrangements. Only one complete autograph can be located with certainty now (K.V. 315c), although parts of others and photographs of still others are extant.[116]

Most of these solo keyboard sonatas were composed as vehicles for Mozart's own playing during his travels, and not, as so often said, "merely for teaching purposes." We are naturally so preoccupied with Mozart the composer today that we tend to forget how much of his

---

540, 644, and III 1281 for other references to keyboard instruments in the family letters (as culled by Broder).

111. Cf. the picture in Badura-Skoda/MOZART 32; also, Leopold's letter of March 12, 1785 (Anderson/MOZART III 1325) and King/MOZART 245-247.

112. Steglich/MOZART is a detailed study of the "Mozart piano."

113. Broder/MOZART-m (with preface on ornaments, a facs., and pictures; revised in 1960); cf. the review of recent eds. in PIANO QUARTERLY XVI (1956) 21-23 and 29 (Newman); also, the list of discrepancies in recent eds., according to the autographs, in Badura-Skoda/MOZART 304-317.

114. For collations of 19th-c. eds. cf. Challier/TABELLE.

115. Mod. ed. of both: Werner/MOZART-m, with preface.

116. Cf. the recent lists in Badura-Skoda/MOZART 324-325 and 336; also, Broder/MOZART-m vi-vii. Facs. published up to 1945 are listed in the 1947 ed. of Köchel/MOZART.

Mozart's Piano Sonatas

K. V. no., revised (and original)	Saint-Foix no.	Key	Year and place of completion	First printing before 1792	Remarks	D/M pages
189d (279)	209	C	1774, Salzburg		facs., iii/1-28, Bory/MOZART 88	32-36
189e (280)	211	F	"			42-46
189f (281)	212	B♭	"			39-42
189g (282)	215	E♭	"			36-39
189h (283)	213	G	"			46-49
205b (284)	221	D	1775, Munich	Toricella, 1784, Op. 7	"Dürnitz Sonata"	49-52
547a (Anh. 135, Anh. 138a)	cf. 557	F	*ca.* 1778, Paris		arrangement by Mozart doubted in Marguerre/KV. 547; on new dating, cf.	254-256
284c (311)	289	D	1777, Munich and Mannheim	Heina, 1782, Op. 4	chronology from Saint-Foix/MOZART III 18	69-73
300h (330)	323	C	1777, Augsburg	Artaria, 1784, Op. 6	"improvised" Oct. 22, 1777; new date.	65-69
284b (309)	290	C	1777, Mannheim	Heina, 1782, Op. 4	composed for Rosa Cannabich?	74-81
315c (333)	331	B♭	1778, Paris?	Toricella, 1784, Op. 7	on the date and place cf.	117-123
300k (332)	324	F	1778, Paris?	Artaria, 1784, Op. 6	on the date and place cf.	111-117
300d (310)	314	a	1778, Paris	Heina, 1782, Op. 4	facs., i/1-36, Bory/MOZART 107	95-102
300i (331)	317	A	"	Artaria, 1784, Op. 6	"Spring Sonata"; iii is "alla Turca"	102-111
457 —	453	c	1778, Munich?	Artaria, 1785, Op. 11 (with K. V. 475)	new date, place argued . . (in spite of "1784" on MS copy)	123-125 196-206
189i (312)	214	g	*ca.* 1782, Vienna		i ("Allegro") only; re-dated (again!) in	59, 96, 167
498a (Anh. 136)	499	B♭	1786, Vienna		revised and iv completed by A. E. Müller; cf. . . .	256-259
533 & — 494	540, 492	F	1788, '86, Vienna	*ca.* 1790, Hoffmeister	Mozart added iii (1786) to i and ii	243-246
545 —	555	C	1788, Vienna		"A Little Keyboard Sonata for Beginners"	250-252
570 —	588	B♭	1789, Vienna		Vn part added by André or Artaria	252-254
576 —	594	D	1789, Vienna		"Hunt" or "Trumpet Sonata"	246-249

career he spent at the keyboard and what a consummate performer he must have been. From the acutely perceptive, largely negative criticisms of other players (including Clementi) in his letters, from the not so precise accounts of his own playing by contemporaries,[117] and from his expert, ever-felicitous writing for the keyboard, one realizes that if Mozart was not the greatest virtuoso of his time in the athletic sense he certainly must have been one of the most refined, sensitive, expressive, and musically vibrant performers.

117. Good compilations of the principal, much quoted documents may be found (in trans.) in Russell/MOZART and King/MOZART 242-259.

Mozart's Solo Piano Sonatas: Circumstances

To judge by the distribution of keys, hints in letters,[118] and stylistic bonds, the first six sonatas on our foregoing list were planned as a set. However, only the last and most distinctive of them—"the one in D composed for [Baron T. von] Dürnitz,"[119] with its "Rondeau en Polonaise" and its theme-and-variations (K.V. 205b/ii and iii)—achieved publication during Mozart's life. This sonata, Mozart wrote from Munich in 1777, "sounds exquisite on Stein's pianoforte."[120] Dennerlein dubs the set the "home" set because it was composed mostly in Salzburg, in the third creative period, between the grand tours to Italy and to France. In 1778 it was apparently to this set that Mozart referred when he wrote of "my six difficult sonatas," presumably to distinguish them from the earlier lost or accompanied sonatas, since they are decidedly easier to play than nearly all the solo sonatas that followed.[121]

K.V. 547a is included in our list partly because it has been included in certain of the most careful editions. However, recently more serious doubts have been cast both on whether Mozart himself made the transcriptions of the first and third movements (from the violin sonata K.V. 547) and the revision of K.V. 545/iii, and on whether he authorized the addition of the variations as the third movement.[122] Dennerlein calls the next eight sonatas on the list the "travel" sonatas, since they were all supposedly written during the fourth period while Mozart was going to, staying in, or returning from Paris. The first two, K.V. 284c in D and 300h in C, he regards as transitional works that take a fresh approach to the problems raised by the two sonatas in the same keys, from the "home" set.[123] In K.V. 300h in C (rather than K.V. 284b in C) he discovers the sonata that Mozart improvised during a concert in Augsburg October 22, 1777, as described by the composer in a letter written over the next two days: "I then played . . .

118. Cf. Köchel/MOZART 264.

119. Cf. Anderson/MOZART III 1312. But the whole set was intended for Countess Schönborn (sister of the Archbishop Colloredo), according to Dennerlein/MOZART 30.

120. Anderson/MOZART II 480.

121. For Mozart's references cf. Anderson/MOZART II 679 and 913 (or Mueller von Asow II 329 and 600, regarding "meine schweren Sonaten"). In Saint-Foix/MOZART III 23, 92, and 109, the "six sonates difficiles" are taken to mean a later series, beginning with K.V. 284b, but that series would include sonatas composed mostly in Paris well after Mozart first made the remark in Mannheim on Feb. 4, 1778.

122. Marguerre/K.V. 547.

123. Dennerlein/MOZART viii, 64, 72-73, 125-126. The "No. 7" in the autograph of K.V. 284c is one supporting fact for this view.

all of a sudden a magnificent sonata in C major, out of my head, and a Rondo to finish up with."[124]

The remaining six "travel" sonatas, K.V. 284b-457 on our list, are viewed by Dennerlein as a second planned set, different in its make-up from any set found among the same eight works by previous scholars. The set as he finds it avoids the duplication of keys and otherwise seems plausible enough[125]—that is, if his most radical departure from the traditional chronology can be accepted, which is the inclusion of K.V. 457 as a work of the fourth period. Before coming to that work and so as to preserve the new chronology arrived at by Dennerlein, we should start with K.V. 284b, which is now taken to be that sonata about which Mozart is more explicit in his letters than any other. While in Mannheim, he tells his father, in the course of several letters written during November and December, 1777:

I am with [Christian] Cannabich every day. . . . He has a daughter [Rosa] who plays the clavier quite nicely; and in order to make a real friend of him I am now working at a sonata for her, which is almost finished save for the Rondo. . . . The Andante will give us most trouble, for it is full of expression and must be played accurately and with the exact shades of forte and piano, precisely as they are marked. . . . [Mlle Rosa is fifteen and] a very pretty and charming girl. She is very intelligent and steady for her age. She is serious, does not say much, but when she does speak, she is pleasant and amiable. Yesterday she again gave me indescribable pleasure; she played the whole of my sonata—excellently. The Andante (which must *not be taken too quickly*) she plays with the utmost expression. Moreover she likes playing it. . . . Young Danner [son of Christian Danner] asked me how I thought of composing the Andante. I said I would make it fit closely the character of Mlle Rosa. It really is a fact. She is exactly like the Andante. . . .[126]

Leopold, obviously more enthusiastic about the 21-year-old's musical progress than about a possible romance or the fact of the tonal portrait, replies pointedly: "Nannerl plays your whole sonata excellently and with great expression. If you leave Mannheim, *as I now presume you will,* I shall have it copied and enclose a small sheet in every letter, so that you may have it again. Your sonata is a strange composition. It has something in it of the *rather* artificial Mannheim style, but so very little that your own good style is not spoilt thereby."[127] In his mention

124. As trans. in Anderson/MOZART II 498.

125. K.V. 300K is actually labeled "Sonata III" in the autograph. But "Sonata I" appears over K.V. 300h rather than 284b, a contradiction only partly explained in Dennerlein/MOZART 65-66. The 2 early eds. that contain 3 of these sons. each, as shown on our list, do not confirm any one planned set of 6 sons.

126. As trans. in Anderson/MOZART II 520, 549, and 602 (among other references to K.V. 284b).

127. As trans. in Anderson/MOZART II 615 (among other references). A new

of the Mannheim style Leopold undoubtedly refers to the first two movements,[128] where the sighs, "rocket" figures, ornaments, detailed dynamic markings, and other *Manieren* abound.

The second sonata of this presumed "travel" set, K.V. 315c in B♭, has been related to the Sonatas in G and B♭, Op. 17/4 and 6, by Christian Bach, who could have shown them to Mozart in Paris in 1778.[129] There are even resemblances between the openings of the three sonatas. K.V. 300k in F shows a decided advance in the succinctness of the ideas in its first movement,[130] the harmonic depth of its 130a
"Adagio," and the drive of its finale. Still further advances of the same sort are evident at once in K.V. 300d in a, which ranks with Mozart's only other complete solo sonata in minor, K.V. 457 in c, with the contrapuntal "Allegro" movement in g, K.V. 189i, and with the equally contrapuntal Sonata in D, K.V. 576, among Mozart's strongest and most original sonatas. Joining those who regard much of Mozart's music—for example, the movement describing Rosa Cannabich—as an expression of immediate personal experiences, Dennerlein believes this strangely sad, quasi-Schubertian sonata was written while Mozart was still "dreadfully sad and depressed," with periodic "fits of melancholy," after his mother's death in Paris (July 3, 1778) and while he was trying desperately to get control of himself again.[131]

K.V. 300i in A ranks with K.V. 545 in C among Mozart's two most popular sonatas. It is the counterpart of K.V. 205b in D in its unusual make-up, what with its skillful variations,[132] minuet, and "Turkish March" (of which the coda in major was added at the time of publication in 1784, according to Saint-Foix[133]). Dennerlein suggests that in another sense this work was also a counterpart of the preceding sonata.

source MS for this son., which may even be a copy made by Leopold himself, is reported in Zimmerman/MOZART.

128. He had not yet seen the finale when Nannerl first noted this style (letter of Dec. 8, 1777).

129. Einstein/MOZART 120 and 246. A still more striking relationship between an aria by Christian Bach and the "Larghetto" of K.V. 296 (P & Vn) is illustrated in Nys/MOZART 93-94. The attempt to relate Mozart's finale to Emanuel Bach's rondos, in Abert/MOZART I 813-814, seems much less successful.

130. In Mason/MOZART interrelationships between these ideas are brought to light, while in Dennerlein/MOZART 254-256 an interrelationship is noted between these ideas and those of the 2 previous sons. in F (K.V. 189e and 547a).

131. Dennerlein/MOZART 96-97; Anderson/MOZART II 851, 865. In Saint-Foix/MOZART III 85-88, some motivation is sought, too, for such striking advances, but it is found rather in the stimulus of sonatas by Schobert that Mozart had recently procured.

132. Perhaps on the Swabian folksong, "Freu dich mein Herz" (Rietsch/MOZART; Dennerlein/MOZART 102-105; Verchaly/MOZART 68-70, where Schmid also relates the same tune to the "Menuett I" of the acc'd. son. K.V. 9). Mozart's theme is the one used for Reger's monstrous *Variations and Fugue,* Op. 132.

133. Saint-Foix/MOZART II 94; cf., also, D. Bartha in Verchaly/MOZART 175-176.

That is, having given vent to his grief in the other, Mozart now took this tender, loving means of honoring the memory of his departed mother.

As for taking K.V. 457 in c to be the concluding sonata in the "travel" set, Dennerlein's arguments are all circumstantial or subjective. In the absence of any direct evidence, they add up merely to a hypothesis for all his categoricalness, yet a hypothesis that seems at
134a least as acceptable as any other. Only a brief summary can be given here. The autograph can no longer be found.[134] On a MS copy in another hand Mozart himself inserted "Sonata. Per il Pianoforte solo. composta per la Sig^{ra} Teresa de Trattnern dal suo umilissimo servo Wolfgango Amadeo Mozart. Vienna li 14 d'Ottobre 1784." There is no doubt that the "Fantaisie" in c, K.V. 475, was composed in 1785, or that Mozart himself joined K.V. 457 to this work for the Artaria publication of 1785, which is also dedicated to his pupil Thérèse von Trattner.[135] But Dennerlein suggests that the dedication Mozart inserted in the sonata MS in 1784 was merely added to an earlier work as an act of courtesy, perhaps in return for Herr von Trattner's services as a godfather the month before.[136] K.V. 457, he observes, has all the Mannheim characteristics to be found in the "travel" sonatas, it has close ties with K.V. 300d in a, especially in its slow movement, and it employs *fermate* throughout its finale in a sense only characteristic of his earlier writing.[137] Furthermore, a personal crisis that easily could have been the emotional impetus for this remarkable, pre-Beethovian "Sonate pathétique"[138] is seen in Mozart's despair when he returned from Paris by way of Munich to find Aloysia Weber no longer interested in him (Dec., 1778).[139] The association is one he must certainly have preferred to forget by 1784 and after his marriage to Aloysia's sister.[140]

134. Efforts made here to follow the lead in Cincinnati as given in Köchel/MOZART 578 were unsuccessful, as were previous efforts made by Oswald Jonas, Otto Albrecht, and others.

135. Cf. the facs. of the title page in Bory/MOZART 125. In 1799 Constanze mentioned only the dedication of the "Fantaisie" to "Frau von Trattner" (cf. Dennerlein/MOZART 198).

136. Carl Thomas Mozart was born Sept. 21, 1784. There are confirmed instances of Mozart putting a later date on an earlier work—e.g. the duet son. K.V. 375a (cf. Köchel/MOZART 467).

137. Cf. Dennerlein/MOZART 204.

138. The anticipations of mood and style have often been noted, as well as the actual thematic relationships of K.V. 457/ii/24 and 29 to Beethoven's Op. 13/ii/1-2 and i/4-5, etc. See, also, note 67a to p. 514.

139. Cf. Anderson/MOZART II 959, III 1089-1090; Nissen/MOZART 414-415.

140. At any rate, if K.V. 457 did come from the earlier period, Mozart still chose to enter the 1784 dedication date in his own index of his works (Mueller von Asow/VERZEICHNIS 42).

Mozart's remaining solo keyboard sonatas, all from his last two creative periods, do not fall into sets. The authenticity of K.V. 498a has been argued back and forth.[141] By now, enough of this work has been traced to other sources in Mozart's music to leave A. E. Müller the credit chiefly for a well assembled and well "doctored" *pasticcio*.[142] On the other hand, there seems to be no question that Mozart composed and himself joined K.V. 533 and 494 for publication.[143] K.V. 545 in C is often dismissed as "the easy, teaching sonata" by Mozart.[144] Nevertheless, this short work, with its wonderfully expressive though simple "Andante," and especially that other short, late, relatively "easy" sonata, K.V. 570 in B♭, reveal some of Mozart's most characteristic, skillful, and sensitive writing. The latter was long neglected and known only as an accompanied sonata, although the innocuous violin part, still to be found in most collections of Mozart's piano-and-violin sonatas,
was probably the work of an early publisher.[145] Whereas Mozart's 145a
"six difficult sonatas" from his third period are actually among his easier sonatas to play, K.V. 576 in D, apparently the first and only completed sonata from "six easy clavier sonatas for Princess Friederike" that he planned to write in 1789,[146] is actually one of his most difficult to play. The difficulty lies not only in the high artistic demands of all three movements, but in the contrapuntal texture that had increased throughout his music since his further introduction to Baroque music by way of Baron van Swieten. Thus, the skill required of the left hand is quite as exceptional as his own playing with this hand is reported to have been.[147]

Mozart's Four-Hand Sonatas

Mozart began to write keyboard duets and accompanied sonatas
sooner than solo keyboard sonatas—in fact, in his first period.[148] His 148a
first keyboard duet, K.V. 19d in C, a rather elementary but not short sonata in three movements, was scored for a two-manual harpsichord

141. It is regarded as stemming largely from Mozart in Köchel/MOZART 634-635 (where Einstein transfers it from K.V. Anh. 136) and again by Einstein, on stylistic grounds, in the Edwards reprint of 1947 (or cf. MR II [1941] 74 and 330-331). But it had been argued mainly as A. E. Müller's work on stylistic grounds in Haupt/MÜLLER 66-71 and on the basis of complex, resourceful bibliographic discoveries in Hill/NUMBERS 128-129. Cf., also, Girdlestone/MOZART 418.

142. Cf. Dennerlein/MOZART 256-259.

143. Cf. Köchel/MOZART 683.

144. Its quick dismissal in Hutchings/MOZART 48 is typical.

145. Cf. Köchel/MOZART 719; MR II (1941) 155.

146. Cf. Anderson/MOZART III 1384 and 1399.

147. Cf. Kelly/REMINISCENCES I 225.

148. The duets are discussed, among other places, in Moldenhauer/DUO 46-68; Sonnedecker/DUETS 24-42; Dennerlein/MOZART *passim*.

(on which it must be played to avoid clashes).[149] It dates from before its first performance by Mozart and his sister in London on May 13, 1765. But whether it antedates any other duet sonata for one keyboard instrument, as Nissen (probably erroneously) credited Leopold with saying,[150] depends on when such pieces were first composed by Christian Bach—for these could well have been Mozart's models—or
151a by Jomelli and perhaps others.[151] Among the better known duet sonatas, that in D, K.V. 123a,[152] is the one Czerny used to illustrate how much more symphonically the same material in the first movement might have been developed (!)[153] This and the duet Sonata in B♭, K.V. 186c, date from Mozart's third period,[154] while the truly symphonic duet Sonata in F (K.V. 497), his most important work in this category, dates from the seventh period (1786). At the start of the last is one of the rare short, dependent slow introductions in Mozart's sonatas.[155] The relative popularity of his duet sonatas is illustrated by the fact that all the complete ones achieved publication during his lifetime, as did nearly all of the sonatas for keyboard and violin but not quite half of the solo keyboard sonatas.

On a par with the duet Sonata in F is the fine Sonata in D for two pianos, K.V. 375a.[156] Of this work Mozart wrote from Vienna to his father in Salzburg on November 24, 1781: At "Aurnhammer's concert yesterday . . . we played the concerto a due [K.V. 316a] and a sonata for two claviers, which I had composed expressly for the occasion and
157a which was a great success."[157]

Mozart's Ensemble Sonatas

157b Mozart's forty-four sonatas for keyboard and violin are generally less well known than his solo or duet sonatas for one or two keyboard

149. Cf. Mozart/NEUE-m IX/24/2 2 (among mod. eds.) and vi-vii (Rehm). This vol. includes facs. from MSS of the duet sons. K.V. 186c and 521.

150. Cf. Nissen/MOZART 102; King/MOZART 100-101; Anderson/MOZART I 83.

151. Cf. King/PIANO 167. In Cat. BRUXELLES II item 6191, is listed a "Sonatine für vier Hände auf einem Claviere" by Saupe that could well be earlier than Mozart's. K.V. 19d was first reported in Saint-Foix/INCONNUE. The question of whether the English or French ed. of this work came first (*ca.* 1788-89) has stimulated some fascinating bibliographic discussions (cf. King/MOZART 100-111, with further references). A facs. of the French (Roullede) ed. is appended to Ganzer & Kusche/VIERHÄNDIG.

152. New information on the autograph and a facs. of the first page are given in King/MOZART 125-128.

153. Czerny/SCHOOL III 37-46.

154. First published in 1783 (Weinmann/ARTARIA plate no. 25), not 1781-82, as in Köchel/MOZART 174.

155. Two others are found in K.V. 293c and 454 (K & Vn).

156. The ed. of this work in Mozart/NEUE-m IX/24/1 (Schmid) includes a facs. of p. 1 of the autograph. The deeply expressive slow mvt. is underrated in Hutchings/MOZART 55.

157. As trans. in Anderson/MOZART III 1161.

instruments. Yet they represent not only the most numerous category
of his sonatas but the only category that he cultivated in every one of
the eight creative periods outlined earlier.[158] Furthermore, K.V. 300c 158a
in e, 317d in B♭, 526 in A, and other of the later sonatas in this
category must be ranked with some of his finest chamber music of all
types (Ex. 79). These works are best discussed chronologically by the sets in which they were first published. Only the last four of them appeared separately. Otherwise there are only fragments to report (e.g., K.V. 385f) or works like the apparent musical joke for his wife (K.V. 385d)[159] and the "Andante" and "Fuga" once called a "sonata" (K.V. 385e). The growing independence of the Mozart violin part, from an optional, truly dispensable adjunct to a full *concertante* partner, makes a fascinating, significant story in itself.[160] In the original editions and nearly all the MSS the titles of the first three sets list this part as optional and the titles in all the subsequent sonatas list it simply as an accompaniment. But from his fourth period, coincidental with the first option of "Clavecin Ou Forté Piano" in these editions (1778), the equal importance of the violin is no longer in doubt. Flute is made optional to the violin in an early edition of the third set, and it could have been intended rather than violin in two sonatas of the 1778 set (K.V. 293a and 293c).[161] A cello reinforcement of the keyboard bass is also included in the third set.

Mozart's first two sets of two accompanied sonatas each were composed in 1762-64 and published in Paris in 1764 as Opp. 1 and 2 (K.V.
6-7 and 8-9).[162] Leopold, who possibly had a hand in writing the 162a
accompaniments,[163] wrote in 1764 (Feb. 1-3):

> At present four sonatas of M. Wolfgang Mozart are being engraved. Picture to yourself the furore they will make in the world when people read on the title-page that they have been composed by a seven-year-old child . . . In due course you will hear how fine these sonatas are; one of them has an Andante [probably the "Adagio" of K.V. 7] in a quite unusual

158. There is no separate, extended study of these sons. But besides the important individual discussions given to each in Saint-Foix/MOZART there are illuminating surveys in COBBETT II 170-177 (Abert) and Einstein/MOZART 252-260.

159. Cf. Einstein/MOZART 258.

160. This growth is ably pursued, with numerous exx., in Fischer/MOZART; cf., also, Newman/ACCOMPANIED 346-347.

161. Einstein/MOZART 254.

162. Cf. Köchel/MOZART 6 and 10, with dedications and pertinent correspondence; Saint-Foix/MOZART I 36-45 (with facs. of the opening of K.V. 6), 81-83, 47-48, 83-85.

163. Fischer/MOZART 21. Leopold himself referred to these works merely as cembalo sons. in one letter (Dec. 22, 1777; Anderson/MOZART II 641) but included the Vn in his index of the boy's works up to 1768 (Mueller von Asow/VERZEICHNIS 2).

Ex. 79. From the opening of Wolfgang Amadeus Mozart's Sonata in C for piano and violin, K.V. 296 (facs. of the autograph at the New York Public Library).

style. Indeed I can tell you . . . that every day God performs fresh miracles through this child.[164]

The third set, increased to six sonatas, was published the same year in London at Leopold's expense as Op. 3 (K.V. 10-15).[165] And the fourth set, of the same size, was published while Mozart was in The Hague, in 1766, as Op. 4 (K.V. 26-31).[166]

The next set of 6 sonatas for keyboard and violin has been the subject of recurrent controversies over their authenticity from soon after Mozart's death to the present day. "Sonates romantiques" was the title Wyzewa and Saint-Foix gave this set, to signify a romantic crisis experienced by Mozart in 1772-73 (during the third period) while he was in Milan.[167] They found this turning point, among other things, in certain Italian traits and in an element of tragedy common to all 6 sonatas. Related to the tragic element, they felt, was a new emphasis on minor keys (actually, 7 out of 18 mvts.),[168] recalling the "romantic crisis" marked by Haydn's Sonata in c of about the same time (H. XVI/20). But in his edition of Köchel/MOZART (pp. 861-865) Einstein transferred this set from K. 55-60 to the "Anhang" (209c-h), primarily because (1) there is no (correct) record of an autograph; (2) neither Constanze nor Nannerl could confirm these sonatas as authentic,[169] although Breitkopf & Härtel finally did proceed with plans to publish them posthumously (Mozart/OEUVRES-m XVI/1-6).[170]

With "extreme caution," Einstein suggested rather that the "Romantic Sonatas" might be a set by one "Schuster," referred to at least four times in the Mozart letters: "I send my sister herewith six duets for clavicembalo and violin by Schuster, which I have often played here. They are not bad. If I stay on I shall write six myself in the same style, as they are very popular here" (Munich, Oct. 6, 1777).[171] At this point Richard Engländer joined the fray to prove beyond reasonable doubt that the Schuster in question was the Dresden composer Joseph Schuster (as others had already assumed[172]); that Schuster's set in question was not the "Romantic" set nor the MS set

164. As trans. in Anderson/MOZART I 54.

165. Cf. Anderson/MOZART I 76; Köchel/MOZART 12-13, with dedication; Saint-Foix/MOZART I 102-112.

166. Cf. Saint-Foix/MOZART I 150-157.

167. Saint-Foix/MOZART I 502-513, 515-519.

168. In Engel/MOZART statistics are provided on Mozart's use of major and minor keys that help to verify this change.

169. Cf. Anderson/MOZART III 1491-1492; Gärtner/MOZART 30-31 (for a summary of the correspondence). Their authenticity had been argued eloquently in Abert/MOZART I 352-353.

170. They were later included in Mozart/WERKE-m XVIII/1 nos. 17-22.

171. As trans. in Anderson/MOZART I 438-439 (with further references in I 456, II 489 and 589).

172. Cf. Abert/MOZART I 623-626; Saint-Foix/MOZART III 38-46; also, SCE XVI.

of six authentic accompanied sonatas by Schuster (1776?) to be found in Naples, but the MS set of six accompanied "Divertimenti" by Schuster in the Dresden Landesbibliothek; and that the Mozart set written under Schuster's influence must have been the "Mannheim" set of 1778 and could not be the "Romantic Sonatas."[173] Einstein then acknowledged these findings and offered the new possibility that one of Mozart's students may have written the "Romantic Sonatas."[174] Saint-Foix rose to repeat his defense of their authenticity, emphasizing the stylistic arguments and the possible influence of accompanied sonatas by Sammartini (1766) and especially Boccherini (1768).[175] Engländer seconded this view,[176] and, most recently, Gustav Gärtner, came to the same conclusion in a still more detailed style analysis.[177] There the matter now stands, somewhat in favor of the authenticity of K.V. Anh. 209c-h (a conclusion also reached, largely through experience with
177a the music itself, in the present study).

Popular editions of Mozart's sonatas for piano and violin exclude all those listed chronologically up to this point and begin with his first true duos—that is, the "Mannheim" (or "Palatinate" or "Kurfürsten")
177b set of 1778 that was just mentioned as being composed under the influence of Schuster's "Divertimenti." Four of these were composed in Mannheim (K.V. 293a-d) and two in Paris (K.V. 300c and 300l), the whole set being published in Paris in the same year, after much worry on Mozart's part over the costs and engraving.[178] K.V. 300c in e has much in common, emotionally, with K.V. 300d in a, for solo piano, and may also have been composed in the troubled period following his mother's death.[179] Mozart's next published set (Vienna, 1781) includes another sonata composed in Mannheim in 1778 (K.V. 296 in C), one composed perhaps early in 1781 while he was in Munich (K.V. 317d in B♭),[180] and four others written in 1781 during his first year of
180a residence in Vienna (K.V. 373a and 374d-f). Sometimes called the "Auernhammer" set for the dedicatee, who was Mozart's pupil, this set well deserves the review it received in 1783:

> These sonatas are the only ones of this kind. Rich in new ideas and in evidences of the great musical genius of their author. Very brilliant and suited to the instrument. At the same time the accompaniment of the

173. Engländer/MOZART.
174. MR II (1941) 325.
175. Saint-Foix/ROMANTIQUES.
176. Engländer/ECHTHEITSFRAGE.
177. Gärtner/MOZART.
178. Cf. Anderson/MOZART II 737, 850-851, 928, 933-934, 958.
179. On the possible derivation of K.V. 300c from K.V. Anh. 209h (rather than any work by Schuster) cf. Engländer/PROBLEM, with exx.
180. Not Salzburg in 1779, argues Gärtner in MUSICA X (1956) 834-835.

violin is so artfully combined with the clavier part that both instruments are kept constantly on the alert; so that these sonatas require just as skillful a player on the violin as on the clavier. . . .[181]

K.V. 373a in G is of special interest for its bearing on Mozart's creative processes. In a letter to his father of April 8, 1781, he wrote:

To-day (for I am writing at eleven o'clock at night) we had a concert, where three of my compositions were performed—new ones, of course . . . [including] a sonata with violin accompaniment for myself, which I composed last night between eleven and twelve (but in order to be able to finish it, I only wrote out the accompaniment for [the violinist] Brunetti and retained my own [clavier] part in my head); . . .[182]

In an enlightening discussion of such feats Erich Hertzmann has shown how the piano part was first noted in shorthand, then later traced into the autograph.[183]

Regarding the four other, completed sonatas for piano and violin, not originally published together in a set, Mozart wrote K.V. 454 in B♭ (Vienna, 1784) to play with the fine violinist Regina Strinasacchi.[184] K.V. 481 in E♭ was published in 1786 and K.V. 526 in A about 1790,[184a] but the suite-like sonata K.V. 547 remained unpublished during Mozart's lifetime both in this original form and in the piano solo arrangement (K.V. 547a).[184a]

Mozart's "Sonata for Bassoon and Cello" in B♭, K.V. 196c, was a product of his third period and is the only such sonata by any of the three great Viennese Classicists. It was composed early in 1775, apparently for an amateur bassoonist in Munich, being actually an accompanied bassoon solo in three movements. Neglected only because the combination of instruments is infrequently heard, it solves the two-part relationship with all the expected skill and imagination, making a delightful novelty in any chamber music recital (Ex. 80).

Mozart's *"Epistle Sonatas"*

Mozart's 17 "Epistle Sonatas" represent an unusual category of the sonata and of his own music. Though, owing to their particularized

181. Cramer/MAGAZIN I 485, as trans. in Einstein/MOZART 256.
182. As trans. in Anderson/MOZART III 1072-1073.
183. Hertzmann/MOZART 189-190 and 194 (with facs. from the autograph, now in the Library of Congress; cf. Albrecht/CENSUS item 1301). In DMF XIII (1960) 57 and 59-60, K. Marguerre disagrees with Einstein's supposition (Köchel/MOZART 457) that the "Abschrift" is Brunetti's original Vn part but believes it was prepared by some better violinist who had to be "accompanied" by some weaker pianist.
184. Anderson/MOZART III 1304.
184a. For a curiously unperceptive, conservative critique of K.V. 481 in 1788, cf. Mozart/NEUE-m X/34 283 (Deutsch).

Ex. 80. From the first movement of Wolfgang Amadeus Mozart's "Sonata for Bassoon and Cello," K.V. 196c (after Mozart/WERKE-m X/14).

and localized use, they remained unpublished in his own day and are still among the lesser known of his instrumental works, they have not suffered from any lack of interest on the part of the scholars. Besides the usual conscientious discussions that Wyzewa and Saint-Foix provided, O. A. Mansfield made an extended survey of the 15 available sonatas in 1922, beginning with a full consideration of the type of organ used; Erich Schenk went further into the dating and use of the sonatas in 1937; Einstein discovered and prepared editions of the 2 missing autographs (K.V. 241 and 263 [or 259a]) in 1940; Robert Tangeman tabulated the chief style traits of all 17 sonatas in 1946; Dennerlein reexamined their dating, the type of organ used, and their church function in 1953; and, most recently (1957), M. E. Dounias has provided a concise summary of our present information about these sonatas in his
185a excellent new edition of the complete set (among several mod. eds.).[185]
A primary bit of information on these sonatas comes in Mozart's own well-known letter to Padre Martini of September 4, 1776:

> Our church music is very different from that of Italy, since a Mass with the whole Kyrie, the Gloria, the Credo, the Epistle sonata, the Offertory or Motet, the Sanctus and Agnus Dei must not last longer than three quarters of an hour. This applies even to the most solemn Mass said by the Archbishop himself. So you see that a special study is required for this kind of composition. At the same time, the Mass must have all the instruments—trumpets, drums and so forth.[186]

185. Mansfield/MOZART; Einstein/MISSING; Tangeman/MOZART; Dennerlein/KIRCHENSONATEN; Mozart/NEUE-m VI/16 (Dounias), with reference to the Schenk article (p. vii) and facs. from the autographs of 4 of the sons.

186. As trans. in Anderson/MOZART I 386-387.

There follows a chronology of the 17 "Epistle Sonatas" (not including
2 fragments, K.V. 65a and 124c), based on the revised dating, and in- 186a
cluding the scorings as well as a conversion table of the Köchel and
(inaccurately listed!) Saint-Foix numbers:

Mozart's "Epistle Sonatas"

K.V. no., revised (and original)	Saint-Foix no.	Key	Year of composition	Scoring
41h (67)	115	E♭	1772?	2 Vns, Vc, organ?, opt. bassoon
41i (68)	116	B♭	"	" " "
41k (69)	117	D	"	" " "
124a (144)	131	D	1772	2 Vns, Vc, organ, *b.c.*, opt. bassoon
124b (145)	132	F	"	" " " "
212 ———	228	B♭	1775	" " " "
241 ———	missing	G	1776	" " " "
241a (224)	251	F	1776?	" " " "
241b (225)	250	A	"	" " " "
244 ———	252	F	1776	2 Vns, Vc, organ, opt. bassoon
245 ———	253	D	"	" " "
[259a] (263)	missing	C	"	2 Vns, 2 trumpets, organ, Vc, opt. bassoon
271d (274)	278	G	1777	2 Vns, Vc, organ, *b.c.*, opt. bassoon
271e (278)	279	C	"	2 Vns, Vc, 2 oboes, 2 trumpets, timpani, organ, *b.c.*
317a (329)	334	C	1779?	2 Vns, Vc, basses, organ, 2 oboes, 2 horns, 2 trumpets, timpani
317c (328)	338	C	1779?	2 Vns, organ, Vc, opt. bassoon
336d (336)	348	C	1780	2 Vns, Vc, organ, *b.c.*, opt. bassoon

As the chronology suggests, these sonatas are now all placed within Mozart's second decade (third to fifth periods), during his formal paid service in Salzburg and while he was not traveling. The majority fall in the third or "home period" and most were composed for special feast days.[187] The sonatas were played during High Mass between the Gloria and Credo—specifically, between the Epistle and the Gospel. Sometimes the sonata was used in a Mass that was also composed by Mozart (as K.V. 263 in K.V. 259), but more often not. For the reasons Mozart's letter makes clear, these sonatas last not more than 5 minutes (ranging only from 60 to 142 mss.). Mozart's own designation in his letter, "sonata all'Epistola," seems appropriate,[188] as does "church sonata." However, the latter must not be taken to suggest the style and form of the Baroque *sonata da chiesa* in several movements, Mozart's "Epistle Sonatas" all being single movements in Classic "sonata forms" (of considerable variety). The designation "organ sonata" is less appropriate, since the organ part is merely an unrealized

187. Cf. Dennerlein/KIRCHENSONATEN 103-104.
188. Only "Sonata" appears as a title in the MSS.

bass line, with or without figures, in 12 of the 17 sonatas, merely a bare realization of the bass in 3 others, and an actual *concertante* solo only in the last 3 sonatas (coinciding with the time Mozart succeeded Adlgasser as court and cathedral organist). In these last the part is still not elaborate, being predominantly manualiter and not unlike that in most of Handel's organ concertos.[189] In the longest, most fully scored of the sonatas, K.V. 317a in C, there is, in fact, the feel of a Handelian concerto grosso movement. One might call Mozart's "Epistle Sonatas" the nearest counterpart to the later, one-movement orchestral sonatas in Haydn's "Seven Last Words." But the contrasts are again greater than the likenesses, what with the shortness, allegro tempo, homophonic texture, and festive spirit of the former (only K.V. 41h being relatively slow).

Mozart's Place in Sonata History

To sum up Mozart's position in sonata history is less the province of this immediate discussion than of the entire present volume. Mozart is the Classicist of Classicists.[190] From our standpoint, his position is somewhat akin to Corelli's in the Baroque Era in that his sonatas represent an ideal to and from which most of the main trends of the time seem to flow. Put differently, he is the most universal of Classic composers. Indeed, the present-day tendency is to view him as the most universal of *all* composers,[191] which means, one supposes, that he is the composer who has found the most lucid, fluent, clearly organized, accurately controlled, aesthetically meaningful, broadly humanitarian ways to apply music's basic materials.

A frequent explanation for this universality is Mozart's unparalleled exposure to all the musical world of his times had to offer, thanks to the grand tours Leopold so expertly engineered. Included in Wolfgang's experience was not only the music of his own day but that of the near past, especially of Handel and J. S. Bach. To be sure, this much exposure could only be tolerated by a composer with his natural genius for assimilation and rejection. As Einstein very aptly puts it,

> He heard . . . such a quantity of music and received such a quantity of changing impressions that one continues to marvel equally at his receptivity

189. That Mozart himself was capable of much more advanced organ playing is made clear in the chapter on "Mozart and the Organ" in King/MOZART 228-241.

190. In Engel/MOZART he is seen as coming exactly between the Rococo and Romantic movements.

191. Quite apart from the naïvely enthusiastic query in a *Life* magazine feature (Feb. 3, 1947, p. 58) as to whether *Don Giovanni* is not "the world's greatest work of art" (in whatever category), one may note such more professionally restrained statements as occur in King/MOZART 2; Lang/MOZART; and Blume/MOZART 15-16, 20, 25.

and at his powers of resistance—his talent for appropriating what was congenial and rejecting whatever was opposed to his nature. He found congenial material in lesser contemporaries, uncongenial material in greater contemporaries, and *vice versa.* Many impressions left him indifferent.[192]

The nature and bearing of all this experience and stimulation has naturally been a main consideration in many of the discussions of individual composers throughout this volume. The experiences started with Leopold's own teaching and his "Notenbuch für Wolfgang," and with the music of near-by composers like Wagenseil (whom the child already knew at six [SCE XI]). If the music of neither Leopold nor Wagenseil could make any special mark, there is no question that Leopold's shrewd counsel was a significant influence right up to his death in 1787, as in this extract from a letter to Wolfgang in Paris (Aug. 13, 1778) that has weathered innumerable citations in music literature:

> If you have not got any pupils, well then compose something more. . . . But let it be something short, easy and popular. . . . Do you imagine that you would be doing work unworthy of you? If so, you are very much mistaken. Did [Christian] Bach, when he was in London, ever publish anything but such-like trifles? *What is slight can still be great,* if it is written in a natural, flowing and easy style—and at the same time bears the mark of sound composition. Such works are more difficult to compose than all those harmonic progressions, *which the majority of people cannot fathom,* or pieces which have pleasing melodies but are *difficult to perform.* Did Bach lower himself by such work? Not at all. Good composition, sound construction, il filo [natural unfolding]—these distinguish the master from the bungler—even in trifles.[193]

From the time of his first travels, the composers Mozart met and the music he heard add up to a fair cross section of international music history in the later eighteenth century, as becomes so evident in the important studies of his artistic environment, whether native Austrian, German, French, English, or Czech.[194] The proof is not only in the letters but in actual musical consequences such as the early keyboard concertos arranged from keyboard sonatas by Christian Bach, Raupach, Schobert, Honauer, Eckard, and Emanuel Bach (K.V. 21b, 37, 39-41). Besides these men, one may recall, to mention only the better known names, Padre Martini, G. B. Sammartini, Sarti, Boccherini, Galuppi, Rutini, Vento, Mysliveček, Clementi, and, of course, Haydn, whose

192. Einstein/MOZART 110; cf., also, p. 92.

193. As trans. in Anderson/MOZART II 888-889; cf., also, Einstein/MOZART 116-121.

194. Along with Saint-Foix/MOZART, Torrefranca/ORIGINI, and Torrefranca/LONDRA, there have been more recent studies, including Gottron/MAINZER, Racek/TSCHECHISCHEN, and, especially, the 14 comprehensive articles in Verchaly/MOZART.

6 sonatas of 1773, "Op. 13" (H. XVI/21-26) already may have influenced Mozart's "home" set of 1774 (K.V. 189d-h and 205b).[195]

A further reference to Mozart's universality along these same lines would have to include his followers as well as his predecessors—starting with Beethoven, Schubert, and many lesser names that also occur in the present and next volume.[196] At this point we can only stop to note that, as with Haydn, his sonatas have seldom been held in quite the same high esteem as his quartets and symphonies. In the nineteenth century the sonatas were not only branded with that stigma of "teaching pieces" but were regarded, in all their purity of texture, as being too thinly scored. It was after hearing *Die Entführung* in Vienna that Emperor Joseph II said, "Too beautiful for our ears and an extraordinary number of notes, dear Mozart," bringing forth Mozart's model retort, "Just as many, Your Majesty, as are necessary."[197] But now this same composer was being charged with too few notes. Scarcely had the new century started before filled-out arrangements of his sonatas began to appear.[198] For some such reason Grieg felt impelled to add second-piano parts to four of the sonatas (from 1879), Rockstro saw fit to rationalize their bareness, and MacDowell brought them down to their moment of lowest repute by calling them products of "mediocrity . . . in a style of flashy harpsichord virtuosity such as Liszt never descended to. . . ."[199] That the twentieth century has taken a much more sympathetic view of the sonatas and prefers them in their original state hardly need be told to any music lover who is selective about the music he buys, the recordings he hears, and the recitals he attends.

195. Cf. Saint-Foix/MOZART II 166-170.

196. Interest in Mozart from his death to the present day is discussed in King/MOZART 10-54. In his unpub. Ph.D. diss. (Yale University, 1974), William Pressly Robinson has concentrated on "Conceptions of Mozart in German Criticism and Biography, 1791-1828: Changing Images of a Musical Genius."

197. The familiar anecdote was originally told in Niemetschek/MOZART 32.

198. Cf. the eds. listed by E. Lebeau in KONGRESS 1956 (Vienna) 327.

199. Cf. King/MOZART 47 and 42; MacDowell/ESSAYS 193-194, 200, 239, 253.

Chapter XV

Beethoven

Sources, Periods, Works

The third of our three Viennese masters, **Ludwig van Beethoven** (1770-1827), is the composer who is commonly agreed to have contributed most significantly to the sonata not only in the Classic Era but, insofar as such generalizations have meaning, to all sonata history. Actually, Beethoven's career and musical thinking extended deep into the Romantic Era, but his firm foundation in Classic music remains the paramount consideration in any survey of his sonatas.[1] More pertinent than any other evidence for this foundation is, of course, the extent to which he achieved an artistic union of Haydn's and Mozart's styles in the generation after these two men wrote their last sonatas. (It will be recalled, from SCE XIV, that whereas Haydn's chief sonata output fell in the years from 1760-95 and Mozart's in 1774-88, Beethoven's fell in 1795-1822. Clementi's chief output, from 1773 to 1821, began before Mozart's but continued nearly as late as Beethoven's.)

The literature on Beethoven and his music is even greater than that for Mozart, especially as regards the sonatas. Yet it is more hit-or-miss in its coverage and more in need, now, of reorganization.[2] For that matter, there is no comprehensive, up-to-date bibliography of this literature.[3] The status of other basic tools as of this writing (1961)

1. Cf. the conclusions reached in Boyer/BEETHOVEN 426-427 and 438; this study is one of the richest and most illuminating among the numerous studies devoted to Beethoven's relation to and influence on the Romantic Era (cf. MGG I 1545-1551 [Schmidt-Görg]).

2. A survey of Beethoven research, comparable to King/MOZART, is lacking.

3. The most recent attempt is Kastner/BEETHOVENIANA (up to 1924). Most of the more basic studies are listed in GROVE I 573-575 (Lord) and Suppl. 29; also (up to 1949) in MGG I 1562-1565. Although no cumulative list has yet been made from the annual lists in NBJ and BEETHOVEN-JAHRBUCH, these are thorough for the years in which they appear. Typed abstracts by Donald MacArdle of some 4,500 items comprising much of the Beethoven literature are on file (without index) at the Library of Congress, New York Public Library, and the British Museum.

may be summarized briefly. In much the best state are the 1,590 letters,
newly collected and translated in Emily Anderson's unequaled, annotated edition,[4] and the thematic index, prepared by Kinsky and Halm
in a single recent volume that, except for including completed works
only, is fully the peer of Hoboken/HAYDN and Einstein's edition of
5a Köchel/MOZART.[5] The standard biography remains the one that the
American, Alexander Wheelock Thayer, was able to finish through 1816
in Beethoven's life (3 vols. published in German in 1865-79), that
Hermann Deiters and Hugo Riemann revised and completed in 5
volumes (1917-23 in its latest form),[6] and that Henry Edward Krehbiel
reproduced and re-edited in an abridged, 3-volume English version with
further revisions by 1914 (but not published until 1921).[7] Since even
the latest of those alterations and additions are now some 40 years old,
since Krehbiel's share was not free from the ill consequences of haste
and compression, and since much new information along with a changing, larger view of Beethoven have been provided by further generations
of Beethoven scholars during those last 40 years or more, the time is
8a obviously ripe for an entirely new, large-scale biography.[8]

With regard to the nearly 140 "Conversation Books" that remain
out of some 400 inherited by Anton Schindler (Beethoven's quasi-
Boswell), the immediate prospects for a complete edition are still not
9a good.[9] This nondescript, occasionally valuable raw material, which

4. Anderson/BEETHOVEN; but cf. MacArdle's review in NOTES XIX (1962) 243-246. Other eds. of the letters are cited here, chiefly MacArdle & Misch/BEETHOVEN, only when their annotations have special value to us. A new "complete" ed. of the letters in the original German is in progress at the Beethovenhaus in Bonn.

5. Kinsky & Halm/BEETHOVEN. References to specific sons. by Beethoven here follow the pattern set in this index—i.e., op. nos. for works that do have op. nos., and the symbol WoO ("Werke ohne Opuszahl") for the works without op. nos. as numbered on pp. 419-708. In neither class is the order strictly chronological. A few complete works and many fragments are added in Hess/VERZEICHNIS.

6. Thayer & Riemann/BEETHOVEN.

7. Thayer/BEETHOVEN; cf. the "Introduction" in Vol. I vii-xviii.

8. Cf. MacArdle's review of the 1960 reprint of Thayer/BEETHOVEN, in NOTES XVIII (1960) 52-53. Since 1950 Elliot Forbes of Harvard has been working on "a completely revised edition." The time is ripe, too, for a new, satisfactory, adequately documented, shorter biography in English; however, special mention should be made of Schönewolf/BEETHOVEN and Hess/BEETHOVEN among recent shorter biographies in German (cf. DMF XII [1959] 254-255 [Kahl]).

9. A good start (1818-23) was made during World War II in Schünemann/KONVERSATIONSHEFTE, but the 3 vols. in this ed. are not convenient to use for reference purposes because they lack the index that surely would have appeared with the remaining vols. Besides extracts in standard biographies, a selection from all this material is provided in Prod'homme/CAHIERS (again, without an index). Schindler/BEETHOVEN is valuable as an early biography chiefly because so much of it grows out of the actual conversations, with Beethoven's answers often supplied by Schindler (though not always dependably). MacArdle has prepared indices

mostly contains the other person's side of numerous conversations with the deaf Beethoven away from home, is scattered throughout the last nine years of his life.[10] Nor does there seem to be any immediate prospect for the publication of a full collection of other contemporary
documents.[11] On the other hand, under Schmidt-Görg's editorship a 11a
complete edition from the Beethovenhaus in Bonn of the approximately
fifty extant "Sketchbooks" is already under way.[12] These valuable 12a
sources, with their clues to the genesis of Beethoven's ideas and sometimes to the creative evolution of entire works,[13] cover most of Beethoven's creative career and, thanks to the minute examinations of the Beethoven scholars, often contribute importantly to our understanding of styles in the sonatas.[14] By way of summarizing the primary sources of most concern here, we may add to the Conversation Books, early Sketchbooks, and contemporary documents, the personal recollections of men like Wegeler, Ries, Reichardt, and Czerny (as cited later), and the first reviews of Beethoven's music, chiefly in the Leipzig *Allgemeine musicalische Zeitung* (AMZ; from 1798).

A considerable portion of the nineteenth-century literature on Beethoven is taken up with the interpretation of his music in poetic terms, reminding us at once how much more Romantically his music was heard and understood than that of Haydn or Mozart. As we shall see, some of this writing is so florid, also grandiloquent, as to surpass comprehension. The most developed, and in many respects the best, examples of this writing have come in the twentieth century, even though the tendency in recent years has certainly been in the other direction—that

of the Schünemann and Prod'homme vols. (Detroit: Information Service, 1962); his annotated, indexed English trans. of Schindler is our Schindler & MacArdle/BEETHOVEN.

10. Cf. Thayer/BEETHOVEN III 11-13 and (on Schindler's tampering with the evidence) II 376-378, III 273 and 281-282; Schünemann/KONVERSATIONSHEFTE I 1-20.

11. A small assortment, including some letters, has been issued most recently in Rutz/BEETHOVEN. Many of the earliest references (up to about 1812) are quoted in full in Kastner/BEETHOVENIANA 1-8 and many documents are given in full in Frimmel/BEETHOVEN. Since 1955 MacArdle has been working on a new "Beethoven Encyclopedia," with some 4,000 entries projected, on persons and places in Beethoven's life.

12. Cf. Nettl/BEETHOVEN 233-235. Among pertinent eds. from separate Sketchbooks are Nottebohm/SKIZZENBÜCHER (illustrated discussions of 2 Sketchbooks dating from 1801-03; cf. Rolland/BEETHOVEN I 317-320); Shedlock/SKETCH (supplementing Nottebohm); Mikulicz/NOTIERUNGSBUCH (a complete Sketchbook from 1800, with preface); cf., also, Schwarz/BEETHOVENIANA on Sketchbooks now in Russia (including sketches for the Sons. Op. 31/3 and 2/1).

13. Cf. Thayer/BEETHOVEN I 257-261 and 364-365.

14. Among separate studies especially pertinent here are Nottebohm/BEETHOVENIANA and Nottebohm/ZWEITE; Shedlock/SKETCH (with much not in Nottebohm); Mies/SKETCHES; Mies/TEXTKRITISCHE; Schenker/BEETHOVEN-m (an exegesis of 4 of the last 5 piano sons.); Prod'homme/BEETHOVEN; Forte/MATRIX (on Op. 109).

is, toward promoting Beethoven from immortality to mortality (to borrow Walton Hamilton's choice expression). One example is found in the seven illuminating, penetrating, highly subjective volumes by the French scholar Romain Rolland that were published under the general heading of *Beethoven, les grandes époques créatrices* (1928-49 [posthumous]). This set we shall have more than one occasion to cite again. The other example is found in the extraordinary, symbolic interpretations developed throughout almost the same years (*ca.* 1930-41) by the German scholar Arnold Schering. Each of Schering's interpretations derives from some actual Beethoven fact or remark, however tenuous. Since the structural aspects of Beethoven's sonatas were discussed in Chapter VI of the present volume, and since the approach there was not symbolic, we shall have less occasion to refer to Schering's ideas again. But at this point we ought at least to recognize his sort of approach by listing the sonatas he analyzes symbolically along with the literary parallels (or inspirations) that he draws so neatly (often even fitting words to the main musical ideas). Schering's arguments[15] go back to Schindler's well-known report of Beethoven's desire to include the "poetic idea" underlying each of his piano works, in a
16a proposed new edition.[16] Yet Schering wards off the vigorous protests of the musical absolutists by agreeing that Beethoven stubbornly refused, for the most part, to divulge his "poetic ideas."[17] The parallels follow (with S/De for Schering/DEUTUNG; S/Di for Schering/DICHTUNG; S/E for Schering/ERKENNTNIS; S/P for Schering/PATHÉTIQUE; and S/V for Schering/VIOLINSONATEN).

Arnold Schering's Literary Parallels to Beethoven's Sonatas

Op. 2/1 (S/Di 547 [only passing mention]) Ossian, *Colmas Klage*
Op. 10/3 (S/De 63 [only passing mention]) "The Four Humors"
Op. 12/3 (S/V 120-130) Goethe, *Scherz, List und Rache*
Op. 13 (S/Di 547-560) *Hero and Leander* (but in the Musäus, not the Schiller version [S/P])
Op. 23 (S/V 1041-1048) Goethe, *Erwin und Elmire*
Op. 24 (S/V 1307-1318) Goethe, *Claudine von Villa Bella*
Op. 26 (S/E 1-16) Gamera, *Achille*
Op. 27/1 (S/De 63-67) Shakespeare, *The Merchant of Venice*
Op. 27/2 (S/De 68-71) Shakespeare, *King Lear*
Op. 28 (S/De 72-75) Shakespeare, *The Winter's Tale*
Op. 30/2 (S/Di 474-485) Goethe, *Leiden des jungen Werther*
Op. 30/3 (S/V 374-381) Goethe, *Lila*
Op. 31/1 (S/De 76-79) Shakespeare, *The Taming of the Shrew*

15. Defended historically at length in Schering/DICHTUNG 13-119.
16. Schindler/BEETHOVEN II 212-218, 220-224. Cf., also, Shedlock/SONATA 182-191; Nettl/BEETHOVEN 209-210.
17. Schering/DICHTUNG 18.

Op. 31/2 (S/De 80-84) Shakespeare, *The Tempest*
Op. 31/3 (S/E 17-28) Shakespeare, *As You Like It*
Op. 47 (S/Di 449-474) Tasso, *Gerusalemme liberata* (selected strophes)
Op. 53 (S/Di 495-507) Homer, *Odyssey* (Book 23)
Op. 54 (S/De 85-86) Shakespeare, *Much Ado About Nothing*
Op. 57 (S/De 87-93) Shakespeare, *Macbeth*
Op. 96 (S/Di 485-492) Goethe, *Triumph der Empfindsamkeit*
Op. 101 (S/Di 507-520) Bürger, *Lenore*
Op. 102/1 (S/E 61-77) Goethe, *Proserpina*
Op. 106 (S/Di 98-113) Schiller, *Jungfrau von Orleans*
Op. 110 (S/Di 521-547) Schiller, *Maria Stuart*
Op. 111 (S/De 94-97) Shakespeare, *Henry the Eighth*

The first and only "critical" and "complete" edition of Beethoven's
music[18] was published nearly a century ago except for the Supplement 18a
isued in 1887.[19] Willy Hess's list of some 335 complete or fragmentary
works not included in that edition[20] is but one reason for the new
"complete" edition being prepared since 1959 at the Beethovenhaus in
Bonn under Schmidt-Görg's editorship.[21] 21a

Ever since Lenz first published his analysis of Beethoven's piano
sonatas according to three styles (1852) it has been customary to view
Beethoven's life in three (not wholly distinct) creative periods.[22] The 22a
first period is now usually said to extend from about 1782 to 1800, including such representative works as the first symphony (Op. 21), the 6 quartets in Op. 18, and the 11 piano sonatas from Op. 2 to 22; the second period extends from about 1801 to 1814, including the second through the eighth symphonies, the quartets Opp. 59, 74, and 95, and the 16 piano sonatas from Op. 26 to 90; and the third period extends from about 1815 to 1826, including the last symphony, the last 5 quartets, and the last 5 piano sonatas. This division into 3 periods is too broad for a more detailed study of Beethoven's works. Yet it is not easy to arrive at a further subdivision that is altogether satisfactory,

18. For Beethoven's own interest in such an ed. cf. Anderson/BEETHOVEN III 1450; Deutsch/BEETHOVEN.

19. Beethoven/WERKE-m; cf. Heyer/HISTORICAL 30-32 (with further details, references, and partial eds.).

20. Hess/VERZEICHNIS. Under Hess's editorship Breitkopf & Härtel started to bring out these works in 1957 as supplements to BEETHOVEN WERKE-m (cf. NOTES XVII [1960] 306).

21. Hess/VERZEICHNIS; cf. the announcement issued in 1960 by G. Henle Verlag. None of the more than 40 vols. projected in 24 "Abteilungen" has been issued as of this writing. Except for the horn and the mandolin works (in Abteilung V) no sons. are among the first vols. scheduled for early publication. The piano sons. will be in Abteilung VII, and the Vn sons. in IV.

22. Lenz/BEETHOVEN; cf. Blom/BEETHOVEN 168-172. A good opportunity to reconsider these periods, according to more accurate dating, is provided by the single list of all Beethoven's works arranged chronologically by the year of composition, in Kinsky & Halm/BEETHOVEN 741-754.

partly because the external crises in his life do not necessarily correspond with the internal crises in his style, and partly because, as the Sketchbooks show, several compositions of very different styles were often germinating concurrently. A further subdivision into five periods is ventured here, based somewhat on other recent approaches to Beethoven's life and works,[23] and somewhat on special considerations in the
23a sonatas themselves.

The *first or "student" period,* 1782-94,[24] covers Beethoven's last ten years in Bonn and his first two in Vienna (from 1792), including the training under Neefe, the employment as organist at the Bonn electoral court and as violist in the local opera orchestra, the beginning of close friendships with the von Breuning, Lichnowsky, Waldstein, and other highly stationed, well-to-do families remembered both as benefactors and dedicatees of Beethoven, the probable meeting, perhaps even some lessons, with Mozart in Vienna in 1787,[25] the visit of Haydn to Bonn in 1790 and possibly again in 1792,[26] and the lessons with Haydn, among others, in Vienna.[27] The *second or "virtuoso" period,* 1795-1800, is marked especially by the renown Beethoven won as a pianist, including the meetings with Wölfl and J. B. Cramer,[28] and the visits, in 1796, to Nürnberg, Prague, Dresden, and Berlin. Yet this period also includes not the first but the recognized Op. 1 among his publications (the 3 trios, 1795) as well as some 35 other works. The *third or "appassionata" period,* 1801-08, begins with Beethoven's rapidly worsening deafness and the desperate "Heiligenstadt Testament," includes some of his principal love affairs, and ends with the invitation to serve in Kassel, the outcome of which was the annuity guaranteed early in 1809 by three princely friends so long as he remained in Vienna. In this period one senses the greatest, though belated, impress of the *Sturm und Drang* movement on Beethoven. The *fourth or "invasion" period,* 1809-14, extends from the siege and occupation of Vienna by the French to their withdrawal and the festive opening of the Congress of Vienna. During this period came Beethoven's closest contacts with Goethe, his curious dealings with Maelzel, and a more intensified,

23. Especially Prod'homme/BEETHOVEN, Schönewolf/BEETHOVEN, Hess/BEETHOVEN, and the rather loose divisions of subject matter in the 7 vols. of Rolland/BEETHOVEN.

24. The valuable monograph Schiedermair/BEETHOVEN concentrates on the years in Bonn, the earliest compositions, and their background.

25. Cf. Schiedermair/BEETHOVEN 182-189.

26. The second visit is regarded as inadequately documented in Schiedermair/BEETHOVEN 211-212.

27. Cf. Thayer/BEETHOVEN I 150-162.

28. Cf. AMZ I (1798-99) 524-525 (for a comparison of Beethoven and Wölfl); GROVE I 537; Baum/WÖLFL 16-18; Schlesinger/CRAMER 43-48, 175.

personal, deliberate approach to composition. The *fifth or "sublimation" period,* 1815-26, includes the tragic relationship with his nephew Karl and the oppressive domestic annoyances of an increasingly eccentric and hermitic existence. It is in this last period that the gap between the mundane and the sublime, within the same man, becomes almost too great to comprehend.

Over 600 completed or nearly completed works by Beethoven are now known (including some sets of dances or other small pieces). This total is nearly twice that in the original "complete" set, although as regards the sonata there are only 5 "new" items[29] and only the last of these is a complete sonata (Anhang 4 in Kinsky & Halm/BEETHOVEN). Not quite half of the 600 works are instrumental, without voices, and of these more than a fourth are sonatas or related cyclic works. As against Haydn's 283 and Mozart's 90 (relatively shorter) "sonatas," the actual number of Beethoven's completed works called "sonata" or "sonatina" is 57 (not including the 2 well-known but doubtful piano sonatinas, in G and F, Anhang 5).[30] Of these, 37 (or about 65 per cent) are for piano alone, one is for piano duet (Op. 6 in D, 1797), 10 are for piano and violin (18 per cent), 5 are for piano and cello (9 per cent), and there are 4 for other instruments and piano—that is, 2 for mandolin (WoO 43 and 44),[31] one for horn (or cello; Op. 17), and one for flute (if authentic;[32] Anhang 4).

The Piano Sonatas: Overview

Beethoven's piano sonatas span forty years of his life (1782-1822). More than any other category of his music, they give a rounded view of his styles and forms throughout his creative periods. Furthermore, unlike the keyboard sonatas of Haydn and Mozart, they have generally been ranked among the most important works in the total production of their creator. It will be convenient again, here, to provide a list by opus or "WoO" numbers of the piano sonatas in their approximately chronological order of composition, with the dates of composition and of the first publication for each. This time it becomes possible to mark off the creative periods (with horizontal lines). New information on the first editions of Opp. 78, 79, and 81a comes from MacArdle/

29. Items 43, 46, 52, 53, and A-11 in Hess/VERZEICHNIS.

30. Sketches show that at least 2 other sons. were projected (Thayer/BEETHOVEN II 310 and III 141), one for P & Vc and one for P 4 hands (cf., also, Hess in ML XXXIII [1952] 223). Recall the related statistics in Chap. IV, *supra.*

31. In each listing is a "Sonatine" and one other piece. Cf. the 2 chief studies, Bone/GUITAR 21-26 (with complete exx.) and 49, and Buchner/BEETHOVEN, with new information.

32. Cf. Hess/ERSTDRUCK.

32a ENGLAND. A lost (though published!) Sonata in C is not included here
32b (Hess/VERZEICHNIS no. 52). Beyond this list the reader is referred, of course, to the full bibliographic details in Kinsky & Halm/BEETHOVEN (cf. p. xvii), which touch on titles, incipits, autographs (with mention of sketches that have been published and analyzed), facsimile editions of the autographs, early printed editions,[33] location (if any) in BEETHOVEN WERKE-m, pertinent letters, listings in other thematic indices, and discussions in Thayer & Riemann/BEETHOVEN, Frimmel/BEETHOVEN,
33a and a few other basic studies. (Prod'homme/BEETHOVEN is the study most regularly cited on the piano sonatas.)

More than fifty authors have devoted whole books exclusively to Beethoven's piano sonatas or certain aspects of them. About a half of these authors may at least be noted here (with the year of the first edition of each book and an asterisk before each author whose book is listed in the Bibliography of the present study). Among authors of the most comprehensive surveys of the sonatas, including historical, biographic, bibliographic, and analytic material, are *W. von Lenz (1852), C. Reinecke (1893), *W. Nagel (1903-05), Sergio Leoni (1920), *W. Behrend (1923), *G. Scuderi (1933), *J.-G. Prod'homme (1937; generally the most useful of these books, including many references, quotations, and preparatory sketches by Beethoven, though with but little form analysis), and *E. Blom (1938). Authors of books primarily concerned with structural analyses of the sonatas include *A. B. Marx (1863; with general essays on style and performance as well as individual discussions), H. A. Harding (1889), G. Sporck (1907-15), *H. Riemann (1917-19; with his usual personal method of marking phrases and harmony), *F. Volbach (1919), *W. Hutschenruyter (1930; with emphasis on theme structure), *D. Tovey (1935; with ms.-by-ms. analyses), and *R. Rosenberg (1957; with emphasis on
34a melodic relationships).[34]

Authors of books consisting largely of random subjective comments on the piano sonatas include *E. von Elterlein (1856), R. Nesieht (1910), A. Coviello (1935; especially on performance difficulties), A. Kelberine (1939), F. A. Lamond (1944), J. de La Goutte (1951), and E. Fischer (1956).[35] As examples of numerous more specialized

33. Cf., also, HIRSCH MUSIKBIBLIOTHEK IV 103-190; Unverricht/BEETHOVEN (a new study [1960] of autographs and first eds.).

34. Detailed analyses of these sons. are also to be found in books not exclusively devoted to them—e.g., d'Indy/COURS II/1 324-369 and the book derived from it, Selva/SONATE 91-155.

35. Further authors of books on Beethoven's piano sons. include A. Bruers, S. Chenier, J. A. Johnstone, R. Kastner, J. A. Kremlev, E. de La Guardia, H. Leichtentritt, C. E. Lowe, J. B. McEwen, A. F. Milne, L. Moeremans, I. Peters, J. Salisbury, A.-T.-A. Wartel, H. Westerby.

Beethoven's Piano Sonatas

	Op. no. (or WoO)	Key	Original (or acquired) name	Composition dates (*at latest)	First publication	Dedicatee	
I	(47)	E♭	("Kurfürsten")	1782-83	Speyer: Bossler, 1783	Max. Friedrich	
	"	f	"	"	"	"	
	"	D	"	"	"	"	
	(50)	F		*ca.* 1788-90	(Berlin, 1909)		
	(51)	C	("Eleonore")	1791-92	(Frankfurt/M, 1830)	E. von Breuning	
II	2/1	f		*1795	Vienna: Artaria, 1796	Joseph Haydn	
	2/2	A		"	"	"	
	2/3	C		"	"	"	
	49/1	g		1795-98	Vienna: Bureau, 1805		
	49/2	G		"	"		
	7	E♭	("Die Verliebte")	1796-97?	Vienna: Artaria, 1797	A. L. B. von Keglevics	
	10/1	c	("Little Pathétique")	1796-98	Vienna: Eder, 1798	A. M. von Browne	
	10/2	F		"	"	"	
	10/3	D		"	"	"	
	13	c	"Grande Sonate pathétique"	1798-99	Vienna: Eder, 1799	Carl Lichnowsky	35a
	14/1	E		*1798-99	Vienna: Mollo, 1799	Josefine von Braun	
	14/2	G		"	"	"	
	22	B♭		1799-1800	Vienna: Hoffmeister, 1802	Johann von Browne	
III	26	A♭		*1800-01	Vienna: Cappi, 1802	Carl Lichnowsky	
	27/1	E♭	"Sonata quasi una Fantasia"	1800-01	Vienna: Cappi, 1802	J. S. von Liechtenstein	
	27/2	c#	"Sonata quasi una Fantasia" ("Moonlight")	1801	"	Giulietta Guicciardi	
	28	D	("Pastorale")	1801	Vienna: Bureau, 1802	Joseph von Sonnenfels	
	31/1	G		1801-02	Zürich: Nägeli, 1803	A. M. von Browne?	
	31/2	d	("Tempest") ("Gespinnste")	"	"	"	
	31/3	E♭	("La Chasse")	"	Zürich: Nägeli, 1804	"	
	53	C	("Waldstein") ("l'Aurore")	1803-04	Vienna: Bureau, 1805	Ferdinand von Waldstein	
	54	F		1804	Vienna: Bureau, 1806		
	57	f	("Appassionata")	1804-05	Vienna: Bureau, 1807	Franz von Brunsvik	
IV	78	F#	("Therese")	1809	London: Clementi, 1810	Therese von Brunsvik	
	79	G	("Cuckoo")	1809	London: Clementi, 1810		
	81a	E♭	"Lebewohl"	1809-10	London: Clementi, 1811	Archduke Rudolph	
	90	e/E		1814	Vienna: Steiner, 1815	Moritz Lichnowsky	
V	101	A	("Sensitive")	*1816	Vienna: Steiner, 1817	Dorothea Ertmann	
	106	B♭	("Hammerklavier")	1817-18	Vienna: Artaria, 1819	Archduke Rudolph	
	109	E		1820	Berlin. Schlesinger, 1821	Max'e Brentano	
	110	A♭		*ca.* 1821	Paris: Schlesinger, 1822		
	111	c/C		1821-22	Paris: Schlesinger, 1823	Archduke Rudolph?	

studies on the sonatas one might cite J. S. Shedlock's collected essays on the autographs and sketches, or H. R. Chase's dissertation on the tonal aspects, or J. V. Cockshoot's book on the use of fugue, or Ludwig Misch's study of the vital question of over-all unity in the instrumental works (not limited to the piano sons.).[36] 36a

As our list shows, Beethoven was more successful than Mozart or even Haydn in getting his piano sonatas published. Nearly every one

36. The extended section on Beethoven in Georgii/KLAVIERMUSIK 212-252 is also organized according to over-all style traits rather than individual sons.

37a appeared within the year after it was completed.[37] The term "Grande," implying a single large-scale work for (his own?) concert use, precedes "Sonate" in about half the titles through Op. 53, then once more in Op. 106, though with no consistent distinction. Opp. 49/1 and 2 and 79 are called "Sonates faciles" and Op. 79 is also called "Sonatine." Only Opp. 13 and 81a have original programmatic titles.[38]

"Klavier" is specified in the solo sonatas prior to Op. 2. The option of "Clavecin ou Pianoforte" is offered in most of the sonatas
38a from Op. 2 through 27. Otherwise and thereafter, "Pianoforte" alone is specified, except that Beethoven's preference for German inscriptions in his last period caused him to use the equivalent term "Hammerklavier" in one or another of the early copies of four of the last five sonatas (all but Op. 111).[39] Actually, by the time Op. 2/1 was published Beethoven already had a strong predilection for the piano, as shown in his two well-known letters written about then to Johann Andreas Streicher, the piano maker in Augsburg and Vienna.[40] It is true that through Op. 31/3 the old 5-octave compass still held, compelling Beethoven to make numerous adjustments in his ideas when their literal restatements in the highest or lowest octaves would have exceeded this compass.[41] But the required range, resonance, and power increased a little at a time in Opp. 53, 57, 81a (up to f''''), 101 (published less than a year before Beethoven received the heavier, stiffer-action, 6-octave Broadwood piano from London[42]), and 109 (now going down to CC). Usually, Beethoven's loss of practical contact with the piano through deafness is given as the reason for his failure to exploit its sustaining power more, as in the works of the early Romantics, and for writing unresonant combinations of tones, as in the wide spacing of Op. 111/ii/116-119 or the thud at the end of Op. 106 made by the close-position chord in the bass.[43]

37. Replacing such stand-bys as the 19th-c. ed. of Bülow and Lebert as well as the 20th-c. eds. by Casella, Schnabel, and others, the most reliable recent eds. are certainly Tovey/BEETHOVEN-m, Schenker & Ratz/BEETHOVEN-m, and Wallner/BEETHOVEN-m.

38. Cf. Shedlock/BEETHOVEN 42.

39. For Opp. 109 and 110 cf. Kinsky & Halm/BEETHOVEN 311 and 315; MacArdle & Misch/BEETHOVEN 205.

40. Cf. Sonneck/BEETHOVEN 182-190; Prod'homme/BEETHOVEN 153-154. A peripheral study of much interest on Beethoven's piano playing is Kullak/BEETHOVEN; cf., also, Behrend/BEETHOVEN 17-22.

41. E.g., cf. Op. 10/3/i/100-101 and 104-105. Other exx. are cited in Shedlock/BEETHOVEN 33-37; Marx/VORTRAG 45-52 (and in numerous other studies).

42. Cf. Thayer/BEETHOVEN II 390-392; MacArdle/BEETHOVENIANA 48-49.

43. Cf. GROVE 568-569; Schünemann/CZERNY 68.

The First or "Student" Period

The early "Kurfürsten" sonatas have after the title the words "composed by Ludwig van Beethoven, eleven years old," which probably meant that they were composed in 1782 after Neefe's arrival but before Beethoven's twelfth birthday (Dec. 15 or 16). In any case, the publication occurred by the fall of 1783,[44] before he was thirteen, so that we do not have here a clear instance of a two-year discrepancy between Beethoven's actual birth and what his father is supposed to have reported in order further to exploit the youth's undeniable precocity.[45] 45a
Neefe probably had a hand in both the dedication[46] and the music. In Sonata 2 in f, anticipations may already be noted both of the main allegro idea in Op. 13/i and of the way by which this later movement interlocks with its introductory material. Moreover, the early piece in f already helps to illustrate that association of mood and key by which are related Beethoven's further sonatas in f, Opp. 2/1 and 57, or Opp. 10/3, 13, and 111 in c, or Op. 2/3 and 53 in C, and so on.[47] Besides these three "Kurfürsten" sonatas, two slight works of only two movements each are extant from the Bonn years. WoO 50 in F was composed for his friend Franz Gerhard Wegeler and WoO 51 in C, actually completed by another friend, Ferdinand Ries, was the first of numerous sonatas he was to dedicate to lady friends.[48] 48a

The Second or "Virtuoso" Period (Opp. 2-22)

As the first of the thirty-two piano sonatas with opus numbers, the three sonatas Op. 2—respectively, impassioned, gay, and brilliant—make a remarkably fine start. Their dedication to Haydn was a homage by the erstwhile pupil, in spite of the frictions between two strong personalities and some little suspicion as to Haydn's motives, on Beethoven's part.[49] But whether the dedication was also meant to flaunt the fact before the teacher that the pupil had arrived, as suggested by its failure to mention this relationship, and whether there was even a touch of sarcasm in the "Docteur en musique" after Haydn's name,

44. Cf. Kinsky & Halm/BEETHOVEN 493-494; Prod'homme/BEETHOVEN 23-27; Behrend/BEETHOVEN 10-11.

45. Cf. Schiedermair/BEETHOVENIANA 130-132.

46. Quoted in its original form in Schiedermair/BEETHOVEN 170; trans. in Anderson/BEETHOVEN III 1410-1411.

47. Cf. Schiedermair/BEETHOVEN 266-279; Schindler/BEETHOVEN II 166-167; Lenz/BEETHOVEN 74-86; Mies/TONARTEN 211-212.

48. Cf. Behrend/BEETHOVEN 12-13. On the possible derivation of the "Adagio" WoO 51/ii from a Neefe Fantasia cf. Steglich/BEETHOVEN.

49. The relationship is well documented and summarized in MacArdle/HAYDN.

remain moot questions.[50] In any case, there are ideas, sometimes nearly whole pages in these sonatas (especially Op. 2/1/ii and 2/3/i) that go back to a piano quartet Beethoven had written in Bonn at the
51a age of 15 (WoO 36/3).[51] Nor can one overlook the influence of Clementi, whose epochal piano writing had already been made known by the Viennese publisher of Beethoven's Op. 2, Artaria, in many fine sonatas published during the previous 14 years.

Although the Sonata in E♭, Op. 7, is a more easygoing, spacious work than its predecessors, it was composed, according to Carl Czerny, "in a very impassioned mood" (perhaps under the pressure of Napoleonic threats to Vienna,[52] and presumably with thoughts of the young lady student to whom it was dedicated[53]). It was Beethoven's first sonata to be called "Grande Sonate," his first to be published singly,
53a and his first that may be rated a consistent masterpiece. The sketches of the third movement may have been intended originally to become one of Beethoven's bagatelles.[54]

In Op. 10, three well contrasted sonatas are again published together, this time in moods that might be described, respectively—if any one term can at least suggest the outer movements—as driving, sportive, and piquant. The struggles that underlay the increasingly original styles in this music are suggested by the larger number of progressive sketches that remain, although among these the minuets and longer finales planned for the first two sonatas were eventually discarded.[55] That the originality was also the chief cause for concern by Beethoven's public is suggested by the review that appeared in AMZ (the first to be written about his piano sons. in this periodical), in 1799, thirteen months after the sonatas were published.[56] Although the resourcefulness and skill were much admired, the reviewer felt that Beethoven had gone too far, "wildly piling up ideas and grouping them in a somewhat bizarre manner, so that not seldom an obscure artifice or artful obscurity is produced that becomes a detriment rather than a benefit to

50. Cf. Wegeler & Ries/BEETHOVEN 86-87. The latter interpretation is advanced in Shedlock/SONATA 166-167.

51. Cf. Prod'homme/BEETHOVEN 42-43, along with earlier sketches of Op. 2/1/i and iii (pp. 36-42).

52. Cf. Nagel/BEETHOVEN I 64.

53. Thayer/BEETHOVEN II 74. On the confused sources for the valuable remarks and recollections of Czerny, cf. MacArdle/CZERNYS 133-134; 2 further sources are Schindler/BEETHOVEN II 203-373 (*passim*), and CZERNY (trans. of *Erinnerungen* . . .). Cf., also, SSB 180, fn. 34.

54. Cf. Prod'homme/BEETHOVEN 53-56, with sketches from Nottebohm and Shedlock.

55. Cf. Nottebohm/ZWEITE 29-41; Shedlock/SKETCH 462-464.

56. AMZ II (1799-1800) 25-27. Cf. Thayer/BEETHOVEN I 307 (but read Op. 10, not Op. 12!).

the total effect." Especially resourceful and subtle are the four move- 56a
ments of Op. 10/3. According to the uncertain testimony of Schindler, its remarkable slow movement was meant to depict melancholy in all its aspects,[57] while, according to Czerny, its finale was an example of how much could be derived from but a few notes (as, indeed, could have been said of the whole sonata, in spite of the review).[58] Others have attributed the "hopeless brooding" of the slow movement to the composer's first secret recognition of impending deafness.[59] The dedicatee, 59a
a pupil of Beethoven, and her husband were honored by several compositions from the composer. (It was Count von Browne-Camus who rewarded Beethoven with the horse that Beethoven soon forgot he owned, as amusingly related by Ries.[60])

The *Grande Sonate pathétique,* Op. 13, stands with the "Moonlight," "Waldstein," and "Appassionata" among Beethoven's most beloved sonatas. Its conspicuous popularity was shown in Beethoven's own day by the numerous ensemble arrangements that were published of
this work[61] and seems to have started right with its publication in 61a
1799. Thus, the pianist Moscheles recalled that as early as 1801, in Prague, "Although but seven years old, I actually ventured upon Beethoven's Sonate pathétique. Imagine if you can how I played it; imagine also the Beethoven fever, to which I fell a victim in those days. . . ."[62] Quite as today, the emotional drama of this music must have had an immediate appeal for all pianists. The authentic title, calling the noble passions to mind, must have helped to distinguish this work at once, too.[63] The review in AMZ (by Rochlitz?), which appeared this time only a few months after publication (Feb., 1800),[64] begins, "Not incorrectly is this well written sonata called pathetic, for it has a truly distinct emotional character." In a Conversation Book from June and July of 1823 Schindler asked Beethoven about the "two principles" —i.e., dualism or conflict of ideas—in the second movement of Op. 13 (as well as Op. 14/2/i), which "thousands [of people] don't understand."[65] Schindler says that in reply Beethoven went so far as to

57. Schindler/BEETHOVEN II 222 and 243.

58. Cf. Prod'homme/BEETHOVEN 63; Rosenberg/BEETHOVEN I 97-112.

59. As in Behrend/BEETHOVEN 39-41.

60. Wegeler & Ries/BEETHOVEN 120-121; also, Thayer/BEETHOVEN I 200.

61. Cf. Kinsky & Halm/BEETHOVEN 30-31; Schmid/GÖTTWEIGER 893.

62. Moscheles/MOSCHELES I 4; cf., also, Thayer & Riemann/BEETHOVEN II 146-147.

63. Beethoven himself regretted this distinction in later years, especially as he regarded all his works as "pathetic" (Schindler/BEETHOVEN I 182-183).

64. AMZ II (1799-1800) 373-374.

65. Cf. Schünemann/KONVERSATIONSHEFTE III 341 (but add "2" before "Principe"); also, Prod'homme/CAHIERS 271 and Hutschenruyter/BEETHOVEN 44 (with errors). Schindler's remark is the starting point for that valuable study of tonal

describe a dialogue of conflict between a man and a woman in both sonatas of Op. 14, especially the second, which achieves a "reconciliation" only at the end of the "Scherzo." Here was an interpretation that A. B. Marx found totally incompatible with the music (1859).[66] Yet the idea of a personified conflict continued to be read into this "pathetic" music throughout the Romantic Era. Thus, Mathis Lussy's book on Op. 13 (published posthumously in 1912), still was "an attempt to interpret the sonata as a dialogue, 'a contest between an unhappy man and fate.' "[67] It will be recalled that as recently as 1935-36 Arnold Schering chose this work as one of the earliest of Beethoven's sonatas to be interpreted symbolically, finding its inspiration and poetic meaning in Musäus's version of the Hero and Leander story (*supra*; cf., also, Blom/BEETHOVEN 154-159!).

The influence of Mozart's Sonata in c, K.V. 457, on Op. 13 was
67a noted earlier (SCE XIV; it can be found in Op. 10/1, too). Numerous other derivations have also been suggested, including Dussek's Sonata in c, Op. 35/3 (*ca.* 1796)[68] and works by J. B. Cramer, Cherubini, and Grétry.[69] Furthermore, the "Rondo" finale of Op. 13, generally conceded to be the least strong of the three movements, was probably anticipated by Beethoven himself in sketches for piano and violin of about 1797 (Ex. 81) and other sketches that may date back to 1785.[70]

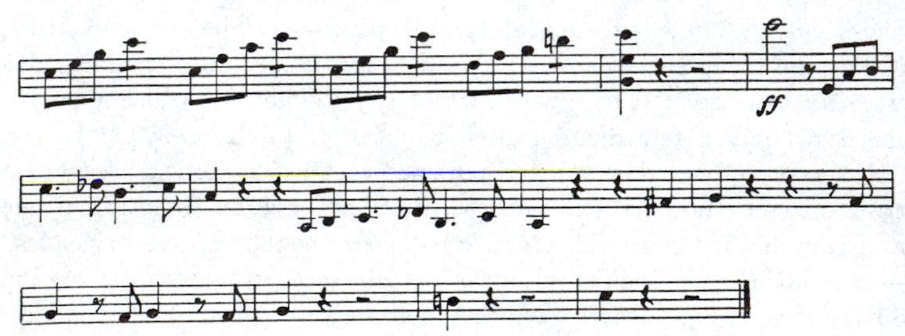

Ex. 81. An early sketch for the finale of Ludwig van Beethoven's *Grande Sonate pathétique* (after Nottebohm/ZWEITE 42).

---

and thematic contrast-within-unity in Beethoven's music, Schmitz/BEETHOVEN (in which, cf. pp. 95-96).

66. Cf. Lenz/BEETHOVEN 170; Prod'homme/BEETHOVEN 88-89; Marx/BEETHOVEN I 128-132 and 134-135 (objecting to the idea); and Schindler/BEETHOVEN II 358-362 and 222-224 (3d ed., with an answer to Marx).

67. Schrade/BEETHOVEN 263.

68. Cf. Blom/BEETHOVEN 56-57, with a further reference. Dussek's second mvt. is called "Adagio patetico ed espressivo."

69. Cf. Prod'homme/BEETHOVEN 72-73.

70. Cf. Shedlock/SKETCH 461.

In the light of these derivations, the only reservation made in that same AMZ review is interesting—that is, to the effect that the thematic material seemed to have been heard before, though just where could not be said. From what Ries tells us about Beethoven's own performance of the finale, the originality may have been partly in the manner of playing it.[71]

The two sonatas of Op. 14 were dedicated to the wife of the Baron von Braun who was to promote the unsuccessful first performance of *Fidelio* in 1805. We have already noted the personified conflict by which Beethoven is reported to have clarified the meaning of these sonatas, which appeared in the same year as Op. 13 (1799). Yet far from being similarly impassioned works, they are relatively quiet and intimate, distinguished rather by their charm, wit, and craftsmanship. Full sketches exist for the Sonata in E (only)[72] that may date as far back as 1795. The earliest ones may have been intended for an instrumental ensemble. At any rate, warning that only the composer can arrange his own works satisfactorily,[73] Beethoven arranged this one
sonata as a string quartet in F.[74] Prod'homme calls the opening idea 74a
of Op. 14/1/i a sort of Beethovian *cantus firmus,* to be found in a sketch
for Op. 10/3/i, in Op. 13/iii/79-81, and finally in the fugue subject of
Op. 110.[75] A similar case might be made for other recurring ideas in
Beethoven's music, such as the slow descending figure heard in Op.
7/ii/84-85, Op. 10/3/ii/9-11, and Op. 22/ii/18-19, finally appearing in 76a
its barest form in Op. 106/ii/170-172 and in its most ornamental form
in the slow movement (mss. 43-46) of the Ninth Symphony.[76]

Op. 22 in B♭ is the sonata that Lenz regarded as ending the first of Beethoven's "three periods"[77]—the last one, that is, in the direct line of Mozart and Haydn and the last one to stay within the bounds of a Classically abstract concentration on the main ideas. Yet, like the Fourth Symphony, written in the same key some six years later, this fine sonata has a new, pre-Mendelssohnian charm and grace and an Italianate lyricism in its lovely "Adagio con molta espressione" that still set it apart from other Beethoven sonatas (perhaps explaining why neither it nor the symphony gets its fair share of performances). Beethoven left no doubt about his own liking for it when he wrote to

71. Wegeler & Ries/BEETHOVEN 106-107; also, Thayer/BEETHOVEN II 90.
72. They are brought together in Prod'homme/BEETHOVEN 78-86.
73. Cf. the incomplete letter of July 13, 1802, as trans. in Anderson/BEETHOVEN I 74-75.
74. Cf. Kinsky & Halm/BEETHOVEN 33; Hess/VERZEICHNIS no. 34.
75. Prod'homme/BEETHOVEN 78, 73, 61, 265.
76. For another recurring idea cf. Shedlock/SONATA 168.
77. Lenz/BEETHOVEN 171-173.

Hoffmeister (about Jan. 15, 1801), "This sonata is a first-rate composition ["hat sich gewaschen"], most beloved and worthy brother!"[78] Full sketches are extant for this work,[78a] some in A rather than B♭ and including an "Alla Marcia" that was discarded. The slow evolution of the "Rondo" finale theme in the sketches seems to contradict W. Nagel's evidence that it derived from a sonata by E. W. Wolf, also in B♭, although the similarity is certainly clear for four measures.[79]

The Third or "Appassionata" Period (Opp. 26-57)

Starting as it does with a set of variations that anticipate his later arabesque style, Beethoven's Sonata in A♭ could have been labeled "quasi una Fantasia" quite as appropriately as the next two sonatas, in Op. 27. Rochlitz wrote a prolix, twenty-eight-page commentary on these variations that goes to a Romantic extreme by interpreting them as the autobiographic confessions of an aging lawyer's clerk.[80] Beethoven himself sought a text for the theme.[81] To be sure, sonatas had been started with variations before, our most recently cited example being Mozart's Sonata in A/i, K.V. 300i. Beethoven's remarkable third movement, "Marcia funebre sulla morte d'un Eroe,"[82] may have been a sketch in spirit for the "Marcia funebre" in the "Eroica" symphony.[83] But it probably did not derive from Paër's *Achille,* as Ries asserted, and after him, Czerny.[84] Whereas the sketches for the entire sonata go back at least to 1800 and perhaps in some instances to 1795, Paër's opera was not produced until 1801.[85] On the other hand, the theme (but not more) of the "Allegro" finale could well have derived from music by the expert pianist J. B. Cramer, who was winning praise in Vienna in 1799-1800, especially for his 3 sonatas Op. 23, dedicated to Haydn and published by Artaria in 1799.[86] Czerny specifically traced Beethoven's theme to Cramer's Op. 23/1/iii in the same key of

78. As trans. in Anderson/BEETHOVEN I 47-48.

78a. They are assembled in Prod'homme/BEETHOVEN 92-96.

79. Cf. Behrend/BEETHOVEN 52-53 (with a quotation from a later ed. of Nagel/BEETHOVEN than that used here).

80. Rochlitz/FREUNDE II 251-268; brief extracts are trans. in Behrend/BEETHOVEN 56-59.

81. Wegeler & Ries/BEETHOVEN 48.

82. Its enthusiastic reception is reflected in the review of Opp. 26 and 27 in AMZ IV (1801-02) 650-653.

83. The former was orchestrated (in b) by Beethoven in 1815 (Kinsky & Halm/BEETHOVEN 65).

84. Wegeler & Ries/BEETHOVEN 80; Thayer & Riemann/BEETHOVEN II 249; Schünemann/CZERNY 60.

85. Cf. Prod'homme/BEETHOVEN 103-108. The full sketches are given in Mikulicz/NOTIERUNGSBUCH *passim* (as indexed on p. 28).

86. Weinmann/ARTARIA item 846. Cf. Schlesinger/CRAMER 43-46.

A♭.[87] The resemblance is not striking. Much closer resemblances to the figure in this theme can be found repeatedly throughout Cramer's études, which Cramer must now have been playing in Vienna if some of them had not already appeared.[88] Well known, of course, are Beethoven's interest in Cramer's playing as well as the annotations made by Schindler on some of Cramer's études and credited to Beethoven (perhaps to be used in Beethoven's projected "Klavierschule").[89] 89a

The three sonatas in Opp. 26 and 27 all appeared at the same time from the same publisher, and were reviewed together (as noted earlier), yet came out as three separate issues. However, since the two sonatas in Op. 27 have the same number and the same qualifying term, "quasi una Fantasia," Beethoven must have intended at least these two to appear as a set. In them the "fantasia" applies equally to the unconventional first movements, the "attacca" connections of the movements, and perhaps some programmatic associations known only to Beethoven. 89b
Presumably these two sonatas appeared separately only because they were dedicated to two different persons. Certainly their fates have been different. Op. 27/1 is one of the least played or sympathetically regarded of Beethoven's sonatas, while Op. 27/2, or at least its first movement, is one of the best known of all musical works, let alone sonatas. Actually, Op. 27/1 may be less accessible for the very reason that it has more of real, improvisatory fantasy in it. All the movements in Op. 27/2 are standard designs that can be readily assimilated by both player and listener, even the first movement being a reasonably clear "sonata form."[90]

As for the dedication of Op. 27/2, only at the last minute was the name of Countess Giulietta Guicciardi transferred to this work from the Rondo in G, Op. 51/2.[91] Therefore, attempts to make a programme out of Beethoven's supposed love for his pupil, then 16 to 17, and fit it to the Sonata in c♯[92] are without support. Nor can this sonata be linked

87. Not Cramer's Op. 23/3/iii in a, as given in Schlesinger/CRAMER 44 and Prod'homme/BEETHOVEN 108. Quotations from Op. 23/1/iii are given in E. Prieger's ed. of the facs. of Beethoven's Op. 26 (Bonn: Beethovenhaus, 1894), Schlesinger/CRAMER Ex. 87 (cf. pp. 131-133), and Shedlock/SONATA 193.

88. In Schlesinger/CRAMER 44, Cramer's "Excercices op. 2" are stated to have been published before the Vienna visit, but without documentation and without further mention on pp. 59-60 or elsewhere.

89. Cf. Wegeler & Ries/BEETHOVEN 99-100; Schindler/BEETHOVEN II 182-183; Schlesinger/CRAMER 45-46. The études in question were edited with their annotations in trans. and a preface, by Shedlock (London: Augener, 1893).

90. It is analyzed as such, ms. by ms., in Krohn/MONDSCHEINSONATE and (less categorically) in Tovey/BEETHOVEN 103-104.

91. Cf. Thayer/BEETHOVEN I 292 and 370.

92. As in Behrend/BEETHOVEN 74-75. The whole question of titles and programmatic assocations is explored, along with style traits, performances, and

especially with the "Eternally Beloved" of the famous mystery letter (July 6 and 7, 1812), whose identity recently has been restored to the realm of free-for-all speculation,[93] whether she was Countess Guicciardi (Schindler's choice[94]), or either of her cousins in the Brunsvik family—
95a Therese (Thayer's choice[95]) and Josephine (the subsequent favorite). Furthermore, there is no special reason for identifying the sonata with "Moonlight," since this familiar title—or "a boat passing the wild scenery of Lake Lucerne in the moonlight," to be more exact—was bestowed on it not by Beethoven but about 1832 by his younger contemporary, the poet and musician H. F. L. Rellstab.[96] On the other hand, what justification is there for quite the hostility toward this title that has been voiced in recent years?[97] Beethoven's objections later (1819) to the literal programmatic interpretations of his symphonies by Dr. Karl Iken in Bremen have often been cited.[98] But as a description of mood "Moonlight" is a no less plausible title for, at least, the first movement of Op. 27/2 than, say, "Clair de lune" for Debussy's almost as well-known piece. At any rate, an association that has lasted so long and held so widely is not likely to die easily, however logical the objections. Beethoven could not have known this title himself,[99] but according to Czerny he seems to have resented the special popularity of Op. 27/2 (as of Op. 13): "Everybody is always talking about the C-sharp minor Sonata! Surely I have written better things. There is the Sonata in F-sharp major—that is something very different."[100]

A little support does exist for the association of Op. 27/2 with a poem about filial devotion, *Die Beterin* by J. G. Seume, a minor poet who reportedly interested Beethoven.[101] But the musical world has not been especially concerned about support for the many extraordinary, varied interpretations of this sonata that followed throughout the nineteenth century. We read of a performance by Liszt in Paris in 1835, in which the first of the three movements was played by an orchestra and the other two by Liszt alone; of Berlioz' association of the work

early history, in the important study in BEETHOVEN-FORSCHUNG VI and VII (1916) 39-102 (Frimmel).

93. Cf. Nettl/GELIEBTEN; Anderson/BEETHOVEN I 373-376; also, Rolland/BEETHOVEN VII 63-98. M. Solomon reviews such speculations in ML LIX (1978) 86-88.

94. Schindler/BEETHOVEN I 92-98; cf., also, Kalischer/BEETHOVEN 31-36; MacArdle/BEETHOVENIANA 45-48.

95. Thayer/BEETHOVEN I 317-347.

96. Lenz/BEETHOVEN 199.

97. E.g., in Blom/BEETHOVEN 108-110.

98. Cf. Schindler/BEETHOVEN II 208-211; Thayer & Riemann/BEETHOVEN IV 206-207; Thayer/BEETHOVEN III 36-37.

99. Cf. Nettl/BEETHOVEN 192, with further references.

100. As trans. in Thayer/BEETHOVEN I 322-323.

101. Cf. Thayer/BEETHOVEN I 292-293.

with sunshine (rather than moonlight) and of other poetic descriptions by him; of a novel in answer to Tolstoy's *Kreutzer Sonata* and of at least two other books inspired by Op. 27/2; of paintings and lithographs; and of much else.[102]

One cannot distinguish between odd- and even-numbered sonatas, as with the symphonies. But Op. 28, coming after Op. 27/2, is typical of Beethoven's tendency to alternate a passionate and driving work with a calm and restful one. It was the last of the four sonatas composed
mostly in 1801 and published in 1802.[103] Few sketches are extant for 103a
either Op. 28 or Op. 27/2.[104] Unlike the "Moonlight" title, the "Pastorale" title could well have been known by Beethoven, since Op. 28 was already so entitled in an English edition (Broderip & Wilkinson) published about three years after the original edition (or about thirty-five years before the Cranz ed. heretofore given as the first use of this title).[105] Czerny said that the "Andante" was long a favorite of Beethoven, who played it often.[106]

The three sonatas of Op. 31 were created about the time of the desperate "Heiligenstadt Testament." Yet only in the second might aesthetic expressions of this mood be argued. The other two sonatas are closer to the spirit of more optimistic products from this same period, such as the Second Symphony or the statement attributed to Beethoven by Czerny, "I am not satisfied with my previous works; from here on I
shall follow a new path."[107] It is not hard to find new paths in the long 107a
ornamental slow movement of Op. 31/1, or the intimate interlocking of slow and fast ideas in Op. 31/2/i,[108] or the deft Scherzo and quasi-
tarantella finale of Op. 31/3. In 1803 Op. 31/1 and 2 made up the 108a
fifth "Suite" (vol.) in the enterprising Anth. NÄGELI-m, Op. 31/3 following as the eleventh "Suite" (along with a reprint of Op. 13) in the next year. Not until 1805 (from Cappi in Vienna) did the three sonatas appear under one opus number and with a dedication to Countess von Browne.[109] Among sketches for all three sonatas are

102. Cf. Prod'homme/BEETHOVEN 123-130.

103. A largely noncommittal review of Op. 28 appeared in AMZ V (1802-03) 189-190.

104. In Kinsky & Halm/BEETHOVEN 69, sketches for Op. 28 are said to be unknown, but a sketch for the "Andante" was published by Frimmel in 1891 (cf. Prod'homme/BEETHOVEN 131, but read 1891).

105. Cf. Kinsky & Halm/BEETHOVEN 70.

106. Cf. Prod'homme/BEETHOVEN 133. The over-all unity of Op. 28 is discussed in Misch/EINHEIT 72-78.

107. Nagel/BEETHOVEN II 1.

108. The problem of analyzing this movement is discussed in Misch/BEETHOVEN 39-53.

109. The dedication is noted only in Prod'homme/BEETHOVEN 151. The op. no. assigned by Cappi was 29, not 31, the confusion still being present in HOFMEISTER

two suggesting that the first movements of Op. 31/1 (originally for string quartet) and Op. 31/2 were conceived almost in one sitting.[110] Well known is Nägeli's deliberate insertion of four extra measures in Op. 31/1/i (after ms. 298), presumably to achieve a more formal symmetry; also, Beethoven's angry reaction.[111] Beethoven's reported reply when Schindler asked what Opp. 31/2 and 57 mean—"Just read Shakespeare's *Tempest*"[112]—accounts for the popular title of the former. If the reply is authentic and significant at all, it can only refer, as with "Moonlight," to a mood. Attempts to relate a literal programme based
113a on the play[113] are obviously doomed from the start.

The "Menuetto" of Op. 31/3 has a strong family resemblance to the theme used for the Septet Op. 20/iv and for Op. 49/2/ii, but its "Trio" is the theme on which Saint-Saëns wrote his 2-piano "Variations" Op. 35. Actually, Op. 49/2/ii preceded Op. 20 (composed 1799-1800), since the "Deux Sonates faciles" were both composed around
114a 1795-96.[114]

Beethoven offered Opp. 53, 54, and 57 to Breitkopf & Härtel at one
115a time,[115] but starting in 1805 each of these and of the 9 further piano sonatas was to appear separately. Op. 53, in certain ways a companion to the "Eroica" symphony, is truly a "grande" sonata, built on a larger scale than any of its predecessors. As a remarkable successor to Beethoven's only other extant piano sonata in C, it also exploits the piano, then enjoying rapid improvements, more than any of its predecessors. (There was to be only one further "easy" sonata, Op. 79.) The dedication of this work to Count von Waldstein, Beethoven's musical friend and benefactor since the early Bonn years, was probably one of the most sincere and heartfelt of any he made. Grouped among sketches for several other significant works (in spite of the fewer significant publications around 1805), the sketches for Op. 53 are especially interesting from the standpoint of thematic gestation.[116]

1815 (Whistling) p. 340. Much headway toward clearing up this and other bibliographic complexities is made in Kinsky & Halm/BEETHOVEN 78-82. Thus, Karl Beethoven's letter of Nov. 23, 1802 proves not to apply to Op. 31/1-3. Nor does Ludwig's letter of April 8, 1802 apply, opposing a request for a "Revolution" sonata (cf. Anderson/BEETHOVEN I 73-74; was a second "Battle of Prague" sought?), although this letter is even used to support a speculation that Op. 31/1 might not be authentic, in Nagel/BEETHOVEN II 4-5.

110. Cf. Prod'homme/BEETHOVEN 137-144. The over-all unity of Op. 31/1 is discussed in Misch/EINHEIT 47-54.

111. Cf. Wegeler & Ries/BEETHOVEN 88-90; Kinsky & Halm/BEETHOVEN 79.

112. Schindler/BEETHOVEN II 221.

113. As in Nagel/BEETHOVEN II 42-45; Behrend/BEETHOVEN 89.

114. Cf. Shedlock/SKETCH 461-462.

115. Letter of Aug. 26, 1804 (in Anderson/BEETHOVEN I 116).

116. Cf. Nottebohm/SKIZZENBÜCHER 59-67; Prod'homme/BEETHOVEN 155-161. On the possible song origin of the finale theme, cf. Rolland/BEETHOVEN I 180-183.

Ries is the first source for the fact that originally a much longer middle movement was written for the sonata but was discarded on the advice of a friend (Ries himself?) that it was too long. This piece was then published separately the same year (WoO 57), soon to be known as the "Andante favori" in F.[117] The pre-Schumannesque "Introduzione, Adagio molto" that replaced this movement is so much shorter and so tied to the long "Rondo" finale that one describes the "Waldstein" sonata more accurately as being in two rather than three movements. Op. 53 also became known as "Aurore," it being another subject of nineteenth-century programmatic interpretations.[118]

Op. 54, like Op. 27/1, has been one of the least played or liked of Beethoven's piano sonatas.[119] Criticized in 1806 chiefly for its "ineffectual peculiarities" and "far-fetched [technical] difficulties," in spite of its originality and skill,[120] it has, for example, been treated harshly by Lenz and Nagel, though more sympathetically by Blom.[121] Coming between two giants, respectively, of virtuosity and passion, and representing one of the seven sonatas with opus numbers to have only two movements (if Op. 53 is included), it is regarded more as an interlude or a biologic sport than as a valid, independent work. Yet its subtleties, humor, and figuration can prove very rewarding to the performer willing and able to follow Beethoven to the outer reaches of his musical personality. There is much satisfaction and interest in the unusual first movement, which combines elements of "sonata form," the minuet, and variation treatment, and in the *moto perpetuo* finale.

Op. 57, greeted by Lenz as something "more than a volcanic explosion,"[122] was regarded by Beethoven himself (according to Czerny) as his "greatest" sonata[123] (prior to Op. 106). Tovey said in particular, "No other work by Beethoven maintains a tragic solemnity throughout all its movements. . . . [Except for Op. 27/2/iii among the piano sons., all] his other pathetic finales show either an epilogue in some legendary

BEETHOVEN/facs.-m (autograph; cf. Weise/WALDSTEINSONATE) is too recent to be listed fully in Kinsky & Halm/BEETHOVEN 125.

117. Wegeler & Ries/BEETHOVEN 101-102; cf. Thayer/BEETHOVEN II 31-32; Rolland/BEETHOVEN I 175-177.

118. Cf. Prod'homme/BEETHOVEN 164.

119. The still unsolved puzzle of "LIme Sonate" in the title of Op. 54 (and "LIV" in Op. 57) is ably summarized in Kinsky & Halm/BEETHOVEN 127-128. The chief extant sketch (finale) is given in Prod'homme/BEETHOVEN 166-167.

120. AMZ VIII (1805-06) 639-640.

121. Lenz/BEETHOVEN 232; Nagel/BEETHOVEN II 102-103; Blom/BEETHOVEN 159-162. Op. 54 is allowed no more than passing mention in Behrend/BEETHOVEN 103 and 124.

122. Lenz/BEETHOVEN 232.

123. Thayer/BEETHOVEN II 74. In Rolland/BEETHOVEN 105-219 a long chapter is dedicated to Op. 57, although most of it concerns Beethoven's previous sons., leaving pp. 188-217 to this work.

or later world far way from the tragic scene . . . or a temper, fighting, humorous, or resigned, that does not carry with it a sense of tragic doom."[124] Op. 57 is now believed to have been completed well before 1806,[125] consistent with Ries's firsthand recollection of a long hike in Döbling in 1804, during which the finale was conceived, but contrary to Schindler's secondhand recollection of Beethoven composing the whole sonata while resting briefly at Count Brunsvik's home, or M. Bigot's story of how his wife sightread the rain-drenched autograph "just composed" before Beethoven quarreled with Prince Lichnowsky and returned abruptly to Vienna.[126] In the review that appeared in AMZ in 1807, the large scope and originality of Op. 57 were recognized, but by now there was a set pattern of objections (often in the same words) to the "great difficulties" and "affected *bizarrerie*," especially in the first movement.[127] No earlier use of the title "Appassionata" is now known than that in the four-hand arrangement published by Cranz in 1838. Yet, the very fact that Cranz's edition was only an arrangement and that Beethoven later did use "Appassionata" at least twice in the headings of movements (Opp. 106/ii and 111/i) suggests that it may well have originated while he could still know about it.[128]

Naturally, the programmatic readings that followed this title and the reference to *The Tempest* (noted with regard to Op. 31/2) were many.[129] In fact, some of the most high-flown of the Romantic and post-Romantic literature on Beethoven was devoted to this work. On the more turgid side are passages such as the following on the first movement, where

> dismal spectral shadows rise, as it were, out of the lowest depths; soft wailings issue from the heart, and fate is heard knocking at the door. Suddenly a mighty storm bursts forth, then there is a painful trembling, and in the second theme in A flat major, there arises a wonderful sympathetic strain of happy consolation. The storm of painful passion begins again, the first flashes of humour disappear, the movement takes the form of convulsive startings, the nightly shadows assume a firmer shape, the inner commotion increases, until the return of another outburst of humour [etc.].[130]

124. Tovey/BEETHOVEN 177-178.

125. Based on a series of letters from Aug. 26, 1804 to June 21, 1805 (as summarized under Op. 53 in Kinsky & Halm/BEETHOVEN 126). The interesting sketches for Op. 57 are quoted in Nottebohm/ZWEITE 436-442 and Prod'homme/BEETHOVEN 173-177.

126. Wegeler & Ries/BEETHOVEN 99; Schindler/BEETHOVEN I 138; Thayer/BEETHOVEN II 31, 68-69, 73-74.

127. AMZ IX (1806-07) 433-436.

128. Czerny thought this title was not strong enough (Thayer/BEETHOVEN II 74).

129. Cf. Schindler/BEETHOVEN II 220-221; Nagel/BEETHOVEN II 164; and Prod'homme/BEETHOVEN 182-184.

130. As trans. in Elterlein/BEETHOVEN 76 (1856).

At best we get a subjective statement such as Rolland could write (backed by his superior technical and historical knowledge of the subject):

> The perfection of the *Appassionata* conceals a danger of a double kind. It is characterised by the emprise of reason over the forces let loose. The tumultuous elements are purified, confined within the strict forms of the classic discipline. These forms, indeed, are enlarged to admit of the entry of a whole world of passions. A sea of blood thunders within them: but the sea is closed with the pillars of Hercules. Beethoven, by a tenacious and superhuman tension, has sealed the hinges and put his shoulder to the gate . . .[131]

Behrend suggests that thoughts of the Countess Guicciardi still underlie this work, but hardly of Therese Brunsvik, whereas Blom suggests that its dualism of physical passion and spiritual peace may reflect a simultaneous interest on Beethoven's part in the two very different sisters, Therese and Josephine.[132] Of course, the dedication itself is to none of these but to the cousin and brother, respectively, Franz Brunsvik, whose "sole passion" was the music of Beethoven.[133]

The Fourth or "Invasion" Period (Opp. 78-90)

Although Beethoven never did dedicate a work solely to Josephine, the next piano sonata, Op. 78 in F♯, was dedicated to Therese von Brunsvik. It was composed along with the dissimilar Opp. 79 and 81a after a break of at least four years in the writing of piano sonatas,[134] perhaps the longest break in the whole series from Op. 2 to 111. Coming at the start of the fourth of the five creative periods that were outlined here, and following, as it did, the Violin Concerto, Fifth Piano Concerto, and Sixth Symphony (among numerous other works), Op. 78 understandably marked a new, more mature style. One notes especially the greater freedom of structure and the frank, pre-Schubertian lyricism. Czerny saw these differences,[135] but Op. 78 was another of the sonatas treated as inferior by most of the further commentators of the nineteenth century.[136] Nagel marks a turning point in criticism of

131. Rolland/BEETHOVEN I 214 (as trans. by Ernest Newman, 1929).
132. Behrend/BEETHOVEN 112 and 114; Blom/BEETHOVEN 163-164.
133. Cf. Rolland/BEETHOVEN I 323-369, on the Brunsvik family and Beethoven's several friendships among them.
134. All 3 sons. were offered to Breitkopf & Härtel in Beethoven's letter of Feb. 4, 1810, Op. 81a to "be published as a separate work" (Anderson/BEETHOVEN I 261). Only 5 months before, he had decided that "I don't like to spend much time composing sonatas for pianoforte solo" (Anderson/BEETHOVEN I 244).
135. According to the statement quoted in Behrend/BEETHOVEN 122 (after what source?).
136. Samples are Elterlein/BEETHOVEN 80; Lenz/BEETHOVEN 238; Marx/VOR-

this work at the start of the present century, saying that it could never become popular in recital (!) but recognizing its depth, subtlety, and tenderness.[137] Today, this work seems like one of the loveliest possible evidences, from inside, of an attachment to Therese,[138] although doubts about the significance of the dedication have been voiced,[139] and the question of whether Beethoven really did prefer Op. 78 to Op. 27/2 has been argued both pro and con.[140]

Op. 79, which Beethoven wanted to be called either "sonate facile"[141] or "sonatine,"[142] is already a neo-Classic work, with syntactic and harmonic surprises[143] and folklike charms that presage Prokofiev's *Classical Symphony* by more than a century.

Op. 81a[144] was very much a product of current times and circumstances. It was composed for Archduke Rudolph soon after the three-way annuity was settled on Beethoven, partly during the invasion of the French that compelled the archduke to leave Vienna from May 4, 1809 to January 30, 1810, and hence that underlay the programme of Op. 81a.[145] The dedication of this work to the royal student, who had begun study with Beethoven about 1804 at the age of 16, was one of more than a dozen dedications to him, from that of the Fourth Piano Concerto on, most of them in works of outstanding importance.[146] That the archduke was honored both more abundantly and more significantly in this way than any other dedicatee, was the consequence as much of a sincere, lasting friendship as of the royal support, with all its advantages and restrictions. ("Dedicated and written from the heart to His Imperial Highness [S. K. H.]" is inscribed in a sketch of Op. 81a.)[147] Clearly, the "Lebewohl" sonata makes no concessions to popular taste, with its increasing fantasy of tempo and structure, and its harmonic daring. In fact, in some early editions, Ries and others

TRAG (no mention at all!). Others (including d'Indy, 1911) are cited in Prod'homme/BEETHOVEN 187-188.

137. Nagel/BEETHOVEN II 143.

138. As is argued in Blom/BEETHOVEN 172-173.

139. Cf. Thayer & Riemann/BEETHOVEN III 171.

140. As in Blom/BEETHOVEN 172 and Behrend/BEETHOVEN 122, respectively.

141. As in the first sketch (in C!); cf. Nottebohm/ZWEITE 269.

142. Letter of Aug. 21, 1810 (Anderson/BEETHOVEN I 285).

143. Cf. Tovey/BEETHOVEN 191-196.

144. The fact that this son. and the Sextet in E♭ were both first published as Op. 81 was only straightened out when they were listed as Op. 81a and b, respectively, in Breitkopf & Härtel's Beethoven *Verzeichnis* of 1851.

145. Cf. Thayer/BEETHOVEN II 143-144, 146. But these dates in the autograph (of which only the first mvt. is now extant) cannot be taken as dates of composition or completion (Thayer & Riemann/BEETHOVEN 173-174).

146. Cf. Kinsky & Halm/BEETHOVEN 137-138 (with further references) and 776; also, Nettl/BEETHOVEN 202-203.

147. Cf. Nottebohm/ZWEITE 100.

deleted the tonic-dominant clashes at the end of the coda of the first movement (mss. 215-218, anticipating the end of R. Strauss's *Tod und Verklärung* written 80 years later).[148]

In a letter to Breitkopf & Härtel of July 2, 1810,[149] Beethoven refers to Op. 81a as (freely) a "sonata characterizing departure [*Abschied*], absence, and reunion." The title of the original edition published by Clementi in London by February 1, 1811, at the latest,[150] was worded slightly differently, in French: *Les Adieux, l'Absence, et le Retour, Sonate caracteristique. . . .*"[151] Breitkopf & Härtel published the work soon after in two simultaneous editions, one with this French title and the other with the German title Beethoven originally and finally preferred: *Lebewohl* [Farewell], *Abwesenheit und Wiedersehn* [i.e., *Wiedersehen*].[152] Beethoven resented the French title and imprecise translation (among other things) in the publication,[153] this work being the very one in which he began, in the last two movements, to use German inscriptions along with the Italian.[154]

"Le-be-wohl" is actually written in the sketches and autograph over the "horn fifths" made by the three opening intervals, perhaps even to suggest the post horns of the traveler's coach.[155] To this extent Op. 81a is more tangibly programmatic than the only other sonata to have an original title, *Sonate pathétique,* and less so than the *Sinfonia pastorale,* with its several specific inscriptions. Beethoven's inscription in the sketches for the latter, to the effect that one will also sense the total meaning without descriptive terms, "more through feeling than tone painting,"[156] certainly applies to Op. 81a.[157] Yet the usual, increasingly specific interpretations began to appear at once from other musicians. These were not merely the sort of literalities that Bülow delighted in finding, as in reference to Op. 81a/iii/5-6: "Even a player with the most deeply rooted antipathy to programs cannot help seeing,

148. Cf. Prod'homme/BEETHOVEN 201-202; Schindler/BEETHOVEN II 254-256; Nagel/BEETHOVEN II 173-174.

149. In Thayer & Riemann/BEETHOVEN III 229-230 (cf. Anderson/BEETHOVEN I 277).

150. MacArdle/ENGLAND.

151. As listed in Cat. ROYAL 41.

152. Cf. M. Unger in ZFM CV (1938) 140-141 and 137 (with facs. of the German title page); Kinsky & Halm/BEETHOVEN 217.

153. Letter of Oct. 9, 1811 (Anderson/BEETHOVEN I 337-338).

154. Cf. Prod'homme/BEETHOVEN 194.

155. Cf. Blom/BEETHOVEN 182-183. The term "Gelegenheitsstück," in the odd, short review of Op. 81a that appeared in AMZ XIV (1812) 67-68, may not have had the flippant sense of a mere occasional piece, as seems to be implied in Schindler/BEETHOVEN I 182, but rather that of a piece written for a particular occasion.

156. Nottebohm/ZWEITE 375.

157. Cf. Prod'homme/BEETHOVEN 203-204; Tovey/BEETHOVEN 197-198.

that in the falling pairs of thirds for the left hand the gesture of beckoning with a handkerchief—the tone-picture of a sign—is illustrated, a sign apprising the coming one of the waiting one's presence."[158] A. B. Marx insisted on reading "incidents in the life of a pair of lovers" into this work, which perversion of the original intention had to be rationalized by a later editor; and Bülow went so far as to hear in the finale "an enunciation of the passionate meeting of Tristan and Isolde" in Wagner's second act.[159]

The publication of Op. 90 in 1815 was announced with the statement, "All connoisseurs and friends of music will surely welcome the appearance of this sonata, since nothing by L. van Beethoven has appeared now for several years."[160] To be exact, not quite four years separated the publication dates of Opp. 81a and 90, a little longer period than separated those of Opp. 57 and 78 (though the break between composition dates may have been less than that between Opp. 57 and 78). The review of Op. 90 early in 1816 was also cordial, beginning, "With much pleasure the reviewer calls attention to this new sonata. It is one of the most simple, melodious, expressive, intelligible, and *mild* among all [the sonatas] for which we are indebted to Beethoven."[161] Perhaps part of this changed attitude may be credited to the musical public, which was beginning to catch up a little more with Beethoven. For Op. 90, with its motivic concentration on the main idea in the first movement and its lyrical finale that extends to a "heavenly length" in Schubertian fashion, is quite as subtle and original in its way as Op. 78 or 81a. It is an exceptionally introspective work, which followed several patriotic works appropriate to the restored freedom in Vienna, and which developed alongside the revision of *Fidelio*.[162] The parallel German and Italian inscriptions over each movement are indicative in themselves: i) "Lively, but with sentiment and expression throughout"; ii) "Not too fast and very songful." The different character of the two movements is emphasized, if nothing else is, by a story from Schindler.[163] Beethoven is supposed to have joked with his dedicatee, Moritz Lichnowsky, to the effect that he had tried to depict the latter's courtship with his second wife. The first movement was to be called "Struggle between head and heart," the second "Conversation with the loved one."

158. As trans. in the G. Schirmer ed. of 1894, vol. II, p. 514.
159. Cf. Thayer & Riemann/BEETHOVEN III 174.
160. Kinsky & Halm/BEETHOVEN 249.
161. AMZ XVIII (1816) 60-61.
162. Sketches for both mvts. are given in Nottebohm/ZWEITE 298 and 366-368.
163. Thayer/BEETHOVEN II 291-292. Cf. Tovey/BEETHOVEN 208.

The Fifth or "Sublimation" Period (*Opp. 101-111*)

During the nearly six years in which the last five piano sonatas were composed (late 1816 to early 1822) they, the "Diabelli Variations," and the *Missa solemnis* (1819-23) were Beethoven's only major works under way and the chief ones from which he led on to the Ninth Symphony and the last quartets. The tradition has been to speak of a marked drop in production during this "last period" and to attribute this drop to his increasing social isolation, ill health, and preoccupation with nephew Karl. But this view is countered at least in part, of course, by the unprecedented creative struggles required to complete the works that he did produce. These works were not only of relatively greater magnitude, both in size and emotional scope, but they continued to lead further and further into the obscurities of uncharted techniques, styles, and forms.[164] Once more, Beethoven's public was left far behind. Now, however, the big difference was a greater effort to understand him, and the best means of understanding seems to have been through increasingly Romanticized, poetic interpretations, as the generally less hostile reviews indicate.[165] To be sure, there were those who saw nothing at all in the later works. One cruel comment, written right while the last two sonatas were in progress, reads: "Beethoven, like Father Haydn formerly, is busy writing out Scotch songs; he seems to be wholly blunted for greater works."[166] But even today a complete acceptance of "late Beethoven" has not been fully accomplished. If Wagner came to prefer the last sonatas in his own last years,[167] W. Nagel was still remarking about incomprehensible and unbeautiful spots, in 1904, and apparently not merely in the sense of questionable sonorities.[168]

The generalizations about the last five sonatas are illustrated well enough in the first of them, Op. 101 in A. In the opening movement of this work, which is the shortest opening movement in all the sonatas with opus numbers, Wagner found an example of what he meant by "endless melody."[169] The second movement replaces the more usual

164. A fundamental contribution to the understanding of all but Op. 106 is made in Schenker/BEETHOVEN-m.

165. An excellent summary of the reactions to Opp. 109, 110, and 111 from this standpoint may be found in Boyer/BEETHOVEN 260-266, with extended quotations from the reviews. The gradual increase in performance of the late sons. (up to a complete series of all "32" in 1873) is traced in Prod'homme/BEETHOVEN 284-288. In the New York Times for Oct. 28, 1962, X/11, H. C. Schonberg cites still earlier series of all 32 sons., including those played by Charles Hallé in London in 1861 and Carl Wolfsohn in Philadelphia and New York in 1863.

166. AMZ XXIII (1821) 539.

167. Cf. Prod'homme/BEETHOVEN 226-227 (from Glasenapp).

168. Nagel/BEETHOVEN II 208.

169. Prod'homme/BEETHOVEN 227 (after Glasenapp).

scherzo with a fanciful march that has suggested Schumann's music to many a commentator, and, indeed, seems to anticipate parts of the powerful middle movement of his *Fantasy* in C, Op. 17 (composed in memory of Beethoven). After the profound, "longing," slow intro-
169a duction, the spirited finale, like the canonic middle section of the "alla Marcia" movement, probably does reflect Beethoven's late interest in Bach.[170] But it is still more interesting as one of his outstanding combinations of the fugal and "sonata form" principles.[171]

Before contenting himself with a simple description of the movements and an almost apologetic mention (with exx.) of several textural perplexities still to be found in the finale, the critic in AMZ wrote about Op. 101:

> Truly, we are filled with admiration and renewed esteem for his 101st work when we [accompany] the great soul painter along strange, untrod paths, as if following Ariadne's thread through labyrinthic windings, where now a fresh brook whispers to us, now a steep rock faces us; here an unknown, sweet-scented flower attracts us, there a thorny path might turn us away.[172]

According to Schindler, Beethoven wanted to call the two slower movements "Dreamlike Sensations."[173] The discussions of this work that followed in the nineteenth century became increasingly flowery.[174] But Lenz liked only the first movement, and even it he found too free to come under the name "sonata."[175]

Schindler reported that Op. 101 was played by a dilettante named Stainer von Felsburg at a concert arranged by the violinist Schuppanzigh in February of 1816, that Beethoven was present, and that this was the only time any sonata by Beethoven was played in public during his lifetime![176] In 1876 Liszt wrote that when he was ten years old—that is, in 1821 when he began to study with Czerny, nearly two years before he met Beethoven—, "Many of Beethoven's sonatas were known and profoundly admired, especially the 'Pathétique,' 'Moonlight,' and 'Appassionata,' but it wasn't the custom to play them in public. Not

170. Cf. Nagel/BEETHOVEN II 209-214; and, especially, Cockshoot/BEETHOVEN 12-27, 179-184, 197-199.

171. Cf. the detailed analysis in Cockshoot/BEETHOVEN 50-69 (including a discussion of the sketches).

172. AMZ XIX (1817) 687. An earlier review, which appeared in Vienna immediately after publication, is cited in Kinsky & Halm/BEETHOVEN 280.

173. Schindler/BEETHOVEN I 240.

174. Cf. the somewhat divergent views in Marx/VORTRAG 230-234 and Elterlein/BEETHOVEN 87-90. Further comments are quoted in Prod'homme/BEETHOVEN 225-227.

175. Lenz/BEETHOVEN 266-269.

176. Schindler & MacArdle/BEETHOVEN 209; but MacArdle's fn. 145 on p. 340 argues that Op. 90, not 101, must have been the son. in question.

until after Beethoven's death did his works circulate everywhere."[177]
Although no conclusive refutations of these statements have been found
in the present study with regard to the piano sonatas,[178] there are 178a
certainly exceptions among his ensemble sonatas. Thus, Beethoven
himself participated at the piano in the first of two public performances
of his horn sonata, Op. 17, in 1800 and 1803.[179] And at least four
instances of public performances of his string sonatas are known.[180] 180a
But we are reminded how rare such opportunities were—hence, how little must have been the public interest in hearing sonatas, at least in Vienna, in those days,[181] and how much depended on private concerts, in which the sonatas did enjoy at least moderate exposure.[182] That Beethoven concert of 1816 was also reported in AMZ, during the next month,[183] with a mention of the cellist Linke as one of the sponsors, too, but without specifying which new piano sonata was played for the first time or making clear that the concert was, in fact, public. Since the date (of completion?) on the autograph of Op. 101—"1816 im Monath November"—would have to be wrong if Op. 101 was played that early, the sonata in question actually may have been the then recently published Op. 90.[184]

Beethoven's letters during the publication of Op. 101 show much concern for minutiae, including the jocular declaration "henceforth" in favor of the German word "Hammerklavier"[185] or whatever word the "language experts" would approve.[186] The type for the heading, the form of the dedication, and the difficulty of the work came up for

177. Trans. here from Prod'homme/BEETHOVEN 249; cf. also, CZERNY 311.

178. A "Sonata, *Pianoforte*," played in Oxford in 1816 by a "Master Reinagle" (according to J. H. Mee, *The Oldest Music Room in Europe* [London: John Lane, 1911], p. 173), seems more likely to have been one of Beethoven's sets of variations for P & Vc.

179. Thayer/BEETHOVEN I 267 (after Wegeler & Ries/BEETHOVEN 82) and II 39 (amplified in Thayer & Riemann/BEETHOVEN II 446). Hanslick/WIEN I 63-79, 120-130, and 273-282 is highly pertinent but adds no instances here. In MacArdle & Misch/MINOR 456-464 is a survey of the but 9 concerts given in Beethoven's lifetime for his own benefit, at none of which were any of his sons. included. A broader survey of what music by Beethoven was performed during his lifetime, and when and where, is much to be desired.

180. E.g., Müller-Reuter/KONZERTLITERATUR 141 (Op. 5/1 or 2), 133 (from Op. 12 or 5), 137 (Op. 47), 143 (Op. 102; cf. Thayer/BEETHOVEN II 338).

181. Cf. Thayer/BEETHOVEN I 166.

182. E.g., cf. Thayer/BEETHOVEN I 186-187.

183. AMZ XVIII (1816) 197.

184. Cf. Thayer & Riemann/BEETHOVEN III 586. The dedication letter of Op. 101 should be dated Feb. 23, 1817, not 1816 (cf. Anderson/BEETHOVEN II 671; Nottebohm/ZWEITE 344; Levinsohn/LEONORE 163-164; Kinsky & Halm/BEETHOVEN 281). The sketches for Op. 101 are extant except for the first mvt., and are brought together in Prod'homme/BEETHOVEN 212-218.

185. Anderson/BEETHOVEN II 654-660, *passim* (Jan., 1817).

186. Cf. MacArdle & Misch/BEETHOVEN 204-206.

discussion, too.[187] The dedicatee was the highly sensitive, capable young pianist Dorothea von Ertmann, who played Beethoven's music by his own preference and was also admired by Reichardt and Mendelssohn, among others.[188]

After Op. 106 once got beyond the mere fact of respectful public recognition and bewildered private astonishment, it soon graduated to its exalted position as the sonata that received the most
188a superlatives in the Beethoven literature. To many, of course, this position was tantamount to that of "the greatest of all sonatas." One notes especially the concurrence with regard to the slow movement. Lenz, for example, called this movement "a mausoleum of the collective sorrow of the world, the greatest adagio for piano in all literature"—a statement that impelled Riemann, who acknowledged equally favorable reactions on his own part, to take Lenz to task for his exuberance.[189] The superlatives have a starting point in the facts of Op. 106, for it is certainly the longest of Beethoven's sonatas (at least 37 minutes in performance), the hardest to play with technical and musical conviction, and the most difficult for the audience to follow. To some, the 12-minute fugue, with its rich assortment of traditional intellectualisms as well as "alcune licenze,"[190] puts Op. 106 in Beethoven's special category of "magnificent failures"—that is, in the company of the "Grosse Fuge" for quartet or even the choral finale of the Ninth Symphony.

Beethoven worked almost steadily for about a year and a half on the composition of Op. 106, his difficult struggles being evident in the hardwon transformations of the sketches.[191] With a letter written in early June, 1819, he sent the first two movements,

> on which I have written that I had in fact composed them last year before Your Imperial Highness's name-day [April 17, 1818] . . . I have added two more [movements], the second of which is a grand Fugato, [all four movements] really amounting to a grand sonata, which will soon be published and which was long ago dedicated entirely *in my heart* to Y. I. H.; *and indeed Y. I. H.'s most recent achievement* [elevation to the rank of archbishop on June 4, 1819] *is not in the least* [not least among the factors?] responsible for it.[192]

187. Cf. Prod'homme/BEETHOVEN 219-221.
188. Cf. Schindler/BEETHOVEN I 240-244; Thayer/BEETHOVEN II 83-84, 364-365, but also p. 383.
189. Riemann/BEETHOVEN III 336.
190. Cf. the helpful analysis in Cockshoot/BEETHOVEN 70-94.
191. Cf. Nottebohm/ZWEITE 123-137. This aspect of Op. 106 is emphasized in the extended analysis, both objective and subjective, in Rolland/BEETHOVEN III 255-349.
192. As trans. in Anderson/BEETHOVEN II 814 and 815.

The last two movements were composed largely in the lovely Austrian resort town of Mödling (where the new Broadwood piano was first delivered to Beethoven[193]). They expanded the work into what Schindler called the "Riesensonate"[194] or "Giant Sonata," a designation that might have stuck had not the later "Hammerklavier" prevailed. Czerny remembered a walk at Mödling during which Beethoven said, "I am now writing a sonata that will be my greatest."[195]

With further regard to the origin and publication of this work as well as the disappearance of the autograph,[196] much bibliographic effort has been expended.[197] Here only certain essentials may be noted. Like Op. 81a, Op. 106 appeared at the same time in two editions from the same publisher, one with a French and the other with a German title page. But otherwise Beethoven already returned to Italian inscriptions in this work. Special interest centers in Beethoven's letters to Ries (then in London), who arranged for the first London edition. Besides having to worry more than usual about the pay he could receive and about the many errors by the engraver,[198] Beethoven asked on April 16, 1819, to have the celebrated introductory measure added to the slow movement, astonishing Ries, first, because so simple a change should seem necessary well after the composition was completed and, second, because just those two double octaves did prove to effect a remarkable improvement.[199] In the same letter he satisfied Ries's request for specific metronome tempos to be inserted over each movement, including both the introduction and fugue of the finale, then later declared himself wholly against the use of the metronome to indicate tempos.[200] 200a
And in one of his letters (*ca.* March 20, 1819), he wrote Ries,

> Should the sonata not be suitable for London, I could send another one; or you could also omit the Largo and begin straight away with the Fugue . . . , which is the last movement; or you could use the first movement and then the Adagio, and then for the third movement the Scherzo—and omit entirely no. 4 with the Largo and Allegro risoluto. Or you could take just the first movement and the Scherzo and let them form the whole sonata. I leave it to you to do as you think best.[201]

193. Thayer/BEETHOVEN II 391.
194. Schindler/BEETHOVEN I 269.
195. Thayer & Riemann/BEETHOVEN IV 53.
196. For this reason Op. 106 was never published in Schenker/BEETHOVEN-m.
197. Cf. Kinsky & Halm/BEETHOVEN 291-296; also, Unger in ZFM CV (1938) 141-145.
198. Cf. MacArdle & Misch/BEETHOVEN 253-258; Anderson/BEETHOVEN II 796-805.
199. Wegeler & Ries/BEETHOVEN 107-108, 148-150; Anderson/BEETHOVEN II 806-807.
200. Schindler/BEETHOVEN II 248-252, with further observations on this matter still overlooked by some literalist performers.
201. As trans. in Anderson/BEETHOVEN II 804-805.

This carte blanche is shocking to everyone who regards the over-all
cycles of Beethoven's instrumental works as inviolable wholes in which
201a every last detail is an indispensable factor. On the other hand, it should
help to deflate some of the most soul-searching literary rationalizations
of renowned two-movement cycles like Op. 111 or Schubert's Unfinished Symphony. Actually, when Op. 106 was first published in
London (still with many errors and soon after Ries got his instructions)
it appeared in two parts, with movements i, iii, and ii in the first part,
202a in that order, and the complete finale in the other part.[202]

202b No early review of Op. 106 is known. Only an announcement
appeared (from Artaria?), "avoiding all the usual eulogies" at the
author's request, but noting its new "contrapuntal style" and "richest and
grandest fantasy" among all his works.[203] Czerny may have been the only
one to master its great difficulties during Beethoven's lifetime,[204] although Liszt said he himself had already played it "with feeling" at
204a the age of ten (1821), however badly. When Liszt did master it
fifteen years later and gave it perhaps its first public performance, in
Paris in 1836, Berlioz followed with an ecstatic review; and in similarly
enthusiastic terms Wagner responded to performances of it by Liszt in
1853 and by Anton Rubinstein in 1881.[205] The orchestration of Op.
106 that Felix Weingartner prepared about 1926[206] was meant to
achieve the mastery of sound and technique that seemed not quite
possible on the piano alone. Yet Beethoven's extraordinary confidence
in the piano is thus misplaced, for the very struggle that the pianist must
make to conquer this work (and that may have provoked Beethoven's
deprecation, "clavicymbalum miserabile,"[207]) is an essential factor in its
strength. One recalls Tovey's observation as to how much its fugue
would have been weakened if "smoother counterpoint" had been employed.[208]

Beethoven's last three piano sonatas are linked in several ways besides the fact of their consecutive opus numbers, from 109 to 111. They were not exactly written "in a single breath," as Beethoven wrote Count Brunsvik,[209] since Op. 109 was already published before the other two were quite finished.[210] But some of the work on all three

202. Cf. Kinsky & Halm/BEETHOVEN 296.

203. R. Klein quotes the announcement and examines the new "contrapuntal" style in BEETHOVEN-JAHRBUCH IX (1973-77) 184-199.

204. Thayer/BEETHOVEN II 376.

205. Prod'homme/BEETHOVEN 248-250.

206. Cf. Prod'homme/BEETHOVEN 252.

207. Behrend/BEETHOVEN 176.

208. Tovey/BEETHOVEN 247-249.

209. According to Schindler/BEETHOVEN II 3; cf. Thayer/BEETHOVEN III 48-50.

210. Cf. Kinsky & Halm/BEETHOVEN 312, 314, and 317. Czerny argued that all 3 were started while Beethoven was still using only a 5½-octave keyboard (Schünemann/CZERNY 63).

was done during another summer at Mödling, in sketches closely intermixed with those for the *Missa solemnis,*[211] and Beethoven originally 211a
negotiated with Schlesinger in Berlin for the publication of all three, even speaking of "a work consisting of three sonatas."[212] All three were, in fact, first published by Schlesinger, although not, of course, as a set, and although the Paris branch of his firm was established after Op. 109 appeared in Berlin, so that Opp. 110 and 111 made their first appearances in the French city.[213]

Furthermore, the chief contemporary review of these sonatas (and the longest contemporary review devoted to Beethoven's sonatas) considers them together.[214] The composer struck out along new paths 214a
some thirty years ago, begins the reviewer. Though he engendered hostility along the way, all that is now stilled (1824), for today no other can touch this great spirit. The reviewer then cites some of the masterworks, including Opp. 90, 96, and 101. His failure to mention Op. 106, which had received no previous review, appears to be deliberate, for after praising the structure, melody, harmony, and rhythm of the last three sonatas he acknowledges their many technical difficulties but emphasizes that none of these is insurmountable; and at the end of the review he only wishes that metronome markings had been supplied with each movement. The main body of the review is taken up by a largely objective description of each movement in each of the three sonatas, much as the reviewer recognizes that such descriptions fail to convey the all-important aspects of spiritual content and the total structure (or *Gestalt,* in more recent terms). From our present viewpoint, one might add to these observations that Opp. 109, 110, and 111, following the grandeur and more regular plan of Op. 106, have in common their intimacy, their introspective fantasy, and their increasing sense of transfiguration, culminating in the otherworldly, transcendant variations that conclude Op. 111.[215]

Beethoven wanted Op. 109 also to be called "Sonate für das Hammerklavier,"[216] but "Pianoforte" was printed in the first edition. Only two German inscriptions survive, both in the profoundly expressive

211. Cf. Kinsky & Halm/BEETHOVEN 311, 314, and 317 for references to the sketches. Forte/MATRIX is a penetrating comparison, along Schenkerian lines, of the sketches and final version of Op. 109 (cf. Newman in *American Music Teacher* for March and April, 1962).

212. Letter of April 30, 1820 (MacArdle & Misch/BEETHOVEN 345 and 347; Anderson/BEETHOVEN II 893).

213. Cf. Kinsky & Halm/BEETHOVEN 312-313 (contradicting the evidence in Prod'homme/BEETHOVEN 257-258 for a first ed. in Paris of Op. 109), 315-316, 319.

214. AMZ XXVI (1824) 213-225. Cf. Boyer/BEETHOVEN 260-266.

215. These qualities of Op. 111/ii were already recognized in Schindler/BEETHOVEN II 3-4 and in an early Berlin review cited there.

216. Letter of March 7, 1821 (Anderson/BEETHOVEN II 916).

variations that make up the finale. In one of these the Italian "Andante molto cantabile ed espressivo" is intensified to "Gesangvoll mit innigster Empfindung" (Op. 109/iii/1). The dedication of Op. 109 to the 21-year-old Maximiliane Brentano honors her parents,[217] who had been benefactors and longtime friends,[218] and was perhaps intended at least to soften the fact that Beethoven was not yet able to make an overdue payment on a debt to her father (Franz).[219] As with previous sonatas, one is impressed by the care and urgency of the corrections that Beethoven submitted to the publisher prior to the work's first appearance.[220] Besides the long review mentioned earlier, there were reviews of Op. 109 alone, in Berlin and Paris, but these were inconsequential.[221] Only the middle movement—the driving, giguelike "Prestissimo"—qualifies as "a regular sonata movement" in the traditional sense. The rhapsodic first movement is unusual not only for its tempo changes but for the fact that they go first from fast to slow (Ex. 82, from the autograph).[222]

Early in 1822 Beethoven planned to dedicate both Opp. 110 and 111 to the wife of Franz Brentano. But he evidently changed his mind, with the result that Op. 110 appeared without dedication and Op. 111 appeared with two dedications, one to Archduke Rudolph in the original Paris edition, of which Beethoven did not apprise him officially until at least a year later,[223] and one to Madame Brentano in the contemporary London edition, published by Clementi.[224] Innovations in style and
225a form continued to appear in Op. 110,[225] including the "Recitativo" (infrequent in Beethoven's music[226]), the well-known "Bebung,"[227] and the extraordinarily sensitive "Arioso dolente" in the slow movement, as well as the fugue finale,[228] with its return to the "Arioso" before the inversion of the fugue, and its ethereal conclusion. Since the fugue is shorter and much more accessible than that in Op. 106, both musically and technically, it is not surprising that Op. 110 is the most rather than least played of the last five sonatas.[229]

217. Letter of Dec. 6, 1821 (Anderson/BEETHOVEN II 931-932).
218. Thayer/BEETHOVEN II 180.
219. Cf. MacArdle & Misch/BEETHOVEN 387-388.
220. E.g., letters of Nov. 13 and 14, 1821 (Anderson/BEETHOVEN II 927-931).
221. Cf. Kinsky & Halm/BEETHOVEN 312; Prod'homme/BEETHOVEN 259.
222. Cf. Tovey/BEETHOVEN 257-260.
223. Cf. Anderson/BEETHOVEN III 1054.
224. The pertinent correspondence is summarized in Kinsky & Halm/BEETHOVEN 316 and 321, and MacArdle & Misch/BEETHOVEN 384-385.
225. The thematic unity of i and the harmonic progressions in ii are explored in Misch/BEETHOVEN 54-75.
226. Cf. Tovey/BEETHOVEN 278-279.
227. Cf. Tovey/BEETHOVEN-m III 216.
228. Analyzed in detail in Cockshoot/BEETHOVEN 95-120.
229. For 19th-century opinions of this work cf. Nagel/BEETHOVEN II 368-373.

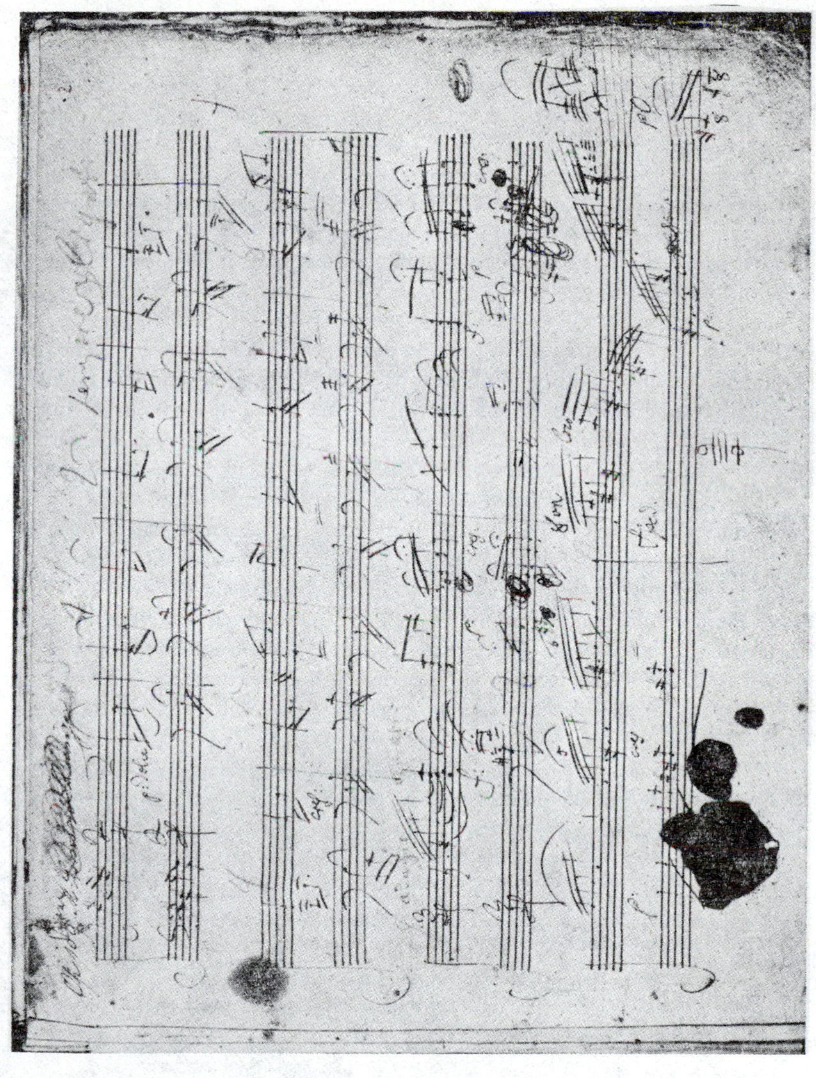

Ex. 82. From the opening of Ludwig van Beethoven's Sonata in E, Op. 109 (facs. of the autograph at the Library of Congress).

Although the history of its first editions remains confused, Op. 111 seems not to have been published by Schlesinger in Paris until April 1823, but in such a faulty edition that it had to be engraved anew, in which form it first appeared in Berlin by Schlesinger's arrangement, later in that same year.[230] This was not only Beethoven's last sonata of any sort, or what Lenz called his "sonate-testament,"[231] but was his last great piano work except for the nearly contemporary "Diabelli Variations." The fact that Op. 111 contains only two movements has occasioned much speculation. Schindler says that in all his innocence he asked the master why he did not add a third movement similar to the first in character, to which Beethoven replied "calmly" that he had been too busy and the long second movement would have to make up for this lack.[232] This reply has generally been treated as facetious,[233] although Beethoven was, in fact, much preoccupied with the *Missa solemnis* at the time,[234] he seems not even to have answered at least two queries from Schlesinger about a third movement,[235] and in the letter to Ries about Op. 106 we have seen what practical considerations could influence his choice and order of movements. Actually, Beethoven did seem to have a third movement in mind originally, for "3tes Stück presto" appears over a sketch of the main idea[236] that eventually served for the first movement. That idea, by the way, is another of the recurring motives in Beethoven's music.[237] It originally appeared in his sketches some twenty years earlier[238] and variants can still be found as late as the string quartets Opp. 131/i/1-4 and 135/iv/15-18 (the "Es muss sein!" motive).

Since Schindler's time there has been less concern about a third movement for Op. 111 than about the meaning of the two movements

230. For the year 1823 and other circumstances of publication, cf. Alan Tyson, "Maurice Schlesinger as a Publisher of Beethoven," in AM XXXV (1963) 182-191, especially p. 185. The previously supposed year of 1822 had been based largely on tentative evidence in correspondence, as in Anderson/BEETHOVEN III 1037-1054 *passim* and as summarized in Kinsky & Halm/BEETHOVEN 319-321. The exceptionally rich, extant sources for Op. 111 have induced an exceptional number of worthwhile mod. studies, including Unverricht/BEETHOVEN (which concludes that the MS sources are generally more authoritative than the printed sources) and 2 recent diss., one by Charles Timbrell (University of Maryland, 1976) and one by William Drabkin (Princeton University, 1977).

231. Lenz/BEETHOVEN 283. Wendell Kretschmar in Thomas Mann's *Dr. Faustus* insists that Op. 111 is the last of *all* sons. (Barford/LAST 323).

232. Schindler/BEETHOVEN II 3-4.

233. As in Shedlock/SONATA 175.

234. E.g., cf. Anderson/BEETHOVEN III 1056-1058 (to Archduke Rudolph).

235. The correspondence is summarized in Kinsky & Halm/BEETHOVEN 320.

236. Nottebohm/ZWEITE 467.

237. Its basic simplicity seems to contradict the effort to attribute it to a motive in Sacchini's opera *Dardanus*, in Frimmel/JAHRBUCH I (1908) 58-62.

238. Nottebohm/SKIZZENBÜCHER I 19.

that he did leave. Lenz, who argued at length that the "Maestoso" in Op. 111 was the only true introduction in all of Beethoven's sonatas (in a long, rambling, and curious discussion of this work),[239] interpreted the two movements as "Resistance" and "Resignation." Philip Barford, who believes a metaphysical, Hegelian approach to Op. 111 is essential to a full understanding of it, prefers not to associate "resignation" with Beethoven.[240] Perhaps "sublimation" or "transfiguration" does come closer to the spiritual sense of the variations.

The String Sonatas

The interest in Beethoven's other main sonatas—the ten for piano and violin and the five for piano and cello—has not been on a par with that in the piano sonatas, of course, although several of these fifteen works continue in strong favor as mainstays of chamber music devotees and concert goers. For purposes of reference and comparison, a tabulation of the fifteen works may be provided similar to that for the piano sonatas earlier in this chapter.

From this list it is obvious that the composing of string sonatas, unlike that of piano sonatas, did not go on almost continuously through-

Beethoven's Sonatas for Piano and Violin

Op. no.	Key	Acquired name	Composition dates	First publication	Dedicatee
12	D		1797-98?	Vienna: Artaria, 1799	Antonio Salieri
"	A		"	"	"
"	E♭		"	"	"
23	a		1800-01?	Vienna: Mollo, 1801	Moritz von Fries
24	F	"Spring"	"	"	"
30	A		1802	Vienna: Bureau, 1803	Alexander I
"	c		"	"	"
"	G		"	"	"
47	A	"Kreutzer"	1802-03	Bonn: Simrock, 1805	Rodolphe Kreutzer
96	G		1812	Vienna: Steiner, 1816	Archduke Rudolph

Beethoven's Sonatas for Piano and Cello

Op. no.	Key	Acquired name	Composition dates	First publication	Dedicatee
5	F		1796	Vienna: Artaria, 1797	Friedrich Wilhelm II
"	g		"	"	"
69	A		1807	Leipzig: Breitkopf & Härtel, 1809	Ingaz von Gleichenstein
102	C		1815	Bonn: Simrock, 1817	Marie von Erdödy
"	D		"	"	"

239. Lenz/BEETHOVEN 283-297.
240. Barford/LAST.

out Beethoven's career. Except for Op. 96, all the violin sonatas were bunched within six years. The cello sonatas would show a little more even distribution if we were to include Beethoven's own preparation, no doubt made for commercial reasons, of an alternative, cello part in his pleasing, effective Horn Sonata in F, Op. 17, which originally appeared with both parts, in 1801.[241] In nearly all of the string sonatas the piano has at least a slight edge in textural and thematic importance. The string part still shows its ancestry in the accompanied keyboard sonata by always coming second in the title, whether the wording is "avec un Violoncelle obligé" (Op. 5), "avec l'Accompagnement d'un Violon" (Op. 30), or simply "et Violoncelle" (Op. 69). (It was in 1800, in reference to the Septet, Op. 20, and during the second or "virtuoso" period when he composed about half of his string sonatas, that Beethoven wrote his celebrated jest, "I cannot compose anything that is not obbligato, seeing that, as a matter of fact, I came into the world with an obbligato accompaniment."[242]) But, of course, these string parts are much more than accompaniments, and, after Op. 5, carry an adequate share of both the solos and the dialogic exchanges.

On the whole, the string sonatas, most of which were written for professional players, are neither as free nor as innovational as the piano sonatas, those in Op. 102 being the chief exception. All have the usual three or four movements. But insofar as the prompt publication of these sonatas is a criterion, they were as successful as the piano sonatas. On the other hand, the subsequent literature on them has been far less.[243]

The two cello sonatas in Op. 5 were products of Beethoven's trip to Berlin in 1796. They were dedicated to the chamber music enthusiast Frederick William II (successor to his uncle Frederick the Great) and were composed for his brilliant first cellist at the Prussian court,
244a Jean Pierre Duport.[244] In the history of the accompanied sonata they
may be regarded as pioneer examples of their type. The renowned Domenico Dragonetti astonished Beethoven by playing Op. 5/2, with
245a him, on his double-bass (1799).[245]

241. The String Trio in E♭, Op. 3 (1796), was published as a "Grande" Son. in E♭ for P + Vc in 1807, but the arrangement was not Beethoven's. Cf. the listings for Opp. 17, 3, and 64 in Kinsky & Halm/BEETHOVEN.

242. Letter of Dec. 15, 1800 (as trans. in Anderson/BEETHOVEN I 42).

243. Excellent factual background material is given in Müller-Reuter/KONZERTLITERATUR. Representative of descriptive accounts are the books listed in GROVE I 573-575, by Midgley (1911), Herwegh (1926), and Engelmann (1931). The descriptions of selected string sons. only, in COBBETT I 87 and 89-92, are too brief to be of much help. Elizabeth Davidson was preparing a diss. on the Vc sons. at the University of California in Berkeley, in 1960.

244. Cf. Wegeler & Ries/BEETHOVEN 109; Müller-Reuter/KONZERTLITERATUR 140-141. Sketches for these sons. are published in Shedlock/SKETCH 649-650.

245. Cf. Thayer/BEETHOVEN I 218 (also, pp. 195 and 205).

The three violin sonatas in Op. 12 were dedicated to Antonio Salieri, one of the four teachers (besides Haydn, Schenk, and Albrechtsberger) with whom Beethoven studied in Vienna, during his second or "virtuoso" period. Op. 12 brought the third review of Beethoven's music and the first of one of his sonatas, in AMZ. The "Leipzig reviewers" (or "oxen"?), whom Beethoven allegedly denounced, set the pattern at once by approving his "talent and industry" but objecting strenuously to the technical difficulties, absence of melody, and "bizarre" effects![246] 246a

Opp. 23 and 24 were originally published under one number, Op. 23, then were separated for reasons of better format.[247] The dedicatee was the wealthy banker and art lover, Moritz von Fries, in whose home, around the time these sonatas were composed, Beethoven improvised in unfriendly competition with Steibelt.[248] In AMZ it was probably the more direct melodic appeal of Opp. 23 and especially 24 that won a more sympathetic response this time, including the statement that "they are among the best Beethoven has written, and that really means generally among the best being written right now. The original, fiery, and bold spirit of this composer could not escape notice even in his earlier works (although these apparently did not get the friendliest reception everywhere, since he himself sometimes raged in an unfriendly, wild, gloomy, and troubled manner). Now this spirit becomes constantly more clear, rejects excesses more and more, and projects ever more agreeably, without loss of character."[249]

Among the three violin sonatas of Op. 30, originally published in three separate issues,[250] the second stands as one of Beethoven's most dramatic and expressive in this category. Indeed, it reveals certain ties with Opp. 13, 67, and 111, among other works in Beethoven's "pathétique" key of c. We have Ries's word as well as good evidence in the sketches to show that the finale of Op. 30/1 was to be the one now known in Op. 47, but that the present variations were substituted to avoid a movement too brilliant for Op. 30/1.[251] 251a

The "Kreutzer" sonata, Op. 47, is one of the best known of all Beethoven's chamber works and undoubtedly deserves its renown. Yet some of this renown must be attributed to the stories associated

246. AMZ I (1798-99) 570-71. Cf. Thayer/BEETHOVEN I 304-306 (but p. 307 refers to Op. 10!); Müller-Reuter/KONZERTLITERATUR 133-134; Anderson/BEETHOVEN I 48. Wetzel's book on Beethoven's violin music (Berlin: Max Hesse, 1924) contains highly personalized analyses of Opp. 12, 23, and 24.

247. Kinsky & Halm/BEETHOVEN 57-58.

248. Wegeler & Ries/BEETHOVEN 81-82; Thayer/BEETHOVEN I 268.

249. AMZ IV (1801-02) 569-570.

250. Kinsky & Halm/BEETHOVEN 75-76.

251. Wegeler & Ries/BEETHOVEN 83; Nottebohm/SKIZZENBÜCHER I 19-27, 29-32.

with the work, from the circumstances of its origin up to the novella by Tolstoy, *The Kreutzer Sonata* (1889), in which the music is the catalytic agent needed to drive a jealous husband to murder. On the autograph, as an apparent quip, is the title "Sonata mulattica,"[252] referring to the outstanding young mulatto violinist George Polgreen Bridgetower. Beethoven reportedly composed the first two movements in great haste for the concert at which he and Bridgetower first played this work, the violinist playing the variations (second mvt.) from the autograph and Beethoven playing his own part mostly from memory and
253a mere sketches.[253] But the finale was ready well ahead, as we have seen in connection with Op. 30/1.

A quarrel over a girl that both Bridgetower and Beethoven were courting is said to have caused the composer to change the dedicatee to the French violinist and composer Rodolphe Kreutzer (whose études are still practiced by every serious violin student). Beethoven thought Kreutzer ideally suited to the performance of Op. 47[254] and, said Czerny, may have derived the "closing theme" of the first movement (the theme that enters first in e) from a published work by Kreutzer.[255] But Berlioz reported in 1844 that "the celebrated violinist could never bring himself to play this outrageously unintelligible composition."[256] Before that remark was made Op. 47 had already been successful enough to be heard in an orchestration in Hamburg, in 1835.[257] Could Berlioz have been influenced by the original review of Op. 47,[258] which Schindler says is "unquestionably in the category of the most abstruse [review] of Beethoven's music"?[259] The reviewer's comments, containing the same tributes and reservations we have now noted so often, may be reduced to the fact that he recognized the presence of genius but had not the slightest idea of what it was all about. Only the closing sentence is short, unqualified, and unambiguous: "The work is very beautifully engraved." As evidence of Beethoven's strong awareness of the duo problem in Op. 47, the long title is worth quoting from the first edition, including a word added here in brackets that was struck

252. Kinsky & Halm/BEETHOVEN 111.

253. Wegeler & Ries/BEETHOVEN 82-83; Thayer/BEETHOVEN II 8-11 (with many details about Bridgetower, including the cadenza he improvised in answer to the piano cadenza in the first mvt., much to Beethoven's delight). Still more on Bridgetower is given in Thayer & Riemann/BEETHOVEN II 389-398.

254. Letter of Oct. 4, 1804 (Anderson/BEETHOVEN I 120).

255. Thayer/BEETHOVEN 112.

256. Trans. from the quotation in Kinsky & Halm/BEETHOVEN 112. Cf. Schwarz/BEETHOVEN 440-441.

257. The arrangement, with the "Scherzo" from Op. 106 added, was made by Brahms' teacher, Eduard Marxsen (Müller-Reuter/KONZERTLITERATUR 138).

258. AMZ VII (1804-05) 769-771.

259. Schindler/BEETHOVEN I 112-113.

out in the autograph: *Sonata per il Pian-forte ed un Violino obligato, scritta in uno stilo [brillante] molto concertante, quasi come d'un Concerto.*

The deeply expressive cello sonata Op. 69 has been said to describe Beethoven's love for Therese Malfatti,[260] another sometime candidate for the "Eternally Beloved."[261] At any rate, it was dedicated to her future brother-in-law Ignaz Gleichenstein, a fine amateur cellist and close friend of Beethoven. In the dedication copy Beethoven wrote in Latin, "Between Tears and Sorrow."[262] 262a

The fine, sensitive violin sonata in G, Op. 96, is a further important work dedicated to Archduke Rudolph. It was composed for another French violinist, Pierre Rode (whose études are also still known to all serious violinists).[263] The archduke and Rode played it for the first 263a
time at the home of Prince Lobkowitz.[264] In the first review of this work, the writer established a more favorable climate at once when he began, "It almost seems as though this great master returns again more to the melodious and, on the whole, more or less cheerful [style] in his newest work."[265] In the rest of the review he recalled Beethoven's more "wild" and "melancholy" styles, he said this work is serious without being unpleasing, he described the four movements briefly, and he noted the equal importance of the two parts.

The two outstanding cello sonatas in Op. 102 were the only large-scale works composed by Beethoven in 1815, the year of the Congress of Vienna.[266] The dedication did not appear in the original edition but was changed from the Englishman Charles Neate, when a planned London edition no longer looked promising, to the Countess Erdödy, a talented pianist and friend of Beethoven.[267] One of the two sonatas was first performed in 1816 in a public concert by Czerny and the esteemed cellist Joseph Linke.[268] In the autograph of Op. 102/1 the title reads "Freje Sonate für Klavier und Violonschell." The "free" was not included in the printed title but might as well have been from the standpoint of the original reviewer of the two sonatas.[269] As with Op. 47, it took the reviewer considerable space to obscure the fact that

260. Nettl/BEETHOVEN 297, 129.
261. Cf. Thayer/BEETHOVEN I 333, 336; II 86, 106, 141, 174-177.
262. Cf. Müller-Reuter/KONZERTLITERATUR 142-143.
263. Cf. Nottebohm/BEETHOVENIANA 28-30; Schwarz/BEETHOVEN 441.
264. Cf. Kinsky & Halm/BEETHOVEN 270.
265. AMZ XIX (1817) 228-229.
266. Cf. the list for 1815 in Kinsky & Halm/BEETHOVEN 750.
267. Kinsky & Halm/BEETHOVEN 283 and 284. Cf. Schindler/BEETHOVEN I 244-245, II 41-42; Thayer/BEETHOVEN II 333-352 *passim.*
268. Thayer/BEETHOVEN II 338.
269. AMZ XX (1818) 792-794.

he could not understand the music. He began by calling it unusual even for Beethoven, then took the different tack of reminding the reader that Bach must have seemed unusual in his day, too. The cello part was observed to be not merely obligatory but of prime thematic significance. In such music each reader must do his own evaluating, the reviewer added. After a brief description of the movements and the difficulties in each part, he closed with the practical note that "the performance would have been much more difficult for both players had not the art-minded publisher put the cello part in small notes on a separate staff throughout the piano part." In fact, as late as 1817 here were the first works of chamber music by Beethoven to be published in score![270]

Historical Perspective

By way of concluding this separate chapter on the most important figure in sonata history, little should be needed here beyond some reminders and cross-references. We have already had occasion to realize how much more attention has been paid to the Romantic aftermath of Beethoven's music than to its eighteenth-century ancestry. Of chief importance in this aftermath, of course, was the sonata itself, which, as Wagner said, was "the transparent veil through which he [Beethoven] seemed to have looked at all music."[271] Actual evidences for the aftermath of Beethoven's sonatas in the nineteenth century will naturally serve as some of the chief points of departure in our next volume.

As for the ancestry of Beethoven's sonatas, among the investigations into this subject one can find a number of efforts such as those of Riemann to link him with the Mannheim school,[272] or of Schiedermair with Neefe, or of d'Indy with Rust, or of Torrefranca even with Platti, as noted earlier, in the discussions of these relatively minor composers. But nothing like the number of antecedents has been found for the style of Beethoven as for that of Mozart or, indeed, of Haydn. Two reasons for this difference may be mentioned. First, there was necessarily considerable eclecticism as well as empiricism in the manner by which Haydn and Mozart had to work their way up from the structural uncertainties and textural diversities of pre-Classic styles to the lucidity and more consistent idioms of high-Classic music. By contrast, a generation later Beethoven could be born into high-Classic styles ready made. Second, the almost explosive originality of Beethoven's genius made him the strong-willed, even stubborn sort of great composer who could accept only from great composers. As stated at the start of this

270. Kinsky & Halm/BEETHOVEN 283.
271. As cited in Blom/STEPCHILDREN 89.
272. Riemann/BEETHOVEN I 28-29 (with further references).

chapter and elsewhere, Haydn and Mozart were the prime influences on Beethoven.[273] Next only to them were Emanuel Bach, whose *Essay* 273a
Beethoven used in his own teaching and whose keyboard sonatas he knew well;[274] J. S. Bach, from whose *Well-Tempered Clavier* Beethoven was already playing at the age of twelve, according to Neefe's testimony, and whose fugal writing we know to have been so much in Beethoven's mind in his late works;[275] Handel, whom Beethoven placed among his favorite composers throughout much of his career;[276] and Clementi, at least in his piano works, which comprised almost the only diet Beethoven would allow for Karl throughout the latter's study with Czerny (SCE XX). How the music of these masters may actually have influenced the styles and forms of Beethoven's sonatas is a question that was kept constantly in view in Chapter VI, on the structure of the Classic sonata.

273. Jalowetz/BEETHOVEN 417-439 surveys their influences during his early years. In Rosenberg/MOZART direct thematic relationships in the works of Mozart and Beethoven are brought to light. Among other things in Schiedermair/BEETHOVEN 286-301, the use of Mozart's Son. in G (K.V. 373a; K & Vn) as a specific model for Beethoven's early Piano Quartet in E♭ (WoO 36/1) is confirmed.

274. Cf. Jalowetz/BEETHOVEN 439-474.

275. Thayer/BEETHOVEN I 69.

276. Thayer/BEETHOVEN II 89; III 182, 277, 289.

Chapter XVI

Minor Austrians and Germans From About 1780 to 1825

In the Shade of the Great Masters

In this chapter are met a good many—seventy, to be exact—of the *Kleinmeister* in Austria and Germany who largely have been lost to view in the blinding light of the three Viennese masters. These men tend to divide loosely into high-Classic contemporaries of Haydn and Mozart, and late-Classic contemporaries of Beethoven. In fact, a surprising number of them actually crossed paths with one, two, or even all three of the latter, as the rich autobiographies and letters of the times reveal. If, then, the reaction of the Viennese master concerned was characteristically one of contempt, even ridicule, we can only acknowledge the vast gaps that separated the great from the little. And we must respect the artistic integrity that compelled the great to speak in complete honesty, at least whenever there was any question of musical values.

Considering these vast gaps, one is more able to understand the way in which nineteenth-century writers elevated Beethoven into Olympian regions quite beyond the reach of his mortal contemporaries. But the gaps were not always so evident. Thus, both Vanhal and Koželuch were more successful, widely published, and—at least with reference to Koželuch—more highly regarded than Mozart while the latter was still alive. Of course, the catch is in the clause, "while Mozart was still alive." The often stereotyped works of *Kleinmeister* like Vanhal, Koželuch, Gyrowetz, Vogler, Sterkel, and Hässler did not outlive their "creators." It is not only that, axiomatically, the contemporary successes of these men were no guarantee of artistic worth. But the *Kleinmeister* were characteristically those who made their best efforts at first, thereafter honoring art less and less as they made increasing concessions to popular demand and to the ease of writing by formulas. (How hungry was the public and how ready were the publishers for such things in those days!) It is to the credit of the contemporary reviewers that usually and eventually they became aware of these concessions and formulas on the part of the *Vielschreiber*. We may laugh today at the inability of some reviewers to keep pace with such an original, forceful genius as Beethoven. But they rarely failed to see through a deteriorating *Kleinmeister* before he had done his last publishing.

All these remarks about the *Kleinmeister* are not to deny that a few remain interesting in their own right. If the curse of most was to compose with little more than high competence, there were occasional figures with enough sparkle, like Rosetti, enough depth, like Mozart's son and namesake, and enough independence, like Reichardt and the posthumously victimized Rust, to show through in spite of the Viennese masters. Otherwise, we meet some of our most obscure names in the present chapter, albeit names too well identified with the sonata in their own day to be left out entirely here. Were it not for the increasing attention to obscure Austro-German names in the later volumes of MGG, or for the continuing thoroughness of German dissertationists, who sometimes have had to scrape pretty close to bottom for their individuals or regions to study, we would be hard pressed to get bibliographic information about the sonatas of these obscure musicians, especially as so many past dictionaries and other sources of information stop at about 1800. But there has been, and is here, less interest in looking into their music, anyway; for as also-rans and epigones they merely confirmed or even fossilized the high-Classic trends of the sonata. They were too late to point the way in a pre-Classic sense, and mostly too early or too unimaginative to have significance as pre-Romanticists. On these accounts and because we saw the same styles and forms to so much better advantage in the sonatas of Haydn, Mozart, and Beethoven, there has seemed to be less reason for more than occasional details of analysis in the present chapter.

A still remarkable number of Czech musicians will be found here to have been active in Austria and southern Germany, partly owing to continuing loose national definitions and close political ties with central European countries. There are still some Italians to be found, too, although more noteworthy is the continuing number of Austrians and Germans who polished off their training in Italy, including some who still went to Tartini and/or Martini. The number of Hungarians and Poles active in Austria and Germany is less conspicuous (or less well investigated). Virtually all of the Austrian sonata activity was centered in Vienna. One may recall that the sonatas Mozart wrote while still in Salzburg were composed mostly in preparation for his travels, and that Michael Haydn found no occasion at all to write sonatas there. As we shall see, a special Viennese development touching the sonata was that of music for the Spanish or the "terz" guitar, which flourished until cheap stunts brought its end by the second quarter of the nineteenth century. In the declining musical center at Mannheim and at other Catholic, south German centers, the number of priests active in music is noteworthy. In central Germany the sphere of J. S. Bach's posthumous influence is still strongly felt, especially in Thuringian and Saxon centers. And both there and in north Germany one becomes aware again of what powerful influences Frederick the Great in Berlin and Emanuel Bach in Hamburg exerted on the sonata (and other music), although in very different ways.

Minor Contemporaries of Haydn and Mozart in Vienna (Dittersdorf)

Carl Ditters von Dittersdorf (1739-99), as relatively minor a figure as he was, must still be called one of the chief contemporaries of Haydn and Mozart in Vienna.[1] Born into his pre-Classic Viennese environment when Wagenseil was still only twenty-four, he made rapid progress on the violin, getting his first court post at eleven. But he did not begin to compose extensively until he was about twenty-five, after traveling to Italy with Gluck and learning to know Haydn well. Ample details of this and Dittersdorf's further career are contained in his autobiography, dictated up to two days before his death, which is as entertaining, nimble, superficially clever, and ingenuous as *Der Apotheker und Doktor* or his other best-known music.[2] We read here for example, what the emperor and he thought of Clementi, Mozart, and Haydn; also, what the emperor thought of Dittersdorf—". . . your composition . . . is a well-furnished, daintily-arranged table. The dishes are well served up. One can take a good helping from each, without risk to the digestion."[3] Dittersdorf knew Mozart personally.[4] But he did not mention the young Beethoven (or the French Revolution, or very much else not directly in his ken).

Dittersdorf was successful primarily in the several varieties of comic opera that he wrote, in his programmatic symphonies, and in his string

1. In MGG VII 1670 (Wessely) is cited a MS diss. of 1910 (not seen here) on the Viennese contemporaries of Haydn and Mozart (1775-1805), by P. Weingarten.

2. DITTERSDORF. The main further source on him is Krebs/DITTERSDORFIANA, with a numbered list of 351 compositions, pp. 55-144. Cf., also, MGG III 588-597 (Wirth); Souper/DITTERSDORF (summarizing the life).

3. DITTERSDORF 250-254.

4. Kelly/REMINISCENCES I 241.

quartets. His works of special interest here include 3 sets of "Sei Sonate a tre" (2 Vns & Vc; Krebs 55-144), of which 2 sets were published in Paris as Opp. 1 and 6 in 1767 and 1771,[5] and are interesting as early string trios without *b.c.* figures;[6] a "Sonata da camera a 5" (2 Vns, Va, Vc, bass);[7] 15 S/bass "soli" (Krebs 220-234), of which only one is actually called "Sonata";[8] and 2 piano sonatas, the only extant one being the autograph that has been at the Library of Congress since 1931 and is headed "Sonata per il Forte piano di Carlo de Dittersdorf, N: II in A, 1799" (Krebs 238).[9] The piano sonata, written in a feeble, tremulous hand, must have been among the "great number of piano compositions" mentioned at the end of his autobiography as being composed in "the last five years" and as being mentioned in the "Neue musikalische Leipziger Zeitung."[10] These last piano compositions included the 12 solo sonatas arranged from quartets and trios (Krebs 260-271; 1796-97), the 6 4-hand sonatas arranged from the programmatic symphonies based on Ovid's *Metamorphoses* (Krebs 254-259; 1797-98), and 12 further 4-hand sonatas (Krebs 242-253; 1796 [not 1769]-97 [arrangements?]), most or all of which were in MSS now lost.[11]

Dittersdorf's trio sonatas Op. 1 are in two movements, F (or M)-minuet, whereas the piano sonata is in three movements, F-minuet-F, and the S/bass "soli" are in three or more movements, often M-F-F.[12] Slow movements are infrequent and keys of more than three sharps or flats are avoided. The main charm of these sonatas lies in their melodic ideas and unexpected harmonic turns (such as the abrupt change from A to F♯ and back in the piano Sonata in A/i/25-35). The main weaknesses are found in the trite passage work, the insufficient textural interest, the lack of true development of material, and the loose, repetitious structures. Gertrude Rigler considers whether the Mannheim or native Viennese composers were the stronger influence on Dittersdorf, deciding in favor of the latter.[13] The style of the early trio sonatas does come closer to the motivic style still often to be found in Wagenseil's

5. Johansson/FRENCH I 24 and 135.

6. Mod. ed.: all of Op. 1, HORTUS MUSICUS-m No. 92 (Noack), with "Nachwort."

7. Rigler/DITTERSDORF 186.

8. Mod. ed.: "Sons." in B♭ and G for Vn/bass and "Son." in E♭ for Va/bass, Mlynarczyk & Lürman/DITTERSDORF-m.

9. Mod. ed.: Newman/THIRTEEN-m, with preface.

10. DITTERSDORF 310; the reference is to AMZ I (1798-99) Intelligenz-Blatt 19-20.

11. Cf. Krebs/DITTERSDORFIANA 101-103.

12. Rigler/DITTERSDORF is a systematic, over-all study of the styles and forms of his chamber music.

13. Rigler/DITTERSDORF 179-185.

music. But the late piano sonata, like the Quartet in E♭ that is still heard, has more of the songful, phrase-grouping style that Dittersdorf could have acquired in Italy and from his training on Italian violin sonatas.[14] And it has some of the melodic chromaticism that Mozart applied so often to passing notes and appoggiaturas.[15] In short, we find not much more than would be expected of a composer who could write candidly, "even if I gave no proof of fiery genius, which never slumbers and sleeps, and seldom does what is told, I am just as well content; for my honest punctuality in time and business stood me in good stead in later life."[16]

The Silesian teacher, theorist, and composer **Emanuel Alois Förster** (1748-1823) came to Vienna around 1776-79, apparently after a period in Prague.[17] He was highly regarded by both Mozart[18] and Beethoven, the latter once referring to him loosely as "his old teacher."[19] The MSS of about 10 solo keyboard, 10 accompanied, and 5 trio sonatas have survived intact or incomplete from before Förster's residence in Vienna (*ca.* 1760-74), and over 25 others were published after he got there, between 1789 and 1808, including 21 for solo piano, one for 4 hands at one piano, and 4 for piano with violin accompaniment.[20] The early sonatas and the light pedagogic works have little interest now, but the 3 piano sonatas in Op. 22 and the *Fantaisie suivie d'une grande sonate* in D, Op. 25, are much stronger. Mozart is obviously the principal influence, especially in the cantilena of the lines, the chromatic inflections, and the feminine cadential appoggiaturas (Ex. 83). In Op. 22/2 the finale seems to be a loose, small-scale copy of the finale of Mozart's "Jupiter" symphony, in texture, structure, and even the shape of the motive. Among the chief differences in Förster's sonata writing are the less interesting accompaniments, the shorter, less developed "development" sections, and the more shallow slow movements. There is only a little of the drama of Beethoven's early sonatas. As Beethoven advanced in his style Förster is said to have cooled toward him.[21] Meanwhile, the reviewers, who had begun by finding the same

14. DITTERSDORF 28, 40-41.
15. Further discussions of Dittersdorf's style may be found in Krebs/DITTERSDORFIANA 36-37; Souper/MUSIC.
16. DITTERSDORF 39.
17. Weigl/FÖRSTER is the only study. Cf., also, MGG IV 453-455 (Orel).
18. Weigl/FÖRSTER 275-276 (but footnote 6 is missing!).
19. Weigl/FÖRSTER 280-281; Thayer & Riemann/BEETHOVEN I 183-184.
20. Cf. the thematic index of the ensemble sons. in DTÖ-m XXXV/1 vii-ix (Weigl, with preface); MGG IV 453-454; Weinmann/ARTARIA items 224, 570, 647; Weinmann/KUNST items 14, 33, 59, 60, 102, 225, 233. The piano sons. are briefly discussed, with exx., in Weigl/FÖRSTER 289-292.
21. Weigl/FÖRSTER 281.

Ex. 83. From the first movement of Emanuel Alois Förster's Sonata in g, Op. 22/2 (after the original ed. of the Bureau d'Arts et d'Industrie at the Library of Congress).

"bizarreries" that they had found in Beethoven, became much more sympathetic toward Förster's Opp. 22 and 25, finding good craftsmanship if not "brilliant originality."[22]

The Abbé **Maximilian Stadler** (1748-1833) knew Haydn and Mozart well although he was not a permanent resident in Vienna until 1796 (and is not to be confused with Anton Stadler, the clarinetist in Mozart's circle).[23] Among his vocal and instrumental works are several sonatas, including some for organ and some for piano.[24] Representative of the latter category are the publications of six sonatinas in 1794, a Sonata in F in 1799, and "Deux Sonates suivies d'une fugue" in 1803 (as "Suite" 8 in Anth. NÄGELI-m). These are sufficient to suggest that a further study of Stadler's instrumental music would be rewarding. The sonatas of 1803, each in only two movements, reveal full textures, decorative passage work, a rich harmonic vocabulary, and that dis-

22. Cf. AMZ I (1798-99) 365-366 (3 Quartets Op. 16) with AMZ V (1802-03) 411-412 and 716-718.

23. Cf. GROVE VIII 35 (Pohl).

24. Cf. the list in Eitner/QL IX 242-244.

armingly simple, forthright melody so characteristic of late-Classic and early-Romantic music.

Franz Anton Hoffmeister (1754-1812), in Vienna from 1768, is remembered today primarily as one of the first and most important publishers of the music of Haydn, Mozart, and Beethoven (all of whom he knew personally), and of J. S. Bach.[25] He himself was active in this capacity in Vienna from 1784-98, in Leipzig from 1800-05 (with Ambrosius Kühnel in the Bureau de musique, immediate ancestor of C. F. Peters), and again in Vienna in a declining way from 1805-07. But in his own day, ephemeral as the reputation proved to be, he was known at least as well as a popular composer. Moreover, he might well be ranked—with Lassus, Telemann, Czerny, and a few others—among the most prolific composers of all time, his vocal and instrumental works being published not only by himself but by nearly all the other main firms of the time.[26] That we know more about Hoffmeister than most of the other minor composers in Vienna is mainly owing to two of those fascinating searches into musical spuriosities, both already mentioned here (SCE XIV). One concerns his publication of Mozart's K.V. 498a under A. E. Müller's name. And the other concerns E. F. Schmid's publication of Hoffmeister's three "Göttweiger" piano sonatas under Haydn's name in 1934, backed by apparently good circumstantial and internal evidence, and his correction of this error three years later following information supplied by Kahl, Steglich, and Larsen.[27]

Hoffmeister contributed to all prevalent sonata types, especially those for piano or harp alone, or with accompaniments variously for flute (his favorite instrument), violin, and cello. But the total output of sonatas was small in relation to his other solo and chamber music. Schmid could only find between 20-26 in all for keyboard alone, including a "Sonata scolastica" and 6 "Sonatines faciles."[28] These 20-26 sonatas date from 1785 to 1803. They have 2 or 3 movements, the finale usually being a rondo in the 3-movement sonatas. In relating the 3 "Göttweiger" sonatas, first published by Hoffmeister himself as Op. 7

25. This aspect of his career is discussed in Schmid/GÖTTWEIGER 761-768, 889-895; Hill/NUMBERS (with cats. after pp. 126 and 128); Weinmann/WIENER 21-22; MGG VI 547-550 (Weinmann).

26. Some idea of the extent and spread of this productivity may be had in HOFMEISTER (no relation) I and II (Whistling), under almost every important category. Cf. Schmid/GÖTTWEIGER 767-768. In Riehl/CHARAKTERKÖPFE I 249-253 the dilettante appeal, good craftsmanship, and great amount of this music are emphasized.

27. Cf. Schmid/GÖTTWEIGER (the main study of Hoffmeister) 760-761, 998-1000, 1116-1117; Hoboken/HAYDN 733.

28. Schmid/GÖTTWEIGER 992-998 and 1117, with a thematic index of 11 of the sons. and full publication details.

between 1787 and 1791, to the style of Haydn, Schmid calls attention especially to their harmonic surprises, wide modulations in the development sections, fresh, wide-spaced themes, ornamental pulsations in the repetitions of themes, melodic sighs in alternation with accompaniment chords, and frequent melodic interest in the bass.[29] A further examination here of other sonatas by Hoffmeister, namely the 3 accompanied sonatas Op. 6 (Hummel in Berlin, 1787), showed the "violon obligé" actually to be a subordinate part, the ideas to be trite, the piano figuration to be brilliant, and the craftsmanship to be both sure and experienced.

This is as good a place as any to take note of the Austrian-born pianist and violinist **Ignaz Joseph Pleyel** (1757-1831), who studied piano with Vanhal and composition with Haydn (*ca.* 1774-79), did further study in Italy, and became active in Strasbourg, London (in competition with Haydn[30]), and lastly in Paris (as a music dealer and as one of the important manufacturers of pianos in the nineteenth century).[31] Pleyel was another extraordinarily prolific composer, who wrote sonatas in all the popular settings of the day and got them published and republished by all the best known publishers of the day.[32] 32a
Most of this music was composed before he reached Paris in 1795 and became a businessman. But little of it has been made known again in recent times,[33] except for elementary teaching pieces. The style and quality may be generalized as high-Classic, light, regularly phrased, skillful, fluent, melodious, and extremely watery, only the earliest works showing any spark of individuality.[34] Until and unless some brave student chooses to explore the vast wasteland still occupied by extant editions of this music, it will be impossible to say more about its quantity, categories, and statistically conspicuous traits. 34a

Obscure Contemporaries of Haydn and Mozart in Vienna

A number of more obscure figures must be passed by rapidly for want of their music or because of its insignificance. **Leopold**

29. Schmid/HOFFMEISTER 1102-1116, with exx.
30. Cf. Landon/HAYDN 126, 128, 132, 134.
31. Cf. GROVE VI 828-830 (Kidson); Riemann & Gurlitt/LEXIKON II 420-421.
32. For sample lists cf. HOFMEISTER 1815 and 1828 *passim* (both Whistling), but not the next vol.; Weinmann/ARTARIA; BRITISH UNION II 791-799.
33. Zeitlin & Goldberger/PLEYEL-m is a 4-hand, one-piano son. in g dated "*ca.* 1815." From Op. 16, 3 acc'd. sons. (P & Fl-or-Vn & Vc) have been issued in ORGANUM-m III Nos. 35-37; the first ed. of Op. 16 was probably that of Artaria in 1789 (plate no. 228).
34. A knowing discussion of Pleyel's "three periods in his artistic development" appears in Riehl/CHARAKTERKÖPFE 239-244. Cf. SCE V, with ex.

Hofmann (1738-93) was a Vienna-born *Hofklaviermeister* and organist who succeeded Wagenseil.[35] Praised by Burney, resented as a "braggart" rival by Haydn, and "assisted" at the organ by Mozart in the latter's last year, Hofmann left a substantial quantity of vocal and instrumental music, little of which achieved publication.[36] None of some 15 extant MS sonatas, for solo keyboard and for small ensembles (including S/- and SS/bass), was available here. But a contemporary keyboard transcription of an early "Sinfonia" in E♭[37] proves to be melodically attractive, light, modern in syntax (for about 1760), and neat though rudimentary in construction.

Two ladies may be noted at this point in the chronicles. **Marianne Martinez** (1744-1812) was a dilettante Viennese harpsichordist and singer of Spanish descent, trained by Haydn and Porpora, and sought out by Mozart as a partner in the playing of his four-hand music.[38] Among her numerous vocal and instrumental works, two of the few publications were cembalo sonatas in E and A that appeared when she was only about eighteen and twenty-one, in Anth. HAFFNER RACCOLTA-m IV no. 3 and V no. 3 (*ca.* 1762 and 1765).[39] These sonatas reveal an advanced knowledge of the keyboard and a marked kinship with the idiom in Haydn's early sonatas, although they are weakened by a surfeit of tonic-dominant harmony. The only other woman composer of sonatas to mention at this time in Vienna was another dilettante keyboardist whom Mozart knew (from at least 1773),[40] **Marianne von Auenbrugger** (?-*ca.* 1786). About 1781 Artaria published her keyboard sonata (H or P), "with an ode by Salieri."[41]

The Bavarian cellist **Franz Xaver Hammer** (?-1813?) served with Haydn in Prince Esterházy's orchestra from 1771-78, as a member of the Vienna Tonkünstler Societät from 1776, and in

35. J. Steffan and L. A. Koželuch also followed Wagenseil in the same or similar posts, leaving some confusion in the records.

36. Cf. BURNEY'S TOURS II 84 and 111; Landon/HAYDN 31; Anderson/MOZART III 1412-1413; MGG VI 561-565 (Prohászka).

37. Anth. SINFONIE-m II no. 20. There is also an SS/bass "Divertimento" in HAUSMUSIK-m No. 156.

38. Cf. Geiringer/HAYDN 42-43; BURNEY'S TOURS II 106-107, 117; Kelly/REMINISCENCES I 252; MGG VIII 1716-1718 (Wessely). Both Burney and Kelly took her for the sister of her father and Kelly caught the name as "Martini."

39. Did her name cause her to be included among the "Ausländer" in this anthology? Mod. ed. of both sons.: Pauer/MEISTER-m VI nos. 59 and 60.

40. Anderson/MOZART I 343.

41. Weinmann/ARTARIA item 14. Mozart regarded as "wretched" the opera by Salieri on a libretto by her father (Anderson/MOZART III 1287).

Schwerin after 1785.[42] He is mentioned here for MSS of a Vc/bass sonata, left in Vienna, and four late examples of viola da gamba sonatas with cello accompaniment, left in Schwerin. One of the latter, which has been made available,[43] returns to the viola da gamba's characteristic double-stops and the old "church" sequence of movements, S-F-M-F. But it is modern in its simple phrase structure and tonal outlines. Considerable melodic charm is to be found here.

The Vienna-born composer of light operas, **Johann Gallus Mederitsch** (called "Gallus"; 1752-1835) was a pupil of Wagenseil, an object of Mozart's ridicule, and the esteemed counterpoint teacher of W. A. Mozart the Younger.[44] He published at least one 44a
4-hand, 3 solo, and 9 accompanied piano sonatas between 1791 and 1813 that remain to be explored. **Franz Jakob Freystädtler** (1768-1841), a pupil of Mozart from 1786 and composer chiefly of songs, published some light solo and accompanied sonatas in Vienna from 1789 to at least 1798.[45] **Franz Grill** (?-1795), probably a German in the service of a Hungarian family, is supposed to have studied with Haydn.[46] He is credited with at least a dozen routine, unoriginal accompanied sonatas (P & Vn) that first appeared in Vienna in 1790-95, then circulated more widely. **Peter Fux** (or Fuchs; 1753-1831), who may have been born in Vienna or Bohemia, was an expert violinist who served under Haydn at Esterház in 1781-82, and in the imperial Chapel in Vienna from 1787.[47] Between 1791 and 1796 he published at least four late examples of Vn/bass sonatas in Vienna, such as only the professional violinists were still writing. In the solo part the double-stops and harmonics point to Fux's full knowledge of his instrument.

Two Italians in Vienna may be given brief mention at this point. **Giovanni Antonio Matielli** (*ca.* 1733-1805) was a skilled keyboardist who studied with Wagenseil.[48] His *Sei Sonate per il cembalo,* Op. 1, published by Toricella in Venice in 1781, were "approvate dal Celebre Sig. Cavaliere de Gluck e Dedicate ai Favorati ed Intendenti della vera

42. Cf. Eitner/QL V 6-7.
43. SCHOTT CELLO-m No. 80 (Döbereiner), but with the 3d mvt. omitted.
44. Cf. MGG VIII 1888-1889 (Pisarowitz); Anderson/MOZART III 1250; Hummel/MOZART 151-153.
45. Cf. MGG IV 935-936 (Orel); Anderson/MOZART III 1346; Weinmann/ARTARIA items 273, 326.
46. Cf. MGG V 913 (Klein).
47. Cf. MGG IV 1175-1176 (Racek).
48. Cf. MGG VIII 1789-1790 (Kollpacker).

Musica," according to the full title. The set succeeded well enough to bring a new one from the same publisher two years later,[49] and an SS/bass arrangement of the original set in 1781. There are still *galant* mannerisms and much use of Alberti and repeated-note accompaniments in this music, its chief virtue being its pathetic, cantilena melody lines. **Giacomo Conti** (*ca.* 1752-1805) was a violinist in Zürich around 1786, at the St. Petersburg court of Prince Potemkin about 1790-91, and in Vienna from at least 1793.[50] But already in about 1788 and in 1790, Artaria had published two sets of Vn/bass sonatas, Opp. 1 and 2.[51] These provide further late examples in Vienna of the old melo/bass setting.

Czech Contemporaries of Haydn and Mozart in Vienna (*Vanhal*)

The very prolific and popular Bohemian composer **Johann Baptist Vanhal** (or Wanhal, etc.; 1739-1813) studied in Vienna with Dittersdorf[52] (from 1760), traveled to Italy, as the latter did, and at least on one occasion[53] played cello in a string quartet that included Haydn on first violin, Dittersdorf on second, and Mozart on viola.[54] A younger contemporary of Haydn, and a composer whose music Mozart played,[55] Vanhal became important first as a symphonist (from *ca.* 1767),[56] later turning more to church and lighter keyboard music (the category in which most of his sons. are written).[57] The researcher Margarethe Dewitz was able to find a total of 72 published keyboard sonatas by Vanhal, which date from a 33-year period, 1779 to 1812.[58]

49. Listed in BRITISH UNION II 661. Discussed in Torrefranca/ORIGINI 658-663 (with exx.) with regard to an Italian genesis of the minuet independent of Haydn. Mod. eds.: Sons. 4/iii, 5/ii, and 5/i, Pauer/MEISTER-m 10, 12, and 14, respectively.

50. Cf. Mooser/ANNALES II 487.

51. Weinmann/ARTARIA items 198 and 302. Op. 2 is listed in BRITISH UNION I 212.

52. DITTERSDORF 225.

53. Kelly/REMINISCENCES I 241.

54. Kelly/REMINISCENCES I 241. Dewitz/VANHAL is a study of the keyboard works, including a short biography (pp. 4-32), analysis of the sons. (pp. 35-65), list of keyboard works (sons. on pp. 123-124 and 134-135), and exx. Cf., also, GROVE VIII 668-669 (Černušak). The curious report in BURNEY'S TOURS II 120-121 was made while Vanhal was suffering mental illness.

55. Cf. Anderson/MOZART II 495.

56. Bryan/VANHAL is a detailed, unpublished diss. on 17 early symphonies, with 6 of these scored in full (vol. II), a helpful biographic summary (vol. I, pp. 1-17) and a summary of style traits (I 197-207), among other sections pertinent here.

57. Some idea of the considerable extent of his compositions may be had from the first 2 vols. of HOFMEISTER (i.e., Whistling); Eitner/QL X 174-178; BRITISH UNION II 1054-1056.

58. For 1779, cf. Johansson/FRENCH II Facs. 85.

About a third of these are easy solo or 4-hand piano sonatinas[59] published mostly in his last decade, a few with accompaniments. Among
the others, some are solos for harpsichord or piano (Opp. 18, 30, 43a,
100), but the majority are accompanied sonatas that qualify as real
duos (H-or-P + Vn ± Vc; Opp. 2, 9, 13, 43b, and others). There 59a
are also several earlier sets of solo/bass sonatas.[60] One of the accompanied sonatas is an early example with clarinet, published by Simrock in Bonn in 1806 (plate no. 473; Ex. 84). There are also a few lit- 60a

Ex. 84. From the opening of Johann Baptist Vanhal's *Sonata per il clavicembalo o piano-forte con clarinetto o violino obligato* (after the original Simrock ed. at the University of North Carolina).

eral programmatic "battle" sonatas for piano, such as "Sonate militaire" or "The Great Naval Battle at Aboukir from August 1 to 3, 1798," which latter starts with the High Admiralty's naming of Sir Horatio Nelson as commander of the fleet and ends with England celebrating its hero.

Neither the number and order of movements nor the individual forms are stereotyped in Vanhal's sonatas. Many have 3 movements,

59. Among mod. eds.: 7 short solo mvts. from Opp. 1 and 2, MAB-m No. 17.

60. Cf. BRITISH UNION II 1055. An "Adagio" from Son. 6 in a London set published in 1765 appears in Anth. CARTIER-m 282.

often with slow introductions leading in dotted rhythms to a dominant cadence, with flexible allegro "sonata forms" in the first movements,[61] with slow or moderate middle movements (frequently a minuet), and with finales in rondo, dance, or variation form. The sonatinas are usually in but 2 movements. Only 5 of the 72 sonatas are in minor keys and only keys of up to 4 sharps and 3 flats are used. By contrast with the "sonata forms" in Vanhal's early symphonies those in the sonatas have more clearly contrasted themes,[62] more actual development of these themes, including harmonic reorientations of them, and more complete recapitulations. Vanhal's melodic ideas are less interesting than Dittersdorf's and he strives less for clever harmonic surprises. But the total effect tends to be more convincing because the structures are more efficiently planned, with less repetition and rambling. Vanhal did write slow movements, although both these and the finales are of less consequence than the first movements. The gist of numerous contemporary reviews is that the sonatas are pleasing, fluent, and rather innocuous.[63]

The once celebrated Bohemian pianist and composer **Leopold Anton Koželuch** (1747-1818) was trained by his older, likewise
64a celebrated cousin J. A. Koželuch and by F. X. Dušek, among others.[64] When he reached Vienna, in 1778, he became another successor to Wagenseil as pianist and teacher, he probably went to Albrechtsberger for further instruction, and he took over Mozart's post at the imperial court in 1792. Among his almost countless works in nearly every category, published mostly in the 30 years between 1780 and 1810, are more than 100 sonatas for piano solo and perhaps as many more with
65a accompaniment or for 4 hands at one piano.[65] Many of these originally appeared in the 20 "Partien" of the periodical that he himself published from 1784 to 1802.[66] Considering the numerous re-editions of these

61. In 56 symphony movements that were analyzed all but 6 had the "basic" elements of "sonata form" (Bryan/VANHAL I 250-253).

62. Similar themes both within and between mvts. are found in the early symphonies (Bryan/VANHAL I 101-107).

63. E.g., AMZ III (1800-01) 628.

64. Cf. the detailed article in MGG VII 1660-1670 (Wessely).

65. Cf. the long list in MGG VII 1661-1666, including more than 2 columns of sonatas alone; also, the entries under almost every category in the first 2 vols. of HOFMEISTER (Whistling). Among mod. eds. (cf. MGG VII 1669 for many others): 2 acc'd. sons. (P & Vn & Vc), Op. 12/1 and 3, ORGANUM-m III Nos. 41 and 54; Son. in E♭ for piano solo, Op. 51/2, ORGANUM-m V No. 5; "Allegro" from Son. in F, Op. 35, MAB-m No. 17, p. 66. The confusion that still exists with the works of the cousin and in the usual problem of conflicting op. nos. could only be relieved by a thematic index. The unpublished diss. on the keyboard sons., by G. Löbl (Vienna, 1937; listed in MGG VII 1670), could not be procured here.

66. Weinmann/KOŽELUCH is a detailed catalogue of this periodical, with preface. The "Partien" include music by other composers, too. Two more "Partien" were issued by Ludwig Maisch in Vienna in 1810.

works in all the main centers of music, it is less surprising to find Gerber, in 1790, calling Koželuch deservedly the most popular living composer, young or old;[67] or to find another writer calling him, 5 years later, "the most celebrated [composer] in all of musical Europe during the past 10 years or so."[68] To be sure, 23 years later (1813) Gerber was already tempering his praise.[69] In fact, by then, Koželuch was fast becoming passé.[70] Although there has been a mild revival of interest in him in recent years, prompted partly by studies in the Classic symphony[71] and concerto and partly by nationalistic interests, one is only reminded how greatly such values can be affected by time and historical perspective.

Yet Gerber does seem justified when in 1790 he explains his admiration for Koželuch's music by viewing it as a compounding of "liveliness and grace, of the noblest melody with the purest harmony, and of the most agreeable organization in respect to rhythm and modulation."[72] Koželuch's sonatas might indeed be called models of Classic perfection in form, line, and fluency (Ex. 85). No skill is lacking, not even that of true "development," which proves to be little more than repetition and transposition in so many of the sonatas of the minor composers. In fact, Koželuch's writing might be called the ideal of the high-Classic style, provided one limits the word classic to mean a perfect balance and co-ordination of the means, and a "moderation in all things." His music is still high- rather than late-Classic because it has not yet settled into a mold. The "sonata forms" and other designs are still variable. So are the cycles as a whole. Sometimes a slow introduction is present (Op. 35/3); sometimes there are only two movements. One cannot expect always to find a more "usual" plan, such as "Allegro," "Poco Adagio," and "Rondeau Presto" (Op. 11/1).

But there is little difference between Koželuch's late and his early sonatas, unless it be a still smoother command of compositional skills in the late ones. In the sense of an original departure from tradition, nothing more unusual occurs throughout his sonatas than the introduction of some Scotch airs (Op. 52). There are gentle passages and strong ones; there are thinly scored passages and fully scored ones

67. Gerber/LEXICON I 750.
68. Trans. from the citation in MGG VII 1666.
69. Gerber/NEUES III 99-100.
70. There are 20 entries on him in AMZ from 1798-1808, one more entry 10 years later, which is his death notice, and not a single mention thereafter! Cf. AMZ II (1799-1800) 206.
71. As in Sondheimer/SINFONIE 99.
72. Gerber/LEXICON I 750. Cf., also, Burney/HISTORY II 960.

Ex. 85. From the opening of Sonata 2 in A, Op. 35, by Leopold Anton Koželuch (after the Bland ed., *ca.* 1793, at the University of North Carolina).

that exploit the instruments' idioms knowingly. But the music flows on essentially untroubled by deeper feelings and with no obstacles for the ready sightreader. In these respects it suggests Mendelssohn's music, or at least all but the greatest of his music. And it must be in these respects that Haydn, Mozart, and Beethoven were all contemptuous of Koželuch,[73] for the Classic ideal in the music of those masters is hardly restricted just to the perfect control and balance of the means.

Anton Kraft (1749-1820) is now remembered as the composer no longer to be credited with the cello Concerto in D that has recently been reinstated as Haydn's.[74] But in his own day he was recognized as one of the foremost cellists by his contemporaries, including Haydn, under whom he played and studied at Esterház.[75] About 1790 were published two sets, Opp. 1 and 2, of 3 Vc/bass sonatas each by Kraft.

73. Cf. Geiringer/HAYDN 74-75; Anderson/MOZART III 1119; Thayer/BEETHOVEN II 219. Koželuch's disregard, in turn, for these men is attributed in MGG VII 1667 partly to his higher social station.
74. Hoboken/HAYDN 529-531.
75. Cf. MGG VII 1679-1680.

In 1799 a reviewer dismissed Op. 2 briefly by saying that the sonatas were long but not important and that Haydn's teaching could hardly be recognized in the music.[76] The successful Singspiel composer **Ferdinand Kauer** (1751-1831), whom Haydn and Mozart knew as a none-too-careful editor for Artaria, left a programmatic *Sonata militaire* (1789),[77] an accompanied sonata (1798?),[78] six harp sonatas, and some teaching sonatas among his many works.[79] Mozart's influence has been noted in his music.[80] The violinist **Franz Christoph Neubauer** (1760-95) knew Haydn and Mozart while he was in Vienna and, in only the last half year of his short life, succeeded Friedrich Bach in Bückeburg. In the early 1790's he left at least four sets of sonatas for two stringed instruments (Vn & Va, Vn-or-Va & Vc, 2 Vns, 2 Vcs). These have considerable sparkle and
technical interest.[81] The three sonatas that were seen here (Op. 8, 81a
ca. 1798),[82] each in three movements in the usual order of F-S-F, give more technical and melodic responsibility to the violin than to the viola. Their revival would enrich the limited literature for this duet setting.

The brothers **Anton** (1761-1820) and **Paul Wranitzky** (1756-1808) were prolific composers and successful violinists well known to both Haydn and Mozart in Vienna (one or both as students of Haydn).[83] Their numerous solo, 4-hand, S/bass, SS/bass, and SS sonatas include a few that were published in the 1790's.[84] These sonatas have not been explored in recent times, but the importance especially of Paul in his own day[85] should justify a special study of them, insofar as their music can still be found.

The organist and violinist **Adalbert Gyrowetz** (1763-1850) was another highly successful, widely published, and extremely prolific musician, whose easy popularity ended almost overnight around 1826.[86]

76. AMZ II (1799-1800) 92-93.
77. Weinmann/KOŽELUCH 11.
78. Weinmann/ARTARIA item 764.
79. Cf. MGG VII 739-746 (Eva Badura-Skoda).
80. MGG VII 746.
81. Granting that these chamber works have more substance, K. M. Komma finds the influence of Haydn but otherwise finds little worth in Neubauer's music (MGG IX 1387-1388). In Riehl/CHARAKTERKÖPFE I 253-258 he is said to have composed himself to death and to have left his best works unpublished.
82. Listed in BRITISH UNION II 728.
83. Cf. Eitner/QL X 304-306; GROVE IX 370-371 (Černušak).
84. Cf. Weinmann/ARTARIA items 418-419 and Weinmann/KUNST item 364 for Anton; BRITISH UNION II 1091 for Paul; and Cat. BRUXELLES II 342 and IV 53 for both.
85. Cf. LaRue in ML XXXVII (1956) 250-252 and 259. The short account of him in Riehl/CHARAKTERKÖPFE 244-249 emphasizes a folk quality throughout his music.
86. It continued longer than 1820 (given by Landon in MGG VII 1156 and 1157),

Unlike Koželuch, he lived on another quarter of a century to realize how completely forgotten he had become, as related in his poignantly ingenuous autobiography published only two years before his death at eighty-seven.[87] Moreover, as compared with Koželuch, Gyrowetz was regarded more sympathetically by Haydn, Mozart, and Beethoven.[88] He wrote in relatively fewer categories of vocal and instrumental music, and his music evinces a little more imagination and independence of personality for all its equally slick, fluent superficiality.[89] He first visited Vienna around 1785 but did not settle there until 1793, after some eight years of travel and study in Italy and successful visits to important centers in other countries, including Paris, London (during Haydn's first visit), and German cities.

Most of Gyrowetz's instrumental works, mainly symphonies and chamber music, were composed by 1804 and most of his vocal works after this year. His almost exclusive contribution to the sonata was to the accompanied setting that led to the piano trio[90]—that is, piano with partially independent violin and rarely independent cello. He published over thirty-five such "sonatas," many for the London market,[91] between about 1790 and 1814.[92] Again, the forms are still not fixed. But typically these sonatas are in the usual three movements, F-S-F, often with a slow movement consisting of variations on a familiar tune (such as "Winde gentle Evergreen" in Op. 18/1/ii) and a rondo or march finale (such as the "Allegro" in rondo form, complete with "Minore," in Op. 25/2/iii). Reading through some of these sonatas in chronological order, one recognizes the successive influence of details in the music of Haydn, Mozart, Clementi, and even Beethoven. For more warmth and originality, and more independence of the cello than most of Gyrowetz's sonatas reveal, the three sonatas of Op. 37 do deserve the exceptional praise given them by a reviewer in 1801.[93]

The violinist **Wenzel Pichl** (1741-1804) was in Vienna from

---

as revealed by AMZ entries through 1826, but the interest in his instrumental music seems to have died out 10 years earlier.

87. Reprinted in Einstein/GYROWETZ, this interesting record of a widely known Classic musician should be made available in English. Cf., also, MGG V 1146-1158, with frequent extracts from the autobiography.

88. Cf. Einstein/GYROWETZ 11-13, 16-17, 75-76, 121.

89. In Riehl/CHARAKTERKÖPFE I 227-235 only the superficiality and great extent of his music are emphasized; cf. *infra,* under Rosetti.

90. A 2-piano son. is favorably reviewed in AMZ XVIII (1816) 208-210.

91. Einstein/GYROWETZ 71, 78, 115.

92. Cf. MGG V 1153-1154. The only pertinent mod. ed. known here is that of a similarly scored "Divertissement" in A (1802? ORGANUM-m III No. 43), although its 5 short mvts. (S-M-M-S-F) make it more like a suite than a son. of that time.

93. AMZ III (1800-01) 490-492. An example of a disdainful, curt review of his sons. (Op. 28) may be seen in AMZ II (1799-1800) 138.

1771-75 and 1796-1804, and in Italy in the twenty-one intervening years.[94] He had previously played under Dittersdorf in Hungary, knew Haydn,[95] and presumably knew Beethoven in Vienna, since he traveled in the same circles. Among his 700 works and wide publications several types of sonatas are extant.[96] These include a set of 6 sonatas for 2 violins alone, Op. 4 (Berlin, *ca.* 1775); 3 accompanied sonatas like those of Gyrowetz that border on the piano trio, Op. 26 (London, 1796); a piano sonata in MS; and 2 SS/bass "Sonate notturne" (Fl, Vn/Vc) in a Milan MS that could well have been modeled after pieces of the same type and title by G. B. Sammartini. The 3 sonatas in Op. 26 show about the same independence in the accompaniments that Gyrowetz's do. They have Mozartean traits—especially the chromaticism, feminine cadences, and thin accurate texture—and are a cut above the average by the minor Viennese composers in their ingratiating ideas and expressive harmony. A new study of this music would be rewarding.[97]

The last in this group of Czechs to mention, Abbé **Joseph Gelinek** (1758-1825) was praised by Mozart for his improvisations at the piano and his counsel was sought by the young Beethoven when the lessons with Haydn were proving unsatisfactory, although this latter relationship quickly deteriorated.[98] Gelinek left only a few original works, including some solo and accompanied piano sonatas published in the decade from 1794 to 1804 and received as agreeable, fluent pieces.[99] He left much more and made more of a reputation in the realm of arrangements, potpourris, and variations based on the music of others.[100] Among these were several further "sonatas." An example is "Grande Sonate pour Le Forte-Piano . . . tirée d'une Symphonie composées par W. A. Mozart" (Artaria, 1806), which proves to be an excellent reduction of the Symphony in g (K.V. 550).[101] Other "sonatas" were arranged, and published as late as 1816, from operas or chamber music by Mozart, Viotti, and Hänsel.[102]

94. Cf. GROVE VI 759-760 (Černušak); AMZ VII (1804-05) 316-317.
95. Cf. Landon/HAYDN 212.
96. Cf. the listings in Eitner/QL VII 439-440; BRITISH UNION II 783-784.
97. An unpublished Vienna diss. (1918) by Robert Kolisko, on Pichl's chamber music, could not be seen here.
98. Cf. MGG IV 1630-1633 (Komma and Vernillat); Nettl/FORGOTTEN 272-276; Nettl/BEETHOVEN 69-70; CZERNY 303-304.
99. Sample listings are items 603, 608, 740, and 1518 in Weinmann/ARTARIA. For a sample review (Op. 2), cf. AMZ I (1798-99) 735.
100. Cf. the long lists in HOFMEISTER I and II (Whistling) *passim*.
101. A copy is still to be found in the Milan Conservatorio de Musica.
102. Cf. Weinmann/KUNST item 51; Weinmann/ARTARIA items 1623, 1791, 1271, 2456.

Viennese Contemporaries of Beethoven (Wölfl)

The brilliant pianist **Joseph Wölfl** (1773-1812) has remained in historical view chiefly because of his rivalry with Beethoven in performance (SCE XV) and because of some largely romanticized and false legends about him.[103] This association with Beethoven and possibly a little polishing from Mozart in 1790[104] explain Wölfl's identification with Vienna. But he was born in Salzburg, did his basic training there with Leopold Mozart and Michael Haydn, and spent much of his short life in other centers, including nearly 4 years in Paris (1801-05) and the last 7 years in London. Along with operas and other vocal music, symphonies, concertos, quartets, trios, and many short piano pieces, he left around 125 sonatas. Most of these last were published, originally in the 15 years from 1795 to 1810. About 48 per cent (or 60) are for piano alone; 44 per cent (or 55) are accompanied by violin or flute, sometimes with cello added; 5 per cent (or 6) are for 4 hands at one piano; and most of the remaining 3 per cent (or 4) are for harp, alone or accompanied.[105]

One of Wölfl's sonatas is his arrangement, for 4 hands and optional violin or flute, of his own Symphony in g. Several incorporate variations on familiar tunes, such as Op. 38 on "Scotch Airs" or Op. 61 on "With the Manly Heart." There are also Op. 14, based on themes
105a from Haydn's *Creation,* and the *Grand Sonata for the Harp, in Which Is Introduced a Favorite Air of* [Mozart's] *Cosi fan tutte.* Beethoven is implied to have respected Wölfl,[106] though he seems to have been contemptuous of the aims and music of men like Gelinek (as we have seen) and Steibelt.[107] As for Wölfl, even before the peak of his pianistic rivalry with Beethoven, in 1799, he had dedicated 3 sonatas to Beethoven (Op. 6 [not 7], 1798), which already show some influences from Beethoven's Op. 2 and which, incidentally, brought him a strongly favorable first review.[108]

The majority of Wölfl's sonatas follow the 3-movement plan of F-S-VF, but a few have a minuet finale, or only 2 movements, or a fugue

103. The 2 best sources on Wölfl and his music are GROVE IX 324-327 (Mee), though portions of the same article as it appeared in the first and 2d eds. are deleted and the original detailed, dated list of works is merely summarized; and Baum/WÖLFL, a diss. (1928) on the keyboard works.

104. HORTUS MUSICUS-m No. 111 2 (Längin).

105. In spite of the care that went into them, the lists of works in the early eds. of GROVE and in Baum/WÖLFL 72-74 and 80 do not tally completely. There are still duplications and conflicting op. nos. that only a thematic index would clarify.

106. Thayer/BEETHOVEN I 216.

107. Thayer/BEETHOVEN I 152 and 268. Cf. Baum/WÖLFL 16.

108. AMZ I (1798-99) 236-238; cf. SCE III. Cf. Baum/WÖLFL 18.

as a fourth movement.[109] Most of the few sonatas in minor keys follow the new Romantic tendency to put the finale in major (as already in Op. 3/3, 1797). The "sonata forms" remain flexible in their thematic relationships and dispositions, with true development being exceptional. In the middle movements—in either dominant or either mediant key—variation or simple song forms are used. The finales, always lighter than the preceding movements, are in rondo or variation forms.

Richard Baum discusses Wölfl's sonatas according to three types: (1) conventional, vapid imitations of Mozart and less distinguished contemporaries (e.g., Op. 27/2); (2) subjective, dramatic expressions of his best creative powers; and (3) virtuoso display pieces.[110] Best known in the last category is the banal Sonata in F, Op. 41, which was first published by Lavenu in London about 1807[111] and could still be heard at the Popular Concerts "several times between 1859 and 1873" (according to Shedlock, who grouped Wölfl with Steibelt and Cramer as mere "sonata-makers" on its account[112]). The oft-repeated story goes that Wölfl dubbed this sonata "Non plus ultra" when the publisher complained that no one else could manage its many double-note passages and other deliberate difficulties, whereupon Dussek's much better and still more difficult Sonata in A-flat, "Le Retour a
Paris," was published in London the next year as "Plus ultra" and 112a
dedicated to "Ne Plus Ultra."[113]

In the subjective category Wölfl demonstrated that he was capable of much better composing. Included here are two of his best sonatas, both significantly in minor keys, and the only two available in modern editions. One is the songful, effective 3-movement Sonata in d, Op. 31, for piano and cello (Paris, 1805), which could well be added to the limited cello repertoire of the period (outside of Beethoven's contributions).[114] The other is the *Sonate précédée d'une Introduction & Fugue* in c for piano, originally published in its entirety as the twelfth volume in Anth. NÄGELI-m (*ca.* 1805, after vol. 11 with Beethoven's Opp. 13 and 31/3).[115] The slow, tonally rich "Introduzione" in this interesting work is but one of numerous late-Classic and early-Romantic pieces that hark back to Mozart's "Fantaisie" in the same key, K.V. 475. The 4-voice "Fuga" on the same idea is skillful and some-

109. Baum/WÖLFL 30-31.
110. Baum/WÖLFL 34-42.
111. GROVE 2d ed. III 389 (Grove).
112. Shedlock/SONATA 192-193.
113. Cf. Shedlock/SONATA 149-150, with further references.
114. Mod. ed.: HORTUS MUSICUS-m No. 111 (Längin), with preface.
115. The "Introduction & Fugue" were first published apart from the son. as Op. 9 (1803? cf. Baum/WÖLFL 37-41). The whole work was later published as Op. 25. Mod. ed.: Newman/THIRTEEN-m 90, with preface (pp. 18-20).

what academic. It may have been included to satisfy Nägeli's desires (cf. SCE II; it is interesting that the finale in the "Non plus ultra" sonata was a set of variations on Nägeli's tune "Freut euch des Lebens"[116]). The "Allegro molto" of the sonata proper has much of the c-minor drive and character of Beethoven's *Sonate pathétique,* although it goes more and farther afield tonally. Next comes one of the many late-Classic slow movements in A♭ that recall the corresponding movement in Beethoven's same work (or in Op. 10/1/ii), but again with more remote modulations. And the finale similarly recalls Beethoven's Op. 13/iii, though the sectional organization is more complex—A-B-A-C-A-D-A-B-C-coda. In this movement the right-hand double-notes and stretches would still be considered difficult to play.

The Bohemian flutist **Antonín Reicha** (1770-1836) still survives in the dictionaries, as a theorist, composer of chamber music, and intimate friend of Beethoven, both in Bonn (from 1788) and in Vienna
117a (1794 and 1802-08).[117] Only a few of Reicha's numerous sonatas
118a can be found now, all for piano with and without accompaniment.[118]
These deserve more of the attention that has been paid to the quintets.[119] They reveal the same melodic wealth, folk elements, and freshness that were noted by a contemporary critic in seven other solo and accompanied sonatas by Reicha.[120] Representative is the theme from an accompanied sonata published in 1804, close to the true piano trio (Ex. 86).

The Bavarian pianist **Franz Xaver Kleinheinz** (1765-1832) was in Vienna from 1799 to 1805 and occasionally later.[121] There he seems to have been well regarded by Beethoven, to have arranged some of the latter's chamber (and keyboard?) music in quartet and accompanied keyboard settings,[122] and to have taught piano, probably on Beethoven's recommendation, in the Brunsvik family. At least seventeen sonatas by Kleinheinz are known, dating from an early work in 1783 to the Vienna publications of 1800-04.[123] These

116. SPOHR I 236.

117. Cf. Thayer/BEETHOVEN I 106-107; GROVE VII 106-108 (Chouquet); Demuth/REICHA; Prod'homme/REICHA (publication of a partial autobiography).

118. E.g., one acc'd. and 5 solo sons. are listed in Cat. BRUXELLES IV 9 and 186. The 10-page "Rondo" of a Piano Son. in B♭, Op. 46, is reprinted in MAB-m No. 20, p. 39. Cf., also, Eitner/QL VIII 160-161 (including several sons. at the Vienna Gesellschaft der Musikfreunde).

119. An unpublished diss. on the quintets was completed in 1952 by M. M. Laing at the University of Michigan.

120. AMZ IX (1806-07) 137-139.

121. Sandberger/AUFSÄTZE II 226-247 is the chief study (including a survey and list of works, pp. 227-228 and 232-237), supplemented by Haraszti/KLEINHEINZ. Cf., also, MGG VII 1207-1208 (Jancik).

122. Cf. Kinsky & Halm/BEETHOVEN 98 and 152; Sandberger/AUFSÄTZE II 232.

123. In addition to the previous references cf. Weinmann/ARTARIA items 938

Ex. 86. From the "Finale" of Antonín Reicha's *Sonata pour piano forte avec accompagnement de violon et violoncelle,* Op. 47 (after the original Breitkopf & Härtel ed. at the British Museum).

include solo and accompanied piano sonatas as well as one each for four hands at one and two pianos. Sandberger regards Kleinheinz's ideas as attractive but sees weaknesses in their working out and organization.[124] He detects Mozart's influence in some of the Viennese sonatas, and Beethoven's in others (especially the acc'd. "Fantaisie Sonate" in E♭, Op. 7 [1801], and the acc'd. Son. Op. 9).

---

and 1633; Weinmann/KUNST items 16, 41, 45. Some of these sons. are preserved at the Gesellschaft der Musikfreunde in Vienna.

124. Sandberger/AUFSÄTZE II 240-245 (including a partly favorable, contemporary review of Op. 5).

The dilettante Count **Wenzel Robert Gallenberg** (1783-1839), who married Giulietta Guicciardi (dedicatee of Beethoven's "Moonlight" sonata), published two piano sonatas in 1802, Opp. 12 and 15.[125] He was a prolific, modish composer, described by one contemporary as a slavish imitator, if not a literal copier, of Mozart and Cherubini.[126] Another prolific, modish composer was **Franz Vinzenz Krommer** (1759-1831), in Vienna from 1794 and one of the most successful Czech emigrants of the late-Classic Era.[127] In two sonatas that could be examined here (Opp. 27 and 32) out of at least ten for one or two strings and piano that were published in the opening years of the nineteenth century, the melodies are well shaped although bordering on the obvious, and the passage work already shows some of the early-Romantic pleasure in salon virtuosity. Another Czech, the capable cellist **Vincenz Hauschka** (1766-1840), in Vienna before 1793, was close to Beethoven and perhaps Haydn, whose music and that of Mozart he did much to promote in Vienna early in the nineteenth century.[128] Among his few extant works are two sets of three Vc/bass sonatas each, Opp. 1 and 2, both published in Vienna in 1803.[129] These are said to exploit the cello well but to be weak in content.[130]

It has not been possible here to see the single publication of nine solo and six accompanied piano sonatas or the once very successful "Battle of Leipzig" sonata among many other works published around 1805-25 by the director and composer **Philipp Jacob Riotte** (1776-1856; in Vienna from 1809).[131] Nor has it been possible to see any of the many light solo and accompanied piano sonatas published about the same time by **Maximilian Joseph Leidesdorf** (1787-1840), a pianist, guitarist,[132] and friend of both Beethoven and Schubert.[133] Leidesdorf was one of the fifty contributors to the "other" set of "Diabelli Variations," which, like Beethoven's great set, was collected and published by another friend of both Beethoven and Schubert, **Anton Diabelli** (1781-1858). Diabelli was born near Salzburg, studied composition with Michael Haydn, began

125. Cf. MGG IV 1274-1276 (Landon); Weinmann/ARTARIA item 1504 and p. 143.
126. AMZ VI (1803-04) 467-468.
127. Cf. MGG VII 1815-1822 (Wessely).
128. Cf. MGG V 1835-1836 (Komma).
129. Weinmann/KUNST items 77 and 217.
130. MGG V 1835-1836.
131. Cf. GROVE VII 181 (Grove); Riemann/LEXIKON II 1524-1525; HOFMEISTER I and II *passim* (Whistling). An intriguing, favorable review of 2 large-scale, "grandes Sonates," Op. 3, appeared in AMZ IX (1806-07) 92-94.
132. Cf. Bone/GUITAR 207.
133. Cf. MGG VIII 515-516 (Schmutzenhofer), including reference to a mod. ed. of 1920 (P & Fl).

teaching piano and guitar[134] in Vienna about 1804, and joined with Cappi in the publishing business in 1818.[135] But though he seems to have composed with the public taste very much in mind, his own firm published but few of the many sonatas and sonatinas for piano, solo and four hands, and for guitar that he composed. These had already begun to appear about 1805 from the Viennese firms of Mechetti, Steiner, and Haslinger.[136] Only Diabelli's hardy little two-movement piano sonatinas, both solo and four-hand, have survived today, still helping to build young students. But it is at least a matter of curiosity to note Diabelli's "Three Anniversary Sonatas" for vocal soloist and guitar accompaniment, both the text and music of which were ridiculed by a critic in 1806;[137] or his "Sonatinas for Piano in All the Major and Minor Keys,"
Op. 50, the first two of which were reviewed more sympathetically;[138] 138a
or the sonatas by him that figure among the many pieces written around Rossini arias in the 1820's.[139]

Mozart's second surviving and only musically successful son, born scarcely fourteen weeks before his father's death, returned to Vienna frequently during his unsettled, migratory career. Renamed by his mother in his father's honor and closely resembling him, **Wolfgang Amadeus Mozart** "the Younger" (1791-1844) apparently found the weight of his heritage to be the chief impediment to his own self-confidence and independent creative abilities.[140] Among nearly sixty instrumental and vocal works credited to him, four sonatas were published between 1808 and 1820, three of which are accompanied (Opp. 7, 15, and 19) and one solo (Op. 10). There is also an unpublished "Rondo" in G for flute and piano from what may have been a Sonata in e.[141] Op. 19, in three movements (F-S-F), provides an alternative cello part for the "Violon obligé," in the then frequent manner. This sonata has more musical substance and breadth than its predecessors, or than most of the other late-Classic sonatas mentioned thus far in this chapter. It would stand up reasonably well in a revival today. Its considerable contrapuntal and dialogic interest reflect the son's training

134. Cf. Bone/GUITAR 96-98.
135. Cf. MGG III 388-391 (Kahl).
136. Cf. HOFMEISTER I and II *passim* (Whistling). Op. 38 was published before 1815, Op. 85 before 1828, and Op. 152 before 1833.
137. AMZ VIII (1805-06) 239-240.
138. AMZ XXVIII (1826) 659-660.
139. Cf. HOFMEISTER II 585 (Whistling).
140. Hummel/MOZART is a full study of both Carl Thomas and this son, including exceptionally rich and interesting documents and a careful list of works (314-319); cf., also, MGG IX 689-692 (Hummel). Several shorter studies of the younger son had been done previously; Geiringer/MOZART includes brief descriptions of the works.
141. Cf. Geiringer/MOZART 468; Hummel/MOZART 318.

Ex. 87. From the first movement of *Grande Sonate* in E, Op. 19, by Wolfgang Amadeus Mozart the Younger (after the original Peters ed. at the Library of Congress).

with Salieri, Albrechtsberger, Mederitsch, and others; and the good keyboard writing reflects Hummel's teaching and his own high skill as pianist and teacher (Ex. 87). But any comparison with his father's music would naturally be to his disadvantage, as was observed in a review of Op. 10.[142] One would point to certain traits, admittedly more common to the late-Classic style, such as a neutral flatness in the ideas, a squareness in the phrase grouping, an emptiness in the passage work, and an ineptness in the development of material.

142. AMZ XI (1808-09) 54-55; in XVI (1814) 764 (or 832!) Op. 15 is reviewed as a pleasing pedagogic piece.

Three More Guitarists in Vienna

Besides Leidesdorf and Diabelli there were several others in Vienna around the same time who were celebrated for their guitar playing and composing, using both the standard Spanish guitar and M. Giuliani's shorter variant known as the "terz chitarra."[143] Much of their music is hard to find today, even in the larger libraries, and much of it is too light and inconsequential to bear a revival. But the fact of its lively cultivation can hardly be overlooked in any historical view of the sonata at this time and place. After all, Beethoven was interested enough to learn well the technicalities of the mandolin and guitar[144] in the two sonatinas that he wrote.

Simon Joseph Molitor (1766-1848) was a German of broad musical training who came to Vienna about 1802 after serving in Venice.[145] Among songs, methods, and other works, he left six separate, three-movement sonatas (F-S-F), of which Opp. 3, 5, 7, and 11 were published in Vienna between 1804 and 1809, while Opp. 12 and 15 were left in MS.[146] The first two of these graceful, light, but not undeveloped pieces are actually violin sonatas with guitar accompaniment, the rest being for guitar alone. In the course of a lengthy historical preface to Op. 7 (1807), "Grand Sonata for the Guitar Alone, [composed] as an example of a better treatment of this instrument," Molitor remarked that he knew of no one who had yet shown in detail, as for other chordal instruments, how to compose the proper harmonic texture for this instrument.[147]

The Bohemian **Wenzeslaus Thomas Matiegka** (1773-1830) and the Italian **Matteo Paolo Bevilaqua** (1772-1849), both in Vienna from about 1800, were two other highly esteemed performers and
composers of guitar sonatas.[148] Finally, **Mauro Giuliani** (1780- 148a
1829) has been called by P. J. Bone "the most renowned of Italian guitarists and one of the most brilliant guitar virtuosi the world has known."[149] He was in Vienna from 1807-21, during which time were

143. Cf. Bone/GUITAR 96-97.

144. Cf. Bone/GUITAR 23 and 26.

145. Zuth/MOLITOR is an excellent published diss. (1919), including documents, analyses, a critical list of works, and an appendix (pp. 69-85) on 22 other guitarists in the Vienna circle. Cf., also., MGG IX 437-438 (Kollpacker), with further references.

146. Cf. Zuth/MOLITOR 19-22 (with facs. of pp. from Opp. 12 and 15 among the unnumbered plates at the end). Mod. ed. of all 6 sons. and a "Rondeau": Zuth/GITARREMUSIK-m.

147. Cf. Zuth/MOLITOR 8.

148. Cf. MGG VIII 1789 (Kramer); Zuth/MOLITOR 69-71; HOFMEISTER I and II *passim* (Whistling); Bone/GUITAR 225-226, 37.

149. Bone/GUITAR 137-145 (much the most thorough account to date). Re-

published numerous sonatas and most of nearly 300 other works for
150a guitar alone or in ensemble.[150] Although this musician, whom even Beethoven admired,[151] implied too much with titles like "Grand Sonata eroica," such examples as could be examined here do reveal more melodic and harmonic character, more originality in the ideas, and more ingenuity in the scoring for guitar than in the guitar music of his Viennese contemporaries.

South German Centers (Rosetti, C. Stamitz, Vogler)

Starting our German survey in the south, as we did in Chapter XI, we may stop first at the busy little court of Öttingen-Wallerstein, where previously we met the dilettante Beecke. This time, with Beecke still alive but often absent, the chief figure of interest to us is the Bohemian composer **Franz Anton Rosetti** (actually Rössler; 1750-92), who came on the scene the same year as Count (soon to be Prince) Kraft Ernst began his reign, in 1773.[152] During the next sixteen years Rosetti advanced from double bass player to *Kapellmeister* (1785), he traveled to Paris (1781-82) and elsewhere, and the court attained its musical heyday in the eighteenth century. Rosetti spent his last three years (1789-92) at the north German court of Mecklenburg-Schwerin in Ludwigslust. Operas, oratorios, symphonies, concertos, and varied types of chamber music comprise the categories of music that he left.[153] Under the last of these categories come his sonatas. All the extant ones, which began to appear about 1781 from London and Paris during his Paris trip,[154] are of the accompanied type (H-or-P & Vn-or-Fl, sometimes with Vc). At least nineteen of these and at least two different published sets have been identified.[155] The violin parts, often marked one degree softer than the keyboard parts, are subordinate to the point of being dispensable. When there is a cello part it merely provides the usual reinforcement of the keyboard bass.

---

garding Giuliani's relation to F. Sor and confusions in the biographies, cf. Sasser/SOR 65 and 67-68.

150. Cf. the many items listed in HOFMEISTER I and II *passim* (Whistling).

151. Bone/GUITAR 139.

152. Rosetti was discussed briefly in 1907 in Schiedermair/WALLERSTEIN 92-96 (cf., also, p. 85); but the principal study of the man and his instrumental music is the detailed preface to DTB-m XII/1 (Kaul), with addenda in DTB-m XXV.

153. A thematic index of the instrumental works, both published and MS, is given in DTB-m XII/1 lix-lxvi.

154. Cf. Johansson/FRENCH II Facs. 86; BRITISH UNION II 901.

155. The lists in DTB-m XII/1 lxv-lxvi (plus 2 more early eds. in XXV xviii) leave much collating, resolving of conflicting op. nos., and checking of further sources to be done; the solo keyboard sons. in these lists are probably acc'd. sons. published without the accompaniments. Mod. ed.: Son. in C (4/b/1/4 in Kaul's list, but called "Trio" here), DTB-m XXV 107.

The number, order, and forms of the movements in Rosetti's sonatas are still in a fluid state. But one can generalize to the effect that the forms are short and clear, the technical requirements are slight, the textures are thin, the melodies are almost naïvely forthright and simple, and the total effect is spontaneous, genuine, happy, and surprisingly telling for its minimal means (such as the start on IV^6_4 in Ex. 88).

Ex. 88. From the final, third movement of Sonata in A (no. 4/c/1/2 in Kaul's index; Op. 6/2 in some eds.) by Franz Anton Rosetti (after the Zatta ed. at the Library of Congress).

The approving judgment by the nineteenth-century German writer W. H. von Riehl still seems valid:

Whoever wants to find a follower of Haydn that is still altogether youthful and still free of the formulas of the Vienna school should study the larger instrumental works of Antonio Rosetti, as against [those of] Gyrowetz, who already marks the decline of this school in his later works. . . . Rosetti seeks to transform into a cheerful overflow of instrumental lyricism all the sweetness, gentleness, and songfulness of the epic poet Haydn. His basic nature is friendly, intimate, youthful delicacy [*Weiblichkeit*]. Where he begins to strike a tone of lamentation or sorrow, it never seems to be really serious with him, and the wag lurks behind it. His writing still does not have any of the mechanical, irksome, conventional formalisms of Haydn's later pupils. His phrase structure is much more often so concisely put together that it recalls Haydn's earliest period, when one was still satisfied if a melodic idea rounded off in four to six measures. He is the German Boccherini. . . . In his smaller works Rosetti is often much weaker in technique than Pleyel. But he was no dull Philistine, such as this other finally became.[156]

Rosetti's smaller works—that is, sonatas—may be less consequential than his symphonies and concertos, as both Riehl and Kaul suggest, but they are certainly deserving of the study they have not yet had.[157]

Our return to Mannheim (SCE XI) finds the "Tonschule" in a state of decline after the transfer of the elector palatine Karl Theodor and his court to Munich in 1778.[158] Yet Mannheim was not without its later generation of active composers, including three who find their places here. The brilliant violinist and older son of Johann Stamitz, **Carl Stamitz** (1745-1801), was actually active in Mannheim only from 1762 to 1770, after which he spent much of his life as a traveling virtuoso in Paris, London, St. Petersburg, and other centers, finally to settle from 1794 in Jena.[159] Moreover, nearly all his publications seem to have appeared after he left Mannheim. Yet his training under his father and Richter, and the fact that no other place can be called his home until late in his life, leave him identified primarily with Mannheim.

Along with many more symphonies, quintets, quartets, SS/bass trios, and a variety of unaccompanied duos, Riemann discovered 31 works called "sonata" by Carl Stamitz, mostly of the accompanied type.[160] About half were published during the composer's lifetime, in the decade from about 1780 to 1790.[161] Included are a set of "Six Sonates en trio," Op. 15 (K & Vn & "basse"); 3 sets of 3, 5, and 6 accompanied sonatas (H-or-P & Vn; Opp. 17 and 20, and MS, respectively), the sixth sonata in Op. 20 being for 2 harpsichords;[162] 2 more sonatas for 2 harpsichords, in MSS;[163] 3 Vn/bass sonatas in MS; a sonata for keyboard and "Alto Viola obligé" in B♭;[164] and 4

156. Trans. from Riehl/CHARAKTERKÖPFE I 235-239.
157. Kaul gives only one paragraph to the sons. in each vol., DTB-m XII/1 liii and XXV xv.
158. Cf. MGG VIII 1598-1599 (Schmitt).
159. Brief summaries of his life are given in DTB-m VII/2 xii-xiii (Riemann) and GROVE VIII 43 (Gradenwitz).
160. A thematic index and a collation of publications are in DTB-m XVI xlvi-li and xx-xxi, respectively.
161. The approximate dates are based on listings in BRITISH UNION II 971-972.
162. Mod. ed.: Sons. 1-5, Op. 20, Riemann/STAMITZ-m.
163. Riemann seems not to have known the son. for 4 hands at one piano listed in Cat. BRUXELLES II item 6211. In 1964 Alan Curtis wrote me that it is lost.
164. Mod. ed.: Lenzewski/STAMITZ-m.

sonatas for viola d'amore and one or more accompanying instruments, two of these using *scordatura* in the solo part.[165]

The "Sonata par la Viola d'amore e Basso" by Carl Stamitz that Riemann published for the first time is a virtuoso, four-movement work that still has elements of the old church sonata and the binary design of its separate movements. By contrast, the sonata with "alto viola obligé" is in three movements, the five accompanied sonatas in Op. 20 are in only two movements, and these are all light pieces, close to Mozart's music in their style, and more modern in their forms. The first movements have the clear second themes and a taste of the development in "sonata form," though the recapitulation usually starts only with the second theme, in the older Mannheim fashion (Son. 4/i being an exception in having a full recapitulation). The finales in Op. 20 are all rondos. Although the violin accompaniments are subordinate, their dialogic interchanges with the piano are missed when these parts are omitted. Carl Stamitz's music moves well but lacks the genuine fresh sparkle of Rosetti's music. Mozart had nothing good to say about him or his younger brother Anton (who also left a few sonatas).[166]

The Abbé **Georg Joseph Vogler** (1749-1814) is another who lived in Mannheim only a few years (1775-80) and published most of his sonatas afterward, yet must remain identified with that center as the starting point for the restless though largely successful career that kept him on the go almost to the end of his life. He was important as a teacher (of Weber and Meyerbeer, among others), organ builder, theorist, organist, and composer, probably in that order. It would be tempting to comment further on him in these capacities or as a world traveler, a romantic adventurer, an iconoclast if not a revolutionary, a pantologist, and even something of a charlatan. But his many compositions, written in most of the usual categories of his day, are hardly important enough in themselves to justify such digressions here, or the numerous books on him that have been written,[167] or Browning's great musical poem honoring the improvisation at the organ by "Abt Vogler."[168]

165. Cf. DTB-m XVI xlix, 113 (mod. ed. of Son. in D); XV xxii-xxiii (explanation of the *scordatura*). Cf. Altmann/KAMMERMUSIK 250 for other mod. eds.

166. Cf. Anderson/MOZART II 838.

167. Cf. the high praise of Vogler, mixed with reflections on the evils of prolificity, in Schubart/IDEEN 133-136.

168. The most comprehensive treatment of the man and his works, both theoretical and musical, is still Schafhäutl/VOGLER, including a full, indexed list of compositions (mostly dated) on pp. 245-286. The 1904 Berlin diss. Simon/VOGLER surveys this music by categories, with brief descriptions of the sons. on pp. 11-13. An extended list of many of the works appears in Nisser/SVENSK 398-431. Cf., also, GROVE IX 38-42 (Mee; with summary of the works); BAKER'S DICTIONARY 1722 (with further bibliography).

In all, 42 works by Vogler that he called "sonata" can be accounted for, most of them accompanied and most of them published in his lifetime, between 1779 and 1796.[169] His first published sonatas appeared in the 3 "Jahrgängen" of his own *Betrachtungen der Mannheimer Tonschule,* 1778-80.[170] There is a set of *Sei sonate facile di cembalo col' accompagnamento d'un violino a piacere* (Op. 2 or 3, 1779), plus 7 more accompanied sonatas in MS. The instances when these accompaniments are important to the texture (as in the dialogic exchanges in the "development" of Op. 3/2/i) are few. There is a set of 6 solo keyboard sonatas with accompaniments of from 1-4 instruments that can be added optionally or can combine to make an independent quartet without the keyboard (Op. 4?[171]). There are 2 sets of 6 accompanied sonatas each (Opp. 6 and 7, 1782?[172]) and 4 more such sonatas in MS, the violin and cello parts of which are independent enough to qualify these sonatas as piano trios. There is a set of 6 sonatas for 2 keyboard instruments (no op. no., 1794?),[173] the last of which turns out to be a fanciful, elaborately edited concerto for 2 pianos with orchestral "ritornelli." And there is a programmatic sonata published twice in 1796, once for piano with string quartet as "La Brouillarie entre mari et femme" (Metzger in Paris), and once for quartet alone as "Der eheliche Zwist" (Breitkopf & Härtel in Leipzig).[174] In this work, the ideal connubial bliss depicted by the gentle, songful introduction is shattered by the furious, scolding quarrel in the allegro first movement, at last to be restored in the calm andante that follows.

Most of Vogler's sonatas are in two movements. In at least one three-movement sonata the finale is in a new key (G instead of B♭).[175] The finale is most often a light rondo, and it is in his rondos that Vogler's best ideas and most convincing designs are to be found (Ex. 89). By sampling such pieces one can well believe that Vogler was influenced by Mysliveček, with whom he studied in Italy. But there are crudities in the writing, especially in his earlier sonatas (Op. 3),

169. The thematic index and the list of publications in DTB-m XVI lviii-lxi and xxiv-xxv give the fullest available information; but Op. 2 was also published as Op. 3, and the 6 sons. for 2 pianos (Bossler, plate no. 265, 1794?) should be added (as listed in BRITISH UNION II 1049).

170. Cf. Schafhäutl/VOGLER 289-292.

171. Cf. DTB-m XVI xxiv.

172. Johansson/FRENCH II Facs. 22.

173. Perhaps the 4-hand sons. published by Boyer in Paris in 1785 (Johansson/FRENCH II Facs. 92) are identical with some or all of these. In 1778 Mozart already mentioned playing Vogler's "tedious engraved sonatas" with Vogler accompanying at another keyboard (Anderson/MOZART II 662). What ed. or set this was is not known.

174. Cf. Schafhäutl/VOGLER 263; Simon/VOGLER 12-13.

175. Simon/VOGLER 12.

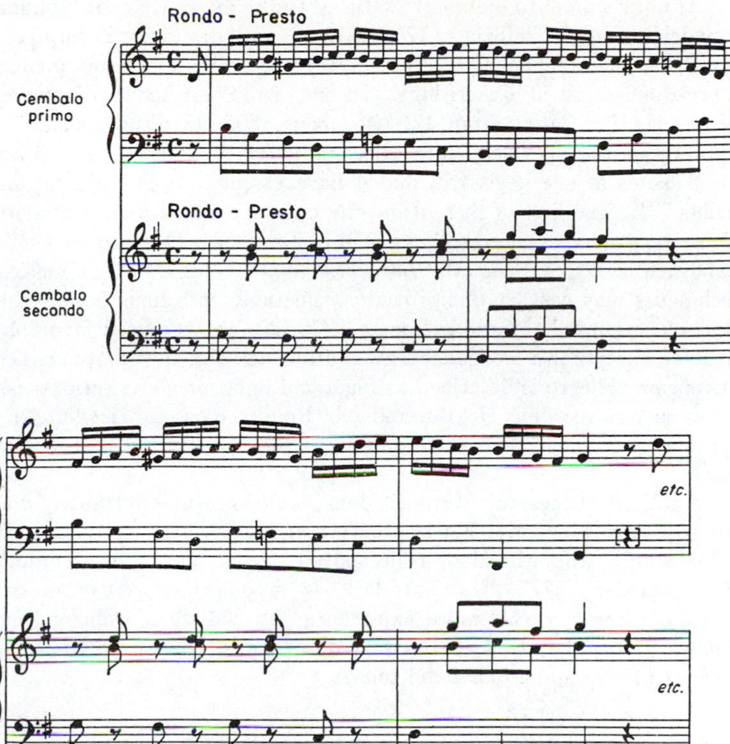

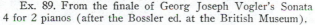

Ex. 89. From the finale of Georg Joseph Vogler's Sonata 4 for 2 pianos (after the Bossler ed. at the British Museum).

that might also be expected of a composer who was impatient with the more solid academic foundation that Vallotti and Martini wanted to give him during those same years in Italy (1773-75).[176] In Vogler's Mannheim years, Mozart felt no better toward him than toward Carl Stamitz, calling the former "a dreary musical jester, an exceedingly conceited and rather incompetent fellow."[177] It is true that whatever originality is to be found in Vogler's sonatas must be classified more as novelty and whimsy than as any fresh insight into musical values. They hardly have the "passionate" quality that would "set the blood in motion," to quote his own standards for the symphony in 1778.[178]

176. Cf. Schafhäutl/VOGLER 7-9.
177. Anderson/MOZART II 522; cf., also, pp. 632 and 662-663.
178. Sondheimer/THEORIE 43.

A final name to connect with Mannheim is that of **Johann Friedrich Hugo Dalberg** (1760-1812). Dalberg was a pupil of Holzbauer in Mannheim, another traveler to Italy, a brilliant pianist, a pre-Romanticist in his writings, and one of the best known dilettantes of his day.[179] Dating from 1779 to about 1805, 17 piano sonatas by him are known, of which 9 are solo, one is for 5 hands (!) and 3 are for 4 hands at one keyboard, and 4 have essential violin "accompaniments."[180] The first of these (and the only one seen here) is a short, elementary, inexperienced solo work in 3 movements (F-minuet-rondo), published in 1779 in Vogler's *Betrachtungen*.[181] But Dalberg's musical techniques may well have improved considerably with time, because his last solo example, a "Grande Sonate," Op. 20, was reviewed favorably, in 1804, except for a few gaucheries and the lack of a slow movement.[182] Its opening allegro is described as fugal and light for all its seriousness, its minuet as recalling Haydn, and its "Rondo, Fantasia" finale as returning, surprisingly and refreshingly, to the free fantasy of Emanuel Bach.

Another successful, though less well-known dilettante, was **Hugo Franz Alexander Karl von Kerpen** (1749-1802), active chiefly in Mainz[183] though also represented by a piece in Vogler's *Betrachtungen* (1778).[184] This last, an accompanied sonata in two fast movements, reveals more experience and skill than Dalberg's example. Otherwise, Kerpen is credited with a set of six accompanied sonatas (1799) and a four-hand sonata.

West Central Germany (*Sterkel*)

In central Germany, not far above Mannheim, the organist and Abbé **Johann Franz Xaver Sterkel** (1750-1817) spent nearly all his life in church positions in the cities of Mainz and his birthplace Würzburg, the chief interruption being a three-year trip to Italy (1779-82). In 1777 Mozart criticized Sterkel's keyboard playing as too fast, unclear, and out of time.[185] Better known is Beethoven's pleasure, in 1791, when he heard an outstanding pianist for the first time, which Sterkel was acknowledged to be by then, and his delight in imitating the delicate refinements of Sterkel's playing when he performed in turn

179. Cf. MGG II 1869-1871 (Komma); Gottron/MAINZER 198-199.
180. Cf. the listings and thematic index in DTB-m XVI xiii and xxxi (incomplete).
181. Cf. Schafhäutl/VOGLER 290; BRITISH UNION I 248.
182. AMZ VI (1803-04) 561-562.
183. Cf. MGG VII 862 (Gottron); Gottron/MAINZER 197-198.
184. Cf. Schafhäutl/VOGLER 290.
185. Anderson/MOZART II 576.

for the latter.[186] A total of 80 sonatas by Sterkel can be accounted for, mostly published in his day, between about 1774-1807.[187] Of these, 66 187a
are accompanied, with occasionally independent violin parts and cello parts that double the piano bass or support the harmony;[188] 7 are for piano duet; and only 7 are for keyboard solo. With regard to the solo sonatas, in 1798 a reviewer greeted one of the best, Op. 36 in C, with the added remark, "This solo sonata is all the more appealing because one can't always have a violinist [on hand] for the accompaniment."[189]

Sterkel's earlier sonatas are mostly in three movements (F-S-F), the later ones in two. Major keys of more than three flats or sharps and minor keys are rare. The harmony and modulations are technically well handled but are not used especially to achieve expressive effects or relationships (as several contemporary reviewers thankfully noted[190]). The forms are clear and well balanced, with undeveloped "development" sections and incomplete "recapitulations" being the chief shortcomings from the standpoint of textbook "sonata form," as usual. Partly because the ideas amount to little more than incidental figures in the prevailing passage work (Ex. 90), the forms seem too long for the content. Some vindictive remarks made by a long-time German rival in Italy about Sterkel's sonatas were published in 1783, evidently cutting him to the quick:[191]

> The keyboardist Abbé Sterkel, known for his, in any case, mediocre sonatas . . . had the nerve to reject [Emanuel] Bach's excellent *Essay* and disparage his [Bach's] compositions, without his being able to play the easiest Bach sonatas acceptably. . . . His [Sterkel's] keyboard sonatas are merely for the ladies, who are satisfied if the ear is enticed with light and

186. Cf. p. 17 in Scharnagl/STERKEL (the main source on the man and his music); Thayer/BEETHOVEN I 113-114; and, especially, Schiedermair/BEETHOVEN 213-215. A summary of his life and works, with exx., is included in Gottron/MAINZER 184-194.

187. Opp. 1 & 2 were announced in 1776 (Johansson/FRENCH I 116), although Op. 1 was already known in Bonn in 1774 (Schiedermair/BEETHOVEN 55). Op. 41 was (favorably) reviewed in 1805 in AMZ VII (1804-05) 244, but no date can be fixed yet for Sterkel's last son., Op. 45 (P & Vn & Vc; Speyer, Vienna). Cf. the lists in Scharnagl/STERKEL 107, 109-111 (without dates); DTB-m XVI xxii-xxiii (publications) and liii-lv (thematic index); BRITISH UNION II 978. Only Eitner/QL IX 283 includes the 3 solo piano sons. that Schott published as Op. 34 in 1798 (plate no. 209), of which a copy is at the Library of Congress.

188. Discussed briefly in Scharnagl/STERKEL 43-47.

189. AMZ I (1798-99) 44-45. Op. 36 is separately analyzed in Scharnagl/STERKEL 37-39.

190. Cf. the review of Op. 30 in 1789, as quoted in Scharnagl/STERKEL 45; or that of Op. 36, noted *supra*.

191. Trans. here after the extract from Cramer/MAGAZIN I (1783) 574 and 969 in Scharnagl/STERKEL 15-16 (cf., also, pp. 75-85 for more on the intriguing correspondence that ensued, with incidental information of value on contemporary performance practices in Italy). The estimate of Sterkel that followed soon after in Burney/HISTORY II 960 acknowledged more spirit than skill or originality.

Ex. 90. From the opening of Johann Franz Xaver Sterkel's Sonata in A, Op. 34/1 (after the original Schott ed. at the Library of Congress).

trifling ideas. But the fair sex does not tell so readily whether one sonata is [merely] like another, whether the harmony is right, whether the bass progresses well, and more of the same. He himself only plays his own pieces with expression . . .

Previously, in the same year, the songful Italianate quality and natural use of the instrument in Sterkel's sonatas had been praised in the same publication.[192] More recently, the chief interest has been in any influence of Sterkel's music on the young Beethoven,[193] although the influence now seems at most to concern a few melodic elegances in Beethoven's earliest sonatas.

The biographically obscure pianist and teacher **Joseph Hemmerlein** (?-1799) was the most prolific composer and probably a member of the family of musicians by this name.[194] Perhaps born in Bamberg, he was active there, in Frankfurt/M (as early as 1753?), and at other central German posts before settling in Paris in his last years. At least seven sets of three accompanied sonatas each (H-or-P + Vn) and four four-hand sonatas by him are extant, published between 1783 and 1795. A reading of the accompanied

192. The remarks are quoted from Cramer/MAGAZIN I (1783) 169 and 346, in Scharnagl/STERKEL 10 and 14.

193. Cf. DTB-m XV xviii (Riemann; emphasizing relationships between their slow mvts.); Schiedermair/BEETHOVEN 270-271, 281-282 (emphasizing influences on Beethoven's "Kurfürsten" sons., with exx.); Scharnagl/STERKEL 29-30, 45-46 (including possible influences of Sterkel's Opp. 17, 18, and 19); Ringer/CLEMENTI 456.

194. Cf. MGG VI 142-146 (Dennerlein), with further references and the title page of a 4-hand son. in facs.

set Op. 5 (Paris: Boyer, 1788[195]) reveals that the language and form are unmistakably high-Classic. The ideas are not without charm and the flow of phrases and passages is compelling. But there is already a sense of pedagogic routine about the procedures, even about the true development in the "development" section; and there is too little harmonic or tonal interest for the full-sized movements.

Two piano virtuosos, successful musicians and writers, in central and west-central Germany, must be passed by because their sonatas have not been available here, although these could well be of interest. **Christian Kalkbrenner** (1755-1806), father and first teacher of Friedrich, was in Kassel when he published three sets of accompanied keyboard sonatas, Opp. 1, 2, and 5, between 1782 and about 1785.[196] **Heinrich Gerhard von Lentz** (or Lenz; *ca.* 1764-1839) was born in Köln, but had an international career and was probably living in Paris (where Christian Kalkbrenner also lived in his later years) in the early 1790's, when more than a dozen solo, four-hand, and accompanied keyboard sonatas were published there.[197]

Central German Descendants of Bach (Hässler, Rust, Müller)

As we move east we come closer once more (as in Chap. XII) to J. S. Bach's posthumous sphere of influence. During the high-Classic Era one of the most productive and knowing sonata composers in this sphere was the skilled organist, clavichordist, and pianist from Erfurt, **Johann Wilhelm Hässler** (1747-1822). In the course of his seventy-five years Hässler underwent and kept pace with changing influences extending from the late-Baroque to the pre-Romantic Eras. He was first given a thorough, traditional foundation in composition and organ playing by his uncle, J. C. Kittel, one of J. S. Bach's last pupils. He then devoted himself, like so many of his central and north German contemporaries, to the music of Emanuel Bach, taking a special interest in the clavichord. Soon he was crossing paths with many of the Germans we meet in the present volume, among them G. Benda, Forkel, Hiller, Türk, E. W. Wolf, Neefe, Löhlein, Naumann, and Dalberg. This portion of Hässler's life we learn about in authentic and captivating detail from his twelve-page autobiography written in 1786 and appended to his 1787 publication of six sonatas.[198] But much more was

195. Johansson/FRENCH II Facs. 101.

196. Cf. MGG VII 445-446 (Sietz). In spite of the listing in BRITISH UNION I 563, Op. 1 cannot now be found at St. John's College in Oxford.

197. Cf. MGG VIII 617 (Lissa). But no sons. are listed in Johansson/FRENCH.

198. Reprinted in facs. in Kahl/SELBSTBIOGRAPHIEN 51-74, with a valuable

to come, including his unsuccessful competition with Mozart at the organ and piano, in Dresden in 1789,[199] in which he might have fared better on the clavichord;[200] and his happier associations with Haydn in London (under whose direction he played a Mozart concerto in 1792).[201] The hard struggles of his career thus far and the taste of greater successes in London must have influenced his bold move to Russia, without his family, in 1792, there to begin a wholly new career (even to starting with Op. 1 again) and to enjoy both prosperity and distinction in Moscow from 1794 throughout his remaining twenty-
202a eight years.[202]

Insofar as works originating during his Russian years can be separated from reprints of earlier works, over 100 keyboard sonatas by Hässler can be identified.[203] Only his published sonatas are known, dating from 1776 to about 1815, 76 being solo,[204] 17 accompanied (Vn-or-Fl, some with Vc);[205] 7 for 4 hands and 3 for 3 hands at one piano,[206] and one for 2 pianos. The earliest of these sonatas come closest to a standardized Classic type, being in the usual 3 movements, F-S-F. However, the "sonata forms" usually have only tentative second themes and incomplete, shortened recapitulations. Emanuel Bach is clearly suggested in the piano writing and specific uses of ornaments (including the trilled turn),[207] but the syntax is more regular. In the several sets of sonatas published in the 1780's the influence of Haydn's rondos and minuets becomes evident, as does the more florid melodic style of Mozart. And in the Russian sonatas the element of virtuosity comes to the fore. Some of these last are introduced by a freer movement, as in "Fantasie et Sonate," or "Prelude . . . ," or "Caprice. . . ."

---

preface (pp. 45-50); also reprinted as a "Beilage" to NAGELS-m No. 20 (Glöder). An English trans. is desirable, for there are many insights into the problems of the 18th-c. composer and performer. For an over-all summary of Hässler's life, cf. MGG V 1299-1304 (Hoffmann-Erbrecht).

199. For what seems like a jealous, excessive condemnation by Mozart, cf. Anderson/MOZART III 1373-1374.

200. Cf. his amusing account of his unfortunate experience with a harpsichord and a piano in recital, Kahl/SELBSTBIOGRAPHIEN 67.

201. Cf. Pohl/MOZART II 140, 190, 196, 200-201.

202. Some new information on his Russian years is given in Mooser/ANNALES II 659-661.

203. Cf. the lists in Eitner/QL 469-471; MGG V 1301-1302.

204. Among mod. eds. (cf. MGG 1303-1304): 3 sons. from 1776, TRÉSOR-m XVI (no. 3 in a is also in Pauer/MEISTER-m 50 and like sets); 6 sons. from 1779 and 4 "Solos" from 1785, TRÉSOR-m IX; 3 "leichte" sons. from 1786, '88, and '90, NAGELS-m No. 20; 6 "leichte" sons. from 1786 and '87, MDMA-m I/11 (Hoffmann-Erbrecht).

205. Among mod. eds.: 2 sons. (K & Fl-or-Vn) from 1786, NAGELS-m No. 11 (Glöder).

206. Among mod. eds.: one of each, NAGELS-m No. 19 (Glöder).

207. Cf. Hässler's mentions of these aspects in Kahl/SELBSTBIOGRAPHIEN 54.

Hässler's tendency toward lighter, shorter, easier sonatas—indicated in the titles for his sets by words like "easy," "very easy," or "half easy, half hard"—undoubtedly reflects awareness of his market.[208] But this tendency and his increasing departure from standardized forms have been taken wrongly as evidence for a gradual cheapening of the content. (There is never any doubt of skilled craftsmanship.) Actually, the later German sonatas, with their irregular, sectionalized, interconnected movements—such as the chorale, allegro, chorale, and presto of Sonata 1 in the 1788 set—show considerably more imagination and character than the first sonatas, in which the ideas themselves are notably lacking in interest. Hässler's own somewhat cryptic remark in 1786 was this: "Mere keyboard sonatas I shall not be writing so much anymore, since I am urged on all sides to [compose] more important works. The overpowering impulse to compose obliges me to write, but I must say in all honesty that all my previous works are merely products of moments [taken off] here and there."[209]

Another fine Thuringian organist brought up in the environment of J. S. Bach was **Johann Gottfried Vierling** (1750-1813) in Schmalkalden.[210] A pupil of Kirnberger (after study with J. N. Tischer and probably Emanuel Bach), Vierling dedicated a set of six keyboard sonatas to Kirnberger in 1781 (Breitkopf), which have not been explored in recent times, although the esteem in which his music was held would justify a study of them.[211]

The pioneer music historian, musicologist, and biographer of J. S. Bach, **Johann Nikolaus Forkel** (1749-1818), lived most of his life in Göttingen.[212] Between 1771 and 1798, he also composed sonatas, including at least 26 solo and 10 accompanied keyboard sonatas in print (mostly at his own expense) or MS. The 2 sonatas from 1779 that have been made available,[213] both in 3 movements (F-S-F), are still *galant* in style and very close to the ornamental, harmonic, syntactic, and textural idioms of Emanuel Bach. They are less advanced in their use of the keyboard, yet do attain a certain depth in the fast as well as the slow movements. From an expressive standpoint they relate to Emanuel's sonatas about as Padre Martini's relate to Scarlatti's, being somewhat heavy and pedantic.

208. Cf. Kahl/SELBSTBIOGRAPHIEN 48-49.
209. Trans. from Kahl/SELBSTBIOGRAPHIEN 73.
210. Paulke/VIERLING is a concise study of the man and his music, with a list of works.
211. Cf. Reichardt/KUNSTMAGAZIN I (1782) 87.
212. Cf. MGG IV 514-520 (Peters-Marquardt & Dürr); Franck/FORKEL.
213. Mod. eds.: Sons. 3 in D and 5 in d from the 2d set of 6 (Breitkopf, 1779; nos. 2 and 4 have opt. Vn & Vc parts), ORGANUM-m V Nos. 11 and 17, with prefaces.

In his writings, which are far more significant, Forkel made numerous references to the sonata, most important here being a seventeen-page discussion in 1784 that starts as a (naturally very enthusiastic) review of Emanuel's Sonata in f in the third "Kenner und Liebhaber set" (W. 57/6).[214] Although the purpose of such discussions, he says near the start, is to give substance and order to our emotional sensations, he is, in later terms, far from being concrete about what goes on in the sonata. The gist of his prolix arguments, with all their repetitions, analogies, and similes, is that the most beautiful ideas are meaningless without their purposeful unification; that only the greatest composers have the necessary logic, taste, and inspiration to achieve such a goal; and that the sonata describes to him the happy or gloomy state of man or the progress from one state to the other (preferably gloomy to happy), the usual three movements being ideal for expressing these states and changes. Only as a problem in rhetoric is "sonata form" hinted in the discussion (p. 32), with references to a main emotional idea, a subordinate one ("Nebenempfindung"), and the necessary release, conflict, and resolution of these ideas.

A surprisingly original and skillful composer of sonatas turns up in **Nathanael Gottfried Gruner** (1732-92), who was active in the Thuringian town of Gera most of his life.[215] His first and second sets of 6 solo keyboard sonatas each were published in 1781 and 1783 (Breitkopf), followed by a set of 3 accompanied sonatas (K & Vn & Vc), Op. 7, published in Lyon. In the first solo set is a short "Vorbericht" to the public and an awe-inspiring subscription list of 1,368 names (among them, Emanuel Bach, Reichardt, Rolle, Schubart, E. W. Wolf, Doles, and many other Germans, as well as 37 Hungarians, and 74 Austrians).[216] The sonatas in this set are like Emanuel Bach's in their 3-movement plan, their great attention to rhythmic and editorial detail, their textural variety, their rather frequent, abrupt feminine cadences, and some of their ornamentation. But they are no slavish copies of Bach's style such as Forkel's sonatas seem to be, and they are still far from the late-Classic stereotypes in Vienna and elsewhere. There is much originality in their multisectional themes (as in the theme of Son. 4/iii, "Villanella alla Rondo"), in the proselike, finely drawn, lyrical "second themes" over a simple Alberti or other chordal bass,

214. Forkel/ALMANACH III (1784) 22-38 (kindly brought to the attention of the present study by Dr. Wolf Franck of New York City). Cf., also, Bitter/BRÜDER I 210-211 and 217-218 (with errors).

215. Cf. MGG V 989-990 (Hoffmann-Erbrecht). No monograph on Gruner is known here.

216. The set was said to have far surpassed the subscribers' expectations, in Reichardt/KUNSTMAGAZIN I (1782) 87.

Ex. 91. From the "development section" of Sonata 4/i in E♭, 1781, by Nathanael Gottfried Gruner (after the original Breitkopf ed. in the New York Public Library).

and in the resourceful harmony (including the good use of the dim.-7th chord in Ex. 91).

Still within J. S. Bach's posthumous sphere of influence and still circling Leipzig, we come to Dessau, where lived one of the most intriguing and notable of the high-Classic Germans, **Friedrich Wil-**

helm Rust (1739-96). Thanks to an autobiographical record he maintained up to about his twenty-fifth year, Rust's extraordinarily rich training is known.[217] He enjoyed the indirect influence of J. S. Bach through his elder brother, who had played violin under Bach's direction in Leipzig, and through another Dessau citizen, Gottlieb Friedrich Müller, who had studied under Bach's pupil Goldberg and himself published a set of six keyboard sonatas in 1762 (Breitkopf).[218] Still better evidence of Bach's influence will be noted in Rust's music and was already demonstrated when he was but thirteen, by his ability to play Book I of *The Well-Tempered Clavier* from memory. In the next fourteen years he enjoyed the further instruction of both Friedemann and Emanuel Bach in keyboard and composition, and Franz Benda in violin. And during a year or more in Italy (1765-66) he enjoyed the counsel, if not the actual teaching, of Georg Benda, Tartini, Nardini, Pugnani, Martini, and others! (Rust's first sonatas and the start of his valuable library of sonatas and other music date from that Italian trip.[219]) Furthermore, he came to know such figures as Neefe,[220] Reichardt, and Goethe, he conducted the symphonies of Haydn and others in Dessau, and he gained a reputation there in Italian opera.[221]

Rudolf Czach's thematic index of Rust's works[222] shows almost 100 sonatas, dating from about 1765 to 1796, of which probably none was published during his lifetime and only one was published during the Classic Era (1797).[223] There are 24 sonatas for solo keyboard (variously specified for harpsichord, clavichord, or piano);[224] 25 for keyboard with optional, obligatory, or discarded violin accompaniments[225]

217. The MS, preserved by a descendant, was utilized in the chief 20th-c. study of the man and his music, Czach/RUST, which is partially summarized in EDML-m I [Czach] v-x and largely but not entirely supersedes Hosäus/RUST (mainly on Rust in the Dessau musical community), Prieger/RUST (mainly quoting evidences of a Rust renaissance *ca.* 1893, created by the grandson), and earlier accounts.

218. Cf. Eitner/QL VII 105.

219. Cf. d'Indy/RUST-m preface; Pfäfflin/NARDINI 27 and 52.

220. Cf. Leux/NEEFE 108-109.

221. Burney/HISTORY II 946.

222. Czach/RUST appendix 3-18.

223. No. 21 in Czach's index, no. 4 in d'Indy/RUST-m (cf. the preface and p. 27). No evidence could be found to support the publication of this work in 1770 (as suggested in Czach/RUST 80; cf., also, pp. 74-75).

224. 2 groups of 6 and 2 sons., respectively, are listed in BREITKOPF MS XI (1776-77) 22 and XV (1782) 48; the first group is probably that listed (wrongly?) as published in Gerber/LEXICON II 353, and accepted as such in Czach/RUST 36. Among mod. eds.: Czach nos. 18, 24, 14, 21, 16, 23, 10, 11, d'Indy/RUST-m nos. 1-4, 8-10, and 12, respectively; Czach nos. 11 and 23, EDML-m I nos. 1 and 2.

225. Among mod. eds.: Czach nos. 30, 32, 41, d'Indy/RUST-m nos. 6, 7, 11; Czach no. 38, EDML-m I no. 4.

and 2 more accompanied by an additional violin and cello;[226] 25 for solo violin and *b.c.*, second violin, or other accompaniment; 3 of the exclusive type for unaccompanied violin, of which that in d is probably Rust's best known work, its 4 movements being so close to corresponding movements from J. S. Bach's unaccompanied Sonata in a and Partita in d as to seem almost like copies;[227] 4 for viola d'amore with and without accompaniment; 4 for viola accompanied by keyboard (or by keyboard, 2 horns & Vc); one for cello and *b.c.*; 5 for lute, of which 3 are accompanied by violin and one is accompanied by viola;[228] one in string quartet setting; and 4 for harp with or without accompaniment.

In spite of the respect Rust won from a select group of contemporary musicians,[229] his music might still be largely unexplored in modern times had not 9 of his most mature solo and accompanied keyboard sonatas as well as the 4 accompanied lute sonatas been brought out, about 1885-92.[230] The "editor" was none other than his grandson, Wilhelm Rust (1822-92), who is now remembered primarily as one of the chief editors for the Bach-Gesellschaft. But in these publications 230a
lay what Calvocoressi summed up in 1914 as "one of the most striking hoaxes to be found in the whole history of musical erudition."[231] In 1893, when Prieger relied on the grandson's editions and ecstatic prefaces to argue for Rust as a significant forerunner of Beethoven, he recognized that editorial changes had been made but assumed that these did not affect the music in any fundamental way.[232] In 1895, describing and quoting from the same editions, Shedlock accepted Prieger's opinion of the changes, though with increased misgivings.[233] But in 1913, the German scholar Ernst Neufeldt related wittily and sarcastically the grand disillusionment that followed his tracking down of the autograph sources in Berlin.[234] Here were no programmatic titles (such as "Sonata erotica" for Czach no. 110), no (admittedly skillful) "Meistersinger polyphony" or full Romantic piano textures, no cyclically treated motives *à la* Liszt Sonata in b (Ex. 92[235]).

226. Mod. ed.: Czach no. 110, d'Indy/RUST-m no. 5.

227. A facs. of the autograph was published by Max Hesse in 1895 for Rust's grandson, apparently as a protest to F. David's arrangement with piano accompaniment, published by Peters in 1867 (Moser/VIOLINSPIEL 332-334; cf. Altmann/KAMMERMUSIK 242). This son. also appears in EDML-m I 51 (with the title changed to "Partite"). It is described in detail in Gates/SOLO 142-152.

228. Mod. eds.: Sons. in d and G for lute and violin, Neemann/RUST-m.

229. Cf. Hosäus/RUST 73-76; Prieger/RUST 4.

230. Cf. HOFMEISTER IX (1880-85) 547, X (1886-91) 642, XI (1892-97) 722.

231. Calvocoressi/RUST 16.

232. Prieger/RUST 3-4.

233. Shedlock/SONATA 152-159.

234. Neufeldt/RUST.

235. Further comparisons of the autographs and revisions will be found in

Ex. 92. From the slow movement of Sonata in D♭ (1777? Czach no. 30), (a) after the autograph by Friedrich Wilhelm Rust, (b) after the "edition" published by his grandson about 1888 (as compared in Neufeldt/CAS).

Furthermore, sections totaling as much as half of a sonata, sometimes whole movements, were missing that Wilhelm Rust later took upon himself to add (even commenting in his prefaces on their great significance as eighteenth-century music!).

Answering Neufeldt at once, Prieger sought variously to apologize, recant, absolve himself, and restate certain arguments.[236] But a vigorous controversy ensued, enhanced by interesting style analyses though not free from bitter recriminations and name calling, when the French-
237a man Vincent d'Indy intervened (still in 1913).[237] D'Indy had previously committed himself unequivocally and at length to the championing of Rust as the missing link leading from Haydn and Mozart to Beethoven.[238] Now he could hardly afford to reverse his views on the basis of the newly discovered liberties and outright deceptions practiced by the grandson. Instead, he prepared a generally faithful edition from the autographs of twelve of Rust's best sonatas and argued that in their original purity these were even more rightly to be viewed as the true precursors of Beethoven's sonatas.[239]

Neufeldt/CAS; Steinitzer/ATLAS-m no. 100 (cf. d'Indy/RUST-m 57 and 55); Shedlock/SONATA 156 (cf. d'Indy/RUST-m 71) and 157 (*not* in d'Indy/RUST-m 130).

236. Prieger/RUSTIANA.

237. D'Indy/RUST, followed by Neufeldt/CAS.

238. D'Indy/COURS II/1 219-230, with several analyses and exx. Although the vol. is dated 1909 both this discussion and the exx. must have been revised in a later, unindicated reprinting, after the controversy; in Calvocoressi/RUST 14-16 the earlier version is cited.

239. D'Indy/RUST-m (1913), with preface and annotations. The chief de-

Finally, in 1914, Calvocoressi summarized "le cas Rust" by drawing morals that should be required reading for everyone who would pinpoint musical styles or who would distinguish historical from aesthetic significance. Also, he judged—rightly, most readers will agree—in favor of Neufeldt insofar as the misdeeds of the grandson are concerned.[240] But at this greater distance and after a survey of the large quantity of mediocre, perfunctory, formulized sonatas of the high-Classic Era, one feels that both more right and more importance should have been granted to the conclusions reached by the highly perceptive musician in d'Indy. Rust does reveal striking similarities to Beethoven, as well as other traits of real interest and distinction. To be sure, the possibility that Rust's MSS were known to Beethoven and could have influenced his writing is slim. If F. W. Rust's son Wilhelm Karl Rust (1787-1855) included any of them among the things he played for Beethoven in Vienna, the latter seems not to have commented on them.[241] In any case, by then, in 1808, Beethoven had already composed the "Waldstein" and "Appassionata" sonatas. F. W. Rust died too soon, of course, to have known any of Beethoven's important sonatas.

Regarding Rust's earliest sonatas (*ca.* 1765-74),[242] the marks of Friedemann and Emanuel Bach are clear, such as the short phrases, the abrupt deceptive cadences, the vacillations of tempo, tonality, and texture, the variable "sonata forms," and sundry other *empfindsam* traits. The first movement of one early keyboard Sonata in F (Czach no. 18) was composed "con variate repetizioni," in the manner of Emanuel Bach's "veränderte Reprisen" sonatas. The sonatas from what d'Indy called Rust's "deuxième époque" (*ca.* 1775-91)[243] seem to show the increasing influence of Haydn, especially in their more piquant ideas and more imaginative development of them. It is "the last five sonatas" (1792-94), as d'Indy pointedly refers to them, that reveal Beethovian traits. D'Indy singles out especially the last three, in C, f♯, and D (Czach nos. 10, 41, and 11), saying that these surpass the

partures from the autographs, aside from errors and some judicious filling out of the harmony in small notes, are the deletions of the accompaniments as unimportant or incomplete in nos. 5-7 and 11, the writing out of many of the ornaments without retaining the original signs, and some rescoring of no. 9 (as shown in the footnotes). Sample facs. of autographs are given in both this ed. and EDML-m I.

240. Calvocoressi/RUST 89-91; on p. 15 is quoted a portion of Rust's Son. in b for Vn & P in the grandson's version. Brenet and others also summarized the controversy, some asking whether the grandson's services as a Bach editor had not now become suspect.

241. Cf. Thayer/BEETHOVEN II 117-118.

242. Discussed in Czach/RUST 74-82.

243. D'Indy/RUST-m preface.

sonatas of Haydn and Mozart and are equalled only by Beethoven's finest works![244]

D'Indy's favorite of all Rust's sonatas, that in f♯, and the last one, in D, still have much *empfindsam* and decorative fantasy in them. Perhaps the value d'Indy found was partly what he read into them, since fine as these two sonatas are they are nevertheless somewhat passive in character. They suffer from rather flat, insipid ideas, which are Rust's chief shortcoming.[245] More positive Beethovian traits, it is felt here, are to be sensed in two other sonatas by Rust, those in e and C (Czach nos. 16 and 10). To the two movements of the Sonata in C Rust's grandson added three others (or some 225 mss. more than the original 286 mss.), including the variations on the Marlborough tune that he assured his readers his grandfather had discovered in Montecassino. But the two sonatas are fine works in their original state, with undeniable suggestions of Beethoven in their creative development, extension, and rhythmic variation of the material; in their treatment of the keyboard, with wide stretches and leaps, modern fingerings (reproduced by d'Indy), hand-crossing to transfer the melody to the bass, and brilliant passages in the Sonata in C that bring Beethoven's "Waldstein" sonata very much to mind. They also suggest Beethoven in their simple harmonic progressions within bold tonal contrasts, and in their sure forms, which hardly attain the scope and intensity of those in Beethoven's major works of a decade or more later, but do have some of the same "fatalistic" inevitability and logic about them. Moreover, Rust has a slow introduction in the Sonata in e, thematic ties between the outer movements in the Sonata in f♯, and the sort of interlocking forms that we know in Beethoven's Opp. 101 and 110, such as a "Fugato" woven into the "Rondo" finale of his Sonata in C, or an alternation of the slow and quick sections that conclude the Sonata in D.

Rust also differs from Beethoven in certain tangible ways, which, combined with the similarities, leave a total impression more like that of Clementi than of any other contemporary sonata composer. Besides the *empfindsam* traits and the less meaningful themes (which make for less telling dualism in the later "sonata forms"), his slow movements are of far less importance and extent than Beethoven's. There are no middle slow movements in Rust's late sonatas in e and C, and only an incipient one in the Sonata in f♯. On the other hand, in the "Fugato" just mentioned, in his unaccompanied violin sonatas, and in several other

244. D'Indy/RUST-m preface, 94, 108, 120. The late sons. are discussed in Czach/RUST 84-89.

245. The attempts to relate themes by Rust and Beethoven in Prieger/RUSTIANA are without significance; cf., also, Czach/RUST 36.

works, Rust was able to come much closer to J. S. Bach's fluent polyphonic style than Beethoven did. The outer movements of his accompanied Sonata in d (Czach no. 32) are actually based on the "royal theme" in Bach's *Musical Offering.* Rust took a special interest in sound effects and may also be called one of the last noteworthy devotees of the clavichord and lute. Besides the lute sonatas and harp sonatas he composed a three-movement Sonata in G (Czach no. 23) that specifies clavichord, is already delightfully neo-Classic in style, and includes detailed instructions for "imitazione de' timpani, del Salterio, e del Liuto."[246]

The well-known pedagogue and theorist **Daniel Gottlob Türk** (1750-1813) trained with J. S. Bach's pupil G. A. Homilius in Dresden and with J. A. Hiller in Leipzig before moving permanently to Halle in 1776.[247] There he taught, directed instrumental and choral groups, wrote (including contributions to AMZ from 1800), and composed. Türk is chiefly remembered for his most successful treatise, the lucid, well-organized *Klavierschule* of 1789.[248] In Chapter II of the present volume this comprehensive work was cited several times, for it often lends perspective to the high-Classic sonata. Noteworthy is its position in history as the last important method founded largely on Emanuel Bach's *Essay,* including a preference for the clavichord (as still meant by "Klavier"), the discussions of fingering and ornaments, and the attitude that the sonata still offered the composer the freest opportunity to indulge his feelings and fancies (reference being made to Forkel's discussion, cited *supra*).[249] But new or changing ideas are also to be found, including the mention of keyboard sonatas first and most importantly among the several instrumental types of sonata, the attempt to distinguish the "Klaviersolo" as a sonata without accompaniment and the (rarely found) "Sinfonie" for "Klavier" as a larger, more imposing type of piece, the illustration of more advanced playing techniques such as hand exchanges and rapid crossing, and the evaluation of contemporary keyboard sonatas according to difficulty (from his own lightest examples to the advanced works of Emanuel Bach).[250]

Türk published 48 solo "Klaviersonaten" in 8 sets of 6 each, be-

246. Cf. the 2 facs. in EDML-m I xiv and xv.

247. Hedler/TÜRK is a detailed diss. on the man, his writings, and his music (with thematic index, pp. 95-111); the birth year of 1756 is still found in all the main recent dictionaries in spite of the correction to 1750 in Hedler/TÜRK 1-2.

248. Summarized and evaluated (along with contemporary opinions) in Hedler/TÜRK 25-34.

249. Türk/KLAVIERSCHULE 4-11, 129-186, 200-331, 390, respectively.

250. Türk/KLAVIERSCHULE 390, 391-392, 186-199, and 16-17 (cf. p. 364), respectively.

tween 1776 and 1793.[251] The first 2 sets (1776 and 1777) were evidently meant for players with some experience, as was the set of 1789, labeled "mainly for connoisseurs."[252] But in his conscientious concern for both the *Liebhaber* and the *Kenner* (as in his preface to the set of 1783) Türk makes clear that the sonatas in the 5 other sets are increasingly "leicht" or "klein."[253] Nearly all of his sonatas are in 3 movements, F-S-F, with "sonata form," more or less, in the outer movements except for those few finales that are rondos or minuets. Minor keys are infrequent, as are keys other than the subdominant or parallel minor for the middle movements. There are traces of Emanuel Bach's style in the first set, which is generally the most interesting set. But the composer tended to keep pace with Haydn and Mozart in the forthrightness and balance of his writing. In none of his sonatas is the use of the keyboard very advanced. His most conspicuous traits are progressions, often block chords, in quarter-note movement, and writing in bare octaves between the hands. In spite of the experience that lies behind these sonatas they have none of Rust's originality or pianistic flair, and must be labeled dull.

In Leipzig itself the one sonata composer of some distinction during the high- and late-Classic Era was the excellent pianist and flutist **August Eberhart Müller** (1767-1817).[254] Müller was in this city from 1794 to 1810, succeeding J. A. Hiller as cantor of the Thomasschule prior to his removal to Weimar at Goethe's recommendation. This overworked man performed widely and often, earned a good reputation as a teacher, contributed to AMZ on occasion, and published a *Fortepiano-Schule* in 1804 (actually a sixth, revised ed. of Löhlein's *Clavier-Schule*).[255] But he probably did most service to music as an enthusiastic performer, conductor, and promoter of the music of J. S. Bach, Haydn, Mozart, and Beethoven, including gratis editorial assistance to Breitkopf & Härtel during the preparation of the first collected editions of Haydn and Mozart.[256]

Müller's nearly 20 sonatas include some 17 for solo piano and 2 with "accompaniments," composed and published between about 1789 and 1814.[257] Three solo sonatas, Op. 3, were published in 1792; three,

251. The sets are surveyed in Hedler/TÜRK 56-75, with exx.

252. Mod. ed.: Son. 1 in a, 1789, ORGANUM-m V No. 19.

253. Mod. eds.: Sons. 4 in e and 5 in C, ORGANUM-m V Nos. 9 and 13.

254. The chief study of the man and his music is Haupt/MÜLLER; cf., also, MGG IX 850-852 (Lidke).

255. Haupt/MÜLLER 8, 12, 27, 14-15, 22.

256. Haupt/MÜLLER 15, 19, 20-22, 23, 26, 27, 34.

257. The sons. are discussed in Haupt/MÜLLER 51-75, with exx., and more summarily, with too much emphasis on Mozart derivations, in Egert/FRÜHROMANTIKER 47-51.

Op. 5, in 1793;[258] three, Op. 7, about 1795; three, Op. 14, about 1797; one, Op. 17, with fairly independent violin and less independent cello "accompaniments," in 1798;[259] one, Op. 26, about 1794,[260] which was credited here largely to Mozart as K.V. 498a (SCE XIV); one, Op. 36, in 1813; and one, Op. 38, with flute, in 1814.[261] The three sonatas Op. 5 and three "Sonatines" Op. 18 are purely pedagogic works, and the three sonatas Op. 14 are weak imitations of Mozart. Müller is heard at his best in his "Grande Sonate pour le Piano-Forte" in f, Op. 36, in which Mendelssohn rather than Mozart is now suggested. The excellent stepwise and disjunct passage work, throughout the pianist's right-hand range, comes close to the bravura treatment in Müller's *Grandes Caprices* for piano. This writing, the frequent enharmonic modulations, and the contrapuntal interest provided by the left hand (with no further use of Alberti bass) are the strongest traits of Op. 36, all three movements being characteristic of early Romantic writing. There is also a hint of the drive of the finale in Beethoven's "Appassionata" sonata in Müller's finale. However, in each movement the ideas themselves have so little independent character, they merge so much into the prevailing, often triplet, passage work, and the tonality shifts so much of the time that the structures tend to lack definition.[262] There is more of dash and promise than of ultimate musical satisfaction in Müller's last sonatas.

Among more obscure composers in Leipzig, the mandolinist and writer **Friedrich August Baumbach** (1753-1813) left several sets of solo and accompanied keyboard sonatas.[263] His set of six accompanied sonatas (K + Vn & Vc) published by Breitkopf in 1780 already shows the full clarity, balance, melodic types, and order of the high-Classic Vienna style, though no special depth. Two others, who composed light popular sonatas that have yet to be investigated in the present day, are the pianist **Christoph August Gabler** (1767-1839)[264] and the flutist **Gottlieb Heinrich Köhler** (1765-1833).[265]

258. Deutsch/NUMBERS 6 (André plate no. 632).
259. A verbose, laudatory review appeared in AMZ I (1798-99) 376-378.
260. Verbal conclusion offered by Richard Hill in 1941, following publication of Hill/NUMBERS 128-129.
261. The last 2 dates are for plate nos. 1091 and 1167 in Deutsch/NUMBERS 13.
262. About the same conclusion was reached in a contemporary review of Op. 36 (AMZ XVI [1814] 91-92).
263. Cf. Eitner/QL I 384-385.
264. Cf. Eitner/QL IV 111; AMZ III (1800-01) 401-402.
265. Cf. MGG VII 1323-1324 (Eller).

Dresden and Near By (Naumann, Seydelmann, Schuster)

In Dresden, where the court of Friedrich August III took a new interest in orchestral and chamber music during the late eighteenth century,[266] three friends, colleagues, and solidly trained composers—Naumann, Seydelmann, and Schuster—concern us here. **Johann Gottlieb Naumann** (1741-1801), who had benefited from study with Tartini, Martini, and Hasse (his predecessor in Dresden) during six years in Italy (1757-63) and who was to spend time later in Italy, Sweden, and Denmark, became something of an international celebrity.[267] His chief importance was as a composer of operas, oratorios, and liturgical music. Within his limited though not uninteresting output of instrumental works over thirty sonatas are known. Three "trio" sonatas with realized keyboard and subordinate second violin were left in MS probably not later than 1761, while Naumann was still in Padua with Tartini.[268] Two of these were later arranged as accompanied sonatas (K & Vn). By about 1775 Naumann composed six accompanied "Sonatines" (K & Oboe-or-Fl & bassoon-or-bass), in at least one of which a movement is arranged from one of his opera scenes.[269] In 1786 this set was published as "Six Quatuors" (H-or-P & Fl, Vn, & bass), Op. 1, very little rearranging being necessary. Before 1781 he composed another set of six accompanied sonatas (K & Vn), published about that time as Op. 2.[270] Most characteristic for Naumann in his later years are his two sets of six sonatas each for glass harmonica or piano, published as "Teil I" and "Teil II" (or Op. 4) in 1786 and 1792.[271] For solo keyboard, four separate sonatas in MS are also known, and possibly three sonatinas.[272]

Naumann's sonatas are rather elementary in their technical range. The keyboard writing is idiomatic enough in Op. 2 but there is none

266. Cf. Engländer/DRESDNER 17-21, 26-36.

267. Cf. Engländer/DRESDNER 37-68; MGG IX 1288-1295 (Engländer); and the posthumous praise by Haydn (at the request of Naumann's widow), trans. in Landon/HAYDN 210-211. Mozart's unguarded opinion of a Naumann Mass was not favorable (Anderson/MOZART III 1372).

268. Discussed in Engländer/DRESDNER 39, 41-43 (with exx., and with facs. from the autograph after p. 68). Listed in Tebaldini/PADOVA 136.

269. Cf. Engländer/DRESDNER 44-48.

270. Discussed in Engländer/DRESDNER 48-51, with exx. But the publication (Hummel, plate no. 433, with the name given as "J. A. Nauman") seems not to have been known to Engländer; an incomplete set (Vn only) is listed in BRITISH UNION II 725.

271. Discussed in Engländer/DRESDNER 54-64, with exx.; listed with details of each mvt. in Nisser/SVENSK 296. Mod. eds.: Teil I, Sons. 2, 5, 6, cf. MGG IX 1294; Teil II, Son. 1, SAMMLUNG SONDHEIMER-m No. 17.

272. Engländer/DRESDNER 51-52.

of the advanced writing for violin that might be expected of a Tartini pupil. Yet the music, in its somewhat conservative, simple, idyllic way, has charm, originality, and delicacy. Christian Bach's sonatas are sometimes brought to mind. One also gets the feeling that more than that one movement might prove to be an arrangement made from Naumann's own operas, or of a folk song, for a naïve folk quality often dominates the melody. This quality is especially evident in the sonatas for glass harmonica, that ethereal invention of the *Empfindsamkeit* (SCE V) with which no composer was more popularly identified than Naumann. When he first heard this instrument in 1776 Naumann found it pleasing though only good for slow, sustained pieces, mainly the expression of grief. But by 1784 he seems to have found it ideal for a much wider range of emotions.[273] All of Naumann's sonatas are in two movements (usually M-F or F-F) except Op. 1/6 and the four MS keyboard sonatas, which are in three movements. The movements are short and rudimentary in structure, tentative "sonata forms" being exceptional (as in Op. 4/3/i, after a slow introduction).

During his second trip to Italy, 1765-68, Naumann was joined by his pupil **Franz Seydelmann** (1748-1806)[274] and their friend Schuster. Serving in Dresden from 1772 as composer, mainly of operas and church music, and as conductor (*Kapellmeister* from 1787), Seydelmann did not acquire the international reputation that Naumann did. But around 1780 and while Naumann was in Sweden, he was the most active instrumental composer in Dresden. Furthermore, his instrumental music, including nearly twenty-five sonatas, has real, intrinsic interest. Baroque and pre-Classic traits are still evident in the earlier sonatas. Thus, two accompanied sonatas (K & Vn), in MSS from about 1768 and 1775, fall between the old violin sonata with realized keyboard and the accompanied keyboard sonata with subordinate violin.[275] In a set of six solo keyboard sonatas in MS, all in three movements in the order F-M-rondo, the idioms of the suite are recalled by the two-part texture and steady 16th- or 8th-notes.[276] A set of six keyboard sonatas with flute accompaniments, of which three were published in 1785, shows *empfindsam* and *galant* traits.[277]

Of more significance among Seydelmann's works are two other, published sets that disclose a serious and progressive approach to the sonata, including pregnant ideas, intensive reaffirmation and develop-

273. Cf. the contemporary documents quoted in Engländer/DRESDNER 56 and 61.
274. Cf. Eitner/QL IX 149-151; Engländer/DRESDNER 84-87.
275. Cf. Engländer/DRESDNER 87-88.
276. Engländer/DRESDNER 117-118.
277. Engländer/DRESDNER 92-93.

ment of them (often through dialogic exchanges), compelling, expressive harmony, and well-knit, compact yet unhurried forms. One of these sets is that of "Six Sonatas for Two Persons at One Keyboard," published by Breitkopf in 1781.[278] The first five sonatas are in major keys and in three movements, the middle or last movement being an expressive andante, or minuet-with-trio, or "Tempo di polacca" (Son. 5/ii), or rondo. Sonata 6 in g is in only two movements, an "Andante" and "Allegro" that comprise a fine expressive prelude and chromatic, four-voice fugue. Richard Engländer emphasizes that this set could have been made known to the young Beethoven in Bonn by way of Neefe.[279] If the resemblances to Beethoven's early sonatas are not striking, one can still agree with Engländer's strong statement that these keyboard duets are among the best examples of this genre from the eighteenth century (Ex. 93).[280] A modern edition of them would enhance the available duet literature. The other set is that of three accompanied sonatas (K & Vn), published as Op. 3 in 1786. Like the duets, which resemble the arrangements of quartets and symphonies by Haydn and Mozart that the Saxon elector himself enjoyed playing,[281] the sonatas in this set are rich in texture and thematic development in the manner of incipient Viennese symphonies.

Joseph Schuster (1748-1812) began service in Dresden in 1772, the same year as Seydelmann, but returned to Italy for two more three-year visits (1774-76 and 1778-81), studying with Martini and Tartini, and composing operas for the Italian stage.[282] We have already met Schuster in connection with Mozart (SCE XIV), as the composer who did not write the contested "Romantic" sonatas and whose "Divertimenti" were almost certainly the models for Mozart's "Mannheim" sonatas, winning Mozart's endorsement in those letters that otherwise are so often caustic and even jealous. Schuster's chamber music, all left only in MSS, includes an early string trio (SSB; *ca.* 1768), a miniature quartet (1779-80), a set of six accompanied "Sonate" (K & Vn; *ca.* 1776), a set of six "Divertimenti da camera a Cembalo e Violino" (called "Duetti a Cembalo e Violino concertato" in another MS; 1777?), and some small keyboard pieces.[283]

278. A facs. of the charming cover appears as the frontispiece in the present volume.

279. Engländer/DRESDNER 87 and 90.

280. Engländer/DRESDNER 118-120. The Breitkopf ed. was still circulating in 1828 (HOFMEISTER II 558 [Whistling]).

281. Engländer/DRESDNER 119, 29, 32.

282. Cf. Eitner/QL IX 100-102; Engländer/DRESDNER 69-71.

283. These works are discussed in Engländer/DRESDNER 71-74, 74, 83-85, 74-83, 114-117, respectively, all with helpful exx.; the incipits of the first mvts. in the 2 sets are listed on pp. 139-141 and all of Divertimento 5 is printed in score on pp.

Ex. 93. From the "development" section of Franz Seydelmann's Sonata 4/i in E for 4 hands at one keyboard (after the original Breitkopf ed. at the British Museum).

Schuster's accompanied "Sonate" are all in two movements, extremely light in texture, with a totally subordinate violin part, and with frequent suggestions of, if not actual borrowings from, his *opere buffe* (Ex. 94). This set was probably composed in Naples, where the MS now remains.[284] The "Divertimenti," which were probably composed during a successful visit to Munich only one year later, when they evidently became known to Mozart, differ markedly in several respects.

143-155. Further mod. eds. are needed. The 2 sets are also described in Engländer/MOZART. The listing in Eitner/QL IX 102 of a MS of 1791 as "6 Sonate per il Cemb. dell'Opera 'Rübenzahl'" is an erroneous reference to the short keyboard pieces (Engländer/DRESDNER 116).

284. But it is not listed in PUBBLICAZIONI NAPOLI.

Ex. 94. From the start of No. 6 in Joseph Schuster's "VI Sonate per il Cembalo accompagnate dal Violino" (after the MS at the R. Conservatorio di Musica in Naples).

Their independent violin parts make them true duets, they are nearly all in three movements (except for No. 3 in 2 mvts.), and they follow no one plan other than the use of a rondo, siciliana, or "Polacca" as the finale. They also exhibit more developed structures, whether in the complete "sonata forms" of several of the first movements or in such relatively free procedures as a "recitativo" and development (like a coda) after the recapitulation (No. 5/i).

Schuster's music has less depth than Naumann's or Seydelmann's, mainly because he was the most modern of the three composers—modern in the sense of coming more under the fluent, songful, *buffa* influences of Austro-Italian music. Actually, in certain respects Schuster anticipates Mozart in style as closely as any eighteenth-century composer except perhaps Mysliveček. Pertinent are his neatly phrased themes that unfold sequentially and are marked by chromatic inflections, slides, and other *buffa*-like ornaments and rhythms.[285] Schuster's good use of the keyboard and relatively early preference for the piano are also noteworthy, as shown in his idiomatic writing[286] and in his "introduction" of the piano in Italy during his second trip there.[287]

Besides these composers in Dresden we may take brief note of **Jean Balthasar Tricklir** (*ca.* 1750-1813), a fine French-born cellist of German descent, trained in Mannheim and Italian centers. At the Dresden court from 1783, he left two sets of six Vc/bass sonatas that were published in the mid 1780's and are interesting for their rich harmony, their good use of the cello, and the late appearance of this setting.[288] There is also an obscure figure who may be mentioned in another Saxon town, Stollberg, fifty miles southwest. The organist **Georg Friedrich Wolf** (*ca.* 1762-*ca.* 1814) was serving there in 1787 when two piano sonatas by him were published in Halle, and in 1794 and 1796 when two separate four-hand sonatas were published by Breitkopf.[289] In addition, he left a successful method for keyboard (1784 and later eds.).[290] The four-hand Sonata in F from 1794 is a short, energetic, transparent work in four movements, "pour les amateurs." It would be welcomed again in a modern edition.

Berlin and Other North German Centers (Reichardt)

With regard to the Berlin school during the high- and late-Classic Era—that is, during the last years of Frederick the Great (d. 1786), throughout the short reign of Frederick William II (d. 1797), and well into the Napoleonic humiliations suffered by Frederick William III (d. 1840)—the most important and renowned musician was **Johann Friedrich Reichardt** (1752-1814). This versatile writer, director, composer, traveler, and free thinker received violin and keyboard instruction early, but never quite overcame his largely empirical training

285. Cf. the incipits in Engländer/DRESDNER; also, Engländer/ECHTHEITSFRAGE 296-297.

286. Cf. Engländer/DRESDNER 111-114.

287. According to Schubart/IDEEN 116.

288. Cf. Straeten/VIOLONCELLO 210-211; BRITISH UNION II 1019; Altmann/KAMMERMUSIK 270 (for 4 sons. in mod. eds.).

289. Cf. Eitner/QL X 294; Gerber/NEUES IV 606.

290. Perhaps from this source comes the 3-mvt. Sonatina in D reprinted (with the year "1788") in Kreutz/SONATINEN 19.

in composition.[291] His life fell into three main periods: (1) the early years in Königsberg (now Kaliningrad) and the first travels (1771-75) "to see the world," (2) the productive though frictional and interrupted years of service as *Kapellmeister* at the Berlin court (1776-94), and (3) the remaining twenty years of writing and travel, especially in Giebichenstein and Vienna.[292] At this point we are interested in the approximately sixty-five sonatas that Reichardt left in MS and print,[293] which originated mostly during the Berlin period. Elsewhere in the present volume there have been numerous occasions to cite the keen and colorful, albeit opinionated travel reports and other essays by him,[294] with regard to the contemporary sonata and its composers. Reichardt knew personally many of the composers of primary importance to the sonata, including Emanuel Bach, Haydn, Mozart, and Beethoven, whose music he revered above that of all others.[295] Today, as in his own lifetime, Reichardt's main claim to a niche in music history remains less that of a composer of sonatas or other instrumental works than of an important figure in the Berlin lieder school, an aesthetician,[296] and an observer of the international musical scene.

About 30, or nearly half, of Reichardt's sonatas are for keyboard alone, and 3 more have largely subordinate accompaniments (no. 52/1, 2, and 4 in Dennerlein's thematic index).[297] Dating from a MS of about 1770 to 3 works composed about 1809 for Beethoven's pupil

291. Extending only to the late 1780's, the most comprehensive study is still Schletterer/REICHARDT (1865); both the unpublished and published (1805) portions of Reichardt's autobiography are included in full (pp. 18-183); besides being unfinished, this study is bulky, disorganized, and without an index. Among several, more recent studies (cf. GROVE VII 109-110 [Loewenberg]; Dennerlein/REICHARDT 3-7), the most pertinent here is Dennerlein/REICHARDT, on the man and his keyboard music (including a thematic index of all movements in all of his available instrumental music).

292. Cf. Schletterer/REICHARDT 17. In Dennerlein/REICHARDT 47-49 appears a chronology of Reichardt's life and works, subdivided into 6 periods.

293. Reichardt's own list of his publications (up to 1791) appeared in Reichardt/KUNSTMAGAZIN I 207-209 and II 124-125.

294. Cf. the list of his writings in Eitner/QL VIII 164-165 (but delete the last item, dated 1812 [Dennerlein/REICHARDT 7]).

295. E.g., on Bach, cf. Reichardt/BERLIN *passim* (written partly to win the Berlin post?) and the oft-cited autobiographic statement in Schletterer/REICHARDT 163-165; on the 3 Viennese masters, cf. Reichardt/PARIS II 34-35 (Haydn) and III 246-247, and the references to Reichardt's important Vienna *Briefe* of 1808-09 in Dennerlein/REICHARDT 36-43 as well as Thayer/BEETHOVEN II 82-83 and 165-166. While Mozart was alive there was some ill feeling between him and Reichardt (Abert/MOZART II 630).

296. Sieber/REICHARDT is a helpful study of Reichardt the aesthetician.

297. The sons., both solo and acc'd., are discussed in chronological order, with many exx. and 2 facs. of title pp., in Dennerlein/REICHARDT 68-104. The solo sons. are also discussed (and listed), with exx., in Stilz/BERLINER 60-72. (Dennerlein and Stilz appear to have worked without knowledge of each other's investigations, both studies appearing in 1930 [as well as Sieber/REICHARDT]; but the analyses are generally similar.)

Dorothea von Ertmann,[298] the solo sonatas include 3 sets of 6, published in 1776, 1778, and 1782, and a set of 4 published in 1793.[299] There are also 7 accompanied sonatas in which the violin is less dispensable, 6 of which appeared as Op. 2 in 1777.[300] There are 8 "solo" violin sonatas, of which 6 have cello or bass accompaniments, but the other 2, Nos. 5 and 6 in a set of 6 "solo" sonatas published in 1778, are actually unaccompanied.[301] There are 2 sonatas for keyboard "con Flauto obligato," one left in MS and the other published in 1787.[302] And there are 17 SSB string trios, of which 14 were originally called "Sonata."[303]

Reichardt's sonatas largely fall into the three-movement plan of a "sonata form," a two- or three-part slow movement, and an A-B-A-B-A rondo. Two notable exceptions are the two extant "Ertmann" sonatas, in which a moderate movement is inserted before the finale. The "sonata forms" are consistent in their ternary design and return to opening material, the latter principle being a significantly conscious one on Reichardt's part as early as 1770:

> How often we [J. A. P. Schulz and I] later laughed over our orthodoxy at that time with regard to the forms sanctified by the Berlin school. As I played my sonata for Schulz up to the second section of the last movement, he would say to me: Now only a good modulation into a related key is lacking, plus a felicitous return in the main key to a restatement of the preferred places in the first section, and the sonata is *comme il faut.*[304]

Reichardt was conservative in his continued insistence, characteristic of Berlin, on but one main *Affekt* in a movement.[305] Even in the late "Ertmann" sonatas the nearest to contrasting themes are accessory ideas heard against the figuration of the main idea (as in Son. in f/i/12 and 51).

Reichardt's early sonatas are rather weak, ungraceful pieces. In them may be detected influences of Emanuel Bach, Georg Benda, and C. F. C. Fasch. As the substance and skill improved—for example, in

298. Mod. ed.: "Grande" Son. in f (first Ertmann son., not published until 1813; Dennerlein no. 57a), Newman/THIRTEEN-m no. 11, with preface.

299. The place and date for Nos. 3 and 4 of this last set are given as "Zerbst, 1799" in Gerber/NEUES III 823, but all 4 sons. in the set at the Library of Congress were published in Berlin, apparently about the same year (1793).

300. Cf. Dennerlein/REICHARDT 80 and 81-82.

301. Dennerlein no. 37/5 and 6. Cf. Moser/VIOLINSPIEL 326-328 and Gates/SOLO 136-142 (both with exx.). Mod. ed.: Sons. 5 and 6 in E♭ and C, NAGELS-m No. 64 (Küster).

302. Cf. Dennerlein/REICHARDT 89. Regarding a mod. ed. of the MS son. in C (Breitkopf & Härtel, 1957) cf. DMF XII (1959) 251.

303. Cf. Dennerlein/REICHARDT 75-76. For a mod. ed. of a Son. in E♭ cf. Altmann/KAMMERMUSIK 78.

304. Trans. from Reichardt/SCHULZ 12-13.

305. E.g., cf. Reichardt/KUNSTMAGAZIN I 25 and II 66; also, the statement of 1792 cited in Dennerlein/REICHARDT 96; Sieber/REICHARDT 95-96.

the accompanied set of 1777—Haydn's mark is suggested more and more, especially in the kind of motivic persistence, refined melodic ornamentation, and tonal surprises. From this point, Reichardt's preference seems already to have changed from the clavichord and harpsichord to the piano, the makes and characteristics of which brought forth numerous comments from him in his later years.[306] His most interesting sonatas are the four of 1793 and the two "Ertmann" sonatas of about 1809. In the former, even though the movements are short, the monothematic and motivic processes sometimes wear out the initial idea and make the "development" section *de trop* (as in Son. 1/i). Dennerlein calls attention to the interconnection of movements by adagio recitative measures (in Son. 1) and to the "parlante" style introduced in these sonatas as part of Reichardt's shift of interest from instrumental to operatic music and to a more personal expression.[307] Every movement of Sonata 2 in G exhibits the short, distinct rhythmic units (often separated by rests) that characterize the "parlante" style (Ex. 95).

Not until fifteen years later did Reichardt turn to the sonata again. Then he wrote his strongest works of this sort, inspired by the performances he heard in Vienna by Beethoven's pupil Dorothea von Ertmann and others in such works as Opp. 13, 26, and 27/2, and

Ex. 95. From the development section in Johann Friedrich Reichardt's Sonata 2/i in G of 1793 (Dennerlein no. 56/2/i; after the original ed. "à Berlin au nouveau Magazin de Musique" at the Library of Congress).

306. Cf. Reichardt/PARIS I 150-152 and III 39; Thayer/BEETHOVEN II 87-88; Dennerlein/REICHARDT 81. The piano is not actually indicated as his alternate choice prior to a title page of 1787 (H-or-P + Fl).

307. Dennerlein/REICHARDT 90-96.

several violin sonatas.[308] Probably he heard Op. 57, too, because the published Sonata in f is more like this than the previous works—in the sudden dynamic contrasts and the coda of its first movement, the somber, low-register chord progressions and quasi-variations of the second movement, and the continuous 16th-note passages in the finale. The added, third movement is an A-B-A "Andante" that slightly anticipates the gentle, songful second and fourth movements of Brahms' piano Sonata in f, Op. 5. Otherwise, Romantic leanings in both "Ertmann" sonatas are found chiefly in the considerable harmonic color, the rich sonorities, and the piano writing that employs chords and octaves. In the first movement of the Sonata in f, the writing becomes thick and clumsy at times, partly because there is a continual pseudopolyphonic filler part. Evidently a motivic unity based on the opening idea was still sought. The counterpoint, harmony, independent musical thinking, and somewhat bland themes in both of the "Ertmann" sonatas bring Rust's sonatas to mind (especially that in e, Czach no. 16),[309] although they do not show Rust's high professional skill. Partly because of the piano treatment, a distinctly unfavorable (and discursive) review of the Sonata in f was written by Reichardt's onetime pupil E. T. A. Hoffmann.[310] Much as it pained him, Hoffmann saw Reichardt as a man of rich and varied talents now living on an island, oblivious of the pianistic marvels created in recent years by Mozart and Beethoven. In particular, he noted that there are still recollections of Emanuel Bach in the sonata under review, that the potentialities of the opening idea are lost in the sameness of the ensuing motivic figuration, and that the movements become progressively weaker. In all of these objections some truth must be acknowledged.

Totally forgotten are the relatively few sonatas published by contemporaries of Reichardt in Berlin. The flutist and pianist **Carl Wilhelm Glösch** (1732?-1809), possibly a pupil of Quantz, left a set of six keyboard "Sonatines," published by Hummel in 1780 and still marked by Emanuel Bach's influence.[311] The violinist and pianist **Friedrich Wilhelm Benda** (1745-1814), eldest son of Franz and pupil of Kirnberger, left a few solo, duet, and accompanied sonatas in MS and print, in the 1780's and 1790's.[312] And the more

308. Cf. Dennerlein/REICHARDT 96-104, 40-41; Thayer & Riemann/BEETHOVEN II 414-415.

309. Cf. Dennerlein/REICHARDT 96-98. The unmistakable signature of Rust is on both the 1776 and 1778 sets of Reichardt's solo sons. at the Library of Congress.

310. AMZ XVI (1814) 344-350. Hoffmann is identified as the author in Stilz/BERLINER 61-62.

311. Cf. MGG V 298-299 (Becker).

312. Cf. Eitner/QL I 435. A 4-hand son., Op. 6, was reviewed favorably, with special praise for some striking modulations, in AMZ I (1798-99) 816.

successful and renowned opera and instrumental composer **Friedrich Heinrich Himmel** (1765-1814), who succeeded Reichardt and had some tiffs with Beethoven in Berlin,[313] left among his many
314a works at least twenty sonatas dating from about 1798 to 1810.[314] Except for a two-piano sonata (played with Wölfl in Paris in 1801[315]) and a sonata for piano and flute, Op. 14, these last are all incipient piano trios, widely published and republished in six sets of three each under the name "sonata," but with fairly independent string and cello parts. Although Op. 14 was reviewed as a "trivial and watery" disappointment,[316] an examination of three of the trios, Op. 16, shows a composer of merit, whose fine piano writing tallies with his reputation as an expert pianist,[317] and whose style, ideas, and developed forms bring him rather near to Mendelssohn.[318]

Only more forgotten sonatas can be found by the obscure composers active in German centers west and north of Berlin during the high- and late-Classic Era. **Johann Friedrich Gottfried Beckmann** (1737-92), outstanding organist and pianist in Celle, left at least sixteen solo or accompanied sonatas of a light popular sort, published between 1769 and 1797 (posthumous).[319] One **N. Scherer** was probably in Schwerin before 1785, where four sets of accompanied sonatas and two of cello sonatas (Vc and bass) are preserved and the first set is dedicated.[320] However, all these sets were published in Geneva (Switzerland), "chez l'auteur." The Baron **Adolph von Münchhausen** (before 1756-1811) was a diplomat and a talented dilettante in music, whose colorful life in various north German centers, partly in the service of Frederick William II, ended in suicide in Paris. His several four-hand and accompanied sonatas were published in the last decade of the eighteenth century.[321] A reading of the two four-hand sonatas published as Op. 2 about 1790 reveals fluent, melodious, fresh

313. Cf. Thayer/BEETHOVEN I 196-197; *The Harmonicon* I/1 (1823) 155.

314. Cf. the list in MGG VI 436 (Pfannkuch).

315. MGG VI 433.

316. AMZ I (1798-99) 735.

317. According to the same review, just cited. A posthumous, more favorable review of a 4-hand arrangement of the first trio in Op. 16 appeared in AMZ XXX (1828) 812.

318. Mendelssohn's teacher Zelter was close to Himmel in Berlin.

319. Gerber/LEXICON I 125; Gerber/NEUES I 304; Eitner/QL I 400-401; Cat. BRUXELLES II item 5918 and III item 12,651.

320. The incipits of the first son. in each set are given in Cat. SCHWERIN II 203-204. Cf. Eitner/QL IX 12.

321. Cf. MGG IX 904 (Langner); Cat. SCHWERIN II 71-72; BRITISH UNION II 715.

music, with a little contrapuntal interest and some challenges for the pianist. **Federigo Fiorillo** (1755-at least 1823), remembered chiefly for his violin studies, was a virtuoso violinist and mandolinist who played in many of the European centers from London and Paris to Riga and St. Petersburg.[322] Born in Braunschweig as the son of a Neapolitan opera composer (Ignatio Fiorillo, 1715-87), who himself had published six cembalo sonatas in Braunschweig in 1750, Federigo left some forty-five sonatas for violin with viola accompaniment, piano alone, or piano with violin accompaniment. Most of these were published along with many other works, between about 1785 and 1820. The six sonatas for violin and viola, Op. 15 (Paris, *ca.* 1795), which were examined here, are all in three movements (F-S-M or F). From both technical and melodic standpoints they would still be of interest to string players.

322. Cf. MGG IV 258-261 (Lehmann); Bone/GUITAR 119-120; Mooser/ANNALES II 198, 204, 365.

Chapter XVII

France From About 1735 to 1780

Pre-Revolutionary Tastes, Trends, and Conditions

The near century of the Classic sonata in France that is surveyed in these next two chapters extends from early in Louis XV's reign to the end of Louis XVIII's. In other words, it embraces that whole cataclysmic segment of French history that saw the rapid deterioration and final collapse of the corrupt, war-ridden, antiquated, financially ruined, feudal monarchy; the ensuing Revolution, with all its own corruptions, disillusionments, terrors, transfers of power, and ultimate failures (1789-99); as well as the sensational rise and stunning fall of the Napoleonic empire (1803-15), ending with the temporary restoration of the French monarchy at the time of the Congress of Vienna (1815). We bump into these hard facts every time we find a sonata composer dedicating his works to Marie Antoinette in one decade, then joining the newest cause to write songs for the Directory in the next decade; or fleeing the country to escape the Revolution; or even, at least in one instance (Edelmann), dying on the guillotine.

To be sure, as fast as the French government deteriorated during the years leading to the Revolution, even faster did the French intellectual life advance. Highly stimulating to the fine arts was that French manifestation of the Age of Reason better known as the Enlightenment, with such immediate outgrowths as the epochal *Encyclopédie* (1751-80) and the naturalistic philosophy of Rousseau. Its effects on music were sometimes less direct and less tangible than on the other arts, but they were felt quite as much. Note how F. M. Grimm, the German litterateur in Paris, seemed compelled to mention current philosophical interests when he described the impact of Gluck's Parisian debut in April, 1774:[1]

1. Trans. from the original French given in Benton/HÜLLMANDEL 3 (in the course of a helpful introductory chap. on "The French Attitude Toward Instrumental Music").

> For fifteen days no one has thought, no one has dreamed of anything but music in Paris. It is the subject of all our disputes, of all our conversations, the essence of all our meals; and it would seem almost ridiculous to [hope to] be able to get interested in something else. To a question of politics one answers you with a detail of harmony; to a moral reflection, by the ritournelle of an ariette; and if you try to recall the interest that a certain work of Racine or Voltaire arouses, one's total answer is to call your attention to the effect of the orchestra in the fine recitative of Agamemnon. Is there any need to add after that that it is the *Iphigénie* of the Chevalier Gluck that has caused all this great turmoil.

Of course, with such a statement we need to recall that from the "Guerre des bouffons" (1752-54) to the feud of the "Gluckists" and "Piccinnists" (1776-79) the long-standing quarrel between the ancients and the moderns was still making itself felt in polemics on Italian (or modern-style) versus French (or older-style) music (SBE 30-32, 352-353; SCE II). Both inside and outside of France there was astonishing hostility toward native French music in the later eighteenth century. We learn of it in no uncertain terms not only from Rousseau, Grimm, d'Alembert, Diderot and the other pro-Italian Encyclopedists but from men like Burney[2] (who for once, while we are on French instrumental music, has only a little to say worth quoting), and from the letters of both Mozarts, father and son.[3] It is true that all of these men were concerned primarily with the nature and singing of French opera. We need to recall, too, that opera, of whatever nationality, was the undisputed center of musical interest in the Paris of the Classic Era. If there were fewer remarks made against the more abstract, French instrumental music of the time it was mainly because fewer writers deigned to discuss it. One who did trouble to comment on it was d'Alembert, who wrote in 1767:[4] "All this purely instrumental music, without plan and without purpose, does not touch the soul and justifies one's asking
with Fontenelle, 'Sonata, what good are you to me?'[5] The authors who 5a
compose instrumental music make nothing but empty noise. . . . It must even be acknowledged that in general the full sense of the music is not perceived until it is allied with words or the dance. . . ."

Yet in spite of this attitude, Classic instrumental music did thrive in France—which for our purposes means, almost exclusively, Paris—and it did enjoy a life of its own. It thrived, in fact, because other conditions were so favorable to its healthy cultivation. For one thing,

2. In BURNEY'S TOURS I 322-326, Scholes summarizes Burney's caustic remarks as part of an intriguing survey of anti-French sentiment at that time.

3. Cf. Anderson/MOZART I 53-54 and II 770, 781, 787.

4. Trans. from the original French as given in Benton/HÜLLMANDEL 5. Recall the longer, similar statement by Rousseau quoted near the end of our Chap. II.

5. On the uncertain origin and the spread of this oft-cited remark, cf. SBE 353.

there was the active concert life.[6] Scarcely a musician we shall meet failed to make one or more appearances as soloist, director, or participant at the Concert spirituel (from 1725), not seldom playing his own concertos or sonatas.[7] The concerts of this organization were public as were those of the Concert des amateurs (from 1769). Many other concerts were privately sponsored in the salons of wealthy amateurs and patrons like the statesman La Pouplinière, among whose directors up to 1762 were Rameau, Gossec, and J. Stamitz;[8] or the Prince de Conti,
8a whom Schobert and Gossec served from the early 1760's, among others; or the Baron de Bagge;[9] or the mistresses of Louis XV, especially Madame de Pompadour.[10]

Another condition favorable to the cultivation of instrumental music was the large number of active publishers in Paris, which made this city at least the equal of London and Amsterdam, and second to no city, in its publishing trade during the later eighteenth century. This distinction applies not only to the number of publishers, the quantity of their publications, the several rich anthologies of eighteenth-century music (such as Anth. VENIER-m or Anth. CARTIER-m), and the several periodicals containing music,[11] but to the wide international spread of the composers listed in the Paris catalogues.[12] It applies, too, to the extent to which the Paris publications are still represented today in all the main libraries throughout Europe.[13]

At the onset of the French pre-Classic Era, in the 1730's, the large number of sonatas and other instrumental works by Italians that were being published[14] was proof that there was no letup in the pro-Italian enthusiasm that had encouraged Couperin to introduce the sonata in France some forty years earlier (SBE 355-366). To this same enthusiasm may be credited the Italian line of melo/bass sonatas in Paris that extended right to the end of the Classic Era and the music of Viotti. The line is defined primarily by French and Italian violinists

6. The chief study of this subject is still Brenet/CONCERTS, in which Chaps. 6-12 of Part II concern the period under discussion here. For convenient summaries cf. MGG VII 1591-1592 (Schaal); Benton/HÜLLMANDEL 78-89.

7. Cf. the description of one complete program in 1770, in BURNEY's TOURS I 16-17.

8. In spite of the basic study Cucuel/LA POUPLINIÈRE, little is known about the actual make-up of La Pouplinière's programs (cf. pp. 356-359).

9. A sample program appears on p. 158 of the fine study Cucuel/BAGGE.

10. Cf. Brenet/CONCERTS 353-355; 216-217.

11. Cf. MGG II 1482-1483 (Sorel-Nitzberg).

12. Cf. Johansson/FRENCH II *passim.*

13. It is interesting, for example, to note, how many were included in the Madrid house of Alba before the library's recent destruction (cf. Subirá/ALBA *passim*).

14. Cf. La Laurencie/ÉCOLE II 5-6.

trained in the Piedmontese school of Pugnani, following the precedent of the late-Baroque violinist Leclair, who had trained under Pugnani's teacher, Somis.[15] The other main line of the sonata in Paris was the more progressive one for keyboard with violin accompaniment. Starting with early but conservative sets of accompanied *pièces de clavecin* by the violinists Mondonville and Guillemain, this other line was continued rather by a series of French organists, clavecinists, and—from about 1770[16]—pianists. But many of its best examples come rather from German and Alsatian residents in Paris, especially Schobert, Eckard, and Hüllmandel. There was also the important set, Op. 5, that Boccherini wrote for the Parisian public in 1768 (as discussed in Chap. VIII).

Disregarding confusions of terminology for the moment, we may note that the accompanied sonata was generally treated more seriously than the even more popular unaccompanied duo in Paris. It was closer in this respect to the keyboard trios (H-or-P & Vn & Vc) and string quartets that were then becoming popular. The sonata was on a par in quantity and often in quality with the two main orchestral forms being cultivated in Paris, the symphony and the solo concerto. The last two types, especially, show the influence of the Mannheim school, and show it for more reasons than Riemann's wide-ranging enthusiasm. In this instance, it will be recalled, there were both the many publications and the actual presence on the scene of J. Stamitz and several of his successors to account for the influence.

Three of the composers in Paris most important to those other chamber and orchestra types just mentioned, as well as to opera, get no special discussion here because they left few or no sonatas now known. **Jean-Philippe Rameau** (1683-1764), the main exponent of the conservative French styles against which the Encyclopedists railed, reportedly wished, after it was too late, that he had taken Pergolesi as his operatic model.[17] At any rate, he at least showed an interest in the newer, though not Italian, style of sonatas when in 1741 he prefaced his *Pièces de clavecin en concert* with an apparent reference to Mondonville's successful accompanied sonatas of 1734: "The success of the sonatas that have appeared recently as clavecin pieces with violin has given me the idea to follow almost the same plan in the new clavecin

15. Cf. SBE 379-384, but add the valuable new, well-oriented diss. Preston/LECLAIR.

16. Cf. BURNEY'S TOURS I 27. Among interesting facts and figures on French musical life in Brook/SYMPHONIE 493-496 are the mentions of listings of some 90 teachers of piano or harpsichord in 1783, 93 of violin, and 42 of cello.

17. Cf. BURNEY'S TOURS I 324; Girdlestone/RAMEAU 439.

pieces that I am presuming to publish today."[18] The Belgian composer **François-Joseph Gossec** (1734-1829) published a youthful, Italianate set of six "trio" sonatas (SS/bass) as his Op. 1 two years after he got to Paris in 1751.[19] Thereafter, except for some unaccompanied duos, his instrumental music consisted of larger chamber ensembles and, especially, the many symphonies for which he is chiefly remembered today. And the other main Belgian, **André Ernest Modeste Grétry** (1741-1813), is supposed to have left two sonatas for two harpsichords in MS,[20] neither of which could be found in the course of the present study. These may have been among the early instrumental works he wrote before leaving Liège in 1759 and before he began his main career ten years later in Paris, in the field of the *opéra comique*.

The contemporary sources on the Classic sonata in France are numerous and often of a specific nature. We shall have several occasions to quote explicit prefaces by the composers themselves, especially from the early accompanied sonatas, and to quote pungent statements by observers like Grimm. Furthermore, much of the contemporary opinion and many of the exact dates come from the copious reviews and announcements in the current Parisian journals and periodicals, of which *Mercure de France* is easily the most important. These reviews and announcements have been culled thoroughly by several twentieth-century writers on French music (and by Cari Johansson in her essential collection of French music publishers' catalogues from the later eighteenth century). The most thorough study for our purposes is still the one relied on most fully in our previous volume—that is, the monumental three-volume study by La Laurencie on the French violin school,[21] published in 1922-24. There is no equally thorough study of the French keyboard school, although the valuable series of articles published by Saint-Foix about the same time[22] would add up to a small volume on this subject. These articles were starting points for Eduard Reeser's important dissertation on the accompanied sonata in Paris (1939)[23] and

18. Trans. from the quotation in La Laurencie/ÉCOLE II 160; cf. *infra* under Guillemain. Rameau's nephew, L. Rameau, published a set of acc'd. sons., Op. 1, in 1788 (Favre/FRANÇAISE 175).

19. Cf. MGG V 545 (Wangermée).

20. Cf. Eitner/QL IV 373 (not in MGG V 827). The 2 acc'd. sons. (H & Vn & Fl & Vc) that are listed as Op. 1 in Cat. BRUXELLES II 379 are arrangements, apparently, from his opera *L'Amitié a l'epreuve,* first produced in Paris in 1770. Perhaps such was the nature, too, of the "Six sonates pour le clavecin" placed in 1768 but reported as inaccessible in Shedlock/SONATA 27.

21. La Laurencie/ÉCOLE.

22. Saint-Foix/PIANISTES (1922-28).

23. Warm thanks are also owing to Dr. Reeser of Bilthoven for various personal communications on this subject.

for George Favre's richly illustrated book on French piano music from about 1770 to 1830 (1953). There are also some still more recent dissertations that contribute significantly to these topics, as noted in the coming pages.[24] The sonatas to be discussed in the next two chapters, by some 40 native and 25 foreign composers, are poorly represented in modern editions. The 12 complete accompanied sonatas and many generous examples in Reeser's book, Reeser's separate edition of Eckard's sonatas, and the sonatas by Schobert that Riemann and later editors have published are the chief exceptions.

Melo/bass Sonatas (*Gaviniès*)

We may begin our discussion of French composers by considering briefly some seventeen men who pointed as much to the past as to the future, although their sonatas appeared as late as the 1780's. The conservatism of these men lay primarily in their adherence to melo/bass settings and their conventional, rather perfunctory approach to problems of harmony and form. Yet, as in Pugnani's sonatas, the styles were 24a
sometimes progressive enough to belie and even absorb the melo/bass settings. Moreover, by the 1770's the bass part often was no longer figured for realization but was intended rather as a true if somewhat subordinate participant in string duos and trios. Although very few added to the scope of violin technique, most of the composers in question were themselves brilliant string players, several performed often at the Concert spirituel, and some of the earlier ones were among those numerous Italian-born violinists from the Piedmont who settled in Paris in the two decades from about 1730. G. B. Somis, teacher of Pugnani, seems to have been one of the principal influences on both the Italian emigrants and the native Frenchmen, like Leclair, Guignon, and Guillemain, who studied with him while they were in Torino (SBE 187-188).

Joseph Canavas (*ca.* 1712-76[25]), born in Torino, was a violinist often heard in the Concert spirituel from 1741. He published two sets of six sonatas each in Vn/bass settings in 1739 and 1763, and another separate sonata of this type in 1767, all in three movements,
F-S-F. The later sonatas are described as revealing much greater 25a
clarity of outline, melodic continuity, and technical exploitation of the violin than the first set.[26] Born in Agen in southwestern

24. The diss. by Barry S. Brook on the related subject of the French symphony in the later 18th c. was not procurable at the time of this study (cf. the "interim report" in Brook/SYMPHONIE).

25. Not *ca.* 1714-66 as in MGG II 740 (Borrel).

26. La Laurencie/ÉCOLE II 91-97.

France, the violinist **Joseph Barnabé Saint-Sevin,** better known as **L'Abbé le fils** (1727-1803), was another frequent performer at the Concert spirituel. A pupil of Leclair, he published two sets of six Vn/bass sonatas each, Opp. 1 and 8 in 1748 and about 1764, that again are reported to reveal distinct advances in style from one set to the next. Several of the sonatas, especially in Op. 1, still have the old church plan of four movements, S-F-S-F. The technical demands—including cadenzas, passages in thirds and sixths, wide stretches, and high positions—are said to equal those
27a of his important teacher.[27] The brothers **Pierre Miroglio** (*ca.* 1715-*ca.* 1763) and **Jean-Baptiste Miroglio** (*ca.* 1725-*ca.* 1785) were two more Piedmontese violinists who settled in Paris, the one eventually going into the employ of La Pouplinière[28] and the other into a stormy music publishing and renting business.[29] Pierre left a set of six Vn/bass sonatas in 1741, dedicated to Geminiani and described as being very advanced technically. Jean-Baptiste's two sets of Vn/bass sonatas and one set of SS/bass sonatas, published in 1749, 1750, and 1753, are described as somewhat less formidable technically, yet still well adapted to the solo instrument and a little more supple and fluent musically.[30]

Nicolas Vibert (*ca.* 1710-72), descended from a French family of luthiers, was active in the Concert spirituel from 1751, and in court and opera productions as well. He published two sets of six sonatas each in 1752, one in SS and one in SS/bass setting. These are interesting for their curious inscriptions such as "Largo ideali" and "Allegro assai bizaria," and for some actual oddities, including unusual chromatic modulations, strangely shaped themes, frequent indications of "solo" and "tutti" (in the SS/bass set), and virtuoso fantasy sections that recall Locatelli.[31] **Julien-Amable Mathieu** (1734-1811), born right in Versailles and a pupil of his father, progressed so rapidly on the violin that at fourteen he was already allowed to succeed a retiring member of the king's "vingt-quatre violons." He published four sets of six sonatas each, two in 1756, in Vn/bass and SS/bass settings, and two in 1764, in SS and Vn/bass settings. After the first set, which abounds in elaborate ornamentations, Mathieu's tendency was to simplify his violin writing and work for clearer, broader designs.[32]

27. Cf. La Laurencie/ÉCOLE II 214-234 and III 249 (reference to a mod. ed. of Op. 1/1 in D); MGG VIII 11-12 (Wirsta).
28. Cf. Cucuel/LA POUPLINIÈRE 354-355.
29. Cf. Hopkinson/PARISIAN 19-20.
30. La Laurencie/ÉCOLE II 200-209 and 288; MGG IX 366-367 (Brook).
31. Cf. La Laurencie/ÉCOLE II 256-261, with exx.
32. Cf. La Laurencie/ÉCOLE II 269-276. The dates of Mathieu's Opp. 1 and 4 are incorrect in MGG VIII 1787 (Raugel).

The most successful, renowned, and representative among these late French composers of melo/bass sonatas was **Pierre Gaviniès** (1728-1800), the son of a Bordeaux luthier who moved to Paris in 1734. Possibly a pupil of Leclair, Gaviniès made his debut at the Concert spirituel when he was thirteen, playing one of Leclair's duets with L'Abbé le fils (then fourteen).[33] A long career of playing before this and other Paris institutions won recognition for him on a par with that of Pugnani (who played in Paris in 1754[34]), J. Stamitz, and his best French contemporaries. Viotti later called him the "French Tartini."[35] He was especially noted for his mastery of the bow, his elegiac projection of melody, his control of the softest tones, his rich ornamentation, and his versatility in all the current schools of violin playing.[36] He seems to have been no less well regarded for his influential teaching and his generosity to both his colleagues and his students.[37]

Along with three sets containing concertos, études, and other string
music by Gaviniès, four sets of sonatas by him are known[38] Opp. 1 and 38a
3 contain six Vn/bass sonatas each, published originally in 1760 and
1764.[39] Op. 5 contains six SS sonatas separately entitled "Duetto,"
published before 1774.[40] And Op. 7, which appeared soon after
Gaviniès' death in 1800 and was dedicated to "son Ami [Rodolphe]
Kreutzer," contains three sonatas for violin with cello accompaniment,
"of which the one in F minor is called his 'Tomb.' "[41] 41a

Gaviniès' sonatas are typical in being almost all in three movements, mostly in the order F-S-M or F (but S-F-M in Op. 1/3). A growing attention to the niceties of execution is suggested in such precise inscriptions over the movements as "Allegro con fuoco ma non troppo" or "Vivace ma affettuoso." When the middle movements are in a different key they are in the relative or dominant. No special effort seems to have been made to relate the movements of a sonata by similar incipits. The finales are in moderate tempos in Op. 1 (including the ever popular

33. The chief study of Gaviniès, superseding previous accounts, is La Laurencie/ÉCOLE II 277-332; on his teachers and debut cf. p. 278. Gaviniès is rated highly in Burney/HISTORY II 976.

34. Pamparato/PUGNANI 228.

35. La Laurencie/ÉCOLE II 282 (with source).

36. Cf. the numerous contemporary tributes cited in La Laurencie/ÉCOLE II 280-283, 310-317. Mentions of Gaviniès by L. Mozart appear in Anderson/MOZART II 698 and 744.

37. Cf. La Laurencie/ÉCOLE II 305-310.

38. Cf. La Laurencie/ÉCOLE II 283, 287, and 317 for full titles; BRITISH UNION I 364 for additional listings and later 18th-c. eds. A further Vn/bass son. and a cembalo son. are listed as being in Paris (in MSS?) in MGG IV 1510 (Borrel).

39. Mod. eds.: Op. 1, complete, Englebert & Gallon/GAVINIÈS-m; Op. 1/2 in g, Alard/VIOLON-m No. 6.

40. That is, before the Sieber reprint (Johansson/FRENCH II Facs. 105).

41. Cf. La Laurencie/ÉCOLE II 302, 317.

minuet, in Son. 1), but several are marked "Presto" in Op. 3. What most of these finales and several other movements do have in common is some use of melodic variations, whether in a numbered series or merely in a written out *da capo* following a "Minore e piano" in a ternary minuet design (Op. 3/5/iii).

Gaviniès' middle movements characteristically have the clear, easy-going melodic flow of that separate violin "Romance" by him that was especially popular in his day.[42] The first movements also reveal well shaped melodic phrases, often in large four-measure arches and always clear in spite of the frequent chromaticism and almost constant rich ornamentation. Only the rather frequent I^6_4-V-I cadences in the sonatas of Op. 1 tend to disrupt the broad flow. When the harmonic rhythm changes at the rate of only one chord per measure, as is frequently true, there is little left for the *b.c.* to do but outline the successive notes of that chord. Second and even third themes are not unusual in the first movements. But since the ideas are almost all lyrical, pathetic, and flowing there is little sense of contrast (Ex. 96). Nor in these

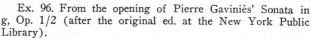

Ex. 96. From the opening of Pierre Gaviniès' Sonata in g, Op. 1/2 (after the original ed. at the New York Public Library).

themes or the many measures of idiomatic passage work is there much of the tension—the thematic concentration, rhythmic intensification, or long-range tonal plan—that makes for the inexorable drive and logic of some of the best Classic sonata forms.

Among the several violinists in Gaviniès' immediate sphere of influence was **Pierre Vachon** (1731?-1803), who may have been

42. Cf. La Laurencie/ÉCOLE II 296-297 and the exx. on pp. 319-323.

born in southeastern France in Arles. Vachon made the first of many appearances as soloist at the Concert spirituel in 1756. In this capacity and especially as a composer of comic operas he met with far less success than that enjoyed by Gaviniès, although he was influential in the development of the French string quartet and seems to have done better after he turned up in Berlin in 1786.[43] Among works pertinent here he left two sets of six sonatas each in Vn/bass setting, Opp. 1 and 3, published in 1760 and 1769,[44] and two sets of six "trios" each in SS/bass setting, Opp. 4 and 5, both published about 1772. Only Op. 4 was published originally not in Paris but in London, probably during Vachon's visit there in 1772.[45] It differs from Op. 5 in that each individual "trio" is called "sonata," and from nearly all the other sonatas or trios in that each sonata has only two movements (F or M and minuet or F) instead of the customary three movements. The brilliant violin writing is, as usual, all in the "solo" sonatas. One finds Gaviniès' rich ornamentation again, with the characteristic turn near the starts of themes,[46] the request for "tasto solo" (unrealized *b.c.*) during the most showy flourishes, and the variation treatment of the finales. One also finds that Gaviniès' sort of clear phrases has sometimes become so symmetrical, square, and harmonically obvious in Vachon's sonatas as to seem almost trite this early in the Classic Era. A Mozartean flavor is imparted when these phrases have chromatic, feminine endings.[47]

The same extreme virtuosity and the same, more obviously phrased melodies are to be found in the six three-movement sonatas in Vn/bass setting, Op. 1, published in 1768 by Gaviniès' pupil **Nicolas Capron** (*ca.* 1740-1784).[48] A frequent soloist at the Concert spirituel from 1761 and an habitué of Parisian musical and literary circles, Capron soon turned to a more popular style based on potpourris of familiar airs after critics praised his technical prowess but lamented the technical inaccessibility of his writing. The Abbé **Alexandre-Auguste Robineau** (1747-1828), who had previously studied with Lolli in Italy, was also a pupil of Gaviniès, a virtuoso soloist at the Concert spirituel (from 1767), and the composer of a single set of six three-

43. The main source on Vachon is La Laurencie/ÉCOLE II 333-346, including the well-known picture of him in a chamber group (after p. 338). He is mentioned favorably in DITTERSDORF 284-285.

44. Cf. La Laurencie/ÉCOLE II 336 for the full titles, and III 252 for the reprint of an "Adagio" in G. The first half of Op. 3/2/i is reprinted in Bücken/ROKOKO 104-105. The date for Op. 1 comes from Johansson/FRENCH II Facs. 45.

45. Cf. Pohl/MOZART II 370.

46. Cf. the exx. in La Laurencie/ÉCOLE II 344-345 and 319-321.

47. Cf. Bücken/ROKOKO 104-105.

48. Cf. La Laurencie/ÉCOLE II 368-379 (with exx.); MGG II 821-823 (Sorel-Nitzberg). Op. 1/1/i ("Allegretto") is in Anth. CARTIER-m 116.

movement Vn/bass sonatas published in 1768.[49] Characterized again by extremely rich, skillful figuration calculated to display all the then violinist's resources, Robineau's sonatas still have some of the elegiac breadth of Gaviniès' writing.[50] But in their pre-Romanticisms and sonorous uses of the violin's lowest tones (as in Son. 6/ii) they anticipate Viotti. In the finale of Sonata 6 the inscription by the good "abbé" reads, "Imitant la voix humaine, avec onction."

Still a third talented pupil of Gaviniès, **Simon Le Duc** the Elder (before 1748?-1777), made his first appearance as a composer in 1768 with a set of six "solo" violin sonatas.[51] Among other works, a second set, Op. 4, appeared three years later, in 1771.[52] Both sets preceded Le Duc's better known activities as publisher (succeeded by his talented younger brother and pupil Pierre) and as codirector of the Concert spirituel (with Gaviniès and Gossec, from 1773). The first set has both a *b.c.* and a *concertante* bass ("alto") part, whereas the second set has an unfigured bass that approaches the status of a duet part about as much as the lower part in Boccherini's Vc/bass sonatas of around 1770 (SCE VIII). Le Duc's style again recalls his teacher's as well as that of the leading Mannheim composers, especially
53a in its melodic mannerisms.[53] Even more than in the sonatas of his contemporaries, the inscriptions in Op. 1 suggest the prevalent concern for a highly refined, sensitive performance, both in their frequency and their choice wording (e.g., "Molto flebile espressivo affettuoso" in Op. 1/6).

By mentioning two remaining violinists who composed melo/bass sonatas before 1780 we are brought to the threshold of Viotti's melo/bass sonatas (which are saved for the start of the next chapter only because of their later date and his influence on still later musicians). Like Viotti, both men trained in Italy. The fine violinist and director **Pierre La Houssaye** (1735-1818) was born in Paris and

49. Cf. La Laurencie/ÉCOLE II 433-435, 437-441 (with exx.); Pincherle/ROBINEAU (with extracts from the fantastic autobiography of this double personality, who called himself Auguste as a painter and Alexandre as a musician; reprinted with minor changes in Pincherle/FEUILLETS 22-39); La Laurencie/ROBINEAU (with further biographic details). Mod. ed.: Son. 3 in f, Alard/VIOLON-m No. 44.

50. They are called the work of a master in Pincherle/ROBINEAU 235.

51. Cf. La Laurencie/ÉCOLE II 380-394. L. Mozart's good opinion of Le Duc's playing is cited in Saint-Foix/MOZART I 52. Cf., also, MQ XLVIII (1962) 498-513 (Brook).

52. Cf. Johansson/FRENCH I 85; on p. 91 a posthumous set (1781) is also listed.

53. The style and technical demands are already much simpler in *Six petits Duos pour deux violons, de la plus grande facilité* (1771), 3 of which were reprinted by B. Schott in 1941 (Doflein).

studied there with Pagin before going to Tartini in Padua and Traetta in Parma.[54] After directing Italian operas in London in 1772 he may have returned to Paris as early as 1773, for in that or the next year his set of six Vn/bass sonatas was published by Sieber.[55] La Laurencie writes of rhythmically fussy themes, advanced exploitation of the violin's techniques, and experiments with sonorities in the first movements of these sonatas; also, of sentimental or pathetic themes in the middle movements. Another fine violinist, **Gioachino Traversa** (*ca.* 1745-?), was, like Viotti, from the Piedmont region and a pupil of Pugnani. He appeared and won favor for his playing at the Concert spirituel in 1770.[56] Along with at least two sets of quartets and another of trios published in Paris between 1772 and 1779,[57] he left a set of 6 Vn/bass sonatas, Op. 2, that were published there, probably early in the decade.[58]

While all these melo/bass sonatas for violin were being produced, the late-Baroque school of cellists in Paris (SBE 388-390) continued to bear a little pre-Classic fruit of its own. All four men to be noted were virtuoso pupils of M. Berteau and all but Tillière can be linked to families with one or more other cellists of some renown at the time. **Jean-Baptiste-Aimé-Joseph Janson** (1742-1803), who made 58a
his debut in the Concert spirituel at thirteen (1755), published two sets of six Vc/bass sonatas, in 1765 and 1768.[59] In these sets the violin is made optional to the cello, as in Boccherini's set of about 1770. The music is described as difficult for its time but grateful for the cellist. **Jean Baptiste Cupis** the Younger (1741-?), who left a cello method and performed widely, published two sets of Vc/bass sonatas about 1765-70.[60]

Berteau's most famous pupil and one of the most important cellists of the later eighteenth century was **Jean Pierre Duport** the Elder (1741-1818). After a debut at the Concert spirituel at the age of twenty and many further Parisian successes, Duport left about 1769 to give concerts in England, Spain, and Italy, finally settling (from 1773) at the court of Frederick the Great, where he

54. Cf. La Laurencie/ÉCOLE II 500-507 (where La Houssaye is the last composer discussed in this monumental survey of French violin music prior to Viotti).

55. Cf. Johansson/FRENCH I 141. A mod. ed. (*ca.* 1900) of Son. 4 in g is cited in Altmann/KAMMERMUSIK 239.

56. Cf. Eitner/QL IX 445; Schmidl/DIZIONARIO II 616; La Laurencie/ÉCOLE III 204, 205.

57. Johansson/FRENCH I 146, II Facs. 56 and 110.

58. That is, sooner than the "c. 1780" in BRITISH UNION II 1018.

59. Cf. MGG VI 1718-1720 (Cotte); Straeten/VIOLONCELLO 267. Both sets are wrongly listed under the younger brother L. A. J. Janson in BRITISH UNION I 554.

60. Straeten/VIOLONCELLO 265-267; GROVE II 562 (Straeten); BRITISH UNION I 343.

stayed on in the service of the latter's successors.[61] L. Mozart knew Duport (and thought him conceited);[62] W. A. Mozart wrote variations on a minuet by him (K.V. 573);[63] Beethoven wrote his two piano sonatas with "Violoncelle obligé," Op. 5, for him, perhaps getting his advice on treatment of the cello while in Berlin (1796); and Schubart was among the many who praised his playing.[64] Duport left three sets of six Vc/bass sonatas each that can
65a be confirmed, published in Paris in 1766, 1771, and 1788.[65] Today these sonatas, in the usual three movements, remain interesting chiefly as fine vehicles for the cellist's art, although their technical problems no longer seem formidable as they once did. Duport knew, of course, how to make the cello sing in the slow movements and more lyrical themes. But the melodies now seem a bit saccharine and the clear phrases a bit obvious.

Somewhat more display of virtuosity and elasticity of phrasing can be found in the short movements of the six sonatas for cello and bass published about 1777 by **Joseph Bonaventure Tillière** (dates unknown). A cellist in Paris chamber and opera ensembles, Tillière was one of the several Frenchmen who wrote cello methods. At the end of his method, first published in 1774 (not 1764), there is a "Suonata" for two cellos in which virtuosity again is a main trait.[66]

Charles de Lusse (*ca.* 1720-at least 1774) may be added here as the composer of two sets of six sonatas each for flute and *b.c.*, both published in 1751. Probably a member of the de Lusse family of wind instrument makers and players, and something of a litterateur, Charles is said to have evinced some Mannheim influence and melodic charm
67a in these sonatas.[67]

61. Cf. MGG III 966-970 (Stephenson), with facs. of the title page of Op. 3 and reference to an unpublished diss. (1922) on the Duport brothers; Straeten/VIOLONCELLO 273-276 (with anecdotes).

62. Anderson/MOZART II 698.

63. Cf. Köchel/MOZART 723.

64. Cited in MGG III 967.

65. Johansson/FRENCH I 72 and 77, II Facs. 38. In BRITISH UNION I 299 the listing of an Op. 3 *ca.* 1765 and an Op. 4 *ca.* 1800, as well as the Op. 4 under the brother J. L. Duport, suggests confusions awaiting clarification or correction. Mod. eds. of 4 sons. are listed in Altmann/KAMMERMUSIK 268 (all with piano accompaniments made from the unfigured bass accompaniment). Cf. SCE V, with ex.

66. Cf. Straeten/VIOLONCELLO 271-273; Johansson/FRENCH II Facs. 108. Mod. ed.: Son. in g, Schroeder/CELLO-m No. 5528.

67. MGG VIII 1330-1332 (Wallon). 1751 would be soon to show "Mannheim influence," although Stamitz "was already in touch with Paris musicians in 1748" (GROVE VIII 41 [Gradenwitz]).

"Accompanied" Sonatas Before 1760 (Mondonville, Guillemain)

Our next composers to discuss for their contributions in Paris take us into more progressive trends. **Jean-Joseph Cassanéa de Mondonville** (1711-72), stood, like Scarlatti and Platti, on the borderline between late-Baroque and pre-Classic music. He was deferred in our previous volume and separated from his principal contemporaries Leclair and "Baptiste" Anet (SBE 367 and 379-385) because of certain anticipations of Classic scorings. An outstanding violinist and a main participant in the Concert spirituel, Mondonville is interesting here not only as the composer of four superior sets of six ensemble sonatas each, Opp. 1-4, but even more for the pioneer position of his Op. 3 in the history of the accompanied keyboard sonata and of the ultimate duo for piano and violin.[68] All of his sonatas were published by Boivin in Paris early in Mondonville's career, by the time he was about twenty-seven, after which he gave himself primarily to church and dramatic music, and to directing. Op. 1, six Vn/bass sonatas, and Op. 2, six *Sonates en trio pour deux violons ou flûtes avec la basse continue,* appeared in 1733 and 1734 during a (first?) visit to Paris from his birthplace of Narbonne in southern France.[69] Op. 3, *Pièces de clavecin en sonates avec accompagnement de violon,* and Op. 4, *Les Sons harmoniques* (6 Vn/bass sons.), were evidently composed in the French-Belgian border town of Lille and appeared probably at the start and end of a four-year gap, 1734-38, largely unaccounted for in Mondonville's life.[70]

Mondonville's melo/bass sonatas are essentially late-Baroque church types in the usual four movements (S-F-S-F).[71] The instrumental 71a
writing from this fine violinist[72] is idiomatic and resourceful. As would be expected, it is technically more advanced in the "solo" than the "trio" sonatas, where exchanges between the upper or all three parts are frequent (the cello occasionally being a *concertante* part independent

68. The chief biographic source, superseding several previous accounts, is La Laurencie/ÉCOLE I 376-423, followed by analyses of Opp. 1-5 on pp. 423-435. Much more detailed analyses of styles and forms, especially in Opp. 3 and 5, are provided in the recent, unpublished, well-conceived diss. Borroff/MONDONVILLE (1958).

69. The full titles of Opp. 1-4 and the dedications of Opp. 2 and 3 are given in La Laurencie/ÉCOLE I 379-380. Facs. of title, dedicatory, and score pp. from Opp. 1-4 (and 5) are scattered throughout Borroff/MONDONVILLE (cf. the "List of Plates" in I xii-xiii).

70. Cf. La Laurencie/ÉCOLE I 380, 381.

71. For mod. eds. of all of Opp. 1/4, 2/3, and 4/5 (Alard/VIOLON-m No. 43) plus a few separate mvts., cf. MGG IX 455-456 (Schwarz), La Laurencie/ÉCOLE III 251, and Borroff/MONDONVILLE I 307-309.

72. Cf. the contemporary tributes cited in La Laurencie/ÉCOLE I 380-383, 419-420.

of the *b.c.*, as in Op. 2/3/i). In the upper "trio" parts the alternative of flutes is actually ruled out much of the time by the range and the uses of double-stops.[73] The motivic, contrapuntal, and harmonic interest in the "solo" sonatas of Op. 1 tends to be greater than that in Op. 4, where the notably early use of harmonics in every sonata takes precedence. The introduction to Op. 4 explains this use of harmonics more as a means of facilitating than of enriching violin playing.[74]

Although violin sonatas with realized keyboard parts had been composed by Bach and others in the Baroque Era (SBE 65, 272, 276, 294), and although doubling of the lines by other instruments had already been invited in the French *Pièces de clavecin* (as by La Guerre),[75] Mondonville showed in his dedication of Op. 3, about 1734, how well aware he was that he was contributing something new: "It is perhaps more than rash to introduce instrumental music to the public today. For several years such a prodigious number of sonatas of all types have been brought to light that there is no one who does not believe this genre is exhausted. However, your Grace, inspired by the support that you accord to my art, I have sought to find something new. . . ." That the public took a special liking to Op. 3 is suggested by the fact that only it among his instrumental sets achieved re-editions while he was alive—two re-editions, in fact[76]—much as only this set has been made available in full in a modern edition.[77] Furthermore, before 1749 Op. 3 was arranged "en grand concerto" by its composer, under the title "Sei Sonate a quattro," to be played as orchestral music at the Concert spirituel;[78] and about 1748 Mondonville was encouraged by the success of Op. 3 to experiment further along the same lines, in the ten (not nine), mostly single-movement *Pièces de clavecin avec voix ou violon,* Op. 5, which might best be described as accompanied solo motets with Psalms in Latin as texts.[79]

Unlike Mondonville's other sonatas, all those in Op. 3 except No. 1

73. Cf. Borroff/MONDONVILLE I 45-46.

74. It is quoted in full in La Laurencie/ÉCOLE I 426-430 (with exx.); the chart of harmonics is reproduced in MGG IX after p. 448.

75. Cf. SBE 361-362; La Laurencie/ÉCOLE I 123 and 232, III 147-148; Rowen/CHAMBER 131-132; Borroff/MONDONVILLE I 289-292.

76. Walsh published it in 1753 (BRITISH UNION II 684) and it also appeared in an ed. with an Italian title but no place, date, or publisher (Pincherle/MONDONVILLE-m 24).

77. Pincherle/MONDONVILLE-m, with preface (cf. Borroff/MONDONVILLE I 310-316 regarding minor departures from the original ed. and differences in the Walsh ed.). Besides La Laurencie/ÉCOLE I 432-433 and Borroff/MONDONVILLE I 115-177, Reeser/KLAVIERSONATE 51-57 includes a discussion of Op. 3, with exx. and a complete reprint of Son. 3 in B♭ (no. 1 in the musical suppl.).

78. Cf. La Laurencie & Saint-Foix/SYMPHONIE 45-49, with exx.

79. Cf. Borroff/MONDONVILLE I 178-284 (full discussion of Op. 5) and II (complete transcription of Op. 5); also, Newman/ACCOMPANIED 339.

(which still begins with an "Overture," marked "Grave") have only three movements each, typically in the order of a fugal or imitative allegro, an "Aria" of moderate tempo in binary design with repeated "halves," and a similarly binary "Giga" in compound meter or "Allegro" in *alla breve* meter. Sonata 6 in A must already have been thought of for orchestra, for its first movement is marked "Concerto," it is based on a unison theme that returns in rondo fashion, and both "Solo" and "Tuti" indications occur in the score. Also, its second movement, marked "Larghetto," differs from the arias in the preceding sonatas in not being in binary design and in having imitative exchanges between the clavecinist's right hand and the violin that recall the middle movements in Vivaldi's concertos for two violins.

The keys of the sonatas in Op. 3 do not exceed two flats or three sharps, and there is no change of tonic in the middle movement, although the mode of the key changes in four of these movements. Mondonville's structures are convincing and the ideas, often piquant and angular in the manner of Scarlatti's ideas, are effective. At most, the fugal writing is fairly concentrated (Son. 1/i), but the left hand is more often a support than a participant with the right hand and violin. When the process is loosely imitative rather than more tangibly fugal, the first movements tend to unfold cursively in two- or four-measure units, quite as in Italy and Germany during the *galant* transition (Ex. 97). In the other movements a larger structural organization is provided by the binary design and by some incorporation of the rondo principle in the arias (as in the tender arias in c and g of Sons. 4 and 5, which recall similar movements by Leclair).

Regarding the ensemble texture of Op. 3, when the writing is fugal or imitative (as in Son. 3/i) the three parts made by clavecin and violin differ little from those in Bach's sonatas with realized keyboard, unless in the slightly slower harmonic rhythm and lesser expressiveness of Mondonville's contrapuntal writing. In other movements a distinction results from the more idiomatic treatment of both clavecin and violin, as in the hand-crossing and string-crossing, respectively, of Sonata 4/iii, or the alternating hands and the chordal bowing slurs in Sonata 5/i. Occasionally the clavecinist is relegated to the role of accompanist (as in Sons. 3/iii, 4/ii, and 5/ii). Less often or consistently the violin may be subordinate (as at the start of Son. 4) or it may double the top clavecin line (as at the start of Son. 6).[80] But the violin is never dispensable. The two upper parts intertwine most of the time, Mondon-

80. The frequent references to this part as a simple accompaniment (as in MGG V 1095) are wrong. Exception must be taken, too, to most of the description of Op. 3 in Girdlestone/RAMEAU 41-42.

Ex. 97. From the first movement of Op. 3/4 by Jean-Joseph Cassanéa de Mondonville (after the Walsh ed. of 1753 at the University of North Carolina).

ville "having so ably married the clavecin to his favorite instrument," as Louis-Claude Daquin wrote in 1752.[81] Consequently, although the resultant texture did not originate as a violin solo with realized accompaniment, it must be said still to resemble that style more than that of the coming keyboard sonata with an actual accompaniment in the sense of a filler, both subordinate and optional.

Another virtuoso violinist deferred in our previous volume because of his association with the origins of the accompanied key-

81. La Laurencie/ÉCOLE I 421.

board sonata was **Louis-Gabriel Guillemain** (1705-70). Guillemain was a neurotic, alcoholic misanthrope, who could not bring himself to perform at the Concert spirituel, squandered his better-than-average earnings, and finally took his own life.[82] After training in Torino under 82a
G. B. Somis, he was active first in Lyon, then in Dijon, where he published his first set of sonatas in 1734. He began serving at court in Versailles and Paris from 1737 or 1738. In all, during the 18 years from 1734 to 1756 he published 10 sets totaling nearly 100 sonatas. These sets included 3 in Vn/bass setting (Opp. 1, 1734; 3, 1739; 11, 1742),[83] 2 in SS/bass setting (Opp. 2, by 1739; 10, 1741), 2 in SS setting (Opp. 4, 1739; 5, 1739), 2 of *Six Sonates en quatuors*[,] *ou conversations galantes et amusantes entre une flûte traversière, un violon, une basse de viole*[,] *et la basse continue* (Opp. 12, 1743; 17, 1756), and the single set of *Pièces de clavecin en* [6] *sonates, avec accompagnement de violon,* published as Op. 13 in 1745.[84]

Guillemain's Vn/bass set, Op. 1, contains his most conservative sonatas in that the prevailing plan of movements is, again, S-F-S-F rather than F-S-F as in most of his later sonatas, there is still some polyphonic writing in double-stops, and there is not yet the clear recapitulation to be found often in the allegros and some other movements of the later sonatas.[85] Op. 1 also contains some of the most difficult examples (short of his *Caprices,* Op. 18) of the wide leaps, rapid figuration, double-stops, intricate bowings, and rich ornamentation that astonished his contemporaries[86] and, in fact, only found their equal at that time in the most virtuosic writing of Leclair and Locatelli. Guillemain intended to make his next Vn/bass set easier for the public, as well as the second unaccompanied SS set (in which double-stops were eliminated so that 2 flutes could be optional in place of 2 violins).[87] But the level of technical demands seems to have remained high throughout his sonatas, especially in the upper instrument of the SS sonatas, which could well have been the works he played variously with Mon-

82. The principal source is the concise account of the man and analysis of most of his instrumental music (though with only cursory remarks, p. 23, on the acc'd. set, Op. 13) in La Laurencie/ÉCOLE II 1-30. A full study of Guillemain's extant instrumental music is needed.

83. "Mod." ed.: Op. 1/2 in C, Alard/VIOLON-m No. 34; this work also appeared in Anth. CARTIER-m III 176-189. A facs. of the title page of Op. 11 is given in Subirá/ALBA 116.

84. This set is briefly described, with exx., in Reeser/KLAVIERSONATE 57-61, 146; all of Op. 13/2 is reprinted as no. 2 in the suppl. A second acc'd. set, haphazardly assembled in a MS in Paris, has also been ascribed to Guillemain (La Laurencie/ÉCOLE II 16).

85. Cf. La Laurencie/ÉCOLE II 16-21, with exx.

86. Cf. La Laurencie/ÉCOLE II 14-15 and 9 for tributes by Marpurg, Daquin, and others.

87. Cf. La Laurencie/ÉCOLE II 4-5.

donville, Guignon, and others.[88] In the first of the two sets "en quators" the composer's "Avertissement" stipulates chamber (solo) rather than orchestral (multiple) performance of the parts, along with other matters of performance.[89] Actually, these sonatas are like "trio" sonatas or accompanied duets, for the "petit clavier" of the clavecin, to which he prefers to restrict the *b.c.* realization, and the "basse de viole" serve mainly to accompany or support the dialogue and the occasionally contrasted ideas presented by the flute and violin.

Guillemain's accompanied set of 1745, Op. 13, contains this historically important "Avertissement":

> When I composed these "pièces en Sonates" my first thought had been to make them only for the clavecin without putting in an accompaniment, having noticed often that the violin covered [the clavecin] a little too much, which keeps one from distinguishing the true melody [*sujet*]. But, to conform to present taste, I did not feel I could do away with the adding of this part, which requires an extreme softness of execution in order to let the clavecin itself be heard readily. If one wishes, one can play these sonatas with or without accompaniment. They will lose none of their melody, since it is all complete within the clavecin part, which [arrangement] will be [all the] more convenient for those who do not always have a violin[-ist?] at hand when they wish to play some of these pieces.[90]

The foregoing preface was written, obviously enough, in full cognizance of the similar preface to Rameau's *Pièces de clavecin en concert avec un violon ou une flûte et une viole ou un 2e violon,* published in 1741.[91] Actually, in the mere eleven years since Mondonville's Op. 3 had appeared, one can detect an evolution toward the optional, dispensable accompaniment. Whereas the solo, *concertante* violin cannot be omitted throughout most of that pioneer set of 1734, the two parts in Rameau's set often only fill out the clavecin part and sometimes simply double it,[92] and now the violin part in Guillemain's set proves, in fact, to be dispensable. Of course, whether it can be discarded with artistic impunity is more a matter of musical opinion. The clavecin part alone does make good sense throughout the six sonatas. But the violin serves as a charming free descant much of the time, since it is above more often than it is below the right-hand clavecin part (this being a main reason why it must be kept soft). Sometimes, too, it provides at

88. Cf. La Laurencie/ÉCOLE II 9, 14.
89. The preface to Op. 12 is quoted in full in La Laurencie/ÉCOLE II 27. The sons. are discussed in La Laurencie & Saint-Foix/SYMPHONIE 34-36 (with ex.).
90. Trans. from the original French, as in La Laurencie/ÉCOLE II 8; on p. 7 are mentioned 2 instances in 1746 in which Guillemain may have "accompanied" in performances of these sonatas.
91. Cf. La Laurencie/ÉCOLE II 159-164; Girdlestone/RAMEAU 43-54.
92. Cf. Newman/ACCOMPANIED 334.

least a rhythmic counterpoint against the clavecin part (Son. 4/iii/21-26) and sometimes some actual melodic imitations (Son. 6/i/1-10). Or it may outline and clarify richer figuration in the clavecin part (Son. 3/i/22-23).

Outwardly similar to Mondonville's accompanied sonatas, Guillemain's consist more of neutral display passages, usually elaborating only the most basic harmonies, in relatively slow harmonic rhythm (Ex. 98). In such writing the addition of an "accompaniment" raises

Ex. 98. From the second (final) movement of Louis-Gabriel Guillemain's Sonata in e, Op. 13/3 (after the original Boivin ed. at the Library of Congress).

no contrapuntal problems. But that he was capable of richer, more expressive writing is shown especially in the gentler arias.[93] Three of these middle movements (Sons. 1, 5, and 6) and one finale (Son. 3) are followed by an "Altro," the two parts comprising typically French A-B-A rondos in each instance, with each part further subdivided into a second rondo form (A-B-A-C-A, as indicated by repeat, *da capo,* and *fine* signs).

Mondonville and Guillemain were joined or soon followed by a

93. Cf. the exx. in Reeser/KLAVIERSONATE 60-61.

swelling stream of others in the writing of accompanied keyboard sonatas during the early pre-Classic years. The organist **Michel Corrette** (1709-95), born in Rouen, was the author of some fifteen pedagogic works that summarize the French knowledge and practice of music from the pre- to the high-Classic Era,[94] and he was a prolific composer.[95] Among his works are 3 sets of sonatas in Vn/bass setting, three in SS setting, one in SS/bass and one in BB/bass setting, and one consisting of six *Sonates pour le clavecin avec un accompagnement de violon*.[96] The first of these sets was Corrette's Op. 1 (Vn/bass), originally published about when he took his first post in Paris, around 1726. The last was his Op. 25 (the acc'd. set), published around 1742.[97] In the accompanied set we are told once more that "these pieces can [also] be played on the clavecin alone" (title page) and that "the violin must play at half volume" (start of score). The same three-movement plan, F-S-F, prevails, but with programmatic titles, like those of Couperin and Rameau, over the first movements and over all three movements of Sonata 6, "Les Voyages d'Ulysse." The writing is skillful though never quite as expressive in the middle "Aria" or "Musette" as that of Mondonville and Guillemain, especially as chordal figures prevail so much of the time. The violin is not really dispensable during imitations (Son. 2/i), during dialogue with the clavecinist's right hand (Son. 1/ii), or when it provides at least rhythmic definition to continuous chordal figures in the clavecin part (as in Son. 1/i, with a very early example of "Alberti bass," but only in the right hand).

Another example of the early French "accompanied" sonata in which much three-part writing still appears is provided by the first work of the clavecinist **Charles-François Clément** (*ca.* 1720-at least 1782), who later became more important as a music editor and arranger. Published in 1743 (not 1755), Clément's *Sonates en trio pour un clavecin et un violon* are all in the usual three movements, F-S-F, except Sonata 3, which is perhaps the first French sonata to have a minuet and trio (actually a first and second minuet, in major and minor) inserted before the finale.[98]

94. His two different violin methods, published in 1738 and 1782, are described in La Laurencie/ÉCOLE III 12-22 and 76-82.

95. Cf. MGG II 1692-1695 (Borrel).

96. A mod. ed. of a son. for viola d'amore and *b.c.* is listed in Altmann/KAMMERMUSIK 246.

97. The date is based on that for Op. 24, the cello method of 1741 (described in Straeten/VIOLONCELLO 268-271), since Corrette's op. nos. seem to fall into a reliable chronological order. Probably the only extant copy of Op. 25 is the one examined here, at the Bibliothèque nationale (Res. F. 889) in Paris.

98. Cf. MGG II 1480-1485 (Sorel-Nitzberg); La Laurencie & Saint-Foix/SYMPHONIE 37; Reeser/KLAVIERSONATE 68-70 (with ex.), 146-147, and no. 3 in the music suppl. (complete reprint of Son. 6 in e).

Simon Simon (*ca.* 1720-at least 1780) earned the post of "Maître de clavecin des Enfants de France," in the service of Louis XV, with the publication around 1750 of his *Pièces de clavecin dans tous les genres avec et sans accompagnement de violon.*[99] These "pièces" are more like suites in their variable number of movements (3-6) and frequent dances, although some tentative "sonata forms" and the placing of movements in different keys, in some instances, are more characteristic of the sonata. The use of Alberti bass (now literally in the bass) and the actual subordination of the violin part much of the time by putting it in the middle of the clavecin texture, help to make this music seem later than Mondonville's or Guillemain's. Of special interest is another of those prefaces bearing on the early stages of the accompanied keyboard sonata:

> Instead of offering the usual suites for the clavecin alone in a single key (which would have made me fall into a sort of uniformity and aridity that it is better to avoid) I have felt I should compose some of them with violin accompaniment. They will be more interesting, because the melody, which loses the smoothness of its contour ["graces de sa rondeur"] in the disunited tones of the clavecin, will be sustained by the spun out tones of the violin.[100]

The violin does provide a sustained outline of the broken clavecin figuration in some portions of these "pièces."[101]

In Simon's Op. 2, *Quatre Sonates et deux concertos pour le clavecin,* published about 1760 in Paris,[102] the title no longer even mentions the violin accompaniment, which appears on a separate staff above the clavecin part. The violin part becomes still more subordinate in the four sonatas, whether as a harmonic filler or a melodic outliner. Only rarely does it show any independence, and then chiefly in imitative exchanges in the slow movements (as in Son. 2). But the scoring is different in the two pieces called "Concerto." When the word "tutti" appears, always over the violin part, the violin takes the lead, with only a figured bass in the clavecin part; when the word "solo" appears, always over the clavecin part, the clavecin takes the lead and is written out, while the violin is entirely subordinate. The sonatas in this set, all in three movements, are like keyboard reductions of Mannheim symphonies in their crisp rhythmic patterns, their considerable prolongation of bare chords over empty, chordal, quasi-orchestral accompaniments, and their frequent repetition of ideas or reiteration of cadential figures in order to fill out the structural rhythm.

99. Cf. Fétis/BU VIII 42; Reeser/KLAVIERSONATE 61-65 (with exx.), 146, 160.
100. Trans. from the extract in Reeser/KLAVIERSONATE 62.
101. Cf. the ex. from No. 2 in Reeser/KLAVIERSONATE 64.
102. Listed in BRITISH UNION II 953.

The Chevalier **d'Herbain** (1730 or 1734?-69) was a versatile short-lived composer in the military. Trained in Italy, he left a set of six SS/bass sonatas in 1755 as well as an accompanied keyboard set published the same or the following year.[103] In the full title of the latter is this explanation: "When one finds double notes in the accompaniment part the upper ones are for the flute and the others are for the violin, whichever the accompanist chooses. When one uses the violin a mute should be applied." The sonatas are in two movements, F-F, or three, F-S-F, with a marked preference for A-B-A-C-A rondo form. The title also notes the dialogue between the upper parts, which refers mainly to the repetition of the opening phrase. Suffering from a surfeit of empty chordal accompaniments, these pieces are described as banal.[104]

Some "German" Clavecinists in the 1760's (*Schobert, Eckard*)

In 1764 Leopold Mozart, always alert to nationality differences, wrote home from Paris,

> There is a perpetual war here between the Italian and French music. The whole of French music is not worth a sou. But the French are now starting to make drastic changes, for they are beginning to waver very much; and in ten to fifteen years the present French taste, I hope, will have completely disappeared. The Germans are taking the lead in the publication of their compositions. Amongst these, Schobert, Eckardt, Honauer for the clavier, and Hochbrucker and Mayr for the harp are favorites.[105]

The anti-French sentiment was noted early in this chapter and the harp sonatas by Christian Hochbrucker (1733-at least 1799) and (presumably) Philipp Jakob Meyer (*ca.* 1737-1819) will occupy us only briefly in later chapters (XVIII and XX, respectively). But the sonatas of the other three, especially **Johann Schobert** (?-1767), invite discussion now, for they are among the most interesting of their sort in pre-Classic France.

To Wyzewa and Saint-Foix and to Riemann, who made the principal attempts to learn about Schobert's background and life, the blank wall that all but blocked these attempts was as tantalizing as it was frustrating.[106] We accept from two letters written by the Baron von Grimm, in 1765 and 1767, the information that Schobert arrived in

103. Cf. MGG VI 180-183 (Briquet).
104. Reeser/KLAVIERSONATE 70-71 (with ex.), 147, 161.
105. As trans. in Anderson/MOZART I 53-54.
106. The information in Saint-Foix/MOZART I 65-80 is largely repeated in Saint-Foix/PIANISTES III but expands the original articles by Wyzewa and Saint-Foix in ZIMG X (1908-09) 35-41 and 139-140. Contemporary with the latter was Riemann's preface to his Schobert anth. in DDT-m XXXIX v-xvi.

Paris by 1760 or 1761,[107] that he was a "young clavecinist" in the employ of the Prince de Conti, that he was a rival of Eckard, that he made "lots of money" from his published "pièces de clavecin," and—what is best known of all—that he died "in the prime of life" in 1767, along with part of his family, by eating poisonous mushrooms. A possible further support for his youth is the evidence that he probably did not marry until he reached Paris, since his wife was French and his oldest known child was "four or five" in 1767.[108] Hence Wyzewa and Saint-Foix guessed 1740 as the approximate year of birth, whereas all dictionaries checked here still follow Schilling/LEXICON (VI 266-267; 1838) in suggesting 1720, and Hans David arrives at a reasonable compromise in 1730.[109]

Slightly more evidence exists regarding Schobert's origin, but it leads off in three very different directions. In both letters, Grimm included the unequivocal statement that Schobert was Silesian, the only other evidence being the existence in Breslau (Wroclaw) of a MS "Divertimento" copied supposedly before it was published in Paris as Sonata 2 of Op. 1.[110]

Schilling followed Gerber/LEXICON (II 441) in saying that Schobert was born in the Alsatian capital of Strasbourg, this time the only other evidences being the record of a gifted dilettante who studied there with Schobert[111] plus the fact that two other of Leopold Mozart's "Germans" (Honauer and Meyer in the letter quoted *supra*) probably came from Strasbourg.[112] And Schubart wrote in his autobiography that the name Schobert was but one of several French spellings of his own name and that the composer was a relative, presumably from Nürnberg![113] Perhaps this possible Bavarian derivation will revive the highly tenuous attempts once made to link Schobert with Wagenseil in Vienna (on stylistic grounds and through the title "Divertimento," *supra*),[114] with the piano maker Stein (and Eckard's birthplace, by the way) in Augs-

107. That is, 5 or 6 years prior to Dec., 1765. The 2 letters are quoted most fully in Saint-Foix/PIANISTES III 127-128 and 129-130.

108. In Saint-Foix/PIANISTES 128-129 is given the birth certificate of Antoine Schobert, born in 1765.

109. David/SCHOBERT 5-6.

110. In Saint-Foix/MOZART I 72 this MS is reported as Op. 1/1, "perhaps autograph"; but cf. David/SCHOBERT 62 and chart of "Werke."

111. Cited in David/SCHOBERT 5.

112. German in origin and speech, Alsace had passed to the French in 1648.

113. SCHUBART I 30. This relationship is not mentioned in the laudatory paragraph on Schobert (including a reference to him as an organist in Versailles) in Schubart/IDEEN 230-231; however, in Gerber/NEUES IV 108 a special point is made of the relationship of the 2 men; cf., also, DDT-m XXXIX vi-vii.

114. Cf. Saint-Foix/MOZART I 72-73; Abert/MOZART I 86 and 90; David/SCHOBERT 58-59 and 61-62 (including even the assumption that Schobert was Wagenseil's pupil).

burg (through the reading of "Chobert," in W. A. Mozart's letter of October 17-18, 1777,[115] as Schobert rather than Schubart),[116] and with the Mannheim school (on stylistic grounds and through the dedication of Op. 3 to an "agent" of "Le Prince Palatin").[117]

The near blank surrounding Schobert's life extends to his publications, too. Only one announcement suitable for dating any of the sonatas appeared in any of the Paris journals. This concerned the serial publication in 1764 of five sonatas, each named for the month of issue and subsequently found in Op. 7 and its apparent sequel, Op. 8.[118] But we also know that Opp. 1 and 19 as well as nearly all the intervening sets list Schobert as the clavecinist of the Prince de Conti and were evidently first published in Paris between about 1760 and 1772,[119] before the numerous re-editions that appeared in London and Amsterdam.[120] Furthermore, according to a eulogistic letter from Goethe's sister Cornelia, (at least) the first fifteen sets were printed by the time of Schobert's death.[121] And all the works through Op. 17 can be validated to the extent that Op. 17 originated before Schobert died, since in 1767 Op. 17/2/i was arranged as a middle concerto movement by the young Mozart (K.V. 39).[122] If Op. 17 was not sold in print by then, Mozart may already have procured a MS copy before he left Paris with his family in 1764.

Out of the 19 sets accepted here as being by Schobert, 11 contain
122a accompanied and only one contains solo keyboard sonatas. There are also 2 sets of accompanied keyboard sinfonias (Opp. 9 and 10)[123] and 5 of keyboard concertos (Opp. 11-13, 15, and 18). If we add a solo

115. Cf. Mueller von Asow/MOZART II 96.

116. E.g., cf. Riemann in DDT-m XXXIX vi; corrected by K. A. Fischer in ZMW XVI (1934) 42-43.

117. Riemann, of course, argued strongly for the Mannheim connection (DDT-m XXXIX vi *et passim*). It is less exclusively and enthusiastically accepted in Saint-Foix/MOZART I 73-76, and largely discredited in David/SCHOBERT 60-61.

118. Cf. Saint-Foix/MOZART I 65 and 68-69; David/SCHOBERT 5 and chart of "Werke."

119. Spurious or not (cf. David/SCHOBERT 20; Reeser/KLAVIERSONATE 79-80), Op. 19 was published by Sieber in Paris in 1772 (Johansson/FRENCH I 138). Op. 20 apparently should be credited to T. Giordani rather than Schobert (BRITISH UNION I 381 and II 931), although it was also once credited to Christian Bach (Saint-Foix/BECK 25).

120. Cf. the (slightly divergent) lists in DDT-m XXXIX xvii-xx (followed by a thematic index of first mvts.); David/SCHOBERT chart of "Werke"; Reeser/KLAVIERSONATE 161-162.

121. Quoted in DDT-m XXXIX xii. Only through Op. 15 were Schobert's publications available "A Paris chez l'auteur."

122. Cf. Saint-Foix/MOZART I 187-192, 195-196; Abert/MOZART I 114-115. The nature of Mozart's changes in his 7 "Pasticci" concertos is ably explored in Simon/MOZART (with ex.).

123. EDMR-m Sonderreihe IV is a mod. ed. of Opp. 9 and 10 complete, with preface (Kramolisch & Becking).

keyboard sonata in Anth. HAFFNER OM-m XII/5 (1766) and 5 others in contemporary printed or MS collections,[124] a total of at least 40 sonatas by Schobert can be reported. These include 21 sonatas for keyboard with optional violin accompaniment, in Opp. 1-3, 5, 8, 14/2-6, 17, and 19 (at the exceptionally low average of only 2-3 sonatas per set);[125] 7 "sonates en trio" for keyboard with optional violin and cello accompaniments in Opp. 6 and 16;[126] 4 "sonates en quatuor" for keyboard with optional accompaniments for 2 violins and cello, in Opp. 7 and 14/1;[127] and the but 2 sonatas for keyboard alone, in Op. 4.[128]

Schobert was a pioneer around 1760 in making his accompaniments optional. At first (from Op. 1) his titles list sonatas "that may be played with violin accompaniment," and later (from Op. 5) he simply qualifies the accompaniment "ad libitum." As usual at that time, some of the re-editions appeared without the accompaniment, and, conversely, the solo sonatas acquired an accompaniment in one re-edition.[129] Melodically the accompaniment is indeed dispensable most of the time, though not always. As a textural filler, as a rhythmic complement, as a color factor in the sonority, it is less dispensable. To take one of Schobert's strongest sonatas, Op. 14/3 in c, as an example, the first movement specifies "Clavecin seul," evidently because any accompaniment would only interfere with the consistent, energetic dotted rhythm of the keyboard solo. In the second movement, except for a couple of imitations (mss. 15 and 17) the violin mainly plays subordinate 8th-notes against the keyboard triplets, and must be kept very soft (or even muted) if it is not to seem obtrusive. But in the "Menuetto" finale the violin helps to define the melodic line. In fact, during its "Trio," it elaborates the line sufficiently to take the lead and to become melodically indispensable. In a few instances, as in Op. 16/1/i/44-47, the keyboard part is actually reduced to a figured *b.c.*

Schobert's use of the keyboard is only moderately advanced for his time. The left hand is limited almost exclusively to Alberti or simpler chordal basses, octaves plain and broken, repeated notes, afterbeats, and occasional scales. The right hand's difficulties consist chiefly of

124. Cf. the "Ergänzung" in David/SCHOBERT chart of "Werke."

125. Mod. eds.: Opp. 1/2 and 17/2, Reeser/KLAVIERSONATE suppl. nos. 4 and 7; Opp. 2/1 and 14/2-5, DDT-m XXXIX 1-54; Op. 3/1/i and ii, Saint-Foix/PIANISTES III suppl.; Opp. 5/1/ii, 14/3-6, and 17/2/i (all without the Vn parts), cf. David/SCHOBERT 74 and chart of "Werke" (also, ZIMG X [1908-09] for Op. 17/2/i); Op. 8/1, Saint-Foix/SCHOBERT-m (without Vn part).

126. Mod. eds.: Op. 16/1 and 4, DDT-m XXXIX 55-82; Op. 16/4, NAGELS-m No. 134 (Schumacher; taken directly from DDT-m XXXIX).

127. Mod. eds.: Opp. 7/1 and 14/1, DDT-m XXXIX 94 and 83; Op. 7/2, COLLEGIUM MUSICUM-m No. 50.

128. "Mod." ed.: Op. 4/1, cf. David/SCHOBERT chart of "Werke."

129. Cf. DDT-m XXXIX viii-ix and David/SCHOBERT chart of "Werke."

quick ornaments, broken-chord figures, rapid passages in triplets, occasional hand-crossing, and occasional double-thirds. Good examples of the uses of all these devices may be seen in the three movements of Op. 17/4. Riemann and Saint-Foix believed Schobert already wrote for the piano.[130] But Schobert's early dates, the lack of any significant textural or editorial evidence (in spite of Riemann's assertions[131]), and the specific statements to the contrary by contemporaries leave little doubt that the harpsichord was primarily intended. Schubart praised his command of the harpsichord ("Flügel") in fast fiery music and only regretted that Schobert did not know the clavichord as well, so he could have written more expressive, ornamented adagios.[132] La Borde called him one of the most astonishing "Professeurs de clavecin" he had ever heard, his works still (1780) being in the fingers of all who take up "le clavecin & le forte piano."[133] Burney's remarks of 1789 are worth quoting almost in full, especially as he leaves the impression that he had known Schobert in person (in spite of errors of time and place, deleted here).[134]

> Schobert is well entitled to a niche in an English history of Music, his pieces for the harpsichord having been for many years the delight of all those who could play or hear them. . . . In 1766, I was the first who brought his works to England from Paris. His style never pleased in Germany so much as in England and France. Those of Emanuel Bach's party allowed him to be a man of genius, but spoiled by his affectation of a new and extraordinary style, accusing him of too frequently repeating himself. The truth is, the spirit and fire of his pieces require not only a strong hand but a *harpsichord,* to give them all their force and effect. They are too rapid, and have too many notes for clavichords or piano fortes, which [now] supply the place of harpsichords in Germany. The novelty and merit of Schobert's compositions seem to consist in the introduction of the symphonic, or modern overture style, upon the harpsichord, and by light and shade, alternate agitation and tranquility, imitating the effects of an orchestra. The general use of piano fortes, for which the present [i.e., today's newest] compositions for keyed-instruments are chiefly written, has more contributed to lessen the favour of Schobert's pieces, than their want of merit.

130. DDT-m XXXIX x; Saint-Foix/PIANISTES III 133-134. Further pros and cons in this question are discussed in David/SCHOBERT 14-16; Brunner/MOZART 44-55; Reeser/KLAVIERSONATE 78-80.

131. "Pia" and "For" indications occur as early as Op. 1/1/i in the keyboard parts, but "pianis," "po-for," "for-pia," and "cresc." appear only in the separate Vn parts, to judge from at least 20 Schobert sons. seen here.

132. Schubart/IDEEN 230.

133. La Borde/ESSAI III 535 (under "Schoberg"). In 1791 Hüllmandel twice identified Schobert with the clavecin rather than the piano (as quoted in Benton/HÜLLMANDEL 289 and 292).

134. Burney/HISTORY II 956-957. Nothing different occurs in BURNEY'S TOURS I 28 and II 121.

Ex. 99. From the finale of Johann Schobert's Sonata in d, Op. 14/4 (after DDT-m XXXIX 43).

Aside from a very few two- or four-movement cycles, Schobert's sonatas are in three movements.[135] The order is not fixed, but the first movement is fast or moderate, the last movement is most often a minuet or "Tempo di Menuet," and the middle movement is usually a moderate, often a dance movement, whether an "Andante" or a polonaise, siciliana, or minuet (when the finale is a faster movement). Keys up to 3 flats or sharps are used in the major, and up to 4 flats

135. Cf. the chart of mvts. and keys on pp. 22-24 of David/SCHOBERT, which is the chief source on the structure of Schobert's sonatas.

but not 4 sharps in the minor. The trio of the minuet may be in the relative key or opposite tonic mode, but in about half the sonatas the middle movement does not change key, and in some not even its mode is changed. At most, this movement is in the relative, dominant, or subdominant key. The interrelation of movements by similar incipits appears not to have interested Schobert.

With his usual shrewd perspicacity Burney seems to have sized up Schobert's music accurately when he spoke of its chief merit as being to bring "the symphonic, or modern overture style" to the harpsichord (*supra*). In his rapid movements, which are easily his most interesting, Schobert found, above all, how to construct strong harmonic progressions and how to bring them to life through simple, telling figuration and plainly balanced rhythms. This is the symphonic trait by which he chiefly justifies Riemann's attempts to link him with the Mannheim school. It is heard in its most developed state in the sonatas of Opp. 14 and 17 (Ex. 99). In many of the rapid movements, especially in these later sonatas, there are no distinct, independent ideas. When such an idea does occur, at the start (Ex. 100) or where the contrasting thought is expected, it sometimes becomes the subject of the "development" after the double-bar (as in Opp. 5/1/i and 17/1/iv). But a sense of "development" is often achieved without it, merely through sequential passages in which the pattern is altered from time to time (Op. 14/2/i).

As these remarks suggest, various approximations of "sonata form"

Ex. 100. From the opening of Johann Schobert's Sonata in B♭, Op. 4/1 (after the early reprint by Longman and Broderip at the University of North Carolina).

are to be met in Schobert's fast movements, whether merely incipient, with a return only to later material of the exposition (Op. 14/4/i), or more complete (Op. 8/1/i). It is true that the Classic "sonata-allegro" drive is present here to a marked degree. One might even call it a *Sturm und Drang,* pre-Beethovian drive.[136] Yet this drive is dissipated to a considerable extent by redundant passage work, circuitous tonal schemes, and excessive length. These traits are most evident in the earliest sets, decreasing thereafter until nearly eliminated, by Op. 17, through a more concentrated, economical handling of the material. There is no corresponding change of style traits in the successive sets. Schobert's writing is always unmistakably *galant,* with its many triplets, its frequent appoggiaturas and turns, its thin texture and simple accompaniments, its progression by short phrases, and its intermittent returns to motivic techniques.

Except for Op. 14, Schobert's moderate movements are shorter, less developed, and less interesting than the fast movements. Clear opening ideas cast in equally clear phrase-and-period structures are not wanting, but these often seem somewhat weak and ungraceful.[137] In Op. 14 the "Andante" of Sonata 4 in d and the "Polonoise" of Sonata 5 are above average for Schobert in their appeal.

If a broad sampling of Schobert's sonatas does produce some surprises and delights, especially in the realm of symphonic drive, one cannot help concluding that these exist largely in the raw. Undoubtedly his influence as a minor tone poet on the young, but only the young, Mozart[138] and the connection that Riemann tried too hard to establish between him and Mannheim school[139] have caused the importance of his music to be exaggerated in its own right. One result has been to obscure the worth of the music by Schobert's contemporaries in Paris that we are about to discuss.

The sonatas of **Johann Gottfried Eckard** (1735-1809) were also known well enough to the young Mozart for one of them (Op. 1/4, in but one movement) to be transcribed as a concerto movement (K.V. 40/ii).[140] Furthermore, the first movement of Mozart's first accompanied sonata (K.V. 6) seems to have been based on the outline and to

136. Cf. Abert/MOZART I 86-90.

137. The negative criticisms in Torrefranca/ORIGINI 638-639 do not seem wholly unwarranted.

138. This influence is emphasized in Saint-Foix/MOZART I 71-72 and 76-80; and in Einstein/MOZART 114-116. Mozart still wrote in 1778 of buying some Schobert sons. for a pupil in Paris (Anderson/MOZART II 805). Actually, Leopold had had some derogatory remarks to make in 1764 about both Schobert's character and his music (Anderson/MOZART I 54-55).

139. DDT-m XXXIV vi *et passim.*

140. Cf. Simon/MOZART 177, 179.

have used the cadence figure from the first and third movements, respectively, of Eckard's first sonata.[141] Born in Augsburg, Eckard largely taught himself, utilizing the first volume of Emanuel Bach's *Essay* (1753), with its six "Probe-Stücken" sonatas.[142] In 1758 Johann Andreas Stein, who had begun about 1755 to add pianos to the instruments he made in Augsburg,[143] took Eckard with him when he moved to Paris. There, thanks to his successes as a performer, Eckard decided to subordinate painting to musical talents.[144] In 1764 Leopold Mozart regarded Eckard's music as the most difficult by the Germans in Paris, and regarded the man himself as honest, in a comparison with *"this mean Schobert."*[145] Grimm saw Eckard as the greater genius of the two, both in performance and composition, but recognized Schobert as being more popular because his music was more facile, more charming, and less complex.[146] High praise for Eckard's playing was also voiced by Schubart, Burney, and La Borde, among others.[147]

Whereas only two of Schobert's sonatas were written for keyboard alone (Op. 4), it is significant in that heyday of the Parisian accompanied sonata that all of the eight sonatas left by Eckard, which represent nearly his entire known output,[148] are of that solo type.[149] Six of these were published as Op. 1 in 1763 (dedicated to Gaviniès), and the other two as Op. 2 a year later. It is also significant that all these sonatas seem already to have been intended for the piano, some five years before its first public use in Paris.[150] Although Op. 1 specifies clavecin and Op. 2 merely gives the choice of "le clavecin ou le piano forte," the copious indications for precisely graduated dynamics and the many new keyboard devices (as in the display passages of Op. 1/6/ii) make fairly clear which instrument is preferred. Further evidence is found in Eckard's oft-quoted "Avertissement" in Op. 1: "I have tried to make this work equally appropriate to the harpsichord,

141. Cf. Saint-Foix/MOZART I 43-44; Reeser/ECKARD 124-125.

142. The chief study of the man and his music is Reeser/ECKARD (summarized in MGG III 1086-1090), including thematic index and list of eds.

143. According to Eva Hertz, as cited in Reeser/ECKARD 100.

144. Cf. Reeser/ECKARD 94-96; the engraving photographed in La Laurencie/ÉCOLE II 426 (cf. p. 425) is shown by Reeser to be the work of a later "Charles Echard."

145. Anderson/MOZART I 55.

146. As cited in Reeser/ECKARD 89-90.

147. Schubart/IDEEN 235-237; Burney/HISTORY II 957; La Borde/ESSAI III 507-508. Cf., also, Reeser/ECKARD 90-93.

148. The concertos and fugues also mentioned in Schubart/IDEEN 236 are not now known.

149. The 8 sons., plus the "Menuet d'Exhaudet" to which Mozart referred (Anderson/MOZART I 372), are all reprinted, along with a helpful "Introduction," annotations, and facs. of the title pp., in Reeser/ECKARD-m.

150. Cf. Brenet/CONCERTS 292-293.

clavichord, and piano. It is for this reason that I have felt obliged to mark the softs and louds so often, which [editing] would have been useless if I had only the harpsichord in mind."[151]

Eckard's treatment of the keyboard may, in fact, be described as outstanding for its time, in originality, diversity, and interest for the performer. In these respects it may be put nearly on a par with Emanuel Bach's writing and well ahead of Schobert's. La Borde saw Eckard mainly as the introducer of the subsequently tedious Alberti bass in France,[152] which view was neither correct nor balanced. In the first place, we have already noted the use of this device some thirteen years earlier by the Frenchman Simon Simon. And in the second place, it was only one of the many styles of accompaniment employed by Eckard. Furthermore, he showed on occasion that he could give it some musical significance of its own (Op. 1/5/49-50 and 80-86), as he did with such other devices as broken octaves (Op. 1/5/123-125), simple double-notes (Op. 1/6/i/29-30), hand-crossing patterns (Op. 1/6/i/31-32), scale figures (Op. 1/1/iii/23-28), and steady quarter-notes (Op. 2/1/i/51-66). In addition, there are many passages where the left hand participates contrapuntally (Op. 1/3/i/1-20 and iii/1-9) or alternates and combines with the right (Ex. 101).

Ex. 101. From the finale of Johann Gottfried Eckard's Sonata in g, Op. 1/2 (after the original ed. at the Library of Congress).

151. In Schubart/IDEEN 236-237 Eckard is stated to have begun with the harpsichord, changed to the piano after several years, and finally preferred the clavichord. Recently, in Paap/ECKARD, the idea that the clavichord was primarily intended in Opp. 1 and 2 is argued informatively though not altogether convincingly.

152. La Borde/ESSAI III 507.

Apart from Eckard's use of Alberti bass, the influence of Emanuel Bach on his style is especially evident in Eckard's first sonata, with its same vocabulary of ornaments, its half-cadences, its leaping syncopated figures that rise or fall sequentially (as in i/9-10), and its moments of *empfindsam* fantasy (i/34-38). Emanuel's influence also can be sensed in the driving dotted rhythm of Eckard's Op. 1/3/i in f, which recalls Emanuel's "Kenner und Liebhaber" sonata in the same key (W. 57/6). A more tangible—in fact, striking—similarity may be noted between Op. 1/3/i and Schobert's Op. 14/3/i in c, as well as between the middle, moderate movements in E♭ in Eckard's Op. 1/1 and Schobert's same sonata. Since Eckard could well have composed his first three sonatas while he was still studying Emanuel's music in Augsburg, the probability is that it was Eckard who influenced Schobert, although the converse is at least possible if we assume that Schobert composed Op. 14 a few years before its publication. At any rate, even after Eckard's style became more regularized and facile in the remaining five sonatas, presumably to meet Parisian tastes half way, his music discloses considerably more imagination and diversity than Schobert's (now bringing Rutini's better sonatas very much to mind). The ideas themselves are of no greater consequence than Schobert's, but the superior development of the material, especially the creative treatment of textures and rhythms, continues throughout Eckard's sonatas.

Eckard was even less disposed than Schobert to stereotyped plans, either in the cycles or the separate movements. Yet the structures seem tighter in both respects. Half of his sonatas are in three movements, whether F-M-F, M-M-F, or F-S-M. Two are in two movements, one of which ends in a "Minuetto con variazioni" (Op. 1/6), and two are in only one, fairly long movement each (Op. 1/4 and 5). The seeker of "sonata form" can find, though not all in the same movement, a second theme in the dominant (Op. 2/1/i/19-40), a convincing development section anticipating the high-Classic manner (Op. 1/2/i/39-69), and, more exceptionally, a clear return at about the two-thirds point in the form (Op. 2/1/i/90, in the tonic minor). On the other hand, Op. 1/6/i, inscribed "Con Discretione," although marked off by repeated halves, is otherwise too free and fantasy-like to submit to such classifications. All in all, Eckard's sonatas make a strong, fresh impression on the reader saturated with later eighteenth-century dilettante music. It is not possible here to accept the surprisingly anti-German evaluation of Wyzewa and Saint-Foix in which the first three sonatas are largely dismissed as mere imitations of Emanuel Bach's sonatas, reflecting inadequate self-training, and the later sonatas as utterly simple, banal works.[153]

The third of the three main "Germans" mentioned by Leopold Mozart in 1764 (*supra*) was **Leontzi Honauer** (?-*ca.* 1790), who seems to have come from Strasbourg and to have entered the employ, by 1761, of Prince Louis de Rohan in Paris (himself a man with Strasbourg connections).[154] No fewer than four of Honauer's sonata movements were transcribed in the "pasticci" keyboard concertos of the young Mozart.[155] Contemporary with Schobert's and Eckard's sonatas are the three sets of six each by Honauer, also first published in Paris and followed by reprints in London and Amsterdam.[156] Opp. (or "Livres") 1/1-5 and 2, which first appeared in 1761 and 1763, consist of solo sonatas, while Opp. 1/6 and 3 consist of accompanied sonatas (H ± Vn; 1764).[157] The close association of Honauer and Schobert 157a
is suggested by the joint collection of a few accompanied sonatas by each that Welcker in London published about 1770.[158] Contemporary praise can also be found for Honauer, both as clavecinist and composer,[159] though it is more modest than that lavished on Schobert or Eckard, and neither Burney nor Schubart saw fit to mention him.

La Borde's remarks about the tedium of the Alberti bass and Wyzewa's and Saint-Foix's about simplicity and banality could have been applied more appropriately to Honauer's than to Eckard's sonatas, for Honauer is unquestionably more obvious and less gifted than Leopold Mozart's other two "Germans." His sonatas often fall into a stereotype. Nearly all are in three movements, F-S-F (exceptions being Opp. 1/3 and 3/4 in 2 mvts.). The Alberti bass goes on almost constantly. When it does not, there is usually some equivalent metric bustle such as the empty right-hand tremolo throughout most of Op. 3/6/i, which helps to suggest almost a parody of the Mannheim symphonies that were then becoming so popular in Paris. The frequent songful melodic lines heard in singing-allegro fashion above the Alberti or similar accompaniments fall into symmetrically balanced phrases. They are sometimes so naïve as to sound like folk tunes (as in the

153. Saint-Foix/MOZART I 42-43.

154. Cf. MGG VI 681-684 (Reeser); David/SCHOBERT 6-7.

155. Honauer's Op. 2 (not 1)/3/i = K.V. 37/iii, Op. 2/1/i = K.V. 40/i, Op. 1/1/i and iii = K.V. 41/i and iii. Cf. Wyzewa and Saint-Foix in ZIMG X (1908-09) 139-140; Saint-Foix/MOZART I 196-200; Simon/MOZART 174, 179.

156. Cf. BRITISH UNION I 490. A set of 4 keyboard quartets followed in 1770.

157. A discussion of Opp. 1/6 and 3, the full titles of Opp. 1 and 3, and a reprint of Op. 3/4 are given in Reeser/KLAVIERSONATE 80-84 (with exx.), 163, and suppl. no. 5. A further study of Honauer is needed.

158. Cf. Reeser/KLAVIERSONATE 80, 83-84, 163.

159. Cf. La Borde/ESSAI III 514-515; Reeser/KLAVIERSONATE 81.

"Siciliana" Op. 1/5/ii or the finale in 6/8 meter Op. 1/2/iii). But there is little melodic contrast or development of material to implement the outlines of "sonata form," which can be found readily.

Occasionally in Honauer's fast movements the melodic lines are replaced by perpetual-motion figuration (Op. 1/5/iii). Although the use of the keyboard is never so advanced or original as in Eckard's sonatas, it does show experience, especially in figures alternated between the hands (as in the variations on the minuet finale of Op. 1/3). The violin parts double the clavecinist's right hand at the unison much of the time (only adding to the considerable amount of unison and octave writing in Honauer's keyboard parts). Otherwise, they outline the melody or accompaniment, but never take an indispensable lead. The relatively few dynamic signs in Honauer's sonatas do not include graduated effects. None of the foregoing remarks should be allowed to obscure the chief virtues of Honauer's music, which show up especially in Op. 3. In addition to the intelligent use of the keyboard (as in Op. 3/4/i), one can find a good command of harmony (as in the modulatory passages of Op. 3/3/ii) and some expressive transparent melody writing of an ornamental sort (as in Op. 3/2/ii) that points to the writing in Mozart's more expressive slow movements.

A lesser-known clavecinist and acquaintance of the Mozarts during their second stay in Paris, in 1766, was **Hermann Friedrich Raupach** (1728-78), who was born in Stralsund (in northeast Germany) and served both in his earlier and last years in St. Petersburg.[160] Grimm called Raupach an outstanding improviser and implied that, as Christian Bach had done in London, Raupach held the little Mozart between his knees while the two improvised alternately at the same harpsichord.[161] As with Honauer, four sonata movements by Raupach, all from Op. 1, were arranged as concerto movements by the young Mozart in 1767.[162] Three sets of sonatas by Raupach were published in Paris, Opp. 1 and 2 having six sonatas each of the accompanied type (1765 or 1766 and 1767) and Op. 3 having four in SS/bass scoring (1767).[163]

160. Cf. GROVE VII 53 (Loewenberg). Raupach gets frequent though only passing mentions in Mooser/ANNALES II and III.

161. As quoted in Saint-Foix/MOZART I 164; Mozart/NEUE-m X/34 55.

162. Raupach's Op. 1/5/i = K.V. 37/i, Op. 1/1/i and iii = K.V. 39/i and iii, Op. 1/1/ii = K.V. 41/ii. Cf. Saint-Foix/MOZART I 195-196, 198-199; Simon/MOZART 175-177, 179, 182 and 185 (exx.). K.V. Anh. 290a in Köchel/MOZART 901 was originally listed as K.V. 61 before it was identified as Op. 1/3 by Raupach; hence, it can readily be examined in MOZART WERKE-m XVIII/1 no. 23.

163. All 3 sets are listed in BRITISH UNION II 874. The dates come from Johansson/FRENCH I 72-73, 24, 27. In Reeser/KLAVIERSONATE 84-86 and 163 may be found a brief discussion of Op. 1, with exx., and its full title.

A reading of the sonatas in Raupach's Op. 1 shows them to be very similar, in form, style, and treatment of the accompaniment, to Honauer's sonatas. Because the tonal outline is broader and simpler, the drive and purpose of the single movements seem a little stronger. On the other hand, Raupach's ideas rarely have enough character to stand out from their context of passage work. A movement like Op. 1/3/i sounds like little more than a series of rhythmically enlivened harmonic progressions. Op. 1/1/ii affords an example of his more expressive writing, which is stiffer and less decorative than Honauer's. Op. 1/2 is interesting for its *galant* traits in all the movements, and for the fact that the most rapid passages are given to the violin in the minuet and trio that comprise the finale. In Op. 1/6, after a pompous chordal introduction in dotted rhythms such as might be expected in a French overture, the first movement proper begins fugally. Though it soon lapses into more homophonic writing, the violin remains fairly independent of the keyboard. The finale (second mvt.) is a naïve display of virtuosity, chiefly for the keyboard. Mozart is brought to mind by the transparent texture and phrase syntax of this music, but only a very watery kind of Mozart.

Some Native French Organists (Séjan)

Our next group of composers consists largely of native French organists. **Armand-Louis Couperin** (1725 or 1727-89), a first cousin once removed of Couperin le Grand, was one of these, being distinguished primarily as an organist[164] and only secondarily for his compositions. Among the compositions is his set with the new compound title *Sonates en pièces de clavecin avec accompagnement de violon ad libitum,* Op. 2, published in Paris in 1765.[165] The six sonatas 165a
in this set are all in three movements, F-S-F, except for the first, which adds a minuet before the finale. Not enough dynamic indications or idiomatic traits are present to confirm a preference for one keyboard instrument over another, although graduated dynamics do occur in the violin part (e.g., Op. 2/3/iii/74). Couperin's forms are compact and flexible, with tentative approaches to the general plan of "sonata form." But especially in the fast movements this Couperin seems to be somewhat ill at ease in his rather independent efforts to keep up with the

164. Cf. BURNEY'S TOURS I 26; Tiersot/COUPERIN 115-123; MGG II 1711 and 1731-1734 (Reimann).

165. Discussed in Reeser/KLAVIERSONATE 88-93 and 148, with exx. and with all of Op. 2/3 reprinted as suppl. no. 6 (also published by Eschig in 1908). Although 3 "Sonates en trio" were announced in 1770 and "a rather large number of sonatas" were left in MS, "some for keyboard alone, others with violin" (Tiersot/COUPERIN 122), only Op. 2 seems to have been explored in recent times.

times, much as was Ernst Bach, another late relative of a great Baroque master. And again the results are rather stiff, stilted, and spare. The conservative influence sometimes persists in the opening or closing ideas of the repeated halves. These do not necessarily fall into balanced members of square phrases (as in Op. 2/5/i/1-8). Instead, they may still unfold into extended, unbroken phrases, supported by more rapid harmonic rhythm and decorated by a degree of exchange and interweaving of the keyboard and violin parts that recalls the "accompanied" textures of Mondonville and Guillemain (Op. 2/3/i/1-6).[166]

Between these unfolding ideas a more modern influence seems to be present in Couperin's sonatas in his almost naïve attempts to fill out an essentially harmonic drive or bridge to the dominant (Op. 2/3/i/7-18). In such passages the violin merely doubles, outlines, or underlies the keyboard part. (In the technically more elaborate passages of the "Aria con variazzione," Op. 2/2/iii, the violin simply repeats a sort of impassive, detached *cantus firmus.*) Couperin seems to be much more at home in his more sectionalized, static middle movements. Here, as in the "Romance" Op. 2/1/ii or the "Rondeau" Op. 2/2/ii, he is free to write the tender, expressive tunes that were so characteristic of the French musical culture even well before the time of Couperin le Grand and Leclair (Ex. 102).

The Parisian organist and inventor of keyboard instruments **De Virbés**[167] left a set of six keyboard sonatas "of which the third [comes] with violin accompaniment" (Paris, 1768). In this three-movement accompanied sonata the violin part is often more independent than other parts we have seen thus far, both as the higher instrument and in dialogue.[168] A more important organist in Paris (from 1762), **Guillaume Lasceux** (1740-1831),[169] published two sets of three accompanied sonatas each, in 1768 and 1772. In the second set the graduated dynamics point to the "forte piano," which is the alternative to the clavecin in the title. The music is described as trite, with excessive Alberti bass and insufficient melodic interest to compensate for it, and with a violin accompaniment that often reduces to afterbeat patterns.[170]

A rewarding surprise awaits the musician who comes upon the

166. Cf. Saint-Foix/PIANISTES III 124-125.
167. Cf. Eitner/QL X 104.
168. Cf. Reeser/KLAVIERSONATE 93-94 (with 2 exx.) and 164.
169. Cf. MGG VIII 240-241 (Bonfils).
170. Reeser/KLAVIERSONATE 94-96 (with 2 exx.), 164. Op. 2/3 is cited in Favre/FRANÇAISE 129 as a rare ex. (recall A. L. Couperin's Op. 2/1) of a 4-mvt. son. (allegro, 2 minuets, and a "Chasse"), but are not the 2 minuets equivalent to a minuet and trio?

Ex. 102. From the second movement of Armand-Louis Couperin's Sonata in e, Op. 2/6 (after the original ed. in the Library of Congress).

nine extant sonatas of **Nicolas Séjan (1745-1819).** He will only hope that this music will be made available soon in a modern edition and that a thorough study will be devoted to it. Séjan was an esteemed, virtuoso church organist often heard at the Concert spirituel. Besides a set of short keyboard pieces (Op. 2, 1784), he left a set of six accompanied "clavecin" sonatas, Op. 1, published not before 1772 in
Paris,[171] and a set of three sonatas for clavecin or piano with obligatory 171a
violin and cello parts for the first and third sonatas, Op. 3, published in Paris in 1784.[172] Op. 3/1 and 3 are described as real piano trios, by virtue of the "obligés" parts.[173] But the "ad libitum" violin part listed in the title of Op. 1, which has been missing in recent years,[174] can hardly have amounted to much, if it ever did exist, for the piano texture and lines seem entirely complete without it. Although the piano is

171. Cf. Saint-Foix/PIANISTES IV 198.

172. The sons. of Op. 1 are discussed, with helpful exx., in Reeser/KLAVIERSONATE 96-100, 153, 164, and in Favre/FRANÇAISE 18-24 (revised, with facs. of the title page, more exx., and less biography, from RDM XVII [1936] 70-78); neither author refers to the other.

173. Favre/FRANÇAISE 23 (with ex. from the piano part of Op. 3/1/ii).

174. Cf. Reeser/KLAVIERSONATE 97.

made optional to the clavecin only in Op. 3, a note on the title page of Op. 1 adds that "some of these pieces may be played on the piano." The dynamic indications are too sparse to furnish clues, but the expressive and dramatic passages in almost every movement and the new wide-spaced scoring often make the piano seem more appropriate than the harpsichord.

All six sonatas in Séjan's first set are in three movements, F-S-F (Sons. 1-3) or F-S-M (with a minuet, rondo, and "Giga" as the finales of Sons. 4, 5, and 6, respectively). The key of the middle movement stays the same, in either mode, or changes to the subdominant or relative of the outer movements. A third of the six home keys—F, A, g, D, E, c—are minor. In Sonata 2 the middle movement leads directly into the finale. The chief strength of these sonatas lies in the quality of their ideas, which is the very trait we have found wanting so often in the other French accompanied sonatas noted thus far. The chief weakness is in the over-all forms, which lack the simple purposeful breadth of, say, Raupach's forms.

Séjan's initial ideas are characteristically extended into notably broad arches, with a wide range of up to two octaves and sufficient leaps and harmonic color to impart a distinct character to each melody (Ex. 103). These ideas are different enough to call up very divergent, if somewhat remote, associations—the gay "ariette" of a French *opéra comique* (Op. 1/4/i/1-16), the chromatic cantabile of a Mozart love aria (Op. 1/4/i/17-20), the delicacy of a Boccherini minuet (Op. 1/4/iii[175]), the serenity of a late Beethoven slow movement (as in Ex. 103), the theme of an impassioned Beethoven allegro (Op. 1/6/i/1-10), or even the expressively harmonized line in 6ths of a Brahms intermezzo (Op. 1/2/ii, after the double-bar).

Séjan's fertility in creating ideas seems to explain a main defect of his forms. Except in the more regularized, dance or rondo movements, there are more ideas than can be digested and co-ordinated in the space of one average-size movement. Thus, after the lyrical idea just noted at the start of Sonata 4, the further lyrical idea starting in measure 17 comes as too much of a good thing. Yet, Séjan could be economical with his material when he chose, using the opening theme again as the "contrasting theme" in the dominant (Op. 1/3/i) or keeping close track of it throughout a movement (Op. 1/1/iii). Unfortunately, his forms are also made lax by the frequently dull texture. Séjan relies largely

175. In Saint-Foix/PIANISTES IV 198-199 neither the parallel drawn between this movement and a Schobert minuet nor that between the "Giga" Op. 1/6/iii and the finale of Christian Bach's Op. 12 in B♭ (i.e., Op. 17/6/iii) seems very fortunate.

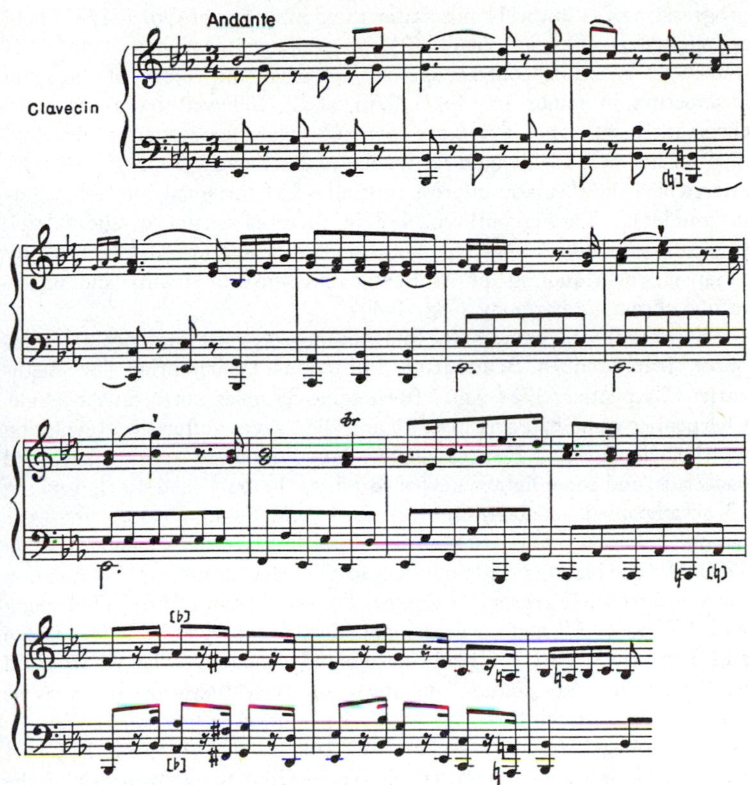

Ex. 103. From the second movement of Nicolas Séjan's Sonata in c, Op. 1/6 (after the original ed. at the Bibliothèque nationale; but the Vn accompaniment is lost).

on Alberti bass and still simpler means of marking time and harmony. He knows how to cross or interchange the hands when he chooses (Op. 1/1/iii and 1/6/iii), or introduce tentative imitations in the left hand (Op. 1/4/i/44-45). Yet he resorts to such devices too seldom to give variety to his forms and relieve the steady patter of a single style of accompaniment (most noticeable when the melodic line also moves largely in steady 16th-notes, as in Op. 1/2/i).

If Séjan's over-all forms are not wholly effective, there are, nevertheless, sections of considerable interest from a structural standpoint. The sense of harmonic propulsion can be strong, whether through chromatic progressions (as in the 11 mss. after the double-bar of Op. 1/1/ii), bold appoggiaturas (Op. 1/1/iii/37-40), or prolonged sequences (Op. 1/2/i/69-79). A telling contrast is achieved when the return of the main idea occurs in minor in Op. 1/2/iii/54-57, followed by a climactic, chromatic excursion. There are moments when the sequential development of his main idea would do justice to Beethoven (Op. 1/3/i/31-40, after which the thematic interest continues but the tonal interest begins to wander). Throughout Op. 1/3/iii there is a hint of the fateful, tragic drive in Beethoven's Op. 27/2/iii. The closing idea in Op. 1/3/i by Séjan is worth quoting for its Beethovian sense of finality and its effective chromatic harmony (Ex. 104).

A friend of Séjan was the outstanding organist and prolific composer **Jean-Jacques Beauvarlet,** known as **Charpentier** (or Beauvarlet-Charpentier; 1734-94). Born some 85 miles north, in Abbeville, Charpentier came to Paris in 1771 and died a year after the Revolution wrecked his career. Besides fugues, liturgical organ works, keyboard concertos, and some lighter keyboard pieces, he published 4 sets totaling 18 accompanied sonatas—Opp. 2, 3, 4, and 8—in about a five-year period, 1773-78, and an unnumbered solo "clavecin" Sonata in c in 1782.[176] The piano is made optional to the clavecin in Opp. 2-4 but not, for any discernible reason, in Op. 8. "Cresc." occurs fairly often along with "F" and "P" and an occasional "fortis." or "pianis." In Opp. 3 and 8 the violin part is already designated "obligé." The violin could not be marked "ad libitum," in any case, since there are passages as early as Op. 2 in which it can hardly be omitted (Op. 2/3/ii/"Trio"). But the "obligé" applies especially to 2 sonatas in Op. 3, one in Op. 4 (no. 3), and all 3 in Op. 8, which are referred to in the titles of the sets as being "dans le gout de la simphonie concertante."

There are differences between Charpentier's sonatas with and without the "obligé" designation and considerable variety of style and form in his sonatas, anyway. The cycles vary between three or two fast, moderate, or dance movements in different orders and the forms are still fluid. Compared with Séjan's sonatas Charpentier's sonatas in Op. 2 reveal not only the need for the violin part but tighter forms, neater

176. Discussions and the full titles of Opp. 2, 4, and 8 may be found in Reeser/KLAVIERSONATE 100-110, 148, and 164-165, among the exx. being complete reprints of Op. 2/2/ii (pp. 101-102) and Op. 2/6 (suppl. no. 8). The solo son. mvt. in c is discussed (including 2 exx.), along with the lighter pieces and concertos, in Favre/FRANÇAISE 24-28. Cf., also, Saint-Foix/PIANISTES IV 196-198 (with sources for the dates of Opp. 2 and 4). Op. 3 is listed in BRITISH UNION I 184. In Eitner/QL I 394-395 all 4 acc'd. sets, which are listed only under "Charpentier," without forename, are attributed to the son Jacques-Marie; but the latter's birth in 1766 surely rules out this possibility even for Op. 8 (*ca.* 1778; cf. Reeser/KLAVIERSONATE 100).

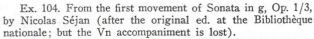

Ex. 104. From the first movement of Sonata in g, Op. 1/3, by Nicolas Séjan (after the original ed. at the Bibliothèque nationale; but the Vn accompaniment is lost).

and crisper ideas that are more obvious yet not without their own charms and similarly broad contours,[177] and a little more contrapuntal texture (as in the canonic passages of Op. 4/1/i). New subtlety,

177. Note how similar are Exx. 53 and 64 in Reeser/KLAVIERSONATE 98 and 109.

warmth, and freedom are reported in the sonatas without the "obligé" part in Op. 4,[178] and there is another example of pre-Beethovian drive in the solo, one-movement Sonata in c, with its unusual, dramatic, slow introduction and frequent diminished-7th chords. But Charpentier's sonatas with "obligé" parts sound like transcriptions of real *concertante* symphonies. They are simpler in construction than their fellows, entirely homophonic, and replete with "solo" and "tutti" indications.

Two other Parisian organists can only be mentioned briefly here because of the scarcity of information and music. One **Joubert** published 2 accompanied sonatas in piano trio setting in 1776 (H-or-P ± Vn & Vc). "A bit short, yet elegant and accurately scored, these pages do not deserve to be totally forgotten."[179] **Jean-François Tapray** (1738-1819) published nearly 40 accompanied and solo sonatas in about 9 sets and singly, between 1770 and 1800. Regarded as mediocre in quality and originality,[180] they are chiefly interesting for their designated scorings, with piano winning out over clavecin in the later solo sonatas. Besides these last and one 4-hand piano sonata published in 1800 as Op. 29 (an infrequent type in France),[181] there are sonatas with violin "obligé," in piano trio setting, and for keyboard with 2 violins and viola. Thus, in 1773, Tapray published a set with the title, *Quatre Sonates pour le clavecin ou le forte-piano . . . première sonate en quatuor, deuxième sonate en trio, la troisième en symphonie, la quatrième sans accompagnement.*"

Two Composers in Bordeaux (Beck)

Before closing this chapter we should also take brief note of two of the very few pre-Classic composers in France who were writing sonatas elsewhere than in Paris. Both were active in Bordeaux. One was the organist **Legrand,** whose set of six accompanied clavecin sonatas was published in Paris about 1755[182] but who apparently should not be confused with the Paris organist from Bordeaux, **Jean-Pierre Legrand** (1734-1809). The latter is perhaps the one represented in Anth. VENIER-m II (*ca.* 1760), the one who left his own set of six solo clavecin sonatas in 1763, and the one whose sonatas were described by Leopold Mozart in 1764 as "now in our style."[183] **Franz Beck** (1723 or be-

178. Cf. Reeser/KLAVIERSONATE 105-106.

179. Favre/FRANÇAISE 38, 130 (ex. from Son. 2 in e).

180. Cf. Saint-Foix/PIANISTES IV 196-197; Favre/FRANÇAISE 13-18 (with exx. and quotations from contemporary announcements).

181. Reviewed unfavorably by Fétis (with ex.) in AMZ II (1799-1800) 743-744.

182. Cf. Saint-Foix/PIANISTES III 124-125; Reeser/KLAVIERSONATE 66-68 (with exx.), 160.

183. Anderson/MOZART I 54. Cf. MGG VIII 474-476 (Bonfils and Durand); Johansson/FRENCH I 107-108; Saint-Foix/MOZART I 61-62.

tween 1730 and 1733-1809) is the much better known violinist and symphonist who first trained under J. Stamitz in Mannheim. After he moved permanently to Bordeaux in 1761 Beck published a set of six solo keyboard sonatas (H-or-P) in Paris about 1772[184] and another like set in Bordeaux, both as Op. 5, between 1774 and 1785.[185] Although Sondheimer, the specialist on Beck's symphonies, did not express a high regard for the sonatas, they should certainly be worth a special study in view of Beck's general importance to pre-Classic instrumental music.[186] Saint-Foix viewed them more sympathetically (after correcting an earlier attribution of the MSS to Christian Bach).[187] He found considerable charm and variety in them, and styles consistent with their period. More recently a brief objective survey of the sonatas was made, in which they are shown to be rather rudimentary and extremely variable in their plans (from 2 to 5 movements), length, and individual forms, with Alberti bass, *galant* traits, and some rhythmic details not found in the symphonies.[188]

184. Johansson/FRENCH II Facs. 56.
185. Saint-Foix/BECK 27.
186. Cf. MGG I 1477-1480 (Sondheimer).
187. Saint-Foix/BECK; Saint-Foix/BACH 87-88.
188. Carrow/MANNHEIM 210-222 and 113-116 (bibliography).

Chapter XVIII

France From About 1780 to 1830

Limits and Changes

In this second, concluding chapter on the sonata in France, neither the start nor the end of the high- and late-Classic phases can be sharply delimited. At the start, the nearly contemporary pianists Edelmann and Hüllmandel, who were otherwise very different, both published accompanied piano sonatas that overlap the pre- and high-Classic Eras in styles as well as time. At the end, the pianists J.-L. Adam and L. Jadin published both accompanied and solo piano sonatas that overlap the late-Classic and pre-Romantic Eras in time and styles.[1] Much more sharply delimited is the violent interruption created by the Revolution (1789-99). Besides this overwhelming historical phenomenon there are some new trends and influences to keep in mind. There is the same tendency toward a lighter, more facile, popular style that we have found in every other country whenever the high-Classic phase is approached. Already in 1765 a Parisian critic wrote,

> we cannot avoid urging all the outstanding performers [*talents*], whatever their instrument, to give preference to pleasing the majority of the public with agreeable and intelligible music [rather than] to the pointless honor of astonishing a small number of rivals or supposed connoisseurs by difficulties that strike others merely as an odd stunt and confusion of sounds; neither the mind nor the heart understands [the latter], any more than the ear that does not have the benefit of being completely musical.[2]

One may also note the almost complete change-over from harpsichord to piano by about 1780;[3] the significant influence of the Parisian symphony and *symphonie concertante*;[4] the direct influence of Gluck's

1. Regarding this second overlap, Schwarz/FRENCH is a detailed, enlightening diss. on French instrumental music "between the revolutions" (1789-1830).
2. Trans. from MERCURE 1765 April, p. 223, as quoted in La Laurencie/ÉCOLE II 369.
3. But the titles were behind the practice, as may be observed in the chronological list of keyboard works from 1771-1829 in Favre/FRANÇAISE 173-182.
4. Cf. Brook/SYMPHONIE.

operas in Paris, from 1774, even on the current piano music (as on that of Edelmann and Hüllmandel); and the still more direct influence of the newer virtuoso pianist-composers who played in Paris, including Dussek, Steibelt, Cramer, and especially Clementi (in 1781 and 1802). Note should be taken, too, of the establishment of the Paris Conservatoire in 1795, during the Revolutionary period and twelve years before the establishment of the Milan Conservatory. A good number of the composers to be discussed here taught at the Conservatoire in their later years.

Some Alsatian Pianists (Edelmann, Hüllmandel)

Johann Friedrich Edelmann (1749-94) began by studying law in Strasbourg, may have spent a few years as a keyboard teacher and performer in Brussels, and traveled in Germany, Italy, and France before settling in Paris about 1775 (rather than 1773). There he enjoyed a highly successful career in music until, reportedly, he participated
discreditably in the Revolution and died on the guillotine.[5] In the 11 5a
years from about 1775 (not 1773[6]) to 1786 some 16 sets of instrumental music by Edelmann were published in Paris, London, Mannheim, and
Offenbach.[7] These include keyboard quartets, concertos, arrangements, 7a
and sonatas for "clavecin" with violin "ad libitum." There are about 40 of the sonatas in at least 10 sets of 2 to 6 each.[8] Contradicting the use only of "clavecin" in the titles are Edelmann's many signs calling for graduated dynamics (right from the first measures of Op. 1) and Gerber's specific reference to him as the one chiefly responsible for making the piano popular in Paris.[9] The violin parts are consistent

5. Cf. Gerber/NEUES II 17-18; Saint-Foix/PIANISTES V 187-189.

6. A favorable review of Op. 1 appeared in MERCURE 1775, March, p. 203 (quoted in Favre/FRANÇAISE 32).

7. In Saint-Foix/PIANISTES V 190, the Mannheim ed. of Op. 6 is reasoned to be what Mozart sight-read on a Stein clavichord in 1777 when he wrote his father about "some very pretty pieces by a certain Edelmann" (Anderson/MOZART II 460).

8. Cf. the lists in MGG III 1097 (Reeser), BRITISH UNION I 312, and DTB-m XVI xiv-xv and xxxiii-xxxiv (Riemann, for whom Edelmann was another in the outer circle of Mannheim composers). But the gaps cannot be filled in nor the conflicting op. nos. fully resolved until a much more complete thematic index is prepared than that in DTB-m XVI xxxiii-xxxiv. The full titles of Opp. 2, 7, and 8 may be found in Reeser/KLAVIERSONATE 165-166. Op. 8/2 is by Edelmann's sister.

9. Gerber/NEUES II 18. The sonatas are discussed in Saint-Foix/PIANISTES V 187-191; Reeser/KLAVIERSONATE 112-120 (with exx.); MGG III 1098-1099. Among too few mod. eds.: Op. 1/1/i, Davison & Apel-m II no. 304; Op. 2/1 and 2 (or Opp. 2/1 and 4/3; but cf. Reeser/KLAVIERSONATE 112), DTB-m XVI 120 and 127; Opp. 2/3/i and 8/1, Reeser/KLAVIERSONATE 114 and suppl. no. 10; Op. 7/2/i and ii, Saint-Foix/PIANISTES V suppl. Only these eds. are cited here for specific illustrations, because of the difficulty in identifying the early English reprints available to this study.

examples of the optional accompaniment in its most subordinated, inconsequential state, there being passages (as in the "Trio" of Op. 2/2/iii) and even whole movements (Op. 2/3/i) in which it is simply marked "tacet."

Before coming to the most distinctive aspect of Edelmann's sonatas, which is their pre-Romantic theatricalism, we may take note of certain more objective traits. Though the number of movements varies from two to four, three movements are found most of the time, as usual, in the order F-M-F or F-M-minuet. No pattern of interrelated movements seems to have been established by the re-use of the "smorz" coda in Op. 2/1/i to end the finale of this sonata. Edelmann's movements fall into sectional forms of considerable variety. All the essentials of textbook "sonata form" can already be found in Op. 1/1/i, although the opening theme does not make a clear melodic landmark because it is purely chordal. In other first movements the design may be simpler (Op. 7/2/i), or without a full recapitulation (Op. 2/2/i), or without the return of the contrasting theme (Op. 2/1/i), and so on. Frequently the "contrasting" theme is simply an adaptation, in the related key, of the opening idea (Op. 8/1/i). Edelmann achieves his phrase grouping much of the time by the soon tiresome method of stating everything twice. Furthermore, he does much padding at the ends of sections in order to fill out the structural rhythm. There is a fair amount of harmonic and tonal color in his sonatas, as in the "development" modulations of Op. 2/3/i,[10] but virtually no contrapuntal interest.

The theatrical character of Edelmann's sonatas clearly reflects, among other influences, his closeness to Gluck,[11] who had become a dominant figure in Parisian opera from 1773. The inscriptions alone, above the movements, would suggest extramusical influences—"avec tristesse," "voluptueusement," "très lentement d'un ton lugubre." There are also programmatic titles of the sort still being taken over from the Baroque French clavecinists—"la Capricieuse," or "la Gémissante" (lamentation)—and one title, "les Adieux de E . . ." (Op. 2/3/i; *ca.* 1776) that anticipates the spirit, although the music does not recall the style, of Emanuel Bach's "Abschied von meinem Silbermannischen Claviere" (1781).[12] Internal signs of theatrical influences are found in pauses for recitative-like passages during fast movements (as in Op. 2/1/iii/38-39) and in the expressive, clearly projected lines of the slow movements, frequently in minor and in *parlante* style (as in Op.

10. The mention of mvts. in F♯ and b♭ in Favre/FRANÇAISE 32 could not be verified here, presumably because of conflicting op. nos.

11. Cf. Saint-Foix/PIANISTES V 189-190.

12. Cf. Reeser/KLAVIERSONATE 113-116.

2/2/ii, with its "Basso sempre piano"). The fast movements often run on, for all the world, like anticipations of corresponding sections of the "Poet and Peasant" overture or other music used to portend disaster in old-time movies (Ex. 105). With quasi-dramatic effect, hammer-

Ex. 105. From the first movement of Johann Friedrich Edelmann's Sonata in c, Op. 2/1 (after DTB-m XVI 120).

stroke cadences and fresh starts occur at every turn in such movements. One gets the recurring impression that he is playing transcriptions of the then contemporary music. Motion is created by Alberti, triplet, or drum basses in the left hand, and by scale and arpeggio passages or tremolo, that hollowest of all piano idioms, in the right hand.

The fine pianist, composer, and author **Nicolas Joseph Hüllmandel** (1756 [not 1751]-1823) shows every evidence of excellent training in composition, whether he got it in his home city of Strasbourg or elsewhere, but there is little in his musical style and nothing in the known facts of his life to confirm the report of Fétis that he studied with Emanuel Bach in Hamburg.[13] There would be much better reason, as regards both styles and facts, to guess that he could have received some instruction from Christian Bach at about the age of fifteen, around 1771, when he is known to have performed under the latter's direction in London.[14] At any rate, after travels in Italy in 1775 that included at least 6 months in Milan, he was definitely settled in Paris in 1776 at the age of twenty. There he quickly made a good name for himself as a virtuoso at the keyboard and, like Naumann and Dussek, on the glass harmonica as well.[15] About 1790 he fled from the Revolution and followed his wealthy wife to London, where he soon gave up composition but became one of the tribe of important "foreign" teachers in residence,[16] including Clementi, J. B. Cramer, Dussek, and F. Ries.

All of Hüllmandel's original compositions are for keyboard with or without violin. Besides some suites and shorter pieces, 7 sets plus 2 single sonatas, totaling 26 sonatas by him, were first published in Paris, between about 1773 and 1788, followed by early reprints variously in Paris, London, Mannheim, and Dublin.[17] Out of this total, 21 sonatas have accompaniments, 17 being "ad libitum" (Opp. 1, 3, 6/1

13. Fétis/BU IV 383-384. Regarding this question, the newly reported birth year, and the order of Hüllmandel's Christian names, cf. pp. 38-47, 98-100, and 90-97 in Benton/HÜLLMANDEL. This new, unpublished diss. (1961), valuable for its broad orientation as well as its thoroughness, supersedes and greatly augments Saint-Foix/PIANISTES IV, Reeser/KLAVIERSONATE 120-128, MGG VI 833-839 (Reeser), Pike/HÜLLMANDEL, and Favre/FRANÇAISE 28-31. In RDM XLVII (1961) 177-194 is an extract from Benton/HÜLLMANDEL.

14. Cf. Terry/BACH 123; Pohl/MOZART II 368. In 1791 Hüllmandel referred to "Emanuel Bach" (as quoted in Benton/HÜLLMANDEL 292), but not as a teacher. In fact, he identified Emanuel curiously and falsely with the early use of the piano in Germany and wrote of his "knowing, agreeable, and piquant music," causing one to wonder whether the wrong name could have slipped in and whether Fétis could have become hazy about any information he may have received in 1808, at the age of 24, when he says he met Hüllmandel. Presumably, Hüllmandel renewed his acquaintance with Christian Bach when Christian came to Paris in 1778 (cf. Benton/HÜLLMANDEL 227-231).

15. Cf. Benton/HÜLLMANDEL 100-102, 112-117 (with contemporary opinions). Hüllmandel could have had Paris connections as early as 1771, since Terry/BACH 123 puts him in the service then of the French royal ambassador in London, Comte de Guînes (cf. La Laurencie/ÉCOLE II 341).

16. Cf. Benton/HÜLLMANDEL 120-125.

17 Cf. Benton/HÜLLMANDEL 129-132, 164-218, and 257-272 for a summary, critical list of original and early eds. (with discussions, many exx., and facs. of title pp.), and thematic index, respectively; also, BRITISH UNION I 514-515.

and 2, 9/1 and 2, 10, and 11[18]) and 4 "obligé" (Opp. 6/3, 8/3, and 9/3, and one published without op. no. by Boyer[19]) ; and 5 are for keyboard alone (Opp. 4/1-3 and 8/1 and 2[20]). A modern edition is needed that will provide a fuller representation of these sonatas than has yet been made available.[21]

Hüllmandel specified the keyboard instrument as "clavecin ou forte piano" through Op. 5 (1780), then reversed the option thereafter except for the Boyer sonata of 1785 (H-or-P) and Op. 11 (P alone). But, once more, the graduated dynamics make the primary intention clear right from Op. 1, as do the sympathetic remarks on the piano quoted in our Chapter V from Hüllmandel's knowing article on the "Clavecin" for the encyclopedia volume *Musique* (1791).[22] The "ad libitum" violin parts are actually purely subordinate, dispensable parts much of the time (as in Op. 3/3/i) ; but, too often for them actually to be omitted, they contribute not a little to the texture through imitations, rhythmic enlivenment, and richer scoring (as in Op. 10/2/i/21-25). The relatively early "obligé" parts (from 1782) certainly leave no question about their domination of the score in many sections (as right at the start of Op. 6/3/i).[23] However, in the sonatas with these parts there is not yet the exchange between instruments of whole phrases and periods such as goes on throughout Beethoven's "Spring" sonata, Op. 24, or that we have found still earlier in "accompanied" sonatas by Boccherini (1768), Friedrich Bach (1777), and Schuster (1777?). Instead, when Hüllmandel does not have the violin dominate completely (Op. 6/3/2) he may assign it a purely subordinate role once more (Op. 8/3/i/1-4 and 10-13), or put it through only a closer, *concertante* (motivic) exchange with the piano (Op. 8/3/i/18-22). It is interesting that even in the "obligé" parts the violin is still marked one degree softer than the keyboard on occasion (Op. 6/2/13-16), suggesting that the early piano posed the same problem of balance that the harpsichord had posed for Mondonville, Guillemain, and others.[24]

Out of Hüllmandel's 26 sonatas 17 are in 3 movements, all F-S(or M)-F, with the middle movement in the same key (in either mode) or

18. Mod. eds.: Op. 1/2, Reeser/KLAVIERSONATE suppl. no. 9; Op. 3/2, Saint-Foix/PIANISTES IV suppl. (without the Vn part).
19. Mod. ed.: Op. 6/3, Reeser/KLAVIERSONATE suppl. no. 12. Op. 8/3 is copied in full in Benton/HÜLLMANDEL 346.
20. Op. 4/3 is copied in full in Benton/HÜLLMANDEL 318.
21. E. Reeser was reported to have one in progress in 1957 (MGG VI 839).
22. Copied in full in French and trans. in Benton/HÜLLMANDEL 280-315.
23. Cf. Benton/HÜLLMANDEL 197-201.
24. Cf. Newman/ACCOMPANIED 339-341.

a nearly related key.[25] The other 9 are in 2 movements, in the same key, one of them having an "Adagio" introduction of 11 measures
25a (Op. 10/3). There are no programmatic associations that bind the cycles and only rarely are there hints of similar incipits (as in Opp. 3/2 and 9/1) or of similar styles (as in the chromaticism and fast harmonic rhythm throughout much of Op. 10/3 in g). Rondo form occurs in 9 finales and 2 middle movements, while the minuet occurs only in one of each. "Sonata form" is applied variously, flexibly, and as an effective structure not only in all the first movements but in many other movements, as well—in fact, in all 3 movements of Opp. 1/1, 3/3, and 10/2. Attention has been called to certain of these "sonata forms" in which the double-bars with repeat signs are absent (Opp. 3/3/ii, 6/3/i, 8/1/ii, 9/2/i).[26] These movements are thought to be the basis for certain rather cryptic remarks by Grétry that were published in 1797:

> However [with regard to an unaffected and natural style], I see almost all instrumental music chained to worn-out forms that are repeated for us without end, and I would wish that a man of genius might change that. Hüllmandel, one of the most perfect composers of this type [of music], was, I believe, the first to connect the two parts of his sonatas so that they do not repeat slavishly; often an interludial passage joins the two parts so as to produce but a single whole.
>
> A sonata is a discourse. What would we think of a man who, cutting his discourse in two, repeated each half?[27]

If anything, the "interludial passage" probably refers to an evaded cadence that leads right on where the exposition normally ends at a double-bar with repeat sign. But this procedure seems to occur only in Opp. 6/3/i and 9/2/i, and, in any case, the examples are too few and haphazard to suggest significant trends.[28]

Compared with Edelmann's sonatas, those of Hüllmandel show distinctly superior craftsmanship. This craftsmanship, which is evident at once in Op. 1 and seems to advance with each opus number, manifests itself especially in the sure command of harmony, the precise voice-leading, and the expert counterpoint in the course of frequent imitations. At times Hüllmandel also depends excessively on the Alberti and other chordal basses (Op. 8/1/i), though with much less frequency than Edelmann, with better voice-leading, and with much other textural interest to counteract the effect. Hüllmandel knows more about piano

25. Cf. Benton/HÜLLMANDEL 142-160, including a table of son. mvts. (pp. 143-145).

26. Cf. Reeser/KLAVIERSONATE 128; Benton/HÜLLMANDEL 148-154.

27. Trans. from the 2d ed. of Grétry's *Mémoires* III 256 as quoted in Benton/HÜLLMANDEL 149.

28. Cf. Saint-Foix/PIANISTES IV 201-202.

writing, finding no need to resort to devices like the tremolo in order to achieve considerable brilliance of a fluent sort (especially in all the fast mvts. of Op. 10). Naturally, the violin writing is more advanced than Edelmann's, too, though even the "obligé" parts offer little challenge to an experienced player. Hüllmandel is not the theatrical pre-Romantic that Edelmann is. Nor is he the abler, expressive pre-Romantic that Séjan is. His melodies are well chiseled and they fall into nicely balanced phrase groupings, within more satisfactorily organized forms. But they do not soar or unfold like the lines of opera arias. In terms of such composers and in spite of some expressive and/or driving movements, one would have to call Hüllmandel cold. He was, indeed, another Koželuch—another master of the high-Classic idiom without enough to say.

Good samples of Hüllmandel's most convincing writing from the standpoints of expression, drive, and skill, can be found in Op. 3/2 in a, among his earlier sonatas, and Op. 10/3 in g, among the later ones. Once more, the best sonatas prove to be those in the minor mode. It was probably Op. 3 or 4 to which Mozart referred when he wrote his father that Hüllmandel's sonatas are "very fine" (1778).[29] In fact, the first movement of Mozart's Sonata in a, K.V. 300d (1778), is said to derive, at least in its second theme, from the corresponding movement and theme of Op. 3/2, although it must be remembered that the second movement of K.V. 300d has been likened to Schobert's Op. 17/2/i (which Mozart had earlier transcribed as K.V. 39/ii).[30] Hüllmandel's Op. 3/2 does open with considerable verve (Ex. 106). Other movements have some pre-Beethovian drive and pathos in them, such as Op. 8/3/i in c[31] or Op. 10/2/ii in d.[32] There is even a foretaste of Schubert in the turn to major and his manner of smiling through tears, during Op. 3/2/ii.

Johann Ludwig (or Jean-Louis) **Adam** (1748-1848), another native of Alsace, trained first in Strasbourg, then settled from at least 1777 in Paris, where he is thought to have furthered his studies under Edelmann (on stylistic grounds).[33] Like Hüllmandel, Adam was an 33a

29. Anderson/MOZART II 827-828.

30. Cf. Saint-Foix/PIANISTES IV 203; Simon/MOZART 183-185; Benton/HÜLLMANDEL 179-186.

31. Hüllmandel himself liked Op. 8/3 well enough to arrange it as a string sextet (Benton/HÜLLMANDEL 204 and 238-240).

32. But the thematic resemblances cited in Pike/HÜLLMANDEL are hardly to be taken seriously.

33. Cf. Saint-Foix/PIANISTES VI 210. In the following discussion Saint-Foix is preferred for his evaluations but the somewhat different bibliographic information in the longer, more comprehensive treatment of Favre/FRANÇAISE 53-60 and 112-117 appears to be more accurate.

Ex. 106. From the opening of Sonata in a, Op. 3/2, by Nicolas Joseph Hüllmandel (after the early reprint by Götz in Mannheim, at the Library of Congress).

author (of two "Méthodes," 1798 and 1804) and a highly influential teacher, serving at the Conservatoire as "Professeur de piano," in fact, for forty-five years, from 1797-1842.[34] The influence of Edelmann—especially his theatrical style, tremolo, and poetic inscriptions—seems to have been a lasting one on Adam. But during his long creative life, from 1778 to 1832, Adam kept pace with the times, reflecting also the strong, successive impressions that Clementi, Dussek, Steibelt, and Cramer made as each played in Paris. Indeed, like the last three, he

34. Cf. Saint-Foix/PIANISTES VI 215; Favre/FRANÇAISE 116-117.

would have been saved here for the Romantic Era were it not that at least the first half of his sonata output still fell in the harpsichord-or-piano style and times. Because that output, all published in Paris, is not to be found in the principal reference works[35] it may be listed here in abbreviated form (except for full titles of special interest):

Johann Ludwig Adam's Sonatas

Op. 1, 3 sons. "dans le genre de Symphonies concertantes," for H-or-P & Vn, 1781; expanded and rearranged from *Deux Symphonies concertantes, pour clavecin et harpe obligé, et violon ad libitum,* 1778.

Op. 2, 6 sons. for H-or-P & Vn, 1781.

Op. 3, 3 sons. "en trio" for H-or-P & Vn & Vc, 1781.

One son. for H-or-P & Vn, without op. no., 1784 (Boyer).

Op. 4, 3 sons. for H-or-P & Vn, 1785.

Op. 6, 3 sons. for P (no. 2 + Vn), 1788.

Op. 7, 3 sons. for P (nos. 1 and 2 ± Vn), 1788.

Op. 7 (or Op. 8 in the Pleyel ed.), 3 sons. for P, 1801.

Op. 10, *Grande Sonate dans le style dramatique, dédiée à Clêmenti,* for P, 1810.

Op. 12, *Grande Sonate* for P, 1810; opt. Vn and Vc parts added later.

Op. 13, *Grande Sonate* for P, *ca.* 1815.

Souvenir et regret de la perte du célèbre pianiste Clémenti, Morceau dramatique pour le piano (a quasi son. in 4 mvts., headed by the words, "The author has wanted to express in this piece the feelings he has experienced in the works of Clementi, to which, in part, he owes his talent for composition"), 1832.

A glance at this list of 29 accompanied or solo keyboard sonatas gives a tabular view of how, in those 54 years, the harpsichord gave way to the piano, how the optional acccompaniment became obligatory and was then discarded (insofar as the piano "soloist" was concerned), how the concepts of "grande" and "dramatique" grew after 1800, and how much one particular composer, Clementi, affected Adam. Adam's earlier sonatas were indeed close to Edelmann's in style, form, and markings. Remembering this fact, one can get at least a small idea of the sharp dynamic contrasts, wide range, new virtuosity, and intensified accompaniments in his style after 1800 by reading a single illustration (Ex. 107). Adam's more lyrical moments give hints of Chopin's cantilena melodies and *fioriture*. It is true that throughout his sonatas Adam's ideas are often somewhat sterile and that his passage work is usually empty, ultimately deteriorating into sheer pyrotechnics and bombast. But there is no denying many fluent, effective sections of piano writing in the sonatas of Op. 8, and many sections that anticipate

35. There is no entry for Adam in either MGG or GROVE. The list in Eitner/QL I 39 is unsatisfactory.

Ex. 107. From the opening of Johann Ludwig Adam's Sonata in f, Op. 8/3 (after the Pleyel ed. at the Library of Congress, but without the narrower-ranged alternative for "Piano ordinaire" in mss. 5 and 6).

the scoring, harmony, technique, melody, and emotionalism of Romantic piano writing.[36]

The one further Alsatian now to be mentioned, **Franz Joseph Hérold** (or François-Joseph Hérold; 1755-1802), is described as having been a "brilliant student" of Emanuel Bach in Hamburg.[37] Father of the much better known Romantic composer Ferdinand Herold, Franz Joseph left at least 10 accompanied sonatas and one of solo
37a piano, issued in 4 publications between 1782 and 1807 (posthumous).

36. Numerous further exx. are given in Favre/FRANÇAISE 55-60 and 113-115.
37. MGG VI 250 (Vigué & Briquet) ; cf., also, Favre/FRANÇAISE 97-98.

The 3 accompanied sonatas that could be examined here (Op. 3, 1803) prove to be facile, fluent, pedagogic works, with an entirely subordinate violin part.

More Foreigners in Paris (Riegel, Sor)

Heinrich Joseph Riegel (or Henri Joseph Rigel; 1741-99) was a minor master of composition, a fine clavecinist, and an esteemed teacher in Paris, whose works are unjustly neglected today and call for further study as well as modern editions.[38] Born in Wertheim (west 38a
of Würzburg), Germany, Riegel was the oldest member of a musical family active up to the mid-nineteenth century, mostly in Paris. He arrived there by 1768 after study with both Richter and Jommelli. Heard often at the Concert spirituel, his compositions included oratorios, light operas, symphonies (led by Gossec), concertos, and sonatas. Of the last, there appear to be (or have been) at least 10 sets of 3 to 6 sonatas each of the accompanied keyboard type, published in Paris roughly in the 15 years from 1770-85.[39] Opp. 1, 8, 13, 18, and 19 are for "clavecin" (or "piano-forte," from Op. 13, 1777) and optional violin (this part now often being lost). Op. 14 has an additional violin 39a
part that permits the sonatas to be played "en quatuor," and Opp. 7, 9, 16, and 17 have optional parts for 2 violins, 2 horns, and cello, thus rightly being called both "Sonates" and "Simphonies."

Riegel's sonatas are mostly in two or three short, concise movements. The first movements generally introduce everything expected of "sonata form," however briefly. The other movements are usually dances or dance-like. Thus, in Op. 13, we find a "Scherzo" in 2/4 meter (No. 1/ii), an "Allemande Stirienne" in 3/8 meter (without the traditional pattern; No. 3/iii), and a "Marcia maëstoso a la Polonese" in *alla breve* meter (No. 4/ii[40]). The wonder of this music, as with that of Rosetti, Sorge, and like minor masters, is that so much can be said, with such originality and skill, yet so simply, lightly, and succinctly (Ex. 108). Riegel's writing is not ornamental but entirely functional and clear. The

38. The only references of consequence here are La Borde/ESSAI III 472; Saint-Foix/PIANISTES V 192-198 and suppl.; Reeser/KLAVIERSONATE 111 (only); Sondheimer/RIGEL (with emphasis on the symphonies). In SAMMLUNG SONDHEIMER Nos. 5, 50, 51, 12, 14, and 18, there are 3 symphonies, and 3 slow mvts. for Vn & K, printed in score.

39. Op. 13, dedicated to Marie Antoinette, appeared in 1777 (Saint-Foix/PIANISTES V 194), and Op. 21 in 1787 (Johansson/FRENCH I 129). The dating is not helped by the fact that Riegel published some of his music, engraved by his wife, at his own expense (Sondheimer/RIGEL 222). The lists of his music in Eitner/QL VIII 233-234 and DTB-m XVI xix are unsatisfactory (including confusions with works by the brother and the son).

40. Reprinted in the suppl. to Saint-Foix/PIANISTES V.

Ex. 108. From Heinrich Joseph Riegel's Sonata in D, Op. 13/3/iii (after the original ed. at the Library of Congress, with the optional Vn part missing).

language is high-Classic.[41] Gluck and Grétry were among those who praised his music.[42] La Borde's remarks, fuller than usual, include these sentences:[43]

> That which characterizes his writing most is a great purity, whether in his melody or use of harmony. All the results are distinct; the biggest sections of the symphony always have a natural, coherent line. M. Rigel, passionately fond of his art, takes pleasure, without envy, in the talent of other composers. An enemy of [all] intrigues, he does not devote himself *exclusively* to any one sort [of music]; but sampling whatever good each style may offer (French, Italian, German), he is one of these foreigners settled in our midst who does the greatest honor to music in France.

The birthplace and life dates are not known for **Valentin Roeser,** a clarinetist active variously in Vienna, Monaco, and Paris (the last perhaps as early as 1764).[44] Riemann assumed he was a pupil of J. Stamitz, since Roeser, too, wrote a set of *Six Sonates a trois ou avec tout l'orchestre,* Op. 1 (1764) and since he arranged Stamitz's set for clavecin alone (1768).[45] A prolific, much published composer, Roeser is also recalled as the author of a book on instrumentation (1764) and of a French translation of Leopold Mozart's *Violinschule.*[46] Other sets of sonatas by him include *Six Sonates pour le forte piano avec accompagnement d'un violon,* Op. 10. Published in Paris probably in 1774,[47] this set may be the first in the Classic Era to specify piano alone without the harpsichord alternative. But its contents are hardly so progressive, for they reveal empty pieces in the style and with the characteristic titles of the antiquated *pièces de clavecin.*[48] There are also unaccompanied duos and melo/bass sonatas by Roeser (both "solo" and "trio" types[49]). However, an examination of the *Douze* [2-mvt.] *Sonates tres facile pour le clavecin ou le forté piano,* Op. 6 (*ca.* 1772[50]), confirms that Roeser's music is plain, square-cut, and trite to a degree that discourages further inspection on purely musical grounds.

41. Although there is no mention of Riegel in the Mozart letters, his apparent influence during Mozart's Paris visit of 1778 is emphasized in Sondheimer/RIGEL.
42. Saint-Foix/PIANISTES V 192-193.
43. Trans. from La Borde/ESSAI III 472.
44. Riemann & Gurlitt/LEXIKON II 526. The year 1764 is suggested only by the first publication in Paris.
45. DTB-m XV xxi. The publication dates come from Johansson/FRENCH I 109 and 27; many more works by Roeser can be found in this source than in the list or thematic index in DTB-m XVI xix and xliv, or the list in BRITISH UNION II 895-896.
46. Cf. Anderson/MOZART II 805.
47. Op. 11 appeared in 1775 (Johansson/FRENCH I 115); cf., also, La Laurencie/ÉCOLE II 413.
48. Cf. Reeser/KLAVIERSONATE 110-111.
49. Perhaps the melo/bass sons. are only arrangements of other composers' works (cf. Johansson/FRENCH I 112).
50. Op. 8 appeared in 1773 (Johansson/FRENCH I 114).

Much fresher were the equally facile sonatas of the pianist **Franz Metzger** (or Mezger; ?-not before 1808), if the two-movement sample in Anth. BLAND-m III No. 32 is a fair sample (Op. 6/6). Another prolific and popular composer in Paris (from about 1785), Metzger came from the Württemberg region (Pforzheim) as did Riegel.[51] Prior to Op. 6, about 1788, he had been one of the few to publish a keyboard sonata "à trois mains."[52]

The Czech composer **Ludwig Venceslav Lachnith** (1746-1820) made his debut at the Concert spirituel in 1773 as soloist in his own horn concerto, and was also a pianist and violinist.[53] This triple performing talent undoubtedly served him well in his Parisian career as teacher, arranger of instrumental works for piano,[54] and compiler of opera *pasticci.* Among his original compositions were published at least seven sets of accompanied sonatas plus two more in piano trio setting, and a set for harp and violin. These works appeared mainly in the 1780's,[55] before the cruel blows that were dealt him by the Revolution. An examination of *Six Sonates concertantes pour clavecin ou forte-piano avec violin,* Op. 14 (*ca.* 1788), reveals full-sized cycles in two or three movements. The forms are clear and the writing is competent. The style is still rather thinly and severely Classic—one might almost say neo-Classic, for one gets the impression that even these pieces might prove, on further investigation, to be *pasticci* of instrumental works by Haydn, Pleyel, Mozart and others especially known to Lachnith. The sonatas are true duos (or appear to be[56]), with those broad exchanges of themes such as did not quite obtain yet in Hüllmandel's sonatas with "obligé" accompaniments.

A reminder of how popular the guitar and the harp were during the high-Classic Era comes with the brief mention of four composers identified with one or the other instrument. The harpist **Christian Hochbrucker** (1733-at least 1799) was another of those "Germans" found by Leopold Mozart in 1764 in Paris (SCE XVII). He may have arrived there before 1762, remaining in the royal service until the Revolution forced him to move to London.[57] At least four sets of solo

51. Cf. Eitner/QL VI 455; DTB-m XVI xviii.
52. BRITISH UNION II 673.
53. Cf. MGG VIII 34-36 (Briquet).
54. Cf. BRITISH UNION II 587.
55. Cf. Johansson/FRENCH II Facs. 111-115.
56. The parts were published separately, as usual. In the copy at King's College in Cambridge the violin part is missing, but the sections in which it takes the lead by answering or anticipating the piano can be determined readily enough from the sections of mere accompaniment in the piano part.
57. A set of 6 harp sons. was already announced in Paris in 1762 (Johansson/FRENCH I 44), which also suggests that "1769" is too late for his move to Paris, as given in MGG VI 500 (Zingel).

or accompanied harp sonatas by Hochbrucker were published in Paris and London between 1762 and 1799. His music is described as of the 57a
salon style, interesting more for its harp techniques and effects than its expressive values.[58]

The outstanding Czech-born harpist and harp innovator **Johann Baptist Krumpholtz** (*ca.* 1745-90) trained in Paris and returned there after recital tours in the 1770's as well as a period of 3 years in Prince Esterházy's orchestra during which he studied composition with Haydn.[59] Between about 1775 and 1789, some 32 sonatas by him, in 11 sets or separate issues, were published and republished in Paris or London.[60] Many of these have violin or flute accompaniments, and 60a
the later ones have programmatic implications, as the title of Op. 15 indicates (*ca.* 1788): *Deux Sonates en forme de scènes di mezzo-carattere pour la harpe, practicables aussi sur le forte-piano, avec un accompagnement d'un violon ad libitum.* The available example (Son. in F, Op. 8[61]) is a fluent, melodious, three-movement work with considerable Alberti bass and a tendency reminiscent of Haydn to develop each idea as it is stated.

Less information and no music could be found here for the popular harpist of Italian descent **Francesco Petrini** (*ca.* 1744-*ca.* 1819), born in Berlin and established in Paris from 1770.[62] Along with a harp method and other works, numerous sonatas are credited to him by Fétis and Schmidl.[63]

The historical significance to the guitar, its playing, and its music, of **José Fernando Macario Sor** (1778-1839) is rightly suggested by Fétis' designation of him as "the Beethoven of the guitar."[64] A native of Barcelona, Sor trained early (*ca.* 1790-95) at Montserrat monastery under Padre Anselmo Viola (whom we met in Chap. IX) and may have done further study under Boccherini during service in the house of Alba in Madrid (after 1798).[65] From 1813 or 1814 he lived alternately in Paris and London, except for about 3 years of travel and a stay in Russia (1823-26). In London (where the smaller, 10-string

58. MGG VI 501.
59. Cf. MGG VII 1840-1843 (Zingel); Landon/HAYDN 266.
60. Cf. the full list in BRITISH UNION I 581-582.
61. NAGELS-m No. 98 (Zingel).
62. Fétis/BU VII 11-12 (with list of works up to Op. 46); Eitner/QL VII 393-394.
63. Schmidl/DIZIONARIO II 264.
64. According to Bone/GUITAR 335. The principal biography is Rocamora/SOR (1957), followed by the helpful, unpublished diss. on the man and his guitar music, Sasser/SOR.
65. Cf. Sasser/SOR 46.

cittern had been known before) Sor introduced the Spanish guitar about 1815,[66] and there, in 1832 or 1833, he may have competed with the Italian guitarist Giuliani (whom we met in Chap. XVI).[67] Along with operas, ballets, oratorios, symphonies, quartets, and other music, Sor wrote over 65 guitar works.[68] In this last category are 3 sonatas, all in C—Op. 15, first published by Meissonier in Paris between 1816 and 1828, and Opp. 22 and 25, each called "Grande Sonate" and first published by Simrock in Bonn between 1829 and 1833.[69] Two lost sonatas for 4 hands at one piano, one based on Swedish folk tunes, are credited to Sor, also, and are supposed to have been written while he was in London in 1822.[70]

The creative worth of Sor's guitar sonatas is high. The ideas, which grow out of the instrument yet stand up well enough apart from it, are fresh and distinctive. The harmony is skillful and surprisingly varied, with bold key changes and with rich modulations in the development sections. The texture is naturally of interest, too, with the melody shifted from top, to bottom, to middle, and frequent contrapuntal bits added. Among the extended forms, the first allegro movements still show considerable flexibility in the application of "sonata form," especially in the larger number of ideas introduced and recalled.[71] For that matter, the style still goes back to that of Haydn and Boccherini, especially in Op. 22/i, which has all the neatness of syntax and accompaniment to be found in a Classic symphony, and Op. 22/iii and iv, which could nicely pass as a minuet and rondo by Haydn. Op. 15 is in one movement, with a development section that is short but effective, both tonally and thematically. Op. 22 is in 4 movements, F-S-M-F, the second being a warmly expressive "Adagio." Op. 25 is in 3 movements—a rather free, pathetic "Andante" in the tonic minor, a gay "Allegro" in 6/8 meter, and a theme-and-variations that recalls the problems publishers were supposed to have had in selling Sor's guitar music to amateurs, so much of it being scored in difficult 4-part textures.[72]

66. Cf. Bone/GUITAR 336-337.
67. Cf. Sasser/SOR 65 and 67-68.
68. Cf. the lists in Rocamora/SOR 121-122; Sasser/SOR 86-92.
69. The dates are based on HOFMEISTER 1828, p. 478 (Whistling) and 1834, p. 80; Sor disappears entirely from the next vol. (1834-38). Mod. eds.: Op. 15, Domandl/SOR-m; Op. 22, Benjamin/SOR-m; Op. 25, Segovia/SOR-m (with considerable changes).
70. DICCIONARIO LABOR II 2054; Sasser/SOR 57 and 88. They are not entered in any vol. of HOFMEISTER.
71. Cf. Sasser/SOR 104-109.
72. Fétis/BU VIII 68; cf. SCE III.

Some Violinists, Mostly French (*Guénin*)

Joseph Boulogne Chevalier de Saint-Georges (1745 [or '49 or '39]-99) was a mulatto born in the French possession of Guadeloupe (in the Caribbean Sea), who came to France before 1766 and Paris about 1770.[73] A professional "Gendarme de la Garde du Roi" most of his life, he participated in music mainly as an enthusiastic amateur. Neither the quality nor the quantity of the extant sonatas quite justify the digression one would like to make into the romantic life of this celebrated fencer, horseman, dancer, actor, and violinist. But his operas, string quartets (which were among the first by a Frenchman[74]), and violin playing were appealing enough to win warm contemporary tributes and the dedication of works to him by other composers like Lolli and Gossec.[75] A total of 7 sonatas by Saint-Georges are known, including a set of 3 for clavecin or piano and violin "obligé," Op. 1, published in 1781;[76] a set of 3 for violin solo with a second, accompanying violin, first book, published posthumously about 1800;[77] and a single sonata in MS for harp with flute accompaniment.[78]

Saint-Georges' accompanied sonatas let the violin "obligé" take the lead more than half the time. Thus, after broad exchanges in the "Minuetto" Op. 1/ii, it becomes the solo instrument for the rest of the movement. The composer seems to be a little at a loss as to how to treat the new duo style. When the piano is in the lead the violin often holds long notes well above it. Sometimes the two instruments run parallel, with either one on top, or make close imitations (Op. 1/2/iii), adding a little needed contrapuntal interest. The piano has an excess of Alberti bass. The violin is treated in a somewhat more advanced fashion, though not with the virtuosity to be found in the posthumous solos supported by an entirely subordinate accompaniment of the second violin. Except for occasional moments of lyricism when the violin dominates (as in Op. 1/3/ii), the ideas, harmony, and structural organization in these sonatas are only mediocre. Each has two movements (F-M) except Op. 1/2 (F-S-M).

From Santo Domingo in the Caribbean Sea came an elder

73. The most detailed scholarly account is that in La Laurencie/ÉCOLE II 449-500.

74. La Laurencie/ÉCOLE II 458.

75. La Laurencie/ÉCOLE II 463-464, 466-467, 474, 454.

76. Discussed in La Laurencie/ÉCOLE II 490-491 (with exx.) and Reeser/KLAVIERSONATE 128-133 (with exx.; cf. pp. 166-167 for the full title).

77. Discussed in La Laurencie/ÉCOLE II 490-492. Mod. ed.: Son. 3 in A, Alard/VIOLON-m No. 37. Only 3 sons. actually exist of the 6 listed in BRITISH UNION II 913.

78. Cf. La Laurencie/ÉCOLE II 490.

colleague of Saint-Georges in Paris, **Michel Paul Guy de Chabanon** (1729-92). Known as a violinist, but even more as an aesthetician (SCE II), litterateur, and friend of Rameau and Gluck, Chabanon published a set of three accompanied sonatas (H & Vn) that may now be lost (1785) and a single solo clavecin Sonata in d (1785).[79] The latter appears to be the sort of elementary, conservative (motivic), though not insensitive nor unskilled work that we have now met several times from the hands of theorists and aestheticians.

In the same year that Saint-Georges published his accompanied sonatas, 1781, another fine French violinist, **Marie-Alexandre Guénin** (1744-1835), also published a set of three (Op. 5), this time simply "Avec Accompagnement de Violon."[80] Born near the Belgian border, Guénin had come to Paris as a prodigy, there to study violin with Capron and Gaviniès and composition with Gossec. From 1771 he became active as an orchestral and solo performer in Paris. His first publication, before 1769, contained *Six Trios* [individually called sonatas[81]], "of which the first 3 are to be played by only 3 and the others by the whole orchestra." The accompanied sonatas of 1781 have numerous passages in which the violin takes the lead, especially, as was often true in these early duos, where the instruments take turns in introducing ideas at the starts of movements (Op. 5/1/i and 5/2/iii). Sometimes such a passage is actually announced by the word "solo" in the score, in concerto fashion. Also, sometimes its good writing for violin gives a hint of Guénin's technical proficiency. But more of the time the violin falls back to its subordinate function of doubling, reinforcing, filling, and complementing. Then both instruments are treated somewhat conservatively, with little resourcefulness in the piano accompaniment, in any case.

There are mannerisms associated with Mozart in Guénin's pleasingly supple melody writing, especially the short phrase members, the chromatic downward slides, the acciaccaturas, and the cadences, both feminine and hammer-stroke. The tonal movement is limited and attenuated, making the long movements seem rather static. Throughout

79. Cf. MGG II 996-1004 (Sorel-Nitzberg), with facs. of title page and first page of score (but neither validates the caption to the effect that this is an acc'd. son.).

80. The full title is given in Reeser/KLAVIERSONATE 167, with discussion and exx. on pp. 133-136 and a complete reprint of Op. 5/3 as suppl. no. 11. A discussion of this set and other works by Guénin (with exx.) may also be found, along with biographic details, in La Laurencie/ÉCOLE II 396-418. The listing of 3 other sets of Vn solos or duos in MGG V 1025 (Borrel) may pertain to authentic works, or these works may be disqualified by Guénin's own statement regarding plagiarisms (so common at the time) as quoted in Reeser/KLAVIERSONATE 133 (trans. in SCE IV).

81. La Laurencie/ÉCOLE II 412.

Guénin's trios, duos, and accompanied sonatas the number of movements varies from two to three according to no set plan of fast and moderate-to-slow tempos.[82] Unusual is Op. 5/3, which should have pleased Grétry (as quoted earlier under Hüllmandel), for it runs on from the start of the first to the end of the third and final movement without repeat signs within the movements or cadential breaks between them.[83]

Joseph Chartrain (?-1793) was a violinist from Liège who played in the Paris opera orchestra and at the Concert spirituel from 1772. Among his several published chamber works were a set of 6 Vn/bass sonatas, Op. 2,[84] and a set of 6 accompanied sonatas Op. 15 (H-or-P & Vn; 1783). The sonatas in Op. 15 all have 2 movements, both fast in 4 instances. The music is described as the conventional, lax sort in which the lightest, shortest movements are the most acceptable.[85] Only Sonata 6 lets the violin take a fair share of the lead.

The precocious, Paris-born violinist **Isidore Bertheaume** (*ca.* 1751-at least 1801) was active in Paris up to the Revolution as one of the principal virtuoso soloists immediately prior to Viotti's triumphal debut in 1782.[86] In 1769 he published a first set of 6 Vn/bass sonatas. Soon after, he composed a 3-movement unaccompanied violin sonata in D "dans le stile de Lolli," whose playing had strongly impressed the Parisian public in 1768. Written in *scordatura* and not published until 1786, this difficult work consists of 3 groups of a total of 16 movements or lesser sections in contrasting tempos.[87] *Scordatura* and a similar complex of movements appears in the second of 2 further unaccompanied sonatas, Op. 4, by Bertheaume, also published in 1786. In addition, one year later he published a set of 3 accompanied sonatas (H-or-P & Vn), Op. 7. But these, as their long full title indicates,[88] are merely arrangements of 2 *Symphonies concertantes* (no. 1 for 2 Vns, no. 2 for Vn & Va), Op. 6, and of Op. 4/2. The surprising effect of the arrangements is completely to subordinate the violin most of the time, although it takes the lead from the keyboard

82. Cf. La Laurencie/ÉCOLE II 412 and 414.
83. Cf. Reeser/KLAVIERSONATE 134.
84. Eitner/QL II 410.
85. Cf. Reeser/KLAVIERSONATE 136-138 (with exx.), 149, 167.
86. The chief account of the man and his music is that in La Laurencie/ÉCOLE II 419-433; the question of the death date (cf. pp. 424-425) is not cleared up in Mooser/ANNALES II 183 and III 738, although Bertheaume can now be placed in St. Petersburg from at least 1798-1801 and the first name can be confirmed as "Isidore."
87. Cf. La Laurencie/ÉCOLE II 420, 422, 426, 429-430 (with exx.).
88. Cf. Reeser/KLAVIERSONATE 167, with discussion and exx. on pp. 138-140 and 154. The exceptionally attractive engraving of the title page of Op. 7 (SCE XVII) is reproduced in La Laurencie/ÉCOLE II 426.

during Op. 7/1/i. Bertheaume's music is of a driving, expressive sort, including recitative passages (Op. 4/2). But the ideas and harmony are of only average interest.

Still another brilliant violinist, **Antoine Lacroix** (1756-1806), was active in Paris from 1780 to 1792, when he fled from the Revolution, gave concerts in Germany and Denmark, and finally settled in Lübeck. Among some 20 works by Lacroix published between 1784 and 1798 in Paris and German centers are a set of 6 accompanied sonatas, Op. 1; a set of 3 violin sonatas with cello accompaniment, Op. 3; a set of 3 sonatas for two unaccompanied violins; and an accompanied sonata, Op. 17, transcribed from an unaccompanied violin duo (Op. 15). Praised by his contemporaries for his brilliant, varied, original compositions, these works have been similarly regarded by one present-day writer,[89] although they remain to be more generally explored.

The last of our French-born violinists to name in Paris, **Rodolphe Kreutzer** (1766-1831) is still remembered for his études and as the unappreciative dedicatee of Beethoven's "Kreutzer" sonata, Op. 47 (SCE XV). Kreutzer was a pupil of J. Stamitz's youngest son, Anton, and an impassioned soloist praised for his original, imaginative style of playing.[90] Not much of this originality seems to have carried over to his compositions. Besides concertos, quartets, and several sets of forgotten Vn/bass sonatas,[91] he published a "Grande" accompanied sonata (P & Vn) in 1799 and a set of three more sonatas of this type in 1802.[92] An examination of the "Grande" sonata reveals a three-movement work with an unexpectedly inconsequential violin part. The piano writing is convenient to play but not especially idiomatic. The outer movements contain much passage work while the middle movement is a setting of a "Romance" by Louis Adam.

Late Organists and Pianists (Méhul, L. Jadin)

Etienne-Nicolas Méhul (1763-1817), important contributor to the eighteenth-century French *opéra comique,* wrote 7 solo and accompanied piano sonatas in his youth that are interesting in their own right. Trained early as an organist, Méhul came to Paris from the department of Ardennes (northeastern France) in 1778. There he studied with Edelmann and, like his teacher, came under Gluck's influence.[93]

89. MGG VIII 43-44 (Karstadt).
90. Cf. MGG VII 1781-1783 (Wirsta), with quotations from contemporaries.
91. Cf. Eitner/QL V 446-447.
92. Weinmann/ARTARIA item 1554.
93. Cf. MGG VIII 1898-1903 (Fréniot; but Op. 2 should be listed as containing acc'd., not solo, sons.).

A set of 3 solo sonatas, still designated "pour le Clavecin ou Piano-Forte," was published as Op. 1 when he was twenty (1783);[94] a set of 3 more sonatas, this time with optional violin accompaniment for the first and third sonatas, appeared 5 years later as Op. 2 (actually "2me Livre"; 1788);[95] and a single, one-movement solo sonata in C, dedicated to Madame Godefroid, appeared about the same time (along with a separate printing of Op. 2/3/iii) in Le Duc's Journal de clavecin.[96]

As early as they came in his total production, Méhul's sonatas must be put with some of the best French examples in the later eighteenth century. Those in Op. 1 show chiefly the concise neatness of ideas and structural clarity that were to be characteristics of his music, but otherwise are a little vapid in their effect. Those in Op. 2 show increasing originality, freedom, and that theatrical style Méhul and Edelmann seem to have derived from Gluck. On occasion Méhul also reaches the dramatic extreme of empty tremolo measures (Op. 2/3/i), but he does not use the poetic inscriptions or quite the number of detailed dynamic indications that Edelmann uses. There is common ground in the imaginative thematic complexes of Méhul (Op. 1/1/ii and iii) and those of Haydn, and in the way both tend to develop the theme before its statement is ended (Op. 1/3/i/1-13). Furthermore, there are suggestions of Beethoven's symphonic drive, even his willfulness, in these same processes.[97]

Nothing about Méhul's sonatas indicates a stereotype, as yet, unless it be the nature of the scoring. Both hands of the pianist are often given reiterative figures related to tremolo or Alberti bass. The right hand plays too often in octaves, and one perpetual-motion movement (Op. 2/3/iii) is little more than an exercise in difficult hand-crossing. The violin accompaniments in Op. 2/1 and 3 are entirely subordinate and dispensable. However, the forms and styles show more independence and imagination. Except for Op. 1/2 in two movements, the sonatas are all in three movements, but the tempos and types of these movements vary considerably. A thematic relationship may have been intended between the dotted patterns that open the outer movements of Op. 2/2, although Méhul was partial to such themes or to still more spasmodic rhythms (Op. 1/2/i/1-7), anyway. The relationship seems more

94. Méhul's sons. are discussed in Saint-Foix/PIANISTES VII 43-46 and Favre/FRANÇAISE 44-52 (with 15 exx.). Mod. ed.: Op. 1/3 in A (the weakest son. of Op. 1!), Pauer/MEISTER-m I 18 (and other "Old Masters" series).

95. A mod. ed. of Op. 2/3 by Mme. Maurice Gallay is cited without further information in Saint-Foix/PIANISTES VII 43.

96. Favre/FRANÇAISE 51.

97. Ringer/MÉHUL explores the relationship of Méhul and Beethoven fruitfully (with further references on pp. 552-553), illustrating in particular some related traits in Méhul's Symphony in g (1809).

positive between the heraldic fanfare that opens Op. 2/3 and the nostalgic, "Adagio" echo of this fanfare at the start of the middle movement. Méhul's first movements are generally more interesting than the others, and bigger to the extent of seeming out of proportion. Only a few of the other movements deserve special mention. The binary "Andante" in A, with variations, in the middle of Op. 2/1 has some of the tender sadness, especially in its minor, second half, that we know in the second movements in that same key in both Beethoven's and Schubert's seventh symphonies. Op. 2/2/iii is a tight, compelling little "Allegretto" in A-B-A design. And Op. 2/3/ii is an "Adagio" of considerable harmonic depth (Ex. 109). Some of the best of these movements are those in minor keys, as usual. On the other hand, a movement like the "Siciliene" in C, Op. 2/2/ii, is too slight in all respects to be of significance, and the "Allegretto Moderato" in A (Op. 2/1/iii), a rondo design, is made dull by its incessant, quasi-tremolo bass.

As for Méhul's first movements, their structural differences give us another reminder of how little codified "sonata form" yet was, even this late. In Op. 2/1/i in D the excess, rambling length results from a prodigality of good ideas, with but a short though telling, contrapuntal development section in which to explore their potentialities. The scalewise opening theme in octaves compels one to wonder whether Beethoven could have been thinking of it when he started to compose his Op. 10/3, in the same key, about ten years later. Before the codetta of the exposition there is one of those "Adagio" recitative moments such as Beethoven liked, too. Op. 2/2/i, in a, recalls the concentrated rhythmic drive and even the style of opening theme in Hüllmandel's sonata in the same key, Op. 3/2 (1777), that was illustrated earlier in this chapter. The "second theme" is but a variant of the first in the relative key, and it is with that variant that the recapitulation begins in the submediant key. The development section in this movement gets as far away as f, a♭, and b♭. The same movement is also noteworthy as another example without repeat signs, although the exposition ends clearly enough on a full cadence.

When a new edition of Méhul's Op. 2 was issued in 1807, about 19 years after the first edition, an overly long and somewhat inconsistent review appeared.[98] It already reflects a change in taste from the Classicism with which Grétry had specifically identified Méhul in 1793.[99] And it reveals a little surprise that such solid and original instrumental music could come from a Frenchman (who is compared here with Gluck), written, at that, while Méhul was still young.

98. AMZ X (1807-08) 11-15.
99. Cf. MGG VII 1031 (Blume).

(Adagio)
Violin
Clavecin or Piano
cresc.
ff
[♭ in source ed.]
p
p

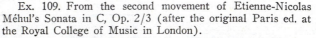

Ex. 109. From the second movement of Etienne-Nicolas Méhul's Sonata in C, Op. 2/3 (after the original Paris ed. at the Royal College of Music in London).

As an organist, **Gervais-François Couperin** (1759-1826), son of Armand-Louis, did honor to his position as one of the last representatives of this great family.[100] As a composer he can be described at best only as competent but uninteresting. Even more than his lighter, partly programmatic piano pieces, his two accompanied sonatas (H-or-P ± Vn & Vc) that were published as Op. 1 in 1788 and his single accompanied sonata (P ± Vn) that appeared as Op. 12 around 1810 lack force and originality.[101]

The brothers **Louis Jadin** (1768-1853) and **Hyacinthe Jadin** (1769-1802) were pianists and prolific composers who taught at the Paris Conservatoire de musique after its establishment in 1795.[102] The younger brother, Hyacinthe, appears to have been the more expressive, brilliant performer of the two, having studied first with Louis, then Hüllmandel. Furthermore, the 9 piano sonatas that he left, in 3 sets—Op. 4, 1795; Op. 5, *ca.* 1795; Op. 6, 1804 (posthumous)—disclose somewhat more Romantic tendencies, in the preference they show for minor keys of 3 or 4 sharps or flats, in their more pathetic and
102a impetuous ideas, and in their more progressive display passages. But, for all his good training, Hyacinthe died too young to develop any significant originality or breadth in his musical thinking. The much longer-lived Louis published more than two dozen sonatas, although most of these appeared while Hyacinthe was still alive. They include four-hand keyboard duets, solo "Sonates faciles," sonatas with violin accompaniments both optional and obligatory, and sonatas in piano trio

100. Cf. MGG II 1734-1736 (Reimann).

101. This music is discussed briefly, with exx. in Favre/FRANÇAISE 73-77. No mod. eds. are known here.

102. Cf. MGG VI 1652-1655 (Ferchault). Brief discussions of their sonatas occur in Saint-Foix/PIANISTES VI 105-109; Favre/FRANÇAISE 61-73 (with titles, dates, and exx.).

setting with a choice of flute or violin in some. Louis' earliest publications, appearing from 1787, are conservative in style. At his best in two accompanied sets (P ± Vn) published in 1795, he neared Clementi in the suppleness of his lines and the brilliance of technical treatment. From his later music, published around 1810, a set of three sonatas for piano, subordinate violin, and a cello reinforcement of the bass was examined here.[103] An approach toward the harmony and idiom of Mendelssohn is now evident. But in spite of Louis' skill and fluency, the blank ideas of the first movement, the weak pathos of the middle movements, and the pure bluster of the finales hardly deserve more than the restrained praise for better-than-average French music that one German critic brought himself to express in 1815.[104] In another of those overly long reviews, the critic discussed a set by Louis similar to the one seen here.

Not seen here were the several solo and accompanied sonatas of **Gabriel Lemoyne** (1772-1815), an esteemed pianist and teacher who had studied with Edelmann and Clementi. Good piano writing and felicitous ideas have been especially noted in these works.[105]

Chiefly Late Melo/bass Sonatas by Foreigners (Viotti)

In these two chapters on France in the Classic Era the fact should be noted that among all the foreigners composing sonatas in Paris only one Italian of consequence, Viotti, can be named. It is true that the **Niccolò Piccinni** (1728-1800) in music history's celebrated operatic feud of the "Gluckists" and "Piccinnists" (1776-79) left, among a few instrumental works,[106] a set of *Tre Sonate e una toccata per il cimbalo* published by Imbault in or before 1792.[107] But these two- and three-movement pieces, in spite of good craftsmanship and a few hints of bigger, more dramatic possibilities (Ex. 110), are too short and too conservative in texture to constitute a valid exception to our statement. And the other Italians in Paris that might be mentioned are more obscure.

There was the opera cembalist **Felice Bambini** (*ca.* 1742-?), who published at least three sets of accompanied sonatas (H-or-P & Vn), in 1771, 1777, and 1788.[108] His textures and phrase syntax already prove to be high-Classic, and there is a freshness about his

103. A Pleyel ed. with the plate no. 1002.
104. AMZ XVII (1815) 297-300.
105. MGG VIII 609-610 (Cotte).
106. Cf. Eitner/QL VII 436.
107. Johansson/FRENCH II Facs. app. 2.
108. Johansson/FRENCH I 33, 38, 99. Cf. Schmidl/DIZIONARIO I 104; BRITISH UNION I 82.

Ex. 110. From the start of Niccolò Piccinni's Sonata 3 in A (after the original ed. at the Library of Congress).

ideas in spite of their slightness. There was the violinist **Antonio Bartolommeo Bruni** (1751-1821), like Viotti a pupil of Pugnani, who left numerous sonatas for violin or viola accompanied only by a second violin, second viola, or cello. Dating from the 1780's in Paris, these sonatas are among his instrumental works reported to be also in the high-Classic language, but still flexible in structure and marked by bold contrasts and other pre-Romanticisms.[109] Along with these obscure Italians there was also the French violinist **Michel Woldemar** (1750-1815), who studied with, and apparently became about as eccentric as, Lolli. In the early 1800's Woldemar published four Vn/bass sonatas each with the title *Sonate*

109. Cf. La Laurencie/BRUNI, especially pp. 271-272.

fantomagique but with a different subtitle, "L'Ombre de Lolli," ". . . de Mestrino," ". . . de Pugnani," and ". . . de Tartini." Though not written for his special five-string "Violon-Alto," these pieces do exploit the violin's capabilities in the style if not the quality of each model.[110]

One of the great violinists of the past, **Giovan Battista Viotti** (1755-1824) was the last and most important representative in Paris of the Piedmontese school fathered first by G. B. Somis, pupil of Corelli, then by Pugnani, pupil of Somis; and he was in turn the single most important influence on violin playing in the nineteenth century.[111] After early study with Pugnani, followed by travels and recitals in the latter's company, as far off as Berlin, Warsaw, and St. Petersburg,[112] Viotti reached Paris late in 1781. His debut at the Concert spirituel early the next year was such that a contemporary wrote in 1783, "From the first day that Viotti was heard, everyone concurred in placing him above all his contemporaries."[113] Among these vanquished contemporaries had been such celebrites as Puppo, Lolli, and Bruni among the Italians, and La Houssaye, Bertheaume, Gaviniès, and Kreutzer among the French. Yet late in 1783 Viotti preferred to quit public performances for the calmer existence and better opportunity to compose that service at the court of Marie Antoinette afforded during the next nine years.[114] He played in public again and prospered for a while after the Revolution forced him to move to London in 1792. But in spite of the lasting friendship of Cherubini in Paris and of the Chinnery family, in London, Viotti's unjust exile to the German town of Schönfeld in 1798, his ill-fated business ventures back in London, from 1801, and his vain attempts to succeed once more in Paris, from 1818, make the later life of this generous, kindly musician an increasingly sad one to relate.

Viotti left mainly concertos, quartets, trios, and duos. His sonatas are relatively few and mostly early, from the 1780's. His violin concertos, for which he is primarily remembered as a composer today, were left in fairly neat bibliographic order. But the chamber works, including the sonatas, appeared under as many as 4 different opus numbers,[115] existed in numerous transcriptions and redesignations[116]

110. Cf. HOFMEISTER 1815 (Whistling), p. 124; Moser/VIOLINSPIEL 404-405.

111. Cf. the charts in Moser/VIOLINSPIEL 574 and 576; also, the historical evaluation in Rinaldi/VIOTTI. Giazotto/VIOTTI (1956), largely superseding previous studies of the man and his music, includes a thematic index (abbreviated to G. here in references to specific sons.), illustrations, facs., and many contemporary documents; Giazotto's treatment of the man is stronger than that of the music.

112. Cf. Mooser/ANNALES II 309-310.

113. Trans. from Giazotto/VIOTTI 54. Cf. Schwarz/BEETHOVEN 432-439 (including possible influences of Viotti's concertos on Beethoven's).

114. Cf. Giazotto/VIOTTI 55-60.

115. Cf. Giazotto/VIOTTI 290.

116. Cf. the listings in Giazotto/VIOTTI for G. 70 and 136.

not necessarily acknowledged or recognized as such, and are often hard to locate today. There is no question about the 15 Vn/bass sonatas that he left, including 2 sets of 6 each first published in Paris in 1782 (G. 26-31 and 35-40) and one set of 3 in 1784 (G. 48-50) [117] But what about the several sets of accompanied sonatas that were left in his name?[118]

Curiously, no mention of Viotti's accompanied sonatas is made throughout Giazotto's recent book on Viotti, and the one such listing in his unfortunately, though understandably, incomplete thematic index is that of a transcribed set of string trios (G. 102). Giazotto does list as composed in London in 1817 and published by Naderman in Paris, "Trois Sonates pour le Violon avec Accompagnement de Forte-Piano" (G. 151), which title, if correct, would be one of the few so worded that have been encountered during the present survey of the Classic Era.[119] Could this set have been a re-edition, with realized bass, of earlier Vn/bass sonatas not otherwise known? Viotti wrote two original piano concertos (G. 91 and 92), later arranged for violin, that reportedly show a fine knowledge of the keyboard.[120] But the two accompanied sets that could be seen here, in spite of some idiomatic piano scoring, have so much two-part and other thin writing, such characteristic cello basses in the left hand, and so many right-hand passages that lie especially well for the violin as to seem suspiciously like arrangements of duos and trios.[121]

All of Viotti's fifteen Vn/bass sonatas are in three movements[122] except the last of the third set (G. 50), which has only two (M-F). Most are in the order F-S-F, with the middle movement in the dominant or subdominant key. All but G. 40 in c are in major keys, although G. 49, with its finale in A, starts with a "Canto Introduzione" and first

117. Briefly discussed in Giazotto/VIOTTI 207-210. Warm thanks for the loan of early Richault eds. of the first 2 sets are owing here to Professor Chappel White of Emory University in Atlanta, who completed a Ph.D. diss. on Viotti's Vn concertos at Princeton University in 1957. A few mod. eds. are listed in Altmann/KAMMERMUSIK 244-245.

118. Conflicting listings of up to 3 sets may be found in HOFMEISTER 1815 (Whistling), p. 318; Johansson/FRENCH II Facs. 78 (1801?); Eitner/QL X 103; Cat. BRUXELLES IV 55.

119. The set is stated to be in the Brussels Conservatoire but is not listed in Cat. BRUXELLES. Under Viotti in HOFMEISTER 1828 (Whistling), p. 152 there is a listing of "3 Divertissemens p. V. avec Pf. Leipz. Br. et Härtel," but even this wording of "V. avec Pf." was infrequent at that time.

120. Giazotto/VIOTTI 220-221.

121. One acc'd. set is listed as an arrangement of Vc duets in BRITISH UNION II 1045. 2 acc'd. sets, "Op. 7" and "Op. 15," are briefly described in Stone/ITALIAN I 224-227 (including exx.), with the incipits of all 17 mvts. in II 102-103, and a complete copy of "Op. 15"/2 in G, except for the Vn & Vc parts, in III 176; the incipits are not among those in Giazotto's index.

122. G. 29 is in 3 mvts., not 4 as suggested in Giazotto/VIOTTI 304.

movement in the tonic minor. Even the middle movements are minor only twice and no movement is in a key of more than four sharps or flats. At first glance, Viotti seems deliberately to have related the incipits of a sonata's movements in many instances. For example, each movement of his Sonata in B♭, G. 29, begins by filling in the descending 5th from the dominant to the tonic scale degrees. That Viotti was fully conscious of such subtle melodic variants is proved repeatedly during his frequent uses of variation techniques. However, the other side of the question is seen in the fact that not only the movements of one sonata but a surprising majority of all the movements begin with an upbeat leap of an ascending 5th followed by a more devious, stepwise descent.

Although the detailed progressions in Viotti's sonata writing are often rhythmically and melodically complex, the over-all forms are clear in their broad outlines. The first movements move in and about "sonata form," without adhering to any set plan. A "second theme" is usually present, but it may actually stand apart as such (G. 39/i/41-57) or not (G. 30/i/17-24). The "development" section does usually deserve to be so called, but the "recapitulation" is less predictable, sometimes beginning its own separately repeated section (G. 35/i), or following a new, charming, independent double-period (G. 29/i), or returning only in a tonal sense, on quite new material (G. 26/i/95). The middle movements are most often in A-B-A design, with long lines that are fragmented by rests and cadences, and are more notable for their elegant melodic, rhythmic, and dynamic refinements than for any considerable expressive warmth. Usually the finales are rondos, providing almost the only tunes with real character in these sonatas (as in G. 36/iii); or they are andantes with virtuoso variations, reminding us that Viotti's Vn/bass sonatas were first of all vehicles for his own display and advancement in the musical world.

Throughout these sonatas Viotti naturally creates much idiomatic passage work of varied interest for the violinist, especially in the last two sonatas of the second set (G. 39 and 40). Some textural interest is provided by the bass (cello), which is unfigured and can even be regarded as an equal partner in a duo (Viotti's favorite type of chamber music) in the few instances when it engages the violin in imitations (as in G. 28/i/64-71) or provides lively rhythmic complements (G. 27/iii/79-83). More often it ranges from the conservative running bass that associates with rapid harmonic rhythm and a relatively complex melodic line (G. 28/i/1-4) to Pugnani's more static kind of bass, in repeated notes or Alberti-bass and other chordal figures, that associates with slower harmonic rhythm and a simpler, more high-Classic type of theme (G. 38/i/21-28). The latter style, along with some Mozartean chromaticism, appears increasingly in Viotti's second set. Somewhere between these styles is the representative theme from the first set that is quoted in Ex. 111. This passage also illustrates Viotti's habit of repeating phrases and his relatively plain harmony. In the "development" sections of two movements, however, the modulations are bold and resourceful, going to the minor dominant and lowered mediant before returning to D in G. 28/i, and to the equivalent keys followed by the tonic minor before returning to G in G. 39/i. G. 39 is perhaps the most original and expressive of all Viotti's sonatas, and the one that brings us closest to his concertos.

Viotti was the last composer of consequence to write melo/bass sonatas. The others, with which our two chapters on the sonata in France are about to conclude, may be given only passing mention. A versatile Alsatian violinist, clarinetist, flutist, bassoonist, and composer of light operas and much chamber music, **Matthieu-Frédéric Blasius** (1758-1829) left at least four sets totaling fifteen "Sonates" or "Sonatines" variously for violin, or flute, or bassoon and bass (Opp. 43, 55, 57, and 58).[123] All published in Paris between about 1800 and 1806, these works were regarded in his own day as pleasant and fluent, without any significant depth or originality, to judge from a contemporary review of Op. 58.[124] The same may be said for the two examples that have been made available[125] from about a half-dozen sets of Vc/bass sonatas and some "trio" sonatas published in the 1780's by **Jean Baptiste Bréval** (*ca.* 1756-
126a 1825).[126] Reported to be an excellent cellist himself, this Frenchman made an early debut at the Concert spirituel, played in the Paris opera orchestra for twenty-five years (from 1781), and taught at the Conservatoire from 1802.

Also on the staff at the Conservatoire was the brilliant flutist **Antoine Hugot** (*ca.* 1761-1803), who published two sets of Fl/bass sonatas in the mid 1790's as well as a set of "Six Sonates faciles" for unaccompanied flute[127] (a rare setting in the Classic Era). These sonatas have not been explored in modern times. Another brilliant flutist, in the same Parisian sphere when he was not on tour, was the German **Christian Karl Hartmann** (1750-1804). In

123. Cf. Eitner/QL II 63-64; BRITISH UNION I 112. Mod. ed.: Vn/bass Son. in G, Alard/VIOLON-m No. 42.

124. AMZ IX (1806-07) 803-804.

125. Son. in C, SCHOTT CELLO-m No. 21; Son. in G, Moffat/CELLO-m No. 4.

126. Cf. Eitner/QL II 188-189; Straeten/VIOLONCELLO 295-298.

127. Cf. MGG VI 870-871 (Cotte).

Maestoso
Violin
Bass (Vc)

Ex. 111. From Giovan Battista Viotti's Sonata in E♭/i, G. 30 (after the early Richault ed. lent by Professor Chappell White).

the 1780's Hartmann published several sets of sonatas, some for flute and cello (or piano) and some of the accompanied keyboard type (H-or-P + Fl or Vn).[128] His first set of the former type has the title *Six Sonates avec des airs variés pour flûte et violoncelle ou accompagnement de forte piano.* Published in Paris in 1783, or thirty-four years before the similar, exceptional Viotti title noted previously, this set of sonatas is actually the earliest encountered here in which the piano is named as the accompanying instrument. And finally may be mentioned a Swiss clarinetist in the Paris opera orchestra and at the Conservatoire, **Jean-Xavier Lefèvre** (1763-1829), who published at least three sets
129a of sonatas for his instrument and *b.c.* early in the 1800's,[129] among many other chamber works and some concertos. These are also early examples of their sort. One of two sonatas by Lefèvre that have been made available, No. 5 in d of 12 that appear in his clarinet method of 1802,[130] is a short, attractive, lyrical work in three movements, making only the modest technical demands on the clarinetist that might be expected in a pedagogic work.

128. Cf. MGG V 1746-1747 (Cotte).
129. Cf. HOFMEISTER 1815 (Whistling), p. 213; Eitner/QL VI 110.
130. Viollier/LEFÈVRE-m, with preface; cf., also, Altmann/KAMMERMUSIK 213 for a mod. ed. of an acc'd. son. in g.

Chapter XIX

Great Britain From About 1740-1780

Attitudes and Milieu

The eighty years in Great Britain's history that are spanned in our next two chapters, from about 1740 to 1820, include part of George II's reign (1727-60) and all of George III's (1760-1820). They fell in a period of relative internal stability, both in spite and because of the strains imposed by the War of the Austrian Succession (1740-48), the Seven Years' War (1756-63), the American Revolution (1775-83), the French Revolutionary Wars (1792-1802), and the Napoleonic Wars (1803-15) with their offshoot in the War of 1812 (1812-15). There were also major adjustments necessitated by a great population increase, new agricultural methods, the Industrial Revolution, and an expanded empire. In the same period arts and letters flourished: it was the great age of English portrait painting, with such figures as Gainsborough, Reynolds, and Lawrence; writers included those as diverse as Johnson, Blake, and Keats; the Scottish school of historians and philosophers, led by Hume, Robertson, and Blair, flourished; and other important figures were Gibbon the historian, Burke the orator, Sheridan the dramatist, and Walpole the letter-writer.

During this period, the musical life to be reported in Great Britain—meaning London most of the time—was significant too.[1] Yet, curiously, as not a few music historians have observed, there were no native English composers of comparable distinction. Already recognized by contemporaries, both native and foreign,[2] this deficiency was probably 2a

1. Among the many accounts of London musical life in the 18th century may be cited Burney/HISTORY II 983-1023; Landon/HAYDN 249-312; Pohl/MOZART *passim*; Terry/BACH *passim*; Unger/CLEMENTI *passim*; Schlesinger/CRAMER, especially pp. 13-23; Loesser/PIANOS 209-283; Elkin/CONCERT; the diss. Helm/ABEL 27-70; Scholes/BURNEY I 118-129, II 164-183; Sadie/CONCERT; and the articles on London in GROVE V 368-381 (Fuller-Maitland) and MGG VIII 1147-1158 (Cudworth; with further bibliography).

2. Cf. the disparagements quoted in OXFORD HISTORY IV 317-318 (Fuller-Maitland) and Schlesinger/CRAMER 13-14.

abetted by an attitude that, for all the cultivation of keyboard, violin, and flute as genteel attainments, music was still no fit pursuit for British gentlemen and ladies.[3] Only the Established Church provided an acceptable basis for a professional career in music. It is no wonder, then, that most of our 17 native British and 6 Anglo-Irish sonata composers—out of a total of 58 composers discussed in these next 2 chapters—figured among "all those obscure English organists" that an American correspondent asked Blom to delete from the new edition of GROVE (I vi).

The importance and brilliance of eighteenth-century musical life in London derived much less from native British musicians than from foreigners. More explicitly, it derived from the fact of this city's being a good paying and publishing host to the many foreign musicians, chiefly Italians and Germans, who visited or resided there. A great deal of this life naturally centered around opera, but the point remains that, from Giuseppe Sammartini to Clementi, London harbored a more active colony of Italians composing instrumental music, including the twenty-three discussed here, than any other center we have visited inside or outside of Italy. The instrumental output of this colony was further graced by that of Italian visitors like Galuppi, Graziani, and Viotti. Within the similarly purposed but competitive German colony[4] Christian Bach and Abel were leaders. German and Austrian visitors included, of course, both Mozart and Haydn (in that order), though not Beethoven in spite of the plans made in his later years.[5] Surprisingly few Bohemians, French, or representatives of other nationalities concern us in London.

Although Bach and Abel gave part of their services to the pro-German court of the music-minded rulers, King George III and Queen Charlotte, the foreign and native musicians in London found more occasion for the composing of solo "lessons" in their teaching and of ensemble sonatas in private groups or in the independent social and public concerts that have been traced as far back as 1672 in that city.[6] In the later eighteenth century these last included the programs of societies like the Academy of Antient Music, its younger rival the Concert of Antient Music, and the Anacreontic Society, meeting characteristically in prominent London taverns. There were also the straight concerts presented in the King's Theatre, Covent Garden, and other

3. Cf. Loesser/PIANOS 209-215, with the well known letter of April 19, 1749, by the fourth Earl of Chesterfield, among other citations; Burney/HISTORY II 983.

4. Cf. Terry/BACH 84-85, 151.

5. E.g., cf. Thayer/BEETHOVEN II 370-372 and 378-379, III 184-188.

6. Cf. H. A. Scott in ML XVIII (1937) 379-390 and MQ XXIV (1938) 194-209. Refer, also, to the sources given earlier in this chapter.

theaters, and in "concert rooms" such as Almack's (where the most successful Bach-Abel concerts were given) and Hickford's Room (where the child Mozart appeared in 1765). And there were the lighter concerts given in the outlying "pleasure gardens," including Vauxhall, Marylebone, and Ranelagh.

The publishing of sonatas by foreign and native musicians continued at an astonishing rate in London, throughout the period in question. One gets some idea of it merely by turning the pages of *The British Union-Catalogue of Early Music,* a source that has already served us so well for musicians on the Continent. The names of Bremner, Welcker, Preston, Longman & Broderip, Dale, Bland, and many others appear on countless sonatas.[7] Their catalogues printed on the covers and flyleaves of this music are an excellent indicator of current tastes.[8] In them it is easy to watch the change-over from harpsichord to piano, the growing preference for the accompanied rather than the solo keyboard sonata, the sudden popularity of the keyboard duet after Burney's first 8a
published examples in 1777, and the considerable frequency of programme, potpourri, and tune (or "favorite air") sonatas toward the end of the century. Of special significance is that change-over from harpsichord to piano, beginning with, if not sooner than, the not uninteresting sonatas of John Burton published in 1766. As we shall see, the sonata composers in London took much interest not only in the playing and writing for this instrument, but in its construction and manufacture—all of which aspects were brought to a peak by one of the most important men to be met in the present volume, Clementi.

The special studies, general surveys, and bibliographies cited thus far in this chapter are representative of a fair, but far from thorough, literature on the Classic sonata in England. More has been made known about the composers and circumstances of the sonatas[9] than about the music itself, much of which seems not to have been examined at all in modern times.[10] Even with regard to the two chief names, there is still no detailed study of Christian Bach's sonatas and much remains to be done on the music as well as the bibliography of Clementi's sonatas. 10a
Furthermore, neither of these composers is adequately represented by

7. Cf. Humphries & Smith/PUBLISHING 24-35.

8. Cf. the analysis of a Bremner catalogue in Scholes/BURNEY 118-129.

9. As in the comprehensive coverage of British composers in the more recent vols. of MGG, especially the many articles by Cudworth.

10. Not available here, except for an abstract, was the recent detailed, unpublished diss., Sadie/BRITISH, on chamber music by British composers from 1720-90, including a full thematic index. However, grateful acknowledgment is made to Dr. Stanley J. Sadie of Wembley and Professor Charles Cudworth of Cambridge for corrections and additions to the present chapter, some of which are cited in subsequent footnotes.

modern editions of their sonatas. Naturally, then, one can only expect to find much less by the more obscure composers. Very scarce and spotty are the modern editions of their sonatas.

A First Group of Italians (*Pescetti, Paradisi*)

Among the first of the many eighteenth-century Italians to publish keyboard sonatas in London was the cembalist and organist **Giovanni Battista Pescetti** (*ca.* 1704-*ca.* 1766), a Venetian who had studied with Lotti and who produced operas in London from at least 1737 to 1744.[11] Pescetti's *Sonate per gravicembalo* appeared in 1739
12a with the city and year, but no publisher[12]—thus, about the same time that D. Scarlatti's *Essercizi* appeared in London (SCE IX) and only 11 to 13 years after G. P. Sandoni's cembalo sonatas were published there (SBE 319). In Pescetti's set are 9 sonatas plus a tenth item, which is a keyboard arrangement of the "Ouverture" to his opera *La Conquista del vello d'oro* (London, 1738) along with other opera excerpts, including some of his "Ariette" with words.[13] In Anth. HAFFNER RACCOLTA-m I/4 another cembalo sonata by Pescetti, in c, was published 17 years later (1756).[14]

Pescetti's 9 sonatas of 1739 have 2 to 4 movements in contrasting
15a tempos but no set order.[15] Notable at this time is the fact that fully half of these sonatas are in minor keys, all the major sonatas being in keys up to 4 sharps and all the minor ones in keys up to 3 flats. The inner movements never change key, but occasionally do change to the opposite mode. Binary design with repeated halves is present in nearly all the movements, exceptions being the quasi fugues (nos. 3/ii and 8/iii in the 1739 set) and a short transitional slow movement (2/ii). In the absence of contrasting ideas, close track is kept of the initial idea, usually with a restatement of it in the dominant or relative key at the start of the second half and sometimes a further statement

11. Cf. Eitner/QL VII 384-385; GROVE VI 685-686 (Fuller-Maitland & Loewenberg).

12. Francesco Degrada reproduces the title page in "Le Sonate per cembalo e per organo di Giovanni Battista Pescetti" (CHIGIANA SETTIMANE XXIII [Nuove Serie N. 3, 1966] 89-108), with new facts (incorporated here).

13. Mod. ed.: Son. 3 in g, Perinello/PESCETTI-m and Tagliapietra/ANTOLOGIA-m XII no. 13; 4 separate mvts. (Sons. 8/iii and iv, 3/ii, and 4/ii, respectively), TRÉSOR-m XX. All of Pescetti's sons. are dismissed as nonoriginal opera arrangements in Schilling/LEXICON V 430, but only item "X" actually applies.

14. Among numerous mod. eds.: Pauer/MEISTER-m VI 2; Oesterle/TREASURY-m V 66; Benvenuti/CEMBALISTI-m 76. Degrada (fn. 12, *supra,* p. 99) reports MSS of this and 5 further cembalo sons. in Dresden and 4 organ sons. in Venice.

15. These sonatas are discussed briefly in Torrefranca/ORIGINI 159-164 (with exx.); Stone/ITALIAN I 80-85 (with exx.; followed by a thematic index of all mvts. in II 57-59; and with a full copy of Son. 7 in G in the 1739 set, in III 1); and Shedlock/SONATA 25-26.

that qualifies as a clear enough return during the second half (as in 2/i but not 6/i).

Pescetti's textures always permit fluent performance, although they range from the skilled polyphony that would be expected of a man also devoted to church music,[16] to a degree of homophony that stands with the most progressive writing of the day. It is true that his fugal movements for keyboard (3/ii and 8/iii) are not consistent in the number of voices and, at times, become almost homophonic themselves, in the Italian manner. But the subject is kept adequately in view, the entries are effectively timed and placed, and there is no lack of such fugal elements as sequential episodes and dominant pedals. As for the more homophonic writing, the accompaniment often runs on like a thinly realized *b.c.* (1/i). At other times it describes chordal figures. In fact, in one movement (throughout the seventh variation of 1/iii) there is one of the earliest uses of literal Alberti bass known here. However, that that device was no standard formula as yet is shown by Pescetti's more frequent use of the related but somewhat more pungent figure that oscillates with a neighbor rather than chord tone (Ex. 112).

Ex. 112. From near the end of the minor second movement of Sonata 7 in G by Giovanni Battista Pescetti (after the original ed. at the Library of Congress).

Although Pescetti made no special point of virtuosity for its own sake, he demonstrated a full knowledge of good keyboard effects, as in the movements that exploit repeated notes (4/ii, "Allegro"), note-against-note quarter-notes (5/iii, "Presto"; scherzando staccato?), chords in dotted rhythm (6/ii, "Spiritoso"), and, of course, hand-

16. Cf. Burney/HISTORY II 911.

crossing (8/i, "Con Spirito," one of his showiest movements). Pescetti's method of progression was the frequent late-Baroque one of starting with a square, four-measure phrase, then following it with a longer, chain or sequential phrase leading to a cadence. He did not yet think in the two-measure units used by Alberti and subsequent Italians. Still, the "Mennuett" that closes Sonata 1 in E shows that he was fully capable of balanced phrase-and-period writing had he chosen to use it more. The variations on this minuet, by the way, are remarkably like those in Handel's "Harmonious Blacksmith" (in the same key), even to the order in which they occur.

In his adagio movements Pescetti could write ornamental cantabile lines in the best Italian manner (2/ii). Otherwise, his ideas and passages are piquant, rather like D. Scarlatti's (2/iii). Characteristically harsh English dissonances occur on occasion, including some surprising false relations (as in the change from the major to the minor dominant harmony soon after the double-bar in 1/ii). However, one must acknowledge a certain routinism in the frequent sequential passages and the many approaches to the dominant key through its dominant and tonic-$^6_4$ harmonies. These late-Baroque traits are less apparent in Pescetti's later Haffner sonata, which fully deserves its survival in the "Old Masters" anthologies. Its imitative, fast, outer movements drive fluently and convincingly to their final cadences, while the middle movement is now a *galant* "Moderato" with pronouncedly *galant* traits such as its incessant light ornaments, triplets, and chordal accompaniment, its short expressive phrases, and its appoggiatura "sighs."

Remarkably little information can be confirmed regarding **Pietro Domenico Paradisi** (or Paradies in some of his own autographs[17] and in the supposedly German corruption; 1707?-91). Torrefranca wonders whether two men discovered to be connected with the Florentine theater in 1719, a scene designer named Domenico Paradisi and a scene painter named Pietro Paradisi, might not be his father and uncle (respectively or not), thus accounting for his compound name.[18] This hypothesis is also plausible with regard to the year; it helps to explain why his first known opera production (*Alessandro in Persia,* 1738) occurred in another, near-by Tuscan city, Lucca; it removes the doubt created by the rarity of the name Paradisi around Naples, where he is usually said to have been born and to have studied with Porpora;[19]

17. Information kindly supplied by Professor Cudworth.

18. Torrefranca/ORIGINI 486-487 (not considered in MGG X 744-745 [Cudworth]).

19. The "napoletano" after Paradisi's name in the Blundell ed. of his sons. is said to prove nothing, in Torrefranca/ORIGINI 486, in view of the "Veneziano"

yet it still leaves the possibility of that Neapolitan training, what with a theatrical family that must have been itinerant. Torrefranca also suggests[20] that the article by C. F. Pohl in the original edition of GROVE[21] confuses two different musicians, our P. D. "Paradies" and a *castrato* singing teacher of doubtful character, Paradisi (without Christian name), who was "old" in 1759 and dead by 1766.[22]

Besides a few operas, sinfonias, and concertos, Paradisi left the set for which he is chiefly remembered—that is, his 12 *Sonate di gravicembalo.* First published by John Johnson in London, in 1754 (according to a Royal Privilege granted on November 28 of that year[23]), this set appeared with almost no changes in at least 4 more London editions and at least 2 Paris editions during the 18th century.[24] A collation follows that equates the numbering of the 18th-century editions (to which all references are made here) with that in the faithful 19th-century edition of 10 of the sonatas in TRÉSOR-m XVII and with that of several of the sonatas separately reprinted in modern times. The original Johnson numbering is retained in the more recent, typically "enriched" and "improved" edition in CLASSICI-m I No. 22 (Benvenuti & Cipollini). Only these 12 sonatas are to be found among 24a
all the early editions and MSS[25] or among the numerous single sonatas by Paradisi in "Old Masters" anthologies.[26] Their decided musical significance and appeal certainly warrant the new, careful, complete edition and full study that they have not yet had.

Torrefranca indulges in one other hypothesis, consistent with his usual effort to establish a date of 1740 or earlier (SCE VII).[27] He guesses that the first six of Paradisi's sonatas were composed before

---

after his name over each son. in another early copy and the frequent misascriptions in other contemporary titles.

20. Torrefranca/ORIGINI 487-488.

21. Previously in Pohl/MOZART I 176-177, and still in the 5th ed. of GROVE (VI 545).

22. Torrefranca then cites the 2 separate articles in Schilling/LEXICON V 374-375, but the 2 (?) men had already been treated separately in Gerber/LEXICON II 78.

23. Copied in full in Stone/ITALIAN I 132.

24. Cf. BRITISH UNION II 761-762; Johansson/FRENCH II Facs. app. 2. The Imbault ed., which appeared in Paris in two books of 6 sons. each, as Opp. 1 and 2, is wrongly credited to the Austrian pianist, singer, and composer Maria Theresia Paradies (1759-1824) in Gerber/NEUES III 654 and MGG X 743 (Ullrich); cf. Eitner/QL VII 316 and Torrefranca/ORIGINI 481. The supposed ed. (by a later Roger?) in Amsterdam *ca.* 1770 (cf. Gerber/LEXICON II 78; Eitner/QL VII 316: Torrefranca/ORIGINI 481) could not be verified here.

25. Cf. Torrefranca/ORIGINI 479.

26. E.g., besides those listed in the ensuing collation: Son. 3 (Johnson numbering), Benvenuti/CEMBALISTI-m 60; Son. 11, Tagliapietra/ANTOLOGIA-m XII no. 19; Son. 2, Paoli/ITALIANE-m 16.

27. Torrefranca/ORIGINI 484-485.

Editions of Paradisi's Cembalo Sonatas

Johnson (1754) Le Clerc (*ca.* 1765) Welcker (*ca.* 1770) Blundell (*ca.* 1781) Preston (*ca.* 1790) Imbault (*ca.* 1791) CLASSICI-m (1920)	TRÉSOR-m (1870)	Single sons. or single mvts. in 2 "mod." eds. (O/T = Oesterle/TREASURY-m; P/M = Pauer/MEISTER-m)
No. 1 in G	No.	O/T V 152; P/M VI 14
2 B♭		ii, O/T V 134
3 E	1	i, O/T V 126
4 c, C	2	ii, O/T V 131
5 F	3	
6 A	4	
7 B♭	5	ii, O/T V 124
8 e	6	ii, O/T V 132
9 a	7	O/T V 136
10 D, d	8	O/T V 144; P/M II 26
11 F	9	O/T V 159; P/M VI 21
12 C	10	O/T V 168; P/M VI 30

his first known production in Venice, *Il Decreto del fato* in 1740, and the other six before his first known production in London, *Phaeton* in early 1747; or, in other words, all twelve go back to that "period from about 1735 to 1740" (!). Torrefranca was also assuming that Johnson had published an earlier edition of Paradisi's sonatas before protecting them with the Royal Privilege in 1754, and that this edition appeared about 1746, when Paradisi is supposed to have arrived in London.[28] If the music of *Phaeton* was as inexperienced and inept as Burney and Busby said it was,[29] then it is more likely (as Burney seems to imply, anyway) that Paradisi's excellent sonatas were products of further experience. Their relatively solid, sometimes contrapuntal style, often close to D. Scarlatti's style, and the use, still, of the conservative term "gravicembalo" in the title (as by Pescetti in 1739 but not Alberti in 1748) do allow for an earlier date than 1754. But there is no bibli-

28. Torrefranca/ORIGINI 483. But the date 1746 that still appears in most of the newest dictionaries (Riemann & Gurlitt/LEXIKON II 369; DIZIONARIO RICORDI 821; BAKER'S DICTIONARY 1206; etc.) traces to a careless antedating of the Blundell ed. by some 35 years in Weitzmann/PIANOFORTE 308 and 313 (in conjunction with the reprinting of Paradisi's Son. 4 in c). When Paradisi left London, presumably to return to Venice, is not at all clear; the Mozarts did not report meeting him in London in spite of their interest in his sons. in 1764 (Mozart/NEUE-m X/34 400) and 1774 (Anderson/MOZART I 364 and 366), so that the "Paradies" reported to be there in 1764-65 in Pohl/MOZART I 63 and 173 may well have been another man.

29. Burney/HISTORY II 846; Torrefranca/ORIGINI 484.

ographic evidence to support an earlier edition and only inconsistent stylistic evidence to support Torrefranca's brief, unillustrated attempt to distinguish between the first six sonatas as being more in the conservative (fugal?) style of Durante in Naples and the other six as being more in the newer Venetian style of Alberti and Galuppi.[30]

Each of Paradisi's twelve sonatas is in the "Italian" plan of two movements, whether both are fast or, less often, either or both are moderate in tempo (as in Sons. 9 and 11, respectively).[31] As the table of these shows (*supra*), keys up to 4 sharps and 2 flats, mostly major, are used, there being no change within the sonatas apart from the three in which the two movements are in the opposite modes. The usual binary design with repeated halves prevails except in two relatively songful finales of moderate tempo that fall into the couplets of a French rondeau (Sons. 3 and 9) and another finale that makes a more continuous rondo (Son. 11). Still another finale is a binary "Minuetto" without trio (Son. 4) and three finales are clever, propulsive gigues with or without the name (Sons. 2, 5, and 12). The rondo finale of Sonata 11 and the other five finales are all short, concentrated, brilliant, quasi-études, of which that in Sonata 6 in A—the so-called "Toccata" that is Paradisi's best known piece—is typical right down to its broken-chord figuration.

In his first movements Paradisi's anticipations of "sonata form," as defined nearly a century later, seem precocious. And, as usual, it has been mainly these anticipations that have occasioned such brief discussions of them as have been written (cited earlier). Yet the anticipations appear too flexibly and irregularly (not to mention naturally) to permit the conclusion that any one design was either sensed or sought. Thus, in the continuous, tortuous yet broadly planned line of Sonata 4/i in c there is no place for a "contrasting theme," although a distinguishable closing figure is provided in the two lines of 8th-notes alternated between the hands (Ex. 113, recalling Scarlatti's Son. in D, K. 29/23-25). A more distinctive closing figure supplies the main contrast in Sonata 6/i/45-52. A contrasting idea, still more of a figure than a theme, appears nearer to the middle of the first section in Sonata 3 in E, entering on the secondary-dominant harmony. An abrupt turn to the dominant minor focuses attention on a more tangible contrasting theme in Sonata 10/i/17-22 (recalling the same Scarlatti son., mss.

30. Torrefranca/ORIGINI 484.

31. Among discussions of the sons., all brief, are those in Eitner/SONATE 169-170; Shedlock/SONATA 108-110; Villanis/CLAVECINISTES 811-812 (with exx.); Hoffmann-Erbrecht/KLAVIERMUSIK 89-91 (with exx.); and Stone/ITALIAN I 129-146 (with exx. and a discussion of Torrefranca's views), II 47-48 (thematic index [in the Johnson order]), III 33 (full copy of Son. 9 in a).

Ex. 113. From the first movement of Sonata 4 in c by Pietro Domenico Paradisi (after Son. "II" in TRÉSOR-m XVII 6).

17-21, and leaving the impression by now that Paradisi could hardly have failed to know this work). In one movement the initial idea becomes the "second" idea by reappearing in the dominant minor (Son. 5/i/48-54). Sometimes there are several different ideas, unfolding, however, in a kaleidoscopic succession that does not make for sharp contrasts (Son. 7/i).

During the modulations after the double-bar Paradisi transposes and sequences his ideas, but only seldom does he also subject them to any of the dissection, expansion, or reorientation of ideas that constitutes "development" in the later sense (Son. 2/i/49-80). In most of the first movements there is a return not to the very first idea (as in Son. 9/i/63) but to material that follows soon after. Sonata 7 in B♭/i does return to the first idea, though in the tonic minor and only to veer away immediately. Sonata 2/i could be called a complete "sonata form" except for the incomplete return (occurring at ms. 83), whereas Sonata 1/i even includes the full return.

More important than these anticipations and approximations of "sonata form" are those intuitive qualities that give Paradisi's sonatas their strength and must explain why they were singled out by men like the Mozarts, or Clementi, or Cramer.[32] His ideas are motivic and short except for the more extended phrases in the rondeau-type movements. Yet they show surprising variety, some being predominantly figural (Son. 4/i/1-2), others ornamental and rhythmically complex (Son. 7/i/1-8), and others more obviously and tunefully disposed (Son. 1/i/1-4). There is fine variety, too, in the amplification of these ideas—in the energetic rhythms (as in the persistent afterbeats in Son. 8/ii/4-5); in the meaningful passage work, often enriched by the movement of an inner part (Son. 8/i/68-72), or by fast harmonic rhythm (Son. 5/ii/7-13), or by frequent appoggiaturas in the line (Son. 4/i/36-40); and in the telling harmony, which includes colorful modulations, bold dissonances, and series of diminished-7th chords (all, for example, in Son. 11/i). And there is fine variety in the euphonious, skillful textures, ranging from imitative accompaniments (Son. 4/i/3-5) to block chords (Son. 9/ii/29-31), arpeggiations, 6-note figures approaching the Alberti bass (Son. 8/i/11-18), and literal Alberti bass in one—significantly, only one—use. (This use is found in both statements of the exceptionally clear second theme on the minor dominant in Son. 12/i/8-15 in C, which begins much as the corresponding theme was to begin at ms. 27 in Beethoven's Op. 2/3/i.)

So much variety of style makes it necessary to place Paradisi rather broadly in pre-Classic sonata history. At times his writing displays the constant triplets and short trills of the *galant* style (Son. 7/i), but the content is never so watery and thin and the flow is never so fragmented as in the average examples of that style in full bloom. More often his writing displays the pseudo-counterpoint, motivic continuation, and keyboard exploitations of D. Scarlatti (including considerable hand-crossing, as in Son. 10/i/9-16). But his logical sense of over-all form, implemented by accurate timing of entries and compelling tonal organization, depends on a somewhat later, more symmetrical approach

32. Cf. Mozart/NEUE-m X/34 400 and Anderson/MOZART I 364; AMZ XXXIV (1832) 655, Unger/CLEMENTI 36, and Stone/ITALIAN I 135 (all 3 with regard to Clementi); Schlesinger/CRAMER 31.

to phrase-and-period syntax. A fine example of the latter occurs at the start of Sonata 6 in A, where the first period of two 5-measure phrases, prolonged by cadence extensions, is repeated in the tonic minor.

Three other early Italians of the pre-Classic Era in London must be dealt with more briefly. If there are any original keyboard sonatas by **Giuseppe Jozzi** (*ca.* 1720-*ca.* 1770), *castrato* "singer-cembalist" from Rome, they have yet to be separated from the sonatas by his probable teacher D. Alberti that he plagiarized. At least three such publications appeared under Jozzi's name in London and Amsterdam (where he probably died), between about 1745 and 1765.[33]

The oboist **Giuseppe Sammartini** (*ca.* 1693-1750[34]), "il londinese," was deferred to the present volume because his music has been so badly confused with that of his younger brother, G. B. Sammartini, "il milanese," and because this music now seems to be merely incidental to the latter's in both significance and quantity. The question of who wrote which sonatas was raised earlier (SCE VIII). Until the needed bibliographic study is done that will clarify the listings one now finds for Giuseppe,[35] one can only summarize to the effect that he published two or more sets of S/- and SS/bass sonatas in the 1730's, soon after his arrival in London in 1727. In any case, it becomes evident in one set that can be confirmed as his—*XII Sonatas for Two German Flutes or Violins With a Thorough Bass* (Walsh, 1727)[36]—that the language is still thoroughly Baroque. The sonatas in this set are in three or four short movements, F-S-F or S-F-S-F. Most often the style recalls that of Handel's less portentous festive music. The writing is generally motivic, continuous, and lightly imitative, with little hint yet of the major style changes that were to lead to the Classic sonata.

Also conservative are the SS/bass sonatas examined here by the successful Italian opera composer **Vincenzo Legrenzio Ciampi** (1719?-62). In London from 1748 to 1756, he published 3 (or 4?) sets of SS/bass sonatas, one of S/bass sonatas, and one of cembalo sonatas, all between 1751 and 1756.[37] All 6 of Ciampi's SS/bass

33. Cf. Torrefranca/ORIGINI 717-719, 693; MGG VII 221-222 (Cudworth); SCE VII (under Alberti). For printed eds. and for MSS under Jozzi's name cf. BRITISH UNION I 561 and II 613; Anth. JOZZI-m; Cat. BRUXELLES II 346, 347, and 320; BRITISH MS III 120 and 130.

34. The year of death, long a matter of wide disagreement, is supported by an item in a newspaper collection left by Burney, as cited by Evelyn B. Lance in "The London Sammartini," MR XXXVIII (1977) 1-14. Miss Lance summarizes this Sammartini's life, style, and identifiable works that survive in print and MS.

35. As in BRITISH UNION II 920-921.

36. Mod. ed., complete: Giesbert/SAMMARTINI-m.

37. Cf. GROVE II 293-294 (Walker); BRITISH UNION I 189-190.

sonatas in his Op. 4 are in the late-Baroque plan of 3 movements, S-F-F. The writing is again primarily motivic and continuous. It is also expressive, contrapuntal, and ornamental, with double-stops and detailed indications for slurs and dynamic contrasts.

Native British Composers (*Avison, Burney*)

There are relatively few pre-Classic composers of sonatas to report among native British musicians. Moreover, what these men wrote is of only minor significance to the Classic sonata. It is not that their sonatas necessarily lack worth but that they are so conservative in style, which fact probably explains the relatively little attention that has been paid to them even by English historians.[38] In our previous volume T. A. Arne (1710-78) was viewed as being on the border between the Baroque and Classic eras, yet was included in that volume (SBE 327-330). The subsequent information that his 8 keyboard sonatas and his 7 "trio" sonatas were published more than a decade later than hitherto supposed—1756 and 1757 rather than *ca.* 1743 and 1740, respectively[39]—would give us at least the chronological justification for transferring him to the Classic side of the border. Yet, assuming the publication dates have some relation to the composition dates, Arne's instrumental style now seems even more conservative for its time.

Except in the strictest terminological sense, Arne's *VIII Sonatas or Lessons for the Harpsichord* of 1756 can no longer be honored as the "first known keyboard sonatas by an English composer" (SBE 328), since the *Eight Setts of Lessons for Harpsichord* by the London organist and choirmaster **James Nares** (1715-83) were published nine years earlier (by J. Johnson in 1747).[40] Yet Arne's sonatas are a bit more 40a
conservative in style than these "lessons" of Nares, and still more so than Nares' later set, in which he does use the term "sonata," although rather to distinguish one ensemble piece, resembling a miniature harpsichord concerto,[41] that is added to five solo "lessons." This later set, published by Nares himself in 1759, is called *Lessons for the Harpsichord With a Sonata in Score for the Harpsichord or Organ* [realization of the *b.c.*].[42] A pupil of Pepusch among others, Nares wrote his "lessons" in three or four movements that still favor Baroque dances,

38. However, Fuller-Maitland's sweeping disavowal of English composition in this period, in OXFORD HISTORY IV 315-318, seems now to have been too harsh and categorical.

39. BRITISH UNION I 49.

40. Cf. BRITISH UNION II 724; MGG IX 1267-1268 (Cudworth).

41. Information kindly supplied by Dr. Sadie.

42. Cf. the listing in Haas/CAT. 20 item 467. Mod. ed.: Lesson 3 in B♭, OXFORD HISTORY IV 329 (previously published as "Sonata" by the Year Book Press [London, 1926], edited by H. G. Ley and Fuller-Maitland).

structural principles, and motivic processes. There are occasional fugal movements (1747/7/ii), preludial movements (1747/1/i), expressive, more ornamented slow movements (1759/3/i), and uses of the allemande (1747/6/i), the minuet (1747/1/iii, with three increasingly showy variations), and, especially as a finale, the "jigg" (1747/4/iii), all much as in Arne's sonatas. Nares' chief style advance appears in his fast movements, where the harmonic rhythm tends to be somewhat slower and there are rare starts toward the Alberti bass (1747/8/i, in the right [!] hand; 1759/3/ii). Yet in these movements his preferred method of continuation is to use a single motive two or three times as the springboard for extended sequential passages, recalling more a process in the concerto grosso than in the contemporary Italian sonata in the *galant* style (Ex. 114).

Related to the keyboard publications of Arne and Nares are the *Eight Setts of Lessons for the Harpsichord* by the London organist **John Jones** (1728-96) that J. Johnson published in 1754, followed by another set "printed for the Author" in 1761.[43] Such samples as were seen here seem gayer and lighter, though not much less conservative in idiom, than the pieces by Arne and Nares.

The organist **Charles Avison** (1709-70) is known best for his pioneer musical criticism in *An Essay on Musical Expression* (London, 1752; 2d, revised ed. in 1753). He spent most of his life in his birthplace in northeastern England, Newcastle-on-Tyne, where he conducted some of the early subscription concerts of consequence in England and published a few of his compositions.[44] But London, as the place where he may have studied with Geminiani and where most of his literary and musical publications appeared, was still a main center for him. Besides several sets of orchestral concertos plus the concertos he arranged from Scarlatti's sonatas in 1743 and 1744, Avison left 4 sets of 6 ensemble sonatas each, first published in the 8 years from 1756 to 1764.[45] The first set, Op. 1 (*ca.* 1757) is in SS/bass scoring. The other 3 sets—Opp. 5, 7, and 8 (1756, 1760, and 1764)—contain some of the earlier accompanied sonatas produced in England, all being composed for harpsichord with distinctly subordinate parts for 2 violins and a cello (but with no alternatives offered). Although concertos by Avison were already published in full score and although he argued for this practice or at least the insertion of cues in the parts,[46] the sonatas appear in the usual separate parts, without cues.

43. Cf. MGG VII 161 (Sadie); BRITISH UNION I 559. Mod. ed.: 3 mvts. in C (including "Sonatina"; from the first set?), Rowley/ENGLISH-m 27.
44. Cf. GROVE I 275 (Rimbault).
45. Cf. BRITISH UNION I 68.
46. Avison/ESSAY 131-138.

Ex. 114. From the opening of Lesson 7 in G (1747) by James Nares (after the 2d ed. of 1757 at the Library of Congress).

Only a partial idea of Avison's musical style can be guessed from his own decidedly independent views of music in his *Essay*. Without using the word "sonata" he makes numerous remarks that are pertinent. He prefers a fugal or imitative style of writing in which one idea prevails and subordinate ideas support it (pp. 28-29, 34, 39-40). He objects to "That Deluge of unbounded *Extravaganzi,* which the unskillful call Invention, and which are merely calculated to shew an Execution without either Propriety or Grace" (p. 35) ; and elsewhere he objects to instrumental abuses such as harmonics and double-stops on the violin (pp. 90-92, 95-96). Among his favorite contemporaries or near predecessors are Corelli, Caldara, D. Scarlatti, B. Marcello, Geminiani, and

Rameau (pp. 51-52, 86-88). Among "the most noted Composers who have erred in the Extreme of an unnatural Modulation" the least objectionable are Vinci, Bononcini, Astorga, and Pergolesi, whose "Faults are lost amidst their Excellencies; and the Critic of Taste is almost tempted to blame his own Severity in censuring Compositions, in which he finds Charms so powerful and commanding" (pp. 43-44). The most objectionable are Vivaldi, Tessarini, Alberti, and Locatelli, "whose Compositions being equally defective in various Harmony and true Invention, are only a fit Amusement for Children; nor indeed for these, if ever they are intended to be led to a just Taste in Music" (p. 42).

However, a somewhat modified attitude is revealed in Avison's message to his public in his last set of sonatas, Op. 8 (1764), explained probably by the practicalities of actual composition, by a slight, perhaps unconscious allowance for the objections to his Essay that William Hayes had raised in 1753,[47] and by the influence that eight years of new styles could have had on him. The first half of this "Advertisement" is interesting enough to quote here (with Avison's footnotes put in parentheses and our annotations added in brackets):

The following SONATAS are composed after the Plan of my fifth and seventh Operas. (See the Advertisements prefixed to those Works [part of that in Op. 7 was quoted in SCE III]).

The accompanied Sonata for the Harpsichord is so far preferable to the Concerto with Symphonies, that the Airs are less tedious—their designs are more compact—and the principal Instrument is better heard [Avison/ESSAY 120: ". . . I shall beg leave to offer an Observation on the Harpsichord Concerto . . . Whereas the Violin Parts should be but few, and contrived rather as Accompanyments than Symphonies; by which means they may assist greatly in striking out some Kind of Expression, wherein the harpsichord is remarkably deficient . . ."].

It is the too frequent Repetition of the Subject which marks the Character of Tedious Music.

When different Instruments repeat the same Air, the Ear is disgusted with the very Thought which at first gave it Pleasure (*Handel's* Concertos for the Harpsichord).

To pursue the same Strain through different Divisions, hath also the same Effect; as the same modulation is perpetually recurring (The *Follia* in the last Solo of *Corelli*), than which nothing can be more tiresome.

To search for other Strains in allowed Modulations, and of a similar Air; the principal Strain returning, like the Intercalary Verse in Pastoral Poetry (The *Minuet* in *Geminiani's* first Concerto, *Opera Secondo*), gives the Ear that Relief which it naturally desires.

Among the various Productions of foreign Composers for the Harpsichord, the Sonatas of SCARLATTI, RAMEAU, and CARLO-BACH [Emanuel Bach], have their *peculiar* Beauties. The *fine fancy* of the Italian

47. Cf. Burney/HISTORY II 1013; LC EARLY 120.

—the *spirited Science* of the Frenchman—and the German's *diffusive Expression* are the distinguishing Signatures of their Music. But if we examine the Lessons of GEMINIANI we shall find them fraught with *every* Beauty, and, therefore, worthy the Attention of Those who would improve a true Taste, and acquire a graceful and fluent Execution (The Lessons here referred to are taken from his second Book of Solos for the Violin, which were first published in *Paris*).

If I have adopted a Method of Composition somewhat different from those excellent Masters, it is chiefly in the Characters of Design and Expression, which distinguish one Composer from another.

What is meant by Design in Musical Composition, is the general Plan of some Whole; whether adapted to the Church or the Theatre, to public Concerts, or the Chamber; which general Plan includes the particular Parts; whether contrived for Voices, or Instruments, either separate or united; such as may best express the intended Sentiment of the Composer. . . .

Unfortunately there is a serious discrepancy between Avison's aims and his musical achievements. One is compelled to endorse Burney's view, even while acknowledging his frequent disinclination to praise fellow Englishmen who practiced music around his time. "With respect to Avison's own musical productions they want force, correctness, and originality, sufficient to be ranked very high among the works of masters of the first class."[48] The sonatas of Op. 8 are in two or three movements without any set plan. There are no really expressive movements (in spite of the detailed dynamic markings), since Avison seems to specialize in marches and rapid passages. The initial and only main idea is usually marchlike and commonplace. As with Nares' music, it leads ordinarily only to passages and sequences. It returns sometimes in the related key at the double-bar and more regularly in the tonic as a clear return in a ternary design. It is not surprising to find traces of Scarlatti, including hand-crossing (Son. 1/ii), but hints of an Alberti bass (as in Son. 2/iii) are rare.[49]

Charles Burney (1726-1814)—music's most quoted traveler and historian of the eighteenth century (and of this volume)—himself left over thirty-five sonatas in print.[50] Here was but one more way by which this internationally beloved gentleman showed his continuing up-to-dateness during his long life of intensive cultural pursuits, inquiries, and exchanges. In 1747, 1754, and 1759 appeared three sets of six sonatas

48. Burney/HISTORY II 1013.

49. Commenting on this paragraph, Dr. Sadie finds Opp. 5 and 7 more interesting than Op. 8 and notes the likely influence of Geminiani's harpsichord style plus the possible influence of Rameau as in the rondeau form of Op. 7/3/i.

50. The chief source on the man and his works is Scholes/BURNEY, which, however, contains relatively little on the sonatas aside from the details in the fine catalogue of his music (II 340-353; but the conflicting dates in BRITISH UNION I 143 are preferred here); cf., also, GROVE I 1027-1032 (Scholes).

each, two sets still being in the older "trio" setting (SS/bass; Opp. 1 and 4) and one set being in duet setting (2 Fls; Op. 3). But in 1761 appeared a set of six solo sonatas for harpsichord, and about 1770[51] two sets of two accompanied sonatas each (H-or-P & Vn & Vc). Furthermore, in 1777 and 1778 appeared two "setts" of *Four Sonatas or Duets for two performers on one Piano Forte or Harpsichord,*[52] and about two years later a harpsichord sonata "à trois mains."

In his literary works Burney's references to his own numerous instrumental compositions are few and modest.[53] His sonatas composed prior to his two grand tours (1770 and 1772) do not seem to justify anything more. They are competent as regards the rules of harmony and voice-leading, but sterile and stiff in their ideas and flow. In the solo harpsichord sonatas the slow movements show a striving toward varied and unusual harmony, whereas the fast movements, while confined to much more rudimentary harmony, skip about naïvely from one favorite Scarlatti keyboard device to another, especially hand-crossing, hand exchanges, and repeated notes. A little use of Alberti bass (as in Son. 6/i/8-10) is the only relief from such devices. It was undoubtedly these fast movements (such as Son. 6/i, again) that provoked the following criticism in 1780: ". . . We can't say much in his favor as a composer, his lessons having nothing in them, but the frequent repetition of one note, which *trick* we think rather ill-adapted to the harpsichord. . . ."[54]

But Burney's duet sonatas, composed after his grand tours, suggest that his musical as well as his historical, social, and literary sensibilities profited from the travels. They reflect especially the extent to which he became enamored of Italian as against French music. They are now not in the three-movement plan of the solo sonatas but in the frequent Italian plan of a moderate and a fast movement. Their first movements simulate the florid lyricism (including free recitative passages) of the Italian opera aria (Ex. 115), and their finales have some of the fluency and dash of the first or last section in the Italian opera sinfonia. Only the fuller texture and careful attention to design betray the scholar, or perhaps some German influence. But if the ideas lack distinction and

51. Or *ca.* 1770 and 1772 (cf. Scholes/BURNEY 347-348).

52. Mod. eds.: Son. 1 in F (1777), Rowley/BURNEY-m; Son. 1 in E♭ (1778), Townsend/DUETS-m 70.

53. In BURNEY'S TOURS I 30 he mentions a vain attempt, while in Paris, to procure a copy of Bremner's second ed. of his solo sons.; and in I 135 he mentions his embarrassment at having to play a "voluntary" (an improvisation) and "a movement of my own composition" on the harpsichord at a social gathering in Italy.

54. As quoted from *A B C Dario* (cf. LC EARLY 5) in Scholes/BURNEY II 345.

Ex. 115. From the first movement of Sonata 3 in B♭ in Charles Burney's first set of "Sonatas or Duets" (after the original ed. at the Library of Congress).

the forms spread out somewhat thinly, the music does not lack warmth and imagination.

There is historical significance, of course, in the fact that in 1777 Burney's duets were "the first that have appeared in print of this kind," as he himself proclaimed in a preface to the first set (only), noteworthy for its full summary of the musical and pedagogic values of duet playing (SCE V). They preceded by one year the first published duet of Christian Bach (Op. 15/6, 1778), although Christian may have composed duets much earlier and Mozart certainly wrote his first not later than 1765 (K. 19d). Burney's duets may be linked directly with the "duet concerts . . . a-la-mode" that his daughter Fanny reported the family was still enjoying in 1775,[55] and with the new 6-octave "Piano Forte" constructed in 1777 at his request expressly "for duets à Quatre Mains."[56] How much Burney must have been thinking about the duet problem is suggested not only by his explicit preface but by his good solutions, already, to the problems of balance, frequent interchanges, and equal responsibilities, in his duet sonatas.

A more obscure English composer of the pre-Classic Era may also be introduced here. The Italian trained violinist at Oxford, **James Lates** (*ca.* 1710-77), left only unaccompanied duets (2 Vns or Fls) and melo/bass "sonatas," "solos," and "trios" (S/- or SS/bass)—in all, thirty sonatas in five sets published between 1761 and about 1775.[57] Op. 5 is notable for being the only English set of the time that is scored for violin, cello, and bass.[58] There is still much of the late-Baroque style in his earlier sonatas, including the fast harmonic rhythm engendered by a "running" *b.c.* and the continuous unfolding and sequences that lead off from an initial motive of no lasting consequence. But an examination of the six SS/bass sonatas in Op. 4 (*ca.* 1775) shows progressivisms, in spite of one "Fuga" (No. 3/ii), that belie the melo/bass style, as is often true in this period. The *b.c.* is frequently chordal or static, making for slower harmonic rhythm. The ideas tend to fall more into phrases and even into phrase groupings. Dynamic gradations, including "Crescendo al For.," are profuse. And the movement plan that prevails is F-S-minuet. Lates' writing is professionally smooth—certainly more so than Avison's or that in Burney's earlier sonatas—and not without charm or force. The student interested in

55. Sonnedecker/DUETS 219.

56. Cf. Scholes/BURNEY II 203-204, 348-349.

57. Cf. BRITISH UNION II 601. Mod. ed.: Son. in G (S/bass, Op. 3, 1764 [not '68]), Moffat/ENGLISH-m No. 1 (with a preface containing about all the readily available information on Lates).

58. According to information kindly supplied by Dr. Sadie.

delving into the little-explored English music of this period will not go unrewarded if he troubles to score some of Lates' sonatas.

A few other Englishmen must be mentioned still more briefly, all of them organists. The friend of Avison and presumed organist from Durham, **John Garth** (*ca.* 1722-1810), published 5 sets of accompanied sonatas for harpsichord, piano, or organ, with subordinate parts for 2 violins and cello, Opp. 2 and 4-7 (1768-82); he also left a keyboard method, now lost, and "Six Easy Lessons or Sonatinas . . ." for harpsichord (1773).[59] A reading of Op. 4 (1772) discloses six 2-movement sonatas in fast or moderate tempos (including a "Tempo di Minuetto," "Tempo di Gavotta," and "Rondeau" among the finales). Bright, purposeful, businesslike passage work prevails.

The outstanding organist and harpsichordist **John Burton** (1730-82), who performed in Germany in 1754, published a set of ten solo sonatas for harpsichord, organ, or piano in London, by Royal Privilege in 1766, followed by several re-editions that attest its popularity; also, a set of 6 accompanied sonatas (with Vn) about 1770, in which the piano is already designated ahead of the harpsichord or organ.[60] The first set proves to be the earliest English composition found here to include the piano as an alternative keyboard instrument. Confirmation of this alternative is supplied not so much by the neat, *galant* keyboard writing as by the copious use of "Pia," "For," "Crescendo," and "Con Espressione."[61] But the musical interest lies in the strong dance and folk elements rather than any expressive moments. Each sonata contains 3 fast or moderate movements except Sonatas 6 and 9 in two movements. No movement is marked slower than "Allegro Andante," although "Pastorale alla Napolitana" (Son. 10/iii) or "Minuetto" (Son. 2/ii) suggests a more moderate tempo. Lively tempos are certainly intended in the "Rondo Presto" (Son. 2/iii) and "Giga in Rondo" (Son. 8/ii). Much of the time Burton writes in 2-measure units of "questions" and "answers" that are frankly but unobjectionably square, he uses "Scotch snaps" and other sprightly rhythms (Son. 1/i), and he makes pronounced modal inflections (like that to the lowered 7th step in Son. 1/iii/3), all of which take us closer to the folk dances than to the sonata styles of the 1760's. Certainly, his sonatas should bring musical delight and some fresh surprises to the English expert on the alert for new applications, as these seem to be, of native folk materials.

The London organist and vocal composer **John Worgan** (1724-

59. Cf. MGG IV 1399-1400 (Cudworth); BRITISH UNION I 361-362.
60. Cf. Marpurg/BEYTRÄGE I 167-168 (praising Burton's playing in Germany); BRITISH UNION I 144; GROVE I 1033-1034 (Straeten); Shedlock/SONATA 228.
61. Cf. Burney/HISTORY II 1018.

90) published a set of six harpsichord sonatas in 1769.[62] Cast in one to three movements, slow or fast according to no set plan, these sonatas display a refreshing freedom and originality in the voice-leading, harmony, and structure that might be charged by some to inexperience were it not for the express note at the start of Sonata 5: "Lest the consecutive fifths at the beginning of the Theme of this movement should escape the Critic, the Author here apprizes him of them." **William Jackson** (1730-1803), organist, vocal composer, writer on music, and painter from Exeter, published six accompanied sonatas in 1760 (H & Vn) and eight more in 1773 as Op. 10 (H & 2 Vns & "a tenor and bass"). In the former set the violin occasionally takes the lead in a manner suggesting the influence of the Giardini sonatas discussed later in this chapter.[63] But Jackson's instrumental music is regarded as being weaker than his secular vocal music in spite of interesting details.[64] Too weak in musical interest to concern us further here are the six "Lessons" for harpsichord or piano (1772) and the three accompanied sonatas "adapted . . . from the favorite songs in his Wags & Oddities" (H-or-P and Vn-or-Fl, *ca.* 1790) by the organist and popular song composer **Charles Dibdin** (1745-1814).[65] In this same paragraph belongs the brilliant organist **Joseph Kelway** (*ca.* 1702-82), whose set of six harpsichord sonatas first published in 1764 was already noted, adversely, under D.
66a Scarlatti (SCE IX).[66]

Christian Bach and Other Germans (Abel)

Among the Germans now to be noted is the composer who is most important to us in pre-Classic London and who, especially in view of his readily demonstrated influence on Mozart, ranks with the chief pre-Classic sonata composers in all regions. He is, of course, **Johann Christian Bach** (1735-82), the eleventh and last son of J. S. Bach and the fourth and last of these sons, or the last of five Bachs, to appear in the present volume.[67] (A sixth Bach, who also wrote sonatas at this

62. Cf. Burney/HISTORY II 1009; GROVE IX 364 (Husk and Squire), with a reference to a detailed study; BRITISH UNION II 1090; Shedlock/SONATA 228.

63. Information kindly supplied by Dr. Sadie.

64. Cf. MGG VI 1596-1599 (Cudworth); also, BRITISH UNION I 551 (but the "favorite" Son., Op. 4, H-or-P alone, proved not to be in the Euing Musical Library in Glasgow).

65. Cf. GROVE II 685-689 (Loewenberg); BRITISH UNION I 272.

66. Cf. MGG VI 825-826 (Cudworth); BRITISH UNION I 568.

67. The chief biography is Terry/BACH (1929; cf. Terry's own summary and list of previous sources, pp. v-viii and xiii-xvi; also, his article in GROVE I 329-331); it supersedes Schwarz/BACH (1900-01) except for the latter's documents in their original languages and a few peripheral details. The interesting survey of the

time, can be found in a grandson of J. S. Bach and son of Friedrich the "Bückeburg Bach," Wilhelm Friedrich Ernst Bach [1759-1845], who worked closely with his uncle Christian from 1778 to the latter's death in 1782; however, little of musical significance is reported in the "Grande Sonate pour le Pianoforte" that this Bach left in MS in 1778, or in the 6 accompanied sonatas that he published about 1785.[68])

There are still many gaps in the records of Christian Bach's life before he reached London. At fifteen, after early training from his father and the latter's death in 1750, he came under the matchless supervision of his half brother Emanuel in Berlin, who, like Friedemann, had left home too early to help or really know Christian in Leipzig. When he was about twenty, the Italian opera that first won Christian's heart in Berlin drew him to Italy. Then, in the course of some seven years, he served as organist at the Milan Cathedral, undoubtedly profit-
ing from his nearness to G. B. Sammartini (as discussed below); he 68a
studied composition with Padre Martini in Bologna; and he produced successful opera in Naples. His desire to compose operas also accounts for his remaining move, to London in 1762, where, like Handel before him, he gave part of his time to royal service. Only the opera productions in Mannheim in 1772 and 1776, and preparations in Paris in 1778 for another production in 1779, resulted in any appreciable absences thereafter from London.

Out of some 450 separate works, large and small, that Christian Bach composed in his nearly 47 years, over two-thirds are instrumental.[69] Out of these instrumental works about a third are symphonies or overtures, about a third (111) are sonatas by actual title, and the remaining third are mostly concertos and chamber works. To carry these statistics one step further, 48 (or over 43 per cent) of the sonatas are accompanied keyboard types, 24 (or less than 22 per cent) are for keyboard alone, 12 (8 per cent) are for 4 hands at one or two keyboards,

---

man and his music in Geiringer/BACH 404-444 (1954) includes a few corrections, new facts, and new views. Cf., also, Reeser/SONS 53-63; MGG I 942-954 (Wirth).

68. Cf. MGG I 916-917 (Benecke); Geiringer/BACH 474-480 (with exx.); BRITISH MS III 125; BRITISH UNION I 78. An "Andante" for 4 hands, one piano, is printed for the first time in Kreutz/VIER-m 18; cf., also, Geiringer/BACH-m 228-248.

69. The thematic index in Terry/BACH 193-361 still comprises the most complete list of all the works, editions, and MSS; it is confused somewhat by double entries and the lack of a numbering system, but it supersedes the much less complete indices of the instrumental works in Schökel/BACH 177-203 and of only the symphonies in Tutenberg/BACH 369-387 (both indices with incipits of first mvts. only). The summary list in GROVE I 331 and the dated list, with the key of each son., in MGG I 950 (but Huberty was still in Paris, not Vienna! [Johansson/FRENCH I 40-42]) are convenient; but in each of the indices now published some of the sons. are missing. Where they differ, the dates in BRITISH UNION I 75-76 are usually preferred here to those in Terry/BACH.

and 27 (24 per cent) are in the older melo/bass or unaccompanied setting.

There follows a chronological summary, by scoring types, of most of Christian's publications and MSS that originally bore the title "sonata,"[70] the dates of the former being for the first of as many as a half-dozen early editions (as of Op. 18, T. 326 [for the page in Terry/BACH on which the title appears]). These first editions appeared during the last 2 decades of his life, 1763-82, except for the few that were posthumous. The publishers' opus numbers are given even though some of them conflict. Not included are arrangements (such as the 4 acc'd. sons. arranged from quartets, T. 330) or spurious works (such as the "Battle of Rosbach" sonata, T. 343,[71] or the "Six Progressive Lessons" published posthumously in 1783, T. 349, which set proves to be simply another re-edition of Emanuel Bach's *Achtzehn Probe-Stücken in sechs Sonaten,* W. 63/1-6). Little more than a fifth of the sonatas, mostly solo keyboard, have been published in modern editions, the most important of which are referred to here.

Christian Bach's Sonatas

A. *Accompanied Keyboard Sonatas*

1. Son. in F for Fl & H "concertato." MS, T. 332; probably composed before Christian left Berlin *ca.* 1755 (Terry/BACH 10).
2. 7 Sons. for H & Vn, MS, T. 332; probably composed before Christian left Milan in 1762 (Terry/BACH 28).
3. 6 Sons. for H & Vn-or-Fl & Vc, Op. 2, London (printed for the author), 1764 (Royal Privilege, Dec. 15, 1763), T. 313; already published in score and parts; dedicated to the Princess Augusta, hence probably composed soon after Christian reached London in 1762. Cf. Terry/BACH 78 (but read "Sonates," not "Trios") and 183-184 (but the announcement on April 9, 1763, of "Six Sonatas or Notturnos" refers to the first set of SSA "trios" [our D. 1., *infra*]).
4. Son. in D for H & Vn, MS dated 1771, T. 331.
5. 6 Sons. for H-or-P & Vn, Op. 10, London (Welcker), 1773, T. 322 (or Op. 7, in different order, T. 316; but Terry gives an entirely wrong incipit, in E, for Son. 4 in A/i in both sets). Among mod. eds. (cf. MGG I 954): Sons. 1-5, Landshoff/BACH-m II.
6. 6 Sons. for H-or-P & Fl-or-Vn, Op. 16, London (Welcker), *ca.* 1776, T 325. Among mod. eds.: Sons. 1, 2, and 4, NAGELS-m Nos. 1 and 103 (both Küster).
7. 4 Sons. for P-or-H & Vn & Vc (and 2 K duets), Op. 15, London (Welcker), 1778, T. 323.
8. 4 Sons. for H-or-P & Vn-or-Fl (and 2 K duets), Op. 18, Paris (Roulledé), *ca.* 1780, T. 326.

70. Without further information one can only guess that 2 items in 18th-c anthologies (BRITISH UNION II 961) are reprints.

71. Cf. Shedlock/SONATA 239; Terry/BACH 344; SBE 299.

9. 6 Sons. for P-or-H & Fl-or-Vn, Op. 19, London (Cooper), 1783, T. 327. The mod. ed. of 2 sons., in A and D, that Fritz Piersig edited for Breitkopf & Härtel (1928) comes not from Op. 19/4 and 3 (as in Terry/BACH 328) but from Opp. 10/4 and 17/1, respectively.

10. 6 Sons. for P-or-H & Vn in 2 sets of 3 each, Op. 20, London (Campbell), 1783, T. 329 (which gives the incipits for only the first set, in the re-edition by Dale; cf. BRITISH UNION I 76).

11. Son. in B♭ for harp & Vn & Vc (or harp & H), London (publisher?), *ca.* 1796, T. 330.

B. *Solo Keyboard Sonatas*

1. 6 Sons. for H-or-P, Op. 5, London (Welcker), *ca.* 1768, T. 338; composed partly or entirely by 1765, which is the year when the young Mozart arranged nos. 2, 3, and 4 as keyboard "Concerti" (K. V. 21b/1-3); the fugue in Son. 6/ii, unique in Christian's son. mvts., and the exceptionally rich texture throughout this son. suggest that it may have been composed while Christian was still under Martini's supervision in Italy. Among mod. eds.: 71a
Sons. 2-5, Landshoff/BACH-m I (with preface); Sons. 3-6, TRÉSOR-m; Son. 6 in c is in numerous "Old Masters" anthologies, such as Pauer/MEISTER-m I 26 and RICORDI ARTE-m IV.

2. "Sonata a Cembalo Solo" in F, MS dated 1768 (but possibly composed during the stay in Milan, where it is found), T. 355.

3. 6 Sons. for H-or-P, Op. 17 (also published as Op. 6 and Op. 12), Amsterdam (Hummel), 1779, T. 341; further published as Op. 1 by André in Offenbach/M (after 1784; copy at the Library of Congress), "con un Violino ad Libitum, composto dal Editore." Among mod. eds.: Sons. 2-6, Landshoff/BACH-m I; Sons. 2, 3, and 6, TRÉSOR-m XVIII (as "Op. 12"); Son. 6 in B♭, Newman/BACH-m 24 (with preface). 71b

4. "Four Progressive Lessons" for H (and 2 duets), London (Longman & Broderip), *ca.* 1780, T. 350 (cf. T. 345).

5. 3 Sons. for H, Op. 21, Paris (Bonin), T. 344 (with incipits for only one mvt. each).

6. 4 sons. in separate MSS, undated, T. 355, 356, 358. Further MS sons. reported in Saint-Foix/BACH proved later to be by Franz Beck (Saint-Foix/BECK).

C. *Four-Hand Duets For One or Two Keyboard Instruments*

1. 2 "Duetts," in G for "Due Cembali obligati" and in C "For two performers on one Pianoforte or Harpsichord," Op. 15/5 and 6; T. 340 (1778; cf. T. 345, T. 323, and our A. 7., *supra*). Mod. eds.: "Duett" in C, NAGELS-m No. 4 (Küster) and Weismann/BACH-m 2.

2. "Deux Duo" for one H-or-P, Op. 18/5 and 6, T. 342 (*ca.* 1780; cf. T. 326 and our A. 8., *supra*). Among mod. eds.: both "Duo," Weismann/BACH-m 18; Op. 18/5 in A, NAGELS-m No. 115 (Küster).

3. "Two Duetts" for one H-or-P, T. 350 (1780; cf. our B. 4., *supra*).

4. 6 Sons. for one H-or-P, undated MS, T. 353. Listed in Cat. BRUXELLES II 298.

D. *Melo/bass and Unaccompanied Sonatas*

1. "Six Trio" for 2 Vns + Va-or-Vc, Op. 2 (or 4), Paris (Huberty), *ca.* 1765 (Johansson/FRENCH II Facs. 27), T. 314; probably preceded by a

lost English ed. (and composed before Christian left Milan, for reasons to be given below), in view of the announcement in the London *Public Advertiser* for April 9, 1763 of "Six Sonatas or Notturnos" (confused in Terry/BACH 183 with our A. 3., *supra*) and A. Hummel's reprint with this title in London *ca.* 1770 (cf. BRITISH UNION I 76); in the A. Hummel ed. the unfigured "alto viola ou basse obligé" becomes a "thorough bass for the harpsichord." Mod. ed.: Sons. 2, 4, and 6, HORTUS MUSICUS-m No. 37 (Upmeyer).
2. About 16 SS/bass sons. (also called "trio" and "divertimento") in undated MSS, T. 317-321; 7 are inscribed "Sig^{re} Bach in Milano" and all have inscriptions in Italian, suggesting composition dates for most or all during Christian's years in Italy; one of these sons. is inscribed "Cembali obbl. e Violini" (T. 321). Cf. Terry/BACH 184-185.
3. One "Sonata a Violino solo col Basso," undated MS, T. 331.
4. 3 "Sonate" for Fl & Vn, undated MS, T. 337.
5. One "Trio" for 2 Fls & Vc (or Fl, Vn, & Vc) in a printed anthology of about 1800, T. 317.

A substantial study has been made of Christian Bach's symphonies, both the *concertante* and the more homophonic songful types.[72] Increasing interest has been shown in his concertos[73] and his chamber music for larger ensembles.[74] And explorations have been made into his Italian operas in order to consider their influence on Mozart's.[75] But thus far only summary discussions have been devoted to the
76a sonatas.[76] The influence of these sonatas on Mozart's music can be demonstrated as tangibly as that of any other works by Christian. Besides the style similarities to be noted shortly and the fact of the concertos that Mozart made from Christian's Op. 5 at the age of nine (cf. our B. 1., *supra*), there are (among numerous other evidences of Mozart's love of Christian's music[77]) the records of his playing Christian's keyboard music as early as 1764 and of sitting on Christian's knees as the two played at the same harpsichord,[78] of his recommending Christian's sonatas to his sister in 1774,[79] of his teaching from them in Mannheim in 1778,[80] and of his father's endorsement of Christian's light instrumental music in the same year.[81]

72. Tutenberg/BACH. Cf., also, Carse/SYMPHONIES 11, 21, 54-55; Carse/SYMPHONIES-m no. 3 (?); Paul Lang in MQ XLIV (1958) 221-227.
73. Daffner/KLAVIERKONZERT 36-45; Geiringer/BACH 426-431.
74. Mod. ed. of 6 Quintets, Op. 11, in EDMR-m III (Steglich), with preface.
75. Cf. Abert in ZFMW I (1919) 313-328.
76. E.g., Schwarz/BACH 436-439; Schökel/BACH 156-162 (in the course of Schökel's over-all survey of Christian's instrumental music); Newman/BACH 236-240 and 245-248; Geiringer/BACH 419-425.
77. Cf., especially, Anderson/MOZART II 736 and 900, III 1193.
78. Anderson/MOZART I 68; Mozart/NEUE-m X/34 55, 90.
79. Anderson/MOZART I 364 and 366.
80. Anderson/MOZART II 711.
81. Anderson/MOZART II 889.

Yet the lesser interest since shown in Christian's sonatas cannot be attributed only to a neglect of them by posterity. The composer himself seems to have thought less of the sonata than of most other categories in which he wrote. He expended less effort on it, treated it more casually as a form, and found less occasion to be imaginative or original in it. In fact, considering that his sonatas were among his most successful publications, it could well have been they that he had in mind when he acknowledged the superiority of Emanuel's music with the oft-quoted retort, "My brother lives to compose and I compose to live."[82] And it could have been they, primarily, that caused this onetime Benjamin of old J. S. Bach already to be viewed in the immediately posthumous remarks of both Forkel and C. F. Cramer as a dilettantish deserter from the great family tradition of professional craftsmanship, a mercenary, and a prostitutor of his own talents.[83] 83a

A routine approach to the sonata, even more than to his other instrumental categories, is shown in Christian's movement plans and key schemes. About 80 per cent of all the sonatas are in 2 movements with no key change, the others being in 3 movements with no key change in more than half of the middle movements and a change only to a nearly related key in the others.[84] Among the published sonatas, almost all of the accompanied type and over 80 per cent of the keyboard solos and duets are in two movements. There are more exceptions among the MSS, including most of the SS/bass sonatas not found in Italy (under our D. 2.) and the 6 duets (C. 4.). The keys are evenly distributed in each set but never exceed 3 flats or 4 sharps and only twice are in minor, both exceptions being 3-movement solo keyboard sonatas in c (Opp. 5/6 and 17/2). Thus, Christian used minor keys less than any other main pre-Classic composer discussed in the present volume.

At least half of Christian's sonatas have minuet or rondo (and "rondeau") finales and more than half of the minuets have trios. Two finales are polonaises, both in a MS set of keyboard duets that also includes a "Siciliano" middle movement (C. 4./1, 4, and 3, respectively). Several of the finales not labeled as dances are like gigues (e.g., in Op. 17/2, 5, and 6). Most of the finales are relatively short, simple binary designs with repeats. Only an occasional one is a theme-and-variations (e.g., B. 4./4 or Op. 5/3).

The initial movement, except for infrequent slow examples (as in

82. Cf. Terry/BACH vi.

83. Cf. Terry/BACH v-vi; Bitter/BRÜDER II 140-149.

84. One is tempted to question the authenticity of the MS "trio" in E♭ for "Cembalo obbl. e Violini," T. 321, in which the second mvt. not only is in the enharmonic equivalent of the lowered submediant key but thus provides the only use of as many as 5 sharps throughout the thematic index in Terry/BACH.

the unusual Sonata in c Op. 5/6 or our D. 1./4/i), is fast in most instances and moderate in a few (e.g., A. 3./4). It reveals the usual, variable approximations of "sonata form" to be found in pre-Classic music. In one such movement (Op. 5/5/i), there is contrast between a first and second theme, but the total effect is merely binary, for although each theme returns in a related key after the double-bar neither ever returns in the home key. In another first movement (Op. 17/5/i), a distinctly contrasting idea is lacking, but the main idea returns in the tonic not only to start the recapitulation but previously, soon after the double-bar, and later, to start a coda or "terminal development," so that the total effect is that of a "sonata-rondo" form. In other first movements there is no return to the initial idea although there is a well-prepared return to the home key (our A. 3./6/i), or the initial idea does return in the home key when it has not been restated after the double-bar in the related key (D. 1./4/i), and so on. Yet Op. 5/2/i contains all the essentials of "sonata form."

The relatively few middle movements in Christian's sonatas are usually moderate in tempo, urbane rather than introspective in content (Op. 17/6/ii), and binary in design, with or without double-bars and repeat signs (as in Opp. 5/2/ii and 17/2/ii, respectively). Exceptionally, Op. 5/5/ii is in ternary design (without repeats) and it is marked "Adagio," although a more moderate tempo still seems to be implied by the simple harmony, longer than usual lines, and slow harmonic rhythm (cf. Ex. 117, *infra*).

Christian's earliest sonata publication (our D. 1.) seems to reflect the influence of G. B. Sammartini in Milan more than that of Padre Martini. There are some external relationships that are probably not mere coincidences. Christian used the rare title *Six Sonatas or Notturnos* only about three years after Sammartini's *Sei Sonate notturne* appeared in Paris (*ca.* 1760; our E. under Sammartini); and he used the equally rare inscription "Allegrino" in a similarly scored MS left in Milan (T. 317), as did Sammartini in Sonata 1/i of his same set. Christian's published set is in the same SS/bass scoring and has the same plan of two movements as in Sammartini's set, although in each of Christian's minuet finales a trio is added. One can also note the similarly tender, delicate style, the same approximate level of pre-Classic syntax, and the frequent use by both men of "Lombardian rhythms" (or "Scotch snaps"; e.g., Sons. 4/i by Sammartini and 6/i by Christian), the latter being discontinued, with only a few exceptions (e.g., Op. 5/1/i), in later sonatas by Christian. But, of course, one becomes less aware of these similarities and more aware of personal differences of style and creative strength after a closer look into the two sets. Hearing the sonatas of Sammartini and Christian alternately is an experience that works to the clear advantage of the older man, for it shows his more subtle, diverse harmony, his freer imagination, and his more active textures as against the rather plain harmony and ideas, and the somewhat perfunctory imitations given to the lower parts in Christian's writing.

Throughout his creative career Christian used much the same materials that are to be found in his first sonata publications (our D. 1. and A. 3). But there are advances in his treatment of these materials, contrary to early deprecations of his music. When C. F. Cramer regretted, in 1783, that Christian's accompanied sonatas and duets in Op. 18 (our Op. 8) lacked the originality of the earlier Sonata in c, Op. 5/6, with its fugue for a second movement, he noted that Christian was using some ideas he had used before. But Cramer was also showing his own conservative tastes.[85] So, presumably, was Emanuel, in the recurring exchanges between himself and Christian that were originally reported by Schubart:[86] "Don't be a child; [in your style of writing?]" "I have to write in monosyllables ['stammeln']," Christian would answer, "so that the children will understand me."[87] Actually, his one fugal venture in his sonatas now recalls not only the skill but a bit of the formalism in Padre Martini's writing (SBE 181-183). He was obviously more at home in the new, lighter, more popular style, and, from our later viewpoint, can hardly be blamed for preferring to live in the then present. In Classic terms, his best—that is, his most meaningful and efficiently organized—sonatas are not his earliest ones, including Op. 5/6, but those in his last important set, Op. 17, especially nos. 2 in c and 4 in G.

To illustrate how the most characteristic features of Christian's ideas are already to be found in his earliest works, we may take note of the opening theme of his first published accompanied sonata, especially its descending quadruplet of conjunct 16th-notes initiated by an appoggiatura, its feminine endings initiated by a chromatic 8th-note appoggiatura, its syncopations on the second beat, its chordal figure in triplets, its short trills, and its elementary—in this instance, note-for-note—accompaniment (Ex. 116). Thus, one can find other and earlier precedents for such a theme as opens Mozart's Sonata in B♭, K.V. 315c,

85. Cramer/MAGAZIN I (1783) 83-84.
86. Schubart/IDEEN 202; in a lengthy statement (pp. 201-204) that blames him for misusing his fine talent, heritage, and training, Schubart called Christian "Georg Bach" and singled out the Son. in "*F* Mol" as a redeeming work, undoubtedly meaning Op. 5/6 in c.
87. Cf., also, Terry/BACH vi.

Ex. 116. From the opening of Sonata 1, Op. 2 (our A. 3.) by Johann Christian Bach (after the original ed. at the Library of Congress).

besides those themes usually cited that open Christian's fine Sonatas in B♭ and G, Op. 17/6 and 4.[88] It is these same traits that account for much of whatever character can be found in Christian's themes, although at most his themes have only a moderate individuality of their own (as in the rondo refrain of the "Pastorale" mvt., Op. 16/4/ii). Sometimes they scarcely stand out from the rather innocuous passage work, which trait is only to be expected in perpetual-motion finales (as in Op. 17/4/ii) but is less satisfactory if clear contrasts are to be required in "sonata form" (Op. 5/5/i). Yet one must not overlook Christian's penchant for lyricism and his ability to spin out an ornamental line in the cantabile manner of the best Italian opera tradition (Ex. 117).

A few examples of pronounced thematic dualism can be cited in Christian's sonatas, as in Op. 5/2/i, where there are sharp contrasts both within the opening theme and between it and a tuneful, well demarcated second theme (Ex. 118). More often, little contrast can be found, because there is no clear change of mood, whether a whole string of themes occurs (Op. 2/6/i) or the initial theme reappears in the dominant key in a form neither quite similar nor quite different enough to indicate any special concern with such matters (Op. 5/4/i/29-36). But Burney's remarks on this aspect of Christian's writing, in the course of a largely enthusiastic statement about him, are well worth quoting, however questionable the reference to Christian's priority may be.[89]

> Bach seems to have been the first composer who observed the law of *contrast*, as a *principle*. Before his time, contrast there frequently was, in the works of others; but it seems to have been accidental. Bach in his symphonies and other instrumental pieces, as well as his songs, seldom failed, after a rapid and noisy passage to introduce one that was slow and soothing. His symphonies seem infinitely more original than his songs or harpsichord pieces, of which [that is, of the symphonies] the harmony, mixture of wind-instruments, and general richness and variety of accompaniment, are certainly the most prominent features.

The advances in Christian's treatment of the materials in his later sonatas have to do not only with the structural transition to high-Classic music that was then in progress everywhere, but with the growing ability to do more with less that almost every composer experiences

88. Cf. Einstein/MOZART 120 and 246 (but there is no sufficient precedent in Christian's sons. for the "Adagio" in Mozart's Son. in F, K.V. 300K); Reeser/BACH 62; and, especially, Lowinsky/MOZART 166-171, in which the extensions of these themes by the 2 composers are fruitfully compared (to Mozart's advantage, of course) from the standpoint of structural rhythm.

89. Burney/HISTORY II 866-867.

Ex. 117. From the opening of the middle movement in the Sonata in E, Op. 5/5, by Johann Christian Bach (after the original ed. at the University of North Carolina).

in his personal development. The kaleidoscope of ideas and the syntax of 2 + 2 + 2 . . . measures to be found often in his earliest sonatas (e.g., D. 1./2/i), change to fewer ideas in larger phrases and periods, as in Op. 17/5/i/1-16, where even the modulatory bridge falls into

Ex. 118. The (a) first and (b) second themes from the first movement of Johann Christian Bach's Sonata in D, Op. 5/2 (after the original ed. at the University of North Carolina).

square groupings. Slightly slower harmonic rhythm and broader, clearer tonal outlines are to be noted in the later works, too. But these observations must not be taken to condemn Christian as an early slave to the "tyranny of the barline." He became, in fact, one of the most subtle masters of phrase syntax. For example, it was only a typical, not an extreme, procedure for him to follow the square 4-measure antecedent phrase that opens the relatively compact Sonata in c, Op. 17/2, with an incomplete consequent of 3 measures, then a complete one of 4.

In the "development" sections of his sonatas Christian never quite worked his materials in the intensive manner made known in high-Classic masterworks. One might suggest that the materials themselves are not pregnant enough to engender such developments, were it not for the minute, simple figures that frequently sufficed for a Haydn, Mozart, or Beethoven. Most often in his "development" sections Christian dealt in passage work rather than main ideas, anyway, his first object being, apparently, to make a modulatory digression in a nearly related minor key. Closer to high-Classic treatments are such sections as those in Op. 2/6/i (or A. 3./6/i), in which the initial idea does undergo some contrapuntal twists; or Op. 5/4/i, in which some of the Beethovian drive by sequential arpeggio flights is anticipated; or Op. 17/5/i, where subordinate figures from the exposition are worked out effectively. But all in all, Christian's "developments" create no more tension than would be expected in forms that are characterized not by drama and passion but by lyricism, charm, fluency, and a certain discursiveness.

Christian's handling of texture in his later sonatas certainly becomes no richer and does not change radically. But it shows a needed increase in variety and an even greater precision in those prime measures of craftsmanship, voice-leading, and balance of sound. There is little unison or open octave scoring such as might suggest the concerto or Mannheim influence (as at the start of Op. 2/3/i), and there is notable moderation, for Christian's time and style, in the use of Alberti bass. But other stock accompaniments of the *galant* style do abound, including different chordal figures in triplets or 16th-notes, repeated notes or double-notes, and the "murky" or "pom-pom" bass. The harmony, though it, too, is expertly handled, does little to add new interest to the texture, for it depends much more on the primary triads that served Rutini so well than on the esoteric, *empfindsam* language of Emanuel. About the most surprise one can find in Christian's sonatas is something like the change from major to minor in Op. 17/3/i/14-20.

Thin as Christian's resulting textures are, it is worth noting that the violin or flute part in the accompanied sonatas always has at least a few measures in which it takes an independent lead, and more generally contributes enough depth and sonority to the texture to keep it from being dispensable. Some recognition of the importance of these parts is suggested by the original publication of Opp. 2, 10, and 16 in score. The cello in Opp. 2 and 15, of course, only doubles the bass. It is pertinent here to quote Burney again, on the subject of Christian's accompaniments and their relation to his own piano playing.[90] Under Emanuel's tutelage

> he became a fine performer on keyed-instruments; but on quitting him and going to Italy, where his chief study was the composition of vocal Music, he assured me, that during many years he made little use of a harpsichord or piano forte but to compose for or accompany a voice. When he arrived in England, his style of playing was so much admired, that he recovered many of the losses his hand had sustained by disuse, and by being constantly cramped and crippled with a pen; but he never was able to reinstate it with force and readiness sufficient for great difficulties; and in general his compositions for the piano forte are such as ladies can execute with little trouble; and the allegros rather resemble bravura songs, than instrumental pieces for the display of great execution. On which account, they lose much of their effect when played without the accompaniments, which are admirable, and so masterly and interesting to an audience, that want of hand or complication in the harpsichord part, is never discovered.
>
> . . . In the sonatas and concertos which he composed for his own playing, when his hand was feeble, or likely to tire, he diverted the attention of the audience to some other [, accompaniment] instrument; and he had Abel, Fischer, Cramer, Crosdil, Cervetto, and other excellent musicians to write for, and take his part, whenever he wanted support.

Christian's keyboard writing does presuppose a command of the articulation, ornaments, fluent passage work, and other niceties of the pre- and high-Classic styles. But the difficulties he poses are seldom any more challenging (even in his piano concertos) than the easy runs, hand exchanges, and hand-crossings to be found in such a movement as the "Rondo" finale of Op. 5/4. As our summary list of his works shows, he already began to specify "piano forte" as an alternative to "clavecin" in Op. 5, about 1768. His preference is implied in that set by the many, musically well justified indications for "p^{o}" and "f^{e}." Indeed, as is still better known in the annals of music history, in that same year he seems to have been the first performer in England, and an early one anywhere, to play a piano solo in public, only a year after a song sung by a Miss Brickler in London had been accompanied by Charles Dibdin "on a new Instrument call'd a Piano Forte."[91]

Prior to Christian Bach the earliest (presumed) German in London to report here is the oboist, clarinetist, and teacher of Samuel Webbe, **Carl Barbandt.** Barbandt's origin and dates are not known but

90. Burney/HISTORY II 866-867.
91. Cf. Terry/BACH 112-113; Parrish/PIANO 326-338. Recall Burton's special priority, *supra.*

his performances and publications place him in London at least between 1752 and 1766.[92] The publications include a set of six SS/bass sonatas, Op. 1, which appeared in 1752; a set of six solo harpsichord sonatas, Op. 5, about 1765; a sonata for harp and violin, 1759; and another for harpsichord solo, 1764.[93] An examination of the solo sonatas in Op. 5 discloses a slightly earlier, more elementary style of texture than Christian wrote, and even more use of triplets, short trills, and other *galant* mannerisms. Although somewhat angular and cut-and-dried, the ideas and their treatment are not devoid of interest. The forms are more condensed than Christian's and the thematic treatment more concentrated, including a nearer approach to an actual development of the main idea after the double-bar in the first movements. Three movements, in the order F-S-minuet or quasi-minuet (with or without trio), are the rule except for a "Vivace" added to an "Alla Polacca" third movement in Sonata 4, and a slow introduction, "Largo Staccato," in Sonata 6.

Closely associated with Christian Bach throughout Christian's two decades in London was the last great virtuoso on the viola da gamba, **Carl Friedrich Abel** (1723-87).[94] Abel was the grandson of Clamor Heinrich Abel (SBE 248), the son of the Christian Ferdinand Abel who had played viola da gamba under J. S. Bach's direction at Köthen, and himself may have known (if not studied with) the latter before or at the start of ten years of service under Hasse at the Dresden court, from 1748. Carl Friedrich arrived in London in 1759. He joined forces with his younger countryman Christian Bach not only in sponsoring the important Bach-Abel public concerts (from 1765), but more personally in a circle of friends that included such notables as the oboist J. C. Fischer[95] and the latter's eventual father-in-law, the painter Thomas Gainsborough.[96]

Besides some 35 symphonies, 15 concertos, 20 quartets, 10 trios, and only a little vocal music, Abel left about as many works originally

92. Cf. Eitner/QL I 332; GROVE I 423 (Straeten).

93. Cf. BRITISH UNION I 83.

94. Cf. Burney/HISTORY II 1018-1020; Terry/BACH 75-76, 92-96, *et passim;* MGG I 22-25 (Redlich); GROVE I 8-9 (Payne, Carr, and Redlich). Helm/ABEL is a comprehensive, unpublished diss. (1953), including biography and environment (Part I), a study of Abel's symphonies (Part II, with extended exx.), and a detailed bibliography of all categories of the instrumental works (Part III, with catalogue, list of mod. eds., thematic index, and "Synoptical Index"), a general bibliography, and a general index (!).

95. Cf. MGG IV 269-271 (Cudworth), including the listing of a published set of 10 Sons. for Fl (or oboe?) & *b.c., ca.* 1780; also, Burney/HISTORY II 1018 and Helm/ABEL 53.

96. His fine paintings of both Christian Bach and Abel are reproduced in Terry/BACH Illustrations 1 and 13.

called "sonata" as Christian did, and during little more than the same 2 decades (*ca.* 1760-84). His known sonatas number 106 (exclusive of several lost, unidentified, and incomplete MSS of the SS/- and S/bass types, as listed mainly under Nos. 33, 34, and 36-39 in Helm/ABEL 312-314). Many of the sonatas enjoyed re-editions, although not those in the most numerous and musically distinguished category—that is, the 32 for viola da gamba and *b.c.* plus another for viola da gamba alone—,[97] which were too passé in their setting even to achieve first editions. Next in quantity to this latter type are Abel's accompanied keyboard, SS/- or SB/bass, S/bass, and solo keyboard types, in that order. Following the same order, Abel's main published sets of sonatas may be listed, with information on the first editions[98] (and with Helm's one or 2 catalogue nos. for each set added in parentheses):

Carl Friedrich Abel's Sonatas

A. *Accompanied Keyboard Sonatas*

1. 6 Sons. for H & Vn-or-Fl & Vc, Op. 2, London (Bremner), 1760 (No. 3).
2. 6 Sons. for H & Vn-or-Fl & Vc, Op. 5, London (Bremner), 1764 (Nos. 6 and 41). In Saint-Foix/MOZART IV 270 and V 319 the main theme of the finale in Mozart's Son. for P & Vn in A, K.V. 526, is "discovered" to derive from that of Op. 5/5 in the same key by Abel, perhaps in memory of the latter's death shortly before K.V. 526 was composed (Aug. 24, 1787 is the date on the autograph). But this supposition, ignored by Einstein and others, and unsupported by any mention in the later Mozart correspondence, seems to be founded on no more than a coincidental relationship of themes and only a slight one, at that. Mod. eds. of Sons. 4 and 5 are published by Hinrichsen in London and Peters in New York.
3. 6 Sons. for H-or-P & Vn, Op. 13, London (Bremner), 1777 (Nos. 15 and 17). For a mod. ed. of Son. 3 cf. MGG I 24.
4. 6 Sons. for H-or-P & Vn, Op. 18, London (Thompson), 1784 (Helm/ABEL 309; No. 23).

B. *SS/- and SB/bass Sonatas*

1. 6 Sons. for 2 Vns, or Fl & Vn, & *b.c.*, Op. 3, Leipzig (Breitkopf), 1762 (Nos. 31 and 4). This set was reproduced in score by the New York Public Library in 1934.
2. 6 Sons. for Vn, Vc, and *b.c.*, Op. 9, London (Bremner), *ca.* 1770 (Nos. 10 and 32).

C. *S/bass Sonatas*

1. 6 Sons. for Fl & *b.c.*, Op. 6, London (Bremner), 1765 (No. 7).

D. *Solo Keyboard Sonatas*

1. *Six Easy Sonattas for the Harpsichord or for a Viola Da Gamba Violin or German Flute with a Thorough-Bass Accompaniment,* Amsterdam

97. Nos. 43 and 44 in Helm/ABEL 315-316. For mod. eds. cf. MGG I 24.
98. For a few of the dates in Helm/ABEL 298-316 the more recent information in BRITISH UNION I 2-3 is preferred.

(Hummel), presumably one of Abel's publications after he reached London (cf. Einstein in ZFMW XIV [1931-32] 114), *ca.* 1760 (No. 42). Mod. ed.: All 6 sons. (in the order of nos. 1, 2, 5, 6, 3, 4), HORTUS MUSICUS-m Nos. 39 and 40 (Bacher & Woehl).

By comparison with Christian Bach, Abel uses the three-movement cycle more often in his sonatas—in fact, about as often as the two-movement cycle; he writes more slow movements and gives them more weight; he chooses minor keys more often, chiefly c and e; and he uses the minuet or "rondeau" as the finale almost as often. Except for this finale, the order of his movements is less predictable. Abel's ideas are similar to, but a little more positive, than Christian's, and their treatment is a little more concentrated. Both traits tend to make for neater, more compact designs, although not without a certain loss of imagination and freshness. If the craftsmanship is no greater, the details of ornamentation, dynamics, and articulation show even more polish in Abel's writing, especially in his viola da gamba and "trio" sonatas, than in Christian's writing. The harmony is often richer, too, with more figures in the *b.c.* parts. But the texture in the accompanied sonatas, the rudimentary accompaniments, the fluency of the keyboard writing short of any real virtuosity, and the moderate use of Alberti bass (Op. 13/2/i) are about the same. There are but a few dynamic signs in Opp. 13 and 18 to show that Abel was actually thinking of the piano as well as the harpsichord.

Although, like Christian's accompanied sonatas, Abel's were published in score, the violin part is purely subordinate more of the time (with infrequent exceptions, such as Opp. 5/5/i or 13/6/ii). It certainly gives little hint of the expert string writing to be found in the viola da gamba sonatas. Only a little better hint of that skill is supplied in the sonatas scored optionally for harpsichord solo or various S/bass groupings (our D. 1.), chiefly in the slower middle movements. This set seems actually to have been intended as much for one scoring as another; it plays equally well in each scoring (assuming the viola da gamba plays an octave lower than the violin or flute, or that the harpsichord alone is provided with a filler part from the figured bass) and yet it is not especially idiomatic in any scoring. More idea of Abel's string writing is found in the "trio" sonatas—that is, in the first violin part, the other parts being only subordinate filler and support parts. In the slow movements of these sonatas we hear him to best advantage (Ex. 119). As Burney wrote in 1779,[99]

99. Burney/HISTORY II 1019-1020; the year is given by Burney in a footnote.

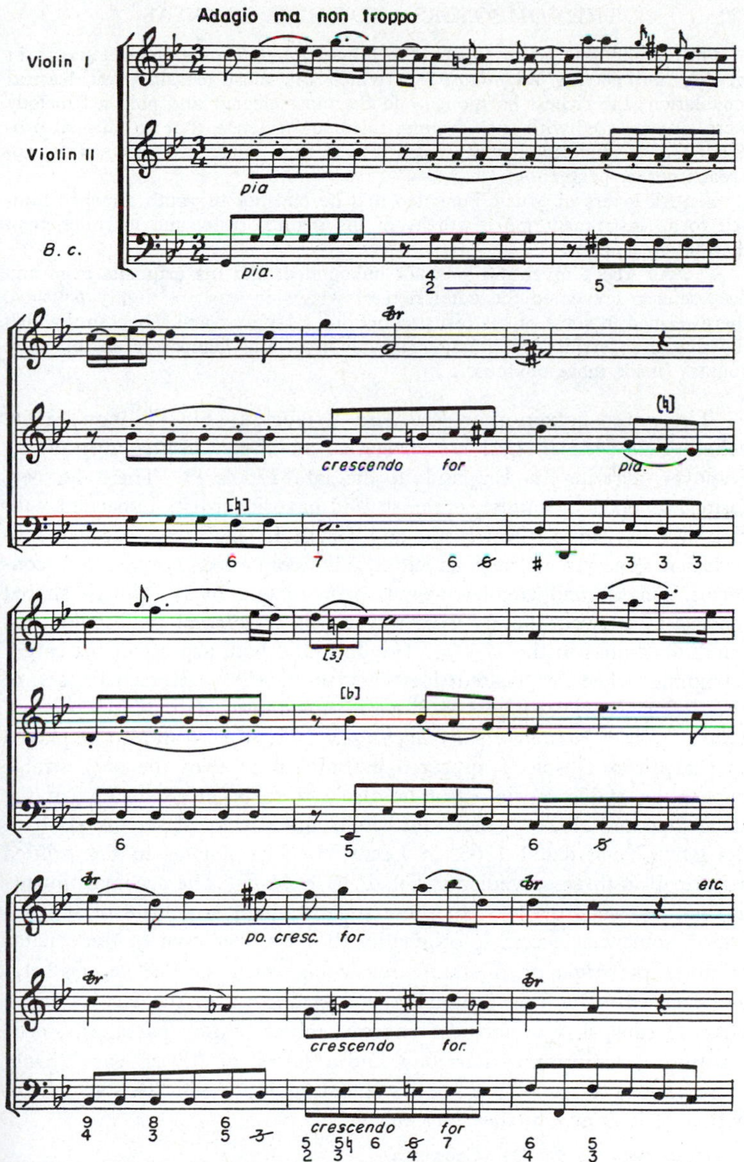

Ex. 119. From the middle movement of Sonata in G, Op. 3/1, by Carl Friedrich Abel (scored from the original ed. at the Library of Congress).

. . . in nothing was he so superior to himself, and to other musicians, as in writing and playing an *adagio;* in which the most pleasing, yet learned modulation; the richest harmony; and the most elegant and polished melody were all expressed with such feeling, taste, and science, that no musical production or performance with which I was then acquainted seemed to approach nearer perfection.

. . . All lovers of Music lamented that he had not in youth attached himself to an instrument more worthy of his genius, taste, and learning, than the *viol da gamba* . . .

. . . As Abel's invention was not unbounded, and his exquisite taste and deep science prevented the admission of whatever was not highly polished, there seemed in some of his last productions a languor and monotony, which the fire and fertility of younger symphonists and composers of his own country, made more obvious. . . .

The noted astronomer **Wilhelm Friedrich** (Sir William) **Herschel** (1738-1822) began his career as an oboist in the military at Hanover, arriving in England in the late 1750's.[100] There he performed as oboist, violinist, organist, and harpsichordist, associated with men like Avison in Newcastle and Garth in Durham, directed subscription concerts in various cities, and composed symphonies, concertos, sonatas and smaller works, before these lively, widely shared musical interests gradually gave way to his concurrent philosophic and scientific studies in the 1780's. Haydn found both aspects of his career intriguing when he visited Herschel in 1792.[101] Herschel's set of *Sei Sonate per il cembalo cogli accompagnamenti di violino e violoncello* [,] *che si possono sonare anche soli* (i.e., which can also be played as [harpsichord] solos) appeared in Bath in 1769 as the only sizable publication of his music. But he also left three more sonatas of the same type and eleven "solos" for violin and *b.c.* in MSS, the sixth of the latter being dated 1763, in Leeds.[102] The sonatas in the printed set are all in three movements, F-S-F or F-M-F. The accompaniments are entirely subordinate. In these sonatas there is a little of the unstifled, somewhat eccentric originality that we have seen in the sonatas of other part-time or dilettante musicians, such as Beecke, Dalberg, and Kerpen. But this originality is meaningless in the face of naïve virtuoso runs, lack of melodic interest, endless empty passages, sterile repetitions, rudimentary harmony, and a surfeit of Alberti bass. Only those curious to see what a great scientist could do with his sonatas will bother to look any further into them.

100. Cf. MGG VI 280-284 (Cudworth).

101. Cf. Landon/HAYDN 254-255.

102. A collection of Herschel's musical autographs and other MSS is listed in Otto Haas's *Catalogue 37* (1959), item 87, including a facs. of the first page of the acc'd. sons. in MS, the style of which is much like that in the printed set.

The organist, pianist, and violinist **Johann Samuel Schroeter** (*ca.* 1752-88) was a member of a musical German family that withdrew to Warsaw during the Seven Years' War, then moved to Leipzig at its end (1763).[103] In Leipzig he may have studied with J. A. Hiller. Perhaps he took a few lessons from Emanuel Bach in Berlin, too, before Emanuel went to Hamburg in 1667.[104] Schroeter made his debut at a Bach-Abel concert in London in 1772, where he eventually "repaid" Christian Bach for his unselfish help and kindly interest by unseating him as pianist in the public eye.[105] Indeed, when Christian died in 1782 Schroeter became the new Music Master in the Queen's Household—that is, during the few months before his strangely contracted marriage to the Rebecca Schroeter whom, in her eventual widowhood, Haydn might have married (in London in 1792 and 1794-95), "if I had been single."[106]

Virtually all of Schroeter's compositions include the instrument he did so much to promote in England, the piano. His piano concertos appealed to Mozart enough for the latter to write cadenzas for three of them fairly late in his career (K.V. 626a D, F, G, H).[107] Schroeter's own piano playing was praised by Burney and others for its refinement, naturalness, delicate nuance, and, as with Abel, its special fitness in adagio movements.[108] Besides concertos, some chamber music, and some arrangements, at least 32 sonatas in 7 sets by Schroeter were published, originally between 1772 and 1789 in London and/or Paris, Edinburgh, and Mainz. Except for his London Op. 1, containing 6
solo keyboard sonatas (H-or-P; Napier, 1775), all of these sonatas 108a
are of the accompanied type, as follows:[109] one set of 6 sonatas for H-or-P with Fl-or-Vn, Op. 4 (Napier, 1772) and one set of 2 for P & Vn, Op. 7 (Corri and Sutherland [in Edinburgh], 1789, posthumous); 2 sets of 6 for H-or-P (or vice versa) with Vn & Vc, Opp. 2

103. The known biographic facts and some new information about Schroeter are brought together in Wolff/SCHROETER, an illuminating article that goes mainly into his concertos and piano style.

104. Wolff/SCHROETER 340.

105. Cf. Geiringer/BACH 415-416; Wolff/SCHROETER 342-343.

106. Cf. Wolff/SCHROETER 344-345; Geiringer/HAYDN 108-110 and 129; Landon/HAYDN 279-286.

107. Cf. his letter of July 3, 1778, in Anderson/MOZART II 827-828; also, Wolff/SCHROETER 338-339.

108. Cf. Wolff/SCHROETER 341-342.

109. The helpful list in Wolff/SCHROETER 347-349 is amended here only to the extent of certain more exact dates and 2 further sets from BRITISH UNION II 933 and Johansson/FRENCH I 150 and II Facs. 114. The programmatic keyboard son., "The Conquest of Belgrade," must be by another "Schroetter," since the event occurred in 1789 (cf. Wolff/SCHROETER 347; BRITISH UNION II 933; Weinmann/ARTARIA item 43).

and 6 (Napier, 1775? and 1786?) and 2 sets of 3 for the same, Opp. 8 and 9 (Sieber [in Paris], both 1788?).

Nearly all of Schroeter's sonatas are in only two movements, although three of the solo keyboard sonatas have three movements. The finales are rondos, minuets, or allegros in binary design with repeated halves. Except for a few slower examples in binary design without repeats (Op. 2/5/i), the first movements are all allegros that approach "sonata form." Some of these have clear returns in the course of the second "half." But more of them are truly binary in the sense that the second "half" is an elongated, tonal mirror of the first half (Op. 4/1/i). There is usually a tuneful, enunciative main theme, followed by a contrasting second theme of considerable lyrical charm. The latter characteristically follows so soon that in one instance where it merely repeats the initial idea it sounds almost like a fugal answer on the dominant (Op. 2/2/i/11-16). The themes have enough traits in common with Mozart's to suggest one main reason for Mozart's interest in Schroeter. In general, Schroeter's forms, like Abel's, are a little more concentrated, symphonic (or purposeful), and tight-knit than Christian Bach's.

In Schroeter's Op. 2 the keyboard writing is about as advanced in style, fluency, and difficulty as Christian Bach's, but reveals nothing to distinguish the composer in this respect from many of his contemporaries or to qualify him as "the first pianist-composer in the modern sense of the term."[110] In fact, this writing proves to be more elementary (and less resourceful) in Op. 4, perhaps as a concession to public taste. The use of Alberti bass is more than moderate throughout Schroeter's sonatas. The violin or flute part is often above the keyboard part or has independent interest, especially in imitative exchanges (Ex. 120).

Last to be named in the same circle is the German violinist and director **Wilhelm Cramer** (1745-95), pupil of J. Stamitz and Cannabich, member of the Mannheim orchestra before he moved to London in 1772 (reportedly, on Christian Bach's urging), and father of the pre-Romantic sonata composer and celebrated pianist, J. B. Cramer.[111] Wilhelm published 2 sets of 6 sonatas each for 2 violins and cello, Opp. 1 and 3, and 2 for one violin and cello, Opp. 2 and 4, as well as some concertos.[112] These all date from the decade of the 1770's. A reading of Op. 4 (*ca.* 1780) corroborates the lesser regard for this outstanding performer as a composer that was expressed by his contemporaries and

110. As in Wolff/SCHROETER 349-353 (after a lead from Burney in Rees/CYCLOPEDIA), but with reference mainly to Schroeter's concertos.

111. The fullest account of Wilhelm is in Schlesinger/CRAMER 11-22.

112. The sons. are variously listed in DTB-m XVI xi-xii and xxviii-xxix (thematic index); BRITISH UNION I 238.

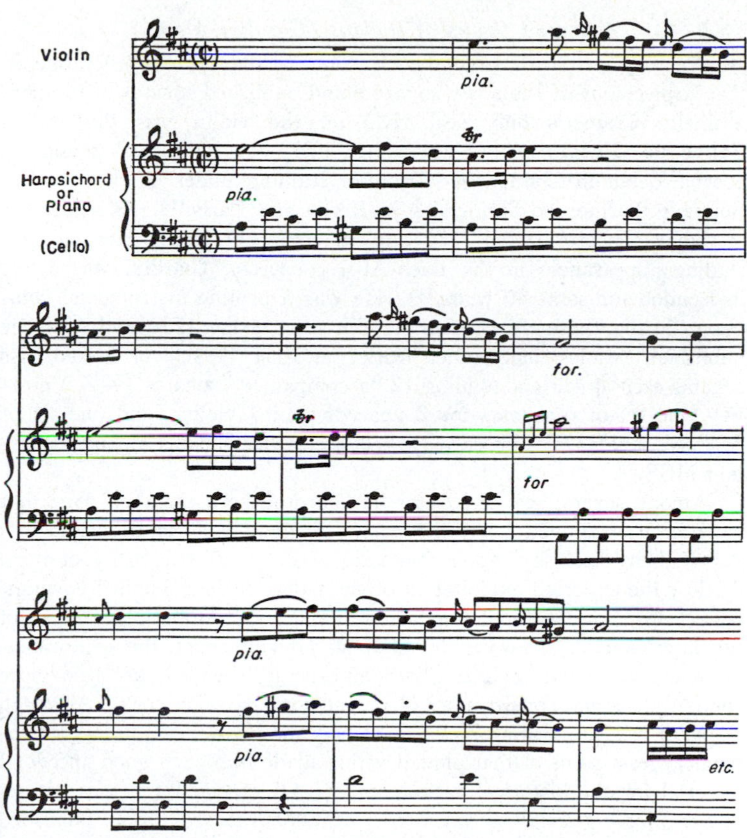

Ex. 120. From the first movement of Johann Samuel Schroeter's Sonata in D, Op. 2/1 (after the original ed. at the Library of Congress).

by later writers.[113] The duos in this set are all in 3 movements, the first 2 being fast and slow, and the finale being a minuet, theme-and-variations, or binary allegro movement. The weakness lies not so much in the ideas, which fall into graceful if obvious phrases, but in an apparent inability to extend those ideas. The resulting impression is often that of a purely additive form in which they are strung end to end without significant integration or interrelation. 113a

113. Cf. Schlesinger/CRAMER 22-23.

A Second Group of Italians (*Giardini, Vento*)

We may now turn from the Germans to the second generation in that large colony of Italians who wrote and published sonatas in London. Wilhelm Cramer's only real rival on the violin was the Italian **Felice de Giardini** (or Degiardino; 1716-96), who had made an epochal debut in London in 1750 after training under G. B. (not L.) Somis in Torino and performing in Berlin and Paris.[114] As a director of public concerts (from 1751), opera composer, and performer (including appearances in the Bach-Abel concerts), Giardini was active in London for some 40 years.[115] He was a prolific instrumental composer during those years, too.[116] Between about 1750 and 1790 he published, besides many other works, at least 11 sets of 6 solo/bass sonatas each, 4 editions totaling 12 "accompanied" sonatas (K & Vn-or-Fl), one set of 6 sonatas for 2 unaccompanied violins, and one set of SS/bass sonatas.[117] There may well be further sonatas among his extant MSS.

Among several sets of sonatas by Giardini, both early and late, that have been examined here, the early sonatas show more originality. All of them disclose a good command of the craft and many of them disclose the expected exploitation of the violin in their detailed bowings, wide leaps, double-stops, ornamental passages, and bariolage.[118] But the later sonatas, showing no stylistic advance over the continuous, motivic style toward which this composer still tended, fall into more routine plans and consist more of perfunctory passage work. Although Giardini was no striking melodist at best, he showed in his earlier sonatas at least some of that piquancy that made him such good anecdotal material for the historical raconteurs.[119] Of special interest is his set of *Sei Sonate di cembalo con violino o flauto traverso,* Op. 3, published by John Cox in London in 1751.[120] These light, witty, fluent sonatas are cast in two movements (F-M or F-F) instead of the three movements in most of his melo/bass sonatas (in which a relatively inexpressive adagio lies between fast or moderate outer movements). They are remarkable for supplying a missing link between the solo/bass and

114. Cf. Avison/ESSAY 103; Burney/HISTORY II 895-896; MGG V 84-88 (Cudworth); Scholes/BURNEY I 120-121.

115. This figure allows for about 6 years in Naples (1784-*ca.* 1789), since Giardini did not go to Moscow (Mooser/ANNALES II 657-658).

116. Cf. MGG V 85-87; BRITISH UNION I 373-375.

117. For mod. eds., cf. MGG V 87.

118. Cf. Moser/VIOLINSPIEL 415-417.

119. Cf. BURNEY'S TOURS I 55; Burney/HISTORY II 896; Landon/HAYDN 257-258.

120. The new, earlier date comes from BRITISH UNION I 375. Mod. ed., complete: CLASSICI-m II No. 3 (Polo), with "Appendice" and editorial additions.

the true duo types. About half the time the violin is clearly the solo instrument, since only a purely supportive *b.c.* is supplied with it. And the rest of the time, except for occasional passages where it still dominates (as in Son. 6/i/116-123), it is subordinate to a realized keyboard part. J. S. Bach had included some short *b.c.* passages in his violin sonatas with realized keyboard (SBE 272), but the difference lies in the polyphonic equality of Bach's upper parts in nearly all the other measures. Besides providing the earliest examples known here of the accompanied setting in England,[121] Giardini's Op. 3 contains early uses of the Alberti bass (as in Son. 2/i/64-72) and reveals the good knowledge he had of the keyboard as well as the violin (as in Son. 3/i).[122] Especially fetching is the giguelike "Allegro" that concludes Sonata 2 in C, with its suggestion of the Piedmontese dance called *monferrina*.[123]

Torrefranca has been able to show that the obscure Neapolitan cembalist and organist **Ferdinando Pellegrini** (or Pellegrino; *ca.* 1715-*ca.* 1767) served in Roman churches from at least 1743 (not 1754), that he was in La Pouplinière's service in Paris at least in 1762, and that the words "Op. X et ultima" appear in the full title of his Op. 10, probably signifying that when that work was published, in 1767 (not 1768[124]), he had already died.[125] Torrefranca goes on to conjecture that Pellegrini moved to London after La Pouplinière's death in 1762, a fact partially supported by the English editions of his works that began to appear, as we now know,[126] in 1763, but not by any mention of him in past or present accounts of music in 18th-century London that are known here. Furthermore, Torrefranca discovered that at least 8 of the 13 movements in the *Sei Sonate per Cembalo* published by Walsh (not Bremner) in 1765 as Op. 2 under Pellegrini's name are actually forgeries of sonatas by Galuppi and Rutini, and that a "Sonata-Fantasia" by Platti appears under Pellegrini's name in Op. 10. ("He had fine taste, this scapegrace of the cembalo!" adds Torrefranca, who believes that it could have been indirectly, through the English editions of Pellegrini, that the young Mozart came to know Galuppi and
Platti.)[127] Torrefranca is on shakier ground when he guesses that 127a
Pellegrini called his first publication, in Paris, "Opera quarta" so as to

121. Cf. Torrefranca/ORIGINI 629-630.
122. Cf. Burney/HISTORY II 895.
123. Cf. Polo in CLASSICI-m II No. 3, p. 75; GROVE V 827-828.
124. Johansson/FRENCH I 23.
125. Torrefranca/ORIGINI 488-492 (including a not wholly accurate list of works) and 716-722; the birth year, *ca.* 1715 is purely speculative. Cf., also, Gerber/LEXICON II 89; Brenet/LIBRAIRIE 448; Cucuel/LA POUPLINIÈRE 254.
126. BRITISH UNION II 767.
127. Torrefranca/ORIGINI 716-722; Torrefranca/LONDRA 361-362.

imply previous experience, thus leaving Opp. 1-3 unassigned numbers until he got to London.[128]

Including forgeries, Pellegrini is credited with 12 solo keyboard sonatas in 2 sets of 6 each (Opp. 2 and 5) and 18 of the accompanied keyboard type in 3 sets of 6 each (Opp. 4, 7, and 10), all published in Paris and/or London in the 8 years between 1759 and 1767. The question naturally arises, Is a man who is once a forger, always a forger? It is hard to examine the 2- and 3-movement sonatas in Opp. 4 and 5 (1759 and 1763) without being suspicious, since the styles in the 2 sets differ considerably.[129] The rather empty bluster of ornamental and display passages throughout Op. 4 and the lack of melodic or expressive interest may well be a true sample of what this composer himself could do, and indeed one clue as to why he felt compelled to commit his forgeries. If so, are the "lessons" in Op. 5 more likely to be the work of others, since they are frequently more lyrical, melodious, and expressive? The 2 sets do have a few traits in common, such as the repeated double-notes, requiring unusually fast right-hand action, in the opening (and other movements) of each. A hint that Pellegrini may have known Giardini's "accompanied" sonatas, Op. 3, is seen in the similar halfway stage of this setting to be found in Pellegrini's Op. 4. In fact, one now finds passages not only of violin and *b.c.* and of violin subordinated to realized keyboard, but of keyboard solo and of considerably more equality of the upper parts through contrapuntal imitations.

Pietro (or Pier Alessandro) **Guglielmi** (1728-1804), Neapolitan-trained master of the *opera buffa,* was in London from 1768 to 1772.[130] During those four years he seems to have been close to Christian Bach[131] and to have written most of his instrumental music, including the "quartettos" for keyboard with accompaniments for two violins and cello[132] and a set of *Six Sonatas for the Harpsichord* or *Forte Piano,* Op. 3, published by Bremner in 1772.[133] All six sonatas are in two

128. But it is true that the Paris ed. of Op. 4 appeared in 1759 (Johansson/FRENCH I 63), whereas that of 6 SS/bass trios, Op. 1 (not known to Torrefranca) appeared not until about 1765 (BRITISH UNION II 767).

129. There are no mod. eds. to report, but Op. 5/5 is copied in full in Stone/ITALIAN III 76 (with thematic index of Opp. 4 and 5 in II 49-51 and brief remarks about these 2 sets in I 194-198).

130. Cf. MGG V 1054-1060 (Zanetti).

131. Cf. Terry/BACH 117, 143, 111-112.

132. Discussed with enthusiasm in Saint-Foix/LONDRES 514-517.

133. Listed in BRITISH UNION I 409. In Eitner/QL IV 413 are listed 10 (more?) solo keyboard sons. in 2 MSS, a set of 6 in Dresden and a set of 4, dated 1771, in Milan. A mod. ed. of Son. 6 in E♭ is listed in MGG V 1059; Son. 3 is copied in full in Stone/ITALIAN III 143 (with thematic index in II 32 and brief discussion in I 231-232).

movements, with a minuet or rondo following a moderate or fast movement. The *opera buffa* composer is revealed in the light, uncomplicated textures and in the saucy, even curt thematic elements, often reiterated as many as a half dozen times. But these elements lack melodic distinction and the broad, compelling organization essential to abstract instrumental forms is lacking in their disposition somewhat as it is in the sonatas of Guglielmi's chief Neapolitan contemporaries in the *opera buffa,* Paisiello and Cimarosa. Originally an orchestral violist, Guglielmi wrote as knowingly for the keyboard as Giardini or Pellegrini. But although he alone entered dynamic contrasts in the keyboard part he showed no more interest in the new piano than these fellow countrymen. Said Burney, fairly enough, "His harpsichord pieces are full of froth and common passages, and have little other merit than *appearing* difficult, though of easy execution; and which, though pert, can never be called dull or tedious."[134]

Giusto Ferdinando Tenducci (*ca.* 1736-at least 1791), a colorful *castrato* "singer-cembalist" from Siena, was in London, Dublin, and Edinburgh much of the time from 1758.[135] He was a close friend of Christian Bach during the latter's last twenty years, and of Mozart during the child's first London trip in 1764-65 and the youth's Paris trip in 1778.[136] Tenducci published *A Collection of Lessons for the Harpsichord or Piano & Forte* about 1768, while he was in Edinburgh.[137] The four "Lessons" in this set, each separately entitled "Sonata," are in two movements, M-minuet, except for No. 3, M-F-minuet (with one variation).[138] They give further examples of the light Italian operatic style at the keyboard, especially the "singing-allegro" style. One may also note that Tenducci's option of harpsichord or piano in Edinburgh, around 1768, was as early as Christian Bach's in London and only two years after John Burton's (*supra*).

Our next Italian in London takes us to the last of Torrefranca's main heroes, and the last of them to be discussed in the present volume, **Mattia Vento** (*ca.* 1735-76).[139] Born and trained in Naples, Vento

134. Burney/HISTORY II 874.
135. Cf. GROVE VIII 392-393 (Marshall).
136. Cf. Terry/BACH 81, 121-122, 161, 168; Anderson/MOZART II 900-902; Mozart/NEUE-m X/34 160, 166.
137. This set is the only one of the sort that he published. The Welcker ed., *ca.* 1770, "for the harpsichord," is a reprint (listed in BRITISH UNION II 1000), as is the set of *Four Sonatas for the Pianoforte* that appeared in 1801 (listed in BRITISH PRINTED II 566). The mention of "six sonatas for harpsichord [published] in Dublin in 1768," in GROVE VIII 393 and elsewhere, is merely a wrong reference to the original set.
138. The sons. are briefly described, with exx. and bibliographic information, in Torrefranca/ORIGINI 705-710.
139. Torrefranca/ORIGINI 492-501 (biographic and bibliographic), 625-658 and 663-704 (style-critical). Cf., also, GROVE VIII 721 (Loewenberg).

went to London in 1763, on the invitation of Giardini, after operatic successes in Rome and Venice. During the remainder of his short life, he was active in London operatic circles, including some collaboration and some competition with Christian Bach.[140] But the bulk of his publications during those 13 years consisted of a set of 6 SS/bass sonatas (*ca.* 1764) and 10 sets of 6 accompanied sonatas each (*ca.* 1764-*ca.* 1775); followed by re-editions and, in the year after his death, by a new set of 5 solo keyboard sonatas.[141] The over-all titles use the word "Sonatas" in the SS/bass sets and in the accompanied sets 1-5 and 9, and "Lessons" in the other sets, but the individual title is always "Sonata." The piano is added as an alternative to harpsichord after the sixth set and relatively sparing dynamic indications are introduced in this same set. At all times the writing for keyboard is experienced and occasionally it is tricky (set 3/5/i). The accompaniment, printed in score with the keyboard, always calls for a violin or flute, which is only seldom essential (2/5/ii/17-29) or needed for textural enrichment (6/4/i/13-16). Although the cello is specified only in the fourth set, its use to double, outline, or embellish the harpsichord bass in any of the accompanied sets can be assumed whenever it was desired and available.[142]

All of Vento's sonatas are in two movements in the same key, most
143a often a moderate or fast movement followed by a rondo or minuet.[143]

140. Cf. Terry/BACH 77, 83, 99-100, 147, *et passim.*

141. The original Welcker eds. of all but the posthumous set, as well as some of the Longman and Broderip re-eds. (from the same careless plates!) are listed in BRITISH UNION II 1037 (but the first 2 acc'd. sets in this list were actually the second and first sets, respectively). The Welcker eds. of sets 1, 2, 3, 5, 6, 7, 10 and the posthumous sons. are in the Library of Congress (thematic index in Stone/ITALIAN II 94-101; but no Vento son. is copied in III as stated in I 193, and the Son. in G listed in II 101 as being in the Bland anth. was originally no. 6 in the third set). Most or all of the sets were published in Paris, too (cf. Johansson/FRENCH I 17, 110, 116, 167, 168).

142. In Torrefranca/ORIGINI 651 and 655-656 the Vc part of the fourth set is assumed to exist separately, even though missing from sets then available, and it is postulated to be something more independent than the usual reinforcement of the bass; but no such separate part was prepared, any more than in any other London eds. of acc'd. sons. printed in score.

143. Little has appeared in mod. eds. and these are scarce themselves (cf. Schmidl/DIZIONARIO II 651; Torrefranca/ORIGINI 643 and 648); but the many generous exx. provided in Torrefranca/ORIGINI 637-658 and 664-685 (*passim*), as well as Torrefranca/LONDRA 352-361, give a good idea of Vento at his best. Reference to these inadequately indexed and labeled exx. and to such full titles and tables of movements as Torrefranca gives can be facilitated by the following page index:

Set	*Full title*	*Table of mvts.*	*Exx.*
1	496, 633	635	637-638, 641-642
2	643	644	645-649
3	496		669-670, 676-677; 352-355 (Torrefranca/LONDRA)
4	650	656-657	652-658, 664-668, 670-675; 356-358

Slow movements (6/4/i), minor keys (2/5), and keys of as many as 4 sharps (1/4) are rare (E♭ being the limit in flats). The usual pre-Classic unformalized variety of near "sonata forms" is found in the first movements, although sometimes such a form occurs in the finale (4/6) and sometimes the first movement is a rondo design (as in the same son., or 7/1). Burney's somewhat harsh remarks about Vento's sonatas are too interesting not to be quoted in full:[144]

> This composer's harpsichord pieces are flimsy, and so much alike, that the invention, with respect to melody and modulation of the eight sets [*sic*], may be compressed into two or three movements. In these sonatas, as well as in his songs, he avoids vulgar passages, and has a graceful, easy, and flowing melody; but his bases are too like Alberti's, and his trebles too like one another, either to improve the hand or delight the ear. He had a great number of scholars, which insured the expence of printing his pieces, though not their general and public favour. One or two sets of such easy compositions would, indeed, have been very useful to scholars in the first stages of their execution; but eight books, in which there is so little variety, can never be wanted, or indeed borne, but by those who think it right implicitly to receive all their master's prescriptions.

Burney's remarks on Vento's sonatas are conspicuously absent from Torrefranca's extended discussions of them, which, though bordering on the idolatrous, are among the most brilliant products of his researches into the "Italian Origins of Musical Romanticism," both in their bibliographic and in their style-critical arguments. As always, Torrefranca sought to establish Italian antecedents for the Mozart style. He maintained that Vento was at the peak of his sonata activity when the child Mozart visited London in 1764-65 (Torrefranca/ORIGINI 689-690), and that Mozart must have profited as much from this Neapolitan and, apparently, Venetian influence as from the Lombardian influence of G. B. Sammartini and Christian Bach, or the Tuscan influence of Rutini and Boccherini (pp. 686-688, 625-628). In Vento's music itself Torrefranca emphasized the symphonic style and form of certain movements (e.g., 4/3/i), which, he said, Riemann would have traced to the Mannheim school but he has traced to Sammartini (pp. 646, 670-671, 680). He emphasized the high quality of the minuets and many rondos (e.g., 4/5/ii and 5/3/ii), ranking them with those of the chief Classicists (pp. 657-658, 668-670). And he called attention to the numerous instances of ternary sonata form (pp. 656-657, 691), to a new type of "harmonic" or chordally diffused theme as distinguished from the "melodic theme" of the previous era (pp. 697-699), to a more expressive

5 668-669; 356
6 678 678-685; 359-361

144. Burney/HISTORY II 884.

second theme than Christian Bach could write (pp. 675-676), to the modulations into minor keys and real working out of the "development" sections (pp. 691-692, 673), and to the broader harmonic outlook, in general (p. 633).

In the over-all view essential to the present survey some justification can be found for the remarks of both Burney and Torrefranca. It is true that there is much sameness throughout Vento's 65 accompanied sonatas that are printed, and that one factor is the elementary keyboard bass, which persists in its simple chordal or repeated-note patterns without compromise. One might observe, also, that his tendency to restate and recast ideas tends to make for somewhat lax forms. But it is also true that some sonatas or separate movements do command more attention than others,[145] and that at least in these instances Vento stands a bit above his fellow Italians in London. Torrefranca has quoted a spirited quasi-tarantella marked "Allegro" (4/1/ii, Torrefranca/ORIGINI 652-653), a fresh "Tempo di Minuetto" (4/5/ii, Torrefranca/ORIGINI 658), a cantabile "Larghetto" (6/4/i, Torrefranca/LONDRA 359-361), and a fairly intensive harmonic and thematic "development" section (3/5/i, Torrefranca/LONDRA 353-354), among many other provocative examples. Here it may help to quote a more nearly average example of a "symphonic passage" in a first movement and another of the refrain from a rondo type of finale, these 2 examples being from the same sonata (Ex. 121).

Pasquale (or "F. P.") **Ricci** (*ca.* 1733-1817) was trained in Milan before his wide travels in the 1760's and 1770's.[146] He was in Paris in 1778 when Leopold Mozart named him among several "lesser lights," "second-rate composers," and "scribblers,"[147] and presumably when he joined with Christian Bach in writing a keyboard method for the Naples Conservatory (not published until about 1790).[148] But his presence in London can only be surmised from the fact that several of his numerous instrumental works were published by Welcker between about 1768 and 1775.[149] These last include one set of 6 SS/bass sonatas, Op. 3 (*ca.* 1775), and one of 6 accompanied sonatas, Op. 4 (1768), with a "violoncello-obligato" as well as a violin. Another accompanied set of 6 sonatas (H & Vn), Op. 6 (*ca.* 1770), was published by "The Author" in The Hague.[150] Most of the sonatas in Ricci's Op. 4 are in 3 move-

145. Torrefranca finds more substance in the even-numbered sets, especially the fourth (1766; Torrefranca/ORIGINI 650, 690).

146. Cf. Eitner/QL VIII 210-211; DIZIONARIO RICORDI 899.

147. Anderson/MOZART II 706.

148. Cf. Terry/BACH 134-135; Johansson/FRENCH II Facs. 75.

149. Cf. BRITISH UNION II 888.

150. A thematic index of Opp. 4 and 6 is in Stone/ITALIAN II 211 and 213.

ments, with a minuet finale, whereas all those in Op. 6 are in 2 movements (not including a "Grave" introduction in Son. 4), with a rondo finale. If his thematic material is somewhat obvious, there is more of interest in the scoring. The violin often exchanges solos with the keyboard in true duo fashion. It is accompanied sometimes by a *b.c.* (Op. 6/6/i) and sometimes by a realized keyboard part, as in Op. 6/2/i/25-31, in which a clear second theme is accompanied only by an Alberti bass divided between the two hands in the treble staff range.

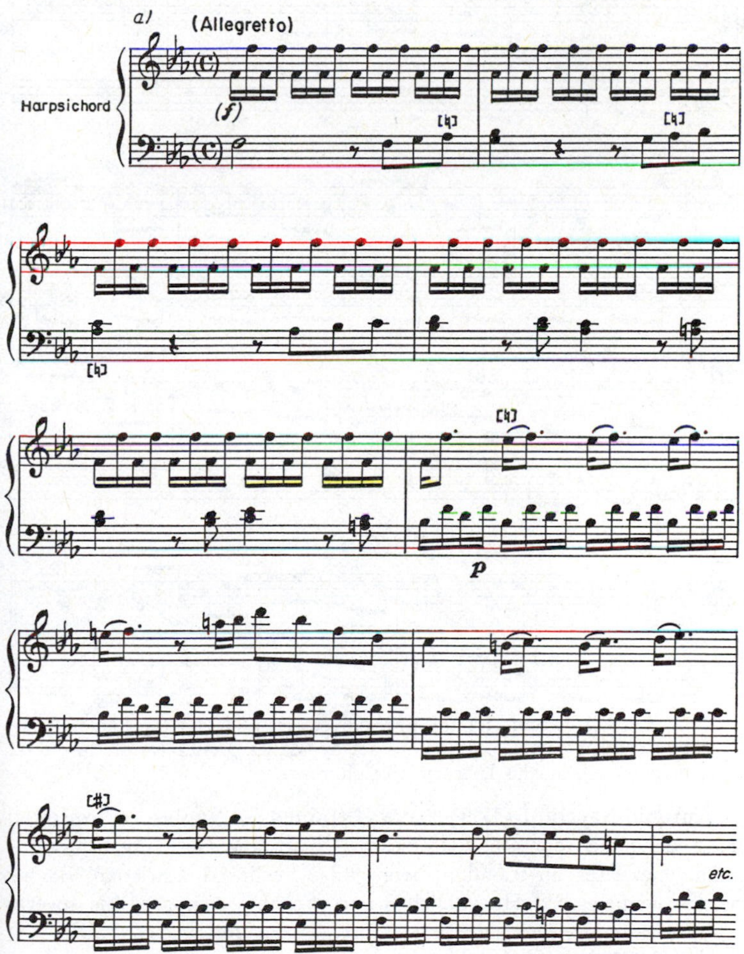

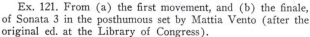

Ex. 121. From (a) the first movement, and (b) the finale, of Sonata 3 in the posthumous set by Mattia Vento (after the original ed. at the Library of Congress).

Antonio Sacchini (1730-86) was trained in Naples and enjoyed almost unequaled operatic successes in Venice and Germany before his similar successes in London, from 1772, eclipsed Christian Bach's operatic ventures.[151] He published and probably composed his several

151. Cf. Burney/HISTORY II 894-895; Terry/BACH 144-145, 157; GROVE VII 347-349 (Marshall).

sets of trios, quartets, and sonatas while he was in London and before the eclipse, in turn, of his own music caused him to spend his last few years (from 1782?) in Paris. The sonatas include the typical Op. 1 made up of 6 sonatas in SS/bass scoring (Bremner, *ca.* 1775), followed by 2 accompanied sets of 6 sonatas each, Opp. 3 and 4 (H-or-P & Vn; first published, respectively, by Bremner in 1779 and Blundell, *ca.* 1780).[152] Although interest has revived lately in the once widely ac- 152a
claimed operas by Sacchini, the sonatas by this all-but-outstanding composer have gone unnoticed since his death.[153] Only one "trio" Sonata in G, from Op. 1, and only two of the accompanied sonatas have been reissued in modern times; and, without acknowledgment, one of the latter (Op. 3/4 in E♭) has been dispossessed of its not unessential accompaniment as well as its finale, while the other (Op. 4/6 in F) has been reduced to a solo piano arrangement.[154] Even Torrefranca viewed Sacchini's sonatas merely as elegant, refined, but unoriginal products of the "second" *galant* style.[155]

But the student looking for new ground to explore will find real musical worth in Sacchini's sonatas, and some new light on high-Classic style and form just at its threshold. The few polite nods that have been made in their direction, based merely on Pauer's solo reduction of Op. 4/6,[156] are misleading. Actually, Sacchini's Opp. 3 and 4 differ appreciably. All 12 sonatas have the same "Italian" plan of 2 movements (F-rondo or minuet). And both sets reveal the same broad, finely drawn melodic arches, the clear phrase-and-period syntax, the expert handling of harmony and voice-leading, and some of the chromaticism that characterize Sacchini's opera arias. Indeed, all of these traits are already to be noted in his "trio" sonatas, as in the ornamental "Largo," middle movement of the Sonata in G edited by Riemann. Such traits, plus some themes compounded of short, pert, *buffa*-like

152. Cf. Eitner/QL VIII 382; BRITISH UNION II 912 (the dates for the Siever eds. in Paris should be close to 1782, rather than "c. 1775," to judge from Johansson/FRENCH II Facs. 111). In Stone/ITALIAN I 237-241, II 88-90, and III 112, respectively, there are a brief discussion of Opp. 3 and 4 (with exx.), a thematic index of these 2 sets, and a complete copy of Op. 3/3 in A (including the Vn part).

153. In all the references to him in BURNEY'S TOURS and Burney/HISTORY there is not the usual incidental mention of instrumental compositions, possibly because these publications appeared too late to get into Burney's notes for those references. They are not mentioned, either, in the exceptionally full accounts in La Borde/ESSAI III 230-232 or Gerber/LEXICON II 357-363, but do get listed, at least, in Gerber/NEUES IV 3-4.

154. These 3 reissues are found, respectively, in COLLEGIUM MUSICUM-m No. 46 (Riemann); Malipiero/ITALIAN-m 3; Pauer/MEISTER-m III 6 (also, RICORDI ARTE-m IV 6 and Köhler/MAÎTRES-m II 80).

155. Torrefranca/ORIGINI 427.

156. As in Eitner/SONATE 183-184 and Villanis/CLAVECINISTES 813.

motives (Op. 3/1/i/1-10), some ingratiating rondos (Op. 3/2/ii), and the excellent piano writing, with dynamic levels and graduations fully indicated, not seldom bring Mozart's writing to mind.

But if Op. 4 reveals more independence of the violin part than Op. 3 (as in Sons. 4/i, 5/i, and 6/i and ii), Op. 3 is more interesting from the standpoint of structure, especially in the greater freedom within the movements and the greater extent of the first movements. For one thing, Sacchini shows himself in Op. 3 to be a master at that fine symphonic art of stretching out a broad simple tonal plan and maintaining the tonal suspense measure after measure, through figure after figure, right up to the moment each tonal goal is attained. For another, he shows himself to be more resourceful and flexible than average in the choice of his tonal plans or, that is, in his solutions to the "sonata-form" problem. Of the first movements in Op. 3, four (all but Sons. 3 and 5) have no repeat signs or internal double-bars and all four are different in their plans. Aside from the absence of an internal double-bar, Sonata 1/i differs from textbook "sonata form" in starting at the "development" section on new material; Sonata 2/i dissolves by chromatic scales into a more intensive, chromatic "development" and returns to the tonic only with the subordinate theme; Sonata 4/i lacks only the subordinate theme in the recapitulation; and Sonata 6/i proceeds directly from a "normal" exposition to a "normal" recapitulation, with no hint of the "normal" development section except for a few extra modulations after the tonic return. Sacchini is resourceful in the composition of his themes, too, a fact that can be but imperfectly illustrated by any one sample (Ex. 122).

Three Italian cellists who published sonatas in London during the 1760's and 1770's are now too obscure to get more than passing mention. Only conjectural is the London residence of the self-taught dilettante **Christian Joseph Lidarti** (1730-at least 1793), a cellist of Italian descent who was born in Vienna and published at least two sets of SS/bass sonatas in London.[157] Only conjectural is the cello playing by **Francesco Zanetti** (or Zannetti; *ca.* 1740-at least 1790?), who could have been in London before as well as after his post in Perugia from 1767-82, in view of his several sets of S/-, SS/bass, and accompanied sonatas published in London from about 1760.[158]

157. Cf. BURNEY'S TOURS I 305, 319; Straeten/VIOLONCELLO 176 and Plate XXIV; MGG VIII 739-740 (Tagliavini), with reference to a mod. ed. of a son. for viola pomposa; BRITISH UNION II 619.

158. Cf. BURNEY'S TOURS I 319; Straeten/VIOLONCELLO 582; Schmidl/DIZIONARIO II 720. The English title of a Welcker ed. of "Trios" published about 1771 (BRITISH UNION II 1100) adds "composed in Italy," possibly to make clear that Zanetti had now left London.

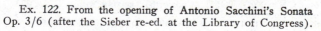

Ex. 122. From the opening of Antonio Sacchini's Sonata Op. 3/6 (after the Sieber re-ed. at the Library of Congress).

Giovanni Battista Cirri (*ca.* 1740-at least 1782), who played in London concerts in which the child Mozart performed, left numerous sets of sonatas for solo cello and *b.c.* and others in SS/bass setting among instrumental works published between 1765 and about 1780.[159]

Two obscure Italian violinists may be given similarly brief mention. **Maddalena Lombardini Sirmen** (*ca.* 1735-at least 1785), remembered only for Tartini's famous letter on violin playing addressed to her in 1760, published a set of unaccompanied violin "Duetts" and another of SS/bass "Trios" or "Sonates" after her two brilliant seasons as a performer in London, 1771-72.[160] **Giovanni Battista Noferi** is known only by his playing and publications during residence in London and Cambridge between about 1757 and 1781.[161] He published several sets of "Solos" for violin and *b.c.*, as well as "Sonatas" in SS and SS/bass settings. Furthermore, he left a set of six "Solos" for guitar and *b.c.* (Op. 3, *ca.* 1765), the only other examples of this sort that were found here in the same period and place being some by one Frederic Schumann from Germany.[162]

Three Other Nationalities

Finally, three other obscure violinists may be added as representatives of three other nationalities in London. **Antonín Kammel** (*ca.* 1740-*ca.* 1788), a Bohemian who reportedly excelled in adagio playing after study with Tartini, lived in the environment and wrote in the styles of Christian Bach and Abel, his many successful publications and re-editions including S/- and SS/bass sonatas and still others in SS and accompanied settings.[163] The Spanish violinist (and/or flutist?) **Jean Oliver y Astorga** left one set each of S/- and SS/bass sonatas, Opp. 1 and 3, first published in 1767 and 1769.[164] And the French virtuoso from Bordeaux, **François-Hippolyte Barthélemon** (1741-1808), who lived a total of some 40 years in London, from 1765, left one set of SS/- and two sets of S/bass sonatas, Opp. 1 (1765), 2 (*ca.* 1765), and 10 (*ca.* 1785), respectively,

159. Cf. Pohl/MOZART 27, 55, 104, 126; Straeten/VIOLONCELLO 167; DIZIONARIO RICORDI 305; BRITISH UNION I 192-193. In Stone/ITALIAN I 214-216 and II 12-14 are exx. from, and a thematic index of, 12 2-manual, 2-mvt. organ sonatas by Cirri's father in Forlì, Ignazio (1720-97), published as Op. 1, *ca.* 1770, by Welcker. In NOTES XIX (1962) 516-518 Igor Kipnis reviews a mod. ed. (Peters) of G. B. Cirri's 6 Vc/bass sons. Op. 16 and quotes his life dates as 1724-1808.

160. Cf. Burney/HISTORY II 880; GROVE VII 821-822 (Rudge & Heron-Allen), with further references; BRITISH UNION II 627; DMF XXXIII (1980) 353.

161. Cf. MGG IX 1550-1551 (Cudworth); BRITISH UNION II 732-733.

162. Cf. Bone/GUITAR 322.

163. Cf. MGG VII 476-477 (Cudworth); BRITISH UNION I 564-565.

164. Cf. GROVE VI 187 (Trend); BRITISH UNION II 742.

as well as "Six Petites Sonates" for piano or harpsichord (*ca.* 1775).[165] Barthélemon, in particular, deserves to be brought out of his obscurity by a reliable modern edition of some of his best "solo" sonatas.[166] The S/bass setting was outmoded by his time, but the pre-Romantic sentiment of his music and his technical exploitation of the violin were more than up to date.

165. Cf. Pohl/MOZART I 163-165; La Laurencie/ÉCOLE II 357-368, including brief exx.; Terry/BACH 87; GROVE I 461-462 (Loewenberg), with reference to a further biographic study by Pincherle; BRITISH UNION I 87-88 (along with listings of solo and acc'd. keyboard sons. by both his wife and daughter).

166. The only "mod." ed. known here is that of Op. 10/2 in e, in Jensen/VIOLIN-m No. 15.

Chapter XX

Great Britain in Clementi's Day

Clementi: Periods, Works, Facts

Our most important Italian in London and our last main composer to discuss in this volume on the Classic sonata is **Muzio Clementi** (1752[1]-1832), the man most nearly entitled to stand alongside, Haydn
1a and Mozart among Beethoven's immediate predecessors. Clementi's life may be divided, at least for our purposes, into seven periods. His period of training began in his native city of Rome, under teachers of no historical renown, and continued some 120 miles southwest of London, apparently as intensive self guidance, when, at the age of fourteen (1766), he was "bought of his father for seven years" by a young English gentleman resident in Dorsetshire.[2] His second period may be said to start with his move to London in 1773 and to include his first publications, performances, and orchestral conducting during the next seven years.[3] His third period, 1780 to 1784, covers his travels to Paris, Vienna (where the celebrated meeting with Mozart took place in 1781), and Lyons (during a prolonged but thwarted love affair[4]). His fourth period, 1784 to 1796, saw some of his most active years (especially 1786) as sonata and symphony composer, performer, and orchestral conductor in London, including close contacts and some rivalry with Haydn, Pleyel, and other musical stars on the scene.[5]

The fifth period, 1797-1802, introduced Clementi the businessman.

1. The principal study of the man and his music is now Plantinga/CLEMENTI, reviewed by W.S. Newman, in NINETEENTH-CENTURY I (1977-78) 261-265 (with author's reply in II 1978-79 192-193), and by J.C. Graue, in JAMS XXXI (1978) 529-535. Previously, from 1913, the principal biographical study had been the pub. diss. Unger/CLEMENTI, digested in English in Saint-Foix/CLEMENTI, along with some further facts and interpretations, but too little noted in standard sources like MGG II 1487-1496 and GROVE II 345-347.

2. Cf. Unger/CLEMENTI 6-11.

3. Cf. Unger/CLEMENTI 11-19. Concrete evidence is lacking for the "most brilliant, hardly precedented success" during these years that is credited to him in GROVE II 345.

4. Cf. Unger/CLEMENTI 44, 49-63; Saint-Foix/CLEMENTI 358-359.

5. Cf. Unger/CLEMENTI 64-89.

Music publishing and instrument manufacturing, chiefly of pianos,[6] were added to his current teaching, transcriptions, writing (including the *Introduction to the Art of Playing On the Piano Forte,* first published by himself in 1801), and some further composing. But now he no longer performed in public.[7] The sixth period, 1802 to 1810, though marred by severe losses both personal and business, found him traveling far and wide again, visiting such main centers as Paris, St. Petersburg, Berlin, Dresden, Leipzig, Rome, and Vienna (where he and Beethoven met in 1807 only after breaking through months of absurd protocol).[8] And the seventh period, 1810 to 1832, which was spent in London except for considerable travel from 1816 to 1827, takes in the late sonatas, symphonies, and other last works composed up to 1825, the final musical activities up to 1828, and his 4 years of retirement.[9]

Since Clementi was born twenty years after Haydn and four before Mozart, yet outlived Beethoven by five years, it is less surprising that we find this eventual octogenarian in close touch and on an almost equal footing with each of the three Viennese masters at one time or another (recall the chart early in SCE XIV). He came somewhat closer to Haydn than to the other two in his character, professional dealings, and increasing successes. In his eightfold capacity as composer, pianist, director, transcriber, teacher, writer, publisher, and manufacturer he was a man of more diverse musical activities than Haydn, as he was a man of broader cultural interests (including a fine command of languages).[10] On the other hand, the scope of his composing was much 10a
narrower, being confined to instrumental music, and to but a few instrumental categories at that—solo and ensemble sonatas, symphonies, a few concertos, and shorter piano works. Furthermore, the extant sonatas by Clementi number well under half of those by Haydn, 123 as against 283, although Clementi left 22 more in the solo, and within 6 as many in the accompanied, keyboard categories.

Specifically, the sonatas by Clementi that can be identified here include 79 of the solo keyboard type (counting in the Sonatinas Op. 36, the "Deux Caprices en forme de sonates," Op. 47, and those many acc'd. sons. that survived only as solos), 35 of the accompanied keyboard type (K & Vn-or-Fl, or K & Vn & Vc), and 9 for 2 players at one or 2 keyboard instruments. To account for these sonatas and provide a reference tool for further discussion it is necessary to make one more

6. Cf. the delightful discussion in Loesser/PIANOS 259-267.
7. Cf. Unger/CLEMENTI 95-113.
8. Cf. Unger/CLEMENTI 114-181; also, Thayer/BEETHOVEN II 23-24, 102-105, 131, 158; Anderson/BEETHOVEN I 243, 267.
9. Cf. Unger/CLEMENTI 182-283.
10. Cf. Unger/CLEMENTI 115-116, 274-275.

of our lists that collates conflicting opus numbers, first editions and
dates, and certain other editions, past and present, insofar as information is now available. One can only hope for an early publication of
the exhaustive thematic index of Clementi's works long in preparation
by the Clementi specialists Walter Howard and Irmgard Auras in
Wenum b/Apeldoorn, the Netherlands.[11] The best such list now
available is the one that fills the second half of Riccardo Allorto's
12a recent book on Clementi's sonatas.[12] This list, arranged in the approximately chronological order of the original opus numbers, gives the
incipit for each first movement (only), the inscriptions and meters of all
movements, and the key of each movement not in the tonic; the publishers, available dates, and varying opus numbers of at least a few of
up to 9 re-editions among some 150 early publications of his works[13]
by at least 45 publishers in 7 countries (SCE IV, with list); the volume,
if any, in which each sonata occurs in the incomplete *Oeuvres complettes*
issued in 13 "cahiers" or volumes by Breitkopf & Härtel under Clemen-
14a ti's supervision between 1804 and about 1819;[14] some representative
modern editions; and numerous phonograph recordings. Although it
supersedes Paribeni's inadequate list, without incipits,[15] Allorto's list
still suffers from errors, omissions, inconsistencies, incomplete references, and the lack of either an index or an independent numbering system to reconcile the conflicting opus numbers.

The following list is arranged according to the approximately
chronological opus numbers of Clementi's presumed first editions, as
16a given by Allorto[16] and as used in subsequent references here. When a
later first edition has a conflicting opus number, the latter has an "a"
added here (as in Op. la published in Paris). When certain sonatas in
a new edition are actually reprints (such as Op. la/2) they are omitted
here except in cross references. Cross references are made here to the
conflicting opus numbers of early re-editions on the Continent, which

11. Cf. MUSICA XIV (1960) 117-118; MEM XV (1960) 40-41 (Howard). Important new bibliographic and biographic information by Mr. Howard has begun to appear serially in *Blätter aus dem Clementi-Archiv* (The Hague: Martinus Nijhoff, 5 issues between Aug., 1961, and Aug., 1962).

12. Allorto/CLEMENTI 67-138. Cf. the reviews by Dale in ML XLI (1960) 58-61, and by LaRue in NOTES XVII (1960) 572-573.

13. MUSICA XIV (1960) 117.

14. CLEMENTI OEUVRES-m; one of the extant sets is at the Library of Congress. Cf. Unger/CLEMENTI 141-145; HOFMEISTER 1828 (Whistling), pp. 475, 523, 582, 616, 1150; HOFMEISTER 1844 II, p. 139; MGG II 1491. For the approximate year of "Cahier" XIII, with plate no. 2840, cf. Deutsch/NUMBERS 9.

15. Paribeni/CLEMENTI 233-240.

16. But read "Op. XXIII" for "Op. XXII," "Bailleux" for "Baillard," and Opp. 37/2, 1, 3 and 38/1, 3, 2, respectively, in Allorto/CLEMENTI 108, 83, 80. Allorto's references to CLEMENTI OEUVRES-m are wrong in 12 instances.

have often become better known than the original numbers and are still used in the convenient though no longer adequate collation of editions of "solo" sonatas (only) in GROVE II 348-349.[17] Cross references are also made to Breitkopf's "Volksausgabe" of 64 solo sonatas in 3 volumes (*ca.* 1855), which though no longer in print is still the most complete edition. And cross references are made to certain other editions, chiefly those now available.[18] The 12 sonatas "composées dans le stile du celebre Scarlati par Muzio Clementi" are not included because they are actually by Scarlatti except for one by Soler and one that remains unidentified; but an earlier edition confirms that Clementi was no plagiarist.[19] Allorto's dates are revised in our list where better or more exact information could be found.[20] In our references to later editions, A. = Taylor/CLEMENTI-m (Augener), B. & H. = Breitkopf & Härtel, C. = CLASSICI-m I No. 8, D. = Dawes/CLEMENTI-m (Schott), G. = Clementi's own *Gradus ad Parnassum*,[21] H. = Hughes/CLEMENTI-m (G. Schirmer), L. & B. = Longman & Broderip, M = Mirovitch/CLEMENTI-m (Marks), O = ORGANUM-m, P. = Piccioli/CLEMENTI-m (Curci), R. = Ruthardt/CLEMENTI-m (the Peters ed. of 24 sons. in 4 vols., of which the 12 sons. in the first 2 vols. correspond to those in the 2 vols. published as G. Schirmer's Library 385 and 386), S. = Schmitt/CLEMENTI-m (Universal), T. = TRÉSOR-m, and Z. = Zeitlin & Goldberger/CLEMENTI-m (G. Schirmer). Note that the sonatas in all these later editions to which cross references are made appear only as keyboard solos, even though our list shows that some (if not still others, including Op. 1) originally had accompaniments. The GROVE list also collates the Holle, Litolff, Cotta, Sénart (Wyzewa & Gastoué/
CLEMENTI-m), and older Schott editions. 21a

Our discussion of Clementi's sonatas may begin with a few random historical circumstances of interest, then proceed to a summary of their structural plans, an examination of their most characteristic style traits, and a consideration of their significance in the larger perspective of

17. Revised from Dale/CLEMENTI 153-154. The less convenient, over-all list in MGG II 1490-1491 includes early eds. Challier/TABELLE 2-4 still provides the best collation of 19th-c. eds. of the solo sons., including incipits of first mvts.

18. Further, less accessible, mod. eds. are given in Allorto's thematic index.

19. Cf. Allorto/CLEMENTI 39-41; Kirkpatrick/SCARLATTI 410. These 12 sons. were included in CLEMENTI OEUVRES-m V/3-14, but with an editorial note explaining the misascription; 2 still appear as his in CLASSICI-m I No. 8, pp. 2-8.

20. Chiefly in BRITISH UNION I 197-200, Johansson/FRENCH *passim*, and Saint-Foix/CLEMENTI. Several eds. published in Clementi's lifetime but after 1800 are listed in HOFMEISTER 1815 and 1828, and in Cat. ROYAL 86-88 (without dates).

21. Composed late in his career, 1816-25, the complete 3 vols. of this important work were still advertised in the Augener catalogue as of this writing (1961).

Clementi's Extant Sonatas

Original op. no. and key	Op. no. used in GROVE (or elsewhere)	Original scoring	Probable first ed.	*Oeuvres complettes* (B. & H.)	*Volksausgabe* (B. & H.)	A few later, more accessible eds.	Index to Allorto/ CLEMENTI
A♭		H	(Paris MS, 1765)				7-8, 69
1/1, E♭		H-or-P	Welcker, 1771?				8, 16, 69-71
1/2, G		"	"				"
1/3, B♭	(1a/2)	"	"				"
1/4, F		"	"				"
1/5, A	33/3 (1a/4)	"	"		II/39		"
1/6, E		"	"				"
2/1, E♭		H-or-P & Fl-or-Vn	Welcker, 1779?	XIII/1			10-16, 71-74
2/2, C	2/1 (30; 37/1)	"	"	III/4	I/1	P. II/8; R. I/1; etc.	"
2/3, G		"	"	XIII/2			"
2/4, A	2/2 (31; 37/2)	"	"	III/5	I/2	T. X/2	"
2/5, F		"	"				"
2/6, B♭	2/4	"	"	III/6	I/3	S. V/26; T. X/3	"
3/1, C	(16/1; 42/1)	P-or-H, duo	Welcker, *ca.* 1780	IV/4		Z. 4	16, 74-77
3/2, E♭	(16/2; 42/2)	"	"	IV/5		Z. 5	"
3/3, G	(16/3; 42/3)	"	"	IV/6		Z. 6	"
3/4, F		K & Fl-or-Vn	"	XIII/3			"
3/5, B♭		"	"	XIII/4			"
3/6, C		"	"	XIII/5			"
4/1, D	(37/2)	P-or-H & Vn & Fl	Welcker, 1780		III/48	(many	16, 49-50, 78-80
4/2, E♭	(37/1)	"	"		II/47	mod. eds.,	"
4/3, C	(37/3)	"	"		III/49	but only	"
4/4, G	(38/1)	"	"		III/50	as solo	"
4/5, F	(38/3)	"	"		III/52	piano	"
4/6, B♭	(38/2)	"	"		III/51	sonatinas)	"
1a/1, F	33/1	P-or-H	Bailleux, 1780	V/15	II/37		17, 80-82
1a/3, G	33/2	"	"	V/16	II/38		"
1a/5, a		"	"			G. III/69	"
1a/6, B♭		2 Ps-or-Hs	"	IV/7		H. no. 2	"
5/1, B♭		P-or-H & Vn	Bailleux, 1782	XII/1			17-18, 83-85
5/2, F		"	"	XII/1			"
5/3, E♭	5/3	"	"	XII/1		M. III, p. 19	"
6/1, C		P-or-H, duo	Bailleux, *ca.* 1782	XII/8		*Edition Peters* 1978a, no. 4	17-18, 85-87

6/2, E♭	35/2 (39)	P-or-H & Vn	“	III/9	II/43	A. IV/19	“
6/3, E		“	“				“
7/1, E♭	7/1	H-or-P	Artaria, 1782	I/11	I/4	T. X/4	18-20, 88-89
7/2, C	7/2	“	“	III/7	I/5		“
7/3, g	7/3	“	“	I/12	I/6	P. III/15; R. IV/20; etc.	‘
8/1, g	30/1 (29/1)	P-or-H	Castaud, 1784	I/8	II/34	T. XVIII/1	26, 89-90
8/2, E♭	30/2 (29/2)	“	“	I/9	II/35	T. XVIII/2	“
8/3, B♭	30/3 (29/3)	“	“	I/10	II/36	T. XVIII/3	“
9/1, B♭	9/1	H-or-P	Artaria, 1783	VI/3	I/7	A. IV/18	20-22, 90-91
9/2, C	9/2	“	“	VI/4	I/8		“
9/3, E♭	9/3	“	“	VI/5	I/9	D. No. 4; T. XVIII/4	“
10/1, A	10/1	H-or-P	Toricella, 1783	VIII/2	I/10	T. XVIII/5	22-25, 92-93
10/2, D	10/2	“	“	VIII/3	I/11		“
10/3, B♭	10/3	“	“	VIII/4	I/12	O. V/4	“
11, E♭	20	P	Kerpen, 1784	VI/7	I/22	A. III/15	26-28, 93-94
12/1, B♭	12/1	P	Preston, 1784	I/1	I/13	R. I/2	28-30, 94-97
12/2, E♭	12/2	P	“	I/2	I/14	A. II/10; R. IV/19, etc.	“
12/3, F	12/3	P	“	I/3	I/15		“
12/4, E♭	12/4	P	“	I/4	I/16	P. II/10; R. III/13; etc.	“
12/5, B♭		2 Ps	“			H. no. 1	“
13/1, G		P & Vn-or-Fl	Clementi, 1785	X/4			30-31, 97-99
13/2, C	13/2	“	“	X/5			“
13/3, E♭		“	“	X/6			“
13/4, B♭	14/1	“	“	X/1	I/17	O. V/18	“
13/5, F	14/2	“	“	X/2	I/18		“
13/6, f	14/3	“	“	X/3	I/19	D. No. 1; M. III, p. 33	“
14/1, C	(16/1)	P, duo	Clementi, 1786	IV/1		ii=G. I/14; Z. 1	30, 32-33, 99-101
14/2, F	(16/2)	“	“	IV/2		Z. 2	“
14/3, E♭	(16/3)	“	“	IV/3		Z. 3	“
15/1, E♭		P+Vn	Clementi, 1786	X/7			30, 32-33, 101-103
15/2, C		“	“	X/8			“
15/3, B♭		“	“	XII/4			“
{16, D “La Chasse”	17	P	L. & B., 1786	XI/4	I/20		33, 103
20, C	19	P-or-H	L. & B., *ca.* 1787	VI/6	I/21		33, 104-105
21/1, D		P-or-H & Fl & Vc	L. & B., 1788	VII/1			33, 105-106

Clementi's Extant Sonatas (Continued)

Original op. no. and key	Op. no. used in GROVE (or elsewhere)	Original scoring	Probable first ed.	*Oeuvres complettes* (B. & H.)	*Volksausgabe* (B. & H.)	A few later, more accessible eds.	Index to Allorto/ CLEMENTI
21/2, G		“	“	VII/2			“
21/3, C		“	“	VII/3			“
21a, F	21	P-or-H	Artaria, 1788	VIII/1	I/23		36, 109-110
22/1, D		P-or-H & Fl & Vc	Dale, 1791	VII/4			33, 106-108
22/2, G		“	“	VII/5			“
{22/3, C "La Chasse"		“	“	VII/6	I/23		“
23/1, E♭	24/1	P-or-H	L. & B., *ca.* 1790	I/5	I/24	A. I; P. III/17	33, 35-36, 108-109
23/2, F	24/2	“	“	I/6	II/25	P. III/14; R. III 14; etc.	“
23/3, E♭	24/3	“	“	I/7	II/26	P. III/16; R. IV/21; etc.	“
25/1, C	25/1	P	Dale, 1791?	II/4	II/27	R. IV/22; S. IV/22; etc.	36-39, 110-113
25/2, G	25/2	P	“	II/5	II/28	P. I/3; R. III/15; etc.	“
25/3, B♭	25/3	P	“	II/6	II/29	S. V/25	“
25/4, A	26/1	P	“	II/1	II/30	P. II/7; R. IV/23; etc.	“
25/5, f#	26/2	P	“	II/2	II/31	P. II/9; R. I/3; etc.	“
25/6, D	26/3	P	“	II/3	II/32	P. I/1; R. I/4; etc.	“
26, F	27	P-or-H	Preston, *ca.* 1792	XI/8	II/33		113-114
27/1, F	(28/1)	P-or-H & Vn & Vc	L. & B., 1792	IX/4			41-43, 114-116
27/2, D	(28/2)	“	“	IX/5		as a "Trio," G. Schirmer	“
27/3, G	(28/3)	“	“	IX/6			“
29/1, C		P & Vn & Vc	Dale, *ca.* 1795	VIII/5		O. V/1	41-43, 116-118
{29/2, E♭ "Chasse"		“	“	VIII/6			“
29/3, G		“	“	VIII/7			“
31/1, F	(33/1; 36/1)	P & Fl-or-Vn ± Vc	Artaria, 1794	VII/8			41-43, 118-119
31/2, D	(33/2; 36/2)	“	“				“
31/3, C	(33/3; 36/3)	“	“	VII/7			“
32/1, A	36/1 (33/1; 34/1)	H-or-P	Artaria, 1794	II/7	II/44	P. I/2; R. I/6; etc.	29, 43-45, 119-121
32/2, F	36/2 (33/2; 34/2)	“	“	II/8	II/45	R. I/7; S. I/7; etc.	“

32/3, C	36/3 (33/3; 34/3)	“	“	II/9	II/46	R. II/8; S. II/8; etc.	“
33/2, G	39/2 (37/2)	P	L. & B., *ca.* 1794	IX/2	III/54	P. I/5; R. III/16; etc.	121-122
33a, C	(35/3)	H-or-P & Fl-or-Vn & Vc	Artaria, 1795				122
34/1, C	34/1 (35/1)	P	Clementi, 1795?	V/1	II/40	P. I/6; R. I/5; etc.	45-47; 123-125
34/2, g	34/2 (35/2)	P	“	V/2	II/41	D. No. 2; S. V/28	“
35/1, F	35/1	P-or-H	Preston, *ca.* 1795	III/8	II/42	A. II/8; P. III/18	125
35a/1, C	(36/1)	P ± Vn ± Vc	Preston, 1796	XIII/9			126-127
35a/2, G	(36/2)	“	“	XIII/10			“
35a/3, D “Chasse”	(36/3)	“	“	XIII/11			“
36/1, C		P	L. & B., 1798?	XI/1		(many mod. eds.)	47-50, 127-129
36/2, G		P	“	XI/2		“	“
36/3, C		P	“	XI/3		“	“
36/4, F		P	“	XI/4		“	“
36/5, G		P	“	XI/5		“	“
36/6, D		P	“	XI/6		“	“
37/1, C	39/1 (41/1)	P	L. & B., 1798	IX/1	III/53	R. IV/24; S. IV/24	50-52, 129-131
37/3, D	39/3 (41/3)	P	“	IX/3	III/55	R. III/17; S. III/17	“
40/1, G	40/1 (41/1; etc.)	P	Clementi, 1801-02	III/1	III/56	R. II/9; S. II/9; etc.	52-54; 131-133
40/2, b	40/2 (41/2; etc.)	P	“	III/2	III/57	P. II/11; R. II/10; etc.	“
40/3, d & D	40/3 (41/3; etc.)	P	“	III/3	III/58	P. II/12; R. II/11; etc.	“
41/1, E♭	47/1 (43/1)	P	Mollo, 1804	VI/1	III/60		26-27, 54-57, 133-134
41/2, B♭ “Magic Flute”	47/2 (24/2; 43/2)	P	Storace, 1789	VI/2	III/61	P. I/4; R. II/12; etc.	“
46, B♭	46	P	Clementi, 1820		III/59		57, 134-135
47/1, e	“Capriccio”	P	Clementi, *ca.* 1821		III/60	S. V/31	57-59, 135-136
47/2, C & b	“Capriccio”	P	“		III/61	D. No. 3; C., p. 62 (i only); S. V/32	“
50, 1, A	50/1	P	Clementi, 1821		III/62	S. V/30	59-62, 136-138
50/2, d	50/2	P	“		III/63	S. V/27	“
50/3, g “Didone abbandonata”	50/3	P	“		III/64	P. III/13; R. III/18; etc.	“

22a sonata history.[22] On the autograph of the "Sonata per Cembalo" in A♭ that was composed at the age of 13, opening our list of Clementi's sonatas, is written "No. 20." Since the 3 movements of this work are reported already to show competent workmanship,[23] it is not hard to believe that the long, 56-year span of his known sonata production, from 1765 to 1821, may actually have been heralded by still earlier sonatas. Presumably the sonatas of Op. 1, dedicated to his young English protector, were composed in England, although they, too, prove still to be marked only by the competence, not yet virtuosity and expressive qualities, that were to distinguish Clementi's piano writing. It is possible that Clementi's accompanied sonatas Op. 2 were written in cognizance of Christian Bach's solo sonatas Op. 5 (*ca.* 1768),[24] and his accompanied and duet sonatas Op. 3 in cognizance of the latter's similar sets Opp. 15 and 18 (1778 and *ca.* 1780). Presumably Clementi's accompanied sonatas Opp. 5 and 6 were composed to suit Paris tastes, and his solo sonatas Opp. 7, 9, and 10 to suit Viennese tastes, all during the travels of his "third period."

It was at the Vienna imperial court on December 24, 1781 that the well-known encounter between Clementi and Mozart took place, as prearranged by Francis Joseph II and as first reported in print in
25a 1805.[25] Among the pieces played by Clementi on that occasion were his Sonata in B♭, Op. 41/2 (to use, as always, the number preferred in our foregoing list), followed by the Toccata in the same key, Op. 11/2, a single movement in "sonata form" that is chiefly interesting for

22. The principal studies of Clementi's sons. besides Allorto/CLEMENTI are Paribeni/CLEMENTI (1921) and the (woefully unindexed) diss. Stauch/CLEMENTI (1930), both being substantial, interesting books, though marred by (opposite) chauvinistic slants. Shorter surveys of interest are to be found in Shedlock/SONATA 131-142, the general preface and preface to each of the 20 sons. in Wyzewa & Gastoué/CLEMENTI-m, Girdlestone/CLEMENTI, Saint-Foix/FORERUNNER (superseding the article in RDM II [1918] 149-161), Egert/FRÜHROMANTIKER 21-31, and Dale/CLEMENTI. Dalrymple/CLEMENTI is a master's thesis in which a detailed style-critical analysis is made of 6 sons. (Opp. 41/2, 33/2, 25/5, 40/2, 40/3, and 50/3, in the numbering of our foregoing list). More recent is the unpublished Ph.D. diss. by Sister Alice Eugene Tighe, "Muzio Clementi and his Sonatas Surviving as Solo Piano Works" (University of Michigan, 1964).

23. Saint-Foix/CLEMENTI 353-354. Cf. the preface to Wyzewa & Gastoué/CLEMENTI-m I; Allorto/CLEMENTI 7-8.

24. But cf. Allorto/CLEMENTI 11-12.

25. Cf. Unger/CLEMENTI 25-31. In chronological order, the main, only slightly divergent, contemporary reports include 1) an account published while Clementi was in Berlin in 1805 with his new, ill-fated bride, this account being the basis for 2 further accounts published in Vienna in 1813 (Unger/CLEMENTI 26); 2) Clementi's own version (partly trans. in Saint-Foix/CLEMENTI 357), as related in 1806 to his pupil L. Berger but not published until 1829, in Berger/CLEMENTI; 3) a version published by the Italian writer G. Bridi (cf. Unger/CLEMENTI 30-31); and 4) the version in columns 657-658 of the extended necrological account in AMZ XXXIV (1832) 653-664.

its exploitation of double-3ds, -4ths, -5ths, and -6ths.[26] Clementi confirmed his playing of these 2 works in his note appended to the title of Op. 41/2 in its first and later editions, adding specifically that Mozart was present. But this first edition did not appear until 1804, 13 years after Mozart's death and 23 years after their encounter, explaining the late opus number of the sonata and the late publicizing of the encounter. The purpose of Clementi's note, supposedly, was to establish priority for the opening idea of Op. 41/2, composed 10 years before the main idea of the "Ouverture" in E♭ to *Die Zauberflöte* by Mozart (K.V. 620). However, as numerous authors have variously concluded, the thematic relationship is not especially significant, since the idea itself is characteristic of the period and can be found in similar guises elsewhere, the resemblance lasts only 2 measures, and Clementi merely states or restates the idea homophonically whereas Mozart extends it and develops it fugally.[27]

In general, the encounter between Clementi and Mozart was reported to have ended with about equal honors for both.[28] Yet nothing has done more damage to Clementi's reputation than Mozart's vindictive, oft-quoted letters written soon after the encounter, unless it be the distorted view imparted since about 1865 by Tausig's infamous edition of the *Gradus ad Parnassum* (containing only the 29 most mechanical of its 100 masterpieces of piano technique, science, and poetry). Mozart's first two, almost identical disparagements of Clementi as a mere "mechanicus," in the letters of January 12 and 16, 1782,[29] are incorporated in another letter he still chose to write two and a half years later (June 7, 1783):

> Well, I have a few words to say to my sister about Clementi's sonatas. Everyone who either hears them or plays them must feel that as compositions they are worthless. They contain no remarkable or striking passages except those in sixths and octaves. And I implore my sister not to practice these passages too much, so that she may not spoil her quiet, even touch and that her hand may not lose its natural lightness, flexibility and smooth rapidity. For after all what is to be gained by it? Supposing that you do play sixths and octaves with the utmost velocity (which no one can accomplish, not even

26. On the confusion of op. nos. cf. Allorto/CLEMENTI 26-28, 93-94, 133-134. The Toccata may be found in TRÉSOR-m XVIII 124; RICORDI ARTE-m V (not III) no. 14; CLASSICI-m I No. 8, p. 17; etc.

27. The resemblance was first specifically noted in Berger/CLEMENTI 240. Cf. Abert/MOZART I 427-428; Stauch/CLEMENTI 43-44; Heuss in ZFM XIII (1931) 187-188; Egert/FRÜHROMANTIKER 26-28; King/MOZART 143-144; Allorto/CLEMENTI 55-56.

28. The emperor's slight nod in Mozart's direction is reported in DITTERSDORF 251 (originally published in 1801).

29. Anderson/MOZART III 1180 and 1181-1182 (with further details of the encounter).

> Clementi) you only produce an atrocious chopping effect and nothing else whatever. Clementi is a *ciarlatano,* like all Italians. He writes *Presto* over a sonata or even *Prestissimo* and *Alla breve,* and plays it himself *Allegro* in 4/4 time. I know this is the case, for I have heard him do so. What he really does well are his passages in thirds; but he sweated over them day and night in London. Apart from this, he can do nothing, absolutely nothing,
> 30a for he has not the slightest expression or taste, still less, feeling.[30]

To be sure, in 1806 Clementi acknowledged to his pupil L. Berger that preoccupation with brilliance, the novelty of double-note passages, and extemporizations did still characterize his playing at the time of the encounter, and that only later, after hearing outstanding singers and knowing the improved, rounder-toned English pianos, did he turn to nobler, more lyrical styles.[31]

Op. 13 was the first of the many sets Clementi published himself. Opp. 14 and 15 were dedicated to the young lady in Lyons, "M.lle M. V. Imbert Colomés," whose father had blocked their elopement.[32] The piano duet movement Op. 14/1 (not 3)/ii was republished as a solo in *Gradus ad Parnassum* I no. 14, with Clementi's inscription from Virgil, "Tulit alter honores," as a gentle admonishment to his former pupil J. B. Cramer. Cramer had plagiarized this movement as he had
33a Op. 2/2.[33] The Sonata in D Op. 16 was but one of at least 4 sonatas by Clementi called "La Chasse" (including Opp. 22/3, 29/2, and 35a/3). Op. 32/1 in A reportedly was one of Clementi's own favorites.[34] Opp. 32/3 and 34/1 were arranged from concertos by the composer, and Opp. 34/2 and 40/3 from symphonies.[35] The first of Clementi's sonatas to be reviewed in the Leipzig *Allgemeine musikalische Zeitung*—Opp. 37/1, 33/2, and 37/3, reprinted as Op. 39/1-3—were greeted by Rochlitz chiefly as being free of double-note difficulties and other, earlier *bizarrerie* (the same word with which Beethoven was so often stigmatized), yet with no sacrifice of originality or force; only the currently popular but too frequent imitations of the Scottish bagpipe were "to be censured" (especially in Op. 37/3/iii).[36]

Between Op. 41 in 1804 and Op. 46 in 1820 there was an unbroken gap of 15 years in Clementi's publication of sonatas.[37] The last and

30. As trans. in Anderson/MOZART III 1267-1268.

31. Berger/CLEMENTI 239, written in 1829 in answer to Nissen/MOZART 449, where Mozart's opinion, in his letter of Jan. 16, 1782, was first published (1828).

32. Cf. Saint-Foix/CLEMENTI 358-359; Saint-Foix/FORERUNNER 89, 91.

33. Cf. Unger/CLEMENTI 213, 34-35; Saint-Foix/CLEMENTI 374-375.

34. Unger/CLEMENTI 135; Saint-Foix/CLEMENTI 368.

35. Cf. Allorto/CLEMENTI 29, 45-47; Unger/BEETHOVENIANA 158-160 (but the original English title and dedication of Op. 40 suggest that this fine set was composed in London well before Clementi's arrival in Vienna in late 1802).

36. AMZ I (1798-99) 86-88 (with thematic incipits in order "to avoid confusion").

37. Clementi's return to sonata writing is warmly welcomed in the en-

perhaps the finest set, Op. 50, was dedicated, significantly enough, to his most important Italian contemporary and musical complement, Cherubini, who was 8 years younger than he.[38] In this set the outstanding Sonata in g, no. 3, was the swan song of his sonata publications, although it may have been composed well before Op. 50/2 in d.[39] Since the title "La Chasse" goes only skin-deep into the rhythm and figuration of the 4 sonatas that bear it, the title of Op. 50/3, "Didone abbandonata, Scena tragica," must be recognized as the only truly programmatic title in Clementi's sonatas. But a more detailed programme is not offered in this work, no more than in Tartini's S/bass sonata Op. 1/10, published 87 years earlier (1734; SBE 192), in the same key, with the same title, and with some curiously similar ideas (e.g., cf. Tartini/ii/49-54 and Clementi/i/5-8). One can only assume that the first allegro, with the inscription "deliberando e meditando," concerns the brooding of Dido over the fateful departure of Aeneas; that the second movement, "Adagio dolente," concerns the desolate loneliness without him; and that the finale, "Allegro agitato e con disperazione," concerns the desperate, suicidal course Dido decides she
must take.[40] 40a

Clementi: Styles, Forms, Significance

A statistical tabulation of Clementi's sonatas shows a slight majority of 3- as against 2-movement sonatas. The latter are found especially in the earlier and the accompanied sets. It is interesting that during the revision of his earlier sonatas for the *Oeuvres complettes,* Clementi decided to amplify the "Italian plan" of Op. 2/2 in C by adding a middle movement, a "Larghetto cantabile in F" (which has yet to appear in its proper place with this son.).[41] Only rarely did Clementi use 4 movements, as he did in Op. 40/1 in G, in the order F-S-F-F. But slow introductions occur in 7 sonatas, including such fine works as Opp. 40/2, 47/2, and 50/3. In the 2-movement sonatas, both movements are usually fast or moderate in tempo, although the order S-F occurs occasionally, too (as in Op. 6/2). The order F-S-F pre-

---

thusiastic, full reviews of Opp. 46 and 47 in AMZ XXIII (1821) 261-264 and 285-288.

38. Cf. Riehl/CHARAKTERKÖPFE II 245.

39. Cf. Wyzewa & Gasṭoué/CLEMENTI-m II/20; Allorto/CLEMENTI 60.

40. Schindler questioned Clementi on the meaning of this work in 1827 and used his findings to preface a new ed. of it issued by André in 1856 (Schindler/BEETHOVEN 223). In a detailed, laudatory review of all 3 sons. in Op. 50 Rochlitz did not attempt to impute any further literalities to Op. 50/3 (AMZ XXIV [1822] 629-635); cf., also, Riehl/CARAKTERKÖPFE II 242-243, Shedlock/SONATA 140-142, Allorto/CLEMENTI 60-62.

41. Cf. pp. 107 and 113 in Simon/CLEMENTI, which is an interesting survey of Clementi MSS at the Library of Congress.

dominates in the 3-movement sonatas, the chief exceptions being F-F-F (as in Op. 37/3) and S-F-F (as in Op. 29/2).

In these last exceptions the key remains the same for all movements. Otherwise the middle movement is most often in the subdominant key and sometimes in the dominant. It is in the opposite mode occasionally, as in Op. 40/3, which is in d (slow introduction), D, d, and D-d-D (finale). It is also in the submediant occasionally, as in both "Caprices" Op. 47. The modulatory slow introduction to the second of these "Caprices" starts in C, in a "Neapolitan" or lowered-second-step relationship to the home key of b. Over 90 per cent of Clementi's sonatas are in major keys, with strong preference shown for C, E♭, G, F, B♭, and D (in that order). Yet, as usual, among the few examples in minor keys, most of them late works, are some of his finest sonatas. None of his keys has more than 4 sharps or flats. Clementi shows some (but not a marked) tendency to interrelate the outer movements of a sonata thematically. In Op. 13/6 in f, the "fate" or ". . .—" motive occurs in these movements, as again in Op. 41/2 in B♭, where reminders of the (eventual) "Magic Flute" theme in the first movement are also heard in the finale.

In a broad sense, "sonata form" prevails without question in Clementi's first movements and in most of the later finales that are no longer rondos. But his "sonata form" is a flexible, personal application, with no feeling of formalism or conscious obligation to any particular design that was to become standard in nineteenth-century textbooks.[42] His pleasure in concentrating on a single idea is a main clue to these forms. They are often almost monothematic. To be sure, there are clearly contrasted themes from time to time, as in Op. 37/1/i/33-53 or Op. 34/1/i/37-48 (Ex. 123). But more often the "second theme" derives directly from the first, as already in Op. 9/2/i,[43] or it relates so closely in its rhythmic pattern that it easily slips back into the first theme as in Op. 40/2/i, mss. 4-6, 39-40, and 56-57 of the "Allegro . . ."

The desire to explore such themes to the fullest causes Clementi to add further, sometimes highly discursive episodes to already intensive developments, as is true right up to the finale of Op. 50/3 in g, where 30 measures in and around the key of C are inserted near the middle of a movement that seldom loses sight of the initial theme. But this discursiveness must not be dismissed peremptorily as a fault. If

42. Nearly the opposite view is maintained in Barford/FORMALISM (especially p. 207), with explicit but quite unsupported references to an "eighteenth-century conception of sonata-form."

43. Cf. Allorto/CLEMENTI 22-25 (with exx.); Stauch/CLEMENTI 41-42 (with exx.).

Ex. 123. From the first movement of Muzio Clementi's Sonata in C, Op. 34/1 (after Ruthardt/CLEMENTI-m I 62).

Schubert can be allowed his "heavenly length" Clementi must be allowed many pages of delectable length, too. After all, he proved how direct, 43a
simple, and efficient he could be in those impeccable little Sonatinas Op. 36, which must be regarded as both the Classic and the classic model for all sonatinas.[44] Other personal applications of "sonata form" by 44a
Clementi may be traced to his love of harmonic and tonal surprises. Thus, the warmly expressive, sensitive Sonata in f, Op. 13/6, prepares for the return of the opening idea in the first movement by a cadence and pause on the dominant (mss. 82-83), but elides that return by skipping directly to the similar "second theme" in the relative major key. In Op. 16 in D the return occurs on the lowered seventh step, with the restoration of the home key delayed until the second theme returns.

The slow movements in Clementi's most telling solo sonatas are relatively short and more in the nature of florid, introspective adagios than steady, fluent andantes.[45] If they never show quite the originality and ingenuity of the fast movements, the finest of them still reveal much

44. Cf. Allorto/CLEMENTI 47-50.
45. Cf. Stauch/CLEMENTI 68-71.

that is deeply expressive and both melodically and harmonically distinguished. An example is the middle movement in the Sonata in f♯, Op. 25/5, which movement inspired a Romantic interpretation in poetry by the late 19th-century Italian Antonio Fogazzaro.[46] The "Largo" in Op. 12/2 already reveals some of the dramatic runs and sharp dynamic contrasts of Beethoven's slow movements for piano. Whereas this and other earlier slow movements by Clementi are in simple binary or ternary forms, the later ones are more likely to be rondo forms with more returns of the main idea (Op. 40/1/ii).

Many of Clementi's finales are rondos, some without the title (such as the "Presto" in Op. 32/3). Since the tendency in these is to make the episodes out of recastings and developments of the main idea (as in Op. 25/6/iii), and since the tendency in his sonata forms, as we have seen, is to return to the initial idea rather than oppose it with an entirely different one, the two forms often approach each other.[47] In the earlier and lighter sonatas the next most frequent finale is the minuet, with or without trio (as in the acc'd. sons. Opp. 4/1 and 4, respectively, known now as the solo Sonatinas Opp. 37/2 and 38/1).[48] The minuet serves occasionally as a middle movement, too, as still in Op. 29/3. Other dances found more rarely in this position are the polonaise (Op. 27/2) and the siciliana (Op. 27/1). Several sets of variations occur as finales or middle movements (as in Opp. 1a/3 and 22/1, respectively).[49] The themes are mostly ingratiating English airs, such as "Since Then I'm Doom'd This Sad Reverse of Fate to Prove," used in Op. 12/1/iii. But this form drew from Clementi little more than effective *pièces d'occasion.* Attention has been called to the scherzando character of certain movements—especially Opp. 32/1/ii, 32/2/ii, 37/3/ii, and 40/1/iii—as being in the style, though not in the designs or with the title, of the scherzos in Beethoven's Op. 2/2 and 2/3. Clementi did use the title later, in his *Gradus ad Parnassum* (vol. III, nos. 70, 82, and 97). However, apart from the uncertain question of priority,[50] Clementi's scherzando writing has less of the jocular crispness of Beethoven's (or the elfin deftness of Mendelssohn's) than the swift but intense fluency of Brahms's scherzando writing (Ex. 124).

A reading of Clementi's sonatas in chronological order brings home

46. The poem is quoted in full in Allorto/CLEMENTI 38-40.
47. Cf. Stauch/CLEMENTI 65-67.
48. Cf. Stauch/CLEMENTI 72-73.
49. Cf. Stauch/CLEMENTI 73-74; Allorto/CLEMENTI 30, 35-36.
50. Since Clementi's Op. 32 was published by Artaria in 1794, 2 years before Beethoven's Op. 2, Stauch/CLEMENTI 73 is rightly corrected in Allorto/CLEMENTI 43-44, but the composition dates could have been considerably earlier for either or both sets (cf. Kinsky & Halm/BEETHOVEN 7-8).

Ex. 124. From the finale of Muzio Clementi's Sonata in A, Op. 32/1 (after Ruthardt/CLEMENTI-m I 93).

the remarkable evolution that his composing underwent during his long creative career and focuses attention on the principal traits of his style. Before noting these traits individually, we should not overlook a certain consistency of style in spite of the almost diametric changes between Opp. 1 and 50. It might best be summarized as a containment within the bounds of Classic taste. Romantic tendencies have been seen in the chromatic harmony, irregular rhythmic groupings, subjective inscriptions, and other details of his writing.[51] Yet, even in the most surprising and captivating modulations of his late sonatas (as in Op. 47/2/i) Clementi never lets the tonal plan get out of Classic bounds. And even more in his late than his early sonatas there is an economy of texture, a devotion to counterpoint, and a succinctness and neat definition of ideas that set this writing apart from that of Weber, Dussek, Field, and the other young Romantics. Its conservatism in these respects makes all the more noteworthy the warm reception given to his last sonatas by the Romantic-minded critics around 1820 (as cited earlier).[52] He seems

51. E.g., cf. Dale/CLEMENTI 150-152; Egert/FRÜHROMANTIKER 28-31.

52. But misgivings were to be voiced about "the contrapuntal, often cold music" (Schumann/SCHRIFTEN I 11 and II 64, 1834 and 1842), "the stereotyped

never to have forsaken completely the composers who chiefly influenced him from the start (most of whom were still represented in the 50 "Lessons" of his *Introduction to . . . the Piano Forte* of 1801 and in the 4 volumes of his *Practical Harmony,* 1803-1815[53])—that is, D. Scarlatti, J. S. Bach, Friedemann Bach, Emanuel Bach, Handel, and such compatriots in London as Pescetti, Paradisi, Galuppi, and perhaps Vento, Sacchini, and other "moderns."[54]

Between his early and late works Clementi's themes grew in individuality and variety through a richer, more trenchant use of foreign tones, a subtler, more diversified harmonic palette, a finer, more imaginative toying with the rhythmic patterns (but less interest in dance rhythms or dance movements), and a freer, more malleable phrase syntax. Thus, compare the wide-spaced chordal theme in Op. 2/1/i/1-19[55] (starting almost like the opening idea of Brahms's Concerto in d, Op. 15) with the equally wide-spaced and chordal, yet curiously dissonant theme in Op. 50/3/i/16-45. But certain thematic traits do
55a recur often throughout his works, besides that wide spacing. One thinks, for example, of the anacrustic or internal group of four 16th-notes that we have found to be so characteristic of Christian Bach's and Mozart's sonata themes (as in Clementi's Op. 36/6/i/1 and 25/5/i/1 and 3, not to mention the "Magic Flute" theme, again). Or one recalls how the gaiety of the *opera buffa* aria exudes from the many quick themes, early and late, that depend on pert triplet figures, as in nearly all of Op. 25/6/i in D, which is of the same Italian stuff that engendered Figaro's "Largo al factotum . . ." less than a generation later (Ex. 125).

In no respect is Clementi's evolution so clearly manifested, of course,
55b as in his piano writing. He ranks with Frescobaldi and Scarlatti before him as one of the three greatest Italian innovators of the keyboard. Himself a first-class performer praised for his brilliance, precision, nuance, phrasing, and specific technical feats,[56] Clementi well deserves his reputation as the composer who first revealed the potentialities of the

sonata form of old" in Op. 50/3 (Schindler/BEETHOVEN II 223, 1860), and "some of the writing [, which] is formal and old-fashioned, and, at times, too thin . . ." for "the present day" (Shedlock/SONATA 141, 1895).

53. Clementi/HARMONY-m; cf. Heyer/HISTORICAL 61-63. The contents of the *Introduction* are discussed by B. Becherini in RM XLIII (1939) 55-71, and in Parrish/PIANO 219-224.

54. Cf. Allorto/CLEMENTI 8-9.

55. Cf. Allorto/CLEMENTI 23-25 (with exx.).

56. Cf. Gerber/LEXICON I 288; Siebigk/CLEMENTI 7-10 (1801); also, the further contemporary tributes quoted in MGG II 1492 (1784); Unger/CLEMENTI 68 (1786), 70 (1788), 86-87 (1796?); Saint-Foix/FERRARI 460.

Ex. 125. From the contrasting theme in Op. 25/6/i by Muzio Clementi (after Ruthardt/CLEMENTI-m I 49).

piano.[57] Op. 2 (though not yet Op. 1) at once steps boldly into the virtuoso's world of fast octaves, broken octaves and 6ths, double-3ds and -6ths, broken chords, cadenzas invited by *fermata* signs,[58] and rapid passage work in both hands. But by the late 1780's, when he was already discontinuing public performances—that is, during his fourth period, as we have outlined his life—Clementi was shifting his interest from the virtuosic to the purely musical capabilities of the piano. The transformation that he later reported to Berger (as noted previously) and the unquestionable impact of the encounter with Mozart are reflected in the songful melody supported in rich, low sonorities at the start of Op. 34/1/ii, or the essential lyricism throughout a sonata like Op. 25/5 in f♯. Difficult double-3ds still occur in the finale of the latter work, but now they have a harmonic and color interest almost as do those in Chopin's magical "Double-Third Etude."

Following Berger's advice that Opp. 32/3, 34/1, and 40/3 were

57. This aspect of his writing is surveyed, with exx., in Parrish/PIANO 338-357; cf., also, Schlesinger/CRAMER 27-32.

58. As in Op. 2/1/ii/68 or Op. 41/2/37; cf. Berger/CLEMENTI 240; also, SCE V, with ex.

transcriptions of orchestral works,[59] Saint-Foix took the increased color, variety, and textural interest of Clementi's piano writing as evidence that many if not most of the later sonatas originated as orchestral works.[60] However, such thoroughly idiomatic treatment of the piano as prevails in these sonatas hardly comes by accident or at second hand. Another view seems preferable,[61] to the effect that Clementi had orchestral colors and sonorities in mind when he wrote for the piano. In any case, as his texture became almost aseptically spare in the last sonatas, each remaining voice took on increasing significance. What was once a static, murky, or similar keyboard accompaniment, and the weakest feature of the early sonatas, now became an equal participant in the texture. At the same time the violin parts in the accompanied sonatas were elevated from the subordinate status in the early works (including even the "obligato" part in Op. 15) to only slightly more independent parts in Opp. 27 and 29,[62] then dropped entirely after Op. 35a (1796). By the time of the late sonatas, Clementi, even more than Beethoven, became absorbed in polyphony. If not so many examples are afforded as in the more forward-looking *Gradus ad Parnassum,* especially the late, third volume, one can still point to a recherché *fugato* in the sonatas (Op. 40/3/i, at the episode in C) or to several strict canons (as in the 2 canons, direct and by inversion, that comprise Op. 40/1/iii, or the canonic episode in Op. 50/1/ii).

In Riehl's sympathetic, broadly oriented appraisal of Clementi's historical position, published originally in 1861,[63] a statement appears with which the conclusions reached in the present study tally fully:

> I label Clementi the "master of the sonata," not because he wrote the unqualifiedly best but rather the most sonatalike [*sonatenhaftesten*] sonatas; for his entire artist's career was concentrated and resolved in the sonata, and he alone lived and worked with the modern sonata throughout all of its three main periods [pre-, high-, and late-Classic]. One rightly names Haydn, Mozart, Beethoven, and Clementi in a single breath as the chief exponents of the Classic piano sonata. But the three first-named were much too universal for their mastery of the sonata to become the sole signature of their entire artistic reaches. This [restriction] is the case only with Clementi; he stands and falls with the sonata; it marks, in a word, his greatness as [it does] his limitations.[64]

59. Cf. Allorto/CLEMENTI 45; Unger/BEETHOVENIANA 160.

60. Saint-Foix/CLEMENTI 361 and 364 (with special reference to Opp. 32 and 40, as numbered in our list).

61. As in Allorto/CLEMENTI 29, 32.

62. Casella made the cello part anachronistically independent in the "Trio" he arranged from Op. 27/2 (Allorto/CLEMENTI 42, 116; cf., also, pp. 33 and 38).

63. Riehl/CHARAKTERKÖPFE II 231-259.

64. Trans, from Riehl/CHARAKTERKÖPFE II 232-233.

Riehl might have added that Clementi was a less universal sonata composer than the other three because he developed a more precious, restricted style than they. Perhaps because the delicate subtleties of his late works presuppose a specially cultivated taste, the relatively few ardent enthusiasts who have been trying all along to win greater interest in his music are still far from getting a universal response.[65] Perhaps, too—to complete the vicious circle—the response to this music will be greater when the way is better paved by editions of his music and literary guides to it that are more nearly commensurate with the major publications that have been dedicated to Haydn, Mozart, and Beethoven.[66]

As against the more recent pro-Italianism of Paribeni (in line with Torrefranca) and pro-Germanism of Stauch,[67] it is comforting to find Riehl allowing unreservedly for international derivations and influences, as in his references to Clementi's Italianate melody and to his Teutonic harmony, counterpoint, and structural (or intensive developmental) techniques.[68] Furthermore, much as Clementi trained himself on composers of different styles and nationalities, so he exerted his influence on pupils and close followers of different styles and nationalities. J. B. Cramer, John Field, A. S. A. Klengel, and L. Berger were among his most important pupils; I. Moscheles, L. Adam, and F. Kalkbrenner were among his close followers.[69] Whether he was close at some time to F. W. Rust before the latter died in 1796 is not known. But as suggested earlier (SCE XVI, under Rust), the two men resemble no other composers in their mature styles so much as each other, especially in their more poetic, *empfindsam* pages (as in the Sonatas in f♯ by each).

Our chief interest lies, naturally, in Clementi's relationship to the three Viennese masters. Clementi himself was said to have made as his goal the fusion of Haydn's and Mozart's styles.[70] As early as 1783 Haydn thanked Artaria for some "pianoforte Sonatas" by Clementi, presumably the solo sonatas Op. 7 or 9, with the words, "they are very

65. The most successful kind of "propaganda" has been the recording, such as the fine performance of Opp. 13/6, 25/5, and 34/2 by V. Horowitz (Victor LM-1902 [1955], with interesting "Notes" by A. Loesser).

66. It is worth recalling that before CLEMENTI OEUVRES-m, Breitkopf & Härtel had attempted similar publications only of Mozart's and Haydn's works.

67. E.g., cf. Paribeni/CLEMENTI 170 and 193 with Stauch/CLEMENTI 73 and 75-78.

68. Riehl/CHARAKTERKÖPFE II 246. A curious summary of French and Italian derivations in Clementi's art, written in Bern in Oct., 1784, is quoted in Schindler/BEETHOVEN II 233. Something of a balance between Paribeni and Stauch is struck in Allorto/CLEMENTI 63-64.

69. Cf. Unger/CLEMENTI 34-38, 90-93, 132-138, 156-160, 175-177, *et passim*.

70. Cf. the hostile criticism of his symphonies and the vigorous rebuttal in AMZ XIX (1817) 149 and 461-462 (repeated in Unger/CLEMENTI 204-210; summarized in Saint-Foix/CLEMENTI 373-374).

beautiful."[71] Haydn had derived his second from his first theme some ten years earlier (as in H. XVI/21/i), although we have seen too many instances of this practice in the pre-Classic era to make this priority a matter of special concern here.[72] On the other hand, there is an increasing element of dash and display in Haydn's later sonatas (as in H. XVI/50, including double-thirds and octaves) that suggests a full cognizance of his younger contemporary's writing. Certainly the two men were well aware of each other while Haydn was still writing sonatas, in London.[73]

In the years after the encounter with Mozart in 1781, Clementi is known to have thought highly of him.[74] Yet nothing Clementi wrote in a later period comes closer to Mozart's style than the Sonata in B♭, Op. 41/2, brought forth on that occasion. On the other hand, in spite of harsh objections to Clementi in Mozart's letters Mozart could not fail to derive some gain from the brilliance and skill of Clementi's writing. Wyzewa and Saint-Foix believed, for example, that he was influenced by Clementi's ability to work and vary a single idea almost indefinitely.[75]

It is the relationship between Clementi and Beethoven that has evoked the most discussion and reveals the most demonstrable musical significance.[76] The influence worked almost entirely one way in this instance, from the Anglo-Italian to the younger, German composer. After Clementi finally met Beethoven in 1807 and became one of the latter's many publishers he had yet to write only the last of his own sonatas. But by then he was much too strong an individual himself to adapt to trends other than those that were already a part of his nature.[77] Schindler is unequivocal about Beethoven's fondness for Clementi's music. Whereas Beethoven had little interest in Mozart's keyboard music and had nothing by Haydn in the meager library of his last years,

71. Landon/HAYDN 42. The relationship and influences between Haydn and Clementi are the subject of Saint-Foix/HAYDN.

72. It is a matter of concern in Paribeni/CLEMENTI 179-181 and Stauch/CLEMENTI 39-42.

73. Haydn's negative comment on a Clementi symphony, in 1795 (Landon/HAYDN 288), is well known.

74. King/MOZART 18.

75. Saint-Foix/MOZART II 416. In Stauch/CLEMENTI 49-51 this view is expanded, but with reference more to K.V. 533 and 576 than 498a.

76. First emphasis is placed on this relationship throughout Stauch/CLEMENTI. Cf., also, Paribeni/CLEMENTI 177-191 (with exx.); Saint-Foix/FORERUNNER; Parrish/PIANO 349-353 (with exx.); Ringer/CLEMENTI (on sources for the "Eroica" Symphony; with exx.).

77. Clementi probably did compose Op. 40/3 after he had a chance to know Beethoven's "Pathétique" Sonata (first published in 1799), as maintained in Unger/BEETHOVENIANA 158-160; but his slow introduction is not enough like the latter's to justify any claim of clear influence.

says Schindler, "almost all of Clementi's sonatas were on hand. For these he had the greatest preference and placed them in the front rank of pieces appropriate to [the development of] fine piano playing, as much for their lovely, pleasing, fresh melodies as for the well-knit, fluent forms of all the movements."[78] No doubt Beethoven's interest in these sonatas explains his desire that Clementi's relatively inconsequential *Introduction to . . . the Piano Forte* be used in Czerny's instruction of nephew Karl, in preference to Czerny's own or other more detailed methods.[79]

Beethoven may well have heard and played Clementi's sonatas while he was still a youth in Bonn, for as early as 1786 Clementi's accompanied set Op. 13 was known there.[80] At any rate, the "pre-Beethovenisms," as Saint-Foix calls them, can be heard fairly early in Clementi's sonatas, if not already in his Op. 2/1. We have previously noted the suggestions of Beethoven in the dramatic "Largo" of Op. 12/2, in the scherzando movements of Op. 32/1 and 2 (even if not quite Beethoven's sort), and in the persistent ". . .—" motive of Opp. 13/6 and 41/2. Among numerous examples of the last is the clearer one of Op. 34/2 in g, which, deriving from a symphony, is all the more likely to have been an influence on Beethoven's Fifth Symphony. The slow introduction—and an expressive, Beethovian one, at that—already appears in Op. 32/2. In Op. 12/2/i one hears a figure of four 16th-notes, some trills, and some broken octaves like those in Beethoven's Op. 2/3/i. In Op. 32/1/i one hears a development figure and in Op. 34/1 some of the drive in the first movement of Beethoven's "Waldstein" Sonata. In the canons of Op. 40/1/iii are hints of the canonic trio section in Beethoven's Op. 101/ii. But such anticipations can be found almost without end—throughout much of Opp. 7/3[81] and 37/1, for example—because the two composers were, in fact, so close in time and spirit.

Other Italians

The other high- and late-Classic Italians in London left music that is generally agreeable but innocuous, and of much less consequence to the sonata than is Clementi's music. The violinist **Luigi Borghi** (*ca.* 1745-at least 1792), born perhaps in Bologna, studied with Pugnani

78. Schindler/BEETHOVEN II 182. But the works of Haydn and Mozart were also recommended by Beethoven for nephew Karl (Anderson/BEETHOVEN II 495).

79. Cf. Schindler/BEETHOVEN II 183-184; Anderson/BEETHOVEN III 1250, 1308, 1323; Thayer/BEETHOVEN II 375, III 214. In spite of the slight rebuff, Czerny himself was able to write that "Clementi's sonatas . . . will always remain the best school for the pianist, *if one knows how to study them in his spirit*," and that he was able to use them to good effect in teaching Karl (CZERNY 315).

80. Cf. Schiedermair/BEETHOVEN 70 and 370.

81. Cf. Ringer/CLEMENTI.

and may have traveled with him on recital tours. He was in London, except for visits or stays in Munich and Berlin, from at least 1772 to 1792.[82] Torrefranca was interested primarily in Borghi's solo violin concertos Op. 2 (1775), especially Op. 2/2 in E as arranged for harpsichord alone by "il mediocre sonatista" J. S. Schroeter (1782).[83] He argued at length that these concertos, more than the piano concertos of Christian Bach, offered all the ingredients of the Mozart style. And, to justify such a digression in a book devoted to the keyboard sonata, he pointed to Schroeter's reduction as one evidence that the late eighteenth-century keyboard sonata was little more than an imitation of either the symphony or concerto.[84] Torrefranca did not find quite enough support for his Mozart derivations in Borghi's two sets of six S/bass "Solos" or "Sonates" each, first published in 1772 and 1783.[85]

Borghi's style in his "solo" violin sonatas is Mozartean chiefly in the clear phrase grouping, frequent feminine incises based on appoggiaturas, intermittent melodic chromaticism, and occasional specific melodic patterns. There is charm in the melodic ideas and an increase in structural breadth and purpose in Op. 4 as against Op. 1. But there is none of Mozart's genius for original melodic turns, subtle harmonic inflection, or structural inevitability. In their over-all plans, Borghi's sonatas employ the 3-movement sequence most often used by his teacher, F-S-minuet or rondeau (Op. 1/3/iii being a "Rondeau" in "Tempo di Minuet"). But they no longer employ very many of the latter's *galant* mannerisms, especially in Op. 4. Op. 1/5/iii, which is in 3/8 meter and is marked "Presto," comes even closer than the finales in Clementi's Op. 32/1 and 2 to the scherzando style of Beethoven. Borghi's technical exploitation of his instrument is moderate, including such devices as bariolage and *ondeggiando* (Op. 1/6/iii).

The prolific composer of operas and instrumental music, **Tommaso Giordani** (*ca.* 1730-1806), came from Naples to London with

82. These and a few other details about this obscure musician are supplied in Torrefranca/ORIGINI 548, 563; Unger/CLEMENTI 40, 72, 77; DIZIONARIO RICORDI 184; Moser/VIOLINSPIEL 247.

83. Torrefranca/ORIGINI 548-568 and Torrefranca/LONDRA 340-352 (both with extended exx.); the concertos are briefly compared with Schroeter's (to the latter's advantage) in Wolff/SCHROETER 354-356 (with exx.). The publication dates in the present discussion come from BRITISH UNION I 124 and Johansson/FRENCH I 43-44.

84. Torrefranca/ORIGINI 548.

85. For mod. eds. of 6 separate sons. from the 2 sets cf. Altmann/KAMMERMUSIK 234. The sons. are discussed briefly in Moser/VIOLINSPIEL 247-248, but the "Op. 5" mentioned there and in Eitner/QL II 134 is probably the no. given to the Paris and Amsterdam reprints of Op. 4. In Stone/ITALIAN I 223-224 and II 8-9 (thematic index) brief mention is made of 3 acc'd. sons. by Borghi (H-or-P & Vn), which prove to be Napier's re-edition in this scoring of Op. 1/2, 4, and 6 without the middle mvts.

his parents in 1753, spending the rest of his life there and in Dublin.[86] His long list of instrumental works, most of them published and republished between 1770 and 1790, includes numerous sets of keyboard duets, solo keyboard "lessons" and "sonatinas," solo keyboard sonatas, accompanied keyboard sonatas, and SS/bass sonatas. The keyboard option is sometimes the triple one of "harpsichord, pianoforte, or organ" (Op. 10). In the solo and accompanied sonatas examined here, all in two movements, the *galant* traits, simple left-hand figures, melodic grace, degree of passage work for both instruments, and occasional independence of the violin (when marked "Solo") are all reminiscent of the music of Christian Bach (with whom Giordani often crossed paths[87]). But there are not the occasional signs of a potentially stronger composer that are to be found in Bach's sonatas.

Venanzio Rauzzini (1746-1810) was a popular *castrato* who won praise from Burney as "not only a charming singer, a pleasing figure, and a good actor; but a more excellent contrapuntist, and performer on the harpsichord, than a singer is usually allowed to be, as all kind of application to the harpsichord, or composition, is supposed, by the Italians, to be prejudicial to the voice."[88] As a young man Rauzzini sang music composed by Mozart for him in Italy, as an older man he knew Haydn in England, and while he was still in Rome he may have trained alongside Clementi, whom he certainly knew while he was in London, from 1774 to 1781 and intermittently thereafter.[89] At least 25 sonatas by Rauzzini were published in London, between 1777 and 1799.[90] These include 6 accompanied keyboard sonatas (P-or-H & Vn) Op. 1 (1777), 6 more Op. 8 (1781), 3 more and a keyboard duet Op. 15 (1786), 3 other duets Op. 12 (1783), and 6 solo piano sonatas (1799).[91] Nearly all in 2 movements, these sonatas, especially those after Op. 1, rise above the level of Borghi's and Giordani's. They disclose broader melodic arches, more development of ideas, and a more advanced handling of the keyboard. Clementi's possible influence is suggested not only in the generally clean, thin writing but in the

86. Cf. GROVE III 647-648 (Loewenberg); MGG V 143-148 (Cudworth), with detailed list of works (cf., also, BRITISH UNION I 381-382). In Stone/ITALIAN I 232-236, II 23-26, and III 96 are, respectively, a discussion of the acc'd. sets Opp. 4 and 17 and the solo set Op. 10, a thematic index of these sets, and a copy of Op. 10/3 in full.

87. Cf. Terry/BACH *passim*.

88. BURNEY'S TOURS II 47; cf., also, p. 54 in this same vol. and Burney/HISTORY II 880.

89. Cf. GROVE VII 54-55 (Loewenberg); Landon/HAYDN 295; Unger/CLEMENTI 15-16.

90. Cf. BRITISH UNION II 875.

91. Opp. 1, 8, and 15 are briefly discussed in Stone/ITALIAN I 236-237; with thematic index in II 67-70, and a full copy of Op. 1/5 in III 83.

octaves and other double-notes, the hand exchanges, and the further keyboard techniques. Though the violin accompaniments are usually subordinate, they sometimes share in a real duo with the keyboard (Ex. 126).

Clementi's influence is also evident in the many sonatas published between 1788 and about 1810 by the Neapolitan-trained opera composer **Giacomo Gotifredo** (or Gotifredo Jacopo) **Ferrari** (1763-1842). Ferrari was in Paris from 1787 to 1792 and spent most of the rest of his life in London.[92] He left numerous sets of solo keyboard sonatas, "sonates très faciles,"[93] and accompanied sonatas, as well as assortments like *Four Sonatinas For the Pedal Harp, the Three First With an Accompaniment for the Violin, the Last With an Accompaniment for the Pianoforte ad Libitum* (London, *ca.* 1795).[94] Ferrari was a competent though sterile composer. His sonatas are only interesting as the products of a musician who revered Mozart, admired Pleyel and Clementi, and left valuable recollections of his travels and experiences during the late-Classic Era, in the two volumes of his entertaining, surprisingly reliable *Aneddoti* (London, 1830).[95]

The number and choice of movements vary considerably in Ferrari's sonatas, with obvious leanings, in all but the first movements, toward the dances and other light movements then in favor (for instance, an "Anglaise," "Rondo Presto," or "Scherzando"). The first movements go through all the motions and have the requisite dualism within and between themes of textbook "sonata form." Their chief weakness is not so much in the ideas as in the empty passage work between landmarks in the design and in the persistence of Alberti bass or similar figures. Ferrari was an avowed antimodernist and had refused to teach piano in Paris in the face of the new piano styles being spread by Clementi's pupils.[96] But his own piano writing became at least technically more advanced after he became a close friend of Clementi and played the latter's sonatas for him.[97]

We may also take note at this point of the London-born organist, presumably of Italian descent, **Joseph Mazzinghi** (1765-1844), who had

92. Cf. GROVE III 71 (Loewenberg); MGG IV 75-77 (Barblan).
93. A Son. in G in this category was published by Summy-Birchard of Evanston in 1959.
94. Cf. BRITISH UNION I 331 (but delete the 6 S/bass sons., Op. 6, dated *ca.* 1765); HOFMEISTER 1815 (Whistling), p. 353 *et passim.*
95. Reprinted in Palermo in 1920; surveyed in Saint-Foix/FERRARI.
96. Cf. MGG IV 77 and 76.
97. Cf. Saint-Foix/FERRARI 464. In Op. 10 (not before 1793), as a note on the title page explains, octave signs are used to designate adaptations for the new six-octave piano.

Ex. 126. From the opening of Sonata in A, Op. 8/4, by Venanzio Rauzzini (after the original edition at the British Museum).

the advantage of training under both Christian Bach and Sacchini.[98] He, too, left many sonatas, published between about 1787 and 1810,[99] most of them of the accompanied piano type "with or without the additional keys." Included are a "battle" sonata on Lord Nelson's Victory (1798) and many sonatas in which "are introduced several favorite Airs." Thus, in Op. 9/1 (1793) we get "Dumfriss House," "The Caledonian Hunt," "Haddington Assembly," and "Madame Cassey," all in the first movement; Paisiello's "Nel cor più," under the heading only of "Ah che nel petto," in the second movement; and "Our trade to work in clay began," with a "Pas Russe" thrown in, in the finale. These sonatas were written for Mazzinghi's pupils, who included the Princess of Wales. The treatment of the tunes is "correct" but trivial.

Some Native British Composers (*Hook*)

The best known of several minor, native English composers near the end of the 18th century, mostly organists, was the organist from Norwich, **James Hook** (1746-1827). Hook was active in London music circles for more than a half century, from 1769 or 7 years after the arrival of Christian Bach.[100] A versatile, prolific musician who had been the precocious pupil of Burney for 7 months, he left a large quantity of songs, light operas, sonatas, and other instrumental works. The sonatas, published in numerous sets between 1775 and 1805, include the usual accompanied keyboard settings, solo keyboard pieces ranging from 2 sets of 12 "Sonatinos" each (Opp. 12 and 13, 1776 and 1779) to
101a *A Masquerade Sonata* (Op. 101, *ca.* 1802), and 4-hand duets.[101]
Though the short "Sonatinos" are all in only 2 moderate or fast movements each, many of Hook's sonatas have 3 movements, in the order F-S-F. The accompaniments are generally not essential, but do add contrapuntal and harmonic interest.[102] At best Hook's sonatas present some regularly phrased melodies of appreciable, childlike charm (as in all 3 mvts. of Bergmann/HOOK-m). But most of them present nothing more than a happy, businesslike disposition of unprogressive clichés over unrelieved Alberti and murky basses or like accompaniments.[103]

98. Cf. GROVE V 643 (Husk); MGG VIII 1861-1862 (Evans).
99. Cf. BRITISH UNION II 664-665.
100. Cf. GROVE IV 348-351 and MGG VI 692-698 (both by Cudworth).
101. Cf. the lists in MGG VI 696-697; BRITISH UNION I 504-505. Among mod. eds.: "Sonatinas" in D and G, Rowley/ENGLISH-m 10 and 16; acc'd. son. in G from Op. 99, Bergmann/HOOK-m; acc'd. sons. in F and C from Op. 54, Salkeld/HOOK-m. The "Sonata for Three Flutes" published in miniature score by Boosey & Hawkes (1941) is Hook's "Trio" Op. 83/4 for 3 Fls-or-Vns, or Fl & Vn & "Tenor."
102. Cf. Newman/ACCOMPANIED 344-345, with ex. from Op. 16/1.
103. In MGG VI 697 Cudworth says only one instance can be confirmed in certain charges of plagiarism against Hook and indicates that such "ideas" were

Hook's first London employment was with another organist, **Samuel Arnold** (1740-1802), whose prolificity as a composer seems moderate only alongside Hook's.[104] Beside his many operas and songs, Arnold left among his instrumental works 4 sets totaling 27 sonatas that were published, plus some pedagogic "progressive lessons." Two sets of "Eight Lessons for the Harpsichord or Piano Forte" were published as Opp. 7 and 10 about 1770 and 1778, with "Sonata" as the individual title of each, according to the usual equation. A "Third Sett of Eight Sonatas" was published as Op. 11 about 1780, with a violin accompaniment added. And 3 more solo sonatas, qualified by an early use of the term "grand," were published as Op. 23 in 1783. Arnold's sonatas have no more melodic, harmonic, or accompanimental interest, either in the violin or keyboard bass, than Hook's. Furthermore, they are a little less purposeful and light. In both of these latter traits one detects a clinging Baroque orientation. This holder of the highest church organ posts, this editor of English *Cathedral Music* and of the first attempt, incomplete and inaccurate, at a complete set of Handel (1786), still thought largely in continuously unfolding, sequential lines, making the lack of harmonic and tonal interest all the more conspicuous in his sonatas.

The London organist and master of the catch and glee, **Samuel Webbe** the Elder (1740-1816), left a set of *Six Sonatas* [each separately called "Lesson"] *for the Forte Piano or Harpsichord,* which Welcker published about 1780.[105] Except for the unrelenting Alberti bass, Webbe's sonatas, all in two movements, have a little more individuality than Hook's or Arnold's from the standpoints of melody, melodic ornamentation, harmony, and the use of the keyboard. But a sense of symphonic development, which is not likely to be fostered by catches and glees, in any case, is certainly no more present in these than in the others' sonatas.

On the other hand, symphonic development is one of the most pronounced traits in the unexpectedly good set of *Three Sonatas for the Pianoforte Composed & Dedicated by Permission to Mr. Haydn,*
Op. 3, by **Christian Ignatius Latrobe** (1758-1836).[106] Latrobe was 106a

---

common property in the late 18th century. One might add, indeed, that, at least in some 3 dozen sons. seen here, there is rarely anything distinctive enough for such charges to be argued, pro or con.

104. Cf. GROVE I 218-220 (Rimbault, Colles, and Loewenberg); BRITISH UNION I 51-55 (as against I 490-505).

105. Cf. GROVE IX 193-194 (Husk); BRITISH UNION II 1060 (followed, on p. 1061, by a listing of 4 harp sons. by the similarly active son, Samuel Webbe the Younger [1770-1843], published by Clementi in 1799).

106. Cf. GROVE V 83-84 (Husk); MGG VIII 308-309 (Cudworth). He was the brother of the American architect, Benjamin Latrobe.

Ex. 127. From the opening of Christian Ignatius Latrobe's Sonata 1 (after the original Bland ed. at the British Museum).

a Moravian missionary and amateur musician best known for his fruitful *Selection of Sacred Music*. His dedication of sonatas to Haydn, mentioned in Haydn's "London Notebooks" for 1791-92,[107] reflects the strong influence the latter made on him during his first visit to London, the sonatas being published about that time (1791?) by Bland.[108] The music of these sonatas, in which there is enough artistic

107. Landon/HAYDN 263.

108. The date "c. 1790" in BRITISH UNION II 602 would therefore be a year or so too early. Further references to Op. 3 may be found in Schmid/HAYDN 301 and, especially, Holmes/LATROBE. In the latter source a letter of 1828 from Latrobe to Vincent Novello is printed, including these sentences (p. 256): "On enquiry, hearing from a friend, that I had ventured to compose some sonatas for the pianoforte, he [Haydn] desired to hear them. As he observed, that they ought to be printed, I agreed, if he would permit me to dedicate them to him.

interest and skill to justify a modern edition, reflects Haydn's influence even more. The first is unusual in having the four-movement plan of Haydn's later symphonies, F-S-minuet-F. The third begins with a short "Adagio molto," then an "Andante Pastorale," by way of a slow introduction. The main ideas are simple (Ex. 127) but these are developed intensively and with convincing drive not only in the "development" section but throughout the first movements. The ornamentation in both slow and fast movements and the melodic conduct also bring Haydn to mind often.

Another devotee of Haydn was the violinist and pianist **Thomas Haigh** (*ca.* 1769-1808), who actually studied with the master during his first London trip.[109] Haigh's published sonatas, dating from about 1790 to 1817, include many of both the accompanied and solo types. Along with the more straightforward examples are tune sonatas, such as that for the piano "in which are Introduced two favorite Airs from the Beggar's Opera" (*ca.* 1800). Each air in this work is extended into a movement by repetitions, additions, and slight variations. The second movement, for instance, is a "Rondo Allegretto" with Macheath's air, "If the Heart of a Man . . . ," used as the recurring refrain, and with pleasing episodes created, evidently, by Haigh himself.

Two other native English composers are of too little consequence to us to permit more than the mention of their names—the harpsichordist and violinist **Charles Rousseau Burney** (?-1819), nephew of the historian and composer of two sets of accompanied and duet sonatas (1781 and 1786);[110] and the organist **Matthew Camidge** (1758-1844), who published numerous accompanied sonatas from about
1796.[111] 111a

Other Nationalities (Kocžwara, Cogan)

Among composers of other nationalities active in London during the high- and late-Classic Era only very minor names can be cited. But they deserve at least passing mention, if only in the interest of a balanced view of the total sonata output. **Louis von Esch,** who probably moved to London from Paris around the time of the Revolution, published at least five sets of accompanied sonatas in piano trio setting between 1781 and about 1798 (Opp. 1, 5, 9, 12,

---

Of this he has made mention in his own account of his visits in England. These sonatas, with many compositions of better masters, have long ago swam down the stream of oblivion, and made room for a younger fry."

109. Cf. MGG V 1329-1331 (Cudworth), with a long list of works.

110. Cf. Scholes/BURNEY *passim;* BRITISH UNION I 144.

111. Cf. GROVE II 30 (Husk); BRITISH UNION I 154-155. Mod. ed.: "Sonatina" in G, Rowley/ENGLISH-m 21.

and 13).[112] Op. 5 uses flute and horn instead of violin and cello. An examination of Op. 12 reveals late-Classic speech and piano writing, totally subordinate accompaniments, and endless dominant preparations for significant statements that never come. The sonatas of **Valentin Nicolai** (?-*ca.* 1800), who was in Paris and London at about the same time as Esch, were both more numerous and more popular, judging by their many re-editions.[113] They are all in four-hand duet or accompanied piano settings. Although no less vapid in substance, the samples seen here are a little more melodious and less pretentious than Esch's.

Also in Paris and London was the theologian from Strasbourg, **Philippe-Jacques Meyer** (the elder; 1737-1819), who studied harp with Hochbrucker in Paris. He left at least two sets of solo sonatas for his instrument, plus one set with violin and one with string quartet accompaniment, published between 1768 and 1800 or later and described as being "in a pleasing and simple style."[114] "Light," "superficial," and "trivial" are terms applied to the music of the Belgian pianist in London from about 1780, **John Lewis Hoebe-rechts** (*ca.* 1760-*ca.* 1820).[115] This composer left numerous solo and accompanied sonatas between 1786 and about 1805, some based on "favorite airs." Nothing better is said for the several sets of accompanied sonatas published between 1786 and 1799 by the Thuringian organist **Karl Friedrich Horn** (1762-1830), who is remembered as an early copyist (?), editor, and champion of *The Well-Tempered Clavier* in
116a London.[116]

From Prague came the cellist **Jan Stiastný** (1764-at least 1820), who served variously in Nürnberg and Mannheim as well as London. Stiastný left a number of duets, solos, sonatas, *divertissements,* and other pieces for his instrument, published around the turn of the century. The known quantity is small and hard to find, but the quality is described as of outstanding "originality and purity."[117] The "Andante Cantabile" in C for cello and piano that has been made available[118] does indeed reveal music of considerable melodic breadth and harmonic color,

112. Cf. Eitner/QL III 352-353; BRITISH UNION I 319. Op. 12, "Printed for the Author" *ca.* 1797, is marked "le premier Publié en Angleterre" and contains a list made up almost entirely of English "Souscripteurs."

113. Cf. MGG IX 1455-1456 (Unverricht); BRITISH UNION II 730; Cat. SCHWERIN II 97.

114. MGG IX 247 (Vernillat). For Meyer's London publications (up to 1800) cf. BRITISH UNION II 673.

115. MGG VI 506-507 (Sadie). Cf. BRITISH UNION I 485.

116. MGG VI 716-718 (Redlich). Cf. BRITISH UNION I 505.

117. GROVE VIII 87-88 (Herbert).

118. Schroeder/CELLO-m No. 5509. Cf., also, Altmann/KAMMERMUSIK 106.

whetting the appetite for more and for a better knowledge of this composer.

The only other Bohemian in London to report is the versatile performer **Franz Kočzwara** (or Kotzwara; *ca.* 1750-91), who composed numerous solo, duet, S/bass, SS/bass, and accompanied keyboard sonatas first published between about 1775 and 1791.[119] But aside from his dissolute life and lurid hanging,[120] Kočzwara is remembered for the most celebrated and republished of all battle sonatas. *The Battle of Prague, a Favourite Sonata,* was originally published in Dublin about 1788 and originally scored for piano or harpsichord with subordinate violin and cello accompaniments.[121] It eventually became most popular as a piano solo. Although the composer was capable enough to pass off other of his own works as Haydn's, Mozart's, or Pleyel's, the utter banality and triteness of this sonata rule out any consideration of musical worth. But its programme referring loosely to an actual battle during the Seven Years' War some three decades earlier, may be noted as typical of the many battle sonatas of the eighteenth century. After a "Slow March" introduction, the "Word of Command" is given, followed by "Signal Cannon" in the bass, then "The Bugle Horn call for the Cavalry" in the treble. "The Attack" pits the "Prussians" (chords and runs in the treble) against the "Imperialists" (Alberti bass), punctuated by "Cannon" (hand-crossing) and succeeded by other battle effects. A "Grave" section in the tonic minor mode is labeled "Cries of the Wounded," but quickly gives way to the "Trumpet of Victory." At last, to round off the piece and insure full value, we have "God Save the King," then a "Quick Step" labeled "Turkish Music," a "Finale" marked "Allegro," and a closing fanfare beginning with the irrelevant if not irreverent instruction, "Go to bed Tom." Kočzwara also wrote a sonata "potpourri," *The Agreeable Surprize,* and the first part of *Siege of Quebec, a Sonata,* both of which were popular in the 1790's.[122]

One **J. D. Benser** himself published or had published at least 19
sonatas in the 15 years from about 1775 to 1790.[123] Nearly all of the 123a
accompanied type, these also include a "Duetto" and a two-movement "Sonata; the Storm." The last, although of more musical value than Kočzwara's programme sonatas, proves to be interesting mainly for its subtitle, "For the Pianoforte ONLY," and for the absence of

119. Cf. GROVE IV 794-795 (Grove); MGG VII 1305-1306 (Cudworth).
120. Cf. Pohl/MOZART II 136; Landon/HAYDN 269.
121. Cf. Loesser/PIANOS 243-244, 279.
122. A facs. of the first page of the latter appears in MGG VII 502.
123. Cf. GROVE I 630 (Straeten); BRITISH UNION I 101.

programmatic inscriptions or even any clear musical suggestion of its title.

Outside of London the only name of consequence to mention is that of the German cellist who was in Edinburgh from 1772 to the end of his life, **Johann Georg Christoff Schetky** (1740-1824).[124] Schetky left numerous solos for his instrument and unfigured bass, as well as several sets of sonatas for harpsichord or piano "with an arbitrary accompanyment of a violin and violoncello" or with violin only. Much of this music was published in London and Edinburgh in the decade from 1776.[125] Representative is the set of six "Solos" for cello and bass Op. 13 (*ca.* 1785), each with three movements in the order F-S-rondo finale. Wide ranges, double-stops, bariolage, and cadenzas confirm the composer's knowledge of the cello, as do the long, lyrical lines. The ideas themselves are not distinguished and their treatment is rather stiff and formalistic.

Finally, we may go outside of Great Britain far enough to include Dublin, since what concerns us there is the Anglo-Irish music of the governing, English-speaking classes rather than the native, essentially
126a different Irish music.[126] The lively musical activities in that city, which had gained new vigor from the first performance of *Messiah* in 1742, included, by the end of the century, the extensive publication and sale of keyboard sonatas by Haydn, Mozart, Clementi, Dussek, and Cramer. Chief among the Anglo-Irish sonata composers was the organist **Philip Cogan** (or Coogan; 1748-1833), who came to Dublin in 1772 after training in his home city of Cork.[127] In all, at least 19 keyboard sonatas by Cogan were published and republished in Dublin or London between about 1780 and 1805, including a set of 6 (Op. 2) with subordinate violin accompaniments for all but one, 3 sets of 3 each for piano or harpsichord, and 4 single solo sonatas.[128] Two of the last are tune sonatas. One is *A Favourite Lesson and . . . Rondo of the Favourite Air of The Dargle,* "The Dargle" being a country dance tune. Another is *Mr. Cogan's Capital Sonata With the Favorite Air of Colin With Variations.* "Colin" proves to be the French tune "Lison dormait." In his later sonatas Cogan, whose own "execution" on the "piano-forte" was described as "astonishing" by his pupil Michael Kelly,[129] came in-

124. Cf. GROVE VII 482 (Kidson).

125. Cf. BRITISH UNION II 927; but the 2 sets indicated as being in The University Library in Glasgow could not be found in August, 1960.

126. Warm thanks are owing to Mrs. Ita Beausang of Dublin for generously contributing much of the information in the remainder of this chapter.

127. Cf. GROVE II 365 (Crawford, Loewenberg, and O'Broin).

128. All are listed in BRITISH UNION I 203 except a single son. Op. 11, and another dedicated to Lady Earlsfort.

129. Kelly/REMINISCENCES I 11.

creasingly close to Clementi. Clementi was, in fact, both the dedicatee and publisher of Op. 8. One notes the brilliant, sonorous, technically advanced writing for the piano, the expressive depth achieved in slow movements through artfully economical means, the freedom of structure in certain "sonata forms" (Opp. 7/3/i and 8/3/i), the fugal finale in a sonata dedicated to Lady Earlsfort, and the slow introductions.[130]

The student interested in going further into the Anglo-Irish sonata would want to see the keyboard sonatas from about this same period by the precocious Dublin emigrant **Thomas Carter** (1769-1800),[131] and by four other obscure composers represented in the National Library of Ireland in Dublin—**Patrick Corbett, William Heron,** and "Mr." **Elfort,**[132] as well as **George Buchanan.**

130. Just as this 3d ed. of SCE is going to press I am indebted to Professor Evelyn C. Barry of Wellesley College for the opportunity to examine the careful critical edition of all 23 (not 19) extant sons. by Cogan that she has prepared for pub. in the Wellesley Edition. Included are essential notes on biography, performance, sources, and revisions.

131. Cf. GROVE II 98 (Flood); BRITISH UNION I 169.

132. Cf. BRITISH UNION I 215, 479, and 315, respectively.

Chapter XXI

Outlying Regions, East, North, and West

Terra infirma

This final chapter touches on the Classic sonata in regions beyond those where we have traced its main currents, schools, and composers. At best, the chapter can be only an introduction to the subject. In spite of the excellent basic studies to be found in at least certain of these regions, little has been done in any of them toward a rounded view of our particular interest. What does exist often has failed to reach our more accessible libraries or even our standard bibliographies and often presents a language barrier that few of us can cross without special help. In short, the survey that is submitted here can only go as far as its available and translatable sources.

The "outlying" regions to be visited here are Switzerland, Czechoslovakia, Russia, Holland, Belgium, Denmark, Sweden, and America. Ireland was visited briefly at the end of the previous chapter. Poland and Hungary are among regions not included, although a better knowledge of such regions would undoubtedly turn up further sonata activities of interest. Certainly some composers deserving of attention will have been overlooked. Yet among the nearly sixty names that do figure in this chapter not one can be regarded as of prime importance to the sonata and a surprising number are marked by conservative, even late-Baroque, styles and forms, leaving some doubt as to how important any of the neglected names may be. One must remember that the composers most likely to take a strong interest in the sonata were generally those who soon emigrated to centers like Vienna, Mannheim, Berlin, Paris, and London, where the sonata was enjoying its principal cultivation. Indeed, it is in such centers that we have already met many more Czechs than we find in Prague. After all, the sonata was native, first, to Italy, Germany, and France rather than to any of those outlying regions. Many of the composers we are about to meet in those regions either came from Italy, Germany, or France or were still going to men like Tartini, Martini, or Emanuel Bach for their training. It is mainly our policy of meeting the composer where he wrote his sonatas and/or exercised his influence rather than where he was born that causes us to take this final excursion into other regions.

Geneva

Geneva, the first home of Rousseau and the last of Voltaire, was in a state of unrest during much of the eighteenth century and enjoyed only a modest concert activity, chiefly under French influence.[1] In 1766-67 Grétry was active there, but the only resident composer of consequence was the outstanding violinist **Kaspar Fritz** (1716-83). A pupil of G. B. Somis in Torino, Fritz appeared three times in 1756 at the Concert spirituel in Paris and still played "with as much spirit as a young man of twenty-five" when Burney visited him in 1770.[2] His known works, except for six late symphonies (1773), are all sonatas in melo/bass and SS settings first published in London and Paris between 1742 and 1759.[3] They include *Sei Sonate a quattro* (2 Vns, Va, K-or-Vc), Op. 1; two sets of S/bass sonatas, Opp. 2 and 3; one set of SS/bass sonatas, Op. 4; and one set of sonatas for two violins alone (without op. no.). These sonatas are generally in three movements in no fixed order of tempos. Burney says Fritz "was so obliging as to play me one of his own solos, which, though extremely difficult, was pleasing. . . ." This reference, presumably to a sonata in Op. 2 or 3, is understandable enough, for in these sets one finds the advanced use of the violin, the wide range, and the rich ornamentation of a Leclair or a Guillemain. Fritz's long, pathetic lines and sure sense of harmonic direction bespeak an experienced, superior composer. The continuous, sequential unfolding of these lines, free from dualistic contrasts, bespeaks an orientation that is still Baroque.

Otherwise, we can report in Geneva, from 1771 to not later than 1791, only a Piedmontese violinist named **Giuseppe Demachi** (or Demacchi), brought perhaps at the instigation of Fritz, since Demachi was in Torino in 1740.[4] Melo/bass sonatas by him, in "solo" and "trio" settings, were published in Paris in 1769, 1770, and 1781.[5]

1. Cf. BURNEY'S TOURS I 40; MGG IV 1747-1749 (Tappolet) and 976 (Giegling).
2. BURNEY'S TOURS I 40-41.
3. Cf. the lists in MGG IV 976-977, including mod. eds. of most of the sons.; BRITISH UNION I 353.
4. Cf. Eitner/QL III 170; Schmidl/DIZIONARIO I 430-431.
5. Johansson/FRENCH I 24, 111-112, 119.

Prague

The mention of names like Mysliveček, Stamitz, Filtz, Richter, Vanhal, Koželuch, the Bendas, and Kocžwara should remind us how many Bohemian and other Czech composers we have met in the foregoing chapters. But in Prague itself, already the center of the vital Czech musical culture for nearly ten centuries, relatively few, mostly obscure composers of sonatas can be found in the later eighteenth century (not counting temporary residents like Rutini). Too many, like some of those just named, left for greener pastures elsewhere or fled to escape the French and Prussian occupations and bombardment during the War of the Austrian Succession and the Seven Years' War.[6] Of those who stayed, some wrote no sonatas known here, as is true of the organist **František Xaver Brixi** (1732-71), composer of much church and a little instrumental music. The Czech scholar Vladimír Helfert called Brixi "an immediate precursor of Haydn and Mozart" and "the most important representative of Czech musical Classicism."[7] A "Presto" in c and an "Andante" in A in two harpsichord "Partitas" by him that have been made available reveal the melodic arches, *galant* traits, and "singing-allegro" style of a composer who was certainly up-to-date around 1760.[8]

The first pre-Classic sonata composer in Prague that has turned up in the present survey is the more obscure, presumably Czech-born musician, the "Abbiate" **Paul Fischer.**[9] Fischer is known only by two harpsichord sonatas in Anth. HAFFNER OM-m II/2 and III/2 (1756 and 1757), and a set of six more published by Breitkopf in Leipzig in 1768. The earlier, Haffner sonatas are in three and two movements, respectively (F-S-F and M-F). Not without a bit of individuality, these light, smoothly flowing sonatas are like Brixi's pieces in style, yet already show more of the simple Classic breadth of design and a more developed use of the keyboard.

Prior to J. L. Dussek and J. V. Tomašek, both of whom were just enough over the border in their pre-Romantic styles to be deferred to our next volume, the most noteworthy sonata composer in Prague was the excellent, crippled pianist **František Xaver Dušek** (Dussek

6. For representative summaries of Czech music activities in the 18th century cf. BURNEY'S TOURS II 132-135; Helfert/CZECHOSLOVAK 15-23; Quoika/BÖHMEN 77-103. Racek/TSCHECHISCHEN is a study of Czech precedents for the Mozart style. Further sources are cited in MAB-m No. 14, p. 8.

7. Helfert/CZECHOSLOVAK 18 and Helfert & Steinhard/TCHÉCOSLOVAQUE 22. Cf. GROVE I 957 (Černušak); Eitner/QL II 195-196.

8. MAB-m No. 14, pp. 15 and 19.

9. Cf. Eitner/QL III 470.

Duschek, etc.; 1731-99).[10] Dušek, who evidently was no relative of J. L. Dussek, moved to Prague from his Bohemian birthplace, Chotěborky, at the age of seventeen. A pupil of Wagenseil and teacher of Koželuch, he and the fine soprano he married were well acquainted with Mozart, whom they met in Salzburg in 1777 and welcomed at their home in Prague in 1787 during the memorable launching of *Don Giovanni*.[11] Only a few sonatas by Dušek were published, all in the 5 years between 1792 and 1797, including 3 piano duets and 2 piano solos.[12] Somewhat more were left in MS, including a set of 8 that have been made available,[13] and some others from which 4 separate movements have been printed.[14] The set of 8 sonatas consists mostly of 3-movement cycles of diminutive, sonatina proportions, in the order F-S-F. The separate movements are on a slightly larger, technically more advanced scale. In these sonatas one finds fresh ideas and imaginative rhythms, skillfully expressed in *galant* and high-Classic speech, with not a few resemblances to Mozart's style. But one senses a structural deficiency. After each phrase is stated and perhaps repeated there is seldom any further development of its idea. The excessive variety that results from the continuous succession of new ideas tends, parodoxically, toward monotony.

St. Petersburg and the Baltic Region (Manfredini)

The cultural growth in Russia that had been fostered earlier in the eighteenth century by Peter the Great reached new heights during the reign, from 1762-96, of another Western-minded, benevolent despot, Empress Catherine the Great (or Catherine II). At her court and in the salon of the Grand Duchess Maria Féodorovna, among related establishments in St. Petersburg, special encouragement was given to French literature and Italian music. German and French musicians were to be found there, too, chiefly and respectively as performers (like J. W. Hässler) and as exponents of the *opéra comique*. But there can be no question about the preference for Italians where composition as well as teaching and performance were concerned.[15] One only needs to recall the more notable composers from earlier chapters who were active there during visits or longer stays, including Galuppi, Rutini,

10. Cf. MGG III 1005-1006 (Kahl), with quotations from contemporary tributes; Racek's preface in MAB-m No. 8 (with further references).
11. Cf. Anderson/MOZART I 408, 535, 1135, 1138, 1369, 1437, *et passim.*
12. MGG III 1005.
13. MAB-m No. 8, with preface.
14. MAB-m No. 14, p. 24 and No. 17, pp. 30 and 41.
15. Cf. Mooser/ANNALES I 8-9. For our purposes, Mooser's monumental survey, which has already been cited many times here, supersedes all previous studies of 18th-c. Western music in Russia.

Cimarosa, Sarti, Paisiello, Lolli, and Viotti. As usual, opera was the primary interest. But good opportunities were provided for a healthy, if much smaller cultivation of instrumental music, by dealers who sold Western publications, by new, local publishers, by a chamber music group in the service of Catherine the Great, by an interest in keyboard
16a music at court, and by not infrequent public concerts.[16] Yet, as in Prague, the resident composers of sonatas to report in St. Petersburg are few and of no great consequence. Most of them were violinists rather than keyboardists.

Following the outstanding Baroque violinist from Padua, Domenico Dall'Oglio (*ca.* 1700-64), who left at least two sets of S/bass sonatas that were published,[17] the most important Italian sonata composer in Russia was the violinist **Vincenzo Manfredini** (1737-99). Manfredini was born in Pistoia and trained under G. A. Perti in Bologna, came to Moscow in 1758, and about a year later replaced the German composer H. F. Raupach in St. Petersburg, a composer we met in Paris.[18] But by 1765 he was demoted from his post as *maestro di cappella* by Catherine the Great, who had concluded that his work was mediocre and now preferred the newly arrived Galuppi. And by 1769 Manfredini returned to Bologna, only to come back to St. Petersburg for the last eleven months of his life. In the present survey we place him in St. Petersburg because it was there in 1765 that his only known sonatas were published, a set of six for harpsichord with a flowery dedication to Catherine the Great.[19]

A still worse opinion of Manfredini's music was expressed in a long, detailed review of his sonatas by J. A. Hiller in Leipzig in 1766 (reprinted in Hamburg in 1767).[20] A sample of the biting remarks is sufficient:

> Well! Well! An Italian, a *maestro* of the imperial Russian chapel! And he writes no better sonatas! That is sad! You, unfortunate principles of order, symmetry, rhythm, modulation, and proper and pure harmony! Mr. Manfredini must not yet have judged you worthy of making his acquaintance and getting into his confidence! . . . An inharmonious jangle is met almost everywhere here, with those broken chords in the left hand, thanks to which the Italian keyboard sonatas have so often nauseated us. . . .

16. Mooser/ANNALES *passim.*

17. Cf. Eitner/QL VII 230; Mooser/ANNALES I 131-136, 389-390, Figs. 19-21.

18. The fullest account of Manfredini is that in Mooser/ANNALES I 317-322, II 20-40 and 69, and III Figs. 3-8 (all overlooked in MGG VIII 1579-1580 [Giegling]).

19. Facs. of the title page, dedication, and first page of Son. 1 in E♭ are given in Mooser/ANNALES III Figs. 6-8; the set is listed in Cat. BOLOGNA IV 54. Mod. ed.: Son. in d, Benvenuti/CEMBALISTI-m 28.

20. Partly quoted, in French trans., in Mooser/ANNALES II 39, from which the shorter extracts quoted here are further trans.

The melody itself might be good if it were not constantly impaired by the accompaniment in the bass, and if one hadn't heard it a hundred times. . . . Aren't the works of [Emanuel] Bach, [Georg] Benda, Wagenseil, Kunz [!], Binder, and other German masters known in Russia?

Notwithstanding its nationalistic tinge, Torchi, Torrefranca, and others evidently have preferred not to question Hiller's judgment of Manfredini's sonatas.[21] Yet the available examples are certainly no weaker than the average run of *galant* sonatas we have been examining throughout this survey (Ex. 128), including those in Anth. HAFFNER OM-m. *Galant* in style is just what they are. They do not have the

Ex. 128. From the opening of Vincenzo Manfredini's Sonata 1 in E♭ (after the facs. of the original ed. in Mooser/ANNALES III Fig. 8).

21. Torchi/ISTRUMENTALE 257-258; Torrefranca/ORIGINI 604; Schmidl/DIZIONARIO II 24.

harmonic subtlety of the *empfindsam* style nor, as might be expected, the structural breadth of Emanuel Bach's sonatas. The uncompelling forms may be, in fact, Manfredini's chief weakness. But the melodic quality begrudgingly acknowledged by Hiller is more convincing than that in Wagenseil's writing. Furthermore, the accompaniment is less limited than Hiller suggests and there are no conspicuous gaucheries in the writing. After all, Manfredini was able enough to publish a comprehensive, respected theory treatise, including a full discussion and examples of fugal as well as more "modern" procedures (SCE II).

The only other Italian in Russia to name is the violinist **Carlo Canobbio** (1741-1822), supposedly from Venice. Canobbio moved permanently to St. Petersburg in 1779, perhaps at Paisiello's instigation. Among Canobbio's works were a set of six duets for flute and violin or for two violins, and a set of six guitar sonatas accompanied by "violin with mute." These unexplored sets were published, respectively, about 1780 and in 1797.[22]

Among Germans in St. Petersburg was the skilled Prussian violinist **Franz Adam Veichtner,** who had studied with Franz Benda and Riepel, and taught Reichardt.[23] Veichtner travelled and composed before he moved permanently to St. Petersburg in 1797, where in that same year he published at least two sets of six sonatas each for violin and cello. His music is described as capable but not especially imaginative.[24] The only other resident German composer of any consequence was **Johann Gottfried Wilhelm Palschau** (*ca.* 1743-1813), who had been greeted as a keyboard prodigy in London in 1754 (the year that Paradisi's sonatas appeared).[25] But the only sonatas by him that are known are the two that appeared in Anth. HAFFNER OM-m VI/6 and VII/4 about 1760-61. At that time Palschau was in Copenhagen, and it would be some 17 years before he reached St. Petersburg (1777), to become one of the few professional players in the empress' private chamber music group. The Haffner sonatas reveal competent handling of form, textures, and keyboard, with unprepossessing ideas. The chief interest lies in the chromaticism, both melodic and harmonic, making for a degree of expressive depth in the slow movements. The first of these sonatas is in 4 movements, S-F-S-F, and the other in 3, F-S-F.

Among native Russians the first notable violinist, both as virtuoso and composer, and the only one to write sonatas at this time so far as

22. Cf. Mooser/ANNALES II 250-252; Johansson/FRENCH I 124.
23. Cf. Mooser/ANNALES III 785-786; GROVE VIII 714 (Straeten).
24. Moser/VIOLINSPIEL 338-339.
25. Cf. Pohl/MOZART I 96; Eitner/QL VII 305-306; Mooser/ANNALES II 278-280 and III Fig. 57 (silhouette).

could be learned here, was **Ivan Evstafiévitch Khandochkine** (1747-
1804).[26] Khandochkine was taught by Italians in Russia and possibly 26a
in Italy[27] before he entered the imperial service about 1765. Lolli is
said to have made a strong impression on him in St. Petersburg in 1774.
The subject of many anecdotes, Khandochkine himself gave frequent
concerts, playing on occasion (1780) in *scordatura.* A set of six sonatas by him was published in Amsterdam in 1781, scored for two
violins (as were the Russian folk songs he later arranged), and three
"solo" violin sonatas were left (in MS or print?) around 1800. Only
the latter sonatas seem now to be extant.[28] 28a

In the Prussian center of Königsberg, the Baltic seaport that is now Kaliningrad in the Soviet Union, lived the versatile instrumentalist **Christian Wilhelm Podbielski** (1740?-92). This composer, who stemmed indirectly from J. S. Bach, who won the esteem of Reichardt, and who was a teacher of E. T. A. Hoffmann,[29] left two sets of six keyboard sonatas each, originally published in Riga in 1780 and 1783.[30] The sonatas were highly praised by Gerber and are reported to be very much in the style of Emanuel Bach's sonatas.[31] In another Prussian center, Breslau (now Wroclaw) lived the Bohemian musician **F. S. Sander** (?-1796). Sander published three sets of six solo sonatas or "leichte Sonatinen" each for keyboard in 1785, 1786, and 1787, and an accompanied set (H & Vn) of six "Sonates ou Divertimentos" in 1790, the 1785 set being warmly praised by C. F. Cramer.[32] Although all his sonatas are light and short and the accompanied types have only two movements, a three-movement Sonatina in G that has been made available from the 1786 set[33] reveals some of the substantial, hardy qualities that have made classics of the Clementi sonatinas. It also reveals an easy grasp of high-Classic styles.

The Netherlands (Hurlebusch, Maldere)

During music's Classic Era Holland was ruled independently by the House of Orange except for a 20-year period of French control, from

26. Cf. Mooser/ANNALES II 385-392, III Figs. 74 and 75.

27. But he probably was not taught by Tartini in Padua, as the more enthusiastic Soviet scholars have argued (Mooser/ANNALES II 387).

28. A mod. ed. of them, published in Moscow in 1949, is cited in Mooser/ANNALES II 392 but could not be examined here.

29. Cf. Schletterer/REICHARDT 64-66; MGG I 996 (Blume) and VI 528 (Ehinger).

30. Cf. Eitner/QL VIII 1-2; BRITISH UNION II 800.

31. They are individually described in brief (along with further biographic information) in Güttler/KÖNIGSBERG 227-231. Cf., also, Gerber/LEXICON II 164-165; ZFMW V (1922-23) 348 (Kroll).

32. Cramer/MAGAZIN II (1786) 1209. Cf. Eitner/QL VIII 413-414 (including "Sander, H . . . S . . ."); BRITISH UNION II 917.

33. Kreutz/SONATINEN-m 13.

the French conquest in 1795 to Napoleon's defeat in the Belgian town of Waterloo, in 1815. During the same period the Belgian provinces were not independent, being under the control of Austria up to 1792, of France up to 1815, and then of Holland until 1830. The interest in music at this time in both "countries" of the Netherlands was intense. One needs only to recall the private and public concerts in the chief cities, and the international publishing trade that flourished in them.[34] Yet, Pieter Hellendaal, the one native Hollander of some musical distinction and a conservative at that, is said to have moved to England because of too little interest at home.[35] Actually, the situation with regard to creative music in the Netherlands was somewhat as it was in London. There were no longer any native composers of the international stature realized by the great Renaissance masters. The two Classic Netherlanders who did earn substantial reputations abroad as composers—that is, the Belgians Gossec and Grétry—emigrated to Paris. In any case, as we saw early in Chapter XVII, these two did little or nothing for the sonata. Other Netherlanders sufficiently interested in contemporary trends to write sonatas were, for all the individuality and charm of their music, essentially conservative imitators of Italian, French, and German models.

In Holland one of the principal composers was the fine German organist and harpsichordist **Conrad Friedrich Hurlebusch** (1696?-1765), who was born in Braunschweig and was brought up, under his father's tutelage, on the music of Buxtehude, Reinken, and the French clavecinists.[36] Before he reached Amsterdam in 1743, where Locatelli had settled 14 years earlier,[37] Hurlebusch had moved about restlessly in the course of travels and temporary posts that took him to Vienna, Italy, Stockholm, and numerous German centers (especially Hamburg). Among the extant church works, operas, and instrumental collections that he left are 2 sets of *VI Sonate di Cembalo,* Opp. 5 and 6. Both sets were beautifully engraved in Amsterdam, evidently at the author's expense, under a Holland privilege dated 1746, although they could
38a have been composed in the 1730's.[38] There must have been other

34. The surveys of most value to us are the recent ones in Borren/NEDERLANDEN II 9-31 and 132-173, and Closson & Borren/BELGIQUE 201-226; cf., also, Scheurleer/NEDERLAND, MGG IX 1485-1494 (Wangermée), and 1494-1501 (Thijsse).

35. GROVE IV 226 (Blom).

36. Autobiographic material is incorporated in Mattheson/EHREN-PFORTE 120-125 and Seiffert/HURLEBUSCH. Cf., also, MGG VI 971-977 (Bense), including contemporary tributes and further sources.

37. Cf. the somewhat circumscribed view of Amsterdam in 1772 in BURNEY'S TOURS II 224-230 and the rounder view of an earlier generation, in Koole/LOCATELLI; also, Schubart/IDEEN 253-254, SBE 344-349.

38. But these sons. are not among works already mentioned in 1740 in Mattheson/EHREN-PFORTE 124, as implied in Seiffert/HURLEBUSCH 272 and MGG VI 973.

sonatas left in MS, since Mattheson mentioned "Sonate a 4. Stromenti" in 1740 and the "Privilegie" lists 12 sonatas for violin "and other instruments" and 18 "sonatas or suites for keyboard," among many other works, most of which did not get into print.[39]

Only the first set of Hurlebusch's printed sonatas, Op. 5, has a subtitle, which may be translated from his Italian as, "Preserved, like my other compositions, from the *bizarrerie* and confused taste of the present day, etc., etc., dedicated to the professors of this art. . . ." Actually, Op. 5 has a bit more of the unusual than Op. 6, at least with regard to the greater variety of titles in the movements and of distributions of these movements. There is even a "Holanoese" or Dutch dance, in Op. 5/2/v (Ex. 129), which, incidentally, provides one basis for conjectur-

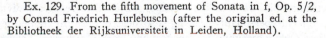

Ex. 129. From the fifth movement of Sonata in f, Op. 5/2, by Conrad Friedrich Hurlebusch (after the original ed. at the Bibliotheek der Rijksuniversiteit in Leiden, Holland).

ing that the sonatas were not composed until Hurlebusch reached Holland in 1743. The sonatas of Op. 6 qualify a bit more as pre-Classic in that their movements have fewer dance rather than tempo titles and even their movements not suggestive of dances fall more often into phrase groupings.

Yet, the chief justification for including Hurlebusch's sonatas in pre-Classic instead of late-Baroque music is only their publication during that conspicuous flowering of so-called "sonatas" for keyboard right

39. The privilege is summarized and the 2 published sets of sons. are listed in BOUWSTEENEN II (1872-74) 197 and III (1874-81) 112, respectively. All the works that got into print are listed on the last page of the original ed. of Op. 6. A 3-mvt. "solo" Vn son. by Hurlebusch, in a Dresden MS, is cited in Studeny/VIOLINSONATE 59.

after 1740. Otherwise, in style and form they are on the border quite as are the sonatas of Arne and Platti. The number of movements ranges from 4 (Op. 5/3) to 7 (Op. 6/1) and their order remains unpredictable. All the movements but the first are usually brief, simple binary designs. As already suggested, there are frequent dances and quasi dances, including especially the "Minuetto," usually with its "Minuetto Alternativo," the "Siciliana," the "Giga," and the "Gavotta." Although in Op. 5/1 in E the "Scherzo" (another frequent movement title) is in the surprising key of the lowered mediant (G), there is usually no key change other than mode. In short, except for their first movements, these sonatas are close to the suites in Hurlebusch's *Compositioni musicali per il cembalo* published about 1735 in Hamburg.[40] In the first movements, especially, the lines are likely to unfold into long, broadly conceived arches over a bass that "runs" in the manner of a thorough bass. The lines are especially bold, wide-ranged, and expressive in Op. 5/2/i in f, a movement that divides into several sections, each with repeat signs. There is a slight sense of formula and routine about Hurlebusch's music and a lack of contrapuntal interest in the keyboard writing. But the melodic content, harmonic force, and rhythmic variety make up for these shortcomings, although it may be just those shortcomings that caused J. S. Bach, reportedly, to smile in kindly tolerance when Hurlebusch visited him in Leipzig and presented some "printed sonatas" (presumably the *Compositioni musicali*) as recommended material for Bach's sons.[41]

Hurlebusch's career was paralleled curiously by that of **Jacob Wilhelm Lustig** (1706-96). Another north German organist whose father trained him on Reinken's music, and another restless individual with a difficult personality, Lustig also held a post in Hamburg for some time (while receiving further training from Mattheson, Telemann, and J. P. Kuntzen!).[42] He moved to Groningen in the northeast tip of Holland in 1728, remaining there to the end of his long life except for a period in England around 1743. Lustig's chief contributions were theoretical treatises based on Mattheson's writings and a translation into Dutch of Burney's travel reports, in 1786. But among the few compositions that have survived out of the many that he listed (as with

40. Mod. ed.: VNM-m No. 32 (Seiffert); note the "Sonata, Villanella" mvt. on p. 69. A further ex. of his writing may be seen in the concerto grosso scored in DDT-m XXIX-XXX 273 (with preface).

41. Cf. the 2 nearly contemporary versions of the story in BACH READER 287 and 334.

42. Cf. MGG VIII 1332-1334 (Reeser), based partly on autobiographic material (again), in Marpurg/BRIEFE II 470-471 (not 740 ff.). A little on both Groningen and Lustig appears in BURNEY'S TOURS II 224; cf. Koole/LOCATELLI 22.

Hurlebusch), a set of *Six Sonates pour le Clavecin,* Op. 1, proves to be not uninteresting. This was published perhaps in 1732, if Lustig's repeated statements are to be accepted,[43] or more probably about 1737, if the plate number 36 of Witvogel in Amsterdam has been correctly placed.[44] The sonatas are about as much on the border between late-Baroque and pre-Classic styles, about as close to suites, and about as much under the influence of the French clavecinists as Hurlebusch's 2 sets of sonatas. But they have more of the unusual—in fact, enough more to suggest that it could have been they that contained the "*bizarrerie* and confused taste of the present day" to which Hurlebusch objected in the Italian rather than French subtitle of Op. 5. Lustig's keyboard writing is more advanced, the forms are freer, the recitative passages are more numerous, the lines are more angular, the rhythms are more diverse, the texture is more varied (including a fugal finale in Son. 3), and the cycles are planned still more flexibly. As a sample of the last, Sonata 1 in c, interrelated by dotted patterns in almost every movement, consists of 9 movements in the same key, with the titles "Ouverture," "Avec Vivacité," "Gravement" and a return to the previous movement, "Vivement," "Allemande," "Courante," "Lentement," "Rondeau" with 3 couplets, and "Menuet" with 3 doubles. The titles "Tendrement" and "Promptement" (as in Son. 2) recur rather often.

Further sonatas bordering on the Baroque were left by **Antoine Mahaut** (or Mahault; ?-at least 1760), a symphonist and author of an up-to-date flute treatise who seems to have been active in Amsterdam except for visits to Paris in 1740 and 1755.[45] Published and republished in Amsterdam, Paris, and London between 1740 and 1775, these sonatas are in Fl/bass, SS/bass, and SS settings.

The chief native Hollander from our standpoint was the violinist **Pieter Hellendaal** (Helendale, etc.; 1721?-99), who was born in

43. Cf. MGG VIII 1333.

44. Deutsch/NUMBERS 27. A later Witvogel ed. is identified as "c. 1740" in BRITISH UNION II 636. Lustig's set was overlooked in Newman/EARLIEST. Madame Leclair's engraving of Lustig's sons., published in Paris in 1742 with the avowed purpose of correcting misattributions, is reported to be partially if not entirely a forgery in Pincherle/LECLAIR 35-36 (and largely accepted as such in SBE 380 and MGG VIII 1333). The evidence is given as identifications by Sorel-Nitzberg of pieces by Scarlatti, Giustini, "etc." (without further details). But in at least a brief check made here no such identifications could be found, and one must note that Son. 2 of Lustig's original ed. (which was too early for any likely Scarlatti forgery) = Son. 5, rearranged, in the Leclair ed., 3 = 6, 4 = 1, 5 = 2, and the other 3 sons. in the Leclair ed. are very similar in style. Leclair was in Holland from 1740-42 (cf. Koole/LOCATELLI 34-35).

45. Cf. MGG VIII 1487-1488 (Cotte); La Laurencie & Saint-Foix/SYMPHONIE 79-81 (with orchestral exx.); BRITISH UNION II 642.

Rotterdam, studied with Tartini in Padua at 15, moved to Amsterdam by 1744, and moved to England in 1752 for the rest of his life.[46] Two sets of 6 Vn/bass sonatas each were published at Hellendaal's own expense in Amsterdam while he was still there—that is, Opp. 1 and 2, dating from about 1744 and 1750. In England appeared another such set, Op. 4, about 1760; a set of 8 Vc/bass sonatas, Op. 5, about 1770;[47] and *Three Grand Lessons for the Harpsichord or Pianoforte With an Accompaniment for a Violin and Violoncello,* Op. 6, about 1790. Other Vn/bass and accompanied sonatas, left in MS by Hellendaal, are lost.[48] Although Hellendaal's later works are said to be more in the *galant* style,[49] the cello sonatas still show a distinct Baroque orientation. Long, elegiac, ornamental lines in Tartini's manner are spun over an active *b.c.* that engenders a relatively quick harmonic rhythm. Even the fast movements are as interesting for their melodic lines as for their decidedly idiomatic string passage work. Several of the sonatas have the 4-movement sequence, S-F-S-F, of the old church sonata. The principal key is major in every sonata. The forms are limited to French rondeaux with couplets or, especially, monothematic binary designs with repeats and frequently a return to the initial idea in the tonic during the second half. There is musical substance in the lines and harmony, and tonal security in the forms. But there is no special individuality in these sonatas unless it be in certain Dutch traits that Borren finds in Sonatas 4 and, particularly, 7 (or nos. 3 and 2 in VNM-m No. 41).[50]

Similar in character, quality, and conservatism, are the 6 Vc/bass sonatas, Op. 9, by the presumed Neapolitan **Francesco Guerini** (1710?-80?[51]), who seems to have been in Holland from about 1740 to 1760 before going to England.[52] Although little else is known about him today, he was popular enough in his own day to have at least 7 sets of sonatas in Vn/bass, Vc/bass, and SS settings pub-

46. Cf. MGG VI 97-100 (Cudworth), including an interesting picture of him in concert, facs. of the title page and dedication of Op. 1, and full bibliographies; also, Borren/HELLENDAAL.

47. Op. 5 is discussed in Borren/HELLENDAAL 344-351, with facs. of the title page after p. 356. Op. 5 is dated *ca.* 1770 in BRITISH UNION I 476 and *ca.* 1780 in MGG VI 99. Mod. ed.: 4 sons., VNM-m No. 41 (Röntgen), but with mvts. transplanted and other disfigurements (cf. Borren/HELLENDAAL 341 and 347, with similar comments on W. Pijper's ed. of Op. 5/3).

48. Cf. MGG VI 99; also, GROVE IV 226 (Blom) for the mention of an ed. of Hellendaal's complete works projected in VNM-m.

49. MGG VI 99.

50. Borren/HELLENDAAL 347-348 and 348-349.

51. The dates are given without question, but also without any basis known here, in Schmidl/DIZIONARIO II 675.

52. Cf. MGG V 1028 (Cudworth), with list of works and of mod. eds. of 4 sons. from Opp. 1 and 2 (Vn/bass) and 9. A facs. of the title page of Op. 1 is in Humphries & Smith/PUBLISHING 215.

lished variously in London, The Hague, Amsterdam, Paris, and Edinburgh, between about 1740 and 1775.[53]

The German-born violinist **Christian Ernst Graf** (or Graaf; *ca.* 1726-*ca.* 1803) was one of the musically active sons and a pupil of that fine musician Johann Graff whom we met in the Baroque Era in Rudolstadt (SBE 281-282). Employed in The Hague from 1762, C. E. Graf left among many other works one set of sonatas in the old setting of violin with realized keyboard, Op. 4; 3 sets in SS/bass setting, Opp. 2, 5, and 10; one accompanied set (K & Vn & Vc); and two 4-hand keyboard duets, Op. 29.[54] These works, unexplored in recent times, were published in The Hague and Amsterdam between about 1765 and 1780.

Besides Guerini the only Italian in Holland to name is the later, obscure pianist (?) **Giovanni Andrea Colizzi** (*ca.* 1740-?), who was in Germany, London, and Paris, and in Holland from 1766 to 1782.[55] Numerous sets of accompanied sonatas or sonatinas by him were published in Amsterdam and London near the end of the century.[56] An examination of one set of "Six Sonatas" published by Preston of London in 1792 (called Op. 8 in another ed.) discloses works of 3 and 4 (not 2 and 3) movements that are slight in length, content, and technical requirements, but are now high-Classic in style.[57]

Another prolific composer of light accompanied sonatas (or "Sonatines," or "Divertissemens," or "Duettino's") in the high-Classic style was the native Dutch pianist **Johann August Just** (*ca.* 1745-*ca.* 1800).[58] Just was a student of Kirnberger in Berlin and of the Holland-born Schwindel whom we met in the "larger" Mannheim circle in Chapter XI. Reportedly born in Groningen, he served in The Hague; then, like Hellendaal, may have moved to London, to judge by his numerous publications with English titles that were printed there.[59] His works were published between about 1770 and 1800, not

53. The "6 Sonate a solo per il pfte" listed in Eitner/QL IV 405 (and only by the composer's last name in MUSIKFREUNDE WIEN II 28) probably refers to Vn/bass sons. arranged in score, as with the thematic index of Op. 1 in Stone/ITALIAN II 30-31.

54. Cf. MGG V 668-669 (Scharnagl & Haase); Scheurleer/NEDERLAND 79, 105 (facs. of title page of Op. 2), 160-161.

55. This much information appears in Schmidl/DIZIONARIO Suppl. 205, but without source. Much confusion appears in Eitner/QL III 12-13.

56. Cf. Eitner/QL III 12-13; BRITISH UNION I 204.

57. This set is briefly described in Stone/ITALIAN I 220, along with a thematic index of it in II 14, and a full copy of Son. 4 in D (without the subordinate Vn part) in III 148.

58. Cf. Eitner/QL V 312-313. The life dates are suggested here only on the basis of the earliest and latest confirmed publications, 1770 and 1799, in BRITISH UNION I 562, no later work being listed in HOFMEISTER 1815 (Whistling).

59. Just was still listed as "a young German" (!) in 1772 among the "fixtures" in The Hague, in BURNEY'S TOURS II 234.

only in London, but in The Hague, Amsterdam, and Berlin. They were performed and publicized at least as far off as Bonn, where the young Beethoven could well have known them among other Dutch works.[60] A reading of two 2-movement "Divertissemens" Op. 12 for keyboard duet (*ca.* 1780) that have been made available[61] suggests that if Beethoven did know Just's music he must have enjoyed it thoroughly, and that Just is wrongly passed by in the standard reference works and histories. The ideas are fresh and expressive enough for all their lightness, and the music moves with convincing verve and drive for all its simplicity.

Other native Dutch composers of light solo, duet, and accompanied sonatas awaiting exploration are **Pieter Soeterijk,** who was in Leiden in 1770,[62] and **Christian Friedrich Ruppe** (*ca.* 1752-at least 1790).[63] In the same musical category is the German-born piano virtuoso and composer of a popular Dutch national song, **Johann Wilhelm Wilms** (1772-1847), who moved to Amsterdam in 1791 and there published most of his music in the early 1800's.[64]

In Belgium the once great center of Brussels was enjoying a certain resurgence of musical activities in the later eighteenth century, especially at the Chapelle royale and court of the Austrian Prince Charles of Lorraine, at the venerable Théâtre de la Monnaie, and at the churches where instrumental groups met.[65] The chief Belgian composer in Brussels at this time, more important to us than either Gossec or Grétry in Paris, was **Pierre van Maldere** (1729-68).[66] One of three brothers serving as violinists at the Chapelle royale, P. v. Maldere was enough of a virtuoso performer to appear in Dublin, Paris, Vienna, and perhaps London between 1752 and 1758.[67] His sonatas consist of a set of 6

60. Cf. Thayer & Riemann/BEETHOVEN I 84; Schiedermair/BEETHOVEN 55.

61. Hillemann/JUST-m.

62. BOUWSTEENEN III 9. An effective light "accompanied" sonata by him with a genuine "obligé" Vn part, published by one Plattner in Rotterdam, is at the Library of Congress.

63. Cf. Eitner/QL VIII 361-363; MGG IX 1500 (Thijsse).

64. Cf. Eitner/QL X 269-270; GROVE IX 910 (Antcliffe); HOFMEISTER 1815 (Whistling), *passim.* In AMZ may be found a favorable review of the piano sons. Op. 13 (X [1807-08] 620); a detailed, unfavorable one, criticizing the "superficiality" of the acc'd. sons. Op. 29 (XV [1813] 643-645); and a short, slightly favorable one on the duets Op. 41 (XVII [1815] 616).

65. Among pertinent surveys, cf. Closson & Borren/BELGIQUE 201-233 (Clercx); BURNEY'S TOURS II 8-10, 17-21; MGG II 388-395 (Borren). The present survey has been somewhat handicapped by the inaccessibility of the incomparable son. collection at the Conservatoire royal de Musique (as only partly listed in Cat. BRUXELLES; cf. GROVE V 163) during the new building program of the past 2 years (1960-61).

66. Clercx/MALDERE is a valuable study of the man and his music. It is very briefly summarized, with minor changes, in MGG VIII 1541-1543 and Closson & Borren/BELGIQUE 215-217.

67. Cf. the brief tributes in Clercx/MALDERE 22; DITTERSDORF 47-48.

in SS/bass setting published by Walsh in London in 1756, 6 more in SS/bass setting in a Milan MS, 3 more out of 6 in SS/bass setting in a Vienna MS of which the other 3 are duplicated in the Walsh set, and 8 in Vn/bass settings in MSS in Brussels and Vienna.[68]

Maldere's "trio" sonatas in the Walsh edition and the Vienna MS are conservative works that give little hint of the significantly pre-Classic traits to be found in his symphonies of 1758 and later, for which he is chiefly remembered.[69] They are in four or three extended movements in the old church or later Baroque plans of S-F-S-F or S-F-F, respectively. Some of the first allegros are fugal (as in Sons. 1 and 6 of the Walsh ed.), revealing Maldere's solid background in harmony and counterpoint, although not any marked individuality. Other first allegros divide into the familiar binary design with repeated halves, and with most of the externals of "sonata form." They may reveal a first and second idea (Ex. 130) as well as the usual closing figure, and a clear return to the first idea in the tonic key, during the second half. But in spite of the *piano* and *forte* signs and the articulation signs that help to demarcate these ideas there is hardly the sense of Classic dualism that has been claimed for the symphonies.[70] The fast harmonic rhythm, imitative texture, and preference for unfolding, often ornamental, lines all still spell Baroque styles. The finales in these "trio" sonatas are quasi-gigues or minuets.

All Maldere's other known sonatas are in three movements, mostly in the order S-F-F. By contrast with the Walsh and Vienna "trio"

68. Cf. the approximately chronological catalogue of works in Clercx/MALDERE 57-59 and 65-68, which requires the following observations: (1) with regard to p. 58, the exact Walsh date of 1756 is given in BRITISH UNION II 645; (2) on p. 57 uncertain evidence is cited for a different, earlier, lost set of 6 SS/bass sons., supposedly published in Dublin in 1752-53 (yet not in BRITISH UNION), but the conservatism of the Walsh set (cf. pp. 58 and 59) suggests that it may be merely a reprint of the Dublin ed.; (3) on pp. 58-59 is noted a Paris reprint of the Walsh set, *ca.* 1765, but an earlier Paris reprint came from De la Chevardière in 1758 (Johansson/FRENCH I 63 and II Facs. 44); (4) on pp. 66-67 the set of 6 Vn/bass sons. listed only as a MS actually seems to have appeared in print, since it probably is the Op. 5 by "Vanmalder" published *ca.* 1767 by De la Chevardière (Johansson/FRENCH I 73; cf., also, Moser/VIOLINSPIEL 380 and Eitner/QL VI 287); (5) on pp. 65-66 the listing of a set of "Sonates pour le clavecin ou piano-forte Op. VII" that is still to be found (as in GROVE V 530 [Corbet]) is rightly shown to be an incorrect title for 3 genuine piano "Trios" with realized keyboard (& Vn & Vc), published in Paris, but the Berlin MS of this set is overlooked (Eitner/QL VI 287).

Mod. ed.: Sons. 6 and 2 in the Walsh set of 1756, Etsen/MALDERE-m (with errors).

69. The year 1758 rather than *ca.* 1760 for his first symphonies comes from Johansson/FRENCH I 63. Carse/SYMPHONIES-m includes a mod. ed. in score of Maldere's Symphony in B♭, Op. 4/3. The sons. are discussed in some detail, with exx., in Clercx/MALDERE 73-102.

70. Cf. Clercx/MALDERE 149-150, 108, *et passim.*

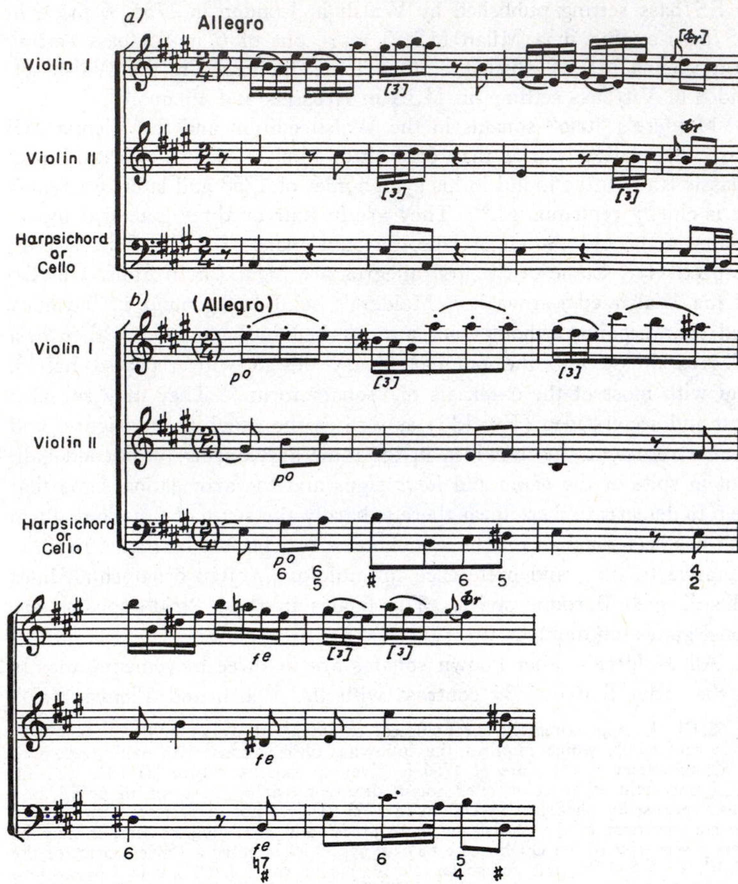

Ex. 130. From (a) the first idea and (b) the second idea in the second movement in Pierre van Maldere's published "trio" Sonata 3 in A (after the Walsh ed. at the Library of Congress).

sonatas, those in the Milan MS are described as a kind of study in more up-to-date Italian styles.[71] They are distinctly less developed, briefer, more *galant* in their specific style traits, and more homophonic. With regard to the homophony, the bass is now unfigured and the second violin part becomes only a filler part made up of the characteristi-

71. Clercx/MALDERE 86-94.

cally vapid figures in *galant* accompaniments. The Vn/bass sonatas in the Brussels and Vienna MSS are also homophonic, with an unfigured bass, and they exhibit a greater tendency toward phrase grouping. But they show a further difference in their advanced, virtuosic treatment of the solo instrument.[72]

Maldere's sonatas, especially the more conservative ones, resemble most closely those of another, somewhat older violinist at the Chapelle royale in Brussels, **Henri-Jacques De Croes** (1705-86). Between 1734 and 1747 two sets of 6 SS/bass sonatas each, Opp. 1 and 3, and one set of 6 SSA/bass sonatas, Op. 4, were published among related instrumental works in Brussels and/or Paris.[73] Cast in 3 movements, F-S-F, or 4 movements in variable order, De Croes's sonatas are decidedly Baroque in their fugal and other polyphonic movements, and late-Baroque in their motivic, lighter, more tuneful movements. A conspicuous trait in these last is the quick 3-note stepwise slide beginning on the strong beat. The music is telling and pleasant, without any significant show of imagination.

Several Belgian composers of pre-Classic sonatas, mostly for keyboard, must be noted still more briefly, for want of their music. **Guillaume Boutmy** (1723-91), member of the Flemish family of musicians by that name and keeper of instruments at the Brussels court, composed a set of 6 harpsichord sonatas that was published in Brussels and Liège around 1755.[74] Cast in 3 movements in the order F-S-F, these sonatas are said to contain monothematic movements in a pre-Classic *galant* style a little later than, but somewhat suggestive of, D. Scarlatti's style, with certain *empfindsam* traits, too.[75]

In Liège, itself an active eighteenth-century music center under strong Italian and French influences,[76] one **Hubert Renotte** (?-1747) published a set of *Six Sonates de clavecin* as early as 1740, in the same 3-movement plan. Renotte's advice that a cellist need play only the lowest note in the chordal bass and the fact that their style suggests the string writing of Vivaldi both indicate that the alternative

72. Cf. Clercx/MALDERE 94-102.

73. Clercx/DE CROES is a full study, including a *catalogue raisonnée* of the works (I 28-40), an analysis of forms (I 42-50, for the sons.); a thematic index (II xxv-xli for the instrumental works); complete reprints in score of Opp. 3/4/i and iii, 1/5/i, 1/6/iii (II lxxvii-xcvii), among other works; exx., documents, and other aids. Clercx's analysis overemphasizes a search for "sonata form." Cf., also, Closson & Borren/BELGIQUE 214-215 and 216; Clercx/MALDERE 78-80.

74. Cf. GROVE I 851 (Blom), summarizing an article on the family by Clercx. The year is approximated on the basis of the style only. This set is incorrectly ascribed to Giacomo Boutmy in Cat. BRUXELLES II 301.

75. Closson & Borren/BELGIQUE 208.

76. Cf. MGG VIII 1292-1293 (Clercx).

scoring allowed in the title—that is, violin or flute and *b.c.*—was intended by the composer at least as much as the keyboard was.[77] A slight MS keyboard sonata entitled "La Partenza di Roma a Napoli" and composed, during Italian travels from 1749 to 1751, by **Jean-Noël Hamal** (1709-78) suggests similarly that strings may have been the original intention; but more idiomatic uses of the keyboard, in the later pre-Classic manner, reportedly appear in a MS set of *Sei Sonate da Cembalo* by the nephew, **Henri Hamal** (1744-1820).[78] Later pre-Classic trends are also noted in the spirited, 3-movement string sonatas by the Neapolitan-trained violinist **Hermann-François Delange** (1715-81), who published a set of 6 Vn/bass sonatas, Op. 1, in Liège about 1765 and left a set of 6 "trio" sonatas in MS around the same time.[79]

Also about this time, virtuoso Vn/bass sonatas and "trio" sonatas in the melodic and harmonic styles of the later pre-Classic Era were left in MSS and print by an outstanding violinist from Antwerp, **Guillaume-Gommaire Kennis** (1717-89). Kennis was active, during most of his career, in Leuven.[80] Not until the 1770's does the change-over from melo/bass to accompanied settings seem to be made in the Belgian sonatas, and then by organists. Examples are the several published and republished sets of accompanied "Divertissements" and sonatas by **Pieter Joseph Van** (or van) **den Bosch** (*ca.* 1736-64) in Antwerp and **Ferdinand Staes** (1748-1809) in Brussels.[81] An examination of Op. 4 by Staes[82] reveals light two-movement pieces with subordinate violin parts. Their ideas and idiom border on the high-Classic. However, since Staes could or would not extend or develop his ideas appreciably, they follow each other not in dualistic opposition but in a pluralistic patchwork that soon grows tiresome.

Copenhagen (*Scheibe, Zink*)

In Scandanavia during the eighteenth century and up to the Napoleonic Wars a state of neutrality existed between Sweden and Denmark while Norway remained a dependency of Denmark. The music of all three countries reflected strong German, French, and Italian in-

77. Cf. Closson & Borren/BELGIQUE 211, with full title, "Avis," and ex.
78. Cf. Closson & Borren/BELGIQUE 210-211; MGG V 1382-1386 (Clercx).
79. The 2 sets are described in some detail in Closson & Borren/BELGIQUE 217-218, with an extended ex. from Op. 1/5 in D.
80. Cf. MGG VII 836-838 (Dehennin); BURNEY'S TOURS II 22.
81. Cf. BURNEY'S TOURS 11, 13, 14; Eitner/QL II 143 and IX 246-247; BRITISH UNION I 125 and II 971; Closson & Borren/BELGIQUE 212.
82. The original ed. at the Library of Congress was used here, but this set was reprinted as late as 1877 by Schott.

fluences.[83] In Denmark itself, where important social reforms were instituted during the later eighteenth-century regimes of Frederick V and Christian VII, Copenhagen's position as one of Europe's leading music centers was enhanced by the cumulating musical organizations within Danish society and the concerts they gave, as well as by the lively operatic productions at the royal theater.[84] Several of the sonata composers we have already met elsewhere were active at one time or another in this city, including Gluck, Sarti, J. G. Palschau (whom we just met in St. Petersburg), J. G. Naumann, and J. A. P. Schulz. Yet no significant resident composer of sonatas can be reported here, and the composers we do find came not from Denmark itself but from Germany, chiefly through direct land contact with north Germany and centers like Hamburg, Mecklenburg-Schwerin, and Berlin.

The earliest resident to come within our focus, overlapping the late-Baroque and pre-Classic eras as they are now defined, was **Johann Adolph Scheibe** (1708-76). Scheibe was the brilliant but quarrelsome, anti-Italian writer whose views on the Baroque sonata we had more than one occasion to quote in our previous volume.[85] Born in Leipzig, he had grown up in the sphere of J. S. Bach, travelled, and lived in Hamburg before he started his checkered career in Copenhagen in 1744. There he composed a large variety of music, as extensive but hardly as important as his writings, including 2 harpsichord sonatas, in E and B♭, in Anth. HAFFNER OM-m III/6 and IV/5 (1757, '58?), and *III Sonate per il cembalo obligato e flauto traverso o violino concertato,* Op. 1, also published by Haffner about 1758 (plate no. 100).[86] Both harpsichord sonatas are well handled, idiomatic keyboard cycles in 3 movements, in the order F-S-F and M-M-F, respectively. Otherwise, they are different in style. The first movement of the Sonata in E is up-to-date in its short, clearly organized phrases, with a well-defined, tonic return to the initial idea during the second half. Rather than a contrasting idea Scheibe writes somewhat formalistic passage work. The second movement, an "Adagio" still in E, returns a little to the expressive motivic style of J. S. Bach. The ensuing "Vivace" makes a fairly fluent finale as German keyboard sonatas of the times go. By contrast, Scheibe's Sonata in B♭ suggests the strong influence

83. Cf. Schubart/IDEEN 240-244.

84. Cf. MGG VII 1606-1609 (Lunn); II 1848-1849 (Schiørring).

85. SBE 27-28 *et passim.* Cf. Mattheson/EHREN-PFORTE 310-315 (autobiography); Eitner/QL VIII 474-476; Riemann & Gurlitt/LEXIKON II 589-590, with bibliography.

86. Cf. Hoffmann-Erbrecht/HAFFNER 122. No support can be found here for the listing of 6 published Fl/bass sons. under the title "Musikalische Erquick[ung]-stunden," in Riemann/LEXIKON II 1606 and BAKER'S DICTIONARY 1430.

of Emanuel Bach's *Probe-Stücken* sonatas, which had appeared about 5 years earlier (1753). Much the same *empfindsam* traits and specific ornaments, including the trilled and the vertical turns,[87] occur in all 3 movements, along with dynamic and tempo changes in the first movement. This time the finale has too great a variety of rhythms, changes of style, and interruptions to be called fluent. But Scheibe's imitation of Emanuel Bach's style (notwithstanding his earlier resentment of J. S. Bach) must be judged not unworthy of the model. There is no special relation between these sonatas and the more conservative, melo/bass types that Scheibe described in his *Critischer musikus* in 1745.

Another German in Copenhagen, from 1766, was **Johann Ernst Hartmann** (1726-93), an outstanding violinist born in Gross-Glogau (Silesia).[88] Hartmann's Op. 1 was a set of 6 SS/bass sonatas, but except for a few string trios (Vn, Vn, & Vc) the few later things by him that have survived are largely directed toward the theater.[89]

Prior to F. D. R. Kuhlau, who would take us into the pre-Romantic sonata, the remaining German to mention is the singer, flutist, organist, and writer **Harnack Otto Conrad Zink** (or Zinck; 1746-1832).[90] Zink was born in the Schleswig-Holstein region, in Husum, only forty miles below the southwestern land strip of Denmark. He is associated chiefly with Copenhagen, but he did not get there until his appointment as singing master at the royal theater in 1787, which was four years after his first published set of sonatas appeared. This set is *Sechs Clavier-Sonaten,* "along with the ode 'Kain am Ufer des Meeres' as a supplement to the sixth sonata," composed while Zink was serving at the Mecklenburg-Schwerin court and published, with an imposing subscription list, in Hamburg in 1783.[91] Four more sonatas of similar character appeared in the Copenhagen music periodical *Sangen og Claveeret* in 1791-93.[92] Zink's long foreword to the first set is worth summarizing.

Noting the French use of inscriptions in their instrumental character pieces, Zink says nevertheless that the Germans have produced the best examples in which particular emotions and sensations are depicted

87. Cf. Bach/ESSAY 121 and 113.
88. Cf. MGG V 1748-1749 (Schiørring).
89. In Cat. SCHWERIN II 76-77 2 keyboard sonatinas by Hartmann are also listed
90. Cf. Eitner/QL X 352-353; GROVE IX 419 (Loewenberg).
91. The title (with the first incipit) and the lengthy foreword (with ex.) are given in full in Cat. SCHWERIN II 326 and 398-399 (but the reference to Lord Byron's *Cain* is a careless anachronism). Winkel/ZINK is primarily a study of these sons., with exx. and a list of all the mvts. (p. 138). Comments on the foreword and references to a review in Cramer/MAGAZIN I (1783) 1263 appear in Sittard/HAMBURG 125.
92. Discussed in Winkel/ZINK 141-143, with exx. and a list of all mvts.

through melody and harmony. Encouraging reactions from friends for whom he tried the sixth sonata prior to publication have led him to believe that a verbal commentary by the composer can help the listener to understand these feelings. He recalls that in spite of training in harmony and various instruments from his father and further studies in Hamburg (with Emanuel Bach?) he did not really learn how to compose until, after great effort, he grasped these principles (that is, how to express feelings through music). How well he has succeeded must await the judgment of these sonatas by those who have already taken an interest in him and by others. As a sample of the sundry moods that inspired these sonatas, he reveals that a conversation of "Madame la Capricieuse with her gentle-hearted husband" underlies the "Andante" of Sonata 3. As for Sonata 6, one day he gave vent to some forgotten anger by brusquely playing a starting theme at the clavier (clavichord?) that recalled, in turn, the start of music he had set a few months previous to "Kain am Ufer des Meeres" ("Cain at the Seashore") by (the *Sturm und Drang* poet) Count (Friedrich Leopold) von Stolberg. The whole episode of the gruesome fratricide then came back to him in all its vivid details, he tells us.

Though Zink's sonatas are all in the usual three movements, F-S-F, they are distinguished by considerable variety and originality. An element of fantasy, certain characteristic ornaments, daring modulations, further traits of the *empfindsam* style, the late preference for the "Clavier" (clavichord), detailed dynamic markings, and the careful indications of fingering (as in Son. 2/iii) all point to another follower of Emanuel Bach. Melodic chromaticism, fast harmonic rhythm, and short concentrated forms are additional marks of Zink's writing. In Sonata 3 in A, the first movement, "Allegro," leads directly into a free "Andante piu tosto allegro" that seems to suggest "Madame la Capricieuse" through its melodic sighs and similar expressive figures. A separate "Scherzando e presto" provides the finale. In three movements of the two minor sonatas, 4/i in c and 6/i and iii in d, the symphonic drive is notable, while in Sonata 5/i in F, marked "Allegro con Brio," the continuous motion of virtuosic passages suggests a toccata. There are no programmatic inscriptions in Sonata 6, although the finale leads right into Zink's simple strophic setting of the ten stanzas in Stolberg's poem. Both the second and third movement are approached with an "attaca," too. Perhaps a passage from the development section of the first movement can give at least a hint of the force of this effective sonata (Ex. 131).

Ex. 131. From the opening movement of Sonata 6 in d by Harnack Otto Conrad Zink (after the original ed. at the Library of Congress).

Stockholm (*Johnsen, Kraus*)

No noteworthy interest in the sonata by composers resident in Norway during the later eighteenth century is known here. The art music that did obtain was again under predominantly German influence. Opera was enjoyed in Oslo, as were public concerts, including performances of works by both Haydn and Mozart in the 1780's. But after the Baroque composer and public official Georg von Bertouch (1668-1743), who left some two dozen ensemble sonatas in MS and print (lost), the most likely candidate for our attention would be the organist **Johann Daniel Berlin** (1714-87). Yet in the way of sonatas not more than a keyboard sonatina or two by Berlin can be identified today.[93]

However, in Sweden during the reigns of Adolphus Frederick, Gustavus III, and Gustavus IV, in the later eighteenth century, the cultivation of the sonata by residents was considerable, by natives as well as foreigners.[94] On the other hand, we meet no Classic composer in Sweden who was of the stature of the Baroque composer, violinist, and "father of Swedish music," J. H. Roman (1694-1758).[95] It was

93. Cf. MGG IX 1580 (Gurvin); Eitner/QL II 14, I 463.

94. Warm thanks are owing to Ingmar Bengtsson, recently appointed Professor of Musicology at the University of Uppsala (1961), and to the students in his fall, 1960 musicology seminar for preparing much of the material on the son. in Sweden that has been summarized here. Repeated use has been made here, too, of Nisser/SVENSK, a detailed catalogue, with summary analyses, of instrumental music composed in Sweden between 1770 and 1830.

95. The monumental study Bengtsson/ROMAN, which appeared in 1955 but

Roman who prepared the way for later eighteenth-century music in Stockholm, by the public concerts he inaugurated[96] and his own fine playing as well as his composing.[97] Nor do we meet any composers superior to those we have already met elsewhere who came from Sweden (Agrell) or visited that country (including Hurlebusch, J. G. Naumann, and Vogler).

One of the main foreign-born composers of sonatas in Sweden during the Classic Era was **Francesco Antonio Baldassare Uttini** (1723-95).[98] Uttini came from Bologna, where he trained under Martini (or Sandoni?) and Perti, and became a "principe" of the Accademia dei Filarmonici before he moved permanently to Stockholm in 1755. Although he made his niche primarily as an opera composer, Uttini left at least 19 sonatas that can still be identified. Twelve of these are in 2 published sets: (1) *VI Sonates pour le clavecin,* printed in Stockholm by L'Imprimerie royale in 1756;[99] and (2) *Six Sonatas for Two Violins and a Bass: the Third and Sixth with Additional Obligato Parts; one Sonata* [No. 3, with an added part] *for the Violoncello, and the other* [No. 6, with an added part] *for the Harpsichord,* Op. 1, published in 1768, while Uttini was in London, by the Swedish printing innovator in that city, Henry Fougt.[100] Another set of 6 SS/bass sonatas, also labeled Op. 1, exists in 2 MSS and may antedate the published set,[101] and there is a Vn/bass sonata in C in MS at the Musikaliska akademiens Bibliotek in Stockholm.

Uttini's solo keyboard sonatas are in three or four, generally short movements of no fixed order. Among the finales are a "Minué," "Giga presto," and "Rondeau Allegro" (Sons. 1, 2, and 4). A "Fuga" appears as the third of four movements in Sonata 4. The signs of the *galant* style in full bloom are everywhere, including the rather flat

---

was not yet at hand during the writing of SBE 349-350, establishes a bibliographic and style-critical foundation for Roman's music much like that supplied by Larsen for Haydn's music. In this way it also throws much light on 18th-c. Swedish instrumental music in general. An extended English "Summary" is given on pp. 423-443.

96. Detailed chronicles of 18th-c. concert life in Stockholm may be found in Vretblad/STOCKHOLM and Norlind/HOVKAPELLETS 65-121. Cf., also, GROVE VIII 94-96 (Norlind). The history of musical commerce, including printing, in Stockholm and other Swedish centers is explored at length in Wiberg/MUSIKHANDELNS.

97. Bengtsson/ROMAN 423, 426.

98. Cf. SOHLMANS IV 1321-1323; Vretblad/STOCKHOLM 31-77, *passim.*

99. Copy at the Lund University Library, according to Professor Bengtsson. Cf. Wiberg/MUSIKHANDELNS 58.

100. Among several extant copies is that listed in BRITISH UNION II 1030. Cf. Wiberg/MUSIKHANDELNS 94-96, with facs. of the title page and Son. 6/i for "Violino primo."

101. Information from Professor Bengtsson. The MSS are in the Uppsala University Library and the Skara Landsbibliothek.

ideas in short phrases, thin texture, chordal accompaniments, light ornaments, frequent triplet passages, and gentle movements of moderate tempo like "Grazioso" and "Affettuoso." The same number and types of movements are found in the "trio" sonatas and the one Vn/bass example, now most often in the sequence M-F-F. Although these sonatas are perhaps a decade later in origin, the *b.c.* makes for more rapid harmonic rhythm and the setting for a somewhat richer texture in more continuous motivic reiteration. At other times the texture is homophonic, with the second violin playing only a filler part.

The organist **Hinrich Philip Johnsen** (1717-79), who was active in Stockholm from 1743, is thought to have been a foreigner, too, probably from north Germany.[102] Except for one Sonata in a, published in Anth. HAFFNER OM-m III/5 (1757),[103] his sonatas remained in undated MSS, now at the Musikaliska akademiens Bibliotek, including a set of 6 for harpsichord[104] and a set of 10 in SS/bass setting. Johnsen's concept of the sonata was fluid and flexible. The Haffner sonata is in 3 movements in the order F-S-F. The "trio" sonatas are in 2 or 3 movements of no set plan, with only an "Ouverture" and "Alla Breve" in Sonata 4, and with a "Dolce" in 3/4 meter, a "Fuga alle breve" in common-time meter, and an "alla Francese" in 6/8 meter in Sonata 8. Each of the harpsichord sonatas in the set of 6 is in one movement. There are conspicuous *galant* traits in Johnsen's sonatas, especially those for keyboard, as in Uttini's sonatas. But in three respects there is a more distinctive, virile composer here. First, his writing for keyboard, though it posed no unprecedented technical problems in his own day, is varied and ingenious, including fast octaves, repeated notes, hand-exchanges, leaps, double-thirds, and other devices exploited by Scarlatti. Second, his knowledge of counterpoint and harmony confirms the praise his craftsmanship won while he was alive,[105] as in the concentrated, chromatic progression of suspensions and resolutions that opens "trio" Sonata 4 in e, or the close imitations at the start of Sonata 6/ii in G. And third, Johnsen was something of a diamond in the rough, as Purcell was three-quarters of a century earlier. If the larger movements do not coagulate fully—as in the first movement of a Haffner sonata, which has more ideas than can be digested successfully—there is still strength in the ideas themselves, in their bold dispositions, and in the originality of their contexts. In

102. Cf. MGG VII 126-127 (Eppstein), with further bibliography. Numerous references to performances by Johnsen appear in Vretblad/STOCKHOLM, including a "Solo f. Clavecin" twice in 1762 (p. 164).

103. Mod. ed.: Eppstein/JOHNSEN-m, with preface.

104. A mod. ed. of one of these is cited in MGG VII 127.

105. MGG VII 126.

this same Haffner sonata, for example, there are cadence extensions in each movement (i/19-21, ii/4-5, and iii/15-19) that could as well come from a nineteenth-century character piece (Ex. 132).

Ex. 132. From the second movement of Hinrich Philip Johnsen's Sonata in a, in Anth. HAFFNER OM-m III/5 (after the original ed. at the Library of Congress).

In the Musikaliska akademiens Bibliotek there is a MS Sonata in D for violin and unfigured cello "obligato," dated 1773, by a successful native Swedish violinist who had studied with Tartini in Padua, **Anders Wesström** (*ca.* 1720-81).[106] On the border of high-Classic phrase-and-period syntax, this work consists of three movements—an "Allegro," a "Cantabile," and a spirited "Polonese Suezeso" (i.e., "Swedish Polonaise") with twenty technically advanced variations.

The German violinist **Joseph Martin Kraus** (1756-92) ranks with Uttini among the chief foreign-born composers of sonatas in Sweden. Born in Miltenberg, he trained 40 miles west in Mannheim, moved to Stockholm in 1778, eventually succeeded Uttini as the head chapel master at court (1788), and similarly made his reputation pri-

106. Cf. SOHLMANS IV 1438; Vretblad/STOCKHOLM 35, 161-162, *et passim.*

marily in opera.[107] Within Kraus's substantial output of vocal and instrumental music, virtually all of which is preserved at the Uppsala University Library, there are at least 9 sonatas.[108] The only real melo/bass sonata, one in d composed before 1777, is scored for violin and *b.c.* A Sonata in D for flute and (unfigured) viola was composed about the same time (*ca.* 1776).[109] One set of 2 piano sonatas with violin accompaniment, in C and D, was composed after 1777, and another, in E♭ and C, in Paris in 1785, while a single piano Sonata in D with violin and cello accompaniments is placed between 1787 and 1790. Finally, there is a set of 2 piano sonatas that was published, by 1790, under a royal privilege.[110] The first, in E, was composed not before 1787,[111] and the second, in E♭, is simply another version of the accompanied sonata in that key.

Except for his Vn/bass sonata, which is in two movements (with sections of contrasting meter and tempo in the second), all of Kraus's sonatas are in three movements, in the order F-S-F, or F-S-M for the piano Sonata in E with its "Andantino con variazioni" as a finale. Variations also occur twice as middle movements. One sonata has a slow introduction (acc'd. Son. 2 in C). Its finale is a "Scherzo Allegretto" in *alla breve* meter, with suggestions of Beethoven's scherzando style and cross rhythms that are worth mentioning. Another finale is a "Ghiribizzo ["Caprice"] Allegro" 282 measures long (Son. in D for P & Vn & Vc). Two finales are rondos, but none is a minuet.

The two sonatas by Kraus that have been made available—the duo for flute and viola and the piano Sonata in E—give ample evidence that he was no *Vielschreiber* and no slave to public taste. A Haydnesque originality and independence prevail both in their large and their small aspects.[112] In the middle movement of the Sonata in E, marked "Adagio," the "B" section of the over-all A-B-A form is itself an a-b-a form marked "Allegretto," and the "A" section undergoes fundamental alterations when it returns. The initial measures of this "A" section show Kraus's characteristic attention to detail, as do the many rhythmic and textural refinements in the highly imaginative variations of the finale. The first movement keeps the main idea well in view, but not merely by exact repetitions, which would only emphasize the lack of

107. Cf. MGG VII 1711-16 (Engländer), with further bibliography; Norlind/HOVKAPELLETS 102-103 *et passim;* Vretblad/STOCKHOLM *passim.*

108. Cf. the full list of his works by categories in AFMW VII (1925) 477-494 and the instrumental list in Nisser/SVENSK 221-245.

109. Mod. ed.: NAGELS-m No. 76 (Winter), with preface.

110. Nisser/SVENSK 228.

111. Mod. ed.: Rosenberg/KRAUS-m.

112. Kraus met Haydn, as well as Gluck and Albrechtsberger, during travels in the 1780's (MGG VII 1711).

clearly contrasted ideas. Instead, this movement allows the main idea to alter its form in plastic fashion, during the outer sections as well as the genuine development section. There are hints of Emanuel Bach's *empfindsam* style in Kraus's abrupt tonal and dynamic contrasts, in the fantasy of his changing tempos, and in occasional deceptive cadences. There is much less of the high-Classic fluency that marks the music of his almost exact contemporary, Mozart. But there is not a little suggestion of Clementi in Kraus's resourceful exploitation of the sonorities and contrasts available on the newly popular piano.

The native Swedish composer, pianist, and stringsman, **Johan Wikmanson** (1753-1800) was a pupil of Johnsen, a disciple of Kraus, and a co-worker of Vogler.[113] His compositions include three cither sonatas published in 1781 and two piano sonatas, in b and C, left in MSS in the Musikaliska akademiens Bibliotek and not printed until recent times.[114] Some of Kraus's caprice and individuality come back in Wikmanson's two piano sonatas, which, however, are less subtle and technically advanced—and less so, evidently, than his own three string quartets Op. 1 dedicated posthumously by his daughter to Joseph Haydn.[115] Most of the movements fall into several repeated sections. The Sonata in b is in three movements, the last being headed "La Capricieuse." The Sonata in C[116] is in four or five movements (depending on where the divisions are made), including an "Alla polacca" and a witty, if naive, programmatic finale labeled "Hönshuset" ("Henhouse").

More prolific was the (German-born?) violinist **Christian Friedrich Müller** (1752-1827).[117] A set of 6 Vn/bass sonatas, Op. 2, by him was composed by 1780 and published by 1784, another set of 3, Op. 3, was published by 1793, and 4 separate sonatas of this type were composed in the later 1780's but 3 of these were not published.[118] He also used the title "Six Sonates" for a set of string quartets composed by 1799.[119] In spite of the old-fashioned scoring, Müller's Vn/bass sonatas, which are nearly all in 3 movements, F-S-F, appear to be spirited works in the high-Classic idiom.

113. Cf. SOHLMANS IV 1481-1483, with further bibliography, including a 1952 diss. by C.-G. S. Mörner.
114. Cf. Nisser/SVENSK 395-397, including references to mod. eds.
115. Cf. Nisser/SVENSK 392-393; Landon/HAYDN 201-202.
116. Not the Son. in b, as in GROVE IX 292 (Dale).
117. His birthplace is given as Rheinsberg in Eitner/QL VII 104 (with a wrong death date), as Braunschweig in Vretblad/STOCKHOLM 70 (cf., also, pp. 123-125, *et passim*), and not at all in SOHLMANS III 1126.
118. Cf. Nisser/SVENSK 276-277 and 284-285, including reference to a mod. ed. of Op. 3/1 in A. Further information comes from Professor Bengtsson.
119. Cf. Nisser/SVENSK 282-283.

Still more prolific was the influential, native Swedish organist, song composer, and music publisher, **Olaf Åhlström** (1756-1835).[120] Åhlström himself published his 2 sets of 3 and 4 accompanied sonatas, Opp. 1 and 2 (K & Vn), in 1783 and 1784, and his 2 sets of 3 solo keyboard sonatas and sonatinas, Opp. 3 and 4, both in 1786.[121] Also, in 1793, 1815, and 1817, 3 other solo sonatas by him were published in the *Musikaliskt Tidsfördrif*.[122] These are all light, fluent, somewhat elementary pieces in the high-Classic idiom, intended for the dilettante.

Five other Classic sonata composers in Sweden can be given only passing mention, including **Johan Adolf Mecklin** (1761-1803), for 2 keyboard sonatas published in 1792 and 1795;[123] the dilettante violinist **Henrik Bratt** (1768-1821), for a set of 6 attractive Vn/bass sonatas with a Mozartean flavor, Op. 1, published in 1806;[124] **Erik Lorens Zebell** (1767-1819), for 3 violin sonatas or "Divertissemens" with unfigured bass, Op. 1, incorporating French Revolutionary songs and published in Paris (1817?);[125] **Conrad Gottfried Kuhlau** (1762-1827; not known to relate to F. D. R. Kuhlau), for a set of 3 accompanied sonatas, Op. 1 (K & Vn), published by 1801, as well as a set of 4 string quartets each individually called "Sonata";[126] and **Thomas Byström** (1772-1839), for another set of 3 accompanied sonatas (H-or-P + Vn), published by Breitkopf & Härtel in Leipzig about 1801.[127]

America (*Reinagle*)

Not until its high-Classic phase in European culture did the sonata make its first small mark on American musical life, and then chiefly by
128a way of England.[128] Understandably, there was little opportunity for such refinements and esoteric diversions before the end of the colonial struggles that underlay the French and Indian Wars (up to 1763), or the American Revolution that at last brought independence (1775-83), or the political insecurity that awaited the agreement on a Federal

120. Cf. SOHLMANS IV 1591-1593; GROVE I 75-76 (Dale) and Suppl. 480.

121. Cf. Nisser/SVENSK 446-448; Wiberg/MUSIKHANDELNS 97-103 (with facs. of the title page of Op. 1).

122. Cf. Nisser/SVENSK 450 and 455-456.

123. Nisser/SVENSK 272.

124. Cf. SOHLMANS I 661; Nisser/SVENSK 65-6

125. Nisser/SVENSK 440-441.

126. Nisser/SVENSK 248-249.

127. Cf. SOHLMANS I 751; Nisser/SVENSK 82.

128. The prime source is still Sonneck/AMERICA. Some additional information appears in Sonneck & Upton/BIBLIOGRAPHY, which includes biographic data (pp. 497-531) and is an indispensable bibliography of early American music, in any case; and further information appears in regional or city studies like PENNSYLVANIA and Johnson/BOSTON.

Constition in 1787 and the inauguration of George Washington, our first president, in 1789. Nor was this young, musically inexperienced country likely to be receptive to something so high-flown as the sonata until the greenhorn, amateur, or dilettante could be met half way or more with a lighter, easier (high-Classic) type certain to be "pleasing
to the ladies."[129] Nor, for that matter, could a foreign importation like 129a
the sonata be transplanted successfully to this country without the help of immigrating professionals, in the 1780's and 1790's, like James Hewitt or Alexander Reinagle.

Under all these circumstances one can hardly expect to discover any significant contribution to the Classic sonata from America during the era of Haydn, Mozart, and Beethoven. Certainly, it would be disproportionate in this over-all survey to dwell at any length on such signs of interest in the sonata as did exist. Yet even these signs may amount to more than some have realized. In any case, we should not conclude our protracted survey without satisfying at least the top layer of curiosity that naturally arises about this corner of our subject.

Probably the most interesting aspect of the Classic sonata in America is not the sonatas themselves but the introduction of the sonata into our musical life. Public concerts are known as far back as the early 1730's in this country—in Charleston, New York, and Boston, with Philadelphia following about 25 years later. But the earliest performance of a sonata that Sonneck reports was that of a "Sonata on the Harpsichord" during a "Performance of Solemn Music, vocal and instrumental,
in the College Hall," in Philadelphia in 1765.[130] And most of nearly 130a
100 further instances that he reports up to 1800 (if we include the use of "Solo" and "Lesson" as in the English models) occurred in the late 1780's and throughout the 1790's. No public performance of a sonata in Boston is reported before 1792,[131] although sonatas were certainly for sale at least 8 years earlier in that city,[132] and they must be presumed to have been taught and played in private still earlier.

Glancing through the early programs in which sonatas, overtures, concertos, solos, and the like were interspersed, one cannot fail to note how often the weight of these is counterbalanced by "sure-fire" sensationalism—prodigies, potpourris of "favorite airs," stunt renditions, even card tricks.[133] Yet by the end of the century the average quality

129. A vivid picture of the musical levels and tastes in America at this time is painted in Loesser/PIANOS 433-458. Cf., also, Chase/AMERICA's 84-145; Howard & Bellows/AMERICA 33-91.

130. Sonneck/AMERICA 66-68.

131. Sonneck/AMERICA 290.

132. Cf. the facs. of the Boston Book-Store's advertisement in Fisher/BOSTON 22.

133. E.g., cf. Sonneck/AMERICA 77 and 22.

of those programs was not appreciably below that in Europe, at least as regards their selectivity and up-to-dateness if not performance.[134] Throughout the programs, the composers of the sonatas are indicated less than half the time, typical being the listing of that first known Boston performance, "A Sonata on the Piano-Forte by a Young Lady." Even when the composer is named, as in "Favorite Sonata of Nicholais on the Piano," the specific opus and number are almost never indicated.[135] For that matter, we may wonder how often the title "Sonata" was used in the program listings merely in the older generic sense of "instrumental piece." There is no such original work as "The Celebrated Sonata of Dr. Haydn, for two performers on one piano-forte," played in Albany in 1797.[136] This could have been Haydn's 4-hand variations, "Il Maestro e lo scolare," first published in London in 1780, but it hardly was any of the arrangements of Haydn's symphonies and quartets that began to appear as 4-hand "sonatas" not before 1796.[137] It is interesting that one of Beethoven's first compositions to be published in this country was his original 4-hand Sonata in D, Op. 6, printed by Bacon in Philadelphia about 1815.[138] But slightly earlier, still about 1815, the same publisher had issued a collection of "Twenty four sonatas for the piano forte, or Elegant extracts from Mozart, Haydn, Beethoven, Steibelt, Koželuch, Pleyel . . . ," in which the 2 "sonatas" by Beethoven prove to be merely arrangements of No. 1 of the "Zwölf Contretänze" (WoO 14) and No. 4 of the "Sieben Ländlerische Tänze" (WoO 11).[139]

Assuming that Reinagle usually played his own works when he played the piano in public,[140] he was far and away the most performed composer of sonatas in early American concert life. Other composers who are identified with sonatas up to 1800 include Haydn, Mozart, Pleyel, Steibelt, (J. B.) Cramer, Schroeter, Prati, Franceschini, Capron, Garth, Moller, Nicolai, Sacchini, Koželuch, and Schetky. Kocžwara's "fav-

134. Cf. Sonneck/AMERICA 91-93 for a defense of the late 18th-c. American programs.

135. The nearest is "Nicolai's Favorite Sonata opera 3d" (Sonneck/AMERICA 59).

136. Listed in Sonneck/AMERICA 249.

137. Cf. Hoboken/HAYDN 807-808, 810-811. An American ed. of 1803 is described in Norton/HAYDN 334-335 and 312 (facs. of title page); this is an illuminating study of early Haydn interest in America.

138. The ed. is not in Kinsky & Halm/BEETHOVEN. Cf. pp. 244-245 (with facs. of title page) in Kinkeldey/BEETHOVEN, a fascinating account of the earliest cultivation of Beethoven in this country; the first public performance of Beethoven is given as 1820 (p. 234) and the earliest from a son. is not until 1838 (p. 244; "Funeral March" from Op. 26).

139. Cf. LC MUSIC 207.

140. There is often a doubt as to whether the program lists the composer or performer when the names are more obscure (cf. Sonneck/AMERICA 129 and 150; Krohn/REINAGLE 144; Norton/HAYDN 312-315).

orite" sonata, *The Battle of Prague,* seems to have been as popular in America as in Europe,[141] being heard in another Schetky arrangement for "full band," too.[142] The majority of the sonatas listed were for piano solo (a kind of fact that the programs do specify almost invariably). But no sonata for piano was listed until 1785, although this instrument had made its appearance in a Boston concert as early as 1771.[143] Besides the harpsichord, used earlier, the instruments or settings listed with the sonatas include piano duet, two pianos, organ, harp, cello, violin, English guitar, Spanish guitar, Italian guitar with violin, salterio, and Italian harmonica.[144] Relatively few of the sonatas seem to have been in either the older Vn/bass or the newer accompanied settings. Otherwise the sonata composers and types made a very representative showing by the 1790's.

This showing is the more noteworthy when one recalls the opposition over here to "modern" innovations like the sonata. In 1765, Benjamin Franklin (1706-90), one of our most important and cosmopolitan statesmen to take a strong interest in music and himself something of a guitarist as well as a developer of the glass harmonica,[145] preferred "the simple tunes sung by a single voice," as revealed in two well-known letters.[146] And 46 years later, in 1811, a reviewer was still writing in the same vein when he paid James Hewitt "a compliment" by saying that "his selection of well-known and favorite pieces for interludes, in preference to the sinfonia and 'sonata' and his taste in modulation from 'gay' to 'grave' and from grave to gay is highly desirable of approbation."[147]

However, there were also strong if somewhat isolated forces working in favor of the sonata and other instrumental music of the sort. After all, under Bohemian and German influence, the Moravians in Bethlehem, 60 miles north of Philadelphia, had started a Collegium musicum as early as 1744 that was to be playing chamber music and symphonies of J. (?) Stamitz, Filtz and further Mannheimers, J. C. Bach, Abel, Haydn, Mozart, and still others of the period before the death of Mozart.[148] One of their members, the Dutch-German organist Johann Friedrich Peter (1746-1813), wrote 6 string quintets in 1789 while in the

141. Cf. Loesser/PIANOS 449-450, 455, 459; Johnson/BOSTON 59.
142. Sonneck/AMERICA 149-150, 250. Cf. Johnson/BOSTON 70-71.
143. Sonneck/AMERICA 81 and 265, respectively. Cf. Loesser/PIANOS 441-442.
144. E.g., cf. Sonneck/AMERICA 22, 196, 52, 307, 234, 86, 229, 83, 175, 76, 175, and 59, respectively.
145. Cf. PENNSYLVANIA III/2 449-463.
146. Printed in full in PENNSYLVANIA III/2 464-472 (with editorial comments).
147. From the quotation in Johnson/BOSTON 38.
148. Cf. PENNSYLVANIA II 155-188; McCorkle/MORAVIAN; Norton/HAYDN 319-320.

Moravian colony in Salem (now Winston-Salem), North Carolina, that are superior in import and skill to any of the sonatas we shall be noting.[149] Another, the Pennsylvania-born minister John Antes (1740-1811), wrote 3 string "Trii," Op. 3, (2 Vns & Vc), which, although composed in Cairo, probably about 1780, after he left his country, represent the first known chamber music by a native American.[150] And the Swabian bishop in Salem, Johannes Herbst (1735-1812), included in his valuable music library such up-to-date items as 2 sets of sonatas each by Hässler and Haydn (H. XVI/21-32) and one set each by E. W. Wolf and Emanuel Bach (W. 53), as well as current "methods" like Türk's *Klavierschule*.[151]

Furthermore, Thomas Jefferson (1743-1826), another of our most important and cosmopolitan statesmen to take a strong interest in music, was much more receptive than Franklin to the new importations. Besides the obvious fact that he lived more than a generation later, he himself was an amateur violinist who enjoyed playing the chamber music of his times and only wished (in a letter from Paris dated Sept. 30, 1785) that he could partake more of the rich musical life in Europe.[152] Ample indications of his knowledge of, and taste for, current chamber music are provided by the careful MS catalogue of his library that he pre-
153a pared between 1783 and 1815.[153] Confining ourselves to composers still remembered and only to those represented by sonatas (with the op. no. often given), we find not only Baroque names like Corelli (complete), Pasquali, Lampugnani (much), Gasparini, Tessarini, Arnold, and Stanley, but more recent ones like G. B. Sammartini (much), Abel, Campioni, Agrell, Giardini, Haydn (much), Pugnani, Schwindel, Kammel, Vanhal, Pleyel, and Boccherini, along with many current "methods" and treatises.

As for actual sonata composers resident in America, the four to whom we shall give chief mention were all foreign-born. Sonatas composed by native Americans in the early 1800's may turn up when that still obscure period in our music history is adequately explored, but none has been found in the course of the present survey.[154] Perhaps the composer who first wrote a sonata in this country that is extant was

149. Reprinted by C. F. Peters in 1954 (David). Cf. David/UNITAS 19-26.

150. Cf. McCorkle/ANTES 486-487, 493-495, 499 (with facs. of the original Bland ed., before 1795; for quartets by Antes cf. JAMS XXXIII (1980) 565-574.

151. Cf. McCorkle/SALEM I 175-176.

152. Cf. Chase/AMERICA'S 83, 85-87, 105.

153. Chaps. 35 and 37 in section 5, on music, in the Coolidge Collection of Jefferson Papers at the Massachusetts Historical Society in Boston.

154. Grateful acknowledgment is made here of source information provided for this survey by the late William Treat Upton, some of which also appears in Sonneck & Upton/BIBLIOGRAPHY.

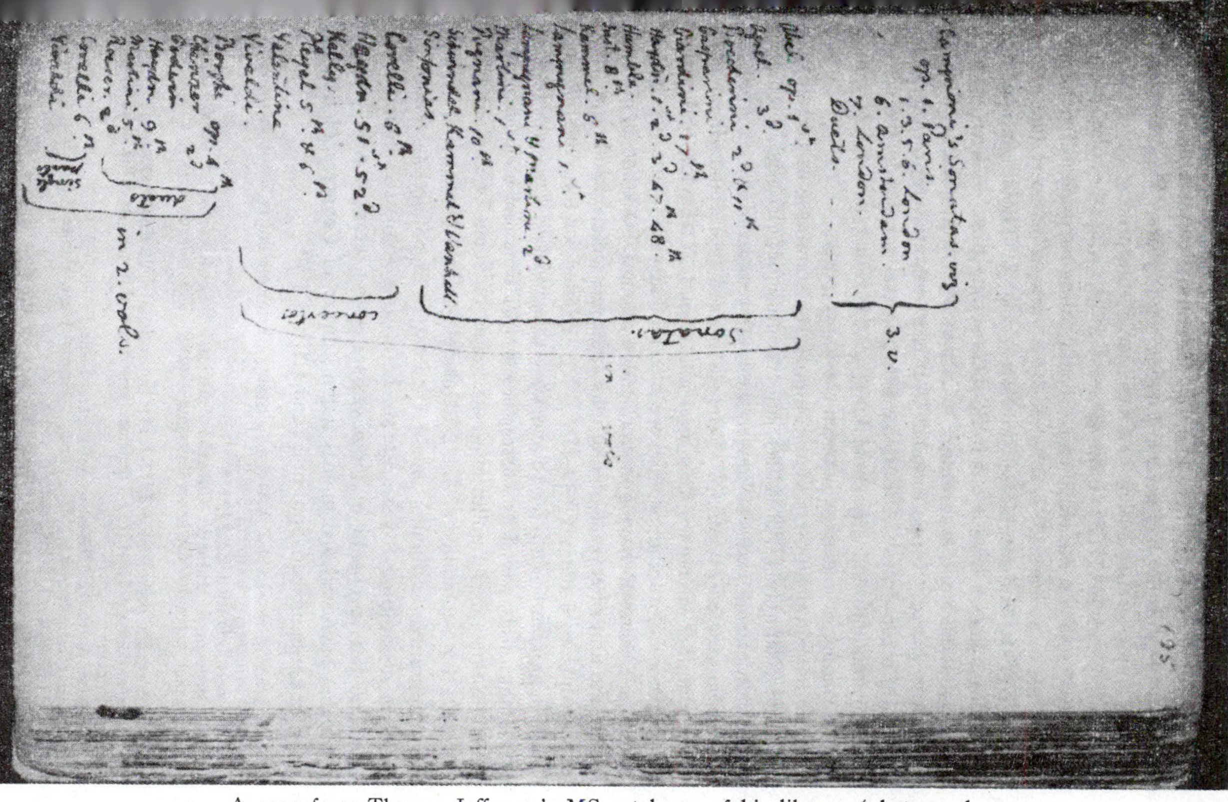

125

Campioni's Sonatas. viz
op. 1. Paris.
1.3.5.6. London
6. Amsterdam.
7. London.
Duets. } 3. v.

Abel op. 1st.
Agrel. 3d.
Boccherini 2d. & 11th.
Gasparini
Giardini. 17th.
Haydn. 1st. 2d. 3d. 47th. 48th.
Humble.
Just. 8th.
Kammel. 5th
Lampugnani 1st.
Lampugnani & Martini. 2d.
Martini. 1st.
Pugnani 10th.
Schwindel, Kammel & Vanhall.
Sinfonias. } Sonatas.

Corelli. 6th.
Haydn. 51st. 52d.
Kelly.
Pleyel 5th. & 6th.
Valentine
Vivaldi. } concertos

} in vols

Borghi op. 4th
Chinzer 2d
Godwin
Haydn. 9th
Martini 5th
Roeser. 2d } duets
Corelli 6th.
Vivaldi } single parts
} in 2. vols.

A page from Thomas Jefferson's MS catalogue of his library (photograph by courtesy of the Massachusetts Historical Socitey).

an Italian violinist and harpsichordist **Gaetano Franceschini.** This musician, who probably had been in London a few years,[155] is otherwise identified only as being active in Charleston's enterprising St. Cecilia Society (founded in 1762) from at least 1774, when he played an unidentified "solo" on the violin and "Sonata on the harpsichord" among other works, to at least 1781, followed by a "benefit" concert that was given in 1783 by and for himself in New York.[156] The single sonata by him that is known here is one in SS/bass setting that has been made known in a phonograph recording.[157] Cast in three movements—"Largo," "Allegro," and "Rondo cantabile"—it is an ingratiating, melodious, competently made work. A Baroque flavor is still present in the continuously unfolding and sequential lines, in the rather active *b.c.*, and in a fair amount of exchange between the upper parts.

The most important resident composer of sonatas was certainly **Alexander Reinagle** (1756-1809), an accomplished English pianist of Austrian descent, who was born in the same year as Mozart and died in the same year as Haydn.[158] Reinagle trained in Edinburgh under another emigrant whom we shall meet in America, R. Taylor, and was the brother-in-law of the Schetky we met in that city in the previous chapter. He seems to have gone to London about 1780—that is, about the time the first of several publications appeared there, including a set of 6 accompanied sonatas (P-or-H & Vn) "Printed for the Author" in 1783.[159] Apparently in 1784 he and his brother visited Emanuel Bach in Hamburg, after which he corresponded with Emanuel about a projected but unrealized publication in London of some of the latter's rondos.[160] By September of 1786, Reinagle was in Philadelphia. His many appearances in public concerts (at least 26 in Sonneck/AMERICA) took place in the next 8 years, before he became engrossed in theater music, and it is probably in those years that he wrote 4 solo piano sonatas that have survived in MS at the Library of Congress (I in D,
161a II in E, an unnumbered Son. in F, and III in C).[161]

155. A set of 6 sons. for 2 Vns by "Giovanni" Franceschini is listed in an ed. of *ca.* 1769 in BRITISH UNION I 346.

156. Sonneck/AMERICA 22, 24, 184.

157. "Instrumental Music in Colonial America," New Records LP 2006, with valuable jacket notes by Carleton Sprague Smith. The source of the music is not given.

158. Cf. BAKER'S DICTIONARY 1323-1324; Sonneck & Upton/BIBLIOGRAPHY 521-522; Chase/AMERICA'S 110-117. The chief article on the man and his sonatas is Krohn/REINAGLE.

159. BRITISH UNION II 884; the Vn part is lost.

160. Cf. Krohn/REINAGLE 143. The 2 letters were printed by Sonneck in SIMG VIII (1906-07) 112-114.

161. Cf. Krohn/REINAGLE 143-149, with a facs. of the first page of Son. III/ii, plus 2 exx., from Sons. I and III; Sonneck & Upton/BIBLIOGRAPHY 393. Mod. ed.:

Ex. 133. From the reprise in the second movement of the Sonata in C by Alexander Reinagle (after the autograph at the Library of Congress).

Reinagle must have been a very impressionable composer, for his 6 accompanied sonatas, in 2 and 3 movements of only moderate musical interest, are said to show the clear influence of Christian Bach,[162] whereas the 4 solo sonatas certainly show the equally clear but very different influence of Emanuel Bach. Each of the 4 solo sonatas is in 3 movements on the same tonic, but with the middle movement of the last 3 sonatas in the minor mode. The first of these sonatas has the order F-F-M, ending with a theme-and-variations.[163] In the other 3 solo sonatas the order is F-S-F. Emanuel Bach's mark is evident in the extended harmonic vocabulary, the free modulations, the numerous half and deceptive cadences, the fantasy character of the passage work, and the specific kinds of ornaments. One might also guess at Haydn's influence (which the music of Peter and Antes shows, too), especially in the charming individuality of Reinagle's best melodic ideas. In all his movements Reinagle achieves decidedly more depth than any other sonata composer of his time in this country (Ex. 133).

Reinagle's teacher, the English organist and singer **Raynor Taylor** (*ca.* 1747-1825), came to this country 6 years later, in 1792,

---

Son. II, Howard/AMERICAN-m, unfortunately abridged by deletions throughout that do serious intrinsic harm to the music; the complete son. is performed on New Records LP 2006 by Arthur Loesser (cf. Franceschini, *supra*).

162. Krohn/REINAGLE 141-142.

163. Cf. Krohn/REINAGLE 143-144 and 145-146, but the supposed additional mvt. (in third place), an Andante in A with variations, is actually Reinagle's separate arrangement of Haydn's "Imperial" Symphony in D, No. 53/ii (Norton/HAYDN 313).

settling in Philadelphia the next year.[164] A set of 6 accompanied
sonatas, Op. 2 (H-or-P & Vn), by Taylor had appeared in London
about 1780,[165] and another such sonata (P & Vn) was published by
166a Carr in Philadelphia in 1797.[166] Also, 6 Vc/bass sonatas, perhaps
written for his friend Schetky, were evidently left in MS, from which
set Sonatas 4 in D and 6 in C have been made available in phonograph
recordings. These last, in 3 movements, F-S-F, belie their era and the
light, witty songs by which Taylor was best known. They come much
closer to a late Baroque cross between the styles of Handel, at whose
grave Taylor mourned, of James Nares, with whom he studied, and of
Samuel Arnold, a fellow chorister. Put differently, they are elegant,
noble, well-conceived pieces composed, without special originality, according to the tried-and-true melodic and harmonic formulas of late-
Baroque writing.

No such redeeming qualities can be found in the sonatas of
another Englishman, the violinist **James Hewitt** (1770-1827), who
166b lived the same years as Beethoven. Hewitt had remained long enough
in London to play under Haydn's direction, coming to New York in
1792.[167] His 3 solo piano sonatas, Op. 5, were published about 1795
168a by the Carr in New York whose music store he soon bought.[168]
They are all in 2 movements, consisting of an allegro and a rondo.
Their style is that of the late, decadent Mannheim School, but more
naïve and not seldom marred by gauche voice-leading and parallelisms.
Unison and octave openings, "singing-allegro" melodies over Alberti
basses, and tremolando chords over trombone-like statements in bass
octaves are Hewitt's stock in trade. A single, similar sonata, "Dedicated to Miss M. Mount" and now at the Library of Congress, was
published by Hewitt himself shortly after 1800. Another piano sonata
by him, *The Battle of Trenton, a Favorite Historical Sonata,* was first
published by Carr in 1797.[169] It includes "Washington's March" and
"Yankee Doodle." The Library of Congress also has by him, *The 4th
of July; a Grand Military Sonata For the Piano Forte, Composed in*

164. Cf. Sonneck & Upton/BIBLIOGRAPHY 527 and BAKER'S DICTIONARY 1622 (but Taylor taught Reinagle in Edinburgh, not London). Some additional and corrected information is provided by C. S. Smith on the jacket of New Records LP 2004, on which 2 Vc/bass sons. by Taylor are recorded.

165. BRITISH UNION II 998.

166. A copy is in the Sibley Music Library at Eastman School of Music in Rochester (Sonneck & Upton/BIBLIOGRAPHY 392).

167. Cf. Howard/HEWITT; Chase/AMERICA'S 120-121; BAKER'S DICTIONARY 708-709.

168. Sonneck & Upton/BIBLIOGRAPHY 395; LC MUSIC 205-206.

169. Sonneck & Upton/BIBLIOGRAPHY 39; Howard/HEWITT 30-31. Cf. Loesser/PIANOS 449-450.

Commemoration of That Glorious Day . . ., published by Hewitt himself about 1805.[170] Here we find sections disparately labeled "Siciliana, 170a
Day Break, and Cannon in the bass," "The General [blurred]," "Fife
and Drum," "Assembling of the People, Maestoso," "Bells," "Distant
March," "Trumpet," "March, The Artillery," "Rifle Music Quick Step,"
"Allegro con Spirito," "Firing Small Arms," "The Reveille," "Shouts
of the Populace," "Hail Columbia," and "Finale," all in 13 pages!

Alongside of sonatas published in this country before 1800 by
Steibelt, Pleyel, Haydn, and especially Nicolai,[171] there are extant
publications by other residents, including the German-born pianist
John Christopher Moller (?-1803),[172] the English organist **Joseph** 172a
Willson, and one **Frederick Rausch** ("Sonatina a quatre mains").
Lost today are the sonatas announced or actually published by "W."
Langdon, the (Dutch?) organist John Henry Schmidt, the (Canadian?)
composer Alexander Juhan, the organist William Selby (1738-98), the 172b
organist Francis Linley (1771-1800), and the English organist Peter 172c
Valton. If Valton's "Six Sonatas for the Harpsichord or Organ," first
proposed for subscription in Charleston in 1768,[173] actually appeared,
they might well be both the first to be composed and the first to be
published in this country.

170. LC MUSIC 206.

171. For the names in this paragraph cf. Sonneck & Upton/BIBLIOGRAPHY 390-397, 497-531.

172. A fine String Quartet in E-flat by Moller is played on New Records LP 2002.

173. Sonneck & Upton/BIBLIOGRAPHY 394.

Addenda

(1972 and 1981 combined)

P. 10. 11a. The listed works by Riegel, Séjan, Hüllmandel, Rutini, Turini, and Wolf have appeared in *Six Keyboard Sonatas from the Classic Era,* ed. by W. S. Newman (Evanston: Summy-Birchard, 1965). Note, also, the anthology ed. by James R. Smart, [10] *Keyboard Sonatas of the Eighteenth* [and early 19th] *Century* (New York: G. Schirmer, 1967), from which mod. eds. are cited where they apply in SCE.

P. 11. 12a. A new series from South Africa, *Contributions to the Development of the Piano Sonata,* has been launched by Karin Heuschneider with a brief survey, *The Piano Sonata of the Eighteenth Century in Italy* (Cape Town: A. A. Balkema, 1967); it consists mainly of analyses with exx., but also includes some notes and bibliography.

P. 11. 13a. More recent is Reinhard G. Pauly, *Music in the Classic Period* (Englewood Cliffs: Prentice-Hall, 1965); cf. W. S. Newman in *Music Educators Journal* LII/4 (Feb.-Mar. 1966) 184-186. NEW OXFORD VII, entitled *The Age of Enlightenment, 1745-1790,* is a more extended treatment; cf. JAMS XXVIII (1975) 384-395 (W. S. Newman).

P. 13. 16a. Imbault's *Catalogue Thématique des ouvrages de musique, ca.* 1792, was reprinted by Minkoff Reprint in Geneva in 1972.

P. 19. 1a. As noted in Plantinga/CLEMENTI 53, William Jackson (SCE 702) distinguished between "sonatas" as having an accompaniment (SCE 98-105) and "lessons" as not having one—an interesting but hardly consistent distinction at the time.

P. 20. 4a. On "divertimento" as a title, often a generic title, see James Webster, "Towards a History of Viennese Chamber Music in the Early Classical Period," in JAMS XXVII (1974) 212-247, especially p. 225.

P. 21. 8a. On the French confusion of "sonate" and "concerto," cf. Howard Brofsky in JAMS XIX (1966) 91.

P. 26. 30a. For more on Koch, Marx, and Czerny, and for further early writers on "sonata form," including F. Galeazzi and A. Reicha, cf. SSB 29-33.

P. 29. 52a. Three light K sons., Op. 7, by Momigny (*ca.* 1801-1805) were ed. by Albert Palm and published by Amadeus of Zürich in 1973; cf. Judith L. Schwartz's review in NOTES XXXI (1974-75) 663-664.

P. 35. 80a. Cf., also, the Ph.D. diss. from the University of Wisconsin–Madison by Betty Hamilton Hosler (1978; projected for pub. by UMI Research Press in 1981), "Changing Aesthetic Views of Instrumental Music in Eighteenth Century Germany."

P. 37. 85a. It is interesting to find that Rousseau's interpretation of Fontenelle's quip is lost by 1811 in Madame de Genlis' *Nouvelle Méthode pour apprendre à jouer de la Harpe* (p. 11 in the Minkoff Reprint [1974] of the original Paris ed.).

P. 43. 2a. Maynard Solomon views "sonata form" as a solution in art to the then unsolvable dilemma of the patronage system in society (in "Beethoven, Sonata, and Utopia," *Telos* 9 [fall 1971] 32-47 and "Beethoven and the Enlightenment," *Telos* 19 [spring 1974] 146-154).

P. 50. 31a. See the express listing of pedagogical values in the preface to Quantz's *Sei Duetti a due Flauti Traversi,* Op. 2 (1759), as trans. by Edward R. Reilly in "Further Musical Examples for Quantz's *Versuch,*" JAMS XVII (1964) 157-169.

P. 55. 49a. Several other accounts of this sort may be found in Otto Erich Deutsch's *Mozart—A Documentary Biography,* trans. by E. Blom, P. Branscombe, and J. Noble (Stanford: Stanford University Press, 1965); cf. JAMS XIX (1966) 254-257 (L. Misch).

P. 69. 22a. Cf. the further study, by Rosemary Hilmar, *Der Musikverlag Artaria & Comp.* (Tutzing: Hans Schneider, 1977), which explores especially historical and archival aspects, but also adds considerable dating information in the period from 1784 to 1801; reviewed by T. F. Heck in NOTES XXXV (1978-79) 78-79.

P. 69. 23a. The material surveyed by Boyden (end of fn. 23) is that in the *Thematic Catalog of a Manuscript Collection of Eighteenth-Century Italian Instrumental Music* by Vincent Duckles and Minnie Elmer (Berkeley: University of California, 1963).

P. 73. 32a. Valuable new information on this question is provided by Klaus Hortschansky in "Pränumerations- und Subskriptionslisten in Notendrucken deutscher Musiker des 18. Jahrhunderts," in AM XL (1968) 154-174, all of which points to a much closer relationship between composer and public then than now.

P. 75. 40a. A notice by Pleyel in 1797 on how the public was being "shamefully deceived by pirating printers" is quoted by Rita Benton in "Pleyel as Music Publisher," JAMS XXXII (1979) 125-140 (see p. 128).

P. 77. 51a. But the publications were often artistically attractive; cf. G. S. Fraenkel, *Decorative Music Title Pages* (New York: Dover, 1968) plates 162 (Manfredini), 168 (C. F. Abel), 170-171 (J. C. Bach), 179 (Haydn), 187 and 189 (Mozart).

P. 82. 6a. Fausto Torrefranca argues unconvincingly that G. B. Platti's Op. 1 anticipated Emanuel Bach's sonatas in the use of the clavichord (in *Platti* 76-82; see note 1a to p. 365).

P. 83. 9a. Remarkable evidence that Giovanni Platti (SCE XII) may have composed his "celebrated sonatas" of 1742 and later for the early piano too (rather than the harpsichord, or even the clavichord as in MQ L [1964] 531-532) appears in the article by Fabbri, pp. 193-194, cited here in fn. 1a to p. 365.

P. 83. 12a. Eva Badura-Skoda finds evidence (p. 78) of a fortepiano recital as early as 1763 in "Prolegomena to a History of the Viennese Fortepiano," in *Israel Studies in Musicology* II (1980) 77-99.

P. 87. 35a. But note the conclusion that Beethoven's allegiance remained with the Viennese pianos, as argued by W. S. Newman in "Beethoven's Pianos Versus His Piano Ideals," in JAMS XXIII (1970) 484-504. Regarding Haydn's and Mozart's uses of the piano, cf. fns. 29a to p. 465 and 109 on p. 482, respectively.

P. 87. 35b. Cf. the illuminating discussion by Herbert Grundmann, "Per il Clavicembalo o Piano-forte," in *Colloquium Amicorum, Joseph Schmidt-Görg zum 70. Geburtstag* (Bonn: Beethovenhaus, 1967) 100-117.

P. 89. 39a. In Plantinga/CLEMENTI 289, Clementi's performance of Op. 2 on the harpsichord is among evidences taken to suggest that Clementi's importance to the early pianoforte has been overstressed. Cf., also, reviews of this book by W. S. Newman in NINETEENTH-CENTURY I (1977-78) 261-265 (with response in II [1978-79] 192-193) and by N. Temperley in ML LIX (1978) 205-209; further, MQ LIV (1968) 259 and W. S. Newman, "The Pianism of Haydn, Mozart, Beethoven, and Schubert Compared," in PIANO QUARTERLY No. 105 (spring 1979) 14-30.

P. 91. 42a. Three unpublished dissertations have done much to amplify the available information on this topic. Two of them, concerning the Baroque Era, are cited in note 11a to p. 54 in SBE. The third is by Gertrude J. Shaw, "The Violoncello Sonata Literature in France During the Eighteenth Century" (Catholic University, 1963).

P. 93. 48a. Cf. the recent diss. by J. M. Bowers (as cited in SBE, p. 376, footnote 41a) for late flowerings of the late-Baroque flute school in France, including discussions and full lists of music by de Lusse, Guillemain, and Corrette (SCE, pp. 616, 621-624).

P. 93. 49a. Cf. Lyle Merriman, "Early Clarinet Sonatas," in *The Instrumentalist* XXI/9 (Apr. 1967) 28-30.

P. 93. 50a. Two further names should be added here (thanks to Jan LaRue in MQ L [1964] 404)—that of the oboist in Parma and

Torino, **Alessandro Besozzi** (1702-93), for numerous ensemble sons. (not including oboe; cf. Eitner/QL II 18-19; G. M. Gatti and A. Basso [eds.], *La Musica—Dizionario* [Torino: Unione Tipografico, 1968-71] I 207-209); and that of the bassoonist in Paris, **Etienne Ozi** (1754-1813), for numerous sonatas and other music for one or more bassoons (cf. MGG X 533-536 [M. Briquet]). N. Casanovas (SCE 286) left rare examples in the Classic Era of sons. for "clarini" (trumpets).

P. 95. 53a. Loft/DUO is a recent, eminently practical survey of the entire span of published literature for violin and one other part, including melo/bass, accompanied-keyboard, and true duo settings.

P. 96. 56a. To these factors should be added the concurrent turn against the *b.c.* accompaniment by north German lieder composers, preceded by Rousseau and other Frenchmen, who wanted the melody to prevail, even to the theoretical extent of no accompaniment at all (cf. NEW OXFORD VII 342-346, *passim* [R. Hughes]).

P. 99. 61a. Add to the literature on the subject the unpublished Ph.D. diss. by Ronald R. Kidd, "The Sonata for Keyboard with Violin Accompaniment in England (1750-1790)" (Yale University, 1967), with extract in AM XLIV (1972) 122-144; also, Hans Hering, "Das Klavier in der Kammermusik des 18. Jahrhunderts," DMF XXIII (1970) 22-37, and David Fuller, "Accompanied Keyboard Music," MQ LX (1974) 222-245.

P. 105. 77a. In NEW OXFORD VII 531, K. Geiringer describes a related halfway stage in Vanhal's *Second Sett of Six Sonatas* (H-or-P+Vn± Vc; London: Longman, *ca.* 1790; cf. BRITISH UNION II 1056). The Vc essentially doubles the K left hand. When the Vn has solo passages they appear in the K part along with a *b.c.* accompaniment. The K player omits the solos and plays the *b.c.* accompaniment only when a Vn player is actually present.

P. 105. 79a. It is noteworthy that the review in AMZ I (1798-99) 570-571 of Beethoven's Op. 12 (3 Sons. "Per il Clavicembalo o Forte-Piano") makes no mention of the Vn part (cf. the trans. in full in Schindler & MacArdle/BEETHOVEN 76-77, 86n. That Beethoven had already distinguished clearly between "violin ad libitum" and "violon obligate" in 1793 is evident in his letter on WoO 40 in Anderson/BEETHOVEN I 7. In 1804 when he offered to supply Breitkopf & Härtel with an "accompaniment" for any of the three solo sons. Opp. 53, 54, or 57 (Anderson/BEETHOVEN I 116), he meant the "ad libitum" type, of course, merely as a concession to popular taste. (He is not known to have followed up this offer.)

P. 107 86a. Regarding the nature and optional scorings of duets (as discussed in a preface by Quantz), see note 31a to p. 50.

P. 110. 94a. Examples accessible in mod. eds. may be seen on pp. 30, 116, 127, and elsewhere in Benedetto Marcello's *Sonates pour Clavecin,* edited by L. Sgrizzi and L. Bianconi as Vol. 28 in Heugel's "Le Pupitre" series.

P. 111. 95a. The filling-in can become objectionable (cf. Kirkpatrick/SCARLATTI 224) and, in any case, is likely to be less in contrapuntal music. In AM XXXIX (1967) 201, Fritz Oberdoerffer emphasizes that the practice of filling-in has never been confirmed (but cf. the references in Gerstenberg/SCARLATTI 96n).

P. 114. 2a. Cf. the discussion along similar lines by Jens Peter Larsen, "Sonatenform-Probleme," in *Festschrift Friedrich Blume zum 70. Geburtstag* (ed. by A. A. Abert and W. Pfannkuch; Kassel: Bärenreiter, 1963) 221-230. Charles Rosen, *Sonata Forms* (New York: W. W. Norton, 1980), is, to me, a large-scale last-ditch effort to modernize, categorize, and chronologize various degrees and stages of Classic "sonata form" and to identify particular style traits in them. The effort is certainly commendable; my doubts about such classifications remain as stated here (SCE 114-117). Somewhat similar doubts are expressed in Joseph Kerman's significant review of Rosen's book in the *New York Review of Books* XXVII/16 (Oct. 23, 1980) 50-52; cf., also, the review by Jan LaRue in JAMS XXXIV (1981) 557-566.

P. 117. 7a. The outer mvts. of the same Mozart quartets are examined for the same purpose and for their interrelationships and like or unlike traits in the Ph.D. dissertation of Werner Hümmeke, *Versuch einer strukturwissenschaftlichen Darstellung der ersten und vierten Sätze der zehn letzten Streichquartette von W. A. Mozart* (Münster, 1970).

P. 119. 14a. More broadly related to the "evolution" of "sonata form" are various efforts to tie it in with philosophical theories. Such is an article by Christopher Ballantine, "Beethoven, Hegel and Marx" (MR XXXIII [1972] 34-46), in which "sonata form" is found to be an ideal example of Hegelian dialect. In particular, Beethoven's "sonata process of exposition, development, and recapitulation [more so than Haydn's or Mozart's]" is seen to reveal "a rough correspondence to the path of the Hegelian search for truth, which sets out from sense-knowledge or sense-certainty, and passes through perception before arriving at understanding and finally self-knowledge" (p. 37).

P. 119. 15a. Attention should be called to Rosen/CLASSICAL, a stimulating, musicianly book that offers numerous valuable insights, in spite of historical shortcomings and of high-level pronouncements incapable of proof or disproof. An article by J. P. Larsen effectively rounds up traditional views, "Alcune considerazioni sull'evoluzione e le carrateristiche della musica strumentale del periodo classico viennese," in *Nuovo Rassegna di studi musicali* II (1978) 79-100 (originally pub. in English in Budapest in 1967). "Approaching Musical Classicism—Understanding Styles and Style Change in Eighteenth-Century Instrumental Music" (*College Music Symposium,* Journal of the College Music Society, XX/1 [spring 1980] 7-48), A. Peter Brown, reviews past efforts to distinguish between late-Baroque and high-Classic styles (including the present one), seeks to reconcile them in an outlined comparison, and provides a full bibliography of them.

P. 119. 15b. In "An Essay by John Marsh" (ML XXXVI [1955] 155-164), Charles Cudworth annotates an anonymous "Comparison" of 1796 (*The* [London] *Monthly Musical Magazine* II 981 ff.) that is remarkably perceptive in its distinction between "ancient" (Baroque) and "modern" (Classic) styles, including the symphony, though not the sonata.

P. 119. 15c. One of the least explored of these elements has been illuminated in the unpublished Ph.D. diss. by Frank E. Lorince, "A Study of Musical Texture in Relation to Sonata-Form as Evidenced in Selected Keyboard Sonatas from C. P. E. Bach Through Beethoven" (University of Rochester and Eastman School of Music, 1966). A discussion of both terrace and graded dynamics that goes well back into the Baroque Era may be read in David Boyden's article, "Dynamics in Seventeenth- and Eighteenth-Century Music," in *Essays on Music in Honor of Archibald Thompson Davison* (Cambridge: Harvard University Depart. of Music, 1957, pp. 185-193).

P. 120. 15d. For a fuller, generally related discussion of the *galant* style, cf. David A. Sheldon, "The Galant Style Revisited and Re-evaluated," in AM XLVII (1975) 240-270.

P. 123. 18a. For a recent diss. on this aspect of Emanuel Bach's style, cf. fn. 54a to p. 423.

P. 123. 18b. Not characteristic of the style (as explored in the present study) is "Ein Thementypus der Empfindsamen Zeit—Ein Beitrag zur Tonsymbolik," as discussed by Rudolf Scholz in AFMW XXIV (1967) 178-198.

P. 129. 27a. Carl Dahlhaus places special emphasis on new legato tendencies in "Cantabile und thematischer Prozess: Der Übergang zum Spätwerk in Beethovens Klaviersonaten," AFMW XXXVII (1980) 81-98, with further references.

P. 135. 30a. Cf. Norbert Stich, "Satzgattungen in Beethovens Instrumentalwerken," in the Schmidt-Görg *Festschrift* of 1967 (see note 35b to p. 87) 379-385.

P. 135. 30b. Cf. Klaus Kropfinger, "Zur thematischen Funktion der langsamen Einleitung bei Beethoven," in the Schmidt-Görg *Festschrift* of 1967 (see note 35b to p. 87) 197-216, and Rudolf Klinkhammer, *Die langsame Einleitung in der Instrumentalmusik der Klassik and Romantik; ein Sonderproblem in der Entwicklung der Sonatenform* (Regensburg: Bosse, 1971 [Ph.D. dissertation, Köln, 1971]); reviewed by Peter Cahn in DMF XXVI (1973) 535-536. A further pub. diss., by Marianne Danckwardt (Tutzing: Hans Schneider, 1977; reviewed somewhat negatively by Peter Brown in JAMS XXXIII [1980] 200-204), concentrates on the slow introduction in Haydn's and Mozart's music.

P. 137. 30c. Cf. R. M. Longyear, "The Minor Mode in the Classic Period," MR XXXII (1971) 27-35, "The Minor Mode in Eighteenth-Century Sonata Form," in *Journal of Music Theory* XV (1971) 182-229.

P. 139. 37a. Cf. Karl Marx, *Zur Einheit der zyklischen Form bei Mozart* (Stuttgart: Ichthys Verlag, 1971); reviewed by H. Federhofer in DMF XXVI (1973) 276-277. Marx's reasoning recalls that in Reti/THEMATIC.

P. 139. 38a. It is explored further (and overstated, in the experience of this study) by Rudolph Réti in *Thematic Patterns in Sonatas of Beethoven,* prefaced and assembled (posthumously) by Jean Réti-Forbes, ed. by Deryck Cooke (New York: Macmillan, 1967); cf. the reviews by Eric Sams in MT CVIII (1967) 908-909 and John Cockshoot in ML XLVIII (1967) 378-380. In progress (as of 1977) at the City University of New York is a Ph.D. dissertation by Meir Wiesel, "Thematic Unity in Beethoven's Sonata Works of the Period 1797-1802."

P. 139. 38b. In Rosen/CLASSICAL 409-434 relationships of the 3d become a main consideration in the analysis of Op. 106/i-iv.

P. 143. 44a. Statistical conclusions about structural procedures are reached in the unpublished Ph.D. diss. by Roger Kamien, "The Opening Sonata-Allegro Movements in a Randomly Selected Sample of Solo Keyboard Sonatas Published in the Years 1742-74 (inclusive)," 2 vols. (Princeton University, 1964); reviewed by Thomas Warburton in *Current Musicology* XI (1971) 118-121. Cf., also, the related article by Kamien, "Style Change in the Mid-18th-Century Keyboard Sonata," JAMS XIX (1966) 37-58. In his Ph.D. diss., "Haydn and Mozart: A Study of Their Mature Sonata-Style Procedures" (University of California at Los Angeles, 1981), John Martin Harutunian compares 5 "central stylistic dimensions": tonic-dominant polarity; tonal digressions, especially between secondary and closing material; tonal shifts at structural junctions; development techniques; and alterations in the recapitulation.

P. 145. 44b. Cf. Rosen/CLASSICAL 395-396; K. F. Heimes, "The Ternary Sonata Principle Before 1742," in AM XLV (1973) 222-248, in particular 239n; and, especially, Michael Broyles, "Organic Form and the Binary Repeat," in MQ LXVI (1980) 339-360.

P. 145. 46a. Besides the article by K. F. Heimes in fn. 44b to p. 145, the unpublished Ph.D. dissertation by his former student Bernése Marais may be cited, "The Ternary Sonata Principle from 1731 to 1765: C. P. E. Bach" (University of Port Elizabeth [South Africa], 1975).

P. 146. 47a. Most recently the theory was advanced by Ernö Lendvai in *Béla Bartók: An Analysis of His Music* (London: Kahn & Averill, 1971); cf. the review by Todd Crow in NOTES XXIX (1972-73) 722-724. Related is Part II in the Ph.D. diss. of Alexander Edward Sidorowicz (Kent State University, 1981), "The Proportional and Space Analysis of the First-Movement Sonata-Allegro Form of Mozart, Haydn, and Beethoven."

P. 149. 55a. Patterns of harmonic rhythm characteristic of each section of "sonata form" are discovered by Shelley Davis in an unpublished M.A. thesis, "Structural Functions of Harmonic Rhythm in Mozart's

Sonata-Allegro Form" (New York University, 1960), partially abstracted in "Harmonic Rhythm in Mozart's Sonata Form," MR XXVII (1966) 25-43.

P. 150. 55b. That Beethoven designed his themes differently, for dialectic treatment in fast movements and cantabile extension in slow movements, is argued by Peter Gülke in "Kantabilität und thematische Abhandlung—Ein Beethovensches Problem und seine Lösungen in den Jahren 1806/1808," in *Beiträge zur Musikwissenschaft* XII (1970) 252-273.

P. 151. 55c. Cf. Friedrich Neumann, "Ein typisches Motiv in Überleitungen von Mozart und Beethoven," in MOZART-JAHRBUCH XII (1962-63) 200-215, with exx.

P. 151. 56a. Cf., also, the unpub. Ph.D. diss. by James Parkinson Farleigh, "Transition and Retransition in Selected Examples of Mozart's Sonata-type Forms" (University of Michigan, 1973).

P. 152. 57a. Cf. Friedrich Neumann, "Zur formalen Anlage des Seitensatzes der Sonatenform bei Mozart," in MOZART-JAHRBUCH XI (1960-61) 219-232, with exx.

P. 153. 60a. Cf. SSB, fn. 24a to p. 31.

P. 155. 61a. Cf. the unpublished Ph.D. dissertation by Marilyn Holt Barnes, "Developmental Procedures in the Sonata Form Movements of the Symphonies of Beethoven, Schubert, Mendelssohn, and Schumann" (Case Western Reserve University, 1973) ; the historical background is surveyed on pp. 1-43; also, Steven Lubin, "Techniques for the Analysis of Developments in Middle-Period Beethoven," unpub. Ph.D. diss. (New York University, 1974).

P. 158. 61b. Schenkerian analyses of recapitulations in Beethoven's son. forms that change appreciably from their expositions are to be found in Roger Kamien's article, "Aspects of the Recapitulation in Beethoven Piano Sonatas," in *Music Forum* IV (1976) 194-235. Cf., also, Beth Shamgar, "On Locating the Retransition in Classic Sonata Form," in MR XLII (1981) 130-143.

P. 159. 62a. But it is worth noting that only Op. 106 among the last fifteen sonatas, from Op. 31/3 through Op. 111, has a slow movement of the sustained, full-length sort to be found in the earlier sonatas.

P. 164. 66a. Cf. the unpublished Ph.D. diss. by Malcolm S. Cole, "The Development of the Instrumental Rondo Finale from 1750 to 1800," 2 vols. (Princeton University, 1964) ; followed by related articles in JAMS XXII (1969) 425-455 and MQ LV (1969) 180-192.

P. 174. 4a. Among further bibliographic aids, add V. Duckles and M. Elmer, *Thematic Catalog* (as cited in note 23a to p. 69).

P. 191. 77a. For a new thematic index cf. note 82a to p. 192.

P. 192. 82a. Among further mod. eds.: *Six Sonatas for Keyboard Instruments* (Nos. 34, 18, 32, 50, 26, 10), ed. by E. Woodcock (New York: Galaxy, 1963) ; [15] *Sonate per cembalo*, I (first vol. of a complete ed.?), ed. by Hedda Illy (Rome: De Santis, 1969), including a thematic index of 103 sons. and 9 concertos, a list of previous eds., and critical apparatus; the first 6 sons. comprise the set of 1785 and the others are previously unpublished MSS. Iris Carunana's ed. of *Dodici Sonate per cembalo* (Padua: Guglielmo Zanzibon, 1974) is reviewed by Arthur Lawrence in NOTES XXXI (1974-75) 869-870, including identification numbers.

P. 192. 85a. Newer eds. include that of F. Piva (Venice: Istituto per la collaborazione culturale, 1964; reported to be erratic by R. Howe in NOTES XXVI [1969-70] 347-348) and another announced by M. Vivarelli ("Bibliopola") of Rome (with a facs. of the MS, too?).

P. 204. 125a. He was also in Dresden by 1747, according to Torrefranca, *Platti* 69 (see note 1a to p. 365).

P. 204. 132a. More details come from MGG XI 1199–1203 (L. F. Tagliavini) and the prefaces (including annotated lists of works) in the mod. eds. of Opp. 3, 5, and 6, complete in 3 vols. ed. by H. Illy (Rome: De Santis, 1965-67; cf. the review by G. Pestelli in *Rivista italiana di musicologia* III [1968] 196-198). The year of publication is 1774 for Op. 9, 1776 for Op. 10, 1778 for Op. 11, 1786 for Op. 14, and 1793 for Op. 18. A facs. of Op. 8 was published by Forni in Bologna in 1969 (revealing that the final mvt. has a vocal text). An Op. 19 exists—a Rondo both for P solo and for P & orchestra—as reported by H. Illy in *Nuova Rivista musicale italiana* III (1969) 1123-1124, with a facs. as a Suppl. Further information, often based on primary sources, appears in the unpub. Ph.D. diss. of Carlo Lombardi, "A Revision of the Instrumental Catalogue and an Examination of the Form-Types of the Six Sonatas for Cembalo, Opus X, of Giovanni Marco Placido Rutini (1723-97)" (New York University, 1972).

P. 218. 16a. Dr. Churgin's diss. was completed through Harvard University in 1963. The jointly authored *Thematic Catalogue of the Works of Giovanni Battista Sammartini* was published by Harvard University Press in 1976 (reviewed by E. K. Wolf in NOTES XXXIV [1977-78] 850-852, with response by authors in NOTES XXXV [1978-79] 456); it includes (thus far?) symphonies and vocal music, along with the most authoritative biographical statement published to date (pp. 1-24 and 33).

P. 219. 17a. New information on Op. 7 appears in JAMS XX (1967) 107-112 (B. Churgin).

P. 228. 46a. Still in progress in 1977 at the University of Maryland was the diss. of R. H. Matthews, "The Instrumental Music of Josef Mysliveček."

P. 233. 70a. Cf., also, Mario Fabbri and Enzo Settesoldi, "Precisazioni biografiche sul musicista pseudolivornese Carlo Antonio Campion [*sic*] (1720-1788)," in *Rivista italiana di musicologia* III (1968) 181-188.

P. 235. 77a. Add the recent unpublished Ph.D. diss. by Virginia Downman Kock, "The Works of Domenico Ferrari (1722-80)," 2 vols. (Tu-lane University, 1969). The attribution of the facs. cited in fn. 77 cannot be confirmed (according to Klaus Häffner of Karlsruhe).

P. 246. 126a. Mod. ed.: Son. I for Vn & K, ed. by F. F. Polnauer (Zürich: Hug, 1966).

P. 248. 133a. A new biography, with further documents and letters, is that of Germaine de Rothschild, *Luigi Boccherini—His Life and Work*, trans. by A. Mayor (from the original French ed. of 1962) (London: Oxford University Press, 1965); but cf. the review in NOTES XXII (1966) 1222-1223 (D. W. Krummel).

P. 250. 148a. A major advance in Boccherini research has been made with the appearance of Yves Gérard's *Thematic, Bibliographical and Critical Catalogue of the Works of Luigi Boccherini,* trans. by A. Mayor (London: Oxford University Press, 1969), with facs., illustrations, chronology of works, and discography; cf. Ellen Amsterdam in JAMS XXIV (1971) 131-133.

P. 250. 148b. In 1968 Yves Gérard (as in note 148a to p. 250, p. xix) was already at work on "a detailed analysis . . . of the structure and aesthetic quality" of Boccherini's music.

P. 260. 4a. In addition to Iberian son. anthologies ed. by Nin and Kastner, as cited *infra,* there may be listed the recent anthology ed. by Gerhard Doderer, *Spanische und portugiesische Sonaten des 18. Jahrhunderts* (Orgel, Cembalo, Klavier), Heidelberg: Willy Müller, 1976; reviewed by Susan Erickson-Bloch in NOTES XXXIV (1977-78) 207. Besides one previously pub. son. each by Seixas and Soler, it includes one each by Baptista, Cordeiro da Silva, Gomes da Silva, Rodríguez, A. Viola, and López.

P. 262. 15a. Two new Italian studies of Scarlatti's sonatas need to be added, both published in 1967 and both concerned with background, structure, and chronology: Giorgio Pestelli, *Le Sonate di Domenico Scarlatti—Proposta di un ordinamento cronologico* (Torino: G. Giappichelli; cf. the reviews by K. Dale in ML XLIX [1968] 183-187, and by A. Basso in *Rivista italiana di musicologia* III [1968] 198-200); and Massimo Bogianckino, *The Harpsichord Music of Domenico Scarlatti,* trans. by John Tickner (Rome: De Santis). Bogianckino wrote in cognizance of Pestelli's study, which is based on a dissertation of 1964. The Apollo paperback reprint (New York, 1968) of Kirkpatrick/SCARLATTI includes some updating. More important is the unpub. diss. by Joel Leonard Sheveloff, "The Keyboard Music of Domenico Scarlatti—A Re-evaluation of the State of Knowledge in the Light of the Sources" (Brandeis University, 1970); reviewed by W. S. Newman in PIANO QUARTERLY No. 79 (fall 1972) 19-20. Besides sources, Sheveloff explores the pairing of the sons., the intended instrument, the notational styles, the dating of the handcrossing, performance practices, the significance of the "great curves" (broad slurs), the authenticity of certain sons., and the chronological order. Some further light comes from Eva Badura-Skoda's discovery of alternate, Vienna MSS of about 200 of Scarlatti's sons., as discussed in the unpub. Ph.D. diss. by Seunghyun Choi, "Newly

Found Eighteenth-Century Manuscripts of Domenico Scarlatti's Sonatas and Their Relationship to Other Eighteenth- and Early Nineteenth-Century Sources" (University of Wisconsin, 1974).

P. 265. 36a. Cf. the mod. ed. of 26 sons. previously unpublished (that is, before *ca.* 1905), as "transcribed for piano" by E. Granados, 2 vols. (Madrid: Union musical espagñol, 1967), with preface by F. Pedrell (trans. into English in the reprint by Associated [New York, 1967]).

P. 265. 37a. The 1970s were blessed by 2 complete authoritative eds. Ralph Kirkpatrick prepared the *Complete Keyboard Works in Facsimile from the Manuscript and Printed Sources,* 18 vols. (New York: Johnson Reprint Corp., 1972); cf. R. Kirkpatrick, "Scarlatti Revisited in Parma and Venice," in NOTES XXVIII (1971-72) 5-15, and W. S. Newman, "Kirkpatrick's *facsimile* Edition of Scarlatti's Keyboard Sonatas," in PIANO QUARTERLY No. 79 (fall 1972) 18-21. Vol. I begins with a complete facs. of the 30 *Essercizi* in its original ed. Kenneth Gilbert's ed. was pub. in 11 vols. in Heugel's "Le Pupitre" series (Nos. 31-41, Paris, 1971-78). In 1978 Vol. I of a 3d new "complete" ed. appeared, ed. by Emilio Fadini for G. Ricordi of Milan; cf. Howard Schott's review of Vol. II in MT CXXII (1981) 186-187.

P. 265. 39a. Among further collections is one of 5 sons. and 3 fugues for organ (Bärenreiter, 1969).

P. 270. 60a. James Dale Unger pursues and extends Kirkpatrick's approach in his unpub. Ph.D. diss., "D. Scarlatti: The Methods and Incidence of Preparation for the Tonal Plateau, the Crux, and the Apex" (University of Port Elizabeth [South Africa], 1976).

P. 273. 70a. On six 4-mvt. sons. in a MS of *ca.* 1758 by an otherwise unknown Italian in Scarlatti's Madrid circle, cf. Giorgio Pestelli, "Sei Sonate per cembalo di Girolamo Sertori (1758)," in *Rivista italiana di musicologia* II (1967) 131-139, with exx. Sheveloff (cf. fn. 15a to p. 262, *supra*) pp. 448-450, 489, and 546-551, suggests that one Sebastiano Albero (Madrid organist in 1749, d. 1756) "may possibly be his [Scarlatti's] nearest disciple" and may have composed K. 142, 143, and 144; cf., also, Pestelli (fn. 15a to p. 262), pp. 224-231, with exx.

P. 273. 71a. In 1965 80 sons. ed. by S. Kastner were published in *Portugaliae musica* A/X (Lisbon: Calouste Gulbenkian); cf. G. Béhague in NOTES XXV (1969) 587-589. In 1967 Klaus F. Heimes completed an unpub. diss. on "Carlos Seixas' Keyboard Sonatas" (Pretoria) and in 1971 his article "Carlos Seixas—Zum Quellenstudium seiner Klaviersonaten," appeared in AFMW XXVIII (1971) 204-216.

P. 278. 85a. Dr. Almonte Howell at the University of Georgia in Athens has kindly reported to me (in 1978) his discovery of a MS in eastern Spain that contains (among 30 K sons. and a "Pastorela") 6 sons.

by V. Rodriguez that are scheduled (as of 1979) for publication. Cf., also, fn. 4a to p. 260, *supra*.

P. 279. 89a. A further discussion occurs in Almarie Dieckow's unpub. Ph.D. diss., "A Stylistic Analysis of the Solo Keyboard Works of Antonio Soler" (Washington University, St. Louis, 1971).

P. 279. 90a. Marvin's ed. seems to have been completed in 4 vols. (41 sons.) in 1971. Rubio's ed. may or may not have been completed in 7 vols. (120 sons.) in 1972, with revisions promised in a re-edition of Vol. III (cf. Judith L. Schwartz's review in NOTES XXXI [1974-75] 651-652).

P. 286. 105a. At least one more son. has been made available in the *Dos sonatas* ed. by J. Climent for *Union Musical Española* in 1970.

P. 286. 109a. Note should be taken, too, of about 15 MS sons. in 2-5 mvts. left about 1800 by a forgotten Madrid organist, thanks to a report by John Gillespie, "The Keyboard Sonatas of **Félix Máximo López**—An Appreciation," in *Studies in Eighteenth-Century Music—A Tribute to Karl Geiringer on His Seventieth Birthday* (New York: Oxford University Press, 1970) 243-252. More information and style analysis occur in the unpub. Ph.D. diss. by Alma O. Espinosa, "The Keyboard Works of Félix Máximo López (1742-1821)" (New York University, 1976). In Antonio Ruiz-Pipó's anthology of obscure Basque composers, *Musica vasca del siglo XVIII para tecla* (Madrid: Union Musical Española, 1972) are included a Son. in C by Joaquín de Oxinaga, Sons. in C, D, G, and D by P. José Larrañaga, a Son. in a by Manuel de Gamarra, a Son. in E♭ by Fr. Agustin Echeverria, and a Son. in D by Juan Andrés Lonbide. *Seis sonatas para clave y fuerte piano* by Joaquin Montero were ed. in 1977 by Linton Powell for Union Musical Española.

P. 287. 112a. On Herrando's Vn method cf. David Boyden, *The History of Violin Playing From Its Origins to 1761* (London: Oxford University Press, 1965) 353 and 362.

P. 295. 18a. Mod. ed. of Son. 4 in g: Newman, *Six Keyboard Sonatas* (cf. note 11a to p. 10).

P. 296. 19a. Responding to this statement, Claudio Sartori has kindly informed me that (as of 1964) both sets exist complete and intact in the private library of Ugo Levi of Venice.

P. 298. 21a. That Rolla taught Paganini is refuted in both Courcy/PAGANINI I 42-43 and Vyborny/PAGANINI 161 (referring to listings in the Bibliography of SSB).

P. 298. 24a. Information kindly supplied by Mr. Joseph A. Kotylo at State University of New York in Binghamton indicates that 6 further solo sons. for P by Pollini were pub. at a "somewhat later date" and that these, primarily in 2 mvts., are of "much higher quality" than the earlier sons.

P. 299. 26a. In personal correspondence, Professor Rey Longyear at the University of Kentucky in Lexington reports a "Sonata per quattromani" in Milan, by B. Asioli, that is actually a transcription of his "Sinfonia compestre." He also reports the Vc part in the acc'd. son. to be more than an accompaniment, finding the work to be on a "scale just below that of the Beethoven cello sonatas," and outstanding among Italian sons. of its time.

P. 300. 32a. The MS has turned up in the catalogue of *The Mary Flagler Cary Music Collection* (New York: The Pierpont Morgan Library, 1970), item 94, with a facs. of the first page on Plate 15.

P. 302. 39a. Cf., also, Mario Fabbri, "Incontro con Ferdinando Rutini, il dimenticato figlio musicista del 'primo maestro di Mozart,'" in CHIGIANA SETTIMANE XX (1963) 195-205.

P. 302. 40a. A helpful article by Jno. L. Hunt, "The Keyboard Works of Giovanni Paisiello" (MQ LXI [1975] 212-232), indicates that this statement "must be amended" for Paisiello because of at least 2 collections of keyboard pieces pub. during his lifetime (pp. 219n and 221). Whether any of those pieces was actually called "sonata" is not clear. The titles in Mola/PAISIELLO-m cannot be confirmed here, either, the source for them being MS A-Wn 12742 at the Nationalbibliothek in Vienna. In 1973 Dr. Hunt had completed an unpub. Ph.D. diss. at the University of Michigan, "The Life and Keyboard Works of Giovanni Paisiello (1740-1816)."

P. 304. 51a. In 1971 Carisch of Milan pub. *31 Sonate* from the same source, with only one duplication (ed. by V. Vitale and Carlo Bruno); cf. Howard Schott's review in ML LVI (1975) 114-115.

P. 304. 53a. Cf. the examination of cycles in the Florence MS, by Lorenzo Bianconi, in RIdM VIII (1973) 254-264.

P. 305. 55a. Cf. MGG XIV 1302-1305 (Francesco Degrada). Out of some 300 sons. or related, single pieces listed in Benedetto Vita's *Catalogo della musica lasciata dal Maestro Niccolò Zingarelli* (Naples, 1837), Professor Rey Longyear at the University of Kentucky (according to information kindly supplied by him) has been able to find 21 son. mvts. for Vc duo (possibly grouping into 3-mvt. sons.), over 100 such mvts. for bass duo (2 of them marked "o contrabasso solo"), and enough seemingly related mvts., labelled "Sonata" or "Sonatina," to comprise about 4 multi-mvt. cycles for organ. Zingarelli frequently used the title "Solfeggio" for the duos, rather than "Sonata" or "Duo."

P. 305. 56a. A mod. ed. has been prepared by Alfred E. Lemmon, S.J., for Union Musical Española (1976).

P. 306. 58a. Further mod. eds.: complete set, ed. by Robert Parris (Madrid: Union musical espagñola, 1963); complete set, ed. by Stewart Gordon, projected for publication by Theodore Presser in 1964; Son. 4 in g, in Smart, *Keyboard Sonatas of the Eighteenth Century* (see note 11a to p. 10). In MR LXI (1980) 197-206, Linton Powell compares this set with that of Joaquín Montero, pub. in 1790 (cf. fn. 109a to p. 286 above).

P. 328. 38a. A substantial contribution is made by the diss. of Roderich Fuhrmann, *Mannheimer Klavier-Kammermusik*, 2 vols. (Philipps-Universität zu Marburg, 1963), the 2d vol. being a "Thematischer Katalog."

P. 329. 44a. Cf. the unpublished M.A. thesis by Stephen Jackson Hill, "The Sonatas of Johann Stamitz" (The University of North Carolina, 1965). I am indebted to Eugene K. Wolf for improvements (growing out of his unpub. diss. on the symphonies and full listings prepared for RISM) that should be entered in the bibliographic table that follows here, including the observations that item C. was originally published by Castagnerie rather than De la Chevardière, that item D. is only a reprint of item C., and that Stamitz may never have had an Op. 4 published by De la Chevardiere (item B). The foregoing details are amplified in Wolf's diss. (New York University, 1972) on pp. 736 ff., p. 40 (Op. 1), p. 51n (the doubtful Op. 4), and pp. 54-55 (Op. 6).

P. 339. 66a. Lines of development from the first Mannheimers to Mozart are emphasized in the unpub. Ph.D. diss. by Marjorie Elizabeth Soutar, "Christian Cannabich (1731-1798): An Evaluation of His Instrumental Works," 3 vols. (University of Aberdeen [Scotland], 1972); representative works in score are included.

P. 342. 82a. We are reminded of another publisher who should have been singled out, too, thanks to Horst Heussner, in "Der Musikdrucker Balthasar Schmid in Nürnberg," in DMF XVI (1963) 348-362, including a new list of plate nos.

P. 350. 112a. Related to the study of this music is the thorough, unpublished Ph.D. diss. by Gayle A. Henrotte, "The Ensemble Divertimento in Pre-Classic Vienna," 2 vols. (The University of North Carolina, 1967), with 29 SSB trios—by G. Porsile, the Monn Brothers, and F. Asplmayer—scored in Vol. II.

P. 350. 113a. Cf. the unpublished M.A. thesis of Patricia Mosely Jackson, "The Keyboard Sonatas of Two Pre-Classic Viennese Composers: Mathias Georg Monn (1717-1750), Johann Christoph Mann (1726-1782); a Style-Critical Analysis" (The University of North Carolina, 1966).

P. 352. 118a. The works for K have been sorted out by Helga Michelitsch in *Das Klavierwerk von Georg Christoph Wagenseil—Thematischer Katalog* (Vienna: Böhlaus, 1966).

P. 354. 137a. Cf. the unpublished Ph.D. diss. by Eva Rose Meyer, "Florian Gassmann and the Viennese Divertimento," 2 vols. (University of Pennsylvania, 1963), Vol. II being a "Musical Appendix."

P. 356. 144a. Cf. note 113a to p. 350.

P. 358. 149a. Mod. eds.: 6 Divertimenti, Op. 1 (1759), 6 Sons., Op 3 (1763), and 3 separately published sons. (1771, 1771, 1776), all in MAB-m No. 64 (D. Šetková, with preface); and 8 previously unpublished sons. (nos. 26-28, 30, 32, 37, 38, and 40 as listed in a Czech study of Steffan's P works by Daňa Šetková [Prague, 1965]), in MAB-m No. 70.

P. 365. 1a. Torrefranca's major work on Platti appeared posthumously, *Giovanni Benedetto Platti e la sonata moderna*, completed by A. Bonaccorsi and enhanced by an appendix on the Schönborn family by Fritz Zobeley (Milan: G. Ricordi, 1963); cf. the reviews by W. S. Newman in *Musica d'oggi* VII (1964) 194-198 and in MQ L (1964) 526-535. The volume includes an *Urtext* ed. (pp. 215-403) of all 18 known sons. for K by Platti, as well as illustrations, facs., and documents (among them, a marriage certificate dated 1723 and the death certificate sought in fn. 4 below). Cf., also, Alfredo Bonaccorsi, "Giovanni Platti (precisazioni sul Settecento)," in CHIGIANA SETTIMANE XX (1963) 66-72, and Mario Fabbri, "Una nuova fonte per la conoscenza di Giovanni Platti e del suo 'Miserere,'" in CHIGIANA SETTIMANE XXIV (Nuova Serie N. 4, 1967) 181-202. Fabbri establishes both Platti's birth year and his apparent intention that his K sons. be played on the early piano.

P. 366. 5a. On the valuable Schönborn library holdings in and around Wiesentheid, cf. the review in NOTES XXIV (1968) 715-716 (W. G. Marigold) of Vol. I (1967) in a 5-vol. catalogue under preparation by Fritz Zobeley. The succeeding vols. have not appeared as of Jan. 1980.

P. 367. 11a. For Torrefranca's complete mod. ed. see note 1a to p. 365.

P. 367. 11b. The final sons. that Torrefranca has made available (see note 1a to p. 365) reveal traits of the later-*galant* style, too.

P. 367. 13a. With further regard to their numbering, cf. pp. 195-196 in Torrefranca, *Platti* (see note 1a to p. 365).

P. 369. 17a. Regarding Platti's apparent interest in the early piano, as against the harpsichord or even the clavichord, cf. fn. 9a to p. 83, *supra*.

P. 374. 23a. An article by Shelley Davis, "J. G. Lang and the Early Classical Keyboard Concerto," includes newly preferred life dates (*ca.* 1722-98) and other biographical information as well as some remarks about Lang's sonatas (especially p. 31).

P. 377. 40a. Mod. ed.: complete set of 1773, ed. by W. Thoene, 2 vols. (Düsseldorf: Schwann, 1961-64; cf. DMF XX [1967] 114-115). It is interesting that Burney's diary for this same year of 1773 already singles out Neefe, among four Leipzig composers, for some "pretty sonatas" (BURNEY'S TOURS II 239).

P. 382. 61a. Cf. the unpublished M.A. thesis by Ellen Singleton Ligon, "An Edition of Ernst Wilhelm Wolff's *Vier affectvolle Sonaten und Ein Dreyzehnmal variirtes Thema* [1785] Together With the Preface, Translated and Annotated" (Cornell University, 1969); the Preface adds light on contemporary performance practices. Mod. ed.: Son. 2 in G (1774): Newman, *Six Keyboard Sonatas* (see note 11a to p. 10).

P. 388. 72a. Cf. MGG XIII 430-431 (L. P. Pruett).

P. 389. 77a. Information has been incorporated here from the helpful, recent, unpub. diss. by Franklin Sherwood Miller, "The Keyboard Music of Georg Andreas Sorge (1703-1778)," completed at Michigan State University in 1974.

P. 389. 79a. Dr. Miller (cf. fn. 77a to p. 389, *supra*) has kindly informed me that the set at the British Library (British Museum) does prove to be complete and includes a pencilled date of 1747; furthermore, that another complete set in the same edition exists at the Bayrisches Staatsbibliothek.

P. 390. 80a. The name should be added here of an obscure organist in Clausthal and pupil of J. S. Bach, **Johann Christoph Ritter** (1715-67), for 3 appealing cembalo sons. published in 1751 and related in style to the sons. just discussed. Mod. ed.: complete set, ed., with valuable preface, by Erwin R. Jacobi (Leipzig: VEB Deutscher Verlag, 1968).

P. 395. 97a. Cf. George Benson Weston, "Some works Falsely Ascribed to Friedemann Bach" (including J. W. Hässler's *Sechs leichte Sonaten* of 1786), with facs., in *Essays on Music in Honor of Archibald Thompson Davison by His Associates* (Cambridge: Harvard University, 1957) 247-251.

P. 405. 1a. The diss. is by Ursula Götze, *Johann Friedrich Klöffler (1725-1790)*, Westfälischen Wilhelms-Universität zu Münster, 2 vols. (published by the author, 1965); with a "Thematisch-bibliographisches Werke-Verzeichnis" in Vol. I and an ed. of Op. 5/3/iii among 2 works in Vol. II.

P. 405. 2a. The name of **August Heinrich Michaelis** (?-1816), cantor in Osnabrück, may be added for 6 pleasing, *galant* Sons. for H & Vn-or-Fl & Vc, Op. 2 (1774), 3 of which have been ed. for publication by Karl Schäfer (Köln: Hans Gerig, 1965).

P. 405. 4a. Cf. Jack Pilgrim, "A Note on G. B. Serini," in MT CV (1964) 581-582, with a new source for autograph MSS and biographic data (including an approximate birth year of 1710).

P. 406. 5a. Another mod. ed.: CLASSICI-m I No. 29.

P. 406. 7a. For a more recent study cf. Hannsdieter Wohlfart, *Johann Christoph Friedrich Bach: Ein Komponist im Vorfeld der Klassik* (Bern: Francke Verlag, 1971); reviewed by E. Helm in JAMS XXVI (1973) 496-498 and by L. Hoffmann-Erbrecht in DMF XXVII (1974) 265-266.

P. 412. 24a. But more recently, in "Johann Gottfried Schwanenberger—Acht Sonaten für Cembalo" (DMF XXVIII [1975] 429-431), Johann Zürcher established a *terminus ad quem* of 1768 for Sons. 1-3 and 6-8 of the 8 sons., indicating that it was Christian Bach who would have had to derive from Schwanenberger, or both from still another source.

P. 413. 29a. A facs. of the original German was published as *Carl Philip Emanuel Bach's Autobiography—1773* (Hilversum: Frits Knuf, 1967), with annotations in English by W. S. Newman; a full trans., with annotations, appears in W. S. Newman, "Emanuel Bach's Autobiography," MQ LI (1965) 363-372.

P. 414. 34a. A fundamental new "Thematic Catalog of the Works of Carl Philipp Emanuel Bach" has been prepared for early publication (as of 1979) by Professor Eugene Helm at the University of Maryland. Cf., also, the intriguing survey of source problems by Darrell M. Berg, "Towards a Catalogue of the Keyboard Sonatas of C. P. E. Bach," in JAMS XXXII (1979) 276-303.

P. 415. 35a. Another study is that of Philip Barford, *The Keyboard Music of C. P. E. Bach* (London: Barrie & Rockliff, 1965), with emphasis on "the rise of the sonata principle" as linked with "the flowering of a metaphysical system" (but cf. the reviews in MT CVII [1966] 35-37 [S. Sadie] and DMF XXII [1969] 120-122 [L. Hoffmann-Erbrecht]).

P. 416. 39a. There is evidence for 1743 as well as 1742 for Schmid's ed. (cf. BJ XXXV [1938] 109 and MT CIV [1963] 788).

P. 416. 39b. A still earlier ed. by G. G. Windter of Nürnberg is argued in AM XXVII (1955) 141-142.

P. 416. 39c. There is now an excellent mod. ed. of the complete set, ed. by Etienne Darbellay (Winterthur: Amadeus [Peters], 1976); cf. A. Seay in NOTES XXXV (1978-79) 161-162.

P. 416. 39d. A somewhat unsatisfactory mod. ed. of the complete set has been ed. by J. M. Rose (Bryn Mawr: Theodore Presser, 1973); cf. Howard Schott in ML LVI (1975) 109-110.

P. 416. 39e. Mod. ed.: "Presto" in B♭, in *The Second Bach*, ed. by O. Jonas

P. 417. 39f. Mod ed.: W. 62/14 in G, in *The Second Bach* (see note 39e

P. 417. 39g. Friedheim's own ed. of 6 K sons. by Emanuel Bach (New York: Galaxy, 1967) includes W. 65/9 in B♭, W. 65/16 in C, W. 65/23 in d, W. 62/19 in G, W. 52/2 in d, and W. 53/4 in b; cf. W. S. Newman in NOTES XXV (1968-69) 132-135.

P. 420. 45a. Cf. the diss. by Marais cited in fn. 46a to p. 145, *supra*.

P. 423. 54a. Darrell M. Berg prefers the term "mannerist" in her recent, unpub. Ph.D. diss., "The Keyboard Sonatas of C. P. E. Bach: An Expression of the Mannerist Principle" (State University of New York at Buffalo, 1975). She sees the style as depending on the paradox of abrupt contrast and as combining "anti-classicism with preciosity." Yet she also sees it as couched in a consistent structural framework and as marked by clear traits of Viennese Classicism.

P. 430. 77a. Peter Brown argues that, in any case, the influence of Emanuel Bach on Haydn in the decade from 1766 to 1776 has been overstated, in "The Earliest English Biography of Haydn," MQ LIX (1973) 339-354, especially pp. 349-354.

P. 432. 89a. Add to mod. eds.: 4 S/bass sons. in MAB-m No. 57 (J. Štědroň), including reprints of the Moffat and Jensen eds. in fn. 89 (as the best available sources!); one Fl/bass son. in MAB-m No. 60

(C. Schoenbaum), from an ed. of 1756 published by Winter in Berlin; 2 S/bass sons. published from MSS by Édition nationale de musique classique (in Paris), Nos. 5396 and 5402.

P. 433. 98a. Cf. Douglas A. Lee, "Some Embellished Versions of Sonatas by Franz Benda," in MQ LXII (1976) 58-71; also, Sonja Gerlach in *Gedenkschrift Günter Henle* (Munich: G. Henle, 1980) 199-212. Lee, who finds a total of as many as 140 sons. by F. Benda, has pub. a mod. ed. of 6 MS sons. complete with original and embellished versions of the Vn part and a valuable overall preface (Madison: A-R Editions, 1981).

P. 437. 116a. The birth document, confirming 1728, is given in the recent, comprehensive, unpublished Ph.D. diss. by Robert G. Campbell, "Johann Gottfried Müthel, 1728-1788," 2 vols. (Indiana University, 1966).

P. 438. 118a. The sons. are among the works discussed by Campbell (see note 116a to p. 437).

P. 444. 142a. A further Ph.D. diss. (unpublished) is that of Douglas Allen Lee, "The Instrumental Works of Christoph Nichelmann," 2 vols. (University of Michigan, 1968), from which has been published *The Works of Christoph Nichelmann: A Thematic Index* (Detroit: Information Coordinators, 1971).

P. 445. 146a. Futher mod. ed.: Son. 5 in E♭ ("Sonata XII" on pp. 52-53 of Lee's *Thematic Index*, as in note 142a to p. 444), ed. by W. Abert, in *Neue Musik-Zeitung* XXXIV (1913), *Beilage*.

P. 452. 175a. Thanks to information from Sister Mary Romana Hertel (author of the unpublished Ph.D. diss., "The Keyboard Concertos of Johann Wilhelm Hertel," Catholic University, 1964), Uldall's reference cited in fn. 175 is shown to be to the father (J. C. Hertel) and not to J. W. Hertel; the error seems to have started with W. Kahl in MGG VI 287.

P. 458. 3a. Two of these sources, Dies and Griesinger, have been made available in annotated English trans. by Vernon Gotwals in *Haydn—Two Contemporary Portraits*, 2d printing (Madison: The University of Wisconsin Press, 1968).

P. 459. 9a. The collection has been revised by H. C. Robbins Landon and Dénes Bartha in the original German as *Joseph Haydn—Gesammelte Briefe und Aufzeichnungen* (Kassel: Bärenreiter, 1965; cf. K. Geiringer in JAMS XIX [1966] 251-254).

P. 459. 11a. Since the 2d ed. of SCE in 1972, new Haydn literature has continued to appear at a remarkable rate. Besides the completion of Hoboken/HAYDN in 1978, with its 3d (final) vol. of indices, additions, and corrections, first mention should be given to the 5 vol. set, completed by 1980, Landon/CHRONICLE. This rich documentary, which largely recapitulates and augments all of H. C. Robbins Landon's previous Haydn studies, takes in the 62 K sons. in Vols. I-III (cf. the reviews in PIANO QUARTERLY nos. 100 and 115 [winter

1977-78 and fall 1981] 43-46 and 46-50 [W. S. Newman]). Note, too, the full bibliography, up to 1972, now available in Brown & Berkenstock/HAYDN.

P. 461. 17a. Georg Feder recognizes one or two of the four-hand sons. as authentic (p. 100 as cited in note 21a to p. 462).

P. 462. 20a. Two important new editions of the K sons. have appeared (cf. Alan Tyson in MT CV [1964] 604-605). One is a selection of 21 sons. in 2 vols. (München-Duisburg: G. Henle, 1963), ed. by Georg Feder in advance of the complete set in Haydn/INSTITUT-m; it includes 2 newly discovered sons. (nos. 1 and 2, both in E♭), published here for the first time. The other is a complete ed. of the 54 sons. now known, in 3 vols. ed. by Christa Landon (Vienna: Universal, 1964-66; cf. H. Ferguson in ML XLVIII [1967] 199-200); it also includes the incipits and a fragment from the 8 "lost" sons. (cf. fn. 20); in addition to the helpful preface, a *Revisionsbericht* is stated to be published separately. Feder's ed. cited above, appeared as 54 sons. in 3 vols. in Haydn/INSTITUT-m XVIII/3/1-3 in 1966-70 (with prefaces but without the *kritische Berichte* yet, as of 1979; cf. NOTES XXVIII [1971-72] 766-767 [K. Geiringer] and again as 3 separate vols. from G. Henle Verlag in 1972. The authenticity of the 2d of Feder's 2 newly discovered sons. (Nos. 8 and 9 in E♭ in Haydn/INSTITUT-m XVIII/3/1, pp. 53-67, the so-called "Raigern Sonatas") has been questioned by C. E. Hatting in DMF XXV (1972) 182-187 and argued further at the international Haydnfest in Washington in 1975 (congress report in progress as of 1979), with Mariano Romano Kayser as one possible alternative composer of the work.

P. 462. 21a. Cf., further, Georg Feder, "Probleme einer Neuordnung der Klaviersonaten Haydns," in *Festschrift Friedrich Blume* 92-103 (see note 2a to p. 114). There are still too many uncertainties to permit the needed revision of the table on p. 464. An orientation to these problems is provided by Peter Brown in "A Re-introduction to Joseph Haydn's Keyboard Works," PIANO QUARTERLY No. 79 (fall 1972) 42-47. The new chronologies of the K sons. in Landon's and Feder's eds. (cf. fn. 20a to p. 462, *supra*) differ considerably, especially in the very uncertain succession of the early sons. (prior to 1774), which Feder prefers only to consider by groups. Each of these eds. has its own helpful thematic index. Some idea of the revised chronologies may be had by comparing the numbering arrived at by Landon with that of Päsler and Hoboken (as in the chart on SCE 464) for those sons. both Landon and Päsler include:

Landon =	Päsler	L =	P	L =	P	L =	P	L =	P	L =	P
1	8	11	2	30	19	38	23	46	31	54	40
2	7	12	12	31	46	39	24	47	32	55	41
3	9	13	6	32	44	40	25	48	35	56	42
5	11	14	3	33	20	41	26	49	36	57	47
6	10	15	13	34	33	42	27	50	37	58	48
8	5	16	14	35	43	43	28	51	38	59	49
9	4	20	18	36	21	44	29	52	39	60	50
10	1	29	45	37	22	45	30	53	34	61	51
										62	52

P. 463. 23a. Two further Ph.D. diss. may be reported: Bettina Wackernagel, *Joseph Haydns frühe Klaviersonaten und die Wiener Klaviermusik um die Mitte des 18. Jahrhunderts* (Universität München, 1966; listed in *Current Musicology* V [1967] 148); Harold L. Andrews, "Tonality and Structure in the First Movements of Haydn's Solo Keyboard Sonatas" (unpublished, The University of North Carolina, 1967). The diss. projected by I. M. Hedrick in JAMS XX (1967) seems not to have been pursued. Wackernagel's diss. cited above has been published by Hans Schneider in Tutzing (1975) and reviewed somewhat negatively by Peter Brown in NOTES XXXIII (1976-77) 69-71 and by I. M. Bruce in *Haydn Yearbook* XI (1980) 206-208; cf., also, the several comments in Landon/CHRONICLE I and II. To be added is Brown's own unpub. Ph.D. diss. in 3 vols. (Northwestern University, 1970), "The Solo and Ensemble Keyboard Sonatas of Joseph Haydn: A Study of Structure and Style" (Vol. III, not filmed by University Microfilms but filed at the Northwestern University Library, contains keyboard works never published). This diss. takes an approach similar to that in SCE, examining Haydn's son. cycles as wholes, then the separate mvts. by types. In an article in MR XXXVI (1975) 102-129, Brown examines "The Structure of the Exposition in Haydn's Keyboard Sonatas" according to five successive creative periods. Scheduled for publication (as of 1980), in Hungarian and probably in English translation, is a significant, new analytic approach to Haydn's K sons. by the Haydn specialist Lászlo Somfai. Related is the provocative study of "Texture and Dynamics in Haydn's [symphonic] Sonata-Allegro Structures," unpub. Ph.D. diss. by Judith K. Fisher, University of Sydney (Australia), 1981. Many pertinent details on Haydn, his sons., and their form, style, and performance are scattered throughout *Haydn Studies: Proceedings of the International Haydn Conference, Washington, D. C., 1975,* edited by J. P. Larsen, H. Serwer, and J. Webster (New York: W. W. Norton, 1981).

P. 465. 29a. Cf. the penetrating study by Horst Walter, "Haydns Klaviere," in *Haydn-Studien* II (1970) 256-288.

P. 465. 32a. On the early popularity of H. XVI/35 in C and 2 different English song settings of it in the late 1780's, cf. Frank Dawes, "William: or The Adventures of a Sonata," in MT CVI (1965) 761-764.

P. 467. 38a. The authenticity of Son. 47, especially its first mvt., was severely doubted by both Georg Feder and Christa Landon at the Haydnfest in Washington in 1975; cf. Landon's ed. III xviii (No. 57).

P. 468. 46a. Further facs. from the autograph of Son. 52 may be seen in Emanuel Winternitz, *Musical Autographs from Monteverdi to Hindemith,* revised from the original ed. of 1955, 2 vols. (New York: Dover, 1965) II Plates 55-56.

P. 470. 51a. Cf. Landon/CHRONICLE III 309-310 for Dies's contemporary account.

P. 470. 52a. A basic start has been made by Georg Feder's article, "Haydns frühe Klaviertrios—Eine Untersuchung zur Echtheit und Chronologie," in *Haydn-Studien* II (1970) 289-316; and much helpful information appears in Ruth Blume's Ph.D. diss., *Studien zur Entwicklungsgeschichte des Klavier-Trios im 18. Jahrhundert* (Universitat Kiel, 1962). H. C. Robbins Landon prefaces his new "Complete Edition" of the trios (fn. 57a to p. 472, *infra*) with a "Foreword," pub. as a separate booklet, that discusses sources and chronology and provides a thematic index; cf. I. M. Bruce's review in *Haydn Yearbook* XI (1980) 221-225.

P. 470. 54a. Cf., also, Alan Tyson, "New Light on a Haydn Trio (XV: 32)," in *Haydn Yearbook* I (1962) 203-205.

P. 472. 55a. The whole question is reviewed and advanced by Rita Benton in "A Resumé of the Haydn-Pleyel 'Trio-Controversy' with Some Added Contributions," in *Haydn-Studien* IV (1978) 114-117.

P. 472. 57a. Authoritative eds. of the trios are at last becoming available in 2 new complete critical eds., both begun in 1970. One is in Reihe XVII of Haydn/INSTITUT-m, ed. by Wolfgang Stockmeier, also appearing separately from G. Henle Verlag; cf. K. Geiringer in NOTES XXVIII (1971-72) 765-768. The other is H. C. Robbins Landon's ed. pub. by Doblinger in Vienna, one vol. for each of the 45 trios he authenticates plus one for a Foreword on sources and chronology; cf. H. L. Andrews in NOTES XXVIII (1971-72) 768-769. Landon's chonology is close to that of Larsen (as in the chart on SCE 472), although Larsen had included fewer trios.

P. 479. 91a. The long needed *Mozart-Bibliographie (bis 1970)*, ed. by R. Angermüller and O. Schneider, was pub. in 1976 as the MOZART-JAHRBUCH for 1975, followed by a supplement in 1978 (up to 1975, with additions and corrections up to 1970), also pub. by Bärenreiter.

P. 479. 93a. The 6th ed., ed. by F. Giegling, A. Weinmann, and G. Sievers, appeared in 1964 (Wiesbaden: Breitkopf & Härtel; U. S. agent, C. F. Peters); cf. the review in NOTES XXI (1964) 531-540, with corrections and additions (B. E. Wilson). Note, also, Otto Schneider and Anton Algatzy, *Mozart-Handbuch: Chronik, Werk, Bibliographie* (Vienna: Brüder Hollinek, 1962).

P. 480. 99a. The complete new ed. in the original German is that of W. A. Bauer, O. E. Deutsch, and J. H. Eibl, *Mozart: Briefe und Aufzeichnungen*, 7 vols. including commentary and detailed indices. Kassel: Bärenreiter, 1962-75. Cf. Neal Zaslaw's review in JAMS XXXI (1978) 367-372.

P. 480. 101a. For the English trans., see note 49a to p. 55. An extensive supplement of additions and corrections to the documentary collection in Mozart/NEUE-m X/34 appeared in 1978 in Mozart/NEUE-m X/31/1 (prepared by J. H. Eibl).

P. 482. 107a. More flexible is the recent text of Richard Rosenberg, *Die Klaviersonaten Mozarts–Gestalt- und Stilanalyse* (Hofheim a/Taunus: Friedrich Hofmeister, 1972), which analyzes 18 solo K sons. individually.

P. 483. 113a. In the present study the preference now (as of 1979) would be for the revision in 1976 by Ernst Herttrich of the 2-vol. ed. originally pub. in 1955 by G. Henle Verlag, mainly because of still further primary sources that have become available (see Herttrich's Preface). The solo sons. have not yet been pub. (as of early 1980) in Mozart/NEUE-m.

P. 483. 113b. Certain years of completion become somewhat later on our chart if we accept Wolfgang Plath's conclusions based on Mozart's handwriting, in "Beiträge zur Mozart-Autographie II, Schrift-chronologie 1770-1780" (MOZART-JAHRBUCH 1976-77, pp. 131-173, especially 144 [fn. 35], 165, and 171). Those years "probably" would be 1775 for K.V. 189d-h, not before 1780 for K.V. 300d, 300i, and 300k, and 1783-84 for K.V. 315c (November of 1783 argues Alan Tyson in *Gedenkschrift Günter Henle* [Munich: G. Henle, 1980] 447-454).

P. 487. 130a. Cf., also, MR XXII (1961) 177-180 (N. Temperley).

P. 488. 134a. Cf. the list of lost autographs, including several sons., in DMF XVII (1964) 152-155.

P. 489. 145a. That K.V. 570 may have been another late *pasticcio* is argued by Hans Eppstein in "Warum wurde Mozarts KV 570 zur Violin-sonate?" in DMF XVI (1963) 379-381.

P. 489. 148a. Cf. Alan Tyson's review in MT CV (1964) 604 of a new edition of the duets, ed. by Christa Landon (Vienna: Universal, 1963).

P. 490. 151a. For still more on the question, cf. Alan Tyson in MR XXII (1961) 222 and A. H. King in MR XXV (1964) 124-126. There is a paragraph (p. 320) on sonatinas and sonatas but no mention of a duet sonata in an article by Walter Hüttel, "Christian Gottlob Saupe, Leben und Werk" (DMF XXIII [1970] 311-321); however, if this is the same Saupe, his indicated birth year of 1763 removes him as a contender for priority.

P. 490. 157a. A newly discovered, incomplete Son. in E♭ for 2 Ps is reported in 2 articles (with facs.) by Gerhard Croll: "Ein überraschender Mozart-Fund," in MOZART-JAHRBUCH 1962-63, pp. 108-110, and "Zu Mozarts Larghetto und Allegro Es-Dur für 2 Klaviere," in MOZART-JARHBUCH 1964, pp. 28-37.

P. 490. 157b. Not all of the 44 sons. for K & Vn are accounted for in the discussion that follows, and the number must remain variable, in any case, because of uncertain attributions (cf. the 6th ed. of the Köchel *Verzeichnis* [see note 93a to p. 479], pp. cxxix-cxxxii).

P. 491. 158a. One analytic study has appeared of the entire output, divided into three creative periods—the unpublished Ph.D. diss. of Carl Earl Forsberg, "The Clavier-Violin Sonatas of Wolfgang Amadeus Mozart" (Indiana University, 1964). Cf., also, NEW OXFORD VII 539-541 (K. Geiringer).

P. 491. 162a. Cf. the excellent new study by Jürgen Hunkemöller, *W. A. Mozarts frühe Sonaten für Violine und Klavier* (Bern: Francke, 1970; publication of a 1968 Ph.D. diss. at Universität Heidelberg).

P. 494. 177a. Friedrich Neumann leans away from their authenticity again in MOZART-JAHRBUCH 1965-66, pp. 152-60, and they are absent not only from Mozart/NEUE-m VIII/23/1-2 (E. Reeser; cf. Band 1, p. xi) but from the projected contents of the Suppl. containing doubtful works (X/29). They are in the Anhang of the latest, 6th, ed. of Köchel/MOZART, pp. 887-888. Indeed, with the discovery of the original MS in a still unidentified hand the possibility of Mozart's authorship now seems to be ruled out once and for all; cf. MOZART-JAHRBUCH 1968-70, pp. 368-373 (W. Plath), and *Mozart Briefe* (fn. 99a to p. 480, *supra*) VI 462 (as kindly called to my attention by Dr. Max Rudolf).

P. 494. 177b. Some details on the dates of composition are given by W. Plath (fn. 113b to p. 483, *supra*), p. 170.

P. 494. 180a. Cf. the listing of, and facs. from, the autograph of K.V. 374d in *The Mary Flagler Cary Music Collection* (see note 32a to p. 300), item 157 and Plate 34; and the facs. of the first page of music in the autograph of K.V. 374f in Kinsky/KOCH (as listed in SSB 807), p. 23 (Plate 5).

P. 495. 184a. The publication of K.V. 526 probably occurred in 1787, according to the 1961 ed. of Deutsch/NUMBERS 14 (Hoffmeister Plate No. 128) and the 6th ed. of the Köchel/VERZEICHNIS (see note 98a tc p. 479), p. 590. Cf., also, W. S. Newman, "The Duo Texture of Mozart's K. 526: An Essay in Classic Instrumental Style," in *Essays in Musicology, in Honor of Dragan Plamenac on His 70th Birthday,* ed. by G. Reese and R. J. Snow (Pittsburgh: University of Pittsburgh Press, 1969) 191-206.

P. 496. 185a. Add Thomas Harmon, "The Performance of Mozart's Church Sonatas," in ML LI (1970) 51-60.

P. 497. 186a. But W. Plath argues for 1780 as the year of composition for K.V. 241a and 241b (MOZART-JAHRBUCH 1976-77, pp. 167-168).

P. 502. 5a. A supplement to Kinsky & Halm/BEETHOVEN has been prepared by Kurt Dorfmüller and pub. by G. Henle Verlag (1978), *Beiträge zur Beethoven-Bibliographie,* including additions and corrections.

P. 502. 8a. Elliot Forbes's revision of Thayer/BEETHOVEN appeared in 1964 in 2 vols., with further revisions in 1967, and slight further revisions in one vol. and in paperback in 1970, all from Princeton University Press. One of the most significant biographies of recent decades is Maynard Solomon's *Beethoven* (New York: Schirmer Books, 1977). It draws important new conclusions about the man, psychological and otherwise, from the known facts of his life; cf. NOTES XXXIV (1977-78) 847-850 (R. Winter), MQ LXIV (1978) 389-394 (E. Rothstein), NINETEENTH-CENTURY III (1979) 79-82 (L. Lockwood).

P. 502. 9a. For the English trans. of Schindler's biography see note 79a to p. 105; this trans. includes an index to all the cited reviews of

Beethoven in AMZ. *An Index to Beethoven's Conversation Books* (as published by Schünemann and Prod'homme), by the late Donald MacArdle, appeared in 1962 (Detroit: Information Service). Since 1968 Karl-Heinz Köhler and Grita Herre of the Deutsche Staatsbibliothek Berlin have been preparing a complete ed. of *Ludwig van Beethovens Konversationshefte* in 12 vols. (including indices); cf. Köhler's article, "Beethovens Gespräche-Biographische Aspekte zu einem modernen Beethovenbild, Bemerkungen zur Edition der noch unveröffentlichen Konversationshefte," in *Beiträge zur Musikwissenschaft* XII (1970) 322-332. Vols. 4, 5, 1, 6, 2, and 7 have appeared biennially in that order up to 1980, marred only by significant new evidence of Schindler's forgeries in them (cf. the insert of 1978 in Vol. 7 as well as 2 articles by Peter Stadlen, in MT CXVIII [1977] 549-552 and in *Österreichische Musikzeitschrift* XXXII [1977] 246-252).

P. 503. 11a. Nearest to a Beethoven encyclopedia among the many Beethoven pubs. of the late MacArdle (d. 1964) is his collection of *Beethoven Abstracts* of articles in more than 400 periodicals, pub. posthumously (Detroit: Information Coordinators, 1973). A good start toward more complete document collections are 2 pubs. timed for the Beethoven bicentennial in 1970, both also rich in illustrations and facs. of early sources, both available in English translations. One is H. C. Robbins Landon's somewhat random assortment organized around Beethoven's life chronology, with indices of names but not topics—*Beethoven* (London: Thames and Hudson). The other is Joseph Schmidt-Görg's and Hans Schmidt's more systematic assortment, organized in an anthology of articles on the various genres of Beethoven's compositions, including many facs. of MSS and documents bearing on the son.—*Ludwig van Beethoven* (Bonn: Beethoven-Archiv, and Hamburg: Deutsche Grammophon Gesellschaft).

P. 503. 12a. For more on Sketchbooks in Russia cf. B. Schwarz in MQ XLIX (1963) 518-526 and M. H. Brown in NOTES XX (1963) 460-463 on a new, 3-vol. ed. of the "Wielhorsky Sketchbook" (including Op. 47); also, B. Schwarz in MQ LVI (1970) 539-550. Sketches for Op. 49/2/i and a possible alternative to Op. 13/iii are among the *Autograph Miscellany, circa 1786 to 1799 . . . (the 'Kafka Sketchbook')*, ed. by Joseph Kerman, 2 vols. (London: The British Museum, 1970). Cf., also, the index of sketches in BEETHOVEN-JAHRBUCH VI (1965-68) 7-128. The facs. of the *Kesslersches Skizzenbuch*, with "Nachwort" and indexes by Sieghard Brandenburg (Munich: Emil Katzbichler, 1976), makes available important sketches for Opp. 30/1-3, 31, and 47, among other works. As of 1979 Dieter Krüger was working in Berlin on "Die Skizzen zu Beethovens späten Klaviersonaten." Further diss. on sketches for individual sons. are cited *supra*, p. 536, fn. 230 (Op. 111), and *infra*, fn. 251a to p. 539 (Op. 30/1-3).

P. 504. 16a. Cf., also, Franziska Lomtano's "poetic clarifications" of Opp. 10/2, 53, and 90 in *Neue Musik-Zeitung* I (1880) Nos. 7, p. 2; 11, p. 1; and 17, pp. 1-2, respectively. Czerny attests to Beethoven's poetic inspirations, too (cf. W. S. Newman, *Performance Practices in Beethoven's Piano Sonatas—An Introduction* [New York: W. W. Norton, 1971] 56-59).

P. 505. 18a. Cf., also, Anderson/BEETHOVEN I 290-291, II 953, and III 1435; Alan Tyson on pp. 486-489 in *The Beethoven Reader,* ed. by D. Arnold and N. Fortune (New York: W. W. Norton, 1971); and W. S. Newman, "A Chronological Checklist of Collected Editions of Beethoven's Solo Piano Sonatas Since His Own Day," in NOTES XXXIII (1976-77) 503-530, especially pp. 506 and 509-510.

P. 505. 21a. The 18 vols. issued by the end of 1979 include all of the string sons., in 3 vols.; all of the K sons. with op. nos. through Op. 57, in 2 vols. (cf. W. S. Newman in PIANO QUARTERLY No. 82 [summer 1973] 37-39, No. 85 [spring 1974] 47-48, No. 86 [summer 1974] 1 and 41, and No. 87 [fall 1974] 42-45); but no "Kritischer Bericht" for any vol. as yet.

P. 505. 22a. The view of three style periods is traced back even earlier, to Czerny in 1837, in JAMS XX (1967) 515 (W. S. Newman); to J. A. Schlosser in 1828, according to the *Beethoven-Jahrbuch,* 2d series, Vol. V (1933) 85; and to Beethoven himself, on his deathbed in 1827, according to Harry Goldschmidt in *Bericht über den Internationalen Beethoven-Kongress 10.-12. Dezember 1970 in Berlin* (Berlin: Verlag neue Musik, 1971) 41 (without documentation). Indeed, as early as 1818 a premature tripartite division of his works was made in an anonymous Viennese article (quoted in Boyer/BEETHOVEN 191-92 and kindly called to my attention by Mr. Maynard Solomon).

P. 506. 23a. The last 4 of the 5 periods also reveal their character in Beethoven's concurrent output of string quartets—the 2d period in Op. 18, the 3d in Op. 59, the 4th in Opp. 74 and 95, and the 5th in the last 5 quartets.

P. 508. 32a. Cf., further, Alan Tyson, *The Authentic English Editions of Beethoven* (London: Faber and Faber, 1963).

P. 508. 32b. Nor is the "Sonata" in E♭ that is transcribed for solo piano, perhaps by Beethoven himself, from his String Trio Op. 3 in E♭; cf. E. Hartzell's preface to his mod. ed. of the transcription (Vienna: Doblinger, 1968).

P. 508. 33a. For a chronological survey of over 130 collected eds. of Beethoven's solo K sons. (outnumbering those of Bach's *Well-Tempered Clavier* by a considerable number) cf. fn. 18a to p. 505, *supra.*

P. 508. 34a. Each sonata is individually discussed at some length in the 5 vols. of Wilhelm von Lenz's *Beethoven: Eine Kunststudie* (Kassel: Ernst Balde, 1855 [Vols. I-III], and Hamburg: Hoffmann & Campe, 1860 [Vols. IV and V]). To the list of authors add E. Stainkamph (1968), J. and B. Massin (1970), P. Badura-Skoda and J. Demus (1970; cf. DMF XXVI [1973] 129 [E. Voss]), Jürgen Uhde (1970; cf. DMF XXVI [1973] 129-130 [E. Voss]), Joachim Kaiser (1975; cf. DMF XXXII [1979] 96-99 [E. Voss]).

P. 509. 35a. That Franz Anton Hoffmeister preceded Eder in the publication of Op. 13 (both in Vienna in 1799) was concluded first by Richard Hill, in NOTES XV (1958) 396-397, and subsequently but independently by Alan Tyson, in MT CIV (1963) 333.

P. 509. 36a. Add the book by W. S. Newman cited in note 16a to p. 504; also, cf. my more specific studies of Beethoven performance problems, including authoritative sources (in the vol. cited in fn. 5a to p. 502, *supra*), pianos and piano writing (fn. 38a to p. 510, *infra,* and fn. 39a to p. 89, *supra*), articulation and rhythmic grouping (fn. 89a to p. 517; also, "Some Articulation Puzzles in Beethoven's Autographs and Earliest Editions," in *International Musicological Society: Report of the Eleventh Congress Copenhagen 1972* II 580-585), trills (in JAMS XXIX [1976] 439-462, MQ LXIV [1978] 98-103, and the *Gedenkschrift Günter Henle* [Munich: G. Henle, 1980] 384-393 [on Op. 96]), tempo ("Tempo in Beethoven's Instrumental Music," DMF XXXIII [1980] 161-183), and Liszt's playing of Beethoven (MQ LVIII [1972] 185-209).

P. 510. 37a. With further regard to eds. of Beethoven's sons., cf. W. S. Newman (as cited in note 16a to p. 504), pp. 24-26.

P. 510. 38a. Cf. W. S. Newman, "Beethoven's Pianos Versus His Piano Ideals," in JAMS XXIII (1970) 484-504.

P. 511. 45a. Cf., also, Maynard Solomon, "Beethoven's Birth Year," in MQ LVI (1970) 702-710.

P. 511. 48a. On sketches for WoO 51, cf. Anderson/BEETHOVEN I 13-14 and MQ LVI (1970) 530-532.

P. 512. 51a. Cf., also, Boris Schwarz, "A Little Known Beethoven Sketch in Moscow," in MQ LVI (1970) 539-550.

P. 512. 53a. On the subsequent critical reception of Op. 7, cf. R. Steglich, "Dokumentarisches zur Lebensgeschichte eines Beethovenschen Sonatensatzes," in *Festschrift Otto Erich Deutsch zum 80. Geburtstag,* ed. by W. Gerstenberg, J. LaRue, and W. Rehm (Kassel: Bärenreiter, 1963) 213-225.

P. 513. 56a. On the theme of Op. 10/1/iii cf. DMF XVII (1964) 174.

P. 513. 59a. Hellmut Federhofer's article, "Zur Analyse des zweiten Satzes von L. van Beethovens Klaviersonate Op. 10 No. 3," in *Festskrift Jens Peter Larsen* (Copenhagen: Wilhelm Hansen, 1972) 339-350, reviews past approaches and offers his own.

P. 513. 61a. A "new" orchestration of Op. 13 was announced in *Neue Zeitschrift für Musik* XXXVII (1852) 116.

P. 514. 67a. Cf. W. S. Newman, "K. 457 and *op.* 13—Two Related Masterpieces in C minor," in MR XXVIII (1967) 38-44.

P. 515. 74a. Cf. Michael E. Broyles, "Beethoven's Sonata Op. 14, No. 1—Originally for Strings?" in JAMS XXIII (1970) 405-419.

P. 515. 76a. Cf. p. 536, *infra;* also, the unpub. Ph.D. dissertation by Leilani Kathryn Lutes, "Beethoven's Re-Uses of His Own Compositions, 1782-1826" (University of Southern California, 1974); also, Otto Brusatti, "Die thematisch-melodische Einheit im Spätwerk Beethovens," in *Musicologica Austriaca* II (1979) 117-140.

P. 517. 89a. Cf. W. S. Newman, "On the Rhythmic Significance of Beethoven's Annotations in Cramer's Etudes," in *Bericht über den internationalen musikwissenschaftlichen Kongress Bonn 1970* (Kassel: Bärenreiter, 1971) 43-47.

P. 517. 89b. Cf. Paul Mies, ". . . Quasi una Fantasia" (exploring its meaning in Op. 27 and other Beethoven uses), in *Festschrift Schmidt-Görg* (as cited in note 35b to p. 87) 239-249.

P. 518. 95a. A link in 1801 (the year when Op. 27/2 was composed) becomes no more likely now that Maynard Solomon has established Antonie Brentano as the "Eternally Beloved" (in MQ LVIII [1972] 572-587; also, cf. fn. 8a to p. 502, ch. 15) to the satisfaction, at last, of most scholars, though not including Joseph Schmidt-Görg (personal communication), who, like Thayer, cannot accept the impropriety of a Beethoven relationship with a married woman, and Harry Goldschmidt (*Um die Unsterbliche Geliebte* [Leipzig: VEB Deutscher Verlag für Musik, 1977], especially pp. 229-241), who still views Josephine Brunsvik as an equal possibility.

P. 519. 103a. Daniel Coren touches on the background and sketches of Op. 28 and analyzes it in "Structural Relations Between Op. 28 and Op. 36," in *Beethoven Studies II*, ed. by Alan Tyson (London: Oxford University Press, 1977).

P. 519. 107a. P. G. Downs examines the "Eroica" Symphony for the meaning of the "new path," which he interprets as "a new humanity," in Paul Lang, *The Creative World of Beethoven* (New York: W. W. Norton, 1970, pp. 83-102). Cf., also, Richard Kramer in JAMS XXXIII (1980) 596-601 (especially 598-600); but recall, too, the fantasy element in Op. 27/1, *supra*.

P. 519. 108a. Cf. Ludwig Finscher, "Beethoven's Klaviersonate opus 31, 3—Versuch einer Interpretation," in *Festschrift für Walter Wiora zum 30. Dezember 1966*, ed. by L. Finscher and C.-H. Mahling (Kassel: Bärenreiter, 1967) 385-396.

P. 520. 113a. Czerny reported that Beethoven conceived the theme of Op. 31/2/iii as he watched a horseman galloping! (P. Badura-Skoda [ed.], *Carl Czerny: Über den richtigen Vortrag der sämtlichen Beethoven'schen Klavierwerke* [Vienna: Universal, 1963] 48).

P. 520. 114a. For more on the sketches of Op. 31/3 cf. B. Schwarz in MQ XLIX (1963) 522-523.

P. 520. 115a. Any one of the three, said Beethoven, could be (but never was) supplied with an "accompaniment"; cf. fn. 79a to p. 105, *supra*.

P. 522. 130a. Cf., also, Grillparzer's poem on Clara Schumann's performance of Op. 57, in *Neue Zeitschrift für Musik* LXXII/1 (1876) 15.

P. 528. 169a. A facs. of the autograph of the slow introduction (2 pp.) appears in Kinsky/KOCH (as listed in SSB 803) 72, Plate 9.

P. 529. 178a. But, among exceptions, Tomaschek heard Beethoven himself play Op. 2/2/ii and iv in 1798 (Thayer/BEETHOVEN I 207 in the Elliot Forbes ed. cited above, note 8a to p. 502) and on Feb. 27, 1819, Sophia Hewitt apparently played Op. 26 in Boston (H. E. Johnson: *Musical Interludes in Boston* [New York: Columbia University Press, 1943] 144).

P. 529. 180a. A fifth instance (Op. 69) is cited in Anderson/BEETHOVEN II 561 (fn. 1). Cf., also, Forbes's ed. of Thayer (fn. 8a to p. 502, *supra*), p. 641; and Beethoven's own comments on public performance in his letter (evidently written in English) to Sir George Smart of *ca.* Oct. 11, 1816 (Anderson/BEETHOVEN II 604-607).

P. 530. 188a. Cf. W. S. Newman, "Some 19th-Century Consequences of Beethoven's 'Hammerklavier' Sonata, Op. 106," in *The Piano Quarterly* No. 67 (spring 1969) 12-18 and No. 68 (summer 1969) 12-17.

P. 531. 200a. But Nottebohm refuted Schindler's arguments, as discussed by W. S. Newman (see note 16a to p. 504), pp. 51-53.

P. 532. 201a. Beethoven had also considered leaving out other movements, especially scherzos, in a contemplated re-edition of his sons., as discussed by W. S. Newman (see note 16a to p. 504), pp. 91-92.

P. 532. 202a. The theory that Beethoven actually intended the slow mvt. to precede the "Scherzo," as in both the first and 2d eds. of 1819 and 1820 from the Regent's Harmonic Institution in London, is the burden, argued more persuasively on "philological" than historical grounds, of a recent book by Ernesto Paolone, *La grande sconosciuta —"Grosse Sonate für das Hammerklavier Op. 106" di Ludwig van Beethoven—Analisi storica e filologica dell'ordine dei tempi* (Cagliari: Edizioni il Solco, 1977). Without knowing Tyson's book on the English eds. (fn. 32a to p. 508, *supra;* pp. 102-107), Paolone had already argued for the greater authority of the London eds., in "L'Edizione originale dell'op. 106 di L. van Beethoven," RIdM V (1970) 148-158. Independently, Johannes Fischer also argues for the inversion of the inner mvts., in *Neue Zeitschrift für Musik* CXXXIII (1972) 186-194, whereas Paul Badura-Skoda answers in favor of the order in the original, Artaria ed. (F-F-S-[S]F), in *Melos/NZ* III (1977) 11-15.

P. 532. 202b· In contradiction to that statement, a review is cited in Boyer/BEETHOVEN 255.

P. 532. 204a. Moscheles seems not to have played Op. 106 until 1845, and then to have responded to the slow mvt. but not to the fugue (Moscheles/MOSCHELES II 138).

P. 533. 211a. Facs. of the autographs of Opp. 110 and 111 have been published, respectively, by Ichthy in Stuttgart (1967, with commentary vol. by K. M. Komma) and by C. F. Peters in Leipzig. Facs. of 3 pp. from the autograph of Op. 109 are in Winternitz (see note 46a to p. 468) II Plates 88-90.

P. 533. 214a. A review of Op. 110 in *The Harmonicon* II/1 (1824) 67 concludes that Beethoven, once so great, has now become all but incomprehensible.

P. 534. 225a. Cf., also, the analytic discussion by Egon Voss, "Zu Beethovens Klaviersonate As-dur," in DMF XXIII (1970) 256-268. In progress at the City University of New York as of 1979 is a Ph.D. diss. by Carl Skoggard, "A Transcription and Analysis of Sketches for Beethoven's Piano Sonata in A-flat, Op. 110."

P. 538. 244a. In *Beethoven-Kolloquium 1977* (Kassel: Bärenreiter, 1978) 175-176 Lewis Lockwood argues for Jean Louis rather than Jean Pierre Duport.

P. 538. 245a. In *The Harmonicon* V/1 (1827) 22, the parallel 5ths that the Vc plays in the finale of Op. 5/1 are reviewed as "striking and beautiful."

P. 539. 246a. Cf. the trans. in MacArdle's ed. of Schindler's biography (as cited in note 79a to p. 105, above) 76-77.

P. 539. 251a. Cf. the important unpub. Ph.D diss. by Richard A. Kramer, "The Sketches for Beethoven's Violin Sonatas, Opus 30: History, Transcription, Analysis," 3 vols. (Princeton University, 1974).

P. 540. 253a. But cf. B. Schwarz in MQ XLIX (1963) 524; also, Sieghard Brandenburg, "Zur Textgeschichte von Beethovens Violinsonate Opus 47," in *Gedenkschrift Günter Henle* (Munich: G. Henle, 1980) 111-124.

P. 541. 262a. Cf. Lewis Lockwood's fascinating search for the definitive text in "The Autograph of the First Movement of Beethoven's Sonata for Violoncello and Pianoforte, Op. 69," in *The Music Forum* II, ed. by W. J. Mitchell and F. Salzer (New York: Columbia University Press, 1970) 1-109 (including facs. of the autograph [also published separately], exx., and other illustrations).

P. 541. 263a. Cf., also, Anderson/BEETHOVEN I 391. An outstanding facs. of the autograph, in the Pierpont Morgan Library in New York, was pub. by G. Henle Verlag in 1977, with a "Geleitwort" by Martin Staehelin. Regarding the MS sources, cf. Mary Rowen Obelkevich, "The Growth of a Musical Idea—Beethoven's Op. 96," in CM XI (1971) 91-114, with exx.; Sieghard Brandenburg, "Bemerkungen zu Beethovens Op. 96," BEETHOVEN-JAHRBUCH IX (1973-77) 11-25; also, my article listed in fn. 36a to p. 509, *supra*.

P. 543. 273a. But according to the uncertain word of Schindler (p. 379 in the trans. cited in note 79a to p. 105), there was nothing by Haydn in Beethoven's library; there were many sonatas by Mozart, but Beethoven had "little liking for Mozart's music"; and, unlike Czerny, he had "the greatest admiration" for Clementi's sonatas.

P. 548. 20a. That further bibliographical clarification is needed is suggested by the questions Rey Longyear has raised about the scoring and even the authorship of some of these sons., in DMF XXVIII (1975) 297-299. Style traits are discussed in Longyear's article "Klassik und

Romantik in Emanuel Förster's Nachlass," *Musicologica Austriaca* II (1978) 108-116, with several exx.

P. 551. 32a. A facs. of the start of Pleyel's autograph of his Son. in C for H & Vn & Vc is in MGG X 1357-1358. Mod. ed. of Son. in B♭, Op. 7/1: in the Smart collection cited in note 11a to p. 10, above.

P. 551. 34a. Cf. Wagner's somewhat disdainful reference to Pleyel, as cited in SSB 381 and 383. The late Rita Benton has paved the way heroically for an exploration of the works in *Ignace Pleyel: A Thematic Catalogue of His Compositions* (New York: Pendragon Press, 1977), with a helpful "Introduction" (cf., also, her preliminary statement in DMF XXIX [1976] 280-287 and her earlier, more general exposition of Pleyel problems in FONTES XVII [1970] 9-15); reviews in NOTES XXXIV (1977-78) 878-879 (S. M. Fry) and XXXV (1978-79) 75-76 (Lenore Coral), and in JAMS XXXIII (1980) 204-207 (F. K. Grave); also, H. C. Robbins Landon in *Haydn Yearbook* XI (1980) 212-213. A valuable Pleyel collection at the University of California in Los Angeles is described by Malcolm S. Cole in NOTES XXIX (1972-73) 215-223.

P. 553. 44a. Theodor Aigner, who provided preliminary information in DMF XXVI (1973) 341-344, presumably still is completing a Ph.D diss. (Universität Salzburg, as of 1979) on Mederitsch's life and works, including a thematic index.

P. 555. 59a. Recall fn. 77a to p. 105, *supra*.

P. 555. 60a. An earlier example by Vanhal, *ca.* 1800, is listed by Merriman (see note 49a to p. 93).

P. 556. 64a. Two new studies of the man and his works should be added. The first is in Czech: Milan Poštolka, *Leopold Koželuh* (Prague: Státní Hudebni Vydavatelství, 1964); cf. *Beiträge zur Musikwissenschaft* VIII (1968) 83-84. The second is a Ph.D. diss. by Christa Flamm, *Leopold Kozeluch—Biographie und stilkritische Untersuchung der Sonaten für Klavier, Violine und Violoncello nebst einem Beitrag zur Entwicklungsgeschichte des Klaviertrios* (Universität Wien, 1968).

P. 556. 65a. Another mod. ed. of a solo P son. is that of Op. 2/3 in c, in Lincoln/FIVE-m.

P. 559. 81a. Cf. the unpub. Ph.D. diss. by Richard Dale Sjoerdsma, "The Instrumental Works of Franz Christoph Neubauer (1760-1795)," 2 vols. (Ohio State University, 1970); a thematic index is included.

P. 562. 105a. Op. 14 is greeted with modest praise and gratitude for fewer technical difficulties, in AMZ III (1800) 448-450, as transl. in Landon/CHRONICLE IV 591-592.

P. 563. 112a. But with that title it apparently was not published until 1810 (according to Craw/DUSSEK [as listed in SSB 791] 353).

P. 564. 117a. On Reicha's theoretical writings about the son., cf. SSB 29n, 32, 33.

P. 564. 118a. A Son. in E♭, Op. 43, is included in *Antonín Rejcha, Ausgewählte Klavierwerke,* ed. by Dana Zahn (Munich: G. Henle Verlag, 1971); reviewed by Paul Mies in DMF XXVI (1973) 287-288. A full thematic index prepared by Olga Šotolová (Prague: Supraphon, 1977) includes 7 P sons., 5 acc'd. sons., and one son. for 4 Fls.

P. 567. 138a. On Diabelli's unwitting plagiarism of duets by J. A. André, cf. *Caecelia* XIII (1831) 106-108.

P. 569. 148a. Add the important unpub. Ph.D. diss. by Thomas F. Heck, "The Birth of the Classic Guitar and Its Cultivation in Vienna, Reflected in the Career and Compositions of Mauro Giuliani (d. 1829)," 2 vols. (Yale University, 1970).

P. 570. 150a. Mod. ed.: Son. in C, Op. 15, in *Mauro Giuliani, Oeuvres choisies pour guitarre,* ed. by T. F. Heck (Paris: Heugel, 1972).

P. 577. 187a. Cf. R. Fuhrmann in *Mannheimer Klavier-Kammermusik* (see note 38a to p. 328) 159-189.

P. 580. 202a. Cf., further, Gerald Seaman, "The First Russian Chamber Music," in MR XXVI (1965) 326-337, especially pp. 329-330.

P. 585. 230a. A review of the grandson's ed. of the Son. in f♯ (Czach no. 41) may be seen in *Neue Zeitschrift für Musik* LXXII/2 (1886) 302.

P. 586. 237a. But d'Indy had been interested at least as early as 1894 (cf. Gustave Samazeuilh [ed.], *Les Ecrits de Paul Dukas sur la musique* [Paris: Société d'Éditions françaises et internationales, 1948] 185-190). Even Debussy was involved, with an article on F. W. Rust in 1913 that accuses historians of overrating forerunners (cf. William W. Austin, *Music in the 20th Century* [New York: W. W. Norton, 1966] 163). The whole question of Rust's sons. and the hoax are examined once more in the recent D.M.A. diss. of Paul Campbell Ridgway (Peabody Conservatory of Music, 1981); included is a critical ed. of 6 sons. not previously so pub.

P. 602. 314a. An early list of his works appears in *The Harmonicon* II/1 (1824) 125-127. A comparison of him and Steibelt is made in Müller/STEIBELT (as listed in SSB 811) 95.

P. 605. 5a. But Diderot did seem to put the sonata on a higher plane than opera (cf. *Beiträge zur Musikwissenschaft* VII [1965] 112).

P. 606. 8a. Cf. Herbert C. Turrentine, "The Prince de Conti: A Royal Patron of Music," in MQ LIV (1968) 309-315.

P. 609. 24a. Cf. Gisella Beckmann, *Die französische Violinsonate mit Basso continuo von Jean-Marie Leclair bis Pierre Gaviniès* (Hamburg K. D. Wagner, 1975).

P. 609. 25a. The title p. of his Op. 1 and the score of Son. 6 may be foun on pp. 327-332 in the pub. cited in fn. 24a to p. 609, *supra.*

P. 610. 27a. A facs. of his *Principes du Violon* (1761), important to per formance practices of the time, was published in Paris in 1961 b Centre de Documentation Universitaire (cf. A. Mell's review i JAMS XVI [1963] 409-411).

P. 611. 38a. A study of the son. styles and scores of all of Op. 5 may be found in the unpub. Ph.D. diss. by Anthony Francis Ginter, "The Sonatas of Pierre Gaviniès" (Ohio State University, 1976).

P. 611. 41a. A facs. of the title page and score of "Le Tombeau" (Son. 1) appear on pp. 345-353 of the pub. cited in fn. 24a to p. 609.

P. 614. 53a. It is presumably Barry Brook in NEW OXFORD VII 423 (cf. p. 419, fn. 1) who calls Le Duc's few completed symphonies "among the best of the eighteenth century."

P. 615. 58a. The diss. by Jean Shaw on French cello music (see note 42a to p. 91) corrects some details and greatly amplifies the discussion that follows here. Among other things she finds (pp. 152 and 157) 2 sets of sons. by L. A. J. Jannson (*sic*), Opp. 1 and 2, published in 1770, and decided stylistic differences between these and the 1768 set (by his brother?). She finds (p. 141) only one set for Vc by Cupis, Op. 1, the other being for Vn. She finds (pp. 179, 180, and 191) 4 sets by J. P. Duport, including Op. 3, and one by J. L. Duport, the former being more advanced in structure, the latter in technique. And she finds (p. 152) another set of 4 sons. by Tillière, Op. 5, *ca.* 1780, but that "his" Son. in g (SCE 616, fn. 66) is actually Op. 42/10 by Bréval (SCE 678).

P. 616. 65a. Another mod. ed., of a single son., is reviewed in NOTES XXVI (1970) 607-608 (A. Cohen).

P. 616. 67a. The name may be added here of a Bohemian violinist in Paris, **Václav Vodićka** (*ca.* 1720-74), for a set of 6 Sons. in Vn/bass setting, originally published in Paris in the 1740's (mod. ed.: MAB-m No. 54 [Racek & Schoenbaum], with preface).

P. 617. 71a. Add to mod. eds.: Op. 1/3 and 4, ed. by F. F. Polnauer (Mainz: B. Schott's Söhne [1967?]); Op. 2, complete, ed. by R. Blanchard (Paris: Heugel, 1967, in the series "Le Pupitre"). Beckman (fn. 24a to p. 609, *supra*) includes facs. on pp. 333-343 of the title page and "Avertissement" of Op. 4 and Son. 6 from that Op.

P. 621. 82a. In 1975 Gerald Richard Custonguay completed an unpub. Ph.D. diss. on Guillemain's orchestral music, at Rutgers University.

P. 628. 122a. Cf. the unpublished Ph.D. diss. by Herbert C. Turrentine, "Johann Schobert and French Clavier Music From 1700 to the Revolution" (State University of Iowa, 1962), including background, analysis, thematic catalogue, and 3 sons. scored in full (Opp. 7/3, 16/2, 17/4).

P. 637. 157a. Carolyn Ann Bridger includes an ed. of Op. 1/5 in D and a thematic index in her unpub. D.M.A. diss., ". . . An Essay on the Solo Clavier Sonatas of Leontzi Honauer" (University of Iowa, 1977).

P. 639. 165a. David Fuller includes 4 of the acc'd. sons. in Vol. II of his ed. of *Armand-Louis Couperin, Selected Works for Keyboard,* 2 vols. (Madison: A-R Editions, 1975); reviewed by W. D. Gudger in NOTES XXXV (1978-79) 410-412.

P. 641. 171a. Mod. ed.: Op. 1/6, in the collection by W. S. Newman cited in note 11a to p. 10.

P. 649. 5a. Cf. Rita Benton, "Jean-Frédéric Edelmann, A Musical Victim of the French Revolution," in MQ L (1964) 165-187 (with doubts, p. 168, about the residence in Brussels).

P. 649. 7a. Cf. Rita Benton, "The Instrumental Music of Jean-Frédéric Edelmann—A Thematic Catalogue and List of Early Editions," in *Fontes artis musicae* XI (1964) 79-88.

P. 654. 25a. Mod. ed. of Op. 10/3 in g: W. S. Newman, *Six Keyboard Sonatas* (as cited in note 11a to p. 10).

P. 655. 33a. According to information kindly supplied by Dr. Rita Benton, the instruction under Edelmann is confirmed in MERCURE for Apr., 1778 (p. 176).

P. 658. 37a. Six MS sons. were published by his granddaughter, Adèle Clamageran, according to Arthur Pougin, *Hérold* (Paris: Librairie Renouard, 1906), p. 124.

P. 659. 38a. In RDM LIX (1973) a diss. by Martin Roche was reported in progress, "L'oeuvre instrumentale d'Henri-Joseph Rigel." No further mention of it has been found here (as of 1979).

P. 659. 39a. Mod. ed.: Op. 13/3 in D, in W. S. Newman, *Six Keyboard Sonatas* (as cited in note 11a to p. 10).

P. 663. 57a. According to DMF XXIV (1971) 204, they were the first harp sons. to be printed in France.

P. 663. 60a. A mod. ed. of a harp son. by him was published by B. Schott in 1966.

P. 672. 102a. Mod. ed.: The "Andante" of Op. 4/1 and all of Op. 6, in Maurice Cauchie, *L'École française de piano* (Monaco: L'Oiseau Lyre, 1957).

P. 678. 126a. These sets include 6 sons. each in Opp. 12, 28, and 40, and 12 sons. in his *Traité*, Op. 42, according to Jean Shaw (see note 42a to p. 91).

P. 680. 129a. Merriman (see note 49a to p. 93) lists 3 sons. Op. 12 and 12 sons. in Lefèvre's *Methode de clarinette*.

P. 681. 2a. For a view contrary to that in fn. 2, cf. Arthur Hutchings, "The Unwritten Burney," in MR XXV (1964) 127-135.

P. 684. 12a. A facs. of the complete set was announced in NOTES XXX (1973-74) 558. Walsh may have printed the original ed., "for the Author," as assumed by Degrada (p. 102), or he may not; cf. Smith & Humphries/WALSH 269.

P. 684. 15a. The article by Degrada (p. 684, fn. 12) includes biographic, bibliographic, and analytic information, plus contemporary opinions and a thematic index of all 19 known K sons.

P. 687. 24a. Charles Cudworth elegantly deplores this *Classici* ed., in MT CXIII (1972) 77-78, in a review of a newer, excellent mod. ed. of the complete set ed. by H. Ruf & Hans Bemmann (Mainz: Schott, 1971 [?]).

P. 693. 40a. Cf. Paul David Andersen, "The Life and Works of James Nares," unpublished Ph.D. diss. (Washington University, 1968).

P. 702. 66a. Other, even more obscure names remain to be explored, such as that of Thomas Hamly Butler (*ca.* 1755-1823; cf. GROVE I 1049 [W. H. Hadow]), who is represented by various collected and single sons., solo and acc'd., in RISM A/I/1 459 and B/II 104 and 114.

P. 703. 68a. That Bach knew and admired Sammartini has been confirmed; cf. MQ LXVII (1982) 237.

P. 705. 71a. On Martini's influence cf. Schökel/BACH 156-157. A facs. of early eds. of all 12 sons. in Opp. 5 and 17, prefaced by Christopher Hogwood, was pub. by Oxford University Press in 2 vols. in 1973.

P. 705. 71b. Cf. fn. 71a to p. 705, *supra*.

P. 706. 76a. Two unpub. diss. have enriched our knowledge of the sons. (and other K music). "The Solo and Ensemble Keyboard Works of Johann Christian Bach," by Beth Anna Mekota (University of Michigan, 1969), is reviewed by Suzanne Forsberg in CM XVII (1974) 115-120. "Die Klavierwerke von Johann Christian Bach," by Ilse Susanne Staral-Baierle (Graz University, 1971), is followed up by the author, in DMF XXVI (1973) 210-216, with a short article on changing tastes as they affected Bach.

P. 707. 83a. Even so, it is worth noting how Christian Bach seems to be paying "tribute to his father" at the start of Op. 10/1 (our A.5./1) by using virtually the same idea as opens Sebastian Bach's Partita 1 in B♭; Karl Geiringer illustrates how Christian Bach transforms the idea "into a classical four-measure phrase" (NEW OXFORD VII 538-539).

P. 721. 108a. Mod. ed.: Op. 1/1 in C, in Lincoln/FIVE-m.

P. 723. 113a. Another German in London may be added here, **George Berg,** from whose *Ten Sonatas for the Harpsichord or Piano Forte, Opera VII* (London, 1768) Son. 2 in A is reprinted in the Smart collection listed in note 11a to p. 10, above.

P. 725. 127a. Cf., also, Torrefranca's posthumous book on Platti (see note 1a to p. 365) 154-158.

P. 728. 143a. Mod. ed.: Sons. 2 and 3 in Op. 5; 1, 3, 4, and 5 in Op 6; and 1 and 3 in Op. 7, ed. by Lucciano Bettarini (Milan: Nazionalmusic, 1969), with preface, facs., and separate Vn part.

P. 733. 152a. A mod. ed. or facs., presumably of Op. 4, was announced in NOTES XXX (1973-74) 559, to be published by Bibliotheca Musica Bononiensis in Bologna.

P. 738. 1a. Add the important contemporary account (1824) in SAINSBURY (as listed in SSB 823) I 160-165, presumably procured at first hand; also, the unpub. diss. of Jerald Curtis Graue, "Muzio Clementi and the Development of Pianoforte Music in Industrial England" (University of Illinois, 1971). The birth year 1752 was long debated, as in Unger/CLEMENTI 1-3, but is confirmed at last in Plantinga/CLEMENTI 1.

P. 739. 10a. Cf., also, the description of Clementi as an aging man in Moscheles/MOSCHELES I 109-110 (1825), 191-192 (1827), 216-217 (1828, including reference to Walter Scott).

P. 740. 12a. A more accurate, thorough listing (without the collations with later eds.) has now been supplied by Alan Tyson's *Thematic Catalogue of the Works of Muzio Clementi* (Tutzing: Hans Schneider, 1967). Cf., also, his article on "Clementi's Viennese Compositions, 1781-82," in MR XXVII (1966) 16-24. Tyson's *Catalogue* is reviewed by L. B. Plantinga in MQ LIV (1968) 257-263 and by K. Dale in ML XLIX (1968) 231-233.

P. 740. 14a. The *Oeuvres complettes* have been reprinted in a facs. ed. of 13 vols. in 5 (New York: Da Capo Press, 1971). According to Appendix II in Tyson's *Thematic Catalogue* (fn. 12a to p. 740, *supra*), only Vol. VI actually came under Clementi's own supervision. Tyson lists the full contents of this set.

P. 740. 16a. All uses of the list should be checked against Tyson's *Thematic Catalogue* (see note 12a to p. 740).

P. 741. 21a. In 1978 G. Henle Verlag in Munich pub. Vol. I of the most authoritative collection of Clementi's sons. to date, ed. by Sonja Gerlach and Alan Tyson. It includes, as numbered in Tyson's *Catalogue* (fn. 12a to p. 740, *supra*), wo 14 and Opp. 2/4, 1/2, 24/2, 7/3, 8/1, 8/3, 9/3, 10/1, and 13/6.

P. 746. 22a. Add to the studies and mod. eds. the unpublished Ph.D. diss. by James Donald Kohn, "The Manuscript Sonatas by Muzio Clementi at the Library of Congress: A Comparative Edition [Vol. II, 4 sons. and a separate mvt.] With [factual] Commentary" (University of Iowa, 1967); the sons. scored in Vol. II are hitherto unpublished revisions by Clementi of Opp. 1a in F, 13/4 in B♭, 13/5 in F, 13/6 in f, and 2/2/ii from the Son. in C, over each of which Kohn has placed the original published version in the *Oeuvres complettes* for comparison. The revision of Op. 13/6 has appeared (as Op. 14/3) in a mod. ed., ed. by Sandra Rosenblum (Boston: E. C. Schirmer, 1968), with preface.

P. 746. 25a. Cf., also, MacArdle's ed. of Schindler's *Beethoven* (see note 79a to p. 105) 414-415.

P. 748. 30a. In "'Celerio, le Dieu de Clavecin:' an Appraisal of Clementi?"

(MT CXX [1979] 645-647) Peter Brown reprints a description of a pianist, dating from 1790-92 and originally published in 1796. He believes it probably does apply to Clementi, in which case we would have a second opinion not unlike Mozart's. Cf., also, Leon B. Plantinga, "Clementi, Virtuosity, and the 'German Manner,'" in JAMS XXV (1972) 303-339.

P. 748. 33a. Cf., also, Schlesinger/CRAMER 66 and 157. Interest in this incident has continued, with the more recent tendency being to view Cramer's share as parody rather than plagiarism. Cf. Alan Tyson, "A Feud Between Clementi and Cramer," ML LIV (1973) 281-288; Jerald C. Graue, "The Clementi-Cramer Dispute Revisited," ML LVI (1975) 47-54; Plantinga/CLEMENTI 126-127 and 284-285.

P. 749. 40a. Further enlightenment on the programme occurs in a long, detailed, laudatory review of Op. 50/3 in the *Quarterly Musical Magazine and Review* for 1822, a review that Clementi himself may well have written (as discussed in Plantinga/CLEMENTI 263-264 and 269-270).

P. 751. 43a. Cf. SSB 135-136.

P. 751. 44a. The 6th ed. of Op. 36 (1821?) has been reprinted (Chapel Hill, N.C.: Hinshaw, 1978) with a preface by Maurice Hinson on the changes made in that ed. by Clementi, including extensions of range (for the newest pianos), minor alterations of text, and the addition of copious fingerings and pedal markings. (Hinson writes more on these changes, which go back at least to a 5th ed. [1813?], in *Gendenkschrift Günter Henle* [Munich: G. Henle, 1980] 237-243.)

P. 754. 55a. In JAMS XXXI (1978) 529-535 J. C. Graue cites a forthcoming article by himself, "Clementi's Self-Borrowings: the Refinement of a Manner."

P. 754. 55b. Throughout this par. recall fn. 39a to p. 89, *supra.*

P. 764. 101a. Further items are listed in WOLFE (as listed in SSB 836) I, items 4137 and 4211-4213A.

P. 765. 106a. Add the comprehensive, unpublished Ph.D. diss. by Charles Edgar Stevens, "The Musical Works of Christian Ignatius Latrobe" (The University of North Carolina, 1971), including background, biography (with a corrected birth year of 1758), correspondence with Burney, thematic index of works, and chapter on the 3 sons. (pp. 121-148). Additional published information on Latrobe may be found in the *Moravian Music Foundation Bulletin* X/1 (1965; E. V. Nolte) and X/2 (1965; F. Blandford). Mod. ed.: 3 Sons., complete, ed. by C. E. Stevens (New York: Boosey and Hawkes, 1970), with preface and facs. of cover of original ed.; also, Op. 3/1 in A, in Lincoln/FIVE-m.

P. 767. 111a. The London organist **Joseph W. Holder** (1765-1832) should be added for 6 Sons. for P-or-H & Vn (*ca.* 1785; cf. BRITISH UNION I 488), one of which, in E♭, appears in the Smart collection listed in note 11a to p. 10, above.

P. 768. 116a. A presumed Frenchman in London, **A. Quintin Buée** (*ca.* 1765-*ca.* 1825), should be added for 3 Sons. for P, the 3d for 4 hands (*ca.* 1797; cf. BRITISH UNION II 869), of which No. 2, in a, appears in the Smart collection listed in note 11a to p. 10, above.

P. 769. 123a. Cf., also, Schlesinger/CRAMER 142 (fn. 148).

P. 770. 126a. Add the Ph.D. diss. by Ita Margaret Hogan, *Anglo-Irish Music, 1780-1830* (Cork: Cork University Press, [1966]); reviewed by Stanley Sadie in MT CVIII (1967) 41-42.

P. 776. 16a. Cf. Seaman's article as listed in note 202a to p. 580.

P. 779. 26a. The name is transliterated "Handoschkin" in Asaf'ev/RUSSIAN (as listed in SSB 778) 140, 141, and 306. Cf., also, Seaman/RUSSIAN (as listed in SSB 827) 82-83.

P. 779. 28a. Another mod. ed. (under "Handoshkin") is listed in Altmann/KAMMERMUSIK 114.

P. 780. 38a. Mod. ed.: Opp. 5 and 6, complete, 2 vols., ed. by Agi Jambor (Philadelphia: Elkan-Vogel, 1966), with preface.

P. 800. 128a. Two important new contributions (both as listed in SSB 836-837) are WOLFE (extending Sonneck & Upton/BIBLIOGRAPHY to 1825) and Wolverton/KEYBOARD (covering keyboard music up to 1830 and including complete sons. among the exx.).

P. 801. 129a. Also, some of Rousseau's discomfort with independent instrumental music (SCE 36-37) is echoed in a statement attributed to the young William Billings in 1764 by Gillian B. Anderson (p. 51 in "Eighteenth-Century Evaluations of William Billings; a Reappraisal," *Quarterly Journal of the Library of Congress* XXXV/1 [Jan. 1978] 48-58):

> Concertos and Sonatas have their Praise, and they deserve it; but it is to the Appropriations of Sounds to Sense, that the supreme Honors of the Science always have been and always will be paid.

P. 801. 130a. For possible earlier performances, cf. John W. Molner, "A Collection of Music in Colonial Virginia: The Ogle Inventory," in MQ XLIX (1963) 150-162.

P. 804. 153a. Cf. Helen Cripe, *Thomas Jefferson and Music* (Charlottesville: University of Virginia Press, 1974), including his catalogue of 1783 (Appendix I) and "Collections of Jefferson Family Music" (Appendix II); reviewed in MQ LXI (1975) 151-153 (J. R. Heintze).

P. 806. 161a. Mod. ed.: Robert Hopkins (ed.), *Alexander Reinagle, the [4] Philadelphia Sonatas* (Madison: A-R Editions, 1978). An unpub. D.M.A. diss. completed at Peabody Conservatory in 1976 by Susan R. Duer is entitled "An Annotated Edition of Four Sonatas by Alexander Reinagle (1756-1809)." Hopkins' ed. includes a valuable preface; also the opinion that the unnumbered Son. in F probably once had an accompaniment, and so did at least 2 mvts. of the other 3 sons.

P. 808. 166a. Mod. ed.: W. T. Marrocco and H. Gleason (eds.), *Music in America* (New York: W. W. Norton, 1964) 204.

P. 808. 166b. Cf. the unpublished Ph.D. diss. by John Waldorf Wagner, "James Hewitt: His Life and Works," 2 vols. (Indiana University, 1969).

P. 808. 168a. A facs. of Son. 2 in the Carr ed. appears in Wolverton/KEYBOARD (as listed in SSB 836-837) 469.

P. 809. 170a. The cover is reproduced as the back endpaper of Vol. II in WOLFE (as listed in SSB 836).

P. 809. 172a. A facs. of an early unidentified ed. of a 2-page "Sonata VIII" in D appears in Wolverton/KEYBOARD (as listed in SSB 832-833) 479.

P. 809. 172b. In the course of writing a Ph.D. diss. in progress on music in Norfolk, Virginia, James Hines at The University of North Carolina has discovered 3 Sons. for H-or-P, Op. 1, by Juhan, published in Charleston, South Carolina (without date). In Wolverton/KEYBOARD (as listed in SSB 836-837) 60-64 are reports of Selby playing his own sons.

P. 809. 172c. On Linley, cf. Wolverton/KEYBOARD (as listed in SSB 836-837) 196-98.

P. 833.* The contents of the 18th-century instrumental anthologies that follow and many others are itemized in RISM (*Répertoire international des sources musicales* [München-Duisburg: G. Henle, 1964]) B II.

Bibliography

Note: All the short-title references in the present book, including some initials used only in this Bibliography to represent the most cited periodicals, will be found in the one approximately alphabetical listing that follows. References with a lower-case "-m" at the end indicate sources made up primarily of music. Articles in GROVE and MGG and single volumes in the various "Denkmäler" series do not have separate entries in the Bibliography, but their authors or editors are cited where the first references occur in the text.

Abbott/FORM — William W. Abbott, Jr., "Certain Aspects of the Sonata-Allegro Form in Piano Sonatas of the 18th and 19th Centuries," unpublished Ph.D. diss., Indiana University, 1956.

Abert/HAYDN — Hermann Abert, "Joseph Haydns Klavierwerke," ZFMW II (1919-20) 553-573 and III (1920-21) 535-552.

Abert/MOZART — ———, *W. A. Mozart, neubearbeitete und erweiterte Ausgabe von Otto Jahns Mozart,* 6th ed., 2 vols. Leipzig: Breitkopf & Härtel, 1923-24. Cf. King/MOZART 66-77. An unaltered 7th ed. appeared in 1955-56, with a reference to a 3d vol. projected by Anna Amalie Mozart to bring the study up to date.

Abert/WOLFGANG-m — ——— (ed.), *Leopold Mozart's Little Music Book given to his Son Wolfgang Amadeus Mozart on His Seventh Birthday* (with introduction transl. by Kurt Oppens). New York: Kalmus, 1950.

Adler/MUSIKGESCHICHTE — Guido Adler (author and ed.), *Handbuch der Musikgeschichte,* 2d ed., 2 vols. Berlin: Max Hesse, 1930.

Adler/WIENER — ———, "Die Wiener klassische Schule," Adler/MUSIKGESCHICHTE II 768-795.

AFMF — *Archiv für Musikforschung.* 1936-43. Superseded ZFMW.

AFMW — *Archiv für Musikwissenschaft.* 1918-27, 1952—.

Alard/VIOLON-m — Delphin Alard (ed.), *Les Maîtres classiques du violon.* Leipzig: B. Schott's Söhne, [1863-84]. Much of this set was reprinted around 1917 by Schott, under the editorship of O. Kelly.

Albrecht/CENSUS — Otto E. Albrecht, *A Census of Autograph Music Manuscripts of European Composers in American Libraries.* Philadelphia: University of Pennsylvania Press, 1953.

Albrecht/TONKUNST — Johann Lorenz Albrecht, *Gründliche Einleitung in die Anfangslehren der Tonkunst.* Langensalza: J. C. Martini, 1761.

Allorto/CLEMENTI — Riccardo Allorto, *Le Sonate per pianoforte di Muzio Clementi, studio critico e catalogo tematico.* Florence: Olschki, 1959.

Altmann/KAMMERMUSIK — Wilhelm Altmann, *Kammermusik-Katalog,* 6th ed. (to Aug., 1944). Leipzig: Friedrich Hofmeister, 1945; Suppl., 1944-58, ed. by J. F. Richter, 1960.

AM — *Acta musicologica.* 1928—.

AMZ — *Allgemeine musikalische Zeitung.* 3 series: 1798-1848, 1863-65, 1866-82. Cf. GROVE VI 669; Hedler/TÜRK 16-17; Haupt/MÜLLER 13-14.

Anderson/BEETHOVEN — Emily Anderson (ed.), *The Letters of Beethoven,* 3 vols. London: Macmillan, 1961. Cf. NOTES XIX (1962) 243-246 (MacArdle).

Anderson/MOZART — ———, *The Letters of Mozart and His Family,* 3 vols. London: Macmillan, 1938. A revised, 2d ed., not cited in SCE, appeared in 1966 as prepared by A. H. King and M. Carolan (also pub. in New York by St Martin's Press); cf. B. E. Wilson in NOTES XXIII (1967) 512-515.

Anglès & Gerhard/SOLER-m — Robert Gerhard (ed.), *Antoni Soler: Sis Quintets,* with an "Introducció i estudi bibliografic" (pp. ii-lxxii) by Higinio Anglès. Barcelona: Institut d'Estudis Catalan, 1933.

ANNÉE — *L'Année musicale.* 1911-13.

Anth. ALLERLEY-m — *Musikalisches Allerley von verschiedenen Tonkünstlern,* an anthological weekly (edited by Marpurg?) in 9 collections totaling 270 pp. Berlin: Birnstiel, 1761-63. Cf. Eitner/QL II 52-53; WOLFFHEIM MUSIKBIBLIOTHEK I item 1223; Cat. BRUXELLES II 344. *

Anth. BACH-m — *III Sonates pour le Clavecin, composées par Mrs C. P. E. Bach, C. S. Binder et C. Fasch.* Nürnberg: Winterschmidt, [1770]. Cf. Wotquenne/BACH 25; Cat. BRUXELLES II 343; MGG III 1860.

Anth. BLAND-m — *Bland's Collection of Sonatas, Lessons, Overtures, Capricios, Divertimentos &c &c, for the Harpsichord or Piano Forte, without Accomp.ts, by the most Esteem'd Composers,* 48 issues in 4 vols.

London: J. Bland, [1790-94]. Cf. Newman/ACCOMPANIED **329 and 347.**

Anth. CARTIER-m — Jean-Baptiste Cartier, *L'Art du Violon, ou Division des ecoles choisies dans les sonates itallienne, françoise et allemande,* 3d ed. Paris: Decombe, [1801]. Cf. GROVE II 98-99 (David); Cat. BRUXELLES III 128.

Anth. HAFFNER COLLECTION-m — Johann Ulrich Haffner (ed.), *Collection recreative contenant vi sonates* [in each vol.] *pour le clavessin,* 2 vols. Nürnberg: Haffner, [*ca.* 1760-61]. Cf. Eitner/QL IV 473; WOLFFHEIM MUSIKBIBLIOTHEK item 1353; Hoffmann-Erbrecht/HAFFNER 122.

Anth. HAFFNER OM-m — ———, *Oeuvres mêlées contenant vi sonates* [in each vol.] *pour le clavessin,* 12 vols. Nürnberg: J. U. Haffner, (vol. I [plate no. LXXI], 1755; II [LXXV], 1756; III [LXXXIX], 1757; IV [XCV], 1758?; V [CII], 1759?; VI [CV], 1760?; VII [CVII], 1761; VIII [CXI], 1761; IX [CXXII], 1763?; X [CXXVI], 1764; XI [CXXXI], 1765; XII [CXXXIII], 1766). Cf. Faisst/CLAVIERSONATE 55-83 (analysis); Eitner/QL IV 473; Cat. BRUXELLES IV 331 (with complete contents, including identifications of the anonymous sons. in vol. I); DTB-m IX/2 lvi; Riemann/LEXIKON I 692; Hoffmann-Erbrecht/HAFFNER; SCE XI.

Anth. HAFFNER RACCOLTA-m — ———, *Raccolta musicale contenente VI sonate* [in each vol.] *per il cembalo solo d'altretanti celebri compositori italiani . . . ,* 5 vols. Nürnberg: Haffner, [1756, '57, '59?, '62?, '65]. Cf. Eitner/QL IV 473; Cat. BOLOGNA IV 27; Torrefranca/ORIGINI 189-191; Hoffmann-Erbrecht/HAFFNER 122-123 Benvenuti/CEMBALISTI-m.

Anth. HARPSICHORD-m II — *The Harpsichord Miscellany, Book Second, Composed by Alberti, Pasquali, and Nardini.* London Bremner, [1763]. Cf. BRITISH UNION I 449.

Anth. HILL LESSONS-m — *Six Easy Lessons for the Harpsichord.* London Joseph Hill, [*ca.* 1765]. Cf. BRITISH UNION II 61

Anth. JOZZI-m — *A Collection of Lessons for the Harpsichord com pos'd by Sig. Jozzi, St. Martini of Milan, Agre and Alberti, never before printed,* 3 vols. London I. Walsh, 1761, '62, '64. Cf. Saint-Foix/SAM MARTINI 320.

Anth. MAGAZIN-m — *Musikalisches Magazin, in Sonaten, Sinfonie Trios und andern Stücken für das Clavier beste hend.* Leipzig: Breitkopf, 1765. Cf. Cat. BRU ELLES II 345; Eitner/QL II 183.

Anth. MANCHERLEY-m — *Musikalisches mancherley,* 48 keyboard pieces ar songs, 4 quarterly issues. Berlin: Winter, 176 63. Cf. Eitner/QL X 274; WOLFFHEIM MUSI BIBLIOTHEK I item 1428; Cat. BRUXELLES II 345.

Anth. NÄGELI-m	Johann Georg Nägeli (ed.), *Repertoire des clavecinistes,* 17 "Suites" (vols.). Zürich: Nägeli, 1803-10. Cf. AMZ V (1802-03) Intelligenz-Blatt 97-100; HIRSCH MUSIKBIBLIOTHEK IV item 1012; Heyer/HISTORICAL 278; MGG IX 1245-1248 (Schanzlin & Walter) and VIII 961; SCE II.
Anth. SINFONIE-m	*Raccolta delle megliore sinfonie di piu celebri compositori di nostro tempo, accomodate all' clavicembalo,* 4 vols. Leipzig: Breitkopf, 1761-62. Cf. Mennicke/HASSE 73-74; Eitner/QL II 183 (item 8.; add Library of Congress).
Anth. STEFFANN-RUTINI-m	(J. A.) Steffan(n) and (G. M. P.) Rutini, *Six Sonates choisies pour le clavecin ou le forte piano avec un accompagnement de violon ad libitum.* Paris: Le Menu, [1772] (cf. Saint-Foix/MOZART II 167).
Anth. THOMPSON LESSONS-m	*A Collection of Lessons for the Harpsichord, Compos'd by Sig^r Kunzen, Kellery, Agrell & Hoppe.* London: Thompson, [1762]. Cf. BRITISH UNION II 613.
Anth. VENIER-m	*XX Sonate per cembalo da vari autori,* 2 vols. (Opp. 1 and 2). Paris: Venier, *ca.* 1758 and *ca.* 1760. Cf. Cucuel/LA POUPLINIÈRE 370; Torrefranca/SAMMARTINI (XX) 293-294; Johansson/FRENCH I 157, II Facs. 118-125; BIBLIOTHÈQUE NATIONALE VIII 34; Cat. BRUXELLES II 346.
Anth. VIELERLEY-m	*Musikalisches Vielerley,* ed. by Emanuel Bach. Hamburg: M. Chr. Bock, 1770. Cf. Eitner/QL I 286; Cat. BRUXELLES II 345; WOLFFHEIM MUSIKBIBLIOTHEK I item 1241.
ANUARIO	*Anuario musical.* 1946—.
Apel/DICTIONARY	Willi Apel, *Harvard Dictionary of Music.* Cambridge: Harvard University Press, 1944.
Auerbach/CLAVICHORDKUNST	Cornelia Auerbach, *Die deutsche Clavichordkunst des 18. Jahrhunderts.* Leipzig: Robert Noske, 1930.
Aulabaugh/HAYDN	Alan Richard Aulabaugh, "An Analytical Study of Performance Problems in the Keyboard Sonatas of F. J. Haydn," unpublished Ph.D. diss., State University of Iowa, 1958.
Avison/ESSAY	Charles Avison, *An Essay on Musical Expression.* London: C. Davis, 1752.
Bach/ESSAY	Carl Philipp Emanuel Bach, *Essay on the True Art of Playing Keyboard Instruments* (1753-62), translated and edited by William J. Mitchell. New York: W. W. Norton, 1949.

BACH READER	Hans David and Arthur Mendel (eds.), *The Bach Reader*. New York: W. W. Norton, 1945. Supplemented by "More for *The Bach Reader*," MQ XXXVI (1950) 485-510.
Bach/WERKE-m	*Johann Sebastian Bach's Werke*, 47 vols. Leipzig: Bach-Gesellschaft (Breitkopf & Härtel), 1851-99 and 1926.
Badura-Skoda/MOZART	Eva and Paul Badura-Skoda, *Mozart-Interpretation*. Stuttgart: Eduard Wancura, 1957. An English trans. is reviewed in MT CIII (1962) 472-473 (Dart).
BAKER'S DICTIONARY	Nicolas Slonimsky (ed.), *Baker's Biographical Dictionary of Musicians*, 5th ed. New York: G. Schirmer, 1958.
Barblan/ORCHESTRE	Guglielmo Barblan, "Le Orchestre in Lombardia all'epoca di Mozart," KONGRESS 1956 (Vienna) 18-21.
Barblan/PUGNANI	———, "Ansia preromantica in Gaetano Pugnani," CHIGIANA SETTIMANE XVI (1959) 17-26.
Barblan/SANMARTINI	———, "Sanmartini e la scuola sinfonica milanese," CHIGIANA SETTIMANE XV (1958) 21-40.
Barford/BACH	Philip Barford, "Some Afterthoughts by C. P. E. Bach," MMR XC (1960) 94-98.
Barford/FORMALISM	———, "Formalism in Clementi's Pianoforte Sonatas," MMR LXXXII (1952) 205-208, 238-241.
Barford/LAST	———, "Beethoven's Last Sonata," ML XXXV (1954) 320-331.
Barford/SONATA	———, "The Sonata-Principle: A Study of Musical Thought in the Eighteenth Century," MR XIII (1952) 255-263.
Bartlett/BASSOON	Loren Wayne Bartlett, "A Survey and Checklist of Representative Eighteenth-Century Concertos and Sonatas for Bassoon," unpublished Ph.D. diss., State University of Iowa, 1961.
Baum/WÖLFL	Richard Baum, *Joseph Wölfl, sein Leben und seine Klavierwerke*. Kassel: Bärenreiter, 1928.
BBM	*Bolletino bibliografico musicale*. 1926-52.
Becker/HAUSMUSIK	Carl Ferdinand Becker, *Die Hausmusik in Deutschland in dem 16., 17. und 18. Jahrhunderte*. Leipzig: Fest'sche Verlagsbuchhandlung, 1840.
BEETHOVEN/facs.-m	*Ludwig van Beethoven: Klaviersonate in C-Dur, Op. 53* (*Waldsteinsonate*). Bonn: Beethovenhaus, 1954. Cf. MQ XLII (1956) 399-400; Weise/WALDSTEINSONATE.
BEETHOVEN-FORSCHUNG	*Beethoven-Forschung*, edited by T. von Frimmel, 10 fascicles. 1911-25.

BEETHOVEN-JAHRBUCH — *Beethoven-Jahrbuch* (3d series). Bonn: Beethovenhaus, 1954—.

BEETHOVEN KONGRESS — *Beethoven-Zentenarfeier, internationaler musikhistorischer Kongress.* Vienna: Universal, 1927.

BEETHOVEN WERKE-m — *L. van Beethoven's Werke,* 25 Series, including Supplement. Leipzig: Breitkopf & Härtel, 1864-67 and '87. Cf. Hess/VERZEICHNIS.

Behrend/BEETHOVEN — William Behrend, *Ludwig van Beethoven's Pianoforte Sonatas,* trans. from the Danish (1923) by Ingeborg Lund. London: J. M. Dent, 1927.

Bell/HAYDN — A. Craig Bell, "An Introduction to Haydn's Piano Trios," MR XVI (1955) 191-197.

Bellasis/CHERUBINI — Edward Bellasis, *Cherubini: Memorials Illustrative of His Life.* London: Burns and Oates, 1874.

Bengtsson/ROMAN — Ingmar Bengtsson, *J. H. Roman och hans Instrumentalmusik,* with an English summary. Uppsala: Almqvist & Wiksells, 1955.

Benjamin/SOR-m — Anton J. Benjamin (ed.), *Fernando Sor: Op. 22, Grand Sonata for Guitar.* London: published by the ed., 1957.

Benton/HÜLLMANDEL — Rita Benton, "Nicolas Joseph Hüllmandel and French Instrumental Music in the Second Half of the Eighteenth Century," unpublished Ph.D. diss., State University of Iowa, 1961.

Benton/SCARLATTI — ———, "Form in the Sonatas of Domenico Scarlatti," MR XIII (1952) 264-273.

Benvenuti/CEMBALISTI-m — Giacomo Benvenuti (ed.), *Cembalisti italiani del settecento, diciotto sonate* (all of Anth. HAFFNER RACCOLTA-m I-III except for one substitution in each vol.). Milan: G. Ricordi, 1926.

Benvenuti/GALUPPI-m — ———, *Baldassare Galuppi: Dodici Sonate per il cembalo.* Bologna: F. Bongiovanni, 1920.

Berger/CLEMENTI — Ludwig Berger, "Erlaüterung eines Mozartschen Urtheils über Muzio Clementi," CAECILIA X (1829) 238-240.

Bergmann/HOOK-m — Walter Bergmann (ed.), *James Hook: Sonata in G for Descant Recorder and Pianoforte* (arranged from Op. 99). London: Schott, 1948.

Berten-Jörg/BENDA — Francis Berten-Jörg, *Franz Benda, sein Leben und seine Kompositionen.* Essen: C. W. Haarfeld, 1928.

Beurmann/BACH — Erich Herbert Beurmann, "Die Klaviersonaten Carl Philipp Emanuel Bachs," unpublished Ph.D. diss., Georg-August Universität, Göttingen, 1952.

Beurmann/REPRISENSONATEN — ———, "Die Reprisensonaten Carl Philipp Emanuel Bachs," AFMW XIII (1956) 168-179.

BIBLIOGRAPHIE MUSICALE — *Bibliographie musicale de la France et de l'étranger, ou répertoire général systématique de tous les traités et oeuvres de musique vocale et instrumentale. . . .* Paris: Niogret, 1822.

BIBLIOTHÈQUE NATIONALE — Jules Ecorcheville (ed.), *Catalogue du fonds de musique ancienne de la Bibliothèque nationale,* 8 vols. Paris: Terquem, 1910-14.

Bitter/BRÜDER — Carl Hermann Bitter, *Carl Philipp Emanuel und Wilhelm Friedemann Bach und deren Brüder,* 2 vols. Berlin: Wilhelm Müller, 1868.

BJ — *Bach-Jahrbuch.* 1904—.

Blom/BEETHOVEN — Eric Blom, *Beethoven's Pianoforte Sonatas Discussed.* London: J. M. Dent, 1938.

Blom/STEPCHILDREN — ———, *Stepchildren of Music.* London: G. T. Foulis, [1923].

Blume/MOZART — Friedrich Blume, "Mozart's Style and Influence," in Landon & Mitchell/MOZART 10-31.

Boghen/CIMAROSA — Felice Boghen, "Sonates de Cimarosa pour le fortepiano," RM V (July 1, 1924) 95-96 and "Supplément musical."

Boghen/CIMAROSA-m — ——— (ed.), *D. Cimarosa: 32 Sonates* (piano), 3 vols. Paris: Max Eschig, 1925-26.

Bonaccorsi/BOCCHERINI — Alfredo Bonaccorsi, "Luigi Boccherini, nota bibliografica," RAM XVI (1943) 224-227.

Bonaccorsi/CONTRIBUTO — ———, "Contributo alla storia di Boccherini," RAM XXVIII (1958) 196-203.

Bonaccorsi/INEDITA — ———, "Una Sonata inedita di Boccherini per due violoncelli," RAM XII (1939) 208-212.

Bonaccorsi/QUINTETTI — ———, "Di alcuni 'Quintetti' di G. G. Cambini," RAM XX (1950) 32-36.

Bonaventura/BOCCHERINI — Arnaldo Bonaventura, *Boccherini.* Milan: Fratelli Treves, 1931.

Bonaventura/CANTATA — ———, "Una 'Cantata' inedita di Luigi Boccherini," RMI XXXVI (1929) 243-258.

Bonaventura/LIVORNESI — ———, *Musicisti livornesi.* Livorno: S. Belforte, 1930.

Bone/GUITAR — Philip J. Bone, *The Guitar and Mandolin,* 2d ed. London: Schott & Co., 1954.

Borren/GALUPPI — Charles van den Borren, "Contribucion au catalogue thématique des sonates de Galuppi," RMI XXX (1923) 365-370.

Borren/HELLENDAAL — ———, "Pieter Hellendaal," DE MUZIEK II (1927-28) 341-351.

Borren/NEDERLANDEN — ———, *Geschiedenis van de Muziek in de Nederlanden,* 2 vols. Amsterdam: Wereldbibliothek, 1949 and '51.

Borris/KIRNBERGER — Siegfried Borris, *Kirnbergers Leben und Werk und seine Bedeutung im Berliner Musikkreis um 1750*. Kassel: Bärenreiter, 1933.

Borroff/MONDONVILLE — Edith Borroff, "The Instrumental Works of Jean-Joseph Cassanéa de Mondonville," 2 vols., unpublished Ph.D. diss., University of Michigan, 1958.

Bory/MOZART — Robert Bory, *La Vie et l'oeuvre de Wolfgang-Amadeus Mozart par l'image*. Geneva: Les Editions contemporaines, 1948.

BOUWSTEENEN — *Bouwsteenen, Jaarboek der Vereeniging voor Noord-Nederlands Muziekgeschiedenis*, 1869-81.

Boyden/KIRKPATRICK — David Boyden, review of Kirkpatrick/SCARLATTI-m, MQ XL (1954) 260-266.

Boyer/BEETHOVEN — Jean Boyer, *Le "Romantisme" de Beethoven*. Paris: H. Didier, 1938.

Brainard/TARTINI — Paul Brainard, "Die Violinsonaten Giuseppe Tartinis," unpublished Ph.D. diss., Georg-August Universität, Göttingen, 1959.

Branberger/KLAVIERKUNST — Jan Branberger, "Die Klavierkunst der böhmischen Meister aus der vorklassischen Zeit," trans. by Viktor Joss, *Der Auftakt* XIII (1933) 133-138.

Breitkopf SCARLATTI-m — *Domenico Scarlatti: Sixty Sonatas for Piano, Unedited* (Leipzig: Breitkopf & Härtel, 1866-67). New York: Kalmus, [1953?].

BREITKOPF MS — *Catalogo* [thematic] *delle sinfonie* [*soli*, etc.] *che si trovano in manuscritto nella officina musica di Giovanno Gottlob Immanuel Breitkopf*, 6 parts in one vol. Leipzig: 1762-65; 16 Supplements, 1766-87. Cf. HIRSCH MUSIKBIBLIOTHEK IV item 1098 (with facs.); Landon/SYMPHONIES 1-2 (for trans. of statement by Breitkopf); Meyer/BREITKOPF (evaluation as a research tool). Mod. ed. by Barry S. Brook (New York: Dover, 1966), with valuable preface and indexes.

BREITKOPF WERKE — *Verzeichniss musicalischer Werke . . . welche nicht durch den Druck bekannt gemacht worden*, 4 vols. Leipzig: Breitkopf, 1761-80. Cf. HIRSCH MUSIKBIBLIOTHEK IV item 1097.

Brenet/CLASSIQUES — Michel Brenet (Marie Bobillier), "Les grands Classiques," ENCYCLOPÉDIE I/2 1014-1060.

Brenet/CONCERTS — ———, *Les Concerts sous l'ancien régime*. Paris: Librairie Fischbacher, 1900.

Brenet/LIBRAIRIE — ———, "La Librairie musicale en France de 1653 à 1790, d'aprés les Registres de privilèges," SIMG VIII (1906-07) 401-466.

Brijon/MUSIQUE — C. R. Brijon, *Réflexions sur la musique, et la vraie manière de l'exécuter sur le violon*. Paris: Chez l'auteur, 1763.

BRITISH MS	Augustus Hughes-Hughes (ed.), *Catalogue of Manuscript Music in the British Museum,* 3 vols. London, 1906-09.
BRITISH PRINTED	W. Barclay Squire, *Catalogue of Printed Music . . . in the British Museum,* 2 vols. (incl. First Supplement). London, 1912; Second Supplement, 1940.
BRITISH UNION	Edith B. Schnapper (ed.), *The British Union Catalogue of Early Music,* printed before the year 1801, 2 vols. London: Butterworth, 1957.
Brockt/WOLF	Johannes Brockt, *Ernst Wilhelm Wolf, Leben und Werke.* Breslau: Striegauer Anzeiger, 1927.
Broder/MOZART	Nathan Broder, "Mozart and the 'Clavier,'" MQ XXVII (1941) 422-432.
Broder/MOZART-m	——— (ed.), *Mozart: Sonatas and Fantasies for the Piano,* . . . "from the autographs and earliest printed sources." Bryn Mawr: Theodore Presser, 1956, revised 1960.
Brook/SYMPHONIE	Barry S. Brook, "The *Symphonie concertante:* an Interim Report," MQ XLVII (1961) 493-516.
Brown & Berkenstock/ HAYDN	A. Peter Brown and James T. Berkenstock, "Joseph Haydn in Literature: A Bibliography" [to 1972], in *Haydn-Studien* III (1973-74) 173-352.
Brunner/MOZART	Hans Brunner, *Das Klavierklangideal Mozarts und die Klaviere seiner Zeit.* Augsburg: Benno Filser, 1933.
Bryan/VANHAL	Paul Robey Bryan, "The Symphonies of Johann Vanhal," 2 vols., unpublished Ph.D. diss., University of Michigan, 1956.
Buchner/BEETHOVEN	Alexander Buchner, "Beethovens Kompositionen für Mandoline," BEETHOVEN-JAHRBUCH 1957-58, pp. 38-50.
Bücken/GALANTE	Ernst Bücken, "Der galante Stil," ZFMW VI (1923-24) 418-430.
Bücken/ROKOKO	———, *Die Musik des Rokokos und der Klassik,* vol. 4 in *Handbuch der Musikwissenschaft* series. Potsdam: Akademische Verlagsgesellschaft Athenaion, 1927.
Bukofzer/BAROQUE	Manfred Bukofzer, *Music in the Bdroque Era.* New York: W. W. Norton, 1947.
Bukofzer/CLASSIC	———*Music of the Classic Period, 1750-1827,* University of California Syllabus Series ZT, revised ed. Berkeley: University of California, 1955.
BULLETIN AMS	*Bulletin of the American Musicological Society.* 1936-48.

Buonamici/CHERUBINI-m — Giuseppe Buonamici (ed.), . . . *Luigi . . . Cherubini: Sei Sonate per Cimbalo.* Florence: Genesio Venturini, 1903.

Burney/HISTORY — Charles Burney, *A General History of Music* (originally in 4 vols., 1776, '82, '89, and '89), with critical and historical notes by Charles Mercer, 2 vols. New York: Harcourt, Brace, 1935. Cf. Scholes/BURNEY I 306-315.

BURNEY'S TOURS — Percy A. Scholes (ed.), *Dr. Burney's Musical Tours in Europe,* 2 vols. (I, France and Italy, 1771 and '73; II, Central Europe and the Netherlands, 1773 and '75), including material previously unpublished. London: Oxford University Press, 1959.

CAECILIA — *Caecilia, eine Zeitschrift für die musikalische Welt.* 1824-48.

Caffi/STORIA — Francesco Caffi, *Storia della musica sacra nella già Cappella ducale di San Marco in Venezia dal 1318 al 1797,* 2 vols. Venice: G. Antonelli, 1854-55.

Calvocoressi/RUST — Michael D. Calvocoressi, "Friedrich Rust, His Editors and His Critics," and "The Rust Case: Its Ending and Its Moral," MT LV (1914) 14-16 and 89-91.

Canave/BACH — Paz Corazon G. Canave, *A Re-Evaluation of the Role Played by Carl Philipp Emmanuel Bach in the Development of the Clavier Sonata.* Washington, D.C.: The Catholic University of America Press, 1956. Cf. Newman/CANAVE.

Carpani/HAYDINE — Giuseppe Carpani, *Le Haydine, ovvero lettere su la vita e le opere del celebre maestro Giuseppe Haydn.* Milano: C. Buccinelli, 1812.

Carroll/SOLER — Frank Morris Carroll, "An Introduction to Soler," unpublished Ph.D. diss., University of Rochester, 1960.

Carrow/MANNHEIM — Burton Stimson Carrow, "The Relationship Between the Mannheim School and the Music of Franz Beck, Henri Blanchard, and Pierre Gavaux," 2 vols., unpublished Ph.D. diss., New York University, 1956.

Carse/XVIIIth — Adam Carse, *The Orchestra in the XVIIIth Century.* Cambridge (England): W. Heffer, 1940.

Carse/SYMPHONIES — ———, *18th Century Symphonies.* London: Augener, 1951.

Carse/SYMPHONIES-m — ——— (ed.), *Early Classical Symphonies,* 12 vols. up to 1951. London: Augener, 1935—. Cf. Carse/SYMPHONIES 1-4, 51-56, (76).

Castil-Blaze/DICTIONNAIRE — François-Henri-Joseph Blaze, *Dictionnaire de musique moderne,* 2d ed. (first ed. in 1821), 2 vols. Paris: Adrien Égron, 1825.

Cat. BARCELONA — Felipe Pedrell (ed.), *Catàlech de la Biblioteca musical de la Diputació de Barcelona,* 2 vols. Barcelona: Palau de la Diputació, 1908-09.

Cat. BASEL — *Katalog der Musikabteilung der oeffentlichen Bibliothek der Universität Basel.* Basel: Universitätsbibliothek, 1925.

Cat. BOLOGNA — *Catalogo della Biblioteca del Liceo musicale in Bologna,* 5 vols. Bologna: Federico Parisini, 1890-1905, 1943. A reprint of Vols. I-IV and a separate vol. of corrections were announced by Arnold Forni Editore in 1961.

Cat. BRUXELLES — Alfred Wotquenne (ed.), *Catalogue de la Bibliothèque du Conservatoire royal de musique de Bruxelles,* 4 vols. Brussels: J. J. Coosemans, 1898, 1902, '08, '12.

Cat. HAUSBIBLIOTHEK — Georg Thouret, *Katalog der Musiksammlung auf der Königlichen Hausbibliothek im Schlosse zu Berlin.* Leipzig: Breitkopf & Härtel, 1895.

Cat. MADRID — Higinio Anglès & José Subirá, *Catálogo musical de la Biblioteca nacional de Madrid,* 3 vols. Barcelona: Instituto Español de Musicología, 1946-51.

Cat. ROYAL — *Catalogue of Printed Music in the Library of the Royal College of Music,* edited by W. Barclay Squire. London: Novello, 1909.

Cat. SCHWERIN — Otto Kade, *Die Musikalien-Sammlung des Grossherzoglich Mecklenburg-Schweriner Fürstenhauses aus den letzten zwei Jahrhunderten,* 2 vols. Schwerin: Sandmeyer, 1893.

Cesari/GIULINI — Gaetano Cesari, "Giorgio Giulini, musicista; contributo alla storia della sinfonia in Milano," RMI XXIV (1917) 1-34, 210-271.

Cesari/SANMARTINI — ———, "Sei Sonate notturne di G. B. Sanmartini," RMI XXIV (1917) 479-482.

Cesari/TRIO — ———, "Origini del trio con pianoforte," in Franco Abbiati (ed.), *Gaetano Cesari: Scritti inediti* (Milan: Carisch, 1937) 183-198.

Challier/TABELLE — Ernst Challier, *Sonaten-Tabelle, eine nach Tonarten alphabetisch geordnete Aufstellung sämmtlicher Clavier Sonaten von Clementi, Haydn, Mozart in allen Ausgaben.* Leipzig: Fr. Volckmar, 1882.

Chase/AMERICA'S — Gilbert Chase, *America's Music From the Pilgrims to the Present.* New York: McGraw-Hill, 1955.

Chase/BEETHOVEN — Howard Randolph Chase, "Tonality and Tonal Factors in the Piano Sonatas of Beethoven," unpublished Ph.D. diss., University of Michigan, 1952.

Chase/SPAIN — Gilbert Chase, *The Music of Spain,* 2d ed. New York: Dover, 1959.

Cherbuliez/MOZART — Antoine E. Cherbuliez, "Sequenztechnik in Mozarts Klaviersonaten," MOZART-JAHRBUCH 1952, pp. 77-94.

CHESTERIAN — *The Chesterian.* 1915-19, 1919-40, 1947-61.

Chiesa/CIMAROSA — Maria Tibaldi Chiesa, *Cimarosa e il suo tempo.* Milan: Aldo Garzanti, 1939.

CHIGIANA GALUPPI — *Accademia musicale chigiana: B. Galuppi detto "Il Buranello" (1706-1785).* Siena: N. Ticci, 1948.

CHIGIANA SETTIMANE — Guido Chigi Saracini (ed.), *Accademia musicale chigiana: Ente autonomo per le settimane musicale senesi. Ca.* 1943—.

Choron/DICTIONNAIRE — Alexandre Étienne Choron and François Joseph Marie Fayolle, *Dictionnaire historique des musiciens,* 2 vols. Paris: Chimot, 1817.

Choron/PRINCIPES — Alexandre Étienne Choron, *Principes de composition des écoles d'Italie,* 3 vols. Paris: Le Duc, 1808. This work is not a trans. of N. Sala, as implied in MGG II 1402 (Borrel), nor did it appear in 1803, as in GROVE II 277 (Chouquet).

CLASSICI-m I — *I Classici della musica italiana,* 36 vols. Milan: Istituto editoriale italiano, 1919-21. Cf. Heyer/HISTORICAL 58-60.

CLASSICI-m II — *I Classici musicali italiani,* 15 vols. Milan: Fondazione Eugenio Brevi, 1941-43. Cf. Heyer/HISTORICAL 60.

Clementi/HARMONY-m — [Muzio] *Clementi's Selection of Practical Harmony for the Organ or Pianoforte,* 4 vols. London: W. C. Bates, [1803-15]. Cf. Heyer/HISTORICAL 61-63.

CLEMENTI OEUVRES-m — *Oeuvres complettes de Muzio Clementi,* 13 "Cahiers." Leipzig: Breitkopf & Härtel, [1804-*ca* 1819].

Clercx/DE CROES — Suzanne Clercx, *Henri-Jacques De Croes,* 2 vols. Brussels: Palais des Académies, 1940.

Clercx/MALDERE — ———, *Pierre van Maldere, virtuose et maître des concerts de Charles de Lorraine (1729-1768).* Brussels: Palais des Académies, 1948.

Closson & Borren/BELGIQUE — Ernest Closson and Charles van den Borren (eds.), *La Musique en Belgique du Moyen Age a nos jours.* Brussels: La Renaissance du Livre, 1950.

CM — *Current Musicology,* 1965—.

COBBETT — Walter Willson Cobbett (ed.), *Cobbett's Cyclopedic Survey of Chamber Music,* 2 vols. London: Humphrey Milford, 1929.

Cockshoot/BEETHOVEN — John V. Cockshoot, *The Fugue in Beethoven's Piano Music.* London: Routledge & Kegan Paul, 1959.

Coli/ASIOLI — D. Antonio Coli, *Vita di Bonifazio Asioli.* Milan: G. Ricordi, 1834.

COLLEGIUM MUSICUM-m — *Collegium Musicum, A Collection of Old Chamber Music* . . . adapted for general use by H. Riemann, M. Seiffert, P. Klengel, and others. Leipzig: Breitkopf & Härtel, from 1903.

Coover/LEXICOGRAPHY — James B. Coover, *Music Lexicography, Including . . . a Bibliography of Music Dictionaries.* Denver: Denver Public Library, 1958.

Corrette/CLAVECIN — Michel Corrette, *Le Maitre de clavecin pour l'accompagnement.* Paris: L'Auteur, 1753.

Cramer/MAGAZIN — Carl Friedrich Cramer (ed.), *Magazin der Musik.* 1. Jahrgang, 1783; 2. Jahrgang, 1784 and '86. Cf. WOLFFHEIM MUSIKBIBLIOTHEK I item 137; Forkel/LITTERATUR 470.

Cucuel/BAGGE — Georges Cucuel, "Un Mélomane au XVIIIe siècle: Le Baron de Bagge et son temps (1718-1791)," ANNÉE I (1911) 145-186.

Cucuel/DOCUMENTS — ———, "Quelques documents sur la librairie musicale au XVIIIe siècle," SIMG XIII (1911-12) 385-392.

Cucuel/LA POUPLINIÈRE — ———, *La Pouplinière et la musique de chambre au XVIIIe siècle.* Paris: Librairie Fischbacher, 1913.

Cudworth/GALANTE — Charles L. Cudworth, "Cadence Galante: The Story of a Cliché," MMR LXXIX (1949) 176-178.

Cudworth/SPURIOSITY — ———, "Ye Olde Spuriosity Shoppe, or Put It in the Anhang," NOTES XII (1955) 25-40, 533-553.

Cuming/HAYDN — Geoffrey Cuming, "Haydn: Where to Begin," ML XXX (1949) 364-375.

Czach/RUST — Rudolf Czach, *Friedrich Wilhelm Rust.* Essen: Julius Kauermann, 1927.

CZERNY — Carl Czerny, "Recollections From My Life," trans. from "Erinnerungen aus meinem Leben" by Ernest Sanders, MQ XLII (1956) 302-317.

Czerny/SCHOOL — ———, *School of Practical Composition,* Op. 600, trans. from the original German by John Bishop (with "Memoir" of author and list of works through Op. 798 plus MSS), 3 vols. London: Robert Cocks, [1848?]. Cf. SSB 29-32.

Daffner/KLAVIERKONZERT — Hugo Daffner, *Die Entwicklung des Klavierkonzerts bis Mozart.* Liepzig: Breitkopf & Härtel, 1906.

Dagnino/MONTECASSINO — Eduardo Dagnino, *L'Archivio musicale di Montecassino.* Montecassino ("Estratto di Casinensia," pp. 273-296), 1929.

Dale/CLEMENTI — Kathleen Dale, "Hours With Muzio Clementi," ML XXIV (1943) 144-154.

Dalrymple/CLEMENTI — Mary Alice Dalrymple, "Six Representative Clementi Sonatas," unpublished M.A. thesis, University of North Carolina, 1957.

Danckert/GIGUE — Werner Danckert, *Geschichte der Gigue.* Leipzig: Fr. Kistner & C. F. W. Siegel, 1924.

DANSK — *Dansk Musiktidsskrift.* 1925—.

David/UNITAS — Hans T. David, *Musical Life in the Pennsylvania Settlements of the Unitas Fratrum,* reprinted from *Transactions of the Moravian Historical Society,* 1942. Winston-Salem: The Moravian Music Foundation, 1959.

Dart/KIRKPATRICK — Thurston Dart, review of Kirkpatrick/SCARLATTI, ML XXXV (1954) 144-147 (with reply pp. 397-398).

David/PLEYEL-m — Ferdinand David (ed.), *Ignace Pleyel: Six Little Duets for Two Violins,* Op. 59. New York: G. Schirmer, 1898.

David/SCHOBERT — Hans T. David, *Johann Schobert als Sonatenkomponist.* Leipzig: Robert Noske, 1928.

David/VIOLINSPIEL-m — Ferninand David (ed.), *Die Hohe Schule des Violinspiels,* 3 vols. Leipzig: Breitkopf & Härtel, 1867.

Davison & Apel-m — Archibald Thompson Davison and Willi Apel (eds.), *Historical Anthology of Music,* 2 vols. Cambridge: Harvard University Press, 1946 and '50.

Dawes/CLEMENTI-m — Frank Dawes (ed.), *Muzio Clementi: Works for Pianoforte* (Opp. 13/6, 34/2, 47/2, 9/3), 4 vols. London: Schott, 1958.

DDT-m — *Denkmäler deutscher Tonkunst,* erste Folge, 65 vols., 1892-1931.

Della Corte/GALUPPI — Andrea Della Corte, *Baldassare Galuppi, profilo critico.* Siena: N. Ticci, 1948.

Della Corte/PAISIELLO — ———, *Paisiello, con una tavola tematica* (or rather, a numbered list of his works). Torino: Fratelli Bocca, 1922.

Della Corte & Pannain/STORIA — A. Della Corte and G. Pannain, *Storia della musica,* 2d ed., 3 vols. Torino: Editrice Torinese, 1944.

DE MUZIEK — *De Muziek.* 1926—.

Demuth/REICHA — Norman Demuth, "Antonín Reicha," ML XXIX (1948) 165-172.

Dennerlein/KIRCHENSONATEN — Hanns Dennerlein, "Zur Problematik von Mozarts Kirchensonaten," MOZART-JAHRBUCH 1953, pp. 95-104.

Dennerlein/MOZART — ———, *Der unbekannte Mozart; die Welt seiner Klavierwerke,* 2d ed. (with revisions). Leipzig: Breitkopf & Härtel, 1955.

Dennerlein/REICHARDT	———, *Johann Friedrich Reichardt und seine Klavierwerke.* Münster: Helios, 1930.
Dent/HAYDN	Edward Joseph Dent, "Haydn's Pianoforte Works," MMR LXII (1932) 1-4.
Dent/OPERA	Edward J. Dent, "Italian Opera in the Eighteenth Century, and Its Influence on the Music of the Classical Period," SIMG XIV (1912-13) 500-509.
Deutsch/BEETHOVEN	Otto Erich Deutsch, "Beethovens gesammelte Werke," ZFMW XIII (1930-31) 60-79.
Deutsch/NUMBERS	———, "Music Publisher's Numbers" (reprint from *The Journal of Documentation* I and II [1946]). London: Association of Special Libraries and Information Bureaux, 1946. A revised, German ed. (Berlin: Merseburger, 1961) appeared too late for use here.
Deutsch/SCHUBERT	———, *The Schubert Reader, A Life of Franz Schubert in Letters and Documents,* trans. by Eric Blom. New York: W. W. Norton, 1947.
Dewitz/VANHAL	Margarethe von Dewitz, *Jean Baptiste Vanhal, Leben und Klavierwerke.* Munich: Ludwig Maximilians Universität, 1933.
DICCIONARIO LABOR	Joaquín Pena and Higinio Anglès, *Diccionario de la música labor,* 2 vols. Barcelona: Editorial Labor, 1954.
DICCIONARIO PORTUGUEZES	Ernesto Vieira, *Diccionario biographico de musicos portuguezes,* 2 vols. Lisbon: Mattos Moreira & Pinheiro, 1900.
DITTERSDORF	*The Autobiography of Karl von Dittersdorf,* translated from the German (first ed., Leipzig, 1801) by A. D. Coleridge. London: Richard Bentley, 1896.
DIZIONARIO RICORDI	Claudio Sartori (ed.), *Dizionario Ricordi della musica e dei musicisti.* Milan: G. Ricordi, 1959.
DM	*Die Musik.* 1901-41.
DMF	*Die Musikforschung.* 1948—.
Döllmann/NICHELMANN	Heinz Döllmann, *Christoph Nichelmann (1717-1762), ein Musiker am Hofe Friedrichs des Grossen.* Löningen: Friedrich Schmücker, 1938.
Doflein/BACH-m	Erich Doflein (ed.), *Carl Phillip Emanuel Bach: Sechs Sonaten/Achtzehn Probe-Stücke zu dem Versuch . . .* (1753). Mainz: B. Schott's Söhne, 1935.
Domandl/SOR-m	Willy Domandl (ed.), *Fernando Sor: Op. 15, Sonate für Gitarre.* Hamburg: N. Simrock, [no date].
DTB-m	*Denkmäler der Tonkunst in Bayern* (DDT-m, 2d series), 36 vols., 1900-31.
DTÖ-m	*Denkmäler der Tonkunst in Österreich.* 1894—.

EDML-m — *Das Erbe deutscher Musik, Landschaftsdenkmale* (2d series). 1936—. Cf. Heyer/HISTORICAL 101-103.

EDMR-m — *Das Erbe deutscher Musik, Reichsdenkmale* (1st series). 1935—. Cf. Heyer/HISTORICAL 99-101 and 103-104.

Egert/FRÜHROMANTIKER — Paul Egert, *Die Klaviersonate der Frühromantiker* (Vol. I [diss., 1929] of "Die Klaviersonate im Zeitalter der Romantic," not published to date). Berlin: R. Niedermayr, 1934.

Eggebrecht/TERMINOLOGIE — Hans Heinrich Eggebrecht, *Studien zur musikalischen Terminologie*. Wiesbaden: Franz Steiner, 1955.

Einstein/GLUCK — Alfred Einstein, *Gluck,* trans. by Eric Blom. London: J. M. Dent, 1936.

Einstein/GYROWETZ — ——— (ed.), *Lebensläufe deutscher Musiker von ihnen selbst erzählt; Band III/IV. Adalbert Gyrowetz (1763-1850)*. Leipzig: C. F. W. Siegel, (1915).

Einstein/MISSING — Alfred Einstein, "Two Missing Sonatas by Mozart" (organ sons. K.V. 241 and 263), ML XXI (1940) 1-17.

Einstein/MOZART — ———, *Mozart, His Character, His Work.* New York: Oxford University Press, 1945.

Einstein/RUTINI-m — G. M. P. Rutini: Opp. 1, 3, 5, 6, 7 in Vol. XI and Opp. 8, 13 (and the cantata *Lavinia e Turno*) in Vol. XII of "A MS collection of Italian and German instrumental music of the 16th-18th centuries prepared in score by Alfred Einstein [*ca.* 1899-1903] and presented to Smith College Library."

EITNER MISCELLANEA — Hermann Springer, Max Schneider, and Werner Wolffheim, *Miscellanea musicae bio-bibliographica* [1904-13] . . . *als Nachträge und Verbesserungen zu Eitners Quellenlexikon,* 2d ed. New York: Musurgia, 1947.

Eitner/QL — Robert Eitner, *Biographisch-bibliographisches Quellenlexikon der Musiker und Musikgelehrten* . . . , 10 vols. Leipzig: Breitkopf und Härtel, 1899-1904. Cf. EITNER MISCELLANEA; Göhler/GESCHICHTSFORSCHUNG 365-373.

Eitner/SONATE — ———, "Die Sonate, Vorstudien zur Entstehung der Form," MFMG XX (1888) 163-170 and 179-185.

Elkin/CONCERT — Robert Elkin, *The Old Concert Rooms of London.* New York: St Martin's Press, 1955.

Elterlein/BEETHOVEN — Ernst von Elterlein, *Beethoven's Pianoforte Sonatas,* trans. from the German of 1856 by E. Pauer. London: W. Reeves, 1879.

ENCYCLOPÉDIE	*Encyclopédie de la musique et dictionnaire du conservatoire,* 11 vols. Paris: Delagrave, 1913-31.
Engel/KLASSIK	Hans Engel, "Haydn, Mozart und die Klassik," MOZART-JAHRBUCH 1959, pp. 46-79.
Engel/MOZART	———, "Mozart zwischen Rokoko und Romantik," MOZART-JAHRBUCH 1957, pp. 63-77.
Engel/QUELLEN	———, "Die Quellen des klassischen Stiles," KONGRESS 1961 (New York) 285-304.
Engländer/DRESDNER	Richard Engländer, *Die Dresdner Instrumentalmusik in der Zeit der Wiener Klassik.* Uppsala: Almqvist & Wiksells, 1956.
Engländer/ ECHTHEITSFRAGE	———, "Die Echtheitsfrage in Mozarts Violinsonaten KV 55-60," DMF VIII (1955) 292-298.
Engländer/MOZART	———, "Les Sonates de violon de Mozart et les 'Duetti' de Joseph Schuster," RDM XX (1939) 6-19.
Engländer/PROBLEM	———, "Problem kring Mozarts Violinsonat i E-moll, K. 304," STFMF XXXIII (1951) 127-135.
Englebert & Gallon/ GAVINIÈS-m	Y. O. Englebert and Jean Gallon (eds.), *Gaviniès: Six Sonates pour violon et piano* (Op. 1), 2 vols. Paris: Senart, 1922.
Eppstein/JOHNSEN-m	Hans Eppstein (ed.), *Henrik Filip Johnsen: Sonat* (in a; after Anth. HAFFNER OM-m III/5). Stockholm: Nordiska, 1950.
Etsen/MALDERE-m	Julius van Etsen (ed.), *Pieter van Maldere: Twee Sonaten voor twee Violen en Klavier.* Antwerp: De Ring, [*ca.* 1949].
Faisst/CLAVIERSONATE	Imanuel Faisst, "Beiträge zur Geschichte der Claviersonate von ihrem ersten Auftreten bis auf C. P. Emanuel Bach" (Berlin, 1845), reprinted (from CAECILIA XXV [1846] 129-158 and 201-231, XXVI [1847] 1-28 and 73-83) in NBJ I (1924) 7-85.
Falck/BACH	Martin Falck, *Wilhelm Friedemann Bach,* 2d ed. Leipzig: C. F. Kahnt, 1919.
Farnsworth/ PSYCHOLOGY	Paul R. Farnsworth, *The Social Psychology of Music.* New York: Dryden Press, 1958.
FASQUELLE ENCYCLOPÉDIE	François Michel and others (eds.), *Encyclopédie de la musique,* 3 vols. Paris: Fasquelle, 1958-61.
Favre/FRANÇAISE	George Favre, *La Musique française de piano avant 1830.* Paris: Didier, 1953.
Feder/HAYDN	Georg Feder, "Bemerkungen über die Ausbildung der klassischen Tonsprache in der Instrumentalmusik Haydns," KONGRESS 1961 (New York) 305-313.

FESTSCHRIFT FISCHER *Festschrift Wilhelm Fischer zum 70. Geburtstag überreicht im Mozartjahr 1956.* Innsbruck: Universität Innsbruck, 1956.

FESTSCHRIFT NEF *Festschrift Karl Nef zum 60. Geburtstag (22. August* 1933). Zürich: Hug, 1933.

FESTSCHRIFT RIEMANN *Hugo Riemann zum sechzigsten Geburtstage, überreicht von Freunden und Schülern.* Leipzig: Max Hess, 1909.

FESTSCHRIFT SCHMIDT-GÖRG *Festschrift Joseph Schmidt-Görg zum 60. Geburtstag,* edited by Dagmar Weise. Bonn: Beethovenhaus, 1957.

Fétis/BU François-Joseph Fétis, *Biographie universelle des musiciens* . . . , 2d ed., 8 vols.; suppl., 2 vols. Paris: Firmin Didot, 1860-65; 1878-80.

Fischer/BACH Kurt von Fischer, "C. Ph. E. Bachs Variationwerke," RBDM VI (1952) 3-31.

Fischer/INSTRUMENTALMUSIK Wilhelm Fischer, "Instrumentalmusik von 1750-1828," in Adler/MUSIKGESCHICHTE II 795-833.

Fischer/MOZART ———, "Mozarts Weg von der begleiteten Kloviersonate zur Kammermusik mit Klavier," MOZART-JAHRBUCH 1956, pp. 16-34.

Fischer/SARTI Kurt von Fischer, "Sind die Klaviervariationen über Sartis 'Come un'agnello' von Mozart?" MOZART-JAHRBUCH 1958, pp. 18-29.

Fischer/SONATE-m Hans Fischer, *Die Sonate,* vol. 18 in *Musikalische formen in historischen Reihen.* Berlin: Chr. Friedrich Vieweg (1937). References are made to this first ed. rather than the radically altered 2d ed. (Wolfenbüttel: Möseler, 1957).

Fischer/WIENER Wilhelm Fischer, "Zur Entwicklungsgeschichte des Wiener klassischen Stils," SZMW III (1915) 24-84.

Fisher/BOSTON William Arms Fisher, *Notes on Music in Old Boston.* Boston: Oliver Ditson, 1918.

Fleischer/BINDER Heinrich Fleischer, *Christlieb Siegmund Binder.* Regensburg; Gustav Bosse, [1942].

FLORILEGIUM-m Gustav Scheck and Hugo Ruf (eds.), *Florilegium musicum, Eine Werkreihe alter* [instrumental ensemble] *Musik.* Lörrach/Baden: Deutscher Ricordi Verlag, 1954—.

Floros/CAMPIONI Constantin Floros, "Carlo Antonio Campioni als Instrumentalkomponist," unpublished Ph.D. diss., University of Vienna, 1955.

FONTES *Fontes artis musicae.* 1954—.

Forkel/ALMANACH Johann Nikolaus Forkel, *Musikalischer Almanach für Deutschland,* 4 vols. Leipzig: Schwickert, 1782, '83, '84, and '89.

Forkel/BIBLIOTHEK — ———, *Musikalisch-kritische Bibliothek,* 3 vols. Gotha: C. W. Ettinger, 1778-79.

Forkel/LITTERATUR — ———, *Allgemeine Litteratur der Musik.* Leipzig: Schwickert, 1792.

Forte/MATRIX — Allen Forte, *The Compositional Matrix* (on the sketches for Beethoven's Op. 109). New York: The Music Teachers National Association, 1961.

Franck/FORKEL — Wolf Franck, "Musicology and Its Founder, Johann Nicolaus Forkel (1749-1818)," MQ XXXV (1949) 588-601.

Frey/SONATINA-m — Martin Frey (ed.), *The New Sonatina Book.* London: Schott, 1936.

Friedlaender/MOZART — Max Friedlaender, "Leopold Mozarts Klaviersonaten," DM IV/1 (1903-04) 38-40.

Frimmel/BEETHOVEN — Theodor von Frimmel, *Beethoven-Handbuch,* 2 vols. Leipzig: Breitkopf & Härtel, 1926.

Frimmel/JAHRBUCH — ——— (ed.), *Beethoven-Jahrbuch,* 2 vols. Leipzig: Georg Müller, 1908-09.

Frotscher/ORGELSPIEL — Gotthold Frotscher, *Geschichte des Orgelspiels und der Orgelkomposition,* 2 vols. Berlin-Schöneberg: Max Hesses Verlag, 1935-36.

Fruchtman/BARYTON — Efrim Fruchtman, "The Baryton Trios of Tomasini, Burgksteiner, and Neumann," unpublished Ph.D. diss., University of North Carolina, 1960.

Fürstenau/SACHSEN — Moritz Fürstenau, *Zur Geschichte der Musik und des Theaters am Hofe der Kurfürsten von Sachsen und Könige von Polen,* 2 vols. Dresden: Rudolf Kuntze, 1861 and '62.

Gärtner/MOZART — Gustav Gärtner, "Stilkritische Argumente für die Echtheit der 'romantischen Violinsonaten' W. A. Mozarts," MOZART-JAHRBUCH 1958, pp. 30-43.

GALUPPI/facs.-m — Baldassare Galuppi, *Passa Tempo al cembalo* (1785), facs. of autograph MS S.S.B.2.5 in the Biblioteca del Liceo musicale Paganini, Genova. Siena: Accademia musicale chigiana, 1948.

Ganzer & Kusche/VIERHÄNDIG — Karl Ganzer and Ludwig Kusche, *Vierhändig.* Munich: Ernst Heimeran, 1937.

Gates/SOLO — Willis Cowan Gates, "The Literature for Unaccompanied Solo Violin," unpublished Ph.D. diss., University of North Carolina, 1949.

Gatti/LOLLI-m — Carlo Gatti(ed.), *A. Lolli: Sei Sonate per violino Op. 1.* Milan: G. Ricordi, [1912].

Geiringer/BACH — Karl Geiringer, *The Bach Family.* London: George Allen & Unwin, 1954.

Geiringer/BACH-m ——— (ed.), *Music of the Bach Family, an Anthology.* Cambridge (Mass.): Harvard University Press, 1955.

Geiringer/BÜCKEBURGER ———, "Unbeachtete Kompositionen des Bückeburger Bach," FESTSCHRIFT FISCHER 99-107.

Geiringer/HAYDN ———, *Haydn, a Creative Life in Music.* New York: W. W. Norton, 1946. Cf. Marion M. Scott in MT LXXXIX (1948) 9-11.

Geiringer/MOZART ———, "W. A. Mozart the Younger," MQ XXVII (1941) 456-473.

Georgii/KLAVIERMUSIK Walter Georgii, *Klaviermusik,* 2d ed. Zürich: Atlantis-Verlag, 1950.

Gerber/LEXICON Ernst Ludwig Gerber, *Historisch-biographisches Lexicon der Tonkünstler,* 2 vols. Leipzig: Breitkopf, 1790-92.

Gerber/NEUES ———, *Neues historisch-biographisches Lexikon der Tonkünstler,* 4 vols. Leipzig: A. Kühnel, 1812-14.

Gericke/WIENER Hannelore Gericke, *Der Wiener Musikalienhandel von 1700 bis 1778.* Graz: Hermann Böhlaus, 1960.

Gerstenberg/KIRKPATRICK Walter Gerstenberg, review of Kirkpatrick/SCARLATTI, DMF VII (1954) 342-344.

Gerstenberg/SCARLATTI ———, *Die Klavierkompositionen Domenico Scarlattis.* Regensburg: Heinrich Schiele, [1933].

Gerstenberg/SCARLATTI-m ——— (ed.), *Domenico Scarlatti: 5 Klaviersonaten* (K. 452, 453, 204a, 204b, 357). Regensburg: Gustav Bosse Verlag, 1933 (as "Notenbeilage" for Gerstenberg/SCARLATTI).

Giazotto/VIOTTI Remo Giazotto, *Giovan Battista Viotti.* Milan: Curci, 1956.

Giegling/SOLO-m Franz Giegling (ed.), *The Solo Sonata* (in *Das Musikwerk* series). Köln: Arno Volk Verlag, 1960.

Giesbert/SAMMARTINI-m Franz Julius Giesbert (ed.), *G*[iuseppe]. *Sammartini: Zwölf Sonaten für zwei Altblockflöten in f' (Violinen) und Cembalo (Klavier), Gambe (Violoncello) ad lib.,* 3 vols. Mainz: B. Schott's Söhne, 1935.

Girdlestone/CLEMENTI Cuthbert Girdlestone, "Muzio Clementi," ML XIII (1932) 286-297.

Girdlestone/MOZART ———, *Mozart's Piano Concertos.* London: Cassell, 1948.

Girdlestone/RAMEAU ———, *Jean-Philippe Rameau, His Life and Work.* London: Cassell, 1957.

Glasenapp/LÖHLEIN — Franzgeorg von Glasenapp, *Georg Simon Löhlein, sein Leben und seine Werke, insbesondere seine volkstümlichen Musiklehrbücher.* Halle: Frommhold & Wendler, 1937.

Göhler/GESCHICHTSFORSCHUNG — Karl Albert Göhler, "Die Messkataloge im Dienste der musikalischen Geschichtsforschung," SIMG III (1901-02) 294-376.

Göhler/MESSKATALOGEN — ———, *Verzeichnis der in den Frankfurter und Leipziger Messkatalogen der Jahre 1564 bis 1759 angezeigten Musikalien,* 4 vols. in one. Leipzig: C. F. Kahnt, 1902.

Gottron/MAINZER — Adam Gottron, *Mainzer Musikgeschichte von 1500 bis 1800.* Mainz: Schmidt, 1959.

Gradenwitz/FAMILY — Peter Gradenwitz, "The Stamitz Family; Some Errors, Omissions, and Falsifications Corrected," NOTES VII (1949) 54-64.

Gradenwitz/STAMITZ — ———, *Johann Stamitz, I. Das Leben* (the 2d, unpublished vol., "Thematic Catalog," exists in a copy at the New York Public Library). Brünn: R. M. Rohrer, 1936.

Gradenwitz/STYLE — ———, "Mid-Eighteenth-Century Transformations of Style," ML XVIII (1937) 265-275.

Gradenwitz/SYMPHONIES — ———, "The Symphonies of Johann Stamitz," MR I (1940) 354-363.

Grétry/MÉMOIRES — André Ernest Modeste Grétry, *Mémoires, ou essai sur la musique.* Paris: chez l'auteur, 1789.

Griesinger/HAYDN — Georg August Griesinger, *Biographische Notizen über Joseph Haydn* (reprinted from AMZ XI [1808-09] 641-781 *passim*), annotated by Franz Grasberger. Vienna: Paul Kaltschmid, 1954.

Grosley/MEMOIRES — [Pierre Jean Grosley], *Nouveaux Memoires ou observations sur l'Italie et sur les Italiens,* [in 1758] *par deux gentilshommes suédois,* 3 vols. London: Jean Nourse, 1764.

GROVE — Eric Blom (ed.), *Grove's Dictionary of Music and Musicians,* 5th ed., 9 vols. and Suppl. New York: St Martins Press, 1954 and '61. References are to this ed. unless an earlier ed. or the new 6th ed. (1980) is specified.

Güttler/KÖNIGSBERG — Hermann Güttler, *Königsbergs Musikkultur im 18. Jahrhundert.* Kassel: Bärenreiter, (1925).

Güttler/WÜRFELSPIEL — ———, "Musik und Würfelspiel," ZFM CIII (1936) 190-193.

Haas/AUFFÜHRUNGSPRAXIS — Robert Haas, *Aufführungspraxis der Musik.* Potsdam: Akademische Verlagsgesellschaft Athenaion, 1931.

Haas/BERTONI — Ingrid Haas, "Ferdinando Bertoni: Leben und Instrumentalwerke," unpublished Ph.D. diss., University of Vienna, 1958.

Haas/CAT. 20 — Otto Haas, *Catalogue 20: The Valuable Music Library Formed by Alfred Moffat, Esq.* London, [*ca.* 1945].

Hadow/SONATA — William Henry Hadow, *Sonata Form.* London: Novello, [1896].

Hanslick/WIEN — Eduard Hanslick, *Geschichte des Concertwesens in Wien,* 2 vols. Vienna: Wilhelm Braumüller, 1869-70.

Haraszti/KLEINHEINZ — Émile Haraszti, "Les Compositions inconnues de Xavier François Kleinheinz," RM XI/102 (March, 1930) 229-244.

Hase/BACH — Hermann von Hase, "Carl Philipp Emanuel Bach und Joh. Gottl. Im. Breitkopf," BJ VIII (1911) 86-104.

Haupt/MÜLLER — Günther Haupt, *August Eberhard Müllers Leben und Klavierwerke.* Leipzig: Breitkopf & Härtel, 1926.

Hausswald/WAGENSEIL — Günter Hausswald, "Der Divertimento—Begriff bei Georg Wagenseil," AFMW IX (1952) 45-50.

HAYDN/facs.-m — Jens Peter Larsen (ed.), *Joseph Haydn: Klaviersonate A-Dur, Faks.* (H. XVI/26). Munich: Henle Verlag, 1958.

Haydn/INSTITUT-m — Jens Peter Larsen and others (eds. for the Joseph Haydn-Institut in Köln), *Joseph Haydn: Werke,* projected in 34 *Reihen* (of one or more vols. each), each with its separate *Kritischer Bericht.* Munich: Henle Verlag, 1958—.

Haydn/OEUVRES-m — *Oeuvres complettes de Joseph Haydn,* 12 vols. Leipzig: Breitkopf & Härtel, [1800-06].

Haydn/WERKE-m — Eusebius Mandyszewski and others (eds.), *Joseph Haydns Werke,* 11 vols. (incomplete). Leipzig: Breitkopf & Härtel, [1907-33].

Haydn/WORKS-m — Jens Peter Larsen and others (eds.), *Joseph Haydn: The Complete Works,* 4 vols. (incomplete). Boston: The Haydn Society; Leipzig: Breitkopf & Härtel, 1950-51.

Hedler/TÜRK — Gretchen Emilie Hedler (Thieme), *Daniel Gottlob Türk (1750-1813).* Leipzig: Robert Noske, 1936.

Helfert/CZECHOSLOVAK — Vladimír Helfert and others, *Czechoslovak Music.* Prague: Orbis, 1946.

Helfert/SONATENFORM — Vladimír Helfert, "Zur Entwickelungsgeschichte der Sonatenform," AFMW VII (1925) 117-146.

Helfert & Steinhard/TCHÉCOSLOVAQUE — Vladimír Helfert and Erich Steinhard, *Histoire de la musique tchécoslovaque.* Prague: Orbis, 1936.

Helm/ABEL — Sanford M. Helm, "Carl Friedrich Abel, Symphonist," unpublished Ph.D. diss., University of Michigan, 1953.

Helm/FREDERICK — Ernest Eugene Helm, *Music at the Court of Frederick the Great.* Norman: University of Oklahoma Press, 1960.

Hermann/HAYDN-m — Friedrich Hermann (ed.), *Joseph Haydn: Trios für Pianoforte Violine u. Violoncell,* 3 vols. Leipzig: C. F. Peters, [1876].

Herrmann/BACH-m — Kurt Herrmann (ed.), *C. Ph. E. Bach: Sonaten und Stücke.* Leipzig: C. F. Peters, [1938].

Herrmann/LEHRMEISTER-m — Kurt Herrmann (ed.), *Lehrmeister und Schüler Joh. Seb. Bachs,* 2 vols. Leipzig: Hug, 1935.

Hertzmann/MOZART — Erich Hertzmann, "Mozart's Creative Process," MQ XLIII (1957) 187-200.

Hess/BEETHOVEN — Willy Hess, *Beethoven.* Zürich: Büchergilde Gutenberg, 1956. Cf. DMF XII (1959) 254-255.

Hess/ERSTDRUCK — ———, "Der Erstdruck von Beethovens Flötensonate," NBJ VI (1935) 141-158.

Hess/VERZEICHNIS — ———, *Verzeichnis der nicht in der Gesamtausgabe veröffentlichten Werke Ludwig van Beethovens.* Wiesbaden: Breitkopf & Härtel, 1957.

Heuss/DYNAMIK — Alfred Heuss, "Uber die Dynamik der Mannheimer Schule," FESTSCHRIFT RIEMANN 433-455.

Heuss/DYNAMIK II — ———, "Die Dynamik der Mannheimer Schule; II. Die Detail-Dynamik, nebst einer dynamischen Analyse von Mozarts Andante aus der Mannheimer Sonate (Köchel V. Nr. 309)," ZFMW II (1919-20) 44-54.

Hey/BACH — Gotthold Hey, "Zur Biographie Johann Friedrich Bachs und seiner Familie," BJ XXX (1933) 77-85.

Heyer/HISTORICAL — Anna Harriet Heyer, *Historical Sets, Collected Editions and Monuments of Music.* Chicago: American Library Association, 1957; 3d, rev. ed., 1980.

Hieronymus/RUTINI — Bess Hieronymus, "Rutini, the Composer of Pianoforte Sonatas, Together with Thematic Index of the Sonatas," unpublished M.A. thesis, Smith College (Northampton, Mass.), 1948.

Hill/NUMBERS — Richard S. Hill, "The Plate Numbers of C. F. Peters' Predecessors," PAPERS AMS 1938 113-134.

Hill/SOLER — ———, review of Marvin/SOLER-m, Rubio/SOLER-m, Kastner/SOLER-m, and other Soler eds., NOTES XVI (1958) 155-157.

Hillemann/JUST-m — Willi Hillemann (ed.), *Johannes A. Just: Zwei kleine Sonaten für Klavier zu vier Händen* (Op. 12). Mainz: B. Schott's Söhne, 1950.

HIRSCH MUSIKBIBLIOTHEK — Kathi Mayer and Paul Hirsch (eds.), *Katalog der Musikbibliothek Paul Hirsch,* 4 vols. Frankfurt am Main, 1928-47.

Hoboken/HAYDN — Anthony van Hoboken, *Joseph Haydn: Thematisch-bibliographisches Werkverzeichnis, Instrumentalwerke,* vol. I (the first of 4 projected *Abtheilungen*). Mainz: B. Schott's Söhne, 1957.

Hoffmann/CAMERLOHER-m — Adolf Hoffmann (ed.), *P. v. Camerloher: Vier Sonaten* (SS/bass), 2 vols. Mainz: B. Schott's Söhne, 1939.

Hoffmann/TRIOSONATE — Hans Joseph Karl Hoffmann, *Die norddeutsche Triosonate des Kreises um Johann Gottlieb Graun und Carl Philipp Emanuel Bach.* Kiel: Walter G. Mühlau, 1927.

Hoffmann-Erbrecht/HAFFNER — Lothar Hoffmann-Erbrecht, "Der Nürnberger Musikverleger Johann Ulrich Haffner" and "Nachträge," AM XXVI (1954) 114-126 and XXVII (1955) 141-142.

Hoffmann-Erbrecht/KLAVIERMUSIK — ———, *Deutsche und italienische Klaviermusik zur Bachzeit* [1720-60]. Leipzig: Breitkopf & Härtel, 1954. Cf. JAMS X (1957) 52-54 (Ringer).

Hoffmann-Erbrecht/STURM — ———, "Sturm und Drang in der deutschen Klaviermusik von 1753-1763," DMF X (1957) 466-479.

HOFMEISTER — *Hofmeisters Jahresverzeichnis.* Leipzig: Friedrich Hofmeister, from 1829, preceded by Carl Friedrich Whistling's *Handbuch der musikalischen Litteratur* for 1815 and 1828. Cf. MGG VI 576-577 (Virneisel).

Holmes/LATROBE — Edward Holmes, "The Reverend Christian Ignatius Latrobe," MT IV (1850-51) 249-250 and 255-256.

Hopkinson/PARISIAN — Cecil Hopkinson, *A Dictionary of Parisian Music Publishers, 1700-1950.* London: Printed for the author, 1954.

HORTUS MUSICUS-m — *Hortus musicus, die neue Ausgabenreihe erlesener Haus- und Kammermusik* . . . . Kassel: Bärenreiter-Verlag, 1948—.

Hosäus/RUST — Wilhelm Hosäus, *Friedrich Wilhelm Rust und das Dessauer Musikleben,* 1766-96. Dessau: Emil Barth, 1882.

Howard/AMERICAN-m — John Tasker Howard (ed.), *A Program of Early American Piano Music.* New York: J. Fischer, 1931.

Howard/HEWITT — ———, "The Hewitt Family in American Music," MQ XVII (1931) 25-39.

Howard & Bellows/AMERICA — John Tasker Howard and George Kent Bellows, *A Short History of Music in America.* New York: Thomas Y. Crowell, 1958.

Hughes/CLEMENTI-m — Edwin Hughes (ed.), *Clementi: Two Sonatas, Two Pianos, Four Hands* (Opp. 12/5 and 1/6). New York: G. Schirmer, 1929.

Hummel/SÖHNE — Walter Hummel, *W. A. Mozarts Söhne.* Kassel: Bärenreiter, 1956.

Humphries & Smith/PUBLISHING — Charles Humphries and William C. Smith, *Music Publishing in the British Isles.* London: Cassell, 1954.

Hutchings/MOZART — Arthur Hutchings, "The Keyboard Music [of Mozart]," in Landon & Mitchell/MOZART 32-65.

Hutschenruyter/BEETHOVEN — Wouter Hutschenruyter, *De Sonates van Beethoven geänalyseerd en Toegelicht,* 2 vols. The Hague: J. Philip Kruseman, 1930.

d'Indy/COURS — Vincent d'Indy, *Cours de composition musicale,* with collaboration of A. Sérieyx and De Lyoncourt, 3 vols. Paris: Durand, 1909-50.

d'Indy/RUST — ———, "Une Mystification musicale, le cas Rust," SIM IX/4 (Apr., 1913) 47-50.

d'Indy/RUST-m — ——— (ed.), *F. W. Rust: Douze Sonates pour piano.* Paris: Rouart, Lerolle, [1913].

ISTITUZIONI-m — *Istituzioni e monumenti dell' arte musicale italiana,* 6 vols. (up to 1961). 1931—.

Jahn/MOZART — Otto Jahn, *Life of Mozart,* trans. from the second German ed. by Pauline D. Townsend, 3 vols. London: Novello, Ewer, 1882.

Jalowetz/BEETHOVEN — Heinrich Jalowetz, "Beethoven's Jugendwerke in ihren melodischen Beziehungen zu Mozart, Haydn und Ph. E. Bach," SIMG XII (1910-11) 417-474.

James/HAYDN — Philip James, "Haydn's Clavichord and a Sonata Manuscript," MT LXXI (1930) 314-316.

JAMS — *Journal of the American Musicological Society.* 1948—.

Janetzky/BACH-m — Kurt Janetzky (ed.), *C. P. E. Bach: 6 Sonatas for 2 Flutes, 2 Clarinets, 2 Horns and Bassoon,* score and parts (W. 184/1-6). London: Musica Rara, 1958.

Jensen/VIOLIN-m — Gustav Jensen (ed.), *Classical Violin Music . . . .* London: Augener, (*ca.* 1890), reprinted by Schott (*ca.* 1911).

JMP — *Jahrbuch der Musikbibliothek Peters.* 1894—.

Johansson/FRENCH — Cari Johansson, *French Music Publishers' Catalogues of the Second Half of the Eighteenth Century,* 2 vols. Stockholm: Publications of the Royal Swedish Academy of Music II, 1955. Cf. Krummel/JOHANSSON; FONTES VII (1960) 61-64; JAMS XI (1958) 62-64.

Johnson/BOSTON — H. Earle Johnson, *Musical Interludes in Boston.* New York: Columbia University Press, 1943.

Jones/FLUTE — William John Jones, "The Literature of the Transverse Flute in the Seventeenth and Eighteenth Centuries," unpublished Ph.D. diss., Northwestern University, 1952.

Junker/COMPONISTEN — Carl Ludwig Junker, *Zwanzig Componisten.* Bern: Typographische Gesellschaft, 1776.

Kaestner/ROLLE — Rudolf Kaestner, *Johann Heinrich Rolle.* Kassel: Bärenreiter, 1932.

Kahl/SELBSTBIOGRAPHIEN — Willi Kahl, *Selbstbiographien deutscher Musiker des XVIII. Jahrhunderts.* Köln: Staufen-Verlag, 1948.

Kamieński/MANNHEIM — Lucian Kamieński, "Mannheim und Italien," SIMG X (1908-09) 307-317.

Kastner/CONTRIBUCIÓN — Santiago Kastner, *Contribución al estudio de la musica española y portuguesa.* Lisbon: Ática, 1941.

Kastner/CRAVISTAS-m — ——— (ed.), *Cravistas portuguezes,* 2 vols. Mainz: B. Schott's Söhne, 1935 and 1950.

Kastner/SEIXAS — Santiago Kastner, *Carlos de Seixas.* Coimbra: Coimbra Editora, 1947.

Kastner/SILVA-m — ——— (ed.), *Silva ibérica de música para tecla de los siglos XVI, XVII y XVIII.* Mainz: B. Schott's Söhne, 1954.

Kastner/SOLER — Santiago Kastner, "Algunas cartas del P. Antonio Soler dirigidas al P. Giambattista Martini," ANUARIO XII (1957) 235-241.

Kastner/SOLER-m — ——— (ed.), *P. Antonio Soler: 2 x 2 Sonatas for Keyboard Instruments.* London: Schott & Co., 1956.

Kastner & Kapp/BEETHOVEN — Emerich Kastner (ed.), *Ludwig van Beethovens sämtliche Briefe,* revised by Julius Kapp. Leipzig: Hesse & Becker, [1923].

Kaul/WÜRZBURGER — Oskar Kaul, *Geschichte der Würzburger Hofmusik im 18. Jahrhundert.* Würzburg: C. J. Becker, 1924.

Keller/BOCCHERINI — Hans Keller, "Mozart and Boccherini," MR VIII (1947) 241-247.

Keller/SCARLATTI — Hermann Keller, *Domenico Scarlatti, ein Meister des Klaviers.* Leipzig: Edition Peters, 1957.

Keller & Weismann/SCARLATTI-m — Hermann Keller & Wilhelm Weismann, *D. Scarlatti:* [150] *Sonaten . . . nach den Quellen,* 3 vols. Leipzig: Edition Peters, 1957.

Kelly/REMINISCENCES — Michael Kelly, *Reminiscences . . . including a period of nearly a half century* (i.e., *ca.* 1775-1825), 2 vols. London: Henry Colburn, 1926. Mod. reprints, including new prefaces, of 2d ed., also 1826; Da Capo Press, 2 vols. (New York City, 1968; facs.); Oxford University Press (London, 1975).

Kenyon/HARPSICHORD Max Kenyon, *Harpsichord Music.* London: Cassell, 1949.

Kenyon/MOZART ———, *Mozart in Salzburg.* London: Putnam & Co., 1952.

Kern/BUTTSTETT Hans Kern, *Franz Vollrath Buttstett, eine Studie zur Musik des Spätbarock.* Würzburg: Triltsch, 1939.

King/MOZART A. Hyatt King, *Mozart in Retrospect.* London: Oxford University Press, 1955.

King/PIANO ———, "Mozart's Piano Music," MR V (1944) 163-191.

Kinkeldey/BEETHOVEN Otto Kinkeldey, "Beginnings of Beethoven in America," MQ XIII (1927) 217-248.

Kinsky & Halm/BEETHOVEN Georg Kinsky, *Das Werk Beethovens, thematisch-bibliographisches Verzeichnis seiner sämtlichen vollendeten Kompositionen,* completed by Hans Halm. Munich: G. Henle Verlag, 1955; Suppl., prepared by Kurt Dorfmüller, 1978 (cf. fn. 5a to p. 502).

Kirkpatrick/SCARLATTI Ralph Kirkpatrick, *Domenico Scarlatti.* Princeton: Princeton University Press, 1953. See note 15a to p. 262.

Kirkpatrick/SCARLATTI-m ——— (ed.), *Domenico Scarlatti: Sixty Sonatas,* 2 vols. New York: G. Schirmer, 1953.

Kirnberger/SONATEN Johann Philipp Kirnberger, *Methode Sonaten aus'm Ermel zu schüddeln.* Berlin: Birnsteil, 1783.

KJ *Kirchenmusikalisches Jahrbuch.* 1896—.

Klauwell/SONATE Otto Klauwell, *Geschichte der Sonate.* Leipzig: H. vom Ende's Verlag, [1899].

Koch/ANLEITUNG Heinrich Christoph Koch, *Versuch einer Anleitung zur Composition,* 3 vols. Leipzig: Adam Friedrich Böhme, 1782, '87, and '93.

Koch/LEXIKON ———, *Musikalisches Lexikon.* Frankfurt/M: Bey August Hermann dem Jüngern, 1802.

Köchel/MOZART Ludwig Ritter von Köchel, *Chronologisch-thematisches Verzeichnis sämtlicher Tonwerke Wolfgang Amade Mozarts,* 3d ed., revised by Alfred Einstein. Leipzig: Breitkopf & Härtel, 1937. Additions and corrections in the reprint by Edwards (Ann Arbor, 1947). Cf., also, Saint-Foix in RDM XIX (1938) 1-6; King/MOZART 55-65; MGG IX 827. Unless otherwise indicated, references in SCE are to the 3d ed. rather than the 6th ed. that appeared in 1964.

Köhler/MAÎTRES-m Louis Köhler, *Les Maîtres du clavecin,* 2 vols. Braunschweig: Litolff, [1860-73]. Cf. HOFMEISTER VI 193 and VII 234.

Kollmann/ESSAY Augustus Friedrich Christopher Kollmann, *An Essay on Practical Musical Composition.* London: printed for the author, 1799. Cf. Michael Kassler's

	review of the 1973 reprint by Da Capo Press of New York, in NOTES XXXI (1974-75) 296-297.
Kolneder/MOTIVISCHE	Walter Kolneder, "Motivische Gliederung und Form," SMZ XCIII (1953) 253-257.
Komma/ZACH	Karl Michael Komma, *Johann Zach und die tschechischen Musiker im deutschen Umbruch des 18. Jahrhunderts.* Kassel: Bärenreiter-Verlag, 1938.
KONGRESS 1924 (Basel)	*Bericht über den Musikwissenschaftlichen Kongress in Basel . . . 1924.* Leipzig: Breitkopf & Härtel, 1925.
KONGRESS 1925 (Leipzig)	*Bericht über den I. Musikwissenschaftlichen Kongress der Deutschen Musikgesellschaft in Leipzig, 1925.* Leipzig: Breitkopf & Härtel, 1926.
KONGRESS 1949 (Basel)	*Basel . . . 1949, Kongressbericht, Internationale Gesellschaft für Musikwissenschaft, vierter Kongress.* Basel: Bärenreiter-Verlag, [1951].
KONGRESS 1952 (Utrecht)	*Kongress-Bericht, Internationale Gesellschaft für Musikwissenschaft, Utrecht, 1952.* Amsterdam: Vereniging voor nederlandse Muziekgeschiedenis, 1953.
KONGRESS 1956 (Vienna)	*Bericht über den Internationalen Musikwissenschaftlichen Kongress Wien Mozartjahr 1956.* Graz-Köln: Hermann Böhlaus, 1958.
KONGRESS 1961 (New York)	*International Musicological Society, Report of the Eighth Congress, New York, 1961, Volume I, Papers.* Kassel: Bärenreiter, 1961.
Koole/LOCATELLI	Arend Koole, *Leven en Werken van Pietro Antonio Locatelli da Bergamo.* Amsterdam: Jasonpers Universiteitspers, 1949.
Krebs/BACH-m	Carl Krebs (ed.), *Carl Philipp Emanuel Bach: Die sechs Sammlungen von Sonaten, freien Fantasien und Rondos für Kenner und Liebhaber,* 2d ed., revised by Lothar Hoffmann-Erbrecht. Leipzig: Breitkopf & Härtel, [1954].
Krebs/DITTERSDORFIANA	Carl Krebs, *Dittersdorfiana.* Berlin: Gebrüder Paetel, 1900.
Kreutz/BACH-m	Alfred Kreutz (ed.), *Carl Philipp Emanuel Bach: Zwei Sonaten für Klavier* (W. 64/1 and a Son. in E♭ not in Wotquenne/BACH). Mainz: B. Schott's Söhne, 1938.
Kreutz/SONATEN-m	———, *Leichte Clavier-Sonaten unterschiedlicher Tonkünstler des 18. Jahrhundert.* Mainz: B. Schott's Söhne, [1941].
Kreutz/SONATINEN-m	———, *Clavier-Sonatinen für Liebhaber und ungeübte Spieler (18. Jahrhundert).* Mainz: B. Schott's Söhne, [1941].

Kreutz/VIER-m ———, *Zwo Stücke für vier Hände* (E. W. Wolf and W. F. E. Bach). Mainz: B. Schott's Söhne, [1940].

Krohn/MONDSCHEINSONATE Ilmari Krohn, "Die Form des ersten Satzes der Mondscheinsonate," BEETHOVEN KONGRESS 58-65.

Krohn/REINAGLE Ernst C. Krohn, "Alexander Reinagle as Sonatist," MQ XVIII (1932) 140-149.

Krummel/JOHANSSON Donald W. Krummel, review of Johansson/FRENCH, NOTES XVII (1960) 234-235.

Kullak/BEETHOVEN Franz Kullak, *Beethoven's Piano-Playing, With an Essay on the Execution of the Trill,* trans. by Theodore Baker from the preface to the Steingräber ed. (1881) of Beethoven's piano concertos. New York: G. Schirmer, 1901.

La Borde/ESSAI (Jean Benjamin de La Borde), *Essai sur la musique ancienne et moderne,* 4 vols. Paris: P.-D. Pierres, 1780.

La Laurencie/BLANCHETON Lionel de La Laurencie, *Inventaire critique du fonds Blancheton de la Bibliothèque du Conservatoire de Paris,* 2 vols. Paris: Librairie E. Droz, 1930-31.

La Laurencie/BRUNI ———, "Un Musicien italien en France a la fin du XVIIIe siècle" [A. B. Bruni], RDM XII (1931) 268-277.

La Laurencie/ÉCOLE ———, *L'École française de violon de Lully a Viotti,* 3 vols. Paris: Delagrave, 1922-24.

La Laurencie/ROBINEAU ———, "A Propos de l'abbé Robineau," RM VI (July, 1925) 34-44.

La Laurencie & Saint-Foix/SYMPHONIE Lionel de La Laurencie and Georges de Saint-Foix, "La Symphonie française vers 1750," ANNÉE I (1911) 1-123.

Landon/CHRONICLE H. C. Robbins Landon, *Haydn: Chronicle and Works,* Vols. I-V. Bloomington: Indiana University Press, 1976-80. Cf. fn. 11a to p. 459, *supra.*

Landon/HAYDN Howard Chandler Robbins Landon (ed. and trans.), *The Collected Correspondence and London Notebooks of Joseph Haydn.* London: Barrie and Rockliff, 1959. See note 9a to p. 459.

Landon/SYMPHONIES Howard Chandler Robbins Landon, *The Symphonies of Joseph Haydn.* London: Universal Ed. and Rockliff, 1955; Supplement, 1961.

Landon & Mitchell/MOZART Howard Chandler Robbins Landon and Donald Mitchell (eds.), *The Mozart Companion.* London: Rockliff, 1956.

Landshoff/BACH-m I Ludwig Landshoff (ed.), *Johann Christian Bach: Zehn Klavier Sonaten* (Opp. 5/2-6 and 17/2-6). Leipzig: C. F. Peters, 1925.

Landshoff/BACH-m II ———, *Johann Christian Bach: Sonatas for Violin and Piano* (Op. 10/1-5, 1773), 2 vols. London: Hinrichsen, [revised, 1961].

Lang/MOZART Paul Henry Lang, "Mozart After 200 Years," JAMS XIII (1960) 197-205.

Lang/WESTERN ———, *Music in Western Civilization.* New York: W. W. Norton, 1941.

Lange/SÜDWESTDEUTSCHEN Martin Lange, *Beiträge zur Entstehung der südwestdeutschen Klaviersonate im 18. Jahrhundert.* Berlin: Lankwitzer Anzeiger, 1930.

Larsen/KATALOGE Jens Peter Larsen, *Drei Haydn Kataloge in Faksimile.* Copenhagen: Einar Munksgaard, 1941. Cf. Landon/SYMPHONIES 4-12; NOTES XXXVII (1980-81) 69.

Larsen/QUELLE ———, "Eine bisher unbeachtete Quelle zu Haydns frühen Klavierwerken," FESTSCHRIFT SCHMIDT-GÖRG 188-195.

Larsen/ÜBERLIEFERUNG ———, *Die Haydn-Überlieferung.* Copenhagen: Einar Munksgaard, 1939. Cf. Landon/SYMPHONIES 10-15.

LaRue/JOHANSSON Jan LaRue, review of Johansson/FRENCH, JAMS XI (1958) 62-64.

LaRue/RESEMBLANCE ———, "Significant and Coincidental Resemblance Between Classical Themes," JAMS XIV (1961) 224-234.

LC EARLY Julia Gregory (ed.), *Library of Congress Catalogue of Early Books on Music (Before 1800).* Washington: Government Printing Office, 1913; *Supplement* (to 1942) by Hazel Bartlett (ed.), 1944.

LC MUSIC *The Library of Congress, Division of Music,* [report for] 1929-30. Washington: United States Government Printing Office, 1931.

Lee/SCARLATTI-m Robert Charles Lee (ed.), *A Second Collection of* [7] *Rare and Unpublished Keyboard Sonatas by Domenico Scarlatti.* Seattle: reproduction of MS by R. C. Lee, 1961. Regarding the first collection, cf. SCE IX.

Lenz/BEETHOVEN Wilhelm von Lenz, *Beethoven et ses trois styles* (originally 1852). Paris: Gustave Legouix, 1909.

Lenzewski/STAMITZ-m Gustav Lenzewski (ed.), *Karl Stamitz: Sonate in B-Dur für Viola (Violine) und Pianoforte.* Berlin: Friedrich Vieweg, [1926].

Lerma/MOZART Dominique-René de Lerma, "Wolfgang Amadeus Mozart: The Works and Influences of His First Ten Years," unpublished Ph.D. diss., Indiana University, 1958.

Lerma/NANNERL ———, "The Nannerl Notebook," MR XIX (1958) 1-5.

Leuchter/GASSMANN Ervin Leuchter, "Die Kammermusikwerke Fl. L. Gassmanns," unpublished Ph.D. diss., University of Vienna, 1926.

Leux/NEEFE Irmgard Leux, *Christian Gottlob Neefe (1748-1798)*. Leipzig: Fr. Kistner & C. F. W. Siegel, 1925.

Levinsohn/LEONORE Albert Levinsohn, "Die Enstehungszeit der Ouverture zu Leonore Nr. 1, mit anschliessenden kritischen Bemerkungen zu Nottebohm's Beethoveniana," VFMW IX (1893) 128-165 (pp. 163-165 on Op. 101).

Lincoln/FIVE-m Stoddard Lincoln (ed.), *Five Eighteenth-Century Piano Sonatas,* with prefaces (J. S. Schroeter, J. J. P. Küffner, L. A. Koželuch, C. I. Latrobe, J. Kirkman). London: Oxford University Press, 1975.

Lindfors/AGRELL Per Lindfors, "En Studie över Johan Agrells Liv och musikaliska Stil," STFMF XIX (1937) 99-112.

Lindsay & Smith/BOCCHERINI J. M. Lindsay and W. Leggat Smith, "Luigi Boccherini (1743-1805)," ML XXIV (1943) 74-81.

LISTENER *The Listener.* 1929—.

Lochner/KREISLER Louis P. Lochner, *Fritz Kreisler.* New York: Macmillan, 1950.

Löffler/'BACHE' Hans Löffler, "'Bache' bei Seb. Bach," BJ XXXVIII (1949-50) 106-124.

Löhlein/CLAVIER-SCHULE *Georg Simon Löhleins Clavier-Schule,* 2 vols. Leipzig: Waisenhaus und Frommann, 1779 (3d, revised ed.) and '81.

Loesser/PIANOS Arthur Loesser, *Men, Women and Pianos.* New York: Simon and Schuster, 1954.

Loft/DUO Abram Loft, *Violin and Keyboard: The Duo Repertoire,* 2 vols. New York: Grossman, 1973. Cf. the review by Sonya Monosoff in NOTES XXXI (1974-75) 56-59.

Longo/SCARLATTI-m Alessandro Longo (ed.), *D. Scarlatti: Opere complete per clavicembalo,* 10 vols. and "Supplemento." Milan: G. Ricordi, [1906]; *Indice tematico,* 1937. Cf. Gerstenberg/SCARLATTI 39-41; Kirkpatrick/SCARLATTI 237-241, 305, 412.

Lowinsky/MOZART Edward E. Lowinsky, "On Mozart's Rhythm," MQ XLII (1956) 162-186.

Lustig/INLEIDING Jacob Wilhelm Lustig, *Inleiding tot de Muzykkunde.* Groningen: Hindrik Vechnerus, 1751.

MAB-m Jan Racek (ed.), *Musica antiqua bohemica,* 40 vols. up to 1959. Prague: Artia, since *ca.* 1934.

MacArdle/BEETHOVENIANA	Donald W. MacArdle, "Minor Beethoveniana II," MQ XLVI (1960) 41-55.
MacArdle/CZERNYS	———, "Beethoven and the Czernys," MMR LXXXVIII (1958) 124-135.
MacArdle/ENGLAND	———, "First Editions of Beethoven Published in England," MMR XC (1960) 228-229.
MacArdle/HAYDN	———, "Beethoven and Haydn," MMR LXXXIX (1959) 203-211.
MacArdle & Misch/BEETHOVEN	Donald W. MacArdle and Ludwig Misch, *New Beethoven Letters.* Norman: University of Oklahoma Press, 1957. Cf. ML XXXVIII (1957) 271-274.
MacArdle & Misch/MINOR	———, "Minor Beethoveniana," MQ XLI (1955) 446-465.
MacDowell/ESSAYS	Edward MacDowell, *Critical and Historical Essays.* Boston: A. P. Schmidt, 1912.
McCorkle/ANTES	Donald M. McCorkle, "John Antes, 'American Dilettante,'" MQ XLII (1956) 486-499.
McCorkle/MORAVIAN	———, "The Moravian Contribution to American Music," NOTES XIII (1955-56) 597-606.
McCorkle/SALEM	———, "Moravian Music in Salem," unpublished Ph.D. diss., 2 vols., Indiana University, 1958.
Mainwaring/HANDEL	(John Mainwaring,) *Memoirs of the Life of the late George Frederic Handel.* London: R. and J. Dodsley, 1760.
Malipiero/ITALIAN-m	Gian Francesco Malipiero (ed.), *18th Century Italian Keyboard Music.* Bryn Mawr: Theodore Presser, 1952.
Manfredini/REGOLE	Vincenzo Manfredini, *Regole armoniche o sieno precetti ragionati per apprender la musica,* revision of the original ed. of 1775. Venice: Adolfo Cesare, 1797.
Mansfield/CHERUBINI	Orlando A. Mansfield, "Cherubini's String-Quartets," MQ XV (1929) 590-605.
Mansfield/MOZART	———, "Mozart's Organ Sonatas," MQ VIII (1922) 566-594.
Marchi/SPAGNOLI-m	Giuliana Marchi (ed.), *Le più belle pagine dei clavicembalisti spagnoli.* Milan: G. Ricordi, 1955.
Marco/ALBERTI	Guy A. Marco, "The Alberti Bass before Alberti," MR XX (1959) 93-103.
Marguerre/KV. 547	Karl Marguerre, "Die Violinsonate KV. 547 und ihre Bearbeitung für Klavier allein," MOZART-JAHRBUCH 1959, pp. 228-233.
Marks/SONATA	F. Helena Marks, *The Sonata, Its Form and Meaning, as Exemplified in the Piano Sonatas by Mozart.* London: William Reeves, [1921].

Marpurg/BEYTRÄGE Friedrich Wilhelm Marpurg, *Historisch-kritische Beyträge zur Aufnahme der Musik,* 5 vols. Berlin: G. A. Lange, 1754-78.

Marpurg/BRIEFE (Friedrich Wilhelm Marpurg), *Kritische Briefe über die Tonkunst . . . ,* 3 vols. Berlin: F. W. Birnstiel, 1760-64. Cf. LC EARLY 139.

Marpurg/CLAVIERSTÜCKE-m Friedrich Wilhelm Marpurg, *Clavierstücke, mit einem practischen Unterricht für Anfänger und Geübtere,* 3 vols. Berlin: Haude und Speuer, 1762-63. Cf. Eitner/QL VI 342.

Martienssen/HAYDN-m Carl Adolf Martienssen (ed.), *Joseph Haydn: Sonaten für Klavier zu zwei Händen,* 5 vols. (including *Sechs leichte Divertimenti*). Leipzig and New York: Peters, 1936-37 and '52.

Marvin/SOLER-m Frederick Marvin (ed.), *Antonio Soler:* [34] *Sonatas for Piano,* 3 vols. London (and New York): Mills, 1957-61. See note 90a to p. 279.

Marx/BEETHOVEN Adolf Bernhard Marx, *Ludwig van Beethoven, Leben und Schaffen* (originally 1859), 5th ed., 3 books in 2 vols. Leipzig: Adolph Schumann, 1902.

Marx/VORTRAG ———, *Anleitung zum Vortrag Beethovenscher Klavierwerke* (originally 1863). Regensburg: Gustav Bosse, 1912.

Mason/MOZART Wilton Mason, "Melodic Unity in Mozart's Piano Sonata, K. 332," MR XXII (1961) 28-33; 177-180 (response by N. Temperley).

Mattheson/EHREN-PFORTE Johann Mattheson, *Grundlage einer Ehren-Pforte* (Hamburg: In Verlegung des Verfassers, 1740), ed. by Max Schneider. Berlin: Leo Liepmannsohn, 1910.

Mazza/DICIONÁRIO José Mazza, *Dicionário biográfico de músicos portugueses* (late 18th c.), ed. with preface and notes by José Augusto Alegria. Lisbon: extract from the periodical *Ocidente* for 1944-45.

MDMA-m *Mitteldeutsches Musikarchiv, Veröffentlichungen des musikwissenschaftlichen Seminars der Friedrich-Schiller-Universität Jena.* Leipzig: Breitkopf & Härtel, 1953—.

MDO *Musica d'oggi.* 1919—.

MEM *Mens en Melodie.* 1946—.

MÉNESTREL *Le Ménestrel.* 1833—.

Mennicke/HASSE Carl Mennicke, *Hasse und die Brüder Graun als Symphoniker.* Leipzig: Breitkopf & Härtel, 1906.

MERCURE *Mercure galant,* succeeded by *Mercure de France.* 1683-1790.

Merian/MOZART Wilhelm Merian, "Mozarts Klaviersonaten und die Sonatenform," FESTSCHRIFT NEF 174-201.

Mersmann/AUFFÜHRUNGSPRAXIS — Hans Mersmann, "Beiträge zur Aufführungspraxis der vorklassichen Kammermusik in Deutschland," AFMW II (1919-20) 99-143.

Mersmann/BACH — ———, "Ein Programmtrio Karl Philipp Emanuel Bachs," BJ XIV (1917) 137-170.

Mersmann/PHÄNOMENOLOGIE — ———, "Versuch einer Phänomenologie der Musik," ZFMW V (1922-23) 226-269.

Meyer/BREITKOPF — Kathi Meyer, "Early Breitkopf & Härtel Thematic Catalogues of Manuscript Music," MQ XXX (1944) 163-173.

MFMG — *Monatshefte für Musikgeschichte.* 1869-1905.

MGG — *Die Musik in Geschichte und Gegenwart,* 17 vols. (including Suppl. in 2 vols. and Register [in progress] in one vol.). Kassel: Bärenreiter-Verlag, 1949—.

Midgley/BEETHOVEN — Samuel Midgley, *Handbook to Beethoven's Sonatas for Violin and Pianoforte.* London: Breitkopf & Härtel, 1911.

Mies/SKETCHES — Paul Mies, *Beethoven's Sketches, An Analysis of His Style Based on a Study of His Sketch-Books,* trans. by Doris L. Mackinnon. London: Oxford University Press, 1929.

Mies/TEXTKRITISCHE — ———, *Textkritische Untersuchungen bei Beethoven.* Bonn: Beethovenhaus, 1957.

Mies/TONARTEN — ———, *Der Charakter der Tonarten.* Köln: Staufen, 1948.

Miesner/GÖNNER — Heinrich Miesner, "Graf v. Keyserlingk und Minister v. Happe, zwei Gönner der Familie Bach," BJ XXXI (1934) 101-115.

Miesner/NACHLASS — ———, "Philipp Emanuel Bachs musikalischer Nachlass," BJ XXXV (1938) 103-136 (Emanuel's instrumental works), XXXVI (1939) 81-112, and XXXVII (1940-48) 161-181.

Mikulicz/NOTIERUNGSBUCH-m — Karl Lothar Mikulicz (ed.), *Ein Notierungsbuch von Beethoven (1800).* Leipzig: Breitkopf & Härtel, 1927.

Mirovitch/CLEMENTI-m — Alfred Mirovitch (ed.), *Clementi: Rediscovered Masterworks,* 3 vols. New York: Edward B. Marks, 1957, '59, and '59.

Misch/BEETHOVEN — Ludwig Misch, *Beethoven Studies.* Norman: University of Oklahoma Press, 1953.

Misch/EINHEIT — ———, *Die Faktoren der Einheit in der Mehrsätzigkeit der Werke Beethovens.* Munich: G. Henle, 1958.

Mishkin/QUARTETS — Henry G. Mishkin, "Five Autograph String Quartets by Giovanni Battista Sammartini," JAMS VI (1953) 136-147.

Mishkin/SAMMARTINI ———, "The Published Instrumental Works of Giovanni Battista Sammartini: A Bibliographical Reappraisal," MQ XLV (1959) 361-374.

Mitchell/HAYDN William J. Mitchell, "The Haydn Sonatas" (a collation of the eds. of Päsler, Zilcher, and Martienssen). PIANO QUARTERLY NO. 7 (1954) 13-17.

Mitjana/ESPAGNE Rafaël Mitjana, "La Musique en Espagne" (1914), ENCYCLOPÉDIE I/4 1913-2351.

Mizler/BIBLIOTHEK Lorenz Christoph Mizler von Kolof, *Neu eröffnete musikalische Bibliothek oder gründliche Nachricht nebst unpartheyischem Urtheil von musikalischen Schriften und Büchern,* 16 parts in 4 books (5 vols.). Leipzig: Mizler, 1739-54.

ML *Music and Letters.* 1920—.

Mlynarczyk & Lürman/DITTERSDORF-m Hans Mlynarczyk and Ludwig Lürman (eds.), *C. D. von Dittersdorf: Drei Sonaten* (Vn & *b. c.* in B♭ and G, Va in E♭), 3 vols. Leipzig: Hofmeister, 1929.

MMR *Monthly Musical Record.* 1871—.

Moffat/CELLO-m Alfred Moffat (ed.), *Sammlung klassicher Violoncello-Sonaten berühmter Komponisten des 17. und 18. Jahrhundert.* Berlin: N. Simrock, from 1904. Cf. Heyer/HISTORICAL 189-190.

Moffat/ENGLISH-m ———, *Old English Violin Music.* London: Novello, from 1906.

Moffat/TRIO-SONATEN-m ———, *Trio-Sonaten alter Meister für zwei Violinen und Piano.* Berlin: N. Simrock, from 1902. Cf. Heyer/HISTORICAL 190.

Moffat/VIOLIN-SONATEN-m ———, *Sammlung klassicher Violin-Sonaten berühmter Komponisten des 17. und 18. Jahrhunderts.* Berlin and Leipzig: N. Simrock, from *ca.* 1920. Cf. Heyer/HISTORICAL 189.

Mola/PAISIELLO-m Corradina Mola (ed.), *G. Paisiello: 6 Sonate per cembalo o pianoforte.* Milan: Carisch, 1941.

Moldenhauer/DUO Hans Moldenhauer, *Duo-Pianism.* Chicago: Chicago Musical College Press, 1950.

Momigny/COURS Jérôme-Joseph de Momigny, *Cours complet d'harmonie et de composition,* 3 vols. Paris: Chez l'auteur, 1806.

Mooser/ANNALES R.-Aloys Mooser, *Annales de la musique et des musiciens en Russie au XVIIIe siècle,* 3 vols. Geneva: Mount-Blanc, [1948-51].

Morini/ACCADEMIA Nestore Morini, *La R. Accademia filarmonica di Bologna.* Bologna: L. Cappelli, 1930.

Moscheles/MOSCHELES Charlotte Moscheles, *Life of Moscheles, With Selections From His Diaries and Correspondence,* trans. by A. D. Coleridge, 2 vols. London: Hurst and Blackett, 1873.

Moser/CORELLI — Andreas Moser, "Arcangelo Corelli und Antonio Lolli," ZFMW III (1920-21) 415-425.

Moser/LEXIKON — Hans Joachim Moser, *Musik Lexikon,* 4th ed., 2 vols. Berlin: Max Hesse, 1955.

Moser/VIOLINSPIEL — Andreas Moser, *Geschichte des Violinspiels.* Berlin: Max Hesses Verlag, 1923.

MOZART-JAHRBUCH — *Mozart-Jahrbuch.* Salzburg: Internationale Stiftung Mozarteum, 1950—.

Mozart/NEUE-m — *Wolfgang Amadeus Mozart: Neue Ausgabe sämtlicher Werke,* projected in 10 series comprising 35 classes in 120 vols. Kassel: Bärenreiter, 1955—. Cf. MGG IX 825-826.

Mozart/OEUVRES-m — [*W. A. Mozart: Oeuvres complettes*], 17 "cahiers." Leipzig: Breitkopf & Härtel, [1798-1806]. Cf. HIRSCH MUSIKBIBLIOTHEK; Köchel/MOZART 910-912.

Mozart/REISE — Arthur Schurig (ed.), *Leopold Mozart: Reiseaufzeichnungen,* in facs. Dresden: Laube, 1920.

Mozart/WERKE-m — *Wolfgang Amadeus Mozart's Werke,* 24 series. Leipzig: Breitkopf & Härtel, 1877-1905.

MQ — *The Musical Quarterly.* 1915—.

MR — *The Music Review.* 1940—.

MT — *The Musical Times.* 1844—.

Mueller von Asow/MOZART — H. and E. H. Mueller von Asow, *Wolfgang Amadeus Mozart Briefwechsel und Aufzeichnungen,* 2 vols. (1769-79). K. G. Frisch & Perneder: Lindau im Bodensee, 1949.

Mueller von Asow/VERZEICHNIS — E. H. Mueller von Asow (ed.), *Wolfgang Amadeus Mozart: Verzeichnis aller meiner Werke und Leopold Mozart: Verzeichnis der Jugendwerke W. A. Mozarts.* Vienna: Doblinger, 1956.

Müller-Reuter/KONZERTLITERATUR — Theodor Müller-Reuter, *Lexikon der deutschen Konzertliteratur, Nachtrag zu Band I* (1909). Leipzig: C. F. Kahnt, 1921.

Müry/PUGNANI — Albert Müry, *Die Instrumentalwerke Gaetano Pugnanis.* Basel: G. Krebs, 1941.

Muns/CLIMAX — George E. Muns, Jr., "Climax in Music," unpublished Ph.D. diss., University of North Carolina, 1955.

Munter/BEECKE — Friedrich Munter, "Ignaz von Beecke (1733-1803) und seine Instrumentalkompositionen," ZFMW IV (1921-22) 586-603.

MUSICA — *Musica.* 1947—.

MUSIKFREUNDE WIEN — R. von Perger, R. Hirschfeld, and E. Mandyczewski, *Geschichte der K. K. Gesellschaft der Musikfreunde in Wien,* 2 vols. (including suppl.). Vienna: Adolf Holzhausen, 1912.

Nagel/BEETHOVEN — Wilibald Nagel, *Beethoven und seine Klaviersonaten,* 2 vols. Langensalza: Hermann Beyer, 1903-05.

Nägeli/VORLESUNGEN — Hans Georg Nägeli, *Vorlesungen über Musik.* Stuttgart: J. G. Cotta, 1826.

NAGELS-m — *Nagels Musik-Archiv.* Hannover: Adolph Nagel, from 1929 (continued under same title by Bärenreiter in Kassel). For contents up to No. 203 cf. No. 156 (W. F. Bach).

NBJ — *Neues Beethoven-Jahrbuch,* 10 vols. 1924-42.

Neemann/RUST-m — Hans Neemann (ed.), *Fr. W. Rust: Sonate in d-moll . . . , Sonate G-dur für Laute und Violine,* 2 separate issues. Berlin: Friedrich Vieweg, (1925).

Nettl/BEETHOVEN — Paul Nettl, *Beethoven Encyclopedia.* New York: Philosophical Library, 1956.

Nettl/FORGOTTEN — ———, *Forgotten Musicians.* New York: Philosophical Library, 1951.

Nettl/GELIEBTEN — ———, "Auf den Spuren von Beethovens 'unsterblicher Geliebten,'" MUSICA XII (1958) 14-19. Cf., also, DMF XII (1959) 255; NOTES XVII (1960) 242; BEETHOVEN-JAHRBUCH 1955-56, pp. 12-13.

Neufeldt/CAS — Ernst Neufeldt, "Le Cas Rust," SIM IX/11 (Nov., 1913) 8-26 and IX/12 (Dec., 1913) 14-24 (including reply by V. d'Indy).

Neufeldt/RUST — ———, "Der Fall Rust," DM XII/1 (Dec., 1912) 339-344.

Neumann/MOZART — Friedrich Neumann, "Der Typus des Stufenganges der Mozartschen Sonatendurchführung," MOZART-JAHRBUCH 1959, pp. 247-261.

NEW OXFORD — J. A. Westrup, Gerald Abraham, & others (eds.), *The New Oxford History of Music,* 11 vols. London: Oxford University Press, 1954—. Cf. OXFORD HISTORY, *infra.*

Newman/ACCOMPANIED — William S. Newman, "Concerning the Accompanied Clavier Sonata," MQ XXXIII (1947) 327-349.

Newman/BACH — ———, "The Keyboard Sonatas of Bach's Sons and Their Relation to the Classic Sonata Concept," *Proceedings for 1949* of the Music Teachers National Association 236-248.

Newman/BACH-m — ——— (ed.), *Sons of Bach* [W. F., C. P. E., and J. C. Bach]: *Three Sonatas for Keyboard.* New York: Music Press (succeeded by Mercury Music), 1947.

Newman/CANAVE — William S. Newman, review of Canave/BACH, NOTES XIV (1957) 363-364.

Newman/CLIMAX — ———, "The Climax of Music," *The University of North Carolina Extension Bulletin* XXXI/3

(Jan., 1952) 22-40; abridged in MR XIII (1952) 283-293.

Newman/EARLIEST ———, "A Checklist of the Earliest Keyboard 'Sonatas' (1641-1738)," NOTES XI (1954) 201-212, with "Correction" in XII (1954) 57.

Newman/HAFFNER ———, "Further on the Nürnberg Music Publisher Johann Ulrich Haffner," to be published in AM XXXIV/4 (1962).

Newman/KIRNBERGER ———, "Kirnberger's 'Method for Tossing Off Sonatas,'" MQ XLVII (1961) 517-525.

Newman/MARCELLO ———, "The Keyboard Sonatas of Benedetto Marcello," AM XXIX (1957) 28-41; "Postcript," AM XXXI (1959) 192-196.

Newman/THEORISTS ———, "The Recognition of Sonata Form by Theorists of the 18th and 19th Centuries," PAPERS AMS 1941 (printed 1946) 21-29.

Newman/THIRTEEN-m ——— (ed.), *Thirteen Keyboard Sonatas of the 18th and 19th Centuries* (by Barrière, Platti, D. Alberti, G. Benda, Agrell, Neefe, Blasco de Nebra, Dittersdorf, Wölfl, E. T. A. Hoffmann, Reichardt, K. Loewe, and Moscheles). Chapel Hill: The University of North Carolina Press, 1947.

Newman/UNDERSTANDING William S. Newman, *Understanding Music,* 2d ed. New York: Harper, 1961.

Newton/SCARLATTI Richard Newton, "The English Cult of Domenico Scarlatti," ML XX (1939) 138-156.

Niemetschek/MOZART Franz Niemetschek, *Life of Mozart* (1798), trans. by Helen Mautner. London: Leonard Hyman, 1956.

Nin/ESPAGNOLS-m Joaquín Nin (ed.), *Seize Sonates* . . . and *Dix-sept Sonates et pièces anciennes d'auteurs espagnols,* 2 vols. Paris: Max Eschig, 1925 and '29.

Nin/HERRANDO-m ———, *Dix Pièces de José Herrando* for Vn and unfigured *b. c.* (realized for P), 10 separate issues. Paris: Max Eschig, 1937-38.

Nin/SOLER Joaquín Nin, "The Bi-Centenary of Antonio Soler," CHESTERIAN XI (1930) 97-103.

NINETEENTH-CENTURY *19th Century Music.* 1977—.

Nissel-Nemenoff/BENDA Elfriede Nissel-Nemenoff, *Die Violintechnik Franz Benda's und seiner Schule.* Kassel: Bärenreiter, 1931.

Nissen/MOZART George Nikolaus von Nissen, *Biographie W. A. Mozart's,* completed by Constanze [Mozart] Nissen. Leipzig: Breitkopf & Härtel, 1828.

Nisser/SVENSK Carl Nisser, *Svensk Instrumentalkomposition 1770-1830, Nominalkatalog.* Stockholm: Gothia, 1943.

NMJ — *Neues Mozart-Jahrbuch,* 3 vols. Regensburg: Gustav Bosse, 1941-43.

Nohl/BRIEFE — Ludwig Nohl, *Musiker-Briefe.* Leipzig: Duncker und Humblot, 1867.

Norlind/HOVKAPELLETS — Tobias Norlind and Emil Trobäck, *Kungl. Hovkapellets Historia, 1526-1926.* Stockholm: Wahlström & Widerstrand, 1926.

Norton/HAYDN — M. D. Herder Norton, "Haydn in America (before 1820)," MQ XVIII (1932) 309-337.

Noske/HAYDN — Frits Noske, "Le Principe structural génétique dans l'oeuvre instrumental de Joseph Haydn," RBDM XII (1958) 35-39.

NOTES — *Music Library Association Notes,* Second Series. 1943—.

Nottebohm/BEETHOVENIANA — Gustav Nottebohm, *Beethoveniana: Aufsätze und Mittheilungen.* Leipzig: C. F. Peters, 1872.

Nottebohm/SKIZZENBÜCHER — ———, *Zwei Skizzenbücher von Beethoven aus den Jahren 1801 bis 1803* (originally published in 1865 and '80, respectively), with preface by Paul Mies. Leipzig: Breitkopf & Härtel, 1924.

Nottebohm/ZWEITE — ———, *Zweite Beethoveniana: nachgelassene Aufsätze.* Leipzig: Rieter-Biedermann, 1887.

Nys/MOZART — Carl de Nys, "Mozart et les fils de Jean-Sebastien Bach," in Verchaly/MOZART 91-115.

Oberdörffer/BENDA-m — Fritz Oberdörffer (ed.), *Georg Benda: Zwölf Sonatinen und eine Sonate.* Berlin: Chr. Friedrich Vieweg, [1937].

Oberdörffer/GENERALBASS — Fritz Oberdörffer, *Der Generalbass in der Instrumentalmusik des ausgehenden 18. Jahrhunderts.* Kassel: Bärenreiter, 1939.

Oesterle/TREASURY-m — Louis Oesterle (ed.), *The Golden Treasury of Piano Music,* 5 vols. New York: G. Schirmer, 1904-09.

ORGANUM-m — Max Seiffert, succeeded by Hans Albrecht (eds.), *Organum; Ausgewählte ältere vokale und instrumentale Meisterwerke.* Leipzig, subsequently Lippstadt: Kistner & Siegel, from 1923. The 3d series is chamber music and the 5th keyboard. Cf. Heyer/HISTORICAL 229-234.

OXFORD HISTORY — *The Oxford History of Music,* 2d ed., 7 vols. London: Humphrey Milford, 1929-34. Cf. NEW OXFORD, *supra.*

Paap/ECKARD — Wouter Paap, "De Klaviersonates van Joh. G. Eckard," MEM XII (1957) 109-112.

Pamparato/PUGNANI — Cordero di Pamparato, "Gaetano Pugnani violinista torinese," RMI XXXVII (1930) 38-58, 219-230, 350-371, 551-561.

Paoli/ITALIANE-m — Domenico de Paoli (ed.), *Sonate italiane del sec: XVIII per cembalo o pianoforte.* London: J. & W. Chester, 1939.

PAPERS AMS — *Papers . . . of the American Musicological Society.* 1936-41.

Paribeni/CLEMENTI — Giulio Cesare Paribeni, *Muzio Clementi nella vita e nell'arte.* Milan: Il primato editoriale, 1922.

Parrish/CRITICISMS — Carl Parrish, "Criticisms of the Piano When It Was New," MQ XXX (1944) 428-440.

Parrish/HAYDN — ———, "Haydn and the Piano," JAMS I (1948) 27-34.

Parrish/PIANO — ———, *The Early Piano and Its Influence on Keyboard Technique and Composition in the Eighteenth Century* (diss., Harvard University, 1939). Superior (Wisconsin): Research Microfilm Publishers, 1953.

Pauer/MEISTER-m — Ernst Pauer (ed.), *Alte Meister, Sammlung wertvoller Klavierstücke des 17. und 18. Jahrhunderts,* 6 vols. Leipzig: Breitkopf & Härtel, [1868-85]. Cf. Eitner/SONATE; Torrefranca/ORIGINI 83-85.

Paulke/VIERLING — Karl Paulke, "Johann Gottfried Vierling," AFMW IV (1922) 439-455.

Paumgartner/MOZART — Bernhard Paumgartner, *Mozart.* Zürich: Atlantis-Verlag, 1940.

Pedrell/SOLER — Felipe Pedrell, "P. Anton Soler y ramos," RMCA V (1908) 177-178, 201-203, 225-226; VI (1909) 3-5.

Pelikant/WAGENSEIL — Irene Pelikant, "G. Ch. Wagenseils Klavierwerke," unpublished Ph.D. diss., University of Vienna, 1926.

PENNSYLVANIA — *Church Music and Musical Life in Pennsylvania in the Eighteenth Century,* 3 vols. in 4 parts. Philadelphia: Pennsylvania Society of the Colonial Dames of America-IV, 1926-47.

Perinello/PESCETTI-m — Carlo Perinello (ed.), *G. B. Pescetti: Sonata per cimbalo* (no. 3 in g from the 1739 set). Milan: A. & G. Carisch, 1922.

Perinello/RUTINI-m — ———, *Giovanni Rutini: Sonate per cimbalo* (Op. 3, Nos. 3-5; Op. 5, Nos. 1 & 5), 5 vols. Milan: A. & G. Carisch, 1922.

Pfäfflin/NARDINI — Clara Pfäfflin, *Pietro Nardini, seine Werke und sein Leben.* Stuttgart: Friedrich Find, [1935].

PIANO QUARTERLY — *Piano Quarterly* (edited by Mary Vivian Lee), founded as *Piano Quarterly Newsletter.* 1952—.

Piatti/BOCCHERINI-m — Alfredo Piatti (ed.), *L. Boccherini: Sei Sonate per violoncello.* Milan: G. Ricordi, [1864-65, 1874].

Piccioli/CLEMENTI-m — Giuseppe Piccioli (ed.), *Clementi: 18 Sonate per pianoforte,* 3 vols. Milan: Curci, 1949.

Piccioli/GALUPPI-m — Giuseppe Piccioli, *Baldassare Galuppi: Quattro Sonate* [4 mvts.!] *per pianoforte (o clavicembalo)*. Milan: Suvini Zerboni, 1952.

Picquot/BOCCHERINI — Louis Picquot, *Notice sur la vie et les ouvrages de Luigi Boccherini* (Paris: Philipp, 1851), 2d ed., emended with "notes et documents nouveaux" by Georges de Saint-Foix. Paris: R. Legouix, 1930.

Pike/HÜLLMANDEL — D. E. Pike, "Hüllmandel," ML XXI (1940) 75-83.

Pincherle/CORELLI — Marc Pincherle, *Corelli, His Life, His Work*, trans. by H. E. M. Russell. New York: W. W. Norton, 1956.

Pincherle/FEUILLETS — ———, *Feuillets d'histoire du violon*, 2d ed. Paris: G. Legouix, 1935.

Pincherle/LECLAIR — ———, *Jean-Marie Leclair l'aîné*. Paris: La Colombe, 1952.

Pincherle/MONDONVILLE-m — ——— (ed.), *J.-C. de Mondonville: Pièces de clavecin en sonates* (Op. 3), Series I, Vol. IX of the Publications de la Société française de musicologie. Paris: E. Droz, 1935.

Pincherle/OSPITALI — Marc Pincherle, "Vivaldi and the *Ospitali* of Venice," MQ XXIV (1938) 300-312.

Pincherle/ROBINEAU — ———, "Le Peintre-violiniste ou les aventures de l'Abbé Robineau," RM VI (March, 1925) 235-246.

Pincherle/VIVALDI — ———, *Antonio Vivaldi et la musique instrumentale*, 2 vols. Paris: Floury, 1948.

Piovano/GALUPPI — Francesco Piovano, "Baldassare Galuppi, note bio-bibliografische," RMI XIII (1906) 676-726, XIV (1907) 333-365, and XV (1908) 233-274.

Plamenac/BACH — Dragan Plamenac, "New Light on the Last Years of Carl Philipp Emanuel Bach," MQ XXXV (1949) 565-587.

Plantinga/CLEMENTI — Leon B. Plantinga, *Clementi: His Life and His Music*. London: Oxford University Press, 1977. Cf. SCE 738, fn. 1.

PMA — *Proceedings of the (Royal) Musical Association*. 1874—.

Pohl/HAYDN — Carl Ferdinand Pohl, *Joseph Haydn*, 3 vols. (completed by Hugo Botstiber). Berlin: A. Sacco, 1875; Leipzig: Breitkopf & Härtel, 1885, 1927.

Pohl/MOZART — ———, *Mozart und Haydn in London*, 2 vols. Vienna: Carl Gerold's Sohn, 1867.

Porter/BOCCHERINI — Emily G. Porter, "The Violoncello Concertos of Luigi Boccherini," unpublished master's thesis, University of North Carolina, 1948.

Preston/LECLAIR — Robert Elwyn Preston, "The Sonatas for Violin and Figured Bass by Jean-Marie Leclair l'Aîné," 3 vols., unpublished Ph.D. diss., University of Michigan, 1959.

Prieger/RUST — Erich Prieger, *Friedrich Wilhelm Rust, ein Vorgänger Beethovens.* Köln: P. J. Tonger, 1894.

Prieger/RUSTIANA — ———, "Rustiana," DM XII/2 (1913) 269-277.

Prod'homme/BEETHOVEN — Jacques-Gabriel Prod'homme, *Les Sonates pour piano de Beethoven.* Paris: Delagrave, 1937.

Prod'homme/CAHIERS — ——— (ed. and trans.), *Cahiers de conversation de Beethoven (1819-27).* Paris: Corrêa, 1946.

Prod'homme/REICHA — Jacques-Gabriel Prod'homme, "From the Unpublished Autobiography of Antoine Reicha," MQ XXII (1936) 339-353.

Prosniz/HANDBUCH — Adolf Prosniz, *Handbuch der Klavier-Literatur,* 2 vols. (1450-1830, 1830-1904). Leipzig: L. Doblinger, 1908 (2d ed.), 1907.

PUBBLICAZIONI — *Bollettino dell'Associazione dei musicologi italiani.* 1909—.

PUBBLICAZIONI AMBROSINI — Biblioteca dell'Avv. Raimondo Ambrosini (in Series II).

PUBBLICAZIONI FILARMONICA — Archivio della R. Accademia filarmonica (in Series II).

PUBBLICAZIONI FIRENZE — Biblioteca del R. Conservatorio di musica (in Series IV).

PUBBLICAZIONI MODENA — Biblioteca estense di Modena (Series VIII).

PUBBLICAZIONI NAPOLI — Biblioteca del R. Conserv. di musica di S. Pietro a Majella (in Series X).

PUBBLICAZIONI PARMA — Citta di Parma (in Series I).

PUBBLICAZIONI PETRONIO — Archivio di S. Petronio di Bologna (in Series II).

PUBBLICAZIONI PISTOIA — Archivio capitolare della Cattedrale (in Series IV).

PUBBLICAZIONI TORINO — Biblioteca nazionale di Torino (in Series XII).

PUBBLICAZIONI VENEZIA — Biblioteca di S. Marco di Venezia (in Series VI).

Pujol/MONTSERRAT-m — David Pujol (ed.), *Mestres de l'escolania de Montserrat, Música instrumental,* 2 vols. Monestir de Montserrat (near Barcelona), 1934, '36.

Quantz/VERSUCH — Johann Joachim Quantz, *Versuch einer Anweisung die Flute traversière zu spielen,* facs. of 3d ed. (Berlin, 1789; first ed. in 1752). Kassel: Bärenreiter, 1953. Page references are to the foregoing rather than to the subsequent, excellent transl. by Edward R. Reilly (New York: Free Press, 1966; new ed. in progress); cf. Reilly's 3 studies in *Quantz and His "Versuch"* (New York: Galaxy, 1971).

Quoika/BÖHMEN — Rudolph Quoika, *Die Musik der deutschen in Böhmen und Mähren.* Berlin: Merseburger, 1956.

Raabe/GALUPPI — Felix Raabe, *Galuppi als Instrumentalkomponist* (Ph.D. diss., 1926). Frankfurt/O: F. Müller, 1929.

Racek/TSCHECHISCHEN — Jan Racek, "Zur Frage des 'Mozart-Stils' in der tschechischen vorklassichen Musik," KONGRESS 1956 (Vienna) 493-524.

Radcliffe/HAYDN — Philip Radcliffe, "The Piano Sonatas of Joseph Haydn," MR VII (1946) 139-148.

RAM — *Rassegna musicale.* 1928—.

Randebrock/BACH — Ekkehard Randebrock, "Studie zur Klaviersonate Carl Phil. Emanuel Bachs," unpublished Ph.D. diss., Westfälische Wilhelms-Universität, (Münster) 1953.

Rangoni/ESSAI — Giovanni Battista Rangoni, *Essai sur le gout de la musique, avec le caractère des trois célèbres joueurs de violon, Messieurs Nardini, Lolli, & Pugnani,* in both the original French and the Italian trans. (Livorno: T. Masi, 1790). Milan: Bolletino Bibliografica Musicale (facs.), 1932.

Ratner/HARMONIC — Leonard Ratner, "Harmonic Aspects of Classic Form," JAMS II (1949) 159-168.

Ratner/THEORIES — ———, "Eighteenth-Century Theories of Musical Period Structure," MQ XLII (1956) 439-454.

RBDM — *Revue belge de musicologie.* 1946—.

RDM — *Revue de musicologie,* founded in 1917 as *Bulletin de la société française de musicologie.*

Rees/CYCLOPEDIA — Abraham Rees, *Cyclopedia; or Universal Dictionary of Arts, Sciences, and Literature,* 41 vols. plus 6 vols. of plates. New York: P. A. Mesier, 1810-24. Music articles by Charles Burney (cf. GROVE I 1030 [Scholes]).

Reeser/ECKARD — Eduard Reeser, "Johann Gottfried Eckard, 1735-1809," TVNM XVII/2 (1949) 89-127.

Reeser/ECKARD-m — ——— (ed.), *Johann Gottfried Eckard: Oeuvres complètes pour le clavecin ou le piano forte.* Kassel: Bärenreiter, 1956.

Reeser/KLAVIERSONATE — Eduard Reeser, *De Klaviersonate met Vioolbegeleiding in het parijsche Muziekleven ten Tijde van Mozart,* with a suppl. of 12 complete sons. Rotterdam: W. L. & J. Brusse, 1939.

Reeser/SONS — ———, *The Sons of Bach,* trans. by W. A. G. Doyle-Davidson. Stockholm: The Continental Book Co., [1947].

Reich/HAYDN — Willi Reich, *Joseph Haydn.* Luzern: Josef Stocker, 1946.

Reichardt/BERLIN — Johann Friedrich Reichardt, *Schreiben über die Berlinische Musik.* Hamburg: Carl Ernst Bohn, 1775.

Reichardt/KUNSTMAGAZIN — *J. F. Reichardt's Musikalisches Kunstmagazin,* 8 issues. Berlin: Im Verlage des Verfassers, 1782-91. Cf. LC EARLY 192.

Reichardt/PARIS — *Johann Friedrich Reichardt's vertraute Briefe aus Paris geschrieben,* 3 vols. Hamburg: B. G. Hoffmann, 1804.

Reichardt/SCHULZ — Johann Friedrich Reichardt, *Johann Abraham Peter Schulz,* reprinted from AMZ III (1800-01) 153 ff., by Richard Schaal. Kassel: Bärenreiter, 1948.

Reichardt/SELBSTBIOGRAPHIE — "Noch ein Bruchstück aus J. F. Reichardt's Autobiographie; sein erster Aufenthalt in Hamburg," AMZ XVI (1814) 21-34.

Reti/THEMATIC — Rudolph Reti, *The Thematic Process in Music.* New York: Macmillan, 1951.

RICORDI ARTE-m — *L'Arte antica e moderna, scelta di composizioni per pianoforte,* 21 vols. Milan: G. Ricordi, *ca.* 1890-*ca.* 1910. Cf. Cat. BOLOGNA IV 180.

RIdM — *Rivista italiana di musicologia.* 1966—.

Riehl/CHARAKTERKÖPFE — Wilhelm Heinrich von Riehl, *Musikalische Charakterköpfe,* 4th ed., 2 vols. Stuttgart: J. G. Cotta, 1868 and '75.

Riemann/BEETHOVEN — Hugo Riemann, *L. van Beethoven's sämtliche Klavier-Solosonaten,* 3 vols. Berlin: Max Hesse, 1917-19.

Riemann/LEXIKON — Alfred Einstein (ed.), *Hugo Riemann's Musik Lexikon,* 11th ed., 2 vols. Berlin: Max Hesses Verlag, 1929.

Riemann/PRÄLUDIEN — Hugo Riemann, *Präludien u. Studien,* 3 vols. Leipzig: Hermann Seemann Nachfolger, 1895-1901.

Riemann/SÖHNE — ———, "Die Söhne Bachs," in Riemann/PRÄLUDIEN III 173-184.

Riemann/STAMITZ-m — ——— (ed.), *Karl Stamitz: Fünf Klaviersonaten mit begleitender Violine.* Leipzig: Peters, [1908].

Riemann & Gurlitt/LEXIKON — Wilibald Gurlitt (ed.), *Riemann Musik Lexikon,* 12th ed., 2 vols. (to date). Mainz: B. Schott, 1959, 1961.

Riepel/TONORDNUNG — Joseph Riepel, *Grundregeln zur Tonordnung.* Ulm: Christian Ulrich Wagner, 1755.

Riess/SCHULZ — Otto Riess, "Johann Abraham Peter Schulz' Leben," SIMG XV (1913-14) 169-270.

Rietsch/MOZART — Heinrich Rietsch, "Ein Sonatenthema [K. V. 300i] bei Mozart," ZIMG XIV (1912-13) 278-280.

Rigler/DITTERSDORF — Gertrude Rigler, "Die Kammermusik Dittersdorfs," SZMW XIV (1927) 179-212.

RIM — *La Revue internationale de musique.* 1938 (irregular)—.

Rinaldi/VIOTTI — Mario Rinaldi, "Missione storica di Giovanni Battista Viotti," in CHIGIANA SETTIMANE XVI (1959) 27-34.

Ringer/CHASSE — Alexander L. Ringer, "The Chasse of the 18th Century," JAMS VI (1953) 148-159.

Ringer/CLEMENTI — ———, "Clementi and the *Eroica*," MQ XLVII (1961) 454-468.

Ringer/MÉHUL — ———, "A French Symphonist at the Time of Beethoven: Etienne Nicolas Méhul," MQ XXXVII (1951) 543-565.

RISM — *Répertoire international des sources musicales.* Munich: G. Henle, Kassel: Bärenreiter, 1960—. Cf. AM XLIV (1972) 171-180 (F. Blume).

RM — *La Revue musicale* (founded by Prunières). 1920—.

RMCA — *Revista musical catalana.* 1904-36.

RMI — *Rivista musicale italiana.* 1894—.

Rocamora/SOR — Manuel Rocamora, *Fernando Sor.* Barcelona: Enrique Tobella, 1957.

Rochlitz/FREUNDE — Friedrich Rochlitz, *Für Freunde der Tonkunst*, 4 vols., 3d ed. Leipzig: Carl Cnobloch, 1868. (The first ed. appeared 1824-32).

Rolland/BEETHOVEN — Romain Rolland, *Beethoven: les grandes époques créatrices,* 7 vols. Paris: Sablier, 1928-49.

Roncaglia/CAMBINI — Gino Roncaglia, "Di Giovanni Giuseppe Cambini, quartettista padre," RAM VI (1933) 267-274.

Roncaglia/QUARTETTISTA — ———, "G. G. Cambini, quartettista romantico," RAM VII (1934) 423-432.

Roncaglia/SAMMARTINI — ———, "Una Sonata inedita di G. B. Sammartini," RMI XLII (1938) 492-494.

Rosen/CLASSICAL — Charles Rosen, *The Classical Style—Haydn, Mozart, Beethoven.* New York: W. W. Norton, 1972 (with revisions in the edition of 1971 from Viking Press). Cf. the enthusiastic review by Roger Fiske in ML LII (1971) 327-329; also, fn. 15a to p. 119 in SCE.

Rosenberg/BEETHOVEN — Richard Rosenberg, *Die Klaviersonaten Ludwig van Beethovens,* 2 vols. Lausanne: Urs Graf-Verlag, 1957.

Rosenberg/KRAUS-m — Hilding Rosenberg (ed.), *Joseph Martin Kraus: Sonata* (in E, for piano). Stockholm: Nordiska, (1925).

Rosenberg/MOZART — Richard Rosenberg, "Mozart-Spuren in Beethovens Klaviersonaten," BEETHOVEN-JAHRBUCH 1957-58, pp. 51-62.

Rousseau/DICTIONNAIRE — Jean-Jacques Rousseau, *Dictionnaire de musique,* 2 vols. (reprint of the 1768 ed.). Amsterdam: Marc Michel Rey, 1772.

Rowen/CHAMBER — Ruth Halle Rowen, *Early Chamber Music.* New York: King's Crown Press, 1949.

Rowley/BURNEY-m — Alec Rowley (ed.), *Charles Burney: Sonata for Two Performers Upon One Instrument* (1777). London: Schott & Co., 1952.

Rowley/ENGLISH-m — ———, *Early English Sonatinas.* London: Boosey & Hawkes, 1918.

Rubio/SOLER-m — Samuel Rubio (ed.), *P. Antonio Soler . . . : Sonatas para instrumentos de tecla,* 6 vols. up to 1962. Madrid: Union Musical Española, 1957—.

Russell/MOZART — John F. Russell, "Mozart and the Pianoforte," MR I (1940) 226-244.

Ruthardt/CLEMENTI-m — Adolf Ruthardt (ed.), *Clementi: Sammlung von [24] berühmter Sonaten.* Leipzig: C. F. Peters, *ca.* 1905.

RUTINI/facs.-m — Giovanni Marco Rutini, *Tre Sonate da cimbalo, e violino obbligato,* Op. 14 [no publisher, place, or date], facs. of printed ed. in the Archivio musicale di Montecassino. Milano: Bolletino Bibliografico Musicale, 1933.

Rutz/BEETHOVEN — Hans Rutz, *Ludwig van Beethoven, Dokumente seines Lebens und Schaffens,* 2d ed. Munich: C. H. Beck, 1957.

Rutz/HAYDN — ———, *Joseph Haydn, Dokumente seines Lebens und Schaffens.* Munich: C. H. Beck, 1953.

Sadie/BRITISH — Stanley J. Sadie, "British Chamber Music, 1720-1790," 3 vols., unpublished Ph.D. diss., Cambridge University (England), 1957.

Sadie/CONCERT — ———, "Concert Life in Eighteenth Century England," PMA LXXXV (1958-59) 17-30.

Saint-Foix/BACH — Georges de Saint-Foix, "A propos de Jean-Chrétien Bach," RDM VII (1926) 83-91.

Saint-Foix/BECK — ———, "Le Symphoniste Franz Beck et le pianoforte," RDM XIII (1932) 24-28.

Saint-Foix/CLEMENTI — ———, "Muzio Clementi," MQ IX (1923) 350-382.

Saint-Foix/FERRARI — ———, "A Musical Traveler: Giacomo Gotifredo Ferrari (1759[1763!]-1842)," MQ XXV (1939) 455-465.

Saint-Foix/FORERUNNER — ———, "Clementi, Forerunner of Beethoven," MQ XVII (1931) 84-92.

Saint-Foix/HAYDN — ———, "Haydn and Clementi," MQ XVIII (1932) 252-259.

Saint-Foix/INCONNUE — ———, "Une Sonate inconnue de Mozart" (K.V. 19d), RM II/7 (May 1, 1924) 99-110.

Saint-Foix/LONDRES — ———, "Les Maîtres de l'opéra bouffe dans la musique de chambre, à Londres," RMI XXXI (1924) 507-526.

Saint-Foix/MOZART — Theodore de Wyzewa (vols. I and II only) and Georges de Saint-Foix, *Mozart,* 5 vols. Paris: Desclée de Brouwer, 1912-46. On vols. I and II cf. Abert/MOZART I xii-xv; King/MOZART 38-39.

Saint-Foix/MYSLIWECZEK — Georges de Saint-Foix, "Un Ami de Mozart: Joseph Mysliweczek," RM IX/5 (March, 1928) 124-128.

Saint-Foix/PAISIELLO — ———, "Autour de Paisiello," RMI XLVIII (1946) 243-250.

Saint-Foix/PIANISTES — ———, "Les premiers Pianistes parisiens," RM III (Aug., 1922) 121-136 and Suppl.: "Jean Schobert," IV (April, 1923) 193-205 and Suppl.: "Nicolas-Joseph Hüllmandel," V (June, 1924) 187-198 and Suppl.: "Edelmann (Jean-Frédéric)" and "Rigel (Henri-Joseph)," VI (June, 1925) 209-215: "Jean-Louis Adam," VI (Aug., 1925) 105-109: "Les Frères Jadin," VII (Nov., 1925) 43-46: "Les six Sonates de Méhul," VII (Feb., 1926) 102-110: "Boieldieu," VIII (Nov., 1926) 13-20: "Ignace-Antoine Ladurner," IX (Aug., 1928) 321-332: "A. P. F. Boëly."

Saint-Foix/ROMANTIQUES — ———, "Les six Sonates, dites 'romantiques,' pour piano et violon, de Mozart," RM XX (April, 1946) 81-89.

Saint-Foix/SAMMARTINI — ———, "La Chronologie de l'oeuvre instrumentale de Jean Baptiste Sammartini," SIMG XV (1913-14) 308-324.

Saint-Foix SAMMARTINI-m — ——— (ed.), *J. B. Sammartini: Sonata II pour piano* (from Anth. JOZZI-m II). Paris: Senart, 1923.

Saint-Foix/SCHENK — Georges de Saint-Foix, review of Schenk/PAGANELLI, RDM X (1929) 303-304.

Saint-Foix/SCHOBERT-m — ——— (ed.), *J. Schobert: Sonate pour clavecin* [Vn omitted], Op. 8/1. Paris: Maurice Senart, 1923.

Saint-Foix/TORREFRANCA — Georges de Saint-Foix, "A Proposito dello scritto: Torrefranca, La fortuna di Ph. E. Bach nell'ottocento" (RMI XXV [1918] 402-447), RMI XXVI (1919) 332-337.

Saint-Foix/TRIOS — ———, "Histoire de deux trios ignorés de Michel Haydn; leur influence sur Mozart," RDM XII (1931) 81-88.

Saint-Foix/VIOLON — ———, "Les Sonates pour violon et alto de Haydn," RM XIII/128 (1932) 81-84.

Salkeld/HOOK-m — Robert Salkeld (ed.), *James Hook: Sonatina No. 1 in F for Treble Recorder and Pianoforte, Sonatina No. 2 in C . . .*, 2 vols. (both arranged from Op. 54). London: Schott, 1951.

Salter/SCARLATTI — Lionel Salter, "Scarlatti's Violin Sonatas," LISTENER XXXVIII (1947) 116.

Salter/SCARLATTI-m — ——— (ed.), *Domenico Scarlatti: Sonatas for Violin and Clavier,* 8 vols. London: Augener, 1947-50.

SAMMLUNG SONDHEIMER-m — Robert Sondheimer (ed.), *Sammlung Sondheimer, Werke aus dem 18. Jahrhundert,* 52 vols. Basel: Bernoulli, 1922-39. Cf. Heyer/HISTORICAL 309-310.

Sandberger/AUFSÄTZE — Adolf Sandberger, *Ausgewählte Aufsätze zur Musikgeschichte,* 3 vols. Munich: Drei Masken, 1921, '24, '34.

Sandberger/HAYDN — ———, "Zur Enstehungsgeschichte von Haydns 'Sieben Worten des Erlösers am Kreuze,'" JMP X (1903) 45-59.

Sartori/DIZIONARIO — Claudio Sartori, *Dizionario degli editori musicali italiani.* Florence: Leo S. Olschki, 1958.

Sartori/SAMMARTINI — ———, "Giovanni Battista Sammartini e la sue corte," MDO March, 1960, pp. 106-121.

Sasser/SOR — William Gray Sasser, "The Guitar Works of Fernando Sor," unpublished Ph.D. diss., University of North Carolina, 1960.

SBE — William S. Newman, *The Sonata in the Baroque Era,* vol. I in *A History of the Sonata Idea.* Chapel Hill: University of North Carolina Press, 1959.

SCE — ———, *The Sonata in the Classic Era* (for cross references within the present vol.).

Schaefer-Schmuck/TELEMANN — Käte Schaefer-Schmuck, *Georg Philipp Telemann als Klavierkomponist.* Leipzig: Robert Noske, 1934.

Schaeffner/LA LAURENCIE — André Schaeffner, review of La Laurencie/ÉCOLE, MÉNESTREL LXXXVI (1924) 9-11, 21-22.

Schafhäutl/VOGLER — Karl Emil von Schafhäutl, *Abt Georg Joseph Vogler.* Augsburg: M. Huttler, 1888.

Scharnagl/STERKEL — Augustin Scharnagl, *Johann Franz Xaver Sterkel.* Würzburg: Konrad Triltsch, 1943.

Scheibe/CRITISCHER — Johann Adolph Scheibe, *Critischer musikus,* revised, collected ed. of the weekly issues that had appeared irregularly from 1737-40. Leipzig: B. C. Breitkopf, 1745.

Schenk/MOZART — Erich Schenk, *Mozart and His Times.* London: Secker & Warburg, 1960.

Schenk/PAGANELLI — ———, *Giuseppe Antonio Paganelli* (Ph.D. diss., 1925). Vienna: Waldheim-Eberle, 1928.

Schenk/TRIOSONATE-m ——— (ed.), *Die italienische Triosonate* (in *Das Musikwerk* series). Köln: Arno Volk-Verlag, [1954?].

Schenker/BEETHOVEN-m Heinrich Schenker (ed.), *Die letzten fünf Sonaten von Beethoven: Kritische Ausgabe mit Einführung und Erläuterung,* originally issued in 4 separate vols. (with Op. 106 missing because Schenker could not find the autograph). Vienna: Universal, 1913 (Op. 109), 1914 (Op. 110), 1916 (Op. 111), 1921 (Op. 101).

Schenker/TONWILLE Heinrich Schenker, *Der Tonwille; Flugblätter zum Zeugnis unwandelbarer Gesetze der Tonkunst einer neuen Jugend dargebracht,* 10 issues of an irregular periodical. Vienna: Tonwille-Verlag (A. J. Gutmann), 1921-24.

Schenker & Ratz/BEETHOVEN-m ——— (ed.), *Beethoven: Klaviersonaten, nach den Autographen und Erstdrucken,* revised by Erwin Ratz, 4 vols. Vienna: Universal, 1946-47.

Schering/BEISPIELE-m Arnold Schering (ed.), *Geschichte der Musik in Beispielen.* Leipzig: Breitkopf & Härtel, 1931.

Schering/DEUTUNG Arnold Schering, *Beethoven in neuer Deutung.* Leipzig: C. F. Kahnt, 1934.

Schering/DICHTUNG ———, *Beethoven und die Dichtung.* Berlin: Junker und Dünnhaupt, 1936.

Schering/ERKENNTNIS ———, *Zur Erkenntnis Beethoven.* Würzburg: Triltsch, 1938.

Schering/PATHÉTIQUE ———, "Zu Beethovens Sonate pathétique," AFMF I (1936) 366-367.

Schering/REDENDE ———, "Carl Philipp Emanuel Bach und das 'redende Prinzip' in der Musik," JMP XLV (1938) 13-29.

Schering/VIOLINSONATEN ———, "Zu Beethovens Violinsonaten," ZFM CIII (1936) 1041-48, 1307-18; CIV (1937) 374-381; CV (1938) 121-130.

Scheurleer/CATALOGUS Daniel François Scheurleer (ed.), *Muziekhistorisch Museum* [in The Hague], *Catalogus van de Muziekwerken en de Boeken over Muziek,* 3 vols. The Hague: Martin Nijhoff, 1923-25.

Scheurleer/NEDERLAND Daniel François Scheurleer, *Het Muziekleven in Nederland.* The Hague: Martinus Nijhoff, 1909.

Schiedermair/BEETHOVEN Ludwig Schiedermair, *Der junge Beethoven.* Leipzig: Quelle & Meyer, 1925.

Schiedermair/MOZART ———, *Die Briefe Mozarts und seiner Familie,* 5 vols. Munich: G. Müller, 1914.

Schiedermair/WALLERSTEIN ———, "Die Blütezeit der Öttingen-Wallerstein'schen Hofkapelle," SIMG IX (1907-08) 83-130.

Schilling/LEXICON — Gustav Schilling (ed.), *Encyclopädie der gesammten musikalischen Wissenschaften oder Universal-Lexicon der Tonkunst,* 6 vols. Stuttgart: F. H. Köhler, 1835-38. *Supplementband,* 1842.

Schindler/BEETHOVEN — Anton Schindler, *Ludwig van Beethoven* (from 3d ed., 2 vols., 1860), 5th ed., edited by Fritz Volbach. Münster: Aschendorff, 1927.

Schindler & MacArdle/BEETHOVEN — Anton Felix Schindler, *Beethoven as I Knew Him,* trans. by Constance S. Jolly and annotated by Donald W. MacArdle from the 3d ed. of 1860, 2 vols. in one. Chapel Hill: The University of North Carolina Press, 1966. Cf. MT CVIII (1967) 40-41 (J. Kerman); also, fn. 9a to p. 502, *supra.*

Schlesinger/CRAMER — Thea Schlesinger, *Johann Baptist Cramer und seine Klaviersonaten.* Munich: Knorr & Hirth, 1928.

Schletterer/BOCCHERINI — Hans Michel Schletterer, "Luigi Boccherini," Waldersee/VORTRÄGE IV 105-156.

Schletterer/REICHARDT — ———, *Joh. Friedrich Reichardt, sein Leben und seine musikalische Thätigkeit* (first published in Augsburg in 1865). Leipzig: Breitkopf und Härtel, 1879.

Schletterer/WIDMUNG — ———, "Eine Widmung an Joh. Seb. Bach," MFMG XI (1879) 65-67.

Schmid/BACH — Ernst Fritz Schmid, *Carl Philipp Emanuel Bach und seine Kammermusik.* Kassel: Bärenreiter, 1931.

Schmid/GÖTTWEIGER — ———, "Franz Anton Hoffmeister und die 'Göttweiger Sonaten,'" ZFM CIV (1937) 760-770, 889-895, 992-1000, 1109-1117.

Schmid/GÖTTWEIGER-m — ——— (ed.), *Joseph Haydn* [actually F. A. Hoffmeister]: *Die Göttweiger Sonaten,* 3 sons. (in C, A, and D) in 3 separate issues. Wolfenbüttel: Verlag für musikalische Kultur und Wissenschaft, 1934. Cf. HOFMEISTER 1934 p. 49; Schmid/GÖTTWEIGER 760-761, 998, 1116-1117.

Schmid/HAYDN — Ernst Fritz Schmid, "Joseph Haydn und Carl Philipp Emanuel Bach," ZFMW XIV (1931-32) 299-312.

Schmid/MOZART — ———, "Mozart and Haydn," MQ XLII (1956) 145-161.

Schmidl/DIZIONARIO — Carlo Schmidl, *Dizionario universale dei musicisti,* 2 vols. and "Supplemento." Milan: Sonzogno, 1926 and 1938.

Schmitt/CLEMENTI-m — Hans Schmitt (ed.), *Clementi:* [32] *Sonaten für Pianoforte,* 5 vols. Vienna: Universal, [1901].

Schmitz/BEETHOVEN — Arnold Schmitz, *Beethovens "Zwei Principe," ihre Bedeutung für Themen- und Satzbau.* Berlin: Ferd. Dümmler, 1923.

Schneider/ELEMENTS — Frederick Schneider, *The Elements of Musical Harmony and Composition,* trans. from the German ed. of 1827. London: Clementi, 1828.

Schneider/SALZBURG — Constantin Schneider, *Geschichte der Musik in Salzburg von der ältesten Zeit bis zur Gegenwart.* Salzburg: Verlag R. Kiesel, 1935.

Schökel/BACH — Heinrich Peter Schökel, *Johann Christian Bach und die Instrumentalmusik seiner Zeit.* Wolfenbüttel: Georg Kallmeyer, 1926.

Schönewolf/BEETHOVEN — Karl Schönewolf, *Beethoven in der Zeitenwende,* 2 vols. Halle: Mitteldeutscher Verlag, 1955.

Scholes/BURNEY — Percy A. Scholes, *The Great Dr. Burney,* 2 vols. London: Oxford University Press, 1948.

SCHOTT ANTIQUA-m — *Antiqua, eine Sammlung alter Musik Meisterwerke des 13-18. Jahrhunderts.* Mainz: B. Schott's Söhne, 1933—.

SCHOTT CELLO-m — *Cello-Bibliothek, klassische Sonaten.* Mainz: B. Schott's Söhne, [*ca.* 1930-35].

Schrade/BEETHOVEN — Leo Schrade, *Beethoven in France, the Growth of an Idea.* New Haven: Yale University Press, 1942.

Schroeder/CELLO-m — Carl Schroeder (ed.), *Classical Violoncello Music by Celebrated Masters of the 17th and 18th Centuries.* London: Augener, [1895].

SCHUBART — Christian Friedrich Daniel Schubart, *Schubart's Leben und Gesinnungen von ihm selbst, im Kerker aufgesetzt,* 2 vols. Stuttgart: Mäntler, 1791 and '93.

Schubart/IDEEN — ———, *Ideen zu einer Ästhetik der Tonkunst* (written in 1784-85; SCE XI). Vienna: J. V. Degen, 1806.

Schueller/QUARREL — Herbert M. Schueller, "The Quarrel of the Ancients and the Moderns," ML XLI (1960) 313-330.

Schünemann/BACH — Georg Schünemann, "Johann Christoph Friedrich Bach," BJ XI (1914) 45-165.

Schünemann/BACH-m — ——— (ed.), *Friedrich Bach: Sonata per il cembalo ô piano forte, violino e viola* (in G). Leipzig: C. F. W. Siegel, 1920. Cf. Wohlfarth/BACH 404-405, 409 (VII/5).

Schünemann/CZERNY — Georg Schünemann, "Czernys Erinnerungen an Beethoven," NBJ IX (1939) 47-74.

Schünemann/KONVERSATIONSHEFTE — ——— (ed.), *Ludwig van Beethovens Konversationshefte,* 3 vols. (1818-23). Berlin: Max Hesse, 1941-43.

Schumann/SCHRIFTEN Robert Schumann, *Gesammelte Schriften über Musik und Musiker,* 2 vols., 5th ed. Leipzig: Breitkopf & Härtel, 1914.

Schwarz/BACH Max Schwarz, "Johann Christian Bach (1735-1782)," SIMG II (1900-01) 401-454.

Schwarz/BEETHOVEN Boris Schwarz, "Beethoven and the French Violin School," MQ XLIV (1958) 431-447.

Schwarz/BEETHOVENIANA ———, "Beethoveniana in Soviet Russia," MQ XLVII (1961) 4-21.

Schwarz/FRENCH ———, "French Instrumental Music Between the Revolutions (1789-1830)," unpublished Ph.D. diss., Columbia University, 1950.

Scott/HAYDN Marion M. Scott, "Haydn's Chamber Music," MT LXXIII (1932) 213-217 (with rejoinder by A. T. Froggatt, pp. 741-742).

Scuderi/BEETHOVEN Gaspare Scuderi, *Beethoven: Le Sonate per pianoforte.* Milan: Sonzogno, 1933.

Segovia/SOR-m Andres Segovia (ed.), *Fernando Sor: 2a Sonata, Op. 25.* Buenos Aires: Ricordi Americana, 1956.

Seiffert/HURLEBUSCH Max Seiffert, "Konrad Friedrich Hurlebusch, (*ca.* 1695-1756), *biographische Skizze,*" TVNM VII (1904) 264-277.

Seiffert/KLAVIERMUSIK ———, *Geschichte der Klaviermusik* (completed only to 1750 but published as 3d ed. of Weitzmann/PIANOFORTE). Leipzig: Breitkopf & Härtel, 1899.

Selva/SONATE Blanche Selva, *La Sonate.* Paris: Rouart, Lerolle, 1913.

Serrins/TEXTBOOK David Serrins, "The Validity of Textbook Concepts of 'Sonata Form' in Late String Quartets of Haydn and Mozart," unpublished M.A. thesis, University of North Carolina, 1950.

Shedlock/BEETHOVEN John S. Shedlock, *Beethoven's Pianoforte Sonatas, the Origin and Respective Value of Various Readings.* London: Augener, [1918].

Shedlock/SKETCH ———, "Beethoven's Sketch Books," MT XXXIII (1892) 331-334, 394-397, 461-465, 523-525, 589-592, 649-652, 717; XXXIV (1893) 14-16; Second Series: XXXV (1894) 13-16, 449-452, 596-600.

Shedlock/SONATA ———, *The Pianoforte Sonata.* London: Methuen, 1895. Facs. reprint, with preface by W. S. Newman (New York: Da Capo), 1964.

Sieber/REICHARDT Paul Sieber, *Joh. Friedr. Reichardt als Musikästhetiker.* Strasbourg: Heitz, 1930.

Siebigk/CLEMENTI Ludwig Anton Leopold Siebigk, *Muzio Clementi, nebst einer kurzen Darstellung seiner Manier.* [Breslau: A. Schall], 1801.

SIM — *Societé internationale de musique* (issued by th French section of the International Musical Socie ty), 1907-14.

SIMG — *Sammelbände der Internationalen Musikgesellschaf* 1900-14.

Simon/CLEMENTI — Heinrich Simon, "The Clementi Manuscripts at th Library of Congress," MQ XXVIII (1942) 105-114

Simon/ENGLÄNDER — Edwin J. Simon, review of Richard Engländer *Die Dresdner Instrumentalmusik in der Zeit de Wiener Klassik,* in JAMS XII (1959) 251-252.

Simon/MOZART — ———, "Sonata into Concerto, a Study of Mozart' First Seven Concertos," AM XXXI (1959) 170-185

Simon/VOGLER — James Simon, *Abt Voglers kompositorisches Wirke mit besonderer Berücksichtigung der romantische Momente.* Berlin: Universitäts-Buchdruckerei 1904.

Sittard/HAMBURG — Josef Sittard, *Geschichte des Musik- und Concert wesens in Hamburg vom 14. Jahrhundert bis au die Gegenwart.* Leipzig: A. C. Reher, 1890.

Smith & Humphries/WALSH — William C. Smith & Charles Humphries, *A Bibliography of the Musical Works Published by the Firm of John Walsh During the Years 1721-1766.* London: The Bibliographical Society, 1968. Cf. the listing for SMITH-WALSH in SBE.

SMT — *Svensk Musiktidning.* 1881-1913.

SMZ — *Schweizerische Musikzeitung.* 1861—.

SOHLMANS — *Sohlmans Musiklexikon,* 4 vols. Stockholm: Sohlmans Förlag, 1951-52.

Solar-Quintes/BOCCHERINI — Nicolás A. Solar-Quintes, "Nuevos documentos sobre Luigi Boccherini," ANUARIO II (1947) 88-98

Sondheimer/BEETHOVEN — Robert Sondheimer, "On Performing Beethoven's Third and Fifth Symphonies," MR II (1941) 36-62

Sondheimer/BOCCHERINI — ———, "Boccherini, la Sinfonia in do magg., Op 16, n. 3," RMI XXVII (1920) 561-601.

Sondheimer/HAYDN — ———, *Haydn, a Historical and Psychologica Study Based on His Quartets.* London: Bernoulli 1951.

Sondheimer/RIGEL — ———, "Henri Joseph Rigel," MR XVII (1956) 221-228.

Sondheimer/SAMMARTINI — ———, "Giovanni Battista Sammartini," ZFMW III (1920-21) 83-110.

Sondheimer/SINFONIE — ———, "Die formale Entwicklung der vorklassischen Sinfonie," AFMW IV (1922) 85-99.

Sondheimer/THEORIE — ———, *Die Theorie der Sinfonie und die Beurteilung einzelner Sinfoniekomponisten bei den Musikschriftstellern des 18. Jahrhunderts.* Leipzig:

Breitkopf & Härtel, 1925 (with index, ed. by Gene Wolf and Jan LaRue, in AM XXXVII [1965] 79-86); cf. SCE 22, fn. 14.

onneck/AMERICA — Oscar George Theodore Sonneck, *Early Concert-Life in America (1731-1800)*. Leipzig: Breitkopf & Härtel, 1907.

onneck/BEETHOVEN — ———, *Beethoven Letters in America*. New York: The Beethoven Association, 1927.

onneck & Upton/BIBLIOGRAPHY — ———, *A Bibliography of Early Secular American Music,* revised and enlarged by William Treat Upton. Washington: The Library of Congress, 1945. Revisions and addenda appear in Richard J. Wolfe's *Secular Music in America, 1801-1825,* 3 vols. (New York: New York Public Library, 1964) III 1001-1033.

onnedecker/DUETS — Donald I. Sonnedecker, "Cultivation and Concepts of Duets for Four Hands, One Keyboard, in the Eighteenth Century," unpublished Ph.D. diss., Indiana University, 1953.

ouper/DITTERSDORF — Frances O. Souper, "Dittersdorf: His Fame and Fall," MMR LIX (1929) 43-45.

ouper/MUSIC — ———, "The Music of Dittersdorf," ML XI (1930) 141-145.

peer/MARVIN — Klaus Speer, review of Frederick Marvin's recording (Decca DL 9937) of 9 sons. and the "Fandango" by A. Soler, MQ XLIV (1958) 414-416.

POHR — *Louis Spohr's Autobiography,* trans. from the German (of 1860-61), 2 vols. London: Longman, Green, 1865.

tassoff/SANTINI — Wladimir Stassoff, *L'Abbé Santini et sa collection musicale à Rome*. Florence: Félix le Monnier, 1854.

tauch/CLEMENTI — Adolf Stauch, *Muzio Clementi's Klavier-Sonaten im Verhältnis zu den Sonaten von Haydn, Mozart und Beethoven*. Köln: Universitätsköln, 1930.

teglich/BACH — Rudolf Steglich, "Karl Philipp Emanuel Bach und der Dresdner Kreuzkantor Gottfried August Homilius im Musikleben ihrer Zeit," BJ XII (1915) 39-145.

teglich/BEETHOVEN — ———, "Zum Adagio der Eleonorensonate Beethovens," FESTSCHRIFT SCHMIDT-GÖRG 309-314.

teglich/MOZART — ———, "Studien an Mozarts Hammerflügel," NMJ I (1941) 181-210.

teglich/SCHWANENBERGER — ———, "Eine Klaviersonate Johann Gottfried Schwanbergs (Schwanenberg[er]s) in der Joseph Haydn-Gesamtausgabe," ZFMW XV (1932-33) 77-79.

Steinitzer/ATLAS-m — Max Steinitzer (ed.), *Musikgeschichtlicher Atlas eine Beispielsammlung . . . mit erlaüterndem Text* Freiburg: Carl Ruckmich, 1908.

Stephenson/KLASSIC-m — Kurt Stephenson (ed.), *Die musikalische Klassik* (in *Das Musikwerk* series). Köln: Arno-Volk-Verlag, [1954?].

STFMF — *Svensk Tidskrift för Musikforskning.* 1919—.

Stilz/BERLINER — Ernst Stilz, *Die Berliner Klaviersonate zur Zeit Friedrichs des Grossen.* Saarbrücken: Friedrich-Wilhelms Universität, 1930.

Stone/ITALIAN — David Stone, "The Italian Sonata for Harpsichord and Pianoforte in the Eighteenth Century (1730-1790)," 3 vols., unpublished Ph.D. diss., Harvard University, 1952.

Straeten/VIOLONCELLO — Edmund S. J. van der Straeten, *History of the Violoncello, the Viola da Gamba, Their Precursors and Collateral Instruments, With Biographies of All the Most Eminent Players of Every Country.* London: William Reeves, [1915].

Strunk/BARYTON — W. Oliver Strunk, "Haydn's Divertimenti for Baryton, Viola, and Bass (After Manuscripts in the Library of Congress)," MQ XVIII (1932) 216-251.

Strunk/HAYDN — ———, "Notes on a Haydn Autograph," MQ XX (1934) 192-205.

Studeny/VIOLINSONATE — Bruno Studeny, *Beiträge zur Geschichte der Violinsonate im 18. Jahrhundert.* Munich: Wunderhorn-Verlag, 1911.

Subirá/ALBA — José Subirá, *La Música en la casa de Alba.* Madrid: Sucesores de Rivadeneyra, 1927.

Subirá/HISTORIA — ———, *Historia de la música española e hispanoamericana.* Barcelona: Salvat Editores, 1953.

Subirá & Donostia/MANALT-m — José Antonio de Donostia (ed), *Francisco Manalt: Sonatas I-II para violín y piano,* with a "Prólogo" by José Subirá. Barcelona: Instituto Español de Musicologia, 1955.

Sulzer/ALLGEMEINE — Johann Georg Sulzer, *Allgemeine Theorie der schönen Künste,* 4 vols. Leipzig: Weidmann, 1773-75. The music articles from A-R are largely by Kirnberger, from S-Z by J. A. P. Schulz. Cf. Riess/SCHULZ 189-194.

SZMW — *Studien zur Musikwissenschaft, Beihefte* of DTÖ-m, **1913-34, 1955—.**

Tagliapietra/ANTOLOGIA-m — Gino Tagliapietra (ed.), *Antologia di musica antica e moderna,* 18 vols. Milan: G. Ricordi, 1931.

Tagliapietra/PAGANELLI-m — ——— (ed.), *G. A. Paganelli: Sei Sonate* [*Sonatines,* 1757] *per pianoforte.* Milan: G. Ricordi, 1936.

Tangeman/MOZART — Robert S. Tangeman, "Mozart's Seventeen Epistle Sonatas," MQ XXXII (1946) 588-601.

Tangeman/TRANSITION — ———, "The Transition Passage in Sonata Form Movements of the Viennese Classical Period (With Special Reference to the Works of Haydn, Mozart, and Beethoven)," 2 vols., unpublished Ph.D. diss., Harvard University, 1947.

Tans'ur/GRAMMAR — William Tans'ur, *A New Musical Grammar*. London: Jacob Robinson, 1746.

Taylor/CLEMENTI-m — Franklin Taylor (ed.), *Clementi:* [20] *Sonatas for the Pianoforte,* 4 vols. London: Augener, 1908.

Tebaldini/PADOVA — Giovanni Tebaldini, *L'Archivio musicale della Cappella Antoniana in Padova.* Padova: Libreria Antoniana, 1895.

Temperley/DOMESTIC — Nicholas Temperley, "Domestic Music in England, 1800-1860," PMA LXXXV (1958-59) 31-47.

Terry/BACH — Charles Sanford Terry, *Johann Christian Bach.* London: Oxford University Press, 1929.

Thayer/BEETHOVEN — Alexander Wheelock Thayer, *The Life of Ludwig van Beethoven,* edited . . . from the original English manuscript and the German editions . . . by Henry Edward Krehbiel, 3 vols. New York: The Beethoven Association, 1921. See note 8a to p. 502.

Thayer & Riemann/BEETHOVEN — ———, *Ludwig van Beethovens Leben,* revised by Hugo Riemann from the German transl. by H. Deiters, 5 vols. Leipzig: Breitkopf & Härtel, 1917-23.

Thoor/RIEMANN — Alf Thoor, "Hugo Riemann, Mannheimskolan och 'Denkmälerstriden,'" STFMF XXXIV (1952) 5-27.

Tiersot/COUPERIN — Julien Tiersot, *Les Couperin.* Paris: Félix Alcan, 1926.

Titus/CLARINET — Robert A. Titus, "The Solo Music for the Clarinet in the Eighteenth Century," unpublished Ph.D. diss., State University of Iowa, 1961.

Tobel/KLASSISCHEN — Rudolf von Tobel, *Die Formenwelt der klassischen Instrumentalmusik.* Bern: Paul Haupt, 1935.

Tobin/MOZART — J. Raymond Tobin, *Mozart and the Sonata Form.* London: William Reeves, [1916].

Torchi/ISTRUMENTALE — Luigi Torchi, *La musica istrumentale in Italia nei secoli XVI, XVII e XVIII.* Torino: Fratelli Bocca, 1901. Cf. Torrefranca/ORIGINI 442.

Torrefranca/GALUPPI — Fausto Torrefranca, "Per un Catalogo tematico delle sonate per cembalo di B. Galuppi detto il Buranello," RMI XVI (1909) 872-881.

Torrefranca/LONDRA — ———, "Influenza di alcun i musicisti italiani vissuti a Londra su W. A. Mozart (1764-65)," KONGRESS 1924 (Basel) 336-362.

Torrefranca/MAESTRO ———, "Il primo Maestro di W. A. Mozart (Giovanni Maria Rutini)," RMI XL (1936) 239-253.

Torrefranca/ORIGINI ———, *Le Origini italiane del romanticismo musicale: i primitivi della sonata moderna.* Torino: Fratelli Bocca, 1930. Cf. Saint-Foix/TORREFRANCA; Sondheimer/SAMMARTINI 83; Raabe/GALUPPI 10-11, 18; Bücken/ROKOKO 19; Stone/ITALIAN I 7-9 *et passim;* SCE VII.

Torrefranca/PLATTIANO ———, "Prime Ricognizioni dello stile violoncellistico plattiano," KONGRESS 1949 (Basel) 203-211.

Torrefranca/SANMARTINI ———, "Le Sinfonie dell'imbrattacarte (G. B. Sanmartini)," RMI XX (1913) 291-346, XXI (1914) 97-121 and 278-312, XXII (1915) 431-446.

Tovey/ANALYSIS Donald Francis Tovey, *Essays in Musical Analysis,* 7 vols. London: Oxford University Press, 1936-44.

Tovey/BEETHOVEN ———, *A Companion to Beethoven's Pianoforte Sonatas.* London: Associated Board to the Royal Schools of Music, 1935.

Tovey/BEETHOVEN-m ——— (ed.), *Beethoven: Sonatas for Pianoforte,* 3 vols. London: The Associated Board of the Royal Schools of Music, [1931].

Townsend/DUETS-m Douglas Townsend (ed.), *Piano Duets of the Classical Period for One Piano, Four Hands.* Bryn Mawr: Theodore Presser, 1956.

TRÉSOR-m *Le Trésor des pianistes,* 20 vols. Paris: Aristide and Louise Farrenc, 1861-72. For contents cf. GROVE 2d ed. V 148-149; Heyer/HISTORICAL 110-111 (but with a different grouping, in 23 vols.).

Türk/KLAVIERSCHULE Daniel Gottlob Türk, *Klavierschule, oder Anweisung zum Klavierspielen für Lehrer und Lernende.* Leipzig: Schwickert, 1789.

Tutenberg/BACH Fritz Tutenberg, *Die Sinfonik Johann Christian Bachs.* Berlin: Georg Kallmeyer, 1928.

TVNM *Tijdschrift der Vereeniging voor nederlandsche Muziekgeschiedenis.* 1882—.

Tyson/HAYDN Alan Tyson, "Haydn and Two Stolen Trios," MR XXII (1961) 21-27.

Uldall/KLAVIERKONZERT Hans Uldall, *Das Klavierkonzert der Berliner Schule.* Leipzig: Breitkopf & Härtel, 1928.

Unger/BEETHOVENIANA Max Unger, "Nova Beethoveniana," DM XII/1 (1912-13) 147-162, 214-225.

Unger/CLEMENTI ———, *Muzio Clementis Leben.* Langensalza: Hermann Beyer & Söhne, 1913 (1914 in some copies).

UNIVERSAL CONTINUO-m *Continuo, Sammlung alter Spielmusik.* Vienna: Universal Edition, from 1936.

Unverricht/BEETHOVEN Hubert Unverricht, *Die Eigenschriften und die Originalausgaben von Werken Beethovens in ihrer Bedeutung für die moderne Textkritik.* Kassel: Bärenreiter, 1960.

Valentin/AGRELL Karl Valentin, "Johan Agrell," SMT 1911/4 25-26.

Valentin/NANNERL-m Erich Valentin (ed.), *Leopold Mozart: Nannerl Notenbuch, 1759.* Munich: Hermann Rinn, 1956. Cf. Lerma/NANNERL.

Vallas/LYON Léon Vallas, *La Musique a l'Académie de Lyon au dix-huitième siècle.* Lyon: Revue musicale de Lyon, 1908.

Verchaly/MOZART André Verchaly (ed.), *Les Influences étrangères dans l'oeuvre de W. A. Mozart* (1956). Paris: Centre National de la Recherche Scientifique, 1958.

VFMW *Vierteljahrsschrift für Musikwissenschaft,* 10 vols. 1885-94.

Vignal/HAYDN Marc Vignal, "L'Oeuvre pour piano seul de Joseph Haydn," RM XXX (1961) *Carnet critique* no. 249, pp. 5-20.

Villanis/CLAVECINISTES Luigi Alberto Villanis, "Les clavecinistes," ENCYCLOPÉDIE I/2 798-814.

Villanis/CLAVICEMBALO ———, *L'Arte del clavicembalo.* Torino: Fratelli Bocca, 1901.

Viollier/LEFÈVRE-m Renée Viollier (ed.), *Xavier Lefèvre: 5ème Sonate pour clarinette.* Geneva: Richli, 1949.

VNM-m *Vereeniging voor nederlandsche Muziekgeschiedenis.* Amsterdam: G. Alsbach, from 1869.

Volbach/BEETHOVEN Fritz Volbach, *Die Klaviersonaten Beethovens.* Köln: P. J. Tonger, 1919.

Volk/EICHNER Alois Volk, "Ernst Eichner, sein Leben und seine Bedeutung für die Entwicklung der Kammermusik und des Solokonzerts," unpublished Ph.D. diss., University of Köln, 1943.

Vretblad/STOCKHOLM Patrik Vretblad, *Konsertlivet i Stockholm under 1700-Talet.* Stockholm: P. A. Norstedt, 1918.

Waldersee/VORTRÄGE Paul Graf Waldersee, *Sammlung musikalischer Vorträge,* 5 vols. Leipzig: Breitkopf & Härtel, 1879-98.

Waldkirch/SINFONIEN Franz Waldkirch, *Die konzertanten Sinfonien der Mannheimer im 18. Jahrhundert.* Ludwigshafen: Julius Waldkirch, 1931.

Walker/MOTIVATION Alan Walker, "Unconscious Motivation in the Composing Process," MR *XX* (1959) 277-281. But see, also, R. L. Jacobs' review in MR XXIV (1963) 349-351 of a subsequent book by Walker on the same topic.

Wallace/LETTERS — *Letters of Distinguished Musicians: Gluck, Haydn, P. E. Bach, Weber, Mendelssohn,* trans. from the German by Lady Grace Wallace. London: Longmans, Green, 1867.

Wallner/BEETHOVEN-m — Bertha A. Wallner (ed.), *Beethoven: Klavier-Sonaten, nach Eigenschriften und Originalausgaben,* 2 vols. Munich: G. Henle, [1952-53].

Walther/BACH-m — Kurt Walther (ed.), *Wilhelm Friedemann Bach: . . . Sechs Duette für 2 Flöten,* 2 vols. Leipzig: Breitkopf & Härtel, 1939.

Wasielewski/VIOLINE — Joseph Wilhelm von Wasielewski, *Die Violine und ihre Meister,* 5th ed., revised and enlarged by Waldemar von Wasielewski. Leipzig: Breitkopf & Härtel, 1910.

Weckbecker/MAICHELBEK-m — Wilhelm Weckbecker (ed.), *F. A. Maichelbek: Zwei Klavier-Sonaten.* Vienna: Universal-Edition, 1923.

Wegeler & Ries/BEETHOVEN — Franz Gerhard Wegeler and Ferdinand Ries, *Biographische Notizen über Beethoven.* Koblenz: K. Bädeker, 1838.

Weigl/VIOLONCELL — Bruno Weigl, *Handbuch der Violoncell-Literatur,* 3d ed. Vienna: Universal-Edition, 1929.

Weigl/FÖRSTER — Karl Weigl, "Emanuel Aloys Förster," SIMG VI (1904-05) 274-314.

Weinmann/ARTARIA — Alexander Weinmann, *Vollständiges Verlagsverzeichnis Artaria & Comp.* Vienna: Ludwig Krenn, 1952.

Weinmann/KOŽELUCH — ———, *Verzeichnis der Verlagswerke des Musikalischen Magazins in Wien, 1784-1802, "Leopold Koželuch."* Vienna: Österreichischer Bundesverlag, 1950.

Weinmann/KUNST — ———, "Vollständiges Verlagsverzeichnis der Musikalien des Kunst- und Industrie Comptoirs in Wien (1801-1819)," SZMW XXII (1955) 217-252.

Weinmann/WIENER — ———, *Wiener Musikverleger und Musikalienhändler von Mozarts Zeit bis gegen 1860.* Vienna: Rudolf M. Rohrer, 1956.

Weise/WALDSTEINSONATE — Dagmar Weise, "Zum Faksimileausdruck von Beethovens Waldsteinsonate," BEETHOVEN-JAHRBUCH 1955-56, pp. 102-111.

Weismann/BACH-m — Wilhelm Weismann (ed.), *Johann Christian Bach: Drei Sonaten für Klavier zu vier Händen* (Opp. 15/6 and 18/5 and 6). C. F. Peters, 1943.

Weitzmann/PIANOFORTE — Karl Friedrich Weitzmann, *A History of Pianoforte Playing,* translated from the 2d German edition of 1879 by Theodore Baker. New York: G. Schirmer, 1897.

Werner/MOZART-m — Jack Werner (ed.), *Mozart: Two Two-Part Sonatas K. 46^{d-e}.* London: J. Curwen, 1958.

Werra/ORGELSPIEL — Ernst von Werra, "Beiträge zur Geschichte des katholischen Orgelspieles," KJ XII (1897) 28-36.

Werra/ROSSI — ———, "Michelangelo Rossi, ein Komponist des 17. Jahrhunderts," MFMG XXVIII (1896) 123-131, 140-148.

Westphal/HAYDN — Kurt Westphal, "Die Formung in Haydns Sonaten," DM XXIV (1931-32) 419-424.

Westrup/HAYDN — Jack Allan Westrup, "New Light on Haydn," MT CII (1961) 85-86.

Wetzel/BEETHOVEN — Hermann Wetzel, "Beethovens Sonate Op. 110, eine Erläuterung ihres Baues," Frimmel/JARHBUCH II 75-154.

Wiberg/MUSIKHANDELNS — Albert Wiberg, *Den svenska Musikhandelns historia.* Stockholm: Victor Petterson, 1955.

Wiel/CATALOGO — Taddeo Wiel, *Catalogo delle opere in musica rappresente nel secolo XVIII in Venezia (1701-1750).* Venice: 1892.

Winkel/ZINK — Erling Winkel, "H. O. C. Zinks klaversonater," DANSK XXVI (1951) 137-143.

Wiora/VOLKSMUSIK — Walter Wiora, *Europäische Volksmusik und abendländische Tonkunst.* Kassel: Johann Philipp Hinnenthal, 1957.

Wirth/MOZART — Helmut Wirth, "Mozart et Haydn," in Verchaly/MOZART 49-57.

Wise/MODE — Wayne Wilmar Wise, "Tonal Relationship Through Interchangeability of Mode in the Music of the Eighteenth and Nineteenth Centuries," unpublished Ph.D. diss., Indiana University, 1956.

Wörmann/ALBERTI — Wilhelm Wörmann, "Die Klaviersonate Domenico Albertis," AM XXVII (1955) 84-112.

Wohlfarth/BACH — Hannsdieter Wohlfarth, "Neues Verzeichnis der Werke von Johann Christoph Friedrich Bach," DMF XIII (1960) 404-417.

Wolff/SCHROETER — Konrad Wolff, "Johann Samuel Schroeter," MQ XLIV (1958) 338-359.

WOLFFHEIM MUSIKBIBLIOTHEK — *Versteigerung der Musikbibliothek des Herrn Dr. Werner Wolffheim,* 2 vols. Berlin: Martin Breslauer & Leo Liepmannsohn, 1928.

Wotquenne/BACH — Alfred Wotquenne, *Thematisches Verzeichnis der Werke von Carl Philipp Emanuel Bach.* Leipzig: Breitkopf & Härtel, 1905. Cf. Miesner/NACHLASS (BJ XXXV) 103; MGG I 930.

Wyler/BACH — Robert Wyler, *Form- und Stiluntersuchungen zum ersten Satz der Klaviersonaten Carl Philipp Emanuel Bachs* (from Ph.D. diss., Zürich, 1955). Biel: Graphische Anstalt Schüler AG, 1960.

Wyzewa & Gastoué/CLEMENTI-m — Théodore de Wyzewa and Amédée Gastoué (eds.), *Clementi: 20 Sonates et caprices,* 2 vols. Paris: Sénart, 1917.

Zeitlin & Goldberger/CLEMENTI-m — Poldi Zeitlin and David Goldberger (eds.), *Clementi: Six Sonatas,* [one] *Piano, Four Hands* (Opp. 3/1-3 and 14). New York: G. Schirmer, 1960.

Zeitlin & Goldberger/PLEYEL-m — ———, *Ignaz Joseph Pleyel: Sonata* (4 hands, 1 P, g minor; *ca.* 1815). New York: C. F. Peters, 1961.

Zelter/FASCH — Carl Friedrich Zelter, *Biographie von Karl Friedrich Christian Fasch.* Berlin: Unger, 1801.

ZFM — *Zeitschrift für Musik,* originally *Neue Zeitschrift für Musik,* 1834—.

ZFMW — *Zeitschrift für Musikwissenschaft.* 1918-35. Superseded by AFMF.

Zilcher/HAYDN-m — Hermann Zilcher (ed.), *Joseph Haydn: Sämtliche Sonaten für Pianoforte zu zwei Händen,* 4 vols. Leipzig: Breitkopf & Härtel, 1932.

ZIMG — *Zeitschrift der internationalen Musikgesellschaft.* 1900-14.

Zimmermann/MOZART — Ewald Zimmermann, "Eine neue Quelle zu Mozarts Klaviersonate KV 309 (284b)," DMF XI (1958) 490-493.

Zschinsky-Troxler/BOCCHERINI — Elsa Margherita v. Zschinsky-Troxler, "Mozarts D dur-Violinkonzert und Boccherini," ZFMW X (1927-28) 415-422.

Zschinsky-Troxler/PUGNANI — ———, *Gaetano Pugnani, 1731-1798.* Berlin: Atlantis-Verlag, 1939.

Zuth/GITARREMUSIK-m — Joseph Zuth (ed.), *Alt-wiener Gitarremusik* (6 sons. and a "Rondeau" by S. Molitor). Vienna: Anton Goll, 1919.

Zuth/MOLITOR — Joseph Zuth, *Simon Molitor und die wiener Gitarristik (um 1800).* Vienna: Anton Goll, [1919].

Index

Note: The index includes nearly every reference to persons' names in both the text proper and the footnotes. But it usually includes other subjects and specific bibliographic references only when these get some mention in their own right. In the longer index entries the page numbers in italics distinguish the main discussions. The page numbers in quotation marks refer to statements quoted verbatim from the persons indexed (on the topics added in parentheses).